EXPLORING STRATEGY

TEXT AND CASES

ELEVENTH EDITION

GERRY JOHNSON
Lancaster University Management School

RICHARD WHITTINGTON
Saïd Business School, University of Oxford

KEVAN SCHOLES
Sheffield Business School

DUNCAN ANGWIN
Lancaster University Management School

PATRICK REGNÉR
Stockholm School of Economics

With the assistance of
JASON EVANS
CLIVE KERRIDGE
STEVE PYLE

Pearson

Harlow, England • London • New York • Boston • San Francisco • Toronto • Sydney • Dubai • Singapore • Hong Kong
Tokyo • Seoul • Taipei • New Delhi • Cape Town • Sao Paulo • Mexico City • Madrid • Amsterdam • Munich • Paris • Milan

100638778

658.
401
2
JOH

Pearson Education Limited
Edinburgh Gate
Harlow CM20 2JE
United Kingdom
Tel: +44 (0)1279 623623
Web: **www.pearson.com/uk**

First edition (print) published under the Prentice Hall imprint 1984
Fifth edition (print) published under the Prentice Hall imprint 1998
Sixth edition (print) published under the Financial Times Prentice Hall imprint 2002
Seventh edition (print) 2005
Eighth edition (print) 2008
Ninth edition (print) 2011
Tenth edition published (2013) (print and electronic)
Eleventh edition published (2017) (print and electronic)

© Simon & Schuster Europe Limited 1998 (print)
© Pearson Education 2002, 2011 (print)
© Pearson Education Limited 2014, 2017 (print and electronic)

The rights of Gerry Johnson, Richard Whittington, Kevan Scholes, Duncan Angwin and Patrick Regnér to be identified as authors of this work have been asserted by them in accordance with the Copyright, Designs and Patents Act 1988.

Contains public sector information licensed under the Open Government Licence (OGL) v3.0. http://www.nationalarchives.gov.uk/doc/open-government-licence/version/3/.

Pearson Education is not responsible for the content of third-party internet sites.

The Financial Times. With a worldwide network of highly respected journalists, *The Financial Times* provides global business news, insightful opinion and expert analysis of business, finance and politics. With over 500 journalists reporting from 50 countries worldwide, our in-depth coverage of international news is objectively reported and analysed from an independent, global perspective. To find out more, visit www.ft.com/pearsonoffer.

Text only
ISBN: 978-1-292-14517-4 (print)
      978-1-292-19149-2 (PDF)
      978-1-292-19150-8 (ePub)

Text and cases
ISBN: 978-1-292-14512-9 (print)
      978-1-292-14513-6 (PDF)
      978-1-292-14514-3 (ePub)

British Library Cataloguing-in-Publication Data
A catalogue record for the print edition is available from the British Library

Library of Congress Cataloging-in-Publication Data
A catalog record for the print edition is available from the Library of Congress

10 9 8 7 6 5 4 3 2 1
20 19 18 17 16

Print edition typeset in 10/12.5pt Sabon MT Pro by SPi Global
Printed and bound by L.E.G.O. S.p.A., Italy
NOTE THAT ANY PAGE CROSS REFERENCES REFER TO THE PRINT EDITION

WELCOME TO
EXPLORING STRATEGY

Strategy is a crucial subject. It's about the development, success and failure of all kinds of organisations, from multinationals to entrepreneurial start-ups, from charities to government agencies, and many more. Strategy raises the big questions about these organisations – how they grow, how they innovate and how they change. As a manager of today or tomorrow, you will be involved in shaping, implementing or communicating these strategies.

Our primary aim with *Exploring Strategy* is to give you a comprehensive understanding of the issues and techniques of strategy. We can also help you get a great final result in your course. You can make the most of the text by:

- Exploring hot topics in cutting-edge issues such as competition, corporate governance, innovation and entrepreneurship and strategy in practice.

- Engaging with our new 'Thinking Differently' sections to access novel and distinctive perspectives on core themes in strategy.

- Using the 'strategy lenses' to think critically and originally about key topics and to set you on your way to better grades in your assignments and exams.

- Pursuing some of the recommended readings at the end of each chapter. They're specially selected as accessible and valuable sources that will enhance your learning and give you an extra edge in your course work.

We want *Exploring Strategy* to give you what you need: a comprehensive view of the subject, an ambition to put that into practice, and – of course – success in your studies. We hope that you'll be as excited by the key issues of strategy as we are!

So, read on and good luck!

Gerry Johnson
Richard Whittington
Kevan Scholes
Duncan Angwin
Patrick Regnér

Gerry Johnson BA, PhD is Emeritus Professor of Strategic Management at Lancaster University School of Management. He has also taught at Strathclyde Business School, Cranfield School of Management, Manchester Business School and Aston University. He is the author of numerous books and his research has been published in many of the foremost management research journals in the world. He is also a partner in the consultancy partnership Strategy Explorers (see **www.strategyexplorers.com**), where he works with senior management teams on issues of strategy development and strategic change.

Richard Whittington MA, MBA, PhD is Professor of Strategic Management at the Saïd Business School and Millman Fellow at New College, University of Oxford. He is author or co-author of nine books and is an Associate Editor of the *Strategic Management Journal*. He has had full or visiting positions at the Harvard Business School, HEC Paris, Imperial College London, the University of Toulouse and the University of Warwick. He is a partner in Strategy Explorers and active in executive education and consulting. His current research focuses on strategy practice and 'open strategy'.

Kevan Scholes MA, PhD, DMS, CIMgt, FRSA is Principal Partner of Scholes Associates – specialising in strategic management. He is also Visiting Professor of Strategic Management and formerly Director of the Sheffield Business School, UK. He has extensive experience of teaching strategy to undergraduate and postgraduate students inside and outside the UK, as well as of management development work in private- and public-sector organisations. He has been an advisor on management development to a number of national bodies and is a Companion of the Chartered Management Institute.

Duncan Angwin MA, MPhil, MBA, PhD is the Sir Roland Smith Professor of Strategic Management and Director of the Centre for Strategic Management at Lancaster University. He is author of eight books and many journal articles and serves on the editorial boards of several journals including *Journal of Management Studies.* He has taught strategy in over 20 countries and is active internationally in executive education and consulting. His current research focuses on mergers and acquisitions, strategy practices and international management.

Patrick Regnér BSc, MSc, PhD is Professor of Strategic Management at Stockholm School of Economics. He has published in leading journals like the *Strategic Management Journal*, *Journal of International Business*, *Human Relations*, etc. and serves on the editorial boards of *Journal of Management Studies*, *Organization Studies* and *Strategic Organization*. He has extensive experience of teaching strategy on all levels at several international institutions. He does executive teaching and consulting with organisations active worldwide and is senior advisor at strategy advisory firm Value Formation. His current research focuses on strategy and institutions.

The case collection has been managed by Jason Evans, Clive Kerridge and Steve Pyle.

BRIEF CONTENTS

CONTENTS

PART I
THE STRATEGIC POSITION

PART II
STRATEGIC CHOICES

PART III
STRATEGY IN ACTION

CASE STUDIES

ILLUSTRATIONS AND THINKING DIFFERENTLY

ILLUSTRATIONS

THINKING DIFFERENTLY BY CHAPTER

FIGURES

TABLES

PREFACE

We are delighted to offer this eleventh edition of *Exploring Strategy*. With sales of previous editions now well over one million, we believe we have a tried and tested product. Yet the strategy field is constantly changing. For this edition, therefore, we have introduced a new chapter, and thoroughly refreshed all the remaining chapters, with new concepts, new cases and new examples throughout. Here we would like to highlight four particular changes, while recalling some of the classic features of the book.

The eleventh edition's principal changes are:

- **Extended coverage of the macro-environment.** We now have a whole chapter on the macro-environment, allowing us to cover increasingly important nonmarket aspects of strategy, such as politics and regulation, and to provide students with the tools to analyse the mega-trends that will drive organisational strategy in the future.

- **A new treatment of business models.** We have developed the treatment of business models, important to students in a start-up culture of rapid technological change.

- **Enhanced emphasis on entrepreneurship.** As entrepreneurial opportunities become increasingly attractive to readers, we have raised the prominence of entrepreneurship, and introduced new materials on opportunity recognition and the entrepreneurial process.

- **New 'Thinking Differently' sections.** At the end of each chapter, we introduce new material designed to encourage students to approach issues from a different point of view to the conventional wisdom of the chapter itself: for example, using crowdsourcing to predict environmental change, or one force rather than five to analyse industries.

At the same time, *Exploring Strategy* retains its longstanding commitment to a comprehensive and real-world view of strategy. In particular, this entails a deep concern for:

- **Process.** We believe that the human processes of strategy, not only the economics of particular strategies, are central to achieving long-term organisational success. Throughout the book, we underline the importance of human processes, but in particular we devote Part III to processes of strategy formation, implementation and change.

- **Practice.** We conclude the book with a chapter on the practice of strategy (Chapter 16), focused on the practicalities of managing strategy. Throughout the book, we introduce concepts and techniques through practical illustrations and applications, rather than abstract descriptions. **MyStrategyExperience** simulation gives students a chance to apply the frameworks of the book to a dynamic, realistic simulation of strategy in the advertising industry (visit https://uk.pearson.com/higher-education-educators/products-and-services/course-resources-and-content/simulations.html).

Many people have helped us with the development of this new edition. Jason Evans, Clive Kerridge and Steve Pyle have led in coordinating the case collection. We have also consulted carefully with our Advisory Board, made up of experienced adopters of the book and other leading academics in the field of strategy. Many other adopters of the book provide more informal advice and suggestions – many of whom we have had the pleasure of meeting at our annual teachers' workshops. This kind of feedback is invaluable and we hope you will keep the comments flowing. Also, our students and clients at Lancaster University, Oxford University, Oxford Brookes, Stockholm School of Economics, Sheffield Hallam and the many other places where we teach are a constant source of ideas and stimulus. We also gain from our links across the world, particularly in Austria, Ireland, the Netherlands, Denmark, Sweden, France, Canada, Australia, New Zealand, Hong Kong, Singapore and the USA. Many contribute directly by providing case studies and illustrations and these are acknowledged in the text.

Finally, we thank those organisations that have been generous enough to be written up as case studies. We hope that those using the book will respect the wishes of the case study organisations and *not* contact them directly for further information.

Gerry Johnson (gerry.johnson@lancaster.ac.uk)
Richard Whittington (richard.whittington@sbs.ox.ac.uk)
Kevan Scholes (KScholes@scholes.u-net.com)
Duncan Angwin (d.n.angwin@lancaster.ac.uk)
Patrick Regnér (patrick.regner@hhs.se)
October 2016

Advisory Board

Special thanks are due to the following members of the Advisory Board for their valued comments:

Mike Davies	University of Winchester
Alison De Moraes	Royal Holloway University of London
Dr Maria Emmanouilidou	University of Kent
Dr Andrew Jenkins	University of Huddersfield
Adrian Myers	Oxford Brookes University
Sarah Owens	Swansea University
Nick Papageorgiadis	University of Liverpool
Adam Raman	Kingston University
Dr Andrew Wild	Nottingham University
Steve Wood	Leeds Beckett University

EXPLORING STRATEGY FEATURES

This eleventh edition of *Exploring Strategy* builds on the established strengths of this best-selling textbook. A range of in-text features and supplementary features have been developed to enable you and your students to gain maximum added value from the teaching and learning of strategy.

- *Outstanding pedagogical features.* Each chapter has clear learning outcomes, practical questions associated with real-life illustrations and examples which students can easily apply to what they have learnt.
- *Flexibility of use.* You can choose to use either the Text and Cases version of the book, or – if you don't use longer cases (or have your own) – the Text-only version. The provision of Thinking Differently sections, Commentaries and Strategy 'Lenses' allows you to dig deeper into the tensions and complexity of strategy.

The two versions are complemented by a concise version of the text, *Fundamentals of Strategy,* and instructors also have the option of further customising the text. Visit www.pearsoned.co.uk/CustomPublishing for more details.

- *Up-to-date materials.* As well as a new chapter on the macro-environment, we have fully revised the other chapters, incorporating new research and updating references so that you can easily access the latest research.
- *Encouraging innovative and critical thinking.* The Strategy Lenses and Commentaries are designed to encourage critical thinking, while each chapter ends with a Thinking Differently section, introducing students to new and distinctive approaches to key issues of the chapter.

Our 'three circles' framework – depicting the overlapping issues of strategic position, strategic choices and strategy in action – also challenges a simple linear, sequential view of the strategy process.

- *Case and examples.* A wide range of Illustrations, Case Examples and (in the Text and Cases version) longer Case Studies are fresh and engage with student interests and day-to-day experience. The majority of these are entirely new to this edition; we have extensively revised the remainder. Finally, we draw these examples from all over the world and use examples from the public and voluntary sectors as well as the private.
- *Teaching and learning support.* You and your students can access a wealth of resources detailed in the *Exploring Strategy* Online section that follows this.
- *Teachers' workshop.* We run an annual workshop to facilitate discussion of key challenges and solutions in the teaching of strategic management. Details of forthcoming workshops can be found at https://heuk.pearson.com/events.html

EXPLORING STRATEGY ONLINE

A wide range of supporting resources are available at: www.pearsoned.co.uk/johnson

For students

- **Multiple choice questions** that test your understanding of key content.
- **Key concept audio summaries** that you can download or listen to online.
- **Video cases** that show managers talking about strategic issues in their own organisations.
- **Revision flashcards** to help you prepare for your exams.
- **A multi-lingual online glossary** to help explain key concepts.
- Guidance on **how to analyse a case study.**
- **Links** to relevant sites on the web so you can explore more about the organisations featured in the case studies.
- **Classic cases** – over 30 case studies from previous editions of the book.

For instructors

- An **Instructor's Manual** which provides a comprehensive set of teaching support, including guidance on the use of case studies and assignments, and advice on how to plan a programme using the text.
- **PowerPoint slides,** containing key information and figures from the book.
- **Classic cases,** from previous editions of the book.

MyStrategyExperience is an engaging and rigorous simulation designed to bring together the theory and practice of strategy-making in the realistic environment of a dynamic organisation and industry. The simulation puts students on the board of directors in a global advertising agency and allows them to make a strategic analysis of the business, put together a business plan and then make a number of challenging decisions on the future strategy of the company.

As students set and implement strategy, they will see the impact of their decisions on financial and non-financial measures of performance within the simulated company. Your students will need to balance strategic opportunities with inherent risk thus gaining knowledge and insights relevant to their strategic studies.

For more information, contact your local sales representative or visit https://uk.pearson.com/higher-education-educators/products-and-services/course-resources-and-content/simulations.html

Follow the authors' latest comments on the strategy issues of this book at https://twitter.com/ExploreStrategy

EXPLORING STRATEGY

1

INTRODUCING STRATEGY

Strategic position

Strategic choices

Strategy in action

Learning outcomes

After reading this chapter you should be able to:

- Summarise the strategy of an organisation in a '*strategy statement*'.

- Distinguish between *corporate*, *business* and *functional* strategies.

- Identify key issues for an organisation's strategy according to the *Exploring Strategy Framework*.

- Understand different people's roles in *strategy work*.

- Appreciate the importance of different *organisational contexts*, *academic disciplines* and *theoretical lenses* to practical strategy analysis.

Key terms

business-level strategy p.11

corporate-level strategy p.10

Exploring Strategy Framework p.11

functional strategies p.11

mission statement p.7

objectives p.8

statements of corporate values p.8

strategic choices p.13

strategic position p.12

strategy p.4

strategy in action p.14

strategy lenses p.21

strategy statements p.8

three-horizons framework p.6

vision statement p.8

1.1 INTRODUCTION

Claudia, a junior at a leading firm of strategy consultants, had just arrived with two senior colleagues at the headquarters of a medium-sized company considering its next strategic move. The CEO began the meeting by outlining the business the company was in and some of the history behind the firm's significant success in European markets. The recent entry into Europe of new aggressive competitors threatened their performance and the Board was wondering whether the company should globalise. The CEO then asked how the consultants might approach this problem. The consulting partner explained they would carry out a systematic strategic analysis of the company's situation and Claudia knew this would be her responsibility – to gather and analyse appropriate data. She would need to understand how the company had been so successful to date, the challenge posed by competitors and the broader opportunities and threats from the wider environment. She knew she could access key company executives to understand what resources, processes and people were supporting the current strategy and also what might support international expansion. She would have to consider the direction in which the business might expand, the methods of expansion that might be most appropriate as well as other strategic options. Through this analysis, she would hope to inform the CEO's decision about what the strategy for the company might be and perhaps gain further work to help implement a strategic direction.

The problem presented by the CEO to the consultants is one of strategy. It is concerned with key issues for the future of the organisation. For instance, how should the company compete in the future with aggressive new entrants? What growth options are there for the company? If going global is a good strategy, what would be the optimal method to achieve this outcome and what might be the resourcing implications? All of these strategy questions are vital to the future survival of the organisation.

Strategy questions naturally concern entrepreneurs and senior managers at the top of their organisations. But these questions matter more widely. Middle managers also have to understand the strategic direction of their organisations, both to know how to get top management support for their initiatives and to explain their organisation's strategy to the people they are responsible for. Anybody looking for a management-track job needs to be ready to discuss strategy with their potential employer. Indeed, anybody taking a job should first be confident that their new employer's strategy is actually viable. There are even specialist career opportunities in strategy, for example like Claudia, as a strategy consultant or as an in-house strategic planner, often key roles for fast-track young managers.

This book takes a broad approach to strategy, looking at both the economics of strategy and the people side of managing strategy in practice. It is a book about 'Exploring', because the real world of strategy rarely offers obvious answers. In strategy, it is typically important to explore several options, probing each one carefully before making choices. The book is also relevant to any kind of organisation responsible for its own direction into the future. Thus the book refers to large private-sector multinationals and small entrepreneurial start-ups; to public-sector organisations such as schools and hospitals; and to not-for-profits such as charities or sports clubs. Strategy matters to almost all organisations, and to everybody working in them.

1.2 WHAT IS STRATEGY?[1]

In this book, **strategy is the long-term direction of an organisation**. Thus the long-term direction of Amazon is from book retailing to internet services in general. The long-term direction of Disney is from cartoons to diversified entertainment. This section examines the practical implication of this definition of strategy; distinguishes between different levels of strategy; and explains how to summarise an organisation's strategy in a 'strategy statement'.

1.2.1 Defining strategy

Defining strategy as the long-term direction of an organisation implies a more comprehensive view than some influential definitions. Figure 1.1 shows the strategy definitions of several leading strategy theorists: Alfred Chandler and Michael Porter, both from the Harvard Business School, Peter Drucker from Claremont University, California and Henry Mintzberg, from McGill University, Canada. Each points to important elements of strategy. Chandler emphasises a logical flow from the determination of goals and objectives to the allocation of resources. Porter focuses on deliberate choices, difference and competition. Drucker suggests that it is a theory about how a firm will win.[2] Mintzberg, however, takes the view that strategy is less certain and uses the word 'pattern' to allow for the fact that strategies do not always follow a deliberately chosen and logical plan, but can emerge in more ad hoc ways. Sometimes strategies reflect a series of incremental decisions that only cohere into a recognisable pattern – or 'strategy' – after some time.

In this book, strategy is defined as 'the long-term direction of an organisation'. This has two advantages. First, the long-term direction of an organisation can include both deliberate, logical strategy and more incremental, emergent patterns of strategy. Second, long-term direction can include both strategies that emphasise difference and competition, and strategies that recognise the roles of cooperation and even imitation.

The three elements of this strategy definition – the long term, direction and organisation – can each be explored further. The strategy of Tesla Motors illustrates important points (see Illustration 1.1):

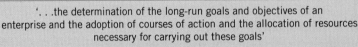

'. . .the determination of the long-run goals and objectives of an enterprise and the adoption of courses of action and the allocation of resources necessary for carrying out these goals'
Alfred D. Chandler

'Competitive strategy is about being different. It means deliberately choosing a different set of activities to deliver a unique mix of value'
Michael Porter

'a firm's theory about how to gain competitive advantages'
Peter Drucker

'a pattern in a stream of decisions'
Henry Mintzberg

'the long-term direction of an organisation'
Exploring Strategy

Figure 1.1 Definitions of strategy

Sources: A.D. Chandler, *Strategy and Structure: Chapters in the History of American Enterprise*, MIT Press, 1963, p. 13; M.E. Porter, 'What is strategy?', *Harvard Business Review,* November–December 1996, p. 60; P.F. Drucker, 'The theory of business', *Harvard Business Review,* September–October 1994, pp. 95–106; H. Mintzberg, *Tracking Strategies: Towards a General Theory,* Oxford University Press, 2007, p. 3.

ILLUSTRATION 1.1   Tesla Motors: the future is electric!

Tesla car
Source: Jim West/Alamy Images.

The Tesla Roadster is a staggeringly quick car with a difference. There's no wheel-spin, no traction control stutter, no driveline shutter. As soon as one stamps on the throttle the driver gets 686 lbs of torque immediately, rocketing the car from 0–60 mph in 3.2 seconds and with negligible noise – the car is electric.

The Tesla Roadster is the main product of Tesla Motors. Its charismatic chairman and main funder is PayPal co-founder, and SpaceX CEO, Elon Musk. Barely a decade old, Tesla Motors is already gigantic, $33bn (£20bn, €25bn) market capitalisation and adored. It's been called 'the world's most important automotive company'[1] and the Tesla's Model S, 'the Most Loved Vehicle in America'[1] – outselling Mercedes S-class and BMW 7 series. And yet the last successful American car start-up was Ford, founded 111 years ago. How can Tesla Motors be so successful?

Tesla is the brain-child of three Silicon Valley engineers convinced by global warming arguments and looking for alternative fuel sources for cars. Co-founder Martin Eberhard asked: 'How much of the energy that comes out of the ground makes your car go a mile?'[1] He observed: 'Hydrogen fuel cells are terrible – no more efficient than gas. Electric cars were superior to everything.'[1] He then discovered a bright yellow, all-electric, two-seater bullet car with zero emissions, 'tzero', built by AC propulsion. Inspired, Eberhard kept saying to potential recruits – 'try and touch the dashboard.'[1] He would then hit the accelerator – they couldn't! With Lamborghini-level acceleration, this demonstrated electric cars didn't have to be golf carts.

But industry logic said electric cars would never succeed. GM spent $1bn (£0.6bn, €0.75bn), developing the EV-1 which was then scrapped. Battery technology had not improved in a hundred years. But Eberhard realised lithium-ion batteries were different – improving 7 per cent p.a. So Tesla was positioned to ride the current of technological history.

The founders had no experience making cars, but realised car companies now outsourced everything, even styling. Manufacturing partners were ready to be connected with; a 'fab-less' car company was possible.[3] Production began 2008. The business plan described the Roadster as 'disruptive' technology[1] – a high-end sports car with lower price and emissions than competitors – and a lower resource cost to the planet.

Roadster

0–60 mph < 3.9 seconds; 100mpg; world-class handling; zero tailpipe emissions; 300 mile range; zero maintenance for 100,00 miles (other than tyres); 50% price of the cheapest competitive sports car.[1]

Tesla's strategy was:

to enter at the high end of the market, where customers are prepared to pay a premium, and then drive down market as fast as possible to higher unit volume and lower prices with each successive model. . . . all free cash flow is plowed back into R&D to drive down the costs and bring the follow on products to market as fast as possible. When someone buys the Tesla Roadster sports car, they are actually helping pay for development of the low cost family car.[2]

Tesla aimed to provide zero emission electric power generation from their 'giga' battery factory in line with their 'overarching purpose . . . to help expedite the move from a mine-and-burn hydrocarbon economy towards a solar electric economy.'[2] In 2015, Tesla Energy was launched selling batteries for home and business use.

Edison didn't invent the light bulb, but he made it affordable and accessible through his electric system.[3] Tesla is also offering an energy system for a world of electric vehicles, homes and businesses, using batteries.

Sources: (1) E. Musk, 'The Secret Tesla Motors Master Plan (just between you and me)', 2 August 2006; (2) D. Baer, 'The making of Tesla: invention, betrayal, and the birth of the Roadster', *Business Insider*, 11 November 2014; (3) J. Suskewicz, 'Tesla's new strategy is over 100 years old', *Harvard Business Review*, May 2015.

Questions

1 How does Tesla Motor's strategy fit with the various strategy definitions in Figure 1.1?

2 What seems to account for Tesla's success?

- *The long term.* Strategies are typically measured over years, for some organisations a decade or more. The importance of a long-term perspective on strategy is emphasised by the 'three horizons' framework in Figure 1.2. The **three-horizons framework suggests organisations should think of themselves as comprising three types of business or activity, defined by their 'horizons' in terms of years.** *Horizon 1* businesses are basically the current core activities. In the case of Tesla Motors, Horizon 1 includes the original Tesla Roadster car and subsequent models. Horizon 1 businesses need defending and extending, but the expectation is that in the long term they will likely be flat or declining in terms of profits (or whatever else the organisation values). *Horizon 2* businesses are emerging activities that should provide new sources of profit. For Tesla, that might include the new mega-battery business. Finally, there are *Horizon 3* possibilities, for which nothing is sure. These are typically risky research and development (R&D) projects, start-up ventures, test-market pilots or similar: at Tesla, these might be further solar electric initiatives, rockets and space transportation. For a fast-moving organisation like Tesla, *Horizon 3* might generate profits a few years from the present time. In a pharmaceutical company, where the R&D and regulatory processes for a new drug take many years, *Horizon 3* might be a decade ahead. While timescales might differ, the basic point about the 'three-horizons' framework is that managers need to avoid focusing on the short-term issues of their existing activities. Strategy involves pushing out Horizon 1 as far as possible, at the same time as looking to Horizons 2 and 3.

- *Strategic direction.* Over the years, strategies follow some kind of long-term direction or trajectory. The strategic direction of Tesla Motors is from the original electric car to a diversified set of solar power offerings. Sometimes a strategic direction only emerges as a coherent pattern over time. Typically, however, managers and entrepreneurs try to set the direction of their strategy according to long-term *objectives*. In private-sector businesses, the objective guiding strategic direction is usually maximising profits for shareholders. However, profits do not always set strategic direction. First, public-sector and charity organisations may set their strategic direction according to other objectives: for example, a sports club's objective may be to move up from one league to a higher one. Second, even in the private sector profit is not always the sole criterion for strategy. Thus family

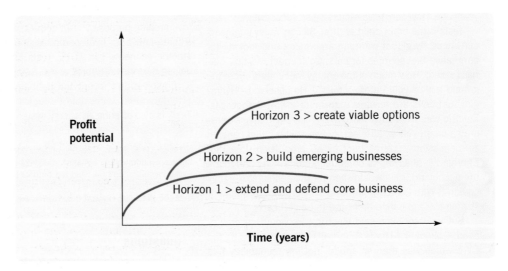

Figure 1.2 Three horizons for strategy

Note: 'profit' on the vertical axis can be replaced by non-profit objectives; 'business' can refer to any set of activities; 'time' can refer to a varying number of years.

Source: M. Baghai, S. Coley and D. White, *The Alchemy of Growth,* Texere Publishers, 2000, Figure 1.1, p. 5.

businesses may sometimes sacrifice the maximisation of profits for family objectives, for example passing down the management of the business to the next generation. The objectives behind strategic direction always need close scrutiny.

- *Organisation*. In this book, organisations are not treated as discrete, unified entities. Organisations involve many relationships, both internally and externally. This is because organisations typically have many internal and external *stakeholders*, in other words people and groups that depend on the organisation and upon which the organisation itself depends. Internally, organisations are filled with people, typically with diverse, competing and more or less reasonable views of what should be done. At Tesla, co-founder and original CEO Martin Eberhard was fired by new Chairman Elon Musk. In strategy, therefore, it is always important to look *inside* organisations and to consider the people involved and their different interests and views. Externally, organisations are surrounded by important relationships, for example with suppliers, customers, alliance partners, regulators and investors. For Tesla, relationships with investors and advertisers are crucial. Strategy therefore is also vitally concerned with an organisation's external *boundaries:* in other words, questions about what to include within the organisation and how to manage important relationships with what is kept outside.

Because strategy typically involves managing people, relationships and resources, the subject is sometimes called 'strategic management'. This book takes the view that managing is always important in strategy. Good strategy is about the practicalities of managing as well as the analysis of strategising.

1.2.2 The purpose of strategy: mission, vision, values and objectives

What is a strategy for? Harvard University's Cynthia Montgomery[3] argues that the core of a strategist's job is defining and expressing a clear and motivating purpose for the organisation. Even for private-sector organisations this is generally more than simple profit-maximisation as long-term prosperity and employee motivation usually require expressions of purpose that go beyond just profits. According to Montgomery, the stated purpose of the organisation should address two related questions: *how* does the organisation make a difference; and *for whom* does the organisation make that difference? If the stakeholders of an organisation can relate to such a purpose it can be highly motivating. Indeed, research by Jim Collins and Jerry Porras suggests that the long-run success of many US corporations – such as Disney, General Electric or 3M – can be attributed (at least in part) to the clear guidance and motivation offered by such statements of purpose.[4]

There are four ways in which organisations typically define their purpose:

- A **mission statement aims to provide employees and stakeholders with clarity about what the organisation is fundamentally there to do.** This is often expressed in the apparently simple but challenging question: 'What business are we in?' Two linked questions that can clarify an organisation's 'business' are: 'What would be lost if the organisation did not exist?'; and 'How do we make a difference?' Though they do not use the term 'mission statement', Collins and Porras[5] suggest that understanding the fundamental mission can be done by starting with a descriptive statement of what the organisation actually does, then repeatedly delving deeper into the organisation purpose by asking 'why do we do this?' They use the example of managers in a gravel and asphalt company arriving at the conclusion that its mission is to make people's lives better by improving the quality of built structures. At Southampton University the mission includes educating students, training the next generation of researchers and addressing social issues.

- A **vision statement is concerned with the future the organisation seeks to create.** The vision typically expresses an aspiration that will enthuse, gain commitment and stretch performance. So here the question is: 'What do we want to achieve?' Porras and Collins suggest managers can identify this by asking: 'If we were sitting here in twenty years what do we want to have created or achieved?' They cite the example of Henry Ford's original vision in the very early days of automobile production that the ownership of a car should be within the reach of everyone. For the Swedish music site Spotify, the vision is to become 'the Operating System of music', a universal platform for listening just as Microsoft is for office software.

- **Statements of corporate values communicate the underlying and enduring core 'principles' that guide an organisation's strategy and define the way that the organisation should operate.** For example, Alphabet (previously Google) famously includes in its values 'you can be serious without a suit', 'fast is better than slow' and 'don't be evil'. It is important that these values are enduring, so a question to ask is: 'Would these values change with circumstances?' And if the answer is 'yes' then they are not 'core' and not 'enduring'. An example is the importance of leading-edge research in some universities. Whatever the constraints on funding, such universities hold to the enduring centrality of research. On the other hand, as Alphabet has grown and diversified, some critics wonder whether the company still abides by its principle of 'don't be evil' (see Chapter 13 end case).

- **Objectives are statements of specific outcomes that are to be achieved.** These are often expressed in precise financial terms, for instance, the level of sales, profits or share valuation in one, two or three years' time.[6] Organisations may also have quantifiable market-based objectives, such as market share, customer service, repeat business and so on. Sometimes objectives focus on the basis of competitive advantage: for example, low-cost airlines such as RyanAir set objectives on turnaround time for their aircraft because this is at the core of their distinctive low-cost advantage. Increasingly, organisations are also setting objectives referred to as 'the triple bottom line', by which is meant not only economic objectives such as those above, but also environmental and social objectives to do with their corporate responsibility to wider society (see Section 5.4.1).

Although visions, missions and values may be liable to become bland and too wide-ranging,[7] they can offer more enduring sources of direction and motivation than the concrete nature of objectives. It is therefore crucial that vision, mission and values are meaningful when included in strategy statements.

1.2.3 Strategy statements

David Collis and Michael Rukstad[8] at the Harvard Business School argue that all entrepreneurs and managers should be able to summarise their organisation's strategy with a 'strategy statement'. **Strategy statements should have three main themes: the fundamental *goals* (mission, vision or objectives) that the organisation seeks; the *scope* or domain of the organisation's activities; and the particular *advantages* or capabilities it has to deliver all of these.**

Mission, vision and objectives have been described in Section 1.2.2 so here we concentrate on the other two main themes, *scope* and *advantage*, with examples of all five given in Illustration 1.2:

- *Scope.* An organisation's scope or domain refers to three dimensions: customers or clients; geographical location; and extent of internal activities ('vertical integration'). For a university, scope questions are two-fold: first, which academic departments to have (a business

ILLUSTRATION 1.2   Strategy statements

Both Samsung Electronics, the Korean telecommunications, computing and TV giant, and Southampton University, a leading British university, publish a good deal about their strategies.

Samsung Electronics

At Samsung, we follow a simple business philosophy: to devote our talent and technology to creating superior products and services that contribute to a better global society.

Every day, our people bring this philosophy to life. Our leaders search for the brightest talent from around the world, and give them the resources they need to be the best at what they do. The result is that all of our products – from memory chips that help businesses store vital knowledge to mobile phones that connect people across continents – have the power to enrich lives. And that's what making a better global society is all about.

As stated in its new motto, Samsung Electronics' vision [. . .] is, 'Inspire the World, Create the Future'. This new vision reflects Samsung Electronics' commitment to inspiring its communities by leveraging Samsung's three key strengths: 'New Technology', 'Innovative Products' and 'Creative Solutions'. As part of this vision, Samsung has mapped out a specific plan of reaching $400 billion in revenue and becoming one of the world's top five brands by 2020. To this end, Samsung has also established three strategic approaches in its management: 'Creativity', 'Partnership' and 'Talent'.

As we build on our previous accomplishments, we look forward to exploring new territories, including health, medicine, and biotechnology. Samsung is committed to being a creative leader in new markets, becoming No. 1 business in the Global IT industry and in the Global top 5.

Southampton University strategy

The university's core mission is to change the world for the better. It is an exceptional place whose people achieve remarkable things. We are a world-leading, research-intensive university, with a strong educational offering, renowned for our innovation and enterprise. Our strategy is about our aspirations – building our reputation and being simply better than our competitors.

We will increase our rankings to be in the top 10 (UK) and top 100 internationally. This will increase our reputation, which will increase our ranking.

A reputation for delivering excellence and an exemplary student experience will lead to greater demand from the best student applicants, sustained support from research funders and strong support from our alumni. We aim to achieve:

1 *Collegiality*: providing excellent staff experience, improving management and leadership throughout, developing agile governance, increasing risk appetite.

2 *Internal quality*: improve student experience to amongst the best in the UK's National Student Survey, develop high quality systems and infrastructure, improve quality of research applications, develop £5m+ strategic partnerships, raise admission standards, increase international student numbers, improve student employability, recruit and retain high quality staff.

3 *National and international recognition*: improve league table rankings and reputation, improve quality of education, grow international alumni community, deliver impactful research.

4 *Sustainability*: deliver the ability to invest, develop sustainable smooth income, improve research overhead recovery, improve productivity, increase revenue from other sources.

Sources: Edited extract from the University of Southampton *Simply Better: The University Strategy*, www.southampton.ac.uk.

Questions

1 Construct short strategy statements covering the goals, scope and advantage of Samsung and the Southampton University. How much do the different private- and public-sector contexts matter?

2 Construct a strategy statement for your own organisation (university, sports club or employer). What implications might this statement have for change in your organisation?

school, an engineering department and so on); second, which activities to do internally themselves (vertically integrate) and which to externalise to subcontractors (for example, whether to manage campus restaurants in-house or to subcontract them).

- *Advantage.* This part of a strategy statement describes how the organisation will achieve the objectives it has set for itself in its chosen domain. In competitive environments, this refers to the *competitive* advantage: for example, how a particular company or sports club will achieve goals in the face of competition from other companies or clubs. In order to achieve a particular goal, the organisation needs to be better than others seeking the same goal. In the public sector, advantage might refer simply to the organisation's capability in general. But even public-sector organisations frequently need to show that their capabilities are not only adequate, but superior to other rival departments or perhaps to private-sector contractors.

Collis and Rukstad suggest that strategy statements covering goals, scope and advantage should be no more than 35 words long. *The three themes are deliberately made highly concise.* Brevity keeps such statements focused on the essentials and makes them easy to remember and communicate. Thus for Tesla, a strategy statement might be: 'To accelerate the advent of a sustainable solar economy by developing and incorporating superior battery-based technologies into compelling mass market electric products and bringing them to market as soon as possible.' The strategy statement of Swedish multinational group IKEA is a little more specific: 'To create a better everyday life for the many people [by offering] a wide range of well-designed, functional home furnishing products at prices so low that as many people as possible will be able to afford them.' Of course, such strategy statements are not always fulfilled. Circumstances may change in unexpected ways. In the meantime, however, they can provide a useful guide both to managers in their decision-making and to employees and others who need to understand the direction in which the organisation is going. The ability to give a clear strategy statement is a good test of managerial competence in an organisation.

As such, strategy statements are relevant to a wide range of organisations. For example, a small entrepreneurial start-up can use a strategy statement to persuade investors and lenders of its viability. Public-sector organisations need strategy statements not only for themselves, but to reassure clients, funders and regulators that their priorities are the right ones. Voluntary organisations need persuasive strategy statements in order to inspire volunteers and donors. Thus organisations of all kinds frequently publish materials relevant to such strategy statements on their websites or annual reports. Illustration 1.2 provides published materials on the strategies of two very different organisations: the technology giant Samsung from the private sector and Southampton University in the UK from the public sector.

1.2.4 Levels of strategy

So far we have considered an organisation as a whole, but inside an organisation, strategies can exist at three main levels.

- **Corporate-level strategy** is concerned with the overall scope of an organisation and how value is added to the constituent businesses of the organisational whole. Corporate-level strategy issues include geographical scope, diversity of products or services, acquisitions of new businesses, and how resources are allocated between the different elements of the organisation. For Tesla, moving from car manufacture to battery production for homes and businesses is a corporate-level strategy. Being clear about corporate-level strategy is important: determining the range of businesses to include is the basis of other strategic decisions, such as acquisitions and alliances.

- **Business-level strategy is about how the individual businesses should compete in their particular markets** (this is often called 'competitive strategy'). These might be stand-alone businesses, for instance entrepreneurial start-ups, or 'business units' within a larger corporation. Business-level strategy typically concerns issues such as innovation, appropriate scale and response to competitors' moves. For Tesla this means rolling out a lower cost electric car to build volume and capture market share in advance of potential competitor entry. In the public sector, the equivalent of business-level strategy is decisions about how units (such as individual hospitals or schools) should provide best-value services. Where the businesses are units within a larger organisation, business-level strategies should clearly fit with corporate-level strategy.

- **Functional strategies are concerned with how the components of an organisation deliver effectively the corporate- and business-level strategies in terms of resources, processes and people.** For example, Tesla continues to raise external finance to fund its rapid growth: its functional strategy is partly geared to meeting investment needs. In most businesses, successful business strategies depend to a large extent on decisions that are taken, or activities that occur, at the functional level. Functional decisions need therefore to be closely linked to business-level strategy. They are vital to successful strategy implementation.

This need to link the corporate, business and functional levels underlines the importance of *integration* in strategy. Each level needs to be aligned with the others. The demands of integrating levels define an important characteristic of strategy: strategy is typically *complex*, requiring careful and sensitive management. Strategy is rarely simple.

1.3 THE *EXPLORING STRATEGY* FRAMEWORK

This book is structured around a three-part framework that emphasises the interconnected nature of strategic issues. The *Exploring Strategy* Framework **includes understanding *the strategic position* of an organisation; assessing *strategic choices* for the future; and managing *strategy in action*.** Figure 1.3 shows these elements and defines the broad coverage of this book. Together, the three elements provide a practical template for studying strategic situations. The following sections of this chapter will introduce the strategic issues that arise under each of these elements of the *Exploring Strategy* Framework. But first it is important to understand why the framework is drawn in this particular way.

Figure 1.3 could have shown the framework's three elements in a linear sequence – first understanding the strategic position, then making strategic choices and finally turning strategy into action. Indeed, this logical sequence is implicit in the definition of strategy given by Alfred Chandler (Figure 1.1) and many other textbooks on strategy. However, as Henry Mintzberg recognises, in practice the elements of strategy do not always follow this linear sequence. Choices often have to be made before the position is fully understood. Sometimes too a proper understanding of the strategic position can only be built from the experience of trying a strategy out in action. The real-world feedback from launching a new product is often far better at uncovering the true strategic position than remote analysis carried out in a strategic planning department at head office.

The interconnected circles of Figure 1.3 are designed to emphasise this potentially non-linear nature of strategy. Position, choices and action should be seen as closely related, and in practice none has priority over another. It is only for structural convenience that this book divides its subject matter into three sections; the book's sequence is not meant to suggest that the process of strategy must follow a logical series of distinct steps. The three

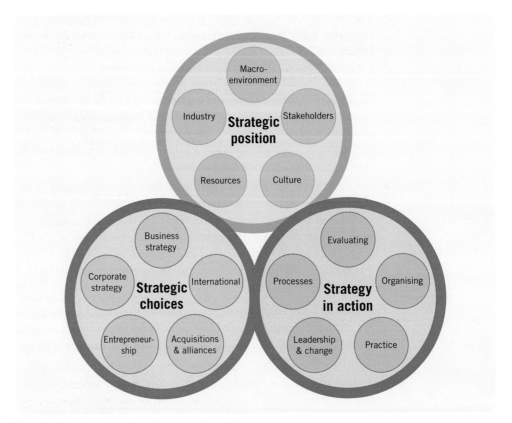

Figure 1.3 The *Exploring Strategy* Framework

circles are overlapping and interdependent. The evidence provided in later chapters will suggest that strategy rarely occurs in tidy ways and that it is better not to expect it to do so.

However, the *Exploring Strategy* Framework does provide a comprehensive and integrated schema for analysing an organisation's position, considering the choices it has and putting strategies into action. Each of the chapters can be seen as asking fundamental strategy questions and providing the essential concepts and techniques to help answer them. Working systematically through questions and answers provides the basis for persuasive strategy recommendations.

1.3.1 Strategic position

The **strategic position** is concerned with the impact on strategy of the macro-environment, the industry environment, the organisation's strategic capability (resources and competences), the organisation's stakeholders and the organisation's culture. Understanding these five factors is central for evaluating future strategy. These issues, and the fundamental questions associated with them, are covered in the following five chapters of Part I of this book:

- *Macro-environment*. Organisations operate in complex multi-level environments. At the macro level, organisations are influenced by political, economic, social, technological, ecological and legal forces. The macro-environment varies widely in terms of its dynamism. The fundamental question here relates to the *opportunities* and *threats* available to the organisation in complex, changing environments. Chapter 2 provide key frameworks to help in focusing on priority issues in the face of environmental complexity and dynamism.

- *Industry environment*. At the industry level of analysis, competitors, suppliers and customers present challenges to an organisation. A fundamental question is: how can an organisation manage industry forces? Industry environments can vary widely in their attractiveness and present *opportunities* and *threats*. Chapter 3 provides key frameworks to help identify major forces at work in different industries.

- *Strategic capability*. Each organisation has its own strategic capabilities, made up of its *resources* (e.g. machines and buildings) and *competences* (e.g. technical and managerial skills). The fundamental question on capability regards the organisation's *strengths* and *weaknesses* (for example, where is it at a competitive advantage or disadvantage?). Are the organisation's capabilities adequate to the challenges of its environment and the demands of its goals? Chapter 4 provides tools and concepts for analysing such resources and capabilities.

- *Stakeholders*. There are many actors who hold a 'stake' in the future of every organisation – not just owners, but employees, customers, suppliers and more. The fourth fundamental question then is: how can the organisation be aligned around a common purpose? An organisation's key stakeholders should define its purpose. Understanding their different interests to identify this purpose is important. *Corporate governance* then matters as it translates this purpose into strategy: how to ensure that managers stick to the agreed purpose? Questions of purpose and accountability raise issues of *corporate social responsibility* and *ethics:* is the purpose an appropriate one and are managers sticking to it? Chapter 5 provides concepts for addressing these issues of purpose.

- *Culture*. Organisational cultures can also influence strategy. So can the cultures of a particular industry or particular country. These cultures are typically a product of an organisation's *history*. The consequence of history and culture can be *strategic drift*, a failure to create necessary change. A fundamental question here, therefore, is: how does culture fit with the required strategy? Chapter 6 demonstrates how managers can analyse, challenge and sometimes turn to their advantage the various cultural influences on strategy.

The *Exploring Strategy* Framework (Illustration 1.1) points to the following positioning issues for Tesla Motors. What is the future of the company given the growing social, political, ecological and legal demands for businesses to be environmentally sustainable? Are its distinctive capabilities really valued sufficiently by consumers to provide a financial return to investors and to allow sustained investment in further innovative products? How will Tesla cope with rising competition from car industry giants who are now selling electric and hybrid cars?

1.3.2 Strategic choices

Strategic choices involve the options for strategy in terms of both the *directions* in which strategy might move and the *methods* by which strategy might be pursued. For instance, an organisation might have a range of strategic directions open to it: the organisation could diversify into new products; it could enter new international markets; or it could transform its existing products and markets through radical innovation. These various directions could be pursued by different methods: the organisation could acquire a business already active in the product or market area; it could form alliances with relevant organisations that might help its new strategy; or it could try to pursue its strategies on its own. Typical strategic choices, and the related fundamental questions, are covered in the five chapters that make up Part II of this book, as follows:

- *Business strategy and models*. There are strategic choices in terms of how the organisation seeks to compete at the individual business level. For example, a business unit could choose to be the lowest cost competitor in a market, or the highest quality. The fundamental question here, then, is what strategy and what business model should a company use to compete? Key dilemmas for business-level strategy, and ways of resolving them, are discussed in Chapter 7.

- *Corporate strategy and diversification.* The highest level of an organisation is typically concerned with issues of corporate scope, in other words, which businesses to include in the portfolio. This relates to the appropriate degree of *diversification,* with regard to products offered and markets served. Corporate-level strategy is also concerned with internal relationships, both between business units and with the corporate head office. Chapter 8 provides tools for assessing diversification strategies and the appropriate relationships within the corporate portfolio.

- *International strategy.* Internationalisation is a form of diversification, but into new geographical markets. Here the fundamental question is: where internationally should the organisation compete? Chapter 9 examines how to prioritise various international options and key strategies for pursuing them.

- *Entrepreneurship and innovation.* Most existing organisations have to innovate constantly simply to survive. Entrepreneurship, the creation of a new enterprise, is an act of innovation too. A fundamental question, therefore, is whether the organisation is innovating appropriately. Chapter 10 considers key choices about innovation and entrepreneurship, and helps in selecting between them.

- *Mergers, acquisitions and alliances.* Organisations have to make choices about methods for pursuing their strategies. Many organisations prefer to build new businesses with their own resources. Other organisations develop by acquiring other businesses or forming alliances with complementary partners. The fundamental question in Chapter 11, therefore, is whether to buy another company, ally or to go it alone.

Again, issues of strategic choice are live in the case of Tesla Motors (Illustration 1.1). The *Exploring Strategy* Framework asks the following kinds of questions here. Should Tesla continue to produce new higher volume cheaper cars or remain specialised? How far should it widen the scope of its businesses: is producing batteries for homes really helping or detracting from car production? Where should Tesla innovate next?

1.3.3 Strategy in action

Managing **strategy in action is about how strategies are formed and how they are implemented.** The emphasis is on the practicalities of managing. These issues are covered in the five chapters of Part III, and include the following, each with their own fundamental questions:

- *Strategy performance and evaluation.* Managers have to decide whether existing and forecast performance is satisfactory and then choose between options that might improve it. The fundamental evaluation questions are as follows: are the options *suitable* in terms of matching opportunities and threats; are they *acceptable* in the eyes of significant stakeholders; and are they *feasible* given the capabilities available? Chapter 12 introduces a range of financial and non-financial techniques for appraising performance and evaluating strategic options.

- *Strategy development processes.* Strategies are often developed through formal *planning* processes. But sometimes the strategies an organisation actually pursues are *emergent* – in other words, accumulated patterns of ad hoc decisions, bottom-up initiatives and rapid responses to the unanticipated. Given the scope for emergence, the fundamental question is: what kind of strategy process should an organisation have? Chapter 13 addresses the question of whether to plan strategy in detail or leave plenty of opportunities for emergence.

- *Organising.* Once a strategy is developed, the organisation needs to organise for successful implementation. Each strategy requires its own specific configuration of *structures* and *systems.* The fundamental question, therefore, is: what kinds of structures and systems are required for the chosen strategy? Chapter 14 introduces a range of structures and systems and provides frameworks for deciding between them.

- *Leadership and strategic change.* In a dynamic world, strategy inevitably involves change. Managing change involves *leadership,* both at the top of the organisation and lower down. There is not just one way of leading change, however: there are different *styles* and different *levers* for change. So the fundamental question is: how should the organisation manage necessary changes entailed by the strategy? Chapter 15 therefore examines options for managing change, and considers how to choose between them.

- *Strategy practice.* Inside the broad processes of strategy development and change is a lot of hard, detailed work. The fundamental question in managing this work is: who should do what in the strategy process? Chapter 16 thus provides guidance on which *people* to include in the process; what *activities* they should do; and which *methodologies* can help them do it. These kinds of practicalities are a fitting end to the book and essential equipment for those who will have to go out and participate in strategy work themselves.

With regard to strategy in action, the *Exploring Strategy* Framework raises the following kinds of questions for Tesla. How will Tesla return value to shareholders going forwards? How will the rate of innovation at Tesla be maintained? Should Tesla move towards a more disciplined strategy development process rather than depend on the vision of Elon Musk? Does Tesla need more structure and systems? As Tesla grows, how should any changes that may be necessary be managed?

Thus the *Exploring Strategy* Framework offers a comprehensive way for analysing an organisation's position, considering alternative choices, and selecting and implementing strategies. In this sense, the fundamental questions in each chapter provide a comprehensive checklist for strategy. These fundamental questions are summed up in Table 1.1. Any assessment of an organisation's strategy will benefit from asking these questions systematically. The frameworks for answering these and related questions can be found in the respective chapters.

The logic of the *Exploring Strategy* Framework can be applied to our personal lives as much as to organisations. We all have to make decisions with long-run consequences for our futures and the issues involved are very similar. For example, in pursuing a career strategy, a job-seeker needs to understand the job market, evaluate their strengths and weaknesses, establish the range of job opportunities and decide what their career goals really are (positioning issues). The job-seeker then narrows down the options, makes some applications

Table 1.1 The strategy checklist

Sixteen fundamental questions in strategy		
Strategic position	**Strategic choices**	**Strategy in action**
• What are the macro-environmental opportunities and threats? • How can the organisation manage industry forces? • How are stakeholders aligned to the organisational purpose? • What resources and capabilities support the strategy? • How does culture fit the strategy?	• How should business units compete? • Which businesses to include in a portfolio? • Where should the organisation compete internationally? • Is the organisation innovating appropriately? • Should the organisation buy other companies, ally or go it alone?	• Are strategies suitable, acceptable and feasible? • What kind of strategy-making process is needed? • What are the required organisation structures and systems? • How should the organisation manage necessary changes? • Who should do what in the strategy process?

and finally gets an offer (choice issues). Once the job-seeker has chosen a job, he or she sets to work, adjusting their skills and behaviours to suit their new role (strategy in action). Just as in the non-linear, overlapping *Exploring Strategy* Framework, experience of the job will frequently amend the original strategic goals. Putting a career strategy into action produces better understanding of strengths and weaknesses and frequently leads to the setting of new career goals.

1.4 WORKING WITH STRATEGY

Strategy itself is a kind of work, and it is something that almost all levels of management have to engage in, not just top decision-makers. Middle and lower-level managers have to understand their organisation's strategic objectives and contribute to them as best they can. Managers have to communicate strategy to their teams, and will achieve greater performance from them the more convincing they are in doing so. Indeed, as responsibility is increasingly decentralised in many organisations, middle and lower-level managers play a growing part in shaping strategy themselves. Because they are closer to the daily realities of the business, lower-level managers can be a crucial source of ideas and feedback for senior management teams. Being able to participate in an organisation's 'strategic conversation' – engaging with senior managers on the big issues facing them – is therefore often part of what it takes to win promotion.[9]

For many managers, then, strategy is part of the job. However, there are specialist strategists as well, in both private and public sectors. Many large organisations have in-house strategic planning or analyst roles.[10] Typically requiring a formal business education of some sort, strategic planning is a potential career route for many readers of this book, especially after some functional experience. Strategy consulting has been a growth industry in the last decades, with the original leading firms such as McKinsey & Co., the Boston Consulting Group and Bain joined now by more generalist consultants such as Accenture, IBM Consulting and PwC, each with its own strategy consulting arm.[11] Again, business graduates are in demand for strategy consulting roles, such as that of Claudia in the opening example.[12]

The interviews in Illustration 1.3 give some insights into the different kinds of strategy work that managers and strategy specialists can do. Galina, the manager of an international subsidiary, Chantal, a strategy consultant, and Paul, heading a strategy office in a not-for-profit organisation, all have different experiences of strategy, but there are some common themes also. All find strategy work stimulating and rewarding. The two specialists, Chantal and Paul, talk more than Galina of analytical tools such as scenario analysis, sensitivity analysis and hypothesis testing. Galina discovered directly the practical challenges of real-world strategic planning, having to adapt the plan during the first few years in the UK. She emphasises the importance of flexibility in strategy and the value of getting her managers to see the 'whole picture' through involving them in strategy-making. But Chantal and Paul too are concerned with much more than just analysis. Chantal emphasises the importance of gaining 'traction' with clients, building consensus in order to ensure implementation. Paul also realises that delivering recommendations is just the beginning of the strategy process and getting buy-in from key stakeholders is critical for implementation. He sees strategy and delivery as intimately connected, with people involved in delivery needing an understanding of strategy to be effective, and strategists needing to understand delivery.

ILLUSTRATION 1.3 — Strategists

For Galina, Chantal and Paul, strategy is a large part of their jobs.

Galina

At the age of 33, after a start in marketing, Galina became managing director of a Russian-owned British IT company. As well as developing the strategy for her local business, she has to interact regularly with headquarters: 'Moscow is interested in the big picture, not just the details. They are interested in the future of the business.'

She had to adapt substantially the subsidiary's strategic plans:

'When we first came here, we had some ideas about strategy, but soon found the reality was very different to the plans. The strategy was not completely wrong, but in the second stage we had to change it a lot: we had to change techniques and adapt to the market. Now we are in the third stage, where we have the basics and need to focus on trends, to get ahead and be in the right place at the right time.'

Galina works closely with her management team on strategy, taking them on an annual 'strategy away-day' (see Chapter 16): 'Getting people together helps them see the whole picture, rather than just the bits they are responsible for. It is good to put all their separate realities together.'

Galina is enthusiastic about working on strategy:

'I like strategy work, definitely. The most exciting thing is to think about where we have come from and where we might be going. We started in a pub five years ago and we have somehow implemented what we were hoping for then. Strategy gives you a measure of success. It tells you how well you have done.'

Her advice is: 'Always have a strategy – have an ultimate idea in mind. But take feedback from the market and from your colleagues. Be ready to adjust the strategy: the adjustment is the most important.'

Chantal

Chantal is in her early thirties and has worked in Paris for one of the top three international strategy consultancies since graduating in business. Consulting was attractive to her originally because she liked the idea of helping organisations improve. She enjoys strategy consulting because 'I like solving problems. It's a bit like working on a mystery case: you have a problem and then you have to find a solution to fit the company, and help it grow and to be better.'

The work is intellectually challenging:

'Time horizons are short. You have to solve your case in two to three months. There's lots of pressure. It pushes you and helps you to learn yourself. There are just three to four in a team, so you will make a significant contribution to the project even as a junior. You have a lot of autonomy and you're making a contribution right from the start, and at quite a high level.'

Consulting work can involve financial and market modelling (see Chapters 3 and 12), interviewing clients and customers, and working closely with the client's own teams. Chantal explains:

'As a consultant, you spend a lot of time in building solid fact-based arguments that will help clients make business decisions. But as well as the facts, you have to have the ability to get traction. People have to agree, so you have to build consensus, to make sure that recommendations are supported and acted on.'

Chantal summarises the appeal of strategy consulting: 'I enjoy the learning, at a very high speed. There's the opportunity to increase your skills. One year in consulting is like two years in a normal business.'

Paul

In his early forties, Paul is a UK ex-pat in Saudi Arabia heading up a key part of the Strategy and Planning Office in a large hospital with a multi-million pound investment responsibility.

'Rational linear analysis is very important here. We have an abundance of data from all the major consultancies and a number of high-profile US academic advisors and need to assemble it for forecasting and trend analysis purposes. A great deal of time is taken crafting documents for key stakeholders. Informally we used a range of strategy tools and techniques including statistical analysis, scenario analysis (see Chapter 2), sensitivity analysis (see Chapter 12), hypothesis testing (see Chapter 16) and also carry out many internal surveys to monitor implementation progress.'

Paul has been surprised by the sheer amount of time and effort needed to consult key internal and external stakeholders personally: 'I have to consult every project manager and director and, more importantly, politically powerful and rich external stakeholders, regardless of their knowledge – and they have to be flattered to get buy-in.'

What Paul likes about the job is making a difference by 'changing people's perceptions, getting powerful individuals to make decisions and understand the reasons – rather than hiding behind endless committees (see Chapter 16).'

Source: interviews (interviewees anonymised).

Questions

1 Which of these strategy roles appeals to you most – manager of a business unit in a multinational, strategy consultant or in-house strategy specialist? Why?

2 What would you have to do to get such a role?

Strategy, therefore, is not just about abstract organisations. It is about linking analysis with implementation on the ground. It is complex work that real people do. An important aim of this book is to equip readers to do this work better.

1.5 STUDYING STRATEGY

This book is both comprehensive and serious about strategy. To understand the full range of strategy issues – from analysis to action – it is important to be open to the perspectives and insights of key disciplines such as economics, finance, sociology and psychology. To be serious about strategy means to draw as far as possible on rigorous research about these issues. This book aims for an evidence-based approach to strategy, hence the articles and books referenced at the end of each chapter.[13]

This book therefore covers equally the three main branches of strategy research: conventionally, these are known as strategy *context*, strategy *content* and strategy *process*. In terms of the *Exploring Strategy* Framework (Figure 1.3), context broadly relates to positioning, content to choice and process to action. Each of these branches contains various research streams whose lessons can be readily applied to practical questions of strategy issues. Figure 1.4 shows the three branches and their respective research streams: these are listed in the approximate historical order of their emergence as strong research streams, the arrows representing the continuously developing nature of each. In more detail, the three branches and the characteristic analytical approaches of their main research streams are as follows:

- *Strategy context* refers to multiple layers of environment, internal and external to organisations. All organisations need to take into account the opportunities and threats of their external environments. *Macro-environmental analysis* has been an enduring theme in strategy with early recognition of multiple pressures upon industries in the 1960s. Subsequently, researchers have focused upon various additional themes including institutional pressures establishing the 'rules of the game' within which companies operate. *Industry analysis* took off as a research tradition in the early 1980s, when Michael Porter showed

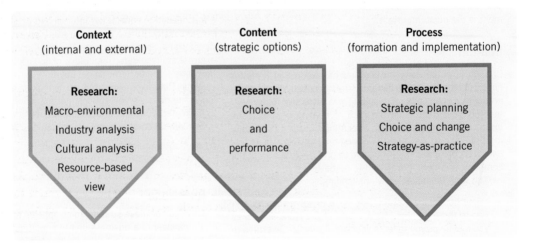

Figure 1.4 Strategy's three branches

how the tools of economics could be applied to understanding what makes industries attractive (or unattractive) to operate in.[14] From the 1980s too, *cultural analysts* have used sociological insights into human behaviour to point to the importance of shared cultural understandings about appropriate ways of acting. In the internal context, cultural analysts show that strategies are often influenced by the organisation's specific culture. In the external context, they show how strategies often have to fit with the surrounding industry or national cultures. *Resource-based view* researchers focus on internal context, looking for the unique characteristics of each organisation.[15] According to the resource-based view, the economic analysis of market imperfections, the psychological analysis of perceptual or emotional biases, and the sociological analysis of organisational cultures should reveal the particular characteristics (resources) that contribute to an organisation's specific competitive advantages and disadvantages.

- *Strategy content* concerns the content (or nature) of different strategies and their probability of success. Here the focus is on the merits of different strategic options. *Strategy and performance* researchers started by using economic analysis to understand the success of different types of diversification strategies. This research continues as the enduring central core of the strategy discipline, with an ever-growing list of issues addressed. For example, contemporary strategy and performance researchers examine various new innovation strategies, different kinds of internationalisation and all the complex kinds of alliance and networking strategies organisations adopt today. These researchers typically bring a tough economic scrutiny to strategy options. Their aim is to establish which types of strategies pay best and under what conditions. They refuse to take for granted broad generalisations about what makes a good strategy.

- *Strategy process,* broadly conceived, examines how strategies are formed and implemented. Research here provides a range of insights to help managers in the practical processes of managing strategy.[16] From the 1960s, researchers in the *strategic planning* tradition have drawn from economics and management science in order to design rational and analytical systems for the planning and implementing of strategy. However, strategy involves people: since the 1980s, *choice and change* researchers have been pointing to how the psychology of human perception and emotions, and the sociology of group politics and interests, tend to undermine rational analysis.[17] The advice of these researchers is to accept the irrational, messy realities of organisations, and to work with them, rather than to try to impose textbook rationality. Finally, *strategy-as-practice* researchers have recently been using micro-sociological approaches to closely examine the human realities of formal and informal strategy processes.[18] This tradition focuses attention on how people do strategy work, and the importance of having the right tools and skills.

From the above, it should be clear that studying strategy involves perspectives and insights from a range of academic disciplines. Issues need to be 'explored' from different points of view. A strategy chosen purely on economic grounds can easily be undermined by psychological and sociological factors. On the other hand, a strategy that is chosen on the psychological grounds of emotional enthusiasm, or for sociological reasons of cultural acceptability, is liable to fail if not supported by favourable economics. As underlined by the four strategy lenses to be introduced later, one perspective is rarely enough for good strategy. A complete analysis will typically need the insights of economics, psychology and sociology.

1.6 EXPLORING STRATEGY FURTHER

So far we have stressed that strategic issues are typically complex, best explored from a number of points of views. There is no simple, universal rule for good strategy. This section introduces two further ways of exploring strategy: one depending on context, the other depending on perspective.

1.6.1 Exploring strategy in different contexts

Although the basic elements of the *Exploring Strategy* Framework are relevant in most circumstances, how they play out precisely is likely to differ according to organisational contexts. To return to Illustration 1.2, both Samsung and Southampton University share some fundamental issues about how to compete and what activities they should have in their portfolio. However, for a Korean electronics company and a British university, the role of institutions, particularly government, varies widely, affecting the freedom to choose and the ability to change. In applying the *Exploring Strategy* Framework, it is therefore useful to ask what kinds of issues are likely to be particularly significant in the specific context being considered. To illustrate, this section shows how issues arising from the *Exploring Strategy* Framework can vary in three important organisational contexts.

- *Small businesses.* With regard to positioning, small businesses will certainly need to attend closely to the environment, because they are so vulnerable to change. But, especially in small entrepreneurial and family businesses, the most important positioning issue will often be strategic purpose: this will not necessarily just be profit, but might include objectives such as independence, family control, handing over to the next generation and maybe even a pleasant lifestyle. The range of strategic choices is likely to be narrower: for a small business, acquisitions may not be affordable, though they may have to decide whether to allow themselves to be acquired. Some issues of strategy in action will be different, for example strategic change processes will not involve the same challenges as for large, complex organisations.

- *Multinational corporations.* In this context, positioning in a complex global marketplace will be very important. Each significant geographical market may call for a separate analysis of the business environment. Likewise, operating in many different countries will raise positioning issues of culture: variations in national culture imply different demands in the marketplace and different managerial styles internally. Strategic choices are likely to be dominated by international strategy questions about which geographical markets to serve. The scale and geographical reach of most multinationals point to significant issues for strategy-in-action, particularly those of organisational structure and strategic change.

- *Public sector and not-for-profits.* Positioning issues of competitive advantage will be important even in these contexts, but have a different flavour. Charitable not-for-profits typically compete for funds from donors; public-sector organisations, such as schools and hospitals, often compete on measures such as quality or service. The positioning issue of purpose is likely to be very important too. In the absence of a clear, focused objective such as profit, purpose in the public sector and not-for-profits can be ambiguous and contentious. Strategic choice issues may be narrower than in the private sector: for example, there may be constraints on diversification. Strategy in action issues often need close attention, leadership and change typically being very challenging in large public-sector organisations.

In short, while drawing on the same basic principles, strategy analysis is likely to vary in focus across different contexts. As the next section will indicate, it is often helpful therefore to apply different lenses to strategy problems.

1.6.2 Exploring strategy through different 'strategy lenses'

Exploring means looking for new and different things. Exploring strategy involves searching for new angles on strategic problems. A comprehensive assessment of an organisation's strategy needs more than one perspective. We introduce 'the strategy lenses' as distinct, theoretically-informed perspectives on strategy. **The strategy lenses are ways of looking at strategy issues differently in order to generate additional insights.** Different perspectives will help you criticise prevailing approaches and raise new issues or solutions. Thus, although drawn from academic theory, the lenses should also be highly practical in the job of doing strategy.

The four lenses are described fully at the end of Part I, after you have had a chance to take on board some key strategy frameworks for analysing strategic position. We shall return to them as well through brief *commentaries* at the end of Parts II and III. The following is therefore just a brief introduction to the lenses:

- *Strategy as design* views strategy development as 'designed' in the abstract, as an architect might design a building using pens, rulers and paper. Taking a design lens to a strategic problem means valuing hard facts and objectivity. It's about being systematic, analytical and logical.

- *Strategy as experience* recognises that an organisation's future strategy is often heavily influenced by its experience and that of its managers. Taken-for-granted assumptions and ways of doing things, embedded in people's personal experience and in organisational culture, will drive strategy. Strategy is likely to build on rules of thumb, appeals to precedent, standard fixes, biases and routines of key decision-makers.

- *Strategy as variety.*[19] Neither of the above lenses is likely to uncover radical new ideas in strategy as a design approach risks being too rigid and top-down and experience builds too much on the past. The variety lens sees strategy as emergent from within and around organisations as new ideas bubble up through an unpredictable process in response to an uncertain and changing environment.

- *Strategy as discourse* focuses attention on the ways managers use language to frame strategic problems, make strategy proposals, debate issues and then finally communicate strategic decisions. Strategy discourse becomes a tool for managers to shape 'objective' strategic analyses in their favour and to gain influence, power and legitimacy – strategy 'talk' matters.

None of these lenses is likely to offer a complete view of a strategic situation. The point of the lenses is to encourage the exploration of different perspectives: first from one point of view and then from another. This might help in recognising how otherwise logical strategic initiatives might be held back by cultural experience, unexpected ideas and self-interested strategy discourse.

SUMMARY

- Strategy is the *long-term direction* of an organisation.

- The work of strategy is to define and express the purpose of an organisation through its *mission*, *vision*, *values* and *objectives*.

- Ideally a *strategy statement* should include an organisation's *goals*, *scope* of activities and the *advantages* or *capabilities* it brings to these goals and activities.

- *Corporate-level strategy* is concerned with an organisation's overall scope; *business-level strategy* is concerned with how to compete; and *functional strategy* is concerned with how corporate- and business-level strategies are actually delivered.

- The *Exploring Strategy* Framework has three major elements: understanding the *strategic position*, making *strategic choices* for the future and managing *strategy in action*.

- Strategy work is done by *managers* throughout an organisation, as well as specialist *strategic planners* and *strategy consultants*.

- Research on strategy *context*, *content* and *process* shows how the analytical perspectives of economics, finance, sociology and psychology can all provide practical insights for approaching strategy issues.

- Although the fundamentals of strategy may be similar, strategy varies by *organisational context*, for example, small business, multinational or public sector.

- Strategic issues can be viewed critically from a variety of perspectives, as exemplified by the four *strategy lenses* of *design*, *experience*, *variety* and *discourse*.

WORK ASSIGNMENTS

✱ Denotes more advanced work assignments.
* Refers to a case study in the Text and Cases edition.

1.1   Drawing on Figure 1.2 as a guide, write a strategy statement for an organisation of your choice (for example, the Airbnb end of chapter case, or your university), drawing on strategy materials in the organisation's annual report or website.

1.2   Using the *Exploring Strategy* Framework of Figure 1.3, map key issues relating to strategic position, strategic choices and strategy in action for either the Airbnb or Glastonbury* cases, or an organisation with which you are familiar (for example, your university).

1.3   Go to the website of one of the major strategy consultants such as Bain, the Boston Consulting Group or McKinsey & Co. (see reference 11 below). What does the website tell you about the nature of strategy consulting work? Would you enjoy that work?

1.4✱   Using Figure 1.3 as a guide, show how the elements of strategic management differ in:

(a) a small or family business (e.g. Adnams*)

(b) a large multinational business (e.g. SABMiller or AB InBev in the Megabrew* case, Kraft Foods in the Mondelez* case)

(c) a non-profit organisation (e.g. Aurizon or King Faisal Hospital*).

RECOMMENDED KEY READINGS

It is always useful to read around a topic. As well as the specific references below, we particularly highlight:

- Two stimulating overviews of strategic thinking in general, aimed particularly at practicing managers, are C. Montgomery, *The Strategist: Be the Leader your Business Needs*, Harper Business, 2012; and R. Rumelt, *Good Strategy/Bad Strategy: the Difference and Why it Matters*, Crown Business, 2011.

- Two accessible articles on what strategy is, and might not be, are M. Porter, 'What is strategy?', *Harvard Business Review*, November–December 1996, pp. 61–78; and F. Fréry, 'The fundamental dimensions of strategy', *MIT*

Sloan Management Review, vol. 48, no. 1 (2006), pp. 71–75.

- For contemporary developments in strategy practice, consult business newspapers such as the *Financial Times, Les Echos* and the *Wall Street Journal* and business magazines such as *Business Week, The Economist, L'Expansion* and *Manager-Magazin*. Several of these have well-informed Asian editions. See also the websites of the leading strategy consulting firms: www.mckinsey.com; www.bcg.com; and www.bain.com.

REFERENCES

1. The question 'What is strategy?' is discussed in R. Whittington, *What Is Strategy – and Does it Matter?*, International Thomson, 1993/2000; and M.E. Porter, 'What is strategy?', *Harvard Business Review*, November–December 1996, pp. 61–78.

2. T. Zenger, 'What is the theory of your firm?', *Harvard Business Review*, June 2013, pp. 72–80.

3. Cynthia A. Montgomery, 'Putting leadership back into strategy', *Harvard Business Review*, January 2008, pp. 54–60.

4. See J. Collins and J. Porras, *Built to Last: Successful Habits of Visionary Companies*, Harper Business, 2002.

5. J. Collins and J. Porras, 'Building your company's vision', *Harvard Business Review*, September–October 1996, pp. 65–77.

6. See Sayan Chatterjee, 'Core objectives: clarity in designing strategy', *California Management Review*, vol. 47, no. 2 (2005), pp. 33–49. For some advantages of ambiguity, see J. Sillince, P. Jarzabkowski and D. Shaw, 'Shaping strategic action through the rhetorical construction and exploitation of ambiguity', *Organization Science*, vol. 22, no. 2 (2011), pp. 1–21.

7. For example, see B. Bartkus, M. Glassman and B. McAfee, 'Mission statements: are they smoke and mirrors?', *Business Horizons*, vol. 43, no. 6 (2000), pp. 23–8.

8. D. Collis and M. Rukstad, 'Can you say what your strategy is?' *Harvard Business Review*, April 2008, pp. 63–73.

9. F. Westley, 'Middle managers and strategy: microdynamics of inclusion', *Strategic Management Journal*, vol. 11, no. 5 (1990), pp. 337–51.

10. For insights about in-house strategy roles, see D. N. Angwin, S. Paroutis and S. Mitson, 'Connecting up strategy: are strategy directors a missing link?' *California Management Review*, vol. 51, no. 3 (2009), pp. 74–94.

11. The major strategy consulting firms have a wealth of information on strategy careers and strategy in general: see www.mckinsey.com; www.bcg.com; www.bain.com.

12. University careers advisers can usually provide good advice on strategy consulting and strategic planning opportunities. See also www.vault.com.

13. For reviews of the contemporary state of strategy as a discipline, see J. Mahoney and A. McGahan, 'The field of strategic management within the evolving science of strategic organization', *Strategic Organization*, vol. 5, no. 1 (2007), pp. 79–99; and R. Whittington, 'Big strategy/small strategy', *Strategic Organization*, vol. 10, no. 3 (2012), pp. 263–68.

14. See M.E. Porter, 'The Five Competitive Forces that shape strategy', *Harvard Business Review*, January 2008, pp. 57–91.

15. The classic statement of the resource-based view is J. Barney, 'Firm resources and sustained competitive advantage', *Journal of Management*, vol. 17, no. 1 (1991), pp. 91–120.

16. A recent review of strategy process research is H. Sminia, 'Process research in strategy formation: theory, methodology and relevance', *International Journal of Management Reviews*, vol. 11, no. 1 (2009), pp. 97–122.

17. Psychological influences on strategy are explored in a special issue of the *Strategic Management Journal*, edited by T. Powell, D. Lovallo and S. Fox: 'Behavioral strategy', vol. 31, no. 13 (2011).

18. For a review of strategy-as-practice research, see E. Vaara and R. Whittington, 'Strategy-as-practice: taking social practices seriously', *Academy of Management Annals*, vol. 6, no. 1 (2012), pp. 285–336.

19. In earlier editions, this lens was called the 'ideas lens'.

The rise of a unicorn – Airbnb

Duncan Angwin

Airbnb logo

Source: Russell Hart/Alamy Images.

A unicorn is a mythical animal that has been described since antiquity as a horse with a large pointed spiral horn. Legend has it unicorns are very rare and difficult to tame. It is a name that has been adopted by the US venture capital industry to denote a start-up company whose valuation exceeds \$1bn (£0.6bn, €0.75bn). Airbnb, founded in 2007, was one of these rare and valuable unicorns, already valued at \$25bn in 2015. How could this start-up become so successful, so fast?

Origins

The original founders of Airbnb, Joe Gebbia and Brian Chesky, first met at Rhode Island School of Design. Five years later, both aged 27, they were struggling to pay their rent when a design conference came to San Francisco. All the hotels were fully booked, so they set up a simple website with pictures of their loft-turned-lodging space – complete with three air mattresses on the floor and the promise of a home-cooked breakfast in the morning. This site got them their first three paying guests at \$80 each. It dawned on them this could be the start of something big. They both wanted to be entrepreneurs and Brian already had some experience having designed a cushion for back sufferers and built a website.[1] Next day they created a website, www.airbedandbreakfast.com.

They decided to target conferences and festivals across America, getting local people to list their rooms on a website created by former flatmate and computer programmer, Nathan Blecharczyk. In the summer of 2008, Barack Obama was due to speak in Denver at the Democratic Party National Convention. Eighty thousand people were expected to attend and Joe and Brian thought there would be a shortage of hotel rooms. They rushed to complete their website in time and recorded 800 listings in one week. However, it did not make any money. To survive they had to make use of their entrepreneurial skills, buying cereal in bulk and designing packaging such as 'Obama's O's' and 'Cap'n McCain' cereal; jokey references to the two Presidential candidates of the year. However, they soon added a payment facility to their website allowing them to charge up to 15 per cent of the booking (the host pays 3 per cent and the traveller between 6 and 12 per cent). By April 2009, they were breaking even.

Growth

Attracting funding for their start-up was not easy. Investors saw Gebbia and Cesky purely as designers, which did not fit the traditional start-up profile. Funders thought there would not be much demand for listings that mostly advertised sleeping on airbeds.

Nonetheless, in 2009 Airbnb received its first funding of \$20,000 from angel investor, Paul Graham, co-founder of Y Combinator (a start-up mentoring programme), who was impressed with their inventiveness and tenacity. The company was renamed Airbnb and it provided an app and website that connects people seeking lodging with renters who have listed their personal houses, apartments, guest rooms on either platform. Further funding followed: in November 2010 Airbnb raised an additional \$7.2m. This allowed the company to expand to 8000 cities worldwide, to increase the number of employees to 500 and to move out of the founders' flat – where staff had been making sales calls from the bathroom and holding conferences in the kitchen – to offices in the design district of San Francisco. The early history of Airbnb is illustrated in Figure 1.

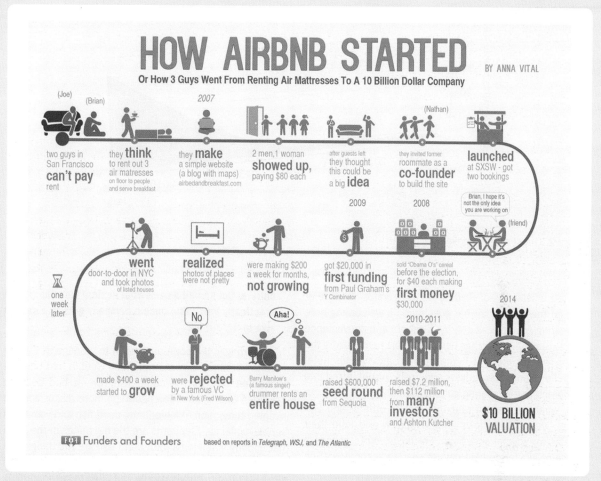

Figure 1 Airbnb early growth story

Source: Funders and Founders, Inc., image courtesy of Anna Vital.

However, in 2010 Airbnb was experiencing sluggish listings in New York. Joe and Brian booked spaces with 24 hosts and flew out to try to understand the problem. They soon realised hosts were doing a very poor job of presenting their properties. They immediately rented a $5000 camera and took as many photos of New York apartments as possible. Listings in the city suddenly doubled. From there on hosts could automatically schedule a professional photographer. This was an immediate hit and by 2012 there were 20,000 freelance photographers being employed by Airbnb around the world. The photos also built trust for guests as they verified addresses. The company also introduced Airbnb Social Connections, which leverages users' social graphs via Facebook Connect. This shows whether friends have stayed with the host or are friends with the host and it allows guests to search for hosts based on other characteristics, like alma mater. Again this reassured potential guests.

Further venture funding of $112m was received in July 2011. Airbnb expanded through acquisitions with a deal in Germany and the purchase of their largest UK-based competitor Crashpadder just in time for the 2012 Summer Olympics in London. Offices were opened in Paris, Barcelona and Milan. Airbnb's growth was explosive with a higher valuation than Hyatt and Wyndham hotel groups by 2014 and more guest nights booked than Hilton Hotels (see Figure 2). By 2016 Airbnb was valued at $25bn – more than any other hotel group. The company justified its valuation by claiming that, when its price ($25bn) to sales ratio of 27.8 (based on estimated sales of $900m for 2015) is divided by its high growth rate of 113 per cent per year, the resulting value for the group is broadly in line with the sector.[2] Airbnb forecasts $10bn of revenues by 2020, with $3bn of profits before tax.

Airbnb proved attractive to guests and hosts as its listings were far superior to others available at the time, such as Craigslist – they were more personal, with better descriptions and nicer photos that made them more appealing for people searching for vacation rentals. The rooms provided by Airbnb were also cheaper than equivalent ones at hotels and had more of a personal flavour. For instance, in a recent stay in Paris a user noted the host

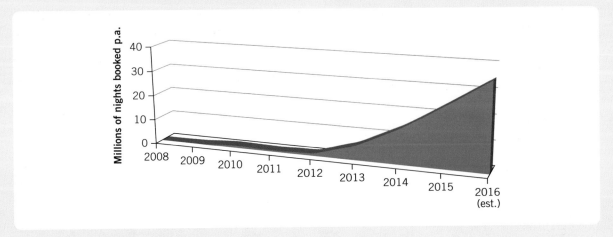

Figure 2 Guest nights booked

had left a selection of food in the refrigerator, a bottle of wine on the counter for her guests and a welcoming note suggesting good places nearby to eat out and convenience shops. Staying in another person's apartment makes the visitor feel far more at home than an anonymous hotel room. For many young guests and hosts, Airbnb fitted into the contemporary sharing culture exemplified by Easy car club, where users can rent their car to others, and Girl Meets Dress, that allows girls to borrow and lend their dresses for special occasions. For hosts, rents provide a source of income to help pay for soaring accommodation costs in many major cities.

Managing growth

Founder and CEO Brian Chesky penned a memo in 2013 to his top management team, as follows:[3]

Hey team,

Our next team meeting is dedicated to Core Values, which are essential to building our culture. It occurred to me that before this meeting, I should write you a short letter on why culture is so important to [co-founders] Joe, Nate, and me.

. . . In 2012, we invited Peter Thiel [a major investor] to our office. This was late last year, and we were in the Berlin room showing him various metrics. Midway through the conversation, I asked him what was the single most important piece of advice he had for us.

He replied, 'Don't f* up the culture.'**

This wasn't what we were expecting from someone who just gave us $150m. I asked him to elaborate on this. He said one of the reasons he invested in us was our

culture. But he had a somewhat cynical view that it was practically inevitable once a company gets to a certain size to 'f* it up.'**

Accordingly, the company began to manage its culture more deliberately. For example, Joe Gebbia had become concerned that as the company grew, it had become less open to dialogue. To encourage more discussion, he invented the notion of 'elephants, dead fish and vomit'. As Gebbia explains: 'Elephants are the big things in the room that nobody is talking about, dead fish are the things that happened a few years ago that people can't get over, and vomit is that sometimes people just need to get something off their mind and you need someone to just sit there and listen'.[4] All three need to be aired. Airbnb also established a series of annual meetings called One Airbnb, bringing together employees (called 'Airfam') from all around the world to the San Francisco base for four-day conferences at which everyone can meet the founders, discuss strategy and also talk about both their work roles and their hobbies. The company has 'ground control' staff in every office in the world dedicated to making the company culture 'come alive', organising pop-up birthday celebrations, anniversary parties or baby showers. The company is rigorous in its recruitment policy, committed to hiring 'missionaries, not mercenaries'.

At the same time, founders Joe Gebbia, Brian Chesky and Nathan Blecharczyk had begun to ask themselves again: 'What is our mission? What is the big idea that truly defines Airbnb?'. As they recalled in their own words: 'It turns out the answer was right in front of us. For so long, people thought Airbnb was about renting houses. But really, we're about home. You see, a house is just a space, but a home is where you belong. And what makes this global community so special is that for the very first time, you can belong anywhere. That is the idea at the core of our company.'[5]

Airbnb in 2016

In 2016, Airbnb had over 1.5 million listings in 34,000 cities in 192 countries, with 40 million total guests. Anyone anywhere in the world can list spare space from a room to a tree house, from a castle to an island in Fiji, with prices ranging from $50 to $2000 per night. Airbnb received 30 million page views per month. The headquarters' walls were covered with world maps dotted with hundreds of coloured pins, charting world domination. Airbnb was so popular that one of their rooms was booked every two seconds.[6]

The company was now focused on the whole travel trip with an emphasis on delivering local experiences. This focus on hospitality was not just about where you stay, but what you do – and whom you do it with – while you're there. To this end they introduced Airbnb Neighbourhoods and local lounges, partnering with local coffee shops that can offer free wifi, a comfortable setting and local guidebooks. They also acquired a small start-up that connects guests with locals who can answer their questions. They also offer cleaning services.

Airbnb was providing a strong challenge to hotels with prices 30–80 per cent lower than local operators. San Francisco hotels were having to slash prices to protect their occupancy rates. Incumbents in the industry fought back by arguing Airbnb were dangerous and unsafe in terms of health and safety and quality assurance as it was unregulated. Although one must have a permit to rent for under 30 days, San Francisco residents were still illegally listing personal homes and apartments. Similar problems were being experienced in New York where an 'illegal hotel law' was passed preventing people from subletting apartments for less than 29 days. There was also a question mark over hosts not paying tax on earnings.

During 2016, Airbnb redesigned its website and apps with subtle animations and flashier imagery. This huge rebranding represented a transition from a hotel service to a lifestyle brand. Airbnb wanted their logo to be seen on a variety of products, houses and businesses, so people understood that owners supported their ideal and their brand. Airbnb's focus was now firmly on 'belonging'. This rebranding may not have been before time, as competition was brewing in the US from vacation rental site Home-Away Inc. (owned by Expedia), Roomorama, HouseTrip, Flipkey and Travel Advisor holiday rentals. Indeed, websites have sprung up such as www.airbnbhell.com that list a string of internet accommodation providers. Nonetheless, at the time of writing Airbnb was rumoured to be the hottest IPO (an initial public offering of its stock to investors) tip for 2016.

References

1. Salter, J. (2012) 'Airbnb: The story behind the $1.3bn room-letting website', *The Telegraph*, 7 September; Lee, A. (2013) 'Welcome to The Unicorn Club: learning from billion-dollar startups', *TechCrunch*, 2 November, https://techcrunch.com/2013/11/02/welcome-to-the-unicorn-club/
2. A ratio of price/sales to revenue growth rate gives Airbnb a figure of 24.6 against Marriott at 19.2, Wyndham at 34.1 and Expedia at 12.2 (Guest post, ' Why that crazy-high AirBnB valuation is fair, www.valuewalk.com, 1 January 2016).
3. https://medium.com/@bchesky/dont-fuck-up-the-culture-597cde9ee9d4\#.5wd5kwtdm.
4. B. Clune, 'How Airbnb is building its culture through belonging', *Culture Zine*.
5. http://blog.airbnb.com/belong-anywhere/.
6. Zacks.com, 'Investing in resting: is Airbnb a top 2016 IPO candidate?', 11 December 2015.

Questions

1 Sticking to the 35-word limit suggested by Collis and Rukstad in Section 1.2.3, what strategy statement would you propose for Airbnb?

2 Carry out a 'three-horizons' analysis (Section 1.2.1) of Airbnb, in terms of both existing activities and possible future ones. How might this analysis affect its future strategic direction?

3 Using the headings of environments, strategic capability, strategic purpose and culture seen in Section 1.3.1, identify key positioning issues for Airbnb and consider their relative importance.

4 Following on from the previous questions and making use of Section 1.3.2, what alternative strategies do you see for Airbnb?

5 Converting good strategic thinking into action can be a challenge: examine how Airbnb has achieved this by considering the elements seen in Section 1.3.3?

PART I
THE STRATEGIC POSITION

This part explains:

- How to analyse an organisation's position in the external environment – both macro-environment and industry or sector environment.

- How to analyse the determinants of strategic capability – resources, competences and the linkages between them.

- How to understand an organisation's purposes, taking into account corporate governance, stakeholder expectations and business ethics.

- How to address the role of history and culture in determining an organisation's position.

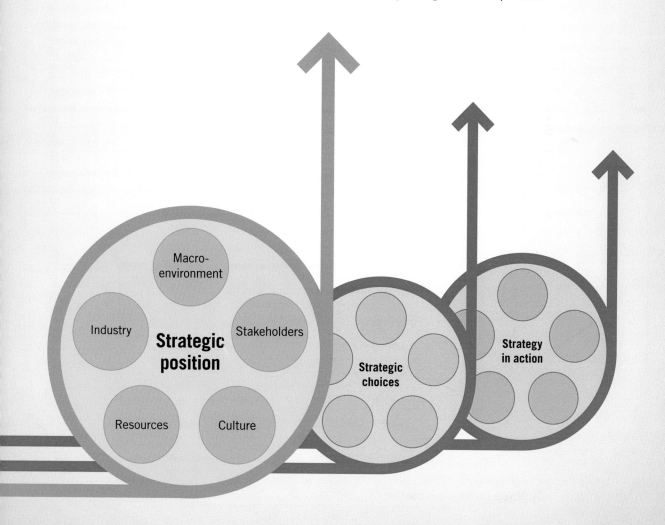

This part of the book is concerned with understanding the strategic position of the organisation. There are five chapters, organised around two themes. The first theme is the organisation's strategic *potential,* in other words what it *can* do. The second theme is the organisation's strategic *ambitions,* what it actually *seeks* to do, sometimes deliberately and sometimes not so deliberately (see Figure I.1).

Strategic potential is addressed as follows:

- Chapters 2 and 3 consider how different environments can be more or less rich in opportunities or hostile, imposing threats and constraints.
- Chapter 4 considers how each organisation has its own particular strategic capabilities (resources and competences), and how these can enable or constrain strategies.

Organisational ambitions are addressed in the following two chapters:

- Chapter 5 is about ambition in terms of the stakeholders' objectives, and the governance mechanisms to ensure their delivery.
- Chapter 6 examines how an organisation's history and culture may shape the ambitions of an organisation, often in taken-for-granted and hard-to-change ways.

There is an important strategic dilemma that runs through Chapters 2, 3 and 4. How much should managers concentrate their attention on the external market position and how much should they focus on developing their internal capabilities? On the external side, many argue that environmental factors are what matter most to success: strategy development should be primarily about seeking attractive opportunities in the marketplace. Those favouring a more internal approach, on the other hand, argue that an organisation's specific strategic capabilities should drive strategy. It is from these internal characteristics that distinctive strategies and superior performance can be built. There can be a real trade-off here. Managers who invest time and resources in developing their external market position (perhaps through acquiring companies that are potential competitors) have less time and resources to invest in managing their internal capabilities (for example, building up research and development). The same applies in reverse.

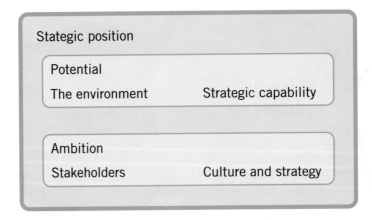

Figure I.1 Strategic position

Chapters 5 and 6 raise another underlying issue. To what extent should managers' ambitions for their organisations be considered as free or constrained? Chapter 5 explains how the expectations of investors, regulators, employees and customers can often influence strategy. Chapter 6 raises the constraints on managers exercised by organisational history and culture. Managers may be only partially aware of these kinds of constraints and are often in danger of underestimating the hidden limits to their ambitions.

Understanding the extent of managers' freedom to choose is fundamental to considering the issues of strategic choice that make up Part II of this book. But first Part I provides a foundation by exploring the question of strategic position.

2

MACRO-ENVIRONMENT ANALYSIS

Learning outcomes

After reading this chapter you should be able to:

- Analyse the broad macro-environment of organisations in terms of *political, economic, social, technological, ecological* and *legal* factors (*PESTEL*).
- Evaluate different approaches to environmental *forecasting*.
- Construct alternative *scenarios* in order to address possible environmental changes.

Key terms

forecasting p.47

key drivers p.47

macro-environment p.33

organisational field p.40

PESTEL analysis p.34

scenarios p.51

2.1 INTRODUCTION

The environment creates both opportunities and threats for organisations. Some organisations have been transformed by environmental change: think how traditional cable and satellite TV services such as Comcast and Sky are being challenged by the digital technologies of players such as Netflix or Amazon. Some organisations have sprung suddenly to global scale: take for example the end of chapter case, the Alibaba trading company, whose massive growth in less than two decades has been facilitated by a combination of new technologies, Chinese political and economic change and international regulations. Although the future can never be predicted perfectly, it is clearly important that entrepreneurs and managers try to analyse their environments as carefully as they can in order to anticipate and – if possible – take advantage of such environmental changes.[1]

Environments can be considered in terms of a series of 'layers', as summarised in Figure 2.1. This chapter focuses on organisations' *macro-environments*, the outermost layer. **The macro-environment consists of broad environmental factors that impact to a greater or lesser extent many organisations, industries and sectors.** For example, the effects of macro-environmental factors such as the internet, economic growth rates, climate change and aging populations go far beyond one industry or sector, impacting a wide range of activities from tourism to agriculture. The *industry,* or *sector,* makes up the next layer within this broad macro-environment. This layer consists of organisations producing the same sorts of products or services, for example the automobile industry or the healthcare sector. The third layer is that of specific *competitors and markets* immediately surrounding organisations. For a company like Nissan, this layer would include competitors such as Ford and Volkswagen; for a hospital, it would include similar facilities and particular groups of patients. Whereas this chapter focuses on the macro-environment, Chapter 3 will analyse industries and sectors and competitors and markets. Chapters 4 and 5 examine the individual organisations at the heart of Figure 2.1.

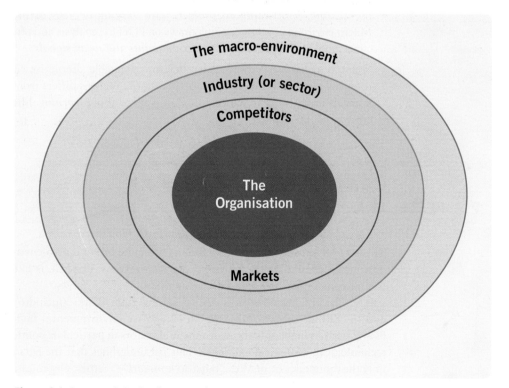

Figure 2.1 Layers of the business environment

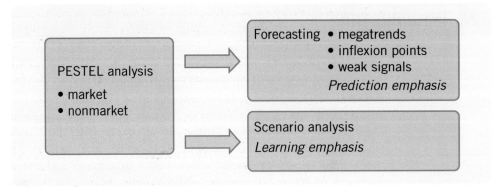

Figure 2.2 Analysing the macro-environment

Macro-environmental changes can often seem too big, complex or unpredictable for managers to grasp. The result is that changes can creep up on them until it is too late to avoid threats or take advantage of opportunities. Thus many traditional retailers, banks and newspapers were slow to seize the opportunities of the internet; many oil and steel producers underestimated the potential impact of China's slowing economic growth. While managers are always liable to some biases and inertia (see Chapter 5), this chapter introduces a number of analytical tools and concepts that can help keep organisations alert to macro-environmental change. The point is to minimise threats and to seize opportunities. The chapter is organised in three main sections:

- *PESTEL* factors which examine macro-environmental factors according to six key types: political, economic, social, technological, ecological and legal. These factors include both *market* and *nonmarket* aspects.

- *Forecasting,* which aims to predict, with varying degrees of precision or certainty. Macro-environmental forecasting draws on PESTEL analysis and often makes use of three conceptual tools: *megatrends, inflexion points* and *weak signals.*

- *Scenario analysis,* a technique that develops plausible alternative views of how the environment might develop in the future. Scenario analysis differs from forecasting because it avoids predictions about the future; it is more about *learning* different possibilities for environmental change.

The structure of this chapter is summarised in Figure 2.2.

2.2 PESTEL ANALYSIS

This section introduces a key tool for analysing the broad macro-environment of an organisation: PESTEL analysis. Providing a wide overview, PESTEL is likely to feed into both environmental forecasts and scenario analyses.

The PESTEL framework is one of several frameworks (including the similar 'PEST' and 'STEEPLE' frameworks) which categorise environmental factors into key types.[1] **PESTEL analysis highlights six environmental factors in particular: political, economic, social, technological, ecological and legal.** This list underlines that the environment includes not only the economics of markets, but also *nonmarket* factors. Organisations need to consider both market and nonmarket aspects of strategy:[2]

- The *market environment* consists mainly of suppliers, customers and competitors. These are environmental participants with whom interactions are primarily economic. Here, companies typically compete for resources, revenues and profits. Pricing and innovation are often key strategies here. The market environment is discussed extensively in Chapter 3, but issues such as economic cycles are also considered in this chapter (Section 2.2.2).

- The *nonmarket environment* involves primarily the social, political, legal and ecological factors, but can also be impacted by economic factors. Key participants in the nonmarket environment are not just other businesses, but non-governmental organisations (NGOs), politicians, government departments, regulators, political activists, campaign groups and the media. In the nonmarket environment, organisations need to build reputation, connections, influence and legitimacy. Lobbying, public relations, networking and collaboration are key nonmarket strategies.

Nonmarket factors are obviously important for government and similar organisations reliant on grants or subsidies, for example schools, hospitals and charities. However, nonmarket factors can be very important for business organisations too. For example, nonmarket factors are particularly important where the government or regulators are powerful (for instance in the defence and healthcare sectors); where consumer sensitivities are high (for instance in the food business); or in societies where political, business and media elites are closely interconnected (typically smaller countries, or countries where the state is powerful).

The following sections consider each of the PESTEL elements in turn, providing key analytical concepts and frameworks for each. Meanwhile, Illustration 2.1 on oil giant BP provides examples of various PESTEL factors, showing how in practice they often inter-relate.

2.2.1 Politics

The political element of PESTEL highlights the role of the state and other political factors in the macro-environment. There are two important steps in political analysis: first, identifying the importance of political factors; second carrying out political risk analysis.

Figure 2.3 is a matrix that distinguishes two variables helpful to identifying the importance of political factors:

- The role of the *state*. In many countries and sectors, the state is often important as a direct economic actor, for instance as a customer, supplier, owner or regulator of businesses.

- Exposure to *civil society* organisations. Civil society comprises a whole range of organisations that are liable to raise political issues, including political lobbyists, campaign groups, social media or traditional media.

To take an example from Figure 2.3, the defence industry faces a highly politicised environment. Defence companies typically have high direct state involvement: national armed services are of course key customers, while states are often owners of their national defence companies. At the same time, defence companies are often highly exposed to groups from civil society, for instance campaigners against the international arms trade. By contrast, food companies face less direct state involvement: most food companies are privately-owned and operate in private-sector markets. However, the political environment is still important for food companies, as they are typically exposed to pressures from civil society in the form of fair trade campaigners, labour rights organisations and health lobbying groups. Pressures from civil society organisations can increase state involvement by demanding additional regulation, for instance health standards for food products. Canals are often state-owned but nowadays are not highly exposed to political pressures from civil society organisations. Industries can rapidly change positions: thus revelations about internet monitoring by

ILLUSTRATION 2.1　BP's PESTEL

In 2016, the world's oil industry was facing a toughening macro-environment.

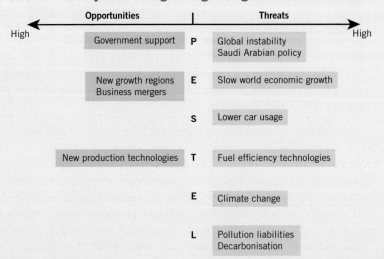

A PESTEL analysis can be done using published sources (e.g. company annual reports, media articles and consultants' reports) or more extensively by direct discussion with managers, customers, suppliers, consultants, academics, government officials and financial analysts. It is important not to rely just on a firm's managers, who may have limited views. A PESTEL analysis of the world oil industry in 2016 based on published sources shows a preponderance of threats over opportunities. In the figure above, the scale of Opportunities and Threats on each of the PESTEL dimensions is indicated by the relative extent of the bars. Just taking 12 issues for illustration, the figure shows more and longer bars on the Threats side than the Opportunities side. Thus:

- *Political.* Global instability raised potential threats to supply and distribution, with tensions in oil-producing regions such as Russia and the Middle East, and in major oil-consuming regions, such as the South China Sea. Short-term, prices were depressed by Saudi Arabian policy to maintain output despite declining demand: oil prices had halved during 2015. The main opportunity was various measures of government support, particularly in favour of shale oil production in China and the West.
- *Economic.* During 2014–15, the world had recorded declining economic growth, with only a modest upturn forecast for 2016. High growth regions such as India and Africa still offered opportunities and Western oil companies were reducing their costs through mergers.

- *Social.* In the West, car usage is declining; in the USA, the number of car passenger miles has fallen by more than 10 per cent since 2007.
- *Technological.* More fuel-efficient cars were also reducing demand, with average miles per gallon improving by 40 per cent since the early 1980s. More positively, technology offered oil producers opportunities to reduce costs: e.g. more efficient production using digital sensors.
- *Ecological.* Climate change raised indirect legal and political threats, but also posed direct threats, as global warming changed demand patterns and threatened production and distribution infrastructure with more extreme weather events.
- *Legal.* Oil companies were facing higher legal penalties for pollution: in 2015, BP had to pay $18.7bn (£11.2bn, €14bn) in fines for the Deepwater Horizon disaster. Global agreements such as the 2015 Paris Climate Change Conference were increasing legal measures to promote decarbonisation.

Questions

1. In the light of this analysis, what strategic options would you advise a Western oil producer such as Shell or BP to consider?

2. Have the Opportunities and Threats changed since 2016? How would you update this analysis?

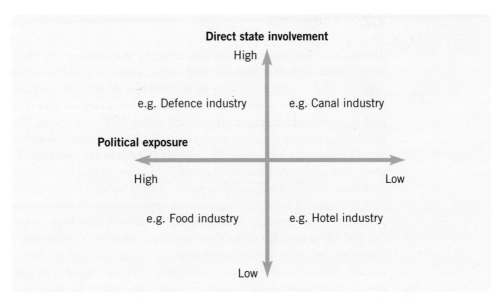

Figure 2.3 The political environment

national security agencies has placed companies such as Apple and Facebook much more under scrutiny by governments, civil liberties groups and consumers.

Organisations that face politicised environments need to carry out *political risk analysis*, the analysis of threats and opportunities arising from potential political change. There are two key dimensions to political risk analysis:[3]

- The *macro–micro* dimension. The macro dimension of political risk refers to the risks associated with whole countries – for instance China, France or Nigeria. Many specialist organisations publish relative rankings of countries' macro political risks. Western European countries are typically ranked low in terms of macro political risk, as even changes of government following elections do not bring fundamental change. On the other hand, some Middle Eastern countries rank high in terms of macro political risk, because changes of government there can be sudden and radical.[4] However, there is also an important micro dimension of political risk, relating to the specific risk of particular organisations or sectors within a country. It is important to distinguish between macro political risk and specific micro-level risk. China is typically ranked medium political risk on the macro dimension, but for some Japanese companies operating there the micro dimension is higher and variable. For many Chinese consumers, resentment of Japan is strong and Japanese car companies are from time to time targeted by nationalist boycotts.

- The *internal–external* dimension. The internal dimension of political risk relates to factors originating within the countries, for example government change or pressure from local campaigning groups. These can be relatively easy to monitor, requiring attention to election dates and opinion polls, for example. However, there are also external political risks, the knock-on effects of events occurring outside particular countries' national boundaries. For example, a fall in oil prices driven by the internal politics of Saudi Arabia is liable to have negative economic and political impacts on other big oil-producing countries such as Russia and Venezuela. On the other hand, oil price falls can produce political benefits in energy-importing countries such as India or Japan. External political risk analysis involves careful analysis of economic, political and other linkages between countries around the world.

2.2.2 Economics

The macro-environment is also influenced by macro-economic factors such as currency exchange rates, interest rates and fluctuating economic growth rates around the world. It is important for an organisation to understand how its markets are affected by the prosperity of the economy as a whole. Managers should have a view on how changing exchange rates may affect viability in export markets and vulnerability to imports. They should have an eye to changing interest rates over time, especially if their organisations have a lot of debt. They should understand how economic growth rates rise or fall over time. There are many public sources of economic forecasts that can help in predicting the movement of key economic indicators, though these are often prone to error because of unexpected economic shocks.[5]

A key concept for analysing macro-economic trends is the *economic cycle*. Despite the possibility of unexpected shocks, economic growth rates have an underlying tendency to rise and fall in regular cycles. These cycles can also link to other important economic variables. For example, severe downturns in economic growth are often followed by falls in interest rates and exchange rates. Awareness of cycles reinforces an important pattern in the macro-environment: good economic times do not last forever, while bad economic times lead eventually to recovery. The key is to identify cyclical turning points.

Overall cycles in economic growth are made up of three principal sub-cycles, each of varying length (and named after the economists who originally identified them):[6]

- *The Kitchin or 'stock' cycle* is the shortest cycle, tending to last about three to four years from one cyclical peak to the next. This short cycle is driven by the need for firms to build up stocks of raw materials and parts as economies emerge from recessions. The build-up of stocks gives an additional boost to economic growth for a year or so, but the boost fades as firms no longer need to build their stocks. As economic growth slows, firms tend to run down their stocks by buying-in less, which reinforces the downward trend. A Kitchin cycle turning point comes when stocks are totally run down and firms fuel the upturn by building-up stocks again.

- *The Juglar or 'investment' cycle* is a medium-term cycle, typically stretching over 7–11 years. The cycle is driven by surges of investment in capital equipment, for instance plant and machinery. The Juglar downturn comes once these investments have been made across an economy and firms are able to cut back on further investment until the equipment is worn out. These investment cut-backs drain demand from the economy. The economy only reaches a new turning-point when wear and tear or innovation forces firms to spend again by investing in a new generation of capital equipment.

- *The Kuznets or 'infrastructure' cycle* is the longest, lasting between 15 and 25 years. These cycles follow the life-spans of infrastructural investments, for example in housing or transport. Kuznets cycles are triggered by initial surges of infrastructure investment, which then ease off as infrastructural needs are met, perhaps for a decade or so. The cyclical upturn comes when the last generation of infrastructure is worn out or outdated, and a new surge of investment is required.

The three sub-cycles add together to determine overall cycles of economic growth. Thus in Figure 2.4, year 1 corresponds with simultaneous low-points in all three of the Kitchin, Juglar and Kuznets cycles: this could be expected to be a very bad year for economic growth. Year 8, on the other hand, corresponds with low growth on both the Kitchin and Juglar cycles, but an approaching peak in the Kuznets cycles: this would be a less bad year.

Managers making long-term strategic decisions should assess where they stand in the overall economic cycle. For example, it might be tempting after several years of rising growth to launch major investments in new capacity. Such new capacity might not be needed in the

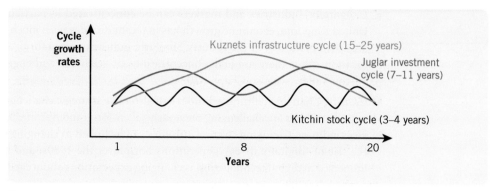

Figure 2.4 Economic cycles

subsequent slowdown. On the other hand, two or three years of slowing growth might make firms over-cautious about new investment. As the economy recovers in the following years, rivals who had invested in extra capacity or innovation might be able to seize the advantage, leaving over-cautious firms struggling to catch up. In assessing the economic environment, therefore, it is crucial not to assume that current economic growth rates will continue.

Some industries are particularly vulnerable to economic cycles. For example:

- *Discretionary spend* industries. In industries where purchasers can easily put off their spending for a year or two, there tend to be strong cyclical effects. Thus housing, restaurants and cars tend be highly cyclical because many people can choose to delay or curtail spending on these for a while. After a period of curtailed spending, there is liable to be a strong upturn as pent-up demand is finally released into the market.

- *High fixed cost* industries. Industries such as airlines, hotels and steel suffer from economic downturns because high fixed costs in plant, equipment or labour tend to encourage competitive price-cutting to ensure maximum capacity utilisation when demand is low. For example, an airline might try to fill its seats in the face of falling demand simply by offering cheap tickets. If its competitors do the same, the resulting price-war will result in low profits for all the airlines.

2.2.3 Social

The *social* elements of the macro-environment have at least two impacts upon organisations. First, they can influence the specific nature of demand and supply within the overall economic growth rate. Second, they can shape the innovativeness, power and effectiveness of organisations.

In the first place, there are a number of key aspects of the social environment that can shape demand and supply. These can be analysed under the following four headings:

- *Demographics*. For example, the ageing populations in many Western societies create opportunities and threats for both private and public sectors. There is increasing demand for services for the elderly, but diminishing supplies of young labour to look after them.

- *Distribution*. Changes in wealth distribution influence the relative sizes of markets. Thus the concentration of wealth in the hands of elites over the last 20 years has constrained some categories of 'middle-class' consumption, while enlarging markets for certain luxury goods.

- *Geography*. Industries and markets can be concentrated in particular locations. In the United Kingdom, economic growth has in recent decades been much faster in the London area than in the rest of the country. Similarly, industries often form 'clusters' in particular locations: thus there are high concentrations of scientists and engineers in California's Silicon Valley (see also Chapter 10).[7]

- *Culture*. Changing cultural attitudes can also raise strategic challenges. For example, new ethical attitudes are challenging previously taken-for-granted strategies in the financial services industry. Changing cultural attitudes can be linked to changing demographics. Thus the rise of 'digital natives' (generations born after the 1980s, and thus from childhood immersed in digital technologies) is changing expectations about media, consumption and education.

A second important social aspect of the macro-environment is organisational networks, with significant implications for innovativeness, power and effectiveness. These networks are frequently described as 'organisational fields'.[8] An **organisational field is a community of organisations that interact more frequently with one another than with those outside the field.** These organisational fields are partly *economic* as they include competing organisations within the industry or sector, as well as customers and suppliers in the marketplace (see Chapter 3). However, the concept of organisational fields also emphasises *social* interactions with other organisations and actors that exercise an influence on the focal organisation. These might include political organisations such as governments and campaign groups, legal entities such as regulators, and other social groups, such as professions and trade unions. Sometimes key actors in the field might even be particularly influential individuals, for example politicians. The organisational field is therefore much broader than just industries or markets. Because of the importance of social networks, managers need to analyse the influence of a wide range of organisational field members, not just competitors, customers and suppliers.

Networks and organisational fields can be analysed by means of *sociograms,* maps of potentially important social (or economic) connections.[9] For a new hi-technology enterprise, important network connections might be links to leading universities, powerful firms and respected venture capitalists, for example. Maps can help assess the effectiveness of networks and identify who is likely to be most powerful and innovative within them. Three concepts help to understand effectiveness, power and innovativeness:

- *Network density* typically increases network effectiveness. Density refers to the number of interconnections between members in the network map. Effectiveness is increased by density because the more interconnections there are, the better the communication of new ideas between network members. Everybody is talking to each other, and nobody with potentially useful information is isolated.

- *Central hub positions,* where a particular organisation is responsible for connecting many network members, are relatively powerful within a network. Hubs have power because network members rely on them for interconnection with other members. Hubs are also potentially innovative because they can collect ideas from the whole network, and they hear about what is going on in one part of the network before most other parts.

- *Broker positions,* where a particular organisation connects otherwise separate groups of organisations, are associated with innovativeness. Brokers' innovation advantage stems from their ability to link the most valuable information from one group of organisations with the most valuable information from the other group. Because they provide the connection between the two groups, they are able to exploit this combination of information before anybody else.

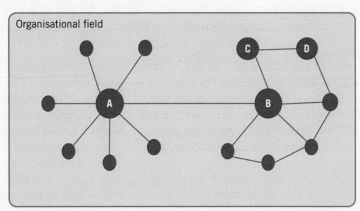

A is a more central hub than B; both A and B are brokers; B's immediate network is denser than A's.

Figure 2.5 Sociogram of social networks within an organisational field

Figure 2.5 provides an illustrative sociogram of two organisations' networks, A and B. Together these networks constitute a shared organisational field, although there are two relatively distinct groups within it. Because they link the two groups of organisations, organisation A and B can both be seen as brokers. Moreover, organisation A occupies a central hub position in its immediate network, connecting to seven other organisations, including organisation B. Organisation B is also a hub, though it links directly to only five organisations: to connect with organisation D, for instance, it passes through organisation C. Because organisation B is a less central hub, the sociogram suggests that it is likely to be relatively less powerful and innovative in its immediate group than organisation A. On the other hand, organisation B is likely to be more powerful and innovative than organisation C, because of its hub position and its role as broker. Moreover, although organisation B might be relatively less powerful and innovative in its group than organisation A, the overall effectiveness of its group might be greater than organisation A's. Organisation B's immediate network is denser, with more interconnections between individual members: all B's group have at least two or three connections. This density of connections means that ideas are more likely to pass quickly between group members, saving the problems involved in always going through a central hub. In this sense, organisation B may individually have less advantage relative to its group than organisation A, but collectively its network may perform better.

Sociograms can be drawn for key people as well as organisations: individuals are often the link between organisations anyway. Personal networks are important in many societies, for example the network of former consultants at the elite McKinsey & Co. consulting firm, or networks of company directors, or the interpersonal *guanxi* networks that prevail in China. Illustration 2.2 describes the network that has emerged from the armed service backgrounds of many Israeli entrepreneurs. The crucial issue in analysing social networks is how hub positions, brokering roles and network density are likely to affect a particular organisation's power, innovativeness and overall effectiveness.

Some organisational fields can be characterised as 'small worlds'.[10] *Small worlds* exist where the large majority of a network's members is closely connected, either just one step away (as C is from B in Figure 2.5) or one or two more steps away (as D is from B). Small

ILLUSTRATION 2.2 — Intelligence Unit 8200 and the small world of Israeli hi-tech

Israel, a nation of just eight million people, exports more than $6bn worth of cybersecurity products a year, accounting for about 10 per cent of the global cybersecurity market. At the heart of this success is Unit 8200, the largest unit of the Israeli Defence Force and the equivalent of America's National Security Agency.

Unit 8200's alumni have produced more hi-tech start-ups per capita than the University of Stanford. Some of the successful companies originating with Unit 8200 include Check Point, with 2900 employees and a pioneer in Virtual Private Networks; NICE Systems, with 2700 employees and a pioneer in telephone recording technology; and Palo Alto Networks, with 3000 employees and a pioneer in computer firewall technology. Unit 8200 recruits are drawn from young Israelis doing their national military service: because this is compulsory only for Jews, few Arabs join. Recruitment into Unit 8200 is highly selective (in the Israeli Defence Force, only pilot training is harder to enter) and favours skilled computer science students and linguists. Recruits come disproportionately from the richer and more highly educated Tel Aviv area of Israel, and from elite schools such as Leyada, the semi-private Hebrew University High School in Jerusalem (where the founder of Check Point was a student). Alumni of Unit 8200 go not only into hi-tech business; many pursue successful careers in politics, the judiciary, the media and academia. For example, the former CEO of NICE Systems became director general of the Israeli Ministry of Finance.

Unit 8200's young recruits are intensively trained and work long hours in small groups applying the latest technology to security matters that might involve life and death. To maximise security, Unit 8200's technology systems – from analytics to data mining, intercept and intelligence management – are designed and built in-house. This experience prepares Unit 8200 alumni well for futures in hi-tech business. Avi Hasson, Chief Scientist at the Israeli Economy Ministry and himself an alumnus of Unit 8200, describes the working environment: 'When it comes to managing a startup, Unit 8200 is a fantastic school. . . . The unit encourages independent thought. It's something that was adopted later by many companies, a little like the culture in Google, in which good ideas can come from anywhere.'

Because recruitment in hi-tech tends to favour a 'buddy-system', alumni are often sought out for employment by other alumni. Experience of this intense, elitist organisation in the formative years of youth creates strong social bonds. The 8200 alumni association has more than 15,000 members, and hosts networking events and community outreach programmes, including start-up accelerators.

By 2020, Unit 8200 is due to move adjacent to the Advanced Technology Park at Be'er Sheva in southern Israel's Negev Desert. In 2013, Israel's President Benjamin Netanyahu had declared that Be'er Sheva would become the 'cybercenter of the Western hemisphere'. Be'er Sheva already had the advantage of the local Ben-Gurion University and its Cyber Security Research Centre. The National Cyber Bureau, a newly created agency advising the government on cyber policies, moved to Be'er Sheva in 2015. Companies already with operations in the Advanced Technology Park included many leading foreign firms such as Deutsche Telecom, IBM, Lockheed Martin, Oracle, PayPal and EMC. Venture capital firm JVP, with more than $1bn (£0.6bn, € 0.75bn) funding available, was also running a local 'cyberincubator' for start-ups. One of its first ventures was sold to PayPal.

Sources: Haaretz, 18 April and 24 April 2015; Financial Times, 10 July 2015; TechCrunch, 20 March 2015.

Questions

1 Identify at least one important hub and one important broker in the Unit 8200 network.

2 If you were a foreign cybersecurity company, what would you do to access Israel's expertise?

worlds typically give members a good deal of protection and effectiveness, due to their density. However, outsider organisations (for example foreign firms) will have difficulty penetrating small world networks on their own, and will typically require the help of insiders. Small worlds are particularly likely in societies where economic activity is geographically concentrated or where social elites share common backgrounds (for example, the French elite is often characterised as living in the same exclusive parts of Paris and as graduating from the same higher education institutions, the so-called Grandes Ecoles). Thus an important aspect of social analysis is the extent of small worlds in the macro-environment.

2.2.4 Technology

Further important elements within the macro-environment are *technologies* such as the internet, nanotechnology or new composite materials, whose impacts can spread far beyond single industries. As in the case of internet streaming, new technologies can open up opportunities for some organisations (e.g. Spotify and YouTube), while challenging others (traditional music and broadcasting companies). Chapter 10 will discuss specific strategies surrounding innovative new technologies in more detail.

Meanwhile, it is important to carry out the macro-environmental analysis of technology in order to identify areas of potential innovative activity. There are five primary indicators of innovative activity:[11]

- *Research & development budgets.* Innovative firms, sectors or countries can be identified by the extent of spending on research, typically reported in company annual reports and government statistics.
- *Patenting activity.* Firms active in patenting new technologies can be identified on national patent registers, the most important being the United States Patents and Trademarks Office.
- *Citation analysis.* The potential impact of patents and scientific papers on technology can be measured by the extent to which they are widely cited by other organisations, with data available from Google Scholar for instance.
- *New product announcements.* Organisations typically publicise their new product plans through press releases and similar media.
- *Media coverage.* Specialist technology and industry media will cover stories of the latest or impending technologies, as will various social media.

Although there is some variation between firms, sectors and countries in how far their innovative activity is reflected by these kinds of indicators, generally they will help to identify areas of rapid technological change and locate centres of technological leadership. For example, an analysis for the new material graphene (a material just one atom thick, but both strong and highly flexible) reveals that the annual number of published scientific papers multiplied by four between 2010 and 2014. Clearly graphene is likely to be of growing importance in the coming years. However, technological leadership is not clear. Western Europe accounts for 34 per cent of the scientific papers, but just 9 per cent of the patents. China accounts for 40 per cent of the patents and Samsung is the single firm with the largest number of patents. In terms of graphene application areas, patenting is greatest in electronics and composite materials.[12]

Many organisations also publish technology roadmaps for their sectors going forward.[13] *Technology roadmaps* project into the future various product or service demands, identify technology alternatives to meet these demands, select the most promising alternatives and then offer a timeline for their development. Thus they provide good indicators of future technological developments. Figure 2.6 provides a simplified technology roadmap for

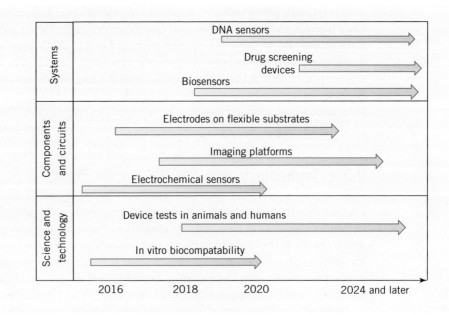

Figure 2.6 Technology roadmap for graphene technology in electronics
Source: Substantially simplified from A. Ferrari, 'Science and technology roadmap for graphene', *Nanoscale*, vol. 7 (2015), pp. 4598–810 (Figure 121, p. 4759).

applications of graphene in electronics, both components and circuits and electronic systems. The roadmap suggests that tests of graphene devices in live animals and humans will be underway by 2018, with products like drug-screening devices and ultra-sensitive sensors emerging around 2020. This kind of roadmap has implications that go beyond the electronics industry, to include pharmaceuticals and every sector where detecting product characteristics is important, from retails to logistics.

2.2.5 Ecological

Within the PESTEL framework, *ecological* stands specifically for 'green' macro-environmental issues, such as pollution, waste and climate change. Environmental regulations can impose additional costs, for example pollution controls, but they can also be a source of opportunity, for example the new businesses that emerged around mobile phone recycling.

When considering ecological issues in the macro-environment, there are three sorts of challenges that organisations may need to meet:[14]

- *Direct pollution obligations* are an obvious challenge, and nowadays typically involve not just cleaning up 'at the end of the pipe' (for example, disposing of waste by-products safely), but also minimising the production of pollutants in the first place. Having clean processes for supply, production and distribution is generally better than managing the consequences of polluting after the fact.

- *Product stewardship* refers to managing ecological issues through both the organisation's entire value chain and the whole life cycle of the firm's products. Stewardship here might involve responsibility for the ecological impact of external suppliers or final end-users. It will also involve responsibility for what happens to products at 'end of life', in other words how they are disposed of when consumers have no more use for them. Thus car manufacturers are increasingly responsible for the recycling and safe disposal of old cars.

- *Sustainable development* is a criterion of increasing importance and refers not simply to reducing environmental damage, but to whether the product or service can be produced indefinitely into the future. This sustainability criterion sets constraints on the over-exploitation of particular sources of raw materials, for instance in developing countries, and often raises issues regarding the economic and social well-being of local communities.

In assessing the macro-environment from an ecological point of view, all three criteria of pollution, stewardship and sustainability need typically to be considered.

The extent to which these ecological criteria are important to organisations relies on three contextual sources of pressure, the first two arising directly from the macro-environment:

- *Ecological*. Clearly ecological issues are more likely to be pressing the more impactful they are: a chemical company may have more to worry about than a school. However, there are three less obvious characteristics to consider. First, ecological issues become more salient the more *certain* they are. For example, as doubts have reduced about the facts of global warming, so the pressures on organisations to act on it have increased. Pressures are also likely to be greater the more *visible* ecological issues are: aircraft pollution is more salient as an issue than shipping pollution because aircraft are more obvious to ordinary citizens than pollution done far out to sea. Similarly, the *emotivity* of the issue is liable to be a factor: threats to polar bears generally get more attention than threats to hyenas.

- *Organisational field*. Ecological issues do not become salient just because of their inherent characteristics. The extent of pressure is influenced by how ecological issues interact with the nature of the organisational field. An organisational field with highly *active* regulators or campaign groups will clearly give saliency to ecological issues. However, high levels of field *interconnectedness* will also increase the importance of ecological issues: within densely interconnected networks, it is harder to hide damaging behaviour and peer pressure to conform to ecological standards is greater.

- *Internal organisation*. The personal *values* of an organisation's leadership will clearly influence the desire to respond to ecological issues. Actual responsiveness will rely on the effectiveness of managerial *systems* that promote and monitor behaviours consistent with ecological obligations.

Although ecological issues can exercise unwelcome pressure, there are potentially strong organisational motives to respond. As in Figure 2.7, the three kinds of contextual pressure can satisfy a variety of motives. Fundamentally, there is of course a sense of ecological *responsibility:* thus the personal values of the organisation's leaders might stimulate ecological initiatives, or routine production systems might reduce pollution. However, another outcome can be *legitimacy,* as reflected in regulatory compliance and a good reputation with consumers. Finally, responding to ecological issues can even enhance *competitiveness*. For example, minimising waste in production processes for pollution reasons can reduce costs. Green products are attractive in the marketplace and often command a price premium.

2.2.6 Legal

The final element in a PESTEL analysis of the macro-environment refers to *legal* aspects. These can cover a wide range of topics: for example, labour, environmental and consumer regulation; taxation and reporting requirements; and rules on ownership, competition and corporate governance. In recent years, the relaxation of legal constraints through deregulation has created many new business opportunities, for example for low-cost airlines and

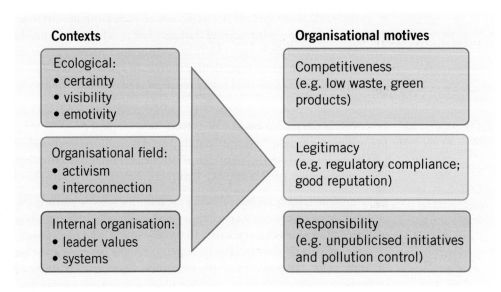

Figure 2.7 Contexts and motives for ecological issues

Source: Substantially adapted from P. Bansal and K. Roth, 'Why companies go green: a model of ecological responsiveness', *Academy of Management Journal,* vol. 43, no. 4 (2000), pp. 717–36 (Figure 2, p. 729).

'free schools' in various countries. However, regulations can also handicap organisations: Illustration 2.3 shows how the taxi-hailing app company Uber ran into important legal issues as it entered new markets and regulators struggled to keep up with the new technology.

Legal issues form an important part of the *institutional environment* of organisations, by which is meant the formal and informal 'rules of the game'.[15] This concept of institutional environment suggests that it can be useful in a PESTEL analysis to consider not only formal laws and regulations but also more informal norms: the 'L' can be stretched to cover all types of rule, formal and informal. Informal rules are patterns of expected ('normal') behaviour that are hard to ignore. Thus, regardless of the law, there are fairly explicit norms regarding proper respect for the ecological environment. Organisations ignoring these norms would risk outrage amongst consumers or employees, regardless of the legal situation.

Formal and informal rules vary sufficiently between countries to define very different institutional environments, sometimes known as 'varieties of capitalism'.[16] These *varieties of capitalism* have implications for the ways in which business and management are done in those environments and the prospects for success, both for insiders and for outsiders. Although every country differs in detail, three broad varieties of capitalism have been identified, whose formal and informal rules lead to different ways of doing business:

- *Liberal market economies* are institutional environments where both formal and informal rules favour competition between companies, aggressive acquisitions of one company by another and free bargaining between management and labour. Companies in these liberal market economies tend to raise funds from the financial markets and company ownership is either entrepreneurial or, for older companies, widely dispersed amongst many shareholders. These economies tend to support radical innovation and are receptive to foreign firms. Although neither is perfectly representative, the United States and the United Kingdom correspond broadly to this type of institutional environment.

- *Coordinated market economies* encourage more coordination between companies, often supported by industry associations or similar frameworks. There are legal and normative constraints on hostile acquisitions on the one hand, and various supports for consensual

ILLUSTRATION 2.3   Uber drives into trouble

The Uber taxi-hailing company has often run up against local regulations.

The inspiration for the Uber's taxi-hailing app came on a snowy night in Paris in 2008, when co-founders Travis Kalanick and Garrett Camp couldn't find a cab. Uber began business in Kalanick's home state of California, launching in San Francisco in 2011. With early funding from renowned investment bank Goldman Sachs and Google Ventures, Uber expanded rapidly. At the end of 2015, the company was able to celebrate its billionth ride. It was operating in about 400 cities around the world, from Abu Dhabi to Zurich.

Uber's hectic growth was in part aimed at pre-empting competitors. It is technically fairly easy to launch a local taxi-hailing app. Some of Uber's regional competitors grew rapidly, for example Lyft in the USA, Didi Kuaidi in China, Ola in India and GrabTaxi in Southeast Asia. In December 2015, these four rivals to Uber declared a strategic alliance, promising to share technologies and offer common services to customers travelling from one region to another.

The pursuit of growth has frequently got Uber into legal trouble. There are three areas in which Uber's strategy is particularly controversial. First, there is the contention that the company does not employ its drivers, but just offers a technology platform on which drivers and passengers freely interact. With drivers considered independent contractors, the company appears absolved from costly obligations such as insurance, minimum wages, overtime pay and pensions. This has helped Uber undercut the prices of traditional taxi services: in New York, the traditional yellow cabs saw a 14 per cent drop in business after the local launch of Uber. In several localities, including its home state of California, the independent contractor status of Uber's drivers has faced legal challenges, leading to local bans or fines.

Second, by comparison with becoming a licensed taxi-driver, it is relatively easy for people to become Uber drivers. This creates safety risks, with cases of Uber drivers even assaulting passengers. In 2015, an Uber driver in Delhi was convicted of raping a passenger. Uber was accused of failing to conduct adequate background checks after it emerged the rapist had been previously accused of assaulting women. The victim lodged a lawsuit in San Francisco (later dropped) and Uber was temporarily banned by the Delhi local authorities.

A third source of controversy is Uber's apparent aggression. The motto of the company's growth team is: 'it is easier to ask for forgiveness than permission'. Uber is often careless of local regulations. Local officials regarded by Uber as obstructive have allegedly become the targets of systematic attack. A hostile official in Virginia, United States, was flooded with emails and calls after Uber distributed his personal contact information to all of its users in the state. A senior vice president of Uber was widely reported to have suggested that Uber hire a team with a million-dollar budget to dig into the personal lives and backgrounds of media reporters critical of Uber: the company was obliged to disown the suggestion. During a bitter dispute in Portland, Oregon, the transportation commissioner called Uber management 'a bunch of thugs'.

In early 2016, CEO Travis Kalanick gave his view of Uber's approach to the *Times of India*: The way of an entrepreneur is the way of an adventurer. . . . . It can be conveyed as aggressive, but it is doing things people think is against conventional wisdom. . . . Ultimately, all rules have to bend towards people and progress.

Main sources: *Financial Times*, 15 September 2015; *Times of India*, 19 January 2016; *Forbes*, 17 August 2015.

Questions

1 Using the concept of 'varieties of capitalism', in which countries would you expect Uber to be most successful and in which less so?

2 What are the costs and benefits of Uber's aggressive approach to growth?

and collective arrangements between management and labour on the other. Companies in these coordinated market economies tend to rely on banks for funding, while family ownership is often common. These economies support steady innovation over the long-run and, because of coordination networks, are typically less easy for foreign firms to penetrate. Again, neither is perfectly representative, but Germany and Japan correspond broadly to this type of institutional environment.

- *Developmental market economies* tend to have strong roles for the state, which will either own or heavily influence companies that are important for national economic development. Formally or informally, the state will often encourage private-sector firms to coordinate between themselves and with national economic policy-makers. Labour relations may be highly regulated. Banks, often state-owned, will be a key source of funding. Long-term, infrastructural and capital-intensive projects may be favoured, but foreign firms will often be at a disadvantage. Although each is very different in its own way, Brazil, China and India all have aspects of this developmental market economy environment.

A macro-environmental analysis of any particular country should therefore include an assessment of the local variety of capitalism and the extent to which it favours particular kinds of firm and strategy.

2.2.7 Key drivers for change

The previous sections have introduced a variety of concepts and frameworks for analysing each of the PESTEL factors, particularly at a macro-level. As can be imagined, analysing these factors, together with their interrelationships, can produce long and complex lists of issues. Rather than getting overwhelmed by a multitude of details, it is necessary to step back to identify the *key drivers for change* in a particular context. **Key drivers for change are the environmental factors likely to have a high impact on industries and sectors, and the success or failure of strategies within them.**

Key drivers thus translate macro-environmental factors to the level of the specific industry or sector. Thus social and legislative changes discouraging car use might have different and greater effects on supermarkets than, for example, retail banks. Identifying key drivers for change in an industry or sector helps managers to focus on the PESTEL factors that are most important and which must be addressed most urgently. Without a clear sense of the key drivers for change, managers will not be able to take the strategic decisions that allow for effective responses. To return to the example above, the supermarket chain might address reduced car use by cutting the number of out-of-town stores and investing in smaller urban and suburban sites. It is important that an organisation's strategists consider each of the key drivers for change, looking to minimise threats and, where possible, seize opportunities.

2.3 FORECASTING

In a sense, all strategic decisions involve forecasts about future conditions and outcomes. Thus a manager may decide to invest in new capacity because of a forecast of growing demand (condition), with the expectation that the investment will help capture increased sales (outcome). PESTEL factors will feed into these forecasts, for example in tracking economic cycles or mapping future technologies. However, accurate forecasting is notoriously difficult. After all, in strategy, organisations are frequently trying to surprise their competitors. Consequently, **forecasting takes three fundamental approaches based on varying degrees** of certainty: **single-point, range and multiple-futures forecasting.** This section explains these three approaches and also introduces some key concepts that help explore the direction of future change.

2.3.1 Forecast approaches

The three approaches to forecasting are explored in the following and illustrated in Figure 2.8:[17]

- *Single-point forecasting* is where organisations have such confidence about the future that they will provide just one forecast number (as in Figure 2.8(i)). For instance, an organisation might predict that the population in a market will grow by 5 per cent in the next two years. This kind of single-point forecasting implies a great degree of certainty. Demographic trends (for instance the increase in the elderly within a particular population) lend themselves to these kinds of forecasting, at least in the short term. They are also often attractive to organisations because they are easy to translate into budgets: a single sales forecast figure is useful for motivating managers and for holding them accountable.

- *Range forecasting* is where organisations have less certainty, suggesting a range of possible outcomes. These different outcomes may be expressed with different degrees of probability, with a central projection identified as the most probable (the darkest shaded area in Figure 2.8(ii)), and then a range of more remote outcomes given decreasing degrees of likelihood (the more lightly shaded areas). These forecasts are often called 'fan charts', because the range of outcomes 'fans out' more widely over time, reflecting growing uncertainty over the longer term. These 'fan charts' are often used in economic forecasting, for example economic growth rates or inflation.

- *Alternative futures forecasting* typically involves even less certainty, focusing on a set of possible yet distinct futures. Instead of a continuously graduated range of likelihoods, alternative futures are discontinuous: they happen or they do not, with radically different outcomes (see Figure 2.8(iii)). These alternatives might result from fundamental policy decisions. For example, for a country facing possible exit from a currency union (for instance the Euro), outcome A might reflect the consequences for growth or unemployment of staying in the union; outcome B might reflect the consequences of exiting the union; and outcome C would be a further alternative outcome, consequent on a decision

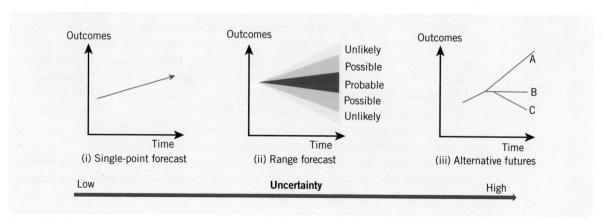

Figure 2.8 Forecasting under conditions of uncertainty

that followed the initial decision pointing towards outcome B (for instance, to adopt trade barriers as well as to exit the currency union). For a business, outcome A might represent expected sales if a competitor business did not invest in a new machine or similar capacity; outcome B is a consequence of the competitor making that investment; and outcome C is a consequence of the competitor both making that investment and then slashing prices to make full use of the new capacity. It is possible to put probabilities to each of these outcomes too: for example, outcome A might have a 40 per cent probability, while outcomes B and C would be 30 per cent each. These kinds of alternative futures are often fed into scenario analyses (see Section 2.4), though not as simple forecasts.

2.3.2 Directions of change

It is helpful in forecasting to keep an eye on the fundamental directions of likely change. Managers need to check their forecasts are consistent with major trends and to be alert to possible turning points. Three concepts help focus both on major trends and on possible turning points that might invalidate existing forecasts:

- *Megatrends* are large-scale political, economic, social, technological, ecological or legal movements that are typically slow to form, but which influence many other activities and views, possibly over decades.[18] A megatrend typically sets the direction for other factors. Thus the social megatrend towards ageing populations in the West influences other trends in social care, retail spending and housing. The megatrend towards global warming affects agriculture, tourism and, with more extreme climatic events, insurance. It is important to identify major megatrends because they influence so many other things. Forecasts should be checked for consistency with such trends.

- *Inflexion points* are moments when trends shift in direction, for instance turning sharply upwards or downwards.[19] For example, after decades of stagnation and worse, in the early twenty-first century sub-Saharan Africa may have reached an inflexion point in its economic growth, with the promise of substantial gains in the coming decade or so. Internet retailing may also have put urban shopping on a path to significant decline in advanced economies. Inflexion points are likely to invalidate forecasts that extrapolate existing trends. Clearly it is valuable to grasp the inflexion point at the moment when trends just start to turn, in order either to take advantage of new opportunities early or to act against escalating decline as soon as possible.

- *Weak signals* are advanced signs of future trends and are particularly helpful in identifying inflexion points.[20] Typically these weak signals are unstructured and fragmented bits of information, often perceived by observers as 'weird'. A weak signal for the worldwide financial crisis that began in 2008 was the rise in mortgage failures in California the previous year. An early weak signal foreshadowing the current success of Asian business schools was the first entry of the Hong Kong University of Science and Technology into the *Financial Times*' ranking of the top 50 international business schools in the early 2000s. It is important to be alert to weak signals, but it is also easy to be overwhelmed by 'noise', the constant stream of isolated and random bits of information without strategic importance. Some signs of truly significant weak signals (as opposed to mere noise) include: the repetition of the signal and the emergence of some kind of pattern; vehement disagreement among experts about the signal's significance; and an unexpected failure in something that had previously worked very reliably.

2.4 SCENARIO ANALYSIS

Scenarios offer plausible alternative views of how the macro-environment might develop in the future, typically in the long term. Thus scenarios are not strategies in themselves, but alternative possible environments which strategies have to deal with. Scenario analysis is typically used in conditions of high uncertainty, for example where the environment could go in several highly distinct directions.[21] However, scenario analyses can be differentiated from alternative futures forecasting (Section 2.3.1), as scenario planners usually avoid presenting alternatives in terms of finely calculated probabilities. Scenarios tend to extend too far into the future to allow probability calculations and besides, assigning probabilities directs attention to the most likely scenario rather than to the whole range. The point of scenarios is more to learn than to predict. Scenarios are used to explore the way in which environmental factors inter-relate and to help keep managers' minds open to alternative possibilities in the future. A scenario with a very low likelihood may be valuable in deepening managers' understanding even if it never occurs.

Illustration 2.4 shows an example of scenario planning for information technology to 2030, published by the international advisory firm Gartner. Rather than incorporating a multitude of factors, Gartner focused on two key drivers which are clearly differentiated on the dimensions of the *scenario cube* in terms of having (i) high potential impact; (ii) high uncertainty; (iii) high independence from each other (see Figure 2.9 and below). The first of these two drivers are technological, in other words the extent to which information technologies are more interconnected; the second is regulatory, with regard to the extent to which technologies are controlled. Both of these drivers may produce very different futures, which can be combined to create four internally consistent scenarios for the next decade and a half. Gartner does not predict that one scenario will prevail over the others, nor do they allocate relative probabilities. Prediction would close managers' minds to alternatives, while probabilities would imply a spurious kind of accuracy over this period of time.

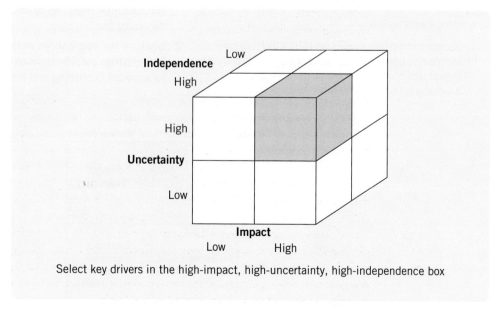

Select key drivers in the high-impact, high-uncertainty, high-independence box

Figure 2.9 The scenario cube: selection matrix for scenario key drivers

ILLUSTRATION 2.4   Datatopia?

In 2014, Gartner, a leading information technology and research company, published a major report on four scenarios for IT developments to 2030.

Gartner had identified a major switch to digitisation of products and services in the world and wanted to consider the alternative implications of this change. Accordingly, the company used crowdsourcing to get ideas for future scenarios, bringing in 132 responses from volunteers across the world. The most frequent terms in the responses were initially analysed using a word cloud, in which words such as 'privacy' and 'trust' and 'personalization' were prominent. Next a form of PESTEL analysis was used to group assumptions by different factors, subdividing them into 'utopian' (positive) and 'dystopian' (negative) groups. Gartner then derived two basic dimensions for scenario analysis:

1. The extent to which the world would be 'connected' or 'conflicted'. In a connected world, technologies would interact easily with each other, and goals would be aligned. In a conflicted world, technologies would often be used to block each other, with conflicting goals.
2. The extent to which the world would be 'controlled' or run 'amok'. In a controlled world, society would be able to manage the direction of technological developments, but in an 'amok' world, technologies would run beyond society's control.

These two dimensions yielded four scenario stories, as summarised in the figure below. Briefly, the four scenarios were as follows:

1. *Society, Inc.* extends today's world, in which big corporations and governments control reams of data about individuals. Surveillance will be the norm and privacy disappears. Both organisations' and individuals' data will be regulated (independent storage mechanisms such as USB sticks might even be banned).
2. *Sorcerer's Apprentice* takes its title from the Disney story in which brooms come to life but run out of control. Technologies can talk to each other, so that people's identities will be easy to track. Regulation of data usage will continuously be behind what new entrepreneurial companies dream up for their own profit.
3. *Digital Wild West* describes a world where public outcry over data abuses stimulates new technologies that protect individuals, for instance widespread use of encryption. Companies will charge fees for privacy, a form of 'protection money'.
4. *Datatopia* is a utopian scenario in which privacy problems are solved by new technologies such as randomly fragmented storage, with personal keys necessary to reintegrate the information. All information is protected by copyright law. All activities – from power to parking – will be 'smart'.

Source: Adapted from Gartner Inc., 'Last Call for Datatopia . . . Boarding Now! Four future scenarios on the role of information and technology in society, business and personal life, 2030', 2014.

Questions

1. Which scenario would companies like Google and Facebook most desire and which would they most fear?
2. What are the implications of these scenarios for industries outside information technology, for example publishing and hotels?

	Conflicted	Connected
Control	Society, Inc. 'Whatever'	Datatopia 'Aspiring creativity'
Amok	Digital Wild West 'State of nature'	Sorcerer's Apprentice 'Ruled by machines'

Source: Adapted from Gartner Inc. (2014), p. 6.

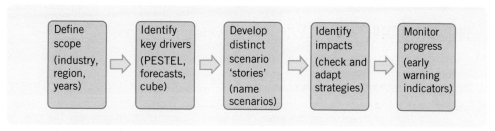

Figure 2.10 The scenario process

While there are many ways to carry out scenario analyses, the process often follows five basic steps (summarised in Figure 2.10):[22]

- *Defining scenario scope* is an important first step in the process. Scope refers to the subject of the scenario analysis and the time span. For example, scenario analyses can be carried out for a whole industry globally, or for particular geographical regions and markets. While businesses typically produce scenarios for industries or markets, governments often conduct scenario analyses for countries, regions or sectors (such as the future of health-care or higher education). Scenario time spans can be either a decade or so (as in Illustration 2.4) or perhaps just five years ahead. The appropriate time span is determined partly by the expected life of investments. In the energy business, where oil fields, for example, might have a life span of several decades, scenarios often cover 20 years or more.

- *Identifying the key drivers for change* comes next. Here PESTEL analysis can be used to uncover issues likely to have a major *impact* upon the future of the industry, region or market. In the information technology, key drivers range from regulation to innovation. The *scenario cube* (Figure 2.9) helps identify the most significant key drivers. As well as the size of impact, the scenario cube underlines two additional criteria for key drivers: *uncertainty,* in order to make different scenarios worthwhile (there's no point in developing alternative scenarios when only one outcome is likely); and *mutual independence,* so that the drivers are capable of producing significantly divergent or opposing outcomes (there's no point in considering factors individually if they lead to the same outcome anyway). In the oil industry, for example, political stability in the oil-producing regions is one major uncertainty; another is the development of new exploration technologies, enabling the quick and efficient identification of new oil fields. These could be selected as key drivers for scenario analysis because both are uncertain and regional stability is not closely correlated with technological advance.

- *Developing scenario 'stories'*. As in films, scenarios are basically stories. Having selected opposing key drivers for change, it is necessary to knit together plausible stories that incorporate both key drivers and other factors into a coherent whole. These stories are often encapsulated with striking titles: for example, oil company Shell launched two opposing scenarios entitled simply 'Oceans' and 'Mountains', the first describing a more free-market world with solar power important, the second a more government-led world, with gas power important.[23] Striking titles help to communicate scenarios and embed them in strategic discussions (see also Illustration 2.4).

- *Identifying impacts* of alternative scenarios on organisations is the next key stage of scenario building. For example, in Illustration 2.4, the possibility of private data would pose major challenges to companies making their living from the assembly, analysis and sale of data. It is important for an organisation to carry out *robustness checks* in the face of each plausible scenario and to adapt strategies that appear vulnerable and develop contingency plans in case they happen.

THINKING DIFFERENTLY   The crowdsourced forecast

Do we need experts to forecast anymore?

We usually think of forecasts as the product of small groups of experts. But there is a different way. Forecasts can be 'crowdsourced', using the collective judgement of many different kinds of people, not just experts. There are two principal ways of using the 'wisdom of crowds' in forecasting: prediction markets and internet media analysis.

Prediction markets are markets designed specifically to combine the scattered information of many participants into values (for instance, market prices or betting odds) that can be used to make predictions about specific future events.[24] An example is the Iowa Electronic Market (IEM) for betting on the outcome of American Presidential elections. Market participants buy a contract that pays a dollar if, for instance, a Democrat wins the election. The more money participants are prepared to pay for that contract, the more likely it appears that a Democrat will indeed win that election. Google uses similar prediction markets to forecast the success of possible new products: if many people within the company are prepared to bet on their

success, then probably the new products will indeed turn out well. The bets of many employees may be more reliable than the self-interested forecasts of the product's own developers.

Internet media such as Twitter and Google can also provide forecasts, drawing on the inputs of many thousands of users. For example, Google Trends analyses the frequency with which people search about flu symptoms to predict the onset of flu epidemics. Others analyse the mix of positive and negative sentiments expressed by ordinary people in Twitter feeds to forecast the direction of financial markets, up or down.[25] Data about what people are interested in, or how they feel, provides valuable clues to what will happen next.

Question

Why might experts make bad forecasters in the case of (i) Presidential elections; (ii) new product developments?

- *Monitor progress.* Once the various scenarios are drawn up, organisations should monitor progress over time, to alert themselves to whether and how developments actually fit scenario expectations. Here it is important to identify indicators that might give early warning about the final direction of environmental change, and at the same time set up systems to monitor these. Effective monitoring of well-chosen indicators should facilitate prompt and appropriate responses. In Illustration 2.4, a clear indicator of a coming Sorcerer's Apprentice world would be relaxation of data-protection laws.

Because debating and learning are so valuable in the scenario-building process, and they deal with such high uncertainty, some scenario experts advise managers to avoid producing just three scenarios. Three scenarios tend to fall into a range of 'optimistic', 'middling' and 'pessimistic'. Managers naturally focus on the middling scenario and neglect the other two, reducing the amount of organisational learning and contingency planning. It is therefore typically better to have two or four scenarios, avoiding an easy mid-point. It does not matter if the scenarios do not come to pass: the value lies in the process of exploration and contingency planning that the scenarios set off.

SUMMARY

- Environmental influences can be thought of as layers around an organisation, with the outer layer making up the *macro-environment,* the middle layer making up the *industry or sector* and the inner layer *strategic groups* and *market segments.*

- The macro-environment can be analysed in terms of the *PESTEL factors* – political, economic, social, technological, ecological and legal.

- Macro-environmental trends can be *forecast* according to different levels of uncertainty, from single-point, through ranges to multiple-futures.

- A PESTEL analysis helps identify *key drivers of change,* which managers need to address in their strategic choices. Alternative *scenarios* about the future can be constructed according to how the key drivers develop.

WORK ASSIGNMENTS

✱ Denotes more advanced work assignments.
* Refers to a case study in the Text and Cases edition.

2.1 For an organisation of your choice, carry out a PESTEL analysis and identify key opportunities and threats. Use Illustration 2.1 as a model. For simplicity, choose an organisation that is focused on a limited number of industries.

2.2 For your own country, or any other country with which you are familiar, look up the political risk as assessed by Aon, the Economist Intelligence Unit or similar (see references in endnote 4). How far do you agree with this assessment?

2.3 For the last year or two, review the forecasts for economic growth made by key forecasting organisations such as the OECD or the World Bank (see references in endnote 5). How accurate were they? What accounts for any difference between forecast and outcomes?

2.4✱ For the same organisation as in 2.1, and using Illustration 2.4 as a model, construct four scenarios for the evolution of its macro-environment (or main industry or sector). What implications are there for the organisation's strategy?

Integrative assignment

2.5 Carry out a full analysis of an industry or sector of your choice (using for example PESTEL and scenarios). Draw also on the five forces and strategic groups analyses of Chapter 3. Consider explicitly how the industry or sector is affected by globalisation (see Chapter 9, particularly Figure 9.2 on drivers) and innovation (see Chapter 10, particularly Figure 10.5 on product and process innovation).

RECOMMENDED KEY READINGS

- For an overview of techniques for thinking ahead, see P. Tetlock and D. Gardner, *Superforecasting: The art and science of prediction,* Crown, 2015. For approaches to how environments change, see K. van der Heijden, *Scenarios: The art of strategic conversation,* 2nd edn, Wiley, 2005; and R. Ramírez, J.W. Selsky and K. Van der Heijden (eds),

Business Planning for Turbulent Times: New methods for applying scenarios, Taylor & Francis, 2010.

- A collection of academic articles on PEST, scenarios and similar is the special issue of *International Studies of Management and Organization,* vol. 36, no. 3 (2006), edited by Peter McKiernan.

REFERENCES

1. PESTEL is an extension of PEST (Politics, Economics, Social and Technology) analysis, taking more account of ecological ('green') and legal issues. PEST is sometimes called STEP analysis. PESTEL is sometimes called PESTLE and is also sometimes extended to STEEPLE in order to include Ethical issues. For an application of PEST analysis to the world of business schools, see H. Thomas, 'An analysis of the environment and competitive dynamics of management education', *Journal of Management Development,* vol. 26, no. 1 (2007), pp. 9–21.

2. D. Bach and D. Allen, 'What every CEO needs to know about nonmarket strategies', *Sloan Management Review,* vol. 51, no. 3 (2010), pp. 41–8; J. Doh, T. Lawton and T. Rajwani, 'Advancing nonmarket strategy research: institutional perspectives in a changing world', *Academy of Management Perspectives,* August (2012), pp. 22–38.

3. I. Alon and T. Herbert, 'A stranger in a strange land: micro political risk and the multinational firm,' *Business Horizons,* vol. 52, no. 2 (2009), pp. 127–37; J. Jakobsen, 'Old problems remain, new ones crop up: political risk in the 21st century', *Business Horizons,* vol. 53, no. 5 (2010), pp. 481–90.

4. Organisations such as the insurance company Aon, and economic media such as the Economic Intelligence Unit and Euromoney, publish regular rankings of country political risk.

5. Macroeconomic forecasts can be found at: http://www.oecd.org/eco/outlook/; http://www.imf.org/external/; http://www.worldbank.org/.

6. For a summary, see B. de Groot and P.H. Franses, 'Stability through cycles', *Technological Forecasting and Social Change,* vol. 75, no. 3 (2008), pp. 301–11. Economists sometimes also highlight the 50-year long Kondratieff 'innovation' cycle: in this perspective, the world economy may still be on the upswing of the internet innovation cycle.

7. M.E. Porter, 'Clusters and the new economics of competition', *Harvard Business Review,* vol. 76, no. 6 (1997), pp. 77–90.

8. A useful review of research on this topic is R. Suddaby, K.D. Elsbach, R. Greenwood, J.W. Meyer, and T.B. Zilber, 'Organizations and their institutional environments – bringing meaning, values, and culture back in: Introduction to the special research forum', *Academy of Management Journal,*

vol. 53, no. 6 (2010), pp. 1234–40. For a more general review, see G. Johnson and R. Greenwood, 'Institutional theory and strategy' in M. Jenkins and V. Ambrosini (eds), *Strategic Management: a Multiple-Perspective Approach,* V. Palgrave, 3rd edn, 2015.

9. R.S. Burt, M. Kilduff and S. Tasselli, 'Social network analysis: foundations and frontiers on advantage', *Annual Review of Psychology,* vol. 64 (2013), pp. 527–47.

10. M.A. Sytch, A. Tatarynowicz and R. Gulati, 'Toward a theory of extended contact: the incentives and opportunities for bridging across network communities', *Organization Science,* vol. 23, no. 6 (2012), pp. 1658–81.

11. J. Hagedoorn and M. Cloodt, 'Measuring innovative performance: is there an advantage in using multiple indicators?', *Research Policy,* vol. 32, no. 8 (2003), pp. 1365–79.

12. A.C. Ferrari, F. Bonaccorso, V. Falko, K.S. Novoselov, S. Roche, P. Bøggild and S. Borini, 'Science and technology roadmap for graphene, related two-dimensional crystals, and hybrid systems', *Nanoscale,* vol. 7, no. 11 (2015), pp. 4598–810.

13. J.H. Lee, H.I. Kim and R. Phaal, 'An analysis of factors improving technology roadmap credibility: a communications theory assessment of roadmapping processes', *Technological Forecasting and Social Change,* vol. 79, no. 2 (2012), pp. 263–80.

14. S.L. Hart and G. Dowell, 'A natural-resource-based view of the firm: fifteen years after', *Journal of Management,* vol. 37, no. 5 (2010), pp. 1464–79.

15. J. Cantwell, J.H. Dunning and S.M. Lundan, 'An evolutionary approach to understanding international business activity: the co-evolution of MNEs and the institutional environment', *Journal of International Business Studies,* vol. 41, no. 4 (2010), pp. 567–86.

16. M.A. Witt, and G. Redding, 'Asian business systems: institutional comparison, clusters and implications for varieties of capitalism and business systems theory', *Socio-Economic Review,* vol. 11, no. 2 (2013), pp. 265–300; M.R. Schneider and M. Paunescu, 'Changing varieties of capitalism and revealed comparative advantages from 1990 to 2005: a test of the Hall and Soskice claims', *Socio-Economic Review,* vol. 10, no. 4 (2012), pp. 731–53.

17. U. Haran and D.A. Moore, 'A better way to forecast', *California Management Review*, vol. 57, no. (2014), pp. 5–15; H. Courtney, J. Kirkland and P. Viguerie, 'Strategy under uncertainty', *Harvard Business Review*, vol. 75, no. 6 (1997), pp. 67–79.

18. R.A. Slaughter, 'Looking for the real megatrends', *Futures*, October (1993), pp. 823–49.

19. A. Grove, *Only the Paranoid Survive*, Profile Books, 1998.

20. S. Mendonca, G. Caroso and J. Caraca, 'The strategic strength of weak signals', *Futures*, 44 (2012), pp. 218–28; P. Schoemaker and G. Day, 'How to make sense of weak signals', *Sloan Management Review*, vol. 50, no. 3 (2009), pp. 81–9.

21. For a discussion of scenario planning in practice, see R. Ramirez, R. Osterman and D. Gronquist, 'Scenarios and early warnings as dynamic capabilities to frame managerial attention', *Technological Forecasting and Strategic Change*, vol. 80 (2013), pp. 825–38. For how scenario planning fits with other forms of environmental analysis such as PESTEL, see G. Burt, G. Wright, R. Bradfield and K. van der Heijden, 'The role of scenario planning in exploring the environment in view of the limitations of PEST and its derivatives', *International Studies of Management and Organization*, vol. 36, no. 3 (2006), pp. 50–76. For the grid method, see R. Ramirez and A. Wilkinson, 'Rethinking the 2 × 2 scenario method: grid or frames?' *Technological Forecasting and Social Change*, vol. 86 (2014), pp. 254–64.

22. Based on P. Schoemaker, 'Scenario planning: a tool for strategic thinking', *Sloan Management Review*, vol. 36 (1995), pp. 25–34.

23. http://www.shell.com/global/future-energy/scenarios/new-lens-scenarios.html.

24. G. Tziralis and I. Tatsiopoulos, 'Prediction markets: an extended literature review', *Journal of Prediction Markets*, vol. 1, no. 1 (2012), pp. 75–91 and K. Matzler, C. Grabher, J. Huber and Füller, J. 'Predicting new product success with prediction markets in online communities', *R&D Management*, vol. 43, no. 5 (2013), pp. 420–32.

25. P. Wlodarczak, 'An approach for big data technologies in social media mining', *Journal of Art Media and Technology*, vol. 1, no. 1 (2015), pp. 61–6.

Alibaba – the Yangtze River Crocodile

Richard Whittington

In May 2015, the Alibaba Group – China's largest e-commerce company – got a new Chief Executive. Daniel Zhang was 43 years old, with a career in the accounting firms Arthur Andersen and PwC before joining Alibaba in 2007. Zhang's experience in international firms was reflected in an early statement: 'We must absolutely globalize,' he said during a company-wide strategy session. 'We will organize a global team and adopt global thinking to manage the business and achieve the goal of *global buy and global sell*.'

Zhang's appointment as CEO came at a difficult time. Alibaba had undergone the largest ever Initial Public Offering (IPO) on the New York Stock Exchange in September 2014, achieving a total valuation of $231bn (£138.6bn, €173.3bn). But the first quarter of 2015 had seen profits at half those of the same period in the previous year. The Group's share price was down a third from its post-IPO peak. Zhang's predecessor as CEO had been dismissed after just two years in the job.

The man who appointed Zhang was Jack Ma, founder of Alibaba just 16 years earlier. Alibaba started as China's first business-to-business portal connecting domestic manufacturers with overseas buyers. Since then, the Group had grown in many directions. 1688.com was founded for business-to-business trade within China. Alibaba's Taobao Marketplace serves small businesses and individuals. Tmall.com provides electronic shop fronts to help overseas companies such as Nike, Burberry and Decathlon to reach Chinese consumers. Juhuasuan offers daily deals on everything from toys to laptops. There is also Alipay, effectively under Ma's personal control but functioning as the Group's equivalent to PayPal, which processes 75 per cent of Group transactions. One way or another, it is possible for Alibaba's customers to trade almost anything: the American security services have even set up a sting operation on Alibaba to catch traders selling uranium to Iran. At the start of 2015, Alibaba had approaching 80 per cent of the e-commerce market in China, the largest e-commerce market in the world, and also had strong positions in Brazil and Russia. International e-commerce represented nearly 10 per cent of the company's total sales of 76.2bn Yuan in the financial year ending 2015 (about $12.3bn, £11.2bn, €8.2bn: see Table 1).

Alibaba had always had an international bent. Founder Jack Ma had started his career as an English language teacher in the city of Hangzhou, not far from Shanghai. As early as 2000, Ma had persuaded both the leading American investment bank Goldman Sachs and the Japanese internet giant Softbank to invest. The then ascendant America internet company Yahoo had bought nearly a quarter of the Group in 2005. Post-IPO, SoftBank still held 32.4 per cent of the shares and Yahoo 15 per cent. The Alibaba Group board counted as members Yahoo's founder Jerry Yang, Softbank's founder Masayoshi Son and Michael Evans, former vice-chairman of Goldman Sachs. Even so, Jack Ma was ambivalent about Western investors: 'Let the Wall Street investors curse us if they wish!,' Ma had proclaimed at a staff rally. 'We will still follow the principle of customers first, employees second and investors third!'

Strictly, overseas investors do not directly own stakes in the Alibaba Group, instead owning shares in a shell company – a so-called variable interest entity (VIE) – that has a contractual claim on Alibaba's profits. This VIE structure is a common way for Western-listed Chinese firms to get around Beijing's foreign-ownership rules. But the Chinese government could close the loophole at any

Table 1 Key statistics

	2010	2011	2012	2013	2014	2015
Alibaba Group Sales Yuan bn	6.7	11.9	20.0	34.5	52.5	76.2
Chinese GDP Yuan Tr.	40.4	48.4	53.4	58.8	63.6	66.8
Chinese ecommerce market Yuan Tr.	4.6	6.4	8.1	10.5	13.4	16.2
Per cent of Chinese using Internet	34.3	38.3	42.3	45.8	49.3	51.3

Sources: iResearchChina.com; InternetLiveStats.com; Statista.com.

time, and it gives foreign shareholders limited recourse against abuses by Chinese companies' managers. Ironically, the most notorious VIE controversy so far involved Alibaba's Jack Ma, who in 2011 separated Alipay from the rest of the Group without board approval. Ma said new Chinese regulations forced him to make the move. Yahoo was only told about the spin-off five weeks after it had happened. A fund-raising round for Alipay's new parent company valued Alipay at nearly $50bn.

Alibaba's relationship with the Chinese government is hard to read. Jack Ma insists that he has never taken loans or investment from the Chinese government or its banks: he had gone to overseas investors instead. However, given that a third of Chinese business activity is carried out within state-owned enterprises, the government is bound to be in close liaison with the dominant national player in e-commerce. Ma explained his philosophy as: 'Always try to stay in love with the government, but don't marry them.' The Alibaba Group has built up its political connections. Tung Chee-hwa, Hong Kong's first chief executive after its return to China, served on its board of directors. Alibaba has also allied with several so-called 'princelings', children of important political leaders. Princeling investors include Winston Wen, son of a former Chinese premier; Alvin Jiang, grandson of a former Chinese President; He Jinlei, son of a former Politburo member and a senior manager of the state Chinese Development Bank; and Jeffrey Zang, son of a former vice premier and a senior manager at China's state sovereign wealth fund, Citic Capital.

Given Chinese President Xi Jinping's sweeping political and economic reform campaign, there are no guarantees of Alibaba's position domestically. In 2015, princeling investor He Jinlei's older brother was under house arrest because of accusations of corruption. The beginning of the year had also seen the publication of an investigation by China's State Administration for Industry and Commerce into counterfeit goods and fake listings on the Group's Taobao site, leading to a 10 per cent fall in Alibaba's share price. Jack Ma commented on his relations with Chinese regulators: 'Over the past two years, not only was I a very controversial figure, but also these days, the disputes are bigger and bigger.' He continued, 'I, too, felt puzzled, sometimes wronged – how did things become this way?' Nonetheless, Ma promised to clean up the site. Even so, just a few months later, fake Apple Watches were on sale on Taobao weeks before their official launch in the United States.

President Xi Jinping's reform campaigns were partly in response to changing economic conditions in China. After three decades of double-digit growth, China's growth rate has slowed to around 7 per cent a year (see Table 1). Such growth is very respectable by world standards. Besides, faced with rising domestic concern about the environment, President Xi was happy to restrain the expansion of high polluting industries such as cement, coal and steel. At the same time, the Chinese government was promoting e-commerce as a key area for future economic growth. However, there were causes for concern. Many local authorities and firms had borrowed heavily on expectations of higher growth, and there were fears that financial institutions had over-lent. Some warned of a consequent crash. Moreover, it was hard to see China's growth rate picking up again, on account of an ageing population and the drying up of the traditional supply of young labour from rural villages: by 2015, the Chinese workforce was falling by about three million workers a year. Although the government relaxed the famous one-child per family rule in 2013, Chinese parents are still reluctant to have more children because of the cost of housing and a good education in the main urban centres. It is predicted that by the early 2030s, about a quarter of China's population will be over 65 (against 17 per cent in the United Kingdom). Slower economic growth in China overall is being matched by some slowing in the rate of growth of the Chinese e-commerce market (see Table 1).

At the same time, Alibaba faces greater competition. A decade ago, Alibaba had seen off an attack by American rival eBay in the Chinese market with a fierce price-war. Jack Ma had proclaimed: 'EBay is a shark in the ocean; we are a crocodile in the Yangtze River. If we fight in the ocean, we will lose, but if we fight in the river, we will win.' A combination of cultural, linguistic and government policy factors kept Western internet companies at arm's length in the Chinese market: Google has been reduced to a market share of about one per cent, while Amazon eventually chose to list on Alibaba's TMall site after a decade pushing its own venture in China.

But now Alibaba's home-market dominance is facing a local challenge from the aggressive JD.com. While Alibaba still depends on China's unreliable postal service to get its goods to customers' doors, JD.com has been more like Amazon in investing in its own distribution centres and delivery services. As a result, JD.com can promise same-day delivery in 43 of China's biggest cities. Moreover, JD.com is well-placed to benefit from the shift to smartphones for e-commerce. Tencent, China's largest social networking and online games company, has taken a 15 per cent stake in JD.com, giving the challenger access to more than 400 million users of its WeChat phone messaging app. WeChat allows users to scan product bar codes with their smartphone cameras to make instant purchases through JD.com. Alibaba too has been entering smartphone e-commerce, and in early 2015, smartphone sales accounted for half of its retail Chinese sales, twice the proportion of a year earlier. But smartphone screen-sizes are less attractive to advertisers, an important part of Alibaba's traditional PC-based business model. JD.com's domestic growth in the year to 2015 has been twice that of Alibaba's. Although JD.com was still only about 15 per cent of its rival's size, founder and chief executive Richard Liu has declared a goal of beating Alibaba to the top position: 'The competition makes the two companies stronger. I'm actually enjoying competing.'

Thus Alibaba's new chief executive Daniel Zhang faced many opportunities and threats in 2015. There were already promising signs in favour of the globalisation strategy, though. Alibaba's international flagship AliExpress had rapidly taken the number one position in Russia and the number three position in Brazil, with local users delighted to have direct access to cheap Chinese goods.

One target now is the United States, only second to China in market size. The Yangtze River crocodile is aiming to attack the ocean sharks in their home seas.

Sources: *China Daily*, 8 and 13 May 2015; *eMarketer*, 23 December 2014; *Financial Times*, 16 June and 9 September 2014; *South China Morning Post*, 12 February 2015; *Washington Post*, 23 November 2014. With thanks to Mariya Eranova and Robert Wright for comments on an earlier version of this case.

Questions

1 Carry out a PESTEL analysis of Alibaba at the time of the case. Evaluate the balance of opportunities and threats, using the same kind of figure as in Illustration 2.1.

2 Draw a basic sociogram of Alibaba's network (see Section 2.2.3 and Figure 2.5). Explain why this network may be useful.

3

INDUSTRY AND SECTOR ANALYSIS

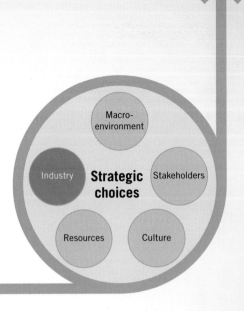

Learning outcomes

After reading this chapter you should be able to:

- Use *Porter's Competitive Five Forces Framework* to analyse industries or sectors: rivalry, threat of entrants, substitute threats, customer's power and supplier power.

- On the basis of the five competitive forces and *complementors* and *network effects*, define *industry attractiveness* and identify ways of managing these.

- Understand different *industry types* and how industries develop and change in *industry life cycles* and how to make five force analyses dynamic through *comparative industry structure analysis*.

- Analyse strategic and competitor positions in terms of *strategic groups, market segments* and the *strategy canvas*.

- Use these various concepts and techniques together with those from Chapter 2 in order to recognise *threats* and *opportunities* in the industry and marketplace.

Key terms

Blue Oceans p.86

complementors p.69

critical success factors p.85

industry p.63

market p.63

market segment p.84

network effects p.71

Porter's Five Forces Framework p.64

strategic groups p.81

strategic lock-in p.71

strategy canvas p.85

value net p.70

3.1 INTRODUCTION

In the last chapter, we considered how the broad macro-environment influences opportunities and threats. The impact of these general factors tends to surface in the immediate environment of the specific industry or sector. The immediate and direct opportunities and threats of this environment are the focus of this chapter. For example, Samsung's strategy depends on the smartphone industry: here it must take account of competitors' strategies, customers' needs and the supply of phone components, for example microchips. Similarly, a hospital needs to consider actors in the healthcare sector including clients, other healthcare providers and the supply of healthcare inputs such as pharmaceuticals. This suggests that it is crucial for managers to examine the industry or sector and the actors these involve carefully in order to determine what strategy to pursue.

The focus here is thus on the middle 'industry' and 'sector' layer in Figure 2.1 (see the last chapter), which involves central actors that influence an organisation's long-term survival and success including competitors, customers or clients, and suppliers. An **industry is a group of firms producing products and services that are essentially the same.**[1] Examples are the automobile industry and the airline industry. Industries are also often described as 'sectors', especially in public services (e.g. the health sector or the education sector). Industries and sectors are often made up of several specific markets or market segments. A **market is a group of customers for specific products or services that are essentially the same (e.g. a particular geographical market).** Thus the automobile industry has markets in North America, Europe and Asia, for example.

This chapter examines three main topics and provides different frameworks and concepts for understanding the industry or sector:

- Industry analysis through the use of the *Competitive Five Forces Framework,* which examines five essential industry forces: competitors, customers, potential entrants, suppliers and substitutes. Two additional factors are *complementors* and *network effects.* Together these forces and factors provide an understanding of industry attractiveness and competitive strategy.

- Fundamental industry structures and dynamics, which include examinations of underlying economic *industry types* and how industries evolve through *industry life cycles,* which might influence changes in the five forces that can be examined with a *comparative five force analysis.*

- Competitor groups and segments including examinations of *strategic groups,* groups of organisations with similar strategies and of *market segments,* groups of customers with similar needs. This focus provides a more fine-grained understanding of competition within an industry or sector.

The structure and topics of this chapter are summarised in Figure 3.1.

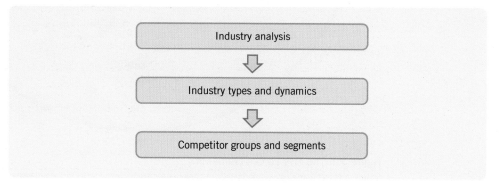

Figure 3.1 Industry and sector environments: the key topics

3.2 THE COMPETITIVE FORCES

Industries vary widely in terms of their attractiveness, as measured by how easy it is for participating firms to earn high profits. A key determinant of profitability is the extent of competition and the strength of buyers and suppliers, and this varies between industries. Where competition and buyer and supplier strengths are low, and there is little threat of new competitors, participating firms should normally expect good profits. Profitability between industries can thus vary considerably; for example, the pharmaceutical industry has performed very well while others, like the airline industry, have underperformed.[2]

Porter's Five Forces Framework[3] helps to analyse an industry and identify the attractiveness of it in terms of five competitive forces: (i) extent of rivalry between competitors (ii) threat of entry, (iii) threat of substitutes, (iv) power of buyers and (v) power of suppliers. These five forces together constitute an industry's 'structure' (see Figure 3.2), which is typically fairly stable. Porter's main message is that where the five forces are high and strong, industries are not attractive. Excessive competitive rivalry, powerful buyers and suppliers and the threat of substitutes or new entrants will all combine to squeeze profitability.

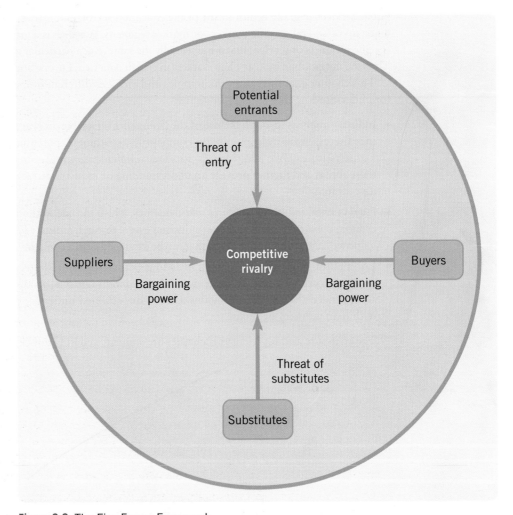

Figure 3.2 The Five Forces Framework

Source: Adapted from *Competitive Strategy: Techniques for Analyzing Industries and Competitors* by Michael E. Porter, copyright © 1980, 1998 by The Free Press. All rights reserved.

Although initially developed with businesses in mind, the five forces framework is relevant to most organisations. It can provide a useful starting point for strategic analysis even where profit criteria may not apply. In the public sector, it is important to understand how powerful suppliers can push up costs; in the charity sector, it is important to avoid excessive rivalry within the same market. Moreover, once the degree of industry attractiveness has been understood, the five forces can help set an agenda for action on the various critical issues that they identify: for example, what specific strategy to pursue in order to control excessive rivalry in a particular industry? Managers should try to finds positions where the organisation can best defend itself against strong competitive forces or where they can influence them in its favour. The rest of this section introduces each of the five forces in more detail and discusses industry definition and the implications of the forces. Illustration 3.3 at the very end of this section summarises industry and sector analysis and provides an overview of its various steps.

3.2.1 Competitive rivalry

At the centre of five forces analysis is the rivalry between the existing players – 'incumbents' – in an industry. The more competitive rivalry there is, the worse it is for incumbents. *Competitive rivals* are organisations aiming at the same customer groups and with similar products and services (i.e. not substitutes). In the European airline industry, Air France and British Airways are rivals; high-speed trains are a 'substitute' (see below). Five factors tend to define the extent of rivalry in an industry or market:

- *Competitor concentration and balance.* Where competitors are numerous or of roughly equal size or power there is the danger of intensely rivalrous behaviour as competitors attempt to gain dominance over others, through aggressive price cuts, for example. Conversely, less rivalrous industries tend to have one or two dominant organisations, with the smaller players reluctant to challenge the larger ones directly (e.g. by focusing on niches to avoid the 'attention' of the dominant companies).

- *Industry growth rate.* In situations of strong growth, an organisation can grow with the market, but in situations of low growth or decline, any growth is likely to be at the expense of a rival, and meet with fierce resistance. Low-growth markets are therefore often associated with price competition and low profitability. The *industry life cycle* influences growth rates, and hence competitive conditions: see Section 3.3.2.

- *High fixed costs.* Industries with high fixed costs, perhaps because they require high investments in capital equipment or initial research, tend to be highly rivalrous. Companies will seek to spread their costs (i.e. reduce unit costs) by increasing their volumes: to do so, they typically cut their prices, prompting competitors to do the same and thereby triggering price wars in which everyone in the industry suffers. Similarly, if extra capacity can only be added in large increments (as in many manufacturing sectors, for example a chemical or glass factory), the competitor making such an addition is likely to create short-term over-capacity in the industry, leading to increased competition to use capacity.

- *High exit barriers.* The existence of high barriers to exit – in other words, closure or disinvestment – tends to increase rivalry, especially in declining industries. Excess capacity persists and consequently incumbents fight to maintain market share. Exit barriers might be high for a variety of reasons: for example, high redundancy costs or high investment in specific assets such as plant and equipment which others would not buy.

- *Low differentiation.* In a commodity market, where products or services are poorly differentiated, rivalry is increased because there is little to stop customers switching between competitors and the only way to compete is on price. Petrol is a commodity market, for instance.

3.2.2 The threat of entry

How easy it is to enter the industry influences the degree of competition. The greater the threat of entry, the worse it is for incumbents in an industry. An attractive industry has high barriers to entry that reduce the threat of new competitors. *Barriers to entry* are the factors that need to be overcome by new entrants if they are to compete in an industry. Illustration 3.1 describes the entry barriers into the banking industry and the obstacles they provide for new entrants. Five important entry barriers are:

- *Scale and experience.* In some industries, *economies of scale* are extremely important: for example, in the production of automobiles or the advertising of fast-moving consumer goods (see Chapter 7). Once incumbents have reached large-scale production, it will be very expensive for new entrants to match them and until they reach a similar volume they will have higher unit costs. This scale effect is increased where there are high *capital investment requirements* for entry, for example research costs in pharmaceuticals or capital equipment costs in automobiles. Barriers to entry also come from *experience curve* effects that give incumbents a cost advantage because they have learnt how to do things more efficiently than an inexperienced new entrant could possibly do (see Section 7.2.1). Until the new entrant has built up equivalent experience over time, it will tend to produce at higher cost. In some industries there are 'demand or buyer side' economies of scale or *network effects* as buyers value being in a 'network' of a large number of other customers (see Section 3.2.6 below).

- *Access to supply or distribution channels.* In many industries manufacturers have had control over supply and/or distribution channels. Sometimes this has been through direct ownership (vertical integration), sometimes just through customer or supplier loyalty. In some industries this barrier has been overcome by new entrants who have bypassed retail distributors and sold directly to consumers through e-commerce (e.g. Dell Computers and Amazon).

- *Expected retaliation.* If an organisation considering entering an industry believes that the retaliation of an existing firm will be so great as to prevent entry, or mean that entry would be too costly, this is also a barrier. Retaliation could take the form of a price war or a marketing blitz. Just the knowledge that incumbents are prepared to retaliate is often sufficiently discouraging to act as a barrier.

- *Legislation or government action.* Legal restraints on new entry vary from patent protection (e.g. pharmaceuticals), to regulation of markets (e.g. pension selling), through to direct government action (e.g. tariffs). Of course, organisations are vulnerable to new entrants if governments remove such protection, as has happened with deregulation of the airline industry over the last couple of decades.

- *Incumbency advantages.* Incumbents may have cost or quality advantages not available to entrants including access to proprietary technology, raw material sources and geographical locations or an established brand identity. The medical instruments industry is, for example, protected by many patents and Coca Cola and Pepsi have brand loyalties developed over decades that few can overcome.

3.2.3 The threat of substitutes

Substitutes are products or services that offer the same or a similar benefit to an industry's products or services, but have a different nature. For example, aluminium is a substitute for steel; a tablet computer is a substitute for a laptop; charities can be substitutes for

ILLUSTRATION 3.1   Busted banking barriers?

The barriers to entry into the retail banking industry have traditionally been very high, but there are signs they could possibly be tumbling.

The high barriers to entry in financial services include two economic categories. First are the *structural* barriers due to basic industry conditions, and in this industry they include economies of scale, network effects and regulation. The last is significant; to protect the safety and stability of the financial system there are high regulatory walls. Second, incumbents may deliberately promote *strategic* barriers to keep or drive competitors out, like setting prices artificially low or spending heavily on product and brand advertising. The latter has some importance in banking, but the former does not. However, structural regulation barriers could be considered strategic in this industry as incumbents tend to exploit and lobby for them to their own advantage to keep competitors out.

In the UK, these barriers have resulted in the 'Big Five' domination: HSBC, Barclays, Royal Bank of Scotland, Lloyds and Santander. Other markets are very similar with a 'Big Five' in Canada, 'Big Threes' in Spain and the Netherlands and a 'Big Four' in Sweden. It seemed as if regulators would lower barriers to increase competition. However, in the aftermath of the 2008 financial crisis regulations have increased. The dilemma for regulators is that they have two partly conflicting objectives. First, to secure the stability of the financial system they need to increase capital requirements regulation for banks. The second aim is to deliver more efficiency and more services for customers through increased competition. To act on this second objective, regulators have started to encourage more entrants and assist them to find cracks in the barriers without totally breaking them. For example, Britain's Payment Systems Regulator has proposed that banks should cut their ownership stakes in the core payment systems as Managing Director Hannah Nixon confirms:

'There needs to be a fundamental change in the industry to encourage new entrants to compete on service, price and innovation in an open and transparent way.'

The UK's financial regulators have even launched a start-up unit to help new players to enter as Andrew Bailey, former CEO of the Prudential Regulation Authority explained:

'The New Bank Start-Up Unit builds on the work we have already done to reduce the barriers to entry for prospective banks, which has led to twelve new banks now authorised since April 2013.'

It remains to be seen if competition will increase, but adding to the regulators' aspirations is a new breed of potent rivals that may prove more powerful. Helped by new IT technologies, software and mobile banking there are over a hundred so-called 'fintech' (finance and technology) start-ups as confirmed in a Deloitte report:

'New, agile and hitherto unregulated players are emerging and are disintermediating the traditional incumbents.'

Even if incumbents also try to jump on this fintech bandwagon they may not be able to dominate it. In contrast to the flourishing fintech start-ups, they are not only behind the entry barriers, but bound by them as the report continued:

'Regulation is making it harder to innovate and grow, whilst legacy strategy, infrastructure and thinking, are preventing the existing players from responding aggressively from this threat.'

Sources: E. Robinson, *BloombergBusiness*, 16 February 2016; H. Jones, *Reuters*, 25 February 2016; Financial Conduct Authority, 20 January 2016; J. Cumbo, *Financial Times*, 6 December 2015; FCA, 25 February 2016; Deloitte, 'Digital disruption: threats and opportunities for retail financial services', 2014.

Questions

1 Evaluate the strengths of the banking industry's entry barriers according to Porter's criteria.

2 How would you evaluate the ethical behaviour of banks trying to keep competition out?

public services. Managers often focus on their competitors in their own industry, and neglect the threat posed by substitutes. Substitutes can reduce demand for a particular type of product as customers switch to alternatives – even to the extent that this type of product or service becomes obsolete. However, there does not have to be much actual switching for the substitute threat to have an effect. The simple risk of substitution puts a cap on the prices that can be charged in an industry. Thus, although Eurostar has no direct competitors in terms of train services from Paris to London, the prices it can charge are ultimately limited by the cost of flights between the two cities.

There are two important points to bear in mind about substitutes:

- *The price/performance ratio* is critical to substitution threats. A substitute is still an effective threat even if more expensive, so long as it offers performance advantages that customers value. Thus aluminium is more expensive than steel, but its relative lightness and its resistance to corrosion gives it an advantage in some automobile manufacturing applications. It is the ratio of price to performance that matters, rather than simple price.

- *Extra-industry effects* are the core of the substitution concept. Substitutes come from outside the incumbents' industry and should not be confused with competitors' threats from within the industry. The value of the substitution concept is to force managers to look outside their own industry to consider more distant threats and constraints. If the buyers' *switching costs* for the substitute are low the threat increases and the higher the threat, the less attractive the industry is likely to be.

3.2.4 The power of buyers

Buyers are the organisation's immediate customers, not necessarily the ultimate consumers. If buyers are powerful, then they can demand low prices or costly product or service improvements.

Buyer power is likely to be high when some of the following four conditions prevail:

- *Concentrated buyers.* Where a few large customers account for the majority of sales, buyer power is increased. This is the case for items such as milk in the grocery sector in many European countries, where just a few retailers dominate the market. If a product or service accounts for a *high percentage of total purchases* of the buyer their power is also likely to increase as they are more likely to 'shop around' to get the best price and therefore 'squeeze' suppliers more than they would for more trivial purchases.

- *Low switching costs.* Where buyers can easily switch between one supplier and another, they have a strong negotiating position and can squeeze suppliers who are desperate for their business. Switching costs are typically low for *standardised and undifferentiated products* like commodities such as steel. They are also likely to be low when the buyers are *fully informed* about prices and product performance.

- *Buyer competition threat.* If the buyer has the capability to supply itself, or if it has the possibility of acquiring such a capability, it tends to be powerful. In negotiation with its suppliers, it can raise the threat of doing the suppliers' job themselves. This is called *backward vertical integration* (see Section 8.5), moving back to sources of supply, and might occur if satisfactory prices or quality from suppliers cannot be obtained. For example, some steel companies have gained power over their iron ore suppliers as they have acquired iron ore sources for themselves.

- *Low buyer profits and impact on quality.* For industrial or organisational buyers there are two additional factors that can make them price sensitive and thus increase their threat: first, if the buyer group is unprofitable and pressured to reduce purchasing costs and, second, if the quality of the buyer's product or services is little affected by the purchased product.

It is very important that *buyers* are distinguished from *ultimate consumers*. Thus for companies like Procter & Gamble or Unilever (makers of shampoo, washing powders and so on), their buyers are retailers such as Carrefour or Tesco, not ordinary consumers. Carrefour and Tesco have much more negotiating power than an ordinary consumer would have. The high buying power of such supermarkets is a strategic issue for the companies supplying them. It is often useful therefore to distinguish '*strategic customers*', powerful buyers (such as the retailers) towards whom the strategy should be primarily orientated. In the public sector, the strategic customer is typically the provider of funds, rather than the consumer of services: for a pharmaceutical company, the strategic customer is the hospital, not the patient.

3.2.5 The power of suppliers

Suppliers are those who supply the organisation with what it needs to produce the product or service. As well as fuel, raw materials and equipment, this can include labour and sources of finance. The factors increasing supplier power are the converse to those for buyer power. Thus *supplier power* is likely to be high where there are:

- *Concentrated suppliers.* Where just a few producers dominate supply, suppliers have more power over buyers. The iron ore industry is now concentrated in the hands of three main producers, leaving the steel companies, still relatively fragmented, in a weak negotiating position for this essential raw material.

- *High switching costs.* If it is expensive or disruptive to move from one supplier to another, then the buyer becomes relatively dependent and correspondingly weak. Microsoft is a powerful supplier because of the high switching costs of moving from one operating system to another. Buyers are prepared to pay a premium to avoid the trouble, and Microsoft knows it.

- *Supplier competition threat.* Suppliers have increased power where they are able to enter the industry themselves or cut out buyers who are acting as intermediaries. Thus airlines have been able to negotiate tough contracts with travel agencies as the rise of online booking has allowed them to create a direct route to customers. This is called *forward vertical integration,* moving up closer to the ultimate customer.

- *Differentiated products.* When the products or services are highly differentiated, suppliers will be more powerful. For example, although discount retailers like Walmart are extremely powerful, suppliers with strong brands, like P&G with Gilette, still have high negotiating power. Also, if there is no or few substitutes for the input the supplier group will be more powerful, like pilots' unions in the airline industry.

Most organisations have many suppliers, so it is necessary to concentrate the analysis on the most important ones or types. If their power is high, suppliers can capture all their buyers' own potential profits simply by raising their prices. Star football players have succeeded in raising their rewards to astronomical levels, while even the leading football clubs – their 'buyers' – struggle to make money.

3.2.6 Complementors and network effects

The five forces framework has to be used carefully and is not necessarily complete. Some industries may need the understanding of a 'sixth force', organisations that are complementors rather than simple competitors. **An organisation is your complementor if it enhances your business attractiveness to customers or suppliers.**[4] On the *demand side,* if customers value a product or service more when they also have the other organisation's product there is a complementarity with respect to customers. For example, app providers are complementors to Apple and other smartphone and tablet suppliers because customers value the iPhone and iPad more if there are a wide variety of appealing apps to download. This suggests that Apple and other actors in this industry need to take the app providers into consideration when forming their strategies. On the *supply side*, another organisation is a complementor with respect to suppliers if it is more attractive for a supplier to deliver when it also supplies the other organisation. This suggests that competing airline companies, for example, can be complementary to each other in this respect because for a supplier like Boeing it is more attractive to invest in particular improvements for two customers rather than one.

Complementarity implies a significant shift in perspective. While Porter's Five Forces sees organisations as battling against each other for share of industry value, complementors may *cooperate* to increase the total value available.[5] Opportunities for cooperation can be seen through a **value net: a map of organisations in a business environment demonstrating opportunities for value-creating cooperation as well as competition.** In Figure 3.3 Sony is a

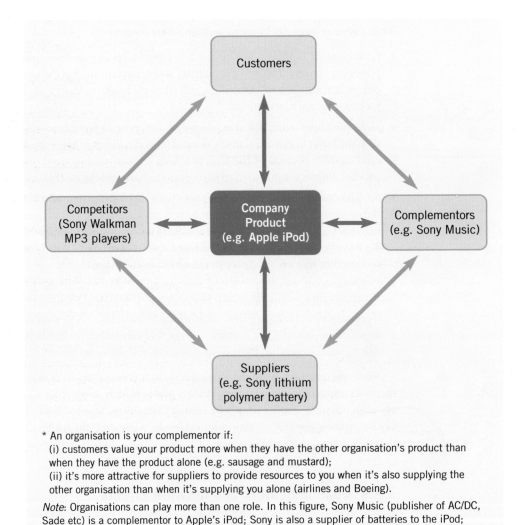

* An organisation is your complementor if:
  (i) customers value your product more when they have the other organisation's product than when they have the product alone (e.g. sausage and mustard);
  (ii) it's more attractive for suppliers to provide resources to you when it's also supplying the other organisation than when it's supplying you alone (airlines and Boeing).

Note: Organisations can play more than one role. In this figure, Sony Music (publisher of AC/DC, Sade etc) is a complementor to Apple's iPod; Sony is also a supplier of batteries to the iPod; Sony also competes with its own MP3 players.

Figure 3.3 The value net

Source: Reprinted by permission of *Harvard Business Review*. From 'The Right Game' by A. Brandenburger and B. Nalebuff, July–August 1996, pp. 57–64. Copyright © 1996 by the Harvard Business School Publishing Corporation. All rights reserved.

complementor, supplier and competitor to Apple's iPod. Sony and Apple have an interest in cooperating as well as competing.

Customers may not only value a product more if they also have another product or service as discussed above, but if other customers use the same product or service. When this is the case the product or service shows network effects or network externalities. **There are network effects in an industry when one customer of a product or service has a positive effect on the value of that product for other customers.** This implies that the more customers that use the product, the better for everyone in the network.[6] For example, the value of the online auction site eBay increases for a customer as the network of other sellers and buyers grows on the site. The more goods that are offered on the site, the better for customers and this makes eBay's site and services more attractive to users than smaller competitors. Network effects are very important for Facebook too (see in Illustration 3.2). Network effects can make an industry structurally attractive with high barriers to entry, low intensity of rivalry and power over buyers as entrants and rivals can't compete with other companies' larger networks and buyers become locked into them. If these effects are present in an industry they need to be carefully considered in addition to the five forces when trying to understand industry structure and strategic positioning.[7] For hardware and software computer products the number of users in a network is often referred to as an 'installed base'.

In some industries complementors and network effects work in tandem. In the smart-phone and tablet industries, for example, they operate in two steps. First, app providers are complementors to Apple as customers are more attracted to the iPhone and iPad if there are many apps. Second, when more customers are attracted to these products the network of users grows, which increases the user value even further. For Apple then the complementary app providers attract more users and this in turn provide for network effects that attract even further users. Other industries where competitors need to consider both complementors and network effects are video gaming (e.g. Nintendo) and computer operating systems industries (e.g. Microsoft).

Both complementors and network effects can create lock-ins. **Strategic lock-in is where users become dependent on a supplier and are unable to use another supplier without substantial switching costs.**[8] Strategic lock-in is related to the concept of path dependency (see Section 6.2.1) and is particularly valuable to differentiators. With customers securely locked in, it becomes possible to keep prices well above costs. For example, customers that bought music on Apple's iTunes store could earlier only play it on Apple's own iPod players. To switch to a Sony player would mean losing access to all the iTunes music previously purchased. Network effects can also create lock-in because when more and more users use the same product and technology it becomes more expensive to switch to another product or service. Sometimes companies are so successful that they create an industry standard under their own control. Microsoft built this kind of proprietary standard with its Windows operating system, which holds more than 90 per cent of the market. For a business to switch to another operating system would mean retraining staff and translating files onto the new system, while perhaps creating communications problems with network members (such as customers or suppliers) who had stuck with Windows.

3.2.7 Defining the industry

The first step in an industry analysis is to define the industry and there are several issues to consider here. First, and most generally, the industry must not be defined too broadly or narrowly. For example, if an entrepreneur considers starting a taxi business in Stockholm it would be much too broad to define the industry as 'the personal

ILLUSTRATION 3.2　Facebook's network fears

Considering Facebook's dominance they should have nothing to fear, but internet history is littered with fast rising and fast falling social networks.

A Statista survey found that with 1.5 billion users Facebook is not only the largest social network globally, but they control the second, third and seventh largest networks: WhatsApp (900m users), Facebook Messenger (800m) and Instagram (400m). It seems they are well ahead of everyone else in network effects and have created high switching costs for users to move to another social network. When users have built up a set-up of perhaps hundreds of friends and have archives of their whole life including photos they don't easily switch to another company and network just because it's something fresh.

Nevertheless, despite Facebook's clear lead, history shows it's far from obvious that any social network incumbent can stay relevant and dominate long term. Friendster pioneered the online community in 2002, three years before Facebook, and gained over three million users within a year; attracting tens of millions of users at its height. It was, however, soon overtaken by MySpace that appealed to even more and younger users with their more hip feature-filled environment including music and music videos. By 2008, it was the leading US social networking site with over 75 million users and consistently ahead of Facebook in traffic. However, soon Facebook started to attract teenagers with their new features with corresponding losses for MySpace. This overview illustrates that networks can quickly gain millions of users and huge valuations, but can just as quickly face slowing growth, users leaving in millions and final implosion. Further back in internet history, there are several other implosions of those with social network ambitions: BBS, CompuServe, AOL, etc.

Founder and CEO Mark Zuckerberg has, however, seen the threats and taken action. Instagram was acquired in 2012 when they were becoming the biggest mobile photo-sharing service with many younger users posting content there rather than on Facebook's own web-based photo service. Next was WhatsApp, the biggest messaging service globally; it was bought in 2014 as users started to move their activities to mobile platforms. To fence off LinkedIn they have launched 'Facebook at Work'. Not even Google has managed to remove Facebook from the social networking throne. Google's first social networking effort was Buzz, based on its Gmail service, but it never managed to attract enough users. Many Facebook users tried Google's next and even bigger bet, but soon discovered that not many of their friends followed so they returned and Google Plus, although still existing in another format, also flopped.

As of 2016, Facebook remains unbeaten and has perhaps learnt from social networking history. With their current valuation they can possibly continue to make defensive acquisitions as users are attracted to competing platforms, content and media, like Snapchat. But how long will it last? Some question Facebook's staying power and claim it's quite possible they will be overtaken. However, as reported by Forbes, Mark Zuckerberg, however, only sees this as inspiration to build Facebook even stronger:

'This is a perverse thing, personally, but I would rather be in the cycle where people are underestimating us. It gives us latitude to go out and make big bets that excite and amaze people.'

Sources: Statista 2016; R. Waters, *Financial Times,* 29 January 2016; J. Gapper, *Financial Times,* 12 April 2015; J. Bercovici, *Forbes,* 11 September 2012; A. Liu, digitaltrends.com, 5 August 2014; R. Waters, *Financial Times,* 21 February 2014; and J. Gapper, *Financial Times,* 3 October 2013.

Questions

1 Why are network effects important for Facebook? Would you switch to another social network if it had better features even if it was considerably smaller?

2 What other social media networks and apps do you use that you think could beat Facebook? Why?

transportation industry' while 'the minicab industry in central Stockholm' would be too narrow. The first definition would include such a wide variety of actors that the analysis would become meaningless, while the second risks excluding important competitors (e.g taxi firms from the suburbs).

Secondly, the broader industry value chain needs to be considered. Different industries often operate in different parts of a value chain or value system and should be analysed separately (see Section 4.4.2 for a discussion of value systems). For example, the iron ore industry (including companies like Vale, Rio Tinto and BHP Billiton) delivers to the steel manufacturing industry (including companies like Mittal Steel and Tata Steel) that in turn deliver to a wide variety of industries such as automobiles and construction. These three stages in the broader value chain or system should be analysed separately.

Thirdly, most industries can be analysed at different levels, for example different geographies, markets and even different product or service segments within them (see Section 3.4.2 below). Thus the airline industry has different geographical markets (Europe, China and so on) and it also has different service segments within each market (e.g. leisure, business and freight). The competitive forces are likely to be different for each of these markets and segments, with distinct buyers, suppliers and barriers, etc. Michael Porter has his own rule of thumb here and suggests that you are likely dealing with distinct industries if there are differences between them in more than one force, or where differences in any force are large.[9] In brief, it is important to consider both to what extent a market is national, regional or global (see Section 9.4 for a discussion of degree of internationalisation) and if product and service segments differ.

Larger corporations are often organised based on diverse markets and segments and would thus analyse each separately. For example, Electrolux, the Swedish appliance manufacturer, organises its major appliances (refrigerators, washing machines, etc.) in regional geographical markets, but also has two global business segments (small appliances and professional products) and would analyse all of these separately. The specific strategy question or organisation at issue might also provide a good indication of how to define the industry. Sometimes there is no ideal way of drawing the industry borders. Under these circumstances, the important thing is to draw the industry borders clearly. They have to be drawn consistently when it comes to what actors are inside and outside the industry. In particularly complex cases it might be necessary to try out both more narrow definitions to identify details and broader ones to avoid overlooking important actors.

3.2.8 Implications of the Competitive Five Forces

The Competitive Five Forces Framework provides several useful insights into the forces and actors at work in the industry or market environment of an organisation. The objective is more than simply listing the strength of the forces and their underlying driving factors. The ultimate aim is rather to determine whether the industry is a good one to compete in or not and to what extent there are strategic positions where an individual organisation can defend itself against strong competitive forces, can exploit weak ones or can influence the forces in its favour. The aim of the five force analysis is thus an assessment of the *attractiveness* of the industry and any possibilities to *manage strategies* in relation to the forces to promote long-term survival and competitive advantage. These considerations make up the last three steps in an industry analysis together with an assessment of industry change, which is discussed in the next section. See Illustration 3.3 for the different steps in an industry analysis. When each of the five forces has been evaluated, the next step is thus to understand the implications of these:

- *Which industries to enter (or leave)?* One important purpose of the five forces framework is to identify the relative attractiveness of different industries: industries are attractive when the forces are weak. In general, entrepreneurs and managers should invest in industries where the five forces work in their favour and avoid, or disinvest from, markets where they are strongly unfavourable. Entrepreneurs sometimes choose markets because entry barriers are low: unless barriers are likely to rise quickly, this is precisely the wrong reason to enter. Here it is important to note that just one significantly adverse force can be enough to undermine the attractiveness of the industry as a whole. For example, powerful buyers can extract all the potential profits of an otherwise attractive industry structure by forcing down prices. Chapter 8 further examines these *strategic choices* and *corporate strategy* and what to consider when deciding to invest into or divest out of various industries.

- *How can the five forces be managed?* Industry structures are not necessarily fixed, but can be influenced by deliberate managerial strategies. Managers should identify strategic positions where the organisation best can defend itself against strong competitive forces, can exploit weak ones or can influence them. As a general rule, managers should try to influence and exploit any weak forces to its advantage and neutralise any strong ones. For example, if barriers to entry are low, an organisation can raise them by increasing advertising spending to improve customer loyalty. Managers can buy up competitors to reduce rivalry and to increase power over suppliers or buyers. If buyers are very strong, an organisation can try to differentiate products or services for a specific customer group and thus increase their loyalty and switching costs. Managing and influencing industry structure involves many issues relating to *strategic choices* and *business strategy* and will be a major concern of Chapter 7.

- *How are competitors affected differently?* Not all competitors will be affected equally by changes in industry structure, deliberate or spontaneous. If barriers are rising because of increased R&D or advertising spending, smaller players in the industry may not be able to keep up with the larger players, and be squeezed out. Similarly, growing buyer power is likely to hurt small competitors most. Strategic group analysis is helpful here (see Section 3.4.1).

Although originating in the private sector, five forces analysis can have important implications for organisations in the public and charity sectors too. For example, the forces can be used to adjust the service offer or focus on key issues. Thus it might be worth switching managerial initiative from an arena with many crowded and overlapping services (e.g. social work, probation services and education) to one that is less rivalrous and where the organisation can do something more distinctive. Similarly, strategies could be launched to reduce dependence on particularly powerful and expensive suppliers, for example energy sources or high-shortage skills.

3.3 INDUSTRY TYPES AND DYNAMICS

The five forces framework is the most well-known strategy tool for industry analysis, but it has to be used carefully. First, industry types and their underlying economic characteristics should be considered as there will have major implications on industry attractiveness and what competitive strategies are available. Second, even though industry structures are

ILLUSTRATION 3.3 — Steps in an industry analysis

There are several important steps in an industry analysis before and after analysing the five forces.

Emily wants to start a coffee shop and perhaps even try to grow the business into several outlets. She needs to consider the following steps and questions:

1 **Define the industry clearly.** Do the actors in the industry face the same buyers, suppliers, entry barriers and substitutes?
   - *Vertical scope*: What stages of the industry value chain/system?
   - *Product or service scope*: What products or services? Which ones are actually parts of other, separate industries? What segments?
   - *Geographic scope*: local, national, regional or global competition?

Emily should consider that many diverse businesses serve coffee. They include not only local cafés and coffee shop chains, but fast food chains, kiosks and restaurants. The definition also depends on whether Emily intends to start in an urban or rural area.

2 **Identify the actors of each of the five forces and, if relevant, define different groups within them and the basis for this.** Which are the . . .
   - competitors that face the same competitive forces? (compare point 1 above)
   - buyers and buyer groups (e.g. end customers vs intermediaries, individual vs organisational)?
   - suppliers and supplier groups (e.g. diverse supplier categories)?
   - potential entrants?
   - substitutes?

Provided there is a clear industry definition the identification of the actors for each force should be rather straightforward for Emily, but groups within them need to be considered. On the supplier side, for example, they include not only inputs like coffee but also the location of the premises and labour supply.

3 **Determine the underlying factors and total strength of each force.**
   - Which are the main underlying factors for each force? Why?
   - Which competitive forces are strong? Which are weak? Why?

Not all underlying factors on the five force checklists will be equally relevant for Emily. With respect to buyers, for example, the products' degree of standardisation and prices matters most, while others are less important.

4 **Assess the overall industry structure and attractiveness.**
   - How attractive is the industry? Why?
   - Which are the most important competitive forces? Which control profitability?
   - Are more profitable competitors better positioned in relation to the five forces?

For Emily several of the forces are quite strong, but some are relatively more important for profitability. In addition, some competitors, like large coffee chains, are better positioned versus the five forces than others.

5 **Assess recent and expected future changes for each force.**
   - What are the potential positive/negative changes? How likely are they?
   - Are new entrants and/or competitors changing the industry structure in any way?

For example, Emily needs to consider the proliferation of coffee chains during the last few years and that pubs and bakers have improved their coffee offerings lately. Maybe she can also spot possible changes in consumer trends and growth.

6 **Determine how to position your business in relation to the five forces.** Can you:
   - exploit any of the weak forces?
   - neutralise any of the strong forces?
   - exploit industry change in any way?
   - influence and change the industry structure to your advantage?

To cope with the forces Emily could possibly identify a concept that would attract a certain group of customers even if buyers have many choices in urban areas. This could neutralise threats from competition and entry somewhat and perhaps provide loyalty from some customers.

Sources: M.E. Porter, 'The five competitive forces that shape strategy', *Harvard Business Review*, vol. 86, no. 1 (2008), pp. 58–77; J. Magretta, *Understanding Michael Porter: The Essential Guide to Competition and Strategy*, Harvard Business Review Press, 2012.

Questions

1 Help Emily and go through each step above. Answer the questions and make a complete analysis. What is your assessment of the industry?

2 Based on your analysis: How should Emily handle the different forces? What strategic options should she consider?

often stable they do change, and some can be in flux for considerable periods of time. This suggests that basic industry types and industry dynamics in competitive forces need to be considered. This section thus first examines fundamental industry types and then industry change and dynamics.

3.3.1 Industry types

The five forces framework builds on theories in economics[10] and it helps to identify main types of industry structure. These vary from consolidated industries with just one or a few firms with high profitability to fragmented ones with many, sometimes thousands, as firms with lower profitability (see Table 3.1). In practice, particular industries are typically not pure representatives of these types, but none the less it is helpful to have these broad categories in mind in order to compare the attractiveness of industries and likely broad patterns of competitive behaviour within them. Three basic types are:

- *Monopoly industries.* A monopoly is formally an industry with just one firm with a unique product or service and therefore no competitive rivalry. Because of the lack of choice between rivals and few entrants, there is potentially very great power over buyers and suppliers. This can be very profitable. Firms can still have monopoly power where they are simply the dominant competitor: for example, Google's 65 per cent share of the American search market gives it price-setting power in the internet advertising market. Some industries are monopolistic because of economies of scale: water utility companies are often monopolies in a particular area because it is uneconomic for smaller players to compete. For this reason, the government sometimes gives one firm the right to be the only supplier of a product or service. Other industries are monopolistic because of 'network effects', where a product is more valuable because of the number of other people using it: Facebook and Microsoft Office are so powerful precisely because so many are already users.[11] See Illustration 3.2 for a discussion of Facebook's dominance.

- *Oligopoly industries.* An oligopoly is where just a few often large firms dominate an industry, with the potential for limited rivalry and threat of entrants and great power over buyers and suppliers. With only a few competitors the actions of any one firm are likely highly influential on the others: therefore all firms must carefully consider the actions of all others. The iron ore market is an oligopoly, dominated by Vale, Rio Tinto and BHP Billiton. In theory, oligopoly can be highly profitable, but much depends on the extent of

Table 3.1 Industry types

Industry structure	Characteristics	Competitive five forces threats
Monopoly	– One firm – Often unique product or service – Very high entry barriers	Very low
Oligopoly	– Few competitors – Product and service differences vary – High entry barriers	Varies
Perfect competition	– Many competitors – Very similar products or services – Low entry barriers	Very high

rivalrous behaviour, the threat of entry and substitutes and the growth of final demand in key markets. Oligopolistic firms have a strong interest in minimising rivalry between each other so as to maintain a common front against buyers and suppliers.[12] Where there are just two oligopolistic rivals, as for Airbus and Boeing in the civil airline industry, the situation is a *duopoly.*

- *Perfectly competitive industries.* Perfect competition exists where barriers to entry are low, there are countless equal rivals each with close to identical products or services, and information about prices, products and competitors is perfectly available. Competition focuses heavily on price, because products are so similar and competitors typically cannot fund major innovations or marketing initiatives to make them dissimilar. Under these conditions, firms are unable to earn more profit than the bare minimum required to survive. Agriculture often comes close to perfect competition (e.g. potatoes, apples, onions, etc.) and so do street food vendors in major cities. Few markets, however, are absolutely perfectly competitive. Markets are more commonly slightly imperfect so that products can be differentiated to a certain degree and with information not completely available for everyone. A number of small firm service industries have this character, like restaurants, pubs, hairdressers, shoe repairs, but also the shampoo, cereal and toothpaste markets.[13]

It has also been argued that there are '*hypercompetitive industries*'. Hypercompetition occurs where the frequency, boldness and aggression of competitor interactions accelerate to create a condition of constant disequilibrium and change.[14] Under hypercompetition, rivals tend to invest heavily in destabilising innovation, expensive marketing initiatives and aggressive price cuts, with negative impacts on profits. Hypercompetition often breaks out in otherwise oligopolistic industries. Competitive moves under conditions of hypercompetition are discussed in Section 7.3.1.

Industry structures change over time and industries can evolve from one type to another depending on the macro-environment and the degree of industry maturity with consequences for competitive force strengths. These industry dynamics are discussed next.

3.3.2 Industry structure dynamics

Industry structure analysis can easily become too static: after all, structure implies stability.[15] However, industries are not always stable. To begin with, industry borders can change over time and this needs to be considered when first defining an industry. For example, many industries, especially in high-tech arenas, are converging. Convergence is where previously separate industries begin to overlap or merge in terms of activities, technologies, products and customers.[16] Technological change has brought convergence between the telephone, photographic and the PC industries, for example, as mobile phones have become smartphones and include camera and video, emailing and document editing functions. Hence, companies that once were in separate industries, like Samsung in mobile phones, Sony in cameras and Microsoft in PC software, are now in the same smartphone industry.

As discussed in the previous chapter, the broader macro-environment also tends to influence the more specific industry environment through changes in the industry structure. These key drivers for change are likely to alter the industry, and scenario analyses can be used to understand possible impacts (see Section 2.4). An illustration of changing industry structure, and the competitive implications of this, is provided by Illustration 3.4 on the UK charity and public sector. This sub-section examines two additional approaches to understanding change in industry structure: the *industry life-cycle* concept and *comparative five forces analyses.*

ILLUSTRATION 3.4   Consolidation across the UK charity and public sectors

Consolidating the structure of the UK charity sector and of public-sector organisations may help improve efficiency and services.

The UK charity sector is fragmented with over 180,000 charities including multiple charities for similar causes; 700 charities for blindness, 900 for the armed forces, 500 for animal welfare, etc. These charities compete for the same fund-raising and resources and some argue that fragmentation has resulted in questionable fund-raising techniques, poor governance and outdated business processes. It has therefore been proposed that restructuring and consolidation of the sector is needed to help improve efficiency and services. As stated in a report of the Charity Commission, the regulator for charities in England and Wales:

> 'Some people believe that there are too many charities competing for too few funds and that a significant amount of charitable resource could be saved if more charities pooled their resources and worked together . . . '[1]

Consolidation of charities has started and, according to one report,[2] 129 charities carried out mergers with a transfer of £110m (€132m, $165m) to form new organisations in 2014/15. While many of the mergers or takeovers are smaller – an average of £2.4m income – there have been larger strategic deals. For example, Addaction (focused on drug and alcohol problems) took mental health provider KCA and Breast Cancer Campaign and Breakthrough Breast Cancer joined forces. Many small charities are forced into takeovers due to financial distress because of the overcrowded sector. Leisure trusts have been very active consolidators with three of the top ten deals, representing 5 per cent of all leisure trusts in England and Wales. Despite this, consolidation activity is still at an early stage as reported in *The Good Merger Index* (2013/14):

> 'The emerging picture was one of a small number of large transformative mergers, and a comparatively long-tail of local small mergers.'[2]

Richard Litchfield writing for *Charity Times* commented that:

> 'This shows trustees aren't proactively exploring merger and giving their charities space to think strategically about the future. Boards should look objectively at their charity's position in an increasingly volatile sector, and plan in the best interest of beneficiaries – could we maximise our reach and impact by joining forces, and indeed are our services better housed elsewhere?'[3]

The public sector is also changing to increase efficiencies and improve services. One significant merger was the creation in 2013 of the combined Scottish Fire and Rescue Service, enabling a budget saving of £13m.[4] This new national service for Scotland involved the merger of the eight former local fire authorities. The NHS has also experienced considerable consolidation activities. For example, 25 mental health trusts in London have been consolidated into ten that also work in a network of partnership with each other.

Charity and public-sector consolidations are not without problems, however, and, as with private-sector mergers, integration difficulties can be severe. Nevertheless, there are also other forms of collaborations that offer opportunities to find efficiencies and improved services across charities and public-sector organisations. For example, joint procurement, sharing facilities, equipment and administration and combining different service deliveries to clients.

Sources: (1) 'RS 4a – Collaborative working and mergers: Summary', http://www.charitycommission.gov.uk/publications/rs4a.asp; (2) *The Good Merger Index,* Eastside Primetimers, 2014/15 and 2013/14; (3) R. Litchfield, *Charity Times,* 'Trustees need more help looking at mergers', 13 November 2015; (4) 'Fire and rescue collaboration', Grant Thornton, 26 March 2014.

Questions

1 How would you describe the current charity industry structure? How could it change if consolidation increases and what would be the benefits and disadvantages?

2 Which of Porter's five forces are creating problems for the UK's charity sector?

The industry life cycle

The industry life-cycle concept proposes that industries start small in their development or introduction stage, then go through a period of rapid growth (the equivalent to 'adolescence' in the human life cycle), culminating in a period of 'shake-out'. The final two stages are first a period of slow or even zero growth ('maturity'), and then the final stage of decline ('old age'). The power of the five forces typically varies with the stages of the industry life cycle.[17]

The *development stage* is an experimental one, typically with few players, little direct rivalry and highly differentiated products. The five forces are likely to be weak, therefore, though profits may actually be scarce because of high investment requirements. The next stage is one of *high growth*, with rivalry low as there is plenty of market opportunity for everybody. Low rivalry and keen buyers of the new product favour profits at this stage, but these are not certain. Barriers to entry may still be low in the growth stage, as existing competitors have not built up much scale, experience or customer loyalty. Suppliers can be powerful too if there is a shortage of components or materials that fast-growing businesses need for expansion. The *shake-out stage* begins as the market becomes increasingly saturated and cluttered with competitors (see Illustration 3.4). Profits are variable, as increased rivalry forces the weakest competitors out of the business. In the *maturity stage*, barriers to entry tend to increase, as control over distribution is established and economies of scale and experience curve benefits come into play. Products or services tend to standardise, with relative price becoming key. Buyers may become more powerful as they become less avid for the industry's products and more confident in switching between suppliers. Profitability at the maturity stage relies on high market share, providing leverage against buyers and competitive advantage in terms of cost. Finally, the *decline stage* can be a period of extreme rivalry, especially where there are high exit barriers, as falling sales force remaining competitors into dog-eat-dog competition. However, survivors in the decline stage may still be profitable if competitor exit leaves them in a monopolistic position. Figure 3.4 summarises some of the conditions that can be expected at different stages in the life cycle.

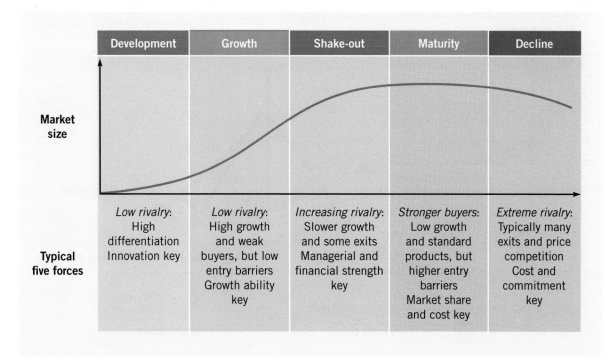

Figure 3.4 The industry life cycle

It is important to avoid putting too much faith in the inevitability of life-cycle stages. One stage does not follow predictably after another. First, industries vary widely in the length of their growth stages. For example, many internet-based industries have matured quickly and moved through the stages in less than a decade, like online travel and dating services. Second, some industries can rapidly 'de-mature' through radical innovation. Thus the telephony industry, based for nearly a century on fixed-line telephones, rejuvenated rapidly with the introduction of mobile and internet telephony. Likewise, since the mobile telephony industry matured it has later been revived by the introduction of smartphones and smartwatches. Anita McGahan of Toronto University warns of the 'maturity mindset', which can leave many managers complacent and slow to respond to new competition.[18] Managing in mature industries is not necessarily just about waiting for decline. However, even if the various stages are not inevitable, the life-cycle concept does remind managers that conditions are likely to change over time. Especially in fast-moving industries, five forces analyses need to be reviewed quite regularly.

Comparative industry structure analyses

The previous section raised the issue of how competitive forces may change over time. The industry life cycle thus underlines the need to make industry structure analysis dynamic. This implies that we not only need to understand the current strength of the competitive forces, but how it may change over time. One effective means of doing this is to compare the competitive five forces over time in a simple 'radar plot'.

Figure 3.5 provides a framework for summarising the power of each of the five forces on five axes. Power diminishes as the axes go outwards. Where the forces are low, the total area enclosed by the lines between the axes is large; where the forces are high, the total area enclosed by the lines is small. The larger the enclosed area, therefore, the greater is the profit potential. In Figure 3.5, the industry at Time 0 (represented by the red lines) has relatively low rivalry (just a few competitors) and faces low substitution threats. The threat of entry is moderate, but both buyer power and supplier power are relatively high. Overall, this looks like only a moderately attractive industry to invest in.

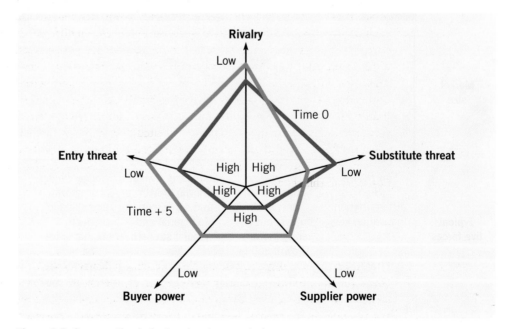

Figure 3.5 Comparative industry structure analysis

However, given the dynamic nature of industries, managers need to look forward, perhaps using scenario analysis. Figure 3.5 represents five years forward by the green lines. Managers are predicting in this case some rise in the threat of substitutes (perhaps new technologies will be developed). On the other hand, they predict a falling entry threat, while both buyer power and supplier power will be easing. Rivalry will reduce still further. This looks like a classic case of an industry in which a few players emerge with overall dominance. The area enclosed by the green lines is large, suggesting a relatively attractive industry. For a firm confident of becoming one of the dominant players, this might be an industry well worth investing in.

Comparing the five forces over time on a radar plot thus helps to give industry structure analysis a dynamic aspect. Similar plots can be made to aid diversification decisions (see Chapter 8), where possible new industries to enter can be compared in terms of attractiveness. The lines are only approximate, of course, because they aggregate the many individual elements that make up each of the forces into a simple composite measure. Notice too that if one of the forces is very adverse, then this might nullify positive assessments on the other four axes: for example, an industry with low rivalry, low substitution, low entry barriers and low supplier power might still be unattractive if powerful buyers were able to demand highly discounted prices. With these warnings in mind, such radar plots can nonetheless be both a useful device for initial analysis and an effective summary of a final, more refined and dynamic analysis.

3.4 COMPETITORS AND MARKETS

An industry or sector may be too high a level to provide for a detailed understanding of competition. The five forces can impact differently on different kinds of players, which requires a more fine-grained understanding. For example, Hyundai and Porsche may be in the same broad industry (automobiles), but they are positioned differently: they are protected by different barriers to entry and competitive moves by one are unlikely to affect the other. It is often useful to disaggregate. Many industries contain a range of companies, each of which have different capabilities and compete on different bases. Some of these competitor differences are captured by the concept of *strategic groups*. Customers too can differ significantly and these can be captured by distinguishing between different *market segments*. Thinking in terms of different strategic groups and market segments provides opportunities for organisations to develop highly distinctive positionings within broader industries. Besides disaggregating the analysis of industry competition, these approaches may help in understanding how value is created differently by different competitors. Competitor differences, both actual and potential, including the identification of entirely new market spaces can also be analysed using the *strategy canvas* and '*Blue Ocean*' thinking, the last topic in this section.

3.4.1 Strategic groups[19]

Strategic groups are organisations within the same industry or sector with similar strategic characteristics, following similar strategies or competing on similar bases. These characteristics are different from those in other strategic groups in the same industry or sector. For example, in the grocery retailing industry, supermarkets, convenience stores and corner shops each form different strategic groups. There are many different characteristics that

It is useful to consider the extent to which organisations *differ* in terms of **characteristics** such as:

Scope of activities

- Extent of product (or service) diversity
- Extent of geographical coverage
- Number of market segments served
- Distribution channels used

Resource commitment

- Extent (number) of **branding**
- **Marketing effort** (e.g. advertising spread, size of salesforce)
- Extent of **vertical integration**
- Product or service **quality**
- **Technological leadership** (a leader or follower)
- **Size** of organisation

Figure 3.6 Some characteristics for identifying strategic groups

distinguish between strategic groups, but these can be grouped into two major categories (see Figure 3.6):[20] first, the *scope* of an organisation's activities (such as product range, geographical coverage and range of distribution channels used); second, the *resource commitment* (such as brands, marketing spend and extent of vertical integration). Which characteristics are relevant differs from industry to industry, but typically important are those characteristics that separate high performers from low performers.

Strategic groups can be mapped onto two-dimensional charts – for example, one axis might be the extent of product range and the other axis the size of marketing spend. One method for choosing key dimensions by which to map strategic groups is to identify top performers (by growth or profitability) in an industry and to compare them with low performers. Characteristics that are shared by top performers, but not by low performers, are likely to be particularly relevant for mapping strategic groups. For example, the most profitable firms in an industry might all be narrow in terms of product range, and lavish in terms of marketing spend, while the less profitable firms might be more widely spread in terms of products and restrained in their marketing. Here the two dimensions for mapping would be product range and marketing spend. A potential recommendation for the less profitable firms would be to cut back their product range and boost their marketing.

Figure 3.7 shows strategic groups among Indian pharmaceutical companies, with research and development intensity (R&D spend as a percentage of sales) and overseas focus (exports and patents registered overseas) defining the axes of the map. These two axes do explain a good deal of the variation in profitability between groups. The most profitable group is the Emergent globals (11.3 per cent average return on sales), those with high R&D intensity and high overseas focus. On the other hand, the Exploiter group

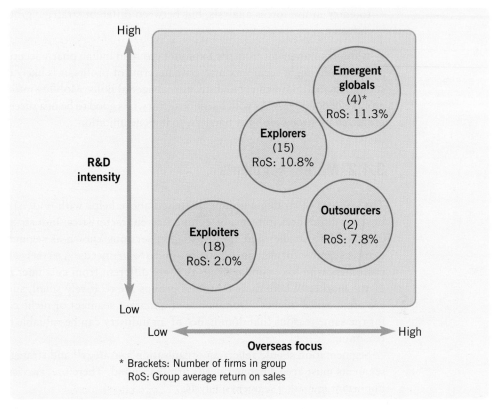

Figure 3.7 Strategic groups in the Indian pharmaceutical industry

Source: Developed from R. Chittoor and S. Ray, 'Internationalisation paths of Indian pharmaceutical firms: a strategic group analysis', *Journal of International Management*, vol. 13 (2009), pp. 338–55.

spends little on R&D and is focused on domestic markets, and enjoys only 2.0 per cent average return on sales.

This strategic group concept is useful in at least three ways:

- *Understanding competition.* Managers can focus on their direct competitors within their particular strategic group, rather than the whole industry as rivalry often is strongest between these. In general, strategic groups are influenced differently by the competitive forces and this focus thus allows for a more specific industry structure analysis. They can also establish the dimensions that distinguish them most from other groups, and which might be the basis for relative success or failure. This suggests that there may be profitability differences between different strategic groups and the differing dimensions can then become the focus of their action.

- *Analysis of strategic opportunities.* Strategic group maps can identify the most attractive 'strategic spaces' within an industry. Some spaces on the map may be 'white spaces', relatively under-occupied. In the Indian pharmaceutical industry, the white space is high R&D investment combined with focus on domestic markets. Such white spaces might be unexploited opportunities. On the other hand, they could turn out to be 'black holes', impossible to exploit and likely to damage any entrant. A strategic group map is only the first stage of the analysis. Strategic spaces need to tested carefully.

- *Analysis of mobility barriers.* Of course, moving across the strategic group map to take advantage of opportunities is not costless. Often it will require difficult decisions and rare resources. Strategic groups are therefore characterised by 'mobility barriers', obstacles to movement from one strategic group to another. These are the equivalent to barriers to entry in five forces analysis, but between different strategic groups within the same industry.

Although movement from the Exploiter group in Indian pharmaceuticals to the Emergent global group might seem very attractive in terms of profits, it is likely to demand very substantial financial investment and strong managerial skills. Mobility into the Emergent global group will not be easy. As with barriers to entry, it is good to be in a successful strategic group protected by strong mobility barriers, to impede imitation.

3.4.2 Market segments

The concept of strategic groups discussed above helps with understanding the similarities and differences in terms of competitor characteristics. Industries can also be disaggregated into smaller and specific market sections known as segments. The concept of market segment focuses on differences in *customer* needs. A **market segment[21] is a group of customers who have similar needs that are different from customer needs in other parts of the market.** Where these customer groups are relatively small, such market segments are often called 'niches'. Dominance of a market segment or niche can be very valuable, for the same reasons that dominance of an industry can be valuable following five forces reasoning.

Segmentation should reflect an organisation's strategy[22] and strategies based on market segments must keep customer needs firmly in mind. Therefore, two issues are particularly important in market segment analysis:

- *Variation in customer needs*. Focusing on customer needs that are highly distinctive from those typical in the market is one means of building a long-term segment strategy. Customer needs vary for a whole variety of reasons – some of which are identified in Table 3.2. Theoretically, any of these factors could be used to identify distinct market segments. However, the crucial bases of segmentation vary according to market. In industrial markets, segmentation is often thought of in terms of industrial classification of buyers: steel producers might segment by automobile industry, packaging industry and construction industry, for example. On the other hand, segmentation by buyer behaviour (e.g. direct buying versus those users who buy through third parties such as contractors) or purchase value (e.g. high-value bulk purchasers versus frequent low-value purchasers) might be more appropriate. Being able to serve a highly distinctive segment that other organisations find difficult to serve is often the basis for a secure long-term strategy.

- *Specialisation* within a market segment can also be an important basis for a successful segmentation strategy. This is sometimes called a 'niche strategy'. Organisations that have built up most experience in servicing a particular market segment should not only have lower costs in so doing, but also should have built relationships which may be difficult for others to break down. Experience and relationships are likely to protect a dominant position in a particular segment. However, precisely because customers value different things in different segments, specialised producers may find it very difficult to compete on a broader basis. For example, a small local brewery competing against the big brands on the basis of its ability to satisfy distinctive local tastes is unlikely to find it easy to serve other segments where tastes are different, scale requirements are larger and distribution channels are more complex.

Table 3.2 Some bases of market segmentation

Type of factor	Consumer markets	Industrial/organisational markets
Characteristics of people/organisations	Age, gender, ethnicity Income Family size Life-cycle stage Location Lifestyle	Industry Location Size Technology Profitability Management
Purchase/use situation	Size of purchase Brand loyalty Purpose of use Purchasing behaviour Importance of purchase Choice criteria	Application Importance of purchase Volume Frequency of purchase Purchasing procedure Choice criteria Distribution channel
Users' needs and preferences for product characteristics	Product similarity Price preference Brand preferences Desired features Quality	Performance requirements Assistance from suppliers Brand preferences Desired features Quality Service requirements

3.4.3 Critical success factors and 'Blue Oceans'

Industry or sector analysis should also include an understanding of competitors and the different ways they offer value to customers. As Michael Porter's five forces framework underlines, reducing industry rivalry involves competitors finding differentiated positions in the marketplace. W. Chan Kim and Renée Mauborgne at INSEAD propose two concepts that help think creatively about the relative positioning of competitors in the environment and finding uncontested market spaces: the strategy canvas and 'Blue Oceans'.[23]

A **strategy canvas compares competitors according to their performance on key success factors in order to establish the extent of differentiation.** It captures the current factors of competition of the industry, but also offers ways of challenging these and creatively trying to identify new competitive offerings. Figure 3.8 shows a strategy canvas for three electrical components companies. The canvas highlights the following three features:

- **Critical success factors (CSFs) are those factors that either are particularly valued by customers (i.e. strategic customers) or provide a significant advantage in terms of cost.** Critical success factors are therefore likely to be an important source of competitive advantage or disadvantage. Figure 3.8 identifies five established critical success factors in this electrical components market (cost, after-sales service, delivery reliability, technical quality and testing facilities). Note there is also a new sixth critical success factor, design advisory services, which will be discussed under the third subhead, value innovation.

- *Value curves* are a graphic depiction of how customers perceive competitors' relative performance across the critical success factors. In Figure 3.8, companies A and B perform well on cost, service, reliability and quality, but less well on testing. They do not offer any design advice. They are poorly differentiated and occupy a space in the market where

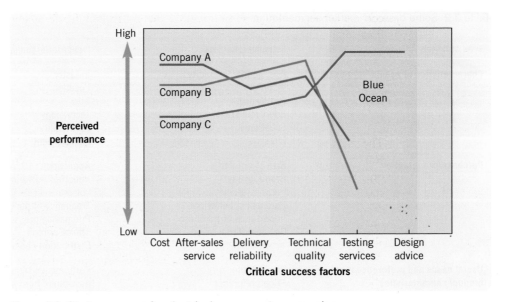

Figure 3.8 Strategy canvas for electrical components companies

Note: cost is used rather than price for consistency of value curves.

Source: Developed from W.C. Kim and R. Mauborgne, *Blue Ocean Strategy*, Harvard Business School Press, 2005.

profits may be hard to get because of excessive rivalry between the two. Company C, on the other hand, has a radically different value curve, characteristic of a 'value innovator'.

- *Value innovation* is the creation of new market space by excelling on established critical success factors on which competitors are performing badly and/or by creating new critical success factors representing previously unrecognised customer wants. Thus in Figure 3.8, company C is a value innovator in both senses. First, it excels on the established customer need of offering testing facilities for customers' products using its components. Second, it offers a new and valued design service advising customers on how to integrate their components in order for them to create better products.

A value innovator is a company that competes in 'Blue Oceans'. **Blue Oceans are new market spaces where competition is minimised.**[24] Blue Oceans contrast with 'Red Oceans', where industries are already well defined and rivalry is intense. Blue Oceans evoke wide empty seas. Red Oceans are associated with bloody competition and 'red ink', in other words financial losses. The Blue Ocean concept is thus useful for identifying potential spaces in the environment with little competition. These Blue Oceans are *strategic gaps* in the marketplace.

In Figure 3.8, company C's strategy exemplifies two critical principles of Blue Ocean thinking: *focus* and *divergence*. First, company C focuses its efforts on just two factors, testing and design services, while maintaining only adequate performance on the other critical success factors where its competitors are already high performers. Second, it has created a value curve that significantly diverges from its competitors' value curves, creating a substantial *strategic gap*, or Blue Ocean, in the areas of testing and design services. This is shrewd. For company C, beating companies A and B in the areas where they are performing well anyway would require major investment and likely provide little advantage given that customers are already highly satisfied. Challenging A and B on cost, after-sales service, delivery or quality would be a Red Ocean strategy, increasing industry rivalry. Far better is to concentrate on where a large gap can be created between competitors. Company C faces little competition for those customers who really value testing and design services, and consequently can charge good prices for them. The task for companies A and B now is to find strategic gaps of their own.

3.5 OPPORTUNITIES AND THREATS

The concepts and frameworks discussed above and in Chapter 2 should be helpful in understanding the factors in the macro-, industry and competitor/market environments of an organisation. However, the critical issue is the *implications* that are drawn from this understanding in guiding strategic decisions and choices. The crucial next stage, therefore, is to draw from the environmental analysis specific strategic opportunities and threats for the organisation. Identifying these opportunities and threats is extremely valuable when thinking about strategic choices for the future (the subject of Chapters 7 to 11). Opportunities and threats form one half of the Strengths, Weaknesses, Opportunities and Threats (SWOT) analyses that shape many companies' strategy formulation (see Section 4.4.5). In responding strategically to the environment, the goal is to reduce identified threats and take advantage of the best opportunities.

lead in to recommendation

The techniques and concepts in this and the previous chapter should help in identifying environmental threats and opportunities, for instance:

- *PESTEL analysis* of the macro-environment might reveal threats and opportunities presented by technological change, or shifts in market demographics or such like factors.

- Identification of *key drivers for change* can help generate different *scenarios* for managerial discussion, some more threatening and others more favourable.

- *Porter's five forces analysis* might, for example, identify a rise or fall in barriers to entry, or opportunities to reduce industry rivalry, perhaps by acquisition of competitors.

- *Blue Ocean* thinking might reveal where companies can create new market spaces; alternatively, it could help identify success factors which new entrants might attack in order to turn 'Blue Oceans' into 'Red Oceans'.

While all these techniques and concepts are important tools for understanding environments, it is important to recognise that any analysis is likely to be somewhat subjective. Entrepreneurs and managers often have particular blinkers with regard to what they see and prioritise. Techniques and concepts can be helpful in challenging existing assumptions and encouraging broader perspectives, but they are unlikely to overcome human subjectivity and biases completely.

THINKING DIFFERENTLY | From five forces to one

A new competition view focuses on how value is created and captured.

A new 'value capture model' based on game theory aspires to replace Porter's competitive forces framework.[25] The power of his five competitive forces defines the opportunities of a firm. The new model rather emphasises how the firm's opportunities depend on how the firm, suppliers and buyers create value together. They then compete for a share of that value based on a single *competition force* that each player has.

Compared to Porter's framework, the emphasis in this model is more on how value is created between parties. The firm and its suppliers and buyers comprise a *value network* of transactions that create value to be shared among them. They then compete for their share based on the single competition force each has: suppliers compete for firms, and vice versa; firms compete for buyers and vice versa. A firm, for example, wants to make transactions with certain suppliers and customers to create value, but also to capture as much of that value as possible. The strength of each

player's competition force then depends on how many others it *could* create value with. For example, if a firm has many alternative suppliers and buyers to create value with, its competition force would go up as it can threaten to make transactions with someone else and thus bargain up its share of the value pie this way. This suggests that value creation and value appropriation are linked in this model. The more value the firm can create with various suppliers and buyers the larger portion of this value it can capture.

> **Question**
>
> How would you compare the 'value capture model' with Porter's five forces when making an industry analysis? What's the benefits and drawback of each?

SUMMARY

- The environment influence closest to an organisation includes the *industry or sector* (middle layer in Figure 2.1).

- Industries and sectors can be analysed in terms of *Porter's five forces* – barriers to entry, substitutes, buyer power, supplier power and rivalry. Together with *complementors* and *network effects,* these determine industry or sector attractiveness and possible ways of managing strategy.

- Industries and sectors are dynamic, and their changes can be analysed in terms of the *industry life cycle* and *comparative five forces radar plots.*

- Within industries *strategic group* analysis and *market segment* analysis can help identify strategic gaps or opportunities (the inner layers in Figure 2.1).

- *Blue Ocean* strategies are a means of avoiding *Red Oceans* with many similar rivals and low profitability and can be analysed with a *strategy canvas.*

WORK ASSIGNMENTS

✱ Denotes more advanced work assignments.
* Refers to a case study in the Text and Cases edition.

3.1 Drawing on Section 3.2, carry out a five forces analysis of the pharmaceutical industry* or SAB Miller's position in the brewing industry (Megabrew*). What do you conclude about that industry's attractiveness?

3.2 Drawing on Section 3.2.7, identify an industry with network effects. Consider what those might involve; why customers prefer certain services, products and companies over others; and why they may not easily switch to other services and companies.

3.3✱ Drawing on Section 3.3, and particularly using the radar plot technique of Figure 3.5, choose two industries or sectors and compare their attractiveness in terms of the five forces (a) today; (b) in approximately three to five years' time. Justify your assessment of each of the five forces' strengths. Which industry or sector would you invest in?

3.4 With regard to Section 3.4.1 and Figure 3.6, identify an industry (e.g. the motor industry or clothing retailers) and, by comparing competitors, map out the main strategic groups in the industry according to key strategic dimensions. Try more than one set of key strategic dimensions to map the industry. Do the resulting maps identify any under-exploited opportunities in the industry?

3.5✱ Drawing on Section 3.4.3, and particularly on Figure 3.8, identify critical success factors for an industry with which you and your peers are familiar (e.g. clothing retailers or mobile phone companies). Using your own estimates (or those of your peers), construct a strategy canvas comparing the main competitors, as in Figure 3.8. What implications does your strategy canvas have for the strategies of these competitors?

Integrative assignment

3.6✱ Carry out a full analysis of an industry or sector of your choice (using, for example, five forces and strategic groups). Consider explicitly how the industry or sector is affected by globalisation (see Chapter 9, particularly Figure 9.2 on drivers) and innovation (see Chapter 10, particularly Figure 10.5 on product and process innovation).

RECOMMENDED KEY READINGS

- The classic book on the analysis of industries is M.E. Porter, *Competitive Strategy*, Free Press, 1980. An updated view is available in M.E. Porter, 'The five competitive forces that shape strategy', *Harvard Business Review*, vol. 86, no. 1 (2008), pp. 58–77.

- For an in-depth discussion of how to apply Porter's Competitive Force Frameworks, see J. Magretta, *Understanding Michael Porter: The Essential Guide to Competition and Strategy*, Harvard Business Review Press, 2012.

- An influential development on Porter's basic ideas is W.C. Kim and R. Mauborgne, *Blue Ocean Strategy: How to Create Uncontested Market Space and Make Competition Irrelevant*, Harvard Business School Press, 2005.

REFERENCES

1. See M.E. Porter, *Competitive Strategy: Techniques for Analyzing Industries and Competitors*, Free Press, 1980, p. 5.

2. See endnote 1 above and see M. Porter, 'The five competitive forces that shape strategy', *Harvard Business Review*, vol. 86, no. 1 (2008), pp. 58–77; and G. Yip, T.M. Devinney and G. Johnson, 'Measuring long-term superior performance: The UK's long-term superior performers 1984-2003', *Long Range Planning*, vol. 42, no. 3 (2009), pp. 390–413. See also http://www.damodaran.com for industry profitability differences in various geographical regions.

3. An updated discussion of the classic framework is M. Porter, 'The five competitive forces that shape strategy', *Harvard Business Review*, vol. 86, no. 1 (2008), pp. 58–77 and 'Strategy and the Internet', *Harvard Business Review*, no. 3 (2001), pp. 62–78. For a discussion and guide to Porter's ideas about strategy see *Understanding Michael Porter: The Essential Guide to Competition and Strategy*, Harvard Business Review Press, 2012. C. Christensen, 'The past and future of competitive advantage', *Sloan Management Review*, vol. 42, no. 2 (2001), pp. 105–9 provides an interesting critique and update of some of the factors underlying Porter's five forces. A critical overview of Porter's thinking is also provided in R. Huggins and H. Izushi (eds), *Competition, Competitive Advantage, and Clusters: The Ideas of Michael Porter*, Oxford University Press, 2011.

4. A. Brandenburger and B. Nalebuff, 'The right game', *Harvard Business Review*, July–August 1995, pp. 57–64.

5. See K. Walley, 'Coopetition: an introduction to the subject and an agenda for research', *International Studies of Management and Organization*, vol. 37, no. 2 (2007), pp. 11–31. On the dangers of 'complementors', see D. Yoffie and M. Kwak, 'With friends like these', *Harvard Business Review*, vol. 84, no. 9 (2006), pp. 88–98.

6. For an overview of recent empirical research of strategy and network effects see D.P. McIntyre and M. Subramaniam, 'Strategy in network industries: a review and research agenda', *Journal of Management* (2009), pp 1–24. For a general discussion of the role of networks externalities and standards, see C. Shapiro and H.R. Varian, *Information Rules: a Strategic Guide to the Network Economy*, Harvard Business Review Press, 2013.

7. If network effects are present, a standard strategic advice for companies has been to move in first and grow fast to capture those effects before anyone else as this would provide an advantage over competitors, but it has recently been demonstrated that there are other issues to consider: H. Halaburda and F. Oberholzer-Gee, 'The limits of scale', *Harvard Business Review*, April 2014, pp. 95–99.

8. W.B. Arthur, 'Increasing returns and the new world of business', *Harvard Business Review*, July–August (1996), pp. 100–109. See also the concept of system lock-in in A. Hax and D. Wilde, 'The Delta Model – discovering new sources of profitability in a networked economy', *European Management Journal*, vol. 19, no. 4 (2001), pp. 379–91.

9. For an in-depth discussion of how to apply Porter's competive forces framework, see J. Magretta, *Understanding Michael Porter: The Essential Guide to Competition and Strategy*, Harvard Business Review Press, 2012.

10. The five forces framework builds on the structure–conduct–performance (SCP) model in industrial organisation economics. It stipulates that the industry *structure* determines firm *conduct* that in turn influences industry *performance*. SCP categorises industry structure into four main types: monopoly, oligopoly, monopolistic competition and perfect competition. See J. Lipczynski, J. Wilson and J. Goddard, *Industrial Organization: Competition, Strategy, Policy*, Prentice Hall/Financial Times, 2009.

11. D. McIntyre and M. Subramarian, 'Strategy in network industries: a review and research agenda', *Journal of Management*, vol. 35 (2009), pp. 1494–512.

12. Explicit cooperation among the firms to limit competition or cartels are prohibited in most developed nations, but there is also 'tacit collusion'. In tacit collusion, companies cooperate to reduce competition without any formal agreement. It is facilitated by a small numer of rivals, a homogenous product or service and costs and high barriers to entry. Tacit collusion can also be illegal under certain circumstances. See Lipczynski, Wilson and Goddard endnote 10.

13. Economists name these markets '*monopolistic competition*' as firms can still create a position or niche for which they have some monopoly power over pricing.

14. This definition is from R. D'Aveni, *Hypercompetition: Managing the Dynamics of Strategic Maneuvering*, Free Press, 1994, p. 2.

15. There is a discussion of the static nature of the Porter model, and other limitations in M. Grundy, 'Rethinking and reinventing Michael Porter's five forces model', *Strategic Change*, vol. 15 (2006), pp. 213–29.

16. See for example F. Hacklin, B. Battistini and G. Von Krogh, 'Strategic choices in converging industries', *MIT Sloan Management Review* vol. 51, no. 1 (2013), pp. 65–73.

17. A classic academic overview of the industry life cycle is S. Klepper, 'Industry life cycles', *Industrial and Corporate Change*, vol. 6, no. 1 (1996), pp. 119–43. See also A. McGahan, 'How industries evolve', *Business Strategy Review*, vol. 11, no. 3 (2000), pp. 1–16.

18. A. McGahan, 'How industries evolve', *Business Strategy Review*, vol. 11, no. 3 (2000), pp. 1–16.

19. For examples of strategic group analysis, see G. Leask and D. Parker, 'Strategic groups, competitive groups and performance in the UK pharmaceutical industry', *Strategic Management Journal*, vol. 28, no. 7 (2007), pp. 723–45; and W. Desarbo, R. Grewal and R. Wang, 'Dynamic strategic groups: deriving spatial evolutionary paths', *Strategic Management Journal*, vol. 30, no. 8 (2009), pp. 1420–39.

20. These characteristics are based on Porter, endnote 1 above.

21. A useful discussion of segmentation in relation to competitive strategy is provided in M.E. Porter, *Competitive Advantage*, Free Press, 1985, Chapter 7. See also the discussion on market segmentation in P. Kotler, G. Armstrong, J. Saunders and V. Wong, *Principles of Marketing*, 5th European edn, Financial Times Prentice Hall, 2008, Chapter 9.

22. For a discussion of how market segmentation needs to be broadly related to an organisation's strategy and not only narrowly focused on the needs of advertising, see D. Yankelovich and D. Meer, 'Rediscovering market segmentation', *Harvard Business Review*, February 2006, pp. 73–80.

23. W.C. Kim and R. Mauborgne, *Blue Ocean Strategy*, Boston, Harvard Business School Press, 2005.

24. W.C. Kim and R. Mauborgne, 'How strategy shapes structure', *Harvard Business Review*, September 2009, pp. 73–80.

25. M.D. Ryall, 'The new dynamics of competition', *Harvard Business Review*, vol. 91, no. 60 (2013), pp. 80–87.

CASE EXAMPLE

Global forces and the advertising industry

Peter Cardwell

*This case is centred on the global advertising industry which faces significant strategic dilemmas driven by the rise of consumer spending in developing economies, technological convergence and pressures from major advertisers for results-based compensation. Strategy in this industry is further explored in **MyStrategyExperience** simulation (https://heuk.pearson.com/simulations/mystrategyexperience.html).*

In the second decade of the new millennium, advertising agencies faced a number of unanticipated challenges. Traditional markets and industry operating methods, developed largely in North America and Western Europe following the rise of consumer spending power in the twentieth century, were being radically reappraised.

The industry was subject to game-changing forces from the so-called 'digital revolution' with the entry of search companies like Google, Bing and Yahoo as rivals for advertising budgets. Changing patterns in global consumer markets impacted on both industry dynamics and structure. Budgets being spent through traditional advertising agencies were being squeezed as industry rivalry intensified.

Overview of the advertising industry

Traditionally, the business objective of advertising agencies is to target a specific audience on behalf of clients with a message that encourages them to try a product or service and ultimately purchase it. This is done largely through the concept of a brand being communicated via media channels. Brands allow consumers to differentiate between products and services and it is the job of the advertising agency to position the brand so that it is associated with functions and attributes which are valued by target consumers. These brands may be consumer brands (e.g. Coca-Cola, Nike and Mercedes Benz) or business-to-business (B2B) brands (e.g. IBM, Airbus Industrie and KPMG). Some brands target both consumers and businesses (e.g. Microsoft and Apple).

As well as private-sector brand companies, governments spend heavily to advertise public-sector services such as healthcare and education or to influence individual behaviour (such as 'Don't drink and drive'). For example, the UK government had an advertising budget of £289m (€347m, $433m) in 2014. Charities, political groups, religious groups and other not-for-profit organisations also use the advertising industry to attract funds into their organisation or to raise awareness of issues. Together these account for approximately three per cent of advertising spend.

Advertisements are usually placed in selected media (TV, press, radio, internet, mobile, etc.) by an advertising agency acting on behalf of the client brand company: thus they are acting as 'agents'. The client company employs the advertising agency to use its knowledge, skills, creativity and experience to create advertising and marketing to drive consumption of the client's brands. Clients traditionally have been charged according to the time spent on creating the advertisements plus a commission based on the media and services bought on behalf of clients. However, in recent years, larger advertisers such as Coca-Cola, Procter & Gamble and Unilever have been moving away from this compensation model to a 'value' or results-based model based on a number of metrics, including growth in sales and market share.

Growth in the advertising industry

Money spent on advertising has increased dramatically over the past two decades and in 2015 was over $180 billion (€166bn, £126bn) in the USA and $569 billion worldwide. While there might be a decline in recessionary years, it is predicted that spending on advertising will exceed $719 billion globally by 2019. Over 2014–15, the Dow Jones stock price index for the American media agencies sector (of which the leading advertising agencies are the largest members) rose about 15 per cent ahead of the New York Stock Exchange average (sources: bigcharts.com and dowjones.com).

The industry is shifting its focus as emerging markets drive revenues from geographic sectors that would not have been significant 5 to 10 years ago, such as the BRICS countries and the Middle East and North Africa. This shift has seen the emergence of agencies specialising in Islamic marketing, characterised by a strong ethical responsibility to consumers. Future trends indicate the

Table 1 Global advertising expenditure by region (US$ million, currency conversion at 2011 average rates)

	2011	2012	2013	2014	2015
N America	164,516	169,277	175,024	183,075	191,130
W Europe	107,520	111,300	114,712	119,531	124,790
Asia Pacific	113,345	122,000	130,711	137,639	145,695
C & E Europe	29,243	32,284	35,514	36,691	37,305
Latin America	31,673	34,082	36,836	38,530	39,226
Africa/ME/ROW	24,150	25,941	28,044	29,334	30,625
World	**470,447**	**494,884**	**520,841**	**544,800**	**568,771**

Source: Zenith, January 2016.

strong emergence of consumer brands in areas of the world where sophisticated consumers with brand awareness are currently in the minority (see Table 1).

In terms of industry sectors, three of the top 10 global advertisers are car manufacturers. However, the two major fmcg (fast-moving consumer goods) producers, Procter & Gamble and Unilever, hold the two top spots for global advertising spend. Healthcare and beauty, consumer electronics, fast food, beverage and confectionery manufacturers are all featured in the top 20 global advertisers. The top 100 advertisers account for nearly 50 per cent of the measured global advertising economy.

Competition in the advertising industry

Advertising agencies come in all sizes and include everything from one- or two-person 'boutique' operations (which rely mostly on freelance outsourced talent to perform most functions), small to medium-sized agencies, large independents to multinational, multi-agency conglomerates employing over 190,000 people. The industry has gone through a period of increasing concentration through acquisitions, thereby creating multi-agency conglomerates such as those listed in Table 2. While these conglomerates are mainly headquartered in London, New York and Paris, they operate globally.

Large multi-agency conglomerates compete on the basis of the quality of their creative output (as indicated by industry awards), the ability to buy media more cost-effectively, market knowledge, global reach and range of services. Some agency groups have integrated vertically into higher-margin marketing services. Omnicom, through its Diversified Agency Services, has acquired printing services and telemarketing/customer care companies. Other agency groups have vertically integrated to lesser or greater degrees.

Mid-sized and smaller boutique advertising agencies compete by delivering value-added services through in-depth knowledge of specific market sectors, specialised services such as digital and by building a reputation for innovative and ground-breaking creative advertising/marketing campaigns. However, they might be more reliant on outsourced creative suppliers than larger agencies.

Many small specialist agencies are founded by former employees of large agencies, such as the senior staff breakaway from Young & Rubicam to form the agency Adam + Eve. In turn, smaller specialist agencies are often acquired by the large multi-agency conglomerates in order to acquire specific capabilities to target new sectors or markets or provide additional services to existing clients, like WPP's acquisition of a majority stake in the smaller ideas and innovation agency AKQA for $540m 'to prepare for a more digital future'.

Table 2 Top five multi-agency conglomerates: 2014, by revenue, profit before interest and tax (PBIT), number of employees and agency brands

Group name	Revenue	PBIT	Employees	Advertising agency brands
WPP (UK)	£11.5 bn	£1.662 bn	190,000	JWT, Grey, Ogilvy, Y&R
Omnicom (US)	$15.32 bn	$1.944 bn	74,000	BBDO, DDB, TBWA
Publicis Groupe (France)	€7.2 bn	€829 m	77,000	Leo Burnett, Saatchi & Saatchi, Publicis, BBH
IPG (US)	$7.54 bn	$788 m	48,700	McCann Erickson, FCB, Lowe & Partners
Havas Worldwide (France)	€1.865 bn	€263 m	11,186	Havas Conseil

Sources: WPP, Omnicom, Publicis Groupe, IPG, Havas.

Recent years have seen new competition in this industry as search companies such as Google, Yahoo and Microsoft Bing begin to exploit their ability to interact with and gain information about millions of potential consumers of branded products.

Sir Martin Sorrell, CEO of WPP, the world's largest advertising and marketing services group, has pointed out that Google will rival his agency's relationships with the biggest traditional media corporations such as TV, newspaper and magazine, and possibly even become a rival for the relationships with WPP's clients. WPP group spent more than $4bn with Google in 2015 and $1bn with Facebook. Sorrell calls Google a 'frenemy' – the combination of 'friend' and 'enemy'. Google is a 'friend' where it allows WPP to place targeted advertising based on Google analytics and an 'enemy' where it does not share these analytics with the agency and becomes a potential competitor for the customer insight and advertising traditionally created by WPP.

With the development of the internet and online search advertising, a new breed of interactive digital media agencies, of which AKQA is an example, established themselves in the digital space before traditional advertising agencies fully embraced the internet. These agencies differentiate themselves by offering a mix of web design/development, search engine marketing, internet advertising/marketing, or e-business/e-commerce consulting. They are classified as 'agencies' because they create digital media campaigns and implement media purchases of ads on behalf of clients on social networking and community sites such as YouTube, Facebook, Flickr, Instagram and other digital media.

Digital search and mobile advertising budgets are increasing faster than other traditional advertising media as search companies like Google and Facebook generate revenues from paid search as advertisers discover that targeted ads online are highly effective (see Table 3). By 2015, Google had a 55 per cent market share of the $81.6 bn spent on online search advertising globally, with Facebook also increasing its share.

Mobile ad spending on sites such as YouTube, Pinterest and Twitter continues to increase at the expense of desktop, taking a bigger share of marketers' budgets. The shift to mobile ad spending is being driven mainly by consumer demand and is predicted to be over 28 per cent of total media ad spending in the US by 2019 which is why Google has made acquisitions in this sector (see Table 4).

Table 3 Global advertising expenditure by medium (US$ million, currency conversion at 2011 average rates)

	2011	2012	2013	2014	2015
Newspapers	93,019	92,300	91,908	90,070	88,268
Magazines	42,644	42,372	42,300	40,185	39,391
Television	191,198	202,380	213,878	210,670	210,459
Radio	32,580	33,815	35,054	34,457	34,130
Cinema	2,393	2,538	2,681	2,767	2,850
Outdoor	30,945	32,821	34,554	36,143	36,324
Internet	70,518	80,672	91,516	130,019	156,543
Total	**463,297**	**486,898**	**511,891**	**544,311**	**567,956**

Note: The totals in Table 3 are lower than in Table 1, since that table includes advertising expenditure for a few countries where it is not itemised by advertising medium.
Source: Zenith, September 2015.

Table 4 US mobile ad spending 2015–2019

	2015	2016	2017	2018	2019
Mobile ad spending (US$bn)	31.59	43.60	52.76	61.20	69.15
% change	65.00%	38.00%	21.00%	16.00%	13.00%
% of digital ad spending	53.00%	63.40%	68.20%	70.70%	72.00%
% of total media ad spending	17.30%	22.70%	26.20%	28.80%	31.00%

Source: eMarketer.com.

The disruptive change in the advertising industry at the beginning of the twenty-first century started with the internet. Many industry experts believe that convergence of internet, TV, smartphones, tablets and laptop computers is inevitable, which in turn will have a further major impact on the advertising industry.

Factors that have driven competitive advantage to date may not be relevant in the future. Traditionally this industry has embodied the idea of creativity as the vital differentiator between the best and the mediocre. Individuals have often been at the heart of this creativity. With the emergence of Google, Yahoo, Facebook and Bing, influencing and changing the media by which advertising messages are being delivered, a key question is whether creativity will be more or less important in the future, in relation to breadth of services and global reach.

Sources: Zenith, September 2015, http://www.zenithoptimedia.co.uk; Advertising Age; Omnicom Group, http://www.omnicomgroup.com; WPP Group, http://www.wpp.com; Publicis, http://www.publicisgroupe.com; Interpublic Group of Companies, http://www.interpublic.com; Havas Conseils, http://www.havas.com/havas-dyn/en/; http://www.financialcontent.com; and http://www.emarketer.com. *See also* MyStrategyExperience: the Strategy Simulation designed for *Exploring Strategy*: https://heuk.pearson.com/simulations/mystrategyexperience.html.

Questions

1 Carry out a five forces analysis of the advertising industry in 2015. What is the strength of the five forces and what underlying factors drive them? What is the industry attractiveness?

2 What are the changes in the industry? Which forces are becoming more negative or positive for the major advertising agencies?

4

RESOURCES AND CAPABILITIES

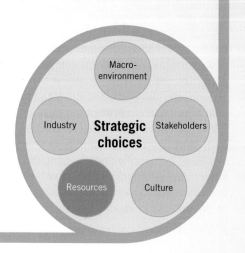

4.1 INTRODUCTION

Chapters 2 and 3 emphasised the importance of the external environment of an organisation and how it can create both strategic opportunities and threats. However, it is not only the external environment that matters for strategy; there are also differences between organisations and companies that need to be taken into account. For example, manufacturers of saloon cars compete within the same industry and within the same technological environment, but with markedly different success. BMW has been relatively successful consistently; Chrysler has found it more difficult to maintain its competitive position. And others, like SAAB in Sweden, have gone out of business (even though the brand as such has been acquired by others). It is not so much the characteristics of the environment which explain these differences in performance, but differences in their company-specific *resources and capabilities*. This puts the focus on variations between companies within the same environment and industry and how they vary in their resources and capabilities arrangements. It is the strategic importance of organisations' resources and capabilities that is the focus of this chapter.

The key issues posed by the chapter are summarised in Figure 4.1. Underlying these are two key issues. The first is that organisations are not identical, but have different resources and capabilities; they are 'heterogeneous' in this respect. The second is that it can be difficult for one organisation to obtain or imitate the resources and capabilities of another. The implication for managers is that they need to understand how their organisations are different from their rivals in ways that may be the basis of achieving competitive advantage and superior performance. These concepts underlie what has become known as the **resource-based view** (RBV) of strategy (sometimes labelled the 'capabilities view') pioneered by Jay Barney at University of Utah: **that the competitive advantage and superior performance of an organisation are explained by the distinctiveness of its resources and capabilities.**[1] Resource – or capabilities – views have become very influential, but it should be borne in mind that while the terminology and concepts employed here align with these views, readers will find different terminology used elsewhere.

The chapter has four further sections:

- Section 4.2 discusses the foundations of what *resources* and *capabilities* are. It also draws a distinction between *threshold* resources and capabilities required to be able to compete in a market and *distinctive* resources and capabilities that may be a basis for achieving competitive advantage and superior performance.

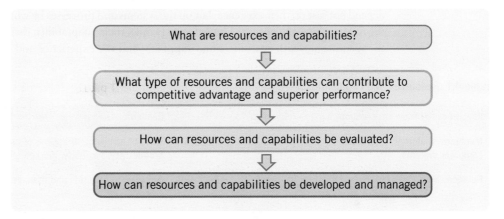

Figure 4.1 Resources and capabilities: the key issues

- Section 4.3 explains the ways in which distinctive resources and capabilities can contribute to *sustained competitive advantage* (in a public-sector context the equivalent concern might be how some organisations sustain relative superior performance over time). In particular, the importance of the *Value, Rarity, Inimitability and Organisational support* (VRIO) of resources and capabilities is explained.

- Section 4.4 moves on to consider different ways resources and capabilities might be diagnosed. These include *VRIO analysis*, *value chain and system analysis*, *activity systems mapping* and *benchmarking*. The section concludes by explaining the use of *SWOT* analysis as a basis for pulling together the insights from the analyses of the environment (explained in Chapter 2 and 3) and of resources and capabilities in this chapter.

- Finally, Section 4.5 discusses some of the key issues of *dynamic capabilities* and how resources and capabilities can be developed and managed.

4.2 FOUNDATIONS OF RESOURCES AND CAPABILITIES

Given that different writers, managers and consultants use different terms and concepts, it is important to understand how concepts relating to resources and capabilities are used in this book. The **resources and capabilities of an organisation contribute to its long-term survival and potentially to competitive advantage.** However, to understand and to manage resources and capabilities it is necessary to explain their components.[2]

4.2.1 Resources and capabilities

Resources are the assets that organisations have or can call upon and capabilities are the ways those assets are used or deployed[3] (earlier editions of this text used the term 'competences' for the latter and these terms are often used interchangeably).[4] A shorthand way of thinking of this is that resources are 'what we *have*' (nouns) and capabilities are 'what we *do* well' (verbs). Other writers use the term *intangible assets* as an umbrella term to include capabilities as well as intangible resources such as brands.

Resources and capabilities are typically related, as Table 4.1 shows. Resources are certainly important, but how an organisation employs and deploys its resources matters at least as much. There would be no point in having state-of-the-art equipment if it were not used effectively. The efficiency and effectiveness of physical or financial resources, or the people in an organisation, depend not just on their existence, but on the systems and processes by which they are managed, the relationships and cooperation between people, their adaptability, their innovative capacity, the relationship with customers and suppliers, and the experience and learning about what

Table 4.1 Resources and capabilities

Resources: what we have (nouns), e.g.		Capabilities: what we do well (verbs), e.g.
Machines, buildings, raw materials, patents, databases, computer systems	Physical	Ways of achieving utilisation of plant, efficiency, productivity, flexibility, marketing
Balance sheet, cash flow, suppliers of funds	Financial	Ability to raise funds and manage cash flows, debtors, creditors, etc.
Managers, employees, partners, suppliers, customers	Human	How people gain and use experience, skills, knowledge, build relationships, motivate others and innovate

ILLUSTRATION 4.1   Resources and capabilities

Executives emphasise the importance of resources and capabilities in different organisations.

The Australian Red Cross

To achieve the vision of improving the lives of vulnerable people, the Australian Red Cross emphasises the crucial role of capabilities in its strategic plan 'Strategy 2015'. 'Capabilities are integral to our overriding strategy to create one Red Cross,' writes CEO Robert Tickner. The Australian Red Cross distinguish between technical competency and behavioural capability. The former refers to specialist skills and may include such competencies as project management, financial management, community development, social work, administrative or information technology skills. Capabilities at the Red Cross refer to the behaviours they expect its people to demonstrate in order to be successful in achieving the objectives. The organisation aims to increasingly invest in the capabilities and skills of Red Cross people and supporters including members, branches and units, volunteers, aid workers, staff and donors. For example, this involves investing in a diverse workforce and supporter base, with strong engagement of 'young people, Aboriginal and Torres Strait Islander people, and other culturally and linguistically diverse people'. The emphasis is on people who are engaged, dynamic, innovative, entrepreneurial and motivated to realise the vision and goals.[1]

Royal Opera House, London

Tony Hall, Chief Executive of the Royal Opera House:

'"World-class" is neither an idle nor boastful claim. In the context of the Royal Opera House the term refers to the quality of our people, the standards of our productions and the diversity of our work and initiatives. Unique? Unashamedly so. We shy away from labels such as "elite", because of the obvious negative connotations of exclusiveness. But I want people to take away from here the fact that we are elite in the sense that we have the best singers, dancers, directors, designers, orchestra, chorus, backstage crew and administrative staff. We are also among the best in our ability to reach out to as wide and diverse a community as possible.'[2]

Infosys

The Indian company Infosys is a global leader in information technology, outsourcing, system integration services and IT consulting. It is listed as one of the world's most reputable companies with close to 150,000 employees worldwide. The company's 'Infosys 3.0 strategy' is taking a further step to provide more advanced IT products and services, which requires investments in new resources and capabilities.[3] Infosys CEO S.D. Shibulal: 'We continue to make focused investments in our organisational capabilities.'[4]

The strategy emphasises innovation and focuses on higher-value software. Innovation abilities are central for this, as stated on the website: 'The foundation of our innovation capability is our core lab network – Infosys Labs – and the new thinking that our team of over 600 researchers brings to the table.'[5] The strategy thus requires human resource and training capabilities including the ability to attract, employ, educate and retain new high-quality engineers. As Srikantan Moorthy, Senior Vice President and Group Head, explains: 'We are currently hiring and developing talent in the areas of cloud, mobility, sustainability, and product development. In addition, a key focus is also consultative skills. All of these are in line with our Infosys 3.0 strategy. We place significant value on continuous learning and knowledge sharing.'[6]

Sources: (1) Australian Red Cross Capability Framework, 2015; (2) Royal Opera House Annual Review 2005–6; (3) *Financial Times*, 12 August 2012; (4) Infosys Annual Report 2011–12; (5) http://www.infosys.com; (6) *SkillingIndia*, 26 September 2012.

Questions

1 Categorise the range of resources and capabilities highlighted by the executives above in terms of Section 4.2 and Table 4.1.

2 To what extent and why might these resources and capabilities be the basis of *sustained* competitive advantage?

3 Imagine you are the general manager of an organisation of your choice and undertake the same exercise as in Questions 1 and 2 above.

works well and what does not. Illustration 4.1 shows examples of how executives explain the importance of the resources and capabilities of their different organisations.

4.2.2 Threshold and distinctive resources and capabilities

A distinction also needs to be made between resources and capabilities that are at a threshold level and those that might help the organisation achieve competitive advantage and superior performance. **Threshold resources and capabilities are those needed for an organisation to meet the necessary requirements to compete in a given market and achieve parity with competitors in that market.** Without these, the organisation could not survive over time. Indeed many start-up businesses find this to be the case. They simply do not have or cannot obtain the resources or capabilities needed to compete with established competitors. Identifying threshold requirements is, however, also important for established businesses. There could be changing *threshold resources* required to meet minimum customer requirements: for example, the increasing demands by modern multiple retailers of their suppliers mean that those suppliers have to possess a quite sophisticated IT infrastructure simply to stand a chance of meeting retailer requirements. Or there could be *threshold capabilities* required to deploy resources so as to meet customers' requirements and support particular strategies. Retailers do not simply expect suppliers to have the required IT infrastructure, but to be able to use it effectively so as to guarantee the required level of service.

Identifying and managing threshold resources and capabilities raises a significant challenge because threshold levels will change as critical success factors change (see Section 3.4.3) or through the activities of competitors and new entrants. To continue the example above, suppliers to major retailers did not require the same level of IT and logistics support a decade ago. But the retailers' drive to reduce costs, improve efficiency and ensure availability of merchandise to their customers means that their expectations of their suppliers have increased markedly in that time and continue to do so. So there is a need for those suppliers continuously to review and improve their logistics resource and capability base just to stay in business.

While threshold resources and capabilities are important, they do not of themselves create competitive advantage or the basis of superior performance. They can be thought of as 'qualifiers' to be able to compete at all with competitors while distinctive resources and capabilities are 'winners' required to triumph over competitors. **Distinctive resources and capabilities are required to achieve competitive advantage.** These are dependent on an organisation having a distinctiveness or uniqueness that are of value to customers and which competitors find difficult to imitate. This could be because the organisation has *distinctive resources* that critically underpin competitive advantage and that others cannot imitate or obtain – a long-established brand, for example. Or it could be that an organisation achieves competitive advantage because it has *distinctive capabilities* – ways of doing things that are unique to that organisation and effectively utilised so as to be valuable to customers and difficult for competitors to obtain or imitate. For example, Apple has distinctive resources in mobile technology and in the powerful brand, but also distinctive capabilities in design and in understanding consumer behaviour.

Gary Hamel and C.K. Prahalad argue that distinctive capabilities or competences typically remain unique because they comprise a *bundle* of constituent skills and technologies rather than a single, discrete skill or technology. They refer to this as *core competences* and the emphasis is thus on the linked set of resources, capabilities, skills and activities.[5] In the Apple example above, it is thus the combination of the resources and capabilities that make them distinctive or core competences in Hamel's and Prahalad's words. Section 4.3 that follows discusses in more depth the role played by distinctive resources and capabilities in contributing to long-term, sustainable competitive advantage. Section 4.3.3 explores further the importance of linkages.

4.3 DISTINCTIVE RESOURCES AND CAPABILITIES AS A BASIS OF COMPETITIVE ADVANTAGE

As explained above, distinctive resources and capabilities are necessary for sustainable competitive advantage and superior economic performance. This section considers four key criteria by which resources and capabilities can be assessed in terms of them providing a basis for achieving such competitive advantage: value, rarity, inimitability and organisational support – or VRIO.[6] Figure 4.2 illustrates these four fundamental criteria and the questions they address.

4.3.1 V – value of resources and capabilities

Valuable resources and capabilities are those which create a product or a service that is of value to customers and enables the organisation to respond to environmental opportunities or threats. There are three components to consider here:

- *Taking advantage of opportunities and neutralising threats.* The most fundamental point is that to be valuable, resources and capabilities need to address opportunities and threats that arise in an organisation's environment. This points to an important complementarity with the external environment of an organisation (Chapters 2 and 3). An opportunity is addressed when a resource or capability increases the value for customers either through lowering the price or by increasing the attractiveness of a product or service. For example, IKEA has valuable resources in its cost-conscious culture and size and in its interlinked capabilities that lower its costs compared to competitors, and this addresses opportunities and customer value of low-priced designer furniture that competitors do not attend to. Using a resource and capability that do not exploit opportunities or neutralise threats does not create value and even risks decreasing revenues and increasing costs.

- *Value to customers.* It may seem an obvious point to make that resources and capabilities need to be of value to customers, but in practice it is often ignored or poorly understood. For example, managers may seek to build on resources and capabilities that *they* may see as valuable but which do not meet customers' critical success factors (see Section 3.4.3). Or they may see a distinctive capability as of value simply because it is unique, although it may not be valued by customers. Having resources and capabilities that are different from those of other organisations is not, of itself, a basis of competitive advantage.

V	**Value:** Do resources and capabilities exist that are valued by customers and enable the organisation to respond to environmental opportunities or threats?
R	**Rarity:** Do resources and capabilities exist that no (or few) competitors possess?
I	**Inimitability:** Are resources and capabilities difficult and costly for competitors to obtain and imitate?
O	**Organisational support:** Is the organisation appropriately organised to exploit the resources and capabilities?

Figure 4.2 VRIO

- *Cost.* The product or service needs to be provided at a cost that still allows the organisation to make the returns expected of it. The danger is that the cost of developing or acquiring the resources and/or capabilities to deliver what customers especially value is such that products or services are not profitable.

Managers should therefore consider carefully which of their organisation's activities are especially important in providing such value and which are of less value. Value chain analysis and activity systems mapping, explained in Sections 4.4.2 and 4.4.3, can help here.

4.3.2 R – rarity

Resources and capabilities that are valuable, but common among competitors, are unlikely to be a source of competitive advantage. If competitors have similar resources and capabilities, they can respond quickly to the strategic initiative of a rival. This has happened in competition between car manufacturers as they have sought to add more accessories and gadgets to cars. As soon as it becomes evident that these are valued by customers, they are introduced widely by competitors who typically have access to the same technology. **Rare resources and capabilities**, on the other hand, **are those possessed uniquely by one organisation or by a few others.** Here competitive advantage is longer-lasting. For example, a company can have patented products or services that give it advantage. Some libraries have unique collections of books unavailable elsewhere; a company can have a powerful brand; or retail stores can have prime locations. In terms of capabilities, organisations can have unique skills or business processes developed over time or make use of special relationships with customers or suppliers not widely possessed by competitors. However, it can be dangerous to assume that resources and capabilities that are rare will remain so. So it may be necessary to consider other bases of sustainability in competitive advantage.

4.3.3 I – inimitability

It should be clear by now that the search for resources and capabilities that provide sustainable competitive advantage is not straightforward. Having resources and capabilities that are valuable to customers and relatively rare is important, but this may not be enough. Sustainable competitive advantage also involves identifying **inimitable resources and capabilities – those that competitors find difficult and costly to imitate or obtain or substitute.** If an organisation has a competitive advantage because of its particular marketing and sales skills it can only sustain this if competitors cannot imitate, obtain or substitute for them or if the costs to do so would eliminate any gains made. Often the barriers to imitation lie deeply in the organisation in linkages between activities, skills and people.

At the risk of over-generalisation, it is unusual for competitive advantage to be explainable by differences in the tangible resources of organisations, since over time these can usually be acquired or imitated (key geographic locations, certain raw material resources, brands, etc., can, however, be exceptions). Advantage is more likely to be determined by the way in which resources are deployed and managed in terms of an organisation's activities; in other words, on the basis of capabilities.[7] For example, as indicated above, it is unlikely that an IT system will improve an organisation's competitive standing in itself, not least because competitors can probably buy something very similar on the open market. On the other hand, the capabilities to manage, develop and deploy such a system to the benefit of customers may be much more difficult and costly to imitate. Compared to physical assets and patents, capabilities tend to involve more intangible imitation barriers. In particular,

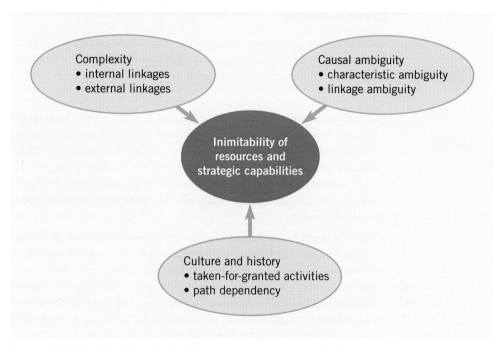

Figure 4.3 Criteria for the inimitability of resources and capabilities

they often include *linkages* that integrate activities, skills, knowledge and people both inside and outside the organisation in distinct and mutually compatible ways. These linkages can make capabilities particularly difficult for competitors to imitate, and there are three primary reasons why this may be so. These are summarised in Figure 4.3 and are now briefly reviewed.

Complexity

The resources and capabilities of an organisation can be difficult to imitate because they are complex and involve interlinkages. This may be for two main reasons:

- *Internal linkages.* There may be linked activities and processes that, together, deliver customer value. The discussion of activity systems in Section 4.4.3 below explains this in more detail and shows how such linked sets of activities might be mapped so that they can be better understood. However, even if a competitor possessed such a map, it is unlikely that it would be able to replicate the sort of complexity it represents because of the numerous interactions between tightly knit activities and decisions.[8] This is not only because of the complexity itself but because, very likely, it has developed on the basis of custom and practice built up over years and is specific to the organisation concerned. For example, companies like IKEA and Ryanair still enjoy competitive advantages despite the availability of countless case studies, articles and reports on their successes.

- *External interconnectedness.* Organisations can make it difficult for others to imitate or obtain their bases of competitive advantage by developing activities together with customers or partners such that they become dependent on them. Apple, for example, has many and intricate linkages with various app developers and actors in the music industry that others may find difficult to imitate.

Causal ambiguity[9]

Another reason why resources and capabilities might be difficult and costly to imitate is that competitors find it difficult to discern the causes and effects underpinning an organisation's advantage. This is called *causal ambiguity*. Causal ambiguity may exist in two different forms:[10]

- *Characteristic ambiguity.* Where the significance of the characteristic itself is difficult to discern or comprehend, perhaps because it is based on tacit knowledge or rooted in the organisation's culture. For example, the know-how of the buyers in a successful fashion retailer may be evident in the sales achieved for the ranges they buy year after year. But this may involve subtleties like spotting new trends and picking up feedback from pioneering customers that may be very difficult for competitors to comprehend so they will find it difficult to imitate.

- *Linkage ambiguity.* Where competitors cannot discern which activities and processes are dependent on which others to form linkages that create distinctiveness. The expertise of the fashion buyers is unlikely to be lodged in one individual or even one function. It is likely that there will be a network of suppliers, intelligence networks to understand the market and links with designers. Indeed, in some organisations the managers themselves admit that they do not fully comprehend the linkages throughout the organisation that deliver customer value. If this is so it would certainly be difficult for competitors to understand them.

Culture and history

Resources and capabilities that involve complex social interactions and interpersonal relations within an organisation can be difficult and costly for competitors to imitate systematically and manage. For example, capabilities can become embedded in an organisation's culture. Coordination between various activities occurs 'naturally' because people know their part in the wider picture or it is simply 'taken for granted' that activities are done in particular ways. We see this in high-performing sports teams or in groups of people that work together to combine specialist skills as in operating theatres. Linked to this cultural embeddedness is the likelihood that such capabilities have developed over time and in a particular way. The origins and history by which capabilities and resources have developed over time are referred to as *path dependency*.[11] This history is specific to the organisation and cannot be imitated (see Section 6.2.1). As explained in Chapter 6, there is, however, a danger that culturally embedded resources and capabilities built up over time become so embedded that they are difficult to change: they become rigidities.

4.3.4 O – organisational support

Providing value to customers and possessing capabilities that are rare and difficult to imitate provides a potential for competitive advantage. However, the organisation must also be suitably arranged to support these capabilities including appropriate organisational processes and systems.[12] This implies that in order to fully take advantage of the resources and capabilities an organisation's structure and formal and informal management control systems need to support and facilitate their exploitation (see Sections 14.1 and 14.2 for further discussions of organisational structure and systems). The question of organisational support works as an adjustment factor. Some of the potential competitive advantage can be lost if the organisation is not organised in such a way that it can fully take advantage of valuable and/or rare and/or inimitable resources and capabilities. For example, if an organisation has a unique patent underlying a product that customers value it may still not be able to convert this into a competitive advantage if it does not have the appropriate sales force to sell the product. Supporting capabilities have been labelled *complementary capabilities* as, by themselves, they are often not enough to provide for competitive advantage, but they are useful in the exploitation of other capabilities that can provide for competitive advantage.[13] In brief, even though an organisation has valuable, rare and inimitable capabilities some of its potential competitive advantage may not be realised if it lacks the organisational arrangements to fully exploit these.

In summary, and from a resource-based view of organisations, managers need to consider whether their organisation has resources and capabilities to achieve and sustain competitive advantage. To do so they need to consider how and to what extent it has capabilities which are (i) valuable, (ii) rare, (iii) inimitable and (iv) supported by the organisation. Illustration 4.2 gives an example of the challenges in meeting these criteria in the context of the internet-based company Groupon.

4.3.5 Organisational knowledge as a basis of competitive advantage

A good example of how both resources and capabilities may combine to produce competitive advantage for an organisation is in terms of organisational knowledge.[14] **Organisational knowledge is organisation-specific, collective intelligence, accumulated through formal systems and people's shared experience.**

The reasons why organisational knowledge is seen as especially important illustrate many of the points made above. As organisations become larger and more complex, the need to share what people know becomes more and more important but increasingly challenging. So organisations that can share knowledge especially well may gain advantage over those that do not. Computerised information systems are available or have been developed by organisations to codify technological, financial and market data that are *valuable* to them; indeed without which they probably could not compete effectively. However, the technology that forms the basis of information systems is hardly *rare*; it is widely available or can be developed. It is therefore less likely that organisations will achieve competitive advantage through such resources and more likely that it will be achieved through the way they manage and develop organisational knowledge more broadly. This may be to do with the capabilities they employ to utilise and develop information technology. But it is also likely to be about how they draw on and develop the accumulated and dispersed experience-based knowledge in the organisation.

The distinction between *explicit* and *tacit organisational knowledge* made by Ikijuro Nonaka and Hiro Takeuchi[15] helps explain why this is important in terms of achieving competitive advantage. Explicit or 'objective' knowledge is transmitted in formal systematic ways. It can take the form of a codified information resource such as a systems manual or files of market research and intelligence. In contrast, tacit knowledge is more personal, context-specific and therefore hard to formalise and communicate. For example, it could be the knowledge of a highly experienced sales force or research and development team; or the experience of a top management team in making many successful acquisitions. It is therefore not only distinctive to the organisation, but likely to be *difficult to imitate* or obtain for the reasons explained in Section 4.3.3 above.

Many organisations that have tried to improve the sharing of knowledge by relying on IT-based systems have come to realise that, while some knowledge can usefully be codified and built into computer-based systems, it can be very difficult to codify the knowledge that truly bestows competitive advantage.[16]

ILLUSTRATION 4.2   Groupon and the sincerest form of flattery

When a firm identifies a new market niche it must also make sure its resources and capabilities are valuable, rare, inimitable and supported by the organisation.

Chicago-based Groupon was launched in 2008 by Andrew Mason with the idea to email subscribers daily deals of heavily discounted coupons for local restaurants, theatres, spas, etc. Groupon sells a coupon for a product and takes up to half of the proceeds, which represent a big discount on the product's usual price. In return, Groupon aggregates demand from customers who receive emails or visit the website and this provides exposure and increased business for local merchants. The venture rapidly became the fastest-growing internet business ever and grew into a daily-deal industry giant. In 2010, Groupon rejected a \$6bn (£3.6bn, €4.5bn) takeover bid by Google and instead went public at \$10bn in November of 2011.

While Groupon's daily deals were valued by customers – the company quickly spread to over 40 countries – they also attracted thousands of copycats worldwide. Investors questioned Groupon's business and to what extent it had rare and inimitable resources and capabilities. CEO Andrew Mason denied in *Wall Street Journal* (*WSJ*) that the model was too easy to replicate:

'There's proof. There are over 2000 direct clones of the Groupon business model. However, there's an equal amount of proof that the barriers to success are enormous. In spite of all those competitors, only a handful is remotely relevant.'

This, however, did not calm investors and Groupon shares fell by 80 per cent at its all-time low. One rare asset Groupon had was its customer base of more than 50 million customers, which could possibly be difficult to imitate. The more customers, the better deals, and this would make customers come to Groupon rather than the competitors and the cost for competitors to acquire customers would go up. Further defending Groupon's competitiveness, the CEO emphasised in *WSJ* that it is not as simple as providing daily deals, but that a whole series of things have to work together and competitors would have to replicate everything in its 'operational complexity':

'People overlook the operational complexity. We have 10,000 employees across 46 countries.

We have thousands of salespeople talking to tens of thousands of merchants every single day. It's not an easy thing to build.'

Mason also emphasised Groupon's advanced technology platform that allowed the company to 'provide better targeting to customers and give them deals that are more relevant to them'. Part of this platform, however, was built via acquisitions – a route competitors possibly also could take.

If imitation is the highest form of flattery Groupon has been highly complimented, but investors have not been flattered. Andrew Mason was forced out in 2013, succeeded by the chairman Eric Lefkofsky. Even though Amazon and many other copycats left the daily-deals business, he struggled to explain how Groupon would fight off imitators and was forced to exit several international markets. In November 2015, he returned to his chairman role and was followed by Rich Williams who stated:

'As CEO, my top priority is to unlock the long-term growth potential in the business by demonstrating everything the new Groupon has to offer.'

Sources: 'Groupon shares crumble after company names new CEO', 3 November 2015, *Forbes*; 'Groupon names Rich Williams CEO', 3 November 2015, *Wall Street Journal*; All Things Digital, 2 November 2012, *Wall Street Journal*; *Financial Times*, 2 March 2013; 'Groupon and its "weird" CEO', *Wall Street Journal*, 31 January 2012.

Questions

1 Andrew Mason admits that Groupon has thousands of copycats, yet his assessment is that imitating Groupon is difficult. Do you agree?

2 Assess the bases of Groupon's resources and capabilities using the VRIO criteria (Figure 4.2 and Table 4.2).

3 If you were the new Groupon CEO, what resources and capabilities would you build on to give the company a sustainable competitive advantage?

4.4 DIAGNOSING RESOURCES AND CAPABILITIES

So far, this chapter has been concerned with explaining concepts associated with the strategic significance of organisations' resources and capabilities. This section now provides some ways in which they can be understood and diagnosed. If managers are to manage the resources and capabilities of their organisation, the sort of diagnosis explained here, the VRIO analysis tool, the value chain and system, activity systems, benchmarking and SWOT, are centrally important. If resources and capabilities are not understood at these levels, there are dangers that managers can take the wrong course of action.

4.4.1 VRIO analysis

One lesson that emerges from an understanding of the strategic importance of resources and capabilities is that it can be difficult to discern where the basis of competitive advantage lies. The strict criteria of the VRIO framework discussed above (see Section 4.3) can conveniently be used as a tool to analyse whether an organisation has resources and capabilities to achieve and sustain competitive advantage. A **VRIO analysis thus helps to evaluate if, how and to what extent an organisation or company has resources and capabilities that are (i) valuable, (ii) rare, (iii) inimitable and (iv) supported by the organisation** . Table 4.2 summarises the VRIO analysis of capabilities and shows that there is an additive effect. Resources and capabilities provide sustainable bases of competitive advantage the more they meet all four criteria. This analysis can be done for different functions in an organisation (technology, manufacturing, purchasing, marketing and sales, etc.) or more fine-grained for individual resources and capabilities (see Table 4.1). Another approach is to evaluate different sections of the value chain or system with this tool (see Section 4.4.2 below).

Sometimes it may be challenging to establish the exact competitive implication, for example when a resource or capability is on the border between sustained or temporary competitive advantage (Illustration 4.2 demonstrates this). However, for managers it is most important to distinguish between sustained or temporary competitive advantage vs competitive parity or competitive disadvantage (see Table 4.2). If it is difficult to discern whether a function or resource or capability provides for sustained competitive advantage, it may help to divide it into subparts. For example, manufacturing in itself may not provide for competitive advantage, but perhaps product engineering or design do. And even if machines and equipment generally do not provide for competitive advantage there may be a particular type of equipment that does.

4.4.2 The value chain and value system

The **value chain describes the categories of activities within an organisation which, together, create a product or service.** Most organisations are also part of a wider **value system, the set of inter-organisational links and relationships that are necessary to create a product or service.** Both are useful in understanding the strategic position of an organisation and where valuable resources and capabilities reside.

Table 4.2 The VRIO framework

Is the resource or capability . . .				Competitive implications
valuable?	rare?	inimitable?	supported by the organisation?	
No	–	–	No	Competitive disadvantage
Yes	No	–	↑	Competitive parity
Yes	Yes	No	↓	Temporary competitive advantage
Yes	Yes	Yes	Yes	Sustained competitive advantage

Source: Adapted from J.B. Barney and W.S. Hesterly, *Strategic Management and Competitive Advantage*, Pearson Education, 2012.

The value chain

If organisations are to achieve competitive advantage by delivering value to customers, managers need to understand which activities their organisation undertakes that are especially important in creating that value and which are not. This can then be used to model the value generation of an organisation. The important point is that the concept of the value chain invites the strategist to think of an organisation in terms of sets of activities. There are different frameworks for considering these categories: Figure 4.4 is a representation of a value chain as developed by Michael Porter.[17]

Primary activities are directly concerned with the creation or delivery of a product or service. For example, for a manufacturing business:

● *Inbound logistics* are activities concerned with receiving, storing and distributing inputs to the product or service including materials handling, stock control, transport, etc.

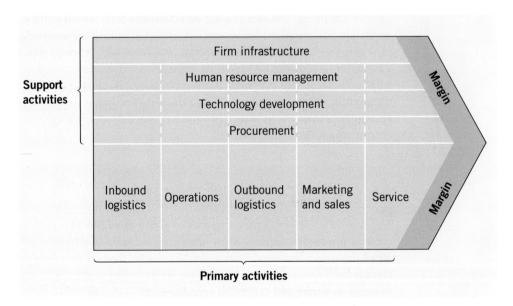

Figure 4.4 The value chain within an organisation

Source: Adapted with the permission of The Free Press, a Division of Simon & Schuster, Inc., from *Competitive Advantage: Creating and Sustaining Superior Performance* by Michael E. Porter. Copyright © 1985, 1998 by Michael E. Porter. All rights reserved.

- *Operations* transform these inputs into the final product or service: machining, packaging, assembly, testing, etc.

- *Outbound logistics* collect, store and distribute the product or service to customers; for example, warehousing, materials handling, distribution, etc.

- *Marketing and sales* provide the means whereby consumers or users are made aware of the product or service and are able to purchase it. This includes sales administration, advertising and selling.

- *Service* includes those activities that enhance or maintain the value of a product or service, such as installation, repair, training and spares.

Each of these groups of primary activities is linked to *support activities* which help to improve the effectiveness or efficiency of primary activities:

- *Procurement*. Processes that occur in many parts of the organisation for acquiring the various resource inputs to the primary activities. These can be vitally important in achieving scale advantages. So, for example, many large consumer goods companies with multiple businesses nonetheless procure advertising centrally.

- *Technology development*. All value activities have a 'technology', even if it is just know-how. Technologies may be concerned directly with a product (e.g. R&D, product design) or with processes (e.g. process development) or with a particular resource (e.g. raw materials improvements).

- *Human resource management*. This transcends all primary activities and is concerned with recruiting, managing, training, developing and rewarding people within the organisation.

- *Infrastructure*. The formal systems of planning, finance, quality control, information management and the structure of an organisation.

The value chain can be used to understand the strategic position of an organisation and analyse resources and capabilities in three ways:

- As a *generic description of activities* it can help managers understand if there is a cluster of activities providing benefit to customers located within particular areas of the value chain. Perhaps a business is especially good at outbound logistics linked to its marketing and sales operation and supported by its technology development. It might be less good in terms of its operations and its inbound logistics.

- In analysing the competitive position of the organisation by using the *VRIO analysis* for individual value chain activities and functions (see Section 4.4.2 above).

- To *analyse the cost and value of activities* of an organisation. This could involve the following steps:

  - *Identify sets of value activities*. Figure 4.4 might be appropriate as a general framework here or a value chain more specific to an organisation can be developed. The important thing is to ask (i) which separate categories of activities best describe the operations of the organisation and (ii) which of these are most significant in delivering the strategy and achieving advantage over competitors? For example, it is likely that in a branded pharmaceutical company research and development and marketing activities will be crucially important.

  - *Assess the relative importance of activity costs internally*. Which activities are most significant in terms of the costs of operations? Does the significance of costs align with the significance of activities? Which activities add most value to the final product or service (and in turn to the customer) and which do not? It can also be important to establish which sets of activities are linked to or are dependent on others and which, in effect, are self-standing. For example, organisations that have undertaken such analyses often find that central services have grown to the extent that they are a disproportionate cost and do not add value to other sets of activities or to the customer.

- *Assess the relative importance of activities externally.* How does value and the cost of a set of activities compare with the similar activities of competitors? For example, although they are both global oil businesses, BP and Shell are different in terms of the significance of their value chain activities. BP has historically outperformed Shell in terms of exploration, but the reverse is the case with regard to refining and marketing.

- *Identify where and how can costs be reduced?* Given the picture that emerges from such an analysis it should be possible to ask some important questions about the cost structure of the organisation in terms of the strategy being followed (or that needs to be followed in the future). For example, is the balance of cost in line with the strategic significance of the elements of the value chain? Can costs be reduced in some areas without affecting the value created for customers? Can some activities be outsourced (see Section 8.5.2), for example those that are relatively free-standing and do not add value significantly? Can cost savings be made by increasing economies of scale or scope; for example, through central procurement or consolidating currently fragmented activities (e.g. manufacturing units)?

The value system

A single organisation rarely undertakes in-house all of the value activities from design through to the delivery of the final product or service to the final consumer. There is usually specialisation of roles so, as Figure 4.5 shows, any one organisation is part of a wider *value system* of different interacting organisations. There are questions that arise here that build on an understanding of the value chain itself:

- The *'make or buy'* or *outsourcing* decision for a particular activity is critical: which activities most need to be part of the internal value chain because they are central to achieving competitive advantage? There may also be activities that do not generate competitive

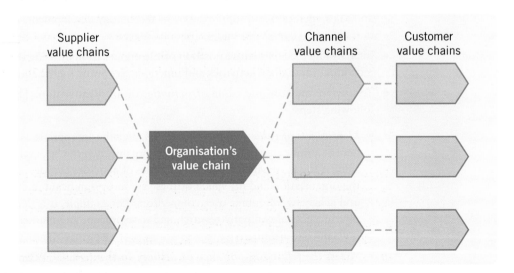

Figure 4.5 The value system

Source: Adapted with the permission of The Free Press, a Division of Simon & Schuster, Inc., from *Competitive Advantage: Creating and Sustaining Superior Performance* by Michael E. Porter. Copyright © 1985, 1998 by Michael E. Porter. All rights reserved.

advantage in themselves, but which the organisation needs to control as they enable the exploitation of competitive advantage in other parts of the value chain, as indicated in Section 4.3.4. Illustration 4.3 shows this in relation to the Nepalese poultry industry. Value system analysis was used by the Valley Group as a way of identifying what they should focus on in securing a steady supply of chicken and developing a more profitable structure. While their analysis resulted in integration along the value system, it is increasingly common to outsource activities as a means of lowering costs (see Section 8.5.2). Just as costs can be analysed across the internal value chain, they can also be analysed across the value system. If activities are less costly when performed by others without any adverse effects, it may make more sense to leave these to others along the value system.

- *What are the activities and cost/price structures of the value system?* Understand the entire value system and its relationship to an organisation's value chain is essential as changes in the environment may require outsourcing or integration of activities depending on changing cost/price structures. The more an organisation outsources, the more its ability to evaluate and influence the performance of other organisations in the value system may become a critically important capability in itself and even a source of competitive advantage. For example, the quality of a cooker or a television when it reaches the final purchaser is influenced not only by the activities undertaken within the manufacturing company itself, but also by the quality of components from suppliers and the performance of the distributors.

- *Where are the profit pools?*[18] **Profit pools** refer to the **different levels of profit available at different parts of the value system.** Some parts of a value system can be inherently more profitable than others because of the differences in competitive intensity (see Section 3.2.1). For example, in the computer industry microprocessors and software have historically been more profitable than hardware manufacture. The strategic question becomes whether it is possible to focus on the areas of greatest profit potential. Care has to be exercised here. It is one thing to identify such potential; it is another to be successful in it given the capabilities an organisation has. For example, engineering firms may recognise the greater profit potential in providing engineering consulting services in addition to or instead of manufacturing. Nonetheless, many have found it difficult to develop such services successfully either because their staff do not have consultancy capabilities or because their clients do not recognise the firms as having them.

- *Partnering.* Who might be the best partners in the various parts of the value system? And what kinds of relationships are important to develop with each partner? For example, should they be regarded as suppliers or should they be regarded as alliance partners (see Section 11.4)?

4.4.3 Activity systems

The discussion so far highlights the fact that all organisations comprise sets of resources and capabilities, but that these are likely to be configured differently across organisations. It is this variable configuration that makes an organisation and its strategy more or less unique. So for the strategist, understanding this matters a good deal.

VRIO and value chain analysis can help with this, but so too can understanding the more fine-grained activity systems of an organisation. As the discussion above in Section 4.3 has made clear, the way in which resources are deployed through the organisation actually takes form in the activities pursued by that organisation; so it is important to identify what these activities are, why they are valuable to customers, how the various activities fit together and how they are different from competitors'.

| ILLUSTRATION 4.3 | An integrated value system in the Nepalese poultry industry |

Integrating the value system under complex conditions.

The Valley Group has moved from backyard farming and selling 13 kilograms of broilers' meat in 1981 to becoming the Nepal poultry market leader despite a context including decades of political insurgency, economic turmoil and social unrest. They have managed the value system and supply chain problems of Nepal's decentralised and scattered poultry-keeping activities. Gradually they have integrated various elements of the value system while leaving supplementary elements to other organisations.

The complex context, including an absence of law and order, frequent general strikes, shortage of supplies and energy and poor transport infrastructure, resulted in irregularities in the supply of commercial chicks, their feeds and medicines. The Valley Group managers recognised that various industrial customers, such as hotels and food processing firms, preferred those suppliers that could meet their steady demand for poultry products. Supply regularity thus emerged as a primary determinant of business success. The managers then vertically and horizontally integrated various parts of the value system. They developed a sustained network of reciprocal interdependence in order to ensure the quality and regularity of poultry products and services thereof, even under the difficult circumstances prevailing.

The poultry value system begins from genetic engineering that passes through the foundation stock, primary breeder (known as grandparents that produce the parent stock – the breeders), parent stock, hatcheries, farm houses, slaughter/processing houses and finally the selling outlets (see table). The primary breeder produces breeder eggs that hatch into breeder chicks, whose eggs further hatch into day-old commercial chicks. These chicks (baby chickens hatched from the breeder eggs) are raised into live broilers (reaching slaughter-weight at between five and seven weeks) in farm houses. The live broilers are then transported to slaughter/

processing houses in order to portion, pack and prepare them for sales outlets.

The Valley Group integrated itself into various parts of the value system in order to secure a regular supply of live broilers to meet the steady demand for poultry products from the market. First, the difficult circumstances made it difficult for poultry farmers to receive live broilers and feed them consistently and this resulted in irregular supply. To address this problem, the Valley Group established Valley Poultry and Valley Feed in order to ensure a steady supply of chicks and feeds, respectively, to the farmers, who could then grow the chicks to live broilers on a regular basis. A second element that prevented regular supply from the farmers was that they were not confident that there would be a steady market demand for their live broilers. This resulted in the Valley Mart that buys live broilers directly from the farmers. The broilers are then slaughtered and processed and, finally, high-quality chicken, chicken sections, processed and packed items are steadily made available in Valley Cold Store.

Source: Prepared by Raj Kumar Bhattarai, Nepal Commerce Campus, Tribhuvan University.

Questions

1 Draw up a value system and value chains for another business and organisation in terms of the activities conducted within each part (see Figure 4.5).

2 Would it make sense to integrate or outsource some of the various value chain activities in this value system in relation to the focal organisation?

3 What are the strategic implications of your analysis – what would you do?

Major actors in the poultry value system					
	Breeding farm	**Valley Poultry**	**Farmers**	**Valley Feed**	**Valley Mart**	**Valley Cold Store**
Input	Primary breeder: – Feed – Medicine and vaccine	Breeder chickens: – Feed – Medicine and vaccine	Chickens: – Feed – Medicine and vaccine	– Food grains and remains – Other items	Live broiler feed	Live broilers
Output	– Breeder eggs – Breeder chickens	– Eggs – Chicks/chickens	– Live broilers – Food grains – Remains	– Feed for poultry and cattle	Live broilers	Poultry: whole chicken, parts and processed items

Some scholars,[19] including Michael Porter, have written about the importance of mapping activity systems and shown how this might be done. The starting point is to identify what Porter refers to as 'higher order strategic themes'. In effect, these are the ways in which the organisation meets the critical success factors determining them in the industry. The next step is to identify the clusters of activities that underpin each of these themes and how these do or do not fit together. The result is a picture of the organisation represented in terms of activity systems such as that shown in Figure 4.6. It shows an activity systems map for the Scandinavian strategic communications consultancy, Geelmuyden.Kiese.[20] The core higher-order theme at the heart of its success is its knowledge, built over the years, of how effective communications can influence 'the power dynamics of decision-making processes'. However, as Figure 4.6 shows, this central theme is related to other higher-order strategic themes (rectangles) as listed below (each of which is underpinned by clusters of supporting activities; see ovals in Figure 4.6):

- The company seeks to work at a *strategic level* based on its own *in-house methodology*, prioritising those clients where such work is especially valued.

- The company takes a *clear stance on integrity of communication,* always advising openness of communication rather than suppression of information and only dealing with clients that will accept such principles.

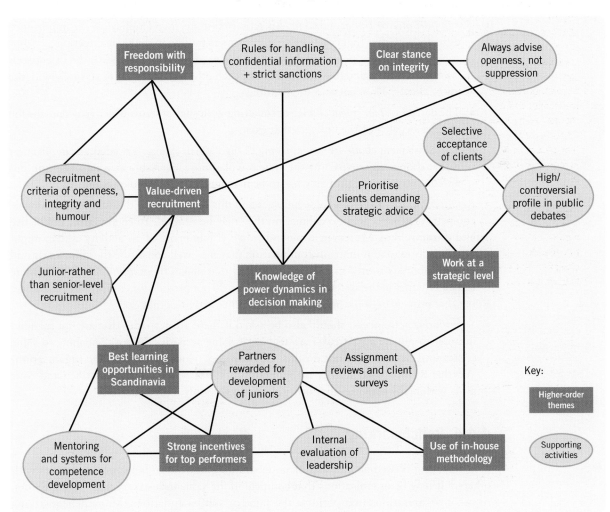

Figure 4.6 Activity systems at Geelmuyden.Kiese

- Staff are given *high degrees of freedom* but with some absolute criteria of responsibility including strict rules for handling clients' confidential information and strict sanctions if such rules are broken.

- Recruitment aims to ensure this responsibility and is carried out largely on the basis of *values of openness and integrity* but also humour. The emphasis is on recruiting junior personnel and developing them based on a mentoring system and, thus, the company believes it offers the best *learning opportunities* in Scandinavia for young consultants.

- There are *strong financial incentives* for top performance, including rewards for the development of junior personnel and based on internal evaluation of leadership qualities and performance.

When mapping activity systems four points need to be emphasised:

- *Relationship to the value chain.* The various activities represented in an activity map can also be seen as parts of a value chain. The in-house methodology is, in effect, part of Geelmuyden.Kiese's operations; its recruitment practices are a component of its human resource management; its stance on integrity and insistence on openness rather than suppression of the information part of its service offering; and so on. However, activity systems mapping encourages a greater understanding of the complexity of resources and capabilities – important if bases of competitive advantage are to be identified and managed.

- *The importance of linkages and fit.* An activity systems map emphasises the importance of different activities that create value to customers pulling in the same direction and supporting rather than opposing each other. So the need is to understand (i) the fit between the various activities and how these reinforce each other and (ii) the fit externally with the needs of clients. There are two implications:

  - The danger of *piecemeal change* or tinkering with such systems which may damage the positive benefits of the linkages that exist.

  - The consequent *challenge of managing change*. When change is needed, the implication is that change to one part of the system will almost inevitably affect another; or, put another way, change probably has to be managed over the whole system.

- *Relationship to VRIO.* It is these linkages and this fit that can be the bases of sustainable competitive advantage. In combination they may be *valuable* to clients, truly distinctive and therefore *rare*. Moreover, while individual components of an activity system might be relatively easy to imitate, in combination they may well constitute the complexity and causal ambiguity rooted in culture and history that makes them *inimitable*. Finally, there can be activities in the system that in themselves do not provide for competitive advantage, but that provide *organisational support* for other activities that do.

- *Superfluous activities.* It should also be asked if there are activities that are not required in order to pursue a particular strategy or if some activities do not contribute to value creation. If activities do not do this, why are they being pursued by the organisation? Whether Ryanair used activity mapping or not, it has systematically identified and done away with many activities that other airlines commonly undertake.

4.4.4 Benchmarking

Benchmarking is used as a means of understanding how an organisation compares with others.[21] It may be organisations that compete in the same industry, typically competitors, or other organisations that perform the same or similar functions. Many benchmarking exercises focus on outputs such as standards of product or service, but others do attempt to take account of organisational capabilities.

Broadly, there are two approaches to benchmarking:

- *Industry/sector benchmarking*. Insights about performance standards can be gleaned by comparing performance against other organisations in the same industry sector or between similar service providers against a set of performance indicators. Some public-sector organisations have, in effect, acknowledged the existence of strategic groups (see Section 3.4.1) by benchmarking against similar organisations rather than against everybody: for example, local government services and police treat 'urban' differently from 'rural' in their benchmarking and league tables. However, an overriding danger of industry norm comparisons (whether in the private or the public sector) is that the whole industry can be performing badly and losing out competitively to other industries that can satisfy customers' needs in different ways.

- *Best-in-class benchmarking*. Best-in-class benchmarking compares an organisation's performance or capabilities against 'best-in-class' performance – from whichever industry – and therefore seeks to overcome some of the above limitations. It may also help challenge managers' mindsets that acceptable improvements in performance will result from incremental changes in resources or capabilities. For example, Southwest Airlines improved refuelling time by studying the processes surrounding Formula One Grand Prix motor racing pit stops.[22]

The importance of benchmarking is, then, not so much in the detailed 'mechanics' of comparison but in the impact that these comparisons might have on reviewing resources and capabilities underlying performance. But it has two potential limitations:

- *Surface comparisons*. If benchmarking is limited to comparing outputs, it does not directly identify the reasons for relative performance in terms of underlying resources and capabilities. For example, it may demonstrate that one organisation is poorer at customer service than another, but not show the underlying reasons.

- *Simply achieving competitive parity*. Benchmarking can help an organisation to develop capabilities and create value in the same way as its competitors and those best-in-class. However, the best performance that can be expected out of this exercise is to achieve a threshold level and competitive parity. For organisations with competitive disadvantage, this can be highly rewarding, but to achieve competitive advantage an organisation needs to move further and develop its own distinctive resources and capabilities.

4.4.5 SWOT[23]

It can be helpful to summarise the key issues arising from an analysis of resources and capabilities discussed in this chapter and the analysis of the business environment discussed in Chapters 2 and 3 to gain an overall picture of an organisation's strategic position. **SWOT provides a general summary of the Strengths and Weaknesses explored in an analysis of resources and capabilities** (Chapter 4) **and the Opportunities and Threats explored in an analysis of the environment** (Chapters 2 and 3). This analysis can also be useful as a basis for generating strategic options and assessing future courses of action.

The aim is to identify the extent to which strengths and weaknesses are relevant to, or capable of dealing with, the changes taking place in the business environment. Illustration 4.4 takes the example of a pharmaceuticals firm (Pharmcare).[24] It assumes that key environmental impacts have been identified from analyses explained in Chapters 2 and 3 and that major strengths and weaknesses have been identified using the analytic tools explained in this chapter. A scoring mechanism (plus 5 to minus 5) is used as a means of getting managers to assess the interrelationship between the environmental impacts and the strengths and weaknesses of the firm. A positive (+) denotes that the strength of the company would help it take advantage of, or counteract, a problem arising from an environmental change or that

ILLUSTRATION 4.4 — SWOT analysis of Pharmcare

A SWOT analysis explores the relationship between the environmental influences and the resources and capabilities of an organisation compared with its competitors.

(a) SWOT analysis for Pharmcare

	Environmental change (opportunities and threats)					
	Healthcare rationing	Complex and changing buying structures	Increased integration of healthcare	Informed patients	+	−
Strengths						
Flexible sales force	+3	+5	+2	+2	+12	0
Economies of scale	0	0	+3	+3	+6	0
Strong brand name	+1	+3	0	−1	+4	−1
Healthcare education department	+3	+3	+4	+5	+15	0
Weaknesses						
Limited capabilities in biotechnology and genetics	−1	0	−4	−3	0	−8
Ever lower R&D productivity	−3	−2	−1	−2	0	−8
Weak ICT capabilities	−3	−2	−5	−5	0	−15
Over-reliance on leading product	−2	−1	−3	−1	0	−7
Environmental impact scores	+7	+11	+9	+10		
	−9	−5	−13	−12		

(b) Competitor SWOT analyses

	Environmental change (opportunities and threats)				
	Healthcare rationing	Complex and changing buying structures	Increased integration of healthcare	Informed and passionate patients	Overall impact
Pharmcare	−2	+6	−4	−2	−2
Big global player suffering fall in share price, low research productivity and post-mega-merger bureaucracy	Struggling to prove cost-effectiveness of new drugs to new regulators of healthcare rationing	Well-known brand, a flexible sales force combined with a new healthcare education department creates positive synergy	Weak ICT and lack of integration following mergers means sales, research and admin are all under performing	Have yet to get into the groove of patient power fuelled by the internet	Declining performance over time worsened after merger
Company W	−4	−4	+0	+4	−4
Big pharma with patchy response to change, losing ground in new areas of competition	Focus is on old-style promotional selling rather than helping doctors control costs through drugs	Traditional sales force not helped by marketing which can be unaccommodating of national differences	Alliances with equipment manufacturers but little work done across alliance to show dual use of drugs and new surgical techniques	New recruits in the ICT department have worked cross-functionally to involve patients like never before	Needs to modernise across the whole company

(b) Competitor SWOT analyses (continued)

	Environmental change (opportunities and threats)				
	Healthcare rationing	Complex and changing buying structures	Increased integration of healthcare	Informed and passionate patients	Overall impact
Organisation X Partnership between a charity managed by people with venture capital experience and top hospital geneticists	+3 Potentially able to deliver rapid advances in genetics-based illnesses	+2 Able possibly to bypass these with innovative cost-effective drug(s)	+2 Innovative drugs can help integrate healthcare through enabling patients to stay at home	+3 Patients will fight for advances in treatment areas where little recent progress has been made	+10 Could be the basis of a new business model for drug discovery – but all to prove as yet
Company Y Only develops drugs for less common diseases	+3 Partnering with big pharma allows the development of drugs discovered by big pharma but not economical for them to develop	0 Focus on small market segments so not as vulnerable to overall market structure, but innovative approach might be risky	+2 Innovative use of web to show why products still worthwhile developing even for less common illnesses	+1 Freephone call centres for sufferers of less common illnesses Company, like patients, is passionate about its mission	+6 Novel approach can be considered either risky or a winner, or both!

Questions

1 What does the SWOT analysis tell us about the competitive position of Pharmcare within the industry as a whole?

2 How readily do you think executives of Pharmcare identify the strengths and weaknesses of competitors?

3 Identify the benefits and dangers (other than those identified in the text) of a SWOT analysis such as that in the illustration.

Source: Prepared by Jill Shepherd, Segal Graduate School of Business, Simon Fraser University, Vancouver, Canada.

a weakness would be offset by that change. A negative (−) score denotes that the strength would be reduced or that a weakness would prevent the organisation from overcoming problems associated with that change.

Pharmcare's share price had been declining because investors were concerned that its strong market position was under threat. This had not been improved by a merger that was proving problematic. The pharmaceutical market was changing with new ways of doing business, driven by new technology, the quest to provide medicines at lower cost and politicians seeking ways to cope with soaring healthcare costs and an ever more informed patient. But was Pharmcare keeping pace? The strategic review of the firm's position (Illustration 4.4a) confirmed its strengths of a flexible sales force, well-known brand name and new healthcare department. However, there were major weaknesses, namely relative failure on low-cost drugs, competence in information and communication technology (ICT) and a failure to get to grips with increasingly well-informed users.

However, in the context of this chapter, if this analysis is to be useful, it must be remembered that the exercise is not absolute but relative to its competitors. So SWOT analysis is most useful when it is comparative – if it examines strengths, weaknesses, opportunities and threats in relation to competitors. When the impact of environmental forces on competitors was analysed (Illustration 4.4b), it showed that Pharmcare was still outperforming its traditional competitor (Company W), but potentially vulnerable to changing dynamics in the general industry structure courtesy of niche players (X and Y).

There are two main dangers in a SWOT exercise:

- *Listing*. A SWOT exercise can generate very long lists of apparent strengths, weaknesses, opportunities and threats, whereas what matters is to be clear about what is really important and what is less important. So prioritisation of issues matters. Three brief rules can be helpful here. First, as indicated above, focus on strengths and weaknesses that differ in *relative* terms compared to competitors or comparable organisations and leave out areas where the organisation is at par with others. Second, focus on opportunities and threats that are directly *relevant* for the specific organisation and industry and leave out general and broad factors. Third, summarise the *result* and draw concrete conclusions.

- *A summary, not a substitute*. SWOT analysis is an engaging and fairly simple tool. It is also useful in summarising and consolidating other analysis that has been explained in this chapter and also in Chapters 2 and 3. It is not, however, a substitute for that analysis. There are two dangers if it is used on its own. The first is that, in the absence of more thorough analysis, managers rely on preconceived, often inherited and biased views. The second is again the danger of a lack of specificity. Identifying very general strengths, for example, does not explain the underlying reasons for those strengths.

SWOT can also help focus discussion on future choices and the extent to which an organisation is capable of supporting these strategies. A useful way of doing this is to use a TOWS matrix[25] as shown in Figure 4.7. This builds directly on the information in a SWOT exercise. Each box of the TOWS matrix can be used to identify options that address a different combination of the internal factors (strengths and weaknesses) and the external factors (opportunities and threats). For example, the top left-hand box prompts a consideration of options that use the strengths of the organisation to take advantage of opportunities in the business environment. An example for Pharmcare might be the re-training of the sales force to deal with changes in pharmaceuticals buying. The bottom right-hand box prompts options that minimise weaknesses and also avoid threats; for Pharmcare, this might include the need to develop its ICT systems to better service more informed patients. Quite likely this would also help take advantage of opportunities arising from changes in the buying structure of the industry (top right). The bottom left box suggests the need to use strengths to avoid threats, perhaps by building on the success of the healthcare education department to also better service informed patients.

	Internal factors	
	Strengths (S)	**Weaknesses (W)**
Opportunities (O)	**SO Strategic options** Generate options here that use strengths to take advantage of opportunities	**WO Strategic options** Generate options here that take advantage of opportunities by overcoming weaknesses
Threats (T)	**ST Strategic options** Generate options here that use strengths to avoid threats	**WT Strategic options** Generate options here that minimise weaknesses and avoid threats

External factors label appears to the left, spanning the Opportunities and Threats rows.

Figure 4.7 The TOWS matrix

4.5 DYNAMIC CAPABILITIES

The previous section was concerned with diagnosing resources and capabilities. This section considers what managers might do to manage and improve resources and capabilities. If resources and capabilities for competitive advantage do not exist, then managers need to consider if they can be developed. Also, if they are to provide a basis for long-term success, resources and capabilities cannot be static; they need to change. University of Berkeley economist David Teece has introduced the concept of **dynamic capabilities**, by which he means **an organisation's ability to renew and recreate its resources and capabilities to meet the needs of changing environments.**[26] He argues that the resources and capabilities that are necessary for efficient operations, like owning certain tangible assets, controlling costs, maintaining quality, optimising inventories, etc., are unlikely to be sufficient for sustaining superior performance.[27] These '*ordinary capabilities*' allow companies to be successful and earn a living now by producing and selling a similar product or service to similar customers over time, but are not likely to provide for long-term survival and competitive advantage in the future.[28]

In other words, there is a danger that capabilities and resources that were the basis of competitive success can over time be imitated by competitors, become common practice in an industry or become redundant as its environment changes. So, the important lesson is that if resources and capabilities are to be effective over time they need to change; they cannot be static. Dynamic capabilities are directed towards that strategic change. They are dynamic in the sense that they can create, extend or modify an organisation's existing ordinary capabilities. Teece suggests the following three generic types of dynamic capabilities:

- *Sensing.* Sensing implies that organisations must constantly scan, search and explore opportunities across various markets and technologies. Research and development and investigating customer needs are typical sensing activities. For example, companies in the PC operating systems industry, like Microsoft, sensed the threats from and opportunities in tablets and smartphones.

- *Seizing.* Once an opportunity is sensed it must be seized and addressed through new products or services, processes, activities, etc. Microsoft, for example, has tried to seize opportunities by launching its own tablet device and software, Surface, and by acquiring the mobile phone company Nokia (now under the brand name Microsoft Lumia).

ILLUSTRATION 4.5 — Dynamic capabilities (and rigidities) in mobile telephone companies

Dynamic capabilities can help firms sense and seize opportunities and reconfigure ordinary capabilities in changing environments.

Companies in the mobile telephone industry have built on their dynamic capabilities in their effort to adapt to environmental changes and dominate the market. They have identified and evaluated new opportunities (sensing); addressed these opportunities with new products (seizing); and renewed and redeployed their capabilities accordingly (reconfiguring). This is illustrated in the table.

The pioneers in mobile telephony, Ericsson and Motorola, managed to sense and explore an entirely new mobile telephony market. They satisfied and captured value in that market by recombining and redeploying telecommunication and radio capabilities. However, they got stuck in these early mobile telephone capabilities and were followed by Nokia. Nokia sensed new opportunities as it realised that mobile phones' awkward design and functionality was not suited to what had become a mass consumer and fashion market. The company seized and addressed these new opportunities, offering improved design and functionality, building on design and consumer behaviour capabilities. Finally, Apple, with a long legacy in consumer products, explored even further opportunities. Apple realised that most phones, even the new smartphones, still maintained a complex and unintuitive interface with limited multimedia functionalities. Apple addressed this by introducing an upgraded multimedia platform smartphone with an intuitive and simple interface combined with complementary services like the App Store and iTunes Music Store. Apple built on a recombination of its prior design, interface and consumer behaviour capabilities and (for them) new mobile phone capabilities.

While the dynamic capabilities of the mobile phone companies helped them adapt, they are no guarantee for keeping ahead permanently as the ordinary capabilities they developed risk becoming rigidities as markets and technologies change even further. If dynamic capabilities do not manage to detect and alleviate rigidities, competitors may emerge over time with more appropriate dynamic capabilities for the constantly changing environment.

Questions

1 What type of dynamic capabilities could help mobile phone companies like Apple and Samsung avoid becoming stuck in their old resources and capabilities?

2 Based on your own experience of using mobile and smartphones:

  a What are the possible future opportunities in mobile telephones?

  b How could they possibly be sensed and seized?

- *Reconfiguring.* To seize an opportunity may require renewal and reconfiguration of organisational capabilities and investments in technologies, manufacturing, markets, etc. For example, Microsoft's inroad into tablets, smartphones and related software and apps requires major changes in its current resources and capabilities. The company must discard some of its old capabilities, acquire and build new ones and recombine them, which may prove quite challenging.

This view of dynamic capabilities relates directly to the framework for this book: strategic position, strategic choices and strategy in action (see Figure 1.3). Sensing capabilities is to do with understanding an organisation's strategic position; seizing opportunities relates to making strategic choices; and reconfiguration is to do with enacting strategies. Illustration 4.5

Companies	Approximate time period	Product	Sensing	Seizing	Reconfiguring
Ericsson (primarily Europe) **Motorola** (primarily the USA)	Mid-1980s–late 1990s	Mobile phones	Need for mobile telephones: fixed telephony did not offer mobility	Creating the first mobile telephone systems and telephones	Creating a new mobile telephone market Acquiring and building mobile telephone capabilities
Nokia	Late 1990s–early 2000s	Mobile phones with improved design and functionality	Need for well-designed and fashionable mobile phones: existing mobile phones were close to their car-phone origins and maintained their awkward design and functionality	Upgrading the mobile phone to provide a richer experience in design, fashion and functionality	Entering the mobile telephone market Acquiring and building mobile telephony capabilities Building design and marketing capabilities
Apple	Late 2000s–	Mobile or smartphones with perfected design, functionality and interface	Need for smartphones with multimedia functionality: existing smartphones maintained a complex and unintuitive interface with limited functionalities	Upgrading the mobile phone to include an intuitive interface and multimedia functionalities containing the App store and iTunes	Entering the mobile telephone market Acquiring mobile telephony capabilities and recombining them with existing design and interface capabilities Cooperating with the music and telephone app industries

provides an example of dynamic capabilities in the context of mobile telephones, but also shows that they are no guarantee for future success.

New product development is a typical example of a dynamic capability and strategic analysis and planning is another. They both involve activities that can sense and seize opportunities and that are intended to reconfigure resources and capabilities. Outlet proliferation by chain retailers such as Starbucks or Zara is another example of a dynamic capability as it extends ordinary capabilities.[29] Dynamic capabilities may also take the form of relatively formal organisational systems, such as reorganisation,[30] recruitment and management development processes and cooperating with others through alliances or acquisitions, by which new skills are learned and developed.[31]

As Teece acknowledges, however, dynamic capabilities are likely to have 'micro-foundations'[32] in people's behaviour within organisations, such as the way in which decisions get taken, personal relationships and entrepreneurial and intuitive skills. This puts the focus on behaviour and the significance of beliefs, social relationships and organisational processes in capability management, which is discussed in 'Thinking Differently' at the end of the chapter.[33]

In brief, dynamic capabilities can change ordinary capabilities in case the environment changes. However, as they are focused on finding solutions beyond and outside current ordinary capabilities there is a trade-off and tension between the two that can make it difficult to achieve an optimal balance between them. This is sometimes referred to as exploration/exploitation trade-offs and they are further discussed in Chapter 15.

As suggested above, dynamic capabilities may take different forms and there are thus many ways in which managers might create, extend or upgrade resources and capabilities including more experimental ones.[34] Several approaches to manage resources and capabilities are discussed in other parts of this book:[35]

- *Internal capability development.* Could resources and capabilities be added or upgraded so that they become more reinforcing of outcomes that deliver against critical success factors? This might be done, for example, by:

  - *Building and recombining capabilities.* Creating entirely new capabilities that provide for competitive advantage requires entrepreneurship and intrapreneurship skills. Managers can build managerial systems and a culture that promote capability innovation or form new venture units outside the rules of ordinary R&D and product development (see Chapter 10).[36]

  - *Leveraging capabilities.* Managers might identify resources and capabilities in one area of their organisation, perhaps customer service in one geographic business unit of a multinational, which are not present in other business units. They might then seek to extend this throughout all the business units, but capabilities might not be easily transferred because of the problems of managing change (see Chapter 15).

  - *Stretching capabilities.* Managers may see the opportunity to build new products or services out of existing capabilities. Indeed, building new businesses in this way is the basis of related diversification, as explained in Chapter 8.

- *External capability development.* Similarly, there may be ways of developing resources and capabilities by looking externally. For example, they could be attained or developed by acquisition or entering into alliances and joint ventures (see Chapter 11).

- *Ceasing activities.* Could current activities, not central to the delivery of value to customers, be done away with, outsourced or reduced in cost? If managers are aware of the resources and capabilities central to bases of competitive advantage, they can retain these and focus on areas of cost reduction that are less significant (see Chapter 7).

- *Awareness development.* One of the lessons of this chapter is that the bases of competitive advantage often lie in the day-to-day activities that people undertake in organisations, so developing the ability of people to recognise the relevance of what they do in terms of how that contributes to the strategy of the organisation is important. This suggests that staffing policies, training and development, including developing employee's awareness of how they contribute to competitive advantage, are all central to capability deployment and development. Together with organisational learning, these issues are discussed in later chapters on organising and leading strategic change (see Chapters 14 and 15).

THINKING DIFFERENTLY   Micro-foundations of capabilities

A new view emphasises the individuals behind capabilities.

In the discussion of dynamic capabilities above (Section 4.5) it was noted that 'micro-foundations' of people's behaviour underlie them, which suggests that strategy is rooted in individual action. From this perspective then the focus is not so much on organisation's resources and capabilities as on the individuals behind them. The emphasis is on how managers' decisions and actions aggregate up to the organisational level and shape resources and capabilities.[37]

The emphasis of this alternative micro-foundations approach is thus on individuals and their social interactions and how they form organisational resources and capabilities. Instead of taking resources and capabilities as the point of departure, micro-foundations starts with individuals' beliefs, preferences, interests and activities. The focus is on the role of key individuals, particularly those at the top, and their ambitions, competences and social networks. It is these individuals' decisions and choices that determine capabilities, strategy and performance.

The focus on micro-foundations suggests that managers should not take resources and capabilities for granted. Instead, they should carefully consider how their skills, activities and choices can develop and change them. For strategy then the focus is primarily on individual managers' capabilities rather than those of the whole organisation. However, it needs to be emphasised that there are limits to how managers can influence resources and capabilities. First, they are often built over extended periods of time (see Chapter 13), even over decades, which often go beyond the tenure of individual CEOs or managers. Second, cognitive and psychological biases often put a limit to managerial judgments and achievements (see Chapter 16).

> **Question**
>
> Pick an organisation mentioned in this chapter (e.g. Apple, IKEA, Microsoft, Ryanair, Starbucks, Zara) or one you admire and would like to work for. What micro-foundations (e.g. individuals and their competences, skills, networks, choices, activities) do you think underlie their resources and capabilities?

SUMMARY

- To be able to compete at all in a market an organisation needs *threshold* resources and capabilities, but to achieve sustained competitive advantage they also need to be unique and *distinctive.*

- To be distinctive and provide for sustainable competitive advantage, resources and capabilities need to fulfil the *VRIO* criteria of being *Valuable*, *Rare*, *Inimitable* and *supported by the Organisation.*

- Ways of diagnosing organisational resources and capabilities include:

  - *VRIO analysis* of resources and capabilities as a tool to evaluate if they contribute to competitive advantage.

  - Analysing an organisation's *value chain* and *value system* as a basis for understanding how value to a customer is created and can be developed.

  - *Activity systems mapping* as a means of identifying more detailed activities which underpin resources and capabilities.

  - *SWOT analysis* as a way of drawing together an understanding of the strengths, weaknesses, opportunities and threats an organisation faces.

  - *Benchmarking* as a means of understanding the relative performance of organisations.

- Managers need to adapt and change resources and capabilities if the environment changes and this can be done based on *dynamic capabilities.*

WORK ASSIGNMENTS

✱ Denotes more advanced work assignments.
 * Refers to a case study in the Text and Cases edition.

4.1 Using Table 4.1 identify the resources and capabilities of an organisation with which you are familiar, your university or school, for example. Alternatively, you can answer this in relation to H&M* or Formula One* if you wish.

4.2✱ Undertake a VRIO analysis of the resources and capabilities of an organisation with which you are familiar in order to identify which resources and capabilities meet the criteria of (a) value, (b) rarity, (c) inimitability and (d) organisational support (see Section 4.3; Figure 4.2 and Table 4.2). You can answer this in relation to H&M* or Formula One* or the end of chapter case, Rocket Internet, if you wish.

4.3✱ For an industry or public service of your choice consider how the resources and capabilities that have been the basis of competitive advantage (or best value in the public sector) have changed over time. Why have these changes occurred? How did the relative strengths of different companies or service providers change over this period? Why? Did dynamic capabilities play any role? Which?

4.4 Undertake a value chain or system analysis for an organisation of your choice (referring to Illustration 4.3 could be helpful). You can answer this in relation to a case study in the book such as Ryanair* or the end of chapter case, Rocket Internet, if you wish.

4.5✱ For a benchmarking exercise to which you have access, make a critical assessment of the benefits and dangers of the approach that was taken.

Integrative assignment

4.6 Prepare a SWOT analysis for an organisation of your choice (see Illustration 4.5). Explain why you have chosen each of the factors you have included in the analysis, in particular their relationship to other analyses you have undertaken in Chapters 2 and 3. What are the conclusions you arrive at from your analysis and how would these inform an evaluation of strategy (see Chapter 12)?

RECOMMENDED KEY READINGS

- For an understanding of the resource-based view of the firm, an early and much cited paper is by Jay Barney: 'Firm resources and sustained competitive advantage', *Journal of Management,* vol. 17 (1991), pp. 99–120. An overview of RBV research is written by Jay B. Barney, David J. Ketchen Jr and Mike Wright: 'The future of resource-based theory: revitalization or decline?', *Journal of Management,* vol. 37, no. 5 (2011), pp. 1299–315.

- A comprehensive book on dynamic capabilities is written by C. Helfat, S. Finkelstein, W. Mitchell, M. Peteraf, H. Singh, D. Teece and S. Winter, *Dynamic*

Capabilities: Understanding Strategic Change in Organisations, Blackwell Publishing, 2007. For a discussion of micro-foundations and dynamic capabilities, see D.J. Teece, 'Explicating dynamic capabilities: the nature and microfoundations of (sustainable) enterprise performance', *Strategic Management Journal,* vol. 28 (2007), pp. 1319–50.

- For a critical discussion of the use and misuse of SWOT analysis, see T. Hill and R. Westbrook, 'SWOT analysis: it's time for a product recall', *Long Range Planning,* vol. 30, no. 1 (1997), pp. 46–52.

REFERENCES

1. The concept of resource-based strategies was introduced by B. Wernerfelt, 'A resource-based view of the firm', *Strategic Management Journal,* vol. 5, no. 2 (1984), pp. 171–80. The seminal and most cited paper is by Jay Barney, 'Firm resources and sustained competitive advantage', *Journal of Management,* vol. 17, no. 1 (1991), pp. 99–120. There are many books and papers that explain and summarise the approach: for example, J. Barney, D.J. Ketchen Jr and M. Wright: 'The future of resource-based theory: revitalization or decline?', *Journal of Management,* vol. 37, no. 5, (2011), pp. 1299–315; and J. Barney and D. Clark, *Resource-Based Theory: Creating and Sustaining Competitive Advantage,* Oxford University Press, 2007.

2. The literature most commonly differentiates between 'resources' and 'capabilities'. See, for example, an early article by Raphael Amit and J.H. Paul Schoemaker: 'Strategic assets and organizational rent', *Strategic Management Journal,* vol. 14 (1993), pp. 33–46; and Jay Barney's book: J.B. Barney, *Gaining and Sustaining Competitive Advantage,* Addison-Wesley, 1997.

3. Please note that we use the terms 'resources' and 'capabilities' as most contemporary strategy texts do and the latter corresponds to what we in earlier editions referred to as 'competences' (earlier we also, somewhat idiosyncratically, used the umbrella term 'strategic capabilities' to refer to resources and capabilities). 'Capabilities' is commonly used in both research and in practice-oriented writings and in discussions within organisations. As Illustration 4.1 shows, organisations frequently refer to their capabilities when describing their strategies. Nevertheless, the term 'competences' is still used by some organisations and managers; 'core competences' in particular. Hence, we also refer to this latter term in the text (see also the next two endnotes).

4. Gary Hamel and C.K. Prahalad popularised the term *core competences* in the early 1990s to refer to an organisation's unique competences. See G. Hamel and C.K. Prahalad, 'The core competence of the corporation', *Harvard Business*

Review, vol. 68, no. 3 (1990), pp. 79–91. Please note, however, that 'capabilities' rather than 'competences' is a more common term today (see also next endnote).

5. G. Hamel and C.K. Prahalad, 'The core competence of the corporation', *Harvard Business Review*, vol. 68, no. 3 (1990), pp. 79–91. This idea of driving strategy development from the resources and capabilities or competences of an organisation is also discussed in G. Hamel and C.K. Prahalad, 'Strategic intent', *Harvard Business Review*, vol. 67, no. 3 (1989), pp. 63–76; and G. Hamel and C.K. Prahalad, 'Strategy as stretch and leverage', *Harvard Business Review*, vol. 71, no. 2 (1993), pp. 75–84.

6. The VRIO criteria were introduced by Jay Barney in J.B. Barney, *Gaining and Sustaining Competitive Advantage*, Addison-Wesley, 1997. Originally the acronym *VRIN* was used to also emphasise non-substitutability and how competitors must not be able to substitute a valuable, rare and inimitable capability for another, but this is now encompassed in the inimitability criterion (see endnote 1; Barney, 1991). See also endnote 12 on VRIN.

7. This is borne out in a meta-study of research on RBV by S.L. Newbert, 'Empirical research on the Resource Based View of the firm: an assessment and suggestions for future research', *Strategic Management Journal*, vol. 28 (2007), pp. 121–46.

8. For an explanation of how complex capabilities and strategies contribute to inimitability, see J.W. Rivkin, 'Imitation of complex strategies', *Management Science*, vol. 46, no. 6 (2000), pp. 824–44.

9. The seminal paper on causal ambiguity is S. Lippman and R. Rumelt, 'Uncertain imitability: an analysis of interfirm differences in efficiency under competition', *Bell Journal of Economics*, vol. 13 (1982), pp. 418–38. For a summary and review of research on causal ambiguity, see A.W. King, 'Disentangling interfirm and intrafirm causal ambiguity: a conceptual model of causal ambiguity and sustainable competitive advantage, *Academy of Management Review*, vol. 32, no. 1 (2007), pp. 156–78.

10. The distinction between and importance of characteristic and linkage ambiguity is explained by A.W. King and C.P. Zeithaml, 'Competencies and firm performance: examining the causal ambiguity paradox', *Strategic Management Journal*, vol. 22, no. 1 (2001), pp. 75–99.

11. For a fuller discussion of path dependency in the context of resources and capabilities, see D. Holbrook, W. Cohen, D. Hounshell and S. Klepper, 'The nature, sources and consequences of firm differences in the early history of the semiconductor industry', *Strategic Management Journal*, vol. 21, nos 10/11, 2000, pp. 1017–42.

12. While the original framework ('VRIN') included 'non-substitutability' ('N') as a separate component, it is now encompassed by the 'Imitation' factor. Hence, in the VRIO framework 'Imitation' encompasses both direct replication of a resource and capability and substitution for it. Direct replication refers to the difficulty or impossibility of replicating resources and capabilities. Substitution refers rather to the difficulty of substituting one resource or capability for another. For example, if it is impossible to replicate a specific marketing expertise of a leading firm a competitor may instead try to substitute for it by cooperating with a marketing consultancy. If neither direct replication nor substitution via consultancy is possible then this capability is inimitable.

13. For an extensive discussion about complementary assets and capabilities, see D. Teece, 'Profiting from technological innovation', *Research Policy*, vol. 15, no. 6 (1986), pp. 285–305.

14. The knowledge-based view was pioneered by B. Kogut and U. Zander, 'Knowledge of the firm, combinative capabilities, and the replication of technology', *Organization Science*, vol. 3, no. 3 (1992), pp. 383–97. The importance of analysing and understanding knowledge is discussed in I. Nonaka and H. Takeuchi, *The Knowledge-creating Company*, Oxford University Press, 1995. More recently, Mark Easterby-Smith and Isabel Prieto have explored the relationships in 'Dynamic capabilities and knowledge management: an integrative role for learning', *British Journal of Management*, vol. 19 (2008), pp. 235–49.

15. See I. Nonaka and H. Takeuchi, endnote 14 above.

16. See S. Gabriel, 'Exploring internal stickiness', *Strategic Management Journal*, vol. 17, no. 2 (1996), pp. 27–43; and D. Leonard and S. Sensiper, 'The role of tacit knowledge in group innovation', *California Management Review*, vol. 40, no. 3 (1998), pp. 112–32.

17. An extensive discussion of the value chain concept and its application can be found in M.E. Porter, *Competitive Advantage*, Free Press, 1985.

18. The importance of profit pools is discussed by O. Gadiesh and J.L. Gilbert, 'Profit pools: a fresh look at strategy', *Harvard Business Review*, vol. 76, no. 3 (1998), pp. 139–47.

19. See M. Porter, 'What is strategy?', *Harvard Business Review*, November–December (1996), pp. 61–78; N. Siggelkow, 'Evolution towards fit', *Administrative Science Quarterly*, vol. 47, no. 1 (2002), pp. 125–59; and M. Porter and N. Siggelkow, 'Contextuality within activity systems and sustainability of competitive advantage', *Academy of Management Perspectives*, vol. 22, no. 2 (2008), pp. 34–56.

20. We are grateful for this example based on the doctoral dissertation of Bjorn Haugstad, *Strategy as the Intentional Structuration of Practice: Translation of Formal Strategies into Strategies in Practice*, submitted to the Saïd Business School, University of Oxford, 2009.

21. See R. Camp, *Benchmarking: the Search for Industry Best Practices that Lead to Superior Performance*, Quality Press, 2006.

22. See A. Murdoch, 'Lateral benchmarking, or what Formula One taught an airline', *Management Today* (November 1997), pp. 64–7. See also the Formula One case study in the case study section of this book (Text and Cases version only).

23. The idea of SWOT as a common-sense checklist has been used for many years: for example, S. Tilles, 'Making strategy explicit', in I. Ansoff (ed.), *Business Strategy*, Penguin, 1968. See also T. Jacobs, J. Shepherd and G. Johnson's chapter on SWOT analysis in V. Ambrosini (ed.), *Exploring Techniques of Strategy Analysis and Evaluation*, Prentice Hall, 1998. For a critical discussion of the (mis)use of SWOT, see T. Hill and R. Westbrook, 'SWOT analysis: it's time for a product recall', *Long Range Planning*, vol. 30, no. 1 (1997), pp. 46–52. For a more recent evaluation of the use of SWOT, see M.M. Helms and J. Nixon. 'Exploring SWOT analysis – where are we now? A review of academic research from the last decade', *Journal of Strategy and Management*, vol. 3, no. 3, 2010, pp. 215–51.

24. For background reading on the pharmaceutical industry see, for example, 'From vision to decision Pharma 2020', PWC, www.pwc.com/pharma, 2012; 'The pharmaceutical industry', Scherer, F.M., *Handbook of Health Economics*, vol. 1 (2000), part B, pp. 1297–336; 'A wake-up call for Big Pharma', *McKinsey Quarterly*, December 2011; and Gary Pisano, *Science Business*, Harvard Business School Press, 2006.

25. See H. Weihrich, 'The TOWS matrix – a tool for situational analysis', *Long Range Planning*, April 1982, pp. 54–66.

26. For summary papers on dynamic capabilities, see I. Barreto, 'Dynamic capabilities: a review of past research and an agenda for the future', *Journal of Management*, vol. 36, no. 1 (2010), pp. 256–80; C.L. Wang and P.K. Ahmed, 'Dynamic capabilities: a review and research agenda', *International Journal of Management Reviews*, vol. 9, no. 1 (2007), pp. 31–52; and V. Ambrosini and C. Bowman, 'What are dynamic capabilities and are they a useful construct in strategic management?', *International Journal of Management Reviews*, vol. 11, no. 1 (2009), pp. 29–49. The most comprehensive book on dynamic capabilities is written by C. Helfat, S. Finkelstein, W. Mitchell, M. Peteraf, H. Singh, D. Teece and S. Winter, *Dynamic Capabilities: Understanding Strategic Change in Organizations*, Blackwell Publishing, 2007.

27. David Teece has written about dynamic capabilities originally in D.J. Teece, G. Pisano and A. Shuen, 'Dynamic capabilities and strategic management', *Strategic Management Journal*, vol. 18, no. 7 (1997), pp. 509–34. More recently, he has expanded his explanation in the book *Dynamic*

Capabilities and Strategic Management – Organizing for innovation and growth, Oxford University Press, 2009.

28. A distinction is made between what is labelled 'ordinary' (sometimes called 'operational') and 'dynamic' capabilities. Sid Winter has explained the difference between ordinary (or operational) and dynamic capabilities in S.G. Winter, 'Understanding dynamic capabilities', *Strategic Management Journal*, vol. 24, no. 10 (2003), pp. 991–5 and David J. Teece, explains the linkage between them in 'The foundations of enterprise performance: dynamic and ordinary capabilities in an (economic) theory of firms', *The Academy of Management Perspectives* vol. 28, no. 4 (2014), pp. 328–52.

29. For a discussion of outlet proliferation as dynamic capability, see S.G. Winter, 'Understanding dynamic capabilities', *Strategic Management Journal*, vol. 24, no. 10 (2003), pp. 991–5.

30. See G. Stephane and R. Whittington, 'Reconfiguration, restructuring and firm performance: dynamic capabilities and environmental dynamism,' *Strategic Management Journal*, online and forthcoming, 2016.

31. For a list of examples of dynamic capabilities, see K.M. Eisenhardt and J.A. Martin, 'Dynamic capabilities: what are they?', *Strategic Management Journal*, vol. 21, no. 10/11 (2000), pp. 1105–21.

32. For a discussion of micro-foundations of capabilities and managerial beliefs, see G. Gavetti, 'Cognition and hierarchy: rethinking microfoundations of capabilities development', *Organization Science*, vol. 16 (2005) pp. 599–617; and for an overview see J.B. Barney and T. Felin, 'What are microfoundations?', *Academy of Management Perspectives*, vol. 27, no. 2 (2013), pp. 138–55.

33. For a discussion of how resources and capabilities relate to strategy practices and processes, see P. Regnér, 'Relating strategy as practice to the resource-based view, capabilities perspectives and the micro-foundations approach', D. Golsorkhi, L. Rouleau, D. Seidl and E. Vaara (eds), in *Cambridge Handbook of Strategy-as-Practice*, London, Cambridge University Press, 2015, pp. 301–316.

34. See J. Teece, 'Explicating dynamic capabilities: the nature and microfoundations of (sustainable) enterprise performance', *Strategic Management Journal*, vol. 28, no. 1, (2007), pp. 1319–50.

35. For a fuller discussion of how managers may manage resources and capabilities, see C. Bowman and N. Collier, 'A contingency approach to resource-creation processes', *International Journal of Management Reviews*, vol. 8, no. 4 (2006), pp. 191–211.

36. For a discussion of how the periphery in organisations can build radically new capabilities, see P. Regnér, 'Strategy creation in the periphery: inductive versus deductive strategy making', *Journal of Management Studies*, vol. 40, no. 1 (2003), pp. 57–82.

37. J.B. Barney and T. Felin, 'What are microfoundations?', *Academy of Management Perspectives* vol. 27, no. 2 (2013), pp. 138–55.

Rocket Internet – will the copycat be imitated?

Patrick Regnér

Introduction

Rocket Internet is a very successful Berlin-based start-up incubator and venture capital firm. It starts, develops and funds e-commerce and other online consumer businesses. With over 700 employees and an additional 30,000 across its network of portfolio companies, the firm has helped create and launch over 100 start-ups and is currently active in more than 70 companies across more than 100 countries.

The company was founded by the Samwer brothers, Alexander, Oliver and Marc. After going to Silicon Valley in the late 1990s they became inspired by the Californian entrepreneurial culture and especially eBay. The brothers contacted eBay offerring to create a German version of the online auction house, but they received no reply from eBay. Instead they launched their own eBay clone, Alando. A month later they were acquired by eBay for $50m (£30m, €37.5m). This was to be their first great online success, but far from the last.

Next the brothers created Jamba, a mobile phone content platform. It was sold to VeriSign, a network infrastructure company, for $273m in 2004. Since then they have become experts in spotting promising business models, especially in the USA, and imitating and scaling them internationally quicker than the originals. This model is the basis of Rocket Internet, which was founded in 2007 and stock listed in Germany in 2014 valued at $8.2bn. Several of their ventures have been acquired by the company with the original idea (see Table 1). Two of their most high-profile ventures after Alando were CityDeal, which was sold off to American Groupon, and eDarling sold to American eHarmony.

The company has frequently been criticised for simply being a copycat machine without any original ideas, and some have even claimed it is a scam that rips off the originals. However, the question remains: if Rocket Internet has been so incredibly successful and what it does is simply copying, why has no one successfully imitated Rocket Internet yet? The brothers, through Oliver Samwer, defend their model in *Wired*:[1]

'But look at the reality. How many car manufacturers are out there? How many washing-machine manufacturers are there? How many Best Buys? Did someone write that Dixons copied Best Buy, or did anyone ever write that Best Buy copied Dixons, or that [German electronics retailer] Media Markt copied Dixons? No, they talk about Media Markt. They talk about Dixons. They talk about Best Buy. What is the difference? Isn't it all the same thing?'

Finance and expert teams

Rocket Internet has strong financial backup from its main investor globally, Kinnevik, a Swedish investment company with a 14 per cent stake. Other investors invest

The Samwer brothers

Source: Dieter Mayr Photography.

Company	Founded	Business	Buyer	Founded	Price, $m	Transaction date
Alando	1999	Online marketplace	eBay	1995	50	1999
cember.net	2005	Online business network	Xing	2003	6.4	2008
eDarling	2009	Online dating	eHarmony	1998	30% stake*	2010
GratisPay	2009	Virtual currency for online games	SponsorPay	2009	*na*	2010
CityDeal	2009	Discount deals for consumers	Groupon	2008	126†	2010
viversum	2003	Online astrology	Questico	2000	*na*	2010

*With option to buy more † Including a stake in Groupon

Source: Attack of the clones, *The Economist*, 6th August 2011, © The Economist Newspaper Limited, London, 2011.

directly in the start-ups and in the later growth stages, among them the American investment bank J.P. Morgan. To work with the investors and structure the financial solutions, Rocket Internet has a large team of finance experts at the Berlin headquarters.

Besides financial skills Rocket Internet also develops the concepts of new ventures, provides the technology platforms and combines various skills necessary for setting up new ventures. It has about 250 specialists working at the Berlin head office. These specialists are part of diverse expert teams. Engineering, including IT software, programming and web design skills, is essential for product development and there are around 200 engineers with access to state-of-the-art technologies.

The expert team in marketing includes experts in customer management, customer relationship marketing and online marketing. Other teams include Operations, Business Intelligence and HR. Apart from this, there is a Global Venture Development programme including a global mobile task force of entrepreneurial talents that can bring further know-how to all international markets. This task force includes venture developers with functional skills in product development, supply management, operations and online marketing. They rotate every 4–6 months to a new venture in another part of the world.

Human resource management and culture

The HR team recruit regular staff support for Rocket Internet and specialists for the expert teams and Global Venture Development programme and, not least, the founders of the ventures. Based on their entrepreneurial spirit they emphasise personal drive rather than good school grades. Head of HR, Vera Termuhlen, explains to VentureVillage.com:[2]

'All in all, it doesn't matter if an applicant is from an elite university. For the area of global venture development, we look for applicants that are hands-on, first-class, have analytical skills, describe themselves as entrepreneurs, have a passion for the online start-up scene along and a willingness to work internationally, often in exotic locations like the Philippines or Nigeria.'

The co-founders and managing directors of the individual ventures establish all operations, build the team around a venture, and develop the business; acting as entrepreneurs and holding personal stakes in the venture's equity. Recruiting them is central and Rocket Internet normally recruits extraordinary, ambitious MBA-level graduates with high analytic skills from within the local regions where the venture is set up. As Alexander Kudlich, Managing Director of Rocket Internet, says:[3]

'We are looking for those who from an analytical point of view understand the beauty of the business model, understand the rationale and understand what a huge opportunity is. Sometimes we say we are looking for analytical entrepreneurs rather than accidental billionaires.'

The company emphasises not only strong expertise, but 'a close cultural connection to Rocket Internet'. Rocket Internet has an intense entrepreneurial working culture that is highly performance driven including high pressure, long working hours, often from 09.00 to 23.00, and little job security. While this is attractive to some, the culture has also been criticised for being too tough and aggressive. Rocket Internet's Managing Director Alexander Kudlich comments on the culture:[3]

'I would describe our culture as very focused, we have young teams – the average age is below 30. There is no place where you get more freedom and where you can take as much responsibility as you want. The only thing we want back is accountability.'

Identification of business models and execution

While some of Rocket Internet's skills are common among other European incubators, the company is more of an international venture builder compared to most. Expertise is shared throughout the portfolio of ventures globally and its best practice can be applied across diverse business models (ranging from online fashion to payments to deals to social networking). Compared to many other incubators, the function of the headquarters is central. While entrepreneurs are hired to oversee individual ventures, overall strategy for Rocket Internet is largely shaped at the head office. The managing directors at head office lead the scanning for and identification of novel and proven online and mobile transaction-based business models that are internationally scalable. Former Managing Director Florian Heinemann explains in *Wired*: 'We take a pretty systematic look at business models that are already out there and we basically try to define whether a model suits our competence and is large enough that it's worth it for us to go in there.'

Another significant aspect of Rocket Internet's centralised model is the speed at which it can launch novel business models internationally. This is different compared to many US and European counterparts. Rocket Internet has an international infrastructure and distribution network with the capacity to build ventures on an international scale in just a few months. As Managing Director Kudlich explains in *Wall Street Journal*:[3]

'When we identify a business model we can, within a few weeks, build a platform out of our central teams. In the meantime the local Rocket offices will have hired or allocated the people who will execute on the ground . . . That gives us the speed. The combination of access to the best talent in each country combined with highly standardised or modular approach in terms of platform and systems which are rolled out by our headquarters.'

In brief, Rocket Internet specialises in execution rather than innovation. This is also how the management defend their model when they are blamed for simply being a clone machine. Oliver Samwer says that they are 'execution entrepreneurs' rather than 'pioneering entrepreneurs'.[4] Managing Director Kudlich explains to *Inc. Magazine*: 'Which is harder: to have the idea of selling shoes online or to build a supply chain and warehouse in Indonesia? Ideas are important. But other things are more important.'[5]

Paradoxically, even though Rocket Internet often builds on others' ideas, it prefers to keep its own ideas for itself as explained by Marc Samwer in the *International Herald Tribune*: 'We really don't like to speak about our investments since our track record encourages people to set up competing sites . . . Ideas travel much faster these days.'[6]

The future

Rocket Internet's success has continued. Zalando, which initially mimicked the online shoe retailing business in the USA by Zappos, now part of Amazon, has expanded into clothing and jewellery. Sales are rising rapidly: annual revenues for 2014 were $2.5bn and $94m in profit; and at its German stock listing the same year it was valued at €5.3bn. Other fashion brands have also been launched under the umbrella Global Fashion Group: Dafiti (Latin America), Jabong (India), Lamoda (Russia), Namshi (Middle East) and Zalora (South East Asia and Australia). After the IPO some investors complained that the company had become too complex to analyse and understand. In the *Financial Times*, Oliver Samwer describes it as a 'killer cocktail' including proprietary software, its training programmes and its 'matter-of-fact and objective' culture and claims: 'I don't think we have to change our successful model because of public investors'.[7]

Rocket Internet has, however, started to attract imitators of its own. One of the operations is Wimdu, a copy of the American Airbnb, which allows individual home and apartment owners to list their properties as holiday accommodation. However, Airbnb quickly formed a partnership with another Berlin incubator, Springstar, and they have since been rolling out Airbnb globally. Similarly, the original company responded swiftly when Rocket Internet imitated Fab.com, a designer deal site, with its Bamarang. Fab acquired Casacanda, a parallel European site, and quickly re-launched it as Fab internationally and Rocket Internet had to close down Bamarang. Rocket Internet is even facing imitators from within. Two of its managing directors have, together with other former employees, left to set up the Berlin incubator 'Project A Ventures'. Internationally there is also increasing competition including The Hut Group in the UK. There are thus signs that Rocket Internet may eventually be imitated itself.

Sources: G. Wiesmann, 'Zalando to set foot in seven new countries', *Financial Times,* 26 March 2012; T. Bradshaw, 'Facebook backers to take stake in Zalando', *Financial Times,* 2 February 2012; R. Levine, 'The kopy kat kids', Cnnmoney.com, 2 October 2007; *The Economist,* 'Attack of the clones', 6 August 2011 and 'Launching into the unknown', 4 October 2014.

References
1. M. Cowan, 'Inside the clone factory', *Wired* UK, 2 March 2012; http://www.economist.com/node/21525394\#.
2. J. Kaczmarek, 'An inside look at Rocket Internet', VentureVillage.com, 18 November 2012.
3. B. Rooney, 'Rocket Internet leads the clone war', *Wall Street Journal,* 14 May 2012.
4. C. Winter, 'How three Germans are cloning the web', *Bloomberg,* 1 March 2012.
5. M. Chafkin, 'Lessons from the world's most ruthless competitor', *Inc. Magazine,* 29 May 2012.
6. T. Crampton, 'German brothers break the mold', *International Herald Tribune,* 3 Decmeber 2006.
7. S. Gordon and D. McCrum, 'Rocket Internet: waiting for the lift-off', *Financial Times,* 19 October 2015.

Questions

1 Based on the data from the case (and any other sources available), use the frameworks from the chapter and analyse the resources and capabilities of Rocket Internet:

 a What are its resources and capabilities?

 b What are its threshold, distinctive and dynamic resources and capabilities?

2 Based on your initial analysis and answers to question 1, carry out a VRIO analysis for Rocket Internet. What do you conclude? To what extent does Rocket Internet have resources and capabilities with sustained competitive advantage?

3 What is the importance of the Samwer brothers? What would happen if they left or sold the company?

Suggested video clip

http://www.youtube.com/watch?v=Tq7WnzY89KE

5

STAKEHOLDERS AND GOVERNANCE

Macro-environment

Industry

Strategic choices

Stakeholders

Resources

Culture

Learning outcomes

After reading this chapter you should be able to:

- Undertake *stakeholder analysis* in order to identify the *power* and *attention* of different stakeholder groups.

- Analyse the strategic significance of different *ownership models* for an organisation's strategy.

- Evaluate the implications for strategic purpose of the *shareholder* and *stakeholder models* of corporate governance.

- Relate *corporate social responsibility* and *personal ethics* to strategy.

Key terms

corporate governance p.141

corporate social responsibility p.150

governance chain p.143

power p.136

stakeholder mapping p.136

stakeholders p.134

5.1 INTRODUCTION

The 2015 controversy surrounding Sepp Blatter, President of the world football's governing body FIFA (Fédération Internationale de Football Associations), points to crucial stakeholder and governance issues in strategy. Blatter's longstanding strategy of developing football outside the traditional heartlands of Western Europe and South America had won him sufficient support from many African, Asian and Caribbean nations to see him elected for a fifth term as FIFA president. Football in these regions had grown hugely thanks to Blatter's support, but controversy about FIFA corruption and the award of the World Cup competitions to Russia and Qatar was damaging the game's image. Powerful World Cup sponsors such as Coca Cola, Visa and McDonalds put FIFA under pressure. A month after his re-election, Sepp Blatter announced his resignation as FIFA President.

At FIFA, *stakeholders* such as Coca Cola were able effectively to reverse the earlier wishes of other stakeholders, even those expressed through the formal *governance* mechanism of the presidential election. The strategy of developing football in previously neglected regions was consequently in question. This chapter will deal with the importance of different organisational stakeholders – including owners, employees, customers, suppliers and communities – and the role of formal governance mechanisms – in FIFA's case, elected officials – in representing these stakeholders. The chapter will conclude with a discussion of *ethics,* a significant issue in FIFA's strategy.

The three issues of stakeholders, governance and ethics recall Chapter 1's discussion of *purpose,* as reflected in organisational missions, visions, values and objectives. The wishes of key stakeholders should define the purpose of an organisation; formal governance mechanisms and ethical considerations should then guide the translation of that purpose into strategy. Figure 5.1 depicts the flow: strategy originates from stakeholders, whose wishes are processed through governance and ethical screens before finally being put into action.

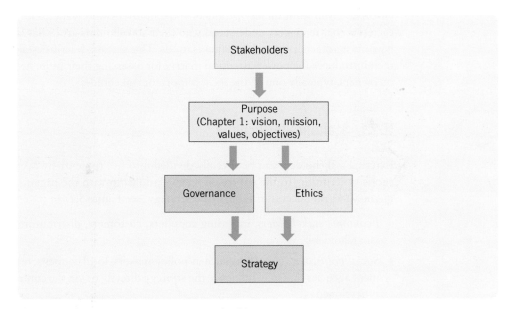

Figure 5.1 Stakeholders, governance and ethics

The chapter continues therefore as follows:

- Section 5.2 introduces the various types of *stakeholder* who may be involved in strategy, and shows how to map their *power* and *attention* using stakeholder analysis. The section then focuses on one crucial set of stakeholders, that is owners (shareholders), and their roles under different *ownership models*.

- Section 5.3 addresses the formal *corporate governance mechanisms* within which organisations operate. Governance is concerned with the way in which legally constituted bodies such as boards of directors influence strategy through formalised processes for supervising executive decisions and actions.

- Section 5.4 is concerned with issues of *social responsibility* and *ethics*. How should managers respond strategically to the expectations society has of their organisations, in terms of both *corporate responsibility* and the *behaviour of individuals* within organisations, not least themselves?

5.2 STAKEHOLDERS[1]

Strategic decisions are influenced by the expectations of stakeholders. Stakeholders are those who have some kind of *stake* in the future of the business. More formally, **stakeholders are those individuals or groups that depend on an organisation to fulfil their own goals and on whom, in turn, the organisation depends.** These stakeholders can be very diverse, including owners, customers, suppliers, employees and local communities. FIFA has stakeholders both in the form of young African footballers who benefit from grants for training facilities, and in the form of major sponsors such as Coca Cola who benefit from association with the World Cup. To the extent their organisations depend on them, managers must take all stakeholders into account. However, stakeholder demands can diverge widely, especially in the short term: for instance, profit maximisation on the part of owners may come at the expense of customers who want quality products and employees who want good jobs. It is important therefore that managers understand who their stakeholders are, what they want and which have most influence upon their organisations. This section describes stakeholders in general, then introduces the power/attention matrix for assessing their influence and finally focuses on owners, typically one of the most important stakeholders.

5.2.1 Stakeholder groups

External stakeholders can be usefully divided into five (potentially overlapping) types, categorised according to the nature of their relationship with the organisation and how they might affect the success or failure of a strategy (see Figure 5.2):

- *Economic stakeholders*, including suppliers, customers, distributors, banks and owners (shareholders).

- *Social/political stakeholders*, such as policy-makers, local councils, regulators and government agencies that may influence the strategy directly or via the context in which strategy is developed.

- *Technological stakeholders*, such as key adopters, standards agencies and ecosystem members supplying complementary products or services (e.g. apps for particular mobile phones).

Figure 5.2 Stakeholders of a large organisation

Source: Adapted from R.E. Freeman, *Strategic Management: A Stakeholder Approach,* Pitman, 1984.

- *Community stakeholders,* who are affected by what an organisation does: for example, those who live close to a factory or, indeed, groups in the wider society. These stakeholders typically have no formal relationship with the organisation but may, of course, take action (e.g. through lobbying or activism) to influence the organisation.

- *Internal stakeholders,* who may be specialised departments, local offices and factories or employees at different levels in the hierarchy.

Individuals may belong to more than one stakeholder group and such groups may 'line up' differently depending on the issue or strategy in hand. External stakeholders may seek to influence an organisation's strategy through their links with internal stakeholders. For example, customers may exert pressure on sales managers to represent their interests within the company.

The influence of these different types of stakeholders is likely to vary in different situations. For example, technological stakeholders will be crucial for strategies of new product development, while the social/political stakeholders are usually particularly influential in the public-sector context or for multinational companies operating in countries with demanding political and legal systems.

Since the expectations of stakeholder groups will differ, it is normal for conflict to exist regarding the importance or desirability of aspects of strategy. In most situations, a compromise will need to be reached. Table 5.1 shows some typical situations which give rise to conflicting stakeholder expectations.

Table 5.1 Some common conflicts of stakeholder interests and expectations

- Pursuit of short-term profits may suit shareholders and managerial bonuses but come at the expense of investment in long-term projects.
- Family business owners may want business growth, but also fear the loss of family control if they need to appoint professional managers to cope with larger-scale operations.
- Investing in growth strategies may require additional funding through share issue or loans, but thereby risk financial security and independence.
- Going public on the stock market may raise funds, but require unwelcome degrees of openness and accountability from management.
- Expanding into mass markets may require a reduction in quality standards.
- In public services, excellence in specialised services might divert resources from standard services used by the majority (e.g. heart transplants come at the cost of preventative dentistry).
- In large multinational organisations, conflict can result because of a local division's responsibilities simultaneously to the company head office and to its host country.

The stakeholder concept, and its sensitivity to different wants, helps in understanding the organisational politics of strategic decision-making. Taking stakeholder expectations and influence into account is an important aspect of strategic choice, as will be seen in Chapter 12. Stakeholder mapping also helps in managing the organisational politics of strategy.

5.2.2 Stakeholder mapping[2]

Given that there are often so many stakeholders, it is useful to categorise them according to their likely influence on strategic decisions. **Stakeholder mapping identifies stakeholder power and attention in order to understand political priorities.** The underlying view is that organisations involve *political coalitions* of stakeholders, each of which has different kinds of power and each of which pays different amounts of attention to issues.[3] It is important therefore to understand the *power* different stakeholders have and their likely *attention* to issues.

These two dimensions form the basis of the power/attention matrix shown as Figure 5.3. The matrix classifies stakeholders in relation to the power they hold and the extent to which they are likely to attend actively to a particular strategic issue. The matrix allows different stakeholders to be plotted either according to the simple dichotomy of low or high, or more subtly according to their relative positions along continuous axes from low to high. The positions of different stakeholders on the matrix are likely to vary according to each issue: stakeholders may have more power in some domains than others, and will care more about some issues than others. Power and attention can be assessed as follows.

Power[4]

In designing strategy, it is important to understand which stakeholders are most powerful. For the purposes of this discussion, **power is the ability of individuals or groups to persuade, induce or coerce others into following certain courses of action.** As Table 5.2 shows, there are different sources of power. Power is not only derived from people's hierarchical position within an organisation or from formal corporate governance arrangements. It could be a function of the resources or know-how they control or the networks they have built up, for example.

Since power is not just a matter of formal rank, it is useful to look for a variety of *indicators of power*. These include: the *status* of the individual or group (such as job rank or reputation); the *claim on resources* (such as budget size); *representation* in powerful positions or committees; and *symbols* of power (such as office size or use of titles and names). For external stakeholders, a key indicator is the organisation's *resource dependence*, for example

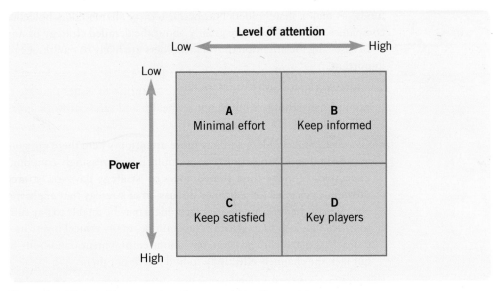

Figure 5.3 Stakeholder mapping: the power/attention matrix

Source: Adapted from R. Newcombe, 'From client to project stakeholders: a stakeholder mapping approach', *Construction Management and Economics,* vol. 21, no. 8 (2003), pp. 841–8.

Table 5.2 Sources and indicators of power

Sources of power	
Within organisations	**For external stakeholders**
• Hierarchy (formal power), e.g. autocratic decision-making • Influence (informal power), e.g. charismatic leadership • Control of strategic resources, e.g. strategic products • Possession of knowledge and skills, e.g. computer specialists • Control of the human environment, e.g. negotiating skills • Involvement in strategy implementation, e.g. by exercising discretion	• Control of strategic resources, e.g. materials, labour, money • Involvement in strategy implementation, e.g. distribution outlets, agents • Possession of knowledge or skills, e.g. subcontractors, partners • Through internal links, e.g. informal influence
Indicators of power	
Within organisations	**For external stakeholders**
• Status • Claim on resources • Representation • Symbols	• Status • Resource dependence • Negotiating arrangements • Symbols

its dependence on particularly large shareholders, lenders, customers or suppliers. One way of assessing resource dependence is to consider the ease with which a supplier, funder or customer could switch away from your organisation or, conversely, you could switch away from them.

Attention

Attention matters as well as power.[5] Stakeholders vary in the attention they pay to the organisation and particular issues within it. Even powerful stakeholders may not attend closely to everything. For example, many companies have institutional shareholders (e.g. pension funds) as major shareholders but, because these shareholders hold shares in many diverse companies, they may not care greatly about the detailed strategy of any single company.

In assessing the attention that stakeholders are likely to pay, three factors are particularly important:

- *Criticality.* Stakeholders will pay more attention to issues that are critical for them. For example, shareholders might not see health and safety at work as critical, but employees very likely will.

- *Channels.* Stakeholders will pay more attention where there are good channels of information and communication. For example, it is increasingly common nowadays for Chief Executives to invite their shareholders to 'strategy days' or 'strategy reviews', thereby providing a channel for a detailed discussion of strategy that might not otherwise be possible.[6] Where channels are poor, stakeholders may be unable to pay sufficient attention even to issues they regard as critical: for example, many ethical investors (such as Church and political groups) care passionately about employment conditions for overseas workers, but lack the channels effectively to find out about them.

- *Cognitive capacity.* Sometimes stakeholders simply do not have the cognitive capacity to process all the information they have. Channels can even be so good that they overwhelm organisations' ability to attend to the flood of information that flows through them. Thus institutional investors may have access to a host of information about the strategies of all the various companies they invest in, but be obliged to reduce complexity by focusing on simple measures such as forecast financial earnings, rather than the details of company strategy.

In order to show the way in which the power/attention matrix may be used, take the example of a business where managers see themselves as formulating strategy by trying to ensure the compliance of stakeholders with their own assessment of strategic imperatives. In this context, the matrix indicates the type of relationship that managers might typically establish with stakeholder groups in the different quadrants. Clearly, the acceptability of strategies to *key players* (segment D) is of major importance. It could be that these are major investors or particular agencies with a lot of power – for example, a major shareholder in a family firm or a government funding agency in a public-sector organisation. Often the most difficult issues relate to stakeholders in segment C. Although these might, in general, be relatively passive, a disastrous situation can arise when their level of attention is underrated and they reposition to segment D and frustrate the adoption of a new strategy. Institutional shareholders such as pension funds or insurance firms can fall into this category. They may show little interest unless share prices start to dip, but may then demand to be heard by senior management. Managers might choose to address the expectations of stakeholders in segment B, for example community groups, through information provision. It may be important not to alienate such stakeholders because they can be crucially important allies in influencing the attitudes of more powerful stakeholders: for example, through lobbying.

The power/attention matrix is a useful tool for analysing potential coalitions of stakeholders for or against particular decisions. Aligning potential supporters for strategic initiatives, and buying-off opponents, are often crucial moves in the process of strategic change (see Chapter 15). Building stakeholder coalitions is at the core of strategy, therefore. Stakeholder mapping can help in three aspects of the coalition-building process:

- Analysing who the key *blockers* and *facilitators* of a strategy are likely to be and the appropriate response.

- *Repositioning* of certain stakeholders is desirable and/or feasible: for example, to lessen the influence of a key player or, in certain instances, to ensure that there are more key players who will champion the strategy (this is often critical in the public-sector context).

- *Maintaining* the level of attention or power of some key stakeholders: for example, public 'endorsement' by powerful suppliers or customers may be critical to the success of a strategy. It may also be necessary to discourage some stakeholders from repositioning themselves. This is what is meant by *keep satisfied* in relation to stakeholders in segment C, and to a lesser extent *keep informed* for those in segment B.

5.2.3 Owners

Owners are typically key stakeholders in strategic decisions. However, their power and attention can vary according to different *ownership models.*

There are many different ways firms are owned, and the boundaries between them often blur.[7] However, it is useful to distinguish four main ownership models, each with different implications for strategy. Figure 5.4 ranges these four models along two axes. The horizontal axis describes the dominant modes of management, ranging from wholly *professional* (with managers employed for their professional expertise) to wholly *personal* (with managers employed because of their personal relationships with owners). The vertical axis describes the extent to which purpose is focused on *profit* as an exclusive goal or on profit as just one of a *mix of motives.* In each case, there is a range along the axes: organisations vary in their relative positioning and sometimes organisations do not conform to the typical behaviour of their ownership model. Nonetheless organisations with particular ownership models do tend to behave in distinctive ways.

The four main ownership models are as follows:

- *Publicly-quoted companies* (often called publicly traded companies or public limited companies) are the most important ownership model in economies such as those of the USA, northern Europe, Japan and many others. These companies' shares are 'quoted' on public stock exchanges. In other words, their shares can be bought and sold by the public, either in the form of individual investors or, frequently, institutions such as pension funds, banks or insurance companies.[8] Usually owners do not manage publicly-quoted companies themselves, but delegate that function to professional managers. In this sense, owners of publicly-quoted companies sacrifice some power, and reduce their attention. However, in principle, company managers work to make a financial return for their owners – that is why the public usually buy the shares in the first place. If shareholders are not satisfied financially, they can either sell the shares or seek the removal of the managers. In terms of Figure 5.4 therefore, most publicly-quoted companies focus strongly on profit. However, profit maximisation is rarely a simple goal for companies. There is often a delicate balance to be struck between short-run profits and long-term survival, for example. Short-term profits might be improved by cutting research budgets or taking advantage of loyal customers, but such action may well be at the expense of the long run. In relation to the vertical axis in Figure 5.4, publicly-quoted companies may therefore vary in how high is their focus on profit objectives.

- *State-owned enterprises* are wholly or majority owned by national or sometimes regional governments. They are very important in many developing economies: about 80 per cent of stock market value is accounted for by state-owned companies in China, 60 per cent in Russia and 40 per cent in Brazil.[9] Privatisation has reduced the role of state-owned enterprises in many developed economies, but quasi-privatised agencies (such as hospital trusts and school academies in the United Kingdom) operate in a similar way. In state-owned enterprises, politicians typically delegate day-to-day control to professional managers, though they may attend more closely to major strategic issues. State-owned enterprises usually have to earn some kind of profit or surplus in order to fund investment and build

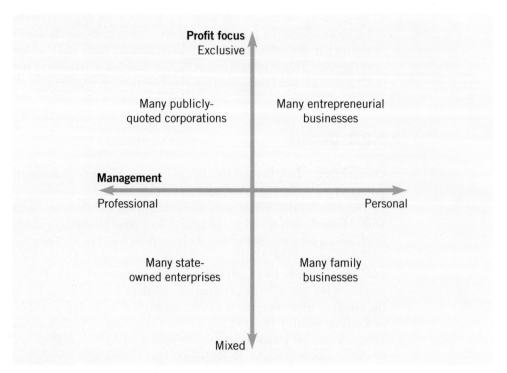

Figure 5.4 Ownership, management and purpose

financial reserves, but they are also likely to pursue a range of other objectives that are in keeping with government policy. For Chinese state-owned enterprises, for example, securing access to overseas resources such as minerals and energy is an important objective, worthwhile sacrificing some profits for.

- *Entrepreneurial businesses* are businesses that are substantially owned and controlled by their founders. Founders are typically very powerful, because of their ownership, the respect they are held in and their deep knowledge of their businesses. Founders head some major companies. For example, Lakshmi Mittal remains chairman and chief executive of his creation, Arcelor Mittal, the largest steel company in the world. Mark Zuckerberg is still CEO of Facebook, which he co-founded in 2004. Nonetheless, as they grow, entrepreneurial businesses are likely both to rely more on professional managers and to draw in external investors in order to fund new opportunities. Typically entrepreneurial companies need to attend closely to profit in order to survive and grow. However, entrepreneurs may attend to some issues more than others.[10] For example, the founders of Twitter have consistently focused on increasing usage, while downgrading the importance of monetising their user-base.

- *Family businesses* are typically businesses where ownership by the founding entrepreneur has passed on to his or her family, on account of the founder's death or retirement for instance. Most family businesses are small to medium-sized enterprises, but they can be very big: Ford, Fiat, Samsung and Walmart, the largest retailer in the world, are all under family ownership and retain significant family involvement in top management roles. Quite often the family retains a majority of the voting shares, while releasing the remainder to the public on the stock market: thus half of stock market-listed companies in the ten largest Asian markets are effectively family-controlled.[11] However, family members may lack the skill and inclination to attend closely to strategy. Family businesses therefore often bring in professional managers, even while retaining ultimate family control: thus the Chief Executive of Ford is a non-family member, but the Executive Chairman is still William Ford Jr. For family businesses, retaining control over the company, passing on management to the next generation and ensuring the company's long-term survival are often very important objectives, and these might rule out profit-maximising strategies that involve high risk or require external finance. Thus a family business might diversify into lots of small businesses rather than engage in one large one, because that would minimise risk and give a chance to younger family members to work in distinct areas of activity.[12]

As well as these four main types of ownership model, there are several other variants that play smaller but still significant roles in the economy.[13] *Not-for-profit* organisations, such as Mozilla (Illustration 5.1), are typically owned by a charitable foundation: they may need to make some kind of surplus to fund investment and protect against hard times, but they fundamentally exist to pursue social missions. The *partnership* model, in which the organisation is owned and controlled by senior employees (its partners), is important in many professional services such as law and accounting. There are also *employee-owned* firms, which spread ownership among employees as a whole. Prominent examples of employee-owned firms include W. L. Gore & Associates, famous for Gore-Tex, the Spanish Mondragon Cooperative, with 75,000 employees, and John Lewis, one of the UK's leading retailers. Typically these not-for-profits, partnerships and employee-owned firms are restricted in their ability to raise external finance, making them more conservative in their strategies. As the Thinking Differently illustration at the end of this chapter indicates, there are also Benefit Corporations in the USA that formally tie themselves to social missions.

Clearly, everybody should know how the ownership of their own organisation relates to its strategy: as above, strategy for a state-owned business is likely to be very different to that for a publicly-quoted company. However, it is also important for managers to understand the ownership of other organisations with which they engage, for example competitors and partners. Different ownership models will drive their strategic decisions in sometimes unconventional directions. Without understanding the relationship between ownership and strategies, it is easy to be surprised by competitors and partners with different priorities to your own. For example, Western public mining companies have often found themselves outbid for overseas mining opportunities by Chinese state-owned companies keen to secure raw material supplies at almost any price.

5.3 CORPORATE GOVERNANCE

The varying power and attention of owners, and their frequent reliance on professional managers, raise issues of corporate governance.[14] **Corporate governance is concerned with the structures and systems of control by which managers are held accountable to those who have a legitimate stake in an organisation.**[15] Key stakeholders in corporate governance are typically the owners, but may include other groups such as employee representatives. Connecting stakeholder interests with management action is a vital part of strategy. Failures in corporate governance have contributed to calamitous strategic choices in many leading companies, even resulting in their complete destruction: in 2014, Portugal's second largest bank, Banco Espirito Sanctu, disappeared after the discovery of financial irregularities involving €5bn losses. With the survival of whole organsations at stake, governance is increasingly recognised as a key strategic issue.

ILLUSTRATION 5.1   Firefox burns out

Is the Mozilla Foundation's army of volunteers enough to save the Firefox browser?

The Mozilla Foundation is a non-profit organisation that originated in the late 1990s from the old web-browser company Netscape. Mozilla's best known product is the Firefox open source web-browser, produced largely for free by volunteer software developers committed to the ideal of an open internet. Four thousand volunteers ('Mozillians') contributed to the original 2003 browser development, each of their names commemorated on a 14-foot high monolith outside Mozilla's San Francisco offices.

Mozilla's mission is summed up by its 'Manifesto' declaration: 'the Internet is a global public resource that must remain open and accessible . . . individuals must have the ability to shape the Internet and their own experiences on it'. Mozilla typically does not patent its innovations. Volunteers meet annually at the so-called MozFest in London to learn from one another and develop new ideas for building the open internet. In early 2016, Mozilla claimed 10,500 active volunteers around the world. Volunteers are able to participate in weekly 'all hands meetings' by global phone conferences. There are also many financial donors (both individuals and large charitable foundations: the MacArthur Foundation gave more than $2m (£1.2m, €1.5m) in 2014) and about 250 paid staff.

The Mozilla non-profit foundation is governed by six directors, chosen from the community by the directors themselves. The Foundation in turn owns the Mozilla Corporation, which directly manages the various Mozilla products and which has a conventional organisational structure with a CEO. In 2014, this structure was challenged when new CEO Brendan Eich was forced to resign by protests from volunteers and donors over his public opposition to gay marriage.

But Mozilla faces a commercial challenge too. Most of its revenue comes from partnerships with search engine companies (e.g. Yahoo and Baidu), who pay to be the Firefox browser's default search engine. Mozilla can offer access to 500 million users all over the world. However, the Firefox browser is losing market share rapidly. In 2009, Firefox had about 30 per cent of the worldwide market; by early 2016, this share was less than 10 per cent.

A major problem for Mozilla has been the switch from desktop computing to mobile computing. The two dominant operating systems (OS), Apple's iOS and Google's Android, come with their own browsers and tightly-integrated applications. Developers are more interested in developing apps for these operating systems than something that will work with Mozilla's declining browser.

In 2011, Mozilla responded by launching its own Firefox OS for smartphones, aiming to offer a lower cost alternative to Apple and Android. Volunteers from Spain's mobile carrier Telefónica offered help to get the new Firefox OS into Spanish America; a designer from Berlin developed a distinctive typeface; a Spaniard in Amsterdam implemented the swipe-function; and a Canadian created more than 600 unique emoji. Alliances were negotiated with chip makers such as Qualcomm, handset makers such as South Korean LG, and carriers in South American, Asia, Eastern Europe and Africa. The new phone launched in 2013.

But the new Firefox OS phone had very limited apps: the philosophy of offering everything for free gave little incentive for app developers. The messaging service WhatsApp only launched on Firefox OS in 2015. Many standard sites like Yelp and LinkedIn performed badly. Google then took Firefox by surprise by slashing prices charged to handset makers for Android. By 2015, the Firefox OS had less than one per cent world market share. In 2016, Mozilla announced it was abandoning the Firefox OS to concentrate its resources on 'the Internet of Things'.

Sources: www.mozilla.org; www.technologyreview.com/s/537661/firefox-maker-battles-to-save-the-internet-and-itself/.

Questions

1 Compare the power and attention of Mozilla's various stakeholders with regard to: (i) the former CEO Brendan Eich's position on gay marriage; (ii) the development of the Firefox OS (see Section 5.2.2).

2 What are the advantages and disadvantages of Mozilla's ownership model (see Section 5.2.3)?

5.3.1 The governance chain

Managers and stakeholders are linked together via the governance chain. The **governance chain shows the roles and relationships of different groups involved in the governance of an organisation**. In a small family business, the governance chain is simple: there are family shareholders, a board with some family members and there are managers, some of whom may be family too. Here there are just three layers in the chain. In large publicly-quoted corporations, however, influences on governance can be complex. Figure 5.5 shows a governance chain for a typical large, publicly-quoted corporation. Here the size of the organisation means there are extra layers of management internally, while being publicly-quoted introduces more investor layers too. Individual investors (the ultimate beneficiaries) often invest in public corporations through investment funds, i.e. institutional investors such as unit trusts or pension funds, which then invest in a range of companies on their behalf. Funds are typically controlled by trustees, with day-to-day investment activity undertaken by investment managers. So the ultimate beneficiaries may not even know in which companies they have a financial stake and have little power to influence the companies' boards directly.

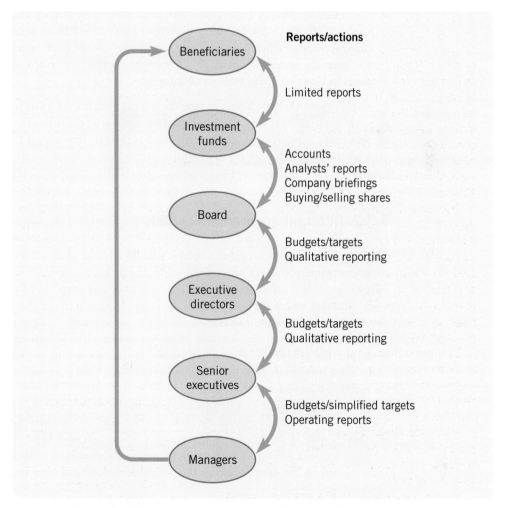

Figure 5.5 The chain of corporate governance: typical reporting structures
Source: Adapted from David Pitt-Watson, Hermes Fund Management.

Economists analyse the relationships in such governance chains in terms of the *principal–agent model*.[16] Here 'principals' employ 'agents' to act on their behalf, just as homeowners pay estate agents to sell their homes. Classically, the principal is simply the owner and the agent is the manager. However, the reality for large publicly-quoted corporations is usually more complex, with principals and agents at every level. In Figure 5.5, the beneficiaries are the ultimate principals and fund trustees and investment managers are their immediate agents in terms of achieving good returns on their investments. Further down the chain, company boards can be considered as principals too, with senior executives their agents in managing the company. Thus there are many layers of agents between ultimate principals and the managers at the bottom, with the reporting mechanisms between each layer liable to be imperfect.

The governance issues in principal–agent theory arise from three problems:

- *Knowledge imbalances.* Agents typically know more than principals about what can and should be done. After all, it is they who are actually doing the job and they have presumably been hired for their expertise.

- *Monitoring limits.* It is very difficult for principals to monitor closely the performance of their agents. This limit is made worse because principals usually have many investments, so their attention is likely to be split several ways.

- *Misaligned incentives.* Unless their incentives are closely aligned to principals' interests, agents are liable to pursue other objectives that reward them better. Principals might introduce bonus schemes in order to incentivise desired performance, but then agents may game the system: for example, they might use their superior knowledge to negotiate bonus targets that are in reality easy to meet.

Principal–agent theory therefore stresses the importance of knowledgeable principals, effective monitoring systems and well-designed incentives in order to make sure that large organisations actually pursue the purposes that their owners set for them. Illustration 5.2 asks what changes at scandal-hit Toshiba would help it avoid governance failures in the future.

5.3.2 Different governance models

The governing body of an organisation is usually a board of directors. Although the legal requirements vary in detail around the world, the primary responsibility of a board is typically to ensure that an organisation fulfils the wishes and purposes of those whom it represents. However, whom the board represents varies. In most parts of the world, private-sector boards primarily represent shareholders, but in some parts of the world they represent a broader or different stakeholder base. In the public sector, the governing body is accountable to the political arm of government – possibly through some intermediary such as a funding body. These differences have implications for organisational purpose and strategy as well as the role and composition of boards.

At the most general level, there are two governance models: the *shareholder* model, prioritising shareholder interests; and the *stakeholder* model, recognising the wider set of actors that have a stake in an organisation's success.[17] These two models are pure types, and there are many variants on each. The question for managers, therefore, is where their organisation is positioned on the range between the pure shareholder and pure stakeholder models of governance.

ILLUSTRATION 5.2 — A load of tosh? Toshiba's accounting scandal

A determination to meet profit targets results in the leading Japanese company misstating its accounts.

Toshiba is one of the largest corporations in Japan, with interests in information technology, power systems, electronic components, consumer electronics, medical and office equipment, lighting and logistics. In 2015, its shares were held roughly equally by foreign investors, individual Japanese investors and Japanese financial institutions. The largest investor, with just under five per cent of the shares, was the Master Trust Bank of Japan, which is a major asset management bank principally owned by the giant Mitsubishi Trust and Banking Corporation and Nippon Life Insurance.

Toshiba was apparently a model of corporate governance. It was one of the earliest adopters of Japanese corporate governance reforms. In 2001, it had introduced three external directors, with the formal authority to name top executives and an auditing committee to monitor company management. In 2013, Toshiba's corporate governance was ranked ninth out of 120 publicly-quoted Japanese companies in a list compiled by the Japanese Corporate Governance Network, a non-profit organisation promoting better governance. One of Japan's biggest law firms, Mori Hamada & Matsumoto, even published a case study of Toshiba as an exemplar of good corporate governance practices.

However, in early 2015, Seiya Shimaoka, an internal auditor in Toshiba, began to ask the head of Toshiba's auditing committee, Makoto Kubo, to examine the accounts of Toshiba's laptop business. Kubo refused to investigate further, warning that doing so would make the company miss its deadline for reporting earnings. It emerged soon after that the laptop business was significantly over-stating its profits. Indeed, in a company where the only significantly profitable business was the semiconductor division, overstatements were rife and longstanding. The total misreported was $1.2bn (£720m, €900m).

It transpired that the head of the audit committee had known about the exaggerated profits since 2008, when the company began to come under pressure after the global financial crisis of that period. The disruption to Toshiba's nuclear power business following the 2011 tsunami and the Fukushima nuclear accident had prompted further large-scale misstatements. Senior management was determined that the company's various businesses would still meet challenging performance targets. An independent panel investigating the accounting scandal explained: 'Within Toshiba, there was a corporate culture in which one could not go against the wishes of superiors. . . . Therefore, when top management presented "challenges", division presidents, line managers and employees below them continually carried out inappropriate accounting practices to meet targets in line with the wishes of their superiors.'

As it became clear that the misstatements had been widely known at the top for several years, September 2015 saw sweeping management dismissals. The company's CEO, Hsiao Tanaka, and Makoto Kubo, the audit head, both resigned. Two further senior board members resigned also, one a former CEO and the other a former company president. The company's share price, having fallen by 20 per cent on the news of the accounting misstatements, recovered some of its losses. As the accounting errors were corrected, Toshiba declared at the end of 2015 losses of $4.5bn and cuts to 6,800 jobs. Small Japanese investors declared that they would sue the guilty senior managers for recovery of their losses. Regulators fined the Japanese branch of accounting firm Ernst & Young, Toshiba's auditor, $17m for its failures.

Sources: BBC News, 21 July 2015 and 21 December 2015; *Financial Times,* 21 July 2015.

Questions

1 Which parts of the governance chain – principals and agents (see Section 5.3.1) – failed at Toshiba?

2 What problems (knowledge, monitoring or incentives) led to the scandal? What would you change to avoid these problems in the future?

A shareholder model of governance

The shareholder model is dominant in publicly-quoted companies, especially in the USA and the UK. Shareholders have priority in regard to the wealth generated by the company, as opposed to employees, for example. The shareholder interest in a company is assumed to be largely financial. Shareholders can vote for the board of directors according to the number of their shares and, in the pure model at least, there are many shareholders so that no single shareholder dominates. Shareholders can also exert control indirectly through the trading of shares. Dissatisfied shareholders may sell their shares, leading to a drop in the company's share price and an increased threat to directors of takeover by other firms.

There are arguments for and against the shareholder model. The argued advantages include:

- *Higher rates of return.* The unambiguous focus on shareholder interests means that investors typically get a higher rate of return than in the stakeholder model. Managers are not distracted by the interests of other stakeholders, and potentially have more money to invest in the future of the organisation.

- *Reduced risk.* Shareholders face less risk in the shareholder model, especially if operating within an economy with an efficient stock market. Shareholders can diversify their risk by using the stock market to buy shares in many different companies. They can also use the stock market to sell the shares of companies that look in danger.

- *Increased innovation and entrepreneurship.* Since the system facilitates higher risk-taking by investors, the shareholder model should promote entrepreneurship, innovation and higher growth. It is easier to attract capital investment where investors know that they can easily diversify their shareholdings and trade their shares.

- *Better decision-making.* Arguably the separation of ownership and management makes strategic decisions more objective in relation to the potentially different demands of various owners. If ownership is widely spread, no one shareholder is likely to exercise undue control of management decisions.

Potential disadvantages of the shareholder model include:

- *Diluted attention.* Where there are many shareholders, each with small stakes and often with many other investments, the principal–agent problem is exacerbated. Any single shareholder may not think it worthwhile monitoring performance closely, but rather assume that other shareholders are doing so. If shareholders all assume that others are monitoring performance, managers may feel free to sacrifice shareholder value to pursue their own agendas. For example, CEOs may further their own egos and empires with acquisition strategies that add no value to shareholders.

- *Vulnerable minority shareholders.* On the other hand, especially where corporate governance regulation is weak, the shareholder model can be abused to allow the emergence of dominant shareholders. Such dominant shareholders may exploit their voting power to the disadvantage of minority shareholders. This is the *principal–principal problem:* the dominant shareholder (principal) may appoint managers, make acquisitions, guarantee debts or sell assets contrary to the interests of the other shareholders (also principals).[18] Minority shareholders do not have enough votes to control abusive majority shareholders.

- *Short-termism.* The need to make profits for shareholders may encourage managers to focus on short-term gains at the expense of long-term projects, such as research and development. Some high-technology public companies such as Alphabet (owner of Google) and Facebook have deliberately adopted a dual-class shareholder structure, where the original founders and their associates have more votes for each of their shares in order to protect these companies' commitment to long-term innovation. Thus the Alphabet founders' B class shares each carry ten times the voting rights of ordinary A class shares, and C class shareholders have no votes at all.

The stakeholder model of governance

An alternative model of governance is the stakeholder model. This is founded on the principle that wealth is created by a variety of stakeholders, all of whom deserve a portion. It is not just shareholders who have a stake in the future of a business. Thus in the stakeholder governance model, management need to attend to multiple stakeholders. In some governance systems, some of these stakeholders, for example banks and employees, may be formally represented on boards (as at Volkswagen, see Illustration 5.3). Moreover, shareholders in the stakeholder model often take larger stakes in their companies than in the pure shareholder model, and hold these stakes longer term.

The argued advantages for the stakeholder model of governance include:

- *Long-term horizons*. It is argued that when shareholders hold large blocks of shares, they are likely to regard their investments as long term. It is harder to dispose of large shareholdings when business is going wrong, and the incentive to get involved in order to maintain the value of the stake is proportionately greater. Thus the predominance of large investors in the stakeholder model reduces the pressure for short-term results as against longer-term performance. It might therefore even increase shareholder returns over the long run.

- *Less reckless risk-taking*. Many stakeholders are more risk-averse than the diversified shareholders typical in the shareholder model. Employees as stakeholders depend entirely on their particular organisation for income and so may avoid risky projects because they fear losing their jobs. Major shareholders have more to lose, and find it harder to exit in the case of difficulty. Local government bodies may face the loss of major employers in their regions. The stakeholder model therefore discourages excessive risk-taking.

- *Better management*. Given stakeholders' concern for the long-term prosperity of the company, there may be a closer level of monitoring of management and greater demands for information from within the firm. Management are under greater pressure to perform. Further, because power may reside with a limited number of large shareholders, it is easier to intervene in the case of management failure.

There are also possible disadvantages to the stakeholder model of governance:

- *Weaker decision-making*. Intervention by powerful stakeholders with different interests could lead to confusion, slowing down of decision processes and the loss of management objectivity when critical decisions have to be made.

- *Uneconomic investments*. Due to lack of financial pressure from shareholders, long-term investments may also be made in projects where the returns may be below market expectations.

- *Reduced innovation and entrepreneurship*. Because investors fear conflicts with the interests of other stakeholders, and because selling shares may be harder, they are less likely to provide capital for risky new opportunities.

The stakeholder model recognises that organisations typically operate within a complex set of relationships, going beyond simple economic ones. As discussed in Chapter 2, organisations participate in *organisational fields* in which *legitimacy* matters, not just profits.[19] Legitimacy typically means more than sticking to the letter of the law; it involves following

ILLUSTRATION 5.3   Volkswagen's governance crisis

Spring 2015 saw a boardroom battle at one of the world's leading car companies; Autumn brought scandal.

The Volkswagen Group was founded in 1937 to manufacture the famous VW Beetle, designed by the engineering genius Ferdinand Porsche. The Porsche family's own car company held an ownership stake that eventually rose to 50.7 per cent by 2009. That year, Volkswagen cemented the relationship by agreeing to take over the Porsche company, creating a single group that became the second largest car company in the world. The German state of Lower Saxony, the location of Volkswagen's huge Wolfsberg factory complex, owns 20 per cent of Volkswagen as well. External investors only hold 12 per cent of the company's voting shares.

The Spring 2015 boardroom battle concerned a member of the Porsche family, Ferdinand Piëch. Piëch had served as Volkswagen CEO from 1993 to 2002, and had then become chairman of the company's supervisory board ('Aufsichtsrat'). Piëch was a cousin of Wolfgang Porsche, who also sat on the supervisory board. Piëch's wife, a former kindergarten teacher, was another member of the supervisory board, as in recent times were two of his nieces. Half the 20 members of the supervisory board are worker representatives; two are representatives of the Lower Saxony government; 17 were either German or Austrian; one represented a Swedish bank, and two more represented investments by the Qatari state.

Ferdinand Piëch had been in dispute over Volkswagen's strategy and performance with the company's CEO since 2007, Martin Winterkorn. On appointment, Winterkorn had announced his 'Strategie 2018', aiming to become the world's largest carmaker by the year 2018. Winterkorn had increased sales by more than 50 per cent, and Volkswagen Group cars had won World Car of the Year awards five times under his leadership. However, Piëch was allegedly disappointed about profit margins, falling sales in the USA and the failure to develop a budget car for China. The dispute was carried out behind closed doors, but finally Winterkorn triumphed and Piëch resigned at the end of April.

The triumphant Martin Winterkorn signalled he wanted to move on from the internal politicking: 'Much has been written about alleged problems and improvements that need to be made . . . [but] don't be fooled. We know what we have to do . . . and we started doing it some time ago. The supervisory board has been a crucial supporter in every step of this journey.'

However, in September 2015, the US Environmental Protection Agency (EPA) issued Volkswagen a notice of violation of the Clean Air Act. The company had been found to have fitted its diesel engines with a so-called 'defeat device' that allowed vehicles' nitrogen oxide (NOx) output to meet US standards during regulatory testing, while emitting up to 40 times more NOx in real-world driving. NOx is a major pollutant, associated with potentially fatal diseases such as emphysema and bronchitis. Volkswagen installed its defeat device in about 11 million cars worldwide between 2009 and 2015. According to some estimates, the cost of legal claims, fixes to cars and regulatory fines could exceed €30 bn (€24bn, $39bn).

A few days after the EPA notice, Martin Winterkorn resigned as CEO. He denied knowing about the defeat devices, but he was the executive ultimately responsible and he was blamed for an expansion strategy that encouraged risk-taking and a corporate culture that was too inward-looking. Volkswagen announced that Hans Dieter Pötsch would become the company's chairman (filling the slot left empty by Piëch in April): Pötsch had been Volkswagen's Chief Financial Officer since 2003. Matthias Müller, who had spent a life-long career in Volkswagen, was appointed CEO.

Sources: *Financial Times*, 26 April 2015, 5 May 2015 and 4 October 2015.

Questions

1 To what extent does Volkswagen reflect the strengths and weaknesses of the stakeholder model of governance (Section 5.3.2)?

2 What should Volkswagen have done with regard to governance and management after the resignation of Martin Winterkorn?

norms of appropriate conduct in the eyes of key members of an organisation's institutional field (e.g. governments, regulators, trade unions and customers, as well as shareholders). Legitimacy is an overarching concept of purpose, where profits, ethical conduct and fairness to stakeholders all play a role. Even if an organisation does not operate explicitly according to a stakeholder model, it is typically important that strategies be legitimate in this wider sense of satisfying all key stakeholders' expectations of appropriate conduct. Firms operating on a shareholder model also need to maintain legitimacy in their field if they are to avoid interference by regulators, consumer boycotts and demoralised employees.

5.3.3 How boards of directors influence strategy

A central governance issue is the role of boards of directors. Since boards have the ultimate responsibility for the success or failure of an organisation, they must be concerned with strategy.

Under the shareholder model there is typically a single-tier board structure, with a majority of 'non-executive' directors, outsiders who do not have day-to-day managerial responsibilities but provide oversight on behalf of shareholders. Outside non-executive directors are supposed to bring greater independence to the primary role of the board, protecting shareholders' interests. However, as explained above, this is not without its problems since the choice of non-executives is often influenced by the executive directors themselves.

The stakeholder model can involve a two-tier board structure. For example, in Germany for firms of more than 500 employees there is a supervisory board (*Aufsichtsrat*) and a management board (*Vorstand*) (see Volkswagen, Illustration 5.3). The supervisory board is a forum where the interests of various stakeholder groups, for instance employees and banks, are represented, as well as shareholders. Strategic planning and operational control are vested with the management board, but major decisions like mergers and acquisitions require approval of the supervisory board. Two-tier boards also exist in other European countries, notably the Netherlands and France.

Two issues are especially significant here:

- *Delegation.* Boards have to delegate a great deal to managers in order to get ordinary business done. Here there is a risk that an organisation's strategy becomes 'captured' by management at the expense of other stakeholders. The two-tier board system seeks to prevent this: the supervisory board has to approve major decisions, while also having the right to interrogate management regarding strategic plans. In the single-board structure typical of the shareholder model, it is more difficult for non-executives to separate themselves sufficiently from executive directors to interrogate them as a group.

- *Engagement.* Non-executive directors may wish to engage in the strategic management process, but face practical problems in terms of the time and knowledge level required to attend effectively to complex strategic issues. This problem can be especially pronounced in organisations such as charities or public bodies with governing boards: these boards are often made up of people passionately committed to the mission of the organisation, but without the time and understanding to get properly involved.

In the guidelines increasingly issued by governments[20] or advocated by commentators there are some common themes:

- Boards must be seen to *operate 'independently' of the management* of the company. So the role of non-executive directors is heightened.

- Boards must be *competent to scrutinise the activities of managers*. So the collective experience of the board, its training and the information available to it are crucially important.

● Directors must have the *time* to do their job properly. So limitations on the number of directorships that an individual can hold are also an important consideration.

However, it is the *behaviour of boards* and their members that are likely to be most significant whatever structural arrangements are put in place.[21] Important, therefore, are respect, trust, 'constructive friction' between board members, fluidity of roles, individual as well as collective responsibility, and the evaluation of individual director and collective board performance.

5.4 SOCIAL RESPONSIBILITY AND ETHICS[22]

Underlying the discussion of corporate governance is an issue highlighted in the introduction to this chapter. Are organisations just for the benefit of a primary stakeholder, such as the shareholders of a company, or do they have a responsibility to a wider group of stakeholders? This section considers, first, *corporate social responsibility:* the role businesses and other organisations might take in society. Second, it considers the *ethics* of the behaviour and actions of people in relation to the strategy of their organisations.

5.4.1 Corporate social responsibility

The sheer size and global reach of many companies means that they are bound to have significant influence on society. In 2015, Facebook had 1.44 billion users worldwide. Further, the widely publicised corporate scandals and failures of the last two decades have fuelled a concern about the role they play. The regulatory environment and the corporate governance arrangements for an organisation determine its minimum obligations towards its stakeholders. However, such legal and regulatory frameworks set minimum obligations and stakeholders typically expect greater responsibility on the part of organisations. **Corporate social responsibility (CSR) is the commitment by organisations to behave ethically and contribute to economic development while improving the quality of life of the workforce and their families as well as the local community and society at large.**[23] CSR is therefore concerned with the ways in which an organisation exceeds its minimum legal obligations.

Different organisations take different stances on CSR. Table 5.3 outlines four basic types to illustrate these differences. They represent a progressively more inclusive 'list' of stakeholder interests and a greater breadth of criteria against which strategies and performance will be judged. The discussion that follows also explains what such stances typically involve in terms of the ways companies act.[24] Illustration 5.4 discusses how leading clothing retailer H&M pursues social responsibility in order to give it a more ethical profile than some of its rivals and pre-empt protests against the clothing industry's traditionally wasteful and exploitative practices.

The *laissez-faire* view (literally 'let do' in French) represents an extreme stance. In this view, organisations should be let alone to get on with things on their own account. Proponents argue that the only responsibility of business is to make a profit and provide for the interests of shareholders.[25] It is for government to protect society through legislation and regulation; organisations need do no more than meet these minimum obligations. Expecting companies to exercise social duties beyond this only confuses decision-making, introduces

Table 5.3 Corporate social responsibility stances

	Laissez-faire	Enlightened self-interest	Forum for stakeholder interaction	Shaper of society
Rationale	Legal compliance: make a profit, pay taxes and provide jobs	Sound business sense	Sustainability or triple bottom line	Social and market change
Leadership	Peripheral	Supportive	Champion	Visionary
Management	Middle-management responsibility	Systems to ensure good practice	Board-level issue; organisation-wide monitoring	Individual responsibility throughout the organisation
Mode	Defensive to outside pressures	Reactive to outside pressures	Proactive	Defining
Stakeholder relationships	Unilateral	Interactive	Partnership	Multi-organisation alliances

additional costs and undermines the accountability of managers to their shareholders. In this view, society benefits anyway from the profits: after all, these can either be used for further investment in the business or be paid out to shareholders, who may be pensioners relying on the income or similar. This laissez-faire stance may be taken by executives who are persuaded of it ideologically or by smaller businesses that do not have the resources to do other than minimally comply with regulations.

Enlightened self-interest is guided by recognition of the potential long-term financial benefit to the shareholder of well-managed relationships with other stakeholders. Here the justification for social responsibility is that it makes good business sense. For most organisations a good reputation in the eyes of customers and suppliers is important to long-term financial success. Working constructively with suppliers or local communities can actually increase the 'value' available for all stakeholders to share: for example, helping improve the quality of marginal suppliers in the developing world is likely to create a stronger overall supply chain; supporting education in the local workforce will increase the availability of skilled labour. Indeed, there is mounting evidence that responsible strategies can also reward shareholders.[26] Thus, like any other form of investment or promotion expenditure, corporate philanthropy or welfare provision might be regarded as sensible expenditure.

Managers with this enlightened self-interest stance take the view that organisations have not only *responsibilities to* society, but also *relationships with* other stakeholders. So communication with stakeholder groups is likely to be more interactive than for laissez-faire-type organisations. They may well also set up systems and policies to ensure compliance with best practice (e.g. ISO 14000 certification, the protection of human rights in overseas operations, etc.) and begin to monitor their social responsibility performance. Top management may also play more of a part, at least insofar as they support the firm taking a more proactive social role.

A *forum for stakeholder interaction*[27] explicitly incorporates multiple stakeholder interests and expectations rather than just shareholders as influences on organisational purposes and strategies. Here the argument is that the performance of an organisation should be measured in a more pluralistic way than just through the financial bottom line. Such organisations adopt the principle of *sustainability* in strategy, one that ensures a better quality of

ILLUSTRATION 5.4   H&M's sustainability strategy

Swedish clothing retailer H&M claims to be pursuing a strategy that delivers profits, environmental gains and worker benefits.

H&M is the world's second-largest clothing retailer, just behind Inditex, owner of Zara. It has 2500 stores worldwide, operating in 44 countries. It sells about 550 million items of clothing per year. As such, it has traditionally been a leader in so-called 'fast-fashion', the retailing of cheap fashion items which are designed to be worn only a few times before disposal.

Fast-fashion is a voracious industry. There are now 30–50 trend-driven fashion seasons a year. Eighty billion garments are made annually worldwide, from virgin resources. There are 40 million garment workers in the world, predominantly making fast-fashion. A garment worker in Bangladesh, a major supplier, earns an average monthly wage of $40 (£24bn, €30bn). A pair of underpants costs about one pence (or roughly a Euro cent) to make in a Third World sweat shop. Fast-fashion is a target of international campaign groups such as the 'Clean Clothes Campaign'.

During 2012, the Clean Clothes Campaign organised mass 'faint-ins' in prominent stores such as Gap, Zara and H&M across Europe, drawing attention to how undernourished women workers frequently faint at work in Third World garment factories. A Clean Clothes spokesperson says: 'The human cost of brands like H&M or Zara paying poverty wages is seen when hundreds of workers pass out due to exhaustion and malnutrition. . . . For decades, global fashion brands have made excuses about why they shouldn't pay a living wage. It's not a choice, it's a pressing necessity. Hiding behind . . . company codes of conduct is no longer acceptable.'

In 2012, H&M launched its new 'Conscious' range of clothing, making use of a large proportion of recycled materials and more environmentally friendly virgin materials such as hemp. The company's website explained the motivation: 'Our vision is that all business operations shall be run in a way that is economically, socially and environmentally sustainable.' This was accompanied by a Sustainability Report with some impressive statistics: for example, 2.5 million shoes were made during 2011 using lower-impact water-based solvents and H&M was the biggest user of organic cotton in the world.

Guardian journalist Lucy Siegle asked H&M's Head of Sustainability, Helena Helmersson, whether she could offer guarantees for the sustainability of the company's products across its ranges. Helmersson responded:

'I don't think guarantee is the right word. A lot of people ask for guarantees: "Can you guarantee labour conditions? Can you guarantee zero chemicals?" Of course we cannot when we're such a huge company operating in very challenging conditions. What I can say is that we do the very best we can with a lot of resources and a clear direction of what we're supposed to do. We're working really hard. . . . Remember that H&M does not own any factories itself. We are to some extent dependent on the suppliers – it is impossible to be in full control.'

Between 2006 and 2012, H&M's share price increased by more than a third, well ahead of the local Stockholm market index. Sales too increased by a third and total operating profit after tax in this period was nearly SEK98bn (€11bn, £9.2bn, $13.75bn). H&M's return on capital employed for year-end 2011 was 47.1 per cent.

Main sources: Clean Clothes Campaign, 18 September 2013; *Guardian*, 7 April 2012; *Ecouterre*, 21 September 2012; www.hm.com; H&M *Conscious Actions and Sustainability Report*, 2011.

Questions

1 Where would you place H&M in terms of the four stances on social responsibility in Table 5.2?

2 What are the kinds of triple-bottom-line measures that would be appropriate for a sustainable strategy in clothing retail (see also Section 12.2.1)?

life by attending to all three dimensions of environmental protection, social responsibility and economic welfare. Social responsibility here can be measured in terms of *the triple bottom line* – social and environmental benefits as well as profits (see Section 12.2.1). Companies in this category might retain uneconomic units to preserve jobs, avoid manufacturing or selling 'anti-social' products and be prepared to bear reductions in profitability for the social good. Sustainability will typically have board-level champions in these kinds of organisations.

Shapers of society regard financial considerations as of secondary importance or a constraint. These are visionary organisations seeking to change society and social norms. Public-sector organisations and charities are typically committed to this kind of stance. There are also *social entrepreneurs* who found new organisations that earn revenues but pursue a specific social purpose (see Chapter 10 and Thinking Differently at the end of this chapter). For example, Traidcraft UK is a public limited company with a chain of retail shops that fights developing world poverty by promoting 'fair trade'. For shapers of society, the social role is the *raison d'être* of the business, not profits (see Illustration 8.1 on Baking Change). Financial viability is important only as providing the means for continuing the social mission.

Table 5.4 provides some questions against which an organisation's actions on CSR can be assessed.

5.4.2 The ethics of individuals and managers

Ethical issues have to be faced at the individual as well as corporate level and can pose difficult dilemmas for individuals and managers. For example, what is the responsibility of an individual who believes that the strategy of his or her organisation is unethical (e.g. its trading practices) or is not adequately representing the legitimate interests of one or more stakeholder groups? Should that person leave the company on the grounds of a mismatch of values; or is *whistle-blowing* appropriate, such as divulging information to outside bodies, for example regulatory bodies or the press?

Given that strategy development can be an intensely political process with implications for the personal careers of those concerned, managers can find difficulties establishing and maintaining a position of integrity. There is also potential conflict between what strategies are in managers' own best interests and what strategies are in the longer-term interests of their organisation and the shareholders. Some organisations set down explicit guidelines they expect their employees to follow. Texas Instruments posed these questions:[28]

Is the action legal? . . . If not, stop immediately.

Does it comply with our values? . . . If it does not, stop.

If you do it would you feel bad? . . . Ask your own conscience if you can live with it.

How would this look in the newspaper? . . . Ask if this goes public tomorrow would you do it today?

If you know it's wrong . . . don't do it.

If you are not sure . . . ask; and keep asking until you get an answer.

Table 5.4 Some questions of corporate social responsibility

Should organisations be responsible for . . .
INTERNAL ASPECTS

Employee welfare

. . . providing medical care, assistance with housing finance, extended sick leave, assistance for dependants, etc.?

Working conditions

. . . job security, enhancing working surroundings, social and sporting clubs, above-minimum safety standards, training and development, etc.?

Job design

. . . designing jobs to the increased satisfaction of workers rather than just for economic efficiency? This would include issues of work/life balance?

Intellectual property

. . . respecting the private knowledge of individuals and not claiming corporate ownership?

EXTERNAL ASPECTS

Environmental issues

. . . reducing pollution to below legal standards if competitors are not doing so?

. . . energy conservation?

Products

. . . dangers arising from the careless use of products by consumers?

Markets and marketing

. . . deciding not to sell in some markets?

. . . advertising standards?

Suppliers

. . . 'fair' terms of trade?

. . . blacklisting suppliers?

Employment

. . . positive discrimination in favour of minorities?

. . . maintaining jobs?

Community activity

. . . sponsoring local events and supporting local good works?

Human rights

. . . respecting human rights in relation to: child labour, workers' and union rights, oppressive political regimes? Both directly and in the choice of markets, suppliers and partners?

THINKING DIFFERENTLY | Benefit corporations

Start-ups are adopting new forms of company in order to reconcile profits with social benefits.

Increasingly, entrepreneurs no longer believe that the profit requirements of an ordinary company are compatible with social objectives. In the USA especially, it is the legal duty of directors to maximise profits for their investors. Ordinarily, investors will allow directors some discretion to pursue social objectives, especially if justified in terms of boosting customer or employee attractiveness. But in hard times, investors are liable to squeeze anything that does not clearly contribute to financial performance.

A new solution for not-for-profit organisations (Section 5.2.3) is to establish their companies as 'benefit corporations' (or community interest companies in the UK). Benefit corporations support non-profit objectives because they must commit themselves not only to commercial goals but to some public benefit, for example environmental sustainability. In hard times, profits and the public benefit have equal claims, hardwired into the legal status of the corporation.[29]

Thus the benefit corporation allows entrepreneurs to raise capital from investors – as a charity typically could not – while guaranteeing public benefit objectives. More than 30,000 new companies have registered as benefit corporations (or equivalent) in the USA. Leading benefit corporations include the trendy Warby Parker glasses company, which donates glasses to people in need, and Patagonia, the outdoors company that supports the environment.

The benefit corporation does have downsides. Corporations must report extensively on how they have delivered their public benefits. Investors may expect lower financial returns and fear they won't be able to realise their investments through the sale of the company to another company. With less investor support, benefit corporations may be able to do less than if they were free to pursue social objectives as and when they could.

> **Question**
>
> What would you argue as a director of a benefit corporation when the survival of your company depended on suspending expenditure on social objectives?

SUMMARY

- The purpose of an organisation will be influenced by the expectations of its *stakeholders*. Different stakeholders exercise different influence on organisational strategy, dependent on the extent of their power and attention. Managers can assess the influence of different stakeholder groups through *stakeholder analysis*.

- The influence of some key stakeholders will be represented formally within the *governance structure* of an organisation. This can be represented in terms of a *governance chain*, showing the links between ultimate beneficiaries and the managers of an organisation.

- There are two generic governance structure systems: the *shareholder model* and the *stakeholder model*, though there are variations of these internationally.

- Organisations adopt different stances on *corporate social responsibility* depending on how they perceive their role in society. Individual managers may also be faced with *ethical* dilemmas relating to the purpose of their organisation or the actions it takes.

WORK ASSIGNMENTS

✱ Denotes more advanced work assignments.
 * Refers to a case study in the Text and Cases edition.

5.1 For Drinking Partners (end of chapter case) or Adnams* or an organisation of your choice, map out a governance chain that identifies the key players through to the beneficiaries of the organisation's good (or poor) performance. To what extent do you think managers are:

    a   knowledgeable about the expectations of beneficiaries;

    b   actively pursuing their interests;

    c   keeping them informed?

5.2 What are your own views of the strengths and weaknesses of the stakeholder and shareholder models of governance?

5.3✱ Identify organisations that correspond to the overall stances on corporate social responsibility described in Table 5.3.

5.4 Identify the key corporate social responsibility issues which are of major concern in the brewing* or advertising (Chapter 3 end case) industries or an industry or public service of your choice (refer to Table 5.4). Compare the approach of two or more organisations in that industry, and explain how this relates to their competitive standing.

5.5✱ Using the stakeholder mapping power/attention matrix, identify and map out the stakeholders for Manchester United*, Aurizon (formerly QR National)* or an organisation of your choice in relation to:

    a   current strategies;

    b   different future strategies of your choice.

    What are the implications of your analysis for the strategy of the organisation?

Integrative assignment

5.6 Using specific examples, suggest how changes in corporate governance and in expectations about corporate social responsibility may require organisations to deal differently with environmental opportunities and threats (Chapters 2 and 3) or develop new capabilities (Chapter 4).

RECOMMENDED KEY READINGS

- A good review of important ideas in both corporate governance and corporate social responsibility is S. Benn and D. Bolton, *Key Concepts in Corporate Responsibility*, Sage, 2011.

- Specifically on corporate governance, a leading guide is B. Tricker, *Corporate Governance: Principles, Policies and Practices*, 2nd edn, Oxford University Press, 2012.

- For a comprehensive review of corporate social responsibility, see A. Crane, A. McWilliams, D. Matten and D. Siegel, *The Oxford Handbook of Corporate Social Responsibility*, Oxford University Press, 2009.

REFERENCES

1. R.E. Freeman, *Strategic Management: A Stakeholder Approach*, Cambridge University Press, 2010 (revised edition). Also see L. Bidhan, A. Parmar and R.E. Freeman, 'Stakeholder theory: the state of the art', *Academy of Management Annals*, vol. 4, no. 1 (2010), pp. 403–45. Our approach to stakeholder mapping has been adapted from A. Mendelow, *Proceedings of the 2nd International Conference on Information Systems*, Cambridge, MA, 1991. See also Graham Kenny, 'From the stakeholder viewpoint: designing measurable objectives', *Journal of Business Strategy*, vol. 33, no. 6 (2012), pp. 40–6.

2. D. Walker, L. Bourne and A. Shelley, 'Influence, stakeholder mapping and visualization', *Construction Management and Economics*, vol. 26, no. 6 (2008), pp. 645–58. In this edition, we have replaced 'interest' by 'attention' in line with recent theoretical literature: for example, D.A. Shepherd, J.S. McMullen and W. Ocasio, 'Is that an opportunity? An attention model of top managers' opportunity beliefs for strategic action,' *Strategic Management Journal* (2016), DOI: 10.1002/smj.2499

3. W. Ocasio, 'Attention to attention', *Organization Science*, vol. 22, no. 5 (2011), pp. 1286–96.

4. D. Buchanan and R. Badham, *Power, Politics and Organisational Change: Winning the Turf Game*, Sage, 1999, provide a useful analysis of the relationship between power and strategy.

5. W. Ocasio, 'Attention to attention', *Organization Science*, vol. 22, no. 5 (2011), pp. 1286–96. See also Chapter 16.

6. R. Whittington, B. Yakis-Douglas and K. Ahn, 'Cheap talk? Strategy presentations as a form of impression management, *Strategic Management Journal* (2016), DOI: 10.1002/smj.2482

7. See for instance M. Nordqvist and L. Melin, 'Entrepreneurial families and family firms', *Entrepreneurship and Regional Development*, vol. 22, no. 3–4 (2010), pp. 211–39.

8. In the UK and associated countries, this kind of corporation is called a public limited company (plc); in Francophone countries, it is the Société Anonyme (SA); in Germany, it is the Aktiengesellschaft (AG).

9. *The Economist*, 'The rise of state capitalism' (21 January 2012); and G. Bruton, M. Peng, D. Ahstrand, C. Stan and K. Xu, 'State-owned enterprises around the world as hybrid organisations', *Academy of Management Perspectives*, vol. 20, no. 1 (2015), pp. 92–114.

10. For a discussion, see R. Rumelt, 'Theory, strategy and entrepreneurship', *Handbook of Entrepreneurship Research*, vol. 2 (2005), pp. 11–32.

11. Credit Suisse, *Asian Family Businesses Report 2011: Key Trends, Economic Contribution and Performance*, Singapore, 2011.

12. I. Le Bretton-Miller, D. Miller and R.H. Lester, 'Stewardship or agency? A social embeddedness reconciliation of conduct and performance in public family businesses', *Organization Science*, vol. 22, no. 3 (2011), pp. 704–21.

13. The Ownership Commission, *Plurality, Stewardship and Engagement*, London, 2012.

14. A useful general reference on corporate governance is: R. Monks and N. Minow (eds), *Corporate Governance*, 4th edn, Blackwell, 2008. Also see Ruth Aguilera and Gregory Jackson, 'The cross-national diversity of corporate governance: dimensions and determinants', *Academy of Management Review*, vol. 28, no. 3 (2003), pp. 447–65.

15. This definition is adapted from S. Jacoby, 'Corporate governance and society', *Challenge*, vol. 48, no. 4 (2005), pp. 69–87.

16. A recent debate on principal–agent theory is D. Miller and C. Sardais, 'Angel agents: agency theory reconsidered', *Academy of Management Perspectives*, vol. 25, no. 2 (2011), pp. 6–13; and V. Mehrotra, 'Angel agents: what we can (and cannot) learn from Pierre Lefaucheux's stewardship of Régie Renault', *Academy of Management Perspectives*, vol. 25, no. 2 (2011), pp. 14–20.

17. S. Letza, X. Sun and J. Kirkbride, 'Shareholding versus stakeholding: a critical review of corporate governance', *Corporate Governance*, vol. 12, no. 3 (2005), pp. 242–62. Within this broad classification, there are other models: see, for example, A. Murphy and K. Topyan, 'Corporate governance: a critical survey of key concepts, issues, and recent reforms in the US', *Employee Responsibility and Rights Journal*, vol. 17, no. 2 (2005), pp. 75–89.

18. M.N. Young, M.W. Peng, D. Ahlstrom, G.D. Bruton and Y. Jiang, 'Corporate governance in emerging economies: a review of the principal–principal perspective', *Journal of Management Studies*, vol. 45, no. 1 (2008), pp. 1467–86.

19. R. Greenwood, M. Raynard, F. Kodeih, E. Micelotta and M. Lounsbury, 'Institutional complexity and organisational responses', *Academy of Management Annals*, vol. 5, no. 1 (2011), pp. 317–71.

20. In the USA: the Sarbanes–Oxley Act (2002). In the UK: D. Higgs, 'Review of the role and effectiveness of non-executive directors', UK Department of Trade and Industry, 2003.

21. J. Sonnenfeld, 'What makes great boards great', *Harvard Business Review*, vol. 80, no. 9 (2002), pp. 106–13.

22. B. Kelley, *Ethics at Work*, Gower, 1999, covers many of the issues in this section and includes the Institute of Management guidelines on ethical management. Also see M.T. Brown, *Corporate Integrity: Rethinking Organisational Ethics and Leadership*, Cambridge University Press, 2005.

23. This definition is based on that by the World Business Council for Sustainable Development.

24. P. Mirvis and B. Googins, 'Stages of corporate citizenship', *California Management Review*, vol. 48, no. 2 (2006), pp. 104–26.

25. Often quoted as a summary of Milton Friedman's argument is M. Friedman: 'The social responsibility of business is to increase its profits', *New York Times Magazine* (13 September 1970). See also A. McWilliams and D. Seigel, 'Corporate social responsibility: a theory of the firm perspective', *Academy of Management Review*, vol. 26 (2001), pp. 117–27.

26. See M. Porter and M. Kramer, 'Creating shared value', *Harvard Business Review*, vol. 89, no. 1/2 (2011), pp. 62–77; and D. Vogel, 'Is there a market for virtue? The business case for corporate social responsibility', *California Management Review*, vol. 47, no. 4 (2005), pp. 19–45. For a sceptical view, see A. Karnani, 'Doing well by doing good: the grand illusion', *California Management Review*, vol. 53, no. 2 (2011), pp. 69–86. For some evidence, see C.E. Hull and S. Rothenberg, 'Firm performance: the interactions of corporate social performance with innovation and industry differentiation', *Strategic Management Journal*, vol. 29 (2008), pp. 781–9.

27. H. Hummels, 'Organizing ethics: a stakeholder debate', *Journal of Business Ethics*, vol. 17, no. 13 (1998), pp. 1403–19.

28. We are grateful to Angela Sutherland of Glasgow Caledonian University for this example.

29. J.E. Hasler, 'Contracting for good: how benefit corporations empower investors and redefine shareholder value', *Virginia Law Review*, vol. 100, no. 6 (2014), pp. 1279–1322.

Drinking Partners – India's United Breweries Holdings Ltd

By 2015, one of India's most powerful and dynamic conglomerates, United Breweries Holdings Ltd (UBHL), was on the brink of disintegration. In the preceding three years, it had been forced to sell down its ownership stakes in India's largest brewery (United Breweries), India's largest spirits company (United Spirits) and a substantial chemicals and fertiliser company, MCF. UBHL's chairman and dominant shareholder, Vijay Mallya, was struggling to retain the last vestiges of control. His key brewing and spirits businesses now depended on partnerships with two Western multinationals, Heineken and Diageo. Relations with the first were amiable; with the second, they were bitterly acrimonious.

King of the Good Times

Vijay Mallya had inherited control of the UBHL conglomerate at the age of 28, upon the death of his father in 1983. He had divested non-core businesses and reorganised the tangle of remaining subsidiaries into a clear divisional structure based on coherent business areas. UBHL grew rapidly and by 2007 Vijay Mallya ranked 664 on the *Forbes* global list of billionaires, with an estimated fortune of $1.5bn (about £950m or €1.2bn).

As it entered the second decade of the twenty-first century, UBHL was selling about 60 per cent of India's spirits and 50 per cent of its beer. The group was organised into four main businesses: brewing, spirits, airlines and chemicals. External shareholders had substantial ownership stakes in each of these businesses, reducing the capital obligations on UBHL. However, Mallya guaranteed effective control of each business by ensuring that in each case UBHL was the largest shareholder, if not the majority owner. Mallya's overall control of the parent company UBHL was assured by dominance of the voting A class shares, while Indian and foreign institutional shareholders held the overwhelming majority of non-voting B class shares. Non-executive directors included Mallya's son, 'Sid' Mallya, pursuing a modelling career in the USA, the British businesswoman Dajlit Mahal, an associate of Mallya's for 22 years, and V K Rekhi, who had been associated with UBHL for nearly 40 years, and was a former president of United Spirits.

Though a shrewd businessman, Mallya was extravagant in his personal life. Playing on the name of his most prominent beer brand, Kingfisher, he often described himself as 'King of the Good Times'. He surrounded himself with beautiful models and actresses, and the annual Kingfisher Calendar became famous in India for its photographs of scantily-clad women. He owned several expensive yachts and a fleet of luxury vintage cars. In 2008, Mallya and a business partner bought a Formula One racing team,

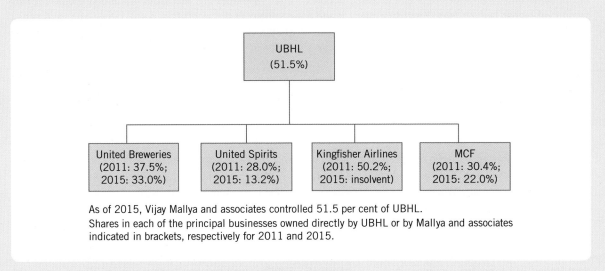

As of 2015, Vijay Mallya and associates controlled 51.5 per cent of UBHL.
Shares in each of the principal businesses owned directly by UBHL or by Mallya and associates indicated in brackets, respectively for 2011 and 2015.

Figure 1 United Breweries Holdings Ltd, principal businesses, 2011

renamed Force India. A similar patriotic theme underpinned his acquisition of the sword of the great Indian leader, Tipu Sultan, captured by the British in the eighteenth century, and his generous assistance with the repatriation of some of the few surviving artefacts owned by Mahatma Gandhi, India's campaigner for Independence. Mallya's personal popularity was reflected in his election to the Upper House of India's federal parliament. But it was Mallya's extravagance in the business realm that finally pushed UBHL to disaster.

Internationalisation and diversification

The first of two fatally extravagant moves had been Mallya's diversification into airlines. To celebrate his son's 18th birthday, Mallya launched Kingfisher Airlines in 2005, with 50.2 per cent of the ownership in his hands. It might have been a good opportunity: the Indian air market was growing fast with increasing economic growth. Mallya gave the new airline a glitzy launch. Promoting its superior food and pretty female staff, Mallya declared that the Kingfisher Airline would have neither business class nor economy class, but its own 'K class' – a rather pricey compromise. In 2008, Kingfisher paid over the odds to buy India's pioneering low-cost carrier, Deccan Airlines. The merged airline boasted 100-plus aircraft, 300 daily flights, over 7,000 employees and a domestic market share of about 30 per cent. With Deccan's track-record, Kingfisher was able to launch international services as well, with an order for the new Airbus A380 superjumbo jet. Mallya, sporting long hair and a beard, did not discourage comparisons with another flamboyant airline boss, Sir Richard Branson of Virgin.

Unfortunately, domestic deregulation brought a surge of new competitors in the Indian airline market. At the same time, fuel prices rose and crowded airports demanded higher landing fees. Kingfisher never made a profit in its whole existence. After failure to pay airports, fuel suppliers and employees, including pilots, over a period of several months, the Indian government suspended Kingfisher's licence to fly in 2012. Kingfisher's total debts and losses stood at about $4.5bn. UBHL had been forced to dilute its ownership to about 12 per cent, and the holding company still guaranteed $2.2bn of the airline's debt.

The second extravagant move by Mallya was into international markets, with the 2007 acquisition of the leading Scottish whisky company Whyte & Mackay for £595m. UBHL's United Spirits business needed access to genuine Scotch whisky brands as its increasingly sophisticated Indian customers sought higher-quality spirits than those traditionally made in India. Acquisition of Whyte & Mackay gave United Spirits control over more than 140 venerable

whisky brands, all genuine Scotch. United Spirits became the third-largest spirits producer in the world, behind Pernod Ricard and Diageo.

But Mallya had paid more for Whyte & Mackay than he could really afford: the United Spirits business was left with heavy debts. In the economic downturn of 2009, Whyte & Mackay was forced to cut about 15 per cent of its jobs. Subsequent years saw difficulties with the organisation of its American export business. At the same time, there was tension over United Spirits' record of trying to sell cheap Indian spirits into European markets. A 2013 partnership with Diageo, the world's largest spirits producer, was leading to regulatory concerns about market power. Needing a cash injection, in 2014 UBHL sold Whyte & MacKay to the Philippines drinks group, Alliance, for just £430m.

Foreign rescuers?

The sale of Whyte & MacKay was just one of a series of disposals. During 2014, Mallya sold key stakes in his chemical company MCF, leaving him with just 22 per cent ownership. The most important deals however were with Diageo, which by 2014 had acquired the majority of shares in United Spirits, and with longstanding partner Heineken, which by 2015 had acquired 43 per cent of United Breweries, leaving UBHL with just 33 per cent.

The Dutch beer company Heineken had first entered into partnership with United Breweries in 2009, acquiring a 37.7 per cent stake. Heineken saw a long-term growth market in India, with 700 million people under 30 years of age and a shift towards premium beers such as Heineken's. United Breweries could give Heineken excellent distribution channels and deep local knowledge, while the Dutch brought new brands and expertise in marketing and manufacturing. Heineken is the only global brewing company in the world that is still family-owned. A senior United Breweries manager commented in 2015 that the relationship between the Dutch and Indian companies was 'great': 'I think Heineken and UBL have enormous respect for each other. Heineken chief executive Jean-Francois van Boxmeer and Vijay Mallya have a great personal equation. The same holds true with the Heineken family.' In 2015, Mallya attended the 61st birthday celebrations of major shareholder, Charlene de Carvalho-Heineken, reputedly the tenth richest woman in the world.

Diageo, a public company based in London, had a more difficult relationship with UBHL. The company's original deal with UBHL in 2013 had been complex, designed to allow Mallya a considerable degree of control. Diageo bought 19.3 per cent of United Spirits' existing shares from Mallya's personal and related holdings, while United Spirits issued new equity, amounting to 10 per cent of the

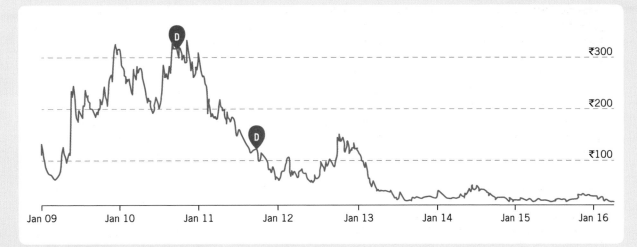

Figure 2 UBHL stock price performance, 2009–16 (rupees)

Source: www.moneycontrol.com, 21 April 2016 ('D' refers to dividend payments).

expanded capital base, to Diageo. Together, these steps gave Diageo an initial 27 per cent of the voting shares in United Spirits. However, Diageo also launched an open offer to external shareholders in United Spirits, in order to take its total holding up to 53.4 per cent. The total deal cost Diageo up to $1.9bn. The price valued United Spirits at 20 times annual earnings (before interest, tax, depreciation and amortisation), about a third more than usual for acquisitions in the international drinks business.

Mallya described the deal as a 'win–win'. Diageo would be able to use United Spirits' unparalleled Indian distribution channels for its high-profile brands, such as the Captain Morgan rum, Johnnie Walker whiskey and Smirnoff vodka. UBHL meanwhile would be able to ease its various debts. Mallya himself would be left in control of 13.5 per cent of United Spirits' expanded equity and was allowed to continue his position as United Spirits chairman. Mallya insisted to the media: 'I have not sold the family silver, or family jewels; I have only embellished them . . . If you have the impression that I have passed on control, and moved out, that is not the correct impression.'

However, Diageo's chief worry as a large multinational was its exposure to the somewhat idiosyncratic Vijay Mallya. In 2011, Diageo itself had been fined $15m by the American Securities and Exchange Commission for bribing government officials in India, Thailand and South Korea. The company had given a pledge to 'cease and

desist' from such corrupt practices, and risked much larger penalties for any repeat offences. Even as a minority partner, Diageo would be liable for any corruption at United Spirits. However, Mallya was set upon maintaining control. He told the Indian *Business Standard* newspaper: 'One must also understand that running an alcohol beverages business in India across 28 cities is not an easy task for a relatively new player (like Diageo). They will require me to run their business effectively and control of the business is one aspect of that.'

Principal sources: *Business Standard*, 27 September 2012; *India Business Journal*, 6 November 2012; *Financial Times*, 9 November 2012; *Times of India*, 11 November 2012 and 12 July 2015.

Questions

1 Consider the governance chain leading from the various shareholders of UBHL to the managers in the main businesses, with particular reference to United Spirits. Why might there be breakdowns in accountability and control in this chain?

2 Group the various key stakeholders discussed in this case (economic, social/political, community and technological). What risks do key stakeholder groups face (including Diageo)?

6

HISTORY AND CULTURE

Learning outcomes

After reading this chapter you should be able to:

- Analyse how *history* influences the strategic position of an organisation, especially via *path dependence*.

- Distinguish different kinds of cultures, *national-geographical*, *field-level* and *organisational*.

- Analyse the influence of an *organisation's culture* on its strategy using the *cultural web*.

- Identify organisations which may be experiencing the symptoms of *strategic drift*.

Key terms

cultural web p.175

legitimacy p.171

organisational culture p.171

organisational identity p.172

paradigm p.172

path dependency p.164

recipe p.170

strategic drift p.180

6.1 INTRODUCTION

The preceding chapters in this section of the book have considered various implications of position for strategy, including the influences of the environment, organisational capabilities and stakeholder expectations. This chapter considers two last important and interconnected aspects of position: organisational history and culture.

Many organisations have long histories. The large Japanese Mitsui Group was founded in the seventeenth century; automobile company Daimler was founded in the nineteenth century; the University of Bologna was founded in the eleventh century. But even newer organisations are marked by their histories: for instance, the airline and consumer group Virgin is still influenced by its hippy origins from the early 1970s (see Chapter 8 end case). Such histories become embedded in organisational cultures, shaping strategic options and decisions. Virgin's culture is very different to that of its rival airline British Airways, which had its origins as a state-owned airline in the 1940s. Sometimes an organisation's cultural heritage can give it a unique advantage, but sometimes it can be a significant barrier to change. Either way, if an organisation's strategy is to be understood, so must the history and culture that influenced it. This is the focus of this chapter, as summarised in Figure 6.1.

The chapter starts in Section 2.2 with history, examining its influence on organisational strategy and considering how that history can be analysed. History shapes culture, so Section 6.3 moves on to examine cultural aspects of organisations, in particular how cultural influences at geographical, institutional and organisational levels impact current and future strategy. This section also explores how a culture can be analysed and its influence on strategy understood. Section 6.4 explains the phenomenon of *strategic drift,* a frequent consequence of historical and cultural influences and hard for managers to correct. Finally, Thinking Differently introduces the conflicts and diversity introduced *institutional logics.*

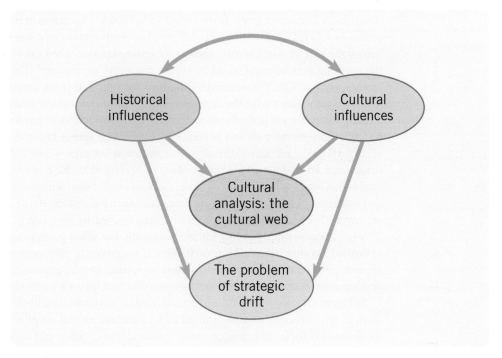

Figure 6.1 The influence of history and culture

The theme of this chapter, then, is the significance of history and culture for strategy. A sense of history is important for environmental analysis, particularly understanding positions on economic cycles (Chapter 2) or industry life cycles (Chapter 3). History and culture are relevant to the capabilities of an organisation (Chapter 4), especially those that have built up over time in ways unique to that organisation. The power and influence of different stakeholders (Chapter 5) are also likely to have historical origins. An understanding of an organisation's history and culture also helps explain how strategies develop (Chapter 12) and informs the challenges of strategic change (Chapter 15).

6.2 WHY IS HISTORY IMPORTANT?

This section starts by introducing the concept of path dependency as one way of examining how history can shape organisations over time. It then brings out positive aspects of history, in terms of it being a managerial resource. The section concludes by describing several ways of analysing an organisation's history.

6.2.1 Path dependency

A useful way of thinking of the influence of history is the concept of **path dependency, where early events and decisions establish 'policy paths' that have lasting effects on subsequent events and decisions.**[1] This suggests that organisational strategies may be historically conditioned. Path dependency has been described as like the ruts made in a dirt track by the passing of vehicle wheels over time. These ruts become deeper and deeper as more and more vehicles go along. Once that happens, vehicles have no option but to continue along those ruts. Future direction is dependent on the paths laid down in the past.

Examples of path dependency often relate to technology. There are many instances where the technology we employ is better explained by path dependency than by deliberate optimisation. A famous example is the layout of keyboard characters in most English-speaking countries: QWERTY. This originated in the nineteenth century as a way of reducing the problem of the keys on mechanical typewriters getting tangled when sales people demonstrated the machine at maximum speed by typing the word 'typewriter'. There are more optimal layouts, but QWERTY has remained with us for over 150 years despite radical changes in keyboard technology with the development of computers, tablets and mobile phones.[2]

Path dependency is not only about technology. It also relates to any form of behaviour that has its origins in the past and becomes so entrenched that it becomes locked-in. 'Lock-in' occurs where the infrastructure of an organisation (or even whole industry) is so strongly entrenched around a technology, product or service that the costs of switching from the established offering become prohibitive. Lock-in could begin with a decision which, of itself, may not appear especially significant, but which then has unforeseen and hard to reverse consequences. For example, airlines easily become 'locked-in' on particular aircraft types (e.g. Boeing), because once systems for crew-training and spare parts availability have become optimised for that particular aircraft type, it is extremely disruptive to start switching to another aircraft type (e.g. Airbus). Thus an initial, maybe chance, decision leads to the development of self-reinforcing mechanisms that lock-in on a particular path.

As Figure 6.2 shows, lock-in can be reinforced by a system of technologies, material objects (such as infrastructure or standardised forms), customers and suppliers in the value system, the day-to-day habits of managers, employees and users, formal and informal industry or professional standards, and the training systems that reproduce appropriate patterns of behaviour.[3] An example is the accounting business, where particular approaches are reinforced by

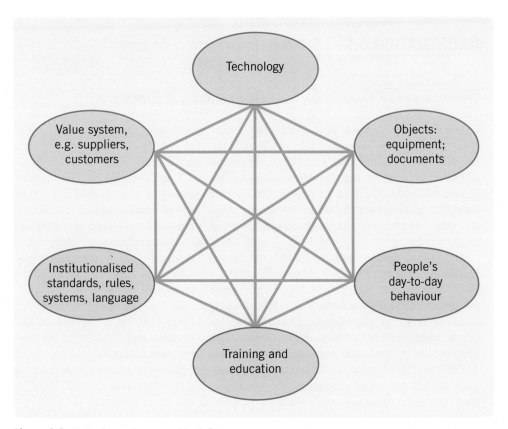

Figure 6.2 Path dependency and lock-in

technologies such as specialised software, by fixed-format forms such as capital expenditure proposals, by the ingrained expectations of customers, by the habits of accountants, by professional standards and by the training of successive generations of accounting practitioners. All these have developed over time and mutually reinforce each other. They also persist despite increasing numbers of experts, both in the accountancy profession and elsewhere, who point to fundamental weaknesses in such systems, not least the failure of accounting to provide measures for many of the factors that account for the market value of firms.[4]

Path dependency tends to reinforce the importance of three aspects of strategy:

- *Comprehensive change.* Because of the system of reinforcing elements, trying to change just one aspect without changing the others is likely to fall short. For an airline to switch from Boeing planes to Airbus planes without changing training and spare parts systems would be highly inefficient and dangerous.

- *Conservatism.* Because the reinforcing elements may make an otherwise maladapted approach work fairly well, it is often not worth the costs of changing everything to gain a small improvement in the performance of one particular element. In India, Japan and the UK roads retain left-hand drive, even though there might be cost advantages for automobile importers and exporters of standardising on the world's dominant right-hand drive approach.

- *Path creation.* Because initial decisions (such as starting with Boeing) can have longstanding repercussions, it is important for managers to recognise that what they choose to do at the start of an initiative or enterprise may lock them into a long-term path. Apple's original investment in graphics capabilities for its computers in the 1980s, and Microsoft's prioritisation of business users in the same period, still resonate in relative market positions three decades or so later.

ILLUSTRATION 6.1   Indian Railways and Empire

The history of an organisation can define culture and strategy.

India's first train journey in April 1853 took 75 minutes to travel 39km on a stretch of rail near Mumbai. More than a century and a half later, the journey still takes 57 minutes. But the Indian railway system has grown enormously since its origins. The network is 64,000km long, with 21,000 trains carrying about 23 million passengers and three million tonnes of freight per day.

The railway system originated under the British Empire (the Raj) and its dependent princely states. It gained impetus with the Indian Mutiny of 1857, when the British learnt the importance of rail for ferrying troops around their vast domain. The railway's restaurant wagons still reflect these origins in the British Empire, with 'Anglo-Indian' food such as omelettes, 'cutlets' and baked beans on the menu. Station baggage carriers are known as 'coolies', the derogatory name for the indentured labourers who served the Raj. Just as colonial officers would travel and stay in railway hotels for free, so too do contemporary politicians and their associates today.

Soon after independence, the various regional railway companies were brought together to form the state-owned Indian Railways in 1951. Socialist-style politics left an enduring mark on the new Indian Railways. Price rises for passengers were extremely rare, with freight used to subsidise transport for 'the common man'. Continuing policies that had been started to support privileged British staff under the Raj, Indian Railways developed a vast social system of employee housing, sports stadia, nursing homes and hospitals, with 2500 doctors by the second decade of this century. Many jobs were passed on almost by family inheritance. All was presided over by a Delhi headquarters (Bhavan) with 140 senior managers. There were 13 levels of hierarchy in every department. Bhavan jobs were sold illegally and many senior managers had never worked outside the Delhi headquarters building. It was said that it took approval from ten departments to change the soap in the first-class carriages.

Although there were pockets of excellence and innovation – for example, the Delhi metro – Indian Railways as a whole stagnated. Its share of passenger traffic declined from 74 per cent in 1951 to 12 per cent in 2011. Indian Railways' productivity trailed international peers: traffic units/employee was 0.84 for India, 1.4 for China and 15.1 for the USA. Bribes were necessary for seat reservations. There were 27,000 railway related deaths in 2014, many involving unguarded crossings and people falling off over-laden trains.

The problems of Indian Railways were well-recognised. A government report of 2015 noted with some irony that there had been 21 government inquiries into the railways since 1951: 'On the positive side, this large number illustrates the importance attached to the railways. On the negative side, repeated reports highlight the non-implementation of recommendations'.

Nonetheless, the government was determined to reform the railways. In 2014, the Chairman of the Railway Board declared: 'The need of the hour is to bring in a total change in the work culture and delivery of railway services by going in for large scale integrated computerisation of major functions of Indian Railways'. A new accounting system was introduced, which began for the first time to record outcomes as well as expenditures. Coolies would be given uniforms, trained in soft skills and renamed as 'sahayaks' ('helpers' in Hindi). Dozens of senior managers were moved out of the Delhi Bhavan. Deloitte Consulting was brought in to do comprehensive work studies. Private investors were allowed to operate services on Indian Railways track. After 16 years of price-freezes and years of financial losses, small price increases were approved.

Sources: Guardian, 30 December 2011; *Economic Times*, 8 July 2014; S. Debroy, 'Interim Report of the Committee for Mobilization of Resources for Major Railway Projects and Restructuring of Railway Ministry and Railway Board', Indian Government publication, 2015.

Questions

1 How would you sum up (i) the strategy (ii) the culture of Indian Railways in the early years of this century?

2 In what ways can you trace this strategy and culture to the Indian Railways' history?

Path dependency is a useful concept because it provides an explanation for why apparently inefficient historical patterns are allowed to continue: in the short term at least, it can be more costly to change than keep things the same. Sometimes though history continues to influence because of managerial inertia or self-interest. These too contribute to the phenomenon of 'strategic drift', as described in Section 6.4. Either way, the hand of history can be heavy. Illustration 6.1 illustrates the lingering influence on Indian Railways of events and strategies from the British Empire, nearly three quarters of a century after independence.

6.2.2 History as a resource

Although historical lock-in does create inflexibility, history can be a useful managerial resource as well. There are at least three ways that managers can use history:[5]

- *Learning from the past.* Understanding the current strategic position of an organisation in terms of the past can provide useful lessons. For example, have there been historical trends or cycles that may repeat themselves? The construction industry for instance has a regular pattern of boom and crisis. Managers in this industry should not expect that good times will continue forever. How have competitors responded to strategic moves in the past? Consumer good companies Unilever and Procter & Gamble have nearly a century's history of move and counter-move from which to learn. These companies' managers can examine past experience in order to predict their rival's likely response to any competitive move.

- *Building capabilities.* In the BMW museum in Munich there is a quote: 'Anyone who wants to design for the future has to leaf through the past.'[6] While the museum is about the history of BMW, it is also about how the lessons of the past can give rise to new ideas and innovation. Indeed the Innovation and Technology Division of BMW is sited next to the museum and the archives of BMW. Innovation may build on historic capabilities in at least two ways. First, as technologies change, firms with experience and skills built over time that are most appropriate to those changes tend to innovate more than those that do not.[7] Or it could be that there are new combinations of knowledge as capabilities built up in adjacent technologies are adapted in innovative ways to new technological opportunities. For example, successful firms in the creation of the TV industry were previously radio manufacturers. They were more effective innovators than the non-radio producers because of their historic capabilities in assembling small components and in mass distribution.[8]

- *Legitimising strategy and change.* History can be used as a resource to legitimise strategies or strategic change. For example, at technology enterprise Hewlett Packard, CEO Carly Fiorina legitimised her strategy by summarising it in terms of 'rules for the garage', referring to the company's famous origins in Dave Packard's garage.[9] Past successes effecting strategic change may also be used as evidence of the organisational potential in managing change and innovation or to encourage commitment to future changes. Thus Microsoft appealed to its earlier success in overcoming the challenge of the internet as it faced the threat of mobile computing.

6.2.3 Historical analysis

If history matters so much, how might managers undertake an historical strategic analysis of their own organisation or of their competitors? There are four ways this may be done:[10]

- *Chronological analysis.* This involves setting down a chronology of key events showing changes in the organisation's environment – especially its markets – how the organisation's strategy itself has changed and with what consequences – not least financial. Organisations will often provide a basic chronology on their websites, but crises and strategic reversals are likely to be underplayed on these, so further analysis using media and other sources will normally be useful.

- *Cyclical influences.* Is there evidence of cyclical influences? These include economic cycles, but perhaps also cycles of strategic activity, such as periods of high levels of mergers and acquisitions. Understanding when these cycles might occur and how industry and market forces can change during such cycles can inform decisions on whether to build strategy in line with those cycles or in a counter-cyclical fashion.

- *Key events and decisions.* History may be regarded as continuous, but historical events can also be significant for an organisation at particular points in time. These could be particularly significant events, in terms of either industry change or an organisation's strategic decisions: for example, Apple remembers the return of founder Steve Jobs in 1997, 12 years after he had previously been sacked. Or they might be policies laid down by a founder or defining periods of time that have come to be seen as especially important: for example, Alex Ferguson's successful years at Manchester United. Key events or decisions could, of course, be for the good: they may help provide a clear overall strategic direction that contributes to the sort of vision discussed in the previous chapter. They can, on the other hand, be a major barrier to challenging existing strategies or changing strategic direction. A famous example is Henry Ford's maxim 'You can have any colour provided it's black', which set a trajectory for mass production and low variety that inhibited the Ford company's response to the more varied cars eventually produced by General Motors and Chrysler in the 1930s.

- *Historical story-telling.* How do people tell their organisation's history? As above, many organisations will have parts of their websites dedicated to their histories, and some even commission business historians to write books on their histories.[11] The stories people tell can offer revealing clues about how the organisation sees its past, not least in terms of the origins of success. IKEA often tells the story of how flat-packed furniture began at the company when a worker of the company disassembled a table to fit inside of a car. And there may be implications in their stories for future strategy development. For IKEA, the story of flat-pack promotes practical improvisation in strategy. Does what people say suggest an organisation with historic capabilities relevant to current markets and customers? Is the organisation capable of innovation and change or so rooted in the glories of the past that it will be difficult to change?

History, then, is important in terms of how it influences current strategy, for better or for worse. History also feeds into organisational culture: history becomes 'encapsulated in culture'.[12] The next section goes on to explain what culture is and how it can be analysed.

6.3 WHAT IS CULTURE AND WHY IS IT IMPORTANT?

There are many ways to define culture, but typically definitions emphasise a set of taken-for-granted beliefs and values that are shared within a particular group. What individual managers believe in and value obviously influences their strategic decisions. Strategy is influenced by culture, therefore. However, because we all belong to many groups, these cultural influences can be very diverse. As in Figure 6.3, we shall analyse three kinds of cultural influences: geographical cultures, field cultures and organisational cultures and subcultures, all of which impinge on individual managers.

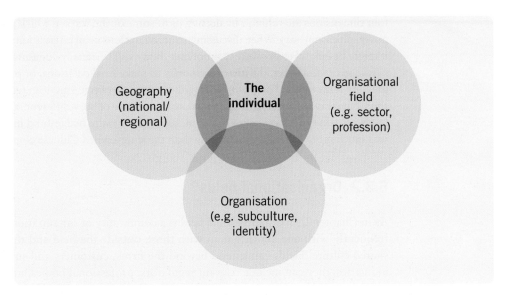

Figure 6.3 Cultural frames of reference

6.3.1 Geographically-based cultures

Many writers – perhaps the most well-known of whom is Geert Hofstede – have shown how attitudes to work, authority, equality and other important factors vary in different geographies, national or regional. Such differences have been shaped by powerful forces concerned with history, religion and even climate over many centuries. Hofstede traces cultural differences between the countries of southern and northern Europe to the boundaries of the Roman Empire 2000 years ago.[13]

According to Hofstede, there are at least four key dimensions upon which national cultures tend to differ:

- *Power distance,* referring to relationships with authority and acceptance of inequality. In Hofstede's studies, and those of his associates, many Asian countries are found to have high power distance, and therefore quite authoritarian management styles. Australia has a low power distance and therefore is more democratic in style.

- *Individualism–collectivism,* referring to the relationship between the individual and the group. According to Hofstede's research, some national cultures are highly individualistic, for example the USA. South American cultures are apparently more collectivist, valuing team approaches.

- *Long-term orientation,* referring to the extent to which people look to the future, something essential to strategy. Hofstede suggests that many Asian cultures tend to be long-term orientated. North American and African cultures are supposedly more short term.

- *Uncertainty avoidance,* referring to tolerance of uncertainty and ambiguity. According to Hofstede, Japan is associated with relatively high intolerance for uncertainty. Chinese culture appears more pragmatic and accepting of uncertainty.

Hofstede's research pioneered understanding about geographical variations in culture, but it has since been criticised for its generalisations about whole countries. After all, countries vary widely within themselves: consider the cultural differences between different regions in Nigeria, Southern and Northern Italy or the East and West Coasts of the USA.[14] Individuals too differ very widely within a particular geographical culture. It is important not to stereotype. Nevertheless, certain national or subnational cultural tendencies can be observed and Hofstede's four dimensions are valuable in alerting us to some of the ways in which people from different geographies may vary. When discussing strategic options in an international management team, it might be helpful to be aware that not everybody will be equally comfortable with *uncertainty,* heroic *individualisism,* the use of *authority* to make final decisions, or projecting far out into the *long-term* future. For example, the joint venture between American tyre-maker Cooper and the Chinese tyre-maker Chengshan fell apart because of very different attitudes to acceptable levels of risk: the American partner, backed by billionaire hedge-fund investor John Paulson, was much more aggressive financially than the state-owned Chinese company.

6.3.2 Organisational fields[15]

As in Chapter 2, an organisational field is a community of organisations that interact more frequently with one another than with those outside the field and that have developed a shared culture. Fields can extend beyond the firms, customers and suppliers in particular industries; they can include relevant regulators, professional bodies, university researchers, specialist media and even campaign groups. An important characteristic of fields is that they involve not just economic transactions, but shared assumptions and beliefs about how the field works.

For example, in the organisational field of 'justice' there are many different types of organisation, such as law firms, police forces, courts, prisons and probation services. The roles of each are different, they all have their own specific organisational cultures and their detailed prescriptions as to how justice should be achieved differ. However, despite their differences, they are all committed to the principle that justice is a good thing which is worth striving for; they interact frequently on this issue; they have developed shared ways of understanding and debating issues that arise; and they operate a set of common routines helping them interact with each other. Similar cultural coherence is common in other organisational fields: for example, professional services such as accountancy and medicine or sectors such as software development or journalism.

Where such shared assumptions and beliefs are powerful, these organisational fields help set the institutional 'rules of the game' (Section 2.2.6) or 'institutional logics' (see final Thinking Differently). Fields influence the ways managers see their activities, define strategic options and decide what is appropriate. Three concepts are useful here:

- *Categorisation.* The ways in which members of an organisational field categorise (or label) themselves and their activities has significant implications for what they do.[16] To categorise a mobile phone as primarily a personal computer or a fashion-statement rather than a phone changes the whole strategy. Over time, members of an organisational field tend to converge on dominant categorisation schemes. For instance, the early car industry had competing categories of 'horseless carriage' and 'automobile'; in computing, there were competing categories of 'pen-computing' and 'tablets' to describe more or less the same thing. Converging on the categories of automobile and tablet helped define the respective industries' subsequent developments.

- *Recipes.* Because of their shared cultures, organisational fields tend to cohere around standard ways of doing things, or 'recipes'. A **recipe is a set of assumptions, norms and routines held in common within an organisational field about the appropriate purposes and strategies of field members.**[17] In effect, a recipe is the 'shared wisdom' about what works best. In English Premier league football, the standard approach is a 'talent-based recipe', where teams compete each year to hire the best players because they believe that individual talent is what delivers results. An alternative recipe, for instance of developing team spirit and skills over the long term as in Germany, is little contemplated in the English Premier league.

- *Legitimacy.* Where categories and recipes have become str⸺ they become the only legitimate way of seeing and behaving. **meeting the expectations within an organisational field in ter⸺ iours and strategies.** By conforming to legitimate norms within secure approval, support and public endorsement, thus increasing t⸺ ping outside that strategy may be risky because important stakeholders ⸺ or bankers) may not see such a move as appropriate. Therefore, organi⸺ *mimic* each other's strategies. There may be differences in strategies betwee⸺ ⸺isa-tions, but those differences tend to be limited to the bounds of legitimacy.[18] L⸺ ⸺imacy helps explain why accounting firms and universities, for example, tend to follow similar strategies to each other, promote similar products and hire similar people.

6.3.3 Organisational culture

Edgar Schein defines organisational culture as the 'basic assumptions and beliefs that are shared by members of an organisation, that operate unconsciously and define in a basic taken-for-granted fashion an organisation's view of itself and its environment'.[19] Related to this are the taken-for-granted 'ways we do things around here'[20] that accumulate over time. So **organisational culture is the taken-for-granted assumptions and behaviours of an organisation's members.** This culture helps make sense of people's organisational context and therefore contributes to how they respond to issues they face.

An organisation's culture can be conceived as consisting of different layers. The four proposed by Edgar Schein[21] are (see Figure 6.4):

- *Values* may be easy to identify in terms of those formally stated by an organisation since they are often explicit, perhaps written down (see Chapter 1). The values driving a strategy may, however, be different from those in formal statements. For example, in the early 2000s, many banks espoused values of shareholder value creation, careful risk

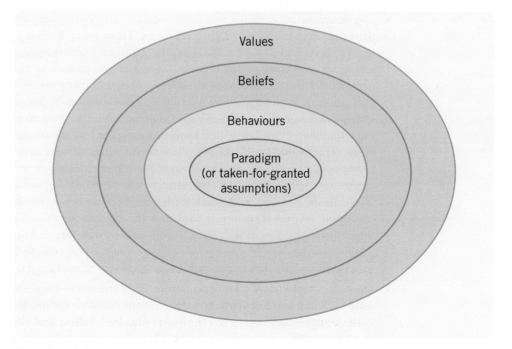

Figure 6.4 Culture in four layers

management and, of course, high levels of customer service. But in practice they indulged in highly risky lending, resulting in the need for huge government financial support in the financial crisis of 2008–09. It is therefore important to delve beneath espoused values to uncover underlying, perhaps taken-for-granted, values that can help explain the strategy actually being pursued by an organisation (see Section 6.3.6 below).

- *Beliefs* are more specific. They can typically be discerned in how people talk about issues the organisation faces; for example, a belief that the company should not trade with particular countries or a belief in the rightness of professional systems and standards.

- *Behaviours* are the day-to-day way in which an organisation operates and that be seen by people both inside and often outside the organisation. This includes the work routines, how the organisation is structured and controlled and 'softer' issues around symbolic behaviours (see Section 6.3.5 below). These behaviours may become the taken-for-granted 'ways we do things around here' that are potentially the bases for inimitable strategic capabilities (see Section 4.3.3) but also significant barriers to achieving strategic change if that becomes necessary (see Chapter 15).

- *Taken-for-granted assumptions* are the core of an organisation's culture which, in this book, we refer to as the organisational *paradigm*. The **paradigm is the set of assumptions held in common and taken for granted in an organisation.** In effect these shared assumptions represent *collective experience* about fundamental aspects of the organisation that, in turn, guide people in that organisation about how to view and respond to different circumstances that they face. The paradigm can underpin successful strategies by providing a basis of common understanding in an organisation but, again, can be a major problem when major strategic change is needed (see Chapter 15). The importance of the paradigm is discussed further in Section 6.3.5.

The concept of culture implies coherence, hence the common expression 'corporate culture'. Illustration 6.2 on the AB InBev brewery describes a company that works hard to create a coherent corporate culture. However, there are at least two ways in which cultures can be subdivided in practice:

- *Organisational subcultures.* Just as national cultures can contain local regional cultures, there are often subcultures in organisations. These subcultures may relate to the structure of the organisation: for example, the differences between geographical divisions in a multinational company, or between functional groups such as finance, marketing and operations. Differences between divisions may be particularly evident in organisations that have grown through acquisition. Also different divisions may be pursuing different types of strategy that require or foster different cultures. Indeed, aligning strategic positioning and organisational culture is a critical feature of successful organisations. Differences between business functions can also relate to the different nature of work in different functions. For example, in a major oil company differences are likely between those functions engaged in 'upstream' exploration, where time horizons may be in decades, and those concerned with 'downstream' retailing, with much shorter market-driven time horizons. Arguably, this is one reason why the oil company Shell took the decision to sell its retail outlets and other downstream activities. In strategic decision-making, therefore, it is important to recognise the different subcultural assumptions managers may be bringing to the processes: finance managers may have different subcultural assumptions to marketing managers, and so on.

- *Organisational identity.* An organisation's culture covers a wide range of aspects, for instance how it sees its environment, but an important part is how the organisation views itself. **Organisational identity refers to what members believe and understand about who they specifically are as an organisation.**[22] Managers and entrepreneurs often try to manipulate organisational identity because it is important for recruiting and guiding employees,

ILLUSTRATION 6.2   Dream. People. Culture.

'Brito', Chief Executive of the world's largest brewery, has culture as one of his three buzzwords.

AB InBev's clumsy name reflects the manner of its growth. It has its origins in the 1999 merger of two Brazilian brewers, Antarctica (founded in 1880) and Brahma (founded in 1886). The new 'AmBev' then merged with Belgian brewer InterBrew to become InBev in 2004, before taking over the American giant Anheuser-Busch in 2008. By 2015, AB InBev was the largest brewer in the world, with its headquarters in Belgium and a 25 per cent share of the global beer business. Its brands included Beck's, Budweiser, Corona and Stella Artois. AB InBev employed 155,000 people in 25 countries. The company had its eyes on taking over one of its last major rivals, the South African brewer SABMiller.

AB InBev's Chief Executive was the Brazilian Carlos Brito, known simply as 'Brito' (never Carlos, never Mr Brito). He had originally begged the former Brazilian tennis champion and investor Jorge Paolo Lemann to fund his MBA at Stanford University. On completion of his MBA, he had joined Brahma, a brewery that Lemann had just bought. By 2004, Brito was CEO of AmBev. With the InterBrew merger, he played second fiddle initially, but by 2005 – aged 45 – he emerged as CEO of the newly-created company InBev.

Brito's three buzzwords, repeated by executives throughout the company, are: 'Dream. People. Culture'. The culture he has sought to create at AB InBev is intense. He himself is away from home travelling on business more than half the year. He claims no hobbies, unless a daily 30 minutes on the treadmill counts. He and his top team fly economy class except on the longest haul flights and they all use mid-market hotels. The top team's desks are placed at the centre of open-plan offices.

Lemann (with a 12.5 per cent stake in the company) describes the culture of AB InBev thus: 'You are always running, always close to the limit. You're working very hard and being evaluated all the time. People either like it or don't like it.' Zero-based budgeting is practised, with all budgets negotiated from scratch at the beginning of each year. Costs and performance are monitored closely. On buying Anheuser-Busch, Brito fired 1400 staff, with the whole top tier of managers going: according to Brito, 'Some were too rich to care, some were too old to work, some wouldn't fit the culture anyway.' Throughout the company, employee metrics are all public and managers are subject to 360 degree feedback systems. The internal joke is that to get promoted, you have to kill three people.

But the rewards are high for good performers, and promotion fast. Young managers rarely spend more than two or three years in a single posting, moved on as soon as they start to get comfortable. In 2014, more than 100,000 people applied for 147 graduate level jobs. Brito personally addresses each class of graduate trainees, looking for talent. He always encourages his trainees to 'dream big'. Luiz Fernando Edmond, head of sales worldwide, was on the company's first management trainee programme in Brazil in 1990. He remarks: 'I came here with nothing. If you work hard, you focus on your results and you work with people, bring people together, promote people better than you, you have a chance to become a CEO of the company.'

Sources: *Fortune*, 15 August 2013; *Financial Times*, June 15 and 16, 2015.

Questions

1 Why do you think that creating a common culture might be important for a company like AB InBev?

2 What mechanisms are used to reinforce such a common culture (see also Chapter 14).

interacting with customers and dealing with regulators. Organisational identity *claims* are often prominent on websites and other official materials. Thus the Danish lager company Carlsberg went through a very deliberate process of changing its claimed identity from a brewer to a fast-moving consumer goods company, with important ramifications for the skills it required. Plausible identity claims are important for entrepreneurial start-ups also: there are significant benefits with customers and investors if they can define themselves as the next generation, rather than a 'me-too'.

6.3.4 Culture's influence on strategy

Mark Fields, President of Ford Motor Company in 2006, famously argued that 'culture eats strategy for breakfast', by which he emphasised the importance of culture for the strategy of the business. The importance of culture does not mean that strategy is irrelevant of course: culture should be seen as *part* of the strategy, something that can be a source of competitive advantage and, to some degree, something that can be adjusted.

The enduring influence of culture on strategy is shown in Figure 6.5.[23] Faced with a stimulus for action, such as declining performance, managers first try to improve the implementation of existing strategy (step 1). This might be through trying to lower cost, improve efficiency, tighten controls or improve accepted ways of doing things. If this is not effective, a change of strategy may occur, but a change in line with the existing culture (step 2). For example, managers may seek to extend the market for their business, but assume that it will be similar to their existing market, and therefore set about managing the new venture in much the same way as they have been used to. Alternatively, even where managers know intellectually that they need to change strategy, they find themselves constrained by path-dependent

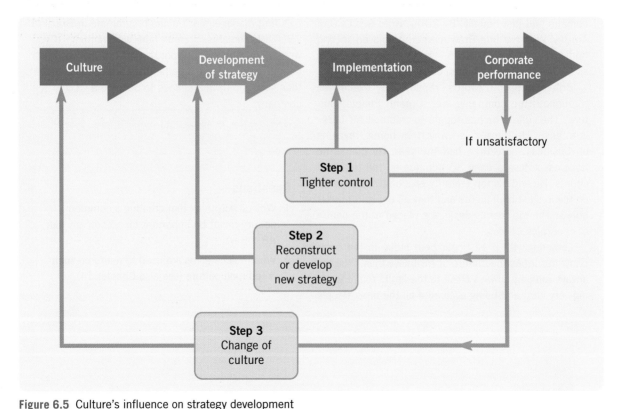

Figure 6.5 Culture's influence on strategy development

Source: Adapted from P. Grinyer and J.-C. Spender, *Turnaround: Managerial Recipes for Strategic Success,* Associated Business Press, 1979, p. 203.

organisational routines and assumptions or political processes, as seems likely in the case of Kodak (see Illustration 6.4 later). This often happens, for example, when there are attempts to change highly bureaucratic organisations to be customer-orientated. Even if people accept the need to change a culture's emphasis on the importance of conforming to established rules, routines and reporting relationships, they do not readily do so. It is a fallacy to assume that reasoned argument necessarily changes deeply embedded assumptions rooted in collective experience built up over long periods of time. Readers need only think of their own experience in trying to persuade others to rethink their religious beliefs, or, indeed, allegiances to sports teams, to realise this. Changes in strategy which entail a fundamental change to an organisation's culture (step 3) are likely to be rare and triggered by dramatic evidence of the redundancy of that culture such as a financial crisis or major loss of market share.

6.3.5 Analysing culture: the cultural web

In order to understand the existing culture and its effects it is important to be able to analyse an organisation's culture. The cultural web[24] is a means of doing this (see Figure 6.6). The **cultural web** shows the behavioural, physical and symbolic manifestations of a culture that inform and are informed by the taken-for-granted assumptions, or paradigm, of an organisation. It is in effect the inner two ovals in Figure 6.4. The cultural web can be used to understand culture in any of the frames of reference discussed above, but it is most often used at the organisational and/or subunit levels in Figure 6.3.[25] The seven elements of the cultural web are as follows:

- The *paradigm* is at the core of Figure 6.6. As previously defined, the paradigm is the set of assumptions held in common and taken for granted in an organisation. The paradigmatic assumptions are, quite likely, very basic. For example, a common problem in technology and engineering firms is the propensity of people to focus on the technical excellence of products rather than customer-perceived needs. Or the paradigm of practitioners in the National

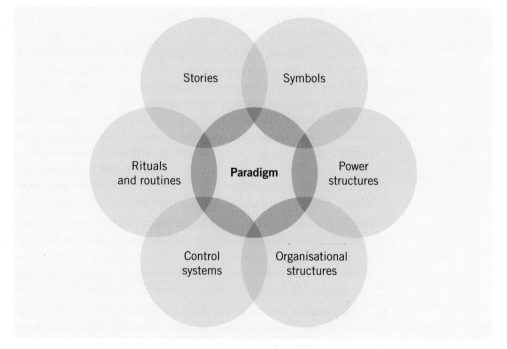

Figure 6.6 The cultural web of an organisation

Health Service in the UK is about curing illnesses. It is quite likely that, even if the rational view is to build a strategy around the engineering business' customer needs or the need for prevention (as distinct from curing) of illnesses, people in those organisations may still interpret issues and behave in line with its paradigm. So it is really important to understand the paradigm and how it informs debate on strategy. The problem is that, since it is unlikely to be talked about, or even be something that people are conscious of, trying to identify it can be difficult, especially if you are part of that organisation. Outside observers may find it easier to identify simply by listening to what people say and emphasise. One way of 'insiders' getting to see the assumptions they take for granted is to focus initially on other aspects of the cultural web because these are to do with more visible manifestations of culture. Moreover these other aspects are likely to act to reinforce the assumptions of the paradigm.

- *Rituals and routines* point to the repetitive nature of organisational cultures. *Routines* refer to 'the way we do things around here' on a day-to-day basis. At their best, routines lubricate the working of the organisation, and may provide a basis for distinctive organisational capabilities. However, they can also represent a taken-for-grantedness about how things should happen which, again, can guide how people deal with situations and be difficult to change. For example, managers trying to achieve greater customer focus in engineering firms often report that customer-facing sales engineers routinely tend to tell customers what they need rather than listening to their needs. The *rituals*[26] of organisational life are particular activities or special events that emphasise, highlight or reinforce what is important in the culture. Examples include training programmes, interview panels, promotion and assessment procedures, sales conferences and so on. An extreme example, of course, is the ritualistic training of army recruits to prepare them for the discipline required in conflict. However, rituals can also be informal activities such as drinks in the pub after work or gossiping around watercoolers. A checklist of organisational rituals is provided in Chapter 15 (see Table 15.2).

- The *stories* told by members of an organisation to each other, to outsiders, to new recruits, and so on may act to embed the present in its organisational history and also flag up important events and personalities. They typically have to do with successes, disasters, heroes, villains and mavericks (who deviate from the norm). They can be a way of letting people know what is conventionally important in an organisation.

- *Symbols* are objects, events, acts or people that convey, maintain or create meaning over and above their functional purpose. For example, offices and office layout, cars and job titles have a functional purpose, but are also typically signals about status and hierarchy. Particular people may come to represent especially important aspects of an organisation or historic turning points. The form of language used in an organisation can also be particularly revealing, especially with regard to customers or clients: defining executive education clients as 'course participants' rather than 'students' makes a significant difference to how teaching staff interact with them. Although symbols are shown separately in the cultural web, it should be remembered that many elements of the web are symbolic. So, routines, control and reward systems and structures are not only functional but also symbolic.

- *Power* was defined in Chapter 5 as the ability of individuals or groups to persuade, induce or coerce others into following certain courses of action. So *power structures* are distributions of power to groups of people in an organisation. The most powerful individuals or groups are likely to be closely associated with the paradigm and long-established ways of doing things. In analysing power, the guidance given in Chapter 5 (Section 5.2.2) is useful.

- *Organisational structures* are the roles, responsibilities and reporting relationships in organisations. These are likely to reflect power structures and how they manifest themselves. Formal hierarchical, mechanistic structures may emphasise that strategy is the province of top managers and everyone else is 'working to orders'. Structures with less emphasis on formal reporting relationships might indicate more participative strategy making. Highly decentralised structures (as discussed in Chapter 14) may signify that collaboration is less important than competition and so on.

- *Control systems* are the formal and informal ways of monitoring and supporting people within and around an organisation and tend to emphasise what is seen to be important in the organisation. They include measurements and reward systems. For example, public-service organisations have often been accused of being concerned more with stewardship of funds than with quality of service. This is reflected in their control systems, which are more about accounting for spending rather than with quality of service. Remuneration schemes are a significant control mechanism. Individually-based bonus schemes related to volume are likely to signal a culture of individuality, internal competition and an emphasis on sales volume rather than teamwork and an emphasis on quality.

Illustration 6.3 describes the culture of the American fund manager Vanguard Asset Management (see also Illustration 7.1). It can be seen that the central paradigm of low-cost investing has been supported by many mutually-reinforcing elements of the cultural web.

6.3.6 Undertaking cultural analysis

When analysing the culture of an organisation, there are important issues to bear in mind:

- *Questions to ask*. Figure 6.7 outlines some of the questions that might help build up an understanding of culture using the cultural web.

- *Statements of cultural values*. As explained in Chapter 1, organisations may make public statements of their values, beliefs and purposes, for example in annual reports, mission or values statements and business plans. There is a danger that these are seen as useful descriptions of the organisational culture. But this is likely to be at best only partially true, and at worst misleading. This is not to suggest that there is any organised deception. It is simply that the statements of values and beliefs are often carefully considered and carefully crafted statements of the aspirations of a particular stakeholder (such as the CEO) rather than descriptions of the actual culture. For example, an outside observer of a police force might conclude from its public statements of purpose and priorities that it had a balanced approach to the various aspects of police work – catching criminals, crime prevention, community relations. However, a deeper probing might reveal that (in cultural terms) there is the 'real' police work (catching criminals) and the 'lesser work' (crime prevention, community relations).

- *Pulling it together*. The detailed 'map' produced by the cultural web can be a rich source of information about an organisation's culture, but it is useful to be able to character-ise the culture that the information conveys. Sometimes this is possible by means of graphic descriptors. For example, managers who undertook a cultural analysis in the UK National Health Service (NHS) summed up their culture as 'The National Sickness Service'. Although this approach is rather crude and unscientific, it can be powerful in terms of organisational members seeing the organisation as it really is – which may not be immediately apparent from all of the detailed points in the cultural web. It can also help people to understand that culture may drive strategy; for example, a 'national sickness service' will prioritise strategies that are about developments in curing sick people above strategies of health promotion and prevention. So those favouring health promotion strategies need to understand that they are facing the need to change a culture.

If managers are to develop strategies that are different from those of the past, they need to be able to challenge, question and potentially change the organisational culture that under-pins the current strategy. In this context, the cultural analysis suggested in this chapter can

ILLUSTRATION 6.3 — The Bogleheads and Vanguard Asset Management

Vanguard's culture of low-cost investing is supported by many elements of the cultural web.

Jack Bogle, founder of Vanguard Asset Management in 1974, tells a story about a summer job as a messenger at a Wall Street broker when he was a student. One of the other messengers said to him: "Let me tell you all you need to know about the investment business". Bogle said, "What's that?" He said, "Nobody knows nuthin'." It was on this principle that investment professionals know nothing that Bogle built what became the largest mutual fund in the world.

Bogle developed a model of index funds in which, instead of trying to pick winners, stocks were chosen simply to match the various stock market indices (for example, the S&P 500). As an investor, he did not claim to know more than other investors. All he did was make sure that his portfolio exactly reflected whatever index he was aiming to follow. There were none of the costs of stock-picking, investment research or frequent trades. His funds would never beat the index, but, unlike the vast majority of funds at the time, his expenses were significantly lower. Moreover, Bogle chose an unusual financial structure for Vanguard: it was owned by its own funds and, as a result, ultimately by the customers investing in the funds. This meant that there were no profits to be paid out to outside investors. Moreover, Bogle refused to pay fees to investment advisers for selling Vanguard products: price and performance should be enough to attract customers.

The result of these policies was what Vanguard describes as 'a culture of low-cost investing'. A Vanguard index fund would charge investors fees of only 0.2 per cent of their investment, against fees approaching 2.0 per cent for an active stock-picker. Between 1983 and 1999, a Vanguard index fund tracking the S&P 500 would turn $10,000 (£6000, €7500) into $81,900, while an active stock-picking fund, allowing for the extra charges, would only make $62,700. Jack Bogle's philosophy eventually attracted 25 million retail American investors, many of them enthusiastically describing themselves as 'Bogleheads'. Each year, these Bogleheads meet at Vanguard's Pennsylvania headquarters to, in their phrase, 'visit their money'. Even in his 80s, Jack Bogle would attend the Boglehead conferences to give his investment advice.

Vanguard's headquarters has some unusual features. There was a prominent mural reproducing a famous picture of the 1798 Battle of the Nile, in which Nelson's ship the *Vanguard* had led the British fleet to a decisive victory over Napoleon. The *Vanguard* is depicted firing upon the French ship *La Fidelité*, a reference to Bogle's great active fund rival Fidelity. All 11 buildings on the Vanguard headquarters are named after Nelson's ships and the restaurant is called the 'galley'. To emphasise the mutual nature of relationships, Bogle insisted that Vanguard employees should be called 'crew'.

The Vanguard crew are chosen carefully. For example, when Vanguard began to expand in the UK, the local head Thomas Rampulla interviewed every one of the first 250 staff personally: Bill McNabb, Vanguard's CEO from 2008, described Rampulla as Vanguard's 'culture carrier'. Employees are under careful performance management, using portfolio attribution analysis to precisely measure their results against relevant indices: low performers are asked to 'walk the plank'. Despite the continuing Bogleheads' adoration of Jack Bogle, who still works in a research role at the headquarters and is sometimes critical of Vanguard's recent policies, Bill McNabb is firmly in control. While his predecessor as CEO fought bitterly with Bogle when the latter retained the executive chairmanship position, McNabb combines the roles of chief executive and company chairman, even though this contradicts the corporate governance arrangements Vanguard preaches for the companies it invests in. McNabb's remuneration is secret and he is politely dismissive of Bogle's criticisms.

Sources: *New York Times*, 11 August 2012; *Financial Times*, 27 May 2015; *Reuters*, 16 September 2014.

Questions

1 Map Vanguard's corporate culture to the cultural web elements of paradigm, stories, symbols, power, organisation structure, control styles and rituals and routine.

2 How do the various elements of the web interrelate? Do any of the elements not fit together?

Stories
- What core beliefs do stories reflect?
- What stories are commonly told, e.g. to newcomers?
- How do these reflect core assumptions and beliefs?
- What norms do the mavericks deviate from?

Symbols
- What objects, events or people do people in the organisation particularly identify with?
- What are these related to in the history of the organisation?
- What aspects of strategy are highlighted in publicity?

Routines and rituals
- Which routines are emphasised?
- Which are embedded in history?
- What behaviour do routines encourage?
- What are the key rituals?
- What assumptions and core beliefs do they reflect?
- What do training programmes emphasise?
- How easy are rituals/routines to change?

Power structures
- Where does power reside? Indicators include:
  (a) status
  (b) claim on resources
  (c) symbols of power
- Who 'makes things happen'?
- Who stops things happening?

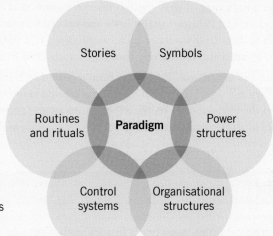

Control systems
- What is most closely monitored/controlled?
- Is emphasis on reward or punishment?
- Are controls rooted in history or current strategies?
- Are there many/few controls?

Organisational structures
- What are the formal *and* informal structures?
- How rigid are the structures?
- Do structures encourage collaboration or competition?
- What types of power structure do they support?

Overall
- What do the answers to these questions suggest are the (few) fundamental assumptions that are the paradigm?
- How would you characterise the dominant culture?
- How easy is this to change?
- How and to what extent do aspects of the web inter relate and re-enforce each other?

Figure 6.7 The cultural web: some useful questions

inform aspects of strategic management discussed in other parts of this book. These include the following:

- *Strategic capabilities.* As Chapter 4 makes clear, historically embedded capabilities are, very likely, part of the culture of the organisation. The cultural analysis of the organisation therefore provides a complementary basis of analysis to an examination of strategic capabilities. In effect, such an analysis of capabilities should end up digging into the culture of the organisation, especially in terms of its routines, control systems and the everyday way in which the organisation runs.

- *Strategy development.* An understanding of organisational culture sensitises managers to the way in which historical and cultural influences will likely affect future strategy for good or ill. It therefore relates to the discussion on strategy development in Chapter 13.

- *Managing strategic change.* An analysis of the culture also provides a basis for the management of strategic change, since it provides a picture of the existing culture that can be set against a desired strategy so as to give insights as to what may constrain the development of that strategy or what needs to be changed in order to achieve it. This is discussed more extensively in Chapter 15 on managing strategic change.

- *Leadership and management style.* Chapter 15 also raises questions about leadership and management style. If one of the major requirements of a strategist is to be able to encourage the questioning of that which is taken for granted, it is likely to require a management style – indeed a culture – that allows and encourages such questioning. If the leadership style is such as to discourage such questioning, it is unlikely that the lessons of history will be learned and more likely that the dictates of history will be followed.

- *Culture and experience.* There have been repeated references in this section to the role culture plays as a vehicle by which meaning is created in organisations. This is discussed more fully in the Commentary on the experience lens and provides a useful way in which many aspects of strategy can be considered (see the Commentaries throughout the book).

6.4 STRATEGIC DRIFT

The influence of an organisation's history and culture on its strategic direction is evident in the pattern of strategy development depicted in Figure 6.8. **Strategic drift**[27] **is the tendency for strategies to develop incrementally on the basis of historical and cultural influences, but fail to keep pace with a changing environment.** An example of strategic drift in Kodak is given in Illustration 6.4. The reasons for and consequences of strategic drift are important to understand, not only because it is common, but also because it helps explain why organisations often seem to stagnate in their strategy development and their performance. Strategic drift also highlights some significant challenges for managers that, in turn, point to some important lessons.

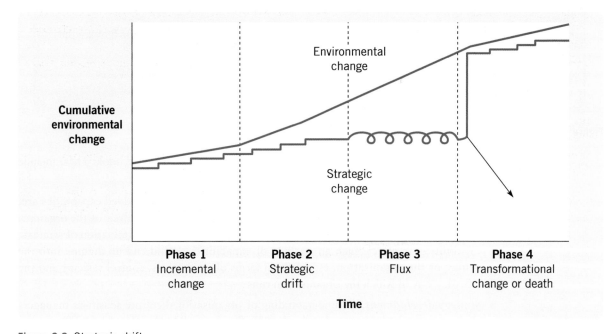

Figure 6.8 Strategic drift

ILLUSTRATION 6.4   Kodak: the decline and fall of a market leader

Knowledge of technological and market changes may not be enough to avoid strategic drift.

In the twentieth century, Kodak, the manufacturer of photographic film and cameras, was one of the world's most valuable brands. Based in Rochester in New York State, by 1976 Kodak had 90 per cent of film and 85 per cent share of camera sales in the USA, and by 1996 turnover was $16bn (£9.6bn, €12bn) and in 1999 profits nearly $2.5bn. Initially known for its innovative technology and marketing, it had developed digital camera technology by 1975, but did not launch digital cameras until the late 1990s by when it was too late.

By 2011, its traditional photography business had been almost entirely eroded, first by digital cameras and then by smartphones. Turnover was only $6bn, it was loss making, the share price had plummeted and in 2012 it filed for bankruptcy protection. How did Kodak miss such a fundamental shift in the market?

According to Steve Sasson, the engineer who invented the first digital camera, the response to his invention in Kodak was dismissive because it was filmless photography. There were similar responses to early internal intelligence reports on digital technology: 'Larry Matteson, a former Kodak executive . . . recalls writing a report in 1979, detailing fairly accurately how different parts of the market would switch from film to digital, starting with government reconnaissance, then professional photography and finally the mass market, all by 2010.'[1] Another internal report in the early 1980s concluded that digital technology would take over the camera industry in about ten years; ten years in which Kodak could work out its response.

The Kodak response was to use digital to enhance the film business. For example, in 1996 Kodak launched a film system using digital technology to provide users with a preview of shots taken and indicate the number of prints required. It flopped.

It was executives in the film division who carried most weight and they were over-confident about Kodak's brand strength. They also misjudged the speed of the change in customer buying preferences. For example, they believed that people in fast-developing markets such as China would buy lots of film, but many moved from no camera at all to digital. The profit margin on digital was also tiny compared with film and there was a real fear of product cannibalisation. Rosabeth Moss Kanter of Harvard Business School also pointed to the Kodak culture: 'Working in a one company town did not help ... Kodak's bosses in Rochester seldom heard much criticism ... '. Moreover, 'executives suffered from a mentality of perfect products, rather than the hi-tech mindset of make it, launch it, fix it.'[1] They also moved slowly: 'Even when Kodak decided to diversify, it took years to make its first acquisition.'[1] Kodak's attempts to diversify by developing the thousands of chemicals its researchers had created for use in film for the drug market also failed.

In 1989, the Kodak board needed to choose a new CEO. The choice was between Kay R. Whitmore, a long-serving executive in the traditional film business, and Phil Samper, who was more associated with digital technology. The board chose Whitmore, who insisted that he would make sure Kodak stayed closer to its core businesses in film and photographic chemicals.[2]

As late as 2007, a Kodak marketing video announced that 'Kodak is back' and 'wasn't going to play grab ass anymore' with digital.[3]

Sources: (1) *The Economist*, 14 January 2012; (2) *New York Times*, 9 December 1989; (3) *Forbes*, 18 January 2012.

Questions

1 Which of the reasons for strategic drift are evident in the Kodak story?

2 Drawing on the lessons from Part I of the book as a whole, how might Kodak's problems have been avoided?

Figure 6.8 identifies four phases in the process of strategic drift, leading either to the organisation's death or to transformational change:

- *Incremental strategic change* is the first phase, involving small changes. In many organisations, there are long periods of relative continuity during which established strategy remains largely unchanged or changes very incrementally. After all, where the environment is changing slowly (as in Figure 6.8 at this point), there is no need for more radical change. Where the pace of environmental change is slow, managers can also experiment with a variety of small-scale responses to change, waiting to see what works before adopting the best solution.

- *Strategic drift* emerges when the rate of environmental change starts to outpace the rate of the organisation's strategic change. Phase 2 of Figure 6.8 shows environmental change accelerating. However, the organisation's rate of change is still incremental, leading to a growing gap with the accumulated environmental change.

- *Flux* is the third phase, triggered by the downturn in performance caused by the growing gap between organisation and environment. In this phase, strategies may change but in no very clear direction: changes may even be reversed, so that strategies loop back on themselves. There may be internal disagreements amongst managers as to which strategy to follow, quite likely based on differences of opinion as to whether future strategy should be based on historic capabilities or whether those capabilities are becoming redundant.

- *Transformation or death* is the final phase in Figure 6.8. As things get worse, there are two possibilities: (a) The organisation may die, either through bankruptcy – as Kodak did in 2012 – or by takeover by another organisation; or (b) the organisation may go through a period of *transformational change,* which brings it back to the level of cumulated environmental change. Such change could take the form of multiple changes related to the organisation's strategy or perhaps a change to its whole business model (see Section 7.4), as well as changes in top management, organisational culture and organisation structure.

Strategic drift is a common phenomenon. The consultants McKinsey & Co. point out that the tendency is for 'most companies to allocate the same resources to the same business units year after year'.[28] It usually takes significant performance decline to prompt transformational change: a study of 215 major UK firms over the 20-year period 1983–2003 identified only four that could be said to have *both* maintained consistently high levels of performance and effected major transformational change over that period.[29] There are three main groups of reasons why it is hard to avoid strategic drift:

- *Uncertainty.* Strategic drift is not easy to see at the time. Chapters 2 and 3 provided ways of analysing the environment, but such analyses are rarely unambiguous. It takes time for managers to be sure of the direction and significance of environmental changes. Changes may be temporary, for instance the result of cyclical downturns that will soon be reversed or fashions that may soon pass. It is easier to see major and irreversible changes with hindsight; it is less easy to grasp their significance as they are happening.

- *Path dependency and lock-in.* As in Section 6.2, the historical trajectory of the organisation might lock organisations into strategies that are costly to change, at least in the short term. For example, capabilities that have historically been the basis of competitive advantage can be difficult to abandon in favour of developing new and untested capabilities. In this sense, old capabilities can become *core rigidities,* rather than core competences capable of supporting new businesses.[30] Similarly, *existing relationships* can become shackles that inhibit significant change.[31] Thus managers may be reluctant to break relationships

THINKING DIFFERENTLY Institutional logics versus organisational cultures

Societal-level institutional logics can be both sources of conflict and sources of inspiration for organisational cultures.

Institutional logics are socially constructed sets of material practices, assumptions, values and beliefs that shape human cognition and behaviour across domains of activity, typically at a societal level.[33] To put it more simply, what we think and how we behave are shaped by the informal rules of the society we live in. These rules come in distinct and coherent sets: for instance, every society has informal rules about how to behave in the different domains of business, the family, national politics and professions. However, we remain sensitive to all these rules even when we are operating in one particular domain.

This notion of institutional logics comes from the institutional theory tradition associated with the concept of organisational fields, with its emphasis on legitimate behaviour (see Section 6.3.2). It has at least two radical implications for the notion of organisational culture. First, organisational cultures can never be wholly 'organisational': they will certainly be impacted – and sometimes distorted – by logics from outside the organisation. Second, organisational cultures can never be entirely coherent and unified: they will always be 'plural', i.e. cross-cut by multiple logics from external society, such as those of the family or profession.

These institutional logics mean that business decisions are rarely purely business decisions. Familial responsibilities may be influential in a family business; professional identities and standards may be influential in a law firm or architectural practice; patriotism or home-country culture may shape local strategic moves in a multinational. These pluralistic logics can be a source of conflict, of course. But institutional logics can also be a source of inspiration for organisations: professionalism or family spirit can be powerful ingredients in organisational cultures.

> **Question**
>
> How might institutional logics shape such strategic choices as diversification, innovation and internationalisation (see Chapters 8, 9 and 10) for (i) a family-business owner looking to pass on the business to the next generation of children; (ii) a state-owned enterprise from a commodity-hungry country such as China; (iii) a growth-seeking professional services firm, in law for example, considering new businesses and new countries to operate in?

with important customers, suppliers and employees built up over many years for the sake of some emerging and uncertain opportunity.

- *Cultural entrenchment.* As in Section 6.3, culture can exert a strong influence over strategy. The paradigmatic set of taken-for-granted assumptions may prevent managers from seeing certain issues: organisational *identities* (such as 'we are a brewing company', not a 'fast-moving consumer goods company') can shape views of environmental opportunities and threats. Performance measures embedded in the organisation's *control systems* can obscure the need for change. Thus many performance measures are lagged: in the early stages of strategic drift, sales figures may hold up because of customer loyalty or long customer waiting lists; profits may be buttressed by simple cost-cutting or staff working harder in an unsustainable way.

- *Powerful people*, whose skills and power bases relate to the old strategy, may naturally resist change too. These kinds of issues are explored further in Chapter 15.

Thus history, culture and genuine uncertainty can easily support strategic drift. Rebecca Henderson of MIT suggested how a Kodak executive might have responded to reports on the threat of digital technology (see Illustration 6.4): '... you are suggesting that we invest millions of dollars in a market that may, or may not exist but that is certainly smaller than our existing market, to develop a product that customers may or may not want using a business model that will almost certainly give us lower margins than our existing product lines ... Tell me again just why we should make this investment?'[32]

SUMMARY

- Historical, *path-dependent processes* may play a significant part in the success or failure of an organisation and need to be understood by managers. There are historical analyses that can be conducted to help uncover these influences.

- *Cultural and institutional influences* both inform and constrain the strategic development of organisations.

- *Organisational culture* is the basic taken-for-granted assumptions, beliefs and behaviours shared by members of an organisation.

- The seven elements of the *cultural web* are useful for analysing organisational cultures and their relationships to strategy.

- Historic and cultural influences may give rise to *strategic drift* as strategy develops incrementally on the basis of such influences and fails to keep pace with a changing environment.

WORK ASSIGNMENTS

✱ Denotes more advanced work assignments.
* Refers to a case study in the Text and Cases edition.

6.1✱ In the context of Section 6.2, undertake a historical analysis of the strategy development of an organisation of your choice and consider the question: When has history mattered for strategy; when has it appeared not to matter?

6.2 Identify an organisation that describes its culture publicly (use a Google search on 'our culture' plus 'business', for example). What do they mean by culture and how does it fit with the description of culture in this chapter?

6.3 Identify a company reputed to have a strong and positive culture (e.g. via Fortune's 'Best Companies', Glassdoor's 'Best Places to Work' or LinkedIn's 'Most In-Demand Employers'). What is attractive about this company's culture, how is it sustained and to what extent is it a competitive advantage?

6.4 Use the questions in Figure 6.8 to identify elements of the cultural web for Barclays Investment Bank (end of chapter case), Adnams* or an organisation of your choice (for example, your business school).

6.5 Identify an organisation that, in your view, is in one of the phases of strategic drift described in Section 6.4 (Google search 'disappointing results' or 'slow growth' plus 'business' or 'company'). How and why did it get into this state?

Integrative assignment

6.6✱ Choose an example of a major change in strategy of an organisation. Explain to what extent and how its strategic capabilities and its organisation culture changed. (Refer to Chapters 4, 6 and 15.)

RECOMMENDED KEY READINGS

- For a historical perspective on strategy, see Manuel Hensmans, Gerry Johnson and George Yip, *Strategic Transformation*: *Changing while Winning*, Palgrave Macmillan, 2013 (summarised in G. Johnson, G. Yip and M. Hensmans, 'Achieving successful strategic transformation', *MIT Sloan Management Review,* vol. 53, no. 3 (2012), pp. 25–32); and John T. Seaman Jr and George David Smith, 'Your company's history as a leadership tool', *Harvard Business Review* (December 2012), pp. 1–10.

- For a summary and illustrated explanation of institutional theory, see Gerry Johnson and Royston Greenwood, 'Institutional theory and strategy', in *Strategic Management*: *A Multiple-Perspective Approach,* M. Jenkins and V. Ambrosini (eds), Palgrave, 2007.

- For a comprehensive and critical explanation of organisational culture see Mats Alvesson, *Understanding Organisational Culture,* 2nd edn, Sage, 2012.

REFERENCES

1. W.B. Arthur, 'Competing technologies, increasing returns and lock in by historical events', *Economic Journal*, vol. 99 (1989), pp. 116–31.

2. P.A. David, 'Clio and the economics of QWERTY', *American Economic Review*, vol. 75, no. 2 (1985), pp. 332–7, but also for a challenge to David's argument see S.J. Liebowitz and S.E. Margolis, 'The fable of the keys', *Journal of Law & Economics*, vol. 30, April (1990), pp. 1–26.

3. For discussions of path dependency in an organisational context, see Jorg Sydow, George Schraeyogg and Jochen Koch, 'Organisational path dependance: opening the black box', *Academy of Management Review*, vol. 34, no. 4 (2009), pp. 689–708. L. Dobusch and E. Schüssler discuss path dependence at Intel and Microsoft in 'Theorizing path dependence: a review of positive feedback mechanisms in technology markets, regional clusters, and organizations', *Industrial and Corporate Change*, vol. 22, no. 3 (2013), pp. 717–46.

4. The world's biggest accounting firms have called for radical reform: 'Big four in call for real time accounts', *Financial Times* (8 November 2006), p. 1.

5. See J.T. Seaman Jr and G.D. Smith, 'Your company's history as a leadership tool', *Harvard Business Review*, December 2012, pp. 1–10.

6. This quote by André Malroux and the story of the BMW museum was provided by the business historian Mary Rose.

7. See D. Holbrook, W. Cohen, D. Hounshell and S. Klepper, 'The nature, sources and consequences of firm differences in the early history of the semiconductor industry', *Strategic Management Journal*, vol. 21, no. 10–11 (2000), pp. 107–42.

8. S. Klepper and K.L. Simons, 'Dominance by birthright: entry of prior radio producers and competitive ramifications in the US television receiver industry', *Strategic Management Journal*, vol. 21, no. 10–11 (2000), pp. 987–1016.

9. S. Paroutis, M. Mckeown and S. Collinson, 'Building castles from sand: unlocking CEO mythopoetical behaviour in Hewlett Packard from 1978 to 2005', *Business History*, vol. 55, no. 7 (2013), pp. 1200–27. See also O. Brunninge, 'Using history in organization: how managers make purposeful reference to history in strategy processes', *Journal of Organizational Change Management*, vol. 22, no. 1 (2009), pp. 8–26.

10. Also see D.J. Jeremy, 'Business history and strategy', in A. Pettigrew, H. Thomas and R. Whittington (eds), *The Handbook of Strategy and Management*, pp. 436–60, Sage, 2002.

11. For good examples of corporate histories see G. Jones, *Renewing Unilever: Transformation and Tradition*, Oxford University Press, 2005; R. Fitzgerald, *Rowntrees and the Marketing Revolution, 1862–1969*, Cambridge University Press, 1995; and T.R. Gourvish, *British Railways 1948–73*, Cambridge University Press, 1986.

12. This quote is from S. Finkelstein, 'Why smart executives fail: four case histories of how people learn the wrong lessons from history', *Business History*, vol. 48, no. 2 (2006), pp. 153–70.

13. See G. Hofstede, *Culture's Consequences*, Sage, 2nd edn, 2001; and M. Minkov and G. Hofstede, 'The evolution of Hofstede's doctrine', *Cross Cultural Management: An International Journal*, vol. 18, no. 1 (2011), pp. 10–20.

14. For a critique of Hofstede's work, see B. McSweeney, 'Hofstede's model of national cultural differences and their consequences: a triumph of faith – a failure of analysis', *Human Relations*, vol. 55, no. 1 (2002), pp. 89–118. For example, differences in regional cultures impacted on the integration of banking mergers in Nigeria, as shown by E. Gomes, D. Angwin and K. Melahi, 'HRM practices throughout the mergers and acquisition (M&A) process: a study of domestic deals in the Nigerian banking industry', *International Journal of Human Resource Management*, vol. 23, no. 14 (2012), pp. 2874–900.

15. A useful review of research on this topic is T. Dacin, J. Goodstein and R. Scott, 'Institutional theory and institutional change: introduction to the special research forum', *Academy of Management Journal*, vol. 45, no. 1 (2002), pp. 45–57. For a more general review, see G. Johnson and R. Greenwood, 'Institutional theory and strategy', in M. Jenkins and V. Ambrosini (eds), *Strategic Management: a Multiple-Perspective Approach*, Palgrave, 2007.

16. For discussion of a classic case, see J.F. Porac, H. Thomas and C. Baden-Fuller, 'Competitive groups as cognitive communities: the case of Scottish knitwear manufacturers revisited', *Journal of Management Studies*, vol. 48, no. 3 (2011), pp. 646–64. See also F.F. Suarez, S. Grodal and A. Gotsopoulos, 'Perfect timing? Dominant category, dominant design, and the window of opportunity for firm entry', *Strategic Management Journal*, vol. 36, no. 3 (2015), pp. 437–48.

17. The term 'recipe' was introduced to refer to industries by J.-C. Spender, *Industry Recipes: the Nature and Sources of Management Judgement*, Blackwell, 1989. We have broadened its use by applying it to *organisational fields*. For a recent application, see P. McNamara, S. I. Peck and A. Sasson, 'Competing business models, value creation and appropriation in English football', *Long Range Planning*, vol. 46, no. 61 (2013), pp. 475–487.

18. D. Deephouse, 'To be different or to be the same? It's a question (and theory) of strategic balance', *Strategic Management Journal*, vol. 20, no. 2 (1999), pp. 147–66.

19. This definition of culture is taken from E. Schein, *Organisational Culture and Leadership*, 3rd edn, Jossey-Bass, 2004, p. 6.

20. This is how Terrence Deal and Alan Kennedy define organisational culture in *Corporate Cultures: the Rites and Rituals of Corporate Life*, Addison-Wesley, 1982.

21. E. Schein (see end note 19) and A. Brown, *Organisational Culture*, Financial Times Prentice Hall, 1998 are useful in understanding the relationship between organisational culture and strategy. For a useful critique of the concept of organisational culture see M. Alvesson, *Understanding Organizational Culture*, Sage, 2002.

22. M.J. Hatch, M. Schultz and A.-M. Skov, 'Organizational identity and culture in the context of managed change: transformation in the Carlsberg Group, 2009–2013', *Academy of Management Discoveries*, vol. 1, no. 1 (2015), pp. 56–87; T. Wry, M. Lounsbury and M.A. Glynn, 'Legitimating nascent collective identities: coordinating cultural entrepreneurship', *Organization Science*, vol. 22. no. 2 (2011), pp. 449–63.

23. Figure 6.5 is adapted from the original in P. Grinyer and J.-C. Spender, *Turnaround: Managerial Recipes for Strategic Success*, Associated British Press, 1979, p. 203.

24. A fuller explanation of the cultural web can be found in G. Johnson, *Strategic Change and the Management Process*, Blackwell, 1987; and G. Johnson, 'Managing strategic change: strategy, culture and action', *Long Range Planning*, vol. 25, no. 1 (1992), pp. 28–36.

25. A practical explanation of cultural web mapping is a 'white paper' by Gerry Johnson, 'Mapping and Re-mapping Organisational Culture: a Local Government Example', www.strategyexplorers.com.

26. See A.C.T. Smith and B. Stewart, 'Organizational rituals: features, functions and mechanisms', *International Journal of Management Reviews*, vol. 13, no. 2 (2011), pp. 113–33; and G. Islam and M.J. Zyphur, 'Rituals in organizations: a review and expansion of current theory', *Group & Organization Management*, vol. 34 (2009), pp. 114–39.

27. For an explanation of strategic drift, see G. Johnson, 'Rethinking incrementalism', *Strategic Management Journal*, vol. 9 (1988), pp. 75–91; and 'Managing strategic change – strategy, culture and action', *Long Range Planning*, vol. 25, no. 1 (1992), pp. 28–36. Also see E. Romanelli and M.T. Tushman, 'Organizational transformation as punctuated equilibrium: an empirical test', *Academy of Management Journal*, vol. 7, no. 5 (1994), pp. 1141–66. They explain the tendency of strategies to develop incrementally with periodic transformational change.

28. S. Hall, D. Lovallo and R. Musters, 'How to put your money where your strategy is', *McKinsey Quarterley* (March 2012).

29. See G. Yip, T. Devinney and G. Johnson, 'Measuring long-term superior performance: the UK's long term superior performers 1984–2003', *Long Range Planning*, vol. 43, no. 3 (2009), pp. 390–413.

30. See D. Leonard-Barton, 'Core capabilities and core rigidities: a paradox in managing new product development', *Strategic Management Journal*, vol. 13 (1992), pp. 111–25.

31. This is a term used by Donald S. Sull in accounting for the decline of high-performing firms (see 'Why good companies go bad', *Harvard Business Review*, July/August 1999, pp. 42–52).

32. John Naughton, 'The lessons we can learn from the rise and fall of Kodak', *Observer Discover*, 22 January 2012.

33. M.L. Besharov and W.K. Smith, 'Multiple institutional logics in organizations: explaining their varied nature and implications', *Academy of Management Review*, vol. 39, no. 3 (2014), pp. 364–81; and for a case of an international law firm, M. Smets, T. Morris and R. Greenwood, 'From practice to field: a multilevel model of practice-driven institutional change', *Academy of Management Journal*, vol. 55, no. 4 (2012), pp. 877–904.

CASE EXAMPLE

Culture clashes at Barclays Bank

Barclays Bank is an international retail and investment bank based in London. It ranks amongst the ten largest banks in the world and has 130,000 employees. In the four years to 2015, it had four separate bosses: the aggressive investment banker Robert Diamond ('Diamond Bob'), the reformist 'Saint' Antony Jenkins, ex-insurance titan John 'Mack the Knife' McFarlane; and lately another American investment banker James ('Jes') Staley.

Quaker origins – and beyond

Barclays Bank traces its origins to 1690. Its early address in Lombard Street – the heart of London's financial district – was 'the Sign of the Black Spread Eagle'. The Spread Eagle remains Barclays' corporate logo even today. The bank's founding families were from the Quaker religious movement, who emphasised sobriety, pacificism and high ethical standards. Their descendants were still in important executive positions in the mid-twentieth century: the last family member served as Chairman during the 1980s. Reinforced by mergers, the company became one of the big four retail bankers in the UK. As the *Financial Times* observed:

> 'In many ways the bank resembled a club and, as so often with British clubs, the thing worked surprisingly well despite its flaws ... It was, in fact, the most innovative of the British clearing banks in the post-war period. In 1967 it installed the world's first automated cash teller machine ... Barclays also came up with the first plastic payment device, Barclaycard, still outstandingly successful.'

Since the early 1800s, Barclays had been accepting bills from other banks to reinvest in businesses – an early form of investment banking. The investment banking business received a huge impetus after the 1986 Big Bang, the liberalisation of London's stock market. Barclays embarked on acquisitions including a leading stock broker, de Zoete Wedd. This became the core of an investment bank, BZW. However, in common with other investment banks who got involved in equities trading, Barclays had great difficulty combining conventional and investment banking in a coherent model. As the *Financial Times* put it:

Bob Diamond, Barclays CEO 2011–12
Source: Jerome Favre/Bloomberg/Getty Images.

> 'The chief problem was culture. As Michael Lewis, author of *Liar's Poker*, a commentary on Wall Street in the 1980s, memorably put it, a commercial banker was someone who had a wife, a station wagon, 2.2 children and a dog that brought him his slippers when he returned home from work at 6 pm. An investment banker, by contrast, was a breed apart, a member of a master race of dealmakers. He possessed vast, almost unimaginable talent and ambition. If he had a dog it snarled. He had two little red sports cars yet wanted four. To get them, he was, for a man in a suit, surprisingly willing to cause trouble.'

Investment banking was notorious for its 'hard work and hard play'. It was common for investment bankers to work through the night, or at least to be seen to be doing so – stories had it that they would own two suit jackets so they could leave one on the back of the chair to pretend they were still in the office working. It was also a 'can-do' mentality which legitimated, for example, a day trip to Australia for a one-hour meeting. No expense was spared on flights, entertainment or accommodation provided a big deal was signed. There was also much visible excess with traders spending thousands of pounds a night at champagne bars. Long hours and intense pressure tended to foster strong loyalties to team-mates, with bankers identifying with their work group rather than with the bank as a whole.

Diamond Bob

The American investment banker Bob Diamond joined Barclays in 1996, with a reputation as a successful trader earned in leading US banks. Throughout the first decade of this century, Bob Diamond grew in influence, becoming head of Barclays' investment banking businesses. A past employee of Barclays' investment arm, interviewed in a BBC *Panorama* programme, claimed that Bob Diamond 'installed Wall Street values into Barclays; it was every man for himself … It was all about doing ever bigger deals' and being willing to take 'extreme risks' to make 'super profits' and generate huge bonuses for the traders involved. In 2008, Diamond was responsible for buying the failed Lehman Brothers Wall Street investment bank. Diamond also grew the much criticised Structured Capital Markets 'tax planning' business, which many saw as just about tax avoidance. Employing only 100 people, by 2010 this business was generating £1 (€1.2, $1.5) billion a year in profits. Bob Diamond also succeeded in growing the trading arm of the bank into a major profit contributor, accounting for 58 per cent of Barclays' overall pre-tax earnings by 2011. Diamond became known as 'Diamond Bob', a reference both to his financial success and to a rather flashy lifestyle which included hanging out with Mick Jagger of the Rolling Stones.

In 2011, Diamond's success was rewarded by appointment as chief executive of the whole bank. But problems were emerging. There were investigations into the mis-selling of payment protection insurance by the retail bank and into the manipulation of the inter-bank lending rate, Libor, in the investment bank. Traders at Barclays were accused of manipulating Californian electricity prices. A mysterious rescue package involving Qatari capital that had saved Barclays from nationalisation during the financial crisis of 2008 came under growing scrutiny. Barclays was criticised for continuing to pay high bonuses to staff even after the financial crisis of 2008–09. BBC's *Panorama* calculated that in 2010–11 payments to shareholders had amounted to £1.4bn while payment of bonuses for staff amounted to £6bn. There was widespread criticism of the bank's tax minimisation activities and public outrage at Bob Diamond's huge remuneration package, estimated to be around £120m between 2007 and 2012. Barclays' reputation was in tatters. Bob Diamond resigned in 2012.

Saint Antony

Antony Jenkins was appointed Chief Executive of Barclays in August 2012. He had actually begun his career in the bank's UK retail business in the early 1980s, before a time at Citigroup. He had returned to Barclays to run the credit card division in 2006, becoming head of retail and business banking in 2009. Jenkins was not an investment banker and declared himself determined to clean up Barclays' reputation.

Jenkins commissioned a prominent City lawyer, Anthony Salz, to review Barclays' culture. The review concluded:

> 'We believe that the business practices for which Barclays has rightly been criticised were shaped predominantly by its cultures, which rested on uncertain foundations. There was no sense of common purpose in a group that had grown and diversified significantly in less than two decades. And across the whole bank, there were no clearly articulated and understood shared values – so there could hardly be much consensus among employees as to what the values were and what should guide everyday behaviours. And as a result there was no consistency to the development of a desired culture.'

The review specifically identified pay, especially in the investment bank, as a source of many problems:

> 'Most but not all of the pay issues concern the investment bank. . . . Based on our interviews, we could not avoid concluding that pay contributed significantly to a sense among a few that they were somehow unaffected by the ordinary rules. A few investment bankers seemed to lose a sense of proportion and humility. . . . Elevated pay levels inevitably distort culture, tending to attract people who measure their personal success principally on compensation. . . . Many interviewees [reported] a sense of an entitlement culture.'

Antony Jenkins' concurred with the criticisms of the Salz review, issuing a memo to all Barclays' staff as follows:

> 'Over a period of almost 20 years, banking became too aggressive, too focused on the short term, too disconnected from the needs of our customers and clients, and wider society. We were not immune at Barclays from these mistakes … Performance assessment will be based not just on what we deliver but on how we deliver it. We must never again be in a position of rewarding people for making the bank money in a way which is unethical or inconsistent with our values.'

All Barclays' staff would receive training on the central importance of five core values: respect, integrity, service, excellence and stewardship. Jenkins became known in the bank as 'Saint Antony', wearing crisp white shirts and plain ties in the Barclays' colour blue. In a saintly gesture, Jenkins waived his first year bonus of £2.75m. He also told his employees that anybody who did not like the new culture should leave.

In his first strategic review, Jenkins examined the performance and reputation of Barclays' 75 business units. The review concluded that 39 business units were in good shape, 15 needed some attention, 17 needed serious attention to avoid closure or sale and four would definitely be sold or closed, one of which was its tax-avoiding Structured Capital Markets unit. Basically though, investment banking would remain intact.

Nonetheless, Jenkins promised to bring pay at the investment bank down as a percentage of income to the mid-thirties. During 2014, however, rival banks started to poach top performers. Jenkins publicly warned of a 'death spiral' if pay did not match competitors'. The investment banking pay ratio increased from 39.6 to 43.2 per cent.

Mack the Knife

In May 2015, John McFarlane took over as Barclays chairman on the retirement of his predecessor. McFarlane had acquired his nickname 'Mack the Knife' when he had despatched his CEO within a few weeks of arriving as chairman of Aviva, the large insurance company. Matters quickly came to a head at Barclays when the board had an off-site meeting in June at an exclusive country house hotel near Bath.

The investment bankers were already disgruntled with Jenkins. The latest irritation was when Jenkins had sent a letter to all staff celebrating the bank's 325th anniversary without mentioning the investment banking division. The Bath meeting was divided between Jenkins and the investment bankers about strategy for the next five years. McFarlane sided mostly with the investment bankers. Consulting with the non-executive directors present, McFarlane decided to dismiss Jenkins. McFarlane declared himself as executive chairman, filling the CEO role until another one could be put in place.

McFarlane did not commit himself to major changes in strategy, only to focus more on execution. He declared that Barclays was only halfway through its cultural change 'journey'. But in almost the same breath, he added: 'What we really need is a high energy, supercharged performance driven approach.' He promised to double the Barclay's share price in three to four years.

The Staley strategy

James Staley joined Barclays as CEO at the end of 2015, with McFarlane returning to a non-executive chairman role. Although recently working at a hedge-fund, Staley had spent his career mostly at JPMorgan, the largest bank in the USA and an investment banking powerhouse since the late nineteenth century. Staley quickly appointed former JPMorgan colleagues as chief operating officer and chief risk officer.

In March 2016, Staley presented his first strategic review to shareholders and analysts. He committed himself to simplifying the international businesses, including the sale of the major African retail business and peripheral international investment banking operations. In order to strengthen the bank's financial position, he cut the dividend payments for the next two years by 50 per cent. The Barclays share price fell by eight per cent on the news. Barclays' market valuation was little more than half what it had been in 2014.

Sources: Barclays Bank, *Salz Review: an Independent Review of Barclays' Business Practices*, April 2013; *Financial Times*, 6 July 2012, 12 February 2012, 12 July 2013, 10 July 2015, 1 March 2016; *Guardian*, 28 June 2012; *Panorama: Inside Barclays: Banking on Bonuses*, 11 February 2013; *Telegraph*, 17 January 2013.

Questions

1 With an eye to elements of the cultural web (Section 6.3.5), analyse the culture of Barclays' investment banking business.

2 Reformist Antony Jenkins could have used Barclays' Quaker history as a resource for change (Section 6.2.2). What might have been the advantages and disadvantages of drawing on this history?

COMMENTARY ON
PART I THE STRATEGY LENSES

The strategy lenses aim to help you explore strategy 'critically'. Critical here is meant constructively: it is about asking better questions, generating new options, building stronger evidence and being more aware of different points of view. Ultimately, thinking critically should help you be more persuasive with regard to your own chosen positions, helping you convince your teachers, your fellow students or your work colleagues.[1] Using the strategy lenses to explore strategic issues critically will help you both to generate additional insights and respond to possible counter-arguments against your own position.

The last few chapters have already introduced many points of view, each offering different insights into what matters in strategy. Some of these reflect a strong economics orientation, for instance macro-economic cycles and the Five Forces in Chapters 2 and 3. Others are more sociological, such as the highlighting of legitimacy in Chapters 2 and 5. Some concepts and frameworks emphasise opportunities for innovation, as in the strategy canvas of Chapter 3. Others stress conservatism in organisations, for example strategic drift and organisational culture in Chapter 6. Generally, the chapters assume objectivity in analysis, but issues such as the principal–agent problem in Chapter 5 warn of the scope for divergent political interests in organisations, while organisational culture too can be a source of bias. What should be clear from these chapters, therefore, is that there are many different ways of seeing strategy. Each of them suggests different questions, generates different kinds of insights and demands different types of evidence.

The strategy lenses organise many of these different perspectives into four basic approaches to exploring strategic issues. Each of these lenses will help you generate distinct kinds of questions, options and evidence. They each have distinct implications for practice too.

The four strategy lenses are as follows:

- **The design lens views strategy development as a logical process of analysis and evaluation**. This is the most commonly held view about how strategy is developed and what managing strategy is about. Options and evidence here are generated by objective analysis using formal concepts and frameworks.

- **The experience lens views strategy development as the outcome of people's taken-for-granted assumptions and ways of doing things**. Strategy through the experience lens puts people, culture and history centre stage in strategy development. Options need to respect the past, and evidence is likely to draw heavily on previous experience.

- **The variety lens* views strategy as the bubbling up of new ideas from the variety of people in and around organisations**. According to this lens, strategy emerges not just from the top, but also from the periphery and bottom of the organisation. It is important to question top management views, and recognise the potential value of options coming from all round the organisation, and even from outside.

- **The discourse lens views language as important both for understanding and changing strategy and for managerial power and identity**. Through this lens, unpicking managers' language can uncover hidden meanings and political interests. Choosing the right language is also important to legitimating options and evidence.

* In earlier editions the variety lens was called the 'ideas lens'. The authors believe that the word 'variety' more accurately encapsulates the concepts explained in this section.

The critical exploration of strategy through these four lenses is useful because they all raise different questions and suggest different approaches. Think of everyday discussions you have. It is not unusual for people to say: 'But what if you looked at it this way instead?' Taking just one view can lead to a partial and perhaps biased understanding. Looking at an issue another way can give a much fuller picture, generating new and different insights. For example, is a proposed strategy the result of objective analysis or is it rather the reflection of the proposer's personal experience or political self-interest? The lenses can also prompt different options or solutions to strategic problems. For example again, should organisations rely just on top managers to create new strategies, or rather look towards the bottom of the organisation to uncover existing experiments and initiatives that have greater potential? Thus, taking a critical perspective on strategy can help managers and students consider a wider range of issues and responses.

The rest of this Commentary explains the lenses in more detail, showing how they each relate to the following three key dimensions of managing strategy:

- *Rationality*: the extent to which the development of strategy is rationally managed. The design lens assumes high rationality, but the other lenses question this.

- *Innovation*: the extent to which strategy is likely to develop innovative, change-oriented organisations, or alternatively consolidate past experience and existing power structures.

- *Legitimacy*: the extent to which strategy analysis and discourse is involved in sustaining managers' power and identities in organisations.

This Commentary concludes with a short case on Nokia, illustrating how the four lenses can be used to explore a real company's strategy. There will be shorter Commentaries later in the book helping readers to reflect on the concepts and frameworks highlighted in Parts II and III. Meanwhile, this Commentary relates mostly to the material in the first six chapters of this book.

The design lens

The design lens evokes an image of the strategist as detached designer, drawing up precise blueprints distant from the messy realities of action. In terms of the three key dimensions, the design lens therefore puts a strong premium on rational analysis and decision-making (see Figure C.i).[2] Because of its overt commitment to optimising the performance of

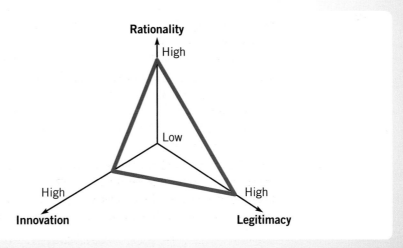

Figure C.i Design lens

organisations, the design lens tends also to be highly legitimate. Rational analysis is what counts, not passion or intuition. However, this commitment to dry analysis can sometimes work against innovation.

The design lens is associated broadly with strategy theorists such as the former Lockheed Corporation strategic planner Igor Ansoff or the economics-trained Harvard Business School Professor Michael Porter.[3] It has its origins in traditional economists' expectations about perfect information and 'rational economic man', and is further informed by management science techniques for resource optimisation. The design lens is also how strategy is often explained in textbooks, by teachers and indeed by managers. The design lens makes the following three assumptions about how strategic decisions are made:

- *Systematic analysis is key.* Although there are many influences on an organisation's performance, careful analysis can identify those that are most significant. In this view, calculating the attractiveness of an industry using Porter's Five Forces (Chapter 3), and identifying strategic capabilities using Valuable, Rare, Inimitable and Organisational support criteria (Chapter 4), would be standard processes for estimating future performance.

- *Analysis precedes action.* In the design lens, strategy is generally seen as a linear process. Decisions about strategy are separate from and precede implementation. From this point of view, therefore, environmental analysis – for example projecting scenarios or forecasting industry life cycles (Chapters 2 and 3) – is the crucial first step in strategy-making.

- *Objectives should be clear.* Rational analysis and decision-making need unambiguous criteria by which to evaluate options. Missions and visions (Chapter 1) should be set in advance as precisely as possible, with little scope for adjustment as new opportunities or constraints are discovered in action.

These design lens assumptions about how decisions should be made are in turn associated with two key views about the nature of organisations:

- *Organisations are hierarchies.* It is the responsibility of top management to plan the destiny of the organisation. The responsibility of the rest of organisation is simply to implement the strategy decided at the top.

- *Organisations work mechanically.* This hierarchical approach implies a view of organisations as engineered systems or even machines. Pulling the right organisational levers should produce predictable results. Principal–agent problems can be controlled by the appropriate gearing of incentives (Chapter 5). Even organisational cultures (Chapter 6) can be designed from above.

Implications

The design lens has practical implications for both managers and students. From the design point of view, it is worth investing extensive time in formal analysis, especially economic forms of analysis. Formal strategic planning and financial calculations are crucial parts of the design lens approach. But even if strategic plans do not always produce the expected results, there are two further reasons for taking a design lens approach:

- *Dealing with complexity and uncertainty.* The design lens provides a means of talking about complex and uncertain issues in a rational, logical and structured way. Even if rational analysis can sometimes over-simplify or convey undue precision, it is usually better than just concluding that everything is all much too complicated for any kind of plan or calculation. Strategy is more than guesswork.

- *Meeting stakeholder expectations.* As well as the sheer analytical value of a design approach, adopting rational procedures is something that important stakeholders (see Chapter 5) such as banks, financial analysts, investors and employees typically expect. For these audiences, analysis is highly legitimate. Taking a design lens approach is therefore an important means of gaining the support and confidence of significant internal and external actors.

Technical and elitist forms of strategy analysis can also have implications for managerial power and personal identity. These side-effects will be discussed further with the discourse lens later.

In summary, the design lens is useful in highlighting the potential value of systematic analysis, step-by-step sequences and the careful engineering of organisational objectives and systems. However, the design lens does have its limits. In particular, a narrow design lens tends to underestimate the positive role of intuition and experience, the scope for unplanned and bottom-up initiatives, and the power effects of strategy analysis. Different lenses can provide useful insights into these other elements of strategy.

Strategy as experience

The experience lens sees strategy as coming less from objective analysis on a clean sheet of paper and more from the prior experience of the organisation's managers. History and culture matter. Strategy is shaped by people's individual and collective taken-for-granted assumptions and ways of doing things. As indicated in Figure C.ii, the experience lens therefore places less emphasis than the design lens on rationality. It also sets low expectations in terms of innovation and change. Legitimacy is important, but this is defined in terms of tradition, routines and culture rather than simple appeal to analysis and 'the facts'.

The experience lens is based on a good deal of research about how strategies actually develop in the real world. As early as the 1950s, Nobel prize winner Herbert Simon was developing the so-called Behavioral Theory of the Firm, based on how managers really behave.[4] Contemporary researchers into 'Behavioral Strategy' underline two kinds of problem for rational analysis in practice:

- *External constraints:* Behavioral Theory points to real-world barriers to rationality: for example, it is difficult to obtain all the information required for comprehensive analysis; it is hard to forecast accurately in an uncertain future; and there are cost and time limits to undertaking complete analyses. In these conditions, managers often 'satisfice' when analysing strategic options: in other words, they settle for adequate solutions rather than the rational optimum.

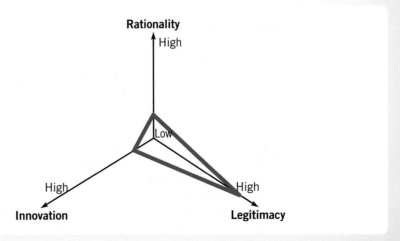

Figure C.ii Experience lens

- *Internal psychological limitations:* Behavioral Theory underlines how managers suffer from 'bounded rationality', human limitations on the intellectual ability to process information and carry out analysis. They are also liable to 'cognitive bias': in other words, managers tend to be selective in the attention they give to issues and often automatically favour some types of solutions rather than others.

Cognitive bias is often based on managers' experience, both individual and collective:

- *Individual experience* can particularly shape managers' taken-for-granted assumptions about what is important and what kinds of actions work best. Influential sources of experience can be education and training. For example, accountants tend to see things differently to engineers; MBAs are often accused of favouring excessively analytical approaches to solving problems. Other kinds of influential individual experience are personal careers. Thus a manager who had spent his or her career in the traditional automobile industry (for instance, Ford or BMW) might find it difficult to take seriously new entrants such as Google or Tesla. Differences in individual experience within an organisation can lead to debate and negotiation between managers with divergent views about what is important and what should be done. Sometimes such negotiation can slow decision-making down and lead to excessive compromise. Stakeholder mapping (Chapter 5) of different managers' power and attention can be useful in resolving divergent views.

- *Collective experience* tends to form habitual patterns of thinking and acting, which can translate into standard responses to strategic issues. One kind of collective experience is encapsulated in organisational culture, as discussed in Chapter 6. Another kind of collective experience is reflected by national culture: so for instance Chinese and American managers may see the world differently (see also Chapter 10). A third kind of collective experience is embodied in industry 'recipes' (Chapter 6), based on years of regular interaction between existing competitors: for example, managers in the clothing industry come to believe over time that style is important to success, even though new ideas from outside the industry imply that new technologies may be the source of competitive advantage in the future. By contrast with individual experience, collective experience tends to suppress debate in management teams, and it becomes hard to challenge the consensus. A consequence can be 'strategic drift' (Chapter 6), with everybody agreeing to continue as before, even in the face of environmental change.

Implications

The experience lens has significant implications for strategy. First there are three important warnings:

- *Analysis is typically biased to some extent.* All managers – and even students – bring their own particular experience to any set of strategic issues. It is very hard to analyse a situation as if from a clean sheet of paper. You should distrust claims to complete objectivity. Ask yourself where people are coming from.

- *Watch out for undue conservatism.* Experience is likely to lead to routinised responses, even to new problems. Tried-and-tested solutions become too legitimate; managers become powerful because of successes experienced in the past. 'Path dependency' and 'lock-in' are enduring risks (Chapter 6). Organisations can end up like old-fashioned generals, always fighting the last war.

- *Change is hard.* Because of conservatism, strategic change is liable to require long and difficult processes of persuasion (see Chapter 15). Continuity is often the default option. Relying on the 'objective analysis' in the business case for change will rarely win over hearts as well as minds.

On the other hand, the experience lens has some positive practical advice:

- *Analysis can cost more than it's worth.* Because good information is hard and expensive to get, and because analysis can consume too much time, sometimes it is sensible simply to cut short information search and analysis. Depending on the availability of information and the ability to analyse it, beyond a certain point it might be sensible just to drop the analysis.

- *Experience may provide the best guide.* If analysis is not going to produce good answers, then relying on the rules-of-thumb ('heuristics') and instincts of experienced managers may be at least as effective. Sometimes a quick response that is half right is better than an analytical response that is only slightly better but much slower.

- *Challenge the consensus.* While established rules-of-thumb can be effective, sometimes it is necessary to challenge the consensus in an organisation. As in Chapter 16, 'groupthink' is a risk. The need to challenge existing approaches is often the motivation for bringing in new leaders from outside the organisation in order to manage strategic change (Chapter 15).

Strategy as variety

The extent to which the design and experience lenses help explain innovation is rather limited. The variety lens, on the other hand, emphasises innovation and change. However, as indicated in Figure C.iii, the variety lens puts low value on rational analysis and tends to give little weight to what is simply legitimate in an organisation. Viewed through the variety lens, strategies are seen as emerging from the different ideas that bubble up from the variety in and around organisations.

The variety lens builds on two theoretical perspectives from the natural sciences, both emphasising spontaneity. First there is *evolutionary theory,* in which natural phenomena evolve through a Darwinian process of Variety, Selection and Retention.[5] Various genetic mutations emerge as more or less random experiments; some variations are selected for success by their environments; and these successful variations may be retained over the long term because of continuing good environmental fit. Second, there is *complexity theory*, where phenomena are characterised by complex, dynamic sets of interactions, so that small events can have surprisingly large effects.[6] An example is the famous butterfly effect, where the flap of a butterfly's wings in Brazil triggers a series of escalating knock-on effects that eventually cause a tornado in far-way Texas. In both evolutionary and complexity theories, variety in the form of many small experiments or interactions can lead to large and enduring outcomes. These outcomes are generated spontaneously, with very little top-down direction.

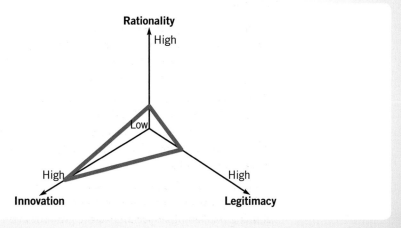

Figure C.iii Variety lens

Moving from nature to strategy, the variety lens de-emphasises the deliberate decision-making of the design lens. Likewise, the emphasis on spontaneity contrasts with the conservatism of the experience lens. For human organisations, the three elements of evolutionary theory work as follows:

- *Variety*. Organisations and their environments offer a rich 'ecology' for the generation of different ideas and initiatives. There are many kinds of people and many kinds of circumstance. Sales people working closely with customers may be able to sense new opportunities at least as well as top managers at headquarters. Since people interact with their environment throughout the organisation, new ideas often come from low down in the hierarchy, not just from the top.[7] Complexity theorist Bill McKelvey refers to this as the 'distributed intelligence' of an organisation.[8] Variety can even come from apparent mistakes, just as genetic mutations come from imperfect genes. A famous example is Post-it notes, which originated from an 'imperfect' glue being applied to paper, but resulted in a semi-adhesive for which the researcher saw market potential.

- *Selection*. In nature, selection is 'blind', determined by environmental fit rather than deliberate intervention. In organisations, selection can be nearly as blind, with strategies selected more according to how they well they match prevailing cultures or standard decision rules, rather than by objective analysis and evaluation. In this view, there is an 'internal ecology' within organisations, with ideas and initiatives winning out against competing ideas and initiatives according to their internal fit.[9] A good idea may fail simply because it does not meet existing selection rules, regardless of its overall merits: for example, a company may apply standard return on capital criteria that are outdated on the basis of the current real cost of capital (see Chapter 12 on strategy evaluation). On the other hand, as in complexity theory, ideas can gain rapid momentum as they attract 'positive feedback': the support of one important set of actors can attract the support of another, and the support of that set of actors attracts the support of still others, and so on in an escalating process. Thus selection mechanisms can be self-reinforcing, speeding the passage of both good and bad ideas.

- *Retention*. As well as processes of selection, there are processes of retention. Retention refers to the preservation and reproduction over time of selected variations.[10] Retention may happen as particular policies or preferences become embedded in the organisation. Retention may be achieved by instituting formal procedures: for example, job descriptions, accounting and control systems, management information systems, training and organisation structure. Often it is done through more informal processes of routinisation, in which simple repetition of certain routine behaviours leads to the eventual imprinting of such routines in the culture and capabilities of the organisation.

Implications

A key insight from the variety lens is that managers need to be wary of assuming that they can wholly control the generation and adoption of new ideas. However, there are a number of things managers can do to foster initiatives and prevent the undue suppression of good ideas. At the same time, the variety lens points both managers and students to distinctive sources of innovation in organisations. We highlight three key implications:

- *Allow for emergence*. Rather than being deliberately designed, strategies often emerge from the bottom and the periphery of organisations, accumulating coherence over time. As in Chapter 1, Henry Mintzberg's definition of strategy as an emergent 'pattern' rather than an explicit statement is widely relevant. Managers and students should not necessarily trust in the stated strategic vision and mission (Chapter 1), but rather look to what is actually happening, especially on the ground. The future of an organisation may well be emerging from somewhere far beyond headquarters' formal initiatives. Indeed, in many industries, large firms frequently watch the interesting experiments and initiatives of small independent firms, and then buy them up.[11]

- *Encourage interaction, experiment and change.* From a variety lens point of view, organisations can be too stable and ordered. To generate variety, managers should promote potentially disruptive interactions across internal and external organisational boundaries: cross-departmental initiatives are important internally and communication with customers, suppliers, partners and innovators should be extensive externally. Alphabet (formerly Google) encourages experiments by giving staff 20 per cent of their time to pursue their own projects. Complexity theorists prescribe regular change in order to stay at the dynamic 'edge of chaos', the delicate balancing point where organisations neither settle down into excessive stability nor topple over into destructive chaos.[12]

- *Attend to key rules.* If strategies tend to get adopted according to their fit with established organisational cultures or investment criteria, then managers need to attend at least as much to setting the context for strategy as to individual strategic decisions. As above, managers should create a context conducive to interaction, experiment and change. But they should particularly attend to the key selection and retention rules by which strategies are allowed to emerge. Drawing on complexity theory, Kathy Eisenhardt encourages the design of 'simple rules', a few clear guidelines for strategy selection and retention.[13] For example, the movie studio Miramax only selects movies that revolve round a central human condition (e.g. love), feature an appealing but flawed central character, and have a clear storyline. The Danish hearing aid company Oticon does not retain projects where any key team member chooses to switch from that project to another.

Strategy as discourse

In many ways, management is about discourse. Managers spend 75 per cent of their time communicating: for example, gathering information, persuading others or following up decisions.[14] In particular, strategy has a high discursive component, involving both talk and text. Strategy is debated in meetings, written as formal plans, explained in annual reports and media releases, presented on PowerPoints, and communicated to employees.[15] The discourse lens recognises this discursive component as central to strategy. Here, as indicated in Figure C.iv, the legitimacy of discourse is particularly important. The importance of legitimacy, however, can work against both objective rationality and organisational innovation.

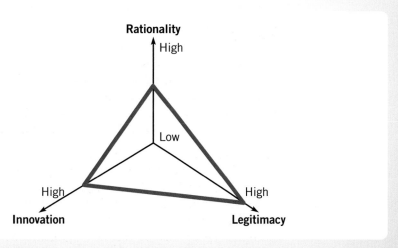

Figure C.iv Discourse lens

An important influence on the discourse lens is the work of the French philosopher Michel Foucault. Foucault stresses the subtle effects that language can have on understanding, power and personal identities. For example, he shows how changing scientific discourses in the seventeenth and eighteenth centuries redefined insanity as treatable illness rather than natural foolishness.[16] The insane now had a new identity, medically ill, and became subject to a new power, the medical doctors with the task of curing them. In a similar way, the 'financialisation' discourse emerging in the 1990s and early 2000s sought to redefine the purpose of the firm as solely about shareholder value, enhancing the power of investors to insist on short-term financial results rather than long-term strategic investments.[17] Those taking a discourse lens are therefore sensitive to how strategy discourse can shape understanding, change personal identities and disseminate power.

These three effects of strategy discourse are explored as follows:

- *Shaping understanding.* The language of strategy has characteristics that make it convincing to others.[18] Its concepts and jargon have high legitimacy in many organisations. Here the discourse lens reveals the design lens in another light. The legitimacy of strategy discourse gives the analytic apparatus of the design lens a persuasiveness that often goes beyond the technical effectiveness of the analysis itself. Drawing on established techniques such as the Porter Five Forces (Chapter 3) or fashionable concepts such as Blue Ocean strategy (Chapter 3) can add to the authority of strategic recommendations. The ability to write inspiring vision and mission statements (Chapter 1) can help motivate a whole organisation. The justification of strategic change by the radical rhetoric of hypercompetition (Chapter 3) or disruptive innovation (Chapter 10) may give legitimacy to radical actions that might otherwise be rejected as excessive. In other words, managers draw on the rhetoric of strategy and the apparent 'rightness' of strategy concepts to convince others they should comply.

- *Defining identities.* How managers talk about strategy also positions them in relation to others, either by their own deliberate choice or as a result of how they are perceived.[19] Discourse therefore influences the identity and legitimacy of managers as 'strategists'. The ability to use the rational analytical language of the design lens helps define managers as legitimate participants in the strategy process. Of course, sometimes other kinds of discursive identity may be appropriate. For example, in some contexts the language of the heroic leader (Chapter 15) or the innovative entrepreneur (Chapter 10) might offer more support for the decision-maker's identity than simple rational analysis. Whatever the precise identity, the assumptions built into strategy discourse are liable to affect behaviour. For example, lower-level managers and professionals who internalise the strategy discourse of competitiveness and performance as part of their identities come to prioritise those values in their everyday work, subordinating to some degree the administrative or professional values (such as equity or care) that might otherwise be important in their roles.

- *Instrument of power.* Here strategy discourse is linked to power and control.[20] By understanding the concepts of strategy, or being seen to do so, top managers or strategy specialists are positioned as having the knowledge about how to deal with the really difficult problems the organisation faces. The possession of such knowledge gives them power over others who do not have it. Design lens discourse, with its commitment to demanding forms of technical analysis, can be particularly elitist and exclusive. Thus mastering the discursive language of the design lens offers a political advantage as well as an analytical one. At the same time, the internalisation of strategy discourse by employees renders them more compliant to the strategy: they see pursuing the strategy as a natural part of their role. In this sense, discourse is associated with power when it attracts followers and is self-reproducing and self-reinforcing. Insofar as strategy discourse serves the interests of the powerful, it may suppress innovation and change and distort objective rational analysis from the point of view of the organisation as a whole.

Implications

The discourse lens suggests the importance of the appearance, as well as the reality, of rational argument. Through the discourse lens, strategies need to be legitimate, not simply correct. Strategy discourse, moreover, helps define legitimate participants in strategic decision-making and gives power to the decisions that are ultimately made. The fundamental lesson for managers and students is that the language of strategy matters.

The implications of the discourse lens have both instrumental and critical aspects:

- *Use strategy discourse skilfully*. The right discourse can add legitimacy to particular strategies or individuals in an organisation.[21] This discourse needs to match particular contexts and circumstances. Justifying a strategy to a potential investor may call for a logical, highly quantitative financial case; explaining the same strategy to employees may involve emphasising implications for job security and career growth. For some organisations, the analytic discourse of the design lens will be a legitimate mode of justification; in other organisations, appeal to technical or professional values may be more effective. The instrumental value of the discourse lens lies in this: using the right language matters both for justifying and imposing strategies and for participating in strategy discussions in the first place.

- *Treat strategy discourse sceptically*. Just as strategy discourse can be used instrumentally, so should managers and students be ready to take a critical perspective towards such discourse. Are concepts and frameworks being used as a smokescreen for some particular individuals or groups to advance their sectional power and interests, as for example 'financialisation' discourse did for investors? Are strengths and weaknesses, threats and opportunities (Chapter 4) being mystified or exaggerated? Are the grandiose ambitions of vision and mission statements just empty rhetoric (Chapter 1)? Seeing strategy as discourse can prompt the healthy questioning of concepts, ideas and rhetorics that might otherwise be taken for granted. The discourse lens encourages managers and students to see through the surface language of strategy to uncover the deeper interests and motives behind it. Adopters of the discourse lens are naturally sceptical.

Conclusion

The core assumptions and the key implications of the four lenses of design, experience, variety and discourse are summarised in Table C.i. They are not offered here as an exhaustive list, but to crystalise the distinctive perspectives of each lens. Indeed, this Commentary as a whole is merely an introduction and you may usefully explore each of the lenses further yourself. After all, each of the lenses presented here actually includes several perspectives themselves. For example, the variety lens builds on both evolutionary theory and complexity theory, each of which offers distinctive points of their own. So, within these lenses there are finer-grained insights to discover. The references at the end of this Commentary should help with deeper exploration of the lenses. In addition, there are whole books written that provide multiple perspectives on strategy, from the four different ones that Richard Whittington offers, to the ten of Henry Mintzberg and his co-authors, or even the 13 'images' provided in the collection by Stephen Cummings and David Wilson.[22]

However, the overarching message that comes from all four lenses is this: in considering a topic like strategy, it is useful to take a critical approach. Being critical involves recognising that one lens is probably not enough, and that every lens has its own value and its own limitations. You should not necessarily be satisfied with just the rational analysis of the design lens. Use the experience lens to consider sources of unconscious bias; take a variety lens approach to be sensitive to spontaneous initiatives from the bottom or periphery; stay sceptical by

Table C.i A summary of the strategy lenses

	Strategy as:			
	Design	**Experience**	**Variety**	**Discourse**
Strategy develops through . . .	A logical process of analysis and evaluation	People's experience, assumptions and taken-for-granted ways of doing things	Ideas bubbling up from the variety of people in and around organisations	Managers seeking influence, power and legitimacy through the language they use
Assumptions about organisations	Mechanistic, hierarchical, rational systems	Cultures based on experience, legitimacy and past success	Complex, diverse and spontaneous systems	Arenas of power and influence shaped by discourse
Role of top management	Strategic decision-makers	Enactors of their experience	Creators of context	Manipulators of language
Key implications	Undertake careful and thorough analysis of strategic issues	Recognise that people's experience is central but also needs challenging	Be sensitive to ideas from the bottom, the periphery and even outside the organisation	See through strategy language to uncover hidden assumptions and interests

interpreting strategy talk through the discourse lens. It is because different perspectives are important that we shall return to the four lenses in the Commentaries at the ends of Parts II and III of this book. Throughout your course, we encourage you to approach the topics of strategy with eyes open to different points of view. To get into the habit, you might now want to consider the short Nokia case through the four strategy lenses.

REFERENCES

1. For a good discussion of the meaning of critical thinking, see S. Michailova and A. Wright, 'Criticality in management learning and education: what it is and what it is not', *Academy of Management annual conference*, Vancouver, Canada, 2015.
2. A useful review of the principles of rational decision making can be found in J.G. March, *A Primer on Decision Making: How Decisions Happen*, Simon & Schuster, 1994, Chapter 1, pp. 1–35.
3. An introduction to Ansoff's thought is R. Moussetis, 'Ansoff revisited', *Journal of Management History*, vol. 17, no. 1 (2011), pp. 102–25. Porter discusses his thinking in N. Argyres and A. McGahan 'An interview with Michael Porter', *Academy of Management Executive*, vol. 16, no. 2 (2002), pp. 43–52.
4. An updated view of the *Behavioral Theory of the Firm* is in G. Gavetti, D. Levinthal and W. Ocasio, 'The behavioral theory of the firm: assessment and prospects', *Academy of Management Annals*, vol. 6, no. 1 (2012), pp. 1–40. A contrast with traditional economics is provided in M. Augier, 'The early evolution of the foundations for behavioral organization theory and strategy', *European Management Journal*, vol. 28 (2012), pp. 84–102.
5. W. P. Barnett and R. Burgelman, 'Evolutionary perspectives on strategy', *Strategic Management Journal*, vol. 17.S1 (2007), pp. 5–19.
6. S. Girod and R. Whittington, 'Change escalation process and complex adaptive systems: from incremental reconfigurations to discontinuous restructuring', *Organizational Science*, vol. 26, no. 5 (2015), pp. 1520–535.

7. See G. Johnson and A.S. Huff, 'Everyday innovation/everyday strategy', in G. Hamel, G.K. Prahalad, H. Thomas and D. O'Neal (eds), *Strategic Flexibility – Managing in a Turbulent Environment*, Wiley, 1998, pp. 13–27. Patrick Regner also shows how new strategic directions can grow from the periphery of organisations in the face of opposition from the centre; see 'Strategy creation in the periphery: inductive versus deductive strategy making', *Journal of Management Studies*, vol. 40, no. 1 (2003), pp. 57–82.

8. Bill McKelvey, a complexity theorist, argues that the variety within this distributed intelligence is increased because individual managers seek to become better informed about their environment: see B. McKelvey, 'Simple rules for improving corporate IQ: basic lessons from complexity science', in P. Andriani and G. Passiante (eds), *Complexity, Theory and the Management of Networks*, Imperial College Press, 2004.

9. R. Burgelman and. A. Grove, 'Let chaos reign, then rein in chaos – repeatedly: managing strategic dynamics for corporate longevity', *Strategic Management Journal*, vol. 28, no. 10 (2007), pp. 965–79.

10. B. McKelvey and H. Aldrich, 'Populations, natural selection, and applied organizational science', *Administrative Science Quarterly*, vol. 28, no. 1 (1983), pp. 101–128.

11. P. Puranam, H. Singh and M. Zollo, 'Organizing for innovation: managing the coordination-autonomy dilemma in technology acquisitions', *Academy of Management Journal*, vol. 49, no. 2 (2006), pp. 263–80.

12. K.M. Eisenhardt and S. Brown, 'Competing on the edge: strategy as structured chaos', *Long Range Planning*, vol. 31, no. 5 (1998), pp. 786–89.

13. C.B. Bingham and K.M. Eisenhardt, 'Rational heuristics: the "simple rules" that strategists learn from process experience', *Strategic Management Journal*, vol. 32, no. 13 (2011), pp. 1437–64.

14. H. Mintzberg, *The Nature of Managerial Work*, Harper & Row, 1973.

15. See A. Spee and P. Jarzabkowski, 'Strategic planning as communicative process', *Organization Studies*, vol. 32, no. 9 (2011), pp. 1217–45. Also W. Küpers, S. Mantere and M. Statler, 'Strategy as storytelling: a phenomenological collaboration', *Journal of Management Inquiry*, vol. 22, no. 1 (2013), pp. 83–100.

16. M. Foucault, *Discipline and Punish*, Vintage, 1995.

17. P. Thompson and B. Harley, 'Beneath the radar? A critical realist analysis of "the knowledge economy" and "shareholder value" as competing discourses', *Organization Studies*, vol. 33, no. 10 (2012), pp. 1363–81.

18. D. Barry and M. Elmes, 'Strategy retold: toward a narrative view of strategic discourse', *Academy of Management Review*, vol. 22, no. 2 (1997), pp. 429–52.

19. S. Mantere and E. Vaara, 'On the problem of participation in strategy: a critical discursive perspective', *Organization Science*, vol. 19, no. 2 (2008), pp. 341–58.

20. C. Hardy and R. Thomas, 'Strategy, discourse and practice: the intensification of power', *Journal of Management Studies*, vol. 51, no. 2 (2014), pp. 320–48.

21. R. Whittington, B. Yakis-Douglas and K. Ahn, 'Cheap talk: strategy presentations as a form of Chief Executive Officer impression management', *Strategic Management Journal* (forthcoming).

22. R. Whittington, *What is Strategy – and Does it Matter?*, Thompson, 2000; H. Mintzberg, B. Ahlstrand and J. Lampel, *Strategy Safari*, Prentice Hall, 1998; S. Cummings and D. Wilson, *Images of Strategy*, Sage, 2003.

Nokia's evolving strategy through the lenses

Nokia, the Finnish telecommunications firm, has pursued a trajectory that, over time, has exemplified all four of the Strategy Lenses.

Nokia started out in 1865 as a Finnish paper pulp mill. The company only began to take its modern form in 1966 when it had merged with the Finnish Rubber Works and the Finnish Cable Company to form a conglomerate with businesses ranging from rubber boots to aluminium parts. The Finnish Cable Works had established a small electronics department in 1960 in one corner of its main factory. This electronics department in turn spawned several businesses, including a mobile phone unit launched in 1979 through a joint venture with another Finnish company, Salora.

During the 1980s, Nokia became committed to an active diversification strategy, especially internationally. Businesses were acquired in the television and computer industries, and Salora itself was taken over in 1984. By 1987, an internal strategic planning document identified over 30 strategic business units in a Boston Consulting Group portfolio matrix (see Chapter 8), with mobile phones labelled one of several 'star' businesses ripe for investment.

But Nokia then hit a very rough patch. Its chairman and CEO committed suicide in 1988, and many of its industrial markets were hit hard by the collapse of the then Soviet Union. There was a period of losses and top management turmoil, from which finally emerged a new CEO, Jorma Ollila. Ollila had only arrived at Nokia in 1985, after an early career in the American investment bank Citibank. Since 1990, he had been head of the mobile phones business, then accounting for only ten per cent of Nokia's total sales.

On appointment as CEO, Ollila had promised continuity. In fact, the company rapidly focused on mobile phones. By 1996, mobile phones accounted for 60 per cent of Nokia sales and two years later Nokia became the world's largest mobile phone company. Other businesses were divested, so that soon the only other substantial business was Nokia telecommunications networks and infrastructure business, merged into a joint venture with Siemens in 2007.

Nokia's phone business flourished for more than a decade, until two cataclysmic events: first, Apple's launch of the iPhone in 2007 and then the 2009 launch of Google's Android operating system supported by companies such as HTC and Samsung. At the same time,

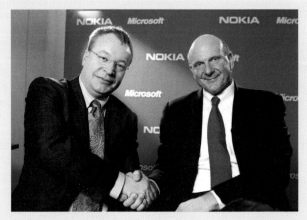

Stephen Elop and Steve Ballmer
Source: Simon Dawson/Bloomberg via Getty Images.

Chinese manufacturers began to attack Nokia's position in low-cost phones, especially in developing markets. In 2010, Nokia responded to the growing pressure by appointing its first non-Finnish CEO, the Canadian Stephen Elop.

Elop's previous company had been Microsoft, another company struggling in the phone market, though he himself had been responsible for Microsoft's Office products business. The new CEO launched a wide-ranging strategic review: 'The very first day I began, I sent out an email to all of the employees and I asked them: what do you think I need to change? What do you think I need not or should not change? What are you afraid I'm going to miss?' A key issue that he and his management team struggled with during the first year was whether Nokia should continue with its own operating system. Operating systems are highly expensive to develop and sustain and need to be attractive to external software developers in order to secure a competitive range of apps. Within a few months, Elop and his team had decided to abandon Nokia's own operating system. There were two alternative operating systems available: Google's or Microsoft's. Elop inclined towards Microsoft. His reasoning was that Microsoft was the weaker of the two, and therefore needed Nokia more than Google did. Nokia also feared being just another Android phone manufacturer competing on the same basis as HTC or Samsung.

In February 2011, Elop released what would become his famous 'burning platform' memo to all employees. Nokia was compared to a man on a burning oil platform, who could only survive by leaping into the sea. Nokia had been too slow, and must now make a dramatic move. Elop told his employees: 'We poured gasoline on our own burning platform. I believe we have lacked accountability and leadership to align and direct the company through these disruptive times. We had a series of misses. We haven't been delivering innovation fast enough. We're not collaborating internally. Nokia, our platform is burning.' Several days later, he announced to the world that he was abandoning Nokia's own operating systems in favour of Microsoft's, sealed by a public handshake with his old boss, Steve Ballmer, CEO of Microsoft. A senior Google executive commented on the Nokia–Microsoft alliance: 'two turkeys do not make an eagle'.

Nokia's first phones with the new operating system were not an immediate success and Nokia's losses deepened. By spring 2012, Stephen Elop was describing Nokia in terms of a famous Finnish long-distance runner, Lasse Virén, who had tripped during a race in 1972 but still won in the end: 'like Virén we are off the grass, on the track and running again.' But Nokia soon ran out of breath. In the autumn of 2013, it was announced that Nokia would be selling its mobile phone business to Microsoft, and that Stephen Elop would be returning to his old company.

Key sources: J. Aspara, J.A. Lamberg, A. Laukia and H. Tikkanen, 'Strategic management of business model transformation: lessons from Nokia', *Management Decision*, vol. 49, no. 4 (2011), pp. 622–647; *Financial Times*, 11 April 2011, 3 May 2012 and 3 September 2013; *Engadget*, 2 August 2011. T. Laamanen, J.-A. Lamberg and E. Vaara, 'Explanations of success and failure in management learning: what can be learnt from Nokia's rise and fall?', *Academy of Management Learning and Education*, vol. 15, no. 1 (2016), pp. 2–25.

Questions

1 How could you use the design lens, the experience lens and the variety lens to account for the development of the mobile phone business within Nokia?

2 How could you use the design lens and the experience lens to explain Stephen Elop's adoption of the Microsoft operating system?

3 Comment on Stephen Elop's changing language from a discourse lens perspective.

PART II
STRATEGIC CHOICES

This part explains strategic choices in terms of:

- How organisations relate to competitors in terms of their competitive business strategies.

- How broad and diverse organisations should be in terms of their corporate portfolios.

- How far organisations should extend themselves internationally.

- How organisations are created and innovate.

- How organisations pursue strategies through organic development, acquisitions or strategic alliances.

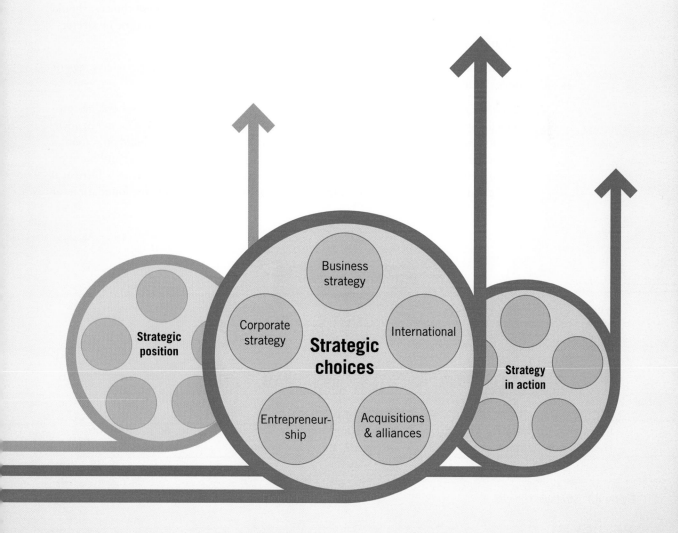

This part is concerned with the strategic choices, or options, potentially available to an organisation for responding to the positioning issues discussed in Part I of the book. There are three overarching choices to be made as shown in Figure II.1. These are:

- Choices as to *how an organisation at a business level positions itself in relation to competitors*. This is a matter of deciding how to compete in a market. For example, should the business compete on the basis of cost or differentiation? Or is competitive advantage possible through being more flexible and fleet-of-foot than competitors? Or is a more cooperative approach to competitors appropriate? These business strategy questions together with business model considerations are addressed in Chapter 7.

- Choices of *strategic direction*: in other words, which products, industries and markets to pursue. Should the organisation be very focused on just a few products and markets? Or should it be much broader in scope, perhaps very diversified in terms of both products (or services) and markets? Should it create new products or should it enter new territories? These questions relate to corporate strategy, addressed in Chapter 8, international strategy in Chapter 9 and innovation and entrepreneurial strategy, as discussed in Chapter 10.

- Choices about *methods by which to pursue strategies*. For any of these choices, should they be pursued independently by organic development, by acquisitions or by strategic alliances with other organisations? This is the theme of Chapter 11.

The discussion in these chapters provides frameworks and rationales for a wide range of strategic choices. But some words of warning are important here:

- *Strategic choices relate back to analysis of strategic position.* Part I of the book has provided ways in which strategists can understand the macro-environment (Chapter 2), identify forces at work in the industry and sector (Chapter 3), identify and build on resources and capabilities (Chapter 4), meet stakeholder expectations (Chapter 5) and build on the benefits, as well as be aware of the constraints, of their organisation's historical and cultural context (Chapter 6). Exploring these issues will provide the foundation for

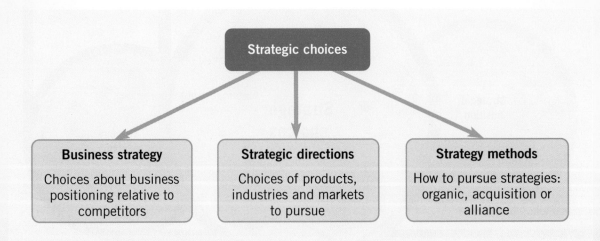

Figure II.1 Strategic choices

considering strategic options. However, the *Exploring Strategy* Framework (Figure 1.3) implies that issues of position, choice and action overlap. Thus working through the choices of Part II is also likely to feed back into the initial analysis of strategic position. Similarly, the potential of some strategic choices will only be revealed in action, the theme of Part III.

- *Key strategic issues.* Choices have to be made in the context of an organisation's strategic position, of course. But here it is important that the analysis of strategic position distinguishes the *key strategic issues* from all the many positioning issues that are likely to arise. Analysis needs to avoid producing a very long list of observations without any clarity of what such key issues are. There is no single 'strategy tool' for this. Identifying key strategic issues is a matter of informed judgement and, because managers usually work in groups, of debate. The analytic tools provided can help, but are not a substitute for judgement.

7

BUSINESS STRATEGY AND MODELS

Business strategy

Corporate strategy · **Strategic choices** · International

Entrepreneur-ship · Acquisitions & alliances

Learning outcomes

After reading this chapter you should be able to:

- Assess business strategy in terms of the generic strategies of *cost leadership*, *differentiation*, *focus* and *hybrid* strategy.
- Identify business strategies suited to *hypercompetitive* conditions.
- Assess the benefits of *cooperation* in business strategy.
- Apply principles of *game theory* to business strategy.
- Identify and apply *business model* components: *value creation*, *configuration* and *capture*.

Key terms

business model p.229

competitive advantage p.210

competitive strategy p.210

cost-leadership strategy p.211

differentiation strategy p.215

focus strategy p.216

hybrid strategies p.219

game theory p.226

strategic business unit p.209

7.1 INTRODUCTION

This chapter is about two fundamental strategic choices: what business strategy and what business model should a company, business unit or other organisation adopt in its market? Business strategy questions are fundamental both to stand-alone small businesses and to all the many business units that typically make up large diversified organisations. Business strategies are about how to compete in a marketplace so that a restaurant for instance has to decide a range of issues such as menus, décor and prices in the light of local competition from other restaurants. Similarly, large diversified corporations typically include many decentralised 'strategic business units' in different product or market areas each with its own business strategy depending on the specific needs of their served market. A **strategic business unit (SBU) supplies goods or services for a distinct domain of activity** (sometimes these SBUs are called 'divisions' or 'profit centres'). For example, Nestlé's ice-cream SBU has to decide how to compete against smaller and local artisanal companies with new imaginative flavours and different customer focus, distribution channels and pricing. These kinds of business strategy issues are distinct from the question as to whether Nestlé should own an ice-cream business in the first place: this is a matter of corporate strategy, the subject of Chapter 8.

Another important choice is to identify the relationship between the value created for customers and other participants, the organisational activities that create this value and how the organisation and other stakeholders can capture value from this – a *business model*. For instance, Amazon was a pioneer with its e-commerce business model that contrasted with bricks-and-mortar retailers. It involved a different customer offering, arrangement of its activities and structure of revenues and costs compared to the traditional retailing model. Over time, however, business models get established and many other retailers also entered into e-commerce. This shows that organisations need to consider what business model to build on; established or new ones or both.

Business strategy and business models are not just relevant to the private business sector. Charities and public-sector organisations also compete and have business models. Thus charities compete between each other for support from donors. Public-sector organisations also need to be 'competitive' against comparable organisations in order to satisfy their stakeholders, secure their funding and protect themselves from alternative suppliers from the private sector. Schools compete in terms of examination results, while hospitals compete in terms of waiting times, treatment survival rates and so on. Likewise, these sectors need to consider what value is created for whom and how organisational activities contribute to this in a business model. Although some of the detailed implications may vary between sectors, wherever comparison is possible with other similar organisations, basic principles of business strategy and models are likely to be relevant. Very few organisations can afford to be demonstrably inferior to peers. Most have to make choices on key competitive variables such as costs, prices and quality.

Figure 7.1 shows the main three themes around business strategy that provide the structure for the rest of the chapter:

- *Generic competitive strategies,* including cost leadership, differentiation, focus and hybrid strategies.
- *Interactive strategies,* building on the notion of generic strategies to consider interaction with competitors, especially in *hypercompetitive environments,* and including both *cooperative strategies* and *game theory.*
- *Business models,* including the three basic components of *value creation, value configuration* and *value capture.*

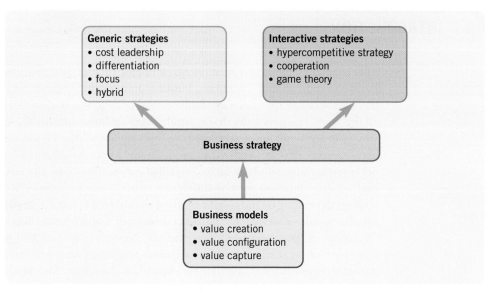

Figure 7.1 Business strategy

7.2 GENERIC COMPETITIVE STRATEGIES

This section introduces the competitive element of business strategy, with cooperation addressed particularly in Section 7.4. **Competitive strategy is concerned with how a company, business unit or organisation achieves competitive advantage in its domain of activity.** Competitive strategy therefore involves issues such as costs, product and service features and branding. In turn, **competitive advantage is about how a company, business unit or organisation creates value for its users which is both greater than the costs of supplying them and superior to that of rivals.** Competitive advantages should underpin competitive strategies. There are two important features of competitive advantage. To be *competitive* at all, an organisation must ensure that customers see sufficient value that they are prepared to pay more than the costs of supply. To have an *advantage,* the organisation must be able to create greater value than competitors. In the absence of a competitive advantage, an organisation's competitive strategy is always vulnerable to competitors with better products or offering lower prices.

Michael Porter[1] argues that there are two fundamental means of achieving competitive advantage. An organisation can have structurally lower *costs* than its competitors. Or it can have products or services that are *differentiated* from competitors' products or services in ways that are so valued by customers that it can charge higher prices that cover the additional costs of the differentiation. In defining competitive strategies, Porter adds a further dimension based on the *scope* of customers that the business chooses to serve. Businesses can choose to focus on narrow customer segments, for example a particular demographic group such as the youth market. Alternatively, they can adopt a broad scope, targeting customers across a range of characteristics such as age, wealth or geography.

Porter's distinctions between cost, differentiation and scope define a set of 'generic' strategies: in other words, basic types of strategy that hold across many kinds of business situations. These three generic strategies are illustrated in Figure 7.2. In the top left-hand corner is a strategy of *cost leadership,* as exemplified in the British food and grocery market by retailers such as Lidl. Waitrose, in contrast, pursues a strategy of *differentiation*, offering

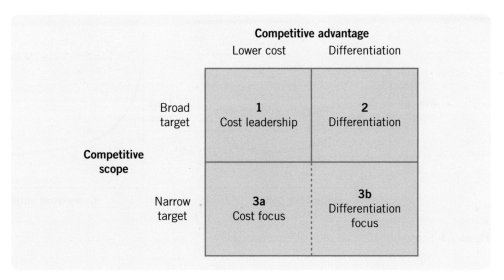

Figure 7.2 Three generic strategies

a range of quality, fresh and environmentally-friendly products focused on the upper market with relatively higher prices. Porter distinguishes between cost focus and differentiation focus, but for him narrow scope is such a distinctive fundamental principle that these two are merely variations on the same basic theme of narrowness. For example, delicatessens target a relatively narrow group of higher-end customers with their high food quality and provenance. They thus often achieve a higher price for their distinctive products through their *differentiation focus* strategy. On the other hand, the product lines of the major supermarkets, like Tesco, target shoppers who are simply looking for good-value standard products for their families, a *cost focus* strategy. The rest of this section discusses these three generic strategies in more detail.

7.2.1 Cost-leadership strategy

Cost-leadership strategy involves becoming the lowest-cost organisation in a domain of activity. For example, Ryanair pursues a relentless low-cost strategy in the European airline industry. The airline saves costs in virtually every aspect of its operation from purchasing a single type of aircraft (without reclining seats) to selling tickets primarily online (over 90 per cent of sales) to low employee costs (second lowest in Europe). There are four key *cost drivers* that can help deliver cost leadership, as follows:

● *Input costs* are often very important, for example labour or raw materials. Many companies seek competitive advantage through locating their labour-intensive operations in countries with low labour costs. Examples might be service call centres in India or manufacturing in South East Asia and China. Location close to raw material sources can also be advantageous, as for example the Brazilian steel producer CSN which benefits from its own local iron-ore facilities.

● *Economies of scale* refer to how increasing scale usually reduces the average costs of operation over a particular time period, perhaps a month or a year. Economies of scale are important wherever there are high fixed costs. Fixed costs are those costs necessary for a

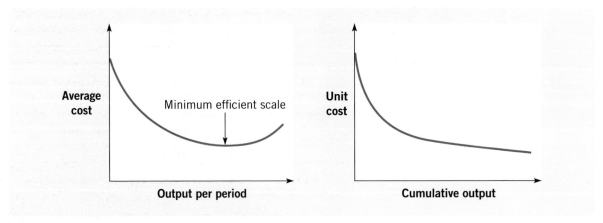

Figure 7.3 Economies of scale and the experience curve

level of output: for example, a pharmaceutical manufacturer typically needs to do extensive R&D before it produces a single pill. Economies of scale come from spreading these fixed costs over high levels of output: the average cost due to an expensive R&D project halves when output increases from one million to two million units. Economies of scale in purchasing can also reduce input costs. The large airlines, for example, are able to negotiate steep discounts from aircraft manufacturers. For the cost-leader, it is important to reach the output level equivalent to the *minimum efficient scale*. Note, though, that *diseconomies of scale* are possible. Large volumes of output that require special overtime payments to workers or involve the neglect of equipment maintenance can soon become very expensive. As to the left in Figure 7.3, therefore, the economies of scale curve is typically somewhat U-shaped, with the average cost per unit actually increasing beyond a certain point.

- *Experience*[2] can be a key source of cost efficiency. The *experience curve* implies that the cumulative experience gained by an organisation with each unit of output leads to reductions in unit costs (see Figure 7.3 to the right). For example, for many electronic components per unit costs can drop as much as 95 per cent every time the accumulated volume doubles. There is no time limit: simply the more experience an organisation has in an activity, the more efficient it gets at doing it. The efficiencies are basically of two sorts. First, there are gains in labour productivity as staff simply learn to do things more cheaply over time (this is the specific *learning curve* effect). Second, costs are saved through more efficient designs or equipment as experience shows what works best. The experience curve has three important implications for business strategy. First, entry timing into a market is important: early entrants into a market will have experience that late entrants do not yet have and so will gain a cost advantage. Second, it is important to gain and hold market share, as companies with higher market share have more 'cumulative experience' simply because of their greater volumes. Finally, although the gains from experience are typically greatest at the start, as indicated by the steep initial curve to the right in Figure 7.3, improvements normally continue over time. Opportunities for cost reduction are theoretically endless. Figure 7.3 compares the experience curve (to the right) and economies of scale (to the left) in order to underline the contrast here. Unlike scale, where diseconomies appear beyond a certain point, the experience curve implies at worst a flattening of the rate of cost reduction. However, completely new production technologies can potentially introduce even steeper experience effects and further improved cost savings.

- *Product/process design* also influences cost. Efficiency can be 'designed in' at the outset. For example, engineers can choose to build a product from cheap standard components rather than expensive specialised components. Organisations can choose to interact with customers exclusively through cheap web-based methods, rather than via telephone or stores. Organisations can also tailor their offerings in order to meet the most important customer needs, saving money by ignoring others. In designing a product or service, it is important to recognise *whole-life costs*: in other words, the costs to the customer not just of purchase but of subsequent use and maintenance. In the photocopier market, for example, Canon eroded Xerox's advantage (which was built on service and a support network) by designing a copier that needed far less servicing.

Porter underlines two tough requirements for cost-based strategies. First of all, the principle of competitive advantage indicates that a business's cost structure needs to be *lowest* cost (i.e. lower than all competitors'). Having the second-lowest cost structure implies a competitive disadvantage against somebody. Competitors with higher costs than the cost-leader are always at risk of being undercut on price, especially in market downturns. For businesses competing on a cost basis, cost leadership is always more secure than being second or third in terms of costs. The US financial investments company Vanguard is a good example of this as discussed in Illustration 7.1 (see also Illustration 6.3).

The second requirement is that low cost should not be pursued in total disregard for quality. To sell its products or services, the cost-leader has to be able to meet market standards. For example, low-cost Chinese car producers exporting to Western markets need to offer not only cars that are cheap, but cars that meet acceptable norms in terms of style, safety, service network, reliability, resale value and other important characteristics. Cost-leaders have two options here:

- *Parity* (in other words, equivalence) with competitors in product or service features valued by customers. Parity allows the cost-leader to charge the same prices as the average competitor in the marketplace, while translating its cost advantage wholly into extra profit (as in the second column of Figure 7.4). The Brazilian steel producer CSN, with its cheap iron-ore sources, is able to charge the average price for its steel, and take the cost difference in greater profit.

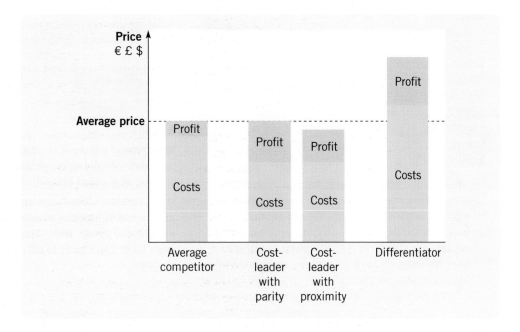

Figure 7.4 Costs, prices and profits for generic strategies

ILLUSTRATION 7.1   Vanguard's low-cost strategy comes to Europe

The US company Vanguard pioneered a distinct low-cost strategy in the mutual fund industry and is now exporting it worldwide.

Mutual funds are managed by investment companies that raise money from multiple customers and invest the money in a group of assets (stocks, bonds, money market instruments, etc.). Each customer, often as part of a retirement plan, then owns shares that represent a portion of the holdings of the fund. They are charged an annual fee or 'expense ratio' that covers investment advisory fees, administrative costs, distribution fees and other operating expenses. The traditional way of competing in the industry was by actively managed and differentiated investments that tried to generate as high returns as possible and thus being able to charge higher fees. The emphasis was on the business performance end of the business by offering differentiated funds with higher returns. Vanguard instead focused on the cost end of the business and offered customers considerably lower annual fees and costs. Most comparisons showed that Vanguard's fees or expense ratios were 65–80 per cent less than the industry average depending on investment asset. The company also launched the industry's first index mutual fund that passively followed a stock market index without ambitions to generate a better performance than the market, but which outperformed many actively managed funds.

Vanguard has started to export its low-cost focus to Europe, and their non-US assets have more than doubled in the last six years, reaching over $90bn (€68bn, £54bn) in Europe. 'Lowering the cost of investing is in our DNA,' blogged Tom Rampulla, former head of Vanguard Europe. Their low-cost strategy involved several components. First, unlike competitors it did not need to make a profit. Tim Buckley, chief investment officer explained:

'We are not a listed company. We're a mutual company. We're owned by our clients. So when we make a profit, we have two choices. We can roll that profit back into the business or we can pay it out to our owners, our clients, in the form of lower expenses. Over the years we have lowered expenses and that has attracted more clients.'[1]

Second, Vanguard distributed their funds directly to customers and did not need to pay commissions of around eight per cent to brokers. Third, the company had internalised investment advisory functions of the funds at cost instead of using external investment advisors that would charge a premium. Fourth, Vanguard relied on a no-nonsense thrifty organisational culture where managers were incentivised to control cost and no one, not even senior executives, flew first class. Fifth, the company had only a few retail centres and spent less on advertising than anyone else in the industry. Last, but not least, as one of the largest asset managers globally they gained large economies of scale.

By 2015, the next step for Vanguard was to do to the financial advisory services industry what they had done to the mutual fund industry. Based on webcam chats and other cost reductions, the aim was to offer advisory services at a fraction of the cost of competitors. They would charge annually 0.3 per cent on assets compared to the industry average of one per cent, according to Vanguard CEO Bill McNabb:[2]

'Can we provide really super-high quality advice at a very low cost and do that in a very large way, and change the market? I think we can. We continue to think of our primary mission to reduce the complexity and cost of investing across the board.'

Sources: (1) D. Oakley, *Financial Times*, 4 March 2015. (2) S. Foley, *Financial Times*, 8 December 2014.

Questions

1 What type of competitive strategy, low-cost, differentiation, focus or hybrid, would you suggest as a way of competing with Vanguard?

2 Using webcam chats is one approach to lower costs in financial advisory services as indicated above. What other ways could there be to lower costs to support a low-cost strategy?

- *Proximity* (closeness) to competitors in terms of features. Where a competitor is sufficiently close to competitors in terms of product or service features, customers may only require small cuts in prices to compensate for the slightly lower quality. As in the third column in Figure 7.4, the proximate cost-leader still earns better profits than the average competitor because its lower price eats up only a part of its cost advantage. This proximate cost-leadership strategy might be the option chosen initially by Chinese car manufacturers in export markets, for example.

7.2.2 Differentiation strategy

The principal alternative to cost leadership is differentiation.[3] **Differentiation strategy involves uniqueness along some dimension that is sufficiently valued by customers to allow a price premium.** For example, German manufacturer Miele pursues a differentiation strategy in the domestic appliance industry. Their European manufactured, high-quality and durable dishwashers, washing machines and stoves are targeted towards higher income households at a price premium. Relevant points of differentiation vary between markets. Within each market too, businesses may differentiate along different dimensions. Thus in clothing retail, competitors may differentiate by store size, locations or fashion. In cars, competitors may differentiate by safety, style or fuel efficiency. Where there are many alternative dimensions that are valued by customers, it is possible to have many different types of differentiation strategy in a market. Thus, even at the same top end of the car market, BMW and Mercedes differentiate in different ways, the first typically with a sportier image, the second with more conservative values. In brief, there are various aspects to consider in pursuing a differentiation strategy and below are three primary differentiation drivers to consider:

- *Product and service attributes*. Certain product attributes can provide *better or unique features* than comparable products or services for the customer. For example, the Dyson vacuum cleaner with its unique technology provides customers with a better suction performance compared to competitors. The possibilities of product differentiation are, however, virtually endless and only limited by the creativity of an organisation. They may include differences in colour, design, speed, style, taste, etc. For vacuum cleaners, other companies may, for example, differentiate themselves on the basis of user convenience or design rather than suction performance. Product innovation and introduction can also be a basis of differentiation. Apple has been able to charge considerable premiums by continuously launching novel products with superior technologies, design and consumer interfaces, including the iPod, iPhone and iPad.

  In building a basis for differentiation it is vital to identify clearly the customer on whose needs the differentiation is based. This is not always straightforward, as discussed in Section 3.4.2. For example, for a newspaper business, the customers could be readers (who pay a purchase price), advertisers (who pay for advertising), or both. Finding a distinctive means of prioritising customers can be a valuable source of differentiation. Considering competitors' offerings is also important when identifying a basis for differentiation and the strategy canvas provides one means of mapping various kinds of differentiation (see Section 3.4.3).

- *Customer relationships*. Besides more tangible differences in product and service characteristics, differentiation can rely on the relationship between the organisation providing the product and the customer. This often relates to how the product is perceived by the customer. The perceived value can increase through *customer services and responsiveness*. This can include distribution services, payment services or after-sales services among other things. For example, Zalando, Europe's leading online retailer for fashion and shoes, offers not only free shipping to the customer but free returns and a 'bill-me-later' service. Products can also be differentiated for the individual customer through *customisation*. This is the case for a variety of consumer goods from athletic shoes to cars, but also for business-to-business goods like enterprise software. For example, the German software company SAP not only sells its standardised software packages, but customises these to meet specific customer needs. Finally, *marketing and reputation,* including emotional and psychological aspects, that an organisation projects can be another basis for differentiation. Starbucks, for example, can charge a premium price for its coffee not only because of its product differences but also because of the ambiance and image that the company displays at its outlets. Building on brand image is common for products that otherwise are difficult to differentiate. This is a foundation for Coca Cola's differentiation strategy for example.

- *Complements.* Differentiation can also build on linkages to other products or services. The perceived value of some products can be significantly enhanced when consumed together with other product or service complements compared to consuming the product alone. This complementarity was discussed in Chapter 3 as these complements can be vital for the profit potential of an industry (see Section 3.2.6). Apple has created the complement services iTunes and App Store free of charge for the consumer, which differentiate its products (iPhone, iPad, etc.) with the possibility to charge a premium. Considering how customers benefit from consuming two products or services in tandem is thus another possible way to differentiate. More generally, this can be thought of as a way of bundling products and services together to increase the value for the customer.

There is an important condition for a successful differentiation strategy. Differentiation allows higher prices, but usually this comes at a cost. To create valuable differentiation typically involves additional investments, for example in R&D, branding or staff quality. The differentiator can expect that its costs will be higher than those of the average competitor. But, as in the fourth column of Figure 7.4, the differentiator needs to ensure that the additional costs of differentiation do not exceed the gains in price. It is easy to add on additional costs in ways that are not valued sufficiently by customers. The historic failures under British ownership of the luxury car companies Rolls-Royce and Bentley against top-end Mercedes cars are partly attributable to the expensive crafting of wood and leather interiors, the full cost of which even wealthy customers were not prepared to pay for. Just as cost-leaders should not neglect quality, so should differentiators attend closely to costs, especially in areas irrelevant to their sources of differentiation. Volvo's differentiation strategy in the Indian bus market in Illustration 7.2 also involved keeping an eye on costs besides differentiation.

7.2.3 Focus strategy

Porter distinguishes focus as the third generic strategy, based on competitive scope. A **focus strategy targets a narrow segment or domain of activity and tailors its products or services to the needs of that specific segment to the exclusion of others.** Focus strategies come in two variants, according to the underlying sources of competitive advantage, cost or differentiation. In air travel, Ryanair follows a *cost focus strategy*, targeting price-conscious travellers with no need for connecting flights. In the domestic detergent market, the Belgian company Ecover follows a *differentiation focus strategy*, gaining a price premium over rivals on account of its ecological cleaning products targeted at environmental conscious customers.

The focuser achieves competitive advantage by dedicating itself to serving its target segments better than others that are trying to cover a wider range of segments. Serving a broad

ILLUSTRATION 7.2 Volvo's different Indian buses

Volvo has a strategy to sell buses at nearly four times the prevailing market price.

The Indian bus market has long been dominated by two subsidiaries of major Indian conglomerates: Tata Motors and Ashok Leyland. They made simple coaches on a design that had hardly changed for decades. On top of a basic truck chassis, the two companies bolted a rudimentary coach body. Engines were a meagre 110–120 horsepower, and roared heartily as they hauled their loads up the steep roads. Mounted at the front, the heat from the over-strained engines would pervade the whole bus. Air conditioning was a matter of open windows, through which the dust and noise of the Indian roads would pour. Suspension was old-fashioned, guaranteeing a shaky ride on pot-holed roads. Bags were typically slung on the top of the bus, where they were easily soiled and at high risk of theft. But at least the buses were cheap, selling to local bus companies at around Rs 1.2m (€15,000, £12,000, $19,500).

In 1997, Swedish bus company Volvo entered, with buses priced at Rs 4m, nearly four times as much as local products. Akash Passey, Volvo's first Indian employee, commissioned a consultancy company to evaluate prospects. The consultancy company recommended that Volvo should not even try. Passey told the *Financial Times*: 'My response was simple – I took the report and went to the nearest dustbin and threw it in.' Passey entered the market in 2001 with the high-priced luxury buses.

Passey used the time to develop a distinctive strategy. His product had superior features. Volvo's standard engines were 240–250 hp and mounted at the back, ensuring a faster and quieter ride. Air conditioning was standard of course. The positioning of the engine and the specific bus design of the chassis meant a roomier interior, plus storage for bags internally. But Passey realised this would not be enough. He commented to the *Financial Times*: 'You had to do a lot of things to break the way business is done normally.'

Volvo offered post-sale maintenance services, increasing life expectancy of buses from three to ten years, and allowing bus operating companies to dispense with their own expensive maintenance workshops. Free training was given to drivers, so they drove more safely and took more care of their buses. The company advertised the benefits of the buses direct to customers in cinemas, rather than simply promoting them to the bus operators. Faster, smoother and more reliable travel allowed the bus operators to increase their ticket prices for the Volvo buses by 35 per cent.

Business people and the middle classes were delighted with the new Volvo services. Speedier, more comfortable journeys allowed them to arrive fresh for meetings and potentially to save the costs of overnight stays. Tata and Ashok Leyland both now produce their own luxury buses, with Mercedes and Isuzu following Volvo into the market. Nonetheless, the phrase 'taking a Volvo' has become synonymous with choosing a luxury bus service in India, rather as 'hoover' came to refer to any kind of vacuum cleaner.

A new state-of-the-art bus factory was opened in Bangalore 2008 and after further investments in 2012 it doubled the annual capacity to 1,500 buses per year. As Volvo's most efficient bus factory worldwide it started to export buses to Europe three years later. In 2016, Volvo continued its distinctive strategy and became the first bus company in India to manufacture and sell hybrid buses running on an electric motor and battery as well as diesel.

Sources: Adapted from J. Leahy, 'Volvo takes a lead in India', *Financial Times*, 31 August 2009; M. Lalatendu, 'Hybrid Volvo bus for Navi Mumbai', *The Hindu*, 15 February 2016.

Questions

1 Rank the elements of Passey's strategy for Volvo in order of importance. Could any have been dispensed with?

2 How sustainable is Volvo's luxury bus strategy?

range of segments can bring disadvantages in terms of coordination, compromise or inflexibility. Focus strategies are, therefore, able to seek out the weak spots of broad cost-leaders and differentiators:

- *Cost focusers* identify areas where broader cost-based strategies fail because of the added costs of trying to satisfy a wide range of needs. For instance, in the UK food retail market, Iceland Foods has a cost-focused strategy concentrated on frozen and chilled foods, reducing costs against discount food retailers with a wider product range and more diverse suppliers which have all the complexity of fresh foods and groceries as well as their own frozen and chilled food ranges.

- *Differentiation focusers* look for specific needs that broader differentiators do not serve so well. Focus on one particular need helps to build specialist knowledge and technology, increases commitment to service and can improve brand recognition and customer loyalty. For example, ARM Holdings dominates the world market for mobile phone chips, despite being only a fraction of the size of the leading microprocessor manufacturers, AMD and Intel, which also make chips for a wide range of computers.

Successful focus strategies depend on at least one of three key factors:

- *Distinct segment needs.* Focus strategies depend on the distinctiveness of segment needs. If segment distinctiveness erodes, it becomes harder to defend the segment against broader competitors. For example, Tesla Motors currently targets a narrow segment with its expensive premium electric vehicles. However, if the boundaries become blurred between Tesla's focus on electric cars used by affluent environmentally conscious consumers and electric cars used by general consumers it could become easier for competitors to also attack this distinctive niche.

- *Distinct segment value chains.* Focus strategies are strengthened if they have distinctive value chains that will be difficult or costly for rivals to construct. If the production processes and distribution channels are very similar, it is easy for a broad-based differentiator to push a specialised product through its own standardised value chain at a lower cost than a rival focuser. In detergents, Procter & Gamble cannot easily respond to the Belgian ecologically friendly cleaning products company Ecover because achieving the same environmental soundness would involve transforming its purchasing and production processes.

- *Viable segment economics.* Segments can easily become too small to serve economically as demand or supply conditions change. For example, changing economies of scale and greater competition have eliminated the traditional town-centre department stores from many smaller cities, with their wider ranges of different kinds of goods from hardware to clothing.

7.2.4 Hybrid strategy

Porter warned that managers face a crucial choice between the generic strategies of cost leadership, differentiation and focus. According to him, it would be unwise to blur this choice. As earlier, the lowest-cost competitor can always undercut the second lowest-cost competitor. For a company seeking advantage through low costs, therefore, it makes no sense to add extra costs by half-hearted efforts at differentiation. For a differentiator, it is self-defeating to make economies that jeopardise the basis for differentiation. For a focuser, it is dangerous to move outside the original specialised segment, because products or services tailored to one set of customers are likely to have inappropriate costs or features for the new target customers. Porter's argument was that managers are generally best to choose which generic strategy they are pursuing and then sticking to it. Otherwise there would be a danger of being *stuck in the middle,* doing no strategy well.

However, Porter's early argument for pure generic strategies was controversial and it has later been acknowledged that a hybrid type of strategy is possible under certain circumstances. A **hybrid strategy combines different generic strategies.** For example, American Southwest Airlines pursues a low-cost strategy with their budget and no-frills offering. However, its brand also signals differentiation based on convenience including frequent departures and friendly service. Another example in the airline industry is Singapore Airlines with a differentiation strategy based on passenger comfort, attentive personal service and amenities. This is, however, combined with a lowest-cost position among its key competitors based on low maintenance costs, standardisation and outsourcing of various activities. Some companies start out with one strategy that is later combined with another. McDonald's first followed a product differentiation strategy, but later its fast-food leader position allowed the company to emphasise scale and low costs as well.

As Porter himself acknowledges there may also be particular circumstances in which the strategies can be combined:[4]

- *Organisational separation.* It is possible for a company to create separate strategic business units (SBUs), each pursuing different generic strategies and with different cost structures. The challenge, however, is to prevent negative spill-overs from one SBU to another. For example, a company mostly pursuing differentiated strategies is liable to have high head office costs that the low-cost SBUs will also have to bear. On the other hand, a cheap cost-leader might damage the brand value of a sister SBU seeking differentiation. Because of these kinds of trade-offs, it can be very difficult to pursue different generic strategies within a single set of related businesses. Despite the success of Singapore Airlines, Europe's leading airline Lufthansa has struggled to combine its low-cost subsidiaries, Eurowings, with its traditional higher-service core business.

- *Technological or managerial innovation.* Sometimes technological innovations allow radical improvements in both cost and quality. Internet retailing reduces the costs of bookselling, at the same time as increasing differentiation by greater product range and, through online book reviews, better advice. Managerial innovations are capable of such simultaneous improvements too. The Japanese car manufacturers' introduction of Total Quality Management led to reductions in production line mistakes that both cut manufacturing costs and improved car reliability, a point of successful differentiation.

- *Competitive failures.* Where competitors are also stuck in the middle, there is less competitive pressure to remove competitive disadvantage. Equally, where a company dominates a particular market, competitive pressures for consistency with a single competitive strategy are reduced.

Hybrid strategies are, however, complex and should be pursued with caution. They require careful considerations as the fundamental trade-off between low cost and differentiation has to be resolved. Porter's warning about the danger of being stuck in the middle provides a useful discipline for managers. It is very easy for them to make incremental decisions that compromise the basic generic strategy. As profits accumulate, the successful cost-leader will be tempted to stop scrimping and saving. In hard times, a differentiator might easily cut back the R&D or advertising investments essential to its long-term differentiation advantage. Consistency with generic strategy provides a valuable check for managerial decision-making. The next section provides a helpful tool in calibrating generic and hybrid strategies.

7.2.5 The Strategy Clock

The Strategy Clock provides another way of approaching generic strategies (see Figure 7.5), one which gives more scope for *hybrid* strategies.[5] The Strategy Clock has two distinctive features. First, it is focused on prices to customers rather than costs to the organisation: because prices are more visible than costs, the Strategy Clock can be easier to use in comparing competitors. Second, the circular design of the clock allows for more continuous choices than Michael Porter's sharp contrast between cost leadership and differentiation: there is a full range of incremental adjustments that can be made between the 7 o'clock position at the bottom of the low-price strategy and the 2 o'clock position at the bottom of the differentiation strategy. Organisations may travel around the clock, as they adjust their pricing and benefits over time.

The Strategy Clock identifies three zones of feasible strategies, and one zone likely to lead to ultimate failure:

- *Differentiation (zone 1).* This zone contains a range of feasible strategies for building on high perceptions of product or service benefits among customers. Close to the 12 o'clock position is a strategy of *differentiation without price premium.* Differentiation without a price premium combines high-perceived benefits and moderate prices, typically used to gain market share. If high benefits also entail relatively high costs, this moderate pricing strategy would only be sustainable in the short term. Once increased market share has been achieved, it might be logical to move to *differentiation with price premium* closer to a 1 or 2 o'clock position. Movement all the way towards the 2 o'clock position is likely to involve a focus strategy. Such a *focused differentiation* strategy targets a niche where the higher prices and reduced benefits are sustainable, for instance because of a lack of competition in a particular geographical area.

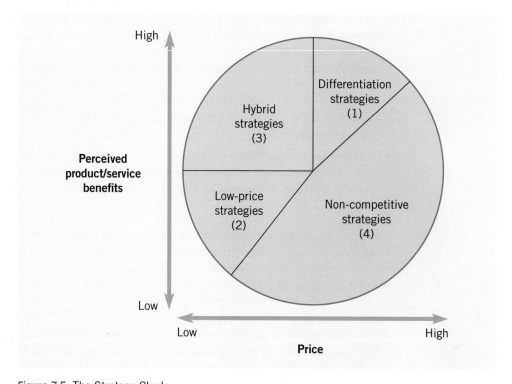

Figure 7.5 The Strategy Clock

Source: Adapted from D. Faulkner and C. Bowman, *The Essence of Competitive Strategy,* Prentice Hall, 1995.

- *Low-price (zone 2).* This zone allows for different combinations of low prices and low perceived value. Close to the 9 o'clock position, a standard *low-price* strategy would gain market share by combining low prices with reasonable value (at parity with competitors). To be sustainable, this strategy needs to be underpinned by some cost advantage, such as economies of scale gained through increased market share. Without such a cost advantage, cuts in benefits or increases in prices become necessary eventually. A variation on the standard low-price strategy is the *no-frills* strategy, close to the 7 o'clock position. No-frills strategies involve both low benefits and low prices, similar to low-cost airlines such as Ryanair.

- *Hybrid strategy (zone 3).* A distinctive feature of the Strategy Clock is the space it allows between low-price and differentiation strategies.[6] Hybrid strategies involve both lower prices than differentiation strategies and higher benefits than low-price strategies. Hybrid strategies are often used to make aggressive bids for increased market share. They can also be an effective way of entering a new market, for instance overseas. Even in the case of innovations with high benefits, it can make sense to price low initially in order to gain experience curve efficiencies or lock-in through network effects (see Section 3.2.6). Some companies sustain hybrid strategies over long periods of time: for example, furniture store IKEA, which uses scale advantages to combine relatively low prices with differentiated Swedish design (see end of chapter case).

- *Non-competitive strategies (zone 4).* The final set of strategies occupies a zone of unfeasible economics, with low benefits and high prices. Unless businesses have exceptional strategic lock-in, customers will quickly reject these combinations. Typically these strategies lead to failure.

The Strategy Clock's focus on price, and its scope for incremental adjustments in strategy, provides a more dynamic view on strategy than Porter's generic strategies. Instead of organisations being fairly fixed in terms of either a cost or a differentiation strategy, they can move around the clock. For example, an organisation might start with a *low-price* strategy to gain market share, later shift to a higher-priced *differentiation with premium* strategy in order to reap profits, and then move back to a *hybrid* strategy in order to defend itself from new entrants. However, Porter's generic strategies do remind managers that costs are critical. Unless an organisation has some secure cost advantage (such as economies of scale), a hybrid strategy of high-perceived benefits and low prices is unlikely to be sustainable for long.

7.3 INTERACTIVE STRATEGIES

Generic strategies need to be chosen, and adjusted, in the light of competitors' strategies. If everybody else is chasing after cost leadership, then a differentiation strategy might be sensible. Thus business strategy choices *interact* with those of competitors. This section starts by considering business strategy in the light of competitor moves, especially in hypercompetition. It then addresses the option of cooperation and closes with game theory, which helps managers choose between competition and more cooperative strategies.

7.3.1 Interactive price and quality strategies

Richard D'Aveni depicts competitor interactions in terms of movements against the variables of price (the vertical axis) and perceived quality (the horizontal axis), similar to the Strategy Clock: see Figure 7.6.[7] Although D'Aveni applies his analysis to the very fast-moving environments he terms 'hypercompetitive' (see Section 3.3.1), similar reasoning applies wherever competitors' moves are interdependent.

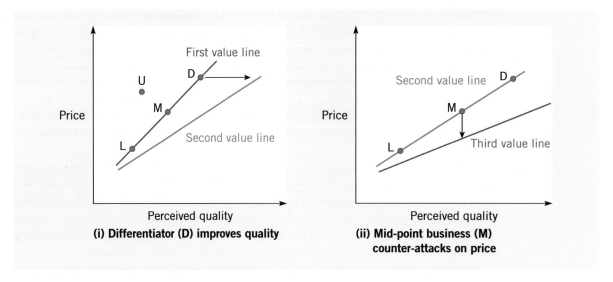

Figure 7.6 Interactive price and quality strategies

Note: axes are not necessarily to linear scales.

Source: Adapted with the permission of The Free Press, a Division of Simon & Schuster, Inc., from *Hypercompetition: Managing the Dynamics of Strategic Maneuvering* by Richard D'Aveni with Robert Gunther. Copyright © 1994 by Richard D'Aveni. All rights reserved.

Figure 7.6 shows different organisations competing by emphasising either low prices or high quality or some mixture of the two. Graph (i) starts with a 'first value line', describing various trade-offs in terms of price and perceived quality that are acceptable to customers. The cost-leading firm (here L) offers relatively poor perceived quality, but customers accept this because of the lower price. While the relative positions on the graph should not be taken literally, in the car market this cost-leading position might describe some of Hyundai's products. The differentiator (D) has a higher price, but much better quality. This might be Mercedes. In between, there are a range of perfectly acceptable combinations, with the mid-point firm (M) offering a combination of reasonable prices and reasonable quality. This might be Ford. M's strategy is on the first value line and therefore entirely viable at this stage. On the other hand, firm U is uncompetitive, falling behind the value line. Its price is higher than M's, and its quality is worse. U's predicament is typical of the business that is 'stuck in the middle', in Porter's terms. U no longer offers acceptable value and must quickly move back onto the value line or fail.

In any market, competitors and their moves or counter-moves can be plotted against these two axes of price and perceived value. For example, in graph (i) of Figure 7.6, the differentiator (D) makes an aggressive move by substantially improving its perceived quality while holding its prices. This improvement in quality shifts customer expectations of quality right across the market. These changed expectations are reflected by the new, second value line (in green). With the second value line, even the cost-leader (L) may have to make some improvement to quality, or accept a small price cut. But the greatest threat is for the mid-point competitor, M. To catch up with the second value line, M must respond either by making a substantial improvement in quality while holding prices, or by slashing prices, or by some combination of the two.

However, mid-point competitor M also has the option of an aggressive counter-attack. Given the necessary capabilities, M might choose to push the value line still further outwards, wrong-footing differentiator D by creating a third value line that is even more demanding in terms of the price-perceived quality trade-off. The starting point in graph (ii) of Figure 7.6 is all three competitors L, M and D successfully reaching the second value line (uncompetitive U has disappeared). However, M's next move is to go beyond the second value line by making radical cuts in price while sustaining its new level of perceived quality. Again, customer expectations are changed and a third value line (in red) is established. Now it is differentiator D that is at most risk of being left behind, and it faces hard choices about how to respond in terms of price and quality.

Plotting moves and counter-moves in these terms underlines the dynamic and interactive nature of business strategy. Economically viable positions along the value line are always in danger of being superseded as competitors move either downwards in terms of price or outwards in terms of perceived quality. The generic strategies of cost leadership and differentiation should not be seen as static positions, but as dynamic trajectories along the axes of price and quality.

A more detailed example of the sequence of decisions and possible options involved in competitive interaction is given in Figure 7.7.[8] This illustrates the situation of a business facing a low-price competitor, for example a high-cost Western manufacturer facing possible attack by cheap imports from Asia. There are three key decisions:

- *Threat assessment.* The first decision point is whether the threat is substantial or not. If there is a threat, the high-cost organisation should not automatically respond to a low-price competitor by trying to match prices: it is likely to lose a price war with its existing cost structure. The high-cost organisation needs a more sophisticated response.

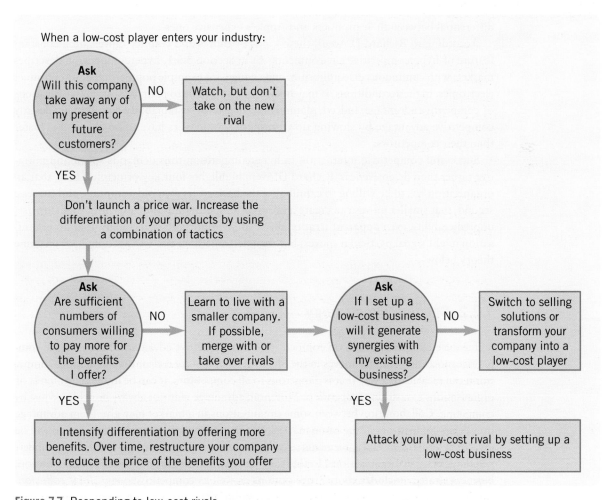

Figure 7.7 Responding to low-cost rivals

Source: Reprinted by permission of *Harvard Business Review.* Exhibit from 'A framework for responding to low-cost rivals' by N. Kumar, December 2006. Copyright © 2006 by the Harvard Business School Publishing Corporation. All rights reserved.

- *Differentiation response.* If there are enough consumers prepared to pay for them, the high-cost organisation can seek out new points of differentiation. For example, a Western manufacturer may exploit its closeness to local markets by improving service levels. At the same time, unnecessary costs should be stripped out. If increased differentiation is not possible, then more radical cost solutions should be sought.

- *Cost response.* Merger with other high-cost organisations may help reduce costs and match prices through economies of scale. If a low-cost business is synergistic with (in other words, has benefits for) the existing business, this can be an effective platform for an aggressive cost-based counter-attack. If there is neither scope for further differentiation or synergy between the existing business and a possible new low-cost business, then the existing business must sooner or later be abandoned. For a Western manufacturer, one option might be to outsource all production to low-cost operators, simply applying its design and branding expertise. Another option would be to abandon manufacturing in favour of becoming a 'solutions provider', aggregating manufactured components from different suppliers and adding value through whole-systems design, consultancy or service.

Equivalent decisions would have to be made, of course, by a low-price competitor facing a differentiator. When Apple entered the phone market with its expensive iPhone, established handset manufacturers had first to decide whether Apple was a serious long-term threat, and then choose how far they should either match the iPhone's features or increase the price differential between their products and Apple's expensive ones.

According to Richard D'Aveni, these kinds of moves and counter-moves are a constant feature of hypercompetitive environments. As in Section 3.3.1, hypercompetition describes markets with continuous disequilibrium and change, for example popular music or consumer electronics. In these conditions, it may no longer be possible to plan for sustainable positions of competitive advantage. Indeed, planning for long-term sustainability may actually destroy competitive advantage by slowing down response. Managers have to be able to act faster than their competitors.

Successful competitive interaction in hypercompetition thus demands speed and initiative rather than defensiveness. Richard D'Aveni highlights four key principles: first, that an organisation has to be willing to cannibalise the basis of its own old advantage and success; second, that smaller moves can create a series of temporary advantages; third, that surprise, unpredictability, even apparent irrationality can be important; and, finally, that an organisation might signal particular moves, but then do something else (see Section 7.3.3 on game theory below).

7.3.2 Cooperative strategy

So far the emphasis has been on competition and competitive advantage. However, the competitive moves and counter-moves in the previous section make it clear that sometimes competition can escalate in a way that is dangerous to all competitors. It can be in the self-interest of organisations to restrain competition. Moreover, advantage may not always be achieved just by competing. Collaboration between some organisations in a market may give them advantage over other competitors in the same market, or potential new entrants. Collaboration can be explicit in terms of formal agreements to cooperate, or tacit in terms of informal mutual understandings between organisations. In short, while organisations need to avoid illegal collusion, business strategy includes cooperative options as well as competitive ones.[9] *Tacit collusion*, where companies agree on a certain strategy without any explicit communication between them, is not uncommon; for example agreeing to avoid price competition. It is facilitated by industries or sectors with few competitors, homogenous products and high entry barriers.

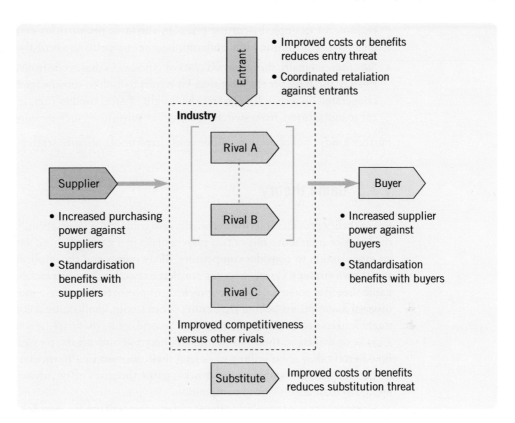

Figure 7.8 Cooperating with rivals

Source: Adapted from *Competitive Strategy: Techniques for Analysing Industries and Competitors*, The Free Press by Michael E. Porter. Copyright © 1980, 1998 by The Free Press. All rights reserved.

Figure 7.8 illustrates various kinds of benefits from cooperation between firms in terms of Michael Porter's five forces of buyers, suppliers, rivals, entrants and substitutes (see Section 3.2). Key benefits of cooperation are as follows:

- *Suppliers.* In Figure 7.8, cooperation between rivals A and B in an industry will increase their purchasing power against suppliers. Sometimes this increased cooperation is used simply to squeeze supplier prices. However, cooperation between rivals A and B may enable them to standardise requirements, allowing suppliers to make cost reductions to all parties' benefit. For example, if two car manufacturers agreed on common component specifications, their suppliers could gain economies through production of the standardised part on a greater scale (this kind of *complementarity* is discussed in Section 3.2.6).

- *Buyers.* Conversely, cooperation between rivals A and B will increase their power as suppliers vis-à-vis buyers. It will be harder for buyers to shop around. Such *collusion* between rivals can help maintain or raise prices, though it may well attract penalties from competition regulators. On the other hand, buyers may benefit if their inputs are standardised, again enabling reductions in costs that all can share. For example, if food manufacturers supplying a retailer agree on common pallet sizes for deliveries, the retailer can manage its warehouses much more efficiently.

- *Rivals.* If cooperative rivals A and B are getting benefits with regard to both buyers and suppliers, other competitors without such agreements – in Figure 7.8, rival C – will be at a competitive disadvantage. Rival C will be in danger of being squeezed out of the industry.

- *Entrants.* Similarly, potential entrants will likely lack the advantages of the combined rivals A and B. Moreover, A and B can coordinate their retaliation strategies against any new entrant, for example by cutting prices by the same proportions in order to protect their own relative positions while undermining the competitiveness of the new entrant.

- *Substitutes*. Finally, the improved costs or efficiencies that come from cooperation between rivals A and B reduce the incentives for buyers to look to substitutes. Steel companies have cooperated on research to reduce the weight of steel used in cars, in order to discourage car manufacturers from switching to lighter substitutes such as aluminium or plastics.

Further kinds of cooperation will be considered under alliance strategy in Section 11.4.

7.3.3 Game theory

Game theory provides important insights into competitor interaction.[10] The 'game' refers to the kinds of interactive moves two players make in a game of chess. **Game theory encourages an organisation to consider competitors' likely moves and the implications of these moves for its own strategy.** Game theorists are alert to two kinds of interaction in particular. First, game theorists consider how a *competitor response* to a strategic move might change the original assumptions behind that move: for example, challenging a competitor in one area might lead to a counter-attack in another. Second, game theorists are sensitive to the *strategic signals,* or messages, their moves might convey to competitors, for example with regard to how fiercely they seem willing to defend their position in a particular market. In the light of possible attacks and counter-attacks, game theorists often advise a more cooperative approach than head-to-head competition.

Game theory is particularly relevant where competitors are *interdependent*. Interdependence exists where the outcome of choices made by one competitor is dependent on the choices made by other competitors. For example, the success of price cuts by a retailer depends on the responses of its rivals: if rivals do not match the price cuts, then the price-cutter gains market share; but if rivals follow the price cuts, nobody gains market share and all players suffer from the lower prices. Anticipating competitor counter-moves is clearly vital to deciding whether to go forward with the price-cutting strategy.

There are two important guiding principles that arise from interdependence:

- *Get in the mind of the competitors*. Strategists need to put themselves in the position of competitors, take a view about what competitors are likely to do and choose their own strategy in this light. They need to understand their competitors' game-plan to plan their own.

- *Think forwards and reason backwards*. Strategists should choose their competitive moves on the basis of understanding the likely responses of competitors. Think forwards to what competitors might do in the future, and then reason backwards to what would be sensible to do in the light of this now.

Game theory insights can be gained through two methods. On the one hand, *war gaming* is helpful where it is important to get stakeholders to deeply appreciate each other's positions through actually playing out their respective roles, and where there is uncertainty about the range of outcomes. Illustration 7.3 provides a public policy example of war gaming and using game theory principles when changing and improving public-sector services. On the other hand, *mathematical game theory* is useful where there is a clear but limited range of outcomes and the values associated with each outcome can be reasonably quantified.

One of the most famous illustrations of mathematical game theory is the *prisoner's dilemma*. Game theorists identify many situations where organisations' strategic decisions are similar to the dilemma of two prisoners accused of serial crimes together and being interrogated in separate prison cells without the possibility of communicating with each other.

ILLUSTRATION 7.3   Game theory in practice in the public sector

Game theory and war gaming can provide insights when changing and improving public sector services.

Game theory has not become a common strategic tool. It has often been considered too theoretical and focused on single solutions to be able to cope with real-world messy managerial problems. However, it has been proposed that instead of using game theory to predict a single optimal solution it can be used to generally understand advantages and disadvantages with different strategic options.

When public-sector organisations try to change and improve public services they frequently need to partner with and interact with a variety of organisations. They need to collaborate with other public-sector organisations, with private companies and not-for-profit organisations. Success therefore depends not only on the public-sector organisation itself, but on several other partners. This requires an insight into partners' intentions and how they may behave. This is central to game theory – understanding what strategic options different players have, what their objectives are and how they will act under different circumstances.

The basic principles of game theory can thus be used to evaluate changes and improvements of public-sector services. The English National Health Service (NHS) has, for example, used war games to better prepare them for government reforms. War gaming began as a military preparation that places players in the positions of different actors (e.g. enemies or allies), and asks them to play out a sequence of moves and counter-moves as if they were the actors themselves. A basic principle underlying the game is that to know your enemy you must become your enemy in the play. Another consideration is that you need to test your own plan and strategy in confrontation with the (played) enemy.

In a war game for healthcare systems, teams are assigned to play the role of different stakeholders including payers, hospitals, physician groups, regulators and suppliers. In a first round the teams are then asked to respond to a given challenge. The actions each team can consider are stipulated by the game's rules, which are based on realistic rules of the health-care system. In subsequent rounds each team reacts to the moves the other teams have made. Through several rounds every team acts on its own strategies and reacts to the moves of other teams. The aim is not primarily to determine a winner, but to develop new insights. War games make participants think carefully about how they would act, react to and interact with others under specific conditions. In this way, participants gain a better understanding of other players' perspectives and possible actions. This helps them to anticipate how various actors will behave under different conditions. The participants also gain a better understanding of their own organisation's strengths and weaknesses in interactions with others.

The principles of game theory can thus be of more general assistance and Timothy Meaklim in the *Guardian* has suggested that public organisations and their leaders should:

1 Be knowledgeable about partners, their strategies, needs and decision-making
2 Be flexible adjusting their own strategies or objectives to meet the overall aim
3 Develop clear lines of partnership communication and decision-making
4 Share the power equally between parties
5 Get agreement on partnership operation and benefits
6 Consider own roles and motives for engaging with the partnership
7 Create partner trust.

Sources: Partly adapted from T. Meaklim, 'Game theory: what prisoners and stags can teach public leaders', *The Guardian*, 27 November 2013 and *International Journal of Leadership in Public Services*, 9(1/2), 2013, pp. 22–31; E. Bury, J. Horn and D. Meredith, 'How to use war games as a strategic tool in health care', *Health International*, 11, 2011, pp. 28–37.

Questions

1 Besides the public sector, can you think of other business situations where war games could be useful?

2 War games could possibly play a role when preparing for strategic change at a university. What stakeholders or players would be relevant and what would their interests be?

The prisoners have to decide on the relative merits of: (i) loyally supporting each other by refusing to divulge any information to their interrogators; and (ii) seeking an advantage by betraying the other. If both stay silent, they might get away with most of their crimes and only suffer some lesser punishment, perhaps for just one or two offences. The interrogators, though, will tempt each of them to divulge full information by offering them their freedom if only they betray their fellow criminal. However, if both betray, then the judge is unlikely to be grateful for the confessions, and will punish them for all their crimes. The dilemma for each of the prisoners is how much to trust in their mutual loyalty: if they both refuse to divulge, they can both get away with the lesser punishment; on the other hand, if one is sure that the other will not betray, it makes even more sense to betray the loyal one as that allows the betrayer to go totally free. The two prisoners are clearly interdependent. But because they cannot communicate, they each have to get in the mind of the other, think forwards to what they might do, and then reason backwards in order to decide what their own strategy should be – stay silent or betray.

The prisoner's dilemma has its equivalence in business where there are two major players competing head-to-head against each other in a situation of tight interdependence. This is the position of Airbus and Boeing in the aircraft business, Sony and Microsoft in the games market, or British Airways and Virgin in transatlantic travel. It would be relevant to the strategic decisions of two such interdependent companies in a range of situations: for example, if one company was thinking about making a major investment in an innovative new product that the other company could match. For two such competitors to communicate directly about their strategies in these situations would likely be judged illegal by the competition authorities. They therefore have to get into each other's minds, think forwards and reason backwards. How will the other company act or react and, in the light of that, what strategy is best?

The kind of situation two interdependent competitors could get into is represented in the prisoner's dilemma matrix of Figure 7.9. Suppose the two main aircraft manufacturers Airbus and Boeing were both under pricing pressure, perhaps because of falling demand. They each have to decide whether to announce radical price cuts or to hold their prices up. If both choose to hold their prices, neither gets an advantage over the other and they both get the returns represented in the top left-hand quadrant of Figure 7.9: for the sake of illustration, each might earn profits of €500m. However, if one competitor pursues the radical price cuts on its own while the other does not, the pattern of returns might be quite different: the radical price-cutter attracts a significantly larger share of airline customers and earns €700m profits through spreading fixed costs over greater sales, while the market-share-losing competitor earns only €100m (as represented in the top-right and bottom-left quadrants).

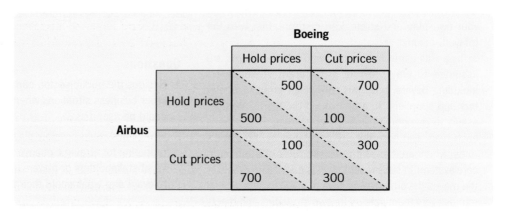

Figure 7.9 Prisoner's dilemma game in aircraft manufacture

This situation might tempt one of the competitors to choose radical price cuts for two reasons: first, there is the prospect of higher profits; but, second, there is the risk of the other competitor cutting prices while leaving it behind. The problem is that if each reason in the same way, the two competitors will *both* cut prices at once. They will thus set off a price war in which neither gains share and they both end up with the unsatisfactory return of just €300m (the bottom-right quadrant).

The dilemma in Figure 7.9 is awkward because cooperation is simultaneously attractive and difficult to achieve. The most attractive strategy for Airbus and Boeing jointly is for them both to hold their prices, yet in practice they are likely to cut prices because they must expect the other to do so anyway. A distinctive feature of game theory is that it frequently highlights the value of a more cooperative approach to competitor interaction, rather than aggressive competition. The cooperation need not be in the form of an explicit agreement: cooperation can be tacit, supported by the recognition of mutual self-interest in not attacking each other head-to-head. Game theory therefore encourages managers to consider how a 'game' can be transformed from lose–lose competition to win–win cooperation. There are various principles to consider here. If players know that their interaction will be repeated this can encourage cooperation. Signalling by responding quickly and aggressively and deterring unwanted strategic moves by competitors can also encourage cooperation and so can a strong commitment to a particular strategy.

7.4 BUSINESS MODELS

Business models have become increasingly popular as internet-based companies like Airbnb, Spotify and Uber have conquered the world with their new models. They are particularly useful when explaining more complex business interrelationships that generate value and profits for more parties than just a buyer and seller. Consequently, the business model concept is commonly discussed in relation to strategy today. Building on David Teece's work, this chapter carefully distinguishes business models from business strategy.[11] A **business model describes a value proposition for customers and other participants, an arrangement of activities that produces this value, and associated revenue and cost structures.**[12] When entrepreneurs in new start-ups have entered old industries with new business models in recent years they have frequently changed industry dynamics and competition in radical ways. The new models often involve more complex interrelationships than traditional models and create value for participants besides the customer and generate profits for more parties than the seller. This shows that both entrepreneurs and managers, whose organisations may be threatened by new start-ups, need to understand business models. Illustration 7.4 discusses how Uber's business model has revolutionised the taxi industry globally. The remainder of this section first discusses three fundamental elements of business models and then some typical business model patterns.

7.4.1 Value creation, configuration and capture

Business models describe business transactions and interrelationships between various parties and are best explained in terms of three interrelated components (see Figure 7.10).[13] The first emphasises *value creation*; a proposition that addresses a specific customer segment's needs and problems and those of other participants. The second component is the *value configuration* of the resources and activities that produce this value. The final *value capture* part explains revenue streams and cost structures that allow the organisation and other stakeholders to gain a share of the total value generated.[14]

ILLUSTRATION 7.4   Uber's ubiquitous business model

The on-demand transportation service that has revolutionised the taxi industry.

With a market value of $50bn (£30bn, €37.5bn) Uber has been predicted to become the world's dominant transportation company without owning a single vehicle. Since its start in San Francisco 2009, it has quickly expanded to over 60 countries and 340 cities worldwide. It now employs 4000, adds 50,000 new partner drivers a month and makes one million trips each day. The company is growing at exponential rates and has received $10bn of equity funding so far. Co-founder and CEO Travis Kalancik claims that they are doubling its size every six months.

Uber's smartphone app is at the centre of their business model. Customers download the app, create an account and put in their credit card information. By tapping the app they request a car and a notification is sent to the nearest driver who can accept or reject the ride and, if rejected, it is sent to another driver in the area. Customers can track the estimated time of arrival and the meter via the app. Payment is made to Uber via the app with a later payment to the driver. The customer gets an option to rate the driver and the driver also has the option to rate the customer.

Through the Uber app customers can search, book, pay and rate the taxi service. They are offered a convenient, reliable and fast taxi service either through luxury rides, priced less than conventional limousine services (Uber Black), or through regular rides priced less than normal taxi fares (UberPop or UberX). The value for drivers is an extra source of income and flexible working hours. The review and rating system is a key difference compared to regular taxis. Customers can avoid drivers with low ratings and drivers can avoid passengers with low ratings.

The basic resources of Uber include their technological platform and app, but they do not own any cars or employ any drivers. Drivers own the cars and are self-employed and apply to Uber to become a driver. Uber's activities are configured to match customers with a nearby driver and car. In addition to matchmaking, the platform and app includes pricing and payment, car tracking and review systems. Uber thus structures the value for both customers and drivers through the development of sophisticated software and algorithms that optimise matchmaking, pricing and reviews for different cities and local markets.

Uber captures their profit and value by typically taking a 20 per cent cut on all rides except for special promotions to customers and/or drivers and in areas where they face competition from similar services. Besides generating a margin, these revenues should cover their expenses to cover R&D, technology development, marketing, local infrastructure and own local employees in each city.

Even though the business model has been a success, there are several significant challenges. The UberPOP service has faced regulatory pushbacks in several European countries and even been forced to shut down in some markets. Uber is also facing an increasing number of competitors with similar business models; Lyft is a significant competitor in the USA and Didi Kuaidi is ahead of Uber in China. As CEO Travis Kalancik explains:

'We're profitable in the USA, but we're losing over $1 billion a year in China.'

Sources: M. Ahmed, 'Uber: Backseat driver', *Financial Times*, 16 September 2015; A. Damodaran, 'A disruptive cab ride to riches: The Uber payoff', *Forbes*, 6 October 2014; J. Narvey, 'Travis Kalanick speaks out: Uber's CEO on risk, regulation, and women in tech', *Betakit*, 16 February 2016.

Questions

1 In terms of Figure 7.10, what are Uber's value creation, value configuration and value capturing?

2 If you were the head of a traditional taxi company, how could you change your business model to compete with Uber?

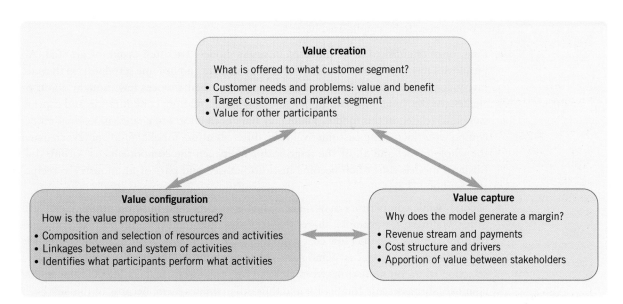

Figure 7.10 Business model components

The business model of the San Francisco-based accommodation broker Airbnb, for example, *creates value* for both the customers that rent the apartment, house or private room and for the hosts that offer their homes for rent. The Airbnb website conveniently provides a platform for exchange activities between the hosts and guests. These activities are *configured* via the web platform so that hosts list, describe and present pictures of their homes and customers are thus offered a wide selection of accommodation to choose from and rent. A review system of both accommodations and guests is available to build references and prevent deception. Finally, both hosts and Airbnb *capture value* from this business model. Hosts receive guest payments and Airbnb gets a 6–12 per cent commission fee on guest reservations, a three per cent to process the payment to the host and also guest credit card processing fees. This points managers and entrepreneurs to three basic and interdependent attributes of business models:

- *Value creation.* A key part of a business model describes what is offered and how value is thus created for the various parties involved: customers, partners and other participants. The main concern here is thus the targeted customer segment and how their needs are fulfilled and their problems solved, but also how to create value for any other parties involved.

- *Value configuration.* A second component explains how various interdependent resources and activities in the value chain underlie the value proposition, for example technology, equipment, facilities, brands, managerial processes, etc. (for a discussion of the value chain see Section 4.4.2). These factors are part of an activity system that not only explains what activities create value, but how they are linked and what participants perform them (for activity systems see Section 4.4.3). While this system is centred on the organisation it can also involve activities conducted by customers, partners, and other participants.[15]

- *Value capture.* A business model also describes the cost structure of resources and activities and the revenue stream from customers and any other parties. In addition, this component shows how the value created will be apportioned between the organisation and any other stakeholders involved. For a company, then, this last component also describes how profit is made while for non-for-profits and the public sector there are of course no expectations of financial gain.[16]

Two points need to be emphasised here:

- First, once established in an industry, business models are often taken for granted. All businesses rely on business models, but as they mature and become standardised they are rarely questioned. Until Airbnb and others started their services few thought about or challenged the 'hotel business model' and how value creation, configuration and capture were interrelated in this model. There may have been efforts to change individual model components, increasing customer value by differentiation, for example, but few changed the whole model and all of the relationships between the components as Airbnb did. Business models thus often become institutionalised and part of an industry's 'recipe' (see Section 6.3.2).

- Second, while competitors may share business models their business strategy can still differ. Walmart, for example, shares the same discount retailer model with several competitors, but has a distinct low cost strategy. Likewise, Airbnb in the example above have the same business model as Wimdu and other competitors. However, Airbnb's extensive selection of accommodations from close to one million listings in 34,000 cities in 200 countries surpasses any competitor and thus differentiates them. Because of this size both customers and hosts are likely to prefer Airbnb over competitors as guests are offered more accommodations and hosts more guests. In addition, the more customers that use their service the better it is for every customer in their network of guests and hosts and Airbnb can thus build on network effects (see Section 3.2.6 for network effects).

7.4.2 Business model patterns

Even though business model patterns often become established within industries over time, companies use them competitively. New entrants often use new business models to be able to compete successfully with established players. Dell, for example, entered the PC and laptop industry many years ago based on a different business model compared to the established one. Instead of going via the middlemen of retailers and wholesalers as HP, IBM and others did, they sold directly to customers. It is thus important for managers to understand what type of business model pattern their businesses built on and how it may differ from other competitors. It should be noted, however, that business model patterns are described at various levels of detail and sometimes only emphasise one or two business model components, such as value capturing.[17] There are many business models around, but three typical patterns include the following:

- *Razor and blade.* This is perhaps the most well-known business model pattern, but its primary focus is on the value capture component, which makes it more of a revenue model. It builds on Gillette's classic model of selling the razors at a very low price and the compatible replacement blades at a quite high price.[18] This model of selling two technically interlinked products separately is quite common. For example, mobile operators offering consumers a cheap or even a free mobile phone and then catching them through a two-year fee-based subscription plan. In other industries it is the services, maintenance and parts that are priced expensively while the basic product is sold at relatively low margins. This is, for example, the case for ink-jet printers; they are sold at relatively low prices, but manufacturers make their margins on selling expensive ink. It is also common in industrial goods with an emphasis on expensive services; for example, Rolls Royce and GE and others in the jet engine industry and Otis and Schindler and other players in the elevator industry.

- *Freemium.* This business model pattern name comes from combining 'free' and 'premium' and it primarily relates to online businesses. It refers to how a basic version of a service or product is offered for free so as to build a high volume of customers and eventually

THINKING DIFFERENTLY | Transient rather than sustainable advantage

Some question to what extent sustainable competitive advantage is possible at all in today's fast-changing world.

Section 7.4.1 indicated that in hypercompetitive environments it may not be possible to form business strategies that provide for sustainable competitive advantage. Some argue that the era of sustainability in competitive advantage is over altogether as most industries today are too turbulent. It is claimed that competitors and customers have become too unpredictable to form any single long-term strategy. Companies with strong and long-lasting positions like IKEA, GE and Unilever are argued to be exceptions. In this view then, it is a waste of effort to invest in sustainable advantages; better to invest in a series of *transient advantages*.[19]

In this new era managers thus need to constantly start new strategic initiatives and have a portfolio of several transient competitive advantages. They need to think of advantages as fleeting and going through a life cycle. Each competitive advantage has a launch stage that identifies an opportunity and raises resources to capitalise on it. Next is a ramp up period in which the

business is brought to scale, which leads into a phase of exploitation where market shares and profits are gained. Finally, there is a phase of inevitable erosion as competitors enter and weaken the advantage, which may force the company to exit. A company thus needs to catch new advantages continuously as old ones expire; freeing up resources from the old to invest in the new. Even if each advantage is temporary a portfolio of several different advantages would always provide an advantage somewhere. Hence, if managers continuously start strategic initiatives and build many transient advantages they could still get ahead of competitors.

Question

If IKEA chose not to build on sustainable competitive advantage, how could they build on many transient advantages?

---

convince a portion of the customers to buy a variety of premium services. Revenue is generated by the premium buying customers. Often only a small portion of the total volume of users, their revenues can be enough for the provider and they can also be used to attract even more users. The photo sharing service Flickr by Yahoo uses this business model pattern. Flickr offers the basic service of uploading and sharing photos for free while generating revenues through extra services for a subscription fee including unlimited uploading and storing of photos. Flickr also uses contextual advertising and cooperation with retail chains and other photo service companies besides subscription fees to generate revenue. Other online businesses that use this business model are the business-oriented social networking service LinkedIn, the video chat and voice call service Skype and the streaming music service Spotify. The aim of freemium, however, is not only to convince premium customers, but to attract a larger volume of customers as the value of the service increases with more users, which means that the enterprise can gain network effects based on a large installed base of adopters (see Section 3.2.6 for network effects).

- *Multi-sided platforms.* This business model pattern brings together two or more distinct, but interdependent groups of customers on one platform. They are interdependent as the platform is of value to each group of customers only if the other group of customers is also present. There are many different enterprises and markets that rely on this pattern (see for example Illustration 7.4), and video games consoles are a typical example. The players are on one side of the platform and favour consoles with a wide variety of games. This makes them dependent on the other side of the platform, the game developers, which in turn favour platforms with a large enough customer group to regain their development costs for the games. This shows that the value of the platform increases for both customer types as more customers use it. It suggests a network effect as each customer has a positive effect on the value of the product or platform for other customers (see Section 3.2.6). Web search companies like Google also rely on a similar pattern. For them the two sides of the platform involve consumer searchers on the one hand and advertisers that sponsor links on the search website on the other. The more searchers that use Google the better for advertisers and the better data for Google to refine search results and the better quality of the searches the better for consumers.

SUMMARY

- Business strategy is concerned with seeking competitive advantage in markets at the *business* rather than *corporate* level.

- Porter's framework and the Strategy Clock define various *generic strategies*, including *cost leadership*, *differentiation*, *focus* and *hybrid* strategies.

- In *hypercompetitive* conditions sustainable competitive advantage is difficult to achieve and competitors need to carefully consider moves and counter-moves.

- *Cooperative strategies* may offer alternatives to competitive strategies or may run in parallel.

- *Game theory* encourages managers to get in the mind of competitors and think forwards and reason backwards.

- A *business model* describes the business logic of an enterprise including the domains of *value creation*, *value configuration* and *value capture*.

WORK ASSIGNMENTS

✱ Denotes more advanced work assignments.
* Refers to a case study in the Text and Cases edition.

7.1   What are the advantages and what are the disadvantages of applying principles of business strategy to public-sector or charity organisations? Illustrate your argument by reference to a public-sector organisation of your choice.

7.2   Using either Porter's generic strategies or the Strategy Clock, identify examples of organisations following strategies of differentiation, low cost or low price, and stuck-in-the-middle or hybrid. How successful are these strategies?

7.3✱ You have been appointed personal assistant to the chief executive of a major manufacturing firm, who has asked you to explain what is meant by 'differentiation' and why it is important. Write a brief report addressing these questions.

7.4✱ Choose a company that you are familiar with (e.g. Spotify, Netflix, Apple). How do the business model components (value creation, configuration and capture) apply to the company?

7.5✱ Drawing on Section 7.3.2 (on cooperative strategies) write a report for the chief executive of a business in a competitive market (e.g. pharmaceuticals* or Formula One*) explaining when and in what ways cooperation rather than direct competition might make sense.

Integrative assignment

7.6✱ Applying game theory ideas from Section 7.3.3 to issues of international strategy (Chapter 9), how might a domestic player discourage an overseas player from entering into its home market?

RECOMMENDED KEY READINGS

- The foundations of the discussions of generic competitive strategies are to be found in the writings of Michael Porter, which include *Competitive Strategy* (1980) and *Competitive Advantage* (1985), both published by Free Press.

- Hypercompetition, and the strategies associated with it, are explained in Richard D'Aveni, *Hypercompetitive Rivalries: Competing in Highly Dynamic Environments*, Free Press, 1995.

- There is much written on game theory, but a good deal of it can be rather inaccessible to the lay reader. Exceptions are R. McCain, *Game Theory: a Non-technical Introduction to the Analysis of Strategy*, South Western, 2003; and P. Ghemawat, *Games Businesses Play*, MIT Press, 1998.

- There is considerably less written on business models, but one introduction including a long list of various business model types is O. Gassman, K. Frankenberger and M. Csik, *The Business Model Navigator*, Pearson, 2014.

REFERENCES

1. This section draws heavily on M. Porter, *Competitive Advantage*, Free Press, 1985. For a more recent discussion of the generic strategies concept, see J. Parnell, 'Generic strategies after two decades: a reconceptualisation of competitive strategy', *Management Decision*, vol. 48, no. 8 (2006), pp. 1139–54.

2. P. Conley, *Experience Curves as a Planning Tool*, available as a pamphlet from the Boston Consulting Group. See also A.C. Hax and N.S. Majluf, in R.G. Dyson (ed.), *Strategic Planning: Models and Analytical Techniques*, Wiley, 1990.

3. B. Sharp and J. Dawes, 'What is differentiation and how does it work?', *Journal of Marketing Management*, vol. 17, nos 7/8 (2001), pp. 739–59, reviews the relationship between differentiation and profitability.

4. C. Markides and C. Charitou, 'Competing with dual business models: a contingency approach', *Academy of Management Executive*, vol. 18, no. 3 (2004), pp. 22–36.

5. See D. Faulkner and C. Bowman, *The Essence of Competitive Strategy*, Prentice Hall, 1995.

6. For empirical support for the benefits of a hybrid strategy, see E. Pertusa-Ortega, J. Molina-Azorín and E. Claver-Cortés, 'Competitive strategies and firm performance: a comparative analysis of pure, hybrid and "stuck-in-the-middle" strategies in Spanish firms', *British Journal of Management*, vol. 20, no. 4 (2008), pp. 508–23.

7. R. D'Aveni, *Hypercompetition: Managing the Dynamics of Strategic Maneuvering*, Free Press, 1994.

8. This analysis is based on N. Kumar, 'Strategies to fight low cost rivals', *Harvard Business Review*, vol. 84, no. 12 (2006), pp. 104–13.

9. Useful books on collaborative strategies are Y. Doz and G. Hamel, *Alliance Advantage: The Art of Creating Value through Partnering*, Harvard Business School Press, 1998; C. Hutham (ed.), *Creating Collaborative Advantage*, Sage, 1996; and D. Faulkner, *Strategic Alliances: Cooperating to Compete*, McGraw-Hill, 1995.

10. For readings on game theory, see B. Nalebuff and A. Brandenburger, *Co-opetition*, Profile Books, 1997; R. McCain, *Game Theory: A Non-technical Introduction to the Analysis of Strategy*, South Western, 2003; and, for a summary, S. Regan, 'Game theory perspective', in M. Jenkins and V. Ambrosini (eds), *Advanced Strategic Management: a Multi-Perspective Approach*, 2nd edn, Palgrave Macmillan, 2007, pp. 83–101. A more recent practical example is in H. Lindstädt and J. Müller, 'Making game theory work for managers', *McKinsey Quarterly*, December 2009.

11. For discussion about business models and how they differ from business strategy, see D.J. Teece, 'Business models, business strategy and innovation', *Long Range Planning*, vol. 43, no. 2 (2010), pp. 172–94; J. Magretta, 'Why business models matter', *Harvard Business Review*, May 2002, pp. 86–92; C. Zott and A. Raphael, 'The fit between product market strategy and business model: implications for firm performance', *Strategic Management Journal*, vol. 29, no. 1 (2008), pp.1–26; and H. Chesbrough and R.S. Rosenbloom, 'The role of the business model in capturing value from innovation: evidence from Xerox Corporation's technology spin-off companies' *Industrial and Corporate Change*, vol. 11, no. 3 (2002), pp. 529–55.

12. In earlier editions we did not emphasise the first value proposition part, but emphasised the arrangement of activities and the revenues and cost structure (business models were discussed in Chapter 9 in the last two editions).

13. Please note that the business model literature is quite young and fragmented. For a couple of reviews of the literature, see C. Zott, A. Raphael and L. Massa, 'The business model: recent developments and future research', *Journal of Management*, vol. 37, no. 4 (2011), pp. 1019–42; and A. Osterwalder, Y. Pinneur and C. Tucci, 'Clarifying business models: origins, present, and future of the concept', *Communications of AIS*, vol. 16, article 1 (2005). For a debate of the value of business models, see R.J. Arend, 'The business model: present and future – beyond a skeumorph', *Strategic Organization*, vol. 11, no. 4 (2013), pp. 390–402; C. Baden-Fuller and V. Mangematin, 'Business models: a challenging agenda', *Strategic Organization*, vol. 11, no. 4 (2013), pp. 418–27; and C. Zott and A. Raphael, 'The

business model: a theoretically anchored robust construct for strategic analysis', *Strategic Organization*, vol. 11, no. 4 (2013), pp. 403–11.

14. For another division of business model components and a description of a wide range of business models, see O. Gassmann, K. Frankenberger and M. Csik, *The Business Model Navigator*, Pearson, 2014.

15. For a discussion about activity systems in business models, see C. Zott and A. Raphael, 'Business model design: an activity system perspective', *Long Range Planning*, vol. 43, no. 2 (2010), pp. 216–26; and R. Casadesus-Masanell and J.E. Ricart, 'From strategy to business models and onto tactics', *Long Range Planning*, vol. 43, no 2 (2010), pp. 195–215.

16. For a discussion of business models for sustainability that also includes non-for profits, see B. Cohen and J. Kietzmann, 'Ride on! Mobility business models for the sharing economy', *Organization & Environment*, vol. 27, no. 3 (2014) pp. 279–96.

17. There are thus multiple labels around and diverse patterns are often combined into a single business model for a particular enterprise. Airbnb's model is an example of this. On the one hand, it is often referred to as a 'multi-sided platform model' as they connect hosts and guests (see this models' specifications below in the text). On the other hand, it is sometimes also called a 'peer to peer model' as it is based on cooperation among individuals who are connected via an app, website or some other online or communication service.

18. The model is sometimes also referred to as a 'cross-subsidisation' model as one basic product is inexpensive and sold at a discount, while the second dependent product or service needed to get the basic product functional is sold at a considerably higher price. Others refer to it as a 'bait and hook' pattern as it lures in consumers in.

19. R. Gunther McGrath, 'Transient advantage', *Harvard Business Review*, vol. 91, no. 6 (2013), pp. 62–70.

The IKEA approach

Kevan Scholes*

'Our business model is to offer a wide range of well-designed, functional home furnishing products at prices so low that as many people as possible will be able to afford them.'

This was the headline in IKEA's yearly summary report for year ending 31 August 2015.[1] It reported a revenue increase of 11.2 per cent to €32.7bn (£26.2bn, $42.5bn),[2] profits of €3.5bn and share gains in most markets. IKEA continued to be the world's largest home furnishings company with some 9500 products in 375 stores in 28 countries.[3] The company had 172,000 co-workers (of which 40,000 were in production and distribution).

The home furnishings market[4]

By the late 2000s home furnishings was a huge market worldwide with retail sales in excess of $US600bn in items such as furniture, household textiles and floor coverings. More than 50 per cent of these sales were in furniture stores. Table 1 compares the geographical spread of the market and IKEA sales by region.

IKEA's competitors

The home furnishings market was highly fragmented with competition occurring locally rather than globally and included competitors of several types:

- Multinational furniture retailers (like IKEA) all of whom were considerably smaller than IKEA. These included, for example, the Danish company Jysk (turnover €2.9bn).
- Companies specialising in just part of the furniture product range and operating in several countries – such as Alno from Germany in kitchens.
- Multi-branch retail furniture outlets whose sales were mainly in one country, such as DFS in the UK. The US

market was dominated by such players (e.g. Bed, Bath & Beyond Inc. with revenues of some $US12bn).
- Non-specialist companies that carried furniture as part of a wider product range. In the UK, the largest operator was the Home Retail Group whose subsidiary Argos offered some 53,000 general merchandise products through its network of 840 stores and online sales. It was number one in UK furniture retailing. General DIY companies such as Kingfisher (through B&Q in the UK and Castorama in France) were attempting to capture more of the bottom end of the furniture market.
- Small and/or specialised retailers and/or manufacturers. These accounted for the biggest share of the market in Europe.

In 2014, it was estimated that the UK market was about £10.2bn[7] of which IKEA had £1.7bn share (16.7 per cent).

IKEA's approach

IKEA had been founded by Ingvar Kamprad in 1943 in the small Swedish town of Älmhult and opened its first furniture store 1958. The company's success had been achieved through the now legendary IKEA business approach – revolutionary in the furnishing industry of its early years (see Table 2). The guiding business philosophy of Kamprad was that of improving the everyday life of people by making products more affordable. This was achieved by massive (more than 20 per cent) reductions in sales prices vs competitors which, in turn, required aggressive reductions in IKEA's costs.

Reasons for success

In his book *The IKEA Edge*[8] published in 2011, Anders Dahlvig reflected on the reasons for IKEA's success

Table 1 The geographical spread of the market and of IKEA sales by region

	Europe (incl. Russia)	Americas	Asia/Pacific
% of global market[5]	52	29	19
% of IKEA sales[6]	72	18	10

*This case was prepared by Kevan Scholes, Emeritus Professor of Strategic Management at Sheffield Business School. It is intended as a basis for class discussion and not as an illustration of good or bad management practice. Copyright Kevan Scholes 2016. Not to be reproduced or quoted without permission.

Table 2 IKEA's 'upside-down' approach

Element of the approach	Traditional furniture retailer	IKEA
Design	Traditional	Modern (Swedish)
Target households	Older, established	Families with children
Style of shop	Small specialist shops	All furnishing items in big stores
Location	City centre	Out-of-town
Product focus	Individual items	'Room sets'
Marketing	Advertising	Free catalogue (213 million in 32 languages in 2015)
Price	High	Low
Product assembly	Ready assembled	Flat pack – self-assembly
Sourcing	Local	Global
Brand	Manufacturers'	IKEA
Financial focus	Gross margin	Sales revenue
Overheads	Often high	Frugal – no perks

before, during and after his period as CEO (1999–2009). He felt IKEA had five success criteria:

'1. Design, function, and quality at low prices; 2. Unique (Scandinavian) design; 3. Inspiration, ideas, and complete solutions; 4. Everything in one place; 5. "A day out", the shopping experience. . . . You may well say that they are similar to those of most companies. The difference, in my opinion, is that IKEA is much better at delivering on these customer needs than are other retailers. . . . Most competitors focus on one or at most two of these customer needs. High-street shops focus on design and inspiration. Out-of-town low-cost retailers focus on price. Department stores focus on choice. The real strength of IKEA lies in the combination of all five.'[9]

IKEA's competitive strategy

Dahlvig explained IKEA's approach to competition:

'You can choose to adapt your company's product range to the markets you are operating in, or you can choose to shift the market's preference toward your own range and style. IKEA has chosen the latter. By doing this, the company can maintain a unique and distinct profile. This is, however, a more difficult path to follow.[10] . . . A significant understanding of the customer's situation at home is the basis for IKEA's product development.[11] . . . For most competitors, having the lowest price seems to mean being five to ten per cent cheaper than the competition on comparable products. At IKEA, this means being a minimum 20 per cent cheaper and often up to 50 per cent cheaper than the competition.'[12]

Managing the value chain

Dahlvig explained that IKEA's strategy crucially requires the 'design' and control of their wider value chain in detail:

'The secret is the control and coordination of the whole value chain from raw material, production, and range development, to distribution into stores. Most other companies working in the retail sector have control either of the retail end (stores and distribution) or the product design and production end. IKEA's vertical integration makes it a complex company compared to most, since it owns both production, range development, distribution, and stores.[13] . . . This included backward integration by extending the activities of Swedwood (IKEA's manufacturing arm) beyond furniture factories, into control over the raw materials, saw mills, board suppliers, and component factories.'[14]

Global expansion

Despite IKEA's strong global position when Dahlvig took over as CEO, he felt there was need for improvement. Earlier growth had come from going 'wide but thin' with limited market shares, but now they would go 'deep' and concentrate on their existing markets.[15]

He explained his reasoning:

'Why make the change? . . . the competition had been very fragmented and local in nature. However, many of the very big retail companies were shifting strategy. From being local, they were looking to a global expansion, not least in the emerging markets like China, Russia, and Eastern Europe . . . [and] broadening their product range . . . with much more muscle than IKEA's traditional competitors. . . . One way to dissuade them from entering into the home furnishing arena was to aggressively reduce prices and increase the company's presence with more stores in all local markets in the countries where IKEA was operating. . . . Another reason for the shift in strategy was cost efficiency. Growing

sales in existing stores is the most cost-efficient way to grow the company.'[16]

China and India

Around 70 per cent of IKEA stores are still in Europe and expansion into Asia was crucial, but the company had come to realise that emerging markets could be particularly challenging. As head of research Mikael Ydholm remarked: 'The more far away we go from our culture, the more we need to understand, learn, and adapt.'[17]

IKEA first opened in China in 1998 and today it is the company's fastest growing market. They now have eight of its ten biggest stores there. The Chinese market was extremely challenging for a company that had built global success through standardisation.[18] The main problems were that in emerging markets IKEA products were expensive relative to local competitors and the consumer shopping expectations were centred on small, local shops and personal service. IKEA thus had to be flexible and presented an image as exclusive Western Europian interior design specialists – popular with younger, affluent, city dwellers. Their shops were smaller than usual for IKEA and typically nearer city centres. Because DIY was not well developed in China they offered home delivery and assembly services. Catalogues were only available *in store*. Crucially, stores were allowed to source almost 50 per cent locally (against company average of about 25 per cent) in order to keep prices competitive.

The Chinese experience would be useful when IKEA entered India. It was announced in 2012 that IKEA was to invest €1.5bn opening 25 stores over 15 to 20 years[19] with the first store opened in Hyderabad 2017. However, India also proved challenging as a third of a retailer chains' merchandise had to be produced locally. IKEA had huge problems to find producers that could live up to their strict corporate social responsibility requirements.

New leadership

Michael Ohlsson succeeded Dahlvig as CEO in 2009 – having already worked for IKEA for 30 years. In turn, he was succeeded in 2013 by another internal appointee – Peter Agnefjäll (18 years at IKEA).

Despite extremely challenging economic conditions after the global financial crash of 2008, the company's success continued with revenue reaching €21.8bn, €27.6bn and €32.7bn in 2009, 2012 and 2015, respectively, with the goal to reach €50bn by 2020. However, the market was changing as IKEA expanded into more countries (43 by 2015).

Growing IKEA and reaching more customers

Although the IKEA approach remained central to the company's strategy, the yearly report for financial year 2015[20] explained how new challenges were being addressed.

'We want to be even more accessible to the many people. This means working hard to ensure we make it easier for customers to shop with us, wherever and whenever they want to visit our stores and shopping centres, or our website and apps.

Shopping centres

We now operate 40 shopping centres and 25 retail parks [in 14 countries] and we have 20 projects in the pipeline across several markets. These family-friendly shopping centres have an IKEA store as one of the main attractions.

Online

Online sales through our website and apps exceeded €1 billion in FY15. [*There were 1.9bn visits to* IKEA.com *and 54 million hits on the IKEA catalogue app – in each case an increase of about 20 per cent from 2014.*] Currently we offer online shopping in 13 of our 28 retail countries. We are continually exploring how we can expand and improve the ways our customers can find out about our products and be inspired by our range through digital channels, such as website, apps and catalogue.

Pick-up and order points

Our three new pick-up and order points in Spain, Norway and Finland enable customers to see and buy selected products from our range, as well as collect pre-ordered purchases.'

Based on their unique approach and the more recent ingredients mentioned above, IKEA continued to take over the world with the same vision as always. CEO Peter Agnefjäll confirmed:

'We're guided by a vision to create a better everyday life for the many people. That is what steers us, motivates us – that is our role . . . We feel almost obliged to grow.'[21]

Questions

1 Identify where (in their value system) and how IKEA have achieved cost leadership.

2 Identify how IKEA have achieved differentiation from their competitors.

3 Explain how IKEA tries to ensure that their 'hybrid' strategy remains sustainable and does not become 'stuck-in-the-middle'.

4 How would you explain IKEA's business model in terms of value creation, configuration and capture?

Suggested Video Clip

http://fortune.com/video/2015/03/10/
ikeas-secret-to-global-success/

Notes and References

1. 'IKEA Group Yearly Summary FY15' from IKEA website (www.ikea.com).
2. The revenue figure consists of €31.9bn sales and €0.8bn rental income on retail property.
3. IKEA had a presence in 43 countries if retail, distribution and production are all included.
4. Data in this section comes from the IKEA website 2015 and from the Data Monitor report on Global Home Furnishings Retail Industry Profile (Reference Code: 0199-2243 Publication date: April 2008).
5. 2008.
6. 2015.
7. British Furniture Manufacturers (www.bfm.org.uk).
8. Anders Dahlvig, *The Ikea Edge,* McGraw Hill, 2011.
9. Ibid., page 62.
10. Ibid., page 63.
11. Ibid., page 63.
12. Ibid., page 74.
13. Ibid., page 75.
14. Ibid., page 83.
15. Ibid., page 120.
16. Ibid., page 123.
17. B. Kowitt, 'How Ikea took over the world', *Fortune,* 15 March, 2015.
18. U. Johansson and A. Thelander, 'A standardised approach to the world? IKEA in China', *International Journal of Quality and Service Sciences,* vol. 1, no. 2 (2000), pp. 199–219.
19. N. Bose and M. Williams, 'Ikea to enter India, invest 1.5 bln euros in stores', Reuters, 23 June 2012.
20. See endnote 1.
21. See endnote 17.

8

CORPORATE STRATEGY AND DIVERSIFICATION

Learning outcomes

After reading this chapter you should be able to:

- Identify alternative strategy options, including *market penetration*, *product development*, *market development* and *diversification*.
- Distinguish between different diversification strategies (*related* and *conglomerate* diversification) and evaluate *diversification drivers*.
- Assess the relative benefits of *vertical integration* and *outsourcing*.
- Analyse the ways in which a *corporate parent* can add or destroy value for its portfolio of business units.
- Analyse *portfolios* of business units and judge which to invest in and which to divest.

Key terms

Ansoff's growth matrix p.244

BCG matrix p.262

diversification (related and unrelated/
    conglomerate) pp.244/245

dominant logic p.250

economies of scope p.250

outsourcing p.254

parental developer p.261

parenting advantage p.244

portfolio manager p.258

synergy p.251

synergy manager p.259

vertical (forward and backward)
    integration p.253

8.1 INTRODUCTION

Chapter 7 was concerned with *competitive strategy* – the ways in which a single business unit or organisational unit can compete in a given market space, for instance through cost leadership or differentiation. However, organisations may choose to enter many new product and market areas (see Figure II.1 in Part II introduction). For example Tata Group, one of India's largest companies, began as a trading organisation and soon moved into hotels and textiles. Since that time, Tata has diversified further into steel, motors, consultancy, technologies, tea, chemicals, power, communications. As organisations add new units and capabilities, their strategies may no longer be solely concerned with *competitive strategy* in one market space at the business level, but with choices concerning different businesses or markets. Corporate strategy is about what business areas to be active in, and this will determine which business unit(s) to buy, the direction(s) an organisation might pursue and how resources may be allocated efficiently across multiple business activities. For Tata, the corporate strategy questions are whether it should add any more businesses, whether it should exit some, and how far it should integrate the businesses it retains. For large public-sector organisations and charities these choices also have to be made. These choices, indicated in Figure 8.1, inform decisions about how broad an organisation should be. This 'scope' of an organisation is central to *corporate strategy* and the focus of this chapter.

Scope is concerned with how far an organisation should be diversified in terms of two different dimensions: products and markets. As the opening example shows, an organisation may increase its scope by engaging in market spaces or products different to its current ones. Section 8.2 introduces a classic product market framework that uses these categories for identifying different growth directions for an organisation. This indicates different *diversification* strategies open to an organisation, according to the novelty of products or markets. Underpinning diversification choices are a range of drivers, which are discussed in Section 8.3, including increasing market power, reducing risk and exploiting superior internal processes. The performance implications of diversification are, then, reviewed in Section 8.4.

Another way of increasing the scope of an organisation is *vertical integration,* discussed in Section 8.5. It allows an organisation to act as an internal supplier or a customer to itself (as

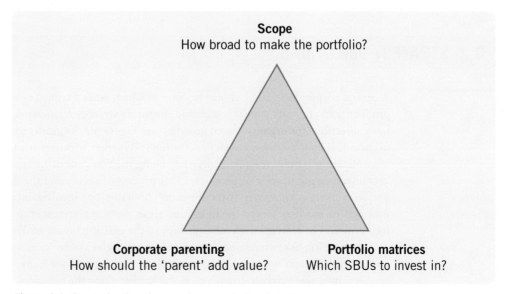

Figure 8.1 Strategic directions and corporate-level strategy

for example an oil company supplies its petrol to its own petrol stations). The organisation may decide to *outsource* certain activities – to 'dis-integrate' by subcontracting an internal activity to an external supplier – as this may improve organisational efficiency. The scope of the organisation may therefore be adjusted through growth or contraction.

Diversified corporations that operate in different areas of activity will have multiple strategic business units (SBUs) with their own strategies for their specific markets for which they can be held accountable in terms of success or failure. SBUs thus allow large corporations to vary their business strategies according to the different needs of the various external markets they serve. Nevertheless, corporate head office, the 'corporate level', needs to manage the selection of SBUs and establish their boundaries, perhaps by market, geography or capability, so they add value to the group.[1] The value-adding effect of head office to individual SBUs, that make up the organisation's portfolio, is termed **parenting advantage** (see Section 8.6). Their ability to do this effectively may make them competitive amongst other corporate parents in acquiring and manage different businesses. But just how do corporate-level activities, decisions and resources add value to businesses? As will be seen at the end of the chapter in the 'Thinking Differently' section, some are sceptical about headquarters' ability to add value.

In order to decide which industries and businesses organisations should invest in or dispose of, the corporate centre needs to assess whether the *portfolio* of businesses is worth more under its management than the individual businesses would be worth standing alone. Section 8.7 reviews portfolio matrices, which are useful techniques to help structure corporate-level choices about businesses in which to invest and those to divest.

This chapter is not just about large commercial businesses. Small businesses may also have different business units. For example, a local building company may be undertaking contract work for local government, industrial buyers and local homeowners. Not only are these different market segments, but the mode of operation and capabilities required for competitive success in each are also likely to be different. Moreover, the owner of that business has to take decisions about the extent of investment and activity in each segment. Public-sector organisations such as local government or health services also provide different services, which correspond to business units in commercial organisations. Corporate-level strategy is also highly relevant to the appropriate drawing of organisational boundaries in the public sector. Privatisation and outsourcing decisions can be considered as responses to the failure of public-sector organisations to add sufficient value by their parenting.

8.2 STRATEGY DIRECTIONS

A central corporate strategy choice is about in which areas a company should grow. **Ansoff's** product/market **growth matrix**[2] **is a classic corporate strategy framework for generating four basic directions for organisational growth** – see Figure 8.2. Typically an organisation starts in zone A. It may choose between *penetrating* still further within zone A (sometimes termed 'consolidation'), or increasing its diversity along the two axes of increasing novelty of markets or increasing novelty of products. This process of increasing the diversity of products and/or markets is known as 'diversification'. **Diversification involves increasing the range of products or markets served by an organisation. Related diversification involves expanding into products or services with relationships to the existing business.** Thus on Ansoff's axes the organisation has two related diversification strategies available: moving to zone B, *developing new products* for its existing markets, or moving to zone C by bringing its existing products into *new markets*. In each case, the further along the two axes, the more diversified the strategy. Alternatively, the organisation can move in both directions at once, following

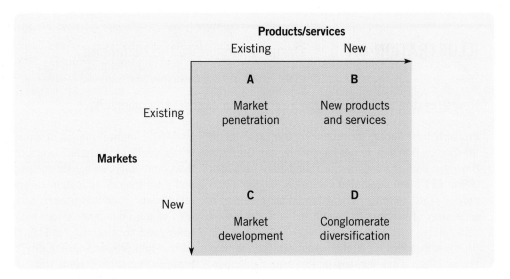

Figure 8.2 Corporate strategy directions

Source: Adapted from H.I. Ansoff, *Corporate Strategy,* Penguin, 1988, Chapter 6 . Ansoff originally had a matrix with four separate boxes, but in practice strategic directions involve more continuous axes. The Ansoff matrix itself was later developed – see Reference 2.

a *conglomerate diversification* strategy with altogether new markets and new products (zone D). Thus **conglomerate (unrelated) diversification involves diversifying into products or services with no relationships to existing businesses.**

Ansoff's axes can be used for brainstorming strategic options, checking that all four zones have been properly considered. Illustration 8.1 traces the evolution of a social enterprise, raising questions about how businesses might think about Ansoff's matrix in choosing their strategic direction. The next section will consider each of Ansoff's four main directions in some detail. Section 8.5 will examine the additional option of *vertical integration*.

8.2.1 Market penetration

For a simple, undiversified business, the most obvious strategic option is often increased penetration of its existing market, with its existing products. Market penetration implies increasing share of current markets with the current product range. This strategy builds on established strategic capabilities and does not require the organisation to venture into uncharted territory. The organisation's scope is exactly the same. Moreover, greater market share implies increased power vis-à-vis buyers and suppliers (in terms of Porter's five forces), greater economies of scale and experience curve benefits.

However, organisations seeking greater market penetration may face two constraints:

- *Retaliation from competitors.* In terms of the five forces (Section 3.2), increasing market penetration is likely to exacerbate industry rivalry as other competitors in the market defend their share. Increased rivalry might involve price wars or expensive marketing battles, which may cost more than any market-share gains are actually worth. The dangers of provoking fierce retaliation are greater in low-growth markets, as gains in volume will be more at the expense of other players. Where retaliation is a danger, organisations seeking market penetration need strategic capabilities that give a clear competitive advantage. In low-growth or declining markets, it can be more effective simply to acquire competitors. Some companies have grown quickly in this way. For example, in the steel industry the Indian company LNM (Mittal) moved rapidly in the 2000s to become the largest global steel producer by acquiring

ILLUSTRATION 8.1   Baking change into the community

How Greyston's diversification transforms a depressed community.

Probably best known for producing the brownies in the famous Ben and Jerry's ice creams, the Greyston Bakery is part of the Greyston Foundation – a $15m (£9m; €11.25m) integrated network of for-profit and not-for-profit entities. The Foundation provides a wide array of services to benefit its local depressed community.

A Zen Buddhist meditation group started the bakery in 1982. They located in the poor neighbourhood of Yonkers, New York, where they perceived a need to create jobs for people in the community who were 'hard to employ' – the homeless, those with poor employment histories, prison records and past substance-abuse problems. Radically they used an 'open hiring' practice that continues today, in which anybody who applies for a job has an opportunity to work, on a first-come, first-hired basis. Employees have to show up for work on time, perform the job and have an appropriate attitude for three months and are then automatically made permanent employees. As SVP David Rome says, 'we judge people based on their performance in the operation, not on their background'. There is high initial turnover but the average tenure is about three years. Greyston considers it a success when an employee moves onto a new job using his or her new skills. According to CEO Julius Walls, 'The company provides opportunities and resources to its employees so they can be successful not only in the workplace but in their personal lives. We don't hire people to bake brownies; we bake brownies to hire people.'

As the bakery expanded it realised that providing jobs to the community was not enough. In 1991, working with governmental agencies, Greyston Family Inn was opened to provide permanent housing for homeless people. Currently there are three buildings, providing 50 housing units. A child day-care centre was also started as after-school care was one of the most pressing needs in the community for working parents. In 1992, Greyston Health Services was formed and in 1997, Issan House opened with 35 permanent housing units for those with

HIV/AIDS, mental illness or chemical dependency. Other ventures included Greyston Garden Project, five community-run gardens on neglected properties, and a technology education centre. In 2011, a local retail bakery/café was opened and in 2012, with the help of the Foundation's real-estate division, a new bakery was constructed, for $10m in a public–private partnership project with the city, on a long-dormant brownfield (contaminated) site.

The Foundation is an umbrella for all Greyston organisations, providing centralised management, fund-raising, real-estate development and planning services. It now comprises four interrelated organisations: bakery, healthcare services, child and family programmes and real-estate development. The Foundation's social mission of supporting low-income people to forge a path to self-sufficiency and community transformation is blended with business collaboration to enable continual growth.

In 2012, Greyston Bakery celebrated its 30th anniversary, and New York State made it a Benefit Corporation, allowing Greyston to demonstrate higher standards of corporate purpose, accountability and transparency. As CEO Steven Brown said, 'Really, we were a benefit corporation long before the term was coined. You're in business for a much larger community that has a stake in what you are doing. Creating value and opportunity is the path out of distress for communities.' Since then Greyston has continued to grow, opening new multi-family housing developments for local working families.

Sources: www.greyston.com; http://1596994.sites.myregisteredsite.com/levpoints/lp52.html#face; *Huffington Post*, 9 December 2012. http://www.youtube.com/watch?v=2WLzV7JfVSc.

Questions

1 What were the motivation(s) for Greyston Bakery's diversifications?

2 Referring to the Ansoff matrix, how would you classify these diversifications?

struggling steel companies around the world. Acquisitions may reduce rivalry, by taking out independent players and controlling them under one umbrella.

- *Legal constraints.* Greater market penetration can raise concerns from official competition regulators concerning excessive market power. Most countries have regulators with the powers to restrain powerful companies or prevent mergers and acquisitions that would create such excessive power. In the UK, the Competition Commission can investigate any merger or acquisition that would account for more than 25 per cent of the national market, and either halt the deal or propose measures that would reduce market power. The European Commission has an overview of the whole European market and can similarly intervene. For example, when it gave approval for the acquisition of the vaccines business of Novartis by GSK, and the creation of a new entity, the decision was conditional upon the divestiture of certain related assets. The Commission had concerns the transaction would have eliminated an important competitor to GSK for the supply of several vaccines and consumer health products, which might lead to price increases for European consumers.[3]

Market penetration may also not be an option where economic constraints are severe, for instance during a market downturn or public-sector funding crisis. Here organisations will need to consider the strategic option of *retrenchment*: withdrawal from marginal activities in order to concentrate on the most valuable segments and products within their existing business. However, where growth is still sought, the Ansoff's axes suggest further directions, as follows.

8.2.2 Product development

Product development is where organisations deliver modified or new products (or services) to existing markets. This can involve varying degrees of diversification along the horizontal axis of Figure 8.2. For Apple, developing its products from the original iPod, through iPhone to iPad involved little diversification: although the technologies differed, Apple was targeting the same customers and using very similar production processes and distribution channels. Despite the potential for benefits from relatedness, product development can be an expensive and high-risk activity for at least two reasons:

- *New resources and capabilities.* Product development strategies typically involve mastering new processes or technologies that are unfamiliar to the organisation. For example, the digital revolution is forcing universities to reconsider the way learning materials are acquired and provided to students and the nature of the student/academic interface. High-quality content available free online and virtual engagement with students now raise the question of how universities should consider redeploying their resources in the future. Success is likely to depend on a willingness to acquire new technological capabilities, to engage in organisational restructuring and new marketing capabilities to manage customer perceptions. Thus product development typically involves heavy investments and can have high risk of project failures.

- *Project management risk.* Even within fairly familiar domains, product development projects are typically subject to the risk of delays and increased costs due to project complexity and changing project specifications over time. For example, Boeing's Dreamliner 787 aircraft made innovative use of carbon-fibre composites but had a history of delays even before launch in 2010, and required $2.5bn (£1.5bn, €1.9bn) write-offs due to cancelled orders. Since then, batteries catching fire has resulted in fleets being grounded.

Strategies for product development are considered further in Chapter 10.

8.2.3 Market development

Product development can be risky and expensive. Market development can be more attractive by being potentially cheaper and quicker to execute. Market development involves offering existing products to new markets. Again, the degree of diversification varies along Figure 8.2's downward axis. Typically, of course, market development entails some product development as well, if only in terms of packaging or service. Nonetheless, market development remains a form of related diversification given its origins in similar products. Market development takes two basic forms:

- *New users.* Here an example would be aluminium, whose original users, packaging and cutlery manufacturers, are now supplemented by users in aerospace and automobiles.
- *New geographies.* The prime example of this is internationalisation, but it would also include the spread of a small retailer into new towns.

In all cases, it is essential that market development strategies be based on products or services that meet the *critical success factors* of the new market (see Section 3.4.3). Strategies based on simply off-loading traditional products or services in new markets are likely to fail. Moreover, market development faces similar problems to product development. In terms of strategic capabilities, market developers often lack the right marketing skills and brands to make progress in a market with unfamiliar customers. On the management side, the challenge is coordinating between different users and geographies, which might all have different needs. *International* market development strategy is considered in Chapter 9.

8.2.4 Conglomerate diversification

Conglomerate (or unrelated) diversification takes the organisation beyond both its existing markets and its existing products (i.e. zone D in Figure 8.2). In this sense, it radically increases the organisation's scope. Conglomerate diversification strategies can create value as businesses may benefit from being part of a larger group. This may allow consumers to have greater confidence in the business units products and services than before and larger size may also reduce the costs of finance. However, conglomerate strategies are often not trusted by many observers because there are no obvious ways in which the businesses can work together to generate additional value, over and above the businesses remaining on their own. In addition, there is often an additional bureaucratic cost of the managers at headquarters who control them. For this reason, conglomerate companies' share prices can suffer from what is called the 'conglomerate discount'– in other words, a lower valuation than the combined individual constituent businesses would have on their own. For instance, shares in Old Mutual, an international financial services group, traded at a 25 per cent discount to its peers since the recession. This underperformance occurred since it moved its business to the UK from South Africa and diversified away from its core focus on Africa and emerging markets. Speculation that the CEO will announce a break-up saw Old Mutual shares rise 7 per cent in trading.

However, it is important to recognise that the distinction between related and conglomerate (unrelated) diversification is often a matter of degree. Relationships that might have seemed valuable in related diversification may not turn out to be as valuable as expected. Thus the large accounting firms have often struggled in translating their skills and client contacts developed in auditing into effective consulting practices. Similarly, relationships may change in importance over time, as the nature of technologies or markets change: see, for example, the decision by TomTom to move into different product offerings (Illustration 8.2).

ILLUSTRATION 8.2   From sat nav to driverless cars

Sat nav manufacturer TomTom diversifies to survive.

Dutch manufacturer TomTom's fortunes dived in 2008 with sales down 36 per cent to €959m (£767m, $1.2bn) (2014) and profits down 71 per cent to €25.4m (2014). From its peak of $15bn, multinational TomTom's market value was just €2.3bn by 2015. How did this decline come about and what could management do about it?

Originally a software developer for business-to-business mobile applications and personal digital assistants (PDAs), TomTom became market leader in PDA software in just two years with navigation applications RoutePlanner and Citymaps. In 2002, the TomTom Navigator was launched, providing European customers for the first time with an easy-to-use, affordable, portable navigation device (PND). Demand was strong for the PND which was not just a new product, but an entirely new consumer electronics category. TomTom GO, launched in 2004, revolutionised the way millions of drivers got from A to B. Affordable and accessible to everyone, it became the fastest selling consumer technology device ever. Since then, over 75 million devices have been sold in 35 countries, guiding drivers over 280 billion kilometres.

During 2008, TomTom's sales fell dramatically due to an increasingly saturated sat nav market, plus smartphone alternatives from Google and Nokia. TomTom was forced to reconsider its business and diversified into fleet management and vehicle telematics, where it is now a recognised leader. TomTom evolved from just a hardware business, selling sat navs to stick on windscreens, to a software and services provider that offered free mapping on smartphones and integrated traffic management systems used by governments to quell traffic and manage roads.

After partnering with Nike on the Nike+ Sport-Watch, TomTom launched its own TomTom Runner and TomTom Multi-Sport watches in 2013, to help runners, cyclists and swimmers keep moving towards their fitness goals, by providing essential performance information at a glance. Both have GPS sensors, allowing them to tap into TomTom's navigation platform. TomTom is now straying further from its roots by launching Bandit, an action camera, to challenge American market leader GoPro. It will contain GPS sensors allowing users to find and tag exciting moments in their video footage, based on speed, altitude, G-force and acceleration. Bandit's real selling point is its video-editing and -sharing capabilities.

Although sat nav devices, sports watches and action cameras may seem unlikely bedfellows, co-founder Vigreux explains that 'TomTom is a bit like a collection of startups under one umbrella. Employees are actively encouraged to be entrepreneurial in product development. . . . We're a tech brand at the end of the day – the only consumer electronics brand to come out of Europe in the last 15 years with a global footprint' and if there is one thing that unites Tomtom products its 'we make things easy for consumers'.

TomTom still feels there is a market for a stand-alone sat nav for people to avoid roaming charges on mobile phones and the need to buy a new car if they want an in-built system. They are also working with car manufacturers to build embedded navigation systems into their vehicles as the era of the 'connected car' – where manufacturers do everything from updating car entertainment to suspension adjustment – has forced automakers into partnerships with technology companies. Competitive concerns mean manufacturers are unwilling to share data with rivals and so rely on third parties for services such as traffic management as it is not always cost-effective for them to make the investment themselves. TomTom is currently collaborating with Volkswagen on real-time map updates for driverless cars although they will face tough competition from Google and Apple.

Sources: http://corporate.tomtom.com; *Telegraph*, 20 August 2015; *Financial Times*, 12 February 2015.

Questions

1 Explain the ways in which relatedness informed TomTom's post-2008 strategy.

2 Were there alternative strategies open to TomTom post 2008?

8.3 DIVERSIFICATION DRIVERS

Diversification might be chosen for a variety of reasons, some more value-creating than others.[4] Growth in organisational size is rarely a good enough reason for diversification on its own: growth must be profitable. Indeed, growth can often be merely a form of 'empire building', especially in the public sector. Diversification decisions need to be approached sceptically.

Four potentially value-creating drivers for diversification are as follows:

- *Exploiting economies of scope.* **Economies of scope refer to efficiency gains made through applying the organisation's existing resources or competences to new markets or services.**[5] If an organisation has under-utilised resources or competences that it cannot effectively close or sell to other potential users, it is efficient to use these resources or competences by diversification into a new activity. In other words, there are economies to be gained by extending the scope of the organisation's activities. For example, many universities have large resources in terms of halls of residence, which they must have for their students but which are under-utilised out of term time. These halls of residence are more efficiently used if the universities expand the scope of their activities into con-ferencing and tourism during holiday periods. Economies of scope may apply to both *tangible* resources, such as halls of residence, and *intangible* resources and competences, such as brands or staff skills.

- *Stretching corporate management competences ('dominant logics').* This is a special case of economies of scope, and refers to the potential for applying the skills of talented corporate-level managers (referred to as 'corporate parenting skills' in Section 8.6) to new businesses. The **dominant logic is the set of corporate-level managerial competences applied across the portfolio of businesses.**[6] Corporate-level managers may have compe-tences that can be applied even to businesses not sharing resources at the operating-unit level.[7] Thus the French luxury-goods conglomerate LVMH includes a wide range of businesses – from champagne, through fashion, jewellery and perfumes, to financial media – that share very few operational resources or business-level competences. How-ever, LVMH creates value for these specialised companies by applying corporate-level competences in developing classic brands and nurturing highly creative people that are relevant to all its individual businesses. See also the discussion of dominant logic at Berkshire Hathaway in Illustration 8.4 later.

- *Exploiting superior internal processes.* Internal processes within a diversified corporation can often be more efficient than external processes in the open market. This is especially the case where external capital and labour markets do not yet work well, as in many developing economies. In these circumstances, well-managed conglomerates can make sense, even if their constituent businesses do not have operating relationships with each other. For example, China has many conglomerates because it is able to mobilise internal investment, develop managers and exploit networks in a way that stand-alone Chinese companies, relying on imperfect markets, cannot. For example, China's largest privately owned conglomerate, the Fosun Group, owns steel mills, pharmaceutical companies and China's largest retailer, Yuyuan Tourist Mart.[8]

- *Increasing market power.*[9] Being diversified in many businesses can increase power vis-à-vis competitors in at least two ways. First, having the same wide portfolio of products as a competitor increases the potential for *mutual forbearance*. The ability to retaliate across the whole range of the portfolio acts to discourage the competitor from making any aggressive moves at all. Two similarly diversified competitors are thus likely to forbear from competing aggressively with each other. Second, having a diversified range of businesses increases the power to *cross-subsidise* one business from the profits of the others. The ability to cross-subsidise can support aggressive bids to drive competitors out of a particular market and, being aware of this, competitors without equivalent power will be reluctant to attack that business.

Where diversification creates value, it is described as 'synergistic'.[10] **Synergies are benefits gained where activities or assets complement each other so that their combined effect is greater than the sum of the parts** (the famous $2 + 2 = 5$ equation). Thus a film company and a music publisher would be synergistic if they were worth more together than separately – if the music publisher had the sole rights to music used in the film company productions for instance. However, synergies are often harder to identify and more costly to extract in practice than managers like to admit.[11]

Indeed, some drivers for diversification involve negative synergies, in other words value destruction. Three potentially value-destroying diversification drivers are:

- *Responding to market decline* is one common but doubtful driver for diversification. Rather than let the managers of a declining business invest spare funds in a new business, conventional finance theory suggests it is usually best to let shareholders find new growth investment opportunities for themselves. For example, Kodak (see Illustration 6.4), the US photo film corporation, spent billions of dollars on diversification acquisitions such as chemicals, desktop radiotherapy, photocopiers, telecommunications and inkjet printers in order to compensate for market decline in its main product. Many of these initiatives failed and the decline of the core business continued until Kodak went bankrupt. Shareholders might have preferred Kodak simply to hand back the large surpluses generated for decades beforehand rather than spending on costly acquisitions. If shareholders had wanted to invest in the chemicals, telecommunications or printers, they could have invested in the original dominant companies themselves.

- *Spreading risk* across a range of markets is another common justification for diversification. Again, conventional finance theory is very sceptical about risk-spreading by diversification. Shareholders can easily spread their risk by taking small stakes in dozens of very different companies themselves. Diversification strategies, on the other hand, are likely to involve a limited range of fairly related markets. While managers might like the security of having more than one market, shareholders typically do not need each of the companies they invest in to be diversified as well – they would prefer managers to concentrate on managing their core business as well as they can. However, conventional finance theory does not apply to private businesses, where owners have a large proportion of their assets tied up in their company: here it can make sense to diversify risk across a number of distinct activities, so that if one part is in trouble, the whole business is not pulled down.

- *Managerial ambition* can sometimes drive inappropriate diversification. For example Vijay Mallya, CEO of UB Group, an Indian conglomerate involved in alcoholic beverages, aviation infrastructure, real estate and fertiliser, diversified further into airlines with Kingfisher Airlines (see Chapter 5 end case). This seemed in keeping with his extravagant lifestyle and pursuit of glamour; fitting his reputation as 'the King of Good Times'. However, there were no obvious synergies, and the airline industry was not competitive – leading to the collapse of Kingfisher and the loss of other key group assets. Managers such as Mallya might gain short-terms benefits in terms of prestige and financial rewards from diversification, but going beyond his areas of true expertise soon brought financial disaster.

8.4 DIVERSIFICATION AND PERFORMANCE

Because most large corporations today are diversified, but also because diversification can sometimes be in management's self-interest, many scholars and policy-makers have been concerned to establish whether diversified companies really perform better than undiversified companies. After all, it would be deeply troubling if large corporations were diversifying simply to spread risk for managers, to save managerial jobs in declining businesses or to generate short-term benefits for managers, as in the case of UB group.

Research studies of diversification have particularly focused on the relative benefits of related diversification and conglomerate or unrelated diversification. Researchers generally find that related or limited diversifiers outperform both firms that remain specialised and those that have unrelated or extensively diversified strategies.[12] In other words, the diversification–performance relationship tends to follow an inverted (or upside-down) U-shape, as in Figure 8.3. The implication is that some diversification is good – but not too much.

However, these performance studies produce statistical averages. Some related diversification strategies fail – as in the case of some accounting firms' ventures in consulting – while some conglomerates succeed – as in the case of LVMH. The case against unrelated diversification is not solid, and effective dominant logics or particular national contexts can play in its favour. For instance, easyGroup, with interests including planes, pizza, cars and gyms, has a strong dominant logic around business model innovation in mature industries. In terms of national contexts, conglomerate diversification may be particularly effective in developing economies as a form of protection against institutional weaknesses such as poor law enforcement, lack of quality labour, capricious political contexts. The conclusion from the performance studies is that, although on average related diversification pays better than unrelated, any diversification strategy needs rigorous questioning on its particular merits.

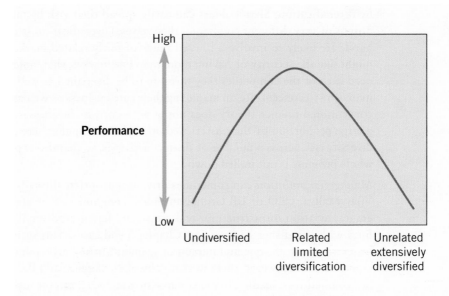

Figure 8.3 Diversity and performance

8.5 VERTICAL INTEGRATION

As well as diversification, another direction for corporate strategy can be vertical integration. **Vertical integration describes entering activities where the organisation is its own supplier or customer.** Thus it involves operating at another stage of the value network (see Section 4.4.2). This section considers both vertical integration and vertical dis-integration, particularly in the form of outsourcing.

8.5.1 Forward and backward integration

Vertical integration can go in either of two directions:

- *Backward integration* is movement into input activities concerned with the company's current business (i.e. further back in the value network). For example, acquiring a component supplier would be backward integration for a car manufacturer.
- *Forward integration* is movement into output activities concerned with the company's current business (i.e. further forward in the value network). For a car manufacturer, forward integration would be into car retail, repairs and servicing.

Thus vertical integration is like diversification in increasing corporate scope. The difference is that it brings together activities up and down the same value network, while diversification typically involves more or less different value networks. However, because realising synergies involves bringing together different value networks, diversification (especially related diversification) is sometimes also described as *horizontal integration*. For example, a company diversified in cars, trucks and buses could find benefits in integrating aspects of the various design or component-sourcing processes. The relationship between horizontal integration and vertical integration is depicted in Figure 8.4.

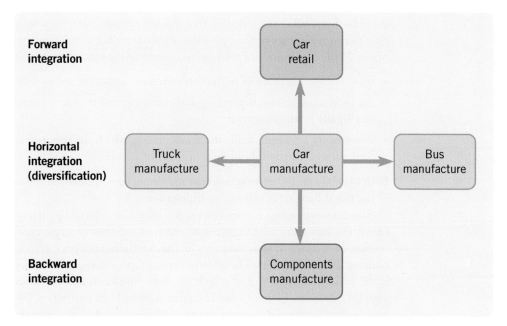

Figure 8.4 Diversification and integration options: car manufacturer example

Vertical integration often appears attractive as it seems to 'capture' some of the profits gained by retailers or suppliers in a value network – the retailers' or suppliers' profits. However there are two dangers. First, vertical integration involves investment. Expensive investments in activities that are less profitable than the original core business will be unattractive to shareholders because they are reducing their *average* or overall rate of return on investment. Second, even if there is a degree of relatedness through the value network, vertical integration is likely to involve quite different strategic capabilities. Thus car manufacturers forwardly integrating into car servicing found managing networks of small service outlets very different to managing large manufacturing plants. Growing appreciation of both the risks of diluting overall returns on investment and the distinct capabilities involved at different stages of the value network has led many companies in recent years to vertically *dis*-integrate.

8.5.2 To integrate or to outsource?

Where a part of vertically integrated operations is not adding value to the overall business, it may be replaced through outsourcing or subcontracting. **Outsourcing is the process by which activities previously carried out internally are subcontracted to external suppliers.** Outsourcing can refer to the subcontracting of components in manufacturing, but is now particularly common for services such as information technology, customer call centres and human resource management (see Illustration 8.3). The argument for outsourcing to specialist suppliers is often based on strategic capabilities. Specialists in a particular activity are likely to have superior capabilities than an organisation for which that particular activity is not a central part of its business. A specialist IT contractor is usually better at IT than the IT department of a steel company.

However, Nobel prize-winning economist Oliver Williamson has argued that the decision to integrate or outsource involves more than just relative capabilities. His *transaction cost framework* helps analyse the relative costs and benefits of managing ('transacting') activities internally or externally.[13] Assessing whether to integrate or outsource an activity, Williamson warns against underestimating the long-term costs of *opportunism* by external subcontractors (or indeed any other organisation in a market relationship). Subcontractors are liable over time to take advantage of their position, either to reduce their standards or to extract higher prices. Market relationships tend to fail in controlling subcontractor opportunism where:

- there are *few alternatives* to the subcontractor and it is hard to shop around;
- the product or service is *complex and changing,* and therefore impossible to specify fully in a legally binding contract;
- investments have been made in *specific assets,* which the subcontractors know will have little value if they withhold their product or service.

Both capabilities and transaction cost reasoning have influenced the outsourcing decisions of the Royal Bank of Scotland, see Illustration 8.3.

This transaction cost framework suggests that the costs of opportunism can outweigh the benefits of subcontracting to organisations with superior strategic capabilities. For example, mining companies in isolated parts of the Australian outback typically own and operate housing for their workers. The isolation creates specific assets (the housing is worth nothing if the mine closes down) and a lack of alternatives (the nearest town might be 100 miles away). Consequently, there would be large risks to both partners if the mine subcontracted housing to an independent company specialising in worker accommodation, however strong its capabilities. Transaction cost economics therefore offers the following advice: if there are few alternative suppliers, if activities are complex and likely to change, and if there are

ILLUSTRATION 8.3   'Out of sight – out of mind'? Outsourcing at Royal Bank of Scotland

In 2012, Royal Bank of Scotland (RBS) experienced a major crisis when its customers could not withdraw cash. Was this the consequence of outsourcing?

In June 2012, RBS encountered severe problems when ten million retail and business customers suddenly found they could not access their cash. This was highly damaging to the bank's reputation and could result in significant customer loss. The problem was faulty updating of CA-7 – critical software that controls the batch processing systems dealing with retail banking transactions. Generally regarded as 'a very common and reliable product, it processes accounts overnight via thousands of pieces of work' such as ATM transactions, bank-to-bank salary payments and so on, and finishes by updating the account master copy with the definitive balance. Described as a huge game of Jenga (the tower game played with interlaced wood blocks), all transactions are related, so everything needs to be processed in order. Thus Tuesday's batch must run before Wednesday's to avoid, for example, penalising someone who has a large sum of money leave their account on Wednesday that might put them in debt but which would be covered by money arriving on Tuesday. In updating CA-7, files were deleted or corrupted so the master copy was wrong for three nights – meaning millions of transactions were not processed. RBS branches had to extend their opening hours to reassure customers about their accounts.

Unions argued that the disaster was due to 'offshoring' UK IT jobs to India. 'RBS has 40 years' experience running this system and banks as a rule don't drop the ball like this,' remarked one bank employee. However, the general banking crisis had pressured UK banks to reduce their costs. RBS, which had suffered badly from the banking crisis, let thousands of UK staff go and transferred their roles to Chennai, India. As one former employee complained, 'We were having to pass 10–20+ years worth of mainframe knowledge onto people who'd never heard of a mainframe outside of a museum . . .'.

Offshore outsourcing was once heralded as the saviour of UK IT departments, cutting costs without compromising quality. Thousands of IT jobs were axed in the name of 'efficiency', many outsourced to India with much lower wages than the UK. Indeed in February 2012, RBS advertised it was urgently seeking computer graduates with several years' experience of using CA-7.

However, India's staff attrition rates in 2012 were at an all-time high with people changing jobs very quickly for just a few extra rupees, leaving insufficient time for adequate cultural awareness training. Quality at call centres suffered. At the same time, the UK was in recession with a devaluing pound greatly reducing wage disparity between India and the UK.

RBS's overseas problems were not uncommon with other banks experiencing loss of private data and in some instances criminal activity. Spanish-owned Santander UK – a bank created from Abbey National, Alliance & Leicester and Bradford & Bingley – also found that outsourced IT systems for these banks could not be trusted and so became the first of the major UK financial institutions to bring back its call centres and software from India to the UK, so that it could take care of its customer base. Ana Botin, Santander UK's Chief Executive, said the move was 'the most important factor in terms of satisfaction with the bank.' This 'inshoring' of strategic assets raises the question of whether strategic assets can afford to be 'out of sight and out of mind'.

Sources: *Guardian*, 25 June 2012; http://www.hrzone.co.uk/topic/business-lifestyle/shoring-new-shoring-call-centres-come-back-uk/112654.

Questions

1 In terms of transaction and capability costs, why might outsourcing be attractive to companies?

2 What might be the risks of 'insourcing'?

significant investments in specific assets, then it is likely to be better to vertically integrate rather than outsource.

In sum, the decision to integrate or subcontract rests on the balance between:

- *Relative strategic capabilities.* Does the subcontractor have the potential to do the work significantly better?

- *Risk of opportunism.* Is the subcontractor likely to take advantage of the relationship over time?

8.6 VALUE CREATION AND THE CORPORATE PARENT

Sometimes corporate parents do not add value to their constituent businesses. Where there is no added value, it is usually best to divest the relevant businesses from the corporate portfolio. Thus in 2016, Toyota Boshoku agreed to sell the automotive interior business of Polytec Holding that the Japanese parts maker had acquired in 2011, at a substantial loss. In the public sector too, units such as schools or hospitals are increasingly being given freedom from parenting authorities, because independence is seen as more effective. Some theorists even challenge the notion of corporate-level strategy altogether. The following section examines how corporate parents can both add and destroy value, and considers three different parenting approaches that can be effective.

8.6.1 Value-adding and value-destroying activities of corporate parents[14]

Corporate parents need to demonstrate that they create more value than they cost. This applies to both commercial and public-sector organisations. For public-sector organisations, privatisation or outsourcing is likely to be the consequence of failure to demonstrate value. Companies whose shares are traded freely on the stock markets face a further challenge. They must demonstrate they create more value than any other rival corporate parent could create. Failure to do so is likely to lead to a hostile takeover or break-up. Rival companies that think they can create more value out of the business units can bid for the company's shares, on the expectation of either running the businesses better or selling them off to other potential parents. If the rival's bid is more attractive and credible than what the current parent can promise, shareholders will back it at the expense of incumbent management.

In this sense, competition takes place between different corporate parents for the right to own and control businesses. In this 'market for corporate control', corporate parents must show that they have *parenting advantage,* on the same principle that business units must demonstrate competitive advantage. They must demonstrate that they are the best possible parents for the businesses they control. Parents therefore must be clear on how they create value. In practice, however, parenting activities can be value-destroying as well as value-creating.

Value-adding activities[15]

There are five main types of activity by which a corporate parent can add value:

- *Envisioning.* The corporate parent can provide a clear overall vision or *strategic intent* for its business units.[16] This should guide and motivate business unit managers to maximise corporation-wide performance through commitment to a common purpose. Envisioning should also provide stakeholders with a *clear external image* about what the organisation as a whole is about: to reassure shareholders about the rationale for having a diversified strategy in the first place.[17] Finally, a clear vision provides a *discipline* on the corporate parent to stop its wandering into inappropriate activities or taking on unnecessary costs.

- *Facilitating synergies.* The corporate parent can facilitate cooperation and sharing across business units, so improving *synergies* from being within the same corporate organisation. This can be achieved through incentives, rewards and remuneration schemes.

- *Coaching.* The corporate parent can help business unit managers develop strategic capabilities, by coaching them to improve their skills and confidence. Corporate-wide management courses are one effective means of achieving these objectives, as bringing managers across the business to learn strategy skills also allows them to build relationships between each other and perceive opportunities for cooperation.

- *Providing central services and resources.* The centre can provide capital for *investment* as well as central services such as treasury, tax and human resource advice. If these are centralised they may have *sufficient scale* to be efficient and can build up *relevant expertise*. Centralised services often have greater *leverage*: for example, combining many business unit purchases increases bargaining power for shared inputs such as energy. This leverage can be helpful in *brokering* with external bodies, such as government regulators, or other companies in negotiating alliances. Finally, the centre can have an important role in managing expertise within the corporate whole, for instance by *transferring managers* across the business units or by creating shared *knowledge management* systems via corporate intranets.

- *Intervening.* Finally, the corporate parent can also intervene within its business units to ensure appropriate performance. The corporate parent should be able to closely *monitor* business unit performance and *improve performance* either by replacing weak managers or by assisting them in turning around their businesses. The parent can also *challenge and develop* the strategic ambitions of business units, so good businesses are encouraged to perform even better.

Value-destroying activities

However, there are three ways in which the corporate parent can inadvertently destroy value:

- *Adding management costs.* Most simply, corporate staff and facilities are expensive. Corporate staff are typically the best-paid managers with the most luxurious offices. It is the actual businesses that have to generate the revenues that pay for them and if corporate centre costs are greater than the value they create, then corporate staff are net value-destroying.

- *Adding bureaucratic complexity.* As well as these direct financial costs, there is the 'bureaucratic fog' created by an additional layer of management and the need to coordinate with sister businesses. These typically slow down managers' responses to issues and lead to compromises between the interests of individual businesses.

- *Obscuring financial performance.* One danger in a large diversified company is that the under-performance of weak businesses can be obscured. Weak businesses might be cross-subsidised by stronger ones. Internally, the possibility of hiding weak performance diminishes the incentives for business unit managers to strive as hard as they can for their businesses: they have a parental safety net. Externally, shareholders and financial analysts cannot easily judge the performance of individual units within the corporate whole. Diversified companies' share prices are often marked down, because shareholders prefer the 'pure plays' of stand-alone units, where weak performance cannot be hidden.[18]

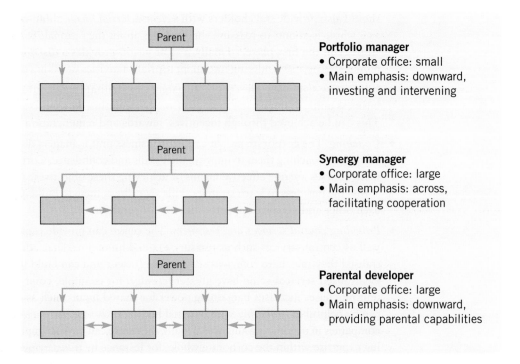

Figure 8.5 Portfolio managers, synergy managers and parental developers
Source: Adapted from M. Goold, A. Campbell and M. Alexander, *Corporate Level Strategy*, Wiley, 1994.

These dangers suggest clear paths for corporate parents that wish to avoid value destruction. They should keep a close eye on centre costs, both financial and bureaucratic, ensuring that they are no more than required by their corporate strategy. They should also do all they can to promote financial transparency, so that business units remain under pressure to perform and shareholders are confident that there are no hidden disasters.

Overall, there are many ways in which corporate parents can add value. It is, of course, difficult to pursue them all and some are hard to mix with others. For example, a corporate parent that does a great deal of top-down intervening is less likely to be seen by its managers as a helpful coach and facilitator. Business unit managers will concentrate on maximising their own individual performance rather than looking out for ways to cooperate with other business unit managers for the greater good of the whole. For this reason, corporate parenting roles tend to fall into three main types, each coherent within itself but distinct from the others.[19] These three types of corporate parenting role are summarised in Figure 8.5.

8.6.2 The portfolio manager

The **portfolio manager** **operates as an active investor in a way that shareholders in the stock market are either too dispersed or too inexpert to be able to do.** In effect, the portfolio manager is acting as an agent on behalf of financial markets and shareholders with a view to extracting more value from the various businesses than they could achieve themselves. Its role is to identify and acquire under-valued assets or businesses and improve them. The portfolio manager might do this, for example, by acquiring another corporation, divesting low-performing businesses within it and intervening to improve the performance of those with potential. Such corporations may not be much concerned about the relatedness (see Section 8.2) of the business units in their portfolio, typically adopting a conglomerate strategy. Their role is not to get closely involved in the routine management of the businesses, only to act over short periods of time to improve performance. In terms of the value-creating activities identified earlier, the portfolio manager concentrates on intervening and the provision (or withdrawal) of investment.

Portfolio managers seek to keep the cost of the centre low, for example by having a small corporate staff with few central services, leaving the business units alone so that their chief executives have a high degree of autonomy. They set clear financial targets for those chief executives, offering high rewards if they achieve them and likely loss of position if they do not. Such corporate parents can, of course, manage quite a large number of such businesses because they are not directly managing the everyday strategies of those businesses. Rather they are acting from above, setting financial targets, making central evaluations about the well-being and future prospects of such businesses, and investing, intervening or divesting accordingly.

Some argue that the days of the portfolio manager are gone. Improving financial markets mean that the scope for finding and investing cheaply in underperforming companies is much reduced. However, some portfolio managers remain and are successful. Private equity firms such as Apax Partners or Blackstone operate a portfolio management style, typically investing in, improving and then divesting companies in loosely knit portfolios. For example, in 2015, Blackstone, with $300bn in assets, owned companies in energy, real estate, water treatment, camera manufacture, banking, railway operation and seed development with more than 616,000 employees around the world. Illustration 8.4 includes a description of the portfolio parenting approach of Warren Buffett at Berkshire Hathaway.

8.6.3 The synergy manager

Obtaining synergy is often seen as the prime rationale for the corporate parent.[20] The **synergy manager is a corporate parent seeking to enhance value for business units by managing synergies across business units.** Synergies are likely to be particularly rich when new activities are closely related to the core business. In terms of value-creating activities, the focus is threefold: envisioning building a common purpose; facilitating cooperation across businesses; and providing central services and resources. For example, at Apple, Steve Jobs' vision of his personal computers being the digital hub of the new digital lifestyle guided managers across the iMac computer, iPod, iPhone and iPad businesses to ensure seamless connections between the fast-developing offerings. The result is enhanced value through better customer experience. A metals company diversified into both steel and aluminium might centralise its energy procurement, gaining synergy benefits through increased bargaining power over suppliers.

However, achieving such synergistic benefits involves at least three challenges:

- *Excessive costs.* The benefits in sharing and cooperation need to outweigh the costs of undertaking such integration, both direct financial costs and opportunity costs. Managing synergistic relationships tends to involve expensive investments in management time.

- *Overcoming self-interest.* Managers in the business units have to want to cooperate. Especially where managers are rewarded largely according to the performance of their own particular business unit, they are likely to be unwilling to sacrifice their time and resources for the common good.

- *Illusory synergies.* It is easy to overestimate the value of skills or resources to other businesses. This is particularly common when the corporate centre needs to justif a new venture or the acquisition of a new company. Claimed synergies often prove ill when managers actually have to put them into practice.

ILLUSTRATION 8.4   Eating its own cooking: Berkshire Hathaway's parenting

The challenge of managing a highly diverse set of businesses for shareholders.

From a small struggling textile business in the 1960s Warren Buffet, Berkshire Hathaway's 85-year-old billionaire Chairman and CEO, had built a $356bn (£219bn; €274bn) conglomerate in 2015. Its businesses were highly diverse including insurance companies (GEICO, General Re, NRG), carpets, building products, clothing and footwear manufacturers, retail companies and private jet service, NetJets. It also held significant long-term minority stakes in Coca-Cola and General Electric and continued to make major cash acquisitions, including BNSF for $34bn in 2009 (the second largest US railway company), Lubrizol (speciality chemicals, $9bn, 2011), Heinz ($23.3bn, 2013), Duracell (batteries, $4.7bn, 2014). In 2015, Precision Castparts, an aircraft components company suffering from falling revenues, profits and a 30 per cent decline in share price, was acquired for $37bn. But, as Buffet remarked, the size of Berkshire Hathaway made finding deals that make a difference, difficult – a bit like 'elephant hunting'.

Annual reports explained how Buffet and Deputy Chairman Charlie Munger ran the business:

'Charlie Munger and I think of our shareholders as owner-partners, and of ourselves as managing partners. (Because of the size of our shareholdings we are also, for better or worse, controlling partners.) We do not view the company itself as the ultimate owner of our business assets but instead view the company as a conduit through which our shareholders own the assets . . . In line with Berkshire's owner-orientation, most of our directors have a major portion of their net worth invested in the company. We eat our own cooking.'

Berkshire has a clear 'dominant logic':

'Charlie and I avoid businesses whose futures we can't evaluate, no matter how exciting their products may be. In the past, it required no brilliance for people to foresee the fabulous growth that awaited such industries as autos (in 1910), aircraft (in 1930) and television sets (in 1950). But the future then also included competitive dynamics that would decimate almost all of the companies entering those industries. Even the survivors tended to come away bleeding. Just because Charlie and I can clearly see dramatic growth ahead for an industry does not mean we can judge what its profit margins and returns on capital will be as a host of competitors battle for supremacy. At Berkshire we will stick with businesses whose profit picture for decades to come seems reasonably predictable. Even then, we will make plenty of mistakes.'

Explaining how they managed their subsidiary businesses, Buffet said:

'We subcontract all of the heavy lifting to the managers of our subsidiaries. In fact, we delegate almost to the point of abdication: though Berkshire has about 340,000 employees, only 25 of these are at headquarters. Charlie and I mainly attend to capital allocation and the care of our key managers. Most are happiest when they are left alone to run their businesses, and that is just how we leave them. That puts them in charge of all operating decisions and of dispatching the excess cash they generate to headquarters. By sending it to us, they don't get diverted by the various enticements that would come their way were they responsible for deploying the cash their businesses throw off. Furthermore, Charlie and I are exposed to a much wider range of possibilities for investing these funds than any of our managers could find.'

Berkshire Hathaway's 50th birthday had financial commentators reviewing its astonishing success. Buffet's investment genius is often cited alongside 'a weirdly intense contagious devotion of shareholders and media' (Munger). Many would like to fully understand the success formula that has stood Berkshire Hathaway in such good stead for so long. In the meantime, Berkshire Hathaway still had a huge cash pile in 2016. Should the ageing billionaire investor reload his 'elephant gun' for another acquisition?

Sources: 'Berkshire Hathaway Owner's Manual', http://brkshr.com/owners.html; http://www.berkshirehathaway.com/letters/2009ltr.pdf.

Questions

1 In what ways does Berkshire Hathaway fit the archetypal portfolio manager (see Section 8.6.2)?

2 Warren Buffet still had $73bn to invest. Suggest industries and businesses he would be unlikely to invest in.

The failure of many companies to extract expected synergies from their businesses has led to growing scepticism about the notion of synergy. Synergistic benefits are not as easy to achieve as would appear. For example, lawsuits between Hewlett Packard and former Autonomy employees following the former's €6.6bn (£5.3bn, $8.8bn) write down of Autonomy, a British software company, have resulted from failure to achieve anticipated integration benefits. Hewlett Packard blamed the former management team of Autonomy for fraudulent misrepresentation during the acquisition process. Nevertheless, synergy continues to be a common theme in corporate-level strategy, as Illustration 8.2 on TomTom shows.

8.6.4 The parental developer[21]

The **parental developer seeks to employ its own central capabilities to add value to its businesses.** This is not so much about how the parent can develop benefits *across* business units or transfer capabilities between business units, as in the case of managing synergy. Rather, parental developers focus on the resources or capabilities they have as parents which they can transfer *downwards* to enhance the potential of business units. For example, a parent could have a valuable brand or specialist skills in financial management or product development. It would seem that McDonald's believed it had identified a parenting opportunity in its acquisition of Chipotle as shown in Illustration 8.5. Parenting opportunities tend to be more common in the case of related rather than unrelated diversified strategies and are likely to involve exchanges of managers and other resources across the businesses. Key value-creating activities for the parent will be the provision of central services and resources. For example, a consumer products company might offer substantial guidance on branding and distribution from the centre; a technology company might run a large central R&D laboratory.

There are two crucial challenges to managing a parental developer:

- *Parental focus.* Corporate parents need to be rigorous and focused in identifying their unique value-adding capabilities. They should always be asking what others can do better than them, and focus their energy and time on activities where they really do add value. Other central services should typically be outsourced to specialist companies that can do it better.

- *The 'crown jewel' problem.* Some diversified companies have business units in their portfolios which are performing well but to which the parent adds little value. These can become 'crown jewels', to which corporate parents become excessively attached. The logic of the parental development approach is: if the centre cannot add value, it is just a cost and therefore destroying value. Parental developers should divest businesses[22] they do not add value to, even profitable ones. Funds raised by selling a profitable business can be reinvested in businesses where the parent can add value.

8.7 PORTFOLIO MATRICES

Section 8.6 discussed rationales for corporate parents of multi-business organisations. This section introduces models by which managers can determine financial investment and divestment within their portfolios of business.[23] Each model gives more or less attention to at least one of three criteria:

- the *balance* of the portfolio (e.g. in relation to its markets and the needs of the corporation);
- the *attractiveness* of the business units in terms of how strong they are individually and how profitable their markets or industries are likely to be; and

ILLUSTRATION 8.5   Chipotle: doing things differently

Struggling to find parenting advantage.

Chipotle Mexican Grill had always done things rather differently to the rest of the restaurant industry. Its outlets were not in the busiest locations, it spent lots on food, rarely added to the menu, didn't serve breakfast, do drive-throughs, franchises, or much advertising. And yet by 2015 it was a $22bn (£13.2bn, €16.5 bn) burrito empire. Despite its success, why did owner McDonald's sell it, especially when McDonald's own sales and stock price had dropped, as it became associated with America's obesity epidemic?

Founded 1993 in Denver, USA by Steve Ells, and relying initially on parents and wealthy friends for initial funding, Chipotle's fast casual dining business soon needed significant capital to expand beyond its 13 stores. In 1998, McDonalds made a $50m investment in Chipotle as part of the group's expansion that included Boston Market, Donatos Pizza, Pret a Manger and Aroma Cafe. It also investigated other businesses such as dry cleaning, a maid service and mowing the lawn.

McDonald's brought distribution systems, real estate expertise, construction knowledge and organisational structure along with its capital investment. To McDonald's, Chipotle brought new products – fresh cilantro, red onions and avocados. One McDonald's executive said: '[Our] Portland distribution centre smelled like a produce house. McDonald's product is fresh, but it's sealed in bags for shelf-life purposes.' Only one product was common to both companies – a five-gallon bag of Coca-Cola syrup.

Coming from a standardised, rules-based, efficiency-oriented culture, McDonald's executives were startled when they first visited Chipotle's headquarters. People brought their dogs into the office and Steve Ells walked around in blue jeans. Shown by Chipotle employees how they scrubbed the grill by hand, one McDonald's executive complained, saying, 'There's got to be a better system. You can't do this by hand all the time,' then suggested a power tool. They showed food could be customised as customers walked down the line. 'If you just want a little bit more salsa or a little bit less rice . . . nobody ever says no to you. . . . They might charge you for it . . . but that customization doesn't slow the throughput.'

By 2005, McDonald's owned 90 per cent of Chipotle. They pressed Chipotle to do drive-throughs, breakfasts and advertising, and suggested the name Chipotle Fresh Mexican Grill. Steve Ells hated the idea and was beginning to be resented at McDonald's for rejecting everything.

Chipotle did franchise eight restaurants for McDonald's, but they didn't succeed, costing a lot to be bought back. Steve Ells explained: 'there are two big things that we do differently. . . . the way we approach food . . . the way we approach our people culture.' McDonald's invited Steve to visit their chicken farm in Arkansas, but he was repelled and soon realised sourcing from small farms dramatically improved the taste of his food. Chipotle food costs ran at 30–32 per cent of total costs, similar to up-market restaurants, and McDonald's executives found this difficult to accept: 'That's ridiculous: that's like a steakhouse.' But Steve Ells was now focusing on ingredients and food integrity.

After seven years, Chipotle's contribution to McDonald's bottom line was small, despite 500 restaurants which investors wanted co-branded. Franchisees were getting distracted and Chipotle's was increasingly unhappy about McDonald's supply chain. Jim Cantalupo, McDonald's CEO, had already begun to sell off partner brands and the stock price had begun to rise. It was time for a McSplit.

Since leaving McDonald's, Chipotle's worth had risen to $15bn (2015), with 1,800 locations and business was booming. Although McDonald's pocketed $1.5bn (after $360m investment), McDonald's shareholders angrily questioned Steve Easterbrook, McDonald's CEO, on Chipotle's disposal.

Sources: Chipotle: the Definitive Oral History, http://www.bloomberg.com/graphics/2015-chipotle-oral-history.

Questions

1 What parenting advantages did McDonald's perceive it might bring to Chipotle?

2 Despite its success, why was Chipotle spun-off?

- the '*fit*' that the business units have with each other in terms of potential synergies or the extent to which the corporate parent will be good at looking after them.

8.7.1 The BCG (or growth/share) matrix[24]

One of the most common and longstanding ways of conceiving of the balance of a portfolio of businesses is the Boston Consulting Group (BCG) matrix (see Figure 8.6). The **BCG matrix uses market share and market growth criteria for determining the attractiveness and balance of a business portfolio.** High market share and high growth are, of course, attractive. However, the BCG matrix also warns that high growth demands heavy investment, for instance to expand capacity or develop brands. There needs to be a balance within the portfolio, so that there are some low-growth businesses that are making sufficient surplus to fund the investment needs of higher-growth businesses.

The growth/share axes of the BCG matrix define four sorts of business:

- A *star* is a business unit within a portfolio that has a high market share in a growing market. The business unit may be spending heavily to keep up with growth, but high market share should yield sufficient profits to make it more or less self-sufficient in terms of investment needs.

- A *question mark* (or problem child) is a business unit within a portfolio that is in a growing market, but does not yet have high market share. Developing question marks into stars, with high market share, takes heavy investment. Many question marks fail to develop, so the BCG advises corporate parents to nurture several at a time. It is important to make sure that some question marks develop into stars, as existing stars eventually become cash cows and cash cows may decline into dogs.

- A *cash cow* is a business unit within a portfolio that has a high market share in a mature market. However, because growth is low, investment needs are less, while high market share means that the business unit should be profitable. The cash cow should then be a cash provider, helping to fund investments in question marks.

- *Dogs* are business units within a portfolio that have low share in static or declining markets and are thus the worst of all combinations. They may be a cash drain and use up a disproportionate amount of managerial time and company resources. The BCG usually recommends divestment or closure.

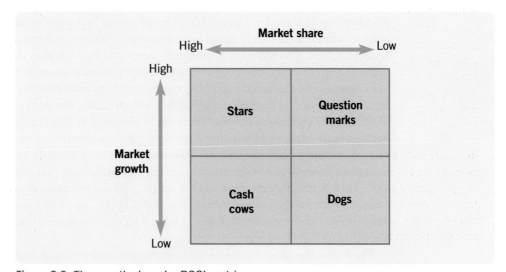

Figure 8.6 The growth share (or BCG) matrix

The BCG matrix has several advantages. It is a good way of visualising different needs and potentials of all the diverse businesses within the corporate portfolio. It warns corporate parents of the financial demands of what might otherwise look like a desirable portfolio of high-growth businesses. It also reminds corporate parents that stars are likely eventually to wane. Finally, it provides a useful discipline to business unit managers, underlining the fact that the corporate parent ultimately owns the surplus resources they generate and can allocate them according to what is best for the corporate whole. Cash cows should not hoard their profits.

However, there are at least four potential problems with the BCG matrix:

- *Definitional vagueness.* It can be hard to decide what high and low growth or share mean in particular situations. Managers are often keen to define themselves as 'high-share' by defining their market in a particularly narrow way (e.g. by ignoring relevant international markets).

- *Capital market assumptions.* The notion that a corporate parent needs a balanced portfolio to finance investment from internal sources (cash cows) assumes that capital cannot be raised in external markets, for instance by issuing shares or raising loans. The notion of a balanced portfolio may be more relevant in countries where capital markets are under-developed or in private companies that wish to minimise dependence on external shareholders or banks.

- *Unkind to animals.* Both cash cows and dogs receive ungenerous treatment, the first being simply milked, the second terminated or cast out of the corporate home. This treatment can cause *motivation problems,* as managers in these units see little point in working hard for the sake of other businesses. There is also the danger of the *self-fulfilling prophecy.* Cash cows will become dogs even more quickly than the model expects if they are simply milked and denied adequate investment.

- *Ignores commercial linkages.* The matrix assumes there are *no commercial ties to other business units* in the portfolio. For instance, a business unit in the portfolio may depend upon keeping a dog alive. These commercial links are less important in conglomerate strategies, where divestments or closures are unlikely to have knock-on effects on other parts of the portfolio.

8.7.2 The directional policy (GE–McKinsey) matrix

Another way to consider a portfolio of businesses is by means of the *directional policy matrix*[25] which categorises business units into those with good prospects and those with less good prospects. The matrix was originally developed by McKinsey & Co. consultants in order to help the American conglomerate General Electric manage its portfolio of business units. Specifically, the directional policy matrix positions business units according to (i) how attractive the relevant market is in which they are operating, and (ii) the competitive strength of the SBU in that market. Attractiveness can be identified by PESTEL or five forces analyses; business unit strength can be defined by competitor analysis (for instance, the strategy canvas); see Section 3.4.3. Some analysts also choose to show graphically how large the market is for a given business units activity, and even the market share of that business unit, as shown in Figure 8.7. For example, managers in a firm with the portfolio shown in Figure 8.7 will be concerned that they have relatively low shares in the largest and most attractive market, whereas their greatest strength is in a market with only medium attractiveness and smaller markets with little long-term attractiveness.

The matrix also offers strategy guidelines given the positioning of the business units. It suggests that the businesses with the highest growth potential and the greatest strength are those

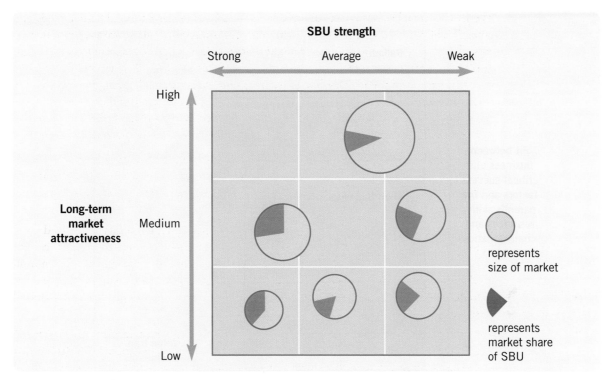

Figure 8.7 Directional policy (GE–McKinsey) matrix

in which to invest for growth. Those that are the weakest and in the least attractive markets should be divested or 'harvested' (i.e. used to yield as much cash as possible before divesting).

The directional policy matrix is more complex than the BCG matrix. However, it can have two advantages. First, unlike the simpler four-box BCG matrix, the nine cells of the directional policy matrix acknowledge the possibility of a difficult middle ground. Here managers have to be carefully selective. In this sense, the directional policy matrix is less mechanistic than the BCG matrix, encouraging open debate on less clear-cut cases. Second, the two axes of the directional policy matrix are not based on single measures (i.e. market share and market growth). Business strength can derive from many other factors than market share, and industry attractiveness does not just boil down to industry growth rates. On the other hand, the directional policy matrix shares some problems with the BCG matrix, particularly about vague definitions, capital market assumptions, motivation and self-fulfilling prophecy and ignoring commercial linkages. Overall, however, the value of the matrix is to help managers invest in the businesses that are most likely to pay off.

So far, the discussion has been about the logic of portfolios in terms of balance and attractiveness. The third logic is to do with 'fit' with the particular capabilities of the corporate parent.

8.7.3 The parenting matrix

The *parenting matrix* (or Ashridge Portfolio Display) developed by consultants Michael Goold and Andrew Campbell introduces parental fit as an important criterion for including businesses in the portfolio.[26]

Businesses may be attractive in terms of the BCG or directional policy matrices, but if the parent cannot add value, then the parent ought to be cautious about acquiring or retaining them.

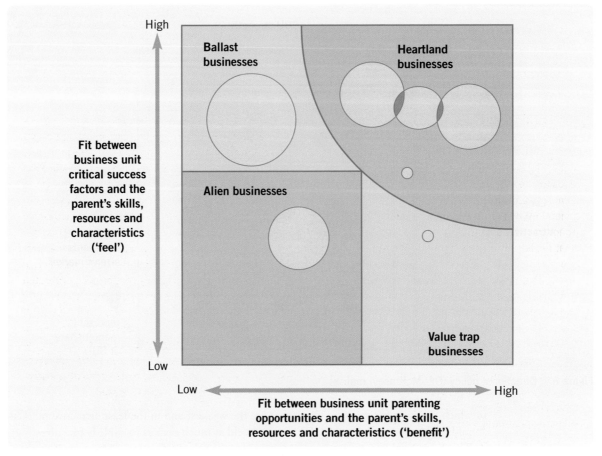

Figure 8.8 The parenting matrix: the Ashridge Portfolio Display

Source: Adapted from M. Goold, A. Campbell and M. Alexander, *Corporate Level Strategy*, Wiley, 1994.

There are two key dimensions of fit in the parenting matrix (see Figure 8.8):

- *'Feel'*. This is a measure of the fit between each business units critical success factors (see Section 3.4.3) and the capabilities (in terms of competences and resources) of the corporate parent. In other words, does the corporate parent have the necessary 'feel', or understanding, for the businesses it will parent?

- *'Benefit'*. This measures the fit between the parenting opportunities, or needs, of business units and the capabilities of the parent. Parenting opportunities are about the upside, areas in which good parenting can benefit the business (for instance, by bringing marketing expertise). For the benefit to be realised, of course, the parent must have the right capabilities to match the parenting opportunities.

The power of using these two dimensions of fit is as follows. It is easy to see that a corporate parent should avoid running businesses that it has no feel for. What is less clear is that parenting should be avoided if there is no benefit. This challenges the corporate parenting of even businesses for which the parent has high feel. Businesses for which a corporate parent has high feel but can add little benefit should either be run with a very light touch or be divested.

Figure 8.8 shows four kinds of business along these two dimensions of feel and benefit:

- *Heartland* business units are ones that the parent understands well and can continue to add value to. They should be at the core of future strategy.

THINKING DIFFERENTLY   Corporate strategy is a fool's errand

Is there a need for corporate strategy at all?

Although this chapter has argued that corporate strategy adds value to the multi-business (see Section 8.6.1), a recent *Harvard Business Review* article by Frank Vermeulen fundamentally challenges this position by asking 'does the headquarters actually add any value?'[27] Other commentators also worry that corporate functions do not generate the value from their activities they expect.[28] Although today's multi-businesses seem to have somewhat related businesses, in reality the various divisions operate completely independently from one another.[29] Also a third of the largest companies in North America and Europe have reported increased numbers of corporate functions with growing influence and yet complaints about that function's performance have increased.[30]

Disparate businesses come from companies growing into adjacent business areas each then requiring their own strategy, management teams and profit and loss responsibility. Corporate top management teams then aim to find synergies between the different divisions, by promoting cooperation, to create extra value as recommended by corporate finance. If none can be found, then headquarters is just managing a portfolio. The alternative view is that those businesses should be spun-off, as investors can diversify for themselves, and money would be saved on expensive headquarters.

Corporate top management may have advantages over external investors, including greater in-depth understanding of their businesses, and they are less likely to be fooled by numbers and charismatic SBU CEOs. They can act as the company's governance mechanism ensuring shareholder funds are wisely spent and strategies are genuine and they can staff divisional management teams with experts they know. However, this may just be rhetoric to conceal portfolio management. Or it may be a genuine attempt to contrive an overarching corporate strategy that seeks to proclaim cross-divisional synergies and cooperation, but is really an expensive illusion, as value is often not created. If the latter, corporate managers should really get out of the way of divisional strategies, rather than trying to set them. And if they are acting as portfolio managers, external investors can do this more efficiently. Therefore corporate strategy is a fool's errand.

> **Question**
>
> Evaluate the arguments for and against corporate strategy for Berkshire Hathaway or the Greystone Foundation.

- *Ballast* business units are ones the parent understands well but can do little for. They would probably be at least as successful as independent companies. If not divested, they should be spared as much corporate bureaucracy as possible.

- *Value trap* business units are dangerous. They appear attractive because there are opportunities to add value (for instance, marketing could be improved). But they are deceptively attractive, because the parent's lack of feel will result in more harm than good (i.e. the parent lacks the right marketing skills). The parent will need to acquire new capabilities if it is to be able to move value trap businesses into the heartland. It might be easier to divest to another corporate parent that could add value, and will pay well for the chance.

- *Alien* business units are clear misfits. They offer little opportunity to add value and the parent does not understand them anyway. Exit is definitely the best strategy.

This approach to considering corporate portfolios places the emphasis firmly on how the parent benefits the business units. This is the question that observers are asking of the Virgin Group in the end of chapter case. It requires careful analysis of both parenting capabilities and business unit parenting needs. The parenting matrix can therefore assist hard decisions where either high-feel or high-parenting opportunities tempt the corporate parent to acquire or retain businesses. Parents should concentrate on actual or potential heartland businesses, where there is both high feel and high benefit.

The concept of fit has equal relevance in the public sector. The implication is that public-sector managers should control directly only those services and activities for which they have special managerial expertise. Other services should be outsourced or set up as independent agencies (see Section 8.5).

SUMMARY

- Many corporations comprise several, sometimes many, business units. Corporate strategy involves the decisions and activities above the level of business units. It is concerned with choices concerning the scope of the organisation.

- Organisational *scope* is often considered in terms of *related* and *unrelated* diversification.

- Corporate parents may seek to add value by adopting different parenting roles: the *portfolio manager*, the *synergy manager* or the *parental developer*.

- There are several portfolio models to help corporate parents manage their businesses, of which the most common are: the *BCG matrix*, the *directional policy matrix* and the *parenting matrix*.

- *Divestment* and *outsourcing* should be considered as well as diversification, particularly in the light of relative strategic capabilities and the transaction costs of *opportunism*.

WORK ASSIGNMENTS

✱ Denotes more advanced work assignments.
* Refers to a case study in the Text and Cases edition.

8.1   Using the Ansoff axes (Figure 8.2), identify and explain corporate strategic directions for any one of these case organisations: CRH*, Air Asia and the Tune Group*, Severstal* and SABMiller or AB InBev in the Megabrew* case.

8.2   Go to the website of any large multi-business organisation (e.g. Alphabet, Google, Megabrew*, Siemens, Tata Group, Virgin Group – see end of chapter case) and assess the degree to which its corporate-level strategy is characterised by (a) related or unrelated diversification and (b) a coherent 'dominant logic' (see Section 8.3).

8.3   For any large multi-business corporation (as in Section 8.2), Alphabet, the Tune Group*, Siemens* or Severstal*, explain how the corporate parent should best create value for its component businesses (as portfolio manager, synergy manager or parental developer: see Section 8.6). Would all the businesses fit equally well?

8.4✱ For any large multi-business corporation (as in 8.2), Megabrew* or the Virgin Group (end of chapter case), plot the business units on a portfolio matrix (e.g. the BCG matrix: Section 8.7.1). Justify any assumptions about the relative positions of businesses on the relevant axes of the matrix. What managerial conclusions do you draw from this analysis?

Integrative assignment

8.5   Take a case of a recent merger or acquisition (see Chapter 11), and assess the extent to which it involved related or unrelated diversification (if either) and how far it was consistent with the company's existing dominant logic. Using share price information (see www.bigcharts.com or similar), assess shareholders' reaction to the merger or acquisition. How do you explain this reaction?

RECOMMENDED KEY READINGS

- An accessible discussion of corporate strategy is provided by A. Campbell and R. Park, *The Growth Gamble: When Leaders Should Bet on Big New Businesses,* Nicholas Brealey, 2005.

- M. Goold and K. Luchs, 'Why diversify: four decades of management thinking', in D. Faulkner and A. Campbell (eds), *The Oxford Handbook of Strategy,* vol. 2, Oxford University Press, pp. 18–42, 2003, provides an authoritative overview of the diversification option over time.

- L. Capron and W. Mitchell, *Build, Borrow or Buy: solving the growth dilemma,* Harvard Business Press, 2012, provides a good review of the arguments for and against different modes of growth.

- A good review of the current state of corporate portfolio management research is provided by M. Nippa, U. Pidua and H. Rubner, 'Corporate portfolio management: appraising four decades of academic research', *Academy of Management Perspectives,* November 2011, pp. 50–66.

REFERENCES

1. For a detailed discussion as to how organisational structures might 'address' an organisation's mix of SBUs, see M. Goold and A. Campbell, *Designing Effective Organizations: How to Create Structured Networks*, Jossey-Bass, 2002. Also K. Eisenhardt and S. Brown, 'Patching', *Harvard Business Review*, vol. 77, no. 3 (1999), p. 72.

2. This figure is an extension of the product/market matrix: see I. Ansoff, *Corporate Strategy*, 1988, Chapter 6. The Ansoff matrix was later developed into the one shown below.

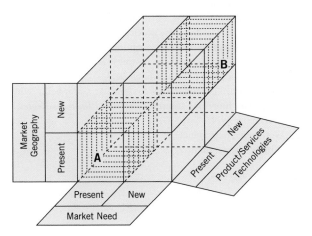

3. For the European Commission competition authority, http://ec.europa.eu/comm/competition; for the UK Competition Commission, see http://www.competition-commission.org.uk/.

4. For discussions of the challenge of sustained growth and diversification, see A. Campbell and R. Parks, *The Growth Gamble*, Nicholas Brealy, 2005; and D. Laurie, Y. Doz and C. Sheer, 'Creating new growth platforms', *Harvard Business Review*, vol. 84, no. 5 (2006), pp. 80–90.

5. On economies of scope, see D.J. Teece, 'Towards an economic theory of the multi-product firm', *Journal of Economic Behavior and Organization*, vol. 3 (1982), pp. 39–63.

6. See R. Bettis and C.K. Prahalad, 'The dominant logic: retrospective and extension', *Strategic Management Journal*, vol. 16, no. 1 (1995), pp. 5–15.

7. F. Neffke and M. Henning, 'Skill relatedness and firm diversification', *Strategic Management Journal*, vol. 34, no. 3 (2013), pp. 297–316 show that internal skills may aid in the diversification process.

8. See C. Markides, 'Corporate strategy: the role of the centre', in A. Pettigrew, H. Thomas and R. Whittington (eds), *Handbook of Strategy and Management*, Sage, 2002. For a discussion of Chinese diversification patterns, see A. Delios, N. Zhou and W.W. Xu, 'Ownership structure and the diversification and performance of publicly-listed companies in China', *Business Horizons*, vol. 51, no. 6 (2008), pp. 802–21. See M.C. Mayer, C. Stadler and J. Hautz, 'The relationship between product and international diversification: the role of experience', *Strategic Management Journal*, vol. 36, no. 10 (2015), pp. 1458–68 for a discussion of the importance of experience in driving diversification.

9. These benefits are often discussed in terms of 'multimarket' or 'multipoint' competition: see J. Anand, L. Mesquita and R. Vassolo, 'The dynamics of multimarket competition in exploration and exploitation activities', *Academy of Management Journal*, vol. 52, no. 4 (2009), pp. 802–21.

10. M. Goold and A. Campbell, 'Desperately seeking synergy', *Harvard Business Review*, vol. 76, no. 2 (1998), pp. 131–45. See also Y.M. Zhou, 'Synergy, coordination costs, and diversification choices', *Strategic Management Journal*, vol. 32, no. 6 (2011), pp. 624–39.

11. A. Pehrson, 'Business relatedness and performance: a study of managerial perceptions', *Strategic Management Journal*, vol. 27, no. 3 (2006), pp. 265–82. See also F. Neffke and M. Henning, 'Skill relatedness and firm diversification', *Strategic Management Journal*, vol. 34, no. 3 (2013), pp. 297–316.

12. L.E. Palich, L.B. Cardinal and C. Miller, 'Curvilinearity in the diversification-performance linkage: an examination of over three decades of research', *Strategic Management Journal*, vol. 21 (2000), pp. 155–74. The inverted-U

relationship is the research consensus, but studies often disagree, particularly finding variations over time and across countries. For recent context-sensitive studies, see M. Mayer and R. Whittington, 'Diversification in context: a cross national and cross temporal extension', *Strategic Management Journal*, vol. 24 (2003), pp. 773–81; and A. Chakrabarti, K. Singh and I. Mahmood, 'Diversification and performance: evidence from East Asian firms', *Strategic Management Journal*, vol. 28 (2007), pp. 101–20. There are also variations by type of diversification – see M. Geoffrey, G.M. Kistruck, I. Qureshi and P.W. Beamish, 'Geographic and product diversification in charitable organizations', *Journal of Management*, vol. 39, no. 2 (2011), pp. 496–530.

13. For a discussion and cases on the relative guidance of transaction cost and capabilities thinking, see R. McIvor, 'How the transaction cost and resource-based theories of the firm inform outsourcing evaluation', *Journal of Operations Management*, vol. 27, no. 1 (2009), pp. 45–63. See also T. Holcomb and M. Hitt, 'Toward a model of strategic outsourcing', *Journal of Operations Management*, vol. 25, no. 2 (2007), pp. 464–81.

14. For a good discussion of corporate parenting roles, see Markides in endnote 8 above. A recent empirical study of corporate headquarters is D. Collis, D. Young and M. Goold, 'The size, structure and performance of corporate headquarters', *Strategic Management Journal*, vol. 28, no. 4 (2007), pp. 383–406.

15. M. Goold, A. Campbell and M. Alexander, *Corporate Level Strategy*, Wiley, 1994, is concerned with both the value-adding and value-destroying capacity of corporate parents.

16. For a discussion of the role of clarity of mission, see A. Campbell, M. Devine and D. Young, *A Sense of Mission*, Hutchinson Business, 1990.

17. T. Zenger, 'Strategy: the uniqueness challenge,' *Harvard Business Review*, November 2013, pp. 52–8.

18. E. Zuckerman, 'Focusing the corporate product: securities analysts and de-diversification', *Administrative Science Quarterly*, vol. 45, no. 3 (2000), pp. 591–619.

19. The first two rationales discussed here are based on M. Porter, 'From competitive advantage to corporate strategy', *Harvard Business Review*, vol. 65, no. 3 (1987), pp. 43–59.

20. See A. Campbell and K. Luchs, *Strategic Synergy*, Butterworth–Heinemann, 1992.

21. The logic of parental development is explained extensively in Goold, Campbell and Alexander (see endnote 15 above). For more on the dynamics of organisational structure see J. Joseph and W. Ocasio, 'Architecture, attention, and adaptation in the multi-business firm: General Electric from 1951 to 2001', *Strategic Management Journal*, vol. 33, no. 6 (2013), pp. 633–60.

22. J. Xia and S. Li, 'The divestiture of acquired subunits: a resource dependence approach', *Strategic Management Journal*, vol. 34, no. 2 (2013), pp. 131–48.

23. A good review of the current state of corporate portfolio management research is provided by M. Nippa, U. Pidua and H. Rubner, 'Corporate portfolio management: appraising four decades of academic research', *Academy of Management Perspectives*, vol. 25, no. 4 (2011), pp. 50–66.

24. For a more extensive discussion of the use of the growth share matrix, see A.C. Hax and N.S. Majluf, 'The use of the industry attractiveness business strength matrix in strategic planning', in R.G. Dyson (ed.), *Strategic Planning: Models and Analytical Techniques*, Wiley, 1990; and D. Faulkner, 'Portfolio matrices', in V. Ambrosini (ed.), *Exploring Techniques of Analysis and Evaluation in Strategic Management*, Prentice Hall, 1998; for source explanations of the BCG matrix, see B.D. Henderson, *Henderson on Corporate Strategy*, Abt Books, 1979.

25. Hax and Majluf (see endnote 24).

26. The discussion in this section draws on Goold, Campbell and Alexander (see endnote 15) which provides an excellent basis for understanding issues of parenting.

27. F. Vermeulen, 'Corporate strategy is a fool's errand', *Harvard Business Review*, March 2013.

28. S. Kunisch, G. Muller-Stewens and A. Campbell, 'Why corporate functions stumbles', *Harvard Business Review*, December 2014.

29. Vermeulen (see endnote 27).

30. Kunisch (see endnote 28).

Virgin – is the brand more than Richard Branson?
by Marianne Sweet

Introduction

The Virgin Group is a highly diversified organisation which runs a range of businesses including mobile telephony, financial services, airlines, railways, music, holidays and health and care services. It has grown to be one of the largest private UK companies, employing around 50,000 people in 50 countries and with revenues in excess of £15bn (€18bn, $22bn). According to the Centre for Brand Analysis, in 2015 Virgin was the number three best-known brand in the UK after British Airways and Apple.

Virgin's flamboyant founder, Sir Richard Branson, is one of the UK's richest and best known entrepreneurs and at the centre of the group's growth. Branson has a flair for publicity and over the past 40 years has generated the interest and awareness that have made Virgin such a strong brand. The Group believes the Virgin brand is so well respected that it adds value to any business that bears the name.

What is difficult to unpick is how much of Virgin's success is down to Branson's entrepreneurial flair and how much is down to the group's unusual structure and business model. Virgin's strategy and business models are not widely understood and, as a result, investors have questioned its sustainability should Branson depart. The parent company describes itself as a leading international investment group. But does Virgin Group add value to the diverse portfolio of SBUs? Does the portfolio of businesses make strategic sense?

Virgin's beginnings and style

Branson founded his first business, a student magazine, after dropping out of school at the age of 15. Virgin began in 1970 when Branson sold music (vinyl records) by mail order. Able to undercut high street retailers, the business grew rapidly. He opened Virgin Record Shop – named to reflect his naivety in business – in Oxford Street, London a year later. Further expansion took the form of backward integration as he moved into recording and publishing music: his first album, *Tubular Bells* by unknown musician Mike Oldfield in 1973, became a worldwide hit. He then controversially signed the Sex Pistols, a punk rock group

Richard Branson

Source: RichardBakerFarnborough/Alamy Images.

who became notorious for their rude anti-establishment behaviour and lyrics. Those two events epitomised the business philosophy Branson would use to build a worldwide brand – a love of risk-taking, irreverence to the 'old school of business', a passion for fun and a flair for publicity.

The common threads uniting this diverse group of companies are the core values of the Virgin brand – as described by Virgin Group itself: customer-driven with an emphasis on value for money, quality, fun and innovation.[1]

Branson is not risk averse, but a core part of his business philosophy is 'protect the downside' – that is limiting possible losses before moving forward with a new business venture. It was a lesson his father taught him when he was 15. His dad agreed to let him drop out of school to start a magazine, but only if he sold £4,000 of advertising to cover printing costs.[2]

It's an approach he repeated in 1984 when launching low-cost transatlantic airline, Virgin Atlantic. To create this new venture, Branson had to battle to procure landing rights at London's Heathrow Airport. Up to that time, the routes had been dominated by British Airways, which led to an intense rivalry between the two carriers, involving a 'dirty tricks' campaign by BA and a very bitter and public court case, which Virgin won, adding fuel to the image of Richard Branson as the underdog, average businessman

Marianne Sweet is Director of Damselfly Communications Limited and lectures on business enterprise and entrepreneurship at the University of Gloucestershire, UK. This case example includes some material and sources from previous cases on Virgin which featured in earlier editions of *Exploring Strategy*, written by Urmilla Lawson and updated by Aidan McQueen and by John Treciockas.

taking on the oppressors, self-interested 'big business' and the traditional establishment.

Branson had to make some tough decisions to support the fledging airline. At the time, Virgin Records was a profitable business and Virgin decided that selling that business was the safest way to raise funds. 'If we continued running both companies, then we risked them both. At that point, it seemed possible that Virgin Atlantic would have had to close, leaving 2,500 people without jobs and our brand's reputation in tatters. By selling Virgin Records, we left both companies in strong positions,' explained Branson in one of his Virgin blogs.[3]

Virgin Records was sold to EMI for £500m. The Group then decided to go on to the London and NASDQ stock markets, offering 35 per cent ownership. But Branson's business style did not suit the accountability needed for a chairman of a public corporation and he returned the group to private ownership in 1988.

Growth of the Virgin brand

The Virgin Group grew rapidly through a series of new start-ups, joint ventures and acquisitions. Branson, as chair of Virgin Group, has overseen approximately 500 companies during the parent group's lifetime.

The rationale behind many of the initiatives can be hard to understand and some appear to be pure whim. For Branson it all made business sense. 'Think of the world as one country – it's a lot more fun to do business that way,' he commented.[4] Initially the group focused on travel/holidays and music. Since the 1990s, it has expanded into a wide variety of businesses (Appendix 1, below, lists a selection of new businesses and key events). Virgin Group has repeatedly demonstrated that it is skilled at environmental scanning, searching for those strategic windows of opportunity – usually created by innovation or changes in legislation – and then taking the market advantage.

For instance, the development of digital technologies enabled Virgin to grow its retail interests, moving into the online sales of music, cars, wine, financial products and internet services. Virgin Mobile was the result of deregulation of the telecommunications sector in the UK and the growing advances in cellular communications. Deregulation of the railways in the UK led to Virgin launching Virgin Rail, first running the passenger train service on the West Coast of England and then, in 2014, in a joint venture with Stagecoach, winning the franchise for the East Coast line, between London and Scotland.

In 2012, Virgin purchased Northern Rock, a medium-sized UK mortgage finance provider, which the Government had temporarily nationalised at the beginning of the financial crisis in 2007. The purchase marked the growth of Virgin as a financial services provider, leading to the eventual flotation of Virgin Money on the London Stock Exchange in 2014.

Branson is also known for his taste for adventure and in 2012 launched Virgin Galactic, intending to provide a passenger service into orbital space. He has often commented that being an adventurer and being an entrepreneur is the same thing – and both involve risk. Although Virgin Galactic suffered a huge setback in 2014, when one of its test planes crashed, the following year Virgin Galactic won a $4.7m contract from NASA to carry more than a dozen satellites into orbit on board its LauncherOne.

Again identifying opportunities from deregulation, this time of health services in the UK, Virgin acquired a 75 per cent stake in Assura Medical, which in 2012 was rebranded as Virgin Care. Since then, Virgin Care has become one of the market leaders in providing healthcare, for example, in 2012 it signed a £500m five-year contract to provide community health services for the National Health Service's Surrey region. The Virgin Care website was able to claim that it was providing more than 230 NHS social care services and since 2006 had treated more than four million people.

Corporate rationale

In 2016, the Virgin Group described itself as a leading international investment group and one of the world's most recognised and respected brands. While the group does not provide an organisational structure chart, it is possible to see a discernible grouping of businesses (see Figure 1) within six categories. The operational companies are all separate strategic business units (SBUs), financed on a stand-alone basis.

Branson believes that companies should succeed within the first year or exit the market. In 2013, Virgin Atlantic launched a UK domestic airline, Little Red, linking London Heathrow with Edinburgh, Aberdeen and Manchester. After 18 months, it was scrapped. Branson claimed the venture had benefited consumers but 'the odds were stacked against us'.

Virgin looks for market opportunities where the Group believes its brand can create competitive advantage, usually in markets where existing customers are not receiving value for money, such as health clubs, cosmetics, weddings, drinks, airlines and clothing. The Virgin brand is perceived as the consumer's champion for value-for-money, good quality, brilliant customer service, innovation, being anti-establishment and fun.

Virgin is a mix of publicly listed and privately owned companies, ranging from start-up ventures through to large corporate businesses. Each is 'ring-fenced' so that lenders to one company have no rights over the assets of another. Each company may have very different strategic

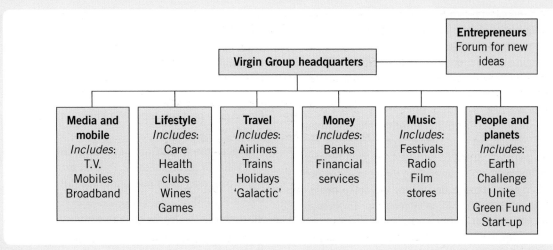

Figure 1

objectives. The larger start-ups are serious strategic moves into new markets. Some may be a method of training and developing managers. Some may be to keep Virgin in the public eye.

Each company has no direct lines of reporting or control in the Group. There are minimal management layers. Companies are linked through a complex network of parent subsidiary relations involving 'holding companies' with the ultimate holding company being registered in the British Virgin Islands – a tax haven. The freedom of the companies and the employees – which mirrors Branson's disrespect for hierarchy – and their separation from the parent company, enables the group to retain a spirit of entrepreneurism.

Managers are trusted, have high levels of responsibility and have financial incentives that could turn them into millionaires. This mirrors Branson's ethos of shaping and building businesses around people. He also believes that trusting others with the day-to-day running of Virgin has enabled him to be more agile as an entrepreneur and to focus on scoping for opportunities to grow the brand. He surrounds himself with people who can turn his ideas into reality.

'The best bit of advice I think I can give to any manager of a company is find somebody better than yourself to do the day-to-day running,' Branson stated in 2015 in an interview with Business Insider UK. 'And then free yourself up to think about the bigger picture. By freeing myself up, I've been able to dream big and move Virgin forward into lots of different areas.'[2]

Virgin is known for its risk-taking when entering the market and its pragmatic approach to exiting. No business is too precious to have its role challenged within the portfolio. The underlying business logic has been summarised by Branson: 'Business opportunities are like buses . . . There's always another coming along'.[5]

Branson wrote in 2016, at the time of the sale of Virgin America: 'In 2007, when the airline started service, 60 per cent of the industry was consolidated. Today, the four mega-airlines control more than 80 per cent of the US market. Consolidation is a trend that sadly cannot be stopped.'[6] In 2015, the Group decided to sell another of its flagship companies, with 80 per cent of its share of the Virgin Active fitness chain going to South African billionaire Christo Wiese, prompting the British health-club chain to cancel plans for a share sale.[7] Of the sale, Virgin stated: 'Our investment strategy is to build businesses of scale and this sometimes means accessing external capital to build them further through sales of stakes to partners or through the public markets.'[8]

The future

While Branson does not mention his departure, he has continued to state that the company has been structured to continue without him. He says that he now devotes the majority of his time and energy to Virgin Unite – a charitable foundation which focuses on environmental and charity activities. Business observers remain divided about the essence of the group's business model: some see it as a private equity organisation (but many of the businesses are start-ups); others see it as a branded venture capital organisation (but the group incubates its own businesses); some suggest that it is a conglomerate. Some critics assert that the Virgin brand has been over-extended.

It is difficult to discover the overall financial position of Virgin because it is made up of so many individual companies and there are no consolidated accounts. Branson has agreed that he is interested in growth, not short-term profits, and builds companies for the long term. There is an emphasis on maximising returns to Virgin Group equity through high financial leverage and the use of equity partners. The financial picture is very mixed: in 2014, Virgin Money reported a £34m statutory profit before tax whereas Virgin Australia reported a AUS$356m ($276m, €245m, £193m) net loss after tax for the same year. A spokesman for Virgin Care, in 2015, said the company had not yet reached 'a state of profitability' and shareholders were still investing in the growth of the business.

Branson remains, as ever, defiant to his critics. Is Virgin a strong enough brand to survive if he steps aside? Would the Virgin Group survive? 'The Virgin brand is not a product; it's an attitude and a way of life to many,' explained Branson in 2012 in an interview for Economia. 'That attitude is about giving customers a better time and better value in a fun way that embraces life. But brands, ultimately, belong to the consumer and while a business can influence its brand by what it does and how it behaves, it is what the customer thinks at the end of the day that is the only important thing.'[9]

Questions

1 What directions of strategic development have been followed by Virgin over the period of the case (use Figure 8.2 as a guide)?

2 Which type of corporate parenting role (as per Figure 8.5) best describes the Virgin Group? Justify your choice.

3 How does the Virgin Group as a corporate parent add value to its businesses? To what extent are these parenting skills relevant to the differing business units?

4 What should the future corporate strategy be? (And how essential is Richard Branson himself to that strategy?)

References
1. http://www.virgin-atlantic.com/tridion/images/companyoverviewnov_tcm4-426059.pdf
2. http://uk.businessinsider.com/how-richard-branson-maintains-the-virgin-group-2015-2?r=US&IR=T
3. https://www.virgin.com/entrepreneur/richard-branson-how-to-find-the-right-funding-for-your-business
4. https://www.virgin.com/entrepreneur/six-things-we-learnt-business-adventure-la
5. https://www.virgin.com/richard-branson/opportunity-missed
6. https://www.virgin.com/richard-branson/virgin-america
7. http://www.bloomberg.com/news/articles/2015-04-16/brait-agrees-to-buy-80-of-virgin-active-for-about-1-billion
8. http://www.theguardian.com/business/2015/apr/16/virgin-active-stake-sold-to-south-africas-brait
9. http://economia.icaew.com/people/november-2012/out-of-this-world

Appendix 1 Strategic developments of the Virgin Group 1970–2016

1970	Branson founds the Virgin business selling records
1971	First Virgin record shop opened
1977	Virgin record label is launched
1984	Virgin Atlantic, a long-haul airline is founded
1985	Virgin Holidays is founded
1986	Virgin Group PLC formed
1987	Virgin Records America is launched
1988–90	Virgin Megastores are opened in prime city locations in Europe, USA and Japan Branson takes Virgin Group PLC private for £248 m
1991	Virgin Publishing formed through merging Virgin Books and WH Allen PLC Virgin Games formed
1992	Virgin Records sold for £510 m
1993	Virgin Games floated as Virgin Interactive Entertainment PLC Virgin Radio commences broadcasting
1994	Virgin Retail acquires Our Price chain of shops
1996	Virgin Net an internet service provider is launched
1997	Virgin Trains is founded to run West Coast rail franchise in the UK Virgin Cosmetics launches with four flagship stores Virgin Radio sold for £87m
1999	Virgin Mobile is launched in joint venture with Deutsche Telekom Virgin Health starts a network of health clubs Virgin Cinemas is sold for £215 m 49 per cent of Virgin Atlantic sold to Singapore Airlines for $500 m
2000	Virgin Mobile launches US wireless phone service (JV with Sprint) Virgin Blue launched (low-cost airline – Australia) Virgin Cars launched to sell online
2001	50 per cent of Virgin Blue sold
2004	Virgin Digital launched to sell online music Virgin Unite, a charitable foundation, launched
2006	Virgin Media is launched in partnership with NTL-Telewest Virgin Fuel launched Virgin Cars closed
2007	Last of Virgin Megastores (125) sold Virgin America (airline) launched Virgin Earth Challenge and World Citizen initiatives are launched
2009	Virgin Green Fund launched
2010	Virgin Hotels launches Virgin Racing launched (Formula One) Virgin Gaming launched Virgin Produced launched (film and TV production company) Virgin Money acquires Church House Trust to acquire UK banking licence Virgin Group acquires majority stake in Assura Medical
2011	Virgin Cosmetics and Virgin Money (USA) are closed Virgin Active acquires Esporta for £80 m Virgin Unite (charitable foundation) launches Branson's Centre for Entrepreneurship
2012	Assura Medical rebrands as Virgin Care Virgin Care signs £500m contract to run Surrey Care Services, part of NHS Surrey
2013	Virgin Money acquires Northern Rock for about £1bn Virgin Media sold to Liberty Global
2014	Virgin Money floated on Stock Exchange Virgin and Stagecoach joint venture wins East Coast mainland rail franchise Virgin Galactic spaceship crashes
2015	Virgin Active sells 80% of its stake Virgin Galactic wins $4.7m NASA contract
2016	Virgin America is sold to Alaska Air for £1.8bn Branson unveils Virgin Galactic's new space tourism rocket plane

Source: Based on www.virgin.com.

9

INTERNATIONAL STRATEGY

Learning outcomes

After reading this chapter you should be able to:

- Assess the *internationalisation drivers and potential* of different markets.

- Identify sources of competitive advantage in international strategy, through both exploitation of *local factors* and *global sourcing*.

- Understand the difference between *global integration* and *local responsiveness* and four main types of international strategy.

- *Rank markets* for entry or expansion, taking into account attractiveness, cultural and other forms of distance and competitor retaliation threats.

- Assess the relative merits of different *market entry strategy modes*, including joint ventures, licensing and franchising and wholly owned subsidiaries.

Key terms

9.1 INTRODUCTION

The last chapter introduced market development as a strategy, in relation to the Ansoff axes (see Section 8.2.3). This chapter focuses on a specific but important kind of market development, operating in different geographical markets. Many types of organisations expand internationally and face new customer needs and are challenged by local economic, regulative, political and cultural institutions that often differ substantially from home. There are of course the large traditional multinationals such as Nestlé, Toyota and McDonald's. But recent years have seen the rise of emerging-country multinationals from Brazil, Russia, India and China. New small firms, like internet-based start-ups, are also increasingly 'born global', building international relationships right from the start. Likewise, not-for-profit organisations like the Red Cross and Doctors without Borders have been working internationally from the beginning. Public-sector organisations also have to make choices about collaboration, outsourcing and even competition with overseas organisations. For example, European Union legislation requires public service organisations to accept tenders from non-national suppliers.

Figure 9.1 identifies the five main themes of this chapter, with international strategy as the core. The themes are as follows:

- *Internationalisation drivers.* Drivers of organisation's internationalisation include market demand, the potential for cost advantages, government pressures and inducements and the need to respond to competitor moves. Given the risks and costs of international strategy, managers need to know that the drivers are strong to justify adopting an international strategy in the first place.

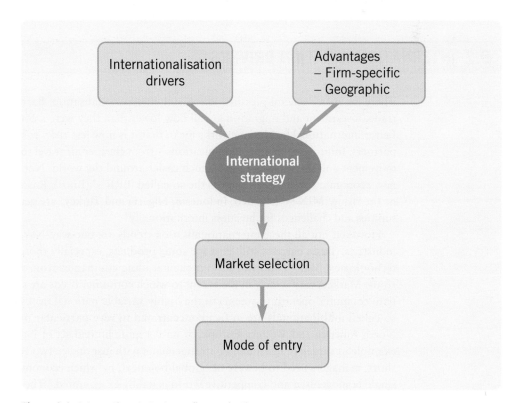

Figure 9.1 International strategy: five main themes

- *Geographical and firm-specific advantages.* In international competition, advantages might come from firm-specific and geographical advantages. Firm-specific advantages are the unique resources and capabilities proprietary to an organisation as discussed in Chapter 4. Geographical advantages might come both from the geographic location of the original business and from the international configuration of their value system. Managers need to appraise these potential sources of competitive advantage carefully: if there are no firm-specific or geographical competitive advantages, international strategy is liable to fail.

- *International strategy.* If drivers and advantages are sufficiently strong to merit an international strategy, then a range of strategic approaches are opened up, from the simplest export strategies to the most complex global strategies.

- *Market selection.* Having adopted the broad approach to international strategy, the next question is which country markets to prioritise and which to steer clear of. Here managers need to consider differences and distances in economic, regulative, political and cultural institutions.

- *Entry strategy mode.* Finally, once target countries are selected, managers have to determine how they should enter each particular market. Again, export is a simple place to start, but there are licensing, franchising, joint venture and wholly owned subsidiary (acquisition or 'greenfield' investments) alternatives to consider as well.

The chapter takes a cautious view on international strategy. Despite the fashionable talk of increasing 'globalisation', there are many challenges and pressures for being local or regional as well.[1] The chapter will therefore distinguish between international strategy and global strategy and consider the financial performance implications of growing internationalisation.[2] **International strategy refers to a range of options for operating outside an organisation's country of origin.** Global strategy is only one kind of international strategy. **Global strategy involves high coordination of extensive activities dispersed geographically in many countries around the world.**

9.2 INTERNATIONALISATION DRIVERS

There are many general pressures increasing internationalisation. Barriers to international trade, investment and migration are all now lower than they were a couple of decades ago. Better international legal frameworks mean that it is now less risky to deal with unfamiliar partners. Improvements in communications – from cheaper air travel to the internet – make movement and the spread of ideas much easier around the world. Not least, the success of new economic powerhouses such as the so-called 'BRICs' (Brazil, Russia, India and China) or the rising 'MINTs' (Mexico, Indonesia, Nigeria and Turkey) are generating new opportunities and challenges for business internationally.[3]

However, not all these internationalisation trends are one-way. Nor do they hold for all industries. Trade barriers still exist for some products, especially those relating to defence technologies. Many countries protect their leading companies from takeover by overseas rivals. Markets vary widely in the extent to which consumer needs are standardising – compare computer operating systems to the highly variable national tastes in chocolate. Some so-called multinationals are in fact concentrated in very particular markets, for example North America and Western Europe, or have a quite limited set of international links, for example in supply or outsourcing arrangements with just one or two countries overseas. In short, managers need to beware of 'global boloney', by which economic integration into a single homogenised and competitive world is wildly exaggerated.[4] The US discount retailer Walmart has learned the hard way that international markets are not only very different from home, but differ significantly from each other (see Illustration 9.1).

ILLUSTRATION 9.1 Walmart: international successes and failures

The biggest retailer in the world has found that internationalisation is considerably more challenging than expansion at home.

Walmart began its international operations 1991 and today the UK, Brazil and China are their largest markets outside the USA. Walmart International is the company's fastest growing unit with sales of $141bn (£85bn, €106bn) in 2015, accounting for about 30 per cent of Walmart's overall sales. It included close to 800,000 employees in over 6,200 stores and 11 e-commerce websites in 28 countries. Internationalisation results have, however, been mixed as Walmart has struggled to understand local buying patterns, culture, competitors and regulations, not the least in emerging markets.

Walmart first entered the Americas and has since expanded into ever more distant geographic markets. The early entry into Canada and Mexico was successful, but South America's largest market, Brazil, has been considerably more challenging. After two decades they are still losing money there. Their challenges include regulatory problems, strong competition from the French supermarket chain Carrefour and being unable to convince shoppers about Walmart's 'everyday low prices' model. In 2016, they restructured the Brazil operations and closed 60 outlets, accounting for 5 per cent of its sales.

European expansion results have similarly been mixed. The acquisition of the ASDA Group in the UK was relative successful while Walmart experienced eight years of struggle in Germany that ended in a market exit. First, they did not have enough scale economies compared to local competitors, like Aldi, with strong relationships with German suppliers and already catering to price-conscious consumers. Second, cultural mistakes were made as customers did not approve of American service practices. A third challenge was Germany's then strict regulations on location and opening hours. German workers also resisted Walmart workplace customs, resulting in labour union conflicts.

Walmart's first Asian expansion into South Korea was similar to the German story with strong local competition and failures to meet local customer needs. It ended in exit after eight years. China has been more of a mixed picture. On the one hand, sales have steadily increased – over 400 stores have been established and they make a profit. On the other hand, the distance, both geographically and culturally, was considerably larger than first anticipated. An early discovery was that Chinese consumers prefer frequent shopping trips in contrast to Walmart's home-based experience where customers drive to out-of-town stores and fill their cars with large multi-packs. While they encountered a completely different international market, they also faced large regional variations in this vast and multi-ethnic country. They have also struggled with local regulations and food safety issues and tough competition from Carrefour.

In a 2014 interview with the *Wall Street Journal*, Walmart International President and CEO David Cheesewright, former CEO of Walmart's UK supermarket chain Asda, admits to the struggles, but explained they would still be the Walmart growth engine. He emphasised four initiatives:

'First, create a platform for sustainable growth in China. . . . Second, turn around our operation in Brazil. . . . Third, we have to rejuvenate Mexico. . . . And, fourth we have to drive e-commerce.'

Sources: Dudely, R., 'Wal-Mart's everyday low prices fail to stir Brazilians', *Bloomberg Business*, 23 April 2014; S. Banjo, 'Wal-Mart's strategy to jump start growth in China', *Wall Street Journal*, 5 August 2014; A. Felsted, 'China set to remain at head of line for grocery sales', *Financial Times*, 23 August 2015; *Thomson Reuters Street Events*, 'Wal Mart Stores Inc. 22nd Annual Meeting for the Investment Community', edited transcript, 14 October 2015; L. Whipp, 'Walmart to close 269 stores as it revamps online presence', *Financial Times*, 15 January 2016.

Questions

1 What are the internationalisation drivers Walmart International has struggled with?

2 What might be the dangers for a large Western retailer in staying out of emerging markets?

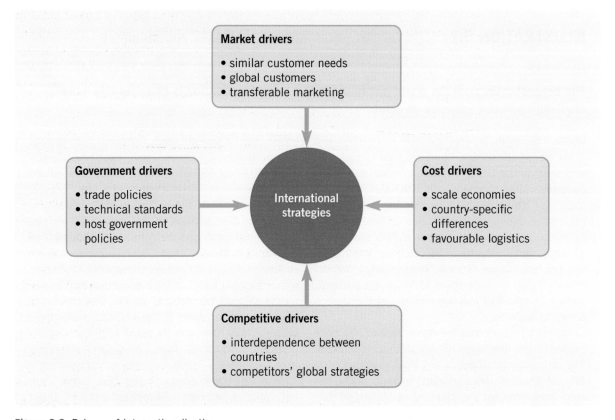

Figure 9.2 Drivers of internationalisation

Source: Adapted from G. Yip, *Total Global Strategy II*, Financial Times Prentice Hall, 2003, Chapter 2.

Given internationalisation's complexity, international strategy should be underpinned by a careful assessment of trends in each particular market. George Yip at Imperial College Business School provides a framework for analysing 'drivers of globalisation'. In the terms of this chapter, these drivers can be thought of as 'internationalisation drivers' more generally. In this book, therefore, **Yip's globalisation framework sees international strategy potential as determined by market drivers, cost drivers, government drivers and competitive drivers** (see Figure 9.2).[5] In more detail, the four internationalisation drivers are as follows:

- *Market drivers.* A critical facilitator of internationalisation is standardisation of market characteristics. There are three components underlying this driver. First, the presence of *similar customer needs and tastes*: for example, the fact that in most societies consumers have similar needs for easy credit has promoted the worldwide spread of a handful of credit card companies such as Visa. Second is the presence of *global customers*: for example, car component companies have become more international as their customers, such as Toyota or Ford, have internationalised and required standardised components for their factories around the world. Finally, *transferable marketing* promotes market globalisation: brands such as Coca-Cola are still successfully marketed in very similar ways across the world.

- *Cost drivers.* Costs can be reduced by operating internationally. Again, there are three main elements to cost drivers. First, increasing volume beyond what a national market might support can give *scale economies*, both on the production side and in purchasing of supplies. Companies from smaller countries such as the Netherlands, Switzerland and Taiwan tend therefore to become proportionately much more international than companies from the USA, which have a vast market at home. Scale economies are particularly important in industries with high product development costs, as in the aircraft industry, where initial development costs need to be spread over the large volumes of international markets. Second, internationalisation is promoted where it is possible to take advantage of variations in *country-specific differences.* Thus it makes sense to locate the manufacture of clothing in Africa or Bangladesh where labour is still considerably cheaper, but to keep design activities in cities such as New York, Paris, Milan or London, where fashion expertise is concentrated. The third element is *favourable logistics,* or the costs of moving products or services across borders relative to their final value. From this point of view, microchips are easy to source internationally, while bulky materials such as assembled furniture are harder.

- *Government drivers.* There are three main factors here that facilitate internationalisation. First, *reduction of barriers to trade and investment* has accelerated internationalisation. During the last couple of decades national governments have reduced restrictions on both flow of goods and capital. The World Trade Organization has been instrumental in reducing trade barriers globally.[6] Similarly, the emergence of regional economic integration partnerships like the European Union (EU), the North American Free Trade Agreement (NAFTA) and the Association of Southeast Asian Nations (ASEAN) Economic Community has promoted this development. No government, however, allows complete economic openness and it typically varies widely from industry to industry, with agriculture and high-tech industries related to defence likely to be particularly sensitive. Second, *the liberalisation and adoption of free markets* in many countries around the globe have also encouraged international trade and investments. Economic and free market reforms in China and later in Eastern Europe and Russia have been followed by market-based reforms in numerous Asian, South American and African economies. A third important government factor is *technology standardisation.* Compatible technical standards make it easier for companies to access different markets as they can enter many markets with the same product or service without adapting to local idiosyncratic standards.

- *Competitive drivers.* These relate specifically to globalisation as an integrated worldwide strategy rather than simpler international strategies (see Section 9.4). These have two elements. First, *interdependence* between country operations increases the pressure for global coordination. Company value chains are increasingly fragmented with suppliers, manufacturing and sales dispersed over a range of different countries facing various competitive and customer pressures. For example, a business with a plant in Mexico that sources parts in Brazil and serves both the US and the Japanese markets has to coordinate carefully between the different locations: surging sales in one country, or a collapse in another, will have significant knock-on effects on the other countries. The second element relates directly to competitor strategy. The presence of *globalised competitors* increases the pressure to adopt a global strategy in response because competitors may use one country's profits to cross-subsidise their operations in another. A company with a loosely coordinated international strategy is vulnerable to globalised competitors, because it is unable to support country subsidiaries under attack from targeted, subsidised competition. The danger is of piecemeal withdrawal from countries under attack, and the gradual undermining of any overall economies of scale that the international player may have started with.[7]

The key insight from Yip's drivers framework is that the internationalisation potential of industries is variable. There are many different factors that can support it as indicated above, but others can inhibit it. For example, customer needs and tastes for many food products inhibit their internationalisation and local governments often impose tariff barriers, ownership restrictions and local content requirements on foreign entrants. An important step in determining an internationalisation strategy is a realistic assessment of the true scope for internationalisation in the particular industry.

9.3 GEOGRAPHIC SOURCES OF ADVANTAGE

A competitor entering a market from overseas typically starts with considerable *disadvantages* relative to existing local competitors, which will usually have superior knowledge of the local market and its institutions, established relationships with local customers, strong supply chains and the like.[8] A foreign entrant must thus have significant firm-specific competitive advantages for it to overcome these inherent advantages of local competitors. Tesco's failure in the USA is an example of this. After seven years and investments of about £1bn (€1.2bn, $1.5bn) in its US Fresh & Easy business Tesco was forced to withdraw. Unlike in the UK, Tesco had limited competitive advantage over the strong US domestic retailers. Internationalisation thus requires building on the sources of sustainable competitive advantage that we have discussed earlier in Chapters 4 and 7 including the organisation's unique strengths in resources and capabilities. While these *firm- or organisation-specific advantages* are important, competitive advantage in an international context also depends on *country-specific or geographic advantages.*[9]

As the earlier discussion of cost drivers in international strategy has shown, the geographical location of activities is a crucial source of potential advantage and one of the distinguishing features of international strategy relative to other diversification strategies. Bruce Kogut at Columbia University has explained that an organisation can improve the configuration of its *value chain and system* (see Section 4.4.2) by taking advantage of country-specific differences.[10] There are two principal opportunities available: the exploitation of particular *locational advantages*, often in the company's home country, and sourcing advantages overseas via an *international value system*.

9.3.1 Locational advantage: Porter's Diamond[11]

Countries and regions within them, and organisations originating in those, often benefit from competitive advantages grounded in specific local conditions. They become associated with specific types of enduring competitive advantage: for example, the Swiss in private banking, the northern Italians in leather and fur fashion goods, and the Taiwanese in laptop computers. Michael Porter has proposed a four-pointed 'diamond' to explain why some locations tend to produce firms with sustained competitive advantages in some industries more than others (see Figure 9.3). Specifically, **Porter's Diamond suggests that locational advantages may stem from local factor conditions; local demand conditions; local related and supporting industries; and from local firm strategy, industry structure and rivalry.** These four interacting determinants of locational advantage work as follows:

- *Factor conditions.* These refer to the 'factors of production' that go into making a product or service (i.e. raw materials, land and labour). Factor condition advantages at a national level can translate into general competitive advantages for national firms in international markets. For example, the linguistic ability of the Swiss has traditionally provided a significant advantage to their banking industry. Cheap energy has traditionally provided an advantage for the North American aluminium industry.

- *Home demand conditions.* The nature of the domestic customers can become a source of competitive advantage. Dealing with sophisticated and demanding customers at home helps train a company to be effective overseas. For example, America's long distances have led to competitive strength in very large truck engines. Sophisticated local customers in France and Italy have helped keep their local fashion industries at the leading edge for many decades.

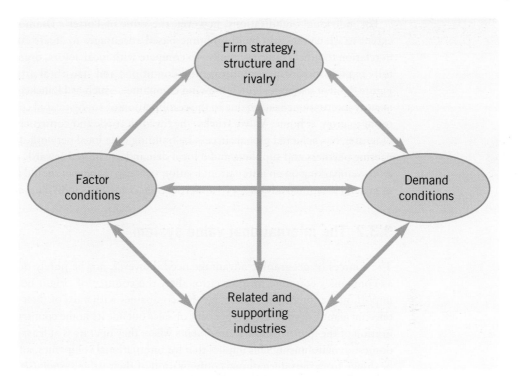

Figure 9.3 Porter's Diamond – the determinants of national advantages

Source: Adapted with permission of The Free Press, a Division of Simon & Schuster, Inc., from *The Competitive Advantage of Nations* by Michael E. Porter. Copyright © 1990, 1998 by Michael E. Porter. All rights reserved.

- *Related and supporting industries.* Local 'clusters' of related and mutually supporting industries can be an important source of competitive advantage. These are often regionally based, making personal interaction easier. In northern Italy, for example, the leather footwear industry, the leatherworking machinery industry and the design services that underpin them group together in the same regional cluster to each other's mutual benefit. Silicon Valley forms a cluster of hardware, software, research and venture capital organisations that together create a virtuous circle of high-technology enterprise.

- *Firm strategy, industry structure and rivalry.* The characteristic strategies, industry structures and rivalries in different countries can also be bases of advantage. German companies' strategy of investing in technical excellence gives them a characteristic advantage in engineering industries and creates large pools of expertise. A competitive local industry structure is also helpful: if too dominant in their home territory, local organisations can become complacent and lose advantage overseas. Some domestic rivalry can actually be an advantage, therefore. For example, the long-run success of Japanese car companies is partly based on government policy sustaining several national players (unlike in the UK, where they were all merged into one) and the Swiss pharmaceuticals industry became strong in part because each company had to compete with several strong local rivals.

Porter's Diamond model underlines the environmental conditions and structural attributes of nations and their regions that contribute to their competitive advantage. It has been used by governments aiming to increase the competitive advantage of their local industries. The argument that rivalry can be positive has led to a major policy shift in many countries towards encouraging local competition rather than protecting home-based industries. Governments can also foster local industries by raising safety or environmental standards (i.e. creating sophisticated demand conditions) or encouraging cooperation between suppliers and buyers on a domestic level (i.e. building clusters of related and supporting industries in particular regions).

For individual organisations, however, the value of Porter's Diamond is to identify the extent to which they can build on home-based advantages to create competitive advantage in relation to others internationally. To compete with local actors, organisations must carefully exploit the distinct environmental conditions and structural attributes illustrated in Figure 9.3. For example, Dutch brewing companies – such as Heineken – had an advantage in early internationalisation due to the combination of sophisticated consumers and limited room to grow at home. Volvo Trucks, the Swedish truck and construction equipment manufacturer, has achieved global success by building on a local network of sophisticated engineering partners and suppliers and a local demand orientated towards reliability and safety. Before embarking on an internationalisation strategy, managers should thus seek out sources of general locational advantage to underpin their company's individual sources of advantage.

9.3.2 The international value system

The sources of geographic advantage need, however, not be purely domestic. In addition, as companies continue to internationalise, the country of origin becomes relatively less important for competitive advantage. For companies with most of their sales abroad, like the telecom giant Ericsson with 95 per cent of sales outside its home country Sweden, the configuration of the international environments where they operate is at least as important as their domestic environment. This implies that for international companies, advantage also needs to be drawn from the international configuration of their *value system* (see Section 4.4.2). Here the different skills, resources and costs of countries around the world can be systematically exploited in order to locate each element of the value chain in that country or region where it can be conducted most effectively and efficiently. This may be achieved through both foreign direct investments and joint ventures but also through **global sourcing: purchasing services and components from the most appropriate suppliers around the world, regardless of their location.** For example, in the UK for many years the National Health Service has been sourcing medical personnel from overseas to offset a shortfall in domestic skills and capacity. Smaller organisations can also build on the broader system of suppliers, channels and customers as demonstrated in Illustration 9.2.

Different locational advantages can be identified:

- *Cost advantages* include labour costs, transportation and communications costs and taxation and investment incentives. Labour costs are important. American and European firms, for example, have moved much of their software programming tasks to India where a computer programmer costs an American firm about one quarter of what it would pay for a worker with comparable skills in the USA. As wages in India have risen, some IT firms have started to move work to even more low-cost locations such as Thailand and Vietnam.

- *Unique local capabilities* may allow an organisation to enhance its competitive advantage. Gradually value-creating and innovative activity becomes geographically dispersed across multiple centres of excellence within multinational organisations.[12] For example, leading European pharmaceuticals company GSK has R&D laboratories in Boston and the Research Triangle in North Carolina in order to establish research collaborations with the prominent universities and hospitals in those areas. Internationalisation, therefore, is increasingly not only about exploiting an organisation's existing capabilities in new national markets, but about developing and drawing on capabilities found elsewhere in the world.

- *National market characteristics* can enable organisations to develop differentiated product offerings aimed at different market segments. American guitar-maker Gibson, for example, complements its US-made products with often similar, lower-cost alternatives produced in South Korea under the Epiphone brand. However, because of the American music tradition, Gibson's high-end guitars benefit from the reputation of still being 'made in the USA'.

ILLUSTRATION 9.2   The international 'Joint Effort Enterprise'

For Blue Skies international strategy is something more than profit alone.

Blue Skies specialises in producing fresh-cut fruit and juice products from a network of factories in Africa and South America. It supplies over 12 major European retailers, including Waitrose in the UK, Albert Heijn in the Netherlands and Monoprix in France. The company has factories in Ghana, Egypt, South Africa and Brazil. Its biggest factory is in Ghana and employs over 2500 people and sources fruit from over 100 small to medium-sized farms. Blue Skies believes in value adding at source whereby the raw materials are processed within the country of origin rather than shipped overseas and processed elsewhere. By doing this, as much as 70 per cent of the value of the finished product stays within the country of origin, compared to as little as 15 per cent if it is processed outside.

Blue Skies works within a framework it has developed called the 'Joint Effort Enterprise' (JEE). While it is their model for a sustainable business, it is not a model which has been introduced to respond to the growing hype around 'sustainability'. Instead, it is a set of principles from the foundation of the business in 1998 to ensure that the organisation would endure. The JEE is principally made up of three strands: a diverse society, a culture of respect and a drive for profit. The latter must not, however, come at the expense of all the other strands. Blue Skies believes that this model ensures that it retains the best people and conserves the resources they rely on, so that they can produce the best quality products and therefore generate the income that keeps the organisation going. Its approach is 'based on fairness in business, respect for each other and above all, trust'. In addition, Blue Skies raised over £1m (€1.2m, $1.5m) in partnership with two European retailers and completed over 40 projects in Ghana and South Africa including the construction of schools, latrines and community centres. The Blue Skies JEE approach has also been awarded a Queens Award for Enterprise in the Sustainable Development Category in 2009, 2011 and 2015.

During the last few years Blue Skies has encountered several international challenges: a world recession, rising energy prices, exchange rate volatility, shortage of raw materials, etc. It realises that these are challenges that an international operation across three continents must be ready and willing to respond to. Accordingly, it has undertaken a number of initiatives:

- Developing products for local and dollar-based markets to reduce exposure to exchange rate losses and supply chain disruption.
- Expanding its supply base around the world to ensure year-round supply of fruit.
- Helping its suppliers achieve agricultural standards such as LEAF (Linking Environment and Farming) to ensure sustainability of supply.
- Growing the Blue Skies Foundation to strengthen its relationship with staff, farmers and their communities.
- Developing plans to generate renewable energy to reduce electricity costs and greenhouse gas emissions.
- Opening a European-based contingency factory to ensure consistency of supply during supply chain disruption.

Source: Prepared by Edwina Goodwin, Leicester Business School, De Montfort University.

Questions

1. What internationalisation drivers (Figure 9.2) do you think were most important for Blue Skies' decision to enter its specific markets?

2. How does Blue Skies' strategy fit into a broader international value system including suppliers, channels and customers (see also Figure 4.5)?

3. To what extent is JEE key to Blue Skies' international strategy and competitive advantage or rather a social entrepreneurship effort?

9.4 INTERNATIONAL STRATEGIES

Given their organisation-specific advantages and the ability to obtain sources of international competitive advantage through geographic home-based factors or international value systems, organisations still face difficult questions about what kind of international strategy to pursue. The fundamental issue in formulating an international strategy is to balance pressures for *global integration* versus those for *local responsiveness*.[13] Pressures for **global integration encourage organisations to coordinate their activities across diverse countries to gain efficient operations.** The internationalisation drivers discussed above (Section 9.2) indicate forces that organisations can build on to achieve lower costs and higher quality in operations and activities on a global scale. However, there are conflicting pressures that also encourage organisations to become locally responsive and meet the specific needs in each individual country (see Section 9.5.1 below). Values and attitudes, economics, political institutions, cultures and laws differ across countries, which imply differences in customer preferences, product and service standards, regulations and human resources that all need to be addressed. These two opposing pressures – global integration vs local responsiveness – put contradictory demands on an organisation's international strategy. High pressure for global integration implies an increased need to concentrate and coordinate operations globally. In contrast, high pressure for **local responsiveness implies a greater need to disperse operations and adapt to local demand.**

This key problem is sometimes referred to as the **global–local dilemma: the extent to which products and services may be standardised across national boundaries or need to be adapted to meet the requirements of specific national markets.** For some products and services – such as TVs – markets appear similar across the world, offering huge potential scale economies if design, production and delivery can be centralised. For other products and services – such as processed food – tastes still seem highly national-specific, drawing companies to decentralise operations and control as near as possible to the local market.

This dilemma between global integration and local responsiveness suggests several possible international strategies, ranging from emphasising one of the dimensions to complex responses that try to combine both. Organisations need to assess to what degree there are potential advantages of cost and quality of global integration and balance those pressures against the need to adapt products and/or services to local conditions. This section introduces four different kinds of international strategy, based on strategic choices about this balance (see Figure 9.4). The four basic international strategies are:[14]

- *Export strategy.* This strategy leverages home country capabilities, innovations and products in different foreign countries. It is advantageous when both pressures for global integration and local responsiveness are low, as shown in Figure 9.4. Companies that have distinctive capabilities together with strong reputation and brand names often follow this strategy with success. Google, for example, centralises its R&D and the core architecture underlying its internet services at its headquarters in California in the USA and exploits it internationally with minor adaptations except for local languages and alphabets. The downside of this approach is the limits of a home country centralised view of the business with risks of skilled local competitors getting ahead. Google, for example, meets strong local rivals in Baidu in China and Naver in Korea with superior mastery of the language and understanding of local consumer behaviour.

- *Multi-domestic strategy.* This is a strategy that maximises local responsiveness. It is based on different product or service offerings and operations in each country depending on local market conditions and customer preferences. Each country is treated differently with considerable autonomy for each country manager to best meet the needs of local

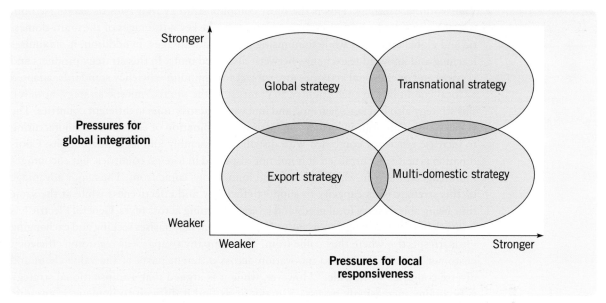

Figure 9.4 Four international strategies

markets and customers in that particular country. As with the export strategy, this strategy is similarly loosely coordinated internationally. The organisation becomes a collection of relatively independent units with value chain activities adapted to specific local conditions. This multi-domestic approach is particularly appropriate when there are strong benefits to adapting to local needs and when there are limited efficiency gains from integration. It is common in food and consumer product industries where local idiosyncratic preferences are significant. Marketing-driven companies often pursue this type of strategy. For example, Frito-Lay, a US branded-snacks company, tailors its global products to local tastes and even creates entirely new snack products for local markets.[15] The disadvantages of a multi-domestic strategy include manufacturing inefficiencies, a proliferation of costly product and service variations and risks towards brand and reputation if national practices become too diverse.

- *Global strategy.* This is a strategy that maximises global integration. In this strategy the world is seen as one marketplace with standardised products and services that fully exploits integration and efficiency in operations. The focus is on capturing scale economies and exploiting location economies worldwide with geographically dispersed value chain activities being coordinated and controlled centrally from headquarters. In these respects, this strategy is the exact opposite to the multi-domestic strategy. A global strategy is most beneficial when there are substantial cost or quality efficiency benefits from standardisation and when customer needs are relatively homogeneous across countries. It is a common strategy for commodities or commodity-like products. For example, Mexican Cemex, one of the largest cement companies in the world, follows a global strategy with centralised and shared services in information technology, R&D, human resources and financial services across countries and regions.[16] Non-commodity companies can also follow a global strategy, like Sweden's furniture retailer IKEA. Based on a strong home base, they standardise products and marketing with limited local adaptation to gain maximum global integration efficiency. The drawback of the global strategy is reduced flexibility due to standardisation that limits possibilities to adapt activities and products to local conditions.[17] This has, for example, led IKEA to make minor modifications of some furniture offerings to suit local tastes.

- *Transnational strategy*. This is the most complex strategy that tries to maximise both responsiveness and integration. Its aim is to unite the key advantages of the multi-domestic and global strategies while minimising their disadvantages. In addition, it maximises learning and knowledge exchange between dispersed units. In this strategy products and services and operational activities are, subject to minimum efficiency standards, adapted to local conditions in each country. In contrast to the multi-domestic strategy, however, this strategy also leverages learning and innovation across units in different countries. The value chain configuration includes an intricate combination of centralised manufacturing to increase efficiency combined with distributed assembly and local adaptations. Coordination is neither centralised at home nor dispersed in foreign countries, but encourages knowledge flows from wherever ideas and innovations come from. The major advantage of this strategy is its capacity to support efficiency and effectiveness while at the same time being able to serve local needs and leverage learning across units. General Electric has been celebrated as having a transnational strategy that emphasises seeking and exchanging ideas irrespective where they come from. The company swaps ideas regarding efficiency, customer responsiveness and innovation across different parts of the value chain and diverse countries worldwide.[18] However, while it is argued that a transnational strategy is becoming increasingly necessary, many firms find it difficult to implement given its complexity and the fundamental trade-off between integration and responsiveness. ABB, the Swiss–Swedish engineering giant, was once identified as the archetypal transnational company, but later ran into serious problems.[19] They have since tried to find the middle ground in a more regional strategy – a compromise discussed below.

In practice, these four international strategies are not absolutely distinct as indicated by the overlapping ovals in Figure 9.4. They are rather illustrative examples of alternative international strategies. Global integration and local responsiveness are matters of degree rather than sharp distinctions. Moreover, choices between them will be influenced by changes in the internationalisation drivers introduced earlier. It is rare that companies adopt a pure form of international strategy; instead they often blend approaches and are located somewhere between the four strategies. As exemplified above, IKEA has a global strategy, but also makes some minor local adaptations, which may eventually move the company towards more of a transnational strategy.

Often regions (e.g. Europe or North America) play a larger role in international strategy than individual countries or global expansion. Thus many multinationals compromise between local and global logics by opting for *regional strategies*.[20] The aim of this strategy is to attain some of the economic efficiency and location advantages while simultaneously reaching local adaptation advantages. Regions are treated as relatively homogenous markets with value chain activities concentrated within them. Sales data suggest that many multinational companies follow this type of strategy focused on one or two regions including the triad of the European Union, the North American Free Trade Agreement and/or Japan/Asia.[21] For example, over 85 per cent of all cars sold within each region of Europe, North America and Japan are built in that same region. This regional approach to international strategy shows that distances and differences between nations are still relatively large (see Section 9.5.1 below), which makes global integration difficult.

These differences can, however, be exploited in arbitrage for value creation. *Arbitrage* implies that multinationals take advantage of price differences between two or more markets by purchasing goods cheaply in one market and selling them at a higher price in another. For example, Walmart is known for sourcing much of what the company sells in the USA from China. Not only price differences, but differences in labour costs, in knowledge, capital and taxes can be exploited by operating in diverse countries. The potential for arbitrage in multinationals is substantial and it has been suggested as a third significant international strategy dimension, besides integration and responsiveness.[22] Finally, different international strategies require diverse organising requirements for success, which are discussed in Chapter 14 (Section 14.2.4).

9.5 MARKET SELECTION AND ENTRY

Having decided on an international strategy built on significant sources of competitive advantage and supported by strong internationalisation drivers, managers need next to decide which countries to enter. There are substantial differences in customer needs and in economic, regulative–administrative, political and cultural institutions that make countries and markets more or less attractive. Thinking Differently at the end of this chapter even considers an entirely new strategy view based on institutions. To an extent, however, countries can initially be compared using standard environmental analysis techniques, for example along the dimensions identified in the PESTEL framework (see Section 2.2) or according to the industry five forces (Section 3.2). However, there are specific determinants of market attractiveness that need to be considered in internationalisation strategy: the intrinsic characteristics of the country and market. A key point is how initial estimates of country attractiveness can be modified by considering *institutional voids* and various measures of *distance*. The section concludes by considering different *entry strategy modes* into national markets.

9.5.1 Country and market characteristics

At least four elements of the PESTEL framework are particularly important in comparing countries for entry:

- *Political.* Political environments vary widely between countries and can alter rapidly. Russia since the fall of communism has seen frequent swings for and against private foreign enterprise. It is important to determine the level of *political risk* before entering a country. Toyota, for example, found itself the subject of an unexpected consumer boycott in China because of political tensions over a territorial dispute between China and Japan. There is also a risk that governments simply take over companies. In 2012, the Argentinian government nationalised the Spanish oil company Repsol's 57 per cent stake in Argentina's largest oil extractor and refinery. Governments can of course also create significant opportunities for organisations. For example, the British government has traditionally promoted the financial services industry in the City of London by offering tax advantages to high-earning financiers from abroad and providing a 'light-touch' regulatory environment.

- *Economic.* Key comparators in deciding entry are levels of gross domestic product and disposable income that help in estimating the potential size of the market. Fast-growth economies obviously provide opportunities, and in developing economies such as China and India growth is translating into an even faster creation of a high-consumption middle class. At the same time, entirely new high-growth markets are opening up in Africa including Nigeria and Ghana.

- *Social.* Social factors will clearly be important, for example the availability of a well-trained workforce or the size of demographic market segments – old or young – relevant to the strategy. Cultural variations also need to be considered, for instance in defining tastes in the marketplace.

- *Legal.* Countries vary widely in their legal regime, determining the extent to which businesses can enforce contracts, protect intellectual property or avoid corruption. Similarly, policing will be important for the security of employees, a factor that in the past has deterred business in some African countries.

A common procedure is to rank country markets against each other on criteria such as these and then choose the countries for entry that offer the highest relative scores. However, Tarun

---

ILLUSTRATION 9.3 Nordic Industrial Park: bridging distance across international markets

---

When a resource-constrained firm enters a high-distance market, it helps greatly if it can utilise a low-distance entry point.

The lure of the Chinese market has led several Western companies to venture into a context that is unfamiliar and bewildering, especially for small and medium-sized enterprises (SMEs) lacking the deep pockets of large multinationals. It is useful for SMEs to have a 'bridge' into a high-distance market. One way to accomplish this is to use a foreign-owned industrial park (i.e. a space designated for industrial use).

Consider the case of the Nordic Industrial Park (NIP) that provides a physical space for offices and light-manufacturing facilities, and a range of value-added services to set up a business in China. These include legal services (e.g. registering the company and drafting contracts), human resource management (e.g. recruitment, payroll and expat relocation), accounting (e.g. financial reporting), and information and communication technology (e.g. internet access).

NIP was co-founded by Ove Nodland, a Norwegian who first came to China in 1994 to manage different ventures. Nodland learnt that even though rules were set in Beijing (the national capital and political centre of China), they were implemented by local officials – and so they mattered greatly. Over the years he invested considerable energies in building close relationships with various officials, and took care to ensure that the ventures he worked for complied with local regulations and aligned themselves with local governmental priorities. Nodland's local *guanxi* (network connections) grew rapidly.

After a decade's experience in China, Nodland realised he was well placed to help European SMEs enter China more broadly. He chose to focus on what he knew best: firms from the Nordic region (Denmark, Finland, Iceland, Norway and Sweden) setting up a base in Ningbo, a port city in Zhejiang province just south of Shanghai (the commercial centre of China) and renowned for its entrepreneurialism. Thus was born the concept of NIP in 2002, which was sold to Silver Rise Hong Kong Pte Ltd, part of China's Yinmao Group, in 2013, with Nodland staying on as consultant. In 2015, NIP was selected by the Zhejiang provincial government as one of the first designated 'international industrial cooperative parks' which further strengthened its local standing. Going forward, NIP has signalled its intent to attract projects from Nordic universities and achieve an output value in excess of RMB 2bn (€280m, £224m, $364m) by 2017.

From the perspective of a European SME entering NIP, there are multiple benefits:

- *Process*: Lower start-up costs. NIP leverages its knowledge of the Chinese business environment by hand-holding clients through the complexities associated with starting and running a business in China, thereby allowing firms to focus their time and energies on core business activities.
- *Physical environment*: A familiar ambience. NIP's architecture and design mimics Scandinavian features that set it apart from standard Chinese buildings. Not only does this give expat managers a sense of the familiar, it is also a symbolic reminder to Chinese employees that they are part of a Western organisation.
- *People*: A like-minded community. By virtue of being part of the largest concentration of Nordic companies in China, expat managers have the opportunity to share experiences with and pick up 'tricks of the trade' from other managers with a similar cultural background through hallway conversations and lunchtime meetings.

Of course, entering a facility like NIP comes at a cost, but offers benefits in terms of 'reducing distance'.

Source: Prepared by Shameen Prashantham, China Europe International Business School.

Questions

1 Consider NIP's services in light of the CAGE framework and analyse how they may help reduce distance.

2 What might be the drawbacks in being located in an industrial park?

Khanna and Krishna Palepu from Harvard Business School have shown that this may not be enough, especially not for emerging markets.[23] These are often equally attractive, but may differ considerably as regards institutional infrastructure. This can be particularly challenging because of the lack of important institutions like regulatory systems, contract and law enforcement mechanisms and 'soft' infrastructure like the availability of market research and employee search firms. The absence of this suggests that these types of *institutional voids* need to be taken into consideration besides country rankings.[24] Pankaj Ghemawat from Spain's IESE Business School also emphasises that what matters is not just the attractiveness of different countries relative to each other. He points out that the compatibility of the countries with the internationalising firm itself and its country of origin is what really matters.[25] Thus Ghemawat underlines the importance of *match* between country and firm. For firms coming from any particular country, some countries are more 'distant' – or mismatched – than others. For example, a Spanish company might be 'closer' to a South American market than an East Asian market and might therefore prefer that market even if it ranked lower on standard criteria of attractiveness. As well as a relative ranking of countries, therefore, each company has to add its assessment of countries in terms of closeness of match.

Ghemawat's 'CAGE framework' measures the match between countries and companies according to four dimensions of distance, reflected by the letters of this acronym. Thus the CAGE framework emphasises the importance of cultural, administrative, geographical and economic distance, as follows:

- *Cultural distance.* The distance dimension here relates to differences in language, ethnicity, religion and social norms (see Section 6.3.1 for four key dimensions upon which national cultures tend to differ). Cultural distance is not just a matter of similarity in consumer tastes, but extends to important compatibilities in terms of managerial behaviours. Here, for example, US firms might be closer to Canada than to Mexico, which Spanish firms might find relatively compatible. Figure 9.5 draws on the GLOBE survey of 17,000 managers from 62 different societal cultures around the world to contrast specifically the orientations of American and Chinese managers on some key cultural dimensions. According to this GLOBE survey, American managers appear to be typically more risk-taking, while Chinese managers are more autonomous. One way to shrink distance is through cooperation with local partners, which is demonstrated in Illustration 9.3.

- *Administrative and political distance.* Here distance is in terms of incompatible administrative, political or legal traditions. Colonial ties can diminish difference, so that the shared heritage of France and its former West African colonies creates certain understandings that go beyond linguistic advantages. Institutional weaknesses or voids – for example, slow or corrupt administration – can open up distance between countries. So too can political differences: Chinese companies are increasingly able to operate in parts of the world that American companies are finding harder, for example parts of Africa and the Middle East.

- *Geographical distance.* This is not just a matter of the kilometres separating one country from another, but involves other geographical characteristics of the country such as size, sea-access and the quality of communications infrastructure. Transport infrastructure can shrink or exaggerate physical distance. France is much closer to large parts of Continental Europe than to the UK thanks to its high-speed rail network and because of the barrier presented by the English Channel and the latter's relatively poor road and rail infrastructure. Another example is the Brazilian mining company Vale, which has developed megaship carriers for its Chinese exports to limit the effect of geographic distances.

- *Economic.* The final element of the CAGE framework refers particularly to wealth distances. There are of course huge disparities in wealth internationally: around the world, there are four billion people beneath the poverty income threshold of less than $2 a day.[26]

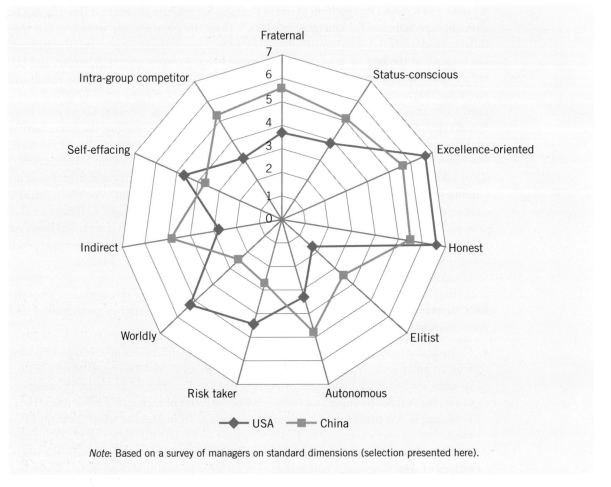

Figure 9.5 International cross-cultural comparison

Source: M. Javidan, P. Dorman, M. de Luque and R. House, 'In the eye of the beholder: cross-cultural lessons in leadership from Project GLOBE', *Academy of Management Perspectives* (February 2006), pp. 67–90 (Figure 4: USA vs China, p. 82). (GLOBE stands for 'Global Leadership and Organisational Behaviour Effectiveness'.)

Multinationals from rich countries are typically weak at serving such very poor consumers. However, these rich-country multinationals are losing out on large markets if they only concentrate on the wealthy elites overseas. C.K. Prahalad pointed out that the aggregated wealth of those at the 'base of the pyramid' in terms of income distribution is very substantial: simple mathematics means that those four billion below the poverty threshold represent a market of more than $2,000bn per year. If rich-country multinationals can develop new capabilities to serve these numerically huge markets, they can bridge the economic distance, and thereby both significantly extend their presence in booming economies such as China and India and bring to these poor consumers the benefits that are claimed for Western goods.[27] See Illustration 9.4 for examples of innovative bases of pyramid strategies.

9.5.2 Competitive characteristics

Assessing the relative attractiveness of markets by PESTEL and CAGE analyses including careful examinations of institutions is a significant first step. However, there is also a second element, which relates to competition. Here, of course, Michael Porter's five forces

ILLUSTRATION 9.4   Base of the pyramid strategies

Base of the pyramid strategy means more than just low prices and involves designing new products, forming partnerships, reshaping distribution channels and introducing novel financing solutions.

Product design

A key problem in the developing world is the poor quality of piped water. Unilever Hindustan, India's largest consumer goods company, owned by Anglo-Dutch Unilever, developed a water filter that makes water as safe as boiling. It is marketed and sold through the wide Unilever distribution network. The filter has attracted over three million households, mainly in India's mega- or middle-sized cities. However, at \$35 (£21, €26) it is still unattainable for millions of Indians who live on less than a dollar a day. In an effort to reach rural customers Unilever has introduced a light-version (lower capacity) of the filter. The success of the product on the Indian market has led Unilever Hindustan to introduce the water filter in other markets in Asia, Eastern Europe and South Africa.

Partnerships

First Energy Oorja started as a partnership between the Indian Institute of Science Bangalore and British Petroleum (BP) Emerging Consumer Market (ECM) division to develop a stove using the 'power of innovation and a strong understanding of consumer energy needs'. It was later acquired by The Alchemists Ark, a privately held business consulting firm. The First Energy Oorja stoves are low-smoke, low-cost stoves, which work on pellets – an organic biofuel made of processed agricultural waste. First Energy Oorja works in close partnership with both local non-governmental organisations and dealer networks in rural markets to distribute and market the stove. This distribution model ensures that the product reaches remote Indian locations and the stove had reached over 3000 households by 2015.

Distribution channels

Bayer CropScience, a global firm that develops and manufactures crop protection products, initiated a Green World venture in Kenya. It introduced small packs of pesticides and trained a network of small, rural agrodealers to guide and educate small farmers on product handling and use. It also provided further support and marketing via radio. Bayer CropScience carefully selected dealers based on their reputation in the community and sales volumes. Today about 25 per cent of its horticultural retail revenues in Kenya now come from Green World stores.

Financial solutions

Cemex, a global cement corporation from Mexico, has been an innovative pioneer in designing a microfinancing system, 'Patrimonio Hoy' (Property Now), for the poor in Mexico and later in the rest of Latin America. In the past, building houses for this group had often proved lengthy and risky because without savings or access to credit, low-income families could only buy small amounts of building material at a time. Patrimonio Hoy is a solution to this. It is a combination of savings and credit schemes in which Cemex provides collateral-free financing to customers via a membership system based on small monthly fees. Customers demonstrate their savings discipline by regular monthly payments and Cemex develops trust in them by delivering building raw materials early on credit. The programme is a success and has reached 265,000 families so far with a further commitment to provide at least 125,000 additional low-income families with affordable housing by 2016.

Sources: Business Call to Action, 2016; Swiss Agency for Development and Cooperation, 2011; Institute for Financial and Management Research, 2012; E. Simanis and D. Duke, 'Profits at the bottom of the pyramid', *Harvard Business Review*, October 2014; A. Karamchandani, M. Kubzansky and N. Lalwani, 'Is the bottom of the pyramid really for you?', *Harvard Business Review*, March 2011; *Business Today*, December 2011.

Questions

1 Can you imagine any risks or dangers that Western companies might face in pursuing base of the pyramid strategies?

2 Is there anything that Western companies might learn from base of the pyramid strategies in emerging markets that might be valuable in their home markets?

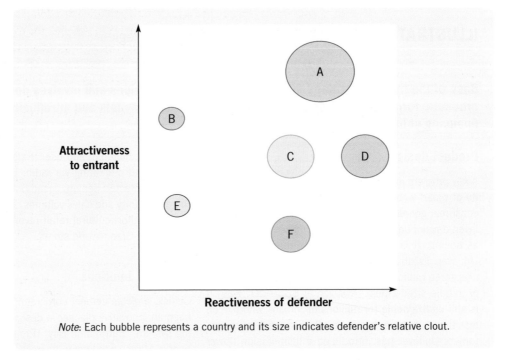

Note: Each bubble represents a country and its size indicates defender's relative clout.

Figure 9.6 International competitor retaliation

Source: Reprinted by permission of *Harvard Business Review*. Exhibit adapted from 'Global gamesmanship' by I. MacMillan, S. van Putter and R. McGrath, May 2003. Copyright © 2003 by the Harvard Business School Publishing Corporation. All rights reserved.

framework can help (see Section 3.3), but it is important to observe that an attractive industry in the home market can be unattractive in another country. For example, country markets with many existing competitors, powerful buyers (perhaps large retail chains such as in much of North America and Europe) and low barriers to further new entrants from overseas would typically be unattractive. An additional consideration is the likelihood of retaliation from other competitors.

In the five forces framework, retaliation potential relates to rivalry and entry, but managers can extend this by using insights directly from 'game theory' (see Section 7.3.3). It takes competitor interdependence including moves and counter-moves into consideration. Here, the likelihood and ferocity of potential competitor reactions are added to the simple calculation of relative country market attractiveness. As in Figure 9.6, country markets can be assessed according to three criteria:[28]

- *Market attractiveness* to the new entrant, based on PESTEL, CAGE and five forces analyses, for example. In Figure 9.6, countries A and B are the most attractive to the entrant.

- *Defender's reactiveness*, likely to be influenced by the market's attractiveness to the defender but also by the extent to which the defender is working with a globally integrated, rather than multi-domestic, strategy. A defender will be more reactive if the markets are important to it and it has the managerial capabilities to coordinate its response. Here, the defender is highly reactive in countries A and D.

- *Defender's clout*, that is the power that the defender is able to muster in order to fight back. Clout is typically a function of share in the particular market, but might be influenced by connections to other powerful local players, such as retailers or government. In Figure 9.6, clout is represented by the size of the bubbles, with the defender having most clout in countries A, C, D and F.

Choice of country to enter can be significantly modified by adding reactiveness and clout to calculations of attractiveness. Relying only on attractiveness, the top-ranked country to enter in Figure 9.6 is country A. Unfortunately, it is also one in which the defender is highly reactive, and the one in which it has most clout. Country B becomes a better international move than A. In turn, country C is a better prospect than country D, because, even though they are equally attractive, the defender is less reactive. One surprising result of taking defender reactiveness and clout into account is the re-evaluation of country E: although ranked fifth on simple attractiveness, it might rank second overall if competitor retaliation is allowed for.

This sort of analysis is particularly fruitful for considering the international moves of two interdependent competitors, such as Unilever and Procter & Gamble or British Airways and Singapore Airlines. In these cases, the analysis is relevant to any aggressive strategic move, for instance the expansion of existing operations in a country as well as initial entry. Especially in the case of globally integrated competitors, moreover, the overall clout of the defender must be taken into account. The defender may choose to retaliate in other markets than the targeted one, counter-attacking wherever it has the clout to do damage to the aggressor. Naturally, too, this kind of analysis can be applied to interactions between diversified competitors as well as international ones: each bubble could represent different products or services.

9.5.3 Entry mode strategies

Once a particular national market has been selected for entry, an organisation needs to choose how to enter that market. Entry mode strategies differ in the degree of resource commitment to a particular market and the extent to which an organisation is operationally involved in a particular location. In order of increasing resource commitment, the four key entry mode types are: *exporting;* contractual arrangement through *licensing or franchising* to local partners; *joint ventures* with local companies, in other words the establishment of jointly owned businesses; and *wholly owned subsidiaries,* through either the acquisition of established companies or 'greenfield' investments, in other words the development of facilities from scratch.

This *staged international expansion* model emphasises the role of experience and learning in determining entry mode strategy. Internationalisation typically brings organisations into unfamiliar territory, requiring managers to learn new ways of doing business.[29] The **staged international expansion model proposes a sequential process whereby companies gradually increase their commitment to newly entered markets, as they build knowledge and capabilities.** Thus firms might enter initially by exporting or licensing, thereby acquiring some local knowledge while minimising local investments. As they gain knowledge and confidence, firms can then increase their exposure, perhaps first by a joint venture and finally by creating a wholly owned subsidiary. For example, the leading Danish wind turbine manufacturer Vestas first entered the US market through exports. Subsequently, Vestas established manufacturing and R&D facilities in Eastern Colorado to strengthen its competitive position versus domestic players and now supplies 90 per cent of components required for the assembly of a final turbine within the USA.

There are advantages and disadvantages for each entry mode strategy depending on a range of factors including resource and investment requirements, control, risks, transport costs, trade barriers, entry speed, etc. Table 9.1 lists some of these fundamental factors that can help guide managers in choosing between market entry modes:

- Export is the baseline option and has the advantages of requiring relatively less investment of resources and entailing lower costs and risks whilst offering speedy entry and the potential to take full advantage of production economies in existing facilities. However, a

Table 9.1 Comparison of entry mode strategies

	Export	Licensing or franchising	Joint ventures	Wholly owned subsidiaries
Resource commitments (financial, managerial, equity, etc.)	Low	Low	Medium	High
Control: technology and quality	High	Low	Low/Medium	High
Control: marketing and sales	Low	Low	Medium	High
Risk (financial, political, etc.)	Low	Low	Medium	High
Entry speed	High	High	Medium	Low/Medium

potential disadvantage is of course transportation costs and the possibility that products can be manufactured cheaper locally. Limited control of marketing and sales and possible international trade barriers are other drawbacks.

- *Licensing or franchising* involves a contractual agreement whereby a local firm receives the right to exploit a product technology or a service concept commercially for a fee during a specific time period. Soft-drink companies like Coca-Cola use license agreements for their drinks and brands internationally and fast food chains like McDonald's use franchise arrangements. Resource commitments can be kept low as local partners bear the primary financial and political risks while entry can be relatively quick. The main disadvantage with this entry mode is potential lack of control over technologies and product and service quality with an apparent risk of technological leakage and poor quality.

- *Joint ventures* are jointly owned companies where the international investor shares assets, equity and risk with a local partner. This implies that resource and financial commitments are limited compared to full ownership, and financial and political risks are also reduced. Another advantage is the ability to build on the local partner's knowledge of customer needs and local institutions. In some countries, China for example, joint ventures may be the only option for foreign investors in certain sectors. An important drawback, however, is the risk of losing control over technologies to the partner even if agreements can be made to lower this risk. Another disadvantage is disagreements and conflicts between the partners when the joint venture evolves and changes over time. Companies balance the trade-offs between these advantages and disadvantages in different ways. For example, Sweden's heavy truck maker Volvo has set up joint ventures in China while its competitor Scania, also headquartered in Sweden, has decided not to enter into Chinese joint ventures due to the risk of losing control of its technological expertise.

- *Wholly owned subsidiaries* involve 100 per cent control through setting up entirely new greenfield operations or by acquiring a local firm. This entry mode has the advantage of giving the company strong control over technologies, operations, sales and financial results. It also allows for exploiting production and coordination economies among diverse units globally. On the negative side, this mode of entry involves substantial commitment of resources and costs and also significant risks, although the latter can be reduced somewhat if a local company is acquired (but acquisitions involve their own challenges, see Section 11.5.2). Acquisitions are a common entry mode in the auto industry and the last decade has seen a whole range of these, from Chinese Geely's acquisition of Volvo Cars to Indian Tata Motors' acquisition of Jaguar and Land Rover to Italian Fiat's mega acquisition of Chrysler.

Case-specific factors other than those discussed above are also liable to enter the calculation of appropriate entry mode. For example, if global coordination of various value chain and system activities across different countries is essential, wholly owned subsidiaries would be the principal entry mode. This entry mode also promotes scale economies as does the export mode for existing facilities.

It should now be clear that each entry mode strategy involves important trade-offs between various factors and that managers need to carefully consider the specific situation and context when trying to choose the optimal entry mode. For example, if entering an entirely new and unknown market a joint venture may be preferable as a local partner could provide valuable market and institutional knowledge. However, if the international investor's products build on unique and patented technologies and the ability to enforce contracts and protect intellectual property is weak then a wholly owned subsidiary may still be the wiser choice.

The gradualism of staged international expansion outlined above has, however, recently been challenged by two phenomena:

- *'Born-global firms'* are new small firms that internationalise rapidly at early stages in their development.[30] New technologies now help small firms link up to international sources of expertise, supply and customers worldwide. For such firms, waiting until they have enough international experience is not an option: international strategy is a condition of existence. For example, companies like Twitter and Instagram internationalised quickly from being small start-ups. Other types of companies may also internationalise fast. Blue Skies in Illustration 9.2 with operations across three continents is an example of a small company that started out as a mini-multinational.

- *Emerging-country multinationals* also often move quickly through entry modes. Prominent examples are the Chinese white-goods multinational Haier, the Indian pharmaceuticals company Ranbaxy Laboratories and Mexico's Cemex cement company mentioned above.[31] Such companies typically develop *unique capabilities* in their home market that then need to be rolled out quickly worldwide before competitors catch up. For example, Haier became skilled at very efficient production of simple white goods, providing a cost advantage that is transferable outside its Chinese manufacturing base. Haier now has factories in Italy and the USA, as well as the Philippines, Malaysia, Indonesia, Egypt, Nigeria and elsewhere round the world. The rapid internationalisation made by emerging multinationals from China has largely been based on acquisitions.[32] These are often high-profile as illustrated by the Chinese conglomerate Wanda buying the second-biggest movie theatre chain in the USA, AMC and the Hollywood film studio, Legendary (see end of chapter case).

9.6 SUBSIDIARY ROLES IN AN INTERNATIONAL PORTFOLIO

International strategies imply different relationships between subsidiary operations and the corporate centre. The complexity of the strategies followed by organisations such as General Electric or Unilever can result in highly differentiated networks of subsidiaries with a range of distinct strategic roles. Subsidiaries may play different roles according to the level of local resources and capabilities available to them and the strategic importance of their local environment (see Figure 9.7):[33]

- *Strategic leaders* are subsidiaries that not only hold valuable resources and capabilities, but are also located in countries that are crucial for competitive success because of, for

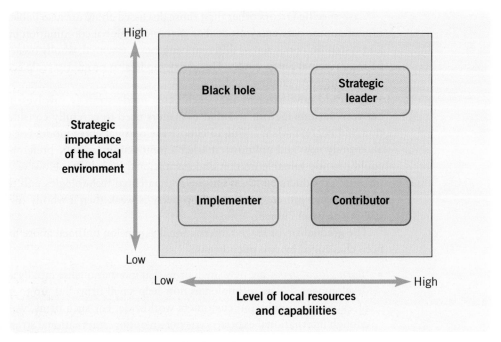

Figure 9.7 Subsidiary roles in multinational firms

Source: Reprinted by permission of Harvard Business School Press. From *Managing Across Borders: The Transnational Solution* by C.A. Bartlett and S. Ghoshal, Boston, MA, 1989, pp. 105–11. Copyright © 1989 by the Harvard Business School Publishing Corporation. All rights reserved.

example, the size of the local market or the accessibility of key technologies. Japanese and European subsidiaries in the USA often play this role. Increasingly, subsidiaries are seen as playing important strategic roles with entrepreneurial potential for the whole multinational organisation.[34] Subsidiaries and subunits are thus either assigned strategic roles or take autonomous strategic initiatives. Hewlett Packard, for example, is known to have used both approaches.[35]

- *Contributors* are subsidiaries located in countries of lesser strategic significance, but with sufficiently valuable internal capabilities to nevertheless play key roles in a multinational organisation's competitive success. The Australian subsidiary of the Swedish telecommunications firm Ericsson played such a role in developing specialised systems for the firm's mobile phone business.

- *Implementers,* though not contributing substantially to the enhancement of a firm's competitive advantage, are important in the sense that they help generate vital financial resources. In this sense, they are similar to the 'cash cows' of the Boston Consulting Group matrix. The danger is that they turn into the equivalent of 'dogs'.

- *Black holes* are subsidiaries located in countries that are crucial for competitive success but with low-level resources or capabilities. This is a position many subsidiaries of American and European firms found themselves in over long periods in Japan. They have some of the characteristics of 'question marks' in the Boston Consulting Group matrix, requiring heavy investment (like an astrophysicist's 'black hole', sucking matter in). Possibilities for overcoming this unattractive position include the development of alliances and the selective and targeted development of key resources and capabilities.

Corporate headquarters often assigns these roles, although subsidiary managers sometimes also take more independent initiatives. The roles thus relate to how subsidiaries are generally controlled and managed, and this is discussed in Chapter 14.

9.7 INTERNATIONALISATION AND PERFORMANCE

Just as for product and service diversity discussed in Section 8.4, the relationship between internationalisation and performance has been extensively researched.[36] Some of the main findings are as follows:

- *An inverted U-curve.* While the potential performance benefits of internationalisation are substantial, in that it allows firms to realise economies of scale and scope and benefit from the locational advantages available in countries around the globe, the combination of diverse locations and diverse business units also gives rise to high levels of organisational complexity. At some point, the costs of organisational complexity may exceed the benefits of internationalisations. Accordingly, theory, and the balance of evidence, suggest an inverted U-shaped relationship between internationalisation and performance (similar to the findings on product/service diversification shown in Section 8.4), with moderate levels of internationalisation leading to the best results. However, Yip's research on large British companies suggests that managers may be getting better at internationalisation, with substantially internationalised firms actually seeing performance improving to the point where international sales are above 40 per cent of total sales.[37] Experience and commitment to internationalisation may be able to deliver strong performance for highly internationalised firms.

- *Service-sector disadvantages.* A number of studies have suggested that, in contrast to firms in the manufacturing sector, internationalisation may not lead to equally improved performance for service-sector firms. There are three possible reasons for such an effect. First, the operations of foreign service firms in some sectors (such as accountants or banks) remain tightly regulated and restricted in many countries; second, due to the intangible nature of services, they are often more sensitive to cultural differences and require greater adaptation than manufactured products which may lead to higher initial learning costs; third, the services typically require a significant local presence and reduce the scope for the exploitation of economies of scale in production compared to manufacturing firms.[38]

- *Internationalisation and product diversity.* An important question to consider is the interaction between internationalisation and product/service diversification. Compared to single-business firms, it has been suggested that product-diversified firms are likely to do better from international expansion because they have already developed the necessary skills and structures for managing internal diversity.[39] At the other end of the spectrum, there is general consensus that firms that are highly diversified in terms of both product and international markets are likely to face excessive costs of coordination and control leading to poor performance. As many firms have not yet reached levels of internationalisation where negative effects outweigh possible gains and because of current scepticism with regard to the benefits of high levels of product diversification, many companies currently opt for reducing their product diversity while building their international scope. Unilever, for example, has been combining a strategy of growing internationalisation with de-diversification.

THINKING DIFFERENTLY   An institution-based view of strategy

A new strategy view focused on institutions rather than competition and capabilities has been proposed.

The primary difference between strategies at home compared to in foreign markets is the lack of knowledge of local customer needs and local institutions. While the emphasis traditionally has been on responding to the former, there has recently been an increased focus on the latter. It was observed in Section 9.5.1 that local economic, regulative, normative, political and cultural-cognitive institutions often differ substantially from those in home markets. They include local market regulations, rules, practices and behaviour that local actors take for granted, but that can be severely constraining and challenging for a foreign company.

It has been argued that current views of strategy largely ignore the importance of institutions despite research demonstrating how institutions significantly influence strategic decision-making. Therefore it has been suggested that strategy needs a new third view in addition to the industry and competitive focused view put forward by Michael Porter (see Chapter 3) and the resource-and-capabilities-based view (see

Chapter 4).[40] The argument is that managerial strategic choices must not only consider these aspects, but also local market's institutional characteristics.

Managers thus need to consider several choices in relation to institutions. For example, if the local institutions work in favour of the organisation then managers can try to reinforce and stabilise them by cooperating with local competitors and regulators. However, if the institutions are constraining and difficult to change, the only choice for the organisation may be to adapt to and follow them. Managers in powerful organisations could possibly choose to actively resist institutions and even change them. For example, they can try to influence local regulations or the legitimacy of various local business practices.[41]

> **Question**
>
> Why would institutions be of particular importance for strategy in emerging economies?

SUMMARY

- Internationalisation potential in any particular market is determined by Yip's *four drivers of internationalisation*: *market*, *cost*, *government* and *competitors' strategies*.

- Besides *firm-specific advantages*, there are *geographic sources of advantage* in international strategy that can be drawn from both national sources of advantage, as captured in *Porter's Diamond*, and global sourcing through the *international value system*.

- There are *four main types of international strategy*, varying according to extent of coordination and geographical configuration: *export strategy*, *multi-domestic strategy*, *global strategy* and *transnational strategy*.

- *Market selection* for international entry or expansion should be based on *attractiveness*, *institutional voids*, *multi-dimensional measures of distance* and *expectations of competitor retaliation*.

- *Entry mode strategies* into new markets include *export*, *licensing* and *franchising*, *joint ventures* and *wholly owned subsidiaries*.

- Subsidiaries in an international firm can be managed by *portfolio methods* just like businesses in a diversified firm.

- Internationalisation has an uncertain relationship to financial performance, with an *inverted U-curve* warning against over-internationalisation.

WORK ASSIGNMENTS

✱ Denotes more advanced work assignments.
* Refers to a case study in the Text and Cases edition.

9.1   Using Figure 9.2 (internationalisation drivers), compare two markets you are familiar with and analyse how strong each of the drivers is for increased international strategy.

9.2✱ Visit the websites of the following companies and try to plot their international strategies in one of the four international strategy types of Figure 9.4 (each company primarily fits one strategy): Nestlé, ABB, Louis Vuitton and Lenovo.

9.3✱ Using the CAGE framework (Section 9.5.1), assess the relative 'distance' of the USA, China, India and France for a British company (or a company from a country of your choice).

9.4   Using the diverse modes of international market entry of Table 9.1, classify the entry mode strategies of H&M*, Teva* or SABMiller or AB InBev* or any other multinational corporation with which you are familiar.

9.5   Critically evaluate the suggestion that globalisation is mostly beneficial for companies.

9.6   Take any part of the public or not-for-profit sector (e.g. education, health) and explain how far internationalisation has affected its management and consider how far it may do so in the future.

Integrative assignment

9.7   As in 9.2, use the four international strategies of Figure 9.4 to classify the international strategy of H&M*, SABMiller or AB InBev (Megabrew* case) or any other multinational corporation with which you are familiar. Drawing on Section 13.2.4, how does this corporation's organisational structure fit (or not fit) this strategy?

RECOMMENDED KEY READINGS

- A useful collection of academic articles on international business is in A. Rugman and T. Brewer (eds), *The Oxford Handbook of International Business*, Oxford University Press, 2003. For a collection of seminal contributions in research on multinational corporations see J.H. Dunning, *The Theory of Transnational Corporations*, vol. 1, Routledge, 1993.

- An invigorating perspective on international strategy is provided by G.S. Yip and G.T. Hult, *Total Global Strategy*, Pearson, 2012.

- A critical evaluation of the emphasis on globalisation and global integration contrasted with a regional focus can be found in A.M. Rugman, *The Regional Multinational: MNEs and 'global' strategic management*, Cambridge University Press, 2005 and P. Ghemawat, *Redefining Global Strategy*, Harvard Business School Press, 2007.

- An eye-opening introduction to the detailed workings – and inefficiencies – of today's global economy today is P. Rivoli, *The Travels of a T-Shirt in the Global Economy: an economist examines the markets, power and politics of world trade*, Wiley, 2006. A more optimistic view is in T. Friedman, *The World is Flat: the globalized world in the twenty-first century*, Penguin, 2006.

REFERENCES

1. For another cautious view, see M. Alexander and H. Korine, 'Why you shouldn't go global', *Harvard Business Review*, December 2008, pp. 70–7.

2. For a discussion that challenges globalisation, see P. Ghemawat, 'Distance still matters', *Harvard Business Review*, September 2001, pp. 137–47.

3. For two different views on globalisation, see T. Friedman, *The World is Flat: the globalized world in the twenty-first century*, Penguin, 2006; and P. Rivoli, *The Travels of a T-Shirt in the Global Economy: an economist examines the markets, Power and Politics of World Trade*, Wiley, 2006.

4. For different viewpoints on the extent to which world markets are globalising, see T. Levitt, 'The globalisation of markets',

Harvard Business Review, May–June 1983, pp. 92–102; S.P. Douglas and Y. Wind, 'The myth of globalization', *Columbia Journal of World Business*, vol. 22, no. 4 (1987), pp. 19–29; P. Ghemawat, 'Regional strategies for global leadership', *Harvard Business Review*, December 2005, pp. 98–108; and A. Rugman and A. Verbeke, 'A new perspective on the regional and global strategies of multinational service firms', *Management International Review*, vol. 48, no. 4 (2008), pp. 397–411.

5. G.S. Yip and G.T. Hult, *Total Global Strategy*, Pearson, 2012.

6. Useful industry-specific data on trends in openness to trade and investment can be found at the World Trade Organization's site, www.wto.org.

7. G. Hamel and C.K. Prahalad, 'Do you really have a global strategy?', *Harvard Business Review*, vol. 63, no. 4 (1985), pp. 139–48.

8. International firms have traditionally been considered to have a 'liability of foreignness' as home and host country environments often differ substantially; not the least in economic, regulative, normative and cultural institutions. See for example W. Henisz and A. Swaminathan, 'Introduction: institutions and international business', *Journal of International Business Studies*, vol. 39, no. 4 (2008), pp. 537–539 and L. Eden and S.R. Miller, 'Distance matters: liability of foreignness, institutional distance and ownership strategy', *Advances in International Management*, vol. 16 (2004), pp. 187–221.

9. For a discussion of firm-specific advantages ('FSAs') and country-specific advantages ('CSAs'), see A.M. Rugman, *The Regional Multinational: MNEs and 'global' strategic management*, Cambridge University Press, 2005; A. Rugman and A. Verbeke, 'Location, competitiveness and the multinational enterprise', in A.M. Rugman (ed.), *Oxford Handbook of International Business*, Oxford University Press, 2008, pp. 150–77 and A. Verbeke, *International Business Strategy*, Cambridge University Press, 2009.

10. B. Kogut, 'Designing global strategies: comparative and competitive value added changes', *Sloan Management Review*, vol. 27 (1985), pp. 15–28.

11. M. Porter, *The Competitive Advantage of Nations*, Macmillan, 1990; M. Porter, *On Competition*, Harvard Business Press, 2008.

12. J.A. Cantwell, 'The globalization of technology: what remains of the product life cycle model?', *Cambridge Journal of Economics*, vol. 19, no. 1 (1995), pp. 155–74; A. Rugman and A. Verbeke (see endnote 9).

13. The integration–responsiveness framework builds on the original works by C.A. Bartlett, 'Building and managing the transnational: the new organizational challenge', in M.E. Porter (ed.), *Competition in Global Industries*, Harvard Business School Press, 1986, pp. 367–401; and C.K. Prahalad and Y. Doz, *The Multinational Mission: Balancing local demands and global vision*, Free Press, 1987.

14. The typology builds on the basic framework of C.A. Bartlett and S. Ghoshal, *Managing Across Borders: the Transnational Solution*, The Harvard Business School Press, 1989 (2nd updated edn, 1998); and S. Ghoshal and N. Nohria, 'Horses for courses: organizational forms for multinational corporations', *Sloan Management Review*, vol. 34 (1993), pp. 23–35.

The typology was later confirmed in a large-scale empirical investigation by A.W. Harzing, 'An empirical analysis and extension of the Bartlett and Ghoshal typology of multinational companies', *Journal of International Business*, vol. 32, no. 1 (2000), pp. 101–20. For a similar typology, see M. Porter, 'Changing patterns of international competition', *California Management Review*, vol. 28, no. 2 (1987), pp. 9–39. For a critical evaluation, see T.M. Devinney, D.F. Midgley and S. Venaik, 'The optimal performance of the global firm: formalizing and extending the integration–responsiveness framework', *Organization Science*, vol. 11, no. 6 (2000), pp. 674–95.

15. For a discussion of companies that build on the multidomestic route, see A. Rugman and R. Hodgetts, 'The end of global strategy', *European Management Journal*, vol. 19, no. 4 (2001), pp. 333–43.

16. For a detailed account of Cemex strategy, see P. Ghemawat, *Redefining Global Strategy*, Harvard Business School Press, 2007.

17. For a discussion of the limits of global strategy, see A. Rugman and R. Hodgetts in endnote 15 above.

18. For a more in-depth discussion of how General Electric (GE) tries to combine a global and multi-domestic ('glocalisation') strategy with innovation in emerging markets, see J.R.I. Immelt, V. Govindarajan and C. Trimble, 'How GE is disrupting itself', *Harvard Business Review*, October 2009, pp. 57–65.

19. For an analysis of the transnational strategy and ABB as an example, see C.A. Bartlett and S. Ghoshal, *Managing Across Borders: the Transnational Solution*, 2nd edn, Harvard Business School Press, 1998, pp. 259–72; and S. Ghoshal and C. Bartlett, *The Individualized Corporation*, Harper Business, 1997.

20. For criticism of the integration–responsiveness framework and its shortcoming in taking regions into account and a detailed discussion of regional strategy, see A.M. Rugman, *The Regional Multinational: MNEs and 'global' strategic management*, pp. 48–53 and 201–12, Cambridge University Press, 2005. Further analysis of regional strategies can be found in P. Ghemawat, 'Regional strategies for global leadership', *Harvard Business Review*, December 2005, pp. 98–108.

21. For an in-depth examination of the regional sales data, see A. Rugman and A. Verbeke, 'A perspective on regional and global strategies of multinational enterprises', *Journal of International Business*, vol. 35 (2004), pp. 3–18; A.M. Rugman, *The End of Globalization*, Random House, 2000; A.M. Rugman and S. Girod, 'Retail multinationals and globalization: the evidence is regional', *European Management Journal*, vol. 21, no. 1 (2003), pp. 24–37; and A.M. Rugman, endnote 20 above.

22. P. Ghemawat, 'Reconceptualizing international strategy and organization', *Strategic Organization*, vol. 6, no. 2 (2008), pp. 195–206.

23. For a framework of how to map institutional contexts, see T. Khanna and K. Palepu, 'Strategies that fit emerging markets', *Harvard Business Review*, June 2005, pp. 63–76; and T. Khanna and K. Palepu, *Winning in Emerging Markets: a road map for strategy and execution*, Harvard Business Press, 2013.

24. For a case study of institutional voids in Bangladesh and how to handle them, see M. Johanna and I. Marti,

'Entrepreneurship in and around institutional voids: a case study from Bangladesh', *Journal of Business Venturing*, vol. 24, no. 5 (2009), pp. 419–35.

25. See P. Ghemawat, 'Distance still matters', *Harvard Business Review*, September 2001, pp. 137–47; and P. Ghemawat, *Redefining Global Strategy*, Harvard Business School Press, 2007.

26. C.K. Prahalad and A. Hammond, 'Serving the world's poor, profitably', *Harvard Business Review*, September 2002, pp. 48–55; Economist Intelligence Unit, 'From subsistence to sustainable: a bottom-up perspective on the role of business in poverty alleviation', 24 April 2009.

27. See also E. Simanis and D. Duke, 'Profits at the bottom of the pyramid', *Harvard Business Review*, October 2014; and A. Karamchandani, M. Kubzansky and N. Lalwani, 'Is the bottom of the pyramid really for you?', *Harvard Business Review*, March 2011.

28. This framework is introduced in I. MacMillan, A. van Putten and R. McGrath, 'Global gamesmanship', *Harvard Business Review*, vol. 81, no. 5 (2003), pp. 62–71.

29. For detailed discussions about the role of learning and experience in market entry, see M.K. Erramilli, 'The experience factor in foreign market entry modes by service firms', *Journal of International Business Studies*, vol. 22, no. 3 (1991), pp. 479–501; and Jan Johanson and Jan-Erik Vahlne, 'The Uppsala internationalization process model revisited: from liability of foreignness to liability of outsidership', *Journal of International Business Studies*, vol. 40, no. 9 (2009), pp. 1411–31.

30. See G. Knights and T. Cavusil, 'Innovation, organizational capabilities, and the born-global firm', *Journal of International Business Studies*, vol. 35, no. 2 (2004), pp. 124–41; and G. Knights and T. Cavusil, 'A taxonomy of born-global firms', *Management International Review*, vol. 45, no. 3 (2005), pp. 15–35.

31. For analyses of emerging-country multinationals, see T. Khanna and K. Palepu, 'Emerging giants: building world-class companies in developing countries', *Harvard Business Review*, October 2006, pp. 60–9; P. Gammeltoft, H. Barnard and A. Madhok, 'Emerging multinationals, emerging theory: macro- and micro-level perspectives', *Journal of International Management*, vol. 16, no. 1 (2010), pp. 95–101; and the special issue on 'The internationalization of Chinese and Indian firms – trends, motivations and strategy', *Industrial and Corporate Change*, vol. 18, no. 2 (2009).

32. For a detailed analysis of the unique aspects of Chinese multinationals, see M.W. Peng, 'The global strategy of emerging multinationals from China', *Global Strategy Journal*, vol. 2, no. 2 (2012), pp. 97–107.

33. See C.A. Bartlett and S. Ghoshal, 'Tap your subsidiaries for global reach', *Harvard Business Review*, November–December (1986), pp. 87–94; C.A. Bartlett and S. Ghoshal, *Managing across Borders: the Transnational Solution*, Harvard Business School Press, 1989, pp. 105–11; and A.M. Rugman and A. Verbeke, 'Extending the theory of the multinational enterprise: internalization and strategic management perspectives', *Journal of International Business Studies*, vol. 34 (2003), pp. 125–37.

34. For a discussion about the strategic role of subsidiaries, see J. Birkinshaw and A.J. Morrison, 'Configurations of strategy and structure in multinational subsidiaries', *Journal of International Business Studies*, vol. 26, no. 4 (1996), pp. 729–94; and A. Rugman and A. Verbeke, 'Subsidiary-specific advantages in multinational enterprises', *Strategic Management Journal*, vol. 22, no. 3 (2001), pp. 237–50.

35. For an analysis of subsidiary and subunit initiatives in multinational corporations, see J. Birkinshaw, *Entrepreneurship and the Global Firm*, Sage, 2000.

36. A useful review of the international dimension is M. Hitt and R.E. Hoskisson, 'International diversification: effects on innovation and firm performance in product-diversified firms', *Academy of Management Journal*, vol. 40, no. 4 (1997), pp. 767–98. For a meta-analytic review of previous studies of multinationality-performance relationships and what the effects depend on, see A.H. Kirca, K. Roth, G.T.M. Hult and S.T. Cavusgil, 'The role of context in the multinationality-performance relationships: a meta-analytic review', *Global Strategy Journal*, vol. 2, no. 2 (2012), pp. 108–21.

37. For detailed results on British companies, see G. Yip, A. Rugman and A. Kudina, 'International success of British companies', *Long Range Planning*, vol. 39, no. 1 (2006), pp. 241–64.

38. See N. Capar and M. Kotabe, 'The relationship between international diversification and performance in service firms', *Journal of International Business Studies*, vol. 34 (2003), pp. 345–55; and F.J. Contractor, S.K. Kundu and C. Hsu, 'A three-stage theory of international expansion: the link between multinationality and performance in the service sector', *Journal of International Business Studies*, vol. 34 (2003), pp. 5–18.

39. See S.C. Chang and C.-F. Wang, 'The effect of product diversification strategies on the relationship between international diversification and firm performance', *Journal of World Business*, vol. 42, no. 1 (2007), pp. 61–79; and C.H. Oh and F.J. Contractor, 'The role of territorial coverage and product diversification in the multinationality-performance relationship', *Global Strategy Journal*, vol. 2, no. 2 (2012), pp. 122–36.

40. M. W. Peng, S. L. Sun, B. Pinkham and H. Chen, 'The institution-based view as a third leg for a strategy tripod', *The Academy of Management Perspectives*, vol. 23, no. 3 (2009), pp. 63–81.

41. See P. Regnér and J. Edman, 'MNE institutional advantage: how subunits shape, transpose and evade host country institutions', *Journal of International Business Studies*, vol. 45, no. 3 (2014), pp. 275–302.

China goes to Hollywood – Wanda's move into the US movie industry

Patrick Regnér

Introduction

Chinese foreign direct investments in the USA have reached record levels and exceeded $10bn (£6bn, €7.5bn) in 2014. Despite this, Wanda's $2.6bn acquisition of US second-largest cinema chain AMC in 2012 and the later $3.5bn acquisition of one of the world's biggest movie producers, Legendary Entertainment in 2016, sent shock waves through the US entertainment industry. The AMC acquisition created the world's largest cinema company by revenues and the Legendary Entertainment acquisition was the biggest China–Hollywood deal ever.

Wanda Cinema Line Corp. is China's largest operator by cinema screens with close to 300 cinemas and 2,550 screens. Through the AMC acquisition, Wanda now controls more than ten per cent of the global cinema market. AMC is the second-biggest cinema chain operator in North America, which is the world's biggest film market with ticket sales of over $10bn. The company has more than 5250 screens and 375 theatres in this market and is the world's largest operator of IMAX and 3D screens including 120 and 2170 screens, respectively.

The AMC and Legendary investments marked a new era as Chinese investment reached into the heart of US entertainment and culture. Although Chinese acquisitions in the USA have proven to be controversial before, they may prove to be even more challenging, and it was speculated that a Hollywood ending was far from certain. According to Chen Zheng, manager of Saga Cinema in Beijing, the AMC deal strengthens Wanda's global status as movie theatre owner:

'Wanda has been the largest theatre owner in the second largest film market in the world. Now the deal makes it also the owner of the second largest theatre chain in the largest film market.'[1]

Another analyst commented on the Legendary deal:

'Buying Legendary Entertainment puts Wanda on the road to becoming a global media company and one of the world's biggest players in movie production.'[2]

Legendary Entertainment is a leading film production company that owns film, television, digital and comics divisions. Its big-budget, action and special-effects global blockbuster type of movie productions has performed very well in China. These include films such as *The Dark*

Gerry Lopez, CEO of AMC Entertainment Holdings, left, shakes hands with Zhang Lin, Vice President of Wanda during a signing ceremony in Beijing, China, Monday, 21 May 2012.

Source: Ng Han Guan/Press Association Images.

Knight batman trilogy, *Jurassic World*, *Inception*, *Pacific Rim* and *Godzilla* – the last two particularly successful in China. The Hollywood studio adds experience and expertise to Wanda's movie production business. Wanda group is constructing a $8.2bn studio in eastern China which is claimed to be the biggest studio complex globally, competing with and even exceeding Hollywood's best studios, but with Chinese costs.

Although the acquisitions are huge, they are relatively small compared with the rest of the Dalian Wanda real-estate conglomerate. Dalian Wanda Group Corp. Ltd includes assets of over $86bn and annual income of about $39bn (2014). Wanda, which means 'a thousand roads lead here', consists of five-star hotels, tourist resorts, theme parks and shopping malls. The 'Wanda Plaza' complexes that combine malls with housing and hotels have been a huge success in China and can be found in more than 60 Chinese cities.

Mr Wang Jianlin, the Founder, Chairman and President of Dalian Wanda, is the richest man in China. He joined the army as a teenager and stayed in the military for 17 years. In 1988, he founded Dalian Wanda and rode the wave of China's phenomenal growth by investing in property. His military background and ties to local officials helped him as large commercial land sales are handled by local governments. As he was willing to take on whatever property the local government was ready to give, he became popular with officials. Soon Wanda was the first property company to work in several cities.

Landmark deals

AMC was considered a 'trophy' acquisition in the American entertainment industry and it was described as a landmark deal by analysts and investors. As announced by the Chairman and President, Mr Wang:

'This acquisition will help make Wanda a truly global cinema owner, with theatres and technology that enhance the movie-going experience for audiences in the world's two largest movie markets.'[3]

Mr Wang considered the AMC deal to be a springboard to expand Wanda's global cinema presence further with the goal to reach 20 per cent of the world movie theatre market by 2020.

At the announcement of the deal Gerry Lopez, Chief Executive Officer and President, explained:

'As the film and exhibition business continues its global expansion, the time has never been more opportune to welcome the enthusiastic support of our new owners. Wanda and AMC are both dedicated to providing our customers with a premier entertainment experience and state-of-the-art amenities and share corporate cultures focused on strategic growth and innovation. With Wanda as its partner, AMC will continue to seek out new ways to expand and invest in the movie-going experience.'[3]

When expanding on its home market Wanda wants to benefit from the know-how of AMC, which operates on a market five times Chinese annual box office sales. AMC has an established worldwide network of cinema theatres and this will give Wanda a reputable brand. There is also a trend for more foreign movies in China and the transaction may allow Wanda to secure more Hollywood movies for distribution in China.

The Legendary Entertainment acquisition was considered as a next bold step towards Wanda's goal of becoming a global film and entertainment company. Besides expertise and intellectual property, it offered potential synergies between film production and screening both between and within China and the USA. It would help the distribution of more films into the tightly controlled Chinese film market. The quota of 34 foreign films per year could be bypassed if Legendary could make films in China. Mr Wang, however, particularly emphasised the business integration benefits:

'The acquisition of Legendary will make Wanda Film Holdings Company the highest revenue-generating film company in the world, increasing Wanda's presence in China and the US, the world's two largest markets. Wanda's businesses will encompass the full scope of film production, exhibition and distribution, enhancing Wanda's core competitiveness and amplifying our voice in the global film market.'[4]

Thomas Tull, the Chairman and CEO of Legendary added:

'Together, Wanda and Legendary will create a completely new international entertainment company. There is an ever growing demand for quality entertainment content worldwide, particularly in China, and we will combine our respective strengths to bring an even better entertainment experience to the world's audiences.'[5]

Wanda's Cultural Industry Group in the USA

Wanda's acquisitions were part of a more general effort to develop China's own home-grown culture and entertainment industry. Cinema is an increasingly popular recreational activity in China and the film market is booming with an amazing increase in box office sales of 50 per cent to $6.7bn during 2015. The market is expected to overtake that of the USA as the world's largest film market by 2017.

Wanda's investments in culture and entertainment align well with China's overall ambition to invest in the sector. The company described the Legendary Entertainment investment as 'China's largest cross-border cultural acquisition to date' and commented on the AMC acquisition:

Signing of the Wanda Cultural Industry Group and Legendary Entertainment merger

Source: Imaginechina/REX/Shutterstock.

'The Wanda Group began to massively invest in cultural industries in 2005. It has entered five industries, including central cultural district, big stage show, film production and projection, entertainment chain and Chinese calligraphy and painting collection. . . . Wanda has invested more than $1.6 billion in cultural industries and become the nation's largest enterprise investor in cultural industries.'[5]

As Wanda's acquisitions were the largest overseas cultural investments of a Chinese private enterprise ever, they raised some concerns in the USA. AMC is a US household name, 'once epitomised as the all-American movie-watching experience'[6] and the Legendary investment reached into the heart of Hollywood. This was a significant expansion of Chinese influence in the American film industry and some were anxious about the effect as many American movies are censored or even banned in China. Mr Wang was after all a Communist Party member, sitting on China's top advisory council. Wanda's acquisitions raised concerns that Chinese-style censorship of politically controversial movies would become commonplace also in the USA. As reported by *USA Today*: 'Beijing is investing heavily in projecting its "soft power", or cultural influence. . . .'[7]

Chinese investments in the USA had been of concern earlier and the US government had rejected investments in the past in the telecommunications and energy industry due to national security concerns. However, cinema was unlikely to be considered a strategic industry for the USA.

Mr Wang insisted that Wanda had 'no plans to promote Chinese films in the United States' and that AMC CEO Lopez 'will decide what movies will be shown' in AMC theatres.[8] It was also made clear that AMC would continue to be operated from its headquarters in Kansas City. Mr Wang said Wanda will retain AMC senior management and would not interfere with everyday operations and programming decisions, which should remain with the US management and claimed 'The only thing that changed is the boss.'[9] On the Legendary Entertainment deal Mr Wang dismissed concerns that it would lead to censorship or alter movie content claiming he is a businessman that buys things '. . . to make money, so I don't really think about government priorities'[10] and the main consideration was instead commercial.

Some claimed, however, that China was already achieving its goal of 'soft power' as Legendary's Chinese arm (Legendary East) had partnered with state-owned China Film Group to co-produce *The Great Wall,* starring Matt Damon and Willem Dafoe alongside Chinese actors such as Andy Lau, Jing Tian and Eddie Peng. The big-budget, Hollywood blockbuster action-fantasy film was the largest film intended for global distribution ever shot entirely in China, starring Chinese actors, and incorporating Chinese myths.

AMC and Legendary Entertainment were not likely to be Wanda's last investments into the global entertainment industry. It acquired Hoyts, Australia's second-largest multiplex chain, 2015 and was rumoured to be looking for a pan-European chain. In the spring of 2016, they announced the intent to acquire Carmike Cinemas. If approved this deal would make them the largest cinema chain in the USA. Wanda also had plans to make the movie theatre operator Wanda Cinema Line Corp public in an initial public offering with the aim to raise money for further worldwide expansion.

Sources: Wanda Group press release, 12 January 2016; *The Diplomat*, 13 January 2016; *Forbes*, 12 January 2016; *Financial Times*, 22–28 May; *Los Angeles Times*, 20 May 2012; *New York Times*, 5 January 2016; *New York Times*, 20 May 2012; *Reuters*, 21 May 2012; *The Washington Post*, 21 May 2012; *Wall Street Journal*, 21 May 2012.

Questions

1 Considering Yip's globalisation framework (Figure 9.2), what drivers of internationalisation do you think were most important when Wanda entered the US market through its AMC and Legendary acquisitions?

2 What national sources of competitive advantage might Wanda draw from its Chinese base? What disadvantages derive from its Chinese base?

3 In the light of the CAGE framework, what challenges may Wanda meet as it enters the US market?

References
1. 'Wanda's AMC deal a ticket to global rule', *Beijing International*.
2. *BBC News*, 12 January 2016.
3. 'Wanda Group to acquire AMC Holdings Inc.', Dalian Wanda press release, 20 May 2012.
4. 'Wanda acquires Legendary for $3.5b in biggest Chinese overseas deal', *ChinaDaily*, 12 January 2016.
5. 'Wanda attends Shenzhen cultural fair', Wanda Group press release, 18 May 2012.
6. L. Hook, 'AMC deal to boost Wanda's global exposure', *Financial Times*, 22 May 2016.
7. C. MacLeod, 'Chinese firm to buy AMC movie chain', *USA Today*, 21 May 2012.
8. J. McDonald, 'Chinese company to buy US movie theatre chain', *Yahoo News*, 21 May 2012.
9. 'Wanda's AMC deal a ticket to golden role', *ChinaDaily*, 22 May 2012.
10. S. Zhang and M. Miller, 'Wanda goes to Hollywood: China tycoon's firm buys film studio Legendary for $3.5 billion', *Reuters,* 12 January 2016.

10

ENTREPRENEURSHIP AND INNOVATION

Learning outcomes

After reading this chapter you should be able to:

- Anticipate key issues facing entrepreneurs in *opportunity recognition*, in making choices during the *entrepreneurial process* and in various *stages of growth*, from start-up to exit.

- Evaluate opportunities and choices facing *social entrepreneurs* as they create new ventures to address social problems.

- Identify and respond to key *innovation dilemmas*, such as the relative emphases to place on technologies or markets, product or process innovations and open versus closed innovation.

- Anticipate and to some extent influence the *diffusion* (or spread) of innovations.

- Decide when being a *first-mover* or an imitator and *follower* is most appropriate in innovation, and how an *incumbent* organisation should respond to innovative challengers.

Key terms

diffusion p.324

disruptive innovation p.328

entrepreneurship p.310

entrepreneurial life cycle p.315

first-mover advantage p.327

innovation p.317

open innovation p.321

opportunity recognition p.310

S-curve p.325

social entrepreneurs p.316

strategic entrepreneurship p.309

10.1 INTRODUCTION

As discussed in Chapter 1, strategy concerns an organisation's long-term direction, and one important dimension of this is to create new value and competitive advantages for the future. Organisations need not only build competitive advantages in relation to current domestic and international competitors, but they need to identify growth opportunities. Hence this chapter is about identifying opportunities and creating new products and services, technologies, resources and capabilities. For example, Apple needs to sustain and develop their existing competitive advantages with the iPhone in the smartphone industry, but they also need to find new opportunities in the market, as with the Apple watch.

Strategic entrepreneurship combines strategy and entrepreneurship and includes both advantage-seeking strategy activities and opportunity-seeking entrepreneurial activities to create value.[1] While strategy supports this by forming competitive advantages, entrepreneurship contributes the identification of new opportunities in the market or environment. The latter involves entrepreneurs that innovate by identifying and exploiting new ideas and inventions that result in innovations. Strategic entrepreneurship and its outcome, innovation, are essential for the long-term survival and success of all organisations and are the focus of this chapter.[2]

Entrepreneurship is fundamental not only for creating value for customers and organisational growth and prosperity, but generally for today's economy. All businesses start with an act of entrepreneurship, but large established firms also practise entrepreneurship to find new innovative products and services in the form of corporate entrepreneurship or 'intrapreneurship', while many people pursue 'social entrepreneurship' for the public good. Innovation is also a key aspect of business-level strategy and models as introduced in Chapter 7, with implications for cost, price, differentiation and sustained competitive advantage. Moreover, it is a dynamic capability that can renew organisational resources and capabilities as discussed in Chapter 4. Promoting greater innovation and entrepreneurship is thus crucial to the improvement of not only all firms, but for public services. But it also poses hard choices. For example, how can new and valuable opportunities be identified and what are the essential considerations involved? Should a company always look to be a pioneer in new technologies, or rather be a fast follower such as Samsung typically is? How should a company react to radical innovations that threaten to destroy their existing revenues, as the Kodak film business had to with the rise of electronic cameras (see Illustration 6.4)? The chapter thus focuses particularly on the choices involved in entrepreneurship and innovation aimed at creating new value that benefit organisations and society.

Figure 10.1 identifies four major themes of this chapter; within this framework this chapter will first examine entrepreneurship then innovation:

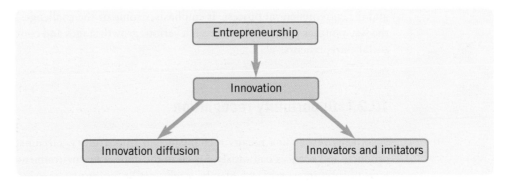

Figure 10.1 Entrepreneurship and innovation: four major themes

- Section 10.2 addresses *entrepreneurship*. The section starts with a discussion of a central step in entrepreneurship, *opportunity recognition*, which captures conditions under which products and services satisfy market needs or wants in the environment. Other steps in the *entrepreneurial process* then follow. They provide a foundation for further entrepreneurial *growth stages* from start-up to growth, maturity and possibly finally to exit. Finally, this section introduces *social entrepreneurship*, which explains how individuals and small groups can launch innovative and flexible new initiatives that larger public agencies are unable to pursue.

- Section 10.3 discusses three fundamental *innovation dilemmas*: technology push as against market pull; product innovation rather than process innovation; and, finally, open versus closed innovation. None of these are absolute 'either-or' dilemmas, but managers and entrepreneurs must choose where to concentrate their limited resources.

- Once created, innovations will be diffused among users over time, and diffusion pace depends on various product and demand features. Section 10.4 considers issues surrounding the *diffusion*, or spread, of innovations in the marketplace. Diffusion processes often follow *S-curve patterns*, raising further typical issues for decision, particularly with regard to tipping points and tripping points.

- Section 10.5 completes the discussion of innovation by considering choices with regard to timing. This includes *first-mover* advantages and disadvantages, the advantages of being '*fast second*' into a market, and the issue of how established *incumbents* can be innovative and respond to innovative challengers.

10.2 ENTREPRENEURSHIP

Understanding and developing a competitive position in relation to competitors and competitive advantages in resources and capabilities is fundamental for the long-term strategic direction of an organisation. However, all organisations also need to explore and find new opportunities for the future. This suggests that strategy is not enough and that organisations also need entrepreneurship. **Entrepreneurship is a process by which individuals, teams or organisations identify and exploit opportunities for new products or services that satisfy a need in a market.**[3] The focus is thus on entirely new opportunities for the organisation and not on current competitive positions. Recognising an opportunity is the very first step in an entrepreneurial process. It is more than a simple business idea and involves a combination of elements that an entrepreneur believes will create value and possibly profit. This section introduces some key issues for entrepreneurial innovators including opportunity recognition and the entrepreneurial process. It emphasises some of the challenges of entrepreneurship, the way ventures tend to evolve through various growth stages and concludes by considering social entrepreneurs.

10.2.1 Opportunity recognition

Opportunity recognition means recognising an opportunity, circumstances under which products and services can satisfy a need in the market or environment. It is central for any form of entrepreneurship whether by small start-up, corporate or social entrepreneurs.[4] This involves an entrepreneur or entrepreneurial team identifying trends in the environment and

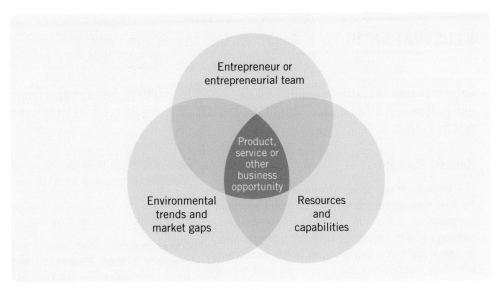

Figure 10.2 Entrepreneurial opportunity recognition

combining resources and capabilities into the creation of new products or services. Opportunity recognition thus involves three important and interdependent elements: the entrepreneur or entrepreneurial team, the environment and resources and capabilities (see Figure 10.2):

- *Entrepreneur or entrepreneurial team.* The entrepreneur or team drives and integrates the various parts of an entrepreneurial process including scanning and spotting trends in the environment (see Section 2.2) linking these to existing resources and capabilities (see Chapter 4) or acquiring appropriate ones and recombining them. Their characteristics differ and entrepreneurs thus come in many different forms and shapes. However, they are often alert to opportunities and able to deal with uncertainty, willing to take risks, highly motivated, optimistic and persuasive as they coordinate resources from their social networks. Entrepreneurship, however, normally includes a team and the managing of relationships with other partners and sometimes other and bigger companies. Beneath the common stereotype of entrepreneurs as heroic individuals, starting their businesses at night in a university laboratory or in a local lock-up garage there can be important external relations (see Illustration 10.1).

- *Environment trends and marketplace gaps.* Building on macro trends and possible marketplace gaps is likely to be central in identifying an opportunity. This includes observing economic, technological, social and political trends (as with PESTEL; see Section 2.2) and linking them to specific customer needs that are currently not satisfied. Spotting macro trends, industry and strategic group analysis and Blue Ocean thinking can be very useful for identifying new market opportunities (see Sections 2.2, 3.2 and 3.4.3). The GPS fitness-tracking app Runkeeper launched in 2008, for example, built on a range of trends and industry developments and now has 45 million users worldwide. These trends included the health awareness and fitness trends, the proliferation of smartphone users and apps, globalisation of markets and the increased possibility to integrate apps across various social media platforms like Facebook and Twitter. It addresses the market gap of runners' needs to be able to track and engage with their progress.

- *Resources and capabilities.* Having access to or being able to obtain resources and capabilities is an important part of opportunity recognition. Various helpful ways of mapping and evaluating them were discussed in Chapter 4 (VRIO, value chain, activity systems, etc.; see Sections 4.3, 4.4.2 and 4.4.3). For small start-ups, the necessary resources and

ILLUSTRATION 10.1 Entrepreneurs, teams and external relationships

Entrepreneurs are often stereotyped as heroic individuals, but entrepreneurship is rarely done alone – it often builds on a team, pre-existing organisational experience and external relationships.

Hewlett Packard

The entrepreneurial team William Hewlett and David Packard, founders of the famous computing and printer company HP, are oft-quoted examples of the garage stereotype. But digging beneath the stereotype soon reveals a more complex story, in which relationships with large companies can be important right from the start. Often entrepreneurs have worked for large companies beforehand, and continue to use relationships afterwards. While Hewlett came fairly directly out of Stanford University's laboratories, Packard worked at General Electric and Litton Industries. They built extensively on their previous social relationships and ties when setting up HP. The company used Litton Industries' foundries early on, and later used relationships at General Electric to recruit experienced managers.

Apple

Steve Jobs has often been celebrated as the heroic innovator and entrepreneur behind Apple, but he too relied heavily on external relationships. From the very beginning Apple computer did not only involve Jobs, but his founding partner Steve Wozniak. They too started in a garage, but similar to HP built heavily on their experiences with more established organisations. Wozniak worked at HP and Jobs at Atari and this helped them gain access to crucial knowledge and contacts for the development of the start-up. When their venture had become more established they left their employers and incorporated Apple Computer. Apple's much later successes with the iPod and later the iPhone and iPad have also relied on important external relationships. The music player application SoundJam MP was externally acquired early on and an external entrepreneur was vital for developing iTunes. Apple also initially worked with the then leading mobile telephone maker Motorola to develop a smart phone.

Facebook

One of today's most successful and well known entrepreneurs is Mark Zuckerberg who started a photo-rating site called Facemash from his dorm room by using Harvard's online student photographs. Zuckerberg did not rely on previous organisational experiences, but built on his programming skills and involved others with complementary skills early on. Based on his previous experience with Facemash, he founded the social networking website Facebook together with other fellow Harvard students to develop and grow the site. The team (Dustin Moskovitz, Chris Hughes and Eduardo Saverin) brought various skills including programming, promotion, graphics, financing and other business expertise. To focus entirely on Facebook and attract further talent and financing to their team, Zuckerberg and Moskovitz abandoned their education at Harvard and moved to California and Silicon Valley. There Zuckerberg continued to build on external business expertise together with venture capitalist investors to further grow the company.

Sources: P. Audia and C. Rider, 'A garage and an idea: what more does an entrepreneur need?', *California Management Review*, vol. 40, no. 1, 2005, pp. 6–28; D. Kirkpatrick, *The Inside Story of the Company That Is Connecting the World*, Simon & Schuster, 2010.

Questions

1 Based on the experiences of HP, Apple and Facebook what elements of skills and expertise do you think a new venture requires?

2 How would you form a venture team if you set up your own start-up?

capabilities frequently arise from and draw upon the knowledge and experiences and competences of the people involved (see Illustration 10.1). However, while existing resources and capabilities can be helpful, they can also be harmful for opportunity recognition, especially for larger established organisations. Incumbent companies are always bound by existing resources and capabilities, activities and vested interests, which can make entrepreneurial behaviours and activities very difficult (see Section 6.4). Given this, many would conclude that the best approach for entrepreneurship is to start up a new venture from scratch. Independent entrepreneurs such as the Samwer brothers of Rocket Internet and Larry Page and Sergey Brin of Google are exemplars of this entrepreneurial approach to innovation (see Chapters 4 and 13 end cases).

10.2.2 Steps in the entrepreneurial process

The first step of opportunity recognition explained above is likely to be followed by five other steps in the development of an entrepreneurial venture. See Figure 10.3 for an overview of these steps.[5] Before developing a *business plan* (see Section 13.2.2) an entrepreneur and start-up can usefully include an initial *feasibility analysis*. This would critically assess an entrepreneurial idea in terms of product or service viability, market opportunity and financing to establish if it can be turned into a business at all. Next, *industry conditions and competitors* are often considered. Competitive positions can be evaluated with the help of five forces and strategic groups analyses (see Sections 3.2 and 3.4), and competitors' potential to imitate the venture's resources and capabilities can be examined with the VRIO analysis (see Section 4.3). One of the most important considerations in the entrepreneurial process is to *choose a business model and strategy* (see Chapter 7).[6] A start-up thus needs to consider how to create value for the customers, how to manage revenues and costs, how to generate a margin and whether to build on an established business model or create a new one. In addition to this, a distinct competitive strategy position and advantage need to be identified. Thus entrepreneurs will typically have to choose between the generic business strategies of differentiation, cost and focus or any possible hybrid strategy (see Section 7.2.4). Finally, the new venture's financial strength in terms of *financing and funding* need to be carefully examined (see Chapter 12).

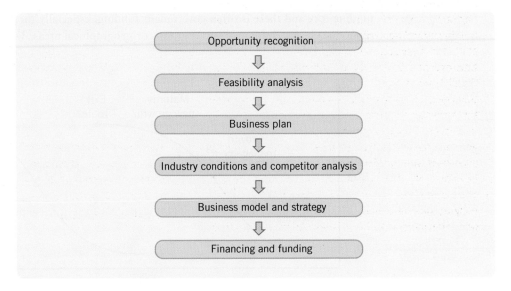

Figure 10.3 Steps in an entrepreneurial process

Source: Adapted from B.R. Barringer and R.D. Ireland, *Entrepreneurship – Successfully launching new ventures*, 4th edn, 2012, Pearson.

While all these entrepreneurial process steps are important, it must be noted that it is an iterative rather than a sequential process and thus not necessarily quite as simple as indicated by Figure 10.3 (see also Thinking Differently at the end of this chapter). The steps do not necessarily neatly follow on from each other and typically include setbacks along the way. The process thus often involves continuous experimentation and the original business itself may evolve quite radically. This is sometimes referred to as a '*pivoting*', which means making major changes in some dimension of the venture based on market and external feedback.[7] For example, Starbucks started off 1971 selling espresso makers and coffee beans rather than brewed coffee. It was after a visit to Italy in 1983 that Howard Schultz (current chairman, president and CEO) started to brew and sell Starbucks coffee in the first coffeehouse. At this time, however, it was a European-style coffeehouse with classical music and waiters, completely different from the type of Starbucks café it eventually evolved into. The important role of experimentation or pivoting also suggests that many entrepreneurs will fail. For every revolutionary entrepreneur that has recognised new opportunities, created new markets and beaten off well-resourced challengers, like Starbucks' Howard Schultz, there are countless forgotten failures (see Illustration 10.2 for an example). No matter how the entrepreneurial process develops or the degree of experimentation and set-backs, ventures develop through diverse growth stages, and this is discussed next.

10.2.3 Stages of entrepreneurial growth

Entrepreneurial ventures are often seen as going through four stages of a life cycle: see Figure 10.4. The **entrepreneurial life cycle progresses through start-up, growth, maturity and exit.** Of course, most ventures do not make it through all the stages – the estimated failure rate of new businesses in their first year is more than one fifth, with two thirds going out of business within six years. However, each of these four stages raises key questions for entrepreneurs:

- *Start-up.* There are many challenges at this stage, but one key question with implications for both survival and growth concerns sources of capital. Loans from family and friends are common sources of funds, but these are typically limited and, given the new-business failure rate, likely to lead to embarrassment. Bank loans and credit cards can provide funding too, and there is often government funding, especially for new technologies or economically disadvantaged social groups or geographical areas. *Venture capitalists* are

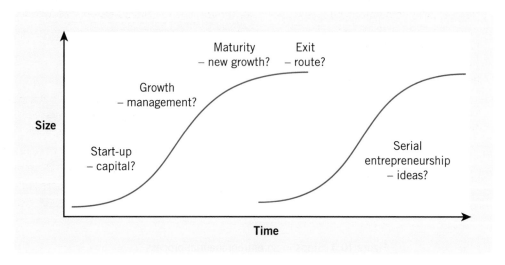

Figure 10.4 Stages of entrepreneurial growth and typical challenges

ILLUSTRATION 10.2 Nearly billionnaires

Adam Goldberg and Wayne Ting had the same idea as Facebook's Mark Zuckerberg – and first.

In 2003, Golderg and Ting were engineering students at the prestigious Columbia University, New York. Goldberg was president of his class and hearing lots of complaints about lack of community spirit. Over the summer, he designed a social network for his fellow engineers. Unlike other existing social networks such as MySpace and Friendster, this was the first network which overlaid a virtual community on a real community. Mark Zuckerberg would try the same idea at Harvard the next year.

Three quarters of Columbia's engineering students signed up to the Columbia network over the summer. Goldberg improved the network and relaunched it as CU Community in January 2004, open to all the University's students. Most Columbia students signed up within a month. CU Community was sophisticated for its time. When Facebook launched in February 2004, it only allowed members to 'friend' and 'poke' each other. CU Community also allowed blogging, sharing and cross-profile commenting. Goldberg did not worry about Facebook: 'I saw it was totally different. It had an emphasis on directory functionality, less emphasis on sharing. I didn't think there was much competition. . . . We were the Columbia community, they were Harvard.'

Then in March Facebook launched in other elite American universities such as Yale, Stanford and Columbia. Goldberg, now joined by Wayne Ting, transformed CU Community into Campus Network and launched in elite American universities as well. But Facebook outpaced the new Campus Network. By summer 2004, Facebook had already overtaken Goldberg and Ting's network even at Columbia.

Goldberg and Ting now plunged into the competition full-time. They suspended their studies and moved to Montreal, hiring three other software developers to help them. But resources were tight. Campus Network refused funds from venture capitalists and turned down some large advertisers, including MTV. The two entrepreneurs slept in the office on air mattresses, hiding them away as the three employees turned up for work so they would not know they were homeless.

Nonetheless, Campus Network developed a sophisticated product, with fully-customisable pages, multiple designs and backgrounds. Facebook was simpler. The feel of Campus Network was a bit like Dungeon and Dragons, unlike the clean aesthetics of early Facebook. Ting commented on the logic behind the early development of Campus Network: 'Why would you go to a site that only had poking and a photo [like Facebook then] when you can share photos, share music and share your thoughts on a blog?' Looking back though he observed: 'A good website should have functionalities that 70 or 80% of users want to use. We had functions that only 10% wanted – nobody blogged, nobody even blogs today.'

Campus Network reached 250,000 users by 2005, but at the same point Facebook had reached one million. Goldberg and Ting decided to wind down the network and returned to Columbia as students in the autumn of 2005. The venture had cost them personally something between $100,000 (£60,000, €75,000) and $200,000, as well as more than a year of their lives. Ting reflected in 2012, when an MBA student at Harvard Business School: 'There are still moments when you feel a deep sense of regret . . . . Could we have succeeded? I think that's a really painful question. . . . There are fleeting moments like that. But I'm much prouder that we took a risk and we learned from it.'

Sources: *Slate*, 29 September 2010; BBC, 21 December 2010.

Questions

1 What do you learn from the experience of Goldberg and Ting which could be useful to launching a new enterprise?

2 Are there any unmet needs in your community, at college or elsewhere, that could be turned into a business opportunity?

specialised investors in new ventures, especially when there is some track record. Venture capitalists usually insist on a seat on the venture's board of directors and may install their preferred managers. Venture capitalist backing has been shown to significantly increase the chances of a venture's success, but venture capitalists typically accept only about one in 400 propositions put to them.

- *Growth.* A key challenge for growth ventures is management. Entrepreneurs have to be ready to move from doing to managing. Typically this transition occurs as the venture grows beyond about 20 employees. Many entrepreneurs make poor managers: if they had wanted to be managers, they would probably be working in a large corporation in the first place. The choice entrepreneurs have to make is whether to rely on their own managerial skills or to bring in professional managers. For example, Groupon's founder Andrew Mason had to step down as chief executive in 2013 after creating the fastest growing internet business ever and leading an IPO of $10bn (see Illustration 4.2).

- *Maturity.* The challenge for entrepreneurs at this stage is retaining their enthusiasm and commitment and generating new growth. This is a period when entrepreneurship can change to *intrapreneurship,* the generation of new ventures from inside the organisation (see Section 10.5.2). An important option is usually *diversification* into new business areas, a topic dealt with in Chapter 8. Amazon.com in the USA has moved from book-selling to automotive parts, groceries and clothing. When generating new ventures at this stage, it is critical to recall the odds on success. Research suggests that many small high-tech firms fail to manage the transition to a second generation of technology, and that it is often better at this point simply to look for exit.

- *Exit.* Exit refers to departure from the venture, either by the founding entrepreneurs, or by the original investors, or both. At the point of exit, entrepreneurs and venture capitalists will seek to release capital as a reward for their input and risk-taking. Entrepreneurs may consider three prime routes to exit. A simple *trade sale* of the venture to another company is a common route. Thus in 2014 the founders of the internet-based mobile texting app WhatsApp sold their company to Facebook for $16bn in combined cash and stock, just four years after starting the company. Another exit route for highly successful enterprises is an *initial public offering* (IPO), the sale of shares to the public, for instance on the American NASDAQ exchange. IPOs usually involve just a portion of the total shares available, and may thus allow entrepreneurs to continue in the business and provide funds for further growth. In 2012, Mark Zuckerberg raised $16bn in Facebook's IPO, while retaining for himself 28 per cent ownership of the company. It is often said that good entrepreneurs plan for their exit right from start-up, and certainly venture capitalists will insist on this.

Entrepreneurs who have successfully exited a first venture often become *serial entrepreneurs.* Serial entrepreneurs are people who set up a succession of enterprises, investing the capital raised on exit from earlier ventures into new growing ventures. For example, the German Samwer brothers of Rocket Internet have started and sold a whole series of companies and then started new ones (see Chapter 4 end case). For serial entrepreneurs, the challenge often is no longer so much funding but good ideas.

10.2.4 Social entrepreneurship

Entrepreneurship is not just a matter for the private sector. The public sector has seen increasing calls for a more entrepreneurial approach to service creation and delivery. The notion of social entrepreneurship has become common. **Social entrepreneurs are individuals and groups who create independent organisations to mobilise ideas and resources to address**

social problems, typically earning revenues but on a not-for-profit basis. Independence and revenues generated in the market give social entrepreneurs the flexibility and dynamism to pursue social problems that pure public-sector organisations are often too bureaucratic, or too politically constrained, to tackle. Social entrepreneurs have pursued a wide range of initiatives, including small loans ('micro-credit') to peasants by the Grameen bank in Bangladesh, employment creation by the Mondragon cooperative in the Basque region of Spain, and fair trade by Traidcraft in the UK. This wide range of initiatives raises at least three key choices for social entrepreneurs.

- *Social mission.* For social entrepreneurs, the social mission is primary. The social mission can embrace two elements: end-objectives and operational processes. For example, the Grameen bank has the end-objective of reducing rural poverty, especially for women. The process is empowering poor people's own business initiatives by providing micro-credit at a scale and to people that conventional banks would ignore.

- *Organisational form.* Many social enterprises take on cooperative forms, involving their employees and other stakeholders on a democratic basis and thus building commitment and channels for ideas. This form of organisation raises the issue of which stakeholders to include, and which to exclude. Cooperatives can also be slow to take hard decisions. Social enterprises therefore sometimes take more hierarchical charity or company forms of organisation. Cafédirect, the fair-trade beverages company, even became a publicly listed company, paying its first dividend to shareholders in 2006.

- *Business model.* Social enterprises typically rely to a large extent on revenues earned in the marketplace, not just government subsidy or charitable donations. Housing associations collect rents, micro-credit organisations charge interest and fair-trade organisations sell produce. Social entrepreneurs are no different to other entrepreneurs, therefore, in having to design an efficient and effective business model (see Section 7.4). This business model might involve innovative changes in the value chain. Thus fair-trade organisations have often become much more closely involved with their suppliers than commercial organisations, for example advising farmers on agriculture and providing education and infrastructure support to their communities.

Social entrepreneurs, just like other entrepreneurs, often have to forge relationships with large commercial companies. Harvard Business School's Rosabeth Moss Kanter points out that the benefits to large companies can go beyond a feel-good factor and attractive publicity. She shows that involvement in social enterprise can help develop new technologies and services, access new pools of potential employees, and create relationships with government and other agencies that can eventually turn into new markets. Kanter concludes that large companies should develop clear strategies with regard to social entrepreneurship, not treat it as ad hoc charity.

10.3 INNOVATION DILEMMAS

One important outcome of entrepreneurship is innovation. It is of importance not only for start-ups, but for all firms, including large companies that continuously need to develop new and innovative products and services to successfully compete. Innovation, however, raises fundamental strategic dilemmas for strategists. Innovation is more complex than just invention. *Invention* involves the conversion of new knowledge into a new product, process or service. **Innovation involves the conversion of new knowledge into a new product, process or** service *and* the putting of this new product, process or service into actual commercial use.[8] The strategic dilemmas stem from this more extended innovation process. Strategists have to make choices with regard to three fundamental issues: how far to follow technological opportunity as against market demand; how much to invest in product innovation rather than process innovation; and how far to open themselves up to innovative ideas from outside.[9]

10.3.1 Technology push or market pull

People often see innovation as driven by technology. In the pure version of this *technology push* view, it is the new knowledge created by technologists or scientists that pushes the innovation process. Research and development laboratories produce new products, processes or services and then hand them over to the rest of the organisation to manufacture, market and distribute. According to this push perspective, managers should listen primarily to their scientists and technologists, let them follow their hunches and support them with ample resources. Generous R&D budgets are crucial to making innovation happen. For example, estimates for making a new drug show that the costs can be as high as $200m (£120m, €150m).

An alternative approach to innovation is *market pull*. Market pull reflects a view of innovation that goes beyond invention and sees the importance of actual use. In many sectors users, not producers, are common sources of important innovations. In designing their innovation strategies, therefore, organisations should listen in the first place to users rather than their own scientists and technologists. There are two prominent but contrasting approaches to market pull:

- *Lead users.* According to MIT professor Eric Von Hippel, in many markets it is lead users who are the principal source of innovation.[10] In medical surgery, top surgeons often adapt existing surgical instruments in order to carry out new types of operation. In extreme sports such as snowboarding or windsurfing, it is leading sportspeople who make the improvements necessary for greater performance. In this view, then, it is the pull of market experts that is responsible for innovation. Managers need to build close relationships with lead users such as the best surgeons or sporting champions. Marketing and sales functions identify the lead users of a field and then scientists and technologists translate their inventive ideas into commercial products, processes or services that the wider market can use. For example, the Danish toy company Lego runs a special 'Ambassador Program' to keep close to 150 specialised user groups around the world; specialist users in design and architecture were responsible for originating the Lego Jewellery and Lego Architecture ranges.

- *Frugal innovation.* At the other end of the user continuum is the pull exerted by ordinary consumers, particularly the poor in emerging markets.[11] Rather than the expensive research-intensive model of the traditional technology push approach, frugality is the guiding principle here. Frugal innovation involves sensitivity to poor people's real needs. Responding not only to these users' lack of money, but also to the tough conditions in which they live, frugal innovation typically emphasises low cost, simplicity, robustness and easy maintenance. The Tata Nano car is a famous example, a simple car produced for the Indian market for only $2,000. Muruganatham's cheap sanitary towels are another example, this time emphasising opportunities to create employment for the economically disadvantaged too (see Illustration 10.3).

The lead user and frugal innovation approaches are opposite ends of a spectrum, one elitist, the other basic. Many organisations will choose somewhere in between. But fundamentally both approaches share a key insight: innovations do not just come from scientific research, but can be pulled by users in the external market.

ILLUSTRATION 10.3   Frugal sanitary towels

Arunachalam Muruganantham aims to transform the lives of Indian women with a fundamental innovation.

High school drop-out and welder Arunachalam Muruganantham has developed a low-cost sanitary towel the hard way. In India, only 12 per cent of women can afford to use sanitary towels for their monthly periods, the rest making do with old rags and even husks or sand. As Muruganantham's wife explained to him, if she bought the expensive sanitary towels on the market, the family would have to do without milk. But the cost for many women is infections and even cervical cancer.

Muruganantham determined to find a cheap way of supplying Indian women with proper sanitary towels. In Indian society, however, the issue was taboo. The local hospital was unhelpful, and even Muruganantham's wife and sisters refused to talk about the problem. A survey of college girls failed. Muruganantham's prototypes were scorned by his wife. At his wits' end, Muruganantham experimented on himself, carrying a bladder inflated with goat's blood while wearing one of his own sanitary towels and women's undergarments. His tests while walking and cycling around the village created a local scandal. His wife moved out.

Muruganantham characterised the issue as a 'triple A problem – Affordability, Availability and Awareness'. But after four years of research, he finally built a machine for producing sanitary towels at less than half the price of those offered by rivals such as Procter & Gamble and Johnson & Johnson. The machines are cheap and hand-operated, enabling small-scale local production by units employing six to ten women each. Muruganantham believes that the small businesses using his machines could create up to one million jobs: 'The model of mass-production is outdated. Now it is about production by the mass of people.'

Muruganantham sells the machines to NGOs, local entrepreneurs, charities and self-help groups, who produce the sanitary towels without fancy marketing. A manual machine costs around 75,000 Indian rupees (£723, €868, $1084) – a semi-automated machine costs more. Often the women who make the towels are the best marketers, passing on the benefits by word-of-mouth. Towels are often sold singly rather than in bulk packets, and are even sold through barter. Muruganantham explains the marketing: 'It's done silently and even the male members of their families don't know.'

Slowly but surely his machines spread all over India with operations in 23 states. By 2015, his company, Jayaashree Industries, had expanded to 17 other countries including Kenya, Bangladesh, Nigeria and Myanmar. He employs over 20,000 women in rural India and the enterprise has been valued at over a billion dollars by some analysts. Muruganantham has become a globally renowned frugal innovator and motivational speaker. His machine was entered in a competition for a national innovation award and came first out of 943 entries; he received the award by the then President of India. He was also ranked by *Time* magazine as one of 100 most influential people in the world in 2014 and was invited to give a lecture at Harvard. His wife has moved back in with him.

Muruganantham was confident about the sustainability of his model: 'We compete very comfortably with the big giants (such as Procter & Gamble). That's why they call me the corporate bomber.'

Sources: BBC World Service, 6 August 2012; *China Daily Asia,* June 5 2015; *Economic Times,* 18 January 2012; *The Hindu,* 9 February 2012, *Vancouver Observer,* 9 July 2015.

Questions

1 Identify the various features of Muruganantham's approach that make his sanitary towel business a typical or not so typical 'frugal innovation'.

2 Could a large company such as Procter & Gamble imitate this strategy?

There are merits to both the technology push and market pull views. Relying heavily on existing users can make companies too conservative and vulnerable to disruptive technologies that uncover needs unforeseen by existing markets (see Section 10.5.2). On the other hand, history is littered with examples of companies that have blindly pursued technological excellence without regard to real market needs. Technology push and market pull are best seen as extreme views, therefore, helping to focus attention on a fundamental choice: relatively how much to rely on science and technology as sources of innovation, rather than what people are actually doing in the marketplace. The key is to manage the balance actively. For a stagnant organisation looking for radical innovation, it might be worth redeploying effort from whichever model currently predominates: for the technology push organisation to use more market pull or for the market pull organisation to invest more in fundamental research.

10.3.2 Product or process innovation

Just as managers must manage the balance between technology and market pull, so must they determine the relative emphasis to place on product or process innovation. *Product innovation* relates to the final product (or service) to be sold, especially with regard to its features; *process innovation* relates to the way in which this product is produced and distributed, especially with regard to improvements in cost or reliability. Some firms specialise more in product innovation, others more in process innovation. For example, in computers, Apple has generally concentrated its efforts on designing attractive product features (for instance, the iPad tablet), while Dell has innovated in terms of efficient processes, for instance direct sales, modularity and build-to-order. Dell's process innovation even underlies a different business model compared to their competitors; selling a differentiated customised product with after-sales services. Business model innovation is still another form of innovation, which was discussed in Chapter 7, and many successful innovations thus do not necessarily rely only upon new science or technology, but can involve reorganising various elements of a business into a new business model.[12]

The relative importance of product innovation and process innovation typically changes as industries evolve over time.[13] Usually the first stages of an industry are dominated by product innovation based on new features. Thus the early history of the automobile was dominated by competition as to whether cars should be fuelled by steam, electricity or petrol, have their engines at the front or at the rear, and have three wheels or four.[14] Industries eventually coalesce around a *dominant design,* the standard configuration of basic features: after Henry Ford's 1908 Model T, cars generally became petrol-driven, with their engines at the front and four wheels. Once such a dominant design is established, innovation switches to process innovation, as competition shifts to producing the dominant design as efficiently as possible. Henry Ford's great process innovation was the moving assembly line, introduced in 1913. Finally, the cycle is liable to start again, as some significant innovation challenges the dominant design: in the case of cars, recently the emergence of electric powered cars with forerunners like Toyota and Tesla.

Figure 10.5 provides a general model of the relationship between product and process innovation over time. The model has several strategic implications:

- *New developing industries* typically favour product innovation, as competition is still around defining the basic features of the product or service.

- *Maturing industries* typically favour process innovation, as competition shifts towards efficient production of a dominant design of product or service.

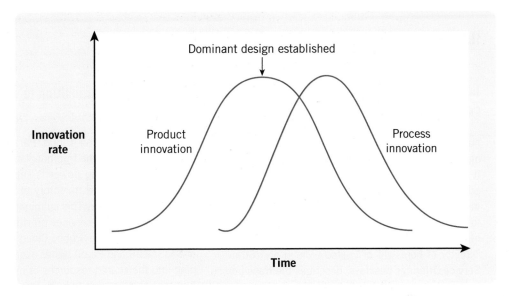

Figure 10.5 Product and process innovation

Source: Adapted from J. Abernathy and W. Utterback, 'A dynamic model of process and product innovation', *Omega*, vol. 3, no. 6 (1975), pp. 639–56, with permission from Elsevier.

- *Small new entrants* typically have the greatest opportunity when dominant designs are either not yet established or beginning to collapse. Thus, in the early stages of the automobile industry, before Ford's Model T, there were more than a hundred mostly small competitors, each with its own combination of product features. The recent challenge to the petrol-based dominant design has provided opportunities to entrepreneurial companies such as the Californian start-up Tesla Motors, which projected sales of 50,000 electric-powered vehicles worldwide in 2015 (see Illustration 1.1).

- *Large incumbent firms* typically have the advantage during periods of dominant design stability, when scale economies and the ability to roll out process innovations matter most. With the success of the Model T and the assembly line, by the 1930s there were just four large American automobile manufacturers, namely Ford, General Motors, Chrysler and American Motors, all producing very similar kinds of cars.

This sequence of product to process innovation is not always a neat one. In practice, product and process innovation are often pursued in tandem.[15] For example, each new generation of microprocessor also requires simultaneous process innovation in order to manufacture the new microprocessor with increasing precision. However, the model does help managers confront the issue of where to focus, whether more on product features or more on process efficiency. It also points to whether competitive advantage is likely to be with small new entrants or large incumbent firms. Other things being equal, small start-ups should time their entry for periods of instability in dominant design and focus on product rather than process innovation.

10.3.3 Open or closed innovation

The traditional approach to innovation has been to rely on the organisation's own internal resources – its laboratories and marketing departments. Innovation in this approach is secretive, anxious to protect intellectual property and avoid competitors free-riding on ideas. This 'closed' model of innovation contrasts with the newer 'open model' of innovation.[16] **Open innovation involves the deliberate import and export of knowledge by an organisation**

ILLUSTRATION 10.4   The disruptive cloud

Japanese computer giant Fujitsu plots a roadmap to navigate the transition to cloud computing.

Fujitsu is the world's third largest information technology services company, after IBM and Hewlett-Packard. It offers a range of products and services in the areas of computing, telecommunications and microelectronics. In 2010, it launched a new cloud computing business to take advantage of the transition from the traditional model of in-house business computing. David Gentle, Director of Foresight at Fujitsu's Cloud and Strategic Service Offerings business, describes the transition as a disruptive innovation: 'It's a bit like a salmon that is swimming upstream and then has to make a leap to get to the next smooth stretch of water.'

Cloud computing relies on the internet to deliver computer services from external suppliers direct to users. Dropbox and Apple's iCloud are consumer cloud services. For business, the cloud comes in three main forms: 'Software as a Service' (SaaS), such as Microsoft Office via the internet; 'Infrastructure as a Service' (IaaS), such as Amazon's EC2 virtual computer capacity; and 'Platform as a Service' (PaaS), which provides a computing platform with operating system, web server and database, such as Google's App Engine.

Fujitsu describes the transition from the traditional model to the Cloud Computing Era in a technology 'roadmap' titled 'The Cloud Paradigm Shift'. The roadmap describes the traditional client-server model, where the computing power is supplied by in-house servers, as offering a trajectory of steadily improving *technology* efficiency. This culminates in the so-called Private Cloud, cloud services provided by the business itself. The shift to the 'Public Cloud' (with full adoption of SaaS, IaaS and PaaS) brings a leap in value. By tapping into the shared resources of external suppliers, a business gains access to huge economies of scale and the innovations possible by specialist suppliers. The new trajectory increases value by improving *business* efficiency.

The shift is disruptive though. Purchasers in IT functions will no longer need such large investments in physical servers and staff. As traditional server products and related services decline, Fujitsu is transitioning its business to meet the demands of the new market. David Gentle explains the function of the roadmap in this context: 'This roadmap is the first slide in any conversation with customers, partners and staff internally. It shows the future, as well as anchoring on the past. It helps get everyone on the same page.'

---

in order to accelerate and enhance its innovation. The motivating idea of open innovation is that exchanging ideas openly is likely to produce better products more quickly than the internal, closed approach. Speedier and superior products are what are needed to keep ahead of the competition, not obsessive secrecy.[17]

Open innovation is being widely adopted. For example, technology giant IBM has established a network of 10 'collaboratories' with other companies and universities, in countries ranging from Switzerland to Saudi Arabia. Swedish music streaming service Spotify arranges 'music hack days' in various locations around the globe where developers are invited for a day of free food, drink and work on discussing and developing new applications. *Crowdsourcing* is an increasingly popular form of open innovation and means that a company or organisation broadcasts a specific problem to a crowd of individuals or teams often in tournaments with prizes awarded to the best solution.[18] Companies such as Procter & Gamble, Eli Lilly and Dow Chemicals use the network company InnoCentive to set innovation 'challenges' (or problems) in open competition over the internet: by 2015, over 1,300 challenges had been solved by a community of around 250,000 'solvers', winning prizes of up to $1m. Similarly, Starbucks crowdsourcing platform has generated close to 200,000 customer ideas and implementation of over 300.

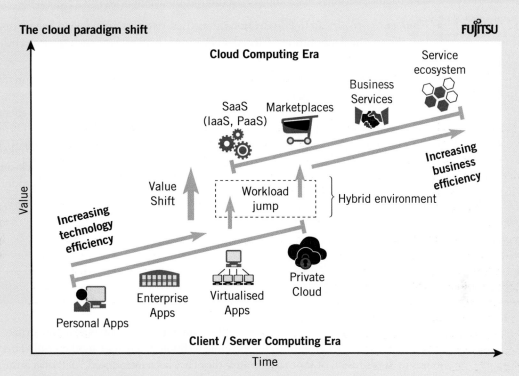

Fujitsu's Cloud Roadmap

Source: Making the Transition to Cloud, Fujitsu Services Ltd (Gentle, David 2011). With permission from Fujitsu Limited UK.

Questions

1 Why might some groups be apprehensive about the cloud computing era?

2 What are the advantages of a visual roadmap of this kind? What are the limitations to this visual approach?

Open innovation typically requires careful support of collaborators. In particular, dominant firms may need to exercise platform leadership. *Platform leadership* refers to how large firms consciously nurture independent companies through successive waves of innovation around their basic technological 'platform'.[19] Intel, whose microprocessors are used by a host of computer, tablet and smartphone companies, regularly publishes 'roadmaps' outlining several years ahead the new products it expects to release, allowing customers to plan their own new product development processes (see Illustration 10.4 for Fujitsu's cloud computing roadmap). Platform high-technology companies often foster *ecosystems* of smaller companies around their platform. Ecosystems are communities of connected suppliers, agents, distributors, franchisees, technology entrepreneurs and makers of complementary products around a platform or company. Apple has created an ecosystem of apps around its iPhone and the app writers get the benefit of a large and often lucrative market. Apple has paid out over $25bn to them up until 2016, more than any other smartphone supplier. Small entrepreneurial firms wishing to participate in such ecosystems have to be skilled in managing relationships with powerful technological leaders.[20]

The balance between open and closed innovation depends on three key factors:

- *Competitive rivalry.* In highly rivalrous industries, partners are liable to behave opportunistically and steal innovations. Closed innovation is better where such rivalrous behaviours can be anticipated.

- *One-shot innovation.* Opportunistic behaviour is more likely where innovation involves a major shift in technology, likely to put winners substantially ahead and losers permanently behind. Open innovation works best where innovation is more continuous, so encouraging more reciprocal behaviour over time.

- *Tight-linked innovation.* Where technologies are complex and tightly interlinked, open innovation risks introducing damagingly inconsistent elements, with knock-on effects throughout the product range. Apple, with its smoothly integrated range of products from computers to phones, has therefore tended to prefer closed innovation in order to protect the quality of the user experience.

10.4 INNOVATION DIFFUSION

This chapter has been concerned with entrepreneurship and its outcome in the form of diverse sources and types of innovation, for example technology push or market pull. This section moves to the diffusion of innovations after they have been introduced.[21] **Diffusion is the process by which innovations spread among users.** Since innovation is typically expensive, its commercial attractiveness can hinge on the pace – extent and speed – at which the market adopts new products and services. This pace of diffusion is something managers can influence from both the supply and demand sides, and which they can also model using the S-curve.

10.4.1 The pace of diffusion

The pace of diffusion can vary widely according to the nature of the products concerned. It took 28 years for the television to reach 50 per cent of ownership and use in the US and the mobile phone only half that time. The pace of diffusion is influenced by a combination of supply-side and demand-side factors, over which managers have considerable control. On the *supply side,* pace is determined by product features such as:

- *Degree of improvement* in performance above current products (from a customer's perspective) that provides incentive to change. For example, 3G mobile phones did not provide sufficient performance improvement to prompt rapid switch in many markets. Managers need to make sure innovation benefits sufficiently exceed development costs.

- *Compatibility* with other factors: for example, HDTV becomes more attractive as the broadcasting networks change their programmes to that format. Managers and entrepreneurs therefore need to ensure appropriate complementary products and services are in place (see Section 3.2.6).

- *Complexity,* either in the product itself or in the marketing methods being used to commercialise the product: unduly complex pricing structures, as with many financial service products such as pensions, discourage consumer adoption. Simple pricing structures typically accelerate adoptions.

- *Experimentation* – the ability to test products before commitment to a final decision – either directly or through the availability of information about the experience of other customers. Free initial trial periods are often used to encourage diffusion.

- *Relationship management,* in other words how easy it is to get information, place orders and receive support. Managers and entrepreneurs need to put in place an appropriate relationship management process to assist new and existing users.

On the *demand side,* simple affordability is of course key. Beyond this, there are three further factors that tend to drive the pace of diffusion:

- *Market awareness.* Many potentially successful products have failed through lack of consumer awareness – particularly when the promotional effort of the innovator has been confined to 'push' promotion to its intermediaries (e.g. distributors).

- *Network effects* refer to the way that demand growth for some products accelerates as more people adopt the product or service. Once a critical mass of users have adopted, it becomes of much greater benefit, or even necessary, for others to adopt it too. With 1.5 billion users, Facebook is practically the obligatory social network for most readers of this book (see Section 3.2.6).

- *Customer propensity to adopt*: the distribution of potential customers from early-adopter groups (keen to adopt first) through to laggards (typically indifferent to innovations). Innovations are often targeted initially at early-adopter groups – typically the young and the wealthy – in order to build the critical mass that will encourage more laggardly groups – the poorer and older – to join the bandwagon. Clothing fashion trends typically start with the wealthy and then are diffused to the wider population.

10.4.2 The diffusion S-curve

The pace of diffusion is typically not steady. Successful innovations often diffuse according to a broad *S-curve* pattern.[22] The shape of the **S-curve reflects a process of initial slow adoption of innovation, followed by a rapid acceleration in diffusion, leading to a plateau representing the limit to demand** (Figure 10.6). The height of the S-curve shows the extent of diffusion; the shape of the S-curve shows the speed.

Diffusion rarely follows exactly this pattern, but nonetheless the S-curve can help managers and entrepreneurs anticipate forthcoming issues. In particular, the S-curve points to four likely decision points:

- *Timing of the 'tipping point'.* Demand for a successful new product or service may initially be slow but then reaches a *tipping point* when it explodes onto a rapid upwards path of growth.[23] A tipping point is where demand for a product or service suddenly takes off, with explosive growth. Tipping points are particularly explosive where there are strong *network effects*: in other words, where the value of a product or service is increased the more people in a network use them (see Section 3.2.6). Being aware of a possible tipping point ahead can help managers plan investment in capacity and distribution. Companies can easily underestimate demand. In the mid-1980s, American companies predicted that by 2000 there would be 900,000 mobile phones worldwide. When that year came 900,000 phones were sold every 19 hours.

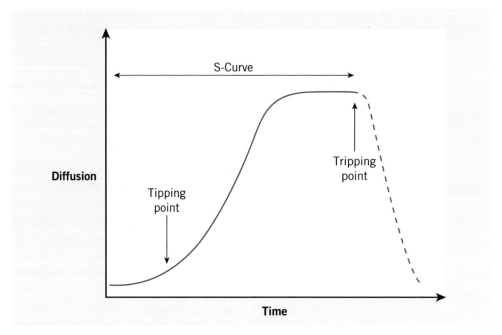

Figure 10.6 The diffusion S-curve

- *Timing of the plateau.* The S-curve also alerts managers to a likely eventual slowdown in demand growth. Again, it is tempting to extrapolate existing growth rates forwards, especially when they are highly satisfactory. But heavy investment immediately before growth turns down is likely to leave firms with over-capacity and carrying extra costs in a period of industry shake-out.

- *Extent of diffusion.* The S-curve does not necessarily lead to one hundred per cent diffusion among potential users. Most innovations fail to displace previous-generation products and services altogether. For example, in music, traditional turntables and LP discs are still preferred over CD and MP3 players by some disc jockeys and music connoisseurs. A critical issue for managers then is to estimate the final ceiling on diffusion, being careful not to assume that tipping point growth will necessarily take over the whole market.

- *Timing of the 'tripping point'.* The tripping point is the opposite of the tipping point, referring to when demand suddenly collapses.[24] Of course, decline is usually more gradual. However, the presence of network effects can lead to relatively few customer defections setting off a market landslide. Such landslides are very hard to reverse. This is what happened to social networking site MySpace, as American and European users defected to Facebook. Facebook, in turn, may have considered this risk themselves when they acquired Instagram as users started to move there (see Illustration 3.2). The tripping point concept warns managers all the time that a small dip in quarterly sales could presage a rapid collapse.

To summarise, the S-curve is a useful concept to help managers and entrepreneurs avoid simply extrapolating next year's sales from last year's sales. However, the tripping point also underlines the fact that innovations do not follow an inevitable process, and their diffusion patterns can be interrupted or reversed at any point. Netflix, for example, has managed to move from a tripping point in DVD rentals to a new S-curve of digital streaming.[25] Most innovations, of course, do not even reach a tipping point, let alone a tripping point.[26]

10.5 INNOVATORS AND IMITATORS

A key choice for managers is whether to lead or to follow in innovation. The S-curve concept seems to promote leadership in innovation. First-movers get the easy sales of early fast growth and can establish a dominant position. There are plenty of examples of first-movers who have built enduring positions on the basis of innovation leadership: Coca-Cola in drinks and Hoover in vacuum cleaners are powerful century-old examples. On the other hand, many first-movers fail. Even the powerful Microsoft failed with its first tablet computer launched in 2001. Nine years later, Apple swept the market with its iPad tablet computer.

10.5.1 First-mover advantages and disadvantages

A **first-mover advantage exists where an organisation is better off than its competitors as a result of being first to market with a new product, process or service.** Fundamentally, the first-mover is a monopolist, theoretically able to charge customers high prices without fear of immediate undercutting by competitors. In practice, however, innovators often prefer to sacrifice profit margins for sales growth and, besides, monopoly is usually temporary. There are five potentially more robust first-mover advantages:[27]

- *Experience curve benefits* accrue to first-movers, as their rapid accumulation of experience with the innovation gives them greater expertise than late entrants still relatively unfamiliar with the new product, process or service (see Section 7.3.1).

- *Scale benefits* are typically enjoyed by first-movers, as they establish earlier than competitors the volumes necessary for mass production and bulk purchasing, for example.

- *Pre-emption of scarce resources* is an opportunity for first-movers, as late-movers will not have the same access to key raw materials, skilled labour or components, and will have to pay dearly for them.

- *Reputation* can be enhanced by being first, especially since consumers have little 'mind-space' to recognise new brands once a dominant brand has been established in the market.

- *Buyer switching costs* can be exploited by first-movers, by locking in their customers with privileged or sticky relationships that later challengers can only break with difficulty. Switching costs can be increased by establishing and exploiting a *technological standard*.

Experience curve benefits, economies of scale and the pre-emption of scarce resources all confer cost advantages on first-movers. It is possible for them to retaliate against challengers with a price war. Superior reputation and customer lock-in provide a marketing advantage, allowing first-movers to charge high prices, which can then be reinvested in order to consolidate their position against late-entry competitors.

But the experience of Microsoft with its tablet computer shows that first-mover advantages are not necessarily overwhelming. Late-movers have two principal potential advantages:[28]

- *Free-riding*. Late-movers can imitate technological and other innovation at less expense than originally incurred by the pioneers. Research suggests that the costs of imitation are only 65 per cent of the cost of innovation.

- *Learning*. Late-movers can observe what worked well and what did not work well for innovators. They may not make so many mistakes and be able to get it right first time.

Given the potential advantages of late-movers, managers and entrepreneurs face a hard choice between striving to be first or coming in later. London Business School's Costas

Markides and Paul Geroski argue that the most appropriate response to innovation, especially radical innovation, is often not to be a first-mover, but to be a '*fast second*'.[29] A fast second strategy involves being one of the first to imitate the original innovator. Thus fast second companies may not literally be the second company into the market, but they dominate the second generation of competitors. For example, the French Bookeen company pioneered the e-book market in the early 2000s, but was soon followed by Amazon's Kindle in 2007. Likewise, the first jet airliner was the British de Havilland Comet with Boeing being a successful follower.[30]

Three factors need to be considered in choosing between innovating and imitating. First, the *capacity for profit capture*, the importance of innovators to capture for themselves the profits of their innovations. David Teece of the University of California Berkeley emphasises that this may be challenging if the innovation is *easy to replicate* and if *intellectual property rights* are weak, for example where patents are hard to define or defend.[31] The second issue that needs to be considered is *complementary assets*, possession of the assets or resources necessary to scale up the production and marketing of the innovation.[32] For organisations wishing to remain independent and to exploit their innovations themselves, there is little point in investing heavily to be first-mover in the absence of the necessary complementary assets. Finally, innovation vs imitation choices depend on whether there are *fast-moving arenas*. Where markets or technologies are moving very fast, and especially where both are highly dynamic, first-movers are unlikely to establish a durable advantage.

10.5.2 The incumbent's response

Definitions of entrepreneurship often emphasise pursuing opportunities and developing innovations without immediately being constrained by the resources under present control. This refers to the fact that incumbent organisations and companies mostly are constrained by their existing resources, capabilities, activities and vested interests. This suggests that for established companies in a market, innovation can be challenging and innovations from others can be a threat. Kodak's dominance of the photographic film market was made nearly worthless by the sudden rise of digital photography (see Illustration 6.4).

As Harvard Business School's Clay Christensen has shown, the problem for incumbents can be two-fold.[33] First, managers can become too attached to existing assets and skills: understandably, as these are what their careers have been built on. Second, relationships between incumbent organisations and their customers can become too close. Existing customers typically prefer incremental improvements to current technologies, and are unable to imagine completely new technologies. Incumbents are reluctant to 'cannibalise' their existing business by introducing something radically different. After all, as in Figure 10.7, incumbents usually have some scope for improving their existing technology, along the steady upwards trajectory described as Technology 1. Innovations on this trajectory are termed 'sustaining innovations', because they at least allow the existing technology to meet existing customer expectations.

The challenge for incumbents, however, is disruptive innovation. A **disruptive innovation creates substantial growth by offering a new performance trajectory that, even if initially inferior to the performance of existing technologies, has the potential to become markedly superior.** This superior performance can produce spectacular growth, either by creating new sets of customers or by undercutting the cost base of rival existing business models. Such disruptive innovation involves the shift from Technology 1 in Figure 10.7 to Technology 2. Disruptive innovations are hard for incumbents to respond to because poor performance in the early days is likely to upset existing customer relationships and because they typically involve changing their whole business model (see Chapter 7). Thus, in the music industry,

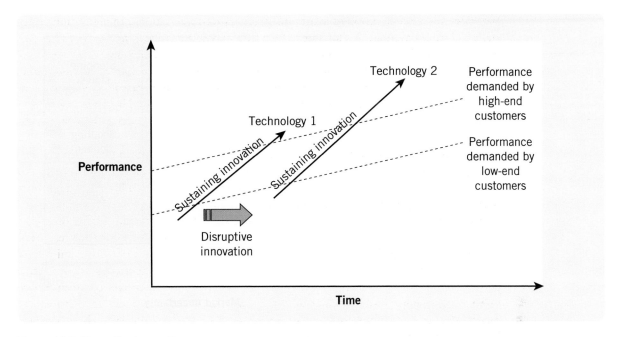

Figure 10.7 Disruptive innovation

the major record companies were long content to keep on selling traditional CDs through existing retailers and responded to online music simply by prosecuting new distribution firms such as Napster. Today, online music downloads and streaming have overtaken CD sales with services such as Apple's iTunes and Spotify as leading players.

Sometimes, however, incumbents do respond. IBM continued to make mainframe computers while launching a new business unit to make PCs, which was a disruptive innovation at the time. The mobile phone disrupted the fixed telephony business, but Ericsson managed to continue its leadership in telephony systems. To encourage innovation and be responsive to potentially disruptive innovations there are three different approaches:

- *Develop a portfolio of real options.* Companies that are most challenged by disruptive innovations tend to be those built upon a single business model and with one main product or service. Columbia's Rita McGrath and Wharton's Ian MacMillan recommend that companies build portfolios of *real options* in order to maintain organisational dynamism.[34] Real options are limited investments that keep opportunities open for the future (for a more technical discussion, see Section 12.3.2). Establishing an R&D team in a speculative new technology or acquiring a small start-up in a nascent market would both be examples of real options, each giving the potential to scale up fast should the opportunity turn out to be substantial. McGrath and MacMillan's portfolio identifies three different kinds of options (Figure 10.8). Options where the market is broadly known, but the technologies are still uncertain, are *positioning options:* a company might want several of these, to ensure some position in an important market, by one technology or another. On the other hand, a company might have a strong technology, but be very uncertain about appropriate markets, in which case it would want to bet on several *scouting options* to explore which markets are actually best. Finally, a company would want some *stepping stone options,* very unlikely in themselves to work, but possibly leading to something more promising in the future. Even if they do not turn a profit, stepping stones should provide valuable learning opportunities. An important principle for options is: 'Fail fast, fail cheap, try again'.

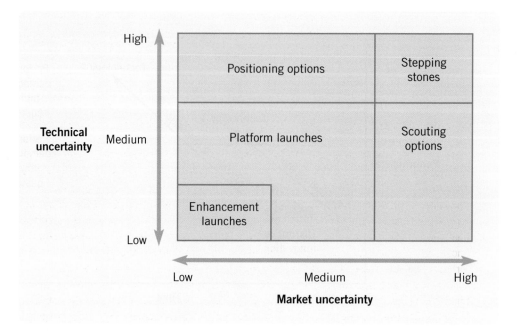

Figure 10.8 Portfolio of innovation options

Source: Reprinted by permission of Harvard Business School Press. From *The Entrepreneurial Mindset* by I. MacMillan and R.G. McGrath, Boston, MA (2000), p. 176. Copyright © 2000 by the Harvard Business School Publishing Corporation. All rights reserved.

- *Corporate venturing.* New ventures, especially when undertaken from a real options perspective, may need protection from the usual systems and disciplines of a core business. It would make no sense to hold the managers of a real option strictly accountable for sales growth and profit margin: their primary objective is preparation and learning. For this reason, large incumbent organisations often establish relatively autonomous 'new venture units', sometimes called new venture divisions, which can nurture new ideas or invest externally and acquire novel and untried businesses with a longer-term view.[35] BMW's has, for example, set up a completely separate business unit to develop its first mass-produced electric car, BMW i. The company was concerned that its current focus on the internal combustion engine would risk the success of the development of the BMW i.

- *Intrapreneurship.* This approach rather emphasises the individual and the ability to perform entrepreneurial activities within a large organisation.[36] Companies can thus encourage employees to be creative and develop entrepreneurial ideas as part of their regular job. Potential entrepreneurs within existing organisations can be found from the top to middle management to those developing or producing products and services. Google have intrapreneurship programmes that aim at creating a start-up culture within the larger corporation. They, for example, let their engineers spend 20 per cent of their work week on projects of their own choice that interest them. Likewise, IBM has various initiatives to encourage intrapreneurship and innovation, like 'Intrapreneurship@IBM' and the 'IBM Jam sessions'. Intrapreneurship, however, can also be autonomous from and in conflict with corporate management and thus need not always be encouraged. Instead, it can be a long hard fight to get entrepreneurial ideas and innovations accepted by corporate management. For example, Ericsson's global leadership in mobile telephone systems initially started out with a group of intrapreneurs in confrontation with corporate strategy and management.

Whether by developing real options, internal venture units or equivalent means, it is clear that established incumbents need to be able to support a spirit of intrapreneurship.[37]

THINKING DIFFERENTLY | Entrepreneurship: discovery or creation?

An alternative view suggests that opportunities are created rather than discovered.

This chapter has emphasised opportunity recognition as one stage in a sequence of entrepreneurial process steps. This builds on the dominating *discovery* perspective of opportunities, but there is also an alternative, *creation* view.[38]

The influential *discovery* perspective argues that opportunities exist independently from entrepreneurs and are generated by external shocks. They can include technological, regulatory or social changes that generate opportunities to be discovered. This perspective suggests there are already seeds of opportunity in industries and markets waiting to be discovered by entrepreneurs.

In contrast, the *creation* view emphasises that opportunities are intimately linked with entrepreneurs and their iterative actions, understanding of and engagement with potential new products. In this view entrepreneurs do not have to wait for external shocks; instead they create opportunities through repeatedly interacting with and developing their beliefs about new products and customer needs. They do this through actively trying out product ideas and forming opportunities around them. Seeds are thus not discovered in

this view; instead, entrepreneurs explore through iterative processes what can grow where and themselves plant and create new seeds of opportunity.

The two views have different implications for how to manage entrepreneurship. The discovery perspective relies on traditional forms of strategic planning and decision-making (see Section 13.2). Entrepreneurs collect and analyse information and carefully make predictions and decisions concerning product market potential. The creation view suggests a more complex process. Entrepreneurs do not so much carefully collect information to get answers; rather they try to ask the right questions, experiment and adapt around potential new products (see Section 13.3).

Question

Google, now Alphabet, is often celebrated as a highly entrepreneurial and innovative company. To what degree do you think they have relied on discovering or creating opportunities?

SUMMARY

- *Opportunity recognition* involves three important and interdependent elements: the *environment*, the *entrepreneur or entrepreneurial team* and *resources and capabilities.*

- Besides opportunity recognition, the *entrepreneurship process* typically involves the development of a *business plan*, making a *feasibility analysis*, considering *industry conditions and competitors*, choosing *business model and strategy* and, finally, examining the venture's *financing and funding.*

- *Social entrepreneurship* offers a flexible way of addressing social problems, but raises issues about appropriate missions, organisational forms and business models.

- Strategists face three fundamental dilemmas in innovation: the relative emphasis to put on *technology push* or *market pull*; whether to focus on *product* or *process innovation*; and finally how much to rely on '*open innovation*'.

- Innovations often diffuse into the marketplace according to *an S-curve model* in which slow start-up is followed by accelerating growth (the tipping point) and finally a flattening of demand. Managers should watch out for 'tripping points'.

- Managers have a choice between being first into the marketplace and entering later. Innovators can capture *first-mover advantages.* However, '*fast second*' strategies are often more attractive.

- Established incumbents' businesses should beware *disruptive innovations.* Incumbents can stave off inertia by developing *portfolios of real options*, by organising autonomous *new venture units* or by encouraging '*intrapreneurship*'.

WORK ASSIGNMENTS

✱ Denotes more advanced work assignments.
* Refers to a case study in the Text and Cases edition.

10.1 Use Figure 10.2 and try to identify the three elements (entrepreneur/team, trends/gaps and resources/capabilities) behind the opportunity recognition in Apple*, Widespace* and Flight Centre*.

10.2 With reference to the entrepreneurial life cycle, identify the position of Rovio (end of chapter case), Flight Centre* or Ningbo Smarter Logistics*. What managerial issues might this case company anticipate in the coming years?

10.3 Use the internet to identify a social entrepreneurial venture that interests you (via www.skollfoundation.org, for example), and, with regard to Section 10.2.4, identify its social mission, its organisational form and its business model.

10.4✱ For a new product or service that you have recently experienced and enjoyed, investigate the strategy of the company responsible. With reference to the dilemmas of Section 10.3, explain whether the innovation was more technology push or market pull, product or process driven, or based on open versus closed innovation.

10.5 Go to a web traffic site (such as alexa.com) and compare over time trends in terms of 'page views' or 'reach' for older sites (such as Amazon.com) and newer sites (such as spotify.com, or any that has more recently emerged). With reference to Section 10.4, how do you explain these trends and how would you project them forward?

10.6✱ With regard to a new product or service that you have recently experienced and enjoyed (as in 10.4), investigate the strategic responses of 'incumbents' to this innovation. To what extent is the innovation disruptive for them (see Section 10.5.2)?

Integrative assignment

10.7 Consider a for-profit or social entrepreneurial idea that you or your friends or colleagues might have. Drawing on Section 16.4.4, outline the elements of a strategic plan for this possible venture. What more information do you need to get?

RECOMMENDED KEY READINGS

- B.R. Barringer and R.D. Ireland, *Entrepreneurship – Successfully launching new ventures,* 4th edn, Pearson, 2012, provides details of all entrepreneurial process steps.

- P. Trott, *Innovation Management and New Product Development,* 5th edn, Financial Times Prentice Hall, 2011, provides a comprehensive overview of innovation

strategy issues. P.A. Wickham, *Strategic Entrepreneurship,* 5th edn, Prentice Hall, 2013, is a standard European text with regard to entrepreneurial strategy.

- Social entrepreneurship is discussed usefully in R. Ridley-Duff and M. Bull, *Understanding Social Enterprise: Theory and Practice,* Sage 2011.

REFERENCES

1. M.A. Hitt, R.D. Ireland, D.G. Sirmon and C.A. Trahms, 'Strategic entrepreneurship: creating value for individuals, organizations, and society', *The Academy of Management Perspectives*, vol. 25, no 2 (2011), pp. 57–75.

2. There is an increased interest in strategic entrepreneurship with both journals and books dedicated to the area: David J. Ketchen, R. Duane Ireland and Charles C. Snow, 'Strategic entrepreneurship, collaborative innovation, and wealth creation, *Strategic Entrepreneurship Journal*, vol. 1, no. 3–4 (2007), pp. 371–85; R. Duane Ireland, Michael A. Hitt and David G. Sirmon, 'A model of strategic entrepreneurship: the construct and its dimensions', *Journal of Management*, vol. 29, no. 6 (2003), pp. 963–89; Donald F. Kuratko and David B. Audretsch, 'Strategic entrepreneurship: exploring different perspectives of an emerging concept', *Entrepreneurship Theory and Practice*, vol. 33, no. 1 (2009), pp. 1–17; and Michael

A. Hitt *et al.* (eds), *Strategic Entrepreneurship: Creating a new mindset*, Wiley-Blackwell, 2002.

3. For a good overview of the academic theories that underpin contemporary entrepreneurship theory, see S.A. Shane, *A general theory of entrepreneurship: the individual-opportunity nexus*, Edward Elgar Publishing, 2000.

4. Opportunity recognition and identification is central to contemporary entrepreneurship theory. See Shane in endnote 3 and A. Ardichvili, R. Cardozo and S. Ray, 'A theory of entrepreneurial opportunity identification and development', *Journal of Business Venturing*, vol. 18, no. 1 (2003), pp. 105–23.

5. For an excellent textbook that provides details of all the steps in the entrepreneurial process, see B.R. Barringer and R.D. Ireland, *Entrepreneurship: successfully launching new ventures*, 4th edn, Pearson, 2012.

6. Please note that business models are now discussed in Chapter 7 (previously discussed in this chapter).

7. For a discussion about lean start-ups and pivoting, see S. Blank, 'Why the lean start-up changes everything', *Harvard Business Review*, vol. 91, no. 5 (2013), pp. 63–72.

8. This definition adapts, in order to include the public sector, the definition in P. Trott, *Innovation Management and New Product Development*, 5th edn, Financial Times Prentice Hall, 2011.

9. For a good discussion of the academic theories that underpin these dilemmas see R. Rothwell, 'Successful industrial innovation: critical factors for the 1990s', *R&D Management*, vol. 22, no. 3 (1992), pp. 221–39.

10. E. von Hippel, *Democratizing Innovation*, MIT Press, 2005; E. von Hippel, 'Lead users: a source of novel product concepts', *Management Science*, vol. 32, no. 7 (1986), pp. 791–805. Y.M. Antorini, A. Muniz and T. Askildsen, 'Collaborating with customer communities: lessons from the Lego Group', *MIT Sloan Management Review*, vol. 53, no. 3 (2012), pp. 73–9.

11. D. Nocera, 'Can we progress from solipsistic science to frugal innovation?', *Daedalus*, vol. 143, no. 3 (2012), pp. 45–52; M. Sarkar, 'Moving forward by going in reverse: emerging trends in global innovation and knowledge strategies', *Global Strategy Journal*, vol. 1 (2011), pp. 237–42.

12. H. Chesbrough, 'Business model innovation: it's not just about technology anymore', *Strategy & Leadership*, vol. 35, no. 6 (2007), pp. 12–17.

13. J. Abernathy and W. Utterback, 'A dynamic model of process and product innovation', *Omega*, vol. 3, no. 6 (1975), pp. 142–60.

14. P. Anderson and M.L. Tushman, 'Technological discontinuities and dominant designs: a cyclical model of technological change', *Administrative Science Quarterly*, vol. 35 (1990), pp. 604–33.

15. J. Tang, 'Competition and innovation behaviour', *Research Policy*, vol. 35 (2006), pp. 68–82.

16. H. Chesbrough and M. Appleyard, 'Open innovation and strategy', *California Management Review*, vol. 50, no. 1 (2007), pp. 57–73; O. Gasman, E. Enkel and H. Chesbrough, 'The future of open innovation', *R&D Management*, vol. 38, no. 1 (2010), pp. 1–9.

17. For an overview of research on open innovation, see: L. Dahlander and D.M. Gann, 'How open is innovation?' *Research Policy*, vol. 39 (2010), pp. 699–709.

18. L.B. Jeppesen and K. Lakhani, 'Marginality and problem solving: effectiveness in broadcast search', *Organization Science*, vol. 21, no. 5 (2010), pp. 1016–33.

19. A. Gawer and M. Cusumano, *Platform Leadership: How Intel, Microsoft and Cisco drive industry innovation*, Harvard Business School Press, 2002.

20. For a discussion of how large corporations can tap into entrepreneurial innovation in start-ups, see T. Weiblen and H.W. Chesbrough, 'Engaging with startups to enhance corporate innovation', *California Management Review*, vol. 57, no. 2 (2015), pp. 66–90 and for a discussion of the general significance of external support and innovation ecosystems, see R. Adner, *The Wide Lens*, Penguin, 2012.

21. Innovation diffusion is discussed in the classic E. Rogers, *Diffusion of Innovations*, Free Press, 1995; C. Kim and R. Maubourgne, 'Knowing a winning idea when you see one', *Harvard Business Review*, vol. 78, no. 5 (2000), pp. 129–38; and J. Cummings and J. Doh, 'Identifying who matters: mapping key players in multiple environments', *California Management Review*, vol. 42, no. 2 (2000), pp. 83–104 (see especially pp. 91–7).

22. J. Nichols and S. Roslow, 'The S-curve: an aid to strategic marketing', *Journal of Consumer Marketing*, vol. 3, no. 2 (1986), pp. 53–64; and F. Suarez and G. Lanzolla, 'The half-truth of first-mover advantage', *Harvard Business Review*, vol. 83, no. 4 (2005), pp. 121–7. This S-curve refers to innovation diffusion. However, the S-curve effect sometimes also refers to the diminishing performance increases available from a maturing technology: A. Sood and G. Tellis, 'Technological evolution and radical innovation', *Journal of Marketing*, vol. 69, no. 3 (2005), pp. 152–68.

23. M. Gladwell, *The Tipping Point*, Abacus, 2000. Tipping points are also important in public policy and can help anticipate emerging problems, for example crime waves and epidemics.

24. S. Brown, 'The tripping point', *Marketing Research*, vol. 17, no. 1 (2005), pp. 8–13.

25. For a discussion of possibilities to 'jump' the S-curve, see P. Nunes and T. Breene, 'Reinvent your business before it's too late', *Harvard Business Review*, vol. 89, no. 1/2 (2011), pp. 80–87.

26. Marketing guru Geoffrey Moore has pointed out that often there is a deep 'chasm' to cross between specialised early-adopters of a product and the mainstream market: *Crossing the Chasm: Marketing and selling high-tech products to mainstream customers*, 2nd edn, Harper Perennial, 2002.

27. C. Markides and P. Geroski, *Fast Second: How smart companies bypass radical innovation to enter and dominate new markets*, Jossey-Bass, 2005; M. Lieberman, and D. Montgomery, 'First-mover (dis)advantages: retrospective and link with the resource-based view', *Strategic Management Journal*, vol. 19, no. 12 (1998), pp. 1111–25.

28. F. Suarez and G. Lanzolla, 'The half-truth of first-mover advantage', *Harvard Business Review*, vol. 83, no. 4 (2005), pp. 121–7. See also S. Min, U. Manohar and W. Robinson, 'Market pioneer and early follower survival risks: a contingency analysis of really new versus incrementally new product-markets', *Journal of Marketing*, vol. 70, no. 1 (2006), pp. 15–33.

29. C. Markides and P. Geroski, *Fast Second*: *How smart companies bypass radical innovation to enter and dominate new markets*, Jossey-Bass, 2005. See also the discussion of B. Buisson and P. Silberzahn, 'Blue Ocean or fast-second innovation?', *International Journal of Innovation Management*, vol. 14, no. 3 (2010), pp. 359–78.

30. J. Shamsie, C. Phelps and J. Kuperman, 'Better late than never: a study of late entrants in household electrical equipment', *Strategic Management Journal*, vol. 25, no. 1 (2004), pp. 69–84.

31. David Teece, the academic authority in this area, refers to the capacity to capture profits as 'the appropriability regime': see D. Teece, *Managing Intellectual Capital*, Oxford University Press, 2000. The key book on intellectual property strategy is A. Poltorak and P.J. Lerner, *Essentials of Intellectual Property*: *Law, economics and strategy*, Wiley, 2009. For a discussion and framework of how intellectual property rights and patent systems varies between different countries, see N. Papageorgiadis, A.R. Cross and C. Alexiou, 'International patent systems strength 1998–2011', *Journal of World Business*, vol. 49, no 4 (2014), pp. 586–97.

32. D. Teece, *Managing Intellectual Capital*, Oxford University Press, 2000.

33. See J. Bower and C. Christensen, 'Disruptive technologies: catching the wave', *Harvard Business Review*, vol. 73, no. 1 (1995), pp. 43–53.

34. R.G. McGrath and I. MacMillan, *The Entrepreneurial Mindset*, Harvard Business School Press, 2000.

35. C. Christensen and M.E. Raynor, *The Innovator's Solution*, Harvard Business School Press, 2003. For various approaches to corporate venturing, see W. Buckland, A. Hatcher and J. Birkinshaw, *Inventuring – Why big companies must think small*, 2003.

36. The original book on intrapreneurship was G. Pinchot, *Intrapreneuring*, London, Macmillan, 1985.

37. There is a growing literature on intrapreneurship or what is often called corporate entrepreneurship or corporate venturing, but there is little consensus on theories and different forms of corporate entrepreneurship. For an overview, see P.H. Phan *et al.*, 'Corporate entrepreneurship: current research and future directions', *Journal of Business Venturing*, vol. 24, no. 3 (2009), pp. 197–205. For various approaches to corporate entrepreneurship, see R.C. Wolcott and M.J. Lippitz, 'For four models of corporate entrepreneurship', *MIT Sloan Management Review*, vol. 49, no. 1 (2007), pp. 73–9 and D.A. Garvin and L.C. Levesque, 'Meeting the challenge of corporate entrepreneurship', *Harvard Business Review*, vol. 84, no. 10 (2006), pp. 102–12.

38. A. Sharon and J.B. Barney, 'Discovery and creation: alternative theories of entrepreneurial action', *Strategic Entrepreneurship Journal*, vol. 1, no. 1–2 (2007), pp. 11–26.

Rovio Entertainment – going back to the entrepreneurial roots

Daryl Chapman (Metropolia Business School)

Revision by Sandra Lusmägi (Metropolia Business School)

Introduction

Rovio Entertainment Ltd is most famous for its *Angry Birds* smartphone game, in which colourful birds are catapulted at egg-stealing pigs. The company is based in Finland, and its key employees comprise Mikael Hed, former CEO and now chairman of Rovio Animation Studios, Niklas Hed, head of Research and Development, and Peter Vesterbacka, the Chief Marketing Officer and self-proclaimed 'Mighty Eagle', the public face of the company around the world. *Angry Birds* became a top-selling app on Apple's App Store in 2010, the start of a stream of business ventures including broadcast media, merchandising, publishing, retail stores and playgrounds. Peter Vesterbacka told *Wired Magazine* that Rovio could follow the world's largest entertainment company and that it would be Disney 2.0?[1] However, after some years of significant growth Rovio faced several challenges.

The team

Rovio was founded in 2003 by Niklas Hed and two classmates at Helsinki University of Technology after they won a game-development competition sponsored by Nokia and Hewlett Packard. The company initially did well in work-for-hire jobs, developing games for Electronic Arts, Nokia and Real Networks. Niklas' cousin Mikael Hed, with an MBA from Tulane University in the USA, soon joined. His father, Kaj Hed, had been a successful software entrepreneur, selling an earlier business for $150m (£100m, €110m). Kaj Hed invested €1m and became company chairman: Kaj still owns 70 per cent of the equity. Peter Vesterbacka only joined full-time in 2010, as *Angry Birds* began to take off. However, Vesterbacka, a business developer from Hewlett Packard active in the Finnish start-up scene for many years, had been encouraging Rovio and helping from the sidelines since 2003.

Although Rovio had been successful at creating games and selling them to established third party companies, the company's ambition was to create a major game success of its own. Niklas Hed thought it would take about 15 tries to create a world-beater, but *Angry Birds* turned out to be Rovio's 52nd attempt. Meanwhile, there were clashes over strategy. In 2005, Mikael Hed left the company after a row with his father, Kaj, whom he accused of being over-controlling. By 2008, Rovio had cut employment from 50 to just 12. But in 2009, Mikael came back, making peace with his father and sensing an opportunity with the new Apple iPhone and its App Store. The combination of the striking *Angry Bird* characters with the success of the Apple iPhone finally created a winning formula.

Rovio used Chillingo, a well-connected British games publisher, to negotiate a deal with Apple and push *Angry Birds* into world markets. In February 2010, Chillingo persuaded Apple to feature *Angry Birds* as the game of the week on the Apple App Store's front page: *Angry Birds* shot to No. 1 in the UK; five months later, it was top of the US charts as well. Chillingo was bought by Electronic Arts during 2010, and Rovio declared that it would no longer use any publishing intermediaries. In October 2010, Rovio launched the free Android *Angry Birds,* winning two million downloads in three days. By 2011, *Angry Birds* and its various branded spin-offs had earned €50m, on the back of a game which originally cost only €100,000 to develop. In March 2011, Mikael Hed was cautiously excited, telling *Wired Magazine*: 'I know how fragile the gaming industry is; I'm super-paranoid. But I feel at the moment that we are walking. We should be running.'[1]

The new Disney?

Like Disney with Mickey Mouse, Rovio saw the potential of transferring its powerful brand to other products. Partnering with the American toy manufacturer Commonwealth Toy & Novelty, Rovio was able to place *Angry Birds* soft toys and T-shirts in US shops. Rovio soon had more than 400 partners, including Coca-Cola, Intel and Kraft. The number of *Angry Birds* products reached 20,000, including board games, fridge magnets and key chains. Rovio receives royalties on sales of its licensed products ranging from 5 to 20 per cent. Rovio said merchandise accounted for 45 per cent of the €152m revenue generated in 2012.[2] Rovio's merchandising business is strongly linked to the games; if they become less popular, so will the toys, notebooks, soft drinks and other items that license the *Angry Birds* brand.

Rovio launched its first *Angry Birds* playground in Finland, with a strategy to mimic Disney's theme parks on a smaller scale. Rovio wanted to create a more 'distributed' means of physical interaction with families and children than the occasional visit to Disneyland: the *Angry Birds* playgrounds are local and can be visited every day. The first *Angry Birds* theme park was opened in Finland in 2012, followed with a theme park in China in 2013. Rovio planned to open theme parks around the globe in the hope of moving beyond the *Angry Birds* mobile game and becoming an entertainment powerhouse, combining both physical and digital media.

Rovio partnered with Samsung to include a motion-controlled *Angry Birds* game on its smart televisions. In November 2012, the company launched the Rovio Channel; letting users of the Samsung TV sets download games as well as the new *Angry Birds Toons* show and a comic-book series. The Rovio channel builds on the success of the *Angry Birds* YouTube channel, which attracted well over two billion views by the end of 2015. Rovio also established a successful books operation in 2011; they have released and licensed hundreds of books, which are sold in over 50 countries.

Stalled growth

The number of employees grew from 40 to over 800 between 2010 and 2012. With amusements parks, toys, books, comics and even a movie announcement, as a result, the parallel with Disney became clearer. In 2011, Rovio was offered a reported $2.25bn from Zynga, the US games company famous for Farmville, but the Finnish company decided not to make a deal with the Farmville creator.[3] However, the business peaked in 2013 – after three years of significant growth, from a mere €6.5m in revenue in 2010 to €152m in 2012. Rovio then reported operating profits of €36.5m in 2013, which fell 73 per cent in the next year, to €10m.[4] Rovio was forced to lay off 110 employees in 2014 and another dramatic cut in 2015 – 260 people were laid off, one third of all employees.[5] The company received a lot of criticism for failing to introduce new characters and industry experts wondered if the *Angry Birds* characters really had the same appeal as Mickey Mouse or Donald Duck. To date, Rovio has released 15 main *Angry Birds* themed title games, including two Star Wars crossovers and a female-focused *Angry Birds Stella.*

Up until 2013, *Angry Birds* had generated revenue through download fees. Kart-racing title *Angry Birds Go!* was released in December 2013, and it was their first game designed from scratch for a freemium model. Nearly all top performing titles today are so-called free-to-play or freemium games, meaning the downloading is free and revenue is generated through in-game purchases. *Angry Birds 2* was released in the summer of 2015 and it was downloaded nearly 50 million times in just a month, but it failed to boost revenues and disappeared from the top

grossing app store charts in a relatively short time. *Angry Birds* games were, however, not originally designed for the freemium model; fans complained about limited game time and intrusive in-app purchase offers which changed the flow of the gameplay. Excessive monetisation and a more complicated game environment are driving away the casual gamers and younger players. The core of the original game was lost in the new freemium games because it was created for a different model. In an attempt to keep up with the mobile gaming trends, the game franchise suffered an identity crisis.

In October 2015, Rovio jumped on the bandwagon of celebrity endorsed games and launched the new game *Love Rocks,* featuring the pop star Shakira, but it did not bring in massive revenues. According to the mobile-app analytics firm App Annie, the game peaked at number 21 in the top grossing charts in the first month of release and fell to a ranking of 304 during the next month.

Restructuring

When the company grew, new support functions had been established, such as a personnel department and licensing department. With this, they lost the flat hierarchy and fast decision-making model of a start-up and as a consequence the original organisational culture vanished.[6] As a result, many ex-Rovio employees ventured out to start their own gaming companies. The brain-drain then continued when growth stalled and many of those who helped to build the original success of Rovio left. Some of the former managers opened up anonymously to a Finnish business and finance magazine (*Talouselämä*), to point out the lack of a shared strategic vision from the family owned business, where each member seems to have a different idea in terms of what kind of company they are building.

Co-founder Mikael Hed stepped down from the CEO position in 2014, but stayed on the board and became chairman of Rovio Animation Studios. The newly appointed CEO Pekka Rantala left the position after only 16 months, after a difficult year of mass job losses and a disappointing response to *Angry Birds 2*. A former head of legal operations, Kati Levoranta, is the newest CEO. She says Rovio is ready to make the most out of the *Angry Birds* movie release in 2016.

The chairman Kaj Hed explained that after extensive layoffs, Rovio aimed to become 'leaner and more agile' with restructuring of its business operations and going back to their entrepreneurial roots.[4] As a part of their restructuring plans, Rovio announced at the beginning of 2016 the spinoff of their education business which includes a preschool concept and digital learning tools and licensing out the *Angry Birds* playgrounds. The books business was spun off as well.

Future plans

Rovio, however, also had plans for the future. An *Angry Birds* 3D movie is planned for release in 2016, after three years in the making. Rovio is financing the entire production of the movie, making it the most expensive Finnish film ever made. They have hired Sony Pictures Imageworks to produce the animation. Hollywood celebrities Jason Sudeikis, Josh Gad and Peter Dinklage, among many others, are acting as voiceovers for the characters. Of the total budget of €175m, €75m is production costs and €100m marketing.[7] Rovio has high hopes that the movie will create the next boost for the company's licencing business. Lego and Spin Master are already on board as toy partners for movie-inspired lines, other new licencing partners include the tech company Painting Lulu and www.SwimOutlet.com with an exclusive *Angry Birds* swim line. By retaining creative control and utilising the global marketing and distribution skills of Sony Pictures Entertainment, Rovio believes they are on track to deliver a hit feature.

Rovio acknowledged they lost focus and tried to do too many things. As the company moves ahead with the movie, they still have the ambition to be a leading entertainment company, with mobile games at its heart, said the CEO Kati Levoranta in 2015. The main focus after the restructuring will be games, media and consumer products. Majority owner Kaj Hed has announced that Rovio has its eye on a possible merger or acquisition, although a public share offering is not up for discussion at the moment. In 2014, Rovio made an operating profit of €10m on sales of €158m, down from profits of €36.5m on sales of 173.5m in 2013. For 2015, Hed expected results to have fallen compared to 2014 due to restructuring costs. Rovio, however, is confident they will see sales growth in 2016 on the back of the new movie, new licensing deals and new games:

> **'We had an exceptional situation a few years ago. I am satisfied with the current situation, because now we don't have false visions.'[4]**

Hed says as the new Hollywood 3D movie is about to be released in May 2016.

Original key sources: The Guardian, Media Network, 15 November 2012; Fast Company, 26 November 2012; The Next Web, 21 December 2012.

References
1. T. Cheshire, 'In depth: how Rovio made Angry Birds a winner (and what's next), *Wired Magazine*, 7 March 2011.
2. Lundgren, 'Angry birds maker Rovio says 2012 sales up 101% to $195m with merchandising, IP 45% of that; net profit $71m', *TechCrunch*, 3 April 2013.
3. M. Lynley, 'Angry birds turned down a $2.25bn takeout offer from Zynga', *Business Insider*, 28 November 2011.
4. J. Rosendahl, 'Angry Birds' maker Rovio limbers up for M&A', *Reuters*, 9 December 2015.
5. R. Dillett, 'Rovio to cut 260 jobs as the Angry Birds franchise becomes irrelevant', *TechCrunch*, 26 August 2015.
6. E. Lappalainen, 'Rovio's ex-managers reveal: serious problems with strategy and management', *Talouselama*, 27 August 2015.
7. J.R. Jensen, 'Angry Birds are expensive ones, too: €75m for the 3D animated movie', *Cineuropa*, 13 April 2015.

Questions

1 What are the advantages and disadvantages of Rovio's current business model?

2 Do you agree with the company chairman Kaj Hed when he says he is satisfied with Rovio's current situation?

11

MERGERS, ACQUISITIONS AND ALLIANCES

Learning outcomes

After reading this chapter you should be able to:

- Identify the key strategic motives for *mergers and acquisitions* and *strategic alliances*.
- Distinguish the key issues in the successful management of *mergers and acquisitions* and strategic alliances.
- Understand how to make appropriate choices between *organic* development, *mergers and acquisitions* and *strategic alliances*.
- Identify the *key success factors* of different growth options.

Key terms

acquisition p.341

co-evolution p.355

collaborative advantage p.351

collective strategy p.351

corporate entrepreneurship p.340

divestiture p.350

merger p.341

organic development p.340

organisational fit p.346

strategic alliance p.351

strategic fit p.346

trust p.355

11.1 INTRODUCTION

Mergers, acquisitions and alliances are all common methods for achieving growth strategies and often in the news. For example, in 2014 Comcast, the world's largest broadcasting and cable company, announced a friendly all-share merger with Time Warner, the world's third largest television network. The deal, worth $45.2bn (€31.9bn; £27.1bn), would result in control of around one third of the US cable and satellite market and one half of the bundled video and internet market. In the same year, Apple and IBM signed an exclusive partnership alliance allowing the former a huge opportunity to tap into the latter's large number of corporate customers and to get them to switch to its iOS platform. Apple planned to launch a 'new class' of more than 100 enterprise solutions as part of the deal. For IBM, the iOS technology would allow it to leverage IBM's leadership in analytics, cloud, software and services. As these cases show, acquisitions and alliances are big business with major implications for the strategic development of the companies.

This chapter therefore addresses mergers, acquisitions and alliances as key methods for pursuing strategic options. It will consider them alongside the principal alternative of 'organic' development, in other words the pursuit of a strategy relying on a company's own resources. Figure 11.1 shows how the main strategic options considered in the previous three chapters – diversification, internationalisation and innovation – can all be achieved through mergers and acquisitions, alliances and organic development. Of course, these three methods can also be used for many other strategies as well, for example consolidating markets or building scale advantages.

The chapter starts with organic development. This is the default option as it is natural for an organisation to rely on its internal resources. The chapter then introduces mergers and acquisitions (often abbreviated as M&A) and then strategic alliances as two principal external growth options. The final section compares these external options against the internal option of organic development. M&A and alliances fail frequently and so a fundamental question is when to acquire, when to ally or when to 'do it yourself'? The final section also considers key success factors in M&A and alliances. At the end of this chapter a new insight into understanding M&A performance is presented.

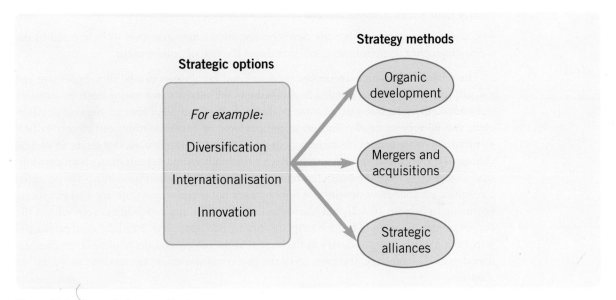

Figure 11.1 Three strategy methods

11.2 ORGANIC DEVELOPMENT

The default method for pursuing a strategy is to 'do it yourself', relying on internal capabilities. Thus **organic development is where a strategy is pursued by building on, and developing, an organisation's own capabilities.** For example, easyGroup's creation of a new subsidiary, easyFoodstore, was organic in nature. Drawing upon and customising internal capabilities, developed from its highly successful startup easyJet, a low-cost competitor in the mature airline industry, easyFoodstore aimed to undercut established supermarkets in a slow-growth industry by offering every food item for 25p (€ 0.30, $0.37). This do-it-yourself (DIY) diversification method was pursued as existing supermarkets were unlikely to want an alliance that would dilute their brands and profitability and also support a new competitor in an already very competitive industry.

There are five principal advantages to relying on organic development:

- *Knowledge and learning.* Using the organisation's existing capabilities to pursue a new strategy can enhance organisational knowledge and learning. Direct involvement in a new market or technology is likely to promote the acquisition and internalisation of deeper knowledge than a hands-off strategic alliance, for example.

- *Spreading investment over time.* Acquisitions typically require an immediate upfront payment for the target company. Organic development allows the spreading of investment over the whole time span of the strategy's development. This reduction of upfront commitment may make it easier to reverse or adjust a strategy if conditions change.

- No *availability constraints.* Organic development has the advantage of not being dependent on the availability of suitable acquisition targets or potential alliance partners. There are few acquisition opportunities for foreign companies wanting to enter the Japanese market, for example. Organic developers also do not have to wait until the perfectly matched acquisition target comes onto the market.

- *Strategic independence.* The independence provided by organic development means that an organisation does not need to make the same compromises as might be necessary if it made an alliance with a partner organisation. For example, partnership with a foreign collaborator is likely to involve constraints on marketing activity in external markets and may limit future strategic choices.

- *Culture management.* Organic development allows new activities to be created in the existing cultural environment, which reduces the risk of culture clash.

The reliance of organic development on internal capabilities can be slow, expensive and risky. It is not easy to use existing capabilities as the platform for major leaps in terms of innovation, diversification or internationalisation, for example. However organic development can be very successful and, as in the example of easyFoodstore, sufficiently radical to merit the term 'corporate entrepreneurship'. **Corporate entrepreneurship refers to radical change in the organisation's business, driven principally by the organisation's own capabilities.**[1] Bringing together the words 'entrepreneurship' and 'corporate' underlines the potential for significant change or novelty not only by external entrepreneurship (see also corporate venturing in Section 10.5.2), but also by reliance on internal capabilities from within the corporate organisation. Thus for easyGroup, easyFoodstore was a radical entrepreneurial step, taking it into a new industry in the hope that its low-cost model might change competitive dynamics landscape and even grow the market in a similar way to some of its earlier start-ups.

The concept of corporate entrepreneurship is valuable because it encourages a creative attitude inside the firm – for example, the creation of low-cost airline Ryanair from inside the aircraft leasing company Guinness Peat. Often, however, organisations have to go beyond their own internal capabilities and look externally for methods to pursue their strategies. This chapter will examine two of these methods, M&A and strategic alliances.

11.3 MERGERS AND ACQUISITIONS

Mergers and acquisitions (M&A) frequently grab the headlines, as they involve large sums of money and can affect a wide range of stakeholders. They can also provide a speedy means of achieving major strategic objectives. However, they can also lead to spectacular failures. For instance, shareholders were shocked in November 2012 when Meg Whitman, Hewlett Packard's CEO, announced they would take a $8.8bn (€6.6bn; £5.3bn) write down following its $11.1bn acquisition of Autonomy, alleging accounting improprieties in the acquired company. Hewlett Packard shares fell from $33 to $11.71 after the revelations and in 2015 it was forced to pay out $100m to its investors in compensation.

11.3.1 Types of M&A

M&A are about the combination of organisations. In an acquisition (or takeover) an acquirer *takes control* of another company through share purchase. Thus **'acquisition' is achieved by purchasing a majority of shares in a target company**. Most acquisitions are *friendly,* where the target's management recommends accepting the deal to its shareholders. Acquirers prefer this, as target management is more likely to work with them to integrate both companies. Sometimes acquisitions are *hostile,* where target management refuses the acquirer's offer. In this circumstance, the acquirer appeals directly to the target's shareholders for ownership of their shares. Hostile deals can be very acrimonious with target company management obstructing efforts to obtain key information and creating problems for post-deal integration. In general, acquirers are larger than target companies although there may be 'reverse' takeovers, where acquirers are smaller than their targets.

A **merger** differs from an acquisition, as it **is the combination of two previously separate organisations in order to form a new company**. For example, with significant changes introduced by government into the UK pensions market, hard-hit annuity providers, Just Retirement and Partnership Assurance lost half their market share and decided to announce their intention to merge in August 2015 to form a £1.6bn (€1.9bn, $2.4bn) company. Merger partners are often of similar size, with expectations of broadly equal status, unlike an acquisition where the acquirer generally dominates. In practice, the terms 'merger' and 'acquisition' are often used interchangeably, hence the common shorthand M&A.

M&A can also happen in the public and non-profit sectors: for example, the Finnish government created the new Aalto University in 2010 by merging the Helsinki School of Economics, the Helsinki University of Art and Design and the Helsinki University of Technology. Publicly owned institutions frequently build up highly distinctive cultures or systems of their own, as if they were in fact independent organisations. Where there are major cultural or systems differences between organisations, the scale and depth of the managerial issues approximate to those that would be involved in a change of ownership. 'Merger' is therefore often used in such cases as that better reflects the scale of the task involved than simply 'reorganisation'.

11.3.2 Timing of M&A

Since records began in the late nineteenth century, M&A have shown a cyclical quality, involving high peaks and deep troughs. Thus 2015 recorded the highest annual total of M&A since records began, with $5.03trn (£3.0trn, €3.7trn) of deals, up 37 per cent from the previous year, and more than double the volume of the global recession of $2.26trn in 2009.[2] M&A cycles are broadly linked to changes in the global economy but are also influenced by new regulations, the availability of finance, stock market performance, technological disturbances and the supply of available target firms. They may also be driven by over-optimism on the part of managers, shareholders and bankers during upturns, and by exaggerated loss of confidence during downturns. This cyclical pattern suggests that some times are better than others for making an acquisition. At the top of a cycle, target companies are likely to be very highly priced, which may reduce the chances of success for an acquirer. For instance, the £5bn merger between house builders Taylor Woodrow and George Wimpey saw a 90 per cent crash in the value of its shares in the following year when the recession started in 2008. These cycles should warn managers that M&A may have a strong fashion element. Especially in an upturn, managers should ask very carefully whether acquisitions are really justified.

Global activity in mergers has traditionally been dominated by North America and Western Europe, whereas it has been much less common in other economies, for example Japan. Many national governance systems put barriers in the way of acquisitions, especially hostile acquisitions (see Section 5.3.2). However, companies from fast-developing economies such as China and India have become very active in large-scale acquisitions in order to access Western markets or technology, or to secure material resources needed for growth. For example, Anbang Insurance Company Group Ltd acquired the Waldorf Astoria hotel in New York in 2014 from Hilton Worldwide Holdings and in 2016 was bidding for further US hotel chains.

11.3.3 Motives for M&A

Motives for M&A can be strategic, financial and managerial[3] (see Illustration 11.1).

Strategic motives for M&A

Strategic motives for M&A involve improving the competitive advantage of the organisation. These motives are often related to the reasons for diversification in general (see Section 8.3). Strategic motives can be categorised in three main ways:[4]

- *Extension*. M&A can be used to extend the reach of a firm in terms of geography, products or markets. For instance, transactions such as Valeant Pharmaceuticals' $55bn purchase of Botox-maker Allergan and Facebook's $22bn acquisition of mobile messaging platform WhatsApp illustrate capturing new products and markets (see Chapter 8).

- *Consolidation*. M&A can be used to consolidate the competitors in an industry. Bringing together two competitors can have at least three beneficial effects. In the first place, it increases market power by reducing competition: this might enable the newly consolidated company to raise prices for customers. Second, the combination of two competitors can increase efficiency through reducing surplus capacity or sharing resources, for instance head-office facilities or distribution channels. Finally, the greater scale of the combined operations may increase production efficiency or increase bargaining power with suppliers, forcing them to reduce their prices. These reasons lie behind the 2015 merger between cement giants Lafarge of France and Holcim of Switzerland.

ILLUSTRATION 11.1   Strategies clash in a contested bid

US hotelier and Chinese insurer contest ownership of Starwood.

In March 2016, struggling US hotel group, Starwood Hotels and Resorts, owner of Weston and Sheraton Hotels, found itself in a bidding war. It had accepted an offer of $10.8bn (€8.1bn, £6.5bn) in cash and stock from US hotelier Marriott International the previous year. Whilst discussing the details of the acquisition, due to close in March 2016, Beijing-based Anbang Insurance Group made an unsolicited offer of $12.9bn. Marriott responded by increasing its offer to $13.6bn and Starwood investors eagerly awaited higher bids.

If Marriott succeeded it would create the world's largest hotel company with 5500 owned or franchised hotels with 1.1 million rooms under 30 brands. Marriott believed it was a compelling bidder having demonstrated multi-year industry-leading growth, powerful brands and consistent return of capital to shareholders, with shares trading consistently above those of its peers. Having already conducted five months of extensive investigation and joint integration planning with Starwood, including careful analysis of the brand architecture, Marriott was confident it could make annual cost savings of $250m, generate greater long-term shareholder value from a larger global presence and offer wider choice of brands to consumers and improved economics to owners and franchisees.

Little known outside of China before 2013, Anbang Insurance Group originated as a small car insurer, before China's move to give insurers greater freedom to invest their money. This allowed Anbang to sell investment products and other services, making them major players in real estate. A slowing Chinese economy and devaluing currency encouraged many domestic companies to invest overseas and Anbang then aggressively pursued overseas deals, largely fuelled by selling high-yield investment products at home. Having spent $2bn on insurers in Belgium and South Korea, Anbang also made many large US acquisitions including the Waldorf Astoria for $1.95bn, the American insurer, Fidelity & Guaranty Life Insurance ($1.6bn) and the biggest-ever acquisition of American property assets by a mainland Chinese buyer, Strategic Hotels and Resorts ($6.5bn), owner of Four Seasons hotels, the Fairmont and Intercontinental hotels and the JW Marriott Essex House hotel. As a late bidder, Anbang had had little time for in-depth investigation of Starwoods but was making its bid in a consortium that included American private equity firm J.C. Flowers & Company. With close personal links to the Chinese Government, commentators believed Anbang could greatly increase Starwood's cash reserves.

On 28 March, Anbang raised its bid to $14bn and analysts wondered whether Marriott would be able to raise its offer further as increasing the cash part of its offer could threaten its investment-grade rating and adding more stock would dilute its earnings per share. Marriott's response was to say that its offer was not just about price. It also questioned whether Anbang had sufficient funds to close the deal and whether the Committee on Foreign Investment (Cfius), which reviews all deals for American companies that involve national security, would intervene as it had with the Waldorf sale, although this had been approved. Starwood properties could be deemed to be near government offices and military bases. This could delay the deal and possibly discourage Anbang's bid. Commentators also wondered whether they had the skills to manage Starwood as the management team at its Belgian acquisition had left quickly amid complaints about Anbang's management style.

Sources: Telegraph, 14 March 2016; nytimes.com, 23 March 2016; *New York Times,* 14 March 2016, 28 March 2016.

Questions

1 How do the bidders' acquisition motives differ?

2 What are the strategic and organisational fit implications of both bids?

- *Capabilities.* The third broad strategic motive for M&A is to increase a company's capabilities. High-tech companies such as Cisco and Microsoft regard acquisitions of entrepreneurial technology companies as a part of their R&D effort. Instead of researching a new technology from scratch, they allow entrepreneurial start-ups to prove the idea, and then take over these companies in order to incorporate the technological capability within their own portfolio. Capabilities-driven acquisitions are often useful where industries are converging (see Section 3.3.2). For example, Alphabet, formerly Google, made substantial acquisitions in order to gain a foothold in the new high-growth mobile advertising market. Alphabet's acquisition of AdMob and, in 2015, acquisition of Agawi, an app streaming specialist, shows commitment to build a notable presence in this market space where there is convergence between telephony and advertising industries.

Financial motives for M&A

Financial motives concern the optimal use of financial resources, rather than directly improving the actual business. There are three main financial motives:

- *Financial efficiency.* An acquirer with a strong balance sheet (i.e. has plenty of cash) may help improve a highly indebted target company (i.e. a weak balance sheet). The target can save on interest payments by using the acquirer's assets to pay off its debt, and it can also get investment funds that it could not have accessed otherwise. The acquirer may also be able to drive a good bargain in acquiring the weaker company. Also, an acquirer with a booming share price can purchase targets very efficiently by offering to pay target shareholders with its own shares (equity), rather than paying with cash upfront.

- *Tax efficiency.* Sometimes there may be tax advantages from bringing together different companies. For example, profits or tax losses may be transferable within the organisation in order to benefit from different tax regimes between industries or countries. In November 2015, US giant Pfizer announced the largest 'tax inversion' deal ever at $160bn (€120bn, £96bn), with the takeover of Irish-based Allergan, to form the world's largest drug company. Pfizer's headquarters would move to Ireland where it would pay 17 per cent tax rather than the 25 per cent it was paying in the USA. Naturally, there are legal restrictions on this strategy and governments may also adjust their tax rates later on.

- *Asset stripping or unbundling.* Some companies are effective at spotting other companies whose underlying assets are worth more than the price of the company as a whole. This makes it possible to buy such companies and then rapidly sell off ('unbundle') different business units to various buyers for a total price substantially in excess of what was originally paid for the whole. Although this is often dismissed as merely opportunistic profiteering ('asset stripping'), if the business units find better corporate parents through this unbundling process, there can be a real gain in economic effectiveness.

Managerial motives for M&A

As for diversification (see Section 8.3), M&A may sometimes serve managers' more than shareholders' interests. 'Managerial' motives are therefore self-serving rather than efficiency-driven. M&A may serve managerial self-interest for two reasons:

- *Personal ambition.* This can take three forms regardless of the real value being created. First, senior managers' personal financial incentives may be tied to short-term growth targets or share-price targets that are more easily achieved by large and spectacular acquisitions than the more gradualist and lower-profile alternative of organic growth. Second, large acquisitions attract media attention, with opportunities to boost personal reputations through flattering media interviews and appearances. Here, there is the so-called 'managerial hubris' (vanity) effect: managers who have been successful in earlier acquisitions become over-confident and embark on more and more acquisitions, each riskier and more expensive than the one before.[5] Finally, acquisitions provide opportunities to give friends and colleagues greater responsibility, helping to cement personal loyalty by developing individuals' careers.

- *Bandwagon effects.* As noted earlier, acquisitions are highly cyclical. In an upswing, there are three kinds of pressure on senior managers to join the acquisition bandwagon. First, when many other firms are making acquisitions, financial analysts and the business media may criticise more cautious managers for undue conservatism. Second, shareholders may fear that their company is being left behind, as they see opportunities for their business being snatched by rivals. Lastly, managers may worry that if their company is not acquiring, it will become the target of a hostile bid itself. For managers wanting a quiet life during a 'merger boom', the easiest strategy may be simply to join in. But the danger is making an acquisition the company does not really need and it can be one reason for paying too much.

In sum, there are bad as well as good reasons for M&A. The general consensus remains that the average performance of deals is unimpressive, with some evidence suggesting that over half fail.[6] It is clearly worth asking skeptical questions about acquisition performance. However, alternative growth methods also exhibit similar problematic levels of performance. Nevertheless, it is worth asking sceptical questions of any M&A strategy. The converse can be true of course: there can be bad reasons for resisting a hostile takeover. Senior managers may resist being acquired because they fear losing their jobs, even if the price offered represents a good deal for their shareholders.

11.3.4 M&A processes

Acquisitions take time. First there is the search to identify an acquisition target with the best possible fit. This process may take years but sometimes can be completed very rapidly indeed. Then there is the process of negotiating the deal: to agree on terms and conditions and the right price. Finally, managers will need to decide on the extent to which the new and old businesses will need to be integrated – and this will have significant implications for the amount of time required to create value. In other words, acquisition should be seen as a process over time. Each step in this process imposes different tasks on managers (see Figure 11.2). This section will consider three key steps: target choice, negotiation and integration.

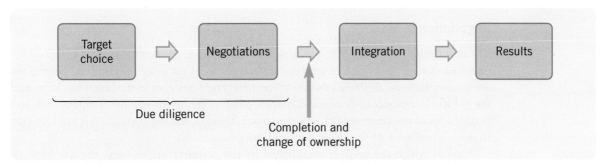

Figure 11.2 The acquisition process

Target choice in M&A

There are two main criteria to apply: strategic fit and organisational fit.[7]

- **Strategic fit. This refers to the extent to which the target firm strengthens or complements the acquiring firm's strategy.** Strategic fit relates to the original strategic motives for the acquisition: extension, consolidation and capabilities. Managers need to assess strategic fit very carefully. The danger is that potential synergies (see Section 8.3) in M&A are often exaggerated in order to justify high acquisition prices. Also, negative synergies ('contagion') between the companies involved are easily neglected[8] where moving from one company's business model to another or amalgamating aspects of each other's business results in value destruction.

- **Organisational fit. This refers to the match between the management practices, cultural practices and staff of characteristics between the target and the acquiring firms.** Large mismatches between the two are likely to cause significant integration problems. International acquisitions can be particularly liable to organisational misfits, because of cultural and language differences between countries[9], although the extent to which there is actual cultural clash will be determined by the extent of integration intended. The bid for Starwood by Anbang raises many questions about organisational fit (see Illustration 11.1). A comparison of the two companies' cultural webs (Section 6.3.5) might be helpful to highlight potential misfit.

Together, strategic and organisational fit determine the potential for the acquirer to add value, the parenting issue raised in Section 8.6. Where there is bad organisational fit, attempts by the acquirer to integrate the target are likely to destroy value regardless of how well the target fits strategically. For instance, the merger between French and American telecoms equipment manufacturers Alcatel and Lucent resulted in significant culture clashes for several years post-deal with losses running into billions of dollars and the departure of the two top executives.

The two criteria of strategic and organisational fit are important components of 'due diligence' – a structured investigation of target companies that generally takes place before a deal is closed. Poor due diligence can lead to serious post-acquisition difficulties as Hewlett Packard's $5bn write down of its Autonomy acquisition shows. Strategic and organisational fit can be used to create a screen according to which potential acquisition targets can be ruled in or ruled out. Note that, because the set of firms that meet the criteria *and* that are actually available for purchase is likely to be small, it is very tempting for managers to relax the criteria too far in order to build a large enough pool of possible acquisitions. Strict strategic and organisational fit criteria are particularly liable to be forgotten after the failure of an initial acquisition bid. Once having committed publicly to an acquisition strategy, senior managers are susceptible to making ill-considered bids for other targets 'on the rebound'.

Negotiation in M&A

The negotiation process in M&A is critical to the outcome of friendly deals. If top managements cannot agree because of personal differences, or if the price or terms and conditions are unacceptable the deal will not take place. In terms of price, offer the target too little, and the bid will be unsuccessful: senior managers will lose credibility and the company will have wasted a lot of management time. Pay too much, though, and the acquisition is unlikely ever to make a profit net of the original acquisition price.

Ways in which the price is established by the acquirer are through the use of various valuation methods, including financial analysis techniques such as payback period, discounted cash flow, asset valuation and shareholder value analysis (see Chapter 12).[10] For acquisition of publicly quoted companies, the market value of the target company's shares can act as a guide. Typically, acquirers do not simply pay the current market value of the target, but have to pay a so-called *premium for control*. This is the additional amount an acquirer has to pay to win control compared to the ordinary valuation of the target's shares as an independent company. Depending on the state of the financial markets, this premium is often around 30 per cent greater than the current market value of target shares. Where the target resists the initial bid, or other potential acquirers join in with their own bids, this premium will rise, and it is very easy for bid prices to escalate well beyond the true economic value of the target.

It is therefore very important for the acquirer to be disciplined regarding the price that it will pay. Acquisitions are liable to the *winner's curse* – in order to win acceptance of the bid, the acquirer may pay so much that the original cost can never be earned back.[11] A famous case of the winner's curse is that of the Royal Bank of Scotland's competition against Barclay's Bank to acquire the Dutch Bank ABN AMRO in 2007. The Royal Bank of Scotland outbid its rival with a price of €70bn (£56bn, $91bn). This was more than it could afford and soon drove the victor into financial collapse and government ownership. The negative effects of paying too much can be worsened if the acquirer tries to justify the price by cutting back essential investments in order to improve immediate profits. In what is called the *vicious circle of overvaluation*, over-paying firms can easily undermine the original rationale of the acquisition by cutting costs on exactly the assets (e.g. brand-marketing, product R&D or key staff) that made up the strategic value of the target company in the first place.

Integration in M&A

The ability to extract value from an acquisition will depend critically on how it is integrated with the acquirer. Integration is frequently challenging because of problems of organisational fit. For example, there might be strong cultural differences (see Section 6.3) or incompatible financial or information technology systems (see Section 14.3). Poor integration can cause acquisitions to fail (see Illustration 11.2 for the way Alphabet has managed its talent acquisition). Getting the right approach to integration of merged or acquired companies is crucial.

INSEAD's Philippe Haspeslagh and David Jemison[12] argue that the most suitable approach to integration depends on two key criteria:

- *The extent of strategic interdependence.* This is the need for the transfer or sharing of capabilities (for example, technology) or resources (for example, manufacturing facilities). The presumption is that significant transfer or sharing through tight integration will enable the 'creation' of value from the acquisition. Of course, some acquisitions 'capture' value purely through the ownership of assets and so there is less need for integration. These unrelated or conglomerate diversifications (see Section 8.2.4) may only be integrated in terms of their financial systems.

- *The need for organisational autonomy.* Where an acquired firm has a very distinct culture, or is geographically distant, or is dominated by prima donna professionals or star performers, integration may be problematic. For this reason, some acquisitions need high levels of organisational autonomy. But in some circumstances it is the distinctiveness of the acquired organisation that is valuable to the acquirer.[13] In this case, it is best to learn gradually from the distinct culture, rather than risk spoiling it by hurried or overly tight integration.

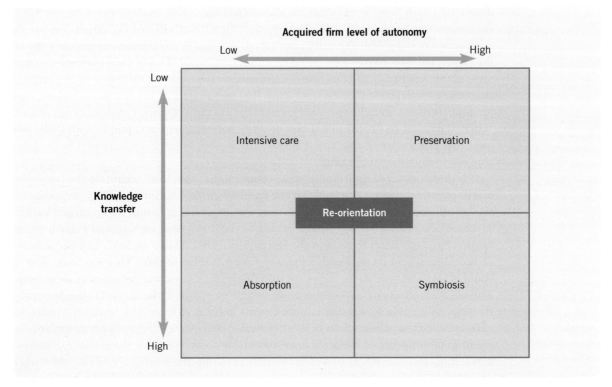

Figure 11.3 Post-acquisition integration matrix

Source: D.N. Angwin and M. Meadows, 'New integration strategies for post acquisition management', *Long Range Planning*, vol. 48, no. 4 (2015), pp. 235–51, with permission from Elsevier.

As in Figure 11.3, therefore, these two criteria result in five integration approaches[14] which have important implications for the length of integration period and choice of top management for the acquired company:

- *Absorption* is preferred where a high level of strategic interdependence is necessary and there is little need for organisational autonomy. Absorption requires rapid adjustment of the acquired company's old strategies and structures to the needs of the new owner, and corresponding changes to the acquired company's culture and systems. In this type of acquisition, it is usual to appoint a new top manager in order to manage the organisation differently.[15]

- *Preservation* is appropriate where the acquired company is well run but not very compatible with the acquirer. The high need for autonomy and low need for integration may be found in conglomerate deals. The preservation style depends on allowing old strategies, cultures and systems to continue in the acquired company much as before. Changes from the acquirer are generally confined to the essential minimum such as adjusting financial reporting procedures for control and carried out in a slow piecemeal fashion. In this situation, it is advisable to retain the incumbent top manager.

- *Symbiosis* is indicated where there is strong need for strategic interdependence, but also a requirement for high autonomy – perhaps in a professional services organisation dependent on the creativity of its staff. Symbiosis implies that both acquired firm and acquiring firm learn the best qualities from the other. This learning process takes significant time and it is often the case that it is best to retain the incumbent top manager in the early stages to stabilise the acquisition before bringing in a new top manager to make far-reaching changes. This is the most complex of the integration approaches.

- *Intensive care* takes place where there is little to be gained by integration. These acquisitions may occur when the acquired company is in poor financial health and very rapid

ILLUSTRATION 11.2 — To deal or not to deal – that's the multi-billion dollar question

To evolve Alphabet needs to acquire big, but does it have the right post-acquisition skills?

With $70bn (£42bn, €53bn) in cash, there was speculation that Alphabet, formerly Google, might make a big acquisition, as shareholders would otherwise press for a special dividend or share repurchase.

Prior to becoming Alphabet, Google had always been a serial acquirer with over 180 deals. Few were in excess of $1bn although the top ten cost more than $24.5bn in total. Many of Google's most well-known products, including Android, YouTube, Maps, Docs and Analytics, came from acquisitions.

Originally, Google did not set a priority on fit between its target companies and its own organisation. Acquisitions were simply ways to enter new markets, gain talent or give Google a stronger foothold where its own efforts had failed. For instance, acquiring You Tube came after Google Video stalled. Soon there were too many separate products, and CEO Larry Page reorganised into seven core product areas in 2011. There were fewer 'acquisition hires' and for a deal to complete it had to pass his 'toothbrush test' – a product you use daily to make your life better. A target must also enhance an existing product and be scalable.

Most of Google's acquisitions had been start-ups. Retaining start-up founders can be very difficult as they think of themselves as entrepreneurs who like doing their own thing. Many acquirers have struggled to retain the expertise they have spent millions acquiring. However, Google has retained at least 221 start-up founders whilst closest competitor Yahoo retained only 110. Google competed with other potential purchasers on offering huge resources to founders to enable them to initiate their product visions faster. Founders were asked what their product would look like with a billion users? For instance, Keyhole's founders were asked to adapt their desktop digital mapping software for urban planning to work on the web. It became Google Maps – the world's largest source of location data. And Google would give entrepreneurs space to innovate, handle contracts, patents and intangibles. However, unless acquisitions were large, few continued to run independently. Often founders were rolled up inside another group in the company and they couldn't make decisions as freely as before. This affected their willingness to remain.

When Google approached Tony Fadell, CEO of Nest, the maker of the learning thermostat, the question was how he wanted to spend his time. He had limited resources for expansion and was working always on managing the day-to-day. Google promised a big payday, retention of the Nest brand name, investment for expansion and time to develop new products. Nest was acquired for $3.2bn to build Google's smart home initiative of connecting devices that anticipate human behaviour. Post-acquisition, Fadell didn't need formal approval for anything although he met regularly with Larry Page.

Alphabet is facing multiple threats with declining share of desktop searches, Facebook taking advertising dollars and Amazon stealing product search queries in the mobile market. It needs new revenue sources to compete effectively and innovate continually – 'it can't all be from within'. Although skilled at acquiring small companies, Google had had less success with larger acquisitions as the biggest, Motorola Mobility, $12.5bn, failed and was later disposed of. With a new company structure of Alphabet as a holding company, and Google as a subsidiary, perhaps a new way of integrating larger acquisitions is possible that may be more appealing to potential targets.

Sources: http://beyondthedeal.net/blog/2012/05/30/google-acquisitions-and-integrations-a-tale-of-two-cities/; *Business Insider*, 2 May 2015; TIME.com, 15 April 2015; *Quartz*, 15 August 2015; Wired.com, 14 January 2014.

Questions

1 Using the post-acquisition integration matrix, Figure 11.3, compare Google's early style of acquisition management with the integration of Nest.

2 How has Google managed to be successful in retaining entrepreneurial talent?

remedial action is required.[16] The acquirer will not integrate the company into its own business to avoid contamination but will impose stringent short-term targets and strategies in order to solve its problems. In more aggressive turnaround cases the incumbent top manager will typically be replaced but otherwise the incumbent is retained for a smoother transition. These businesses may often be for sale.

- *Reorientation acquisitions* occur when the acquired company is in good health and well run, but there is a need to integrate central administrative areas and align marketing and sales functions. Distinctive resources of the acquired company though are left alone and there are few changes to internal operations. In order to drive through changes quickly, a new top manager is generally brought in to run the acquired company.

Especially for absorption, symbiosis and reorientation strategies that require significant organisational interactions, acquisition success will depend upon how well the integration process is managed. Here methods of managing strategic change explained in Chapter 15 will be relevant. However, because acquisitions often involve the loss of jobs, sudden career changes, management relocations and the cancellation of projects, it is argued that organisational justice is particularly important for successful integration.[17]

Organisational justice refers to the perceived fairness of managerial actions, in terms of distribution, procedure and information. Thus:

- *Distributive justice* refers to the distribution of rewards and posts: for example, it will be seen as unfair in a merger between equals if the large majority of senior management posts go to one of the partners, and not the other.

- *Procedural justice* refers to the procedures by which decisions are made: for example, if integration decisions are made through appropriate committees or task forces with representation from both sides, then the perception of fair procedures is likely to be high.

- *Informational justice* is about how information is used and communicated in the integration: if decisions are explained well to all those involved, they are more likely to be accepted positively.

Kraft offended principles of both procedural and informational justice when it assured investors and employees before its 2010 takeover of Cadbury that it would keep open the Somerdale chocolate factory near Bristol, with its 400 workers. Within a month of completing the takeover, Kraft announced that production would be transferred to Poland, causing political controversy and a loss of trust amongst acquired employees.

11.3.5 M&A strategy over time

M&A strategies evolve over time as deals are rarely one-off events for an organisation. Companies that make multiple acquisitions are termed *serial acquirers*. When acquisitions occur closely together, these can be very demanding of managerial time and skills. However, repeating the acquisition process does provide an opportunity for acquiring companies to learn how to do M&A better.[18] Cisco Systems is well known as a successful serial acquirer. By mid-2015 it had made 176 acquisitions since its first deal in 1993; these acquisitions account for at least 50 per cent of revenue. The amount of work in selecting and evaluating targets is significant. In order to make just 50 software acquisitions, IBM had to assess around 500 different potential acquisition targets, choosing not to proceed in the vast majority of cases.[19]

- **When a business no longer fits the corporate strategy it may be sold.** This is termed **divestiture (or divestment)**.[20] This is a central part of 'asset stripping' strategy (see Section 11.3.3), but ought to be on the agenda of every diversified corporation. The key determinant of divestiture is whether the corporate parent has 'parenting advantage': in other words, the corporate parent can add more value to the business unit than other potential owners of the business (see Section 8.6). Where there is no parenting advantage the business should be divested for the best obtainable price. Corporate parents are often reluctant to divest businesses, seeing it as an admission of failure. However, a dynamic perspective on M&A would encourage managers to view divestitures positively. Funds raised by the sale of an ill-fitting business can be used either to invest in retained businesses or to buy other businesses that fit the corporate strategy better. Obtaining a good price for the divested unit can recoup any losses it may have originally made. Sometimes, however, a less positive reason for divestiture is pressure from competition authorities, which may force the sale of businesses to reduce companies' market power. For example, in 2015 BT intended to buy mobile operator EE for £12.5bn (€15bn, $18.6bn). Rivals TalkTalk and Vodafone responded by asking the UK competition authorities to force BT to spin off its Openreach operation to prevent BT dominating the marketplace.

- Acquisitions, therefore, are an important method for pursuing strategies. However, they are not easy to carry out and they are sometimes adopted for misguided reasons. It is important to consider alternatives such as strategic alliances.

11.4 STRATEGIC ALLIANCES

M&A bring together companies through complete changes in ownership. However, companies also often work together in strategic alliances that involve collaboration with only partial changes in ownership, or no ownership changes at all as the parent companies remain distinct. Thus a **strategic alliance is where two or more organisations share resources and activities to pursue a common strategy**. This is a popular method amongst companies for pursuing strategy. Accenture has estimated that the average large corporation is managing around 30 alliances at any one time,[21] and this may account for as much as 26 per cent of large company revenues.[22]

Alliance strategy challenges the traditional organisation-centred approach to strategy in at least two ways. First, practitioners of alliance strategy need to think about strategy in terms of the collective success of their networks as well as their individual organisations' self-interest.[23] **Collective strategy is about how the whole network of alliances, of which an organisation is a member, competes against rival networks of alliances.** Thus for Microsoft, competitive success for its Xbox games console has relied heavily on the collective strength of its network of independent games developers such as Bungie Studios (makers of Halo), Crystal Dynamics (Tomb Raider), Rockstar North (Grand Auto Theft Auto V), Crytek Studios (Crysis 3) and The Coalition (Gears of War). Part of Microsoft's strategy must include developing a stronger ecosystem of games developers than its rivals such as Sony and Nintendo. Collective strategy also challenges the individualistic approach to strategy by highlighting the importance of effective collaboration. Thus success involves collaborating as well as competing. **Collaborative advantage is about managing alliances better than competitors.**[24] For Microsoft to maximise the value of the Xbox, it is not enough for it to have a stronger network than rivals such as Sony and Nintendo, but it must be better at working with its network in order to ensure that its members keep on producing the best games. The more effectively it collaborates, the more successful it will be. Illustration 11.3 describes Apple's approach to collective strategy and collaboration for the iPad.

ILLUSTRATION 11.3   Apple's iPad advantage

Gaining competitive advantage through collaboration?

With much fanfare, a new version of Apple's iPad was launched on 16 March 2012. Apple had dominated the tablet market for two years and iPad's lightweight touchscreen and new operating system, iOS, designed from the ground up for portable performance, had won many admirers. But the first customers were buyers who just couldn't wait to tear the gadget apart.

Market research firm iSuppli's 'teardown' analysis revealed that the €622 (£497, $808), 4G 64GB model cost $409 to make, just 49 per cent of its retail price. They identified Broadcom and Qualcomm as suppliers of Bluetooth and wifi chips, STMicroelectronics the gyroscope, Cirrus Logic the audio chip, three Taiwanese companies touchscreen components, Sony the camera CMOS sensor and Samsung, a direct competitor, the expensive display, battery and processor chip.

Apple was therefore at the heart of a network. However, it had always protected its intellectual property. No hardware was licensed, ensuring control of production and maintenance of its premium pricing policy. It was impossible for any independent company to manufacture cheap iPads, in the way for instance that Taiwanese manufacturers produced cheap IBM/Microsoft-compatible personal computers in the 1980s.

iPad's success attracted a swarm of companies into the accessory market, such as Griffin (USA) and Logitech (Switzerland) supplying attractive add-ons including ultra-thin keyboards, cases and touchscreen stylus. Apple licensed them the necessary technology and benefited from attractive complementary products and royalties. But the relationship was arm's-length, with no advance information about new products.

Apple originally jealously controlled access to iOS. However, for the iPad, it opened up allowing third parties to develop apps, and this stimulated the new App Stores industry. The attractiveness of iOS and strong consumer demand encouraged software developers to produce for Apple first.

Consumers liked the ease of use and vast ecosystem of Apple's iPad, but challenges were mounting. Amazon's low cost 'content consumption device', Kindle, offered a vast library of movies but lacked Apple's beauty and had few apps. Google's low priced Nexus 10 aimed to profit from business services use rather than hardware. Its improved screen resolution and Android operating system challenged iPad's technology and it shared many characteristics of other ecosystems with streaming apps and a consistent user experience. Samsung's own tablet, Galaxy Tab, had similar advantages along with compelling design and openness to non-Apple standards. Microsoft aimed to profit from its hardware, Surface, but was not particularly innovative, lacking a comparable software ecosystem, and its tie to Windows could be a hindrance.

iPad is a phenomenal success with sales in excess of 170 million units. It has evolved to be thinner and smaller and the next evolution may be a larger device targeted at business users. However, Apple remains embroiled in lawsuits against Samsung over its Galaxy Tablet design. Samsung is also counter suing. The lawsuits show the competitive intensity of the sector as companies battle it out amongst their ecosystems – consumers buy the ecosystem rather than the gadget.

Sources: G. Linden, K. Kraemer and J. Dedrick, 'Who captures value in a global innovation network?', *Communications of the ACM*, vol. 52, no. 3 (2009), pp. 140–5; 'Tablet Wars', *The Telegraph*, 6 November 2012; F. MacMahon, 'Tablet Wars', 4 December 2012, BroadcastEngineering. com; A. Hesseldahl, 'Apple's new iPad costs at least $316 to build, IHS iSuppli teardown shows', 16 March 2012, http://allthingsd.com.

Questions

1 What are pros and cons of Apple's tight control of licensing?

2 What role has 'ecosystem' played in Apple's competitive advantage?

11.4.1 Types of strategic alliance

In terms of ownership, there are two main kinds of strategic alliance:

- *Equity alliances* involve the creation of a new entity that is owned separately by the partners involved. The most common form of equity alliance is the *joint venture,* where two organisations remain independent but set up a new organisation jointly owned by the parents. For example, Ethihad Airways, founded in 2004, has grown rapidly to be the fifth largest airline largely through the creation of many equity alliances. These include agreements with Alitalia, Air Berlin, Air Serbia, Air Seychelles, Darwin Airlines and India's Jet Airways. A *consortium alliance* involves several partners setting up a venture together. For example, IBM, Hewlett-Packard, Toshiba and Samsung are partners in the Sematech research consortium, working together on the latest semiconductor technologies.

- *Non-equity alliances* are typically looser, without the commitment implied by ownership. Non-equity alliances are often based on contracts. One common form of contractual alliance is franchising, where one organisation (the franchisor) gives another organisation (the franchisee) the right to sell the franchisor's products or services in a particular location in return for a fee or royalty. Kall-Kwik printing, 7-Eleven convenience stores, McDonald's restaurants and Subway are examples of franchising. Licensing is a similar kind of contractual alliance, allowing partners to use intellectual property such as patents or brands in return for a fee. Long-term subcontracting agreements are another form of loose non-equity alliance, common in automobile supply. For example, the Canadian subcontractor Magna has long-term contracts to assemble the bodies and frames for car companies such as Ford, Honda and Mercedes.

The public and voluntary sectors often get involved in both equity and non-equity strategic alliances. Governments have increasingly encouraged the public sector to contract out the building and maintenance of capital projects such as hospitals and schools under long-term contracts. Individual public organisations often band together to form purchasing consortia as well. A good example of this is university libraries, which typically negotiate collectively for the purchase of journals and books from publishers. Voluntary organisations pool their resources in alliance too. For example, relief organisations in areas suffering from natural or man-made disasters typically have to cooperate in order to deliver the full range of services in difficult circumstances. Although public- and voluntary-sector organisations might often be seen as more naturally cooperative than private-sector organisations, many of the issues that follow apply to all three kinds of organisation.

11.4.2 Motives for alliances

Strategic alliances allow an organisation to rapidly extend its strategic advantage and generally require less commitment than other forms of expansion. A key motivator is sharing resources or activities, although there may be less obvious reasons as well. Four broad rationales for alliances can be identified, as summarised in Figure 11.4:

- *Scale alliances.* Here organisations combine in order to achieve necessary scale. The capabilities of each partner may be quite similar (as indicated by the similarity of the A and B organisations in Figure 11.4), but together they can achieve advantages that they could not easily manage on their own. Thus combining together can provide economies of scale in the production of outputs (products or services). Combining might

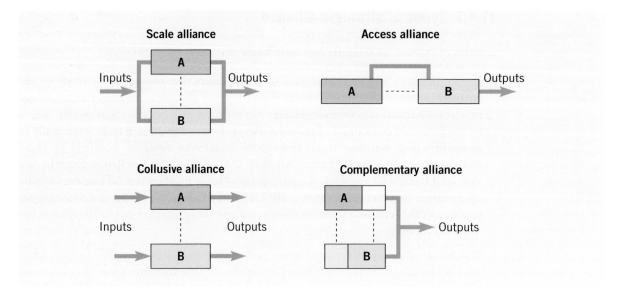

Figure 11.4 Strategic alliance motives

also provide economies of scale in terms of inputs, for example by reducing purchasing costs of raw materials or services. Thus health management organisations often combine together to negotiate better prices with pharmaceutical companies. Finally, combining allows the partners to share risk as well. Instead of organisations stretching themselves to find enough resources on their own, partnering can help each partner avoid committing so many resources of its own that failure would jeopardise the existence of the whole organisation.

- *Access alliances.* Organisations frequently ally in order to access the capabilities of another organisation that are required in order to produce or sell its products and services. For example, in countries such as China and India, a Western company (in Figure 11.4, organisation A) might need to partner with a local distributor (organisation B) in order to access effectively the national market for its products and services. Here organisation B is critical to organisation A's ability to sell. Access alliances can work in the opposite direction. Thus organisation B might seek a licensing alliance in order to access inputs from organisation A, for example technologies or brands. Here organisation A is critical to organisation B's ability to produce or market its products and services. Access can be about tangible resources such as distribution channels or products as well as intangible resources such as knowledge and social/political connections.

- *Complementary alliances.* These can be seen as a form of access alliance, but involve organisations at similar points in the value network combining their distinctive resources so that they bolster each partner's particular gaps or weaknesses. Figure 11.4 shows an alliance where the strengths of organisation A (indicated by the darker shading) match the weaknesses of organisation B (indicated by the lighter shading); conversely, the strengths of organisation B match the weaknesses of organisation A. By partnering, the two organisations can bring together complementary strengths in order to overcome their individual weaknesses. An example of this is the General Motors–Toyota NUMMI alliance: here the complementarity lies in General Motors getting access to the Japanese car company's manufacturing expertise, while Toyota obtains the American car company's local marketing knowledge.

- *Collusive alliances.* Occasionally organisations secretly collude together in order to increase their market power. By combining together into cartels, they reduce competition in the marketplace, enabling them to extract higher prices from their customers or lower prices from suppliers. Such collusive cartels amongst for-profit businesses are generally illegal, so there is no public agreement between them (hence the absence of brackets joining the two collusive organisations in Figure 11.4) and regulators will act to discourage this activity. For instance, mobile phone operators are often accused of collusive behavior. In 2012, Thailand's three largest mobile phone operators bid 41.63bn baht (€1.0bn, $1.3bn) for a 3G license, just 2.8 per cent higher than the minimum price, giving rise to criticism that they had colluded. In not-for profit sectors, collusive alliances do take place and they may also be justified politically in sensitive for-profit industries such as defence or aerospace due to national interests and where the costs of development are far greater than an individual firm can sustain.

It can be seen that strategic alliances, like M&A, have mixed motives. Cooperation is often a good thing, but it is important to be aware of collusive motivations. These are likely to work against the interests of other competitors, customers and suppliers.

11.4.3 Strategic alliance processes

Like M&A, strategic alliances need to be understood as processes unfolding over time. Many alliances are relatively short lived although there are examples of some which last for very long periods indeed. For example, General Electric (USA) and SNECMA (France) have been partners since 1974 in a continuous alliance for the development and production of small aero-engines – this arrangement has been recently extended to 2040. The needs and capabilities of the partners in a long-standing alliance such as this are bound to change over time. However, the absence of full ownership means that emerging differences cannot simply be reconciled by managerial authority; they have to be negotiated between independent partners. This lack of control by one side or the other means the managerial processes in alliances are particularly demanding. The management challenges, moreover, will change over time.

The fact that neither partner is in control, while alliances must typically be managed over time, highlights the importance of two themes in the various stages of the alliance process:

- *Co-evolution.* Rather than thinking of strategic alliances as fixed at a particular point of time, they are better seen as co-evolutionary processes.[25] The concept of **co-evolution underlines the way in which partners, strategies, and capabilities need to evolve in harmony in order to reflect constantly changing environments.** As they change, they need realignment so that they can evolve in harmony. A co-evolutionary perspective on alliances therefore places the emphasis on flexibility and change. At completion, an alliance is unlikely to be the same as envisaged at the start.

- **Trust.** Given the probable co-evolutionary nature of alliances, and the lack of control of one partner over the other, trust becomes highly important to the success of alliances over time.[26] This comprises two parts: structural (which refers to the expectation that a partner will not act opportunistically) and behavioural (the degree of confidence a firm has in its partner's reliability and integrity). All future possibilities cannot be specified in the initial alliance contract. Each partner will have made investments that are vulnerable

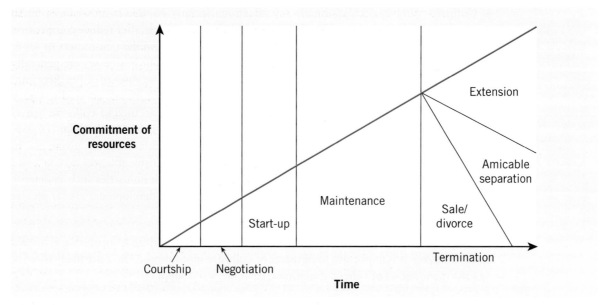

Figure 11.5 Alliance evolution

Source: Adapted from E. Murray and J. Mahon, 'Strategic alliances: gateway to the New Europe', *Long Range Planning,* vol. 26 (1993), p. 109, with permission from Elsevier.

to the selfish behaviour of the other. This implies the need for partners to behave in a trustworthy fashion through the whole lifetime of the alliance. Trust in a relationship is something that has to be continuously earned. Trust is often particularly fragile in alliances between the public and private sectors, where the profit motive is suspect on one side, and sudden shifts in political agendas are feared on the other.

The themes of trust and co-evolution surface in various ways at different stages in the lifespan of a strategic alliance. Figure 11.5 provides a simple stage model of strategic alliance evolution. The amount of committed resources changes at each stage, but issues of trust and co-evolution recur throughout:

- *Courtship.* First there is the initial process of courting potential partners, where the main resource commitment is managerial time. This courtship process should not be rushed, as the willingness of both partners is required. Similar criteria apply to alliances at this stage as to acquisitions. Each partner has to see a strategic fit, according to the rationales in Section 11.3.2. Equally, each partner has to see an organisational fit. Organisational fit can be considered as for acquisitions (Section 11.3.4). However, because alliances do not entail the same degree of control as acquisitions, mutual trust between partners will need to be particularly strong right from the outset.

- *Negotiation.* Partners need of course to negotiate carefully their mutual roles at the outset. In equity alliances, the partners also have to negotiate the proportion of ownership each will have in the final joint venture, the profit share and managerial responsibilities. There is likely to be a significant commitment of managerial time at this stage, as it is important to get initial contracts clear and correct and it is worth spending time working out how disputes during the life of the alliance will be resolved. Although the negotiation of ownership proportions in a joint venture is similar to the valuation process in acquisitions, strategic alliance contracts generally involve a great deal more. Key behaviours required of each partner need to be specified upfront. However, a ruthless negotiation style can also damage trust going forward. Moreover, co-evolution implies the need to anticipate change. In an acquired unit, it is possible to make adjustments simply by managerial authority. In alliances, initial contracts may be considered binding even when starting conditions have changed. It is wise to include an option for renegotiating initial terms right at the outset.

- *Start-up.* This involves considerable investment of material and human resources and trust is very important. First, the initial operation of the alliance puts the original alliance agreements to the test. Informal adjustments to working realities are likely to be required. Also, people from outside the original negotiation team are typically now obliged to work together on a day-to-day basis. They may not have the same understanding of the alliance as those who initiated it. Without the mutual trust to make adjustments and smooth misunderstandings, the alliance is liable to break up. This early period in an alliance's evolution is the one with the highest rate of failure.

- *Maintenance.* This refers to the ongoing operation of the strategic alliance, with increasing resources likely to be committed. The lesson of co-evolution is that alliance maintenance is not a simple matter of stability. Alliances have to be actively managed to allow for changing external circumstances. The internal dynamics of the partnership are likely to evolve as well as the partners build experience. Here again trust is extremely important. Gary Hamel has warned that alliances often become 'competitions for competence.'[27] Because partners are interacting closely, they can begin to learn each other's particular competences. This learning can develop into a competition for competence, with the partner that learns the fastest becoming the more powerful. The more powerful partner may consequently be able to renegotiate the terms in its favour or even break up the alliance and go it alone. If, on the other hand, the partners wish to maintain their strategic alliance, trustworthy behaviour that does not threaten the other partner's competence is essential to maintaining the cooperative relationships necessary for the day-to-day working of the alliance.

- *Termination.* Often an alliance will have had an agreed time span or purpose right from the start, so termination is a matter of completion rather than failure. Here separation is amicable. Sometimes the alliance has been so successful that the partners will wish to extend it by agreeing a new alliance between themselves, committing still more resources. Sometimes too the alliance will have been more of a success for one party than the other, with one partner wishing to buy the other's share in order to commit fully, while the other partner decides to sell out. The sale of one party's interest need not be a sign of failure as their strategic agenda may have changed since alliance formation. However, sometimes it can end in bitter divorce as in the Bharti–Walmart break-up with law suits and counter law suits (see Illustration 11.4). Termination needs to be managed carefully, therefore. Co-evolution implies that mutual trust is likely to be valuable after the completion of any particular partnership. Partners may be engaged in several different joint projects at the same time. For example, Cisco and IBM are partners on multiple simultaneous projects in wireless communications, IT security, data centres and data storage. The partners may need to come together again for new projects in the future. Thus Nokia, Ericsson and Siemens have had mobile telephone technology joint projects since the mid-1990s. Maintaining mutual trust in the termination stage is vital if partners are to co-evolve through generations of multiple projects.

Like M&A, alliances exhibit high rates of failure of up to 70 per cent where they fail to meet the goals of parent companies.[28] There is some evidence that prior experience with joint ventures helps overall performance especially if an alliance capability is created.[29] It may take many years to gradually introduce alliance management processes. For an alliance capability to succeed there needs to be consistent sponsorship and support from top management.

ILLUSTRATION 11.4   Bharti–Walmart break up

Co-evolution is not easy, as Indian and American companies discover.

After a seven-year partnership, Indian retailer Bharti Enterprises and US giant Walmart issued a terse statement at the end of 2013, that their ambitious joint venture was over and their retail dreams would be pursued independently. This surprised commentators as Walmart had been campaigning for the Indian Government to allow 51 per cent foreign holding in multi-brand retail.[1]

Formed in 2007, the 50:50 joint venture's purpose was to build and operate cash and carry superstores in India under the name Best Price Modern Wholesale to sell to hotels, canteens and neighbourhood stores. Twenty superstores were built jointly in major cities such as Amritsar, Zirakpur, Jalandhar, Kota, Bhopal and Ralpur. They identified store locations collaboratively through real estate consultant Cedar Support Services. Independently Bharti ran 'Easy Day', a 212-store multi-brand retail chain.

However, Bharti–Walmart had been going through a rough patch. Retail business entails high costs and narrow margins in India and most big retailers lose money. Bharti–Walmart losses increased 34 per cent from 2011 to 2012 to Rs 372 crore ($59.5m, £41.4m, €52.7m). Although the Government had made regulatory changes/clarifications, allowing foreign supermarkets to take majority ownership of local operations in a market of 1.2 billion people worth $500bn, 90 per cent of trade was still being done at neighbourhood shops. No global supermarket chain had applied to enter the market due to regulatory uncertainty and a condition that multi-brand retailers must source 30 per cent of products locally. This deterred furniture retailer IKEA, as its in-store cafés would make it 'multi-brand'. For Walmart sourcing local textiles and handicrafts might be easy but not electronics. Also some politicians were calling for reversing retail reforms – 'we don't want Walmarts to come'.

In addition, bribery allegations were aimed at Walmart. Its $100m loan to Cedar, Bharti's company, was investigated by the government as breaking foreign investment rules, that 50 per cent of investment must be in back-end infrastructure. Walmart thought it was complying, but subsequent government clarification stated this meant in green-field assets not a loan. Walmart was already involved in a global review of corruption after the *New York Times* highlighted bribery at Mexican, Brazilian and Chinese operations,[2] and India was highlighted as a high corruption risk. In November, Bharti–Walmart suspended employees, including Raj Jain, Chief Finance Officer, during an internal investigation into bribery allegations. This forced the company to put its Indian expansion plans on hold, straining relationships between the two companies. Subsequently, Bharti Enterprises made Jain an advisor to its retail division.

Elsewhere, Bharti Airtel, Bharti Enterprises' flagship operation and India's biggest mobile operator, was struggling with $12bn of debt. After a 14th consecutive quarter of declining profits, Bharti Enterprises wanted to consolidate its position and focus more on Bharti Airtel. Meanwhile, Walmart was aware of a fast-recovering US economy and rapid growth in China where it owned 51 per cent of Yihaodian, an online grocery retailer.

Ending Bharti–Walmart,[3] cost Walmart dear with a net loss of $151m. Now Walmart and Bharti are trying to grow their individual Indian businesses; Bharti investing in 'Easyday' whilst Walmart, without an ally in Asia's third largest economy, has invested an additional 13.3bn rupees ($219m) in its India operations.

Notes:
1. 100 per cent ownership of single brand retail was already allowed.
2. The US Foreign Corrupt Practices Act forbids American firms from paying bribes.
3. The joint venture termination has been hailed as a victory for Indian small traders.

Sources: 'The Bharti-Walmart breakup – where does FDI in Indian go next?' *Knowledge@Wharton;* W. Loeb, 'Walmart: what happened in India,' *Forbes,* 13 October 2015; Bharti Wal-Mart end joint venture, *The Indian Times,* 10 October 2013; S.Shankar, 'Wal-Mart paid nearly to $334m to end Indian partnership with Bharti Enterprises, incurred loss of $151m: Annual Report', *International Business Times,* 28 April 2014.

Question

1 Why did the Bharti–Walmart joint venture break down?

2 What issues should Walmart now take into account pursuing its Indian strategy?

11.5 COMPARING ACQUISITIONS, ALLIANCES AND ORGANIC DEVELOPMENT

It is clear that all three methods of M&A, strategic alliances and organic development have their own advantages and disadvantages. There are also some similarities. This section first considers criteria for choosing between the three methods, and then draws together some key success factors for M&A and alliances.

11.5.1 Buy, ally or DIY?

A large proportion, perhaps as much as half of M&A and strategic alliances, fail. Acquisitions can go wrong because of excessive initial valuations, exaggerated expectations of strategic fit, underestimated problems of organisational fit and all the other issues pointed to in this chapter. Alliances also suffer from miscalculations in terms of strategic and organisational fit, but, given the lack of control on either side, have their own particular issues of trust and co-evolution as well. With these high failure rates, acquisitions and alliances need to be considered cautiously alongside the default option of organic development (do-it-yourself).

The best approach will differ according to circumstances. Figure 11.6 presents a 'buy, ally or DIY' matrix summarising four key factors that can help in choosing between acquisitions, alliances and organic development:[30]

* *Urgency.* Acquisitions are a rapid method for pursuing a strategy. Illustration 11.2 shows how Google expanded rapidly through making many acquisitions – something that might have taken far longer if attempted organically. Alliances too may accelerate strategy delivery by accessing additional resources or skills, though usually less quickly than a simple acquisition. Typically organic development (DIY) is slowest: everything has to be made from scratch.

* *Uncertainty.* It is often better to choose the alliance route where there is high uncertainty in terms of the markets or technologies involved. On the upside, if the markets or technologies

	Buy	**Ally**	**DIY**
High urgency	Fast	Fast	Slow
High uncertainty	Failures potentially saleable	Share losses and retain buy option	Failures likely unsaleable
Soft capabilities important	Culture and valuation problems	Culture and control problems	Cultural consistency
Highly modular capabilities	Avoid buying whole company	Ally just with relevant partner unit	Develop in new venture unit

Figure 11.6 Buy, ally or DIY matrix

turn out to be a success, it might be possible to turn the alliance into a full acquisition, especially if a buy option has been included in the initial alliance contract. If the venture turns out a failure, then at least the loss is shared with the alliance partner. Acquisitions may also be resold if they fail but often at a much lower price than the original purchase. On the other hand, a failed organic development might have to be written off entirely, with no sale value, because the business unit involved has never been on the market beforehand.

- *Type of capabilities.* Acquisitions work best when the desired capabilities (resources or competences) are 'hard', for example physical investments in manufacturing facilities. Hard resources such as factories are easier to put a value on in the bidding process than 'soft' resources such as people or brands. Hard resources are also typically easier to control post-acquisition than people and skills. If Anbang's bid for Starwood (see Illustration 11.1) is entirely about real estate acquisition, then cultural difficulties are likely to be minimal. However greater 'soft' integration might pose the risk of significant cultural problems. Sometimes too the acquiring company's own image can tarnish the brand image of the target company. Acquisition of soft resources and competences should be approached with great caution. Indeed, the DIY organic method is typically the most effective with sensitive soft capabilities such as people. Internal ventures are likely to be culturally consistent at least. Even alliances can involve culture clashes between people from the two sides, and it is harder to control an alliance partner than an acquired unit.

- *Modularity of capabilities.* If the sought-after capabilities are highly modular, in other words they are distributed in clearly distinct sections or divisions of the proposed partners, then an alliance tends to make sense. A joint venture linking just the relevant sections of each partner can be formed, leaving each to run the rest of its businesses independently. There is no need to buy the whole of the other organisation. An acquisition can be problematic if it means buying the whole company, not just the modules that the acquirer is interested in. The DIY organic method can also be effective under conditions of modularity, as the new business can be developed under the umbrella of a distinct 'new venture division' (see Section 10.5.2), rather than embroiling the whole organisation.

Of course, the choice between the three options of buy, ally and DIY is not unconstrained. Frequently there are no suitable acquisition targets or alliance partners available. One problem for voluntary organisations and charities is that the changes of ownership involved in M&A are much harder to achieve than in the private sector, so that their options are likely to be restricted to alliances or organic development in any case. The key message of Figure 11.6 remains nonetheless: it is important to weigh up the available options systematically and to avoid favouring one or the other without careful analysis.

11.5.2 Key success factors

Figure 11.6 indicates that, despite high failure rates, M&A and strategic alliances can still be the best option in certain circumstances. The question then is how to manage M&A and alliances as effectively as possible.

Strategic fit is critical in both M&A and alliances. The target or the partner should suit the desired strategy. As in Section 11.3.4, it is very easy to overestimate synergies – and neglect negative synergies – in alliances as well as M&A. However, *organisational fit* is vital as well, in both cases. In particular, cultural differences are hard to manage, especially where people resources are important. Because of the lack of control, organisational fit issues are liable to be even harder to manage in alliances than in acquisitions, where the ownership rights of the buyer at least provide some managerial authority. *Valuation* likewise is a crucial issue in both

THINKING DIFFERENTLY — From acquiring capabilities to acquiring as capability

How to create value from acquisitions.

Conventional wisdom often emphasises the importance of acquiring resources and capabilities (see Section 11.3.3) in order to create value for the acquirer and to improve its future competitive advantage. Observers generally agree, however, that most acquisitions create little or no value.[31] Even serial acquirers might be expected to perform better than other acquirers, as they have more deal experience, and yet the evidence is not consistent.[32] How might this situation be improved? Research into strategic alliances shows firms with an alliance capability[33] achieve greater success. M&A researchers are therefore examining whether developing an M&A capability, an M&A function, can have a positive impact on M&A performance.

A M&A function's tasks include general strategic decisions via information gathering and analysis, technical execution including target investigation (due diligence), negotiation skills and planning for integration before transacting a deal. To achieve these tasks, the M&A function collects the firm's M&A data, defines a formalised M&A process, developing checklists and templates, establishes M&A committees and roundtables to collect and distribute information, applies accumulated knowledge to transactions and establishes a central, company-wide steering committee to support specific transactions. The M&A function may also be involved in subsequent acquisition integration. Establishing an M&A function enables a firm's M&A knowledge and accumulated experience to be captured. M&A capabilities are developed through articulation, codification, sharing and internalising M&A learning. This allows a firm to be proactive, rather than reactive, about acquisitions and act as a clearing house for potential targets. It might also provide acquisition ideas and have professional know-how for transacting deals. The value of developing acquiring as a capability is supported by recent research showing an M&A function improves M&A performance.[34]

Question

What are the arguments for and against using an M&A function in post-acquisition integration?

M&A and equity alliances. Acquisitions are liable to the 'winner's curse' (Section 11.3.4) of excessive valuation, particularly where there have been bid battles between competitors. But even alliance partners need to assess their relative contributions accurately in order to ensure that they do not commit too many resources with too little return and too little control.

M&A and alliances each raise some very distinct issues to manage. At the start of the process, alliances rely on courtship between willing partners, whereas that need not be the same for M&A. Mergers do require mutual willingness of course, but, if negotiations go poorly, there often remains the option of the *hostile takeover* bid. The process of a hostile bid is principally about persuading shareholders rather than talking with the target's managers. In M&A, a crucial issue is the right approach to *integration:* absorption, preservation, symbiosis, intensive care, re-orientation. In strategic alliances, the option to fully integrate the two partners into a single whole does not exist. Rather the task is the continued maintenance of a partnership between independent organisations that must *co-evolve*. Finally, *divesture* of acquired units and the *termination* of alliances tend to differ. Divestitures are typically one-off transactions with purchasers, with limited consequences for future relationships. On the other hand, the way in which alliances are terminated may have repercussions for important future relationships, as new projects and simultaneous projects often involve the same partners. In sum, it can be seen that the necessity for courtship, co-evolution and sensitive termination frequently makes the strategic alliance process a much more delicate one than simple acquisition.

SUMMARY

- There are three broad methods for pursuing a growth strategy: *M&A, strategic alliances* and *organic development.*

- Organic development can be either continuous or radical. Radical organic development is termed *corporate entrepreneurship.*

- Acquisitions can be *hostile* or *friendly.* Motives for M&A can be *strategic, financial* or *managerial.*

- The acquisition process includes *target choice, valuation* and *integration.*

- Post-acquisition integration depends upon levels of strategic and organisational fit.

- Strategic alliances can be *equity* or *non-equity.* Key motives for strategic alliances include *scale, access, complementarity* and *collusion.*

- The strategic alliance process relies on *co-evolution* and *trust.*

- The choice between acquisition, alliance and organic methods is influenced by four key factors: *urgency, uncertainty, type of capabilities* and *modularity of capabilities.*

WORK ASSIGNMENTS

✱ Denotes more advanced work assignments.
* Refers to a case study in the Text and Cases edition.

11.1 Write a short (about ten lines) statement to a chief executive who has asked you to advise whether or not the company should develop through M&A. Write a similar statement to a chief executive of a hospital who is considering possible mergers with other hospitals.

11.2✱ For a recently announced acquisition, track the share prices (using www.bigcharts.com for example) of both the acquiring firm and the target firm in the period surrounding the bid? What do you conclude from the behaviour of the share prices about how investors regard the bid. Which company's investors are likely to benefit more?

11.3✱ For a recently announced acquisition, or for the acquisition of Argos by Sainsbury in the end of chapter case, or Nest by Google (Illustration 11.2), explain which post-acquisition integration approach might be most appropriate in these situations and why other integration approaches may be less effective.

11.4✱ With reference to either the contested bid for Starwood (Illustration 11.1), SABMiller or AB InBev (in the Megabrew* case), the acquisition of Cadbury by Kraft (Mondelez International*), or end of chapter case 'Future proof', explain why, when the objectives are the mutual creation of value, acquirers chose to make acquisitions rather than alliances.

11.5 Which development approach is a family-owned company likely to prefer? Explain your reasoning.

Integrative assignment

11.6✱ With so many M&A failing, explain why managers continue to transact these deals? In particular, consider alternative methods for strategic re-alignment that may be available to an organisation as well as the possible consequences of a company not using M&A. Now interpret your answer in terms of all the stakeholders who may be affected by an M&A transaction. What conclusions can you draw?

RECOMMENDED KEY READINGS

- A comprehensive book on M&A is S. Sudarsanam, *Creating value from M&A, the challenges*, 2nd edn, FT Prentice Hall, 2010. For some alternative perspectives, see the collection by D. N. Angwin (ed.), *M&A*, Blackwell, 2007.

- A useful book on strategic alliances is J. Child, D. Faulkner and S. Tallman, *Cooperative Strategy: Managing Alliances, Networks and Joint Ventures*, 2nd edn, Oxford University Press, 2005.

- A book which contrasts the benefits of different modes of expansion is L. Capron and W. Mitchell, *Build, Buy, Borrow: Solving the growth dilemma*, Harvard Business Review Press, 2012.

REFERENCES

1. P. Sharma and J. Chrisman, 'Towards a reconciliation of the definitional issues in the field of corporate entrepreneurship', *Entrepreneurial Theory and Practice*, Spring (1998), pp. 11–27; D. Garvin and L. Levesque, 'Meeting the challenge of corporate entrepreneurship', *Harvard Business Review*, October (2006), pp. 102–12.

2. *Financial Times*, 29th February 2012. It is worth noting that the number of deals only fell to 41,000, which suggests that M&A is an important and constant way in which businesses adjust to changing contexts.

3. D.N. Angwin, 'Motive archetypes in mergers and acquisitions (M&A): the implications of a configurational approach to performance', *Advances in Mergers and Acquisitions*, vol. 6 (2007), pp. 77–105. A useful conceptual model of motives and mitigating variables is J. Haleblian, C.E. Devers, G. McNamara, M.A. Carpenter and R.B. Davison, 'Taking stock of what we know about mergers and acquisitions: a review and research agenda', *Journal of Management*, vol. 35 (2009), pp. 469–502.

4. This adapts J. Bower, 'Not all M&As are alike – and that matters', *Harvard Business Review*, March 2001, pp. 93–101.

5. M. Hayward and D. Hambrick, 'Explaining the premiums paid for large acquisitions: evidence of CEO hubris', *Administrative Science Quarterly*, vol. 42 (1997), pp. 103–27. J-Y. Kim, J. Haleblian, and S. Finkelstein, 'When firms are desperate to grow via acquisition: the effect of growth patterns and acquisition experience on acquisition premiums', *Administrative Science Quarterly*, vol. 56, no. 1 (2011), pp. 26–60.

6. C.M. Christensen, R. Alton, C. Rising and A. Waldeck, 'The big idea: the M&A playbook', *Harvard Business Review*, vol. 89, no. 3 (2011) reference a number of studies showing high failure rates in acquisitions. The study by S.B. Moeller, F.P. Schlingemann and R.M. Stultz, 'Wealth destruction on a massive scale: a study of acquiring firm returns in the recent merger wave', *Journal of Finance*, vol. LX, no. 2 (2005), pp. 757–82, suggests greater performance variation based on timing and size effects.

7. This builds on D. Jemison and S. Sitkin, 'Corporate acquisitions: a process perspective', *Academy of Management Review*, vol. 11, no. 1 (1986), pp. 145–63.

8. J.M. Shaver, 'A paradox of synergy: contagion and capacity effects in mergers and acquisitions', *Academy of Management Review*, vol. 31, no. 4 (2006), pp. 962–78.

9. See J. Child, D. Faulkner and R. Pitkethly, *The Management of International Acquisitions*, Oxford University Press, 2001.

10. A useful discussion of valuation methods in acquisitions is in Chapter 9 of D. Sadtler, D. Smith and A. Campbell, *Smarter Acquisitions*, Prentice Hall, 2008.

11. N. Varaiya and K. Ferris, 'Overpaying in corporate takeovers: the winner's curse', *Financial Analysts Journal*, vol. 43, no. 3 (1987), pp. 64–70.

12. P. Haspeslagh and D. Jemison, *Managing Acquisitions: Creating Value through Corporate Renewal*, Free Press, 1991; P. Puranam, H. Singh and S. Chaudhuri, 'Integrating acquired capabilities: when structural integration is (un)necessary', *Organization Science*, vol. 20, no. 2 (2009), pp. 313–28.

13. G. Stahl and A. Voigt, 'Do cultural differences matter in mergers and acquisitions? A tentative model and examination', *Organization Science*, vol. 19, no. 1 (2008), pp. 160–78.

14. D.N. Angwin and M. Meadows, 'New integration strategies for post acquisition management', *Long Range Planning*, vol. 15, August (2015), pp. 235–51.

15. D.N. Angwin and M. Meadows, 'The choice of insider or outsider top executives in acquired companies', *Long Range Planning*, vol. 37 (2009), pp. 239–57.

16. D.N. Angwin and M. Meadows, 'Acquiring poorly performing companies during recession', *Journal of General Management*, vol. 38, no. 1 (2012), pp. 1–22.

17. K. Ellis, T. Reus and B. Lamont, 'The effects of procedural and informational justice in the integration of related acquisitions', *Strategic Management Journal*, vol. 30 (2009), pp. 137–61.

18. A. Nadolska and Harry G. Barkema, 'Good learners: how top management teams affect the success and frequency of acquisitions', *Strategic Management Journal*, vol. 35, no. 10 (2014), pp. 1483–507.

19. R. Uhlaner and A. West, 'Running a winning M&A shop', *McKinsey Quarterly*, March 2008, pp. 106–12.

20. L. Dranikoff, T. Koller and A. Schneider, 'Divesture: strategy's missing link', *Harvard Business Review*, May 2002, pp. 75–83 and M. Brauer, 'What have we acquired and what should we acquire in divesture research? A review and research agenda', *Journal of Management*, vol. 32, no. 6 (2006), pp. 751–85. H. Berry, 'When do firms divest foreign operations?' *Organization Science*, vol. 24, no.1, January/February 2013, pp. 246–61. J. Xia and S. Li, 'The divestiture of acquired subunits: A resource dependence approach', *Strategic Management Journal*, vol. 34, no. 2 (2013), pp. 131–48.

21. Andersen Consulting, *Dispelling the Myths of Strategic Alliances*, 1999.

22. Over 80 per cent of Fortune 1000 CEOs believe that alliances would account for 26 per cent of their companies' revenue in 2007–8, P. Kale, H. Singh and J. Bell, 'Relating well: building capabilities for sustaining alliance networks', in P. Kleindorfer and Y. Wind (eds), *The Network Challenge*, London, Pearson, 2009.

23. R. Bresser, 'Matching collective and competitive strategies', *Strategic Management Journal*, vol. 9, no. 4, pp. 375–85.

24. J. Dyer, *Collaborative Advantage*, Oxford University Press, 2000.

25. A. Inkpen and S. Curral, 'The coevolution of trust, control, and learning in joint ventures', *Organization Science*, vol. 15, no. 5 (2004), pp. 586–99; R. ul-Huq, *Alliances and Co-evolution in the Banking Sector*, Palgrave, 2005.

26. A. Arino and J. de la Torre, 'Relational quality: managing trust in corporate alliances', *California Management Review*, vol. 44, no. 1 (2001), pp. 109–31.

27. G. Hamel, *Alliance Advantage: the Art of Creating Value through Partnering*, Harvard Business School Press, 1998.

28. R. Lunnan and S. Haugland, 'Predicting and measuring alliance performance: a multidimensional analysis', *Strategic Management Journal*, vol. 29, no. 5 (2008), pp. 638–58.

29. P. Kale and H. Singh, 'Managing strategic alliances: what do we know now and where do we go from here?' *Academy of Management Perspectives*, vol. 23, no.3 (2009), pp. 25–62.

30. This draws on J. Dyer, P. Kale and H. Singh, 'When to ally and when to acquire?', *Harvard Business Review*, vol. 82, no. 7/8 (2004), pp. 108–15, and X. Yin and M. Shanley, 'Industry determinants of the merger versus alliance decision', *Academy of Management Review*, vol. 31, no. 2 (2008), pp. 473–91.

31. See Section (11.3.3) and N. Aktas, E. de Bodt and R. Roll, 'Learning, hubris and corporate serial acquisitions', *Journal of Corporate Finance*, vol. 15, no. 5 (2009), pp. 543–61; D.R. King, D.R. Dalton, C.M. Daily and J.G. Covin, 'Meta-analysis of post-acquisition performance: indications of unidentified moderators', *Strategic Management Journal*, vol. 25, no. 2 (2004), pp. 187–200.

32. S.B. Moeller, F.P. Schlingemann and R.M. Stultz, 'Wealth destruction on a massive scale: a study of acquiring firm returns in the recent merger wave', *Journal of Finance*, vol. LX, no. 2 (2005), pp. 757–82.

33. P. Kale and H. Singh, 'Building firm capabilities through learning: the role of the alliance learning process in alliance capability and firm level success, *Strategic Management Journal*, vol. 28, no. 10 (2007), pp. 981–1000.

34. A. Trichterborn, D. zu Knyphausen-Aufsess and L. Schweizer, 'How to improve acquisition performance. The role of a dedicated M&A function, M&A learning process, and M&A capability', *Strategic Management Journal*, vol. 37, no. 4 (2010), pp. 463–73.

Future-proofing business? Sainsbury acquires Argos

Duncan Angwin

Market analysts were stunned when UK supermarket, Sainsbury, announced it was to acquire Argos, a UK general merchandiser for £1.4bn (€1.9bn, $2.1bn). Why would the UK's second largest supermarket want to buy a company famous for its 'laminated book of dreams'[1], its plastic-coated product catalogue? Some analysts said it made no strategic sense whatsoever.

Sainsbury

Sainsbury was the second largest of the big four supermarkets in the UK with 1,304 stores, 161,000 employees and £26bn (€31.2bn, $39bn) of sales for the year to December 2015. Sainsbury held 16.8 per cent of the entire UK food retail market, with the UK's largest retailer Tesco holding 29 per cent, Morrison 11 per cent and Asda 17 per cent. In the run up to Christmas, only Sainsbury, with its relatively prosperous customers, showed sustained increase in sales in a sector which historically had shown slow growth. Although the big four dominated the industry, smaller deep discounters, Aldi and Lidl, had been winning customers at a rapid rate. With sales up 18.9 per cent and 15.1 per cent respectively, Aldi and Lidl had now captured 10 per cent of the market. Also better off customers were turning to Marks & Spencer and Waitrose (5.2 per cent). By March 2016, the supermarket sector had shown a 2 per cent fall in sales overall, year on year, as customers spent less per average shopping trip.

The decline in sales had a mixed effect on the big four. Tesco had experienced a sustained decline in sales and a massive 55 per cent fall, to £345m, in half-year profits to October 2015. However by early 2016, Tesco had begun to turn the corner, reducing a further forecasted fall from 1.8 per cent to 0.8 per cent with renewed focus on price promotions, customer service and product availability even after cutting the number of stores by 50. Morrison had also experienced a heavy fall in profits and a reduction in sales, while Asda reported its worst sales performance in 20 years as a result of the bitter price war against the deep discounters and a resurging Tesco, although managing to increase its operating profit. Sainsbury's increase in sales, its narrowing of the gap between its prices and those of discounters and cutting back on 1100 product lines, helped it maintain good performance rather than relying on a heavy use of discount vouchers, common in the sector. Although its year-end operating profits were down 18 per cent to £720m, Sainsbury's share price remained buoyant to February 2016, whilst the other big supermarket share prices had fallen dramatically. The UK food market remained difficult as food sales declined 1.6 per cent at the beginning of 2016 and the continued pressures on supermarkets caused analysts to predict the Big Four might soon become the Big Three.

In an attempt to reduce costs and woo customers, the supermarkets had embraced online shopping with mixed results. Morrison's online business had grown strongly, but online purchases across the whole UK market accounted for just 5 per cent of total sales. People didn't like to pay delivery fees, delivery slots were inconvenient and the food wasn't always fresh. Indeed for most supermarkets, online transactions were not profitable as they had all the extra costs of picking the food, packing and delivering it. Food items required different temperatures and items were often fragile or bulky making the process more difficult and costly. Also setting up grocery online technology cost tens of millions of pounds and took years to return a profit as online only supermarket Ocado found out, making profits only after 15 years.

Reflecting on how Sainsbury would continue to compete CEO Mike Coupe remarked, 'We're opening one or two stores a week for the next three years.'[2] He also agreed that 'Supermarkets had become too sterile, saying one size fits all is over. Each operator has to be different. In our case we have to be brilliant at being Sainsbury's.'[2] Sainsbury has long had deeply embedded values and goals put in place by its previous outstanding CEO Justin King. These defined the company's aims and standards of behaviour to all employees. In this paternalistic company, supported by excellent training and having won awards for HR management, Sainsbury had an embedded ethos of quality throughout its operations that meant they could concentrate on providing fresh food and great service, with the best people in the business. Sainsbury is also working on customers being able to use their mobile phones to scan and pay. Electronic shopping lists are there to encourage customers to buy cheaper, cater for allergies and to keep a running total of what is spent. What Sainsbury would not do, said Mike Coupe, is 'to use technology for the sake of technology. It has to make the customer experience better.'[2]

A new threat

While the supermarkets remained locked in a price war with no end in sight, struggling with margins and competing on protecting their profitability with supply chain, logistics and store closure programmes, a new threat loomed. Amazon had just launched Pantry – a next day delivery service which charged by the box. It was available to Amazon Prime Members for £79 a year. Although it currently only offered household essentials it was anticipated to be the precursor of a full grocery service – something it already offered in some parts of the USA. A step towards this aim occurred in February 2016 when a deal was struck with Morrison allowing Amazon customers to order hundreds of fresh and frozen food products online. This could herald a big threat to the other supermarkets as Amazon had the capacity to offer a vast range of products. However, alliances in the food retail industry were fairly infrequent and often problematic. The alliance between Waitrose and online retailer Ocado dissolved when they ended up in direct competition with each other, with Ocado claiming only a third of its sales came from Waitrose own-label products and 25 per cent from the products of other suppliers. Ocado's later agreement with Morrison was then renegotiated following the latter's tie up with Amazon.

Argos

Famous for its telephone directory-sized laminated catalogues listing over 60,000 products, Argos is the UK's largest general, non-food, merchandise retailer. With 840 stores in the UK and Ireland and 30,000 employees in 2016, it was the leading multi-channel retailer, allowing purchases of its products from a store, by website as 'click-and-collect', by telephone and catalogue ordering. Argos's just-in-time logistics operations enabled local stores to offer a wide range of products without having to keep a permanent stock of inventory. It also owned a number of discount stores in France and Poland and had recently opened 50 Pep & Co stores in the UK under the banner 'spend a little, get a lot'. Approximately half of Argos stores leases were due for renewal over the next four years.

Argos became vulnerable to a takeover approach after it reported a fall in sales of 2.2 per cent during the crucial Xmas period in 2015. In particular, sales were challenged in the highly competitive electronics market with decline in sales of video games consoles, computer tablets and white goods, such as washing machines. As a result, Argos issued a profits warning and several market commentators felt the company was in long-term structural decline.

Home Retail Group, the owners of Argos, had been turning the subsidiary around by making it into a digital retailer, where the customer offering is as compelling on small screens as big screens, where the transition between devices and stores is seamless and everything promised online is delivered. Order something from Argos before 6pm and it is delivered by 10pm that same day, any day of the week, for £3.95. By March 2016, only 20 per cent of its stores had been transformed into places where customers used iPads to choose their products rather than laminated catalogues. However, 95 digital concessions had been introduced into Home Retail Group subsidiary, Homebase, a home improvement retailer, and ten into Sainsbury and these had helped bolster Argos' overall sales, with growth rates of 5 per cent and 3.1 per cent, respectively, faster than other Argos stores. The fast track delivery service saw an 80 per cent increase in home delivery sales, and just before Christmas 2015 online sales overtook store sales and accounted for 62 per cent of Argos' revenues. Most high street retailers averaged 35 per cent revenues.

The deal

By the time Sainsbury had purchased Home Retail Group, having seen off a South Africa competitor bid, the final price was £1.4bn, a premium of 73 per cent. Homebase was disposed of immediately, leaving Argos, and cash on Home Retail Group's balance sheet and buy-now-pay-later Argos loans to be folded into the loan book in Sainsbury's Bank.

The enlarged Sainsbury would offer 100,000 products from 2000 stores, with £28bn of sales and weekly visits from 25 million shoppers. In terms of general merchandise and clothes, Argos' £4bn and Sainsbury's £2bn sales was larger than John Lewis, Marks & Spencer and even Amazon UK (£5.3bn of sales 2015). Mike Coupe said 'We can bake a bigger cake and do a better job for our customers than we can do as separate businesses' and 'Our customers want us to offer more choice, that choice to be faster than ever, driven by the rise of mobile phones and digital technology.'[3]

Realising the savings and benefits of the acquisition would cost £140m of additional capital expenditure in the first three years. In particular, integrating IT would be important. Argos did not have appropriate IT and supply chain systems for different types of foods and would Sainsbury be prepared to adopt Argos' systems for non-food retail? If two systems remained, however, the Sainsbury customer loyalty Nectar cards for instance would not work for Argos products. Nevertheless, Sainsbury said it would be able to achieve £140m annually in cost savings by 2019.

Not all smooth sailing?

For a deal of this size the Competition Commission could still object to the enlarged group being too dominant in the toy and electrical markets. If an investigation was triggered, it might delay ownership and that could damage trading, and disposals might be needed to lessen Sainsbury's market dominance.

Some analysts were openly sceptical about the deal, seeing Argos as a down-market brand, with stores having a poor appearance and insolent, poorly trained staff depressing customers. Argos had also issued a profits warning and was suffering a like-for-like decline in sales. They worried that Sainsbury's management team could be distracted by the integration just when the supermarket sector was under huge strain. Also analysts remembered the acquisition of Safeway by Morrison that hit major integration problems in terms of brand and IT. Running two IT systems in parallel heavily impacted on performance causing Morrisons to make its first ever loss. Morrisons' systems were then retained, even though Safeway's systems were better, and did not scale well to the enlarged group, causing years of problems for subsequent CEOs.

An analyst at Shore Capital said he was openly torn about the takeover. 'Buying synergies and central overhead savings seem relatively moderate to our minds and so the deal rests to a considerable degree upon revenue synergies, on which we are nervous.'[4] Mike Coupe has dismissed these concerns saying that: 'There's limited risk from an execution point of view because it's largely about property, a core strength of Sainsbury's.'[5]

Yet independent retail veteran Richard Hyman remained sceptical: 'Sainsbury's and its rivals would be better off focusing their attention on their core business: food. However unexciting and old fashioned it may seem it's the products that matter. The delivery system is a support act. There's no uniqueness there. No customer is going to buy a delivery system. It's what is being delivered which is the key. You've got to make sure it's the optimum quality and optimum price.'[1] He also says, 'In the weird world of the stock market, maybe this [deal] could put them into play, but it shouldn't. Before this deal came along I was impressed by what I saw [of Sainsbury].'[6] Maybe buying Argos is not future proofing Sainsbury?

Sources: www.argos.co.uk/about us; A. Armstrong, 'Sainsbury's Argos takeover is as cheap as a Fisher Price toy set', *The Telegraph*, 2 February 2016; J. Bourke and M. Bow, 'Sainsbury's Argos deal dashed as billionaire makes £1.4bn rival bid', *The Independent*, 20 February 2016; G. Hiscott, 'Sainsbury's takeover of Argos likely after drop in sales at high street chain', *The Mirror*, 14 January 2016; M. Lewis, 'Opinion: How could Sainsbury's best integrate Argos' technology?' *Retail Week*, 12 February 2016; B. Marlow, 'How merchandise could further derail £1.3bn "Argosbury" deal', *The Telegraph*, 20 February 2016; S. Reid, 'Which store is top of the supermarket performance league?' *The News*, 9 March 2016.

References
1. K. Hope, 'Why does Sainsbury's want to buy Argos?', *BBC News*, 1 February 2016.
2. C. Blackhurst, 'Sainsbury's Mike Coupe: "I'm not especially anxious when things don't go well"', *Management Today*, 30 June 2015.
3. C. Johnston, 'Sainsbury's to "future-proof" with £1.3bn Argos deal', *BBC News*, 2 February 2016.
4. A. Armstrong, 'Argos sales fall as Homebase enjoys a Christmas surge', *Telegraph*, 14 January 2016.
5. J. Davey and K. Holton, 'Sainsbury's bets on Argos takeover for digital age', *Business*, 2 February, 2016.
6. M. Vandevelde, 'Sainsbury's chief under pressure to deliver', FT.com, 21 February 2016.

Questions

1 Why did Sainsbury bid for Argos?

2 With reference to the post-acquisition integration matrix (see Figure 11.3) consider how Sainsbury might best integrate Argos?

3 With reference to the 'buy, ally or DIY' matrix (see Figure 11.6) consider whether the acquisition of Argos is the best strategy for Sainsbury?

COMMENTARY ON
PART II STRATEGIC CHOICES

The central concern of Part II has been the strategic choices available to organisations, including organic growth business strategy, diversification, internationalisation, new ventures and innovation, acquisitions and alliances. Although the chapters provide various rationales and evidence for these strategic choices, this book recognises that the decisions between them are often not wholly objective and rational. Indeed, the four contrasting 'strategy lenses' (introduced in the Commentary at the end of Part I) each propose very different expectations about strategic decisions. This Commentary applies the same four lenses to the issues raised in Part II, focused on strategic choices. The four lenses raise questions about how to generate the options for strategic choice, assumptions about other organisations, and what is likely to matter in the success of various options.

DESIGN LENS

The design lens places high value on extensive information search and analysis for generating strategic options. Logical, optimal choices are important. The design lens therefore recommends you to:

- *Consider all options*: strategy choices should be made between a large initial range, with techniques such as the Ansoff growth matrix (Section 8.2) used to generate options.
- *Ensure fit between choice and purpose*: preferred options should be checked carefully for consistency with stakeholders' interests and goals (Chapter 5).
- *Maximise returns*: the optimal choice is one that maximises the returns on investment, whether that is investment of capital or effort (Chapter 12).

EXPERIENCE LENS

In this view, strategy develops incrementally based on the past history and culture of the organisation and its members. So the set of strategic options to choose from is unlikely to be comprehensive and cultural factors can generate behaviours different from what might be expected on a simplistically rational point of view. You should therefore:

- *Challenge standard responses*: for example, just because a particular diversification option (Chapter 8) or international entry mode (Chapter 9) has always worked before, does not mean that the same should be done again.
- *Respect cultural differences*: in integrating acquisitions (Chapter 11), cooperating with alliance partners (Chapter 11) or going international (Chapter 9), the experience lens suggests it is very important to take account of the other organisation's history and culture, as well as more objective factors.
- *Adjust competitor analysis*: if experience shapes strategy, simple analyses of competitor interaction, as sometimes in game theory (Chapter 7), may need to be adjusted in order to avoid exaggerating the likely speed of competitors' moves or making excessive assumptions about the rationality of their responses.

This Commentary therefore reconsiders some of the issues of Part II in the light of the four strategy lenses. Note that:

- There is no suggestion here that any one of these lenses is better than the others. It is usually beneficial to explore strategic options using more than one lens, in order to get more than one point of view.
- For a deeper understanding of this Commentary, you might want to review the Part I Commentary, following Chapter 6, which provides a fuller introduction of the four lenses, plus an illustrative case.

VARIETY LENS

The emphasis here is on the variety and spontaneity of strategic options and their possible origins in the organisational periphery. The variety lens is orientated towards innovation. Thus the variety lens encourages you to:

- *Look beyond top management*: from a variety lens point of view, the strategies generated by top management are liable to be limited, so you should look more broadly for ideas about strategic options, for instance by using 'open innovation' or 'market pull' approaches (Chapter 10).
- *Learn from acquisitions and partners*: if the top has no monopoly of wisdom, exploring acquired units or alliance partners (Chapter 11) for underappreciated initiatives or capabilities might uncover new strategic options going far beyond what was planned in the original acquisition or alliance.
- *Expect surprises*: in an environment liable to spontaneous innovation, you should be sensitive to the potential for sudden 'disruptive innovations' and consider holding a strong portfolio of 'real options' (Chapter 10)

DISCOURSE LENS

According to this lens, the strategic options that rise to the surface will typically be shaped by the legitimate discourse of the organisation and the underlying self-interest of various managers. The discourse lens recognises the power of language. So you should:

- *Watch your language*: attend to discursive framing of your strategic options, recognising the emotional resonance of labels such as 'star' and 'dog' in portfolio analyses for instance (Chapter 8) and the different meanings such labels might have in various national cultures (Chapter 9).
- *Distrust others' language*: strategic options that draw heavily on apparently legitimate or fashionable discourses such as synergy (Chapter 8), innovation and entrepreneurship (Chapter 10) or partnership and ecosystems (Chapter 11) should be probed particularly critically for shaky reasoning or self-interested motives
- *Look out for managerial interests*: the discourse with which strategic options are framed may hide managerial self-interest, especially in regard to strategies such as unrelated diversification (Chapter 8) or aggressive acquisitions (Chapter 11) that often perform badly for shareholders.

PART III
STRATEGY IN ACTION

This part explains:

- Criteria and techniques that can be used to evaluate organisational performance and strategic options.

- How strategies develop in organisations; in particular, the processes that may give rise to intended strategies or to emergent strategies.

- The way in which organisational structures and systems of control are important in organising for strategic success.

- The leadership and management of strategic change.

- Who strategists are and what they do in practice.

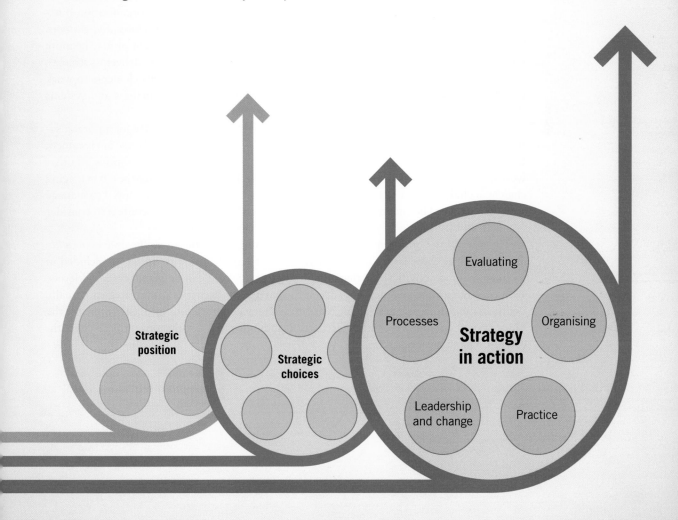

The first two parts of the book have been concerned with how a strategist can think through the strategic position of an organisation and the strategic choices available to it. In this part of the book the focus moves to strategy in action. It is concerned with how a strategy actually takes shape in an organisation and what strategists actually do.

The next chapter explains ways in which managers can assess the performance of the strategic options introduced in Part II and then evaluate alternatives. It stresses both economic and non-economic performance measures and then introduces three criteria to apply in making further choices. *Suitability* asks whether a strategy addresses the key issues relating to the opportunities and constraints an organisation faces. *Acceptability* asks whether a strategy meets the expectations of stakeholders. And *feasibility* invites an explicit consideration of whether a strategy could work in practice. In each case, tools and techniques of evaluation are provided, explained and illustrated.

Chapter 13 examines two broadly different explanations *of how strategies actually develop* in organisations. Do strategies come about in organisations through a sequence of first analysis and then implementation? In other words, do strategies develop on the basis of deliberate intent? Or is strategy more emergent, for example on the basis of people's experience or as a result of responses to competitive action? And what are the implications of these different explanations for managing strategy?

Chapter 14 considers the relationship between strategy and how an organisation functions in terms of people working with each other within different *structures and systems*. These structures and systems may be formally established by management or may be more informal relationships; but they will all affect the organisation's ability to deliver its strategy. The chapter considers how successful organising requires these various elements to work together in order to create mutually reinforcing *configurations* of structures and systems that are matched to an organisation's strategies.

The development of a new strategy may also require significant change for an organisation and this is the theme of Chapter 15. The *leadership of strategic change* is examined, first by acknowledging that managing change is not the same in all organisations; in other words, change context matters. The chapter then examines different approaches to managing change, including styles of managing change and the variety of levers employed to manage strategic change. The chapter concludes by revisiting the importance of context to consider how different levers might be employed in different change contexts.

This part of the book then concludes by discussing *what strategists themselves actually do*. It examines three issues in the practice of strategy. The first is: who gets included in strategy-making activities? Participants in strategy-making can be managers at all levels, with consultants and planners too. Second, what are the activities that strategists actually do: these range fom selling strategic issues to strategy communications. Lastly, there are the kinds of methodologies that strategists use, including strategy workshops, projects, hypothesis testing and business plans.

12

EVALUATING STRATEGIES

12.1 INTRODUCTION

In June 2015, Carlsberg, the Danish brewer, installed a new Chief Executive Cees 't Hart. He replaced Jørgen Buhl Rasmussen who had presided over continued decline in annual profits before tax, 25 per cent fall in share price and continuous underperformance compared to its peers. However, before departure Rasmussen noted that for the year 2014 Carlsberg had achieved organic net revenue growth of 2 per cent to €8.67bn (£6.9bn, $11.3) driven by strong Western Europe and Asia performance and expected it to rise significantly going forwards. Hart had to evaluate why the decline was occurring, what options were available and would be acceptable to stakeholders and which would stand the best chance of being implemented. Amongst the options Hart had to evaluate was whether to cut back on costs to protect the company from tighter regulation and recession in one of its key markets, Russia, and intensifying competition from merging competitors, or broaden its narrow geographic presence by making acquisitions in high growth markets. For Hart, there were two key questions therefore: what level of performance did he need to achieve, and what criteria should he use to evaluate his options?

This chapter is about assessing current organisational performance, evaluating different strategic options. It follows the focus in Part II on various strategic options, such as differentiation, diversification, internationalisation, innovation and acquisitions. Now it is time to consider how to judge these strategies. Managers have to assess how well their existing strategies are performing and evaluate alternatives. This chapter focuses on the use of systematic criteria and techniques for objective analysis – a rational 'Design' perspective (see the Strategy Lenses in the Commentary to Part I). Chapter 13 considers the place of these systematic criteria and techniques within the complex processes of strategy development as a whole.

In this chapter, we consider a range of organisational performance measures, both *economic* measures and broader measures of organisational *effectiveness*. We address the question of performance *comparators*: in other words, what should an organisation's performance be compared to. We also introduce *gap analysis* as a tool for assessing departures from desired levels of performance. Gap analysis can be used as well to identify the scale of the strategic initiatives, major, hard to reverse organisational commitments, that may be needed in order to close the gap between actual and desired levels of performance. The chapter goes on to propose three criteria for evaluating possible strategic initiatives, summarised by the acronym **SAF**e: *Suitability, Acceptability* and *Feasibility*, with the small 'e' in the acronym standing for evaluation.

Figure 12.1 organises the key elements of this chapter. Here managers first assess performance; next they identify the extent of any gap between desired and actual or projected performance; finally they assess the strategic options for filling any such gap. The adopted options themselves eventually feed back into performance in the future.

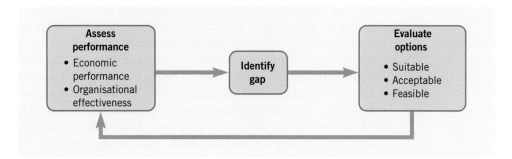

Figure 12.1 Evaluating strategies

12.2 ORGANISATIONAL PERFORMANCE

There are many ways by which to measure organisational performance, with none having clear superiority. This section introduces a range of criteria, both direct economic measures and broader effectiveness measures. It goes on to consider the various comparisons against which performance may be assessed. It finally discusses gap analysis.

12.2.1 Performance measures

We can distinguish between two basic approaches to performance: direct economic performance and overall organisational effectiveness.[1]

- *Economic* performance refers to direct measures of success in terms of economic outcomes. These economic outcomes have three main dimensions. First, there is performance in *product markets*: for example, sales growth or market share. Second, there are accounting measures of *profitability*, such as profit margin or return on capital employed (see Section 12.4.2 below). Finally, economic performance may be reflected in *financial market* measures such as movements in share price. These economic measures may seem objective, but they can be conflicting and need careful interpretation. Sales growth, for example, may be achieved by cutting prices, thereby reducing profit margins. To return to the introductory Carlsberg example, the company was doing badly in profits and share price, but the organic net revenue growth measure was more positive. This potential for economic performance measures to point in different directions suggests that economic performance is best evaluated by more than one measure. It is also why many organisations are now looking to more comprehensive measures of effectiveness as well.

- *Effectiveness* refers to a broader set of performance criteria than just economic, for example measures reflecting internal operational efficiency or measures relevant to stakeholders such as employees and external communities. One important broad measure of effectiveness is the *balanced score card,* which considers four perspectives on performance simultaneously.[2] Thus the balanced scorecard considers the customer perspective, using measures such as customer satisfaction or product quality; the internal business perspective, for instance productivity measures or project management measures; the innovation and learning perspective, measuring new product introductions or employee skills for example; and finally the financial perspective, focused typically on profitability or share-price performance. Another similarly broad measure of performance is the *triple bottom line*, which pays explicit attention to corporate social responsibility and the environment. Thus the triple bottom line has three dimensions: economic measures of performance such as sales, profits and share price; social measures, such as employee training, health and safety and contributions to the local community; and finally environmental measures such as pollution, recycling and wastage targets. For example, the Dutch brewer Heineken publishes a sustainability report[3] showing the company's standing on the Dow Jones sustainability index and lists specific social metrics for employees (reducing accident frequency, training, employee volunteering) and environmental metrics (water usage, CO_2 emissions and energy consumption). Both the balanced scorecard and the triple bottom line share a view that overall effectiveness depends not only on economic performance, but on a range of factors that support the long-term prosperity of the organisation.

12.2.2 Performance comparisons

When considering performance, it is important to be clear about what you are measuring *against*: in other words, performance relative to what? There are three main comparisons to consider:

- *Organisational targets.* A key set of performance criteria are management's own targets, whether expressed in terms of overall vision and mission or more specific objectives, for instance economic outcomes such as sales growth or profitability. Investors are particularly sensitive to performance against financial criteria such as earnings targets. Failure to meet expectations set by these targets often leads to the dismissal of the organisation's Chief Executive or Chief Financial Officer.[4] Returning to the Carlsberg example at the start of this chapter, it was probably the long-term decline in financial performance that precipitated the retirement of CEO Rasmussen and the performance of Aviva that brought about Moss's departure (see Illustration 12.1). Performance against organisational targets can be approached via gap analysis, as in Section 12.2.3 below.

- *Trends over time.* Investors and other stakeholders are clearly concerned about whether performance is improving or declining over time. Improvement may suggest good strategy and increasing momentum into the future. Decline may suggest poor strategy and the need for change. However, it is important to take a relevant time period for comparing trends: except in very fast changing markets, it is typically useful to examine trends over several years in order to smooth out short-run cyclical effects, for example. Note too that performance trends are rarely sustained. It has been shown that only about five per cent of firms are able to sustain superior performance for as long as ten years.[5] From this perspective, one predictor of future declines in performance is an extended period of good performance in preceding years.

- *Comparator organisations.* The final comparison is performance relative to other comparable organisations, as in benchmarking (Section 4.4.4). Comparators are typically competitors but, where there are no competitors, or where it is useful to encourage new approaches, comparators can be other organisations doing equivalent things (for example, a utility company might compare its efficiency in billing and customer service with an insurance company). For established companies, it is often possible to compare with competitors' performance using accounting measures such as profitability or sales growth. Again, the trend over an extended time period is generally useful. Similarly, it is possible for quoted companies to compare their share-price performance against that of specific competitors, or against an index of competitors in the same industry, or against the overall index for the stock market in which they are quoted (this is the stock market in which they are competing for investor support). A sustained decline in relative share price typically implies falling investor confidence in future performance. Note that comparison against individual star performers can often be misleading. Because financial returns are typically related to risk, high performers may simply have undertaken risky strategies, which it might be unwise to imitate.[6] The results of firms that have undertaken similar strategies but finally gone bankrupt or been taken over are unavailable for comparison.

12.2.3 Gap analysis

Gap analysis compares actual or projected performance with desired performance.[7] It is useful for identifying performance shortfalls ('gaps') and, when involving projections, can help in anticipating future problems. The size of the gap provides a guide to the extent to which strategy needs to be changed. Figure 12.2 shows a gap analysis where the vertical axis is some

ILLUSTRATION 12.1   Poor performance?

In 2012, the CEO of Aviva, a large insurance company, lost his job. Looking back from 2016, how fair were the accusations of sustained poor performance at the company?

Aviva is the UK's largest insurance company, and the sixth largest in the world. Its chief executive between 2007 and 2012 was Andrew Moss, formerly the company's Chief Financial Officer. Under his leadership, the company had expanded strongly in Continental Europe, so that the region accounted for about 37 per cent of its insurance business by 2012.

Many observers were disappointed by the results, however. On becoming CEO, Moss had declared a target of doubling earnings per share by the end of 2012, from 48.5 pence in 2007 to 97 pence. In 2011, earning per share were just 5.8 pence. Moss had begun a process of disposing of less successful businesses. Nonetheless, between 2007 and 2012, Aviva's shares steadily underperformed the key indexes of which it was a member, trailing the FTSE 100 index by 52 per cent and the FTSE 350 Insurance Industry index by 47 per cent over the whole period. Comparisons were often made with the Prudential, the UK's third largest insurance company, against which Aviva had launched an unsuccessful acquisition bid in 2006. In the period since that bid, the Prudential had invested heavily in its Asian business, which accounted for more than 40 per cent of its customers by 2012. Since Moss's departure Aviva shares have gone sideways although the £5.6bn (€6.7bn, $8.4bn) takeover of rival Friends Life has greatly strengthened its position in the UK and European markets. The table shows the two companies' sales and operating profits between the years 2007 and 2014.

Moss's departure was not only put down to objective measures of performance, but also to an alienating style of interaction with investors and analysts. One financial analyst commented: 'He was accused of being complacent, arrogant and out of touch. But in terms of strategy, what more could he really have done?' Aviva's chairman, Lord Sharman, defended his own record and that of his CEO, blaming results on the financial crisis since 2008 and disproportionate exposure to Europe's struggling economies: 'I'm not prepared to accept responsibility for the banking crisis or for the European debt crisis. Both have had very significant impacts on the company.' Was Moss paying the price for failings that were outside his control, and that with a bit more personal charm he could have smoothed over?

Main sources: Financial Times, 30 April and 8 May 2012; Aviva and Prudential Annual Reports 2015.

Note: Aviva's share price performance at the appointment of Moss fell nearly 70 per cent from 2007 to 2009, in line with competitors such as Prudential. However, since then Prudential has shown strong growth, more than quadrupling in price from 2009 to 2016 whereas Aviva's share price barely recovered at all during the rest of Moss's tenure, only then growing sluggishly. The acquisition of Friends Life injected new vigour into its shares, but now, one year later, the shares are settling back down to previous levels.

Questions

1 Comment on the measures used to evaluate Moss's performance. What measures would you see as fair and appropriate?

2 Should Andrew Moss and Lord Sharman be held responsible for their strategic bet on European markets rather than Asian markets?

Table Aviva and Prudential sales and operating profits

£bn	2007	2008	2009	2010	2011	2012	2013	2014
Aviva sales	50.2	51.4	45.1	47.1	40.6	46.6	39.3	74.0
Prudential sales	18.1	18.8	20.0	24.2	25.3	29.1	30.5	32.8
Aviva operating profit	2.2	2.3	2.0	2.6	2.3	2.3	2.3	2.2
Prudential operating profit	1.2	1.3	1.6	1.9	2.1	2.5	3.0	3.2

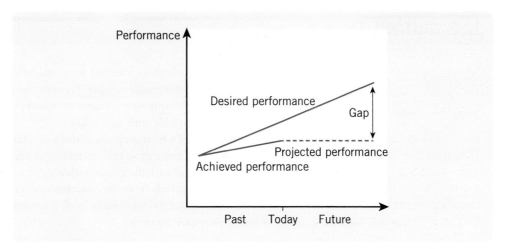

Figure 12.2 Gap analysis

measure of performance (for example, sales growth or profitability) and the horizontal axis shows time, both up to 'today' and into the future. The upper line represents the organisation's desired performance, perhaps a set of targets or the standard set by competitor organisations. The lower line represents both achieved performance to today, and projected performance based on a continuation of the existing strategy into the future (this is necessarily an estimate). In Figure 12.2, there is already a gap between achieved and desired performance: performance is clearly unsatisfactory.

However, the gap in Figure 12.2 is projected to become even bigger on the basis of the existing strategy. Assuming ongoing commitment to the desired level of performance, the organisation clearly needs to adjust its existing strategy in order to close the gap. We shall introduce a number of ways to evaluate strategic options in these and equivalent circumstances later in the chapter.

12.2.4 Complexities of performance analysis

Before considering strategy evaluation, we should underline the complex nature of performance analysis. We have already indicated how some measures might be contradictory in the short term at least: for example, sales growth can be obtained by reducing profit margins. Multidimensional measures of effectiveness such as the balanced scorecard or the triple bottom line are particularly subject to trade-offs: it is easy to see how cutting back on costly environmental protection policies might improve short-term profits.

However, there are three further sources of possible complexity. First, organisations are liable to manipulate outcomes in order to meet key performance indicators.[8] For example, organisations can defer non-urgent expenditures or book sales orders early in order to meet short-term earnings targets. These actions are attractive to companies seeking to be acquired. Second, organisations can legitimately manage performance perceptions and expectations: they are not wholly objective and fixed. For example, CEOs frequently communicate with key investors, financial analysts and the media so as to ensure favourable interpretations of strategies and results.[9] Finally, what matters in terms of performance often changes over time. For example, measures of corporate social responsibility such as the triple bottom line have become more important in recent times and, since the financial crisis, banks have had to attend more to measures of capital adequacy to prove they are secure against bad debts.

12.3 SUITABILITY

The previous section identified gap analysis as a means for considering the extent of new initiatives required to meet desired performance targets. We now turn to how to evaluate possible new initiatives using the SAFe evaluation criteria of suitability, acceptability and feasibility: see Table 12.1. This section deals with suitability.

Suitability is concerned with assessing which proposed strategies address the *key opportunities and threats* an organisation faces through an understanding of the strategic position of an organisation: it is therefore concerned with the overall *rationale* of a strategy. A suitability analysis is therefore likely to draw extensively from the concepts and frameworks introduced in Parts I and II of this book. However, at the most basic level, a suitability analysis involves assessing the extent to which a proposed strategy:

- exploits the *opportunities* in the environment and avoids the *threats*;
- capitalises on the organisation's *strengths* and avoids or remedies the *weaknesses*.

The concepts and frameworks already discussed in Chapters 2 to 6 can be especially helpful in understanding suitability. Some examples are shown in Table 12.2: other frameworks and techniques from Part I could be used in equivalent ways. However, the various techniques will raise many issues. It is therefore important that the really key strategic issues are identified from amongst all these. A major skill of a strategist is to be able to work out what really matters. Strategy is about priorities; long lists should be avoided.

The discussions about possible strategic choices in Part II were concerned not only with understanding what choices might be available to organisations but also providing reasons why each might be considered. So the examples in those sections also illustrate why strategies might be regarded as *suitable*. Table 12.3 summarises these points from earlier sections (particularly Chapters 8 and 11) and provides examples of reasons why strategies might be regarded as suitable. There are, however, also a number of screening techniques that can be used to assess the suitability of proposed strategies by reviewing their relative merits against key opportunities and constraints.

Table 12.1 The SAFe criteria and techniques of evaluation

Suitability	• Does a proposed strategy address the *key opportunities and threats an organisation faces?*
Acceptability	• Does a proposed strategy meet the expectations of stakeholders?
	• Is the level of risk acceptable?
	• Is the likely return acceptable?
	• Will stakeholder reactions be positive?
Feasibility	• Would a proposed strategy *work in practice?*
	• Can the strategy be financed?
	• Do people and their skills exist or can they be obtained?
	• Can the required resources be obtained and integrated?

Table 12.2 Suitability of strategic options in relation to strategic position

Concept	Chapter/ Section	Helps with understanding	Suitable strategies address (examples)
PESTEL	Section 2.2	Key environmental drivers Changes in industry structure	Industry cycles Industry convergence Major environmental changes
Scenarios	Section 2.4	Extent of uncertainty/risk Extent to which strategic options are mutually exclusive	Need for contingency plans or 'low-cost probes'
Five forces	Section 3.2	Industry attractiveness Competitive forces	Reducing competitive intensity Development of barriers to new entrants
Strategic groups	Section 3.4	Attractiveness of groups Mobility barriers Strategic spaces	Need to reposition to a more attractive group or to an available strategic space
Strategic resources and capabilities	Section 4.2	Industry threshold standards Bases of competitive advantage	Eliminating weaknesses Exploiting strengths
Value chain	Section 4.4	Opportunities for vertical integration or outsourcing	Extent of vertical integration or possible outsourcing
Cultural web	Section 6.3	The links between organisational culture and the current strategy	The strategic options most aligned with the prevailing culture

Table 12.3 Some examples of suitability

Strategic option	Why this option might be suitable in terms of:	
	Macro, industry and sector environments	Resources and capabilities
Directions		
Retrenchment	Withdraw from declining markets Maintain market share	Identify and focus on established strengths
Market penetration	Gain market share for advantage	Exploit superior resources and capabilities
New products and services	Exploit knowledge of customer needs	Exploit R&D
Market development	Current markets saturated New opportunities for: geographical spread, entering new segments or new uses	Exploit current products and capabilities
Diversification	Current markets saturated or declining; new opportunities for expansion beyond core businesses	Exploit strategic capabilities in new arenas
Methods		
Organic diversification	Partners or acquisitions not available or not suitable	Building on own capabilities Learning and competence development
Merger/acquisition	Speed Supply/demand	Acquire capabilities Scale and scope economies
Alliance	Speed Industry norm Required for market entry	Complementary capabilities Learning from partners

ILLUSTRATION 12.2   'Refreshing' Heineken

Selecting the most suitable strategic option through ranking.

Dutch brewing giant Heineken, the world's third largest brewer, faced many challenges in 2016. The world beer market was slowing down with the rise of alternative beverages, tighter regulations and global economic slowdown. Craft beers were also on the rise. Nevertheless the developing countries still offered significant growth opportunities – areas in which Heineken was already strong. Heineken was also threatened by AB InBev's bid for SABMiller that would create the world's largest brewer (three times Heineken's size with much higher margins). Heineken's controlling family was fiercely protective of the company's heritage and believed growth and value could continue for shareholders. Nevertheless, how could Heineken 'refresh' its strategy?

Heineken could grow organically, increasing marketing at premier sports events to complement its promotion of world-class tennis at the US Open and Wimbledon. A second option might be to expand its cider and Weiss beer production and distribute globally to address new consumer tastes. Neither option though might be sufficient to compete against a new industry giant. Option three could be to merge with family-owned Carlsberg, fourth largest brewer in the world. A merger would result in 40 per cent of the European market, significantly strengthen their combined Asian presence and build on their joint venture, and achieve sourcing and operations synergies. Although Carlsberg might not be so expensive due to recent poor performance, a merger might not address the rise in beer alternatives and be acceptable to the Carlsberg family. Option four, to merge with Diageo, would give access to a wide range of liquors, spirits and whisky to complement Heineken's beers and provide opportunities in the new mixed drinks sector. However, there could be

ownership concerns as Diageo was twice Heineken's size. This would be less of a problem with a fifth option, merging with Moulson Coors, that would play to Heineken's strengths in brewing and greatly strengthen its US presence with synergies in supply, logistics and distribution. But this would not address the market slowdown or the rise of craft brewers. Option six therefore might be to invest in craft brewers. Heineken could supply capital and distribution as well as brewing know-how. It would keep Heineken close to consumer trends and possibly provide new products. However, this might take time and also being associated with Heineken might make a craft brewer immediately lose their status. It might also set back Heineken's industry-leading efforts in corporate sustainability.

The table opposite relates each strategic option to key strategic factors from a SWOT analysis (see Section 4.4.5). A tick indicates addressing a strategic option (favourable), otherwise an 'x' means unfavourable, or a '?', uncertain. The final column sums the ticks and subtracts the 'x's to indicate a net level of option suitability that can be then ranked. Options can be further debated against the SWOT analysis and then attention can focus upon the most favoured ones in terms of acceptability and feasibility.

Strategic options	Key strategic factors							Ranking
	Slowing global market growth rate	High developing country growth	Creation of AB InBev SABMiller giant	Consumers shifting to craft beers in mature markets	Fit with technical competencies	Fits with sector know-how	Builds on reputation for corporate sustainability	
Grow Heineken Premium beer	?	√	x	x	√	√	√	4-2 (B)
Introduce cider and Weiss beer	√	?	?	√	√	?	?	3-0 (A)
Merge with Carlsberg	√	√	√	x	√	√	?	5-1(A)
Merge with Diageo	√	√	√	√	x	?	?	4-1 (A)
Acquire Moulson Coors (US)	x	√	√	x	√	√	?	4-2 (B)
Fund local craft beers	?	?	x	√	?	?	x	1-2 (C)

√ = favourable x = unfavourable ? = uncertain

A = most favourable, B = possible, C= unsuitable.

Sources: Business Insider, 17 September 2015; Bloomberg, 16 September 2015; *New York Times,* 8 October 2015; http://www.diageo.com; www.theheinekencompany.com/about-us/company-strategy; *Wall Street Journal,* 23 September 2015.

Questions

1 Are there other options or factors Heineken should consider?

2 How could you improve the ranking analysis?

3 Consider the most favoured option in terms of acceptability and feasibility criteria.

12.3.1 Ranking

Here possible strategies are assessed against key factors relating to the strategic position of the organisation and a score (or ranking) established for each option. Illustration 12.2 gives an example. One of the advantages of this approach is that it forces a debate about the implications and impacts of specific key factors on specific strategic proposals. Ranking therefore helps overcome the unconscious biases of each individual manager.

More sophisticated approaches to ranking can assign weightings to factors in recognition that some will be of more importance in the evaluation than others. It should, however, be remembered that assigning numbers, of itself, is not a basis of evaluation; any scoring or weighting is only a reflection of the quality of the analysis and debate that goes into the scoring.

A similar approach can be adopted in relation to examining proposed strategies in terms of the responses of competitors. Section 7.3.3 on game theory emphasised that the viability of a strategy should take into account how competitors might react to a particular strategy. Ranking can be used for this purpose. Each proposed strategy is considered in terms of how competitors might respond. In effect, the key factors are the key competitors' potential responses. Suitability is assessed in terms of which proposed strategy would be most likely to be minimise or blunt adverse competitor responses.

12.3.2 Screening through scenarios

Here strategic options are considered against a range of future scenarios (see Section 2.4). This is especially useful where a high degree of uncertainty exists. Suitable options are ones that make sense in terms of the various scenarios. As a result of such analysis it may be that several strategic options need to be 'kept open', perhaps in the form of contingency plans. Or it could be that an option being considered is found to be suitable in different scenarios. Indeed, a criterion of strategy evaluation for the energy company Shell is that a chosen strategy needs to be suitable in terms of a range of different crude oil prices.

One of the other advantages of screening through scenarios is that, as managers screen the possible strategies in terms of the different scenarios, they come to see which would be most suitable in different environmental contexts. This can then sensitise managers to the need for changes in strategy, or changes in strategic emphasis, given changes in the environment.

12.3.3 Screening for bases of competitive advantage

One of the key issues in evaluating a strategy is whether it is likely to draw on the organisation's bases of competitive advantage. Quite possibly the factors relating to this may already have been built into the ranking exercises explained above. However, if they have not, then it may be sensible to consider this question specifically.

As Chapter 4 shows, the likely bases of competitive advantage reside in the strategic resources and capabilities of an organisation. Screening for bases of competitive advantage therefore requires an analysis of how the proposed strategy is underpinned by resources and capabilities that satisfy the VRIO criteria:

- *Value.* Does the strategy provide value to customers? One test of this is whether the strategy would command a premium price in the marketplace. Alternatively, the strategic capabilities should support a cost advantage.
- *Rarity.* Does the strategy draw on assets that are sufficiently rare to prevent rapid copying by competitors?

- *Inimitability.* If the required assets are not rare, is the strategy sufficiently complex or non-transparent to be difficult for competitors to imitate (or substitute)?
- *Organisational support.* If the strategy is hard to imitate, does the organisation have in place the organisational means actually to implement the strategy (see also the discussion of *Feasibility* in Section 12.5) ?

The various strategic options can be compared systematically against these four VRIO criteria in a simple matrix, with the options as horizontal rows and the individual VRIO criteria as columns.

12.3.4 Decision trees

*Decision tree*s can also be used to assess strategic options against a list of key factors. Here options are 'eliminated' and preferred options emerge by progressively introducing requirements that must be met (such as growth, investment or diversity). Illustration 12.3 provides an example. The end point of the decision tree is a number of discrete development opportunities. The elimination process is achieved by identifying a few key elements or criteria that possible strategies need to achieve. In Illustration 12.3 these are growth, investment and diversification. As the illustration shows, choosing growth as an important requirement of a future strategy ranks options 1–4 more highly than 5–8. At the second step, the need for low investment strategies would rank options 3 and 4 above 1 and 2; and so on. The danger here is that the choice at each branch on the tree can tend to be simplistic. For example, as the illustration points out, answering 'yes' or 'no' to diversification does not allow for the wide variety of options that might exist within this strategy.

12.3.5 Life cycle analysis

A *life cycle analysis* assesses whether a strategy is likely to be appropriate given the stage of the industry life cycle (Section 3.3.2). Table 12.4 shows a matrix with two dimensions. The industry situation is described in five stages, from development to decline. The competitive position has three categories ranging from weak to strong. The purpose of the matrix is to establish the appropriateness of particular strategies in relation to these two dimensions. The consultancy firm Arthur D. Little suggests a number of criteria for establishing where an organisation is positioned on the matrix and what types of strategy are most likely to be suitable:

- *Strong competitive position.* Generally strong competitors should consider aggressive strategies throughout the life cycle. Early on, that implies rapid growth, for instance reinforcing cost advantages through experience curve effects, or extending advantages by broadening scope. Later on, strong competitors may take advantage of their relative strength to drive out weaker competitors by aggressive pricing or innovation, plus acquisitions where appropriate. In maturity, harvesting any weaker activities in the portfolio – through closure or perhaps sale – becomes important. Investment in innovation and differentiation may be less important. In the final stage, strong competitors might aim to be the last remaining player, leaving them the chance to exploit market power through high prices.
- *Middling competitive position.* Early in the life cycle, middling competitors should generally be considering urgent steps to either strengthen their overall position (perhaps by mergers or alliances) or to find a relatively protected niche. Later on, competitors still with

ILLUSTRATION 12.3	A strategic decision tree for a law firm

Decision trees evaluate future options by progressively eliminating others as additional criteria are introduced to the evaluation.

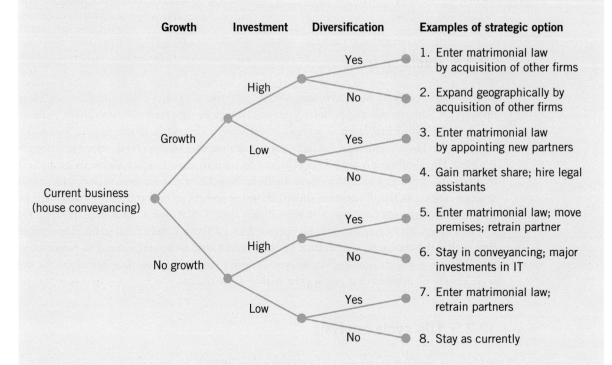

A law firm had most of its work related to house conveyancing (the legal aspects of buying property) where profits had been significantly squeezed. Therefore, it wanted to consider a range of new strategies for the future. Using a strategic decision tree it was able to eliminate certain options by identifying a few key criteria which future developments would incorporate, such as growth, investment (in premises, IT systems or acquisitions) and diversification (for example, into matrimonial law which, in turn, often brings house conveyancing work as families 'reshape').

Analysis of the decision tree reveals that if the partners of the firm wish growth to be an important aspect of future strategies, options 1–4 are ranked more highly than options 5–8. At the second step, the need for low-investment strategies would rank options 3 and 4 above 1 and 2, and so on.

The partners were aware that this technique has limitations in that the choice at each branch of the tree can tend to be simplistic. Answering 'yes' or 'no'

to diversification does not allow for the wide variety of alternatives which might exist between these two extremes, for example *adapting the 'style' of the conveyancing service* (this could be an important variant of options 6 or 8). Nevertheless, as a starting point for evaluation, the decision tree provided a useful framework.

Questions

1 Try reversing the sequence of the three parameters (to diversification, investment and growth) and redraw the decision tree. Do the same eight options still emerge?

2 Add a fourth parameter to the decision tree. This new parameter is development by *internal methods* or by *acquisition*. List your 16 options in the right-hand column.

Table 12.4 The industry life cycle/portfolio matrix

Competitive position	Stages of industry life cycle				
	Development	**Growth**	**Shake-out**	**Mature**	**Decline**
Strong	Fast growth	Attain cost leadership Differentiate Broaden scope	Reinforce cost and differentiation advantages Drive out weaker competitors by innovation or price wars Acquire weaker competitors	Consolidate industry through acquisitions Harvest weaker activities Cut unnecessary costs (e.g. differentiation or innovation)	Drive out remaining competitors Exploit market power Cut unnecessary costs
Middling	Fast growth Differentiate Focus	Catch up Differentiate Focus Find niche	Harvest weaker activities Seek alliances or mergers	Retrench Turnaround Seek alliances or mergers Exit by sale	Seek alliances or mergers Exit by sale or closure
Weak	Find niche Catch up	Turnaround Retrench Seek alliances, mergers or acquirers	Seek alliances, mergers or acquirers Exit	Seek alliances, mergers or acquirers Exit	Seek alliances, mergers or acquirers Exit

Source: Adapted from Arthur D. Little.

a middling position should take seriously the option of selling the business to a stronger rival, one with 'parenting advantage' for example (see Chapter 8).

● *Weak competitive position.* For those competitors with a weak competitive position, the options facing middling competitors are accelerated. If weak competitors cannot rapidly transform their position or find a protected niche, they should promptly consider closure or sale to a stronger competitor.

Whilst this matrix is of use in providing general guidance for evaluating possible strategies over the life cycle, it does not, of itself, provide directive answers. Each organisation must make decisions on their own merits according to its precise individual circumstances. Organisations should beware too that the life-cycle stages are not irreversible. Industries can 'de-mature', so that investments in innovation and differentiation, for example, can again become highly important.

12.4 ACCEPTABILITY

Acceptability is concerned with **whether the expected performance outcomes of a proposed strategy meet the expectations of stakeholders.** These can be of three types, the '3 Rs': *Risk, Return and stakeholder Reactions.* It is sensible to use more than one approach in assessing the acceptability of a strategy.

12.4.1 Risk

The first R is the *risk* an organisation faces in pursuing a strategy. **Risk concerns the extent to which strategic outcomes are unpredictable, especially with regard to possible negative outcomes.** Risk is therefore linked with outcome, return, so that a higher risk is generally associated with the chances of a higher return and a lower risk with lower return – the so-called 'risk-return trade-off'. Risk can be high for organisations with major long-term programmes of innovation, or where high levels of uncertainty exist about key issues in the environment, or where there are high levels of public concern about new developments – such as genetically modified crops.[10] A key issue is to establish the acceptable level of risk for the organisation. Is the organisation prepared to 'bet the company' on a single strategic initiative, risking total destruction, or does it prefer a more cautious approach of maintaining several less unpredictable and lower-stakes initiatives? Formal *risk assessments* are often incorporated into business plans as well as the investment appraisals of major projects. Chosen strategies should be within the limits of acceptable risk for the organisation. Young entrepreneurs may have a higher tolerance for risk than established family businesses, for example. Importantly, risks other than ones with immediate financial impact should be included, such as risk to corporate reputation or brand image. Developing a good understanding of an organisation's strategic position (Part I of this book) is at the core of good risk assessment. However, the following tools can also be helpful in a risk assessment.

Sensitivity analysis[11]

Sometimes referred to as *what-if* analysis, sensitivity analysis allows each of the important assumptions underlying a particular strategy to be questioned and challenged. In particular, it tests how sensitive the predicted performance outcome (e.g. profit) is to each of these assumptions. For example, the key assumptions underlying a strategy might be that market demand will grow by five per cent a year, or that a new product will achieve a given sales level, or that certain expensive machines will operate at 90 per cent loading. Sensitivity analysis asks what would be the effect on performance (for example, profitability) of variations on these assumptions. For example, if market demand grew at only one per cent, or by as much as ten per cent, would either of these extremes alter the decision to pursue that strategy? This can help develop a clearer picture of the risks of making particular strategic decisions and the degree of confidence managers might have in a given decision. Illustration 12.4 shows how sensitivity analysis can be used.

Financial risk[12]

Financial risk refers to the possibility that the organisation may not be able to meet the key financial obligations necessary for survival. Managers need to ensure that strategies meet acceptable levels of financial risk. Two key measures are important here.

First, there is the level of *gearing,* the amount of debt the company has relative to its equity. Strategies that increase the gearing (or 'leverage') of a company also raise the level of financial risk. This is because interest payments on debt are mandatory and inflexible: if performance dips and the interest cannot be paid, the company risks bankruptcy.

A second kind of financial risk measure relates to an organisation's *liquidity.* Liquidity refers to the amount of liquid assets (typically cash) that is available to pay immediate bills. Many businesses fail not because they are inherently unprofitable, but because of a lack of liquid assets, whether their own or obtained through short-term loans. For example, a small manufacturer with a rapid growth strategy may be tempted to take on lots of orders, but then find that they have to pay their suppliers for the raw materials before they actually receive the payments for the goods they have produced. Again, a company that cannot pay its bills risks bankruptcy.

ILLUSTRATION 12.4 — Sensitivity analysis

Sensitivity analysis is a useful technique for assessing the extent to which the success of a preferred strategy is dependent on the key assumptions that underlie that strategy.

In 2016, the Dunsmore Chemical Company was a single product company trading in a mature and relatively stable market. It was intended to use this established situation as a 'cash cow' to generate funds for a new venture with a related product. Estimates had shown that the company would need to generate some £4m (€4.8m, $6m) cash (at 2016 values) between 2017 and 2022 for this new venture to be possible.

Although the expected performance of the company was for a cash flow of £9.5m over that period (the *base case*), management were concerned to assess the likely impact of three key factors:

- Possible increases in *production costs* (labour, overheads and materials), which might be as much as three per cent p.a. in real terms.
- *Capacity-fill,* which might be reduced by as much as 25 per cent due to ageing plant and uncertain labour relations.

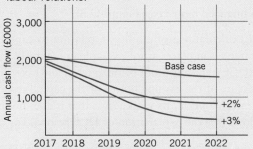

(a) Sensitivity of cash flow to changes in real production costs

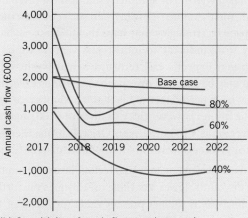

(b) Sensitivity of cash flow to changes in plant utilisation

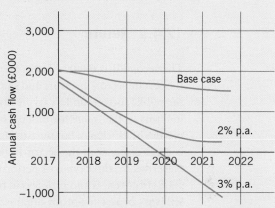

(c) Sensitivity of cash flow to reductions in real price

- *Price levels,* which might be affected by the threatened entry of a new major competitor. This could squeeze prices by as much as three per cent p.a. in real terms.

It was decided to use sensitivity analysis to assess the possible impact of each of these factors on the company's ability to generate £4m. The results are shown in graphs (a), (b) and (c).

From this analysis, management concluded that their target of £4m would be achieved with *capacity utilisation* as low as 60 per cent, which was certainly going to be achieved. Increased *production costs* of three per cent p.a. would still allow the company to achieve the £4m target over the period. In contrast, *price* squeezes of three per cent p.a. would result in a shortfall of £2m.

Management concluded from this analysis that the key factor which should affect their thinking on this matter was the likely impact of new competition and the extent to which they could protect price levels if such competition emerged. They therefore developed an aggressive marketing strategy to deter potential entrants.

Questions

What should the company do if its marketing campaigns fail to stop real price erosion:

1 Push to achieve more sales volume/capacity fill?
2 Reduce unit costs of production?
3 Something else?

Break-even analysis

Break-even analysis[13] is a simple and widely used approach which allows variations in assumptions about key variables in a strategy to be examined. It demonstrates at what point in terms of revenue the business will recover its fixed and variable costs and therefore break even. It can therefore be used to assess the risks associated with different price and cost structures of strategies as shown in Illustration 12.5.

12.4.2 Return

The second R is returns. These are **a measure of the financial effectiveness of a strategy**. In the private sector, investors and shareholders expect a financial return on their investment. In the public sector, funders (typically government departments) are likely to measure returns in terms of the 'value for money' of services delivered. Attention often focuses on financial metrics of efficiency, but measuring return for not-for-profits is notoriously difficult as there is great diversity in the sector in terms of multiple, often conflicting stakeholder interests. Nevertheless, three types of performance metric can be used: success in mobilising resources, staff effectiveness and progress in fulfilling mission. The exact specification of these metrics will vary by not-for-profit organisation.[14]

Measures of return are a common way of assessing proposed new ventures or major projects within businesses. An assessment of the financial effectiveness of any specific strategy should be a key criterion of acceptability.

Financial analysis[15]

There are three common approaches to financial return (see Figure 12.3):

- *Return on capital employed (ROCE)* calculates profitability in relation to capital for a specific time period after a new strategy is in place: as for example in Figure 12.3(a), a ROCE of ten per cent by year 3. The ROCE (typically profit before interest and tax – PBIT– divided by capital employed) is a measure of the earning power of the capital resources used in implementing a particular strategic option. Its weakness is that it does not focus on cash flow or the timing of cash flows (see the explanation of DCF below). For other measures of return see end note.[16]

- The *payback period* assesses the length of time it takes before the cumulative cash flows for a strategic option become positive. In the example in Figure 12.3(b) the payback period is three and a half years. This measure has the virtue of simplicity and is most often used where the difficulty of forecasting is high and therefore risk is high. In such circumstances, this measure can be used to select projects or strategies that have the quickest payback. Thus acceptable payback periods vary from industry to industry. A venture capitalist investing in a high-technology start-up may expect a fast return, whereas public infrastructure projects such as road building may be assessed over payback periods exceeding 50 years. One problem with the basic payback period method is that it assumes that forecast cash flows are equally valuable in the future, however risky or distant: €100 predicted in three years' time is given the same weight as €100 next year. Organisations therefore often use 'discount' methods to allow for greater uncertainty in the more distant future.

- *Discounted cash flow (DCF)* is a widely used investment appraisal technique using common cash-flow forecasting techniques which 'discounts' (gives less value to) earnings the further into the future they are. The resulting measure is the net present value (or NPV) of the project, one of the most widely used criteria for assessing the financial viability of a project. In principle, given limited resources, the project with the best NPV should be selected.

ILLUSTRATION 12.5 — Using break-even analysis to examine strategic options

Break-even analysis can be a simple way of quantifying some of the key factors which would determine the success or failure of a strategy.

A manufacturing company was considering the launch of a new consumer durable product into a market segment where most products were sold to wholesalers which supplied the retail trade. The total market was worth about €4.8m (£3.8m, $6.2m) (at manufacturers' prices) – about 630,000 units. The market leader had about 30 per cent market share in a competitive market where retailers were increasing their buying power. The company wished to evaluate the relative merits of a high-price/high-quality product sold to wholesalers (strategy A) or an own-brand product sold directly to retailers (strategy B).

The table summarises the market and cost structure for the market leader and these alternative strategies.

The table shows that the company would require about 22 per cent and 13 per cent market share respectively for strategies A and B to break even.

Questions

1 Which option would you choose? Why?

2 What would be the main risks attached to that option and how would you attempt to minimise these risks?

3 Create another option (strategy C) and explain the kind of break-even profile which would be needed to make it more attractive than either strategy A or strategy B.

Market and cost structure (€)	Market leader	Strategy A	Strategy B
Price to retailer	10.00	12.00	8.00
Price to wholesaler	7.00	8.40	–
Total variable costs (TVC)	3.50	4.00	3.10
Contribution to profit per unit sold (= Price sold-TVC)	3.50	4.40	4.90
Fixed costs (FC)	500,000	500,000	500,000
Break-even point: no. of units to sell (= FC/Contribution to profit)	142,857	136,363	81,633
Total market size (units)	630,000	630,000	630,000
Break-even point: market share (= Break-even point units/Mkt size)	22.6%	21.6%	13.0%
Actual market share	30.0%	–	–

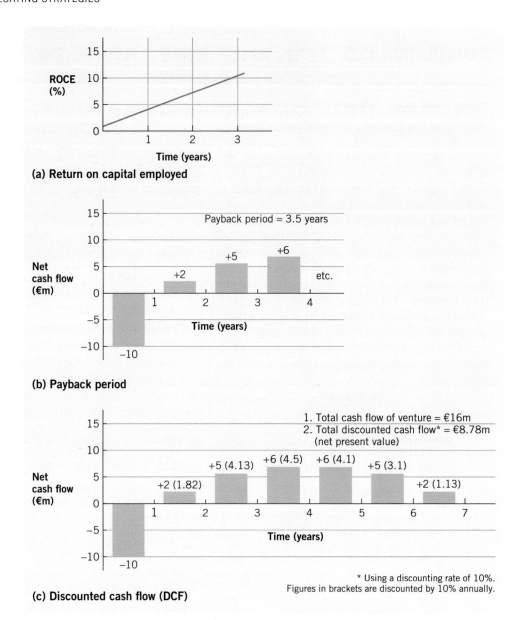

Figure 12.3 Assessing profitability

However, a DCF is only as valid as the assumptions built into it, so it is important to test sensitivity to different evaluations and scenarios. Taking the example of DCF in Figure 12.3(c), once the cash inflows and outflows have been assessed for each of the years of a strategic option they are discounted by an appropriate cost of capital. This cost of capital is the 'hurdle' that projects must exceed. The discount rate reflects the fact that cash generated early is more valuable than cash generated later. The discount rate is also set at a level that reflects the riskiness of the strategy under consideration (i.e. a higher rate for greater risk). In the example, the cost of capital or discounting rate of ten per cent (after tax) reflects the rate of return required by those providing finance for the venture – shareholders and/or lenders. The ten per cent cost of capital shown here *includes* an allowance for inflation of about three to four per cent. It is referred to as the 'money cost of capital'. By contrast, the 'real' cost of capital is six to seven per cent *after* allowing for or *excluding* inflation. The projected after-tax cash flow of £2m (€2.2m, $3m) at the start of year 2 is equivalent to receiving £1.82m now – £2m multiplied by 0.91 or 1/1.10. £1.82m is called the *present value* of receiving £2m at the start of year 2 at a cost of capital of ten per cent. Similarly, the after-tax cash flow of £5m at the start of year 3 has a present value of £4.13m – £5m multiplied by 1/1.10 squared. The *net present value (NPV)* of the venture, as a whole, is calculated by adding up all the annual present values over the venture's anticipated life. In the example, this is seven years. The NPV works out at £8.78m. Allowing for the time value of money, the £8.78m is the extra value that the strategic initiative will generate during its entire lifetime. However, it would be sensible to undertake a sensitivity analysis, for example by assuming different levels of sales volume increases, or different costs of capital in order to establish what resulting NPV measures would be and at what point NPV falls below zero. For example, in Figure 12.3(c) a cost of capital or discounting rate of about 32 per cent would produce a zero NPV. Such sensitivity testing is, then, a way in which DCF can be used to assess risk.

With regard to these three approaches to assessing returns, it is important to remember that there are no absolute standards as to what constitutes good or poor return. It will differ between industries and countries and between different stakeholders. So it is important to establish what return is seen as acceptable by which stakeholders. Views also differ as to which measures give the best assessment of return, as will be seen below. Three further problems of financial analysis are as follows:

- *The problem of uncertainty.* Be wary of the apparent thoroughness of the various approaches to financial analysis. Most were developed for the purposes of investment appraisal. Therefore, they focus on discrete projects where the additional cash inflows and outflows can be predicted with relative certainty: for example, a retailer opening a new store has a good idea about likely turnover based on previous experience of similar stores in similar areas. Such assumptions are not necessarily valid in many strategic contexts because the outcomes are much less certain. It is as strategy implementation proceeds (with the associated cash-flow consequences) that outcomes become clearer (see the discussion of 'real options' below).

- *The problem of specificity.* Financial appraisals tend to focus on direct *tangible* costs and benefits rather than the strategy more broadly. However, it is often not easy to identify such costs and benefits, or the cash flows specific to a proposed strategy, since it may not be possible to isolate them from other ongoing business activities. Moreover, such costs and benefits may have spillover effects. For example, a new product may look unprofitable as a single project. But it may make strategic sense by enhancing the market acceptability of other products in a company's portfolio.

- *Assumptions.* Financial analysis is only as good as the assumptions built into the analysis. If assumptions about sales levels or costs are misguided, for example, then the value of the analysis is reduced, even misleading. This is one reason why sensitivity testing based on variations of assumptions is important.

Shareholder value analysis

Shareholder value analysis[17] (SVA) is a form of financial analysis that poses very directly the question: which proposed strategies would most increase shareholder value? There are several measures of shareholder value, but two are common:

- *Total shareholder return (TSR)* makes use of share price and dividend measures. In any financial year, the TSR is equal to the increase in the price of a share, plus the dividends received per share in that year. This is then divided by the share price at the start of the financial year. A simple example is given as Table 12.5(a). The TSR measure is attractive because it captures both aspects of shareholder value: capital gains (or losses) in the share

Table 12.5 Measures of shareholder value

(a) Total shareholder return (TSR)	(b) Economic profit or economic value added (EVA)
Given	Given
<ul><li>Opening share price, £1</li><li>Closing share price, £1.20</li><li>Dividend per share received during financial year, 5p</li></ul>	<ul><li>Operating profit after tax, £10m</li><li>Capital employed, £100m</li><li>Cost of capital, 8%</li></ul>
Then	Then
<ul><li>Increase in share price (20p) plus dividend received (5p) = 25p</li></ul>	<ul><li>The capital or financing charge required to produce the operating profit after tax is the capital employed of £100m × the cost of capital of 8% = (£8m)</li></ul>
TSR is	EVA is
<ul><li>25p divided by opening share price of £1 expressed as a percentage = 25%</li></ul>	<ul><li>Operating profit (after tax) of £10m less the cost of capital, £8m = £2m</li></ul>

price as well as income in the form of dividends. However, because this measure relies on the availability of a share price, it is inapplicable to privately-held companies and can be only roughly applied to individual business units within a publicly-quoted company. It is also potentially limited as a measure of strategic success because share prices may rise and fall for many reasons outside the responsibility of the company's managers.

- *Economic value added (EVA) or economic profit* relies on accounting data but, unlike accounting profit, which is the difference between explicit costs and revenues, economic profit also includes implicit costs such as opportunity cost of the firm's capital. Specifically EVA uses the 'cost of capital' that consists of (i) cost of equity capital (required dividend and capital gain) and (ii) cost of debt capital (interest rate):

$$\text{EVA} = \text{net operating profit after tax} - \text{cost of capital}$$

If operating profit (after tax) is greater than the cost of the capital required to produce that profit, then EVA is positive. This is normally essential to securing financial support (see Table 12.5(b)). An important feature of EVA is that the cost of capital allows for risk: the higher the risk, the higher the cost of capital. Especially for risky strategies, it is quite possible to be apparently profitable while not actually meeting the cost of capital. EVA does not rely on share prices, so it can be applied to individual business units and projects within a company, with the cost of capital being adjusted according to the risk profile of each individual venture.

Although shareholder value analysis has helped address some of the shortcomings of traditional financial analyses, it has been criticised for over-emphasising short-term shareholder returns and neglecting other stakeholders – customers, employees and communities – that are important to long-run organisational survival.[18] Nevertheless, the idea of valuing a strategy may give greater realism and clarity to otherwise vague claims for strategic benefits. But firms that employ SVA are advised to do so with an eye both to the long term and to the value of the firm as a whole.[19]

Cost–benefit[20]

Profit measures may be too narrow an interpretation of return, particularly where wider benefits than organisational profit are important. This is usually so for major public infrastructure projects for example, such as the siting of an airport or a sewer construction project (see Illustration 12.6). The *cost–benefit* concept suggests that a money value should be put on all the costs and benefits of a strategy, including tangible and intangible returns to people and organisations other than the one 'sponsoring' the project or strategy.

ILLUSTRATION 12.6 Sewerage construction project

Investment in items of infrastructure – such as sewers – often requires a careful consideration of the wider costs and benefits of the project.

Cost/benefit	£m*	£m*
Multiplier/linkage benefits		1.8
Flood prevention		5.0
Reduced traffic disruption		14.4
Amenity benefits		9.2
Investment benefit		47.2
Encouragement of visitors		8.0
Total benefits		85.6
Costs		
Construction cost	36.4	
Less: Unskilled labour cost	(9.4)	
Opportunity cost of construction	(27.0)	
Present value of net benefits (NPV)	58.6	

*(£1m is about €1.2m or $1.5m)

Note: Figures discounted at a real discount rate of 5 per cent over 40 years.

The UK's privatised water companies were monopolies supplying water and disposing of sewage. One of their priorities was investment in new sewerage systems to meet the increasing standards required by law. They frequently used cost–benefit analysis to assess projects. The figures above are from an actual analysis.

Benefits

Benefits result mainly from reduced use of rivers as overflow sewers. There are also economic benefits resulting from construction. The following benefits are quantified in the table:

- The multiplier benefit to the local economy of increased spending by those employed on the project.
- The linkage benefit to the local economy of purchases from local firms, including the multiplier effect of such spending.
- Reduced risk of flooding from overflows or old sewers collapsing – flood probabilities can be quantified using historical records, and the cost of flood damage by detailed assessment of the property vulnerable to damage.
- Reduced traffic disruption from flooding and road closures for repairs to old sewers – statistics on the costs of delays to users, traffic flows on roads affected and past closure frequency can be used to quantify savings.
- Increased amenity value of rivers (for example, for boating and fishing) can be measured by surveys asking

visitors what the value is to them or by looking at the effect on demand of charges imposed elsewhere.
- Increased rental values and take-up of space can be measured by consultation with developers and observed effects elsewhere.
- Increased visitor numbers to riverside facilities resulting from reduced pollution.

Construction cost

This is net of the cost of unskilled labour. Use of unskilled labour is not a burden on the economy, and its cost must be deducted to arrive at opportunity cost.

Net benefits

Once the difficult task of quantifying costs and benefits is complete, standard discounting techniques can be used to calculate net present value and internal rate of return, and analysis can then proceed as for conventional projects.

Source: G. Owen, formerly of Sheffield Business School.

Questions

1 What do you feel about the appropriateness of the listed benefits?

2 How easy or difficult is it to assign money values to these benefits?

Although in practice monetary valuation is often difficult, it can be done and, despite the difficulties, cost–benefit analysis is useful provided its limitations are understood. Its major benefit is in forcing managers to be explicit about the various factors that influence strategic choice. So, even if people disagree on the value that should be assigned to particular costs or benefits, at least they can argue their case on common ground and compare the merits of the various arguments.

Real options[21]

Many of the previous approaches value strategic initiatives on a stand-alone basis. There are, however, situations where the strategic benefits and opportunities only become clear as implementation proceeds. For example, a diversification strategy may develop in several steps: it may take many years for the success of the initial diversification move to become clear and for possible follow-up opportunities to emerge. In these circumstances, the traditional DCF approach discussed above will tend to undervalue an initial strategic move because it does not take into account the value of options that could be opened up by the initiative going forward.[22] In pharmaceuticals, for example, many research projects fail to produce new drugs with the intended benefit. There could, however, be other outcomes of value to a failed project: the research could create valuable new knowledge or provide a 'platform' from which other products or process improvements spring. So a strategy should be seen as a *series* of 'real' options (i.e. opportunities at points in time as the strategy takes shape) that should be evaluated as such. Illustration 12.7 provides an example. A real options approach to evaluation therefore typically increases the expected value of a project because it adds the expected value of possible future options created by that project going forward. There are four main benefits of this approach:

- *Bringing strategic and financial evaluation closer together.* Arguably it provides a clearer understanding of both strategic and financial return and risk of a strategy by examining each step (option) separately.

- *Valuing emerging options.* In taking such an approach, it allows a value to be placed on new options made available by the initial strategic decision. The value of the first step is increased by the opportunities that it opens up.

- *Coping with uncertainty.* Advocates of a real options approach argue it provides an alternative to profitability analyses that require managers to make assumptions about future conditions that may well not be realistic. As such, it can be linked into ways of analysing uncertain futures such as scenario analysis (Section 2.4). Applying a real options approach encourages managers to defer irreversible decisions as far as possible because the passage of time will clarify expected returns – even to the extent that apparently unfavourable strategies might prove viable at a later date.

- *Offsetting conservatism.* One problem with financial analyses such as DCF is that high hurdle or discount rates set to reflect risk and uncertainty mean that ambitious but uncertain projects (and strategies) tend not to receive support. The real options approach, on the other hand, tends to give a higher value to more ambitious strategies. There have, therefore, been calls to employ real options together with more traditional financial evaluation such as DCF. In effect DCF provides the cautionary view and real options the more optimistic view.

Note that a real options approach is more useful where a strategy can be structured in the form of options – for example, where there are stages, as in pharmaceutical development – such that each stage gives the possibility of abandoning or deferring going forward. It would not give the same advantages of flexibility to a project where major capital outlay was required at the beginning.

ILLUSTRATION 12.7   Real options evaluation for developing premium beers in India

A real options approach can be used to evaluate proposed projects with multiple options.

A brewer of premium beers had been exporting its products to India for many years. They were considering an investment in brewing capacity in India. Although it was envisaged that, initially, this would take the form of brewing standard products locally and distributing through existing distributors, there were other ideas being discussed, albeit these were all contingent on the building of the brewery. Management took a real options approach to evaluating the project as set out in the figure below.

The evaluation of the proposal to build the brewery considered three options; to invest now, to invest at a later date, or not invest at all. However, the building of the brewery opened other options. One of these was to cease operating through existing third-party distributors and open up their own distribution network. Again, there were alternatives here. Should they invest in this immediately after the brewery was built, at a later date or not invest in it at all and continue through their current distributors? The investment in the brewery, especially if better distribution systems were to be developed, in turn opened up other options. Currently being discussed, for example, was whether there existed a market opportunity to develop and produce beers tailored more specifically to the Indian market. Again, should there be investment in this soon after the building of the brewery, at a later date, or not at all? It was also recognised that other options might emerge if the project went forward.

The board used a real options approach, not least because they needed to factor in the potential added value of the options opened up by the brewery.

They would employ DCF to evaluate the brewery project. However, they would also evaluate the other options assuming the brewery was built. In each of these evaluation exercises, DCF would also be used, adjusting the cost of capital to the perceived risk of the options. This would give them an indication of NPV for each of those options. The possible positive NPVs of the subsequent options could then be taken into account in assessing the attractiveness of the initial brewery project.

They also recognised that, if they invested in the brewery so as to further develop their presence in India, greater clarity on both costs and market opportunities would emerge as the project progressed. So it would make sense to revisit the evaluation of the other options at later stages as such information became available.

> ### Question
> What are the advantages of the real options approach to this evaluation over other approaches (a) to building the brewery; and (b) to other ideas being considered?

A real options approach to a brewery development

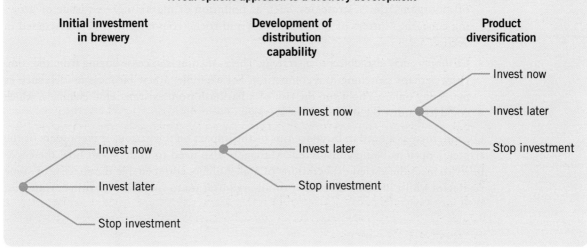

| Initial investment in brewery | Development of distribution capability | Product diversification |

12.4.3 Reaction of stakeholders

The third R is the likely *reaction* of stakeholders to a proposed strategy. Section 5.2.2 showed how *stakeholder mapping* can be used to understand the political context and consider the political agenda in an organisation. It also showed how stakeholder mapping can be used to consider the likely reactions of stakeholders to new strategies and thus evaluate the acceptability of a strategy. There are many situations where stakeholder reactions could be crucial. For example:

- *Owners'* (e.g. shareholders, including private individuals as well as investment funds, venture capitalists, private equity, family owners, the state) financial expectations have to be taken into account and the extent to which these are met will influence the acceptability of a strategy. A proposed strategy might also call for the financial restructuring of a business, for example an issue of new shares, which could be unacceptable, for example to a powerful group of shareholders, since it dilutes their voting power.

- *Bankers* and other providers of interest-bearing loans are concerned about the *risk* attached to their loans and the competence with which this is managed. They normally manage this risk through taking securities against it. A good track record in managing that risk could be regarded as a reason for bankers to invest further with some companies and not others. The extent to which a proposed strategy might affect the capital structure of the company could also be important. For example, would it increase the gearing ratio (of debt to equity), which indicates how sensitive the company's solvency is to changes in its profit position? Interest cover is a similar measure that relates interest payments to profit. Lenders will also be concerned with company *liquidity*. If this deteriorates additional loans may be necessary and the risk profile changed. So the question is: how will the proposed strategy affect liquidity?

- *Regulators* are important stakeholders in industries such as telecommunications, financial services, pharmaceuticals and power. They may have what amounts to decision-making powers over aspects of an organisation's strategy, such as price or geographic expansion.

- *Government agencies* can be important direct and indirect influencers of an organisation's strategies, depending upon national context.

- *Employees and unions* may resist strategic moves such as relocation, outsourcing or divestment if they see them as likely to result in job losses.

- *The local community* will be concerned about jobs but also with the *social cost* of an organisation's strategies, such as pollution or marketing – an issue of growing concern. Matters of business ethics and social responsibility were discussed in Section 5.4.

- *Customers* may also object to a strategy. Their sanction is to cease buying from the company, perhaps switching to a competitor. For example, a new business model, such as marketing online, might run the risk of a backlash from existing retail channels, which could jeopardise the success of the strategy.

Overall, there is a need to be conscious of the impact on the various stakeholders of the strategic options being considered. Managers also need to understand how the capability to meet the varied expectations of stakeholders could enable the success of some strategies whilst limiting the ability of an organisation to succeed with other strategies.

12.5 FEASIBILITY

Feasibility is concerned with whether a strategy could work in practice: in other words, whether an organisation has the capacity to deliver a strategy. An assessment of feasibility is likely to involve two key questions: (i) do the resources and capabilities currently exist to implement a strategy effectively? And (ii) if not, can they be obtained? These questions can be applied to any resource area that has a bearing on the viability of a proposed strategy. Here, however, the focus is on three areas finance, people (and their skills) and the importance of resource integration.

12.5.1 Financial feasibility

A central issue in considering a proposed strategy is the funding required for it. It is therefore important to forecast the *cash flow*[23] implications of the strategy. The need is to identify the cash required for a strategy, the cash generated by following the strategy and the timing of any new funding requirements. This then informs consideration of the likely sources for obtaining funds.

Managers need to be familiar with different sources of funds as well as the advantages and drawbacks of these. This is well explained in standard financial texts.[24] This is not only a matter of the feasibility of a strategy, but also its acceptability to different stakeholders, not least those providing the funds. So the discussion in Section 12.4.3 is relevant here too. Decisions on which funding sources to use will also be influenced by the current financial situation of the organisation such as ownership (e.g. whether the business is privately held or publicly quoted) and by the overall corporate goals and strategic priorities of the organisation. For example, there will be different financial needs if a business is seeking rapid growth by acquisition compared with if it is seeking to consolidate its past performance.

A useful way of considering funding is in terms of which financial strategies might be needed for different 'phases' of the life cycle of a business (as opposed to an industry life cycle): see Table 12.6. In turn, this raises the question as to whether such sources of finance are available and, if not, whether the proposed strategy is both feasible and acceptable.

- *Start-up businesses*[25] are high-risk businesses. They are at the beginning of their life cycle and are not yet established in their markets; moreover, they are likely to require substantial investment. A stand-alone business in this situation might, for example, seek to finance such growth from specialists in this kind of investment, such as venture capitalists who, themselves, seek to offset risk by having a portfolio of such investments. Schemes for private investors (so-called 'business angels') have also become popular. Providers of such

Table 12.6 Financial strategy and the business life cycle

Life cycle phase	Funding requirement	Cost of capital	Business risk	Likely funding source(s)	Dividends
Start-up	High	High	High	Personal debt; Equity (angel and venture capital)	Zero
Growth	High	Medium	High	Debentures and equity (growth investors)	Nominal
Maturity	Low/medium	Low/medium	Low/medium	Debt, equity and retained earnings	High
Exit/Decline	Low/negative	Medium/high	Medium	Debt, retained earnings	High

funds are, however, likely to be demanding, given the high business risk. Thus venture capitalists or business angels typically require a high proportion of the equity ownership in exchange for even quite small injections of funds.

- *Growth businesses* may remain in a volatile and highly competitive market position. The degree of business risk may therefore remain high, as will the cost of capital in such circumstances. However, if a business in this phase has begun to establish itself in its markets, perhaps as a market leader in a growing market, then the cost of capital may be lower. In either case, since the main attractions to investors here are the product or business concept and the prospect of future earnings, equity capital is likely to be appropriate, perhaps by public flotation.

- *Mature businesses* are those operating in mature markets and the likelihood is that funding requirements will decline. If such a business has achieved a strong competitive position with a high market share, it should be generating regular and substantial surpluses. Here the business risk is lower and the opportunity for retained earnings is high. In these circumstances, if funding is required, it may make sense to raise this through debt capital as well as equity, since reliable returns can be used to service such debt. Provided increased debt (*gearing* or *leverage*) does not lead to an unacceptable level of risk, this cheaper debt funding will in fact increase the residual profits achieved by a company in these circumstances.

- *Declining businesses* are likely to find it difficult to attract equity finance. However, borrowing may be possible if secured against residual assets in the business. At this stage, it is likely that the emphasis in the business will be on cost cutting, and it could well be that the cash flows from such businesses are quite strong. Risk is medium, especially if decline looks to be gradual. However, there is the chance of sudden shake-out with battles for survival.

This life-cycle framework does not, however, always hold. In fact it is common for companies to invest in new ventures, services, technologies to develop *new and innovative businesses* in order to survive long term. Doing this on a regular basis might, in effect, be acting as its own venture capitalist, accepting high risk at the business level and seeking to offset such risk by 'cash cows' in its portfolio (see Section 8.7). Or some companies may need to sell off businesses as they mature to raise capital for further investment in new ventures. Public-sector managers know about the need to balance the financial risk of services too. They need a steady core to their service where budgets are certain to be met, hence reducing the financial risk of the more speculative aspects of their service.

12.5.2 People and skills

Chapter 4 showed how organisations that achieve sustainable competitive advantage may do so on the basis of resources and capabilities that are embedded in the skills, knowledge and experience of people in that organisation. Indeed, ultimately the success of a strategy will likely depend on how it is delivered by people in the organisation. These could be managers but they could also be more junior people in the organisation who are nonetheless critical to a strategy, for example as the front-line contact with customers. Three questions arise: do people in the organisation currently have the competences to deliver a proposed strategy? Are the systems to support those people fit for the strategy? If not, can the competences be obtained or developed?

The first step here is the same as suggested in Sections 12.3.3 for the screening for competitive advantage. The need is to identify the key resources and capabilities underpinning a proposed strategy, but specifically in terms of the people and skills required. The second step is to determine if these exist in the organisation. It could be, of course, that the proposed strategy is built on the argument that they do. If so, how realistic is this? Or it could be that the assumption is that these can be obtained or developed. Again, is this realistic?

Many of the issues of feasibility in relation to the structures and systems to support such competence development and people are addressed in Chapter 14 on organising and Chapter 15 on leading strategic change. Other critical questions that need to be considered include:[26]

- *Work organisation.* Will changes in work content and priority-setting significantly alter the orientation of people's jobs? Will managers need to think differently about the tasks that need to be done? What are the critical criteria for effectiveness needed? Are these different from current requirements?

- *Rewards.* How will people need to be incentivised? Will people's career aspirations be affected? How will any significant shifts in power, influence and credibility need to be rewarded and recognised?

- *Relationships.* Will interactions between key people need to change? What are the consequences for the levels of trust, task competence and values congruence? Will conflict and political rivalry be likely?

- *Training and development.* Are current training and mentoring systems appropriate? It may be necessary to take into account the balance between the need to ensure the successful delivery of strategy in the short term and the required future development of people's capabilities.

- *Recruitment and promotion.* Given these issues, will new people need to be recruited into the organisation, or can talent be promoted and supported from below?

12.5.3 Integrating resources

The success of a strategy is likely to depend on the management of many resource areas; not only people and finance, but also physical resources, such as buildings, information, technology and the resources provided by suppliers and partners. It is possible, but not likely, that a proposed strategy builds only on existing resources. It is more likely that additional resources will be required. The feasibility of a strategy therefore needs be considered in terms of the ability to obtain and integrate such resources – both inside the organisation and in the wider value network. Serious problems can result from the failure to think through resourcing needs. Moonpig, an online greeting card and gift firm, experienced a severe wave of customer complaints during March 2016. It failed to honour its promise to deliver on Mothers' Day with flowers arriving damaged or delayed. A wave of complaints appeared on social media with photos of damaged goods. Moonpig apologised profusely and said it was a problem with a supplier, but its reputation had been damaged because it had failed to integrate the resources of its wider value network.

12.6 EVALUATION CRITERIA: FOUR QUALIFICATIONS

There are four qualifications that need to be made to this chapter's discussion of evaluation criteria:

- *Conflicting conclusions and management judgement.* Conflicting conclusions can arise from the application of the criteria of suitability, acceptability and feasibility. A proposed strategy might look eminently suitable but not be acceptable to major stakeholders, for example. It is therefore important to remember that the criteria discussed

THINKING DIFFERENTLY   Misrepresenting strategic projects

Financials play an important role in strategy evaluation (Section 12.4.2) and they can appear to be accurate representations of value, yet should we trust them? Research into mega-strategic projects such as the German Berlin to Hamburg MAGLEV train, Hong Kong's airport, China's Quinling tunnel suggests that many underperform badly with large cost overruns and lower than predicted revenue.[27]

For example, the £4.7bn (€5.6bn, $7bn) England to France Channel Tunnel had cost overruns of 80 per cent, financing cost increase of 140 per cent and less than half projected revenues. Millions in debt were written off for the project to survive. The UK may have been financially better off without it. Retrospectively, commentators often denounce strategic project figures as 'biased', 'seriously flawed', representing deception and lies.

Whilst blamed upon external factors such as unexpected events, stakeholder actions, or regulatory constraints, underperformance may be due to *strategic misrepresentation* that distorts the resource allocation process. It exists as persistent budget overruns and overestimations of benefits on strategic projects ought to have been reduced by now through improved budgeting processes. It cannot be blamed on 'optimism

bias', individual self-deception that results in others being deceived, as it is deliberately designed to deceive others.

Strategic misrepresentation advocates a perfect future, which is unlikely to happen, with benefits that are used to enthuse investors. Whilst Section 12.2.4 recognises that CEOs communicate to ensure favourable interpretations of strategic initiatives, *strategic misrepresentation* is a deliberate distortion of financials based on a future that cannot be realised, to mislead investors to buy-in. Once deceived into committing substantial funds, budgets escalate and investors are locked-in, with no chance of getting a return unless the project is completed.

Be careful that financials are not being used to deceive stakeholders into supporting strategic projects. Look more closely at the fundamental strategic attractiveness of the strategic option to avoid another project 'failure'.

Question

What strategic fundamentals would you consider for an option if you didn't trust the numbers?

---

here are useful in helping think through strategic options but are not a replacement for management judgement. Managers faced with a strategy they see as suitable, but which key stakeholders object to, have to rely on their own judgement on the best course of action, but this should be better informed through the analysis and evaluation they have undertaken.

- *Consistency between the different elements of a strategy.* It should be clear from the chapters in Part II that there are several elements of a strategy, so an important question is whether the component parts work together as a 'package'. So *competitive strategy* (such as low cost or differentiation), strategy *direction* (such as product development or diversification) and *method*s of pursuing strategies (such as organic development, acquisition or alliances) need to be considered as a whole and be consistent. There are dangers if they are not. For example, suppose an organisation wishes to develop a differentiation strategy by building on its capabilities developed over many years to develop new products or services within a market it knows well. There may be dangers in looking to develop those new products through acquiring other businesses which might have very different capabilities that are incompatible with the strengths of the business.

- *The implementation and development of strategies* may throw up issues that might make organisations reconsider whether particular strategic options are, in fact, feasible or uncover factors that change views on the suitability or acceptability of a strategy. This may lead to a reshaping, or even abandoning, of strategic options. It therefore needs to be recognised that, in practice, strategy evaluation may take place through implementation, or at least partial implementation. This is another reason why experimentation, low-cost probes and real options evaluation may make sense.

- *Strategy development in practice.* More generally, it should not be assumed that the careful and systematic evaluation of strategy is necessarily the norm in organisations. Strategies may develop in other ways. This is the subject of Chapter 13 which follows. The final chapter, chapter 16, also explains what managers actually do in managing strategic issues.

SUMMARY

- Performance can be assessed in terms of both *economic* performance and overall organisational *effectiveness*.
- *Gap analysis* indicates the extent to which achieved or projected performance diverges from desired performance and the scale of the strategic initiatives required to close the gap.
- Strategies can be evaluated according to the three SAFe criteria of *suitability* in view of organisational opportunities and threats, *acceptability* to key stakeholders and *feasibility* in terms of capacity for implementation.

WORK ASSIGNMENTS

✱ Denotes more advanced work assignments.
* Denotes case study in the Text and Case edition.

12.1 Identify a quoted company (perhaps a company that you are interested in working for) and assess its share-price performance over time relative to relevant national stock-market indices (e.g. S&P 500 for the USA, CAC 40 for France or FTSE 100 for the UK) and close competitors. (Sites such as Yahoo Finance or MSN.Money provide relevant data for free.)

12.2 Undertake a ranking analysis of the choices available to ITV, Megabrew* or an organisation of your choice similar to that shown in Illustration 12.2.

12.3 Using the criteria of suitability, acceptability and feasibility undertake an evaluation of the strategic options that might exist for ITV, SABMiller or AB InBev (in the Megabrew* case), Mexican NTOs*, HomeCo* or an organisation of your choice.

12.4 Undertake a risk assessment to inform the evaluation of strategic options for an organisation of your choice.

12.5 Write an executive report on how sources of funding need to be related to the nature of an industry and the types of strategies that an organisation is pursuing.

12.6✱ Using examples from your answer to previous assignments, make a critical appraisal of the statement that 'Strategic choice is, in the end, a highly subjective matter. It is dangerous to believe that, in reality, analytical techniques will ever change this situation.' Refer to the Commentary at the end of Part II of the book.

Integrative assignment

12.7✱ Explain how the SAFe criteria might differ between public- and private-sector organisations. Show how this relates to both the nature of the business environment (Chapter 3) and the expectations of stakeholders (Chapter 5).

RECOMMENDED KEY READINGS

- Readers may wish to consult one or more standard texts on finance. For example, G. Arnold, *Corporate Financial Management*, 5th edn, Financial Times Prentice Hall, 2012; P. Atrill, *Financial Management for Decision Makers*, 7th edn, Pearson, 2014.

- A classic paper that considers the relationship between financial approaches to evaluation and 'strategic' approaches is P. Barwise, P. Marsh and R. Wensley, 'Must finance and strategy clash?,' *Harvard Business Review*, September–October 1989.

- R.S. Kaplan and D.P. Norton have been very influential in a series of books providing techniques for evaluation strategy. A useful paper of theirs that examines the link between performance measurement and strategic management is 'Transforming the balanced score card from performance measurement to strategic management: Part I', *Accounting Horizons*, vol. 15, no. 1 (2001), pp. 87–104.

REFERENCES

1. This distinction between economic and effectiveness measures follows the distinction between performance and effectiveness in P. Richard, T. Devinney, G. Yip and G. Johnson, 'Measuring organizational performance: towards methodological best practice', *Journal of Management*, vol. 35 (2009), pp. 718–47.

2. R. Kaplan and D. Norton, 'Using the balanced scorecard as a strategic management system', *Harvard Business Review*, January–February 1996, pp. 75–85.

3. www.sustainabilityreport, Heineken.com.

4. R. Mergenthaler, S. Rajgopal and S. Srinivasan, 'CEO and CFO career penalties to missing quarterly analysts forecasts', *Harvard Business School Working Paper*, no. 14 (2009).

5. R. Wiggins and T. Ruefli, 'Temporal dynamics and the incidence and persistence of superior economic performance', *Organization Science*, vol. 13, no. 1 (2002), pp. 82–105.

6. J. Denrell, 'Selection bias and the perils of benchmarking', *Harvard Business Review*, vol. 83, no. 4 (2005), pp. 114–19.

7. K. Cohen and R. Cyert, 'Strategy: formulation, implementation, and monitoring', *Journal of Business*, vol. 46, no. 3. (1973), pp. 349–67.

8. X. Zhang, K. Bartol and K. Smith, 'CEOs on the edge: earnings manipulation and stock-based incentive misalignment', *Academy of Management Journal*, vol. 51, no. 2 (2008), pp. 241–58.

9. B. Lev, 'How to win investors over', *Harvard Business Review*, November (2011), pp. 53–62.

10. M. Frigo and R. Anderson, 'Strategic risk management', *Journal of Corporate Accounting and Finance*, vol 22, no. 3 (2011), pp. 81–8.

11. For those readers interested in the details of sensitivity analysis, see A. Satelli, K. Chan and M. Scott (eds), *Sensitivity Analysis*, Wiley, 2000.

12. See C. Walsh, *Master the Management Metrics That Drive and Control Your Business*, Financial Times Prentice Hall, 4th edn, 2005.

13. Break-even analysis is covered in most standard accountancy texts. See, for example, G. Arnold, *Corporate Financial Management*, 4th edn, Financial Times Prentice Hall, 2009.

14. J. Sawhill and D. Williamson, 'Measuring what matters in nonprofits', *The McKinsey Quarterly*, vol. 2 (2001), pp. 98–107; M. Epstein and R. Bukovac, *Performance Measurement of Not-For-Profit Organizations*, Management Accounting Guidelines, CMA AICPA, 2009.

15. Most standard finance and accounting texts explain in more detail the financial analyses summarised here. For example see G. Arnold (endnote 13), Chapter 5.

16. There are other measures of return including ROE, ROI, ROA and ROIC. ROE (return on equity) measures the efficiency of the firm in generating profit for each share. ROI (return on investment) shows how profitable a company's assets are in generating revenue. ROIC (return on investment capital) measures the return on money invested. ROIC above an industry's average has been used by strategists such as Michael Porter as an indicator of the success of a company's strategy. M. Porter, 'The five forces that shape strategy', *Harvard Business Review*, vol. 86, no. 1 (2008), pp. 58–77.

17. The main proponent of shareholder value analysis is A. Rappaport, *Creating Shareholder Value: the New Standard for Business Performance*, 2nd edn, Free Press, 1998. See also R. Mill's chapter, 'Understanding and using shareholder value analysis', Chapter 15 in V. Ambrosini with G. Johnson and K. Scholes (eds), *Exploring Techniques of Analysis and Evaluation in Strategic Management*, Prentice Hall, 1998.

18. M.E. Raynor, 'End shareholder value tyranny: put the corporation first', *Strategy & Leadership*, vol. 37, no. 1 (2009), pp. 4–11.

19. This point is made clear in a research study reported by P. Haspeslagh, T. Noda and F. Boulos, 'It's not just about the numbers', *Harvard Business Review*, July–August 2001, pp. 65–73.

20. A 'classic' explanation of cost–benefit analysis is J.L. King, 'Cost–benefit analysis for decision-making', *Journal of Systems Management*, vol. 31, no. 5 (1980), pp. 24–39. A detailed example in the water industry can be found in N. Poew, 'Water companies' service performance and environmental trade-off', *Journal of Environmental Planning and Management*, vol. 45, no. 3 (2002), pp. 363–79.

21. Real options evaluation can get lost in the mathematics, so readers wishing to gain more detail of how real options analysis works can consult one of the following: T. Copeland, 'The real options approach to capital allocation', *Strategic Finance*, vol. 83, no. 4 (2001), pp. 33–7; and P. Boer, *The Real Options Solution: Finding Total Value in a High Risk World*, Wiley, 2002. Also see M.M. Kayali, 'Real options as a tool for making strategic investment decisions', *Journal of American Academy of Business*, vol. 8, no. 1 (2006), pp. 282–7; C. Krychowski and B.V. Quelin, 'Real options and strategic investment decisions: Can they be of use to scholars?', *Academy of Management Perspectives*, vol. 24, no. 2 (2010), pp. 65–78.

22. T. Luehrman, 'Strategy as a portfolio of real options', *Harvard Business Review*, vol. 76, no. 5 (1998), pp. 89–99.

23. See G. Arnold on funds flow analysis (endnote 13), Chapter 3, p. 108.

24. See P. Atrill, *Financial Management for Decision Makers*, 4th edn, Financial Times Prentice Hall, 2006, Chapters 6 and 7; G. Arnold (endnote 13), Part IV.

25. J. Nofsinger and W. Wang, 'Determinants of start-up firm external financing worldwide', *Journal of Banking and Finance*, vol. 35, no. 9 (2011), pp. 2282–94.

26. These issues are based on those identified by C. Marsh, P. Sparrow, M. Hird, S. Balain and A. Hesketh (2009) 'Integrated organization design: the new strategic priority for HR directors', in P.R. Sparrow, A. Hesketh, C. Cooper and M. Hird (eds), *Leading HR*, London, Palgrave Macmillan.

27. This is based upon G. Winch, *Managing Construction Projects*, Oxford, Blackwell Wiley, 2010, and I. Dichev, J. Graham, C.R. Harvey and S. Rajgopal, 'The misrepresentation of earnings', *Financial Analysts Journal*, vol. 72, no. 1 (2016), forthcoming.

CASE EXAMPLE

ITV: DIY, buy or ally?
Duncan Angwin

In 2016, ITV was the UK's largest commercial broadcaster and second only in size to the BBC, a public-sector organisation. ITV produced creative content and broadcasting for different audience targeted channels. Capitalised at £9.6bn (€11.5bn, $14.4bn), the main source of ITV's revenue came from advertisers buying slots to air their advertisements on its channels. Revenues had increased steadily over the five years to 2015, to £2.972bn, a 15 per cent year-on-year improvement, and pre-tax profits to £810m, but ITV was now facing challenges. The television advertising market had become saturated, and new online media was proving attractive to advertisers as viewing habits among the younger generation were changing. There was also the possibility of changes to UK legislation. ITV needed to develop a strategy to address these issues.

ITV's market position

Prior to 2016, ITV had gained its position as the UK's largest commercial broadcaster through a unique blend of content, broadcasting reach and advertising power (see Figure 1). As an integrated producer/broadcaster ITV created value from world-class content that it developed, owned and distributed around the world. The scale of its free and pay platforms and its £1bn annual investment in its programme budget attracted commercial audiences that drove its advertising revenue. It had increased its lead over its main competitors with more than double the TV advertising revenue of public-sector broadcasters (£650m) and Channel 4/S4C (£450m) in 2015, although TV accounted for just over 24 per cent of UK advertising spend and was growing at three per cent per annum whilst digital media attracted just over 50 per cent of advertising spend and this was growing at an annual rate of 9.5 per cent.

ITV attributed its success to the provision of high-quality content as it attracted a high volume of viewers and this enticed advertisers to place their adverts on their channels. Some of ITV's drama and reality shows were already more popular than the BBC with *Downton Abbey* beating *Sherlock* and *Doctor Who*.

It also invested significantly in acquiring intellectual property rights and financed productions on and off ITV to gain global distribution rights. As the UK's biggest marketing platform its channels also enabled it to showcase its own content that could then be sold internationally. As the demand for proven content continued to grow, ITV has been diversifying and driving new revenue streams.

ITV had developed its own online platform in 2007 called ITV Player. Although it had attracted viewers, it was ranked just 8th in the UK in 2015, a long way behind YouTube which dominated the digital services market and the strong number two in the industry BBC iPlayer.

As well as developing its online and pay revenue, it built a global network in the development, production and distribution of content. Through investment in creative pipeline and strategic acquisitions in key creative markets, such as the acquisition of Talpa Media B.V. for £796m that produced *The Voice*, *I Love My Country* and *Dating in the Dark*, it was building scale in its international content business, exploiting programmes and formats that travel.

ITV's resources and capabilities

ITV's strategic assets were high-quality content (ITV Studios), brand and excellent creative, commercial and operational people. In terms of financial performance, revenue from ITV

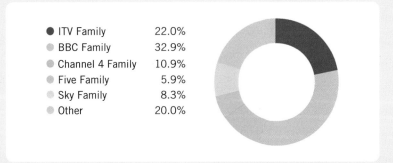

● ITV Family	22.0%
● BBC Family	32.9%
● Channel 4 Family	10.9%
● Five Family	5.9%
● Sky Family	8.3%
● Other	20.0%

Figure 1 The UK television viewing share 2014
Source: BARB.

studios had increased 384 per cent from 2009 to 2014 with 109 percent growth 2013–14 (see Figure 2).

This was driven through purchased international and content and organic productions. International distribution and pay TV also continued to grow but broadcasting and online remained the main source of revenue in 2015 (see Table 1). These supported a strong balance sheet that generated free cash flow of £0.5bn (2015).

In terms of other resources, ITV owned a large content library of 40,000 hours and operated eight network channels, more than any other UK commercial network. Its strong financial resources and large viewing numbers gave it considerable power in winning licences to show live functions and sports events. Investing in a portfolio of channels and digital assets to reach all demographics also extended the brand. Human resources were supported through training and development.

ITV had world-class production capabilities and it owned several production companies and studios. ITV continuously improved their output and quality, providing 60 per cent of ITV's total channel broadcasting output. They also purchased content from external studios. Content, advertising and broadcasting were of central importance to ITV, giving it advantages over competitors such as the BBC with strong content and broadcasting variety but no advertising

and Netflix with much less content and only one medium of distribution.

Online threat

Different entertainment platforms such as online TV and internet had been growing rapidly in the UK. Traditional TV broadcasting industry still had a per annum growth rate of around 3 per cent, but the market was becoming saturated and slowing down. Over the same period, online TV viewing grew by 38 per cent stimulated by recent online video-on-demand (VOD) libraries, such as Netflix, the world's largest VOD provider with 42 million subscribers, capitalised at $33bn, Amazon Prime and Hulu.

Third ranked Hulu, a joint venture with nine million subscribers, worth about $10bn (£6.7bn), was seen as a real threat to Netflix. Although it struggled to find quality content for distribution, its parents, Disney, Fox Broadcasting and NBC Universal, helped to some degree. Hulu had tried to set up a distribution agreement for the UK with ITV in 2010, but it didn't work out. However, in 2016 Time Warner was trying to buy a 25 per cent stake to hedge itself against Hulu's streaming service cannabalising its TV business, although the returns would be low. It would also be a source of cash for Hulu investors seeking to monetise their investment.

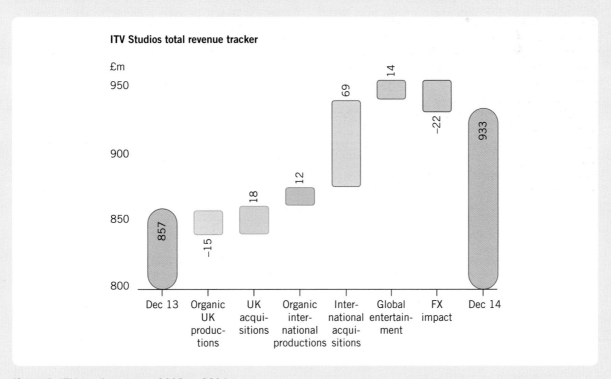

Figure 2 ITV studio revenue 2013 to 2014

Source: ITV Annual Report, 2015.

Table 1 Revenue breakdown

	Source	2015 (£m)	2014 (£m)
Broadcast and online (multiple delivery platforms)	Advertising	1719	1629
	Non-advertising	429	294
ITV Studios (international content business)	Advertising	1045	789
	Non-advertising	192	144
Total		3383	2956

Note: Non-advertising revenue includes sales of shows and online subscriptions.
Source: ITV Annual Report (2015).

By 2015, the internet (43.9 per cent market share) had overtaken television (27.6 per cent) as the biggest advertising platform in the UK. ITV lagged behind in the online content delivery business. There were many complaints and poor reviews about the ITV Platform player, and customers were choosing competing platforms such as BBC iPlayer. This was attributed to technical issues with the catch-up TV platform, ITV Player, and to some extent the advertisements shown while streaming the content. BBC's catch-up TV was superior and so ITV relaunched the ITV player as ITV Hub with new features: live TV along with program catch-up could be aired on all ITV channels so that they could be streamed for 30 days from the day of broadcasting. However, there was strong competition with new platforms from Netflix, Amazon Prime and HBO Go gaining in popularity amongst viewers in the 15–35 age group. ITV therefore considered offering advertisement-free content, for a monthly subscription fee, on a new platform which would cost around £20m to put in place. This would attract viewers who were deterred by earlier ITV online services that had advertisements. This would be a subscription-only service, and would generate income that could reach £100m in five years.

ITV Hub was only for UK audiences and the new platform would be the same. They did not have direct experience and knowledge of global online VOD as they only sold their content to global broadcasting or online VOD companies rather than providing the platform. Amazon Prime and Netflix already operated worldwide and the global online VOD market was likely to be a very important source of growth in the future. However, most VOD operators struggled to obtain

Table 2 ITV SWOT analysis

Strengths	Weaknesses
• Strong brand • Strong balance sheet • Quality content • Combination of content, advertising and distribution	• Underperforming online delivery system • ITV Hub is UK only • CEO about to change

Opportunities	Threats
• Growth of internet distribution and online content delivery • Content diversification • HD and 3D premium content offers • Local television services over digital terrestrial TV (DTT) platforms • Merger possibilities between traditional and chain partners • Consumers prepared to pay for quality content • Privatisation of Channel 4	• Internet as TV substitute • Slow growth UK TV market • Advertisers turning away from TV advertising to internet • Younger generations prefer other media • Demand-side advertising platforms determine pricing • Subscription-based on-demand only providers, e.g. Netflix, Amazon Prime • Potential change to BBC status • Illegal downloads • New non-studio content

large volumes of superior content and all of them were signing deals for specific shows. For instance, Hulu signed up for the rights to distribute Seinfeld for $160m. Alliances and joint ventures were common in the industry and they had the attraction of being relatively cheap to set up, measured in millions of dollars rather than billions, although very complex and time-consuming to negotiate, with the risk of termination along the way.

Regulatory changes

Favourable government policies towards new internet VOD platforms in the UK was one of the major influences on the broadcasting industry. In addition, there was an active public debate about whether legislation concerning the BBC licence fee should be changed. The BBC was entirely funded by the public through the licence fee. If the government decided to end its charter, the BBC would be forced to compete with commercial broadcasters such as ITV and Channel 5. The impact would probably be worse for Channel 5 as a much smaller entity than ITV, although ITV would also be seriously challenged in terms of competing for advertising revenue. Due to the BBC's power in the broadcasting market, prospective changes could impact the whole broadcasting industry, and ITV would probably lose its place as the biggest commercial platform in the UK.

In addition, the government was also considering whether to privatise Channel 4, through a public offering of shares or even sale to another company. Analysts estimated this would bring around £2bn into the government's coffers which would help pay down some of the national debt. Channel 4 had a good reputation for its content quality, had its own content library, recording studios and broadcasting capability and would be attractive to other media operators. Although Channel 4 funded itself through advertising, if the government decided to sell it, this would have major implications for the way its business was run. Channel 4 executives were said

to be concerned that the organisation's ability to take creative risks would be undermined, such that making programmes for unprofitable small audiences that reflected the county's cultural diversity would no longer be viable. As a commercial entity it would have to make a profit.

Future strategy

A SWOT analysis had been prepared for the board (see Table 2) that summarised the main issues facing ITV in 2016.

Faced with the strategic issues raised in the SWOT, the ITV board had to consider whether ITV should pursue organic growth, perhaps through developing its production and online distribution activities, seek to expand through acquisitions and joint ventures or licensing agreements, or consider restructuring the company to specialise in just one activity or perhaps even think about selling the business. Which strategic options should they consider and which one should be pursued in the future?

Sources: ITV plc Annual Report and Accounts, 2015; Ofcom, *The Communications Market*, 2015; C. Williams. 'Changes show ITV is focusing on the bigger picture', *The Telegraph*, 18 January 2016; C. Williams, 'It will be a grand prize for its buyer – but where is the formula to put a value on Channel 4?', *The Telegraph*, 26 December 2015.With thanks to Ana Jesus, Yun-Chin Lee, Caitlin Ormiston, Prateek Singh, MBA students of Lancaster University, Management Shool for their contributions to this case.

Questions

1 Identify the main strategic issues facing ITV.

2 Suggest a number of strategic options that ITV might pursue.

3 Create tables to assess the SAFe of your strategic options (refer to Table 12.1).

4 Rank your strategic options and recommend a strategy for ITV to pursue.

13

STRATEGY DEVELOPMENT PROCESSES

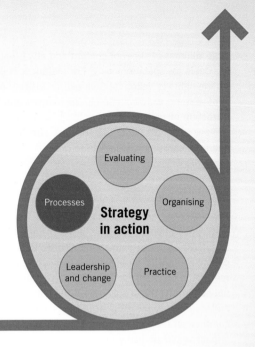

Evaluating

Processes

Strategy in action

Organising

Leadership and change

Practice

Learning outcomes

After reading this chapter you should be able to:

- Understand what is meant by *deliberate* and *emergent* strategy development.
- Identify deliberate processes of strategy development in organisations including: the role *of strategic leadership*, *strategic planning systems* and *externally imposed strategy.*
- Identify processes that give rise to emergent strategy development such as: *logical incrementalism*, *political processes* and *organisational structures and systems.*
- Consider the implications and some of the challenges of *managing strategy development* in organisations.

Key terms

deliberate strategy p.412

emergent strategy p.419

learning organisation p.420

logical incrementalism p.419

political view of strategy
  development p.422

strategic planning p.413

13.1 INTRODUCTION

We are familiar with successful strategies: Google's dominance of internet search; Ryanair becoming one of the most successful airlines in the world; Apple's development of the iPhone and iPad; Zara's internationalisation in the fashion market. We also know about failed strategies: Kodak in photography, the Royal Bank of Scotland in banking; Saab's attempted internationalisation in automobiles. Much of Parts I and II of this book helps us understand this. They addressed how strategists might understand the strategic position of their organisation and what strategic choices are sensible. However, none of this directly addresses the question that is the theme of this chapter: *how do strategies actually develop?* (Chapter 16 then examines in more detail the people involved in these processes and what they actually do in developing strategies.)

According to one source, Steve Jobs' strategy before Apple's entry into the music player and smartphone businesses with the iPod, iTunes and later the iPhone and iPad was 'to wait for the next big thing'.[1] It was not, then, based on brilliant foresight or a clear strategic plan. The strategy rather developed over time in steps some of which were intentional, but some simply materialised over time.

Figure 13.1 summarises the structure of this chapter. It is organised around two main views of strategy development: strategy as deliberate and strategy as emergent.[2] The *deliberate strategy* development view is that strategies come about as the result of the considered intentions of top management. It is related to the *design view* of strategy development explained in the Commentary sections of this book. The second view is that of *emergent strategy* development – that strategies do not develop on the basis of a grand plan, but tend to emerge in organisations over time. The discussion in the Commentaries of the *experience* and *variety* lenses relates to this view. As the chapter will show, however, these two main views of how strategies develop are not mutually exclusive. As Figure 13.1 shows, they are both likely to influence the eventual strategy that actually comes about – the *realised strategy*.

The next section (13.2) of the chapter discusses deliberate strategy development. First, there is an explanation of how strategies may be the outcome of *leadership*, *'command'* or *vision* of individuals. This is followed by a discussion of what formal *planning systems* in organisations might look like and the role they play. The section concludes by explaining

Figure 13.1 Deliberate and emergent strategy development

Source: Adapted from H. Mintzberg and J.A. Waters, 'Of strategies, deliberate and emergent', *Strategic Management Journal,* vol. 6, no. 3 (1985), p. 258, with permission from John Wiley & Sons Ltd.

how strategies might be deliberately *imposed* on organisations from the outside. Section 13.3 of the chapter then switches to views and explanations of how strategies might emerge in organisations. The section offers three views of how this might occur: *logical incrementalism,* the influence of *political processes* in organisations and finally how strategies could be the *outcome of organisational structures and systems.* The final section of the chapter (13.4) raises *implications for managing strategy development* including:

- How different approaches to strategy development may be more or less well suited to different contexts.

- Some of the challenges that arise from managing the processes of deliberate and emergent strategy.

13.2 DELIBERATE STRATEGY DEVELOPMENT

Deliberate strategy involves intentional formulation or planning. Such intentionality may take different forms. It could be the intentionality of a *strategic leader,* for example a CEO or the founder of a firm. It could be through a process of *strategic planning* involving many managers. Or it might be experienced as the *external imposition* of strategy formulated elsewhere.

13.2.1 The role of the strategic leader

An organisation's strategy may be influenced by strategic leaders: individuals or management teams of individuals whose personalities, positions or reputations make them central to the strategy development process. This could be because she or he is the entrepreneur behind, or founder and owner of, the organisation. This is often the case in small businesses and family businesses, but may also persist when a business becomes very large.[3] Such is the case with Richard Branson at Virgin or Ratan Tata of the Tata Corporation. Or it could be that an individual chief executive has played a central role in directing the strategy of an organisation, as with Mark Zuckerberg at Facebook or Michael O'Leary at Ryanair. Research has shown that founder CEOs and CEOs recruited to a firm typically make different contributions to strategic success, at least in terms of market expansion. Founders are more successful at achieving rapid growth in nascent, fast-growing markets, most likely by applying what they have learnt from their previous experience. CEOs that are recruited need more time to build their knowledge and influence but tend to be more successful in complex market conditions.[4]

Strategy, then, may be – or may be seen to be – the deliberate intention of a strategic leader. This may manifest itself in different ways:

- *Strategic leadership as command.* The strategy of an organisation might be dictated by an individual. This is, perhaps, most evident in single owner-managed small firms, where that individual is in direct control of all aspects of the business. Canadian scholars Danny Miller and Isabel Le Breton-Miller[5] suggest there are advantages and disadvantages here. On the plus side it can mean speed of strategy adaptation and 'sharp, innovative, unorthodox strategies that are difficult for other companies to imitate'. The downside can, however, be 'hubris, excessive risk taking, quirky, irrelevant strategies'.

- *Strategic leadership as vision.* It could be that a strategic leader determines or is associated with an overall vision, mission or strategic intent (see Section 1.2) that motivates others, helps create the shared beliefs within which people can work together effectively and guides the more detailed strategy developed by others in an organisation. James Collins and Jerry Porras's study[6] of US firms with long-term high performance concluded that this is a centrally important role of the strategic leader. For example, Ingvar Kamprad, IKEA's founder's, vision, 'To create a better everyday life for the many', has motivated and guided subsequent generations of IKEA managers and staff.

- *Strategic leadership as decision making.* Whichever strategy development processes exist, there could be many different views on future strategy within an organisation and, perhaps, much, but incomplete evidence to support those views. One of the key roles of leaders is to have the ability to weigh such different views, interpret data, have the confidence to take timely decisions to invest in key resources or markets and the authority to get others to buy into those decisions.

- *Strategic leadership as the embodiment of strategy.* A founder or chief executive of an organisation may represent its strategy. This may be unintentional but can also be deliberate: for example, Richard Branson no longer runs Virgin on a day-to-day basis, but he is seen as the embodiment of the Virgin strategy (see Chapter 8 end case) and is frequently the public face of the company.

Illustration 13.1 provides examples of how strategic leaders have influenced different aspects of strategy in their organisations.

13.2.2 Strategic planning systems

A second way in which intended strategies develop is through formalised **strategic planning: systematic analysis and exploration to develop an organisation's strategy.** Larger organisations and corporations often have quite elaborate strategic planning systems. In a study of such systems in major oil companies, Rob Grant[7] of Bocconi University noted the following stages in the planning cycle:

- *Initial guidelines.* The cycle's starting point is usually a set of guidelines or assumptions about the external environment (e.g. price levels and supply and demand conditions) and the overall priorities, guidelines and expectations of the corporate centre.

- *Business-level planning.* In the light of these guidelines, business units or divisions draw up strategic plans to present to the corporate centre. Corporate centre executives then discuss those plans with the business managers usually in face-to-face meetings. On the basis of these discussions, the businesses revise their plans for further discussion.

- *Corporate-level planning.* The corporate plan results from the aggregation of the business plans. This coordination may be undertaken by a corporate planning department that, in effect, has a coordination role. The corporate board then has to approve the corporate plan.

- *Financial and strategic targets* are then likely to be extracted to provide a basis for performance monitoring of businesses and key strategic priorities on the basis of the plan.

Grant found that some of the companies he studied were much more formal and systematised than others (e.g. the French Elf Aquitaine and Italian ENI), with greater reliance on written reports and formal presentations, more fixed planning cycles, less flexibility and more specific objectives and targets relating to the formal plans. Where there was more informality or flexibility (e.g. BP, Texaco and Exxon), companies placed greater emphasis on more general financial targets. Central corporate planning departments also played different roles. In some organisations they acted primarily as coordinators of business plans. In others they were more like internal consultants, helping business unit managers to formulate their plans.

ILLUSTRATION 13.1 The influence of strategic leaders

Founders and chief executives may have a profound effect on an organisation's strategy.

On governance and purpose

On the very first day as Unilever CEO Paul Polman put the shareholders on notice and abandoned quarterly reports along with earnings guidance for the stock market:

'. . . in order to solve issues like food security or climate change, you need to have longer-term solutions. You cannot do that on a quarterly basis . . . I need to create this environment for the company to make the right longer-term decisions. So we stopped giving guidance. We stopped doing quarterly reporting. We changed the compensation for the long term . . . I felt we had to do this to be a long-term viable concern. I don't call it courage. I just call it leadership, which is doing these harder right things versus the easier wrong. It's easy to make a lot of these [short term] decisions, but they are ultimately wrong for the long term . . . I also made it very clear that certain shareholders were not welcome in this company. That created quite some noise.'[1]

On building new businesses

Elon Musk, founder and CEO of electric vehicle manufacturer Tesla Motors and entrepreneur behind PayPal and SpaceX, has provided many innovative ideas, but also led them to execution:

'A company is a group of people that are organized to create a product or service. That's what a company is. So in order to create such a thing, you have to convince others to join you in your effort and so they have to be convinced that it's a sensible thing, that basically there's some reasonable chance of success and if there is success, the reward will be commensurate with the effort involved. And so I think that's it . . . getting people to believe in what you're doing – and in you – is important.'[2]

On changing strategy

NHS England's Chief Executive Simon Stevens announced the need for change as he presented the NHS Five Year Forward View for healthcare in England:

'But the NHS is now at a crossroads – as a country we need to decide which way to go. The Forward View represents the shared view of the national leadership of the NHS, setting out the choices – and consequences – that we will face over the next five years.

It is perfectly possible to improve and sustain the NHS over the next five years in a way that the public and patients want. But to secure the future that we know is possible, the NHS needs to change substantially, and we need the support of future governments and other partners to do so.'[3]

On envisioning the future

Quotes from one of history's most famous fast food retailing leaders reveal what Ray Kroc was thinking as he built McDonald's:[4]

'That night (in 1954) in my motel room I did a lot of heavy thinking about what I'd seen during the day. Visions of McDonald's restaurants dotting crossroads all over the country paraded through my brain.

The McDonald brothers were simply not on my wavelength at all. I was obsessed with the idea of making McDonald's the biggest and the best. They were content with what they had; they didn't want to be bothered with more risks and more demands.'

Sources: (1) Andy Boynton and Margareta Barchan, *Forbes*, 20 July 2015; (2) Alison van Diggelen, *Fresh Dialogues*, 25 January 2013; (3) NHS England, 'NHS Leaders set out vision for healthcare in England', 2014, https://www.england.nhs.uk/2014/10/23/nhs-leaders-vision/; (4) Barbara Farfan, About.com Guide, 8 May 2012.

Questions

1 Can you provide other examples of founders' or chief executives' influence on strategy?

2 What else would you emphasise as an important contribution CEOs make to strategy development?

While larger organisations often have comprehensive strategic planning systems, smaller ones also use strategic planning. A prerequisite for entrepreneurial start-ups that need initial external funding is often to present a detailed strategic business plan. Planning horizons and associated objectives and bases of analysis vary depending on industry and environment conditions. In a complex environment that involves new and emerging technologies, regulations and customer preferences and changing industry borders a new venture may only be able to plan a year ahead. In a fast-moving consumer goods company three- to five-year plans may be appropriate. In companies which have to take very long-term views on capital investment, such as those in the oil industry, planning horizons can be as long as 15 years (in Exxon) or 20 years (in Shell). Illustration 13.2 is a schematic representation of how strategic planning takes form in Siemens, the multinational industrial engineering company. Strategic planning may play several roles and typically four are emphasised:

- *Formulating* strategy by providing means by which managers can understand strategic issues, for example competitive positions (see Chapter 3) and distinctive capabilities (see Chapter 4). Formulation contributes by establishing overall objectives (see Chapter 5), encouraging the use of analytic tools such as those explained in this book and by encouraging a longer-term view of strategy than might otherwise occur.

- *Learning.* Managers can benefit from planning if they see it as a means of learning rather than a means of 'getting the right answers'. Rita McGrath and Ian MacMillan emphasise 'discovery-driven' planning which focuses on the need for questioning and challenging received wisdom and the taken for granted.[8]

- *Integration.* Strategic planning systems may have the explicit purpose of coordinating business-level strategies within an overall corporate strategy. Paula Jarzabkowski and Julia Balogun[9] also show, however, that they can provide a valuable forum for negotiation and compromise and, thus, the reconciliation of different views on future strategy.

- *Communicating* intended strategy throughout an organisation and providing clarity on the purpose and objectives of a strategy or strategic milestones against which performance and progress can be reviewed. Communicating strategy is also a very first step towards strategy implementation.

However, it should be recognised that strategic planning and planning systems may also play other roles. If people are encouraged to be involved in planning processes it can help to create *ownership* of the strategy and thus another way towards implementation.[10] Saku Mantere[11] at McGill University has also shown that it may provide a forum for *middle managers to influence* strategic issues beyond their operational responsibilities (he calls these 'strategy champions'). Strategic planning can also provide a *sense of security* and logic, not least among senior management who believe they should be seen to be proactively determining the future strategy and exercising control over the destiny of their organisation.

Henry Mintzberg has, however, challenged the extent to which planning provides such benefits.[12] Arguably there are five main dangers in the way in which formal systems of strategic planning have been employed:

- *Confusing managing strategy with planning.* Managers may see themselves as managing strategy when what they are doing is going through the processes of planning. Strategy is, of course, not the same as 'the plan': strategy is the long-term direction that the organisation follows – the realised strategy in Figure 13.1 – not just a written document. Linked to this may be confusion between budgetary resource allocation processes and strategic planning processes.[13] The two may come to be seen as the same so that strategic planning gets reduced to resource allocation and financial forecasting rather than thinking through the sort of issues discussed in this book.

ILLUSTRATION 13.2   Strategic planning at Siemens

A planning calendar sets out how strategy is coordinated between the corporate centre and business units.

Siemens is a multinational industrial engineering firm with headquarters in Germany and businesses involved in power generation, power distribution and the application of electrical energy. It operates through ten divisions and 40 business units in 190 countries throughout the world.

The corporate strategy of Siemens forms the basis of a more detailed strategic plan that shows how the strategy is to be put into effect across the divisions and businesses and the projected financial outcome of this. The corporate strategy identifies and defines businesses and markets that Siemens should be in and sets target ranges and five-year growth aspirations. This corporate strategy is developed and decided by the Managing Board supported by the Corporate Strategy Department. More detailed strategic planning occurs at the business unit level with the Corporate Strategy Department working with the divisions to help co-ordinate.

The planning process is summarised in the figure below and has the following stages:

1 Corporate strategists, consulting with divisions and external experts including market research companies, examine global market developments to assess and identify market aspirations for Siemens for the next five years and propose five-year goals by market.

2 Growth aspirations are then passed to divisions together with guidelines on what is required from the businesses to develop a strategic plan for Siemens. This includes prompts on key strategic issues that need addressing such as enhancing performance, fostering growth, strengthening performance, the identification of key market trends, how synergies will be achieved between businesses and a summary SWOT analysis.

3 Combined strategic and financial plans are then developed at the business level with the assistance of divisional strategists who are also responsible for co-ordinating these to produce divisional strategic plans.

4 Towards the end of stage 3 the Corporate Strategy Department facilitates an interim alignment meeting between the divisions and the most important countries on the growth plans of the divisions in the respective countries.

5 The final strategic plans and budget proposals are presented by division and business unit CEOs for review by the management board.

6 The final stage is the agreement by the Siemens managing board. Here an annual agreement of the budget is necessary. An agreement by the supervisory board is only required if extensive changes in strategy and/or the portfolio of the company are planned.

- *Detachment from reality.* The managers responsible for the implementation of strategies, usually line managers, may be so busy with the day-to-day operations of the business that they cede responsibility for strategic issues to specialists or consultants. However, these rarely have power in the organisation to make things happen. The result can be that strategic planning becomes removed from the reality of operations and the experience and knowledge of operating managers. If formal planning systems are to be useful, those responsible for them need to draw on such experience and involve people throughout the organisation. In the absence of such involvement, there is the danger that the resulting strategy is not owned widely in the organisation.

- *Paralysis by analysis.* Ann Langley[14] of HEC Montreal showed that planning can get bogged down in the interminable exchange of analytically-based reports between different parties who do not agree or do not prioritise the same issues. Strategic planning can also become over-detailed in its approach, concentrating on extensive analysis that, while technically sound, misses the major strategic issues facing the organisation. It is not unusual to find companies with huge amounts of information on their markets, but with little

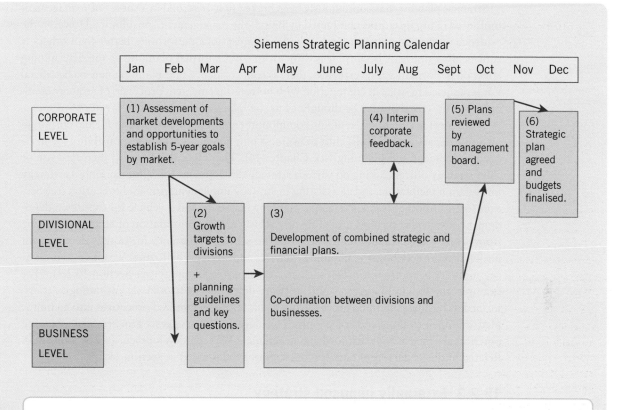

Siemens Strategic Planning Calendar

Questions

1 What types of strategic issues are likely to be most significant at each stage and level of the planning process?

2 How might a planning process differ in other types of organisation (e.g. local government or a university)?

3 How do other processes of strategy development explained in this chapter relate to this planning calendar?

clarity about the strategic importance of that information. The result can be information overload with no clear outcome.

- *Over-complex planning processes.* There is a danger that the strategic planning process is so bureaucratic that it takes too long or, because individuals or groups contribute to only part of it, they do not understand the whole picture. The result can be that the realised strategy at one level, for example the business level, does not correspond to the intended corporate-level strategy. This is particularly problematic in large multi-business firms.

- *Dampening of innovation.* Highly formalised and rigid systems of planning, especially if linked to very tight and detailed mechanisms of control, can contribute to an inflexible, hierarchical organisation with a resultant stifling of ideas and dampening of innovative capacity. This is a reason why new venture units are sometimes set up in larger firms, which do not have to follow their formalised planning systems (see Section 10.5.2).

Strategic planning has continuously been ranked first or second in a survey of management tools used in organisations conducted by Bain,[15] the management consultancy. However, the evidence of strategic planning resulting in organisations performing better than others is equivocal[16] – not least because it is difficult to isolate formal planning as the determining effect on performance. Nevertheless, there is some evidence that planning may be beneficial if it is designed to work in conjunction with bottom-up emergent processes of strategy development a process that may be thought of as the 'planned emergence' of strategy.[17]

While strategic planning remains common, there has been a decline in formal corporate planning departments[18] and a shift to business unit managers taking responsibility for strategy development and planning (see Chapter 16). There has also been an increased use of chief strategy officers taking on various strategy development roles, for example as strategy formulation facilitators and as assisting in strategy implementation and execution (see Section 16.2).[19] Another trend is strategic planning becoming less a vehicle for top-down development of intended strategy and more of a vehicle for the coordination of strategy emerging from below. This includes an increased openness and transparency in strategy development involving more collaborative planning exercises and strategic dialogues. Various social-strategy tools are being tried for this, such as *crowdsourcing* strategy (see Section 10.2.3).[20] For example, the Indian IT services and software development firm HCL Technologies transformed its business planning process from including a few hundred executives into an online platform open to thousands of people. This development suggests that strategic planning practices are increasingly acknowledging emergent strategy development (see Section 13.3). Related to this is the recent concept 'open strategy' discussed in Section 16.2.5.

13.2.3 Externally imposed strategy

Managers may face what they see as the imposition of strategy by powerful external stakeholders. For example, government may dictate a particular strategic direction as in the public sector, or where it exercises extensive regulatory powers in an industry. In the UK public sector, direct intervention has been employed for schools or hospitals deemed to be underperforming badly, with specialist managers being sent in to turn round the ailing organisations and impose a new strategic direction. Alternatively, government may also choose to deregulate or privatise a sector or organisation currently in the public sector with large implications for strategy development. For example, in Scandinavia, and in Sweden in particular, schools, healthcare and public transport have been deregulated and private-sector companies are now actively engaged in their strategy development.

Businesses in the private sector may also be subject to imposed strategic direction, or to significant constraints on their choices. A multinational corporation seeking to develop businesses in some parts of the world may be subject to governmental requirements to do this in certain ways, perhaps through joint ventures or local alliances. An operating business within a multidivisional organisation may also perceive the overall corporate strategic direction of its parent as akin to imposed strategy. For publicly listed companies financial markets also exercise an influence over strategy, not least through so-called 'activists' that take an equity stake in a corporation and put public pressure on its management. For example, activist investor Nelson Peltz bought shares in the US food company Kraft through his Trian Fund Management and pushed the CEO to acquire British confectionary company Cadbury Schweppes and then into splitting the combined company into a global snacks business (Mondelēz) and a US food business (Kraft). Venture capitalists and private equity firms may also impose strategies on the businesses they acquire.[21] When Michael Dell, together with private equity firm Silver Lake Management, acquired Dell and delisted the company's share from NASDAQ, a major objective was to take full control over strategy development from current management and remove pressures from the financial market.

13.3 EMERGENT STRATEGY DEVELOPMENT

Although strategy development is often described as though it is the deliberate intention of top management, an alternative explanation is that of **emergent strategy**: that **strategies emerge on the basis of a series of decisions which form a pattern that becomes clear over time**. This explains an organisation's strategy not as a 'grand plan' but as a developing 'pattern in a stream of decisions'[22] where top managers draw together emerging themes of strategy from various decisions and directions, rather than formulating it directly from the top. The pattern that emerges may then subsequently be more formally described, for example in annual reports and strategic plans, and be seen as the deliberate strategy of the organisation. It will not, however, have been the plan that developed the strategy; it will be the emerging strategy that informed the plan. Emergent strategy may, then, be seen as a basis for learning of what works in search for a viable pattern or consistent strategy.

There are different views of emergent strategy[23] and this section summarises the main ones. They are: logical incrementalism, strategy as the outcome of political processes and strategy as the outcome of organisational systems and routines. All three emphasise that strategy development is not necessarily the province of top management alone, but may be more devolved within organisations. Figure 13.2 shows how the different views can be thought of in terms of a continuum according to how deliberately managed the processes are.

13.3.1 Logical incrementalism

The first explanation of how strategies may emerge is that of *logical incrementalism*. This explanation, in effect, bridges deliberate and emergent processes, as it explains how management may deliberately cultivate a bottom-up, experimental basis for strategies to emerge. **Logical incrementalism** was a term coined by James Quinn in his study of how strategies developed in multinational businesses. It is **the development of strategy by experimentation and learning** 'from partial commitments rather than through global formulations of total strategies'.[24] There are three main characteristics of strategy development in this way:

- *Environmental uncertainty*. Managers realise that they cannot do away with the uncertainty of their environment by relying on analyses of historical data or predicting how it will change. Rather, they try to be sensitive to environmental signals by encouraging constant environmental scanning throughout the organisation.

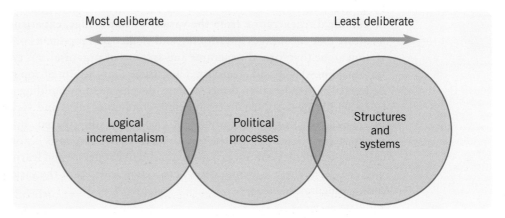

Figure 13.2 A continuum of emergent strategy development processes

- *General goals.* There may be a reluctance to specify precise objectives too early, as this might stifle ideas and prevent innovation and experimentation. So more general rather than specific goals may be preferred, with managers trying to move towards them incrementally.

- *Experimentation.*[25] Managers seek to develop a strong, secure, but flexible, core business. They then build on the experience gained in that business to inform decisions both about its development and experimentation with 'side-bet' ventures. Commitment to strategic options may therefore be tentative in the early stages of strategy development. Such experiments are not the sole responsibility of top management and can thus be autonomous. They emerge from what Quinn describes as 'subsystems' in the organisation – groups of people involved in, for example, product development, product positioning, diversification, external relations and so on. Employees can thus take strategic initiatives and form entrepreneurial ventures from the bottom up with important influence on strategy development.[26] Organisations can also encourage this type of experimentation in different ways (see Section 10.5.2).

Quinn argued that, despite its emergent nature, logical incrementalism can be 'a conscious, purposeful, proactive, executive practice' to improve information available for decisions and build people's psychological identification with the development of strategy. Logical incrementalism therefore suggests that strategy development can be deliberate, whilst relying on organisational subsystems to sense what is happening in the environment and to try out ideas through experimentation. It is a view of strategy development similar to the descriptions that managers themselves often give of how strategies come about in their organisations as Illustration 13.3 shows.

Arguably, developing strategies in such a way has considerable benefits. Continual testing and gradual strategy implementation provide improved quality of information for decision-making and enable the better sequencing of the elements of major decisions. Since change will be gradual, the possibility of creating and developing a commitment to change throughout the organisation is increased. Because the different parts, or 'subsystems', of the organisation are in a continual state of interplay, the managers of each can learn from each other about the feasibility of a course of action. Such processes also take account of the political nature of organisational life, since smaller changes are less likely to face the same degree of resistance as major changes. Moreover, the formulation of strategy in this way means that the implications of the strategy are continually being tested out. This continual readjustment makes sense if the environment is considered as a continually changing influence on the organisation.

Given logical incrementalism's emphasis on learning, it is a view of strategy development which corresponds to the 'learning organisation'[27] – an organisation **that is capable of continual regeneration from the variety of knowledge, experience and skills within a culture that encourages questioning and challenge.** Proponents of the learning organisation argue that formal structures and systems of organisations typically stifle organisational knowledge and creativity. They argue that the aim of top management should be to facilitate rather than direct strategy development by building pluralistic organisations, where ideas bubble up from below, conflicting ideas and views are surfaced and become the basis of debate; where knowledge is readily shared and experimentation is the norm such that ideas are tried out in action. The emphasis is not so much on hierarchies as on different interest groups that need to cooperate and learn from each other. In many respects, there are similarities here to implications of the variety lens discussed in the Commentaries.

ILLUSTRATION 13.3 — An incrementalist view of strategic management

Managers often see strategy as developing through continual adaptation to keep in line with the changing environment.

- 'I begin wide-ranging discussions with people inside and outside the corporation. From these a pattern eventually emerges. It's like fitting together a jigsaw puzzle. At first the vague outline of an approach appears like the sail of a ship in a puzzle. Then suddenly the rest of the puzzle becomes quite clear. You wonder why you didn't see it all along.'[1]

- 'There is a period of confusion before you know what to do about it . . . You sleep on it . . . start looking for patterns . . . become an information hound, searching for [explanations] everywhere.'[2]

- 'We haven't stood still in the past and I can't see with our present set-up that we shall stand still in the future; but what I really mean is that it is a path of evolution rather than revolution. Some companies get a successful formula and stick to that rigidly because that is what they know – for example, [Company X] did not really adapt to change, so they had to take what was a revolution. We hopefully have changed gradually and that's what I think we should do. We are always looking for fresh openings without going off at a tangent.'[3]

- 'The strategy process reflects the company's culture. You can look at it positively or negatively. Positively, it looks like a Darwinian process: we let the best ideas win, we adapt by ruthlessly exiting business; we provide autonomy, and top management is the referee who waits to see who wins and then rearticulates the strategy; we match evolving skills with evolving opportunities. Negatively, it looks like we have no strategy; we have no staying power, we are reactive, try to move somewhere else if we fail; we lack focus'.[4]

- 'We used plenty of trial and error . . . it was ad hoc and informal . . . not systematic at all'; ' . . . what you experience after the fact, as strategy, is often something for the moment'; 'Development is in the everyday business . . . it's a continuous development. It's about socializing with markets and people. This develops competencies. That's where it happens!'[5]

- 'I don't give them [employees] a strategic plan to work to; my job is to discern a strategy from what they tell me and what they are doing. Of course, they don't always agree – why would they, they can't *know* the future either – which means there's a good deal of debate, a good deal of trial and error and a good deal of judgement involved.'[6]

Sources: (1) Management quote from J.B. Quinn, *Strategies for Change*, Irwin, 1980; (2) Management quote: Extract from H. Mintzberg and J.A. Waters, 'Researching the formation of strategies', p. 91 in R. Lamb (ed.), *Competitive Strategic Management*, Prentice Hall, 1984; (3) Management quotes from G. Johnson, *Strategic Change and the Management Process*, Blackwell, 1987; (4) Management quotes from R.A. Burgelman, 'Strategy as vector and the inertia of coevolutionary lock-in', *Administrative Science Quarterly*, vol. 47, no. 2 (2002), pp. 325–57; (5) Management quotes from P. Regnér, 'Strategy creation in the periphery', *Journal of Management Studies*, vol. 40, no. 1 (2003), pp. 57–82; (6) CEO of a hi-tech business in an interview with a co-author.

Questions

1 With reference to these views of strategy development, what are the main advantages of developing strategies incrementally? Are there disadvantages or dangers?

2 Is incremental strategy development bound to result in strategic drift (see Section 6.4)? How might this be avoided?

3 Under what conditions may these approaches to strategy work best?

13.3.2 Strategy as the outcome of political processes

A second explanation of how strategies may emerge is that they are the outcome of the bargaining and power politics that go on between executives or between coalitions within an organisation and its major stakeholders. Managers may well have different views on issues and how they should be addressed; they are therefore likely to seek to position themselves such that their views prevail. They may also seek to pursue strategies or control resources to enhance their political status. The **political view of strategy development**[28] is, then, that **strategies develop as the outcome of bargaining and negotiation among powerful interest groups** (or stakeholders). This is the world of boardroom battles often portrayed in film and TV dramas.

A political perspective on strategic management suggests that the rational and analytic processes often associated with developing strategy (see Section 13.2.2 above and the design lens in the Commentary) may not be as objective and dispassionate as they appear. Objectives may reflect the ambitions of powerful people. Information used in strategic debate is not always politically neutral. A manager or coalition may exercise power over another because they control important sources of information. Powerful individuals and groups may also strongly influence which issues get prioritised. In such circumstances, it is bargaining and negotiation that give rise to strategy rather than careful analysis and deliberate intent. Indeed, strategic planning processes themselves may provide an arena within which managers form coalitions to gain influence.

None of this should be surprising. In approaching strategic problems, people are likely to be differently influenced by at least:

- *Position and personal experience* from their roles within the organisation.
- *Competition for resources and influence* between the different subsystems in the organisation and people within them who are likely to be interested in preserving or enhancing their positions.[29]
- *The relative influence of stakeholders* on different parts of the organisation. For example, a finance department may be especially sensitive to the influence of financial institutions whilst a sales or marketing department will be strongly influenced by customers.
- *Different access to information* given their roles and functional affiliations.

In such circumstances there are two reasons to expect strategy development to build gradually on the current strategy. First, if different views prevail and different parties exercise their political muscle, compromise may be inevitable. Second, it is quite possible that it is from the pursuit of the current strategy that power has been gained by those wielding it. Indeed it may be very threatening to their power if significant changes in strategy were to occur. It is likely that a search for a compromise solution accommodating different power bases will end up with a strategy which is an adaptation of what has gone before.

There are, however, more positive ways of seeing political processes. The conflict and tensions that manifest themselves in political activity, arising as they do from different expectations or interests, can be the source of new ideas[30] (see the discussion on the variety lens in the Commentaries) or challenge old ways of doing things. New ideas may be supported or opposed by different 'champions' who will battle over what is the best idea or the best way forward. Arguably, if such conflict and tensions did not exist, neither would innovation. Further, as Section 15.5.5 shows, the exercise of power may be important in the management of strategic change.

13.3.3 Strategy as the product of structures and systems

A third view of how strategies may emerge is on the basis of an organisation's structures and systems. Rather than seeing strategy development as about foresight and anticipation taking form in directive plans from the top of the organisation, strategy development can be seen as the outcome of managers, often at lower levels, making sense of and dealing with problems and opportunities by applying established ways of doing things. There are echoes here of logical incrementalism, but there is less emphasis on deliberate experimentation. The emphasis is rather on the influence of the structures, systems and routines with which managers are familiar and which guide and constrain their decisions. There are different explanations to consider here: first, strategy may be steered by how resources are allocated; second, structures and systems set up for one strategy may guide later strategies; and third, culture may influence strategy. Each one of these explanations is discussed below.

The way resources are allocated may direct strategy development and there are two views of how this may happen: the resource allocation process[31] (RAP) view of strategy development and the attention-based view[32] (ABV) of strategy development. Both support the argument advanced by Harvard's Joe Bower and Clark Gilbert that: 'The cumulative impact of the allocation of resources by managers at any level has more real-world effect on strategy than any plans developed at headquarters.'[33] In a study of how Intel became a microprocessor company in the 1980s Robert Burgelman at Stanford demonstrated how the resource allocation process can influence strategy.[34] There are two main insights that this view of strategy development offers, shown graphically in Figure 13.3:

- *Organisational systems as a basis for making sense of issues.* Managers are likely to make sense of issues they face on the basis of the systems and routines with which they are familiar and which directly affect them. For example, a finance director will be primarily concerned with the financial systems of the organisation or an operations director with

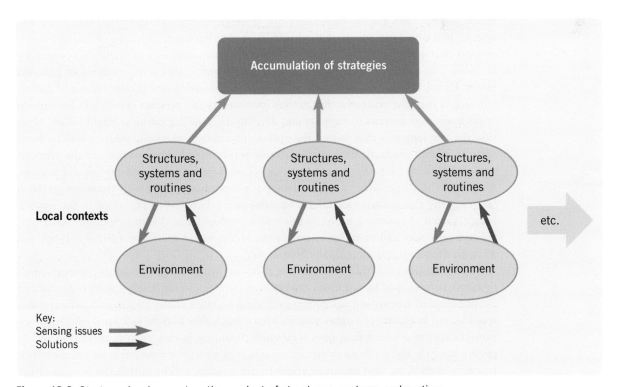

Figure 13.3 Strategy development as the product of structures, systems and routines

operations. Managers within a business unit will be primarily concerned with the systems relating to that business; managers at the corporate level with systems at that level. Targets set by government for those managing public services can result in a focus on some issues at the expense of others.

Vertical reporting relationships in hierarchies will focus managers' attention on issues within their part of the organisation as distinct from cooperating on wider issues across the wider organisation. Managers in a business unit, close to a market, may pay attention to routines and systems to do with competitors and customers whereas senior corporate executives may be concerned with balancing resource allocation across businesses, with systems relating to financial markets and with government regulation.

Whereas top-down explanations of deliberate strategy development assume that managers' focus of attention will readily cohere around clearly identified overarching 'strategic issues', this explanation emphasises that (i) it may not be analysis of an organisation's overall strategic position so much as local systems that surface issues that get attended to; and (ii) such issues are likely to be locally defined.

- *Organisational systems provide bases of solutions to strategic issues.* Systems and routines also provide solutions that managers can draw on when faced with problems. However, responses may differ depending on the context the managers are in and the associated systems and routines. A common example is the way in which different responses emerge as a result of a downturn in company performance. Marketing managers, seeing this as a downturn in the market, may originate solutions that are to do with sales promotion and advertising to generate more sales, research and development managers may see it as a need for product innovation and accountants may see it as a need for tighter controls and cost cutting. Each is drawing on the context in which they find themselves and the associated systems and routines for dealing with such problems.

Another explanation of how strategies may emerge on the basis of structures and systems concentrates on how these may be set up for one strategy, but then also guide later strategies. Strategies may then emerge based on prior strategic decisions and related structures and systems that inform or constrain further strategy development. This type of strategy development can be expected if a strategy is successful, as managers seek to maintain a continuity of strategy in a series of strategic moves, each of which makes sense in terms of previous moves. Figure 13.4 illustrates this. A business may start with a new product idea and the initial success may give rise to further market investments and product extensions. Investment in resources and systems to support and develop the growing business might follow. Over time the company may then launch the product into new markets and perhaps seek to diversify into related products. Each strategic move is informed by the rationale of the previous one, such that over time the overall strategy becomes more and more established. However, sometimes this can result in a sub-optimal path dependency if the early decisions establish 'policy paths' that have lasting effects on subsequent decisions as explained in Section 6.2. Hence, even if the opening move (in this case a product launch) is not especially successful the company may still continue to pursue the strategy that reinforces further sub-optimal strategic decisions; just 'digging the hole deeper'.

Besides the influence from resource allocation and prior strategic decisions, strategy development can be shaped by organisational culture. Strategies may develop as an outcome and continuation of organisational culture including people's taken-for-granted assumptions, routines and behaviours in organisations even though they may be sub-optimal. Organisational culture works to define, or at least guide, how people view their organisation and its environment. It also tends to constrain what is seen as appropriate behaviour and activity. It is very likely, then, that decisions about future strategy will be within the bounds of the culture and that a pattern of continuity will be the outcome, subsequently post-rationalised

Figure 13.4 Strategic direction from the continuity of prior strategic decisions

by managers. Examples of this are given in Chapter 6 together with the potential problems that can arise. Not least among these is that such culturally bounded strategy development can lead to strategic drift (see Section 6.4).

The influence from organisational structures, systems and prior decisions on strategy development does not of course exclude other views and explanations. For example, it helps explain why strategy development is likely to be a political process (Section 13.3.2) since it recognises that there will be different perceptions of strategic issues and different views on solutions. The emphasis on structures and systems does, however, de-emphasise top-down strategic planning and suggests that it is an accumulation of local decisions strongly influenced by local context that accounts for strategy development. It may be, however, that such local decisions are then post-rationalised into an apparently coherent strategy in the form of a strategic plan. There is also evidence that the sponsors of successful exploratory and innovatory local initiatives tend to employ rational justification and draw on formal authority in support of such initiatives.[35]

13.4 IMPLICATIONS FOR MANAGING STRATEGY DEVELOPMENT

It should be clear from the different views and explanations of strategy development processes that they are not discrete or mutually exclusive: multiple processes are likely to be evident.[36] For example, planning systems exist in most large organisations, but there will also undoubtedly be political activity; indeed the planning system itself may be used for negotiating purposes. There will also be established structures, systems and procedures that will affect future decisions. As was explained at the beginning of the chapter, then, the strategy of an organisation is likely to develop in both deliberate and emergent ways. Illustration 13.4 describes what has become a classic case of strategy development in research and teaching;

ILLUSTRATION 13.4 A classic case: Honda entering the US motorcycle market

There are different explanations of successful strategy development.

In 1984, Richard Pascale published a paper that described the success Honda had experienced with the launch of its motorcycles in the US market in the 1960s. It is a paper that has generated discussions about strategy development processes ever since. First he gave explanations provided by the Boston Consulting Group (BCG):

'The success of the Japanese manufacturers originated with the growth of their domestic market during the 1950s. This resulted in a highly competitive cost position which the Japanese used as a springboard for penetration of world markets with small motorcycles in the early 1960s . . . The basic philosophy of the Japanese manufacturers is that high volumes per model provide the potential for high productivity as a result of using capital intensive and highly automated techniques. Their market strategies are therefore directed towards developing these high model volumes, hence the careful attention that we have observed them giving to growth and market share.'

Thus the BCG's account is a rational one based upon the deliberate intention of building up a cost advantage based on volume.

Pascale's second version of events was based on interviews with the Japanese executives who launched the motorcycles in the USA and demonstrates how the serendipitous nature of Honda's strategy shows the importance of learning and culture:

'In truth, we had no strategy other than the idea of seeing if we could sell something in the United States. It was a new frontier, a new challenge, and it fitted the "success against all odds" culture that Mr Honda had cultivated. We did not discuss profits or deadlines for breakeven . . . We knew our products . . . were good but not far superior. Mr Honda was especially confident of the 250cc

and 305cc machines. The shape of the handlebar on these larger machines looked like the eyebrow of Buddha, which he felt was a strong selling point . . . We configured our start-up inventory with 25 per cent of each of our four products – the 50cc Supercub and the 125cc, 250cc and 305cc machines. In dollar value terms, of course, the inventory was heavily weighted towards the larger bikes . . . We were entirely in the dark the first year. Following Mr Honda's and our own instincts, we had not attempted to move the 50cc Supercubs . . . They seemed wholly unsuitable for the US market where everything was bigger and more luxurious . . . We used the Honda 50s ourselves to ride around Los Angeles on errands. They attracted a lot of attention. But we still hesitated to push the 50cc bikes out of fear they might harm our image in a heavily macho market. But when the larger bikes started breaking, we had no choice. And surprisingly, the retailers who wanted to sell them weren't motorcycle dealers, they were sporting goods stores.'

Sources: Based on R.T. Pascale, 'Perspectives on strategy: the real story behind Honda's success', *California Management Review*, vol. 26, no. 3 (1984), pp. 47–72; H. Mintzberg, R.T. Pascale, M. Goold and R.P. Rumelt, 'The Honda effect revisited', *California Management Review*, vol. 38, no. 4 (1996), pp. 78–116.

Questions

1 Are the different accounts mutually exclusive?

2 What different insights can the two accounts provide? How can they be useful?

3 Do you think Honda would have been more or less successful if it had adopted a more formalised strategic planning approach to the launch?

two descriptions of how Honda became incredibly successful when entering the motorcycle market in the USA.[37]

It is also likely that processes of strategy development will be seen differently by different people. For example, senior executives tend to see strategy development in terms of deliberate, rational, analytic planned processes, whereas middle managers see strategy development more as the result of political and cultural processes. Managers in public-sector organisations tend to see strategy as externally imposed more than managers in commercial businesses, largely because their organisations are answerable to government bodies.[38] People who work in family businesses tend to see more evidence of the influence of powerful individuals, who may be the owners of the businesses.

13.4.1 Strategy development in different contexts

Whilst there is no one right way in which strategies are developed, it is helpful if managers recognise the potential benefits and pitfalls of different processes of strategy development. Organisations differ in their size, form and complexity. They also face different environments, so different processes for managing strategy may make sense in different circumstances (see also Thinking Differently at the end of this chapter). Figure 13.5 provides a way of considering this by showing how organisations may seek to cope with conditions that are more or less stable or dynamic and simple or complex:[39]

- *In simple/static conditions,* the environment is relatively straightforward to understand and is not undergoing significant change. The organisation itself is also not overly complex; for example, it may be operating in a single market or with a narrow portfolio. Raw materials suppliers and some mass-manufacturing companies are examples. In such circumstances, if environmental change does occur, it may be predictable, so it could make sense to analyse the environment extensively on an historical basis as a means of trying to forecast likely future conditions. In situations of relatively low complexity, it may also be possible to identify some predictors of environmental influences. For example, in public services, demographic data such as birth rates might be used as lead indicators to determine the required provision of schooling, healthcare or social services. So in simple/

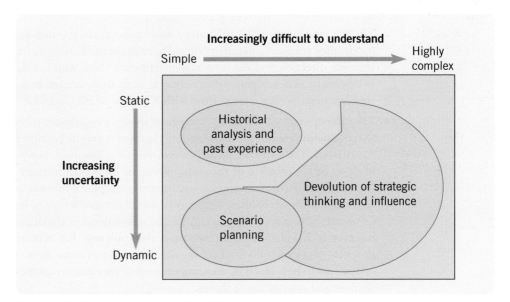

Figure 13.5 Strategy development in different contexts

static conditions systematic strategic planning is possible, perhaps with central planners taking the lead. It is also likely that past experience and prior decisions will be a significant influence since little is changing. The potential problem is, of course, that conditions do change; for example, the environment may become more dynamic and the established processes may not be suited to such conditions.

- *In dynamic conditions,* managers need to consider the environment of the future, not just of the past. The degree of uncertainty therefore increases. They may employ structured ways of making sense of the future, such as scenario planning, discussed in Section 2.4, or they may rely more on encouraging active sensing of environmental changes lower down in the organisation where people are operating closer to the changes that are taking place, for example in the market or in technology. Organisations seek to do this in various ways. For example, through strategy workshops and more open strategy making involving much wider participation in strategy development (see Sections 16.2.5 and 16.4.1) or by seeking to create organisational conditions that encourage individuals and groups to be sensitive to signals from the changing environment, forward thinking and challenging, approximating to logical incrementalism and organisational learning (Section 13.3.1).

- *Organisations in complex situations* face an environment difficult to comprehend. For example, a multinational firm, or a major public service such as a local government authority with many services, is complex because of its diversity. In such circumstances such organisations may seek structural solutions; for example, they may subdivide their organisation into units where managers have particular expertise and have responsibility for strategic decision making within those units (see Section 14.2.2). Such organisations may, of course, also face dynamic conditions and therefore a combination of complexity and uncertainty. With more and more sophisticated technology, there is an increasing move towards this condition of greatest uncertainty. In such circumstances it is simply not feasible for top management to understand all the influences on future strategy so there will be an even greater need to devolve strategy thinking and influence within the organisation. There are various ways of doing this, including the development of a portfolio of real options, corporate venturing and intrapreneurship (see Section 10.5.2).

Considering the ways in which strategy may be developed in different contexts in turn has a number of implications:

- *The top management role in strategy development.* Do top managers see themselves as the detailed planners of strategy throughout the organisation; as the ones who set broad strategic direction and cultivate managers below them who can develop more detailed strategies; or as developing their own capabilities to detect and build upon strategies and strategic ideas as they emerge from within the rest of the organisation?

- *The roles of strategic planning.* Strategic planning has different roles to play. The simpler the conditions faced by the organisation, the more it may be possible for planning to direct the strategy. The more the strategy development is devolved, however, the more there is likely to be the problem of the coordination of an overall strategy for an organisation. In such circumstances, strategic planning may also play a role but as a coordinating and communication mechanism. This may be useful because it may be important that there is a formal explanation of the strategy for the stakeholders of the organisation. The danger, however, is that planning does little more than pull together 'received wisdom' such that it merely post-rationalises where the organisation has come from. If strategic planning systems are to be useful it is, then, important that they encourage the challenge of received wisdom and ways of doing things.

- *Different strategy development roles at different organisational levels.* A study of corporate parents' relationship to their business units or subsidiaries found that there were distinct differences in the strategy development approaches and roles at these different levels.[40] The business units/subsidiaries were playing the experimental role. Highly reliant on informal contacts with their markets, managers' decisions were made largely on the basis of their experience. The executives at the centre were more concerned with the search for order throughout the business and therefore on planning, building on existing resources and refining existing strategy. This study makes the point that managers at different levels will likely play different roles. So the building of productive dialogue between the different levels may be very important.

- *Strategic inflection points.* Robert Burgelman and Andy Grove[41] argue that all organisations face what they call 'strategic inflection points' where there are shifts in fundamental industry dynamics which management need to recognise and act upon. In such circumstances, it may well be that the symptoms are recognised by managers close to such changes who may then press for changes in strategy. The problem may be that other, perhaps top, management may be busily working to maximise their competitive advantage and returns in the prevailing industry structure. The result could be a build-up of 'dissonance' within the organisation. Burgelman and Grove argue that top managers need to learn when to take such dissonance seriously. This relates to the challenge of organisational ambidexterity which is discussed more fully in Section 15.4.4.

13.4.2 Managing deliberate and emergent strategy

This chapter began by drawing the distinction between deliberate and emergent strategy and has shown that in most organisations there are processes at work that are characteristic of both. There are some issues that arise from the recognition of this:

- *Unrealised strategy.* There will, very likely, be aspects of a deliberate strategy that do not come to be realised in practice. There are several reasons for this: the environment changes and managers decide that the strategy, as planned, should not be put into effect; the plans prove to be unworkable or unacceptable in practice; or the emergent strategy comes to dominate. There is, however, a danger. Managers may espouse a deliberate strategy, perhaps the result of a strategic planning process, but the organisation may be following a different strategy in reality. We experience this as customers of organisations that have stated strategies quite different from what we experience – government agencies that are there purportedly to serve our interests but act as bureaucratic officialdom, companies that claim they offer excellent customer service but operate call centres that frustrate customers and fail to solve problems, universities that claim excellence of teaching but are more concerned with their staff's research, or vice versa. It should not, however, be assumed that top managers are always close enough to customers to understand the extent of difference between what is intended as the strategy and what is actually happening. Managers need to take steps to check if the deliberate strategy is actually being realised.

- *Managing deliberate strategy.* Wherever there are processes of deliberate strategy-making feedback should play an important role, not least because it may change that deliberate strategy. Such feedback may take different forms. The first step in strategy implementation – the communication of strategy throughout the organisation – may give rise to immediate feedback from different stakeholders arguing for adjustments to that strategy. Feedback can also come from organisational structures, systems and routines that support strategy implementation (see Chapter 14). For example, control systems set up to monitor

THINKING DIFFERENTLY Different strategy development styles

A new view proposes not two, but four strategy development styles.

It was earlier observed that different strategy processes, like deliberate and emergent, may make sense under different conditions (see Section 13.4.1). A new view has proposed four different processes or 'styles' based on this idea.[42] It suggests that strategy styles depend on two specific dimensions: how predictable an industry's environment is and how easily an organisation can influence it. Four styles are identified based on these dimensions: *classical*, *adaptive*, *shaping* and *visionary*. They are described below (note that the *classical* and *adaptive* styles are quite similar to the deliberate and emergent strategy patterns, respectively).

Some business environments are fairly predictable, but difficult to influence and change, like the oil industry. Here a *classical* approach is appropriate in which a company, Shell for example, uses careful analysis, planning and execution. Other environments are hard to predict, but still difficult to change, like the fast fashion industry. Here an *adaptive* strategy style is appropriate. In this environment a company, like H&M, relies on observing and responding to changes in the environment and experimenting with alternative strategies.

There are two additional types of environments and corresponding styles. Some environments such as certain internet network environments are quite unpredictable, but may still be possible to influence and change. A *shaping* strategy style may work best here. Facebook has used this and it emphasises influencing, engaging and cooperating with other organisations to shape the development of the environment and market. Finally, an environment can be both fairly predictable and possible to influence, like the internet retailing industry. This suggests the need for a *visionary* style similar to the one Amazon used. It relies on seeing long-term opportunities, visualising how to exploit them and then being persistent.

Question

Pick three different industries and environments. What different strategy development styles (classical, adaptive, shaping or visionary) would be appropriate in them?

the progress of a strategy may signal that key objectives are not being met. Similarly, key performance indicators and balanced scorecards may also indicate a need to change the deliberate strategy (see Chapter 12). Organisational culture also plays an important role in strategy implementation (Chapter 6) and if it becomes clear that a strategy requires cultural changes which are too radical it may have to be adjusted.

- *Managing emergent strategy*. The processes of strategy development that give rise to emergent strategy may be rooted in incremental learning, political processes and organisational structures and systems, but they are not unmanageable. Indeed, this is as much about managing strategy as is strategic planning. Political processes can be analysed and managed (see Section 5.2.2 on stakeholder mapping) and organisational structures and resource allocation can be changed. A clear mission or vision can help direct the bottom-up strategy development, and strategic planning systems can help coordinate the outcomes of such processes.

- *The challenge of strategic drift*. A major strategic challenge facing managers was identified in Section 6.4 as the risk of strategic drift: the tendency for strategies to develop incrementally on the basis of historical and cultural influences, but fail to keep pace with a changing environment. The views and explanations of emergent strategy in Section 13.3 of this chapter suggest that such a pattern may be a natural outcome of the influence of political processes, organisational structure and systems and prior strategic decisions. This further highlights that strategy development processes in organisations need to encourage people to have the capacity and willingness to challenge and change their core assumptions and ways of doing things.

SUMMARY

This chapter has dealt with different ways in which strategy development occurs in organisations. The main lessons of the chapter are:

- It is important to distinguish between *deliberate strategy* – the desired strategic direction deliberately planned by managers – and *emergent strategy,* which may develop in a less deliberate way from the behaviours and activities inherent within an organisation.

- Most often the process of strategy development is described in terms of a deliberately formulated intended strategy as a result of *planning systems* carried out objectively and dispassionately. There are advantages and disadvantages of formal strategic planning systems.

- Deliberate strategy may also come about on the basis of central command, the *vision of strategic leaders* or the *imposition of strategies* by external stakeholders.

- Strategies may emerge from within organisations. This may be explained in terms of:

  - How organisations may proactively try to cope through processes of *logical incrementalism and organisational learning.*

  - The outcome of the bargaining associated with *political activity* resulting in a negotiated strategy.

  - Strategies developing because *organisational structures* and *systems* favour some strategy projects over others and strategies often develop on the basis of continuity or organisational culture.

- In managing strategy development processes, managers face challenges including:

  - Recognising that different processes of strategy development may be needed *in different contexts.*

  - Managing the processes that may give rise to *emergent strategy* as well as *deliberate strategy.*

WORK ASSIGNMENTS

✱ Denotes more advanced work assignments.
* Refers to a case study in the Text and Cases edition.

13.1 Read the annual report of a company with which you are familiar as a customer (e.g. a retailer or transport company). Identify the main characteristics of the intended deliberate strategy as explained in the annual report, and the characteristics of the realised strategy as you perceive it as a customer.

13.2 Using the different views in Sections 13.2 and 13.3, characterise how strategies have developed in different organisations (e.g. Alphabet/Google, Siemens* and Mormor Magda*).

13.3✱ Planning systems exist in many different organisations. What role should planning play in a public-sector organisation such as local government, a not-for-profit organisation such as Where should the beds go?* and a multinational corporation such as SABMiller or AB InBev (in the Megabrew* case).

13.4✱ Incremental patterns of strategy development are common in organisations, and managers see advantages in this. However, there are also risks of strategic drift. Using the different views in Sections 13.2 and 13.3, suggest how such drift might be avoided.

13.5 Suggest why different approaches to strategy development might be appropriate in different organisations such as a university, a fashion retailer, a diversified multinational corporation and a high-technology company.

Integrative assignment

13.6✱ Assume you were asked to advise a chief executive of a long-established, historically successful multinational business with highly experienced managers that is experiencing declining profits and falling market share. What might you expect to be the causes of the problems? What processes of strategy development would you propose to address them?

RECOMMENDED KEY READINGS

- A much quoted paper that describes different patterns of strategy development is H. Mintzberg and J.A. Waters, 'Of strategies, deliberate and emergent', *Strategic Management Journal*, vol. 6, no. 3 (1985), pp. 257–72.

- For an overview of different types of strategy development processes and a collection of strategy process articles, see P. Olk (ed.), *Strategy Process*, Edward Elgar, 2010.

- The changing role of strategic planning in the oil industry is explained by Rob Grant; see 'Strategic

planning in a turbulent environment: evidence from the oil majors', *Strategic Management Journal*, vol. 24 (2003), pp. 491–517.

- For two overviews of strategy process perspectives, see T. Hutzschenreuter and I. Kleindienst, 'Strategy-process research: what have we learned and what is still to be explored', *Journal of Management*, vol. 32, no. 5 (2006), pp. 673–720; and S. Elbanna 'Strategic decision making: process perspectives', *International Journal of Management Reviews*, vol. 8, no. 1 (2006), pp. 1–20.

REFERENCES

1. See R. Rumelt, *Good Strategy/Bad Strategy: The difference and why it matters*, Profile Books, 2011.

2. See H. Mintzberg and J.A. Waters, 'Of strategies, deliberate and emergent', *Strategic Management Journal*, vol. 6, no. 3 (1985), pp. 257–72.

3. T. Nelson, 'The persistence of founder influence: management, ownership, and performance effects at initial public offering', *Strategic Management Journal*, vol. 24 (2003), pp. 707–24.

4. D. Souder, Z. Simsek and S.G. Johnson, 'The differing effects of agent and founder CEOs on the firm's market expansion', *Strategic Management Journal*, vol. 33, no. 1 (2012), pp. 23–42.

5. The role of a command style in small businesses is discussed in D. Miller and I. Le Breton-Miller, 'Management insights from great and struggling family businesses', *Long Range Planning*, vol. 38 (2005), pp. 517–30. The quotes here are from p. 519.

6. J. Collins and J. Porras, *Built to Last*, Harper Business, 1994.

7. R. Grant, 'Strategic planning in a turbulent environment: evidence from the oil majors', *Strategic Management Journal*, vol. 24 (2003), pp. 491–517.

8. Rita Gunther McGrath and Ian C. MacMillan, *Discovery Driven Planning*, Wharton School, Snider Entrepreneurial Center, 1995 and Rita Gunther McGrath and Ian C. MacMillan, 'Discovery driven planning', *Harvard Business Review*, vol. 24, no. 3 (1995), pp. 44–54.

9. See P. Jarzabkowski and J. Balogun, 'The practice and process of delivering integration through strategic planning', *Journal of Management Studies*, vol. 46, no. 8 (2009), pp. 1255–88. P. Spee and P. Jarzabkowski, 'Strategic planning as communicative process', vol. 32, no. 9 (2011), pp. 1217–45, also explain how clarity on strategy may emerge as different parties involved iterate versions of the plan.

10. See M. Ketokivi and X. Castaner, 'Strategic planning as an integrative device', *Administrative Science Quarterly*, vol. 49 (2004), pp. 337–65.

11. Saku Mantere, 'Strategic practices as enablers and disablers of championing activity', *Strategic Organization*, vol. 3, no. 2 (2005), pp. 157–84.

12. Many of these dangers are drawn from H. Mintzberg, *The Rise and Fall of Strategic Planning*, Prentice Hall, 1994.

13. The confusion of strategic planning and budgeting is identified as a significant 'bad strategy' practice by Richard Rumelt in *Good Strategy/Bad Strategy: The difference and why it matters*, Profile Books, 2011.

14. Ann Langley, 'Between "Paralysis by Analysis" and "Extinction by Instinct"', *Sloan Management Review*, Spring (1995), pp. 63–76.

15. See http://www.bain.com/publications/articles/management-tools-and-trends-2013.aspx. Also, see evidence from other surveys such as G.P. Hodgkinson, R. Whittington, G. Johnson and M. Schwarz, 'The role of strategy workshops in strategy development processes: formality, communication, co-ordination and inclusion', *Long Range Planning*, vol. 39 (2006), pp. 479–96; also R. Whittington and Cailluet, 'The crafts of strategy', *Long Range Planning*, vol. 41 (2008), pp. 241–7.

16. Studies on the relationship between formal planning and financial performance are largely inconclusive. Some studies have shown benefits in particular contexts. For example, it is argued there are benefits to entrepreneurs setting up new ventures; see F. Delmar and S. Shane, 'Does business planning facilitate the development of new ventures?', *Strategic Management Journal*, vol. 24 (2003), pp. 1165–85. Other studies show the benefits of strategic analysis and strategic thinking, rather than the benefits of formal planning systems; e.g. see C.C. Miller and L.B. Cardinal, 'Strategic planning and firm performance: a synthesis of more than two decades of research', *Academy of Management Journal*, vol. 37, no. 6 (1994), pp. 1649–65.

17. P.J. Brews and M.R. Hunt, 'Learning to plan and planning to learn: resolving the planning school/learning school debate', *Strategic Management Journal*, vol. 20 (1999), pp. 889–913. Others have suggested planning may be beneficial in dynamic environments where decentralised authority for strategic decisions is required, but with a need for coordination of strategies: T.J. Andersen, 'Integrating decentralized strategy making and strategic planning processes in dynamic

environments', *Journal of Management Studies*, vol. 41, no. 8 (2004), pp. 1271–99.

18. See R. Grant, endnote 7.

19. M. Menz and C. Scheef, 'Chief strategy officers: contingency analysis of their presence in top management teams', *Strategic Management Journal*, vol. 35, no. 3 (2014), pp. 461–71; D. Angwin, S. Paroutis and S. Mitson. 'Connecting up strategy: are senior strategy directors a missing link?' *California Management Review*, vol. 51, no. 3 (2009); R. Breene, S. Timothy *et al.*, 'The chief strategy officer', *Harvard Business Review*, vol. 85, no. 10 (2007), pp. 84–93.

20. Daniel Stieger *et al.*, 'Democratizing strategy: how crowd-sourcing can be used for strategy dialogues', *California Management Review*, vol. 54, no. 4 (2012), pp. 44–68.

21. See B. King, 'Strategizing at leading venture capital firms: of planning, opportunism and deliberate emergence', *Long Range Planning*, vol. 41 (2008), pp. 345–66.

22. See H. Mintzberg and J.A. Waters, endnote 2.

23. See S. Elbanna, 'Strategic decision making: process perspectives', *International Journal of Management Reviews*, vol. 8, no. 1 (2006), pp. 1–20. Another examination of extant strategy process research identified four types of strategy development paths: see P. Olk (ed.), *Strategy Process*, Edward Elgar, 2010.

24. See J.B. Quinn, *Strategies for Change*, Irwin, 1980, p. 58.

25. For a more extensive discussion of experimentation, see O. Sorenson, 'Strategy as quasi-experimentation', *Strategic Organization*, vol. 1 (2003), p. 337.

26. For strategic initiatives see R.A. Burgelman, 'Intraorganizational ecology of strategy making and organizational adaptation: theory and field research', *Organization Science*, vol. 2, no. 3 (1991), pp. 239–62 and B. Lovas and S. Ghoshal 'Strategy as guided evolution', *Strategic Management Journal*, vol. 21 (2000), pp. 875–96.

27. The concept of the learning organisation is explained in P. Senge, *The Fifth Discipline: the Art and Practice of the Learning Organization*, Doubleday/Century, 1990. Also M. Crossan, H.W. Lane and R.E. White, 'An organizational learning framework: from intuition to institution', *Academy of Management Review*, vol. 24, no. 3 (1999), pp. 522–37.

28. See V.K. Narayanan and L. Fahey, 'The micro-politics of strategy formulation', *The Academy of Management Review*, vol. 7, no. 1 (1982), pp. 109–40.

29. For an example of how different political coalitions can influence strategy, see S. Maitlis and T. Lawrence, 'Orchestral manoeuvres in the dark: understanding failure in organizational strategizing', *Journal of Management Studies*, vol. 40, no. 1 (2003), pp. 109–40.

30. See P. Regnér, 'Strategy creation in the periphery: inductive versus deductive strategy making', *Journal of Management Studies*, vol. 40, no. 1 (2003), pp. 57–82.

31. The RAP explanation is sometimes known as the Bower–Burgelman explanation of strategy development after two US professors – Joe Bower and Robert Burgelman. Their original studies are J.L. Bower, *Managing the Resource Allocation Process: a Study of Corporate Planning and Investment*, Irwin, 1972; R.A. Burgelman, 'A model of the interaction of strategic behavior, corporate context and the concept of strategy', *Academy of Management Review*, vol. 81, no. 1 (1983), pp. 61–70; and 'A process model of internal corporate venturing in the diversified major firm', *Administrative Science Quarterly*, vol. 28 (1983), pp. 223–44. Also see J.L. Bower and C.G. Gilbert, 'A revised model of the resource allocation process', in L. Bower and C.G. Gilbert (eds), *From Resource Allocation to Strategy*, Oxford University Press, 2005, pp. 439–55.

32. W. Ocasio, 'Towards an attention-based view of the firm', *Strategic Management Journal*, vol. 18 (Summer Special Issue, 1997), pp. 187–206.

33. J.L. Bower and C.G. Gilbert, 'How managers' everyday decisions create or destroy your company's strategy', *Harvard Business Review*, February 2007, p. 2.

34. See *Strategy as Destiny: How Strategy Making Shapes a Company's Future*, Free Press, 2002. Also see R. Burgelman, 'Fading memories: a process theory of strategic business exit in dynamic environments', *Administrative Science Quarterly*, vol. 39 (1994), pp. 34–56.

35. C. Lechner and S.W. Floyd, 'Group influence activities and the performance of strategic initiatives', *Strategic Management Journal*, vol. 33, no. 5 (2012), pp. 478–96.

36. Insights into the importance of multiple processes of strategy development can be found in S.L. Hart, 'An integrative framework for strategy-making processes', *Academy of Management Review*, vol. 17, no. 2 (1992), pp. 327–51. For an overview strategy process research, see T. Hutzschenreuter and I. Kleindienst, 'Strategy-process research: what have we learned and what is still to be explored', *Journal of Management*, vol. 32, no. 5 (2006), pp. 673–720.

37. See R.T. Pascale, 'Perspectives on strategy: the real story behind Honda's success', *California Management Review*, vol. 26, no. 3 (1984), pp. 47–72; and H. Mintzberg, R.T. Pascale, M. Goold and R.P. Rumelt, 'The Honda effect revisited', *California Management Review*, vol. 38, no. 4 (1996), pp. 78–116.

38. For a discussion of the differences between strategy development in the public and private sectors, see N. Collier, F. Fishwick and G. Johnson, 'The processes of strategy development in the public sector', in G. Johnson and K. Scholes (eds), *Exploring Public Sector Strategy*, Pearson Education, 2001.

39. R. Duncan's research, on which this classification is based, can be found in 'Characteristics of organisational environments and perceived environmental uncertainty', *Administrative Science Quarterly*, vol. 17, no. 3 (1972), pp. 313–27.

40. See P. Regnér, endnote 30.

41. R.A. Burgelman and A.S. Grove, 'Let chaos reign, then rein in chaos – repeatedly: managing strategic dynamics for corporate longevity', *Strategic Management Journal*, vol. 28 (2007), pp. 965–79.

42. M. Reeves, C. Love and P. Tillmanns, 'Your strategy needs a strategy', *Harvard Business Review*, vol. 90, no. 9 (2012), pp. 76–83.

Alphabet – who and what drives the strategy?

Phyl Johnson and Patrick Regnér

From Google to Alphabet – twists and turns in Google's strategy development.

Google is one of the few companies whose main product's name became so synonymous with its primary offering that it has become a commonly used verb. Google, which was renamed Alphabet in October 2015, had a market capitalisation of $725bn (£435bn, €544bn) by 2016. With a network of over one million computers worldwide, it was the dominant player in internet search globally (85 per cent market share, way ahead of former giant Yahoo's six per cent and Microsoft's 'Bing' and Chinese Baidu, both with three per cent). Google's internet search-related advertising accounted for 86 per cent of Alphabet's revenues. However, the giant's expansion faced some challenges. People moved to mobiles with lower-priced ads, which limited growth. In contrast to expectations, the YouTube video service was also unable to produce profits. Finally, the company was slowly but surely closing down Google +, its big bet on social networking services. In addition, there were questions concerning the restructuring of Google and renaming it Alphabet;[1] intended as a holding company including the Google search business and an increasingly diversified portfolio.

About Google

Google started life as the brainchild of Larry Page and Sergey Brin when they were students at Stanford University in the USA. When Page and Brin launched their own search engine product, it gained followers and users quickly, attracted financial backing and enabled them to launch their IPO to the US stock market in 2004 raising a massive $1.67bn.

From the beginning Google was different. Instead of using investment banks as dictators of the initial share price for the IPO, they launched a kind of open IPO auction with buyers deciding on the fair price for a share. Page sent an open letter to shareholders explaining that Google was not a conventional company and did not intend to become one; it was about breaking the mould. This continued as Google set up a two-tier board of directors, a model which, though common in some European countries (e.g. the Netherlands), is rare in the USA. The advantage for Page and Brin was the additional distance

it placed between *them* and their shareholders and the increased managerial freedom it offered to them to run their company their way.

Page and Brin also recruited successful CEO Eric Schmidt from Novell Inc. and, between the three of them, shared power at the top. Schmidt dealt with administration and Google's investors and had the most traditional CEO role. Page was centrally concerned with the social structure of Google while Brin took a lead in the area of ethics.

How it was

It could be difficult to work out who was responsible for what inside Googleplex (Google's HQ) in Mountain View, California. There was a famously unstructured style of operating; Eric Schmidt claimed that their strategy was based on trial and error:

> **'Google is unusual because it's really organised from the bottom up . . . It often feels at Google people are pretty much doing what they think best and they tolerate having us around . . . We don't really have a five-year plan . . . We really focus on what's new, what's exciting and how can you win quickly with your new idea.'[2]**

With regard to product development, their approach was to launch a part-finished (*beta*) product, let Google fanatics find it, toy with it, error-check and de-bug it – an imaginative use of end-users but also a significant release of control. Control of workflow, quality and to a large extent, the nature of projects underway at any one time were down to employees and not management. Google was a famously light-managed organisation. It had a 1:20 ratio of employees to managers – half the number of managers than in the average American organisation (1:10) and considerably fewer than some European countries (France 1:7.5).

Engineers worked in small autonomous teams and the work they produced was quality assured using peer review rather than classical supervision or clear strategic guidelines. So there was the potential for these small work teams with their freedom for self-initiated project work to create a situation of project proliferation. Moreover, engineers at Google were allowed to allocate 20 per cent of their work time to personal projects that interested them as a means to stimulate innovation and the creation of new knowledge as well as potential products. However, some commentators suggested that many engineers spent more like 30 per cent of their time on such projects.

Google was proud of its laissez-faire approach to management and product development as explained by former CEO Eric Schmidt:

> 'Google is run by its culture and not by me . . . It's much easier to have an employee base in which everybody is doing exactly what they want every day. They're much easier to manage because they never have any problems. They're always excited, they're always working on whatever they care about . . . But it's a very different model than the traditional, hierarchical model where there's the CEO statement and this is the strategy and this is what you will do, and it's very, very measured. We put up with a certain amount of chaos from that.'[2]

There were, however, some areas of rigidity built into the system. One was that of recruitment. With such a highly rated employment brand, Google could afford to be choosy. Close to 100 talented applicants chased each job. The pay was competitive but not way ahead of the competition. However, perks, including free meals, a swimming pool and massages, all helped attract employees. So too did the 20 per cent of free time engineers could spend on their own interests. In return, Google had rigid recruitment criteria and processes. Engineers had to have either a Masters or Doctorate from a leading university and pass a series of assessment tests and interviews. The criteria for these were derived in a highly scientific manner. In effect, Google recruited against a psychometric profile of *googleness* and could therefore hire and hopefully retain a fairly predictable employee population: much easier to manage.

What it became: Alphabet

In October 2015, Google was restructured and renamed Alphabet, a holding company that included the Google search company and a range of other businesses. The company had acquired over 150 companies spending around $23bn since its IPO in 2004. This included companies like YouTube, Android, Doubleclick and Nest. Besides all these acquisitions, Alphabet also included the semi-secret research and development facility Google X, focused on robotics and artificial intelligence including the company's driverless car. Larry Page became the CEO of Alphabet and Google co-founder Sergey Brin President, and senior VP Sundar Pichai became CEO of Google. Larry Page argued for forming Alphabet in his blog post:

> 'This newer Google is a bit slimmed down, with the companies that are pretty far afield of our main Internet products contained in Alphabet instead. What do we mean by far afield? Good examples are our health efforts: Life Sciences (that works on the glucose-sensing contact lens), and Calico (focused on longevity). Fundamentally, we believe this allows us more management scale, as we can run things independently that aren't very related. Alphabet is about businesses prospering through strong leaders and independence.'[3]

Observers and analysts were somewhat sceptical to a restructuring Google and its new name Alphabet.[1,4] Would it solve the recent challenges the company faced? Influenced by consumers' movement to smartphones with harder to see lower-priced ads, the amount advertisers were prepared to pay click-by-click had been falling. In addition, people didn't use mobile phones to do searches to the same extent as on computers, which offered the easiness of full keyboards and screens. Instead of internet searches, people increasingly used apps on mobiles.

Adding to Google's challenges was the fact that advertisers had not shifted their television ad budgets to internet and YouTube at the pace anticipated. YouTube accounted for about six per cent of Google's overall sales in 2014 and had about one billion viewers, but no profit. In addition, Facebook and Twitter, which regularly send traffic to the site, were building video offerings themselves. Amazon and Netflix were other contenders in the online video business.

The meteoric rise of Facebook, which also sold advertising space, was a third challenge. Google's response had been Google+, which former CEO Eric Schmidt had described as one of Google's most ambitious bets in the company's history. However, in 2015, Google+ was slowly but surely dismantled as customers did not appreciate the company's aim to create a platform that unified its different products. It was then relaunched with an emphasis on ways to join interest groups or 'Communities' and group posts by topics, called 'Collections'.

It seemed that the formation of Alphabet was a way to make each business able to operate more independently. This could possibly help the company focus on the search- and advertising-related businesses without being distracted by all their other businesses and vice versa. The change also made the company's structure clearer to investors as the company would report the core Google business results separately in earnings reports. It could potentially also help manage the company's talent as its various businesses would become more prominent and possibly attractive for employees and new hires.

In addition, the restructuring could, perhaps, persuade entrepreneurs to sell their businesses to Alphabet as they could go on developing them more independently from Google's search business.

The effects of forming Alphabet remained to be seen and it was not quite clear what strategy held the diverse portfolio together, as noted by one observer:

'Projecting a looser corporate structure, meanwhile, will raise the question of why Alphabet's collection of businesses belongs together. If the only things they share in common are the group's ample money and ambition, will this be enough to hold it together?

All of this made the evolution of Google into Alphabet feel more like part of a process than a settled corporate structure.

But as the Google CEO reminded shareholders: "Google is not a conventional company. We do not intend to become one."'[1]

Primary source: B. Girard, *The Google Way: How one company is revolutionising management as we know it,* No Starch Press, 2009.

References

1. Richard Waters, 'Google's Alphabet puzzle is all about perceptions', *Financial Times*, 1 October 2015, http://www.ft.com/cms/s/0/4fad4fa6-6854-11e5-a57f-21b88f7d973f.html.
2. Interview by Nicholas Carlson of Google CEO Eric Schmidt: 'We don't really have a five-year plan', *Washington Post Leadership series*, 20 May 2009.
3. Robert Hof, 'The real reasons Google will become Alphabet', *Forbes*, 8 October 2015, http://onforb.es/1MZ7T2Q.
4. See also https://www.youtube.com/watch?v=blAOPCNCszM.

Questions

1 Explain how Google's strategy has been developed over the years.

2 What are the strengths and weaknesses of its approach?

3 In what ways should Google's approach to strategy development change in the future?

14

ORGANISING
AND STRATEGY

Learning outcomes

After reading this chapter you should be able to:

- Analyse main organisational *structural types* in terms of their strengths and weaknesses.
- Identify key issues in designing organisational *control systems* (such as planning and performance targeting systems).
- Recognise how the three strands of strategy, structure and systems should reinforce each other in *organisational configurations*.

Key terms

configurations p.458

cultural systems p.453

divisional structure p.442

functional structure p.440

market systems p.456

matrix structure p.444

performance targets p.454

planning systems p.451

project-based structure p.448

structures p.439

systems p.439

transnational structure p.446

14.1 INTRODUCTION

Strategies only happen because people do what is required. If the American multinational retailer Walmart wants to achieve its strategy, it needs to get 2.2 million employees spread over 11,000 locations pointing in the right direction. In just the same way, a sports team has to ensure that its members coordinate their game plays. Thus strategies require organising and this involves both structures and systems. If the organisation is not consistent with the strategy, then even the cleverest strategy will fail because of poor implementation.

This chapter examines organising for successful strategy implementation. It focuses particularly on two key elements of organisational 'design': organisational structures and organisational systems. **Structures give people formally defined roles, responsibilities and lines of reporting.** These structures can be seen as the skeletons of organisations, providing the basic frameworks on which everything is built. **Systems support and control people as they carry out structurally defined roles and responsibilities.** Systems can be seen as the muscles of organisations, giving them movement and coherence.

Figure 14.1 expresses the interdependency between strategy, structure and systems. A starting principle of organisational design is that all three should support each other in a circular process of mutual reinforcement. This chapter captures the importance of mutual reinforcement between elements with the concept of *configuration,* explained in Section 14.4. However, the mutually reinforcing nature of configurations can create not only virtuous circles of performance, but also problems of control and adaptability. With regard to control, logically it seems that strategic priorities should determine structure and systems. But the circular nature of Figure 14.1 captures the potential for structures and systems to feed *into* strategy. As discussed in Section 14.2.6, structure and systems are not always the logical supports of strategy; sometimes, they shape it, consciously or not. With regard to adaptability, tightly-interlinked configurations of strategy, structure and systems can actually be a handicap. Section 14.4 will consider how configurations can be made more adaptable by fostering both *agility* and *resilience*.

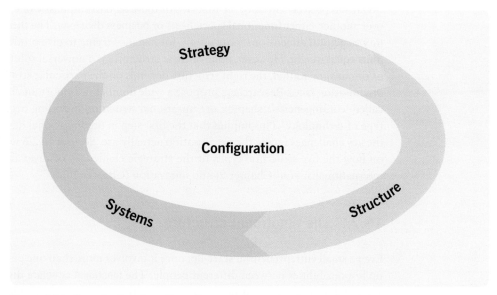

Figure 14.1 Organisational configurations: strategy, structure and systems

The chapter therefore addresses the following topics:

- *Structures*, defining the formal roles, responsibilities and lines of reporting in organisations. The chapter considers the main types of structures, including functional, divisional, matrix, project and transnational structures. Strategy and structure *fit* will be a key theme here.

- *Systems*, supporting and controlling people within and around an organisation. These systems include direct mechanisms such as performance targeting and planning, and more indirect ones such as cultural and market systems.

- *Configurations*, the mutually supporting elements that make up an organisation's design. As well as strategy, structure and systems, these elements can include staff, style, skills and superordinate goals, as encapsulated in the *McKinsey 7-S framework*.

The chapter concludes by considering new *non-hierarchical* structures and systems in Thinking Differently.

14.2 STRUCTURAL TYPES

Managers often describe their organisation by drawing an organisation chart, mapping out its formal structure. These structural charts define the levels and roles in an organisation. They are important to managers because they describe who reports to whom in terms of management and who is responsible for what in terms of activities. Thus structures can have major implications for organisational priorities and interactions in the marketplace. Structures therefore need careful alignment with strategy. One of the strategy discipline's founders, Alfred Chandler, documents how major corporations such as DuPont and General Motors nearly failed not because of ill-chosen strategies, but due to mismatches between their centralised structures and diversified strategies. He sums up the importance of fitting structure to strategy by saying: 'Unless structure follows strategy, inefficiency results.'[1] Qwikster's quick demise (Illustration 14.1) shows the perils of getting structure wrong.

This section reviews five basic structural types: functional, divisional, matrix, transnational and project.[2] Broadly, the first two of these tend to emphasise one structural dimension over another, either functional specialisms or business divisions. The three that follow tend to mix structural dimensions more evenly, for instance trying to give product and geographical units equal weight. However, none of these structures is a universal solution to the challenges of organising. Rather, the right structure depends on the particular strategic challenges each organisation faces. Researchers propose a wide number of important challenges (sometimes called 'contingencies') shaping organisational structure, including organisational size and type of technology.[3] This implies that the first step in organisational design is deciding what the key challenges facing the organisation actually are. Section 14.2.6 will particularly focus on how the five structural types fit the strategic challenges of diversification (Chapter 8), internationalisation (Chapter 9) and innovation (Chapter 10).

14.2.1 The functional structure

Even a small entrepreneurial start-up, once it involves more than one person, needs to divide up responsibilities between different people. The **functional structure divides responsibilities according to the organisation's primary specialist roles** such as production, research and

ILLUSTRATION 14.1 — Structural fault: Qwikster's quick demise

Netflix's introduction of the new Qwikster structure is a multi-billion-dollar failure.

In 2011, Netflix, the USA's largest online DVD rental and internet streaming company, faced a dilemma. Internet streaming of movies was clearly a growth business, one which competitors such as Amazon were beginning to enter. On the other hand, DVD rental by mail was facing long-term decline. In September 2011, Reed Hastings, CEO and joint founder of the company, responded to the dilemma with a structural solution. He proposed to split his business into two separate parts: henceforth streaming would be done exclusively under the Netflix label, while DVD rental would be done exclusively in a new organisational unit called Qwikster. In a blog post, Hastings explained his motivation: 'For the past five years, my greatest fear at Netflix has been that we wouldn't make the leap from success in DVDs to success in streaming. Most companies that are great at something – like AOL dialup or Borders bookstores – do not become great at new things people want (streaming for us) because they are afraid to hurt their initial business. Eventually these companies realise their error of not focusing enough on the new thing, and then the company fights desperately and hopelessly to recover. Companies rarely die from moving too fast, and they frequently die from moving too slowly.'

There were other reasons for the proposed split. The DVD business requires large warehouse and logistics operations, while streaming requires large internet resources. For DVDs, competitors include Blockbuster and Redbox, whereas streaming rivals include Amazon, iTunes and cable TV companies. As a stand-alone unit, managers in the streaming business could promote their alternative model without worrying about protecting the DVD business, still the larger part of Netflix's profits overall.

For customers, though, the split was less attractive. In future, customers would have to deal with two sites to get what they had previously got through one site. The DVD site offered many more movies, and tended to have more recent releases. Movie viewing recommendations for one site would not transfer to the other site. DVD renters would no longer receive the distinctive Netflix DVD envelopes which had strong brand loyalty.

The customer response was hostile. In the month following Qwikster's launch, Netflix lost hundreds of thousands of subscribers. The Netflix share price fell more than 60 per cent, wiping out more than $3bn (£1.8bn, €2.3bn) in value. CEO Reed Hastings joked in a Facebook message that he feared poisoning by some of his investors: 'I think I might need a food taster. I can hardly blame them.'

On 10 October 2011, three weeks after the original Qwikster announcement, Hastings blogged that the new unit would not go ahead after all, and that all business would continue under the Netflix label. Hastings explained: 'There is a difference between moving quickly – which Netflix has done very well for years – and moving too fast, which is what we did in this case.' Despite his reversal of the structural change, repercussions were still being felt a year later: Netflix's market share of DVD rentals in 2012 had dropped from 35 per cent to 27 per cent, and rival Redbox had taken market leadership.

Sources: *Wall Street Journal*, 11 October 2011; *Strategy+Business*, 2 April 2012; *PC Magazine*, 17 September 2012.

Questions

1 How do the pros and cons of the Qwikster structure fit with those associated with the divisional structure (see Section 14.2.2)?

2 In the light of the planning, cultural, market and targeting systems discussed in Section 14.3, what else would Netflix have needed to do to manage the separation of the streaming business and the rental business?

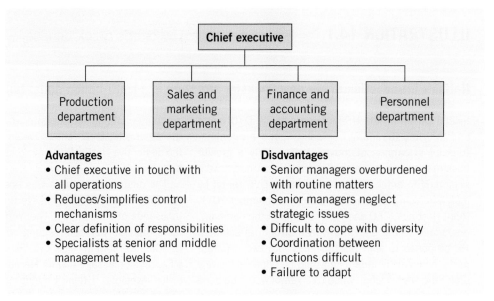

Figure 14.2 A functional structure

sales. Figure 14.2 represents a typical organisation chart for such a functional organisation. This kind of structure is particularly relevant to small or start-up organisations, or larger organisations that have retained narrow, rather than diverse, product ranges. Functional structures may also be used within a multidivisional structure (see below), where the divisions themselves may split themselves up according to functional departments (as in Figure 14.2).

Figure 14.2 also summarises the potential advantages and disadvantages of a functional structure. There are advantages in that it gives senior managers direct hands-on involvement in operations and allows greater operational control from the top. The functional structure provides a clear definition of roles and tasks, increasing accountability. Functional departments also provide concentrations of expertise, thus fostering knowledge development in areas of functional specialism.

However, there are disadvantages, particularly as organisations become larger or more diverse. Perhaps the major concern in a fast-moving world is that senior managers focus too much on their functional responsibilities, becoming overburdened with routine operations and too concerned with narrow functional interests. As a result, they find it hard either to take a strategic view of the organisation as a whole or to coordinate separate functions quickly: marketing managers focus on just marketing, while operations managers focus on operations. Thus functional organisations can be inflexible, poor at adapting to change. Separate functional departments tend also to be inward-looking – so-called 'functional silos' – making it difficult to integrate the knowledge of different functional specialists.[4] Finally, because they are centralised around particular functions, functional structures are not good at coping with product or geographical diversity. For example, a central marketing department may try to impose a uniform approach to advertising regardless of the diverse needs of the organisation's various markets around the world.

14.2.2 The divisional structure

A **divisional structure** is built up of separate divisions on the basis of products, services or geographical areas (see Figure 14.3). Divisionalisation often comes about as an attempt to overcome the problems that functional structures have in dealing with the diversity mentioned

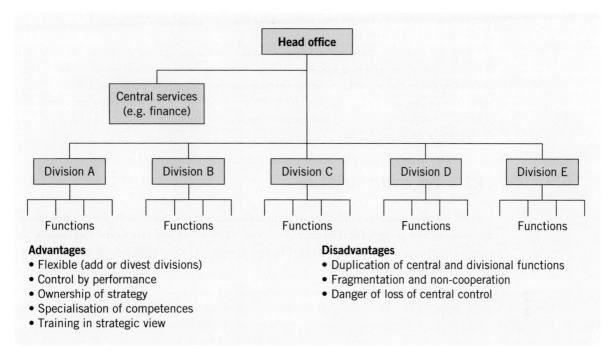

Advantages
- Flexible (add or divest divisions)
- Control by performance
- Ownership of strategy
- Specialisation of competences
- Training in strategic view

Disadvantages
- Duplication of central and divisional functions
- Fragmentation and non-cooperation
- Danger of loss of central control

Figure 14.3 A multidivisional structure

above.[5] Each division can respond to the specific requirements of its product/market strategy, using its own set of functional departments. A similar situation exists in many public services, where the organisation is structured around *service departments* such as recreation, social services and education.

There are several potential advantages to divisional structures. As self-standing business units, it is possible to control divisions from a distance simply by monitoring business performance: top management need only intervene if targets are being missed (see Illustration 14.2 on Google and Section 14.3.3). Having divisions also provides flexibility because organisations can add, close or merge divisions as circumstances change. Divisional managers have greater personal ownership for their own divisional strategies. Geographical divisions – for example, a European division or a North American division – offer a means of managing internationally (see Section 14.2.4). There can be benefits of specialisation within a division, allowing competences to develop with a clearer focus on a particular product group, technology or customer group. For managers expecting to go on to a main board position, management responsibility for a whole divisional business is good training in taking a strategic view.

However, divisional structures can also have disadvantages of three main types. First, divisions can become so self-sufficient that they are *de facto* independent businesses, but duplicating the functions and costs of the corporate centre of the company. In such cases of *de facto* independence, it may make more sense to split the company into independent businesses, and de-mergers of this type are now common. Second, divisionalisation tends to get in the way of cooperation and knowledge-sharing between business units: divisions can quite literally divide. Expertise is fragmented and divisional performance targets provide poor incentives to collaborate with other divisions. Finally, divisions may become too autonomous, especially where joint ventures and partnership dilute ownership. Here, divisions pursue their own strategies almost regardless of the needs of the corporate parent. In these cases, divisional companies become *holding companies,* where the corporate centre effectively 'holds' the various businesses in a largely financial sense, exercising little control and adding little value. Figure 14.3 summarises these potential advantages and disadvantages of a multidivisional structure.

Large and complex divisional companies often have a second tier of *subdivisions* within their main divisions. Treating smaller strategic business units as subdivisions within a large division reduces the number of units that the corporate centre has to deal with directly. Subdivisions can also help complex organisations respond to contradictory pressures. For example, an organisation could have geographical subdivisions within a set of global product divisions (see Section 14.2.4).

14.2.3 The matrix structure

A **matrix structure** combines different structural dimensions simultaneously, for example product divisions and geographical territories or product divisions and functional specialisms.[6] In matrix structures, staff typically report to two managers rather than one. Figure 14.4 gives examples of such a structure.

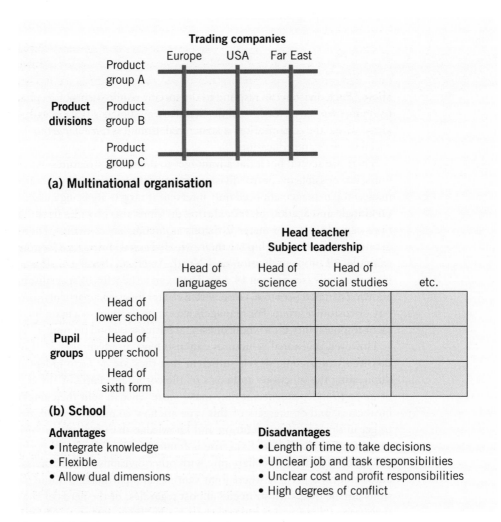

(a) Multinational organisation

(b) School

Advantages	**Disadvantages**
• Integrate knowledge	• Length of time to take decisions
• Flexible	• Unclear job and task responsibilities
• Allow dual dimensions	• Unclear cost and profit responsibilities
	• High degrees of conflict

Figure 14.4 Two examples of matrix structures

Matrix structures have several advantages. They promote *knowledge-sharing* because they allow separate areas of knowledge to be integrated across organisational boundaries. Particularly in professional service organisations, matrix organisations can be helpful in applying particular knowledge specialisms to different market or geographical segments. For example, to serve a particular client, a consulting firm may draw on people from groups with particular knowledge specialisms (e.g. strategy or organisation design) and others grouped according to particular markets (industry sectors or geographical regions). Figure 14.4 shows how a school might combine the separate knowledge of subject specialists to create programmes of study tailored differently to various age groups. Matrix organisations are *flexible*, because they allow different dimensions of the organisation to be mixed together. They are particularly attractive to organisations operating globally, because of the possible mix between local and global dimensions. For example, a global company may prefer geographically defined divisions as the operating units for local marketing (because of their specialist local knowledge of customers). But at the same time it may still want global product units responsible for the worldwide coordination of product development and manufacturing, taking advantage of economies of scale and specialisation. However, because a matrix structure replaces single lines of authority with multiple cross-matrix relationships, this often brings problems. In particular, it will typically take *longer to reach decisions* because of bargaining between the managers of different dimensions. There may also be *conflict* because staff find themselves responsible to managers from two structural dimensions. In short, matrix organisations are hard to control.

As with any structure, but particularly with the matrix structure, the critical issue in practice is the way it actually works (i.e. behaviours and relationships). The key ingredient in a successful matrix structure can be senior managers good at sustaining collaborative relationships (across the matrix) and coping with the messiness and ambiguity which that can bring. It is for this reason that Chris Bartlett and Sumantra Ghoshal describe the matrix as involving a 'frame of mind' as much as a formal structure.[7]

14.2.4 Multinational/transnational structures

Operating internationally adds an extra dimension to the structural challenge. As in Figure 14.5, there are essentially four structural designs available for multinationals. Three are simple extensions of the principles of the divisional structure (Section 14.2.2), so are dealt with briefly. The fourth, the transnational structure, is more complex and will be explained at more length.

The three simpler multinational structures are as follows:

- *International divisions.* An international division is a stand-alone division added alongside the structure of the main home-based business. This is often the kind of structure adopted by corporations with large domestic markets (such as in the USA or China), where an initial entry into overseas markets is relatively small-scale and does not require structural change to the original, much bigger, home businesses. For example, a Chinese car, truck and motorbike manufacturer might have separate divisions for each of its product areas in its home market of China, but run its overseas businesses in a separate 'international division' combining all three product areas together. The international division is typically run from headquarters, but not integrated with the domestic business. As in Figure 14.5, the international division is centralised, but not highly coordinated with other parts of the business.

- *Local subsidiaries.* These subsidiaries typically have most of the functions required to operate on their own in their particular local market, for example design, production and marketing. They are thus a form of geographic divisional structure. They have high

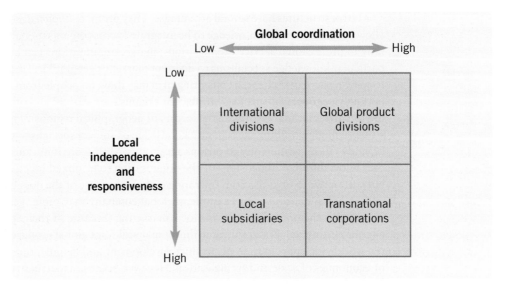

Figure 14.5 Multinational structures

Source: Reprinted by permission of Harvard Business School Press. From *Managing Across Borders: The Transnational Corporation,* 2nd edition by C.A. Bartlett and S. Ghoshal, Boston, MA, 1998. Copyright © 1998 by the Harvard Business School Publishing Corporation. All rights reserved.

local responsiveness and are loosely coordinated. A local subsidiary structure is very common in professional services such as law, accounting and advertising, where there are few economies of scale and responsiveness to local regulations, relationships or tastes is very important. This structure fits the multi-domestic strategy introduced in Section 9.4.

- *Global product divisions.* This kind of structure is often used where economies of scale are very important. Organising the design, production and marketing on the basis of global divisions rather than local subsidiaries typically maximises cost efficiency. It also helps direct central resources to targeted markets and facilitates cross-subsidisation of unprofitable geographical markets. To return to the Chinese car, truck and motorbike manufacturer, there would be just three divisions, each responsible for its particular product area across the whole world, China included. There would be very little scope for adaptation to local tastes or regulations in particular markets. In global product divisions, local responsiveness would typically be very low. This structure fits the global strategy introduced in Chapter 9. It is also similar to Google's basic structural approach (see Illustration 14.2 and Chapter 13 end case).

The international division, local subsidiary and global product division structures all have their particular advantages, whether it is managing relative size, maximising local responsiveness or achieving economies of scale. The fourth structure, however, tries to integrate the advantages of the local subsidiary structure with those of the global product divisional structure.

In terms of Figure 14.5, the **transnational structure combines local responsiveness with high global coordination.**[8] According to Bartlett and Ghoshal, transnational structures are similar to matrices but distinguish themselves by their focus on knowledge-sharing, specialisation and network management, as follows:

- *Knowledge-sharing.* While each national or regional business has a good deal of autonomy, in the transnational they should see themselves as sources of ideas and capabilities for the whole corporation. Thus a good idea that has been developed locally is offered for adoption by other national or regional units around the world.

ILLUSTRATION 14.2   Google gets a new name and a new structure

In August 2015, Google became a subsidiary of Alphabet Inc.

Google had been founded in 1998 as an internet search company by two Stanford PhD students, Larry Page and Sergey Brin. The search activities were funded by advertising (Ads). In the following years, the company had diversified radically, entering for example maps, video (YouTube) and mobile operating systems (Android). It had also established Google X, for so-called 'moonshot' initiatives such as Google Glass, which displays information on a headset (like glasses). Google Ventures invested in start-ups such as Uber. There were also acquisitions such as Nest, involved in home automation. Another major venture was Calico, a health business dedicated to extending lives through better use of information.

In August 2015, Google CEO Larry Page announced a major change of structure. A new parent company Alphabet Inc. would be created, under which Google would become a subsidiary responsible for a group of businesses (Ads, Maps, Search and so on) that would no longer report directly to Page. The Google X, Ventures, Nest and Calico subsidiaries would continue to report directly to Page. Each of the subsidiaries would have their own CEOs (Pichai, Teller, Marris, Fadell and Levinson). Financial results would be reported for each subsidiary, instead of just consolidated for the whole as previously. Brin explained: 'Fundamentally, we believe this allows us more management scale, as we can run things independently that aren't very related. . . . In general, our model is to have a strong CEO who runs each business, with Sergey and me in service to them as needed.' News of the restructuring lifted the Google/Alphabet stock price by seven per cent, an increase worth $29bn (£17.4bn, €21.6bn).

Sources: Business Insider, 11 August 2015; *Financial Times*, 11 August 2015; *Google Press Release*, 10 August 2015.

> ### Questions
>
> 1 In what respects is the change consistent with Alfred Chandler's phrase, 'structure follows strategy'?
>
> 2 Why do investors think that the new Alphabet structure is worth an extra $29bn?

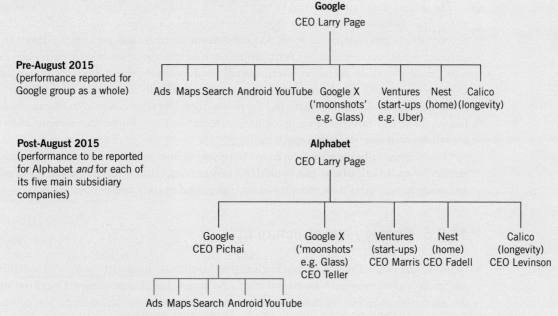

Pre-August 2015
(performance reported for Google group as a whole)

Google
CEO Larry Page

Ads   Maps   Search   Android   YouTube   Google X ('moonshots' e.g. Glass)   Ventures (start-ups) e.g. Uber   Nest (home)   Calico (longevity)

Post-August 2015
(performance to be reported for Alphabet *and* for each of its five main subsidiary companies)

Alphabet
CEO Larry Page

Google CEO Pichai   Google X ('moonshots' e.g. Glass) CEO Teller   Ventures (start-ups) CEO Marris   Nest (home) CEO Fadell   Calico (longevity) CEO Levinson

Ads   Maps   Search   Android   YouTube

Source: Simplified from *Business Insider*, 'One chart that explains Alphabet, Google's new parent company', 11 August 2015, Wright's Media, LLC.

- *Specialisation*. National (or regional) units specialise in areas of expertise in order to achieve greater scale economies on behalf of the whole corporation. Thus a national unit that has particular competences in manufacturing a particular product, for example, may be given responsibility for manufacturing that product on behalf of other units across the world.

- *Network management*. The corporate centre has the role of managing this global network of specialisms and knowledge. It does so first by establishing the specialist role of each business unit, then sustaining the systems and relationships required to make the network of business units operate in an integrated and effective manner.

The success of a transnational corporation is dependent on the ability *simultaneously* to achieve global competences, local responsiveness and organisation-wide innovation and learning. Theoretically the transnational combines the best of local decentralisation with the best of global centralisation. However, the transnational can be very demanding of managers in terms of willingness to work not just at their national business units but for the good of the transnational as a whole. Diffuse responsibilities also make for similar complexities and control problems to those of the matrix organisation.[9]

14.2.5 Project-based structures[10]

Many organisations rely heavily on project teams with a finite life span. A **project-based structure is one where teams are created, undertake a specific project and are then dissolved.**[11] This can be particularly appropriate for organisations that deliver large and expensive goods or services (civil engineering, information systems, films) and those delivering time-limited events (conferences, sporting events or consulting engagements). The organisation structure is a constantly changing collection of project teams created, steered and glued together loosely by a small corporate group. Many organisations use such teams in a more ad hoc way to complement the 'main' structure. For example, projects or *task forces* are set up to make progress on new elements of strategy (for example acquisitions or new business initiatives) or to provide momentum where the regular structure of the organisation is not effective.

The project-based structure can be highly flexible, with projects being set up and dissolved as required. Because project teams should have clear tasks to achieve within a defined period, accountability and control are good. As project team members will typically be drawn from different departments within the firm, projects can be effective at knowledge exchange. Projects can also draw on members internationally and, because project lifespans are typically short, project teams may be more willing to work temporarily around the world. There are disadvantages, however. Organisations are prone to proliferate projects in an ill-coordinated fashion. The constant breaking up of project teams can also hinder the accumulation of knowledge over time or within specialisms.

Overall, project-based structures have been growing in importance because of their inherent flexibility. Such flexibility can be vital in a fast-moving world where individual knowledge and competences need to be redeployed and integrated quickly and in novel ways.

14.2.6 Strategy and structure fit

From the discussion so far, it should be clear that functional, divisional, matrix, transnational and project structures each have their own advantages and disadvantages. Organisational designers, therefore, have to choose structures according to the particular strategic challenges they face. As Chandler said, structures have to fit strategies.[12] This section summarises the effectiveness of the five structures in relation to three key strategies, before going on to consider specific organisation design tests.

Table 14.1 Strategy and structure fit

Strategy/structure	Functional	Multidivisional	Matrix	Transnational	Project
Diversification	*	***	**	**	**
Internationalisation	*	**	***	***	*
Innovation	**	*	**	**	***

* Stars indicate *typical* fits with each strategy, with three stars indicating good fit, two indicating medium fit and one typically less good fit. Fits may vary with industry specific conditions.

Table 14.1 summarises the typical fits between the five structural types and strategies of diversification, internationalisation and innovation (organisations and strategies vary and structures can be adjusted, so outcomes may differ in particular cases). Key points are highlighted in the following:

- *Diversification* raises the corporate strategy challenges of control and accountability within widely different businesses, as discussed in Chapter 8. Divisionalisation should allow business managers enough decentralised responsibility to enact their own strategies, while the corporate parent can exercise control by monitoring business performance. The functional structure is too centralised to allow effective diversification. Matrix structures blur accountability, as divisional business units have horizontal responsibilities as well.

- *Internationalisation* strategies raise dilemmas over global scale, horizontal coordination and local adaptation, as discussed in Section 9.4. Matrix and transnational structures are particularly effective in accommodating both sides of such dilemmas: for example, one dimension could allow for scale, the other could allow for coordination or sharing. Divisional structures tend to resolve these dilemmas more unilaterally, either allowing centralised product divisions for scale or local subsidiaries for local adaptation. They tend to be less good at horizontal coordination and sharing.

- *Innovation* strategies typically require knowledge creation and knowledge-sharing, as discussed in Chapters 4 and 10. Matrix organisations are good for horizontal sharing. Project organisations can bring together teams of relevant experts to focus intensively on innovation initiatives. The functional structure can be effective in innovation because centralisation concentrates resources, particularly research and development.

While Table 14.1 considers the typical fits between strategies and structures, Goold and Campbell provide *nine design tests* to help design tailor-made structural solutions for specific circumstances.[13] The first four tests stress fit with the key objectives and constraints of the organisation:

- The *Market-Advantage Test*. This test of fit with market strategy is fundamental, following Alfred Chandler's classic principle that 'structure follows strategy'.[14] For example, if market advantage depends on integrated services (such as research and development or information technology), then they should probably not be split between different structural units.

- The *Parenting Advantage Test*. The structural design should fit the 'parenting' role of the corporate centre (see Section 8.6). For example, if the corporate centre aims to add value as a synergy manager, then it should design a structure that places important integrative specialisms, such as marketing or research, at the centre.

- The *People Test*. The structural design must fit the people available. It is dangerous to switch completely from a functional structure to a multidivisional structure if, as is likely, the organisation lacks managers with competence in running decentralised business units.

- The *Feasibility Test*. This is a catch-all category, indicating that the structure must fit legal, stakeholder, trade union or similar constraints. For example, after scandals involving biased research, investment banks are now required by financial regulators to separate their research departments from their deal-making departments.

Goold and Campbell then propose five more tests based on good general organisational design principles, as follows:

- The *Specialised Cultures Test*. This test reflects the value of bringing together specialists so that they can develop their expertise in close collaboration with each other. A structure scores poorly if it breaks up important specialist cultures.

- The *Difficult Links Test*. This test asks whether a proposed structure will set up links between parts of the organisations that are important but bound to be strained. For example, extreme decentralisation to profit-accountable business units is likely to strain relationships with a central research and development department. Unless compensating mechanisms are put in place, this kind of structure is likely to fail.

- The *Redundant Hierarchy Test*. Any structural design should be checked in case it has too many layers of management, causing undue blockages and expense. Delayering in response to redundant hierarchies has been an important structural trend in recent years.

- The *Accountability Test*. This test stresses the importance of clear lines of accountability, ensuring the control and commitment of managers throughout the structure. Because of their dual lines of reporting, matrix structures are often accused of lacking clear accountability.

- The *Flexibility Test*. While not all organisations will face the same general rise in environmental velocity as referred to with regard to Table 14.1, a final important test is whether the design will be sufficiently flexible to accommodate possible changes in the future. Here Kathleen Eisenhardt argues for structural 'modularity' (i.e. standardisation) in order to allow easy 'patching' (i.e. transfer) of one part of the organisation to another part of the organisation, as market needs change.[15] For example, if strategic business units are similar in structural size and internal management systems throughout a large organisation, it becomes easy to transfer them from one division to another according to changing business needs.

Goold and Campbell's nine tests provide a rigorous screen for effective structures. However, it is important to realise that in practice managers do not start from scratch in choosing their organisational structures. With regard to the market advantage test, for instance, structure does not always follow logically from strategy; rather, existing structures can shape the strategy. Thus a business with an existing multidivisional structure may continue with an acquisitions and divestments strategy simply because that structure makes it easy just to keep on adding and subtracting various businesses as divisional units. Conversely, a functional organisation might be reluctant to undertake acquisitions because it is hard to integrate within its centralised structure. Thus the structure can reinforce the current strategy, regardless of whether the strategy is a good one.[16] Moreover, not only is it hard to fit strategy and structure as logic seems to dictate, but managers also have to align them with the other key part of the configuration—organisational systems. As in Figure 14.1, systems too should be designed to reinforce strategy and structure.

14.3 SYSTEMS

Structure is a key ingredient of organising for success. But structures can only work if they are supported by formal and informal organisational systems, the 'muscles' of the organisation. Systems help ensure control over strategy implementation. Small organisations may be able to rely on *direct supervision,* where a single manager or entrepreneur monitors activity in person. But larger or more complex organisations typically need more elaborate structures and systems if they are to be effective over time (though see Thinking Differently on non-hierarchical systems, at the end of this chapter). This section considers four systems specifically: planning, performance targeting, culture and internal markets.

Such systems can be subdivided in two ways. First, systems tend to emphasise either control over inputs or control over outputs. Input control systems concern themselves with the *resources* consumed in the strategy, especially financial resources and human commitment. Output control systems focus on ensuring satisfactory *results,* for example the meeting of targets or achieving market competitiveness. The second subdivision is between direct and indirect controls. Direct controls involve *close supervision* or monitoring. Indirect controls are more *hands-off,* setting up the conditions whereby desired behaviours are achieved semi-automatically. Table 14.2 summarises how the four systems of planning, performance targeting, culture and internal markets each emphasise input or output controls and direct or indirect controls.

Organisations normally use a blend of these control systems, but some will dominate over others according to the nature of strategic challenges. As we shall see, direct measures tend to require that the controllers have high levels of knowledge of what the controlled are supposed to do. In many knowledge-intensive organisations, especially those generating innovation and change, controllers rarely have a good understanding of what their expert employees are doing, nor can they easily define what they are potentially capable of doing. In these conditions, it is usually better to rely on indirect controls such as performance targeting: at least they can know when a unit has made its revenue or profitability targets. Direct control works better in simple and stable businesses, where input requirements are stable and well understood, or where key outcomes are unambiguous. Utility businesses supplying power or water might respond well to direct forms of control.

14.3.1 Planning systems

Planning systems plan and control the allocation of resources and monitor their utilisation. The focus is on the direct control of inputs. These might be simple financial inputs (as in budgeting), human inputs (as in planning for managerial succession) or long-term investments (as particularly in strategic planning). This section concentrates on strategic oversight from the corporate centre, developing the discussions in Chapters 8 and 13.

Table 14.2 Types of control systems

	Input	Output
Direct	Planning systems	Performance targeting
Indirect	Cultural systems	Internal markets

Goold and Campbell's[17] typology of three *corporate strategy styles* helps to identify the advantages and disadvantages of planning systems against other methods of corporate central oversight. The three strategy styles differ widely along two dimensions: the *dominant source of planning influence,* either top-down (from the corporate centre to the business units) or bottom-up (from the business units to the centre); and the *degree of performance accountability* for the business units, either tight or reasonably relaxed. As in Figure 14.6, the three corporate strategy styles align themselves on these two dimensions thus:

- The *strategic planning* style is the archetypal planning system, hence its name. In the Goold and Campbell sense, the strategic planning style combines both a strong planning influence on strategic direction from the corporate centre with relatively relaxed performance accountability for the business units. The logic is that if the centre sets the strategic direction, business unit managers should not be held strictly accountable for disappointing results that might be due to an inappropriate plan in the first place. In the strategic planning style, the centre focuses on inputs in terms of allocating resources necessary to achieve the strategic plan, while exercising a high degree of direct control over how the plan is executed by the businesses.

- The *financial control* style involves very little central planning. The business units each set their own strategic plans, probably after some negotiation with the corporate centre, and are then held strictly accountable for the results against these plans. This style differs from the strategic planning style in that control is against financial outputs, similar to a performance targeting system (see Section 14.3.3). If the businesses devised the plans, then they should take full responsibility for success or failure. Business unit managers in the financial control style have a lot of autonomy and typically receive high bonus payments for success. But failure may easily lead to dismissal. The financial planning style fits with the portfolio manager or restructurer roles of the corporate centre referred to in Chapter 8.

- The *strategic control* style is in the middle, with a more consensual development of the strategic plan between the corporate centre and the business units and moderate levels of business unit accountability. Under the strategic control style, the centre will typically act as coach to its business unit managers, helping them to see and seize opportunities

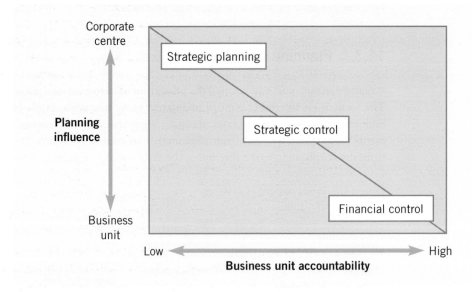

Figure 14.6 Strategy styles

Source: Adapted from M. Goold and A. Campbell, *Strategies and Styles,* Blackwell, 1989, Figure 3.1, p. 39.

in a supportive manner. This style often relies on strong cultural systems to foster trust and mutual understanding (see Section 14.3.3). Consequently, the strategic control style is often associated with the synergy manager or parental developer roles of the corporate centre discussed in Chapter 8.

Thus the three corporate strategy styles vary with regard to their reliance on, and application of, planning systems. The direct control of inputs characteristic of the strategic planning style is only appropriate in certain circumstances. In particular, it makes sense where there are large, risky and long-range investments to be allocated: for example, an oil company typically has to take the decision to invest in the ten-year development of an oilfield at the corporate centre, rather than risk delegating it to business units whose resources and time horizons may be limited. On the other hand, the financial control style is suitable where investments are small, relatively frequent and well understood, as typically in a mature, non-capital-intensive business. The strategic control style is suitable where there are opportunities for collaborating across businesses and there is a need to nurture new ones.

The strategic planning style (not the practice of strategic planning in general) has become less common in the private sector in recent years. The style is seen as too rigid to adapt to changing circumstances and too top-down to reflect real business circumstances on the ground. However, it is important to recognise the internal consistency of all three styles, including strategic planning. Each achieves logical combinations of accountability and strategic influence. Problems occur when organisations construct systems of planning and accountability that depart substantially from the diagonal line in Figure 14.6. Too far below the line (the 'south-west' corner) implies an excessively relaxed combination of weak direction from the centre and low accountability for the businesses. Too far above the diagonal line (the 'north-east' corner) implies a harsh combination of strong direction from the centre and strict accountability in the businesses. In the 'north-east' corner, business managers are held accountable even for mistakes that may have their origins in the centre's own plans.

14.3.2 Cultural systems

Organisations typically have distinctive cultures which express basic assumptions and beliefs held by organisation members and define taken-for-granted ways of doing things (see Chapter 6). Despite their taken-for-granted, semi-conscious nature, organisational cultures can seem a tempting means of managerial control. Managers may therefore try to influence organisational culture through various deliberate mechanisms in order to achieve the kinds of employee behaviour required by their strategy.[18] Such **cultural systems aim to standardise norms of behaviour within an organisation in line with particular objectives.** Cultural systems exercise an *indirect* form of control, because of not requiring direct supervision: it becomes a matter of willing conformity or *self*-control by employees. Control is exerted on the *input* of employees, as the culture defines the norms of appropriate effort and initiative that employees will put into their jobs.

Three key cultural systems are:

- *Selection*. Here cultural conformity may be attempted by the selection of appropriate staff in the first place. Employers look to find people who will 'fit'. Thus some employers may favour recruiting people who have already shown themselves to be 'team-players' through sport or other activities.

- *Socialisation*. Here employee behaviours are shaped by social processes once they are at work. It often starts with the integration of new staff through training, induction and mentoring programmes. It typically continues with further training throughout a career. Symbols can also play a role in socialisation, for example the symbolic example of leaders' behaviours or the influence of office décor, dress codes or language.

- *Reward*. Appropriate behaviour can be encouraged through pay, promotion or symbolic processes (e.g. public praise). The desire to achieve the same rewards as successful people in the organisation will typically encourage imitative behaviour.

It is important to recognise that organisations' cultures are not fully under formal management control. Sometimes aspects of organisational culture may persistently contradict managerial intentions, as with peer-group pressure not to respond to organisational policies. Cynicism and 'going through the motions' are common in some organisations. Sometimes the culture of an organisation may even drive its strategy (see Chapter 6). On the other hand, some cultures can bring about desired results, even without deliberate management intervention. For example, workers often form spontaneous and informal 'communities of practice', in which expert practitioners inside or even outside the organisation share their knowledge to generate innovative solutions to problems on their own initiative.[19] Examples of these informal communities of practice range from the Xerox photocopying engineers who would exchange information about problems and solutions over breakfast gatherings at the start of the day, to the programmer networks which support the development of Linux 'freeware' internationally over the internet.

14.3.3 Performance targeting systems

Performance targets focus on the *outputs* of an organisation (or part of an organisation), such as product quality, revenues or profits. These targets are often known as *key performance indicators* (KPIs) (see Chapter 12). The performance of an organisation is judged, either internally or externally, on its ability to meet these targets. However, within specified boundaries, the organisation remains free on how targets should be achieved. This approach can be particularly appropriate in certain situations:

- Within *large businesses,* corporate centres may choose performance targets to control their business units without getting involved in the details of how they achieve them (as in the financial control style in Section 14.3.1). These targets are often cascaded down the organisation as specific targets for subunits, functions and even individuals.

- In *regulated markets,* such as privatised utilities in the UK and elsewhere, government-appointed regulators increasingly exercise control through agreed key performance indicators (KPIs), such as service or quality levels, as a means of ensuring 'competitive' performance.[20]

- In *the public services,* where control of resource inputs was the dominant approach historically, governments are attempting to move control processes towards outputs (such as quality of service) and, more importantly, towards outcomes (e.g. patient mortality rates in healthcare). See Illustration 14.3 for consideration of performance targets in police, fire and ambulance services.

Many managers find it difficult to develop a useful set of targets. There are at least three potential problems with targets:[21]

- *Inappropriate measures* of performance are quite common. For example, managers often prefer indicators that are easily measured or choose measures based on inadequate understanding of real needs on the ground. The result is a focus on the required measures rather than the factors that might be essential to long-term success. In the private sector, focus on short-term profit measures is common, at the expense of investment in the long-run prosperity of the business.

ILLUSTRATION 14.3   Call fire, police and ambulance

In early 2016, fire, police and ambulance services faced proposals from the UK government for greater collaboration and even merger.

Police officers, firefighters and ambulance paramedics often work closely together in incidents such as major traffic accidents, public disorder or floods and similar natural disasters. Experiments have shown that there is scope for major efficiencies in greater cooperation, for example in the sharing of emergency call facilities or the management of vehicle fleets. It seemed to make sense to the UK government to impose upon the three services a duty of cooperation, and indeed to propose mergers between police and fire services in particular.

However, the three services have previously been controlled by very different organisation structures and have had very different performance metrics and cultures. The police are controlled by directly elected Police and Crime Commissioners for particular localities. They are a uniformed service, with a highly hierarchical quasi-militaristic structure. A key responsibility is to fight crime. The fire services are under the control of local authorities, so without direct accountability to the electorate. They too are a uniformed service, though with a somewhat less militaristic structure. Their job is to prevent and suppress fire and similar types of threat. The ambulance services are the responsibility of local health authorities and are part of the National Health Service. Paramedics see themselves as part of the caring professions.

The government minister responsible told Parliament in January 2016: 'Directly elected Police and Crime Commissioners are clearly accountable to the public and have a strong incentive to pursue ambitious reform and deliver value for money. We will enable them to take on responsibility for fire and rescue services where a local case is made.' It was estimated that savings of about £200m (€240m, $300m) could result from shared back-office activities.

Some were enthusiastic about the possibilities of merger. Adam Simmonds, Police and Crime Commissioner for Northamptonshire, told the *Daily Express* that he saw a day when ambulance services too could be placed under the Police and Crime Commissioner's remit and roles could become more interchangeable:

'You are looking at a single executive figure who has control of a wide range of public services. . . . PCCs certainly have a role to play in wider public service delivery. This merger is . . . about getting a better service for the public. Why not train the workforce in each of the services to do different bits [of each others' jobs] depending on the circumstances? . . . That is the model for the future.'

Others had reservations, especially about where back-office merger and cooperation could eventually lead to. Steve White, chairman of the Police Federation, was reported in the *Daily Express* as warning:

'We can't arrive at the situation where your home has been burgled and you don't know whether a paramedic, a fireman or a police officer is going to turn up. I don't think anybody would want a police car to turn up and then to wheel a hose out of the boot and start putting a fire out. That is utterly barmy.'

Matt Wrack, leader of the Fire Brigades Union, wrote in the *Huffington Post*:

'The fire and rescue service is a separate humanitarian service very distinct from policing. Indeed a more obvious link lies with emergency ambulance services . . . The situation is very different in relation to policing. The police have the power to arrest. Firefighters do not. This is an extremely important aspect of our relations with local communities, especially in an era when firefighters are asking to enter people's homes every day to provide safety.'

Sources: Daily Express, 31 May 2015; *Huffington Post*, 1 January 2016; *Financial Times*, 26 January 2016.

Questions

1 Consider the kinds of cultural and performance targeting systems the police, fire and ambulance services are each likely to have. How compatible are they?

2 Would you agree with Matt Wrack that the more obvious links are between ambulance and fire services?

- *Inappropriate target levels* are a common problem. Managers are liable to give their superiors pessimistic forecasts so that targets are set at undemanding levels, which can then be easily met. On the other hand, superiors may over-compensate for their managers' pessimism and end up setting excessively demanding targets. Unrealistically ambitious targets can either demotivate employees who see no hope of achieving them regardless of their effort, or encourage risky or dishonest behaviours in order to achieve the otherwise impossible.

- *Excessive internal competition* can be a result of targets focused on individual or subunit performance. Although an organisation by definition should be more than the sum of its parts, if individuals or subunits are being rewarded on their performance in isolation, they will have little incentive to collaborate with the other parts of the organisation. The struggle to meet individualistic targets will reduce the exchange of information and the sharing of resources. This kind of individualistic behaviour played a part in the fraud at UBS (Illustration 14.4).

These acknowledged difficulties with targets have led to the development of two techniques designed to encourage a more balanced approach to target-setting. The most fundamental has been the development of the balanced scorecard approach.[22] *Balanced scorecards* set performance targets according to a range of perspectives, not only financial. Thus balanced scorecards typically combine four specific perspectives: the *financial perspective*, which might include profit margins or cash flow; the *customer perspective*, which sets targets important to customers, such as delivery times or service levels; the *internal perspective*, with targets relating to operational effectiveness, such as the development of IT systems or reductions in waste levels; and finally the future-orientated *innovation and learning perspective*, which targets activities that will be important to the long-run performance of the organisation, for example investment in training or research. Attending to targets relevant to all four perspectives helps ensure that managers do not focus on one set of targets (e.g. financial) at the expense of others, while also keeping an eye to the future through innovation and learning.

A second more balanced approach to target-setting is strategy mapping, developing the balanced scorecard idea. *Strategy maps* link different performance targets into a mutually supportive causal chain supporting strategic objectives. Figure 14.7 shows an extract of a strategy map for a delivery company based on the four perspectives of finance, customers, internal processes and innovation and learning. In this map, investments in well-trained and motivated drivers under the heading of 'innovation and learning' lead to on-time deliveries under the heading of 'internal processes', and thence to satisfied customers and finally to profitable growth. The causal chain between the various targets underlines the need for balance between them: each depends on the others for achievement. Thus strategy maps help in reducing the problem of partial measures referred to above; the problems of inappropriate target levels and internal competition are not so easily resolved.

14.3.4 Market systems

Market disciplines (or *internal markets*) can be brought inside organisations to control activities internally.[23] **Market systems typically involve some formalised system of 'contracting' for resources or inputs from other parts of an organisation and for supplying outputs to other parts of an organisation.** Control focuses on outputs, for example revenues earned in successful competition for internal contracts. The control is indirect: rather than accepting detailed performance targets determined externally, units have simply to earn their keep in competitive internal markets.

Internal markets can be used in a variety of ways. There might be *competitive bidding*, perhaps through the creation of an internal investment bank at the corporate centre to support new initiatives. Also, a customer–supplier relationship may be established between a

ILLUSTRATION 14.4 — Rogue banker or rogue bank?

In 2012, Kweku Adoboli was convicted for a fraud involving $2.3bn. But were his actions a product of deep-rooted systems failures at accident-prone UBS?

In 2003, Kweku Adoboli graduated from the University of Nottingham with a degree in Computer Science and Management. Seven years later, he was earning £60,000 (€72,000, $90,000) in salary and £250,000 in bonuses at the London offices of UBS, Switzerland's largest bank. In 2012, he was facing the prospect of seven years in jail, after committing one of the largest frauds in British history.

Adoboli had worked himself up at UBS from so-called back-office jobs (recording and checking trades) to a position as associate director on the elite Delta One desk at UBS. In banking, Delta One desks trade using the bank's own capital, and typically engage in high-risk and innovative deals. As early as 2008, Adoboli had started to create fictitious deals to hide some of his trading losses, taking advantage of his knowledge of back-office systems. The concealment was successful and Adoboli gained a reputation as a star trader, with lavish bonuses to match. It was only in September 2011, as one of UBS's accountants finally began to probe, that Adoboli owned up to his fraud. At that point, UBS had over $10bn at risk through his various trades.

UBS was the creation of a merger between two large Swiss banks in 1998, Union Bank of Switzerland and Swiss Bank Corporation. In 2000, the new bank merged with the leading American stockbroker Paine Webber, launching an aggressive strategy of growth. By 2006, UBS had risen from seventh-largest investment bank in terms of fees, to being one of the top four.

But this growth strategy had an underside. As the financial crisis loomed during 2007, the bank deliberately sold assets to its customers in order to reduce its own liabilities: it would later receive a $150m fine in the USA for this mis-selling. The bank had also taken aggressive positions in the fatally flawed sub-prime mortgage market during the good years, leaving it exposed to losses of $38bn. The Swiss government had to rescue the bank in 2008, firing the then chief executive, with a further 11,000 job losses following. In 2009, the bank had to pay a fine of $781m to the US government for its role in helping American citizens in tax evasion: one scheme had involved bank employees smuggling diamonds out of the country in toothpaste tubes. UBS faced another large fine ($160m) in 2011, due to the rigging of the municipal bonds derivatives market.

In this context, some observers did not think that Adoboli's fraud was an aberration. The bank had been focused on headlong growth, paying rich rewards to those who seemed to deliver it. Top management had not attended to the true merger of the three main component companies. It was commented that Adoboli's Delta One desk had just five staff, working in close proximity to each other, and presumably very aware of what each of their colleagues was doing. A former UBS investment banker told the *New York Times*:

'The problem isn't the culture. The problem is that there wasn't a culture. There are silos. Everyone is separate. People cut their own deals, and it's every man for himself. A lot of people made a lot of money that way, and it fuelled jealousies and efforts to get even better deals. People thought of themselves first, and then maybe the bank, if they thought about it at all.'

Sources: *New York Times*, 24 September 2011; *Financial Times*, 19 September 2012.

Questions

1 In this account, what elements of UBS's systems appear to have been deficient, with regard to Adoboli and more generally?

2 What roles might the merger and growth strategy have played in the various failures at UBS?

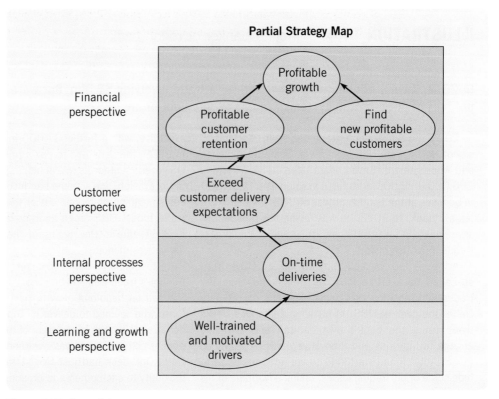

Figure 14.7 A partial strategy map

Source: Exhibit 1: R. Lawson, W. Stratton and T. Hatch (2005), 'Achieving strategy with scorecarding', *Journal of Corporate Accounting and Finance*, March–April, vol. 16, no. 3: p. 64.

central service department, such as training or IT, and the operating units. Typically these internal markets are subject to considerable regulation. For example, the corporate centre might set rules for *transfer prices* between internal business units to prevent exploitative contract pricing, or insist on *service-level agreements* to ensure appropriate service by an essential internal supplier, such as IT, for the various units that depend on it.

Internal markets work well where complexity or rapid change make detailed direct or input controls impractical. But market systems can create problems as well. First, they can increase bargaining between units, consuming important management time. Second, they may create a new bureaucracy monitoring all of the internal transfers of resources between units. Third, an over-zealous use of market mechanisms can lead to dysfunctional competition and legalistic contracting, destroying cultures of collaboration and relationships. These have all been complaints made against the internal markets and semi-autonomous Foundation Trust Hospitals introduced into the UK's National Health Service. On the other hand, their proponents claim that these market processes free a traditionally over-centralised health service to innovate and respond to local needs, while market disciplines maintain overall control.

14.4 CONFIGURATIONS AND ADAPTABILITY

The introduction of this chapter introduced the concept of configurations. **Configurations are the set of organisational design elements that fit together in order to support the intended strategy.** The introductory Figure 14.1 focused on the three mutually supporting elements of strategy, structure and systems, but this section will add more elements in the form of the McKinsey 7-S framework. When all the various elements fit together, they can form a self-reinforcing virtuous circle of superior performance. However, fit can also create problems of adaptability, so this section will also address issues of agility and resilience.

14.4.1 The McKinsey 7-Ss

Developed by the McKinsey consulting company, the *McKinsey 7-S framework* highlights the importance of fit between not just strategy, structure and systems, but also with staff, style, skills and superordinate goals.[24] All seven elements have to be configured together to achieve effectiveness. The elements can therefore serve as a checklist in any organisational design exercise: see Figure 14.8. Because we have already addressed strategy, structure and systems, we shall focus on the remaining four elements of the 7-S framework in the following:

- *Style* here refers to the leadership style of top managers in an organisation. Leadership styles may be collaborative, participative, directive or coercive, for instance (see Chapter 15). Managers' behavioural style can influence the culture of the whole organisation (see Chapter 6). The style should fit other aspects of the 7-S framework: for example, a highly directive or coercive style is not likely to fit a matrix organisation structure.

- *Staff* is about the kinds of people in the organisation and how they are developed. This relates to systems of selection, socialisation and reward (Section 14.3.2). A key

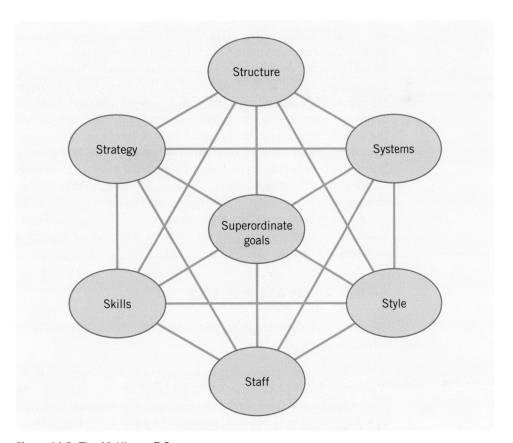

Figure 14.8 The McKinsey 7-Ss.

Source: R. Waterman, T. Peters and J. Phillips, 'Structure is not organisation', *Business Horizons*, June 1980, pp. 14–26: p. 18.

criterion for the feasibility of any strategy is: does the organisation have the people to match (see Section 12.2.4)? A common constraint on structural change is the availability of the right people to head new departments and divisions (the 'People Test': see Section 14.2.6).

- *Skills* relates to staff, but in the 7-S framework refers more broadly to capabilities in general (see Chapter 4). The concept of capabilities here raises not only staff skills but also issues to do with how these skills are embedded in and captured by the organisation as a whole. For example, how do the organisation's training schemes, information technology and reward systems transform the talents of individuals into the organisational capabilities required by the strategy?

- *Superordinate goals* refers to the overarching goals or purpose of the organisation as a whole, in other words the mission, vision and objectives that form the organisational purpose (see Chapter 1). Superordinate (i.e. overarching) goals are placed at the centre of the 7-S framework: all other elements should support these.

The McKinsey 7-S framework highlights at least three aspects of organising. First, organising involves a lot more than just getting the organisational structure right; there are many other elements to attend to. Second, the 7-S framework emphasises fit between all these elements: everything from structure to skills needs to be configured together in order to create virtuous circles of performance. Third, if managers change one element of the 7-S, the concept of fit suggests they are likely to have to change all the other elements as well in order to keep them all appropriately aligned to each other. Changing one element in isolation is liable to break the virtuous circle and make performance worse until overall fit is restored.[25]

Although the concept of configurations and the 7-S framework emphasises the value of mutual fit between elements, in practice this can cause problems in terms of adaptability. First, making everything fit tightly together makes it hard to adapt to specific needs: adjusting to the demands of one particular market is liable to spoil the configuration required to respond to the demands of all the others. One solution to this is to *subdivide* the organisation into different strategic business units, so that one unit is configured optimally according to one set of demands, while the other unit is configured optimally for the others. For example, IBM created its then revolutionary personal computer in a separate new-venture division, configured differently to the traditional mainframe computer business whose principles of hierarchy and efficiency were incompatible with the need to innovate in the new business.[26] Second, as above, configurations create problems for change: tight fits in terms of configurations can make it costly to adapt: changing just a few elements leads to performance declines unless everything else is changed in line. The concepts of agility and resilience are intended to emphasise the importance of adaptability in the face of change.

14.4.2 Agility and resilience

Two concepts help in designing organisations for greater adaptability, the first proactive, the second more after-the-fact:

- Organisational *agility* refers to the ability of organisations to detect and respond to opportunities and threats fast and easily.[27] Agile organisations anticipate environmental shifts and act on them as they emerge. Agility is important because of the growing turbulence of many environments, produced by rapid technological change for example.

- Organisational *resilience* refers to the capacity of organisations to recover from environmental shocks fast and easily after they have happened.[28] Resilient organisations

THINKING DIFFERENTLY   Beyond hierarchy?

There are alternatives to bosses and controls.

This chapter has concerned itself mostly with hierarchical structures and systems, used for top-down control. But there are less hierarchical alternatives which can work as well.

One non-hierarchical way of organising is the 'rule-of-three'.[29] Under the rule-of-three, any project within the organisation can get underway so long as three organisational members agree to do it. The project champion has to persuade two other people that the project is a valid one and worthwhile investing their own work-time into. If the champion can win support from those with the necessary skills to take it forward, the project is deemed worth backing. It does not require the approval of any manager: effectively employees 'vote with their feet'. As the project continues and perhaps attracts more members, nobody is appointed as formal project manager: instead, project 'leads' emerge by informal consensus, these leads changing as project needs evolve. Differences are normally resolved by discussion. The project goes to market when three project members deem it ready.

This rule-of-three is operated by the games company Valve, with 400 employees and responsible for the games portal Steam and games such as *Half-Life* and *Counter Strike.* Although the company operates non-hierarchically, its owner and founder Gade Newell exercises strict control over recruitment and dismissal of employees. Pay is high by industry standards and the company operates a very generous bonus policy. Bonuses are awarded non-hierarchically, according to review by peers. There are thus substantial potential benefits to getting involved in a project creating a successful new game, and large costs to investing time in one that fails. Projects that lose the support of the necessary three members are automatically closed down. Valve is estimated to be worth $2bn (£1.2bn, €1.5bn).

Question

What types of industry or sector would this model be likely to work best in, and in what types might it not work well at all?

---

are good at rebounding from shocks. Resilience is important because of the prevalence of unanticipated events: the collapse of key customers or suppliers, extreme weather events (tsunamis or earthquakes), or sudden changes in government policy, for instance.

Both agility and resilience are facilitated by the existence of *organisational slack*. Such organisational slack provides important spare resources. Slack supports agility by giving organisational members the extra resources necessary to look beyond the immediate business and either to experiment with future possible opportunities or to move against threats. Examples of slack resources supporting agility might be 'blue sky' research and development units or simply financial reserves capable of being used for acquisition opportunities. Similarly, slack can enhance resilience by providing spare resources that can be quickly redeployed to assist or repair parts of the organisation that have suffered an unanticipated shock. Examples of slack resources that enhance resilience might include emergency stocks, spare production capacity or under-used managers. An organisation that is perfectly configured so that everything fits tightly together is unlikely to have much organisational slack. It is therefore important in designing organisations to ask whether their structure and systems have enough slack to allow for adaptability, either in the form of agility or of resilience.

SUMMARY

- Successful organising means responding to the key challenges facing the organisation. This chapter has stressed *control*, *change*, *knowledge* and *internationalisation*.

- There are many *structural types* (e.g. functional, divisional, matrix, transnational and project). Each structural type has its own strengths and weaknesses and responds differently to the challenges of control, change, knowledge and internationalisation.

- There is a range of different organisational *systems* to facilitate and control strategy. These systems can focus on either *inputs* or *outputs* and be *direct* or *indirect*.

- The separate organisational elements, summarised in the *McKinsey 7-S framework*, should come together to form a coherent *reinforcing configuration*. But these reinforcing cycles also raise problems of *agility* and *resilience*, which can be alleviated by the presence of organisational *slack*.

WORK ASSIGNMENTS

✱ Denotes more advanced work assignments.
* Refers to a case study in the Text and Cases edition.

14.1 Go to the website of a large organisation you are familiar with and find its organisational chart (not all organisations provide these). Why is the organisation structured like this?

14.2 Referring to Section 14.2.2 on the divisional structure, consider the advantages and disadvantages of creating divisions along different lines – such as product, geography or technology – with respect to a large organisation you are familiar with or a case organisation such as Siemens A and B*, Academies/ Free Schools* or Unilever*.

14.3✱ Referring to Figure 14.7, write a short executive brief explaining how strategy maps could be a useful management system to monitor and control the performance of organisational units. Be sure to analyse both advantages and disadvantages of this approach.

14.4 As a middle manager with responsibility for a small business unit, which 'strategy style' (Section 14.3.5) would you prefer to work within? In what sort of circumstances or corporate organisation would this style not work so well for you?

Integrative assignment

14.5 Take a recent merger or acquisition (see Chapter 11), ideally one involving two organisations of roughly equal size, and analyse how the deal has changed the acquiring or merged company's organisational structure. What do you conclude from the extent or lack of structural change for the new company going forward?

RECOMMENDED KEY READINGS

- The best single coverage of this chapter's issues is in R. Daftt, *Organization Theory and Design*, 12th edn, Cengage, 2016. G. Tett, *The Silo Effect,* Little and Brown, 2015, is a very readable and stimulating perspective on what can go wrong in organising and some contemporary solutions.

- For a collection of relevant articles, see the special issue 'Learning to design organisations', R. Dunbar and W. Starbuck (eds), *Organisation Science,* vol. 17, no. 2 (2006).

- M. Goold and A. Campbell, *Designing Effective Organisations,* Jossey-Bass, 2002, provides a practical guide to organisational design issues.

REFERENCES

1. A.D. Chandler, *Strategy and Structure*, MIT Press, 1962.

2. Good reviews of recent tendencies in organisation structure are J.R. Galbraith, 'The future of organization design', *Journal of Organization Design*, vol. 1, no. 1 (2012), pp. 3–6; and N. Argyres and T. Zenger, 'Dynamics in organization structure', in A. Grandori (ed.), *Handbook of Economic Organization*, Edward Elgar, 2013.

3. For an introduction to the view that organisations should fit their structures to key challenges ('contingencies'), see B. Luo and L. Donaldson, 'Misfits in organization design: information processing as a compensatory mechanism', *Journal of Organization Design*, vol. 2, no. 1 (2013), pp. 2–10. See also R. Whittington, 'Organisational structure', in *The Oxford Handbook of Strategy*, Volume II, Oxford University Press, 2003, Chapter 28.

4. G. Tett, *The Silo Effect*, Little and Brown, 2015 is an attractive account of the dangers of segmented, silo organisations.

5. This view of divisionalisation as a response to diversity was originally put forward by A.D. Chandler, *Strategy and Structure*, MIT Press, 1962. See R. Whittington and M. Mayer, *The European Corporation: Strategy, Structure and Social Science*, Oxford University Press, 2000, for a summary of Chandler's relevance more recently.

6. For a review of current experience with matrix structures, see S. Thomas and L. D'Annunzio, 'Challenges and strategies of matrix organisations: top-level and mid-level managers' perspectives', *Human Resource Planning*, vol. 28, no. 1 (2005), pp. 39–48; and J. Galbraith, *Designing Matrix Structures that Actually Work*, Jossey-Bass, 2009.

7. See C. Bartlett and S. Ghoshal, 'Matrix management: not a structure, more a frame of mind', *Harvard Business Review*, vol. 68, no. 4 (1990), pp. 138–45.

8. C. Bartlett and S. Ghoshal, *Managing Across Borders*, 2nd edn, Harvard Business School Press, 2008.

9. Research finds that transnational structures generally perform better than either centralised or decentralised structures: see J.-N. Garbe and N. Richter, 'Causal analysis of the internationalization and performance relationship based on neural networks', *Journal of International Management*, vol. 15, no. 4 (2009), pp. 413–31.

10. The classic article on project-based organisations is by R. DeFillippi and M. Arthur, 'Paradox in project-based enterprise: the case of film-making', *California Management Review*, vol. 40, no. 2 (1998), pp. 125–45. For some difficulties, see M. Bresnen, A. Goussevskaia and J. Swann, 'Organizational routines, situated learning and processes of change in project-based organisations', *Project Management Journal*, vol. 36, no. 3 (2005), pp. 27–42.

11. For a discussion of more permanent team structures, see Thomas Mullern, 'Integrating the team-based structure in the business process: the case of Saab Training Systems', in A. Pettigrew and E. Fenton (eds), *The Innovating Organisation*, Sage, 2000.

12. A.D. Chandler, *Strategy and Structure*, MIT Press, 1962.

13. M. Goold and A. Campbell, *Designing Effective Organisations*, Jossey-Bass, 2002. See also M. Goold and A. Campbell, 'Do you have a well-designed organisation?', *Harvard Business Review*, vol. 80, no. 3 (2002), pp. 117–224.

14. A.D. Chandler, *Strategy and Structure*, MIT Press, 1962.

15. This practice of 'patching' or reconfiguring parts of the organisation onto each other according to changing market needs is described in K. Eisenhardt and S. Brown, 'Patching: restitching business portfolios in dynamic markets', *Harvard Business Review*, vol. 75, no. 3 (1999), pp. 72–80. See also S. Girod and R. Whittington, 'Reconfiguration, restructuring and firm performance: dynamic capabilities and environmental dynamism', *Strategic Management Journal*, forthcoming.

16. On the reverse logic of strategy and structure, see T.L. Amburgey and T. Dacin, 'As the left foot follows the right? The dynamics of strategic and structural change', *Academy of Management Journal*, vol. 37, no. 6 (1994), pp. 1427–52.

17. M. Goold and A. Campbell, *Strategies and Styles*, Blackwell, 1987.

18. E.C. Wenger and W.M. Snyder, 'Communities of practice: the organized frontier', *Harvard Business Review*, vol. 78, no. 1 (2000), pp. 139–46.

19. A. Maté, J. Trujillo and J. Mylopoulos, 'Conceptualizing and specifying key performance indicators in business strategy models', *Proceedings of the 2012 Conference of the Center for Advanced Studies on Collaborative Research*, IBM Corp., 5–7 November, pp. 102–15.

20. The value of goals and performance targets has been debated vigorously: see L. Ordonez, M. Schweitzer, A. Galinksy and M. Bazerman, 'Goals gone wild: the systematic side effects of overprescribing goal setting', *Academy of Management Perspectives*, vol. 23, no. 1 (2009), pp. 6–16; and E. Locke and G. Latham, 'Has goal setting gone wild?', *Academy of Management Perspectives*, vol. 23, no. 1 (2009), pp. 17–23.

21. See R. Kaplan and D. Norton, 'Having trouble with your strategy? Then map it', *Harvard Business Review*, vol. 78, no. 5 (2000), pp. 167–76; and R. Kaplan and D. Norton, *Alignment: How to Apply the Balanced Scorecard to Strategy*, Harvard Business School Press, 2006.

22. See Gary Hamel, 'Bringing Silicon Valley inside', *Harvard Business Review*, vol. 77, no. 5 (1999), pp. 70–84. For a discussion of internal market challenges, see A. Vining, 'Internal market failure', *Journal of Management Studies*, vol. 40, no. 2 (2003), pp. 431–57.

23. R. Waterman, T. Peters and J. Phillips, 'Structure is not organization', *Business Horizons*, June (1980), pp. 14–26.

24. R.A. Burgelman, 'Managing the new venture division: implications for strategic management', *Strategic Management Journal*, vol. 6, no. 1 (1985), pp. 39–54.

25. R. Whittington, A. Pettigrew, S. Peck, E. Fenton and M. Conyon, 'Change and complementarities in the new competitive landscape: a European panel study, 1992–1996', *Organization Science,* vol. 10, no. 5 (1999), pp. 583–600.

26. J. Galbraith, 'Organising to deliver solutions', *Organizational Dynamics,* vol. 31, no. 2 (2002), pp. 194–207.

27. Y.L. Doz and M. Kosonen, 'Embedding strategic agility: a leadership agenda for accelerating business model renewal', *Long Range Planning,* vol. 43, no. 2 (2010), pp. 370–82; P.P. Tallon and A. Pinsonneault, 'Competing perspectives on the link between strategic information technology alignment and organizational agility: insights from a mediation model', *MIS Quarterly,* vol. 35, no. 2 (2011), pp. 463–86.

28. G. Hamel and L. Valikangas, 'The quest for resilience', *Harvard Business Review,* vol. 81, no. 9 (2003), pp. 52–65; L. Välikangas and A.G.L. Romme, 'Competing perspectives on the link between strategic information technology alignment and organizational agility: insights from a mediation model', *MIS Quarterly,* vol. 35, no. 2 (2011), pp. 463–86; P. Tallon and A. Pinsonneault, 'Capabilities at "Big Brown Box, Inc."', *Strategy & Leadership,* vol. 4, no. 4 (2012), pp. 43–5.

29. P. Puranam and D. Håkonsson, 'Valve's Way', *Journal of Organization Design,* vol. 4, no. 2 (2015), pp. 2–4; T. Felin, 'Valve Corporation: strategy tipping points and thresholds', *Journal of Organization Design,* vol. 4, no. 2 (2015), pp. 10–11.

One Sony?

Kazuo Hirai's April 2012 appointment as Chief Executive Officer of Sony Corporation would probably have surprised his younger self. After all, Hirai had started out as Japanese translator to the American hip-hop band the Beastie Boys. He had then become a video games designer and later led Sony's PlayStation business in the USA. However, by the time he finally became CEO at the age of 51, Sony was in deep trouble. One of Hirai's first moves was to change Sony's organisational structure. The aim was to create a more integrated business – 'One Sony'. With some adjustments over time, Sony retained this basic structure to at least until 2016.

Business background

Sony's businesses spanned professional electronics such as semiconductors and medical devices, consumer electronics from televisions and mobile phones to computers and the PlayStation, together with 'content' businesses such as movies and music. As such, Sony was pitching against companies like the American success-story Apple and the Korean high-technology giant Samsung. Despite a proud history associated with such brands as the Sony Walkman audio devices or Sony Trinitron televisions, Sony was being left far behind. By 2012, Sony's stock price was less than half it had been five years before, while Apple and Samsung were two or three times as valuable (see Figure 1).

Sony's relative decline has not been for want of trying. In 2003, the company had suffered the so-called 'Sony shock', when both earnings and stock price had plunged simultaneously following a weak response to cheaper Asian electronics firms. The company reduced costs by cutting its workforce by nearly 20 per cent. In 2005, Sony had taken the then-revolutionary step of appointing its first foreigner as CEO, Howard Stringer, a Welsh-American with a background in the music and movie business. Stringer had announced that he would break down the company's vertical management system, which he described as a set of separate 'silos' with little coherence. He sought

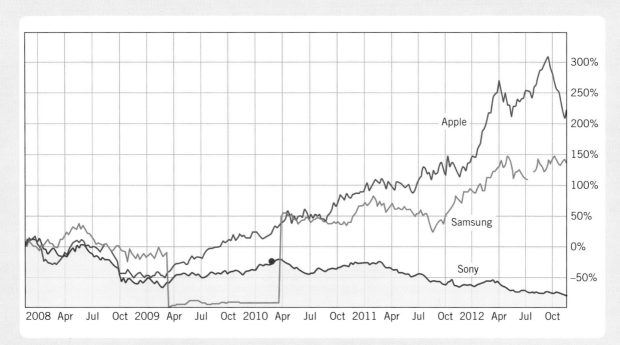

Figure 1 Sony's stock price performance relative to Apple and Samsung, 2008–12

Source: Yahoo Finance. For comparison of price changes, all prices standardised to zero in 2008.

to integrate the company's hardware business, based in Japan, with its various content businesses, led by music and movies in the USA. Stringer's slogan had been 'Sony United'. But Stringer had been neither an engineer nor a Japanese speaker. It was reported that many of his diktats to the Japanese hardware businesses were largely ignored.

The financial results for 2011–12 confirmed Stringer's failure. Without a striking new product to compare with the original Walkman or Trinitron and still heavily reliant on an expensive Japanese manufacturing base, Sony's sales were down nearly ten per cent while profits were negative. The 69-year-old Stringer became Company Chairman. Hirai, Sony's youngest ever CEO and the second non-engineer in a row, set to work.

New strategy and new structure

Hirai insisted that the new Sony would be focused predominantly on five key strategic initiatives. First of all was a strengthening of the core business, by which he meant digital imaging, games and mobile devices, including phones, tablets and laptops. Second, Hirai committed himself to returning the television business back to profitability, after eight years of consistent losses. Third, Sony would develop faster in emerging markets such as India and South America. The fourth initiative was to accelerate innovation, particularly by integrating product areas. Finally, Sony was preparing to realign its business portfolio, with divestments expected of non-core businesses (e.g. the legacy chemicals business).

Hirai supported these strategic initiatives with a new organisational structure, designed to support his concept of 'One Sony'. The old structure had been based on two big groups centred on Japan and predominantly in hardware: the Professional, Device and Solutions Group, responsible for about half of all sales; and the Consumer Products and Services Group, responsible for another fifth of sales. Alongside these two major groups were several stand-alone businesses mostly based abroad, including Music, Pictures (movies) and the Sony–Ericsson joint venture in mobile phones (see Figure 2).

The new structure broke up the big groups, creating 12 stand-alone businesses in all (see Figure 3). The ending of the Sony–Ericsson joint venture in late 2011 allowed the mobile phone business to be brought closer to the VAIO and mobile computing business. Sony's medical-related businesses, previously dispersed across multiple units but now targeted for rapid growth, were folded into a dedicated medical business unit led by an executive at corporate level. The device and semiconductor businesses, including image sensors, became a single business group, Device Solutions. Sony Network Entertainment was strengthened, with all Sony's online offerings now included.

Hirai completed his structural changes by reinforcing headquarters resources and oversight, with several new senior management appointments. The aim was to leverage the company's broad portfolio by creating exclusive content for Sony's own devices. A single corporate-level executive was made responsible for User Experience ('UX'), Product Strategy and the Creative Platform, charged with strengthening horizontal integration and enhancing the experience across Sony's entire product and network service line-up. The same executive would

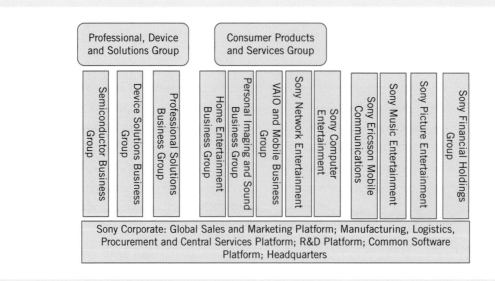

Figure 2 Sony's organisational structure, 2011

Source: Adapted from www.sony.net.

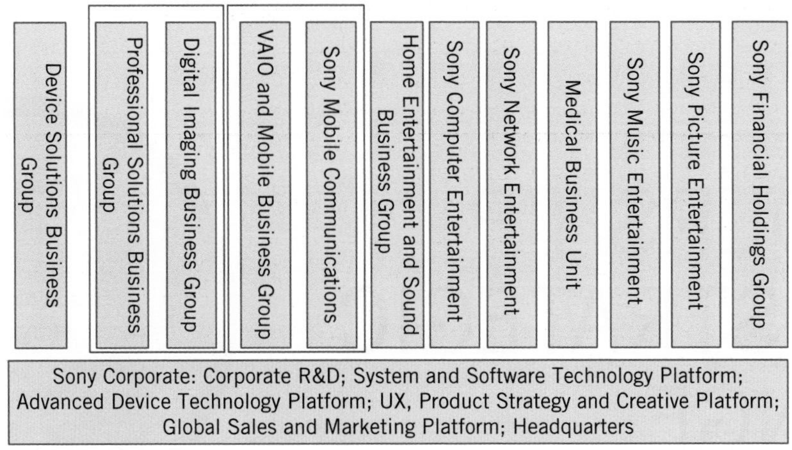

Figure 3 Sony's organisational structure, 2012
Source: Adapted from www.sony.net.

oversee the mobile businesses, including smartphones, tablets and PCs (indicated by the box around the two relevant business groups). Digital Imaging and the Professional Solutions likewise came under the oversight of a single corporate-level executive. Hirai himself was to take direct responsibility for the Home Entertainment Business Group, including the troubled television business, pledging to give it the majority of his time in the coming months.

At an investors' meeting in April 2012, Hirai went beyond strategic and structural changes:

'The other thing is . . . the One Sony/One Management concept. That is really important, because I made sure that as I built my new management team, that everybody in the team is 100 per cent fully committed and also aligned as to what needs to get done and how we're going to get that done. And so we have a lot of discussions internally amongst the management team. Once we make that decision, then everybody moves in the same direction and we execute with speed. And I think that is another area that is quite different from some of the restructurings or the changes that we have made perhaps in the past.'

Results did not come quickly, however. In November 2012, the *Wall Street Journal* observed of Sony's new organisational chart: 'Far from providing clarity of purpose, the diagram should leave investors tearing their hair out. While new Chief Executive Kazuo Hirai shuffles the deckchairs on board the one-time electronics titan, Sony's stock is plunging into deep waters.'

Main sources: *Wall Street Journal*, 2 February 2012; Nikkei Report, 2 March 2012; Sony Corporation press release, Tokyo, 27 March 2012; CQ FD Disclosure, Sony Corporate Strategy Meeting Conference Call for Overseas Investors – Final, 12 April 2012; *Wall Street Journal*, 15 November 2012.

Questions

1 Assess the pros and cons of Hirai's structural changes.

2 What other initiatives beyond structural change might be necessary in order to create 'One Sony'?

15

LEADERSHIP AND STRATEGIC CHANGE

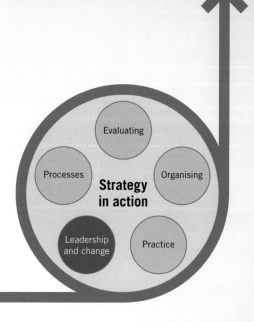

Evaluating

Processes **Strategy in action** Organising

Leadership and change Practice

Learning outcomes

After reading this chapter you should be able to:

- Identify and assess different *leadership styles,* as related to strategic change.

- Use the *change kaleidoscope* and *forcefield analysis* to analyse how *organisational context* might affect strategic change.

- Identify *types* of strategic change, according to speed and scope.

- Assess the value of different *levers* for strategic change.

- Identify the approaches, pitfalls and problems of leading different types of strategic change.

Key terms

forcefield analysis p.476

leadership p.470

organisational ambidexterity p.481

situational leadership p.471

transactional leader p.471

transformational leader p.471

turnaround strategy p.479

15.1 INTRODUCTION

Amazon, the internet retailer, has been led by founder Jeff Bezos for more than two decades. Bezos lays down 'Fifteen Leadership Principles' for the 230,000 people who work for his company around the world. According to these principles, Amazonians should 'Think Big', 'Dive Deep', follow a 'Bias for Action' and 'Have Backbone'. Such principles appear to have helped Bezos manage Amazon's strategic change from online bookstore to diversified technology giant, with interests ranging from cloud infrastructure for business to mobile phones.

The theme of strategic change runs through much of this part of the text. Part I of this book examined pressures for strategic change arising from the organisation's environment and its internal position; Part II looked at the kinds of strategic option that might form part of strategic change, such as diversification, internationalisation or innovation. However, central to strategic change is the leadership task of ensuring that people deliver whatever strategic options are finally chosen. While this leadership role is most often associated with chief executives it may, in fact, occur at different levels in organisations: other senior managers and middle managers too may take leadership roles in change. Indeed, at Amazon, the company's leadership principles are supposed to be followed by all.

Figure 15.1 provides a structure for the chapter. The chapter opens (Section 15.2) by explaining different roles of leaders and different leadership styles. A key task of leadership is strategic change. Leaders need to address two issues in considering their approach to change. First, they have to diagnose the organisational context, the extent to which it is receptive or resistant to change: Section 15.3 particularly addresses the forces blocking or facilitating change. Second, leaders have to identify the type of strategic change required: Section 15.4 differentiates types of change according to speed and scope. Understanding the context, and identifying the required type of change, should help leaders select the appropriate levers for change: Section 15.5 considers levers ranging from symbolic management to political action. Section 15.6 draws many of the issues together by considering common reasons for the failure of strategic change programmes and pointing to the importance of informal change.

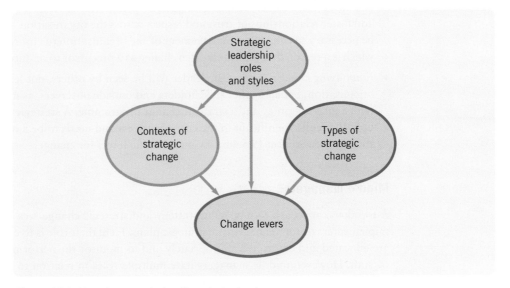

Figure 15.1 Key elements in leading strategic change

15.2 LEADERSHIP AND STRATEGIC CHANGE

Leadership is the process of influencing an organisation (or group within an organisation) in its efforts towards achieving an aim or goal.[1] Without effective leadership the risk is that people in an organisation are unclear about its purpose or lack motivation to deliver the strategy to achieve it. Leadership is associated particularly with strategic change. For example, Harvard's John Kotter argues that 'good management' is about bringing order and consistency to operational aspects of organisations, such as quality and profitability of products and services. Leadership, 'by contrast is about coping with change'.[2] Thus strategic change is a crucial underlying theme in this discussion of leadership.

15.2.1 Strategic leadership roles

While leading strategic change is often associated with top management, and chief executives in particular, in practice it typically involves managers at different levels in an organisation.

Top managers

There are three key roles that are argued to be especially significant for top management, especially a CEO, in leading strategic change:

- *Envisioning future strategy.*[3] Effective strategic leaders at the top of an organisation need to ensure there exists a clear and compelling vision of the future and communicate clearly a strategy to achieve it both internally and to external stakeholders. In the absence of their doing so, those who attempt to lead change elsewhere in an organisation, for example middle managers, are likely to construct such a vision themselves. This may be well-intentioned but can lead to confusion.

- *Aligning* the organisation to deliver that strategy. This involves ensuring that people in the organisation are committed to the strategy, motivated to make the changes needed and empowered to deliver those changes. In doing so, there is a need for leaders to build and foster relationships of trust and respect across the organisation. It can, however, also be necessary to change the management of the organisation to ensure such commitment, which is a reason that top teams often change as a precursor to or during strategic change.

- *Embodying change.* A strategic leader will be seen by others, not least those within the organisation, but also other stakeholders and outside observers, as intimately associated with a future strategy and a strategic change programme. A strategic leader is, then, symbolically highly significant in the change process and needs to be a role model for future strategy (see Section 15.5.4 below on symbolic levers for change).

Middle managers

A top-down approach to managing strategy and strategic change sees middle managers as implementers of top management strategic plans. Here their role is to ensure that resources are allocated and controlled appropriately and to monitor the performance and behaviour of staff. However, middle managers have multiple roles in relation to the management of strategy.[4] In the context of managing strategic change there are four roles to emphasise:

- *Advisers* to more senior management on requirements for change within an organisation. This is because they are often the closest to indications of market or technological changes that might signal the need for change. They are also well-placed to be able to identify likely blockages to change. Middle managers may also provide a useful variety of experience and views that can stimulate thinking on strategy.[5]

- *'Sense making'* of strategy. Top management may set a strategic direction, but how it is explained and made sense of in specific contexts (e.g. a region of a multinational or a functional department) may, intentionally or not, be left to middle managers. If misinterpretation of that intended strategy is to be avoided, it is therefore vital that middle managers understand and feel an ownership of it. They are therefore a crucial *relevance bridge* between top management and members of the organisation at lower levels.[6]

- *Reinterpretation and adjustment* of strategic responses as events unfold (e.g. in terms of relationships with customers, suppliers, the workforce and so on). Middle managers are uniquely qualified to reinterpret and adjust strategy because they are in day-to-day contact with such aspects of the organisation and its environment.

- *Local leadership of change.* Middle managers therefore have the roles of aligning and embodying change, as do top management, but at a local level. This can be particularly important in decentralised organisations, such as chains of retail stores or multinational corporations.

Recognising the leadership role of middle managers can help balance the heroic, top-down and individualist image often associated with leaders, particularly in Anglo-American business cultures. Of course, middle managers can be heroic individuals. However, because they do not have the power or legitimacy of top managers, middle managers are often obliged to adopt more collective or collaborative approaches to leadership.[7] Leaders may need to harness the support and ideas of colleagues in teams. Many top managers also prefer this collaborative approach. In other words, leaders are not always individualistic. There are different styles of leadership.

15.2.2 Leadership styles

Leaders tend to adopt characteristic 'styles' of behaving and intervening. These leadership styles are often categorised in two broad ways:

- **Transformational (or charismatic) leaders emphasise building a vision for the organisation,** creating an organisational identity around collective values and beliefs to support that vision and energising people to achieve it. Organisational founders are often particularly charismatic. Evidence suggests that this approach to leadership has beneficial impact on people's motivation and job performance,[8] and is particularly positive for wider business performance when organisations face uncertainty.[9]

- **Transactional leaders emphasise 'hard' levers of change such as designing systems and controls.** The emphasis here is more likely to be on changes of structures, setting targets to be achieved, financial incentives, careful project management and the monitoring of organisational and individual performance.

In practice, transformational and transactional leadership styles are two ends of a continuum, with many feasible points between. Leaders typically combine elements of the two styles, rather than identifying exclusively with one (see Illustration 15.1). Indeed, the notion of **situational leadership encourages strategic leaders to adjust their leadership style to the context they face.**[10] In other words, there is not just one best way of leading: appropriate leadership style changes according to the specific demands of the situation. The next two sections examine two aspects of such situations: contexts of change and types of change.

ILLUSTRATION 15.1   Leadership styles

Successful top executives talk about their leadership styles.

Learn to lead

'Leadership is a learned skill. Some people are innately good at it, but all can become better. However, this is not to be confused with becoming a great leader – a Ghandi or a Nelson Mandela. . . . [It is] not about how many people report to you, but about how you behave, act, and endeavour to do the right thing. . . . If you are trying to solve complex problems creatively, you can be collaborative . . . If the house is on fire, you don't suggest forming a committee.'

Antony Jenkins, CEO Barclays Bank, 2012–15,
Saïd Business School, Oxford

Select and empower

Interview question: 'What are the most important things that leaders can do to create the conditions for high performance?'

Ursula Burns: 'First, they define the possibilities. They set the agenda, the tone of the organization.

Second, they select. They select the key leaders in the next echelon of the company, help to select the leaders after that, and so on. So, they have a big, big people component.

Third, they empower. After selecting correctly, they have to empower these people to actually do the job.

Next, they set the correct expectation for what excellence looks like, what greatness looks like . . . What's greatness? Greatness is growing a customer base. Greatness is distinguishing ourselves by innovation. Greatness is hitting a certain EPS or revenue growth target or cash target.'

Ursula Burns, Chairman and CEO Xerox Corporation,
December 3, 2012, *triplecrownleadership*

Vision and grit

A leader should never compare his technical skills with his employee's. Your employee should have superior technical skills than you. If he doesn't, it means you have hired the wrong person.

What, then, makes the leader stands out?

1 A leader should be a visionary and have more foresight than an employee.
2 A leader should have higher grit and tenacity, and be able to endure what the employees can't.
3 A leader should have higher endurance and ability to accept and embrace failure.

Jack Ma, Founder of Chinese eCommerce giant,
Alibaba, *VulkanPost*, 25 February 2015

Confidence when you don't know

'One of my favorite episodes of "Star Trek: The Next Generation" is when the captain and the doctor are stranded alone on this planet, and their brains are linked by some kind of alien device so they can read each other's thoughts. They're trying to get somewhere and the captain says, "We're going this way," and the doctor says, "You don't know which way to go, do you?" Because she can read his thoughts.'

'He explains to her that sometimes part of being a leader is just picking a way and being confident about it and going, because people want to be led. I remember that episode, because it rang really true to me. Sometimes you just have to lead, even if you don't have all the answers. In fact, you shouldn't have all the answers. If you think you have all the answers, then you're probably doing something wrong. Good leadership means being willing to have the confidence to move forward, even if you don't have all the answers.'

Biz Stone, Founder of Twitter, 27 May, 2014,
Washington Post

Questions

1 Which leaders are more transformational, which more transactional and which situational (see Section 15.2.1)?

2 Compare the different views of leadership, particularly with regard to knowledge, courage and people. What are the commonalities and differences?

15.3 DIAGNOSING THE CHANGE CONTEXT

The effectiveness of different leadership styles is shaped by the *organisational context* in which change is to occur.[11] A small entrepreneurial business is a very different context to a large, bureaucratic organisation. The 'change kaleidoscope' and forcefield analysis are two ways of assessing organisational receptiveness to change. This will help in the diagnosis of types of change required.

15.3.1 The change kaleidoscope

Julia Balogun (University of Liverpool) and Veronica Hope-Hailey (University of Bath) propose the 'change kaleidoscope' (summarised in Figure 15.2) as a framework for identifying key contextual features to take into account when designing change programmes. Just as a toy kaleidoscope rearranges a set of elements into different patterns, the change kaleidoscope highlights how a set of contextual features can take various forms supporting or resisting change. Figure 15.2 identifies eight contextual features:

- The *time* available for change can differ dramatically. A business may face immediate decline in turnover or profits from rapid changes in its markets. This is a quite different context for change compared with a business where the management may see the need for change as years away and have time to plan it carefully.

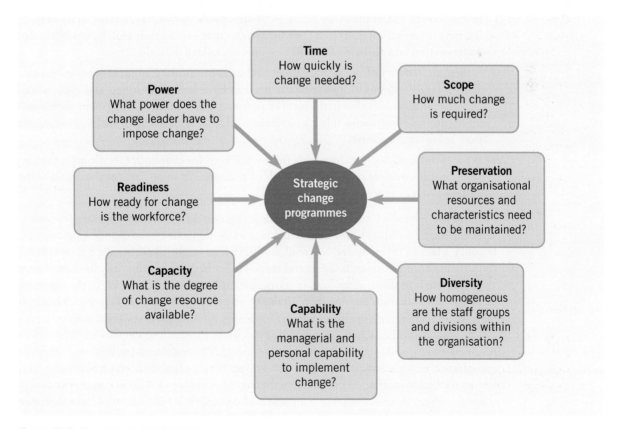

Figure 15.2 The change kaleidoscope

Source: Adapted from J. Balogun and V. Hope Hailey, *Exploring Strategic Change,* 3rd edn, Prentice Hall, 2008.

- The *scope* of change might differ in terms of either the *breadth* of change across an organisation or the *depth* of culture change required. For example, a global business with multiple brands is likely to involve a high breadth of change, while an established organisation with a long cultural heritage is likely to demand depth of change.

- *Preservation* of some aspects of an organisation may be needed. For example, some capabilities may need to be built upon in order to achieve change, while others can simply be abandoned. Alternatively, some established parts of the organisation may need to be retained in order to generate revenues, while waiting for newer parts to build up strength and economic effectiveness. This combination of preservation and change relates to the notion of organisational ambidexterity (Section 15.4).

- A *diversity* of experience, views and opinions within an organisation may help the change process, providing the seeds from which new initiatives can grow. However, if an organisation has followed a strategy for many decades, such continuity may have led to a very homogeneous way of seeing the world, which could hamper change.

- *Capacity* for change in terms of available resources will also be significant. Change can be costly, not only in financial terms, but also in terms of management time. It is likely to be the responsibility of top management (or perhaps owners) to provide such resources.

- Who has the *power* to effect change? Often it is assumed that the chief executive has such power, but in the face of resistance from below, or perhaps resistance from external stakeholders, this may not be the case. It may also be that the chief executive supposes that others in the organisation have the power to effect change when they do not, or do not see themselves as having it. In organisations with *hierarchical power structures* a directive style may be common and it may be difficult to break away from it, not least because people expect it. On the other hand, in '*flatter*' power structures, a more networked or learning organisation described elsewhere in this text (see Section 14.2.3), it is likely that collaboration and participation will be common, indeed desirable.

- Is there a *capability* of managing change in the organisation? Change is complex to manage, so larger organisations especially need to have access to skilled and experienced change managers, whether in the form of in-house organisation development professionals or external consultants. It helps too if the workforce is experienced with change, rather than being set in its ways.

- What is the *readiness* for change? Is there a felt need for change across the organisation, widespread resistance or pockets or levels of resistance in some parts of the organisation and readiness in others?

As in the notion of situational leadership (Section 15.2), the appropriate leadership style will vary according to the contextual factors illuminated by the change kaleidoscope. Urgency, a lack of diversity and low readiness to change might all encourage a transactional style, for instance. However, Balogun and Hope-Hailey highlight particularly how the change approach needs to differ according, in particular, to (i) the capability and (ii) the readiness of employees to change. Bearing in mind these two contextual features, Figure 15.3 suggests that, where there is high readiness but low capability for change, *persuasion,* involving education, training and coaching, may be an appropriate approach to emphasise. Where both readiness and capability are high, an effective focus may be *collaboration,* involving extensive consultation and teamwork in defining the change. Where capability is high but readiness is low, controlled *participation* in managing the change process may help to win over employee support. Where there is both low readiness and capability for change, top-down *direction* may be the most appropriate style, especially if change is urgent. The role of these factors in defining appropriate leadership styles is shown in Illustration 15.2, on Indian banking.

ILLUSTRATION 15.2   Challenges of change in Indian banking

India's public sector banks provide a challenging context for change.

In 2015, India had no less than 27 public-sector banks. Each typically had private investors, but the government owned majority stakes in them all. These banks were enormously important to the Indian economy, lending to large businesses, entrepreneurs, farmers, home-buyers and students needing to fund their education. Comparing India's fragmented state banks with the giant banks of China and Japan, the reformist Indian Prime Minister Narendra Modi demanded 'transformation'.

Indeed, the public-sector banks were failing. New private banks – paying higher salaries to their staff, with greater technological expertise and free of political interference – had driven the public banks' domestic market share down from over 90 per cent in the early 1990s to about 70 per cent by 2015. Return on total assets at private-sector banks was 1.6 per cent compared with just 0.5 per cent for state-run ones, while the state bank non-performing loans were more than five per cent of total loans, against two per cent in the non-state sector. The government directed the public banks to lend into sectors such as steel, power and sugar that were seen as strategically important to India's development but which were also suffering economically. The poorly-paid workforce – 850,000 strong, spread across 50,000 bank branches – was heavily trade-unionised and frequently threatened to strike. Top management was weak, with positions in the smaller banks seen as temporary stepping-stones to more senior positions in the larger banks.

In January 2015, Prime Minister Modi, his finance minister and senior regulators and public officials met with about 60 heads of both private and public financial institutions to discuss reform during a two-day 'retreat'. The official brief for the retreat was to search for 'out-of-the-box' ideas. The Prime Minister insisted that participants arrive in shared coaches rather than private cars, and yoga lessons were scheduled for the second day. Attendees heard presentations from McKinsey & Co management consultants and from the corporate guru Swami Sukhbodhanandji, author of the 'Relax' series of business books, as well as working in round-table teams.

Over the following months, the Modi government considered the various proposals from the retreat, while also heading off a national strike by public bank employees with a new pay settlement. In August 2015, the Finance Minister announced a raft of reforms including: (i) the appointment of more private-sector managers as heads of public-sector banks; (ii) the creation of a Bank Board Bureau to act as a watchdog for public banks' performance and managerial appointments; (iii) the injection of $1.9bn (€1.1bn, €1.4bn) new capital to meet international standards; (iv) allowing public banks to offer managers Employee Stock Ownership Plans to give them a stake in financial success. The Prime Minister announced that he was 'against political interference in the banks, but supports political intervention in the interests of the people'.

Many commentators were disappointed at the modesty of these reforms. The investment bank JP Morgan estimated that the public banks needed $15bn of new capital. Some argued that a proper restructuring of the fragmented sector required ownership by a single holding company with the power to merge smaller banks. Others argued for greater privatisation. The head of one leading private-sector financial institution commented: 'This is purposeful incrementalism. It is not big bang but it is helpful.' There was anxiety about the future of reform, as the Prime Minister's legislative programme faced fierce opposition in the Indian Parliament and the governing party had lost local elections in the Delhi region.

Key sources: Economic Times, 3 January 2015; *CNBC-TV*, 14 August 2015; *Financial Times*, 15 August 2015.

Questions

1 In terms of the eight contextual features in the change kaleidoscope (Figure 15.2), how receptive is the context for strategic change?

2 In the light of capability and readiness (Figure 15.3), what leadership style would be most appropriate to bringing about change?

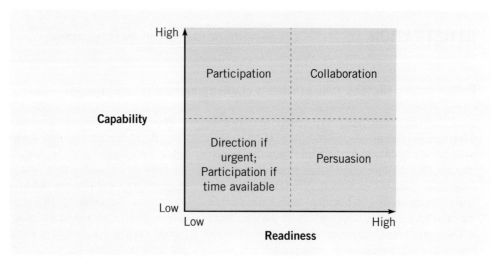

Figure 15.3 Styles of change leadership according to organisational capability and readiness

15.3.2 Forcefield analysis

A second means of approaching the context for change is analysing the balance of forces supporting or resisting change. A **forcefield analysis compares the forces at work in an organisation acting either to prevent or to facilitate change.** Thus forcefield analysis involves identifying those who favour change, those who oppose it and those are more or less neutral. Identifying allies and opponents (actual or potential) helps in the politics of strategic change. The task is to persuade those who are neutral or even against change to move into the camp of those who favour it. The relative weight of the forces finally favouring or opposing change helps also in estimating the effort required to achieve change. The more forces are arrayed against change, the more effort is needed.

Forcefield analysis helps ask some further key questions:

- What aspects of the current situation would block change, and how can these blocks be overcome?

- What aspects of the current situation might aid change in the desired direction, and how might these be reinforced?

- What needs to be introduced or developed to add to the forces for change?

Illustration 15.3 shows how a forcefield analysis was used by managers considering the intention to devolve strategic decisions within the European division of a global manufacturer.

A forcefield analysis can be informed by the change kaleidoscope but also by other concepts and frameworks in the text:

- *Stakeholder mapping* (Section 5.2.2) can provide insight into the power of different stakeholders to promote change or to resist change.

- *The cultural web* (Section 6.3.5). Strategic change often goes hand-in-hand with a perceived need to change the culture of the organisation. The culture web is a means of diagnosing organisational culture and therefore an understanding of the symbolic, routinised as well as structural and systemic factors that may be taken for granted and can act for or against change. It can also be used to envisage what the culture of an organisation would need to look like to deliver future strategy.

- *The 7-S framework* (Section 14.4.1) can highlight aspects of the infrastructure of an organisation that may act to promote or block change.

ILLUSTRATION 15.3   A forcefield analysis for devolving strategy

A forcefield analysis can be used to identify aspects of the organisation that might aid change, blockages to change and what needs to be developed to aid change.

A Japanese multinational manufacturer had always been centralised in terms of strategic direction and, in particular, new product development. It had been hugely successful in Japan and had also developed a global footprint, largely through acquisitions of local manufacturers related to its core business. These acquired businesses operated largely independently of each other as manufacturing units reporting to Japan. Regionally based sales offices were responsible for selling the range of company products and identifying customer needs and, again, reported through to Japan.

In 2012, top management in Japan took the decision to devolve strategic decisions to geographic regional divisions. The decision was based on the desire to grow non-Japanese markets given the changing competitive landscape, especially the growing power of European customers in the world market, but also the need to understand and respond to local markets better. The view was that competitive strategy and innovation needed to originate and develop nearer to regionally based customers rather than centrally in Japan.

Managers in Europe were charged with developing a plan to implement this devolution of strategy. They undertook a forcefield analysis to identify the key issues to be addressed, a summary of which is shown here.

It was market forces and a head office decision that were the main 'pushing forces' for change. But local managers also recognised that their career prospects could be enhanced. The 'resisting forces' were not only a function of the existing organisational structure, but also the lack of any pan-European infrastructure and the lack of European managers with strategic, as distinct from operational, expertise. The forcefield underlined the importance of establishing such an infrastructure and highlighted the need for IT systems to share information and ideas. It also raised the strategic importance of management development at the strategic level.

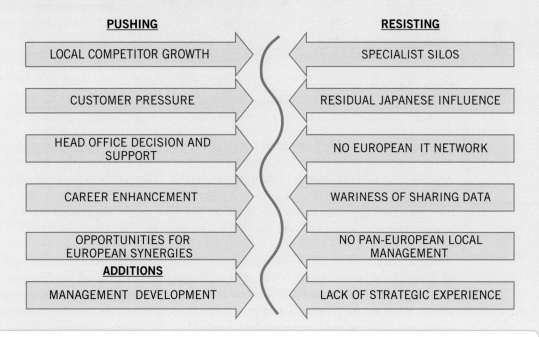

PUSHING | **RESISTING**

PUSHING	RESISTING
LOCAL COMPETITOR GROWTH	SPECIALIST SILOS
CUSTOMER PRESSURE	RESIDUAL JAPANESE INFLUENCE
HEAD OFFICE DECISION AND SUPPORT	NO EUROPEAN IT NETWORK
CAREER ENHANCEMENT	WARINESS OF SHARING DATA
OPPORTUNITIES FOR EUROPEAN SYNERGIES	NO PAN-EUROPEAN LOCAL MANAGEMENT

ADDITIONS

MANAGEMENT DEVELOPMENT	LACK OF STRATEGIC EXPERIENCE

Questions

1 What might the problems be in devolving strategy to a European division?
2 Undertake a forcefield analysis for an organisation of your choice.

As well as helping to identify the current forces acting for and against change, each of these frameworks can also be used to help think through what else might be needed as additional forces to promote change.

15.4 TYPES OF STRATEGIC CHANGE

Julia Balogun and Veronica Hope-Hailey[12] identify four generic types of strategic change. The axes in Figure 15.4 are concerned with (i) the *extent* of change, in other words the desired end result and (ii) the *nature* of the change process, particularly the speed. These two axes relate to the time and scope features of the change kaleidoscope (Figure 15.2).

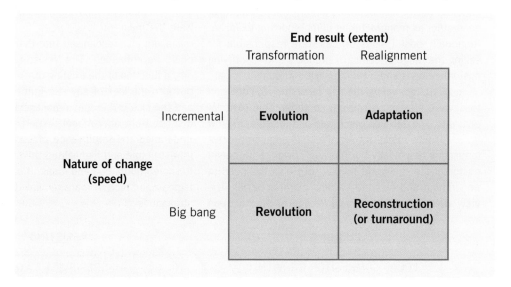

Figure 15.4 Types of change
Source: Adapted from J. Balogun, V. Hope Hailey and S. Gustafsson, *Exploring Strategic Change*, 4th edn, Pearson, 2016, p. 23.

In terms of the *extent* of change, change that occurs in line with the current business model and culture is considered a *realignment* of strategy. More extensive change, going beyond the current business model or culture, is *transformational* change. Many of the tools of analysis in Part I of the text can help identify the extent of change required. For example, does the change require a substantial reconfiguration of the value chain (Section 4.4.2), significant changes in the activities underpinning strategic capabilities (Section 4.4.3) or major cultural change (Section 6.3.5)? Care does, however, need to be taken in considering the significance of new strategies on the extent of change required. For example, a business may launch new products without requiring fundamental changes in the business model or culture of the organisation. On the other hand, some changes in strategy, even if they do not take the form of dramatic product changes, may require culture change. For example, the shift from a production focus for a manufacturer to a customer-led, service ethos may not entail major product changes, but may require significant culture change.

On the other axis in Figure 15.4, the nature of change is concerned with the speed at which change needs to happen. Arguably, it is often beneficial for change in an organisation to be *incremental* since this allows time to build on the skills, routines and beliefs of those in the organisation. It also allows for learning as the change proceeds, enabling adjustments to be made in the light of experience. However, if an organisation faces crisis or needs to change direction fast, a '*big bang*' approach to change might be needed: here everything is attempted all at once.

Together, Figure 15.4's two axes of extent of change and urgency of change define four basic types of strategic change, as follows.

15.4.1 Adaptation

As explained in Section 6.4 and Section 13.3, strategy development is often *incremental* in nature. It builds on rather than fundamentally changes prior strategy. It is what Figure 15.4 refers to as *adaptation*. Change is gradual, building on or amending what the organisation has been doing in the past and in line with the current business model and organisational culture. This might include changes in product design or methods of production, launches of new products or related diversification. This is the most common form of change in organisations. Though less common, the leadership of change is more often associated with the other more fundamental types of change identified in Figure 15.4.

15.4.2 Reconstruction

Reconstruction is rapid change involving a good deal of upheaval in an organisation, but which still does not fundamentally change the culture or the business model. Thus reconstruction might include changes in organisational structure or the introduction of a cost-cutting programme. For a diversified corporation, reconstruction could also involve the acquisition or divestment of a business, something that might involve large assets but which could still be compatible with the basic organisational structure and systems.

The classic reconstruction is a turnaround strategy in the face of radical performance decline. **Turnaround strategies emphasise rapidity in change, cost reduction and/or revenue generation, with the aim of fast recovery.** The priority in turnarounds is actions that give quick and significant improvements. Situations calling for turnarounds include economic recessions, the failure of major investment projects or the sudden collapse of important markets. Turnaround actions go beyond simple cost-cutting. Five key elements of turnaround strategies are:[13]

- *Crisis stabilisation.* The aim is to regain control over the deteriorating position. This requires a short-term focus on cost reduction and/or revenue increase, typically involving some of the steps identified in Table 15.1. There is nothing novel about these steps: many of them are good management practice. The differences are the speed at which they are carried out and the focus of managerial attention on them. The most successful turnaround strategies focus on long-term improvements in direct operational costs and productivity, rather than just cuts to apparent overhead costs, such as research and development or marketing spend.

Table 15.1 Turnaround: revenue generation and cost reduction steps

Increasing revenue	Reducing costs
<ul><li>Ensure marketing mix tailored to key market segments</li><li>Review pricing strategy to maximise revenue</li><li>Focus organisational activities on needs of target market sector customers</li><li>Exploit additional opportunities for revenue creation related to target market</li><li>Invest funds from reduction of costs in new growth areas</li></ul>	<ul><li>Reduce labour costs and reduce costs of senior management</li><li>Focus on productivity improvement</li><li>Reduce marketing costs not focused on target market</li><li>Tighten financial controls</li><li>Tight control on cash expenses</li><li>Establish competitive bidding for suppliers; defer creditor payments; speed up debtor payments</li><li>Reduce inventory</li><li>Eliminate non-profitable products/services</li></ul>

- *Management changes.* Changes in management may be required, especially at the top. This usually includes the introduction of a new chairman or chief executive, as well as changes to the board, especially in marketing, sales and finance, for three main reasons; first, because the old management may well be the ones that were in charge when the problems developed and be seen as the cause of them by key stakeholders; second, because it may be necessary to bring in management with experience of turnaround management; and third, management changes provide the opportunity to bring in new skills and approaches from outside the organisation, different to the old skills and approaches that had led to the original crisis.

- *Gaining stakeholder support.* Poor-quality information may have been provided to key stakeholders. In a turnaround situation it is vital that key stakeholders, perhaps the bank or key shareholder groups, and employees are kept clearly informed of the situation and improvements as they are being made. It is also likely that a clear assessment of the power of different stakeholder groups (see Section 5.2.2) will become vitally important in managing turnaround.

- *Clarifying the target market(s) and core products.* Central to turnaround success is ensuring clarity on the target market or market segments most likely to generate cash and grow profits. A successful turnaround strategy involves getting closer to customers and improving the flow of marketing information, especially to senior levels of management, so as to focus revenue-generating activities on key market segments. Of course, a reason for the poor performance of the organisation could be that it had this wrong in the first place. Clarifying the target market also provides the opportunity to discontinue or outsource products and services that are not targeted on those markets, eating up management time for little return or not making sufficient financial contribution.

- *Financial restructuring.* The financial structure of the organisation may need to be changed. This typically involves changing the existing capital structure, raising additional finance or renegotiating agreements with creditors, especially banks. Reducing debt will increase an organisation's robustness in the face of future crises.

15.4.3 Revolution

Revolution is change that requires rapid and major strategic and cultural change. This could be in circumstances where the strategy has been so bounded by the existing culture that, even when environmental or competitive pressures might require fundamental change, the organisation has failed to respond. This might have occurred over many years (see the discussion of strategic drift in Section 6.4) and resulted in circumstances where pressures for change are extreme – for example, a takeover threatens the continued existence of a firm.

Revolutionary change therefore differs from turnaround (or reconstruction) in two ways that make managing change especially challenging. First, the need is not only for fast strategic change but, very likely, also for deep cultural change. Second, it may be that the need for change is not as evident to people in the organisation as in a turnaround situation, or that they have reasons to deny the need for change. This situation may have come about as a result of many years of relative decline in a market, with people wedded to products or processes no longer valued by customers – the problem of strategic drift. Or it could be that the problems of the organisation are visible and understood by its members, but that people cannot see a way forward. Leading change in such circumstances is likely to involve:

- *Clear strategic direction.* The need to give a clear strategic direction and to undertake decisive action in line with that direction is critical. This may of course include some of the decisions outlined above for turnaround: for example, portfolio changes and greater market focus. This is the type of change where individual CEOs who are seen to provide such direction are often credited with making a major difference. They may well also become the symbol of such change within an organisation and externally.

- *Top management changes.* The replacement of the CEO, senior executives or, perhaps, changes in board membership is common. Existing top management may be embedded within the past culture and their network of colleagues, customers or suppliers. New top managers do not have these established networks, nor are they embedded in the existing culture, so it is more likely that they will bring a fresh perspective and initiate or be ready to adopt new ideas and initiatives.[14] The introduction of new top management also signals the significance of change internally and externally. For similar reasons consultants may also be used not only to provide an analysis of the need for change, but also to signal how meaningful the change process is.

- *Culture change.* It may be possible to work with elements of the existing culture rather than attempt wholesale culture change. This involves identifying those aspects of culture that can be built upon and developed and those that have to be changed – in effect a forcefield approach (see Section 15.3.2).

- *Monitoring change.* Revolutionary change is likely to require the setting and monitoring of unambiguous targets that people have to achieve. Often these will be linked to overall financial targets and in turn to improved returns to shareholders. Although revolutionary change is urgent, some parts of the change – for instance, cultural change – may take longer to bed down than others.

15.4.4 Evolution

Evolution is change in strategy that results in transformation, but gradually. Arguably this is the most challenging type of strategic change since it involves building on and exploiting existing strategic capabilities while also developing new strategic capabilities. As Chapter 6 explains, however, in successful organisations many will see no pressing need for change and there will be a tendency to stick to historic bases of success, so the exploration for new ways of doing things may be limited. Managers and scholars alike have sought to identify ways in which the effective evolution of strategy might occur: how an organisation can change its business model (see Chapter 7) and culture gradually *and* keep pace with a changing environment, thus avoiding strategic drift. One approach is to cultivate organisational ambidexterity.

Human ambidexterity is the ability to use both hands with equal facility. **Organisational ambidexterity is the capacity both to exploit existing capabilities and to search for new capabilities.** It is, of course, appropriate and necessary that an organisation should seek to exploit the capabilities it has built up over time in order to achieve and sustain competitive advantage. However, exploitation will tend to allow only incremental change, since strategy is being built on established ways of doing things. If transformational change is to be achieved, there needs also to be exploration in order to innovate and build new capabilities. This is in line with the lesson from Section 4.5 that organisations need the ability to renew and re-create their capabilities; they need to develop dynamic capabilities.

However, organisational ambidexterity can be challenging because the different processes associated with exploitation and exploration raise contradictory pressures: ambidexterity involves being both focused and flexible, efficient yet innovative, looking forward and looking backward.[15] Four kinds of approach can help manage the pressures of ambidexterity:

- *Structural ambidexterity.* Organisations may maintain the main core of the business devoted to exploitation with tighter control and careful planning but create separate units or temporary, perhaps project-based, teams for exploration (see Section 14.2.5). These exploratory units will be smaller in size, less tightly controlled with much more emphasis on learning and processes to encourage new ideas. As in Illustration 14.2, Alphabet thus restructured in 2015 to place its large and mature search and advertising businesses in the Google subsidiary, while keeping its more exploratory activities apart in the separate Ventures and X subsidiaries.

- *Diversity rather than conformity.* Maintaining a diversity of views within the organisation can help promote ambidexterity, in line with the concept of *organisational learning* (see Section 13.3.1). Such diversity might be based on managers with different experience or different views on future strategy, giving rise to useful debate. Such contesting of strategy may come to be 'normal' at senior levels in an organisation.[16] Stanford University's Robert Burgelman[17] also argues that diverse views can be found close to the market and therefore perhaps at junior levels in an organisation; senior executives need to channel this market or junior-level 'dissonance' into a 'searing intellectual debate' until a clearer strategic pattern emerges.

- *The role of leadership.* In turn this has implications for leadership roles in organisations. Leaders need to encourage and value different views and potentially contradictory behaviours rather than demanding uniformity.[18] This may mean running with new ideas and experiments to establish just what makes sense and what does not. However, they also need to have the authority, legitimacy and recognition to stop such experiments when it becomes clear that they are not worthwhile pursuing and make decisions about the direction that is to be followed, which, once taken, are followed by everyone in the organisation – including those who have previously dissented.

- *Tight and loose systems.* All this suggests that there needs to be a balance between 'tight' systems of strategy development that can exploit existing capabilities – perhaps employing the disciplines of strategic planning – and 'looser' systems that encourage new ideas and experimentation. This combination of loose and tight systems can be given coherence so long as there is some overall common 'glue', perhaps in the form of an organisational mission or vision that allows different units to express the organisation's overall purpose in different ways.

Identifying the type of strategic change in hand will assist in selecting the detailed levers for change to be considered in Section 15.5. Meanwhile, following the logic of situational leadership, it should be noted that appropriate leadership styles are likely to vary according to the types of change being sought. Urgent and limited change – especially the kind of reconstruction associated with turnaround – tend to require a more transactional approach, focused on short-term targets and tight monitoring of performance. Transformational leadership styles are usually more important in broad and longer-term change programmes, for instance evolutionary change.

However, one challenge for leaders is that often one type of change leads to another type of change, requiring different leadership styles. Sometimes this shift between types of change can be managed in stages. For example, short-term turnaround can set the stage for sustained evolutionary change, obliging leaders to transition from a transactional style to a more transformational style. Sometimes, small-scale changes can actually destabilise organisations, leading to larger-scale changes whether or not originally planned or required. It is because changes are not necessarily discrete stand-alone alternatives that Balogun and Hope-Hailey refer to types of change as 'paths', underlining how changes of one kind are liable to lead to more changes of a different kind.[19]

15.5 LEVERS FOR STRATEGIC CHANGE

Having identified both the type of change required and the receptiveness of the context, change leaders must choose between the various levers (or means) for change. Most successful change initiatives rely on multiple levers.[20]

Sometimes these levers are presented as a sequence, as for example in Harvard Business School professor John Kotter's Eight Steps for Change (Figure 15.5).[21] Here the process of change is described as a series of steps, starting from establishing a sense of urgency in the organisation, leading eventually to the institutionalisation of change. These steps provide leaders with a clear progression in the managing of change. However, in practice, many of these levers are likely to be used simultaneously rather than in the kind of logical sequence in Figure 15.5. There are also other levers that can be drawn upon. Some levers for change have already been discussed elsewhere in the text. The importance of strategic vision (a major feature of Figure 15.5) was discussed in Section 6.2 together with the importance of other goals and objectives. The consolidating and institutionalising of change involves the kinds of adjustments of organisational structures and systems described in Chapter 14. This section focuses on seven further levers of change.

15.5.1 A compelling case for change

A starting point must be presenting a convincing case for change. This equates to Kotter's first step, establishing a sense of urgency. However, McKinsey & Co, the consultants,[22] warn that too often the case for change is made in terms of top management's perception of what is important: for example, meeting expectations of shareholders or beating competition. When most managers and employees are asked, however, there are many more factors that motivate them: for example, the impact on society, on customers, on the local working team, or on employees' personal well-being. In making the case for change, transformational leaders especially need to speak to these different bases of motivation, not just to top management perceptions of why change is needed. It may, of course, be difficult for top management

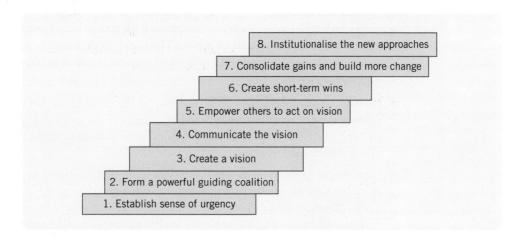

Figure 15.5 Kotter's Eight Steps for Change

Source: J. Kotter, 'Leading change: why transformation efforts fail', *Harvard Business Review,* March–April 1996, p. 61.

to understand and relate to these different needs. In this case, it may make sense to involve employees, themselves, in the creation of stories of change that, in effect, 'translate' corporate imperatives of change into local motivating messages. It is also important that the case for change does not just focus on the understanding of why change is needed, but the action required to deliver it.

15.5.2 Challenging the taken for granted

Often another early key step in managing strategic change is challenging what can be long-standing mindsets or taken-for-granted assumptions – the organisational paradigm, in the terms of Chapter 6. There are different approaches to challenging the paradigm. One view is that gathering enough objective evidence, perhaps in the form of careful strategic analysis, will be enough to challenge and therefore change the paradigm. However, assumptions can be very resistant to change: people find ways of questioning, reconfiguring and reinterpreting objective analyses in order to bring it in line with the existing paradigm. It may take much persistence to overcome this. Another view is that encouraging people to question and challenge each other's assumptions and received wisdom by making them explicit is valuable.[23] Scenario planning (see Section 2.4) is similarly advocated as a way of overcoming individual biases and cultural assumptions by getting people to see possible different futures and the implications for their organisations. There is also research that shows that successful firms able to enact significant strategic changes while also maintaining high levels of performance have questioning and 'contestation' embedded within their cultures: this, for example, has been the case for the French cosmetics firm L'Oréal, where they actually have a presentation theatre called the 'contestation room' (*salle de contestation*).[24]

15.5.3 Changing operational processes and routines

Another lever for strategic change is to start at the bottom, with the basic day-to-day processes and routines of the organisation's operations. These processes and routines might be formalised and codified or they might be less formal 'ways we do things around here'. The ways in which colleagues simply communicate with each other, or interact with customers, or respond to mistakes can all be serious blockages to change. The relationship between strategic change and day-to-day processes and routines is therefore important to consider in at least three respects:

- *Planning operational change.* The planning of the implementation of an intended strategy requires the identification of the key changes in the routines required to deliver that strategy. In effect, strategic change needs to be considered in terms of the re-engineering of organisational processes.

- *Challenging operational assumptions.* Changing organisational processes and routines may also have the effect of challenging the often taken-for-granted assumptions underpinning them. In turn this may have the effect of getting people to question and challenge deep-rooted beliefs and assumptions in the organisation. Richard Pascale argues: 'It is easier to act your way into a better way of thinking than to think your way into a better way of acting';[25] in other words, it is easier to change behaviour and by so doing change taken-for-granted assumptions than to try to change taken-for-granted assumptions as a way of changing behaviour. If this is so, the style of change employed (see Section 15.2.2 above) needs to take this into account: it suggests that attempting to persuade people to change may be less powerful than involving people in the activities of changing.

- *Bottom-up changes to routines.* Even when changes in routines are not planned from the top, people do change them and this may result in wider strategic change. This may occur through trial and error learning as people experiment with different routines associated with doing their jobs.[26] Or it could occur as people learn from and adapt the routines in other organisations.[27] Or it may occur more proactively by managers deliberately and persistently 'bending the rules of the game' till they achieve enough support from different stakeholders such that new routines supporting a shift in strategy become acceptable.[28]

The overall lesson is that changes in routines may appear to be mundane, but they can have significant impact.

15.5.4 Symbolic management[29]

Change levers are not always of an overt, formal nature: they may also be symbolic in nature. Symbols may be everyday things which are nevertheless especially meaningful in the context of a particular situation or organisation. Changing symbols can help reshape beliefs and expectations because meaning becomes apparent in the day-to-day experiences people have of organisations, such as the symbols that surround them (e.g. office layout and décor), the type of language and technology used and organisational rituals. Consider some examples:

- Many *rituals*[30] of organisations are concerned with effecting or consolidating change. Table 15.2 identifies and gives examples of such rituals and suggests what role they might play in change processes. New rituals can be introduced or old rituals done away with as ways of signalling or reinforcing change.

- Changes in *physical aspects* of the work environment are powerful symbols of change. Typical here is a change of location for the head office, relocation of personnel, changes in dress or uniforms, and alterations to offices or office space.

- The *behaviour of managers,* particularly strategic leaders, is perhaps the most powerful symbol in relation to change. So, having made pronouncements about the need for change, it is vital that the visible behaviour of change agents be in line with such change.

- The *language* used by change agents is also important.[31] Either consciously or unconsciously language and metaphor may be employed to galvanise change. Of course, there

Table 15.2 Organisational rituals and change

Types of ritual	Role	Examples in change initiatives
Rites of passage	Signify a change of status or role	Induction to new roles Training programmes
Rites of enhancement	Recognise effort benefiting organisation	Awards ceremonies Promotions
Rites of renewal	Reassure that something is being done Focus attention on issues	Appointment of consultant Project teams and workshops
Rites of integration	Encourage shared commitment Reassert rightness of norms	Celebrations of achievement or new ways of doing things
Rites of conflict reduction	Reduce conflict and aggression	Negotiating committees
Rites of challenge	'Throwing down the gauntlet'	New CEO setting challenging goals

is also the danger that strategic leaders do not realise the significance of their language and, while espousing change, use language that signals adherence to the status quo, or personal reluctance to change.

However, there is an important qualification to the idea that the manipulation of symbols can be a useful lever for managing change. The significance and meaning of symbols are dependent on how they are interpreted. Since they may not be interpreted as intended, their impact is difficult to predict.

15.5.5 Power and political systems

Section 5.2.2 explained the importance of understanding the political context in and around an organisation. Strategic change particularly can be a political process. Illustration 15.4 also gives examples of political processes. To effect change, powerful support may be required from individuals or groups or a reconfiguration of *power structures* may be necessary, especially if transformational change is required. This is equivalent to Kotter's second step in the change process (Figure 15.5), forming a powerful guiding coalition. Table 15.3 shows some of the mechanisms associated with managing change from a political perspective:[32]

- *Controlling or acquiring resources,* being identified with important resource areas or areas of expertise. Such resources might include for example funds, information, key organisational processes or key people. In particular the ability to withdraw or allocate such resources can be a powerful tool in overcoming resistance, persuading others to accept change or build readiness for change.

- *Association with powerful stakeholder groups* (or *elites*), or their supporters, can help build a power base or help overcome resistance to change. Or a manager facing resistance to change may seek out and win over someone highly respected from within the very group resistant to change. It may also be necessary to *remove individuals or groups* resistant to change. Who these are can vary – from powerful individuals in senior positions to whole layers of resistance, perhaps executives in a threatened function or service.

- *Building alliances* and *networks* of contacts and sympathisers may be important in overcoming the resistance of more powerful groups. Attempting to convert the whole organisation to an acceptance of change is difficult. There may, however, be parts of the organisation, or individuals, more sympathetic to change than others with whom support for change can be built. Marginalisation of those resistant to change may also be possible. However, the danger is that powerful groups in the organisation may regard the building of support coalitions, or acts of marginalisation, as a threat to their own power, leading to further resistance to change. An analysis of power and interest using the stakeholder mapping (Section 5.2.2) can, therefore, be useful to identify bases of alliance and likely resistance.

Cynthia Hardy of the University of Melbourne[33] also points out that change leaders may gain power through 'meaning power' by which she means the ability to use symbols, rituals and language to legitimise change, make change appear desirable, inevitable or help build excitement or optimism about change (see Section 15.5.4).

However, the political aspects of change management are potentially hazardous. Table 15.3 also summarises some of the problems. In overcoming resistance, the major problem may simply be the lack of power to undertake such activity. Trying to break down the status quo may become so destructive and take so long that the organisation cannot recover from it. If the process needs to take place, its replacement by some new set of beliefs and the implementation of a new strategy is vital and needs to be speedy. Further, as already identified, in

ILLUSTRATION 15.4	Change levers in action

Emotional change

Karen Addington, 2015 UK Charity Leader of the Year, remembered her third board meeting as CEO of a leading children's diabetes research charity: 'I went into the meeting all fired up to put across a clear business case and persuade the board to invest significant amounts of money in fundraising. But I suddenly realised that I had to manage people's emotional responses as well as their business responses, because at the time the board were all parents of children with diabetes. . . . I was asking them to take money from research in the short term to invest in our mission in the long term. Logically it made sense, but of course our donors hope that the next penny is the one that finds the cure for their children. I realised that it was a huge leap of faith for our trustees and learnt that I must always link the business case back to the impact that it could have on our beneficiaries – their children.'[1]

Not wasting crisis

When Mary Barra became CEO of General Motors at the beginning of 2014, she was immediately confronted by a scandal over faulty switches that, over 12 years, had caused 13 deaths. The company had avoided taking responsibility for all that time, symptomatic of an evasive corporate culture. Barra declared: 'I don't want to set it [the scandal] aside and explain it away, because . . . it uncovered some things in the company that it's critical we challenge . . . ' She continued: 'We didn't have to work too hard to make the case for change because clearly it was deeply troubling. Anytime you want to drive change, you have to have a catalyst . . . and it [the scandal] did provide that. I will also tell you it's made me more impatient.'[2]

Force for change

In November 2015, Ash Carter became new Defense Secretary, determined to reform the Pentagon's personnel systems to create a twenty-first century 'Force for the Future'. Rather than tackling the heated topic of the military's promotion system, he declared his priority to be the 'low hanging fruit'. He approved for immediate action 20 out of the 80 proposals on his desk. Carter said of his plans for change: 'Throughout this process, we've always been mindful that the military is a profession of arms. It's not a business. The key to doing this successfully is to leverage both tradition and change.'[3]

My way or the highway

Since 2013, CEO Tony Hsieh has been trying to reduce management and increase self-organisation at his online retailer, Zappos. Frustrated by slow progress, in 2015 he declared it was time to 'rip the bandaid'. In an internal memo, he told staff to back change or quit: '. . . self-management and self-organization is not for everyone . . . Therefore, there will be a special version of "the offer" on a company-wide scale, in which each employee will be offered at least 3 months' severance . . . if he/she feels that self-management [and] self-organization . . . are not the right fit.'[4]

Designer in Chief

In 2015, Zhang Ruimin, CEO of the giant electricals company Haier, launched a radical decentralization of power in his company. With Haier now a mass of 'micro-enterprises', Zhang would have a reduced role. He commented: 'If one day companies no longer exist, CEOs will also disappear. But I believe organisations will still exist and there may be some role for a person to design the way organisations work and how they grow. Maybe my title can be changed to something like "designer for the organisation".'[5]

Sources: (1) *Third Sector*, 25 June 2015; (2) *Fortune*, 18 September 2014; (3) J. Garamone, 'Carter details force of the future initiatives', US Department of Defense, 18 November 2015; (4) *Quartz*, 26 March 2015; (5) *Financial Times*, 25 November 2015.

Questions

1 Identify the various change levers (Section 15.5) used by these five leaders.

2 Do you think that a diabetes charity or the US military have anything to teach business organisations about change?

Table 15.3 Political mechanisms in organisations

Activity areas	Mechanisms			Problems
	Resources	**Elites**	**Building alliances**	
Building the power base	Control of resources Acquisition of/identification with expertise Acquisition of additional resources	Sponsorship by an elite Association with an elite	Identification of change supporters Alliance building Team building	Time required for building Perceived duality of ideals Perceived as threat by existing elites
Overcoming resistance	Withdrawal of resources Use of 'counter-intelligence'	Breakdown or division of elites Association with change leader Association with respected outsider	Foster momentum for change Sponsorship/reward of change leaders	Striking from too low a power base Potentially destructive: need for rapid rebuilding
Achieving compliance	Giving resources	Removal of resistant elites Need for visible 'change hero'	Partial implementation and collaboration Implantation of 'disciples' Support for 'young Turks'	Converting the body of the organisation Slipping back

implementing change, gaining the commitment of a few senior executives at the top of an organisation is one thing; it is quite another to convert the body of the organisation to an acceptance of significant change.

15.5.6 Timing

How much time is available for strategic change has already been considered as part of the change kaleidoscope (Section 15.3). However, choosing the precise time at which to launch strategic change is another variable. The timing of change is often neglected. Choosing the right time can be tactically vital. For example:

- *Building on actual or perceived crisis* is especially useful the greater the degree of change needed. If there is a higher perceived risk in maintaining the status quo than in changing it, people are more likely to change. Change leaders may take advantages of performance downturns, competitive threats or threatened takeover as catalysts for strategic change.

- *Windows of opportunity* in change processes may exist. The arrival of a new chief executive, the introduction of a new, highly successful product, or the arrival of a major competitive threat on the scene may provide opportunities to make more significant changes than might normally be possible. Since change will be regarded nervously, it may also be important to choose the time for promoting such change to avoid unnecessary fear and nervousness. For example, if there is a need for the removal of executives, this may be best done before rather than during the change programme. In such a way, the change programme can be seen as a potential improvement for the future rather than as the cause of such losses.

- *The symbolic signalling of time frames* may be important. In particular, conflicting messages about the timing of change should be avoided. For example, if rapid change is required, the maintenance of procedures or focus on issues that signal long time horizons may be counter-productive.

15.5.7 Visible short-term wins

A strategic change programme will require many detailed actions and tasks. It is important that some are seen to be successful quickly. In Kotter's model of change (Figure 15.5), creating short-term wins is the sixth step. Identifying some 'low-hanging fruit' – changes that may not be big but can be made easily and yield a quick payoff – can be useful. This could take the form, for example, of a retail chain introducing a new product range and demonstrating its success in the market or the breaking down of a long-established routine and the demonstration of a better way of doing things. In themselves, these may not be especially significant aspects of a new strategy, but they may be visible indicators of a new approach associated with that strategy. The demonstration of such wins can therefore galvanise commitment to the wider strategy.

One reason given for the inability to change is that resources are not available to do so. This may be overcome if it is possible to identify '*hot spots*' on which to focus resources and effort. For example, William Bratton, famously responsible for the 'zero tolerance' policy of the New York Police Department, began by focusing resource and effort on narcotics-related crimes. Though associated with 50–70 per cent of all crimes, he found they only had five per cent of the resources allocated by NYPD to tackle them. Success in this field led to the roll-out of his policies into other areas and to gaining the resources to do so.

In sum, there are many kinds of change lever available. Which levers are most appropriate depends on the type of change being sought and the context in which it is being carried out. Similarly, leadership style needs to be consistent. For example, political approaches are associated with a more transactional leadership style and are more likely to work in unreceptive contexts seeking limited types of change. On the other hand, symbolic management and transformational leadership styles are particularly important when seeking evolutionary or revolutionary change in receptive contexts.

15.6 PROBLEMS OF FORMAL CHANGE PROGRAMMES

Strategic change is often launched as a top-down initiative supported by formal methods of programme and project management. Kotter's Eight Steps for Change (Figure 15.5), with its clear and logical sequence, can lend itself to this kind of formal, top-down approach. However, there are two kinds of potential problem with this formal programmatic approach. First, problems can arise from the process itself. Second, managers may mistake the relative importance of formal and informal change.

15.6.1 Problems in the process

In designing change programmes, it is useful to know in advance common reasons for failure. Researchers identify seven factors that can go wrong in formal change processes, as follows:[34]

- *Death by planning*. The emphasis is put on planning the change programme rather than delivering it. There is a continuous stream of proposals and reports, each one requiring agreement among managers affected by the changes. Subcommittees, project teams and working groups may be set up to examine problems and achieve buy-in. The result can be 'analysis paralysis' and a discourse about change rather than the delivery of change. This may also be linked to the politicisation of the change programme where meetings about change become forums for debate and political game-playing.

- *Loss of focus*. Change is often not a one-off process; it might require an ongoing series of initiatives, maybe over years. However, the risk is that these initiatives are seen by employees as 'change rituals' signifying very little. There is also the risk that the original intention of the change programme becomes eroded by other events taking place: for example, a redundancy programme.

- *Reinterpretation.* The attempted change becomes reinterpreted according to the old culture. For example, an engineering company's intended strategy of achieving differentiation by building on what customers valued was interpreted by the engineers within the firm as providing high levels of technical specification as determined by them, not by the customers.

- *Disconnectedness.* People affected by change may not see the change programme connecting to their reality. Senior executives, as proponents of the change, might not be seen to be credible in terms of understanding the realities of change on the ground. Or perhaps new systems and initiatives introduced are seen as out of line with the aims of the intended change.

- *Behavioural compliance.* There is the danger that people comply with the changes being pursued in the change programme without actually 'buying into' them. Change leaders see specified changes in behaviour, but this is merely superficial compliance. This is like following the letter of the law, rather than its spirit. Because employees do not believe in the behaviours, the result is cynicism and rigid compliance to the rules even when circumstances do not precisely call for them.

- *Misreading scrutiny and resistance.* Change leaders are likely to face either resistance to the change or critical scrutiny of it. Often their response is to see such behaviour as negative and destructive. However, scrutiny and resistance can be seen as ways in which 'change recipients' in the organisation engage with what the changes mean for them. Even if resistance occurs, this is a way of keeping the agenda for change on the table. Moreover, resistance that is explicit is more capable of being addressed than that which is passive or covert. So managers should see scrutiny and resistance as potential positives rather than only negatives. Scrutiny and resistance can be the basis for engaging recipients in the change programme.

- *Broken agreements and violation of trust.* The need for a clear message about the need for and direction of change has been emphasised in this chapter. However, if senior management fail to provide honest assessments of the situation or provide undertakings to employees on which they subsequently renege, then they will lose the trust and respect of employees and, very likely, ensure heightened resistance to change.

15.6.2 What formal programmes forget

Not only can formal change programmes fail, but they often forget what else is going on in the organisation. According to Hari Tsoukas and Robert Chia, from the Universities of Warwick and Glasgow, respectively, a lot of change happens regardless of formal programmes.[35] They argue that change is an inherent property of organisations, as employees continually adapt and learn in response to changing conditions on the ground. Managers are liable not to recognise this inherent, unmanaged change. Indeed, hierarchy and management control often dampen such change. Thus managers underestimate spontaneous, emergent change, while overestimating formal change programmes.

The implication is that top-down planned change programmes can actually get in the way of the local adaptations that employees are always making anyway, and that can be more effective because they are closer to market needs. It is important to remember that strategic change can bubble up from the bottom of the organisation. In this view, management's job is to encourage and multiply successful local adaptations, not just impose strategic change from the top.

THINKING DIFFERENTLY | Women as leaders

Do women lead differently – and better – than men?

Traditionally men have been associated with leadership: think of Winston Churchill or Nelson Mandela. Men too tend still to dominate leadership roles in important spheres from politics to business: in 2015, women still held less than five per cent of CEO roles in the Fortune 500 list of largest American corporations. The implication might seem to be that if women aspire to leadership positions, they should act more like men.

However, increasingly women are taking CEO positions in large corporations across a wide range of industries: for example, Mary Barra at General Motors, Indra Nooyi at PepsiCo, Ginni Rometty at IBM and Cheryl Sandberg at Facebook. Such women leaders do not by any means necessarily lead like men. And their companies tend to perform better than those led by men: over the period 2002–14, leading American companies with women CEOs outperformed those with male CEOs by more than 200 per cent.[36]

Indeed, research suggests that women leaders do lead differently. Women are associated with transformational leadership styles, concerned with collective achievement and energising people, rather than transactional styles, more concerned with structures, systems and incentives (see Section 15.2.2).[37] Moreover, it is often argued that contemporary business, reliant on cooperation between knowledge-workers, demands more transformational leadership styles. Transactional styles do not fit organisations where trust and creativity are important. However, the research also finds very substantial overlaps between male and female leadership styles. Many male leaders display the same traits as women leaders.

Question

Consider two female leaders, in any sphere whether business, politics, education, sport or the arts. How similar are they in style and in what ways is gender important to their style? Could you imagine men leading similarly?

SUMMARY

A recurrent theme in this chapter has been that styles and levers of change need to be tailored to the nature of that change. Bearing in mind this general point, this chapter has emphasised the following:

- There are two main types of leadership style, *transactional* and *transformational*.

- *Situational leadership* suggests that leaders need to adapt their *styles* according to different types and contexts of change.

- The *types of strategic change* can be thought of in terms of the *extent* of change required and its *urgency* – whether it can be achieved through incremental change or requires immediate action (the 'big bang' approach).

- The context for change can be analysed in terms of the c*hange kaleidoscope* and *forcefield analysis*.

- *Levers* for managing strategic change include building a compelling case for change, challenging the taken for granted, changing operational processes, routines and symbols, political processes, timing and quick wins.

WORK ASSIGNMENTS

✱ Denotes more advanced work assignments.
* Refers to a case study in the Text and Cases edition.

15.1 Compare and contrast the different styles of leading change you have read about in the press or in this text (e.g. Sergio Marchionne at Fiat and Chrysler and Steve Jobs and Tim Cook at Apple*).

15.2 Drawing on Section 15.2.2, assess the key contextual dimensions of an organisation (such as Barclays in Chapter 6) and consider how they should influence the design of a programme of strategic change.

15.3 Use a forcefield analysis to identify blockages and facilitators of change for an organisation (such as one for which you have considered the need for a change in strategic direction in a previous assignment). Identify what aspects of the changes suggested by this analysis can be managed as part of a change programme and how.

15.4✱ In the context of leading strategic change in a large corporation or public-sector organisation, to what extent, and why, do you agree with Richard Pascale's argument that it is easier to act ourselves into a better way of thinking than it is to think ourselves into a better way of acting?

15.5✱ There are a number of books by (or about) renowned senior executives who have led major changes in their organisation (for example, Karren Brady, Alex Ferguson, Elon Musk). Read one of these and note the levers and mechanisms for change they employed, using the approaches outlined in this chapter as a checklist. How effective do you think these were in the context that the change leader faced, and could other mechanisms have been used?

Integrative assignment

15.6✱ What would be the key issues for the corporate parent of a diversified organisation with a multi-domestic international strategy (see Chapter 9) wishing to change to a more related portfolio? Consider this in terms of (a) the strategic capabilities that the parent might require (Chapters 4 and 8), (b) the implications for organising and controlling its subsidiaries (Chapter 14), (c) the likely blockages to such change and (d) how these might be overcome (Chapter 15).

RECOMMENDED KEY READINGS

- For a succinct summary of research on effective leadership, including the leadership of change, see G. Yukl, 'Effective leadership behaviour: what we know and what questions need more attention', *Academy of Management Perspectives*, vol. 26, no. 4 (2012), pp. 66–85.

- J. Balogun and V. Hope-Hailey, *Exploring Strategic Change*, Prentice Hall, 4th edn, 2016, builds on and extends many of the ideas in this chapter. In particular, it emphasises the importance of tailoring change

programmes to organisational context and discusses more fully many of the change levers reviewed in this chapter.

- For an understanding of different approaches to leading change, see M. Beer and N. Nohria, 'Cracking the code of change', *Harvard Business Review*, vol. 78, no. 3 (May–June 2000), pp. 133–41. For an understanding of organisational ambidexterity, see G. Johnson, G. Yip and M. Hensmans, 'Achieving successful strategic transformation', *MIT Sloan Management Review*, vol. 53, no. 3 (2012), pp. 25–32.

REFERENCES

1. This definition of leadership is based on the classic by R.M. Stodgill, 'Leadership, membership and organization', *Psychological Bulletin*, vol. 47 (1950), pp. 1–14. Recent reviews of the leadership literature include G. Yukl, 'Effective leadership behavior: What we know and what questions need more attention', *Academy of Management Perspectives*, vol. 26, no. 4 (2012), pp. 66–85; and Jessica E. Dinh, Robert G. Lord, William L. Gardner, Jeremy D. Meuser, Robert C. Liden and Jinyu Hu, 'Leadership theory and research in the new millennium: current theoretical trends and changing perspectives', *Leadership Quarterly*, vol. 25, no. 1 (2014), pp. 36–62.

2. J. Kotter, 'What leaders really do', *Harvard Business Review*, December 2001, pp. 85–96.

3. See D. Ulrich, N. Smallwood and K. Sweetman, *Leadership Code: the five things great leaders do*, Harvard Business School Press, 1999.

4. See S. Floyd and W. Wooldridge, *The Strategic Middle Manager: how to create and sustain competitive advantage*, Jossey-Bass, 1996.

5. See E. Mollick, 'People and process, suits and innovators: the role of individuals in firm performance', *Strategic Management Journal*, vol. 33, no. 9 (2012), pp. 1001–15.

6. See for example J. Balogun and G. Johnson, 'Organizational restructuring and middle manager sensemaking', *Academy of Management Journal*, August 2004, pp. 523–49; and J. Sillence and F. Mueller, 'Switching strategic perspective: the reframing of accounts of responsibility', *Organization Studies*, vol. 28, no. 2 (2007), pp. 155–76.

7. J.A. Raelin, 'Imagine there are no leaders: reframing leadership as collaborative agency', *Leadership* (2014) DOI 1742715014558076.

8. See T.A. Judge and R.F. Piccolo, 'Transformational and transactional leadership: a meta analytic test of their relative validity', *Journal of Applied Psychology*, vol. 89 (2004), pp. 755–68.

9. For this evidence, see D.A. Waldman, G.G. Ramirez, R.J. House and P. Puranam, 'Does leadership matter? CEO leadership attributes and profitability under conditions of perceived environmental uncertainty', *Academy of Management Journal*, vol. 44, no. 1 (2001), pp. 134–43.

10. The discussion on different approaches of strategic leaders and evidence for the effectiveness of the adoption of different approaches can be found in D. Goleman, 'Leadership that gets results', *Harvard Business Review*, vol. 78, no. 2 (March–April 2000), pp. 78–90; and C.M. Farkas and S. Wetlaufer, 'The ways chief executive officers lead', *Harvard Business Review*, vol. 74, no. 3 (May–June 1996), pp. 110–12.

11. For an interesting example of how different contexts affect receptivity to change, see J. Newton, J. Graham, K. McLoughlin and A. Moore, 'Receptivity to change in a general medical practice', *British Journal of Management*, vol. 14, no. 2 (2003), pp. 143–53. And for a discussion of the problems of importing change programmes from the private sector to the public sector, see F. Ostroff, 'Change management in government', *Harvard Business Review*, vol. 84, no. 5 (May 2006), pp. 141–7.

12. This part of the chapter draws on Chapter 3 of *Exploring Strategic Change* by J. Balogun and V. Hope-Hailey, 3rd edn, Prentice Hall, 2008.

13. Turnaround strategy is extensively explained in D. Lovett and S. Slatter, *Corporate Turnaround*, Penguin Books, 1999; and P. Grinyer, D. Mayes and P. McKiernan, 'The sharpbenders: achieving a sustained improvement in performance', *Long Range Planning*, vol. 23, no. 1 (1990), pp. 116–25. Also see V.L. Barker and I.M. Duhaime, 'Strategic change in the turnaround process: theory and empirical evidence', *Strategic Management Journal*, vol. 18, no. 1 (1997), pp. 13–38.

14. See J. Battilana and T. Casciaro, 'Change agents, networks and institutions: a contingency theory of organizational change', *Academy of Management Journal*, vol. 35, no. 2 (2012), pp. 381–98.

15. See W.K. Smith and M. Tushman, 'Senior teams and managing contradictions: on the team dynamics of managing exploitation and exploration', *Organization Science*, vol. 16, no. 5 (2005), pp. 522–36. See also M.L. Tushman and C.A. O'Reilly, 'Ambidextrous organizations: managing evolutionary and revolutionary change', *California Management Review*, vol. 38, no. 4 (1996), pp. 8–30.

16. M. Hensmans, G. Johnson and G. Yip, *Strategic Transformation: changing while winning*, Palgrave, 2013.

17. Robert Burgelman and Andrew Grove, 'Strategic dissonance', *California Management Review*, vol. 38, no. 2 (1996), pp. 8–28.

18. R.A. Burgelman and A.S. Grove, 'Let chaos reign, then rein in chaos – repeatedly: managing strategic dynamics for corporate longevity', *Strategic Management Journal*, vol. 28 (2007), pp. 965–79: also C.A. O'Reilly and M.L. Tushman, 'Organizational ambidexterity in action: how managers explore and exploit', *California Management Review*, vol. 53, no. 4 (2011), pp. 5–22.

19. *Exploring Strategic Change* by J. Balogun and V. Hope-Hailey, 3rd edn, Prentice Hall, 2008. For how incremental changes can tip into transformational change, see S. Girod and R. Whittington, 'Change escalation processes and complex adaptive systems: from incremental reconfigurations to discontinuous restructuring', *Organization Science*, vol. 26, no. 5 (2015), pp. 1520–35.

20. For a review of research that makes this point, see D. Buchanan, L. Fitzgerald, D. Ketley, R. Gallop, J.L. Jones, S.S. Lamont, A. Neath and E. Whitby, 'No going back: a review of the literature on sustaining organizational change', *International Journal of Management Reviews*, vol. 7, no. 3 (2005), pp. 189–205.

21. J. Kotter, 'Leading change: why transformation efforts fail', *Harvard Business Review*, March–April 1995, pp. 59–66.

22. See C. Aiken and S. Keller, 'The irrational side of change management', *McKinsey Quarterly*, no. 2 (2009), pp. 101–9.

23. For an example of this approach, see J.M. Mezias, P. Grinyer and W.D. Guth, 'Changing collective cognition: a process model for strategic change', *Long Range Planning*, vol. 34, no. 1 (2001), pp. 71–95. Also for a systematic approach to strategy making and change based on such surfacing, see

F. Ackermann and C. Eden with I. Brown, *The Practice of Making Strategy*, Sage, 2005.

24. See G. Johnson, G. Yip and M. Hensmans, 'Achieving successful strategic transformation', *MIT Sloan Management Review*, vol. 53, no. 3 (2012), pp. 25–32.

25. This quote is on page 135 of R. Pascale, M. Millemann and L. Gioja, 'Changing the way we change', *Harvard Business Review*, vol. 75, no. 6 (November–December 1997), pp. 126–39.

26. See C. Rerup and M.S. Feldman, 'Routines as a source of change in organizational schemata: the role of trial and error learning', *Academy of Management Journal*, vol. 54, no. 3 (2011), pp. 577–610.

27. See H. Bresman, 'Changing routines: a process model of vicarious group learning in pharmaceutical R&D', *Academy of Management Journal*, vol. 56, no. 1 (2013), pp. 35–61.

28. See G. Johnson, S. Smith and B. Codling, 'Institutional change and strategic agency: an empirical analysis of managers' experimentation with routines in strategic decision-making', in D. Golsorkhi, L. Rouleau, D. Seidl and E. Vaara (eds), *The Cambridge Handbook of Strategy as Practice*, Cambridge University Press, 2010.

29. For a fuller discussion of this theme, see J.M. Higgins and C. McCallaster, 'If you want strategic change don't forget your cultural artefacts', *Journal of Change Management*, vol. 4, no. 1 (2004), pp. 63–73.

30. For a discussion of the role of rituals in change, see D. Sims, S. Fineman and Y. Gabriel, *Organizing and Organizations: an Introduction*, Sage, 1993.

31. See C. Hardy, I. Palmer and N. Phillips, 'Discourse as a strategic resource', *Human Relations*, vol. 53, no. 9 (2000), p. 1231.

32. Table 15.3 is based on observations of the role of political activities in organisations by, in particular, H. Mintzberg, *Power in and around Organizations*, Prentice Hall, 1983; and J. Pfeffer, *Power in Organizations*, Pitman, 1981.

33. C. Hardy, 'Understanding power; bringing about strategic change', *British Journal of Management*, vol. 7, special issue (1996), pp. 3–16.

34. The observations and examples here are largely based on L.C. Harris and E. Ogbonna, 'The unintended consequences of culture interventions: a study of unexpected outcomes', *British Journal of Management*, vol. 13, no. 1 (2002), pp. 31–49; and J.D. Ford, L.W. Ford and A.D. Amelio, 'Resistance to change: the rest of the story', *Academy of Management Review*, vol. 23 (2008), pp. 362–77.

35. H. Tsoukas and R. Chia, 'On organizational becoming: rethinking organizational change', *Organisation Science*, vol. 13, no. 5 (2002), pp. 567–82.

36. *Fortune Magazine*, 'Women-led companies perform three times better than the S&P 500', 3 March 2015.

37. A. Eagly, 'Female leadership advantage and disadvantage: resolving the contradictions', *Psychology of Women Quarterly*, vol. 31 (2007), pp. 1–12; I. Cuadrado, C. García-Ael, and F. Molero, 'Gender-typing of leadership: evaluations of real and ideal managers', *Scandinavian Journal of Psychology*, vol. 56, no. 2 (2015), pp. 236–44.

Sergio Marchionne – motor of change

In 2009, two of America's three largest automotive makers, General Motors and Chrysler, were bankrupt. General Motors was rescued by the US government, with loans and a substantial equity stake. Chrysler was rescued by an Italian company with a decidedly mixed reputation, Fiat. At the head of Fiat was Sergio Marchionne, an Italian–Canadian accountant with just four years' experience in the auto industry. Marchionne undertook radical change at Chrysler, but six years later ended up offering the company for sale to General Motors – and was rejected.

Nonetheless, Marchionne had transformed Chrysler through his energetic leadership style. He is famous for his constant smoking, his heavy consumption of espresso coffees and his informal dress sense, based on sweaters rather than traditional suits. At the same time, Marchionne is a notorious workaholic: no lower than 42 executives report directly to him, he carries six mobile phones, and he works 14–18 hour days, seven days a week. Regarding leadership, he explained to the *Harvard Business Review*: 'My job as CEO is not to make decisions about the business but to set stretch objectives and help our managers work out how to reach them.'[1]

Sergio Marchionne, CEO Fiat Chrysler

Source: Bloxham/LAT/REX/Shutterstock.

Marchionne at Fiat

When Marchionne took over as CEO at Fiat in 2004, he was the fifth CEO since 2001. The company was unprofitable, the products had a reputation for poor quality, its most recent new car launch had been unsuccessful and relationships with the unions were poor.

At Fiat, Marchionne spent his first 50 days touring the business, listening to people and analysing the situation. He found that senior executives were unused to taking responsibility for decisions; everything was referred upwards to the CEO. Executives communicated with each other via their secretaries and spent their time fire-fighting or avoiding problems. The company was dominated by engineers, who would work on new models in isolation. They then passed on their finished designs to sales and marketing, complete with sales targets and price. As well as being inefficient, this procedure caused fierce tensions between departments.

Following initial measures to reduce Fiat's debt level, Marchionne turned his attention to the leadership of the

business. Many senior executives were dismissed and 2000 other managers and staff were retired early. On the other hand, as he toured the company, he had identified young talented managers, often in areas such as marketing that were not the traditional routes to the top, or in geographic areas such as Latin America that were less influenced by head office and where managers tended to behave more autonomously. He drew on this 'talent spotting' to make 20 new leadership appointments as well as other promotions.

Marchionne took a close interest in high potential talent and regarded his personal engagement with them as more valuable than more formal assessment. He also believed that such personal engagement helped develop a top team with strongly held common values. His expectation of this new top cadre of leaders was that they should be given responsibility. He recognised that this was demanding:

'As I give people more responsibility, I also hold them more accountable. A leader who fails to meet an objective should suffer some consequences, but I don't believe that failing to meet an objective is the end of the world . . . (but) if you want to grow leaders, you can't let explanations and excuses become a way of life. That's a characteristic of the old Fiat we've left far behind.'[2]

To achieve greater integration and speed business up, Marchionne also took out several layers of management, eliminated committees and replaced them with a Group Executive Council that brought together executives from disparate operations such as tractors and trucks. To run Fiat Auto he also established a 24-person team with the aim of getting all parts of the company to talk to one another. To further encourage the sharing of ideas, he also began to move executives from one part of the business to another and required his top managers to accept multiple responsibilities for different parts of the business.

Marchionne saw one of his own major roles as the challenging of assumptions. He cites how he asked why it took Fiat four years to develop a new model. The question helped identify processes that could be removed, which meant that the new Cinquecento car was developed and launched in just 18 months in 2006. 'You start removing a few bottlenecks in this way, and pretty soon people catch on and begin ripping their own processes apart.'[3] Such challenging of assumptions and processes was also aided by recruiting managers from outside the car industry and by benchmarking, not just against other car makers but also companies like Apple. At the same time, Marchionne introduced 'World Class Manufacturing', the Japanese approach to lean production.

In 2004, Marchionne's new team had produced a business plan with a stretch target of €2bn (£1.6bn, $2.6bn) profits in 2007. Many thought the target unrealistic, but Marchionne believed that it forced managers to think differently and challenge old ways of doing things. By 2006, Fiat was profitable again. In 2007, Fiat made over €3bn profits. Soon it would be Chrysler's turn to experience Marchionne's leadership style.

Marchionne at Chrysler

By 2009, Chrysler was bankrupt, with potentially 300,000 jobs on the line. Supported by the US government, Fiat Group formed a strategic alliance with Chrysler, taking a 20 per cent ownership stake. Marchionne was appointed CEO, while retaining his role at Fiat. His vision was that Fiat and Chrysler together could create a leading global player in the automobile sector, exploiting synergies in terms of purchasing power, distribution capabilities and product portfolios – Chrysler's Jeeps, mini-vans and light trucks and Fiat's small cars and fuel-efficient engines.

When Marchionne took over at Chrysler in 2009, not only did he inherit a $6bn high-interest government loan, he also found a fearful workforce and a company riddled with bureaucracy. One of his first acts was to point out, in a memo to Chrysler employees, the parallels with Fiat: 'Five years ago, I stepped into a very similar situation at Fiat. It was perceived by many as a failing, lethargic automaker that produced low-quality cars and was stymied by endless bureaucracy.'[4] Like Fiat, Chrysler was highly hierarchical with managers reluctant to take decisions: 'This place was run by a chairman's office . . . the top floor (known as the Tower). It's empty now . . . Nothing happens there. I'm on the floor here with all the engineers.'[5]

Again Marchionne changed the management. As well as bringing in three senior managers from Fiat, Marchionne identified 26 young leaders from two or three levels below top management and made them direct reports in a new flatter organisation structure. One brief for the new managers was to introduce the Japanese-style manufacturing processes that Fiat had already used in its Italian plants. Marchionne also emphasised cost control; for example, the 2009 plan identified savings of $2.9bn by 2014 by sharing parts and engines with Fiat. But there was also an emphasis on product development. Here he drew on the experience of his new executive team to focus on improvements to the product range:

> **'Everyone knew what was wrong with the cars. You ask any employee in the company, they could list ten things that they would do better. And when you're given the chance to do those ten things better, you end up with a product that exceeds the sum of its parts.'[5]**

Another key ambition was to improve product quality. Chrysler had been organised such that each brand had its own quality department. These separate departments were merged and new ways to measure quality introduced to provide greater oversight across all the brands. This attention to product and quality improvement went hand-in-hand with plant modernisation. The result was improved quality ratings for 16 models in 18 months.

An example of Marchionne's bold approach on the ground was the Ram pick-up truck business. In 2009, it had been languishing as part of the Dodge car division, with just 11 per cent share of the US pick-up market. While many expected him to merge brands to save costs, Marchionne made the Ram business a division on its own. A conference room in the basement of Chrysler's headquarters was turned into a 'Ram war room'. Mr Marchionne met monthly with the Ram executives for detailed updates on progress. The Ram division could now approach the market as a truck business rather than part of a car business, and introduced innovations such as fuel-efficient engines, luxury interiors and superior transmission systems that had been denied before. The new manufacturing methods gave a previously alienated workforce a voice in operating decisions. By 2014, Ram held 33 per cent market share.[6]

Ram's success was reproduced elsewhere. Already by 2011 Chrysler was able to announce an operating profit of $2bn (compared with a net loss of $652mn in 2010) and repay all government loans. Fiat increased its stake in Chrysler to 53.5 per cent and in September 2011, Marchionne became the company's Chairman as well as Chief Executive. Chrysler's share in the US automobile market rose from 8.8 per cent in 2009 to 12.2 per cent in 2014. In 2014, Fiat and Chrysler merged entirely to form a new corporation, FCA, headquartered in London and with Marchionne in overall control.

The last lap?

The creation of FCA was marked by the launch in May 2014 of a new five-year plan. Vehicle sales were due to rise from 4.4m in 2013 to 6.3m in 2018, building particularly on the internationalisation of production and marketing of the famous Jeep line of products. However, a stagnant European market was weighing heavily on FCA's performance, with losses at Fiat leading to the accumulation of €10bn debt. Profit margins even in the USA were low, at about four per cent, half those of rivals Ford and General Motors. In 2015, the influential J.D. Powers quality survey rated three FCA brands – Chrysler, Jeep and Fiat – amongst the worst five automotive brands for reliability.

Quality requires investment, and investment requires scale. The *Financial Times* pointed out that, even after the merger, the new FCA was still half the size of world leaders Volkswagen and Toyota.[7] Its US rivals General Motors and Ford were each roughly 50 per cent larger than FCA. Volkswagen was spending more than five times as much as FCA on research and development,

and twice as much on capital investment. At the same time, car prices were falling and worrying new entrants such as Google and Tesla were emerging on the margins. In 2015, Marchionne approached General Motors for a merger. He was turned down. Rumour had it that perhaps a Far Eastern manufacturer would finally take over FCA.

References
1. Sergio Marchionne, 'Fiat's extreme makeover', *Harvard Business Review*, December 2008, p. 46.
2. *Harvard Business Review*, December 2008, p. 46.
3. *Harvard Business Review*, December 2008, p. 47.
4. Peter Gumbe, 'Chrysler's Sergio Marchionne: the turnaround artista', *Time Magazine*, 18 June 2009.
5. Resurrecting Chrysler, *60 minutes,* CBS; interview with Steve Kroft, 25 March 2012, http://www.youtube.com/watch?v=h3ppoyWNN7s.
6. *New York Times*, 18 September 2014.
7. *Financial Times*, 26 May 2015.

Questions

1 In relation to Section 15.3, what were the types of change pursued at Fiat and Chrysler? Were these appropriate to the change contexts?

2 How would you describe the leadership style of Sergio Marchionne? Was this appropriate to the change contexts?

3 What levers for change were employed by Sergio Marchionne? What others might have been used and why?

4 By what criteria would you assess the effectiveness of the change programmes at Fiat and Chrysler?

16

THE PRACTICE OF STRATEGY

Strategy in action

- Evaluating
- Processes
- Organising
- Leadership and change
- Practice

Learning outcomes

After reading this chapter you should be able to:

- Assess who to involve in strategising, with regard particularly to *top managers*, *strategy consultants*, *strategic planners* and *middle managers*.
- Evaluate different approaches to strategising activity, including *analysis*, *issue-selling*, *decision-making* and *communicating*.
- Recognise key elements in various common strategy methodologies, including *strategy workshops*, *projects*, *hypothesis testing* and writing *business cases* and *strategic plans*.

Key terms

business case p.520

hypothesis testing p.518

strategic issue-selling p.509

strategic plan p.520

strategic planners p.501

strategy projects p.517

strategy workshops p.515

16.1 INTRODUCTION

With stalled user growth due to competition from Instagram and WhatsApp, low market share and a stock price below its initial public offering (IPO) level, Twitter parted company with CEO Dick Costolo in 2015. Although Jack Dorsey, the company's co-founder, chairman of the board and first CEO, stepped in as interim CEO, investors wanted a different CEO. Costolo remained on the board with two other ex-CEOs, making appointment of a new CEO difficult. The company had also had five new product heads in a year. Facing strong competitive pressures, possible acquisitive predators such as Google and unhappy investors, how should Twitter develop a strategy to turn things around?

If you were appointed CEO to Twitter, or took on the role of its strategic planner or a strategy consultant, what would you *do* to develop and implement a strategy? How would you manage competing pressures from a changing technological environment and competitor actions as well as handle political and social pressures from competing managers and investors? Formal strategy analysis is valuable here, but multiple dynamic processes and simple chance will make a difference to outcomes. This final chapter recognises that strategy is messy, complex and requires hard work. It is necessary therefore to look at the actual practice of making strategy. Whereas Chapter 13 introduced the overall organisational process of strategy development, and showed that this often does not follow a neat linear sequence, this chapter is about what people do *inside* the process. The aim is to examine the practicalities of strategy-making for top managers, strategic planning specialists, strategy consultants and managers lower down the organisation.

The chapter has three sections as shown in Figure 16.1:

- *The strategists.* The chapter starts by looking at the various people involved in making strategy. It does not assume that strategy is made just by top management. As pointed out in Chapter 13, strategy often involves people from all over the organisation, and even people from outside. Readers can ask themselves how they fit into this set of strategists, now or in the future.

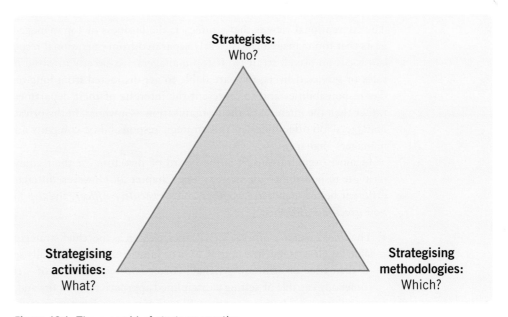

Figure 16.1 The pyramid of strategy practice

- *Strategising activities.* The chapter continues by considering the kinds of work and activity that strategists carry out in their strategy-making. This includes not just the strategy analysis that has been central to a large part of this book, but also the selling of strategic issues, the realities of strategic decision-making and the critical task of communicating strategic decisions throughout the organisation and to external stakeholders.

- *Strategising methodologies.* The final section covers some of the standard methodologies that managers use to carry out their strategising activities. This includes strategy workshops for formulating or communicating strategy; strategy projects and strategy consulting teams; hypothesis testing to guide strategy work; and the creation of strategic plans and business cases.

Figure 16.1 integrates these three sections in a *pyramid of practice*.[1] The pyramid highlights three questions that run through this chapter: *who* to include in strategy-making; *what* to do in carrying out strategising activity; and *which* strategising methodologies to use in this strategising activity. Placing strategists at the top of the pyramid emphasises the role of managerial discretion and skill in strategy-making. It is the strategists who drive both the strategising activity and the strategy methodologies that are at the base of the pyramid. Strategists' choices and skill with regard to activity and methodologies can make a real difference to final outcomes. The rest of the chapter seeks to guide practising strategists through the key choices they may have to make in action.

16.2 THE STRATEGISTS

This section introduces the different types of people potentially involved in strategy. It starts at the top-management level, but also addresses strategic planners, middle managers and consultants. One key issue is who *should* be involved in strategy-making.

16.2.1 Top managers and directors

The conventional view is that strategy is the business of top management. This view suggests that top management is clearly separated from operational responsibilities, so that it can focus on overall strategy.[2] If top managers are directly involved in operations such as sales or service delivery, they are liable to get distracted from long-term issues by day-to-day responsibilities and to represent the interests of their departments or business units rather than the interests of their organisation as a whole. In the private sector at least, top managers' job titles underline this strategic responsibility: company directors' set direction, managers' manage.

In most organisations, it is the board of directors (or their equivalents) which holds ultimate responsibility for strategy (see Chapter 5). However, different roles are played by different board members, whether *chief executive officer*, the *top management team* or *non-executive directors*:

- The *chief executive officer* ('CEO') is often seen as the 'chief strategist', ultimately responsible for all strategic decisions. CEOs of large companies typically spend about one-third of their time on strategy.[3] Michael Porter stresses the value of a clear strategic leader, somebody capable of setting a disciplined approach to what fits and what does not fit the overall strategy.[4] In this view, the CEO (or managing director or equivalent top individual) owns the strategy and is accountable for its success or failure. The clarity of this individual responsibility can no doubt focus attention. However, there are at least two dangers. First, centralising responsibility on the CEO can lead to excessive personalisation. Organisations respond to setbacks simply by changing their CEO, rather than examining deeply the internal sources of failure. Second, successful CEOs can become over-confident, seeing themselves as corporate heroes and launching strategic initiatives of ever-increasing ambition. The over-confidence of heroic leaders often leads to spectacular failures. Jim Collins's research on 'great' American companies that outperformed their rivals over the long term found that their CEOs were typically modest, steady and long-serving.[5]

- The *top management team*, often an organisation's executive directors, also shares responsibility for strategy. They can bring additional experience and insight to the CEO. In theory, they should be able to challenge the CEO and increase strategic debate. In practice, the top management team is often constrained in at least three ways. First, except in the larger companies where there may be senior strategy directors (sometimes called chief strategy officers (CSOs))[6], top managers often carry operational responsibilities that either distract them or bias their strategic thinking: for example, in a business the marketing director will have ongoing concerns about marketing, the production director about production, and so on. In the public sector, the top management team will also, very likely, be heads of operating departments. Second, top managers are also frequently appointed by the CEO; consequently, they may lack the independence for real challenge. Finally, top management teams, especially where their members have similar backgrounds and face strong leadership, often suffer from '*groupthink*', the tendency to build strong consensus amongst team members and avoid internal questioning or conflict.[7] This can be minimised by fostering diversity in membership (for example, differences in age, career tracks and gender), by ensuring openness to outside views, for example those of non-executive directors, and by promoting internal debate and questioning. Organisations with cultures of internal 'contestation' seem to be more able to meet the challenge of strategic change over the long-run.[8]

- *Non-executive directors* have no executive management responsibility within the organisation, and so in theory should be able to offer an external and objective view on strategy. Although this varies according to national corporate governance systems (see Section 5.3.2), in a public company the chairman of the board is typically non-executive. The chairman will normally be consulted closely by the CEO on strategy, as he or she will have a key role in liaising with investors. However, the ability of the chairman and other non-executives to contribute substantially to strategy can be limited as they are often part-time appointments. The non-executive directors' role in strategy is predominantly consultative, reviewing and challenging strategy proposals that come from the top management executive team. They can be very valuable in providing knowledge and contacts about markets and business opportunities, institutional connections and independent thinking.[9] They also have a key governance role to ensure that the organisation has a rigorous system in place for the making and renewing of strategy. It is therefore important that non-executives are independent, authoritative and experienced individuals, and that they are fully briefed before board meetings.

16.2.2 Strategic planners

Strategic planners, sometimes known as strategy directors, strategy analysts or similar, **are those with a formal responsibility for coordinating the strategy process** (see Chapter 13). Although small companies very rarely have full-time strategic planners, they are common in large companies and increasingly widespread in the public and not-for-profit sectors. As in Illustration 16.1, organisations frequently advertise for strategic planning jobs. Here, the personal specifications give a clear picture of the types of role a typical strategic planner might be expected to play. In a large corporation, the scope of a strategic planner's job would not only be working on a three-year strategic plan, but investigating acquisition targets, monitoring competitors, helping business unit managers with their own plans, monitoring implementations and directing strategic initiatives.[10] Thus the role is not just about analysis in the back office. It also involves communications, teamwork and influencing skills.

Although the job in Illustration 16.1 is being advertised externally, strategic planners are often drawn from inside their own organisations. Internal strategic planners are likely to have an advantage in the important non-analytical parts of the job as they bring an understanding of the business, networks with key people in the organisation and credibility with internal audiences. The role can serve as a developmental stage for managers on track for top management positions as it gives them a view of the organisation as a whole and provides exposure to senior management.

Strategic planners do not take strategic decisions themselves. However, they typically have at least three important tasks:[11]

- *Information and analysis.* Strategic planners have the time, skills and resources to provide information and analysis for key decision-makers. This might be in response to some 'trigger' event – such as a possible merger – or as part of the regular planning cycle. Good information and analysis can leave an organisation much better prepared to respond quickly and confidently even to unexpected events. Strategic planners can also package this information and analysis in formats that ensure clear communication of strategic decisions.

- *Managers of the strategy process.* Strategic planners can assist and guide other managers through their strategic planning cycles (see Illustration 13.2). This can involve acting as a bridge between the corporate centre and the businesses by clarifying corporate expectations and guidelines. It could also involve helping business-level managers develop strategy by providing templates, analytical techniques and strategy training. This bridging role is important in achieving alignment of corporate-level and business-level strategies. Researchers[12] point out that this alignment is often lacking; many organisations do not link financial budgets to strategic priorities, or employee performance metrics to strategy implementation.

- *Special projects.* Strategic planners can be a useful resource to support top management on special projects, such as acquisitions or organisational change. Here strategy planners will typically work on project teams with middle managers from within the organisation and often with external consultants. Project management skills are likely to be important.

In addition to these tasks, strategic planners typically work closely with the CEO, discussing and helping refine his or her strategic thinking. Indeed, many strategic planners have their offices physically located close to the CEO. Although strategic planners may have relatively few resources – perhaps a small team of support staff – and little formal power, their closeness to the CEO typically makes them well-informed and influential. Managers throughout an organisation are likely to use them to sound out ideas.

16.2.3 Middle managers

As in Section 16.2.1, a good deal of conventional management theory excludes middle managers from strategy-making. Middle managers are seen as lacking an appropriately objective and long-term perspective, being too involved in operations. In this view, middle managers' role is limited to strategy implementation. This is, of course, a vital role.

ILLUSTRATION 16.1   Wanted: team member for strategy unit

The following job advertisement is adapted from several recent advertisements appearing in the *Financial Times* (exec-appointments.com). It gives an insight into the kind of work strategic planners do and the skills and background required.

Strategy Analyst sought for a fast-paced role in a multinational media business

Reporting to the company's Chief Strategy Officer, the Strategy Analyst will be involved in driving the company's overall growth strategy across the business in Europe. The person appointed will be expected to carry out in-depth analyses of current and potential business strategies, business unit performance, customer markets and segments, and potential acquisition targets or joint venture partners in different territories. The person will probably have a Business Administration, Accounting or similar qualification.

Key responsibilities:

- collection of business and competitor intelligence
- evaluation of business unit performance, actual and potential
- evaluation of new market opportunities and initiatives
- evaluation of possible acquisition targets and joint venture partners
- contribution to strategic planning at the corporate-level
- assistance to business units in preparing their own strategic plans

Essential competences:

- good team player able to work in multicultural environments
- confidence with senior management
- comfortable with complex or ambiguous data and situations
- good project management and work priorisation skills
- excellent strategic and market analysis skills
- financial modelling skills, including DCF
- excellent Excel and PowerPoint skills
- good presentation, communication and influence skills
- prepared for frequent travel

Desirable experience:

The person appointed will be familiar with a multinational corporate environment and be comfortable working in different country contexts. Top-flight academic qualifications and relevant professional qualifications are also highly desirable.

Team:

The person appointed will join an existing team of four junior and senior Strategy Analysts based in the corporate head office in central London. Previous post-holders have progressed to challenging roles elsewhere in the business within two to three years of appointment.

Questions

1 What would be the attractions of this job for you? What would be the disadvantages?

2 What relevant skills and experience do you already have, and what skills and experience would you still need to acquire before you were able to apply for this job?

However, there is a strong case for involving middle managers in strategy-making itself. First, in fast-moving and competitive environments, organisations often need to decentralise strategic responsibilities to increase speed of response: it takes too long to refer everything to the top. Second, in knowledge-intensive sectors (such as design, consulting or finance, but many others too) the key source of competitive advantage is typically the knowledge of people actually involved in the operations of the business. Middle managers at operational level can understand and influence these knowledge-based sources of competitive advantage much more effectively than remote top managers. Many knowledge-intensive firms (e.g. lawyers or accountants) are organised as partnerships, where a significant proportion of staff have a right to consultation on strategic decisions in their formal role as partners, even if they are not themselves members of the top management group.

Against this background, there are at least four strategy roles middle managers can play:[13]

- *Information source.* Middle managers' knowledge and experience of the realities of the organisation and its market is likely to be greater than that of many top managers. So middle managers are a potential source of information about changes in the strategic position of the organisation.

- *'Sense making'* of strategy. Top management may set strategy, but it is often middle managers who have to explain it in the business units.[14] Middle managers are therefore a crucial *relevance bridge* between top management and members of the organisation at lower levels, in effect translating strategy into a message that is locally relevant. If misinterpretation of that intended strategy is to be avoided, it is therefore vital that middle managers understand and feel an ownership of it.

- *Reinterpretation and adjustment* of strategic responses as events unfold. A strategy may be set at a certain point of time, but circumstances may change or conditions in particular units may differ from assumptions held by top management. Middle managers are necessarily involved in strategy adaptation because of their day-to-day responsibilities in strategy implementation.

- *Champions of ideas.* Given their closeness to markets and operations, middle managers may not only provide information but champion new ideas that can be the foundation of new strategies.

Middle managers may increase their influence on strategy when they have:

- *Key organisational positions.* Middle managers responsible for larger departments, business units or strategically important parts of the organisation have influence because they are likely to have critical knowledge, control substantial budgets and may be responsible for large numbers of employees. Also, managers with outward-facing roles (for example, in marketing) tend to have greater strategic influence than managers with inward-facing roles (such as quality or operations).[15]

- *Access to organisational networks.* Middle managers may have little hierarchical power, but can increase their influence by using their internal organisational networks. Information from network members can help provide an integrated perspective on what is happening in the organisation as a whole, something difficult to obtain in a specialised, middle of organisation. Mobilising networks to raise issues and support proposals can give more influence than any single middle manager can achieve on their own. Strategically influential middle managers are therefore typically good networkers.

- *Access to the organisation's 'strategic conversation'.* Strategy-making does not just happen in isolated, formal episodes, but is part of an ongoing strategic conversation amongst respected managers. To participate in these strategic conversations middle managers should: maximise opportunities to mix formally and informally with top managers;

become at ease with the particular language used to discuss strategy in their organisation; familiarise themselves carefully with the key strategic issues; and develop their own personal contribution to these strategic issues.

In the public sector, elected politicians have traditionally been responsible for policy and the public officials are supposed to do the implementation. However, three trends are challenging this division of roles.[16] First, the rising importance of *specialised expertise* has shifted influence to public officials with specialist careers, while politicians are typically generalists. Second, public-sector reform in many countries has led to increased *externalisation of functions* to quasi-independent 'agencies' or 'QUANGOs' (quasi-autonomous non-governmental organisations) which, within certain constraints, can make decisions on their own. Third, the same reform processes have changed *internal structures* within public organisations, with decentralisation of units and more 'executive' responsibility granted to public officials. In short, strategy is increasingly part of the work of public officials too. The end of chapter case, 'Participative strategy in the city of Vaasa', exemplifies some of these issues.

16.2.4 Strategy consultants

External consultants are often used in the development of strategy. Leading strategy consultancies include Bain, the Boston Consulting Group and McKinsey & Co. Most large general consultancy firms also have operations that provide services in strategy development and analysis. There are also smaller 'boutique' consultancy firms and individual consultants who specialise in strategy. Consultants may play different roles in strategy development in organisations:[17]

- *Analysing, prioritising and generating options.* Strategic issues may have been identified by executives, but there may be so many of them, or disagreement about them, that there is lack of clarity on how the organisation should go forward. Consultants may bring a fresh external perspective to help prioritise issues or generate options for executives to consider. This may challenge executives' preconceptions about the strategic issues.

- *Transferring knowledge.* Consultants are carriers of knowledge between clients. Strategy ideas developed for one client can be offered to the next client.

- *Promoting strategic decisions.* Consultants do not take decisions themselves, but their analysis and ideas may substantially influence client decision-makers. A number of major consultancies have been criticised in the past for undue influence on their client decisions, leading to major problems. For example, General Electric blamed McKinsey & Co.'s advice, that the 2008 economic crisis was only temporary, for its decision to delay rationalisation until long after its competitors.

- *Implementing strategic change.* Consultants play a significant role in project planning, coaching and training often associated with strategic change. This is an area that has seen considerable growth, not least because consultants were criticised for leaving organisations with consultancy reports recommending strategies, but taking little responsibility for actually making these happen.

The value of strategy consultants is often controversial. They are often blamed for failures when it is the client's poor management of the consulting process that is ultimately at fault. Many organisations select their consultants unsystematically, give poor initial project briefs, change expectations during the process and fail to learn from projects at the end. To improve strategy-consulting outcomes, client organisations can take three measures:[18]

- *Professionalise purchasing of consulting services.* Instead of hiring consulting firms based on personal relationships with key executives, as is often the case, professionalised purchasing can help ensure clear project briefs, a wide search for consulting suppliers, appropriate pricing, complementarity between different consulting projects and proper review at project-end. The German engineering company Siemens has professionalised its consultancy purchasing, for example, establishing a shortlist of just ten preferred management consulting suppliers.

- *Develop supervisory skills* in order to manage portfolios of consulting projects. The German railway company Deutsche Bahn and automobile giant DaimlerChrysler both have central project offices that control and coordinate all consulting projects throughout their companies. As well as being involved in the initial purchasing decision, these offices can impose systematic governance structures on projects, with clear responsibilities and reporting processes, as well as review and formal assessment at project-end.

- *Partner effectively* with consultants to improve both effectiveness in carrying out the project and knowledge transfer at the end of it. Where possible, project teams should include a mix of consultants and managers from the client organisation, who can provide inside information, guide on internal politics and, sometimes, enhance credibility and receptiveness. As partners in the project, client managers retain knowledge and experience when the consultants have gone and can help in the implementation of recommendations.

16.2.5 Who to involve in strategy development?

Apart from the wide range of people introduced in this chapter who could be involved in strategy, the general trend in recent years has been to include many more people in the strategy process, moving towards more 'open strategy'.[19]

Openness comes in two dimensions: first, including more participants from different constituencies inside and even outside the organisation (for example, middle managers and other staff internally, and key suppliers or partners externally); second, greater transparency about the strategy process itself, in other words what is revealed to both internal audiences, such as staff, and external audiences, such as investors, partners and regulators. Openness is typically a matter of degree and rarely complete. There are pros and cons to greater openness. On the one hand, it can improve strategy formulation by accessing more ideas, and improve implementation by increasing key audiences' understanding and commitment. On the other hand, too many participants can slow down the strategy process and risks the leaking of commercially sensitive information to competitors. The transparency of the process will be dealt with later under Communicating (see Section 16.3.4).

There is no general rule about inclusion or exclusion in strategy-making, but there are criteria that can guide managers. McKinsey & Co.'s research indicates that the people involved should vary according to the nature of the issue (see Figure 16.2). For example, urgent issues that could involve major changes to strategy (such as an acquisition opportunity) are best approached by small special project teams, consisting of senior managers and perhaps planners and consultants. Important, but less urgent, issues (such as deciding on key competitors) can benefit from more prolonged and open strategic conversations, both formal and informal. Urgent issues that do not involve major change (such as responding to competitor threats) require only limited participation. Issues that may involve major changes but require idea generation over time (such as the search for global opportunities) might benefit from more open participation. This might be organised more formally through a series of planned events, such as conferences bringing together large groups of managers in particular geographical regions.

Illustration 16.2 shows one approach to achieving inclusion at Barclay's Bank. The City of Vaasa end of chapter case provides a public-sector example.

ILLUSTRATION 16.2   The Barclays Jam

Barclays Bank used workgroups and 'jamming' to involve all its employees in its new strategy.

In October 2011, Ashok Vaswani became CEO of Barclays' UK Retail and Business Bank. With 35,000 employees and 1600 branches, Barclays was one of the leading retail banks in the country. Like other UK banks, it had been hit both by recession and by accusations of mis-selling of financial products to consumers. However, the global head of retail banking had declared an ambition to make Barclays the 'Go To' bank for consumers, and Ashok set out at once to make this happen.

Ashok launched two initiatives to involve employees in the strategy. He immediately convened six workgroups of graduate trainees and young managers from around the country to address key issues for the implementation of the strategy. With about eight to ten members each, these workgroups were tasked to work on strategic issues such as customers, communications, colleagues and community. Working in their spare time, and mostly communicating virtually, these workgroups produced a flood of ideas, some of them taken up even before the final report-out. The formal reporting took place at a senior management retreat in December, from which a new strategic concept emerged: STAIRS, in other words Speed, Transparency, Access, Information and Results.

Ashok's second initiative was the 'Great Barclays Jam', launched in March 2012 in order to involve all employees in the new STAIRS strategy. Barclays called on IBM's jamming technology, an online collaboration platform designed to facilitate communications and debate amongst large groups of people. The launch of the Jam was preceded by an intensive communications campaign. Ashok first ran a series of leadership days for 400 of the company's senior managers. A 'teaser film', voiced by a well-known British TV personality, was produced, promising employees the chance to discuss the company's future. Over 8000 employees were invited to more than 70 information events held at 16 cinemas across the country, where they saw another specially produced film. Further presentations were held in branches and call centres to reach remaining employees.

With this build-up, the Great Barclays Jam finally took place in March over three days. The Jam gave every employee the chance to debate the practical meaning of the STAIRS strategy and to contribute ideas on how to deliver it. During the Jam, there were live question-and-answer sessions with key executives, including Ashok Vaswani and Bob Diamond, the Barclays Group CEO at the time. Volunteers from across all areas of the business facilitated the discussion, based on the 30th floor of the Barclays head office, easily accessible by the Group's top managers one floor above. The volunteers signposted the most popular threads, highlighted top jammers and alerted participants to senior manager contributions.

The Great Barclays Jam attracted 19,000 registered participants, producing 20,000 comments over the three days. Participants were equally divided between managerial and non-managerial employees and reflected the bank's age distribution. Participation remained high throughout all three days. In all, the Jam produced 650 distinct ideas for business improvement. Ashok Vaswani instituted six new 'Business Councils' focused on various parts of the business with the specific task to implement STAIRS and take forward the most promising ideas from the Jam.

Sources: Interviews with Ashok Vaswani, Julian Davis and Tim Kiy at Barclays, and Richard Mound at IBM.

Questions

1 What do you think were the direct and indirect benefits of Ashok Vaswani's initiatives to involve Barclays' employees in the strategy?

2 If you were a smaller company, without the information technology resources of Barclays and IBM, how might you be able to get employee input into strategy development?

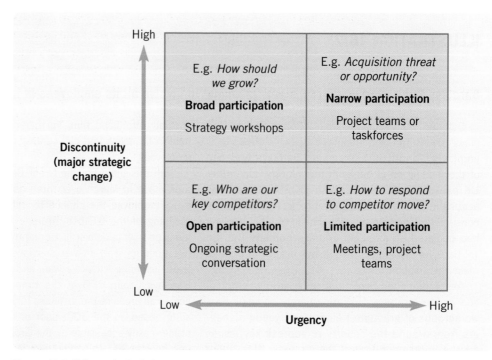

Figure 16.2 Who to include in strategy making?

16.3 STRATEGISING

Whereas the previous section introduced the key strategists, this section concentrates on what these people do – in other words, the activities of *strategising*. The section starts with strategy analysis, then looks at issue-selling, decision-making and strategy communication. In practice, of course, strategy activities rarely follow this logical sequence, or they may not happen at all. As shown in Chapter 13, strategies do not always come about in such ways and strategic decisions are often made without formal analysis and evaluation. This reminds us that strategy development is a messy process.

16.3.1 Strategy analysis

Strategy analysis can be an important input into strategy-making and, although managers often use a limited set of analytical tools, of which SWOT (strengths, weaknesses, opportunities and threats) analysis is by far the most widely used, in practice managers often deviate from the technical ideal.[20] For example, SWOT analysis tends to produce unmanageably long lists of factors (strengths, weaknesses, opportunities and threats), often well over 50 or so. These are rarely probed or refined, little substantive analysis is done to investigate them and they are often not followed up systematically in subsequent strategic discussions. (See the discussion on SWOT in Section 4.4.5).

However, focusing criticism on managers for their analytical limitations may sometimes be misplaced. First, tools themselves contain particular content and methods for structuring thinking – which facilitates and constrains managers. Although this is useful in coping with complexity, where there is uncertainty, tools may offer dangerous oversimplifications.

Second, managers see strategy tools as a means to engage in strategy conversations, but this will be influenced by their different viewpoints, knowledge and goals.[21] Specifically, there are *cost* and *purpose* issues to consider. Analysis is costly in terms of both resources (gathering information using consultants) and time – the risk of '*paralysis by analysis*', where managers spend too long perfecting their analyses and not enough time taking decisions and acting upon them. How much analysis do managers really need? The purpose of analysis is not always simply about providing the necessary information for good strategic decisions. Ann Langley has shown that setting up a project to analyse an issue thoroughly may be a deliberate form of *procrastination*, aimed at putting off a decision.[22] It may be *symbolic*, to rationalise a decision after it has already effectively been made. By asking managers to analyse an issue it may get their *buy-in* to decisions that they might otherwise resist. Analyses may also be *political*, to promote the agenda of a particular manager or part of the organisation.

The different purposes of strategy analysis have two key implications for managers:

- *Design the analysis according to the real purpose.* The range and quality of people involved, the time and budget allowed, and the subsequent communication of analysis results should all depend on underlying purpose, whether informational, political or symbolic. For example, prestigious strategy consulting firms are often useful for political and symbolic analyses. Involving a wide group of middle managers in the analysis may help with subsequent buy-in.

- *Invest appropriately in technical quality.* For many projects, improving the quality of the technical analysis will make a valuable addition to subsequent strategic decisions. On other occasions, insisting on technical perfection can be counter-productive. For example, a SWOT analysis that raises lots of issues may be a useful means of allowing managers to vent their own personal frustrations, before getting on with the real strategy work. It may sometimes be better to leave these issues on the table, rather than probing, challenging or even deleting them in a way that could unnecessarily alienate these managers for the following stages.

16.3.2 Strategic issue-selling

Organisations typically face many strategic issues at any point in time. But in complex organisations these issues may not be appreciated by those involved in developing strategy. Some issues will be filtered out by the organisational hierarchy; others will be sidelined by more urgent pressures. Moreover, senior managers will rarely have sufficient time and resources to deal with all the issues that do actually reach them. So strategic issues compete for attention. What gets top management attention is not necessarily the most important issue.[23] Issues need to be 'sold'.

Strategic issue-selling is the process of gaining the attention and support of top management and other important stakeholders. To gain attention and support of top management, managers need to consider at least four issues:

- *Issue packaging.* Care should be taken with how issues are packaged or framed. Clearly the strategic importance of the issue needs to be underlined, particularly by linking it to *critical strategic goals* or *performance metrics* for the organisation. Generally clarity and succinctness win over complexity and length. It also usually helps if the issue is packaged with *potential solutions*. An issue can easily be put aside as too difficult to address if no ways forward are offered at the same time.

- *Formal and informal channels.* Managers need to balance formal and informal channels of influence. Figure 16.3 indicates some *formal channels* for selling issues in a multidivisional

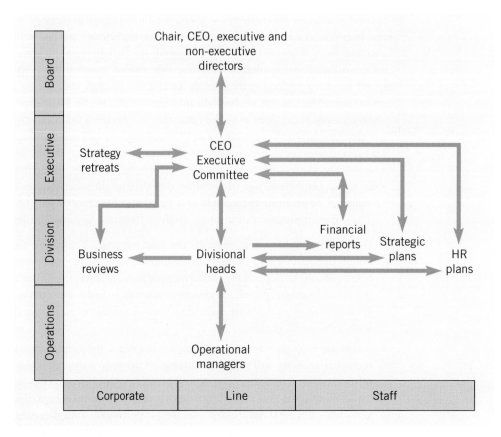

Figure 16.3 Formal channels for issue-selling

Source: Adapted from W. Ocasio and J. Joseph, 'An attention-based theory of strategy formulation: linking micro and macro perspectives in strategy processes', *Advances in Strategic Management*, vol. 22 (2005), pp. 39–62, with permission from Elsevier.

organisation (based on the American conglomerate General Electric). Here formal channels are split between corporate, line and staff. On the corporate side, they include the annual business reviews that the CEO carries out with each divisional head, plus the annual strategy retreats (or workshops) of the top executive team. The line channel involves the regular line interaction of operational managers, divisional heads and the CEO and other executive directors. Finally, there are the various reporting systems to staff functions, including finance, human resources and strategic planning. However, formal channels are rarely enough to sell strategic issues. *Informal channels* can be very important and often decisive. Informal channels might include ad hoc conversations with influential managers in corridors, on journeys or over meals or drinks. Illustration 16.3 shows how informal channels can be important for consultants.

- *Sell alone or in coalitions.* Managers should consider whether to press their issue on their own or to assemble a *coalition of supporters,* preferably influential ones. A coalition adds credibility and weight to the issue. The ability to gather a coalition of supporters can be a good test of the issue's validity: if other managers are unpersuaded, then the CEO is unlikely to be persuaded either. But notice that enlisting supporters may involve compromises or reciprocal support of other issues, so blurring the clarity of the case being put forward.

- *Timing.* Managers should also time their issue-selling carefully. For example, a short-term performance crisis, or the period before the handover to a new top management team, is not a good time to press long-term strategic issues.

ILLUSTRATION 16.3   Dinner with the consultants

Consultants operate through both formal and informal channels to influence strategic thinking.

Locco* was a major European automotive component manufacturer. In the mid-1990s, it began to experience declining profits. The CEO therefore invited consultants to undertake a strategic review of the firm. This consultancy team included a partner, a senior consultant and a junior consultant. Their recommendations led to changes in Locco's product and market strategy.

Like all other consultancy assignments, the consultants undertook extensive analysis of industry data and company data. However, in addition to this more formal work, there was more informal engagement between the consultants and the management, including three dinners held during the period of the project.

At home with the CEO

At the beginning of the assignment the CEO invited the partner and senior consultant to meet senior managers at his home for dinner 'to get together in a more informal way . . . to get to know each other better . . . and . . . learn more about the history of our company', but also to establish trust between the managers and the consultants.

Others saw it differently. For example, the marketing and sales manager viewed it as an attempt by the CEO to influence the outcome of the project: '(he) likes to do this. While dining in his home you can hardly oppose his views.' The consulting partner was somewhat wary, fearing a hidden agenda but nonetheless seeing it as an opportunity to 'break the ice' as well as gaining political insight and understanding of the management dynamics.

Over dinner, discussion was largely between the CEO and the consultants with the CEO setting out some concerns about the project, not least the danger of cost-cutting leading to a loss of jobs. As they mingled over after dinner drinks other sensitive issues were raised by other managers.

At the castle

In the third week of the project the consultant invited the CEO to a restaurant in a converted castle. He saw this as an opportunity to get to know the CEO better, to gain his agreement to the consultants' approach to the project, but also to gain a clearer understanding

of the politics amongst the senior management and establish more insight into the CEO's perceived problems of Locco.

Over the meal the consultant established that there were two management 'camps' with different views of strategy. The consultant also took the opportunity to influence and gain the CEO's approval for the agenda for the next management meeting.

At the pizzeria

Some weeks later the senior consultant invited middle managers who he saw as 'good implementers' for pizza and beer at an Italian restaurant to 'exchange information and get opinions on some of our analyses, see how some of the middle managers react . . . '. Some of those who attended were sceptical about the meeting but went along. Senior managers were not invited.

At the dinner the consultant discussed his initial analysis, particularly on strategic competences. He also raised some issues to do with the political dynamics within the senior management team. The consultant regarded the dinner as a success both in terms of establishing a rapport but also in establishing that 'some (of the managers) know exactly why the company has a problem . . . they already have some ideas for solutions . . . but their voices are not heard'. The managers who attended were, on the whole, also positive about the dinner, many regarding it as 'good fun' though others who were not there felt threatened by their absence.

* A pseudonym used by the researchers.

Source: Adapted from A. Sturdy, M. Schwarz and A. Spicer, 'Guess who's coming to dinner? Structures and uses of liminality in strategic management consultancy', *Human Relations,* vol. 59, no. 7 (2006), pp. 929–60.

Questions

1. Why are informal settings such as dinners useful?

2. Could the consultants have influenced the agenda in more formal ways? How?

3. If you had been one of the managers at the Italian restaurant, what would your views of the meeting been?

16.3.3 Strategic decision-making

Strategic decision-making is not always rational. Nobel prize-winner Daniel Kahneman and colleagues have developed an approach called 'behavioral economics', which seeks to improve decision-making by taking into account real-life human behaviour.[24] Kahneman points out that even senior managers bring 'cognitive biases' to their decisions: their mental processes are liable to neglect, distort or exaggerate certain issues. The trouble with cognitive biases is that, by definition, it is very hard for people to recognise what they are suffering from. However, Kahneman suggests that designing good decision-making processes can help remedy the ill effects of these biases. He highlights five common decision-making biases, along with ways to reduce them:

- *Confirmation bias* is the tendency to seek out data that confirm a favoured course of action, and to neglect information that might disconfirm it. One way to counter this confirmation bias is to insist that alternative options are always considered in decision processes. Then the discussion shifts from whether or not to take a favoured action, to how much better it really is compared to the alternatives.

- *Anchoring bias* is the common error of being tied ('anchored') to one piece of information in making a decision. Anchors are often things that might have been valid in the past, but may not hold true in the future. For example, managers may rely on past sales trends, and neglect the possibility that these trends might change. Sometimes managers will make an initial estimate of a cost or revenue, and allow that value to become entrenched in their decision-making, forgetting that it was only an estimate in the first place. One way of countering anchoring biases is introducing different analytical methods into the process (for instance, a discounted cash flow as well as a pay-back period analysis). A different analysis may surface unacknowledged assumptions or force out new data or insights.

- *Saliency bias* refers to when a particular analogy becomes unduly influential ('salient'). For example, managers may say a particular project is just like a successful project in the past, minimising differences: on the analogy with past experience, they simply expect success to be repeated. It is important here to ask for other analogies, or to seek out possible differences between the successful case and the one being considered. A form of this saliency bias is the so-called 'halo effect', where a manager or organisation that has been successful in one domain is simply assumed to be successful in another: the manager or organisation is treated like a saint (with a 'halo') and assumed to do no wrong. Again, it is important here to check for differences. Just because a manager has been successful in managing a series of acquisitions does not mean he or she will be equally so in managing a joint venture.

- *Affect bias* occurs when managers become too emotionally attached to a particular option (too 'affectionate'). In cases of issue-selling, this is often called *champion's bias*: the likelihood that people will exaggerate the case in favour of their particular proposal. If the proposal comes from a team, it might be worth checking with members individually for signs of discomfort: it may be possible to obtain a more balanced view from the less enthusiastic team members. Having just the lead 'champion' present the proposal on his or her own maximises the danger of hearing the most positive side of the argument.

- *Risk bias* is where managers hold distorted views of risk. Managers are often over-optimistic in assessing their ability to deliver on projects. Here Kahneman recommends that instead of relying on the organisation's own assessment of its capabilities (an 'inside view'), decision-makers also look at the record of *other* organisations undertaking similar projects (an 'outside view'). It is easier to acknowledge the failures of other organisations than to undertake a sceptical review of one's own internal capabilities. On the other hand, managers can sometimes be biased towards pessimism, so-called 'risk aversion'. Their fear of failure may be greater than their appetite for success. Risk aversion can be reduced by reviewing incentives: the rewards of success can be either clarified or increased.

Thus Kahneman's behavioural view leads to concrete methodologies to reduce biases in strategic decision-making. Overall, he encourages hurried managers to 'think slow' – to take the time to ask for additional views, analysis and data. Of course, managers should recognise the danger of paralysis by analysis (see Section 16.3.1): in fast moving environments, the informed intuition of experienced managers may be more effective than thorough but time-consuming analyses.[25] However, Kahneman believes that the costs of error generally outweigh the costs of missed opportunities. It is important too not to exaggerate the importance of decision-making in strategy. As explained in Chapter 16, many strategies are emergent rather than consciously decided anyway.

These insights from behavioural economics underline the potential benefits of constructive *conflict* in decision-making.[26] Conflict can expose champion's biases. It can challenge optimistic self-assessments of managerial competence. Conflict is fostered by having diverse managerial teams, with members prepared to be devil's advocates, challenging assumptions or easy consensus. But productive conflict needs careful management. Table 16.1 uses the idea of 'games with rules' to summarise ways in which this might be done (also see the discussion on 'organisational ambidexterity' in Section 15.4).

16.3.4 Communicating the strategy

Deciding strategy is only one step: strategic decisions need to be communicated. The rise of more open approaches to strategy has put a greater premium on transparency (Section 16.2.5). Managers have to consider which stakeholders to inform (see Chapter 5) and how they should tailor their messages to each. Shareholders, key customers and employees are likely to be particularly central, all with different needs. For every new strategy, there should be a communications strategy to match. It is also important to remember that communication is a two-way process. Harvard's Michael Beer and Russell A. Eisenstat[27] argue

Table 16.1 Managing conflict

Rulebook	• Establish clear behavioural boundaries. • Encourage dissenting voices. • Keep debate professional, not emotional.
Referees	• Ensure the leader is (a) open to differing views, (b) enforces the rules.
Playing field	• Ensure each side of the debate has a chance to win. • Be clear on the basis of resolution (e.g. decision from the top or consensus).
Gaps to exploit	• Does each group have a specific objective to champion?
Relationships	• Ensure individuals (a) deliver on their commitments, (b) behave with integrity. • Ensure leaders throughout the organisation further test perspectives up and down the hierarchy.
Energy levels	• Ensure sufficient tension to promote useful debate, but monitor this. • Do leaders understand what people really care about?
Outcomes	• Ensure leader gives bad news without damaging relationships. • Ensure dignity in losing and risk-taking rewarded.

Source: Reprinted by permission of *Harvard Business Review*. Exhibit from 'How to pick a good fight' by S.A. Joni and D. Beyer, December 2009, pp. 48–57. Copyright © 2009 by the Harvard Business School Publishing Corporation. All rights reserved.

that effective communication needs to involve *both* advocacy of a strategy by senior management *and* inquiry about the concerns of influential internal and external stakeholders. In the absence of the former, there is lack of clarity, confusion and frustration. In the absence of the latter, concerns will surface in any case, but in ways that actively or passively undermine the new strategy.

As a minimum, effective employee communications are needed to ensure that the strategy is understood. Research into the use of strategy communications during mergers and acquisitions shows that strategic communications practices influence outcome.[28] Poor or absent communications are likely to lead to two consequences:

- *Strategic intent will be reinterpreted.* It is inevitable that people in the organisation will interpret intended strategy in terms of their local context and operational responsibilities. The more such reinterpretation occurs, the more unlikely it is the intended strategy will be implemented.

- *Established routines will continue.* Old habits die hard, so top management may underestimate the need to make very clear what behaviours are expected to deliver a strategy. Of course, effective communication is only one way in which change can be managed; the wider lessons of managing strategic change in this regard need to be taken into account (see Chapter 15).

In shaping a communications strategy for employees, four elements need to be considered in particular:[29]

- *Focus.* Communications should focus on the key issues and components of the strategy. If top management cannot show they are clear on these, then it cannot be expected that others will be. It is also helpful to avoid unnecessary detail or complex language. CEO Jack Welch's famous statement that General Electric should be 'either Number One or Number Two' in all its markets is remembered because of this clear focus on the importance of being a dominant player wherever the company competed.

- *Media.* Choosing appropriate media to convey the new strategy matters. Mass media such as e-mails, voicemails, company newsletters, videos, intranets and senior manager blogs achieves '*reach*' with the strategy communication, ensuring all staff receive the same message promptly, helping to avoid damaging uncertainty and rumour-mongering. However, face-to-face communications are important too as they give '*depth*' to the message. Face-to-face demonstrates the personal commitment of managers and allows interaction with concerned staff. One-to-one conversations and team meetings provide greater depth than mass communications. Senior managers may undertake *roadshows*, carrying their message directly to various groups of employees with conferences or workshops at different sites. They may also institute *cascades*, whereby each level of managers is tasked to convey the strategy message directly to the staff reporting to them, who in turn cascade the message to their staff, and so on through the organisation. Of course, to be effective, it is essential the key issues and components of the strategy are clear. Roadshows and cascades may, of course, also raise new issues and should therefore be part of a two-way communication process.

- *Employee engagement.* It is often helpful to engage employees more widely in the communication strategy, so they can see what it means for them personally, how their role will change and to feel the organisation is listening to their concerns. Interchanges through roadshows and cascades can help, but some organisations use more imaginative means to create employee engagement. For example, one UK public-sector organisation invited all its staff to a day's conference introducing its new strategy, at which employees were invited to pin a photograph of themselves on a 'pledge wall', together with a hand-written promise to change at least one aspect of their work to fit the new strategy.[30]

- *Impact*. Communications should be impactful, with powerful and memorable words and visuals. Recent research now shows the power of visuals for conveying strategy to recipients.[31] A strong 'story-line' can help by encapsulating the journey ahead and imagined new futures for the organisation and its customers. One struggling medical centre in New Mexico communicated its new strategy, and inspired its staff, with a story-line representing the organisation as 'The Raiders of the Lost Art', conveying a simultaneous sense of courage in adversity and recovery of old values.[32]

Senior managers spend a great deal of their time in face-to-face meetings over lunch or coffee or in corridors discussing and communicating strategy issues. As Sections 13.3.2 and 13.3.4 explained, in such settings, strategic issues and solutions may arise on the basis of organisational politics or simple chance. This means that strategy managers need political acumen and the ability to build coherent strategic narratives from, often, fragmented discussions.

16.4 STRATEGY METHODOLOGIES

Strategists have a range of standard methodologies to organise and guide their strategising activity. The methodologies introduced here are not analytical concepts or techniques presented earlier in the book, but widely used approaches to managing aspects of strategy work such as issue-selling or decision-making. These could include strategy workshops (or 'away-days') and strategy projects (see below). Strategising output typically has to fit the format of a business case or strategic plan.

16.4.1 Strategy workshops

Strategies are often made through series of managerial meetings. These meetings frequently take the specific form of **strategy workshops** (sometimes called strategy away-days or off-sites).[33] Such workshops usually **involve groups of executives working intensively for one or two days, often away from the office, on organisational strategy**. Such executives are typically senior managers in the organisation, although a wider group of managers can be used. Typically workshops are used to formulate or reconsider strategy, but also to review the progress of current strategy, address strategy implementation issues and to communicate strategic decisions to a larger audience. Workshops can be either ad hoc or part of the regular strategic planning process, and they may be stand-alone or designed as a series of events. As well as facilitating strategy-making, workshops can have additional roles in team-building and the personal development of individual participant. Illustration 16.4 shows how they can contribute to strategy development as well as how they can go wrong.

Strategy workshops can be a valuable part of an organisation's strategy-making activity. However, their form can influence the nature of participants' debate of strategy and its likely success – workshop design matters. Above all, whatever the purpose of the workshop, clarity of purpose is strongly correlated with perceived success. Given this, if the purpose is to *question existing strategy or develop new strategy* successful workshops are likely to involve:

- *Strategy concepts and tools* capable of promoting the questioning of the current strategy.
- *A specialist facilitator to* guide participants in the use of such tools and concepts, free managers to concentrate on the discussion, help keep the discussion focused on the strategic issues and ensure participants contribute equally to discussion.

ILLUSTRATION 16.4   A tale of two workshops

How strategy workshops are designed is a significant influence on their success.

Given the growth of the business, the directors of Hotelco* decided to hold two two-day workshops to re-think the organisational structure needed for the company's future strategic direction. Both workshops were facilitated by an external consultant.

Workshop 1

The first workshop was held in a luxury rural hotel in the South of England far away from Hotelco's modest offices. This was not just to 'get away from the office', but also because: 'It freed up the mind . . . It was a great experience'.

Together with one of the directors, the facilitator had organised the agenda. The 'command style' of the CEO was replaced by a participative approach orchestrated by the facilitator: 'He made it a more level playing field.' He had interviewed staff about the core values of the business and provided a report to the directors as a basis for the discussion: 'Does everyone know what Hotelco stands for?'

The directors became genuinely engaged with the discussion: 'It focused our minds. It made us all understand the things we were good at and . . . the things we were weak at and what we needed to do.' They regarded the workshop as a success, concluding that a change was needed from an authoritarian, command management style to a more structured and devolved approach to management, with responsibility being passed to middle levels, so freeing up the top team to focus more on strategy.

This outcome was not, however, carried forward. On their return to the office, the directors came to the conclusion that what was agreed during the workshop was unrealistic, that they were 'carried away with the process'. The result was significant back-tracking but without a clear consensus on a revised structure for the business.

Workshop 2

The second two-day workshop, two months later, was for the top team and their seven direct reports and used the same facilitator. It took place in

one of the group's own hotels. Again the workshop began with a discussion of the interviews on Hotelco's values. One of the directors then made a presentation raising the idea of an operational board. However, in discussion it emerged that the directors were not uniformly committed to this – especially the CEO. Eventually, as the facilitator explained:

> 'I had to sit the four directors in another room and say: look, until you sort this out; you're just going to create problems. . . . The four directors got into a heated argument and forgot about the other seven.'

This was not, however, how the directors saw it. Their view was that the facilitator was seeking to impose a solution rather than facilitate discussion.

With the directors in one room and the direct reports in another, the comments of each group were transmitted between rooms by the facilitator. It was a situation that satisfied no one. In the afternoon the CEO intervened, replacing the idea of a seven person 'operational board' with an intermediary level of three 'divisional directors'.

No one was content with the workshop. One of the seven who was not to be a divisional director commented: 'I didn't know where I sat any more. I felt my job had been devalued.' A director also recognised: 'We left these people feeling really deflated.'

* Hotelco is a pseudonym for a small UK hotel group.

Questions

1 Evaluate the design of the two workshops in terms of the guidelines in Section 16.4.1.

2 If you were a facilitator, how would you have organised the workshops differently?

3 What benefits (or disadvantages) might such workshops have in comparison with other approaches to strategy development for such an organisation?

- *The visible support of the workshop sponsor* (perhaps the CEO) for the questioning and the facilitator. In the absence of this the workshop is unlikely to succeed.

- *The diminishing of everyday functional and hierarchical roles.* This may be aided by a distinctive off-site location to signal how different from everyday routine the workshop is, help detach participants from day-to-day operational issues and symbolically affirm the occasion is not subject to the usual norms of executive team discussion. Ice-breaking and other apparently playful exercises – sometimes called 'serious play' – at the beginning of a workshop can help generate creativity and a willingness to challenge orthodoxies.[34]

On the other hand, workshops with the purpose of *reviewing the progress of current strategy* are likely to be successful if they have a more operational agenda and if participants maintain functional and hierarchical roles.

Workshops are, however, prone to at least two problems. First, when reduced to a routine part of the strategic planning cycle, and involving the usual group of senior managers every year, workshops may not be able to produce new ideas that significantly challenge the status quo. On the other hand, workshops that are too radically separated from the ordinary routines of the organisation can become detached from subsequent action: it can be difficult to translate radical ideas and group enthusiasm back into the workplace.

In designing workshops that will be closely connected to subsequent action, managers should consider:

- *Identifying agreed actions* to be taken. Time should be set aside at the end of the workshop for a review of workshop outputs and agreement on necessary actions to follow up. However this, of itself, may well not make a sufficiently powerful bridge to operational realities.

- *Establishing project groups.* Workshops can build on the cohesion built around particular issues by commissioning groups of managers to work together on specific workshop-derived tasks and report on progress to senior management.

- *Nesting of workshops.* Especially if a workshop has expected participants to question current strategy and develop radical new ideas, it may be useful to have a series of workshops, each of which becomes more and more grounded in operational realities.

- *Making visible commitment by the top management.* The CEO or other senior manager needs to signal commitment to workshop outcomes not only by their statements but by their actual behaviours.

16.4.2 Strategy projects

Both strategy-making and strategy implementation are often organised in the form of projects or task forces.[35] **Strategy projects involve teams of people assigned to work on particular strategic issues over a defined period of time**. Projects can be instituted in order to explore problems or opportunities as part of the strategy development process. Or they might be instituted to implement agreed elements of a strategy, for example an organisational restructuring or the negotiation of a joint venture. Translating a strategic plan or workshop outcomes into a set of projects is a good means of ensuring that intentions are translated into action. They can also include a wider group of managers in strategy activity.

Strategy projects should be managed like any other project. In particular they need:

- *A clear brief or mandate.* The project's objectives should be agreed and carefully managed. These objectives are the measure of the project's success. 'Scope creep', by which additional objectives are added as the project goes on, is a common danger.

- *Top management commitment.* The continuing commitment of top management, especially the top management 'client' or 'sponsor', needs to be maintained. Top management agendas are frequently shifting, so communications should be regular.

- *Milestones and reviews.* The project should have from the outset clear milestones with an agreed schedule of intermediate achievements. These allow project review and adjustment where necessary, as well as a measure of ongoing success.

- *Appropriate resources.* The key resource is usually people. The right mix of skills needs to be in place, including project management skills, and effort should be invested in 'team-building' at the outset. Strategy projects are often part-time commitments for managers, who have to continue with their 'day jobs'. Attention needs to be paid to managing the balance between managers' ordinary responsibilities and project duties: the first can easily derail the second.

Projects can easily proliferate and compete. Senior management should have careful oversight of the whole portfolio of projects in an organisation, and be ready to merge and end projects according to changing circumstances. Otherwise a proliferation of projects can easily end up with so-called 'initiative fatigue'.

16.4.3 Hypothesis testing

Strategy project teams are typically under pressure to deliver solutions to complex problems under tight time constraints. **Hypothesis testing is a methodology used particularly in strategy projects for setting priorities in investigating issues and options** and is widely used by strategy consulting firms and members of strategy project teams.

Hypothesis testing in strategy is adapted from the hypothesis testing procedures of science.[36] It starts with a proposition about how things are (*the descriptive hypothesis*), and then seeks to test it with real-world data. For example, a descriptive hypothesis in strategy could be that being large-scale in a particular industry is essential to profitability. To test it, a strategy project team would begin by gathering data on the size of organisations in the industry and correlate these with the organisations' profitabilities. Confirmation of this initial descriptive hypothesis (i.e. small organisations are relatively unprofitable) would then lead to several *prescriptive hypotheses* about what a particular organisation should do. For a small-scale organisation in the industry, prescriptive hypotheses would centre on how to increase scale: one would be that acquisitions were a good means to achieve the necessary scale; another would be that alliances were the right way. These prescriptive hypotheses might then become the subjects of further data testing.

This kind of hypothesis testing is ultimately about setting practical priorities in strategy work. Hypothesis testing in business therefore differs from strict scientific procedure (see Illustration 16.5). The aim finally is to concentrate attention on a very limited set of promising hypotheses, not on the full set of all possibilities. Data are gathered in order to support favoured hypotheses, whereas in science the objective is formally to try to refute hypotheses. Business hypothesis testing aims to find a robust and satisfactory solution within time and resource constraints, not to find some ultimate scientific truth. Selecting the right hypotheses can be helped by applying *quick and dirty testing* (QDT). This relies on the project team's existing experience and easily accessed data in order to speedily reject unpromising hypotheses, before too much time is wasted on them.

ILLUSTRATION 16.5 Hypothesis testing at a bank

How to understand stock market irregularities.

The Royal Bank of Canada (RBC) seemed to have a problem. One of its stock market traders, Brad Katsuyama, whose role was to buy and sell stock for investors, reported his computer was behaving strangely. He said that in the past when he wanted to buy shares shown on his screen at a specific price per share, he would push a button and get them for that price. But now when he pushed the button, the offer vanished. He gave the example of one trade when a big investor asked him to sell a large number of shares in a company. His screen showed one million shares of those shares could be sold at a specific price, but when he pressed a button, only a few hundred thousand were sold and then the price fell dramatically leaving his bank with substantial losses. If this was happening to this trader, it might be happening to many traders, costing RBC dear. Why was this happening?

RBC asked Brad if he had tried to solve the problem. He responded by saying he thought it must be due to RBC's new technology system. However, computer support said Brad was the problem and not the technology, even though he was only pressing one button. Brad then spoke to the developers who said the same. They also observed that RBC was in New York and the markets were in New Jersey, and the market data was slow because thousands of people were trading. RBC did not want its losses to continue so gave Brad permission to hire a team to investigate. They conducted a series of experiments costing $10,000 a day. For several months they traded stocks to try to understand why there was a difference between the stock market prices displayed on screen and the actual market price obtained.

Initially the team thought the exchanges were not bundling all the orders they received at the price shown on the screen but were sequencing them. Therefore some orders might not be real, phantom orders, as people might cancel them when Brad's team submitted theirs. To find out, the team sent their orders to just one stock exchange, but were surprised when they were always fulfilled at the screen price. However, when they sent them to many exchanges their success rate dropped quickly with fewer and fewer orders being fulfilled the more exchanges they contacted.

The team had another idea. Maybe the distance from their screens to the different stock markets mattered, even though those distances were measured in milliseconds. They wrote a program that built delayed orders to the nearest exchanges so all orders would arrive simultaneously. It worked as all orders were fulfilled. They ran the tests again comparing delayed and simultaneous orders. They found they were losing around 0.1 per cent on non-delayed trades. This was a tax on RBC's trading activities and amounted to around $160m per day for all US markets.

Operators exploiting millisecond time differences for orders between stock exchanges were causing the pricing variations. These operators, called high frequency traders, noticed the first order for a stock and then bought it at other stock exchanges in anticipation of selling it to the person who had placed the first order, at a higher price. They were making billions of dollars on these trades and couldn't lose. To succeed, high frequency traders needed the fastest routes between stock exchanges and so spent huge sums positioning their machines as close to exchanges as possible, called 'co-location', building direct optical fibre lines (i.e. 4.5 milliseconds time advantage between Chicago and New York) and even microwave towers for a speed advantage.

Source: Michael Lewis, *Flash Boys: Cracking the money code,* Penguin Books, 2015.

Questions

1 Identify the hypothesis testing steps in the illustration.

2 Select an important strategic issue for an organisation you are familiar with and generate some descriptive hypotheses. What data could you collect to test this hypothesis?

16.4.4 Business cases and strategic plans

Strategising activities, such as workshops or projects, are typically oriented towards creating an output in the form of a *business case* or *strategic plan*. Keeping this end goal in mind provides a structure for the strategising work: what needs to be produced shapes the strategising activities. A **business case** usually **provides the data and argument in support of a particular strategy proposal, e.g. investment in new equipment**. A **strategic plan provides the data and argument in support of a strategy for the whole organisation**. It is therefore likely to be more comprehensive, taking an overall view of the organisation's direction over a substantial period of time. Many organisations have a standard template for making business cases or proposing a strategic plan and, where these exist, it is wise to work with that format. Where there is no standard template, it is worth investigating recent successful business cases or plans within the organisation, and borrowing features from them.

A project team intending to make a business case should aim to meet the following criteria:[37]

- *Focus on strategic needs.* The team should identify the organisation's overall strategy and relate its case closely to that, not just to any particular departmental needs. A business case should not look as if it is just an HR department or IT department project, for example. The focus should be on a few key issues, with clear priority normally given to those that are both strategically important and relatively easy to address.

- *Supported by key data.* The team will need to assemble appropriate data, with financial data demonstrating appropriate returns on any investment typically essential. However, qualitative data should not be neglected – for example, striking quotations from interviews with employees or key customers, or recent mini-cases of successes or failures in the organisation or at competitors. Some strategic benefits simply cannot be quantified, but are not the less important for that: information on competitor moves can be persuasive here. The team should provide background information on the rigour and extent of the research behind the data.

- *Provide a clear rationale.* Analysis and data are not enough; make it clear *why* the proposals are being made. The reasons for the choice of recommendations therefore need to be explicit. Many specific evaluation techniques that can be useful in a business cases are explained in Chapter 12.

- *Demonstrate solutions and actions.* As suggested earlier, issues attached to solutions tend to get the most attention. The team should show how what is proposed will be acted on, and who will be responsible. Possible barriers should be clearly identified. Also recognise alternative scenarios, especially downside risk. Implementation feasibility is critical.

- *Provide clear progress measures.* When seeking significant investments over time, it is reassuring to offer clear measures to allow regular progress monitoring. Proposing review mechanisms also adds credibility to the business case.

Strategic plans are similar to business cases in terms of focus, data, actions and progress measures. Strategic plans are, however, more comprehensive, and they may be used for entrepreneurial start-ups, business units within a large organisation, or for an organisation as a whole. Again formats vary. However, a typical strategic plan has the following elements, which together should set a strategy team's working agenda:[38]

- *Mission, goals and objectives statement.* This is the point of the whole strategy, and the critical starting place. While it is the starting place, in practice a strategy team might iterate back to this in the light of other elements of the strategic plan. It is worth checking back with earlier statements that the organisation may have made to ensure consistency. Section 1.2.2 provides more guidance on mission, goals and objectives.

- *Environmental analysis.* This should cover the key issues identified in terms of the whole of the environment, both macro trends and more focused issues to do with customers, suppliers and competitors. The team should not stop at the analysis, but draw clear strategic implications. (See Chapter 2.)

- *Capability analysis.* This should include a clear identification of the key strengths and weaknesses of the organisation and its products relative to its competitors and include a clear statement of competitive advantage. (See Chapter 4.)

- *Proposed strategy.* This should be clearly related to the environmental and organisational analyses and support the mission, goals and objectives. It should also make clear options that have been considered and why the proposed strategy is preferred. Particularly useful here are Chapters 7 to 12.

- *Resources.* The team will need to provide a detailed analysis of the resources required, with options for acquiring them. Critical resources are financial, so the plan should include income statements, cash flows and balance sheets over the period of the plan. Other important resources might be human, particularly managers or people with particular skills. A clear and realistic timetable for implementation is also needed.

- *Key changes.* What does the plan envisage are the key changes required in structures, systems and culture and how are these to be managed? Chapters 14 and 15 are most relevant here.

THINKING DIFFERENTLY   Rethinking the role of strategists

Not all strategists are the same – and that matters.

Early research has uncovered the growing importance of Chief Strategy Officers (CSOs) in US companies. They seem to be prevalent in organisations that need to be more agile in unpredictable environments. CSOs are valuable in providing important interconnections between the economics of the market, the ideas at the core of the business and action. This facilitation allows organisations to adjust, achieving and maintaining strategic momentum.[39]

Recent research, however, has shown that not all strategists are the same. The diversity of challenges facing them has revealed significant differences. A McKinsey survey of 13 facets of the strategist's role, allowed the identification of five types:[40]

- Architect (40 per cent of survey respondents) focused on fact-based analysis to understand company competitive advantage.
- Mobiliser (20 per cent) ran meetings and communicated extensively to build capabilities and deliver special projects.
- Visionary (14 per cent), forecasted trends using big data to spot opportunities.

- Surveyor (14 per cent), scanned for disruptive events and was closely networked with lobbyists, government and regulators.
- Fund manager (12 per cent), optimised corporate portfolio performance and emphasised performance, risk and return.

This suggests that different types of strategist may require different skills in order to be effective in their roles. These may require different educational and life experiences to enable them to be effective in post. It also raises questions about which is the 'right' type of strategist for a particular type of organisation, when should they be used, and whether there are differences between strategists in different countries?

Question

What skills and experiences should a recruiter look for in hiring each of five types of strategist identified above?

SUMMARY

- The practice of strategy involves critical choices about *who to involve* in strategy, *what to do* in strategising activity, and *which strategising methodologies* to use in order to guide this activity.

- Chief executive officers, senior managers, non-executive directors, strategic planners, middle managers and strategy consultants are all involved in strategising. Their degree of appropriate involvement should depend on the nature of the strategic issues.

- Strategising activity can involves *analysing*, *issue-selling*, *decision-making* and *communicating*. Managers should not expect these activities to be fully rational or logical and can valuably appeal to the non-rational characteristics of the people they work with.

- Practical methodologies to guide strategising activity include *strategy workshops*, *strategy projects*, *hypothesis testing* and creating *business cases* and *strategic plans*.

WORK ASSIGNMENTS

✱ Denotes more advanced work assignments.
* Refers to a case study in the Text and Cases edition.

16.1 Go to the careers or recruitment web page of one of the big strategy consultants (such as www. bain.com, www.bcg.com, www.mckinsey.com). What does this tell you about the nature of strategy consulting work? Would you like this work?

16.2 Go to the website of a large organisation (private or public sector) and assess the way it communicates its strategy to its audiences. With reference to Section 16.3.4, how focused is the communication; how impactful is it; and how likely is it to engage employees?

16.3 If you had to design a strategy workshop, suggest who the participants in the workshop should be and what roles they should play in (a) the case where an organisation has to re-examine its fundamental strategy in the face of increased competitive threat; (b) the case where an organisation needs to gain commitment to a long-term, comprehensive programme of strategic change.

16.4✱ For any case study in the book, imagine yourself in the position of a strategy consultant and propose an initial descriptive hypothesis (Section 16.4.3) and define the kinds of data that you would need to test it. What kinds of people would you want in your strategy project team (see Sections 16.2.5 and 16.4.2)?

16.5✱ Go to a business plan archive (such as the University of Maryland's www.businessplanarchive.org or use a Google search). Select a business plan of interest to you and, in the light of Section 16.4.4, assess its good points and its bad points.

Integrative assignment

16.6✱ For an organisation with which you are familiar, or one of the case organisations, write a strategic plan (for simplicity, you might choose to focus on an undiversified business or a business unit within a larger corporation). Where data are missing, make reasonable assumptions or propose ways of filling the gaps. Comment on whether and how you would provide different versions of this strategic plan for (a) investors; (b) employees.

RECOMMENDED KEY READINGS

- For a textbook overview of practice issues in strategy, see S. Paroutis, L. Heracleous and D.N. Angwin, *Practicing Strategy: Text and cases,* 2nd edn, London, Sage, 2016.

- For an overview of research on the practice of strategy, see Eero Vaara and Richard Whittington, 'Strategy as practice: taking practices seriously', *Academy of Management Annals,* vol. 6 (2012), pp. 285–336.

- A practical guide to strategising methodologies is provided by E. Rasiel and P.N. Friga, *The McKinsey Mind,* McGrowhill, 2001.

REFERENCES

1. A theoretical basis for this pyramid can be found in R. Whittington, 'Completing the practice turn in strategy research', *Organization Studies,* vol. 27, no. 5 (2006), pp. 613–34; and P. Jarzabkowski, J. Balogun and D. Seidl, 'Strategizing: the challenges of a practice perspective', *Human Relations,* vol. 60, no. 1 (2007), pp. 5–27.

2. The classic statement is A. Chandler, *Strategy and Structure: Chapters in the History of American Enterprise,* MIT Press, 1962.

3. S. Kaplan and E. Beinhocker, 'The real value of strategic planning', *MIT Sloan Management Review,* Winter 2003, pp. 71–6.

4. M.E. Porter, 'What is strategy?', *Harvard Business Review,* November–December 1996, pp. 61–78.

5. J. Collins, *Good to Great,* Random House, 2001.

6. D.N. Angwin, S. Paroutis and S. Mitson, 'Connecting up strategy; are senior strategy directors a missing link?', *California Management Review,* vol. 51, no. 3 (2009), pp. 74–94.

7. I. Janis, *Victims of Groupthink: a psychological study of foreign-policy decisions and fiascoes,* Houghton Mifflin, 1972; R.S. Baron, 'So right it's wrong: groupthink and the ubiquitous nature of polarized group decision making', in Mark P. Zanna (ed.), *Advances in Experimental Social Psychology,* vol. 37, pp. 219–53, Elsevier Academic Press, 2005.

8. M. Hensmans, G. Johnson and G. Yip, *Strategic Transformation: Changing While Winning,* Palgrave MacMillan, 2012.

9. B. Ni Sullivan and Y. Tang, 'Which signal to rely on? The impact of the quality of board interlocks and inventive capabilities on research and development alliance formation under uncertainty', *Strategic Organization,* vol.11, no. 4 (2013), pp. 364–88.

10. T. Powell and D.N. Angwin, 'One size does not fit all: four archetypes of the Chief Strategy Officer', *MIT Sloan Management Review,* vol. 54, no.1 (2012), pp. 15–16; D.N. Angwin, S. Paroutis and S. Mitson, 'Connecting up strategy; are senior strategy directors a missing link?', *California Management Review,* vol. 51, no. 3 (2009), pp. 74–94; M. Menz and C. Scheef, 'Chief strategy officers: contingency analysis of their presence in top management teams', *Strategic Management Journal,* vol. 35, no. 3 (2013), pp. 461–71; R. Whittington, B. Yakis-Douglas and K. Ahn, 'Strategic planners in more turbulent times: the changing job characteristics of strategy professionals', 1960–2003, *Long Range Planning,* forthcoming.

11. E. Beinhocker and S. Kaplan, 'Tired of strategic planning?', *McKinsey Quarterly,* special edition on Risk and Resilience (2002), pp. 49–57; S. Kaplan and E. Beinhocker, 'The real value of strategic planning', *MIT Sloan Management Review,* Winter 2003, pp. 71–6; D.N. Angwin, S. Paroutis and S. Mitson, 'Connecting up strategy; are senior strategy directors a missing link?', *California Management Review,* vol. 51, no. 3 (2009), pp. 74–94.

12. R.S. Kaplan and D.P. Norton, 'The office of strategy management', *Harvard Business Review,* October (2005), pp. 72–80.

13. S. Floyd and W. Wooldridge, *The Strategic Middle Manager: How to create and sustain competitive advantage,* Jossey-Bass, 1996.

14. See for example J. Balogun and G. Johnson: 'Organizational restructuring and middle manager sensemaking', *Academy of Management Journal,* vol. 47, no. 4 (2004), pp. 523–49.

15. A. Watson and B. Wooldridge, 'Business unit manager influence on corporate-level strategy formulation', *Journal of Managerial Issues,* vol. 18, no. 2 (2005), pp. 147–61; S. Floyd and B. Wooldridge, 'Middle management's strategic influence and organizational performance', *Journal of Management Studies,* vol. 34, no. 3 (1997), pp. 465–85; F. Westley, 'Middle managers and strategy: microdynamics of inclusion', *Strategic Management Journal,* vol. 11 (1990), pp. 337–51; S. Mantere and E. Vaara, 'On the problem of participation in strategy', *Organization Science,* vol. 19, no. 2 (2008), pp. 341–58.

16. See L.S. Oakes, B. Townley and D.J. Cooper, 'Business planning as pedagogy: language and control in a changing institutional field', *Administrative Science Quarterly,* vol. 43, no. 2 (1997), pp. 257–92; and G. Mulgan, *The Art of Public Strategy,* Oxford University Press, 2009.

17. For theoretical discussion of advisers in strategy, see L. Arendt, R. Priem and H. Ndofor, 'A CEO-adviser model of strategic decision-making', *Journal of Management,* vol. 31, no. 5 (2005), pp. 680–99.

18. S. Appelbaum, 'Critical success factors in the client-consulting relationship', *Journal of the American Academy of Business,* March 2004, pp. 184–91; M. Mohe, 'Generic strategies for managing consultants: insights from client companies in Germany', *Journal of Change Management,* vol. 5, no. 3 (2005), pp. 357–65.

19. R. Whittington, B. Basak-Yakis and L. Cailluet, 'Opening strategy: evolution of a precarious profession', *British Journal of Management*, vol. 22, no. 3 (2011), pp. 531–44; D. Stieger, K. Matzler, S. Chatterje and F. Ladstaetter-Fussenegger, 'Democratising strategy', *California Management Review*, vol. 54, no. 2 (2012), pp. 44–68.

20. P. Jarzabkowski, M. Giulietti and B. Oliveira, 'Building a strategy toolkit: lessons from business', AIM Executive briefing, 2009. See also T. Hill and R. Westbrook, 'SWOT analysis: it's time for a product recall', *Long Range Planning*, vol. 30, no. 1 (1997), pp. 46–52.

21. P. Jarzabkowski and S. Kaplan, 'Strategy tools-in-use', *Strategic Management Journal*, vol. 36, no. 4 (2014), pp. 537–58.

22. A. Langley, 'In search of rationality: the purposes behind the use of formal analysis in organisations', *Administrative Science Quarterly*, vol. 34 (1989), pp. 598–631.

23. This draws on the attention-based view of the firm: see J. Joseph and W. Ocasio, 'Architecture, attention and adaptation in the multibusiness firm: General Electric from 1951 to 2001', *Strategic Management Journal*, vol. 33, no. 6 (2012), pp. 633–60.

24. D. Kahneman, D. Lovallo and O. Siboney, 'Before you make that big decision', *Harvard Business Review*, June 2011, pp. 41–60; D. Kahneman, *Thinking, Fast and Slow*, Allen & Unwin, 2012. A good set of papers on 'behavioral strategy' is in the *Strategic Management Journal* special issue on 'the Psychological Foundations of Strategic Management', vol. 32, no. 13 (2011), editors T.C. Powell, D. Lovallo and C. Fox. These ideas are also associated with the Experience Lens, introduced in the Commentary to Part I.

25. K.M. Eisenhardt, J. Kahwajy and L.J. Bourgeois, 'Conflict and strategic choice: how top teams disagree', *California Management Review*, vol. 39, no. 2 (1997), pp. 42–62.

26. R.A. Burgelman and A.S. Grove, 'Let chaos reign, then rein in chaos – repeatedly: managing strategic dynamics for corporate longevity', *Strategic Management Journal*, vol. 28 (2007), pp. 965–79.

27. M. Beer and R.A. Eisenstat, 'How to have an honest conversation', *Harvard Business Review*, vol. 82, no. 2 (2004), pp. 82–9; also for evidence of the effectiveness of strategy communications, see R. Whittington, B. Yakis-Douglas and K. Ahn, 'Cheap talk? Strategy presentations as a form of chief executive officer impression management', *Strategic Management Journal*, forthcoming.

28. D.N. Angwin, K. Mellahi, E. Gomes and E. Peters, 'How communication approaches impact mergers and acquisitions outcomes', *International Journal of Human Resource Management* (2014), pp. 1–28 (in press); B. Yakis-Douglas, D.N. Angwin, K. Ahn and M. Meadows, 'Opening M&A strategy to investors: predictors and outcomes of transparency during organizational transition', *Long Range Planning*, forthcoming.

29. This builds on M. Thatcher, 'Breathing life into business strategy', *Strategic Communication Management*, vol. 10, no. 2 (2006), pp. 14–18; and R.H. Lengel and R.L. Daft, 'The selection of communication media as an executive skill', *Academy of Management Executive*, vol. 2, no. 3 (1988), pp. 225–32. For an academic account, see P. Spee

and P. Jarzabkowski, 'Strategic planning as communicative process', *Organization Studies*, vol 32, no. 9 (2011), pp. 1217–45.

30. R. Whittington, E. Molloy, M. Mayer and A. Smith, 'Practices of strategizing/organizing: broadening strategy work and skills', *Long Range Planning*, vol. 39 (2006), pp. 615–29.

31. S. Cummings, U. Daellenbach and D.N. Angwin, 'How graphical representation helps strategy communication', *Strategic Management Society Special Conference*, December (2014) Sydney, Australia. For examples of how strategy tools and techniques may be used visually in creative ways, see S. Cummings and D.N. Angwin, *The Strategy Builder*, Wiley, 2015.

32. G. Adamson, J. Pine, T. van Steenhoven and J. Kroupa, 'How story-telling can drive strategic change', *Strategy and Leadership*, vol. 34, no. 1 (2006), pp. 36–41.

33. This section builds on the case study research of G. Johnson, S. Prashantham, S. Floyd and N. Bourque, 'The ritualization of strategy workshops', *Organization Studies*, vol. 31, no. 12 (2010), pp. 1589–618. See also B. Frisch and L. Chandler, 'Offsites that work', *Harvard Business Review*, vol. 84, no. 6 (2006), pp. 117–26. Strategy meetings in general have been discussed by P. Jarzabkowski and D. Seidl, 'The role of meetings in the social practice of strategy', *Organization Studies*, vol. 29 (2008), pp. 69–95; and I. Clarke, W. Kwon and R. Wodak, 'A context-sensitive approach to analyzing talk in strategy meetings', *British Journal of Management*, vol. 23 (2012), pp. 455–73.

34. L. Heracleous and C. Jacobs, 'The serious business of play', *MIT Quarterly*, Fall 2005, pp. 19–20.

35. P. Morris and A. Jamieson, 'Moving from corporate strategy to project strategy', *Project Management Journal*, vol. 36, no. 4 (2005), pp. 5–18; J. Kenny, 'Effective project management for strategic innovation and change in an organizational context', *Project Management Journal*, vol. 34, no. 1 (2003), pp. 43–53.

36. This section draws on E. Rasiel and P.N. Friga, *The McKinsey Mind*, McGraw-Hill, 2001; and H. Courtney, *20/20 Foresight: Crafting strategy in an uncertain world*, Harvard Business School Press, 2001.

37. J. Walker, 'Is your business case compelling?', *Human Resource Planning*, vol. 25, no. 1 (2002), pp. 12–15; M. Pratt, 'Seven steps to a business case', *Computer World*, 10 October 2005, pp. 35–6.

38. Useful books on writing a business plan include C. Barrow, P. Barrow and R. Brown, *The Business Plan Workbook*, Kogan Page, 2008; and A.R. DeThomas and S.A. Derammelaan, *Writing a Convincing Business Plan*, Barron's Business Library, 2008.

39. T.R.S. Breene, P.F. Funes and W.E. Shill, 'The Chief Strategy Officer', *Harvard Business Review*, vol. 85, no. 10 (2007), pp. 84–93; D.N. Angwin, S. Paroutis and S. Mitson, 'Connecting up strategy; are senior strategy directors a missing link?', *California Management Review*, vol. 51, no. 3 (2009), pp. 74–94.

40. T. Powell and D.N. Angwin, 'One size does not fit all: four archetypes of the Chief Strategy Officer', *MIT Sloan Management Review*, vol. 54, no.1 (2012), pp. 15–16; M. Birshan, E. Gibbs and K. Strovnik, 'Rethinking the role of stategists', *McKinsey Quarterly*, November 2014.

Participative strategy process in the city of Vaasa

Marko Kohtamäki and Suvi Einola

'Why should businesses, workers, and students choose to come to *our* city?' Like universities or companies, many cities wrestle with the problem – or opportunity – of developing and sustaining their attractiveness. This was exactly the problem faced by the elected representatives and the managers of the apparently successful municipality of Vaasa in western Finland as the effects of global recession began to impact.

Searching for sustainable economic success, municipalities aim to attract companies and a skilled workforce. Municipal authorities try to develop their strategic decision-making to become more effective, agile and responsive than competitors in meeting the expectations of businesses that could establish operations in the region, and of a workforce which could be attracted to move into their city. However, fast and agile decision-making, in parallel with the generic expectations of democracy and equality, poses a unique challenge for public-sector organisations. The city of Vaasa took up that challenge in 2012.

The city of Vaasa

Vaasa is a small but international university city of 67,000 inhabitants, with more than 100 different nationalities. The city organisation employs over 6000 employees in four different sectors (social and healthcare, education and leisure, technical and administration). Vaasa's top management team was renewed almost entirely in the 2010–2012 period, when a new mayor, divisional directors, development director and human resources director were appointed. This organisational renewal, together with the pressures of an economic recession in Finland, led to the city reforming its strategy and strategic decision-making in pursuit of strategic agility.

The city was known for its energy technology and engineering manufacturing companies such as ABB and Wärtsilä. A strong cluster of technology companies had resulted in a low unemployment rate and, by any economic measures, the city was considered highly successful. As a downside, long-term success had led to a situation wherein the city's politicians and officials were relatively satisfied with its current state of affairs – with the attendant risks of *strategic drift* in a context that strategy literature describes as a *learning trap*.[1,2] However, the recessionary economic conditions created an opportunity for the new management team to engage in a broad strategic renewal programme. The city launched a process of strategy making, through which strategy would not only be planned and implemented, but also continuously re-invented.

Strategy workshops and tools

In the beginning of the process, the city's management team set the targets for the strategy work: to develop a city which would be more agile and effective to face the competition for companies and workforce. To generate agility in the long run, the city management believed that the strategy work should be participative and involve personnel throughout the city organisation. An underlying assumption was that participation would facilitate development of a shared understanding about strategy among all stakeholders. However, shared strategy discussions required tools to facilitate interaction, as described by the City Mayor:

'Earlier, we used a system where everything came from top management and we made precise five-year plans, and everything was defined; that will be the outcome, when you do this. But these days, when there are so many external factors which rapidly influence development in the city, you need to be able to create a basic framework inside which new opportunities can emerge.'

(City Mayor, January 2013)

To address the challenge of strategic agility and engaging personnel in the strategy work, a team of researchers together with the top management team built a concept that could be used at different levels and divisions of the Vaasa municipality. The concept included use of three particular strategic management tools: a *strategic capabilities framework*,[3] a *value curve*[4] and a *strategy map*.[5] With the help of these tools, the city's internal developers and the researchers facilitated almost 100 strategy workshops during 2013–2015.

The process of strategy-making was far from straightforward. In the beginning, it was overshadowed by tensions between political parties, and by concerns about the economic recession. Some discussants even questioned whether the city really needed a strategy – and, if there was to be new strategy, whether it should be established for a longer period of time. Eventually, Vaasa's management concluded that the city certainly did need rapid renewal, and that a strategy should be established through a participative process and be updated on a yearly basis. Moreover, they wanted strategy-making to become an integral part of city planning and budgeting, something that would also steer investment decisions, instead of being just a separate annual exercise.

During the strategy process, multiple tensions emerged such as the dilemma between policy-making and effective strategic decision-making, the dilemma between participation and determined implementation, and the dilemma between value creation and service cost-cutting. Extensive participation (100 strategy workshops across a range of different organisational levels) played an important role in coping with and in alleviating those tensions. The strategy workshops offered a platform to develop shared understanding about strategy across intra-organisational boundaries, enabling directors and middle managers to develop a common language building on the selected strategy tools. Thus, throughout the process, middle managers, as well as the city's directors and politicians, were considered as strategists.[6] In strategy workshops, the researchers and development planners acted as facilitators and made notes and interpretations about the

discussions. Facilitation helped workshop participants to concentrate on the key topics and issues, while the discussions were documented (on PowerPoint slides) to 'materialise' the strategy.[7,8]

Building on strategic capabilities

Building on the resource-based view of a firm, the city of Vaasa decided to use a strategic capabilities approach to analyse its core resources and processes over time, to understand upon what capabilities the city was building, and what would be needed in the near future. The strategic capabilities approach was utilised to understand the valuable, rare, inimitable, and non-substitutable (VRIN)[9] resources and processes within the city of Vaasa. The top management team, councillors and city officials mapped the municipality's strategic capabilities in workshops held early in 2013. The workshop groups utilised a mind map technique to create a picture of the municipality's strategic resources and processes with the help of internal developers. The ideas generated were then grouped into five themes and finally synthesised into five descriptions (see Figure 1). This created the first sketch of the core capabilities at the municipality level. Similar processes were later conducted at the level of divisions, business areas and business units. As the process was extended to

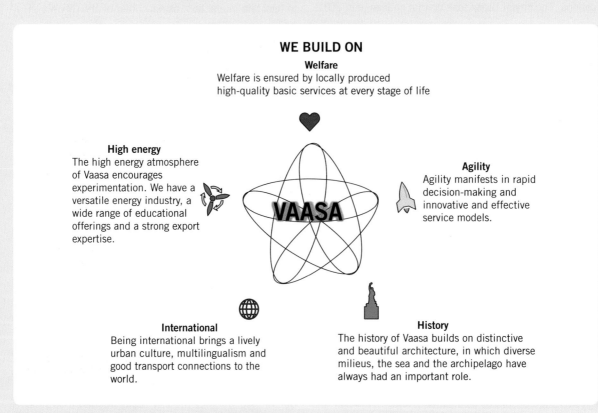

Figure 1 Strategic capabilities of the city of Vaasa

lower levels of the municipality organisation, participants were encouraged to consider how their organisational units could support the city's strategy while developing their strategic capabilities. The role of middle managers was crucial, not only for enriching the discussions with up-to-date knowledge and experience, but also for making sense of the strategic intentions and translating them into unit level actions.

Customer value thinking as part of the strategy

The second strategy tool built on Blue Ocean strategy, with a focus on the components of the customer value proposition. In the city of Vaasa, the value curve was used to identify, develop and explain a shared understanding of the components of the value promise, initially at the municipality level. The city's top management team, along with councillors and city officials, utilised the tool to compare Vaasa's future value promise against the current state of affairs, instead of just comparing its value proposition against competitors. Further, the city focused on its current customers and operations instead of trying to search for 'Blue Oceans' (new non-customers).[10] After finding and deciding on generic key customer segments (companies, citizens, communities), the top management team, councillors and officials built a value curve

to include the components of the value promise for each customer segment (see Figure 2). Interactions in strategy workshops helped to build shared understanding about the key customers, value promises and the current state of affairs, as well as the strategic intent in all organisational levels.

Configuring the strategy map

The strategy map outlines the strategic logic of the city organisation, based on four dimensions from the Balanced Scorecard: (1) the financial perspective, (2) the customer perspective (the components of the value promise/value curve), (3) the process perspective and (4) resources and competencies.[11] The last dimension, originally stated as *learning and growth* in the Kaplan & Norton model, was redefined in the Vaasa strategy map as *resources and competences,* to integrate with the components of the first strategy tool. The strategy map thus builds on the outputs of the two strategy tools used earlier in the process – the strategic capabilities framework and the value curve. The strategy map became the central tool of the strategy development process, enabling management to describe and explain the whole strategic logic of its organisation using only the one visual image. Furthermore, if employed properly, the strategy map would simplify and summarise

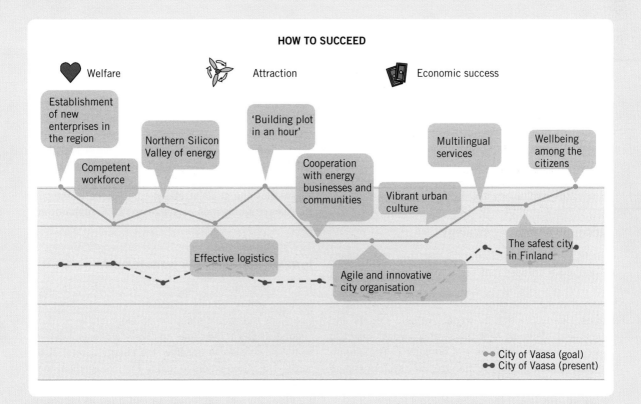

Figure 2 Value curve of the city of Vaasa

VAASA – energy capital of the North

Targets	Top 3 in happiness among cities	Population growth > 1%	Employment > 75%		Debt ratio/citizen < average in cities	Tax revenue top 6 in cities

Value proposition

The happiest and healthiest citizens in the world	Versatile urban culture: 'It happens in Vaasa'	Skilled workforce		Respect for the communities	Interactive expertise
		'Building plot in an hour'	Accessibility and effective logistics		
Trustworthy services	Wide and diverse labour markets	Attractive and functional business environments		Genuine partnership	

Processes and resources

Effective administration of possessions	Managing service processes	Efficient and well-timed decision-making	Long-term strategic business policy	Deliberative democratics	New, innovative partnership models
Service-oriented and competent personnel	Customer-oriented services throughout life		Logistics centers	Recognising the needs of communities	Knowledge of the capabilities and resources in organisations
Functioning service network	Innovation capability	'One stop shop' principle	Cooperation between the city, higher education and companies		
Leisure opportunities	High-level education	Recognising the needs of companies	Land assets	Strengthening the allocated communication	Partnership agreements

Citizens	Companies	Communities

Figure 3 Strategy map of the city of Vaasa

the strategy so that it could be understood throughout the organisation. The map also enabled management to ground the strategy in the organisation, ensuring that it reflected the reality in, and the capabilities of, the municipality – so that strategy was no longer something just planned and instructed by top management. The Vaasa strategy map (see Figure 3) provided an effective tool for discussing and defining the strategic logic of the organisation, bringing strategy into practice.

Execution of the city strategy

Finally, building on their strategy map, the city of Vaasa developed a spreadsheet table to synthesise targets, measures and strategic initiatives which could be summarised on just one slide (Table 1). The city wanted to define clearly the link between strategic targets and investment plans, so that the strategy would begin to steer investment decisions and budgeting. The administration believed that the management system should be developed to facilitate strategy implementation and follow-up. The use of the Excel table summary, for communicating across the organisation, had the additional

benefit of forcing management to decrease the excessive number of key performance indicator (KPI) targets and measures, so that only the important ones were included on the one summary slide. From approximately 70 initial measures, the city decided to focus on just 25 KPIs, with the five measures defined at the top of the strategy map being considered the most vital. Thus, those selected prime metrics became the centrepiece for steering the city's strategy, comparable to the simple rules or guidelines as suggested by Eisenhardt and Sull.[12]

Towards real-time city management

The city organisation began strategy work to increase strategic agility, aiming to create simple practices and guidelines that would steer the development work of different divisions in the same direction – a direction defined by the new vision to become 'the energy capital of the north'. The vision emerged during the management team sessions, reflecting discussions at different levels of the organisation, and was finally settled upon as representing an interpretation of the optimum future for Vaasa.

Table 1 Goals, measures and strategic initiatives

Targets	Measures	Strategic initiatives
ATTRACTION **Attractiveness of the region**	• Population growth/year/ previous year • New vacancies produced by companies/all new vacancies • Tax revenues • Number of national events	• Making energy competence visible in activities and investments • Developing international innovation cluster and R&D platforms in the city of Vaasa area • Strengthening international accessibility through targeted investments in air, ship, rail and road traffic • Two multilingual campuses and learning environments: safeguarding an adequate local shareholder base • The development of city centre, and revitalisation of the islands and beaches • Promoting a diverse urban culture: promoting positive atmosphere, e.g. in the form of international congresses and events
Competitive urban structure	• Amount of plot and plan reserves • Reducing carbon dioxide emissions	• The available plots correspond to the demand: sticking with the housing programme • Review of service networks that observe a life-cycle approach
The employment rate >75%	• Proportion of employed in population (18–64-year-olds)	• Training a competent workforce
WELFARE **Welfare among the population**	• Experienced happiness • Morbidity index • Time limits in basic services and norms within elderly care are kept • Amount of visitors in sports and cultural establishments • Costs of elderly care	• Directing the service network to the main functions: intensifying the library network, early childhood education and the school network • Addressing current special healthcare as a separate issue • Securing the integration of speciality healthcare, basic healthcare and social care: prioritising preventive work • New health centre in the city: centralisation of medical services and other possible services within healthcare • Raising the clients' level of involvement and responsibilities: deliberative democracy, electronic services; utilisation of experience specialists in planning and developing services
Strengthening the democracy	• Trust in decision-making	• Renewal of representative organisation • Local regional government: clarifying the roles of area board and regional councils • Consolidating deliberative democracy practices into the development of services
ECONOMIC SUCCESS **Effective administration of assets**	• Development of premises • Costs of premises/free markets	• Processing the plot possessions • Mapping the use of premises to increase the use; selling unnecessary premises systematically on a tight schedule • Refraining from use of external rented premises
The balance between investments and loans, adjustment of activities	• Gross capital expenditure on same level as depreciation • The level of internal financing of investments • Increasing annual margin	• Developing management systems • Strengthening of state shareholdings in federations of municipalities decision-making • Centralisation of service production and setting the quality standards of services, cost-effective production methods • Outsourcing and purchasing of services: cost accounting and pricing services • Developing IT services
Increasing income	• Income/year/previous year, selling of possessions, payments	• Leasing and selling plots and shares of stock within housing • Developing chargeable services, raising the charges and tariffs
Optimising the personnel structure	• Number of personnel/ services produced/other municipalities • The number of person-years	• Anticipatory personnel planning • Reforming organisations and making the cross-administrative processes more efficient

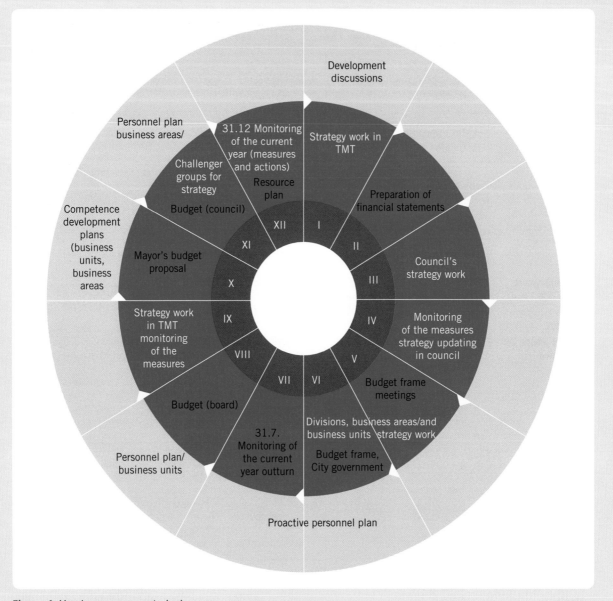

Figure 4 Yearly management clock.

Thus, there was no separate tool or facilitated session for discussion of the vision statement: the vision emerged during the strategy process work, was elaborated on as it emerged, and finally ratified by the municipal parliament. The sequence illustrates the idea behind the way of working during the process – that the strategy can be developed through the discussions, based on a shared understanding of the organisation, its capabilities and its customers: that the strategic logic emerges step-by-step during the rounds of the strategy development process.

Finally, the city also developed a yearly 'management clock' (see Figure 4) to embed strategy updates into the annual management activities' plan. In addition, Vaasa

city management initiated a process to integrate the KPI measures and targets into the annual planning and evaluation tasks. Further action was taken to develop a management system that would support real-time management of the city's organisation. It was recognised that management would require further refinement of the KPIs, to focus on the few most relevant KPIs at the different organisational levels and that could be effectively followed up. However, the involvement of those different organisational levels – and the adoption of the strategy map as the main tool – had facilitated development of a shared understanding about the strategic vision and strategy process across the whole municipality.

Questions

1 Using the pyramid of strategy practice (Figure 16.1), describe strategy-making in the city of Vaasa.

2 Comment on the strategy process being followed at Vaasa. In what ways does this depart from the previous way of doing strategy?

3 What are the advantages and disadvantages of the tools used in this strategy process?

4 Reflect upon the public sector context of this case – in what ways might there be similarities and differences with how strategy is practiced in 'for-profit' contexts?

References

1. K.H. Heimeriks, 'Confident or competent? How to avoid superstitious learning in alliance portfolios', *Long Range Planning*, vol. 43, no. 1 (2010), pp. 57–84.

2. C. Sirén, M. Kohtamäki and A. Kuckertz, 'Exploration and exploitation strategies, profit performance and the mediating role of strategic learning: escaping the exploitation trap', *Strategic Entrepreneurship Journal*, vol. 6, no. 1 (2012), pp. 18–41.

3. C. Long and M. Vickers-Koch, 'Using core capabilities to create competitive advantage', *Organisational Dynamics*, vol. 24, no. 1 (1995) pp. 7–22.

4. C. Kim and R. Mauborgne, 'How strategy shapes structure', *Harvard Business Review*, 87 (September 2009), pp. 73–80.

5. R.S. Kaplan and D.P. Norton, 'Having trouble with your strategy? Then map it', *Harvard Business Review*, vol. 78, no. 5 (2000), pp. 167–76.

6. R. Whittington, 'Strategy practice and strategy process: family differences and the sociological eye', *Organisation Studies*, vol. 28, no. 10 (2007), pp. 1575–586.

7. S. Kaplan, 'Strategy and PowerPoint: an inquiry into the epistemic culture and machinery of strategy making', *Organisation Science*, vol. 22, no. 2 (2011), pp. 320–46.

8. S. Paroutis, A. Franco and T. Papadopoulos, 'Visual interactions with strategy tools: producing strategic knowledge in workshops', *British Journal of Management*, vol. 26, no. 51 (2015), pp. S48–S66.

9. J.B. Barney, 'Firm resources and sustained competitive advantage', *Journal of Management*, vol. 17, no. 1 (1991), pp. 99–120.

10. C.W. Kim and R. Mauborgne, 'Blue ocean strategy: from theory to practice', *California Management Review*, vol. 47, no. 3 (2005), pp. 105–121.

11. R.S. Kaplan and D.P. Norton, 'Having trouble with your strategy? Then map it', *Harvard Business Review*, vol. 78, no. 5 (2000), pp. 167–176.

12. K.M. Eisenhardt and D.N. Sull, 'Strategy as simple rules', *Harvard Business Review*, vol. 79, no. 1 (2001), pp. 106–16.

COMMENTARY ON
PART III STRATEGY IN ACTION

This part of *Exploring Strategy* has considered strategy in action. Although this is the last part, this does not imply that action necessarily follows logically from the analysis of strategic position and choices. Chapter 1 introduced the overall model for this text, made up of three overlapping circles of position, choices and action. The point of the model is that strategy should not be seen as simply a linear process: the issues raised in different parts of this text interact and inform each other. While for purposes of clarity this text presents strategy implementation following strategy formulation in a logical sequence, in practice this is by no means always so.

In this Commentary the strategy lenses are used to explore more deeply this key issue of how formulation and implementation fit together. What are the practical implications of the various lenses for how to put strategy into action?

DESIGN LENS

The design lens builds on the notion that thinking precedes organisational action, so that strategy is, indeed, a linear process. Rational analysis and design are seen as powerful motivators of strategic action. In this view therefore, managers should:

- *Make the business case*: the most important factor in persuading managerial colleagues and other internal and external stakeholders is logical analysis and evidence, for example rigorous evaluation criteria (Chapter 12) and business plans (Chapter 16).
- *Exercise tight change management*: strategies are best implemented through systematic use of the levers for change (Chapter 15) and strict project management (Chapter 16), leaving little scope for improvisation.
- *Reinforce coherent action*: strategies will be most effectively implemented if organisational structures and systems are configured so that they are mutually supporting (Chapter 14).

EXPERIENCE LENS

The experience lens is sceptical about the place of rationality in securing strategy implementation. Managerial biases and organisational conservatism mean that strategy is heavily influenced by the past. The experience lens suggests it is important to:

- *Challenge biases*: strategy evaluation and strategic plans (Chapters 12 and 13) are likely to be shaped by the experience of those who do them, so it is important to challenge what may be taken for granted.
- *Pick your teams carefully*: if strategies are shaped by the people involved in making them, then it really matters who is in your strategy development teams and projects (Chapter 16).
- *Recognise the challenge of change*: given the weight of past experience on organisations, the issues of leadership and change (Chapter 15) are likely to be among the most important and difficult in this whole text.

Note that:

- There is no suggestion here that any one of these lenses is better the others. The point is to avoid using just one. Each lens gives you extra ways to explore strategic issues.
- For a deeper understanding of this Commentary, you might want to review the Part I Commentary, following Chapter 6, which provides a fuller introduction of the four lenses, plus an illustrative case. The Commentary at the end of Part II is also relevant.

VARIETY LENS

According to the variety lens, strategies can bubble up from the periphery and are then often selected and retained according to semi-conscious organisational processes. Innovation does not come simply from top management command. The variety lens therefore encourages you to:

- *Favour inclusiveness*: in deciding who to include in strategy development (Chapter 13 and Section 16.2), innovative strategies are more likely to come – and be implemented – if you include as many people as possible from outside the usual organisational elite.
- *Check the rules*: the variety lens points to the power of taken-for-granted procedures, so it is wise to review standard strategy evaluation criteria and organisational systems for hidden biases in strategy selection and retention (Section 12.3 and Section 14.3).
- *Be ready to go 'off-plan'*: given the role of surprise and spontaneity, flexibility is important and it may be necessary to abandon at least certain aspects of the original strategic plan (Chapter 13).

DISCOURSE LENS

Through this lens, language is highly influential on how strategies are interpreted and implemented. Discourse can both smooth and inhibit putting strategy into action. It is important to recognise that:

- *Words matter*: the symbolic power of language can make the difference between success and failure, for example in leading transformational change (Section 15.4) or justifying performance (Section 12.2).
- *Organisations are political*: discourses can be used to promote sectional interests, so it is important to be sensitive to, and sometimes challenge, the language of issue-selling (Section 16.3) and alliance and network building (Section 13.3) for example.
- *Language is an entry ticket*: for managers and consultants who seek to enter into the organisation's strategy conversation (Section 16.2), it is vital to be able to speak the organisational language of strategy fluently and confidently.

CASE STUDIES

CO-EDITED BY CLIVE KERRIDGE, JASON EVANS
AND STEVE PYLE

GUIDE TO USING THE CASE STUDIES

The main text of this book includes 69 short *illustrations*, 16 *thinking differently* sections and 16 *case examples* which have been chosen to develop and illustrate specific issues in the text and/or provide practical examples of how business and public-sector organisations are managing strategic issues. The *Case Collection* which follows allows the reader to extend this linking of theory and practice further by analysing the strategic issues of specific organisations in much greater depth and proposing 'solutions' to some of the problems or difficulties identified. There are also over 40 *classic cases* on the Companion Website. These are a selection of cases from past editions of the book which remain relevant for teaching.

The case studies are intended to serve as a basis for class discussion and not as an illustration of either good or bad management practice. They provide readers with a core of cases that, together, cover the main issues in the text. They are a useful backbone to a programme of study and could be supplemented by other material. We have provided a mixture of longer and shorter cases to increase the flexibility for teachers. Combined with the *illustrations* and the short *case examples* at the end of each chapter (in both versions of the book), this increases the reader's and tutor's choice. For example, we offer a number of options for exploring the issues in Chapter 2 on the Macro-environment. Thus the case example (Alibaba: the Yangtse River Crocodile) at the end of Chapter 2 provides a short case to test students' core understanding of the main environmental issues. In the case collection, the *Brewing Industry* case offers a concise focus on three companies in the same business environment while the *Global Pharmaceutical Industry* (or *Siemens A*) case has the material needed for a more comprehensive analysis. Some cases are written entirely from published sources but most have been prepared in cooperation with, and with the approval of, the management of the organisation concerned. We would nonetheless also encourage readers and tutors to take every opportunity to explore *live* strategic issues in both their own organisation and others.

The following brief points of guidance should prove useful in selecting and using the case studies provided:

- The summary table that follows indicates the main focus of each of the chosen case studies – together with important subsidiary foci (where appropriate). In general, the sequence of cases is intended to mirror the chapter sequence. However, this should not be taken too literally because, of course, many of these cases cover a variety of issues. The 'classification' provided is therefore for guidance only. We expect readers to seek their own lessons from cases, and tutors to use cases in whichever way and sequence best fits the purpose of their programmes.

- In the commentary at the end of Part I of the book we introduce the concept of 'strategy lenses'. Where there are cases that lend themselves to exploration through different lenses, this is indicated as a secondary focus for those cases.

- Where cases have been chosen to illustrate the issues of strategic choice and strategy in action covered later in the book, it will normally be a prerequisite that some type of analysis of the strategic position is undertaken, using the case material. So care needs to be taken to balance the time taken on such strategic analysis in order to allow the time required to analyse the main issues for which the case has been chosen.

- Where the text and cases are being used as the framework for a strategy programme (as we hope they will), it is important that students undertake additional reading from other sources and that their 'practical' work is supplemented by other material as mentioned above. Frequently company websites can be used to provide additional information, especially the latest financial figures.

- The cases do not have questions attached (although suggested questions are provided in the instructor's manual) in order to allow programme leaders to use the case in the most appropriate way for their own purposes. However, the cases are written in such a way as to suggest the key issues they raise.

- For some of our cases (e.g. Ryanair and Manchester United FC) additional material to supplement cases can be found in the instructor's manual online.

- While every effort has been made to update the cases to incorporate the latest information and developments, inevitably tutors will be using the cases after there have been developments – so we would urge tutors to research and update cases themselves.

GUIDE TO THE MAIN FOCUS OF CASES IN THE BOOK

PAGE NUMBER IN THE BOOK	CASES	Introduction to strategy	The macro-environment context	The industry and sector context	Resources and capabilities	Stakeholders and governance	History and culture	Strategy lenses	Business-level and models strategy	Corporate strategy and diversification	International strategy	Entrepreneurship and innovation	Mergers, acquisitions and alliances	Evaluating strategies	Strategy development	Organising	Leadership for strategic change	The practice of strategy	Public sector/not-for-profit management	Family or small business strategy
541	**Glastonbury:** from hippy weekend to international festival	●	●																	●
545	The **global pharmaceutical industry:** back to the future?		●	●							●		●							
557	**Siemens A:** exploring the future	●	●						●											
563	The **'pub':** decline of a British institution – how the brewers fought back	●	●							●			●							
568	**Ricoh Canada Inc.:** printing the future or recycling the past?		●	●					●											
576	**H&M** in fast fashion: continued success?				●				●	●										
584	The **Formula 1 constructors:** capabilities for success.				●		●		●			●								
593	**'Access to Healthcare'** integrating a CSR programme in **Coloplast**					●											●		●	
600	**Manchester United FC:** competing with Europe's elite clubs	●	●			●		●												
608	**Adnams:** a living company					●	●	●	●						●		●			●
616	**Widespace:** managing growth and culture within a maturing technology venture								●		●					●				●
622	**Ryanair:** the low fares airline – 'always getting better'?	●	●	●					●	●	●		●	●			●			
633	**Flight Centre Limited:** competing to provide the lowest air fares						●		●	●	●						●			
639	**Megabrew:** creating an undisputed global brewing champion?									●	●		●							
651	**AirAsia and the Tune Group:** diversifying across industries									●	●							●	●	
659	**Severstal:** growth and consolidation strategies in a turbulent global steel industry		●	●						●	●									

538

Page	Cases	Introduction to strategy	The macro-environment context	The industry and sector context	Resources and capabilities	Stakeholders and governance	History and culture	Strategy lenses	Business-level and models strategy	Corporate strategy and diversification	International strategy	Entrepreneurship and innovation	Mergers, acquisitions and alliances	Evaluating strategies	Strategy development	Organising	Leadership for strategic change	The practice of strategy	Public sector/not-for-profit management	Family or small business strategy
667	**Indian Premier League:** glitz, glamour and globalisation		●	●							●●									
671	**Handelsbanken:** banking done differently						●				●●								●	
680	**Ningbo Smarter Logistics:** innovating in partnership with IBM in China											●●	●							
684	Leadership and Innovation at **Apple Inc:** entering the post-Jobs era						●					●●					●	●		
690	All change at **Teva**						●			●	●●		●●							
695	**Mondelēz International:** 'Are you going to stick around, Irene?'						●			●	●●		●●							
705	**CRH plc:** leveraging corporate strategy for value creation and global leadership									●●	●●		●●							
713	Evaluating the **Mexican narco-trafficking** problem					●			●	●				●●						●
722	Where should the beds go? Infrastructure planning in **NHS England**				●									●●	●				●●	
729	Strategic planning at **King Faisal Hospital and Research Centre** Saudi Arabia													●●					●●	
734	**Mormor Magda's** ice cream: can you be hot in a cool market?						●					●		●●					●	●
739	**Academies and free schools:** the future of education?						●								●●				●●	
744	**Siemens B:** implementing the strategy														●	●●	●●	●		
750	Paul Polman: turnaround and development of strategy at **Unilever**						●			●	●		●				●●			
758	**Aurizon:** managing change in a complex environment	●				●				●	●						●●		●	
764	In the boardroom at **HomeCo**					●				●					●				●●	●

Key: ●● = major focus ● = important subsidiary focus

Classic Cases on the Companion Website

In addition to the 32 cases provided in this textbook you can view over 40 more classic cases on the Companion Website at **www.pearsoned.co.uk/johnson**. These are a selection of cases from past editions of the book which remain relevant for teaching. A full list of these cases appears in the Guide to Classic Cases immediately before the Glossary on page 770.

Glastonbury: from hippy weekend to international festival

Steve Henderson, Leeds Beckett University

This case considers an increasingly important international music festival market that started from simple beginnings and intentions. It explores the diversifying nature of these events in terms of the entertainment they offer, their income sources and the breadth of objectives pursued by organisers. Using the long established Glastonbury Festival as an example, key strategic issues are revealed.

Background

Following on from the iconic twentieth-century Woodstock Festival that took place in New York State, USA, many have been inspired to create their own music festival. Whilst some of these events have come and gone, the longevity and location of Fuji Rock Festival in Japan, Roskilde in Denmark, Coachella in the USA and Rock al Parque in Colombia illustrate the established international nature of this market (see Table 1).

The early days of festivals like Woodstock were rooted in hippy counterculture with arguments that these music events should be free. To this day, some festivals can include free elements that, for example, involve the local community. However, the estimated crowd at Woodstock

of 400,000 clearly highlighted the mass appeal of these gatherings – and the potential commercial possibilities. From a health and safety perspective alone, ticketing of these events makes sense to control attendee numbers but, of course, these tickets may also be sold to add to the festival's income.

Rock al Parque in Bogotá still offers free entry to the festival even though it has developed from youth music meetings to an event for nearly 90,000 attendees. Organised by Bogotá's City Hall, their early efforts focused on providing a forum for local musicians to develop. Realising that musicians from outside Colombia would provide learning opportunities as much as further performance possibilities, the festival evolved from youth

Table 1 International music festivals

Festival	Country	Started	Estimated capacity[1]	Pricing
Woodstock	USA	1969	400,000	Priced/Free
Glastonbury	UK	1970	130,000	£230 (weekend)
Reading/Leeds Festival	UK	1971[2]/1999	162,000	£213 (weekend)
Roskilde	Denmark	1971	133,000	£204 (eight days)
Rock am Ring/Rock im Park	Germany	1985/1993	150,000	£144 (weekend)
Rock al Parque	Colombia	1995	88,000	Free
Benicassim	Spain	1995	55,000	£124 (four days)
V Festival: Weston Park/Hylands Park	UK	1996	160,000	£189 (weekend)
Fuji Rock	Japan	1997	More than 100,000	£286 (three days)
Coachella	USA	1999	75,000	£255 (three days)
Peace & Love	Sweden	1999	22,000	£127 (three days)

[1]Based on daily capacity
[2]Existed from 1961 as a jazz festival

music meetings to include not only performance stages but also workshops, lectures and networking opportunities within conference-style sessions.

Bogotá is able to finance Rock al Parque from a combination of public-sector support and private-sector sponsorship. For most festivals, this is a key combination of income sources that needs to be managed alongside any ticket income. In some instances, the majority of income comes from sponsorship which is reflected by, for example, the brewers Tuborg being involved with Roskilde Festival and the car company Seat working with Rock am Ring.

Glastonbury

One of the longest established is the Glastonbury Festival where The Rolling Stones, Beyoncé and Adele were recently added to the long list of headliner acts (from Paul McCartney to Oasis) that have appeared there. It started in 1970 when 1500 hippy revellers paid £1 for their ticket and gathered on Worthy Farm near Glastonbury Tor to be plied with free milk and entertainment from a makeshift stage. Now, Glastonbury is a major international festival that attracts close to 200,000 attendees. Without any knowledge of the line-up, the 2016 festival tickets priced at over £230 ($330, €280) sold out within a few hours.

In those early days, the vision was developed by local farmer, Michael Eavis, whose passion for music and social principles led to a weekend of music as a means of raising funds for good causes. It was a social mission rooted in the hippy counterculture of the 1960s and events such as Woodstock. Today, the Glastonbury Festival attendee finds that those early days of hippy idealism are a long way off. The scale of the organisation demands strong management to support the achievement of the festival's social aims. It has long-established relationships with the worthy causes of Oxfam, Greenpeace and Water Aid, all of which have a prominent place in the promotion of the event. They indicate that they are 'working together for a greener, fairer Glastonbury'.

A continued expansion has resulted in a festival with over ten stages covering jazz, dance, classical, world music and other genres. Added to this, there is comedy, poetry, circus, theatre and children's entertainment alongside more esoteric street theatre performances. Much of this is organised into specific grassy field areas where, for example, the Dance Village uses a number of tents dedicated to different types of dance music. Indeed, such is the range of entertainment on offer that some attendees spend the whole weekend at the festival without seeing a single live music act. Though the Eavis family remain involved with the main programme, much of the other

entertainment is now managed by others. Reflecting this shift towards more diverse entertainment, the name of the festival was changed from Glastonbury Fayre (reflecting the ancient cultural heritage of the area) to the Glastonbury Festival for Contemporary Performing Arts.

In some years, like 2012, the festival has been forced to take a year off to allow the farmland to recover from the trampling of thousands of pairs of feet. Not only is this wise from an agricultural viewpoint but it also gives the local residents a rest from the annual invasion of festival goers. Such issues around sustainability, particularly the environment, have become common criticisms of festivals: the need to effectively build a temporary city for the vast numbers of attendees is likely to result in some damage to the environment. Add to this the fact that many of the attendees will travel a long distance to a festival event and this can be seen to be quite a problem, especially if, like Glastonbury, the festival occurs in a rural location with limited transport links.

Glastonbury's social perspective has made the organisers very aware of this and they run a social responsibility campaign called 'Love Worthy Farm, Leave No Trace'. This includes specific elements such as 'Take It, Don't Leave It' which encourages attendees to take home their tents rather than leaving them on site at the end of the festival, resulting in their disposal in a land-fill. Also, Glastonbury has formed relationships with the National Express company in an effort to encourage 'green travellers' to chose to travel by bus from one of over 70 different locations in the UK.

Despite the efforts to achieve social aims, the festival has met with a number of controversies such as when a large number of gatecrashers spoilt the fun in 2000. This caused the festival to be fined for exceeding the licensed attendance and for excessive noise after the event. Furthermore, health and safety laws now require the event management to have a 'duty of care' to everyone on the festival site. To address these health and safety concerns, a steel fence was erected around the perimeter to allow better management of the festival area itself. Reflecting the ups and downs of managing a festival, in 2015, Michael Eavis hinted that Glastonbury may need to find a new site due to 'complications' over land ownership and, in the same year, he said the farm must come first as festivals can come and go 'in a wink'.

Elsewhere in the world of live entertainment, the success of Glastonbury has not gone unnoticed and the music festival market has shown considerable growth. Some of the other festivals aim to capitalise on features that Glastonbury could not offer. For example, Glastonbury is famous for its wet weather with pictures of damp revellers and collapsed tents being commonplace. However, various inner-city based festivals in large open spaces such as London's Hyde Park have developed, offering the opportunity to sleep under a roof at home or in a hotel, as opposed to risking the weather outdoors. Alternatively, Benicassim in southern Spain offers an annual festival with top acts and an excellent chance of sunshine for the price of a low-cost airline ticket. Other festivals noted that Glastonbury attendees enjoyed the wider entertainment at the event. In doing this, they realised that many festival goers were attracted by the whole social experience. So, sidestepping major acts and their related high fees, smaller festivals have been created for just a few thousand attendees. These offer entertainment in various formats, often, in a family-friendly atmosphere or, at least, with an emphasis on the social aspects.

Freddie Fellowes, organiser of the Secret Garden Party, describes this 'boutique' type of festival as a chance 'to be playful, to break down barriers between people and create an environment where you have perfect freedom and perfect nourishment, intellectually and visually'. Similarly, Rob da Bank, a BBC DJ, put together Bestival on the Isle of Wight where the attendees are encouraged to join in the fun by appearing in fancy dress. Quite clearly, audiences are now being presented with a wide range of festivals to consider for their leisure time entertainment.

Many of these festivals attract sponsors with some becoming prominent by acquiring naming rights on the festival, e.g. the Virgin brand's support of V Festival. Others have low-profile arrangements involving so-called 'contra' deals as opposed to sponsorship payments. These work by firms such as drink suppliers offering their products 'in kind' to boost their brand via the added publicity and, sometimes, exclusivity offered by the festival. Though these commercial relationships are sometimes spurned by the smaller festivals that see the branding as an intrusion on their social environment, larger festivals often need such relationships to survive. In order to attract sponsors, large festivals are turning to radio and television broadcasters as a means to expand the audience and offer wider exposure for the sponsor. Indeed, in 2014, the BBC sent around 300 staff members down to Glastonbury to create a broadcasting experience aimed at satisfying the interest of the armchair viewer/listener.

With such huge demand for their talents, artists can have a lucrative summer moving between festivals. Some have also begun to realise that this may not only include performance fees but their filmed performance has commercial value for which they can negotiate the commercial rights. In addition, artists are finding not only that the festivals offer a good source of income but that private parties and corporate entertainment have emerged as alternative, often greater, income opportunities. One newspaper claimed that George Michael pocketed more than £1.5m to entertain revellers at the British billionaire-retailer Sir Philip Green's 55th birthday party in the Maldives. However, those artists with the largest profiles can spurn appearances at festivals and opt for playing stadium concerts at venues such as Wembley Stadium where Ed Sheeran sold out three times over in 2015. Hence, for major artists, the summer has become a case of 'cherry picking' their favourite festivals or seeking out the most lucrative opportunities.

A common complaint in 2015 from festival promoters is that the pool of headlining artists is not only able to be more selective of where they play but is shrinking in size. Pointing to the reducing incomes of record companies and their consequent lack of investment in artists, some suggest that the life span of a popular music artist is reducing. Indeed, Harvey Goldsmith, promoter of Live Aid, goes as far as to suggest that the music festival industry is looking forward to a period of decline because of the lack of suitable headline acts.

Nevertheless, in recent years, Glastonbury has sold all its tickets and managed to keep prices moving ahead of inflation – as has the comparable Danish Roskilde Festival, albeit to a lesser extent (see Figure 1). At the same time, it continues to make donations to its worthy causes, confirming the financial viability of the current business model. Indeed, the festival's iconic status has helped it to become a rite of passage for many young music fans. Despite this, in 2015, the booking of Kanye West as a headliner caused a stir amongst the public with over 100,000 people signing a petition to replace the headliner with a rock music act. This view was countered by those sneering at an ageing audience who said the festival was catering for the 'hip-op' audience rather than the 'hip-hop' fans.

Source: Roger Cracknell 01/classic/Alamy Images.

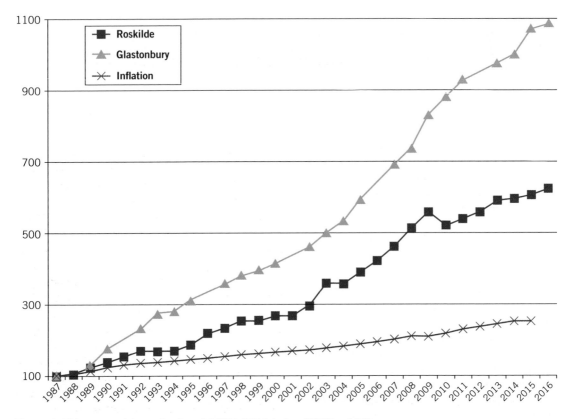

Figure 1 Thirty-year ticket price trend 1987–2016 index (1987 = 100)

Over time, the shift from small, homespun event to corporate-controlled festival has provided awkward situations for Michael Eavis – from the difficulties with establishment politicians who felt the event was out of control to the demands of countercultural groups such as the travelling hippies. Along the way, the festival has maintained the aim of supporting its worthy causes and, in the mind of the audience, this has helped position the festival as a fun event with a social conscience. However, audiences and artists are the two key factors that underpin financial success at their event. Despite the fact that Michael's daughter, Emily Eavis, and her husband are taking on more of the workload, and Michael himself has become more of a figurehead for this event, there are trends in the festival market that suggest some difficult times ahead for Glastonbury and the other events.

Sources: The history of Glastonbury is charted on their website (http://www.glastonburyfestivals.co.uk/history) whilst ownership and finances are available through Companies House. Most of the background to the festival and related market has been drawn from online news resources such as the BBC, *Times Online*, *The Independent* and *The Guardian*, or industry magazines such as *Music Week*. More information on UK festivals is available from Mintel.

CASE STUDY

The global pharmaceutical industry: back to the future?

Sarah Holland

A CEO's dilemma

In April 2015, Olivier Brandicourt started work as CEO of French pharmaceutical and vaccine giant Sanofi, after a profit warning and the abrupt departure of his predecessor Chris Viehbacher had sent the share price tumbling the previous October. Viehbacher had revitalised Sanofi's R&D, notably through the acquisition of Genzyme in 2011, but fallen foul of the largely French board by reportedly acting without consultation, and by moving his domicile back to the USA. A French native with a strong track record at Bayer and Pfizer, Brandicourt's appointment was viewed positively. Sanofi was a top five global pharmaceutical company with $40bn in annual revenues, but the company faced the imminent loss of patent protection on Lantus, one of the world's biggest selling drugs, which contributed over $8bn[1] to sales. Sanofi had also disclosed that sales in the core diabetes franchise would be held flat by strong pricing pressure in the USA. An analyst commented that 'the organisation is just moving too slowly and is not innovative enough.' It was clear that Brandicourt needed to act swiftly, but how?

Industry evolution

As described in Box 1, the pharmaceutical industry is characterised by a highly risky and lengthy research and development (R&D) process, intense competition for *intellectual property*, stringent government regulation and powerful purchaser pressures. How has this unusual picture come about?

The origins of the modern pharmaceutical industry date from the late nineteenth century, when dyestuffs were found to have antiseptic properties. Penicillin was a major discovery, and R&D became firmly established within the sector. The market developed some unusual characteristics. Decision-making was in the hands of medical practitioners whereas patients (the final consumers) and payers (governments or insurance companies) had little knowledge or influence. Consequently, medical practitioners were insensitive to price but susceptible to the efforts of sales representatives.

Two important developments occurred in the 1970s. First, the thalidomide tragedy (an anti-emetic for morning sickness that caused birth defects) led to much tighter regulatory controls on clinical trials. Second, legislation was enacted to set a fixed period on patent protection – typically 20 years. On patent expiry, rivals could launch *generic* medicines with exactly the same active ingredients as the original brand, but at a lower price. The dramatic impact of generic competitors is illustrated by Merck's top-selling asthma and allergy drug Singulair, which lost 90 per cent of US sales just four weeks after patent expiry in 2012. Generics had a major impact on the industry, driving innovation and a race to market, since the time during which R&D costs could be recouped was drastically curtailed.

The pharmaceutical industry is unusual since in many countries it is subject to a 'monopsony' – there is effectively only one powerful purchaser, the government. From the 1980s on, governments focused on pharmaceuticals as a politically easy target in efforts to control rising healthcare expenditure. Many introduced price or reimbursement controls. The industry lacked the public or political support to resist these changes.

Business environment

Ageing populations create pressure on healthcare systems, since 'over-65s' consume four times as much healthcare per head as younger people. Combined with an epidemic of chronic disease linked to obesity, this created an unsustainable situation, further exacerbated by the global financial crisis.

In response to these pressures, government and private payers (such as insurance companies) use a

---

BOX 1 The drug development process

The pharmaceutical industry has long new product lead times, with the period from discovery to marketing authorisation typically taking almost 12 years (Figure 1). New product development can be divided into distinct research and development phases. The research phase produces a new chemical entity (NCE) with the desired characteristics to be an effective drug. Development encompasses all of the formulation, toxicology and clinical trial work necessary to meet stringent regulatory requirements for marketing approval.

During all of these phases 'attrition' occurs, as promising agents fail particular hurdles, so most R&D projects never result in a marketed drug. Late-stage failures are particularly costly and not uncommon – in 2014, Roche announced the failure of bitopertin for schizophrenia and onartuzumab for cancer, in both cases after heavy investment in broad Phase III programmes. Of those drugs that reach the market, 80 per cent fail to recoup their R&D investment. When the costs of all the projects that do not reach fruition are considered, it becomes clear that pharmaceutical R&D is a very high-stakes game indeed.

Given the enormous risks and considerable investment involved, it is not surprising that pharmaceutical companies compete fiercely to establish and retain *intellectual property* rights. Only by securing a patent that can be defended against imitators can the value of all this R&D be recouped.

The industry is subjected to rigorous regulatory scrutiny. Government agencies such as the Food and Drug Administration (FDA) in the USA thoroughly examine all of the data to support the purity, stability, safety, efficacy and tolerability of a new agent. The time taken is governed by legislation and typically averages 12 months. Obtaining marketing approval is no longer the end of the road in many countries, as further hurdles must be overcome in demonstrating the value of the new drug to justify price and/or reimbursement to cost-conscious payers.

	Discovery/ preclinical testing		Clinical trials			FDA	Phase IV
			Phase I	Phase II	Phase III		
Years	6.5		1.5	2	3.5	1.5	
Test population	Laboratory and animal studies	File IND at FDA	20 to 100 healthy volunteers	100 to 500 patient volunteers	1,000 to 5,000 patient volunteers	File NDA/BLA at FDA	Additional post-marketing testing required by FDA
Purpose	Access safety, biological activity and formulations		Determine safety and dosage	Evaluate effectiveness, look for side effects	Confirm effectiveness, monitor adverse reactions from long-term use	Review process/ approval	
Success rate	5,000 compounds evaluated		5 enter trials			1 approved	

Figure 1 Creating new pharmaceuticals: it takes 10–15 years on average for an experimental drug to travel from the lab to patients

Source: PhRMA, Medicines in Development – Biotechnology – 2006 Report, p. 51.

Table 1 Methods used to control pharmaceutical spending

Controls on suppliers	Mixed effect	Controls to influence demand
Negotiated prices	Partial reimbursement at price negotiated with manufacturer	Patient co-payments*
Average pricing		Treatment guidelines
Reference pricing	Generic substitution	Indicative or fixed budgets
Positive and negative lists		Incentives to prescribe or dispense generics or parallel imports
Constraints on wholesalers and pharmacists		
Imposed price cuts		Transfer from prescription-only to over-the-counter
Pay for performance		e-prescribing tools
Indication-based pricing		

*Where the patient pays some of the drug cost.

variety of methods to control pharmaceutical spending (see Table 1). Some put the emphasis on the manufacturer and distributor, others on the prescriber and patient. Controls are designed to reward genuine advances – price and/or reimbursement levels are based on perceived innovation and superior effectiveness.

In countries with supply-side controls, negotiating price or reimbursement can take up to a year. In those with demand-side controls, market penetration is delayed while negotiating with bodies such as the *National Institute for Clinical Excellence* (NICE) in the UK. NICE typifies a general trend towards *evidence-based medicine,* where payers expect objective evidence of effectiveness to justify funding new therapies. The impact of NICE decisions reverberates beyond the UK, as countries collaborate internationally on value assessments. Where new drugs are approved for funding, this is increasingly in the context of formal patient selection and treatment guidelines, so their use is carefully controlled and individual prescribers have limited decision-making power.

Switching to generics is one way to cut drug expenditure. Countries are experimenting with 'e-prescribing' where physicians are presented with recommended options. Payers are increasingly effective in establishing generic drugs as first-line treatment for chronic diseases such as osteoporosis, asthma and depression, with patented drugs only used if generics fail to work. In volume terms, generic drugs are growing and patented drugs are in decline – falling from 50 per cent of US prescriptions in 2005 to barely over 12 per cent by 2014 – so sales growth for patented drugs relies on securing ever higher prices for innovation.

The industry has adopted a number of strategic responses to these challenges. *Pharmacoeconomic* evaluations are conducted to demonstrate the added value offered by a new drug due to improved efficacy, safety, tolerability or ease of use. For example, a study of the cost of diabetes – the fastest-growing chronic disease in the world – found that 60 per cent was driven by hospitalisations, which could often be avoided by correct outpatient use of medicines. Companies have introduced *disease management initiatives,* which focus on the goals of the healthcare system for a specific disease. Firms then offer a broad-based service to improve disease outcomes, positioning their products as part of the solution. Another approach is the 'pay for performance' deal; for example, UK reimbursement of the cancer drug Velcade was linked to disease response. An innovative deal was struck in Italy, where Roche agreed to be paid different amounts for the cancer drug Avastin depending on the type of cancer for which it was prescribed, based on its varying cost-effectiveness.

Payers value '*real-world evidence*', i.e. how drugs perform in real populations rather than the artificial populations studied in trials. One challenge in demonstrating real-world drug performance is that counterfeit products are a growing problem, putting patient safety and lives at risk. In 2012, tainted steroids killed 11 people near Boston and sickened another 100.[2] More than 27 million counterfeit medicine articles were seized at EU borders in 2011, and at least one to two per cent of global sales, or over $100bn were estimated to be counterfeits by 2012.[3] Drug manufacturers and distributors are forced to invest in countermeasures, such as traceability and authentication technologies.

Government price controls create another challenge for the industry in the form of 'parallel trade'. The principle of free movement of goods across the EU mean that distributors are free to source drugs in low price markets and ship them to high price markets, pocketing the difference. EU parallel trade was estimated at €5.4bn in 2013, with the highest penetration in Denmark where it accounted for nearly a quarter of pharmacy sales.[4]

Industry sectors

Prescription-only or *ethical* drugs contribute about 85 per cent ($865bn) of the $1trn global pharmaceutical market by value and 50 per cent by volume. Ethical products divide into conventional pharmaceuticals and more complex *biopharmaceutical* agents and vaccines (see Box 2). The other 15 per cent of the market comprises *over the counter* (OTC) medicines, which may be purchased without prescription. Both ethical and OTC medicines may be patented or generic.

The typical cost structure of ethical pharmaceutical companies comprises manufacturing of goods (25 per cent), research and development (16–24 per cent), administration (10 per cent), and medical education, marketing and sales (25 per cent). The key strategic capabilities of these companies are R&D and medical education, marketing and sales. Pressure on margins created an incentive to restructure manufacturing, rationalising and relocating production sites and outsourcing to *contract manufacturing organisations* (CMOs).

Manufacturing and distribution efficiency is key for generics manufacturers, whose operating margins are typically less than half that of ethical companies. In the 1990s, US generics prices collapsed, accompanied by a shakeout to determine cost leadership. The speed and aggression of generic attacks on branded products increased sharply. Economies of scale, including finance to support complex patent disputes, proved decisive and the sector consolidated, with only four companies holding nearly half the global market by 2014. Given the number of blockbusters undergoing patent expiry and markets with still untapped potential (e.g. Spain, France, Japan), not surprisingly growth in generics outstrips the overall market. The global market for generics is projected to increase from $260bn in 2012 to over $400bn by 2017, with a compound annual growth rate of 11 per cent, contributing half of absolute market growth.

A new type of industry player appeared in the 1980s – small biotechnology start-ups backed by venture capital to exploit the opportunities created by molecular biology and genetic engineering. Initially, *biotechs* were associated with biologics (see Box 2). Biotechs now pursue a huge variety of core capabilities, creating an extraordinarily diverse and innovative sector. Because of the long product development cycle, most biotechs take years to reach profitability, if at all, and revenues are

---

BOX 2 Biologics – the industry saviour

Biopharmaceuticals or '*biologics*' are large molecules that behave like natural substances, such as proteins and monoclonal antibodies. The discovery and design of biologics entails optimising specificity and affinity and making the molecules as close to human substances as possible to avoid provoking an immune response. Produced through large-scale fermentation in costly plants, biologics are given by injection and used to treat specialist conditions such as cancer and rheumatoid arthritis. Biologics are much more specific in their action than small molecules; this avoids unexpected 'off target' side-effects and increases success rate from Phase I to launch from 7 per cent to 12 per cent.[5] Because of their benefits and use in high-unmet-need diseases, biologics generally secure higher prices than small molecules.

Initially associated with biotechs, biologics became mainstream – contributing $230bn in 2014 – and were expected to provide six of the top ten brands by 2020. Companies that invested early benefited from this rapid growth. Others noted their success and many acquired biologics capabilities. Sanofi entered into a strategic partnership with US *biotech* Regeneron in 2007, extended in 2009 and further built on in 2015 after Olivier Brandicourt arrived as CEO. The marketed drugs Zaltrap and Praluent, as well as a number of late-stage assets, were fruits of this deal, and Sanofi hoped that the latest agreement would catapult the company into a competitive position in the exciting field of immuno-oncology.

In addition to lower attrition and superior pricing, biologics are at less risk from generic threat. The sophisticated capabilities required to develop and manufacture a complex *biosimilar* product take substantial investment. Furthermore, regulators were slow to clarify requirements for approval. However, top generics companies clearly saw the potential. Sandoz led the way with human growth hormone and erythropoietin in the EU, and scored the first US approval of a biosimilar in 2015. The lure of stealing sales from blockbuster biologics attracted non-traditional players into the field, such as GE Healthcare, Celltrion and Samsung. Even so, serious biosimilar competition was not expected before 2018 and although markets with tender systems saw rapid penetration, price erosion was likely to be more gradual and less severe than with small molecule generics.

concentrated in a tiny subgroup of highly profitable firms. During the global credit squeeze biotech IPOs became very rare and, as access to venture and debt funding dried up, corporate venture funds of *big pharma* companies became an important source of start-up funding. Investment picked up in 2011, as scientific breakthroughs reignited belief in the sector, and reached record levels by 2014. An amazing 41 FDA approvals of novel drugs in 2014 encouraged an IPO boom: 50 companies raised over $50bn in the first half of 2015, leading to fears of a 'biotech bubble'.

OTC medicines are bought by consumers without a prescription. The global OTC market was estimated at $120bn in 2014, with the top ten manufacturers accounting for more than half. Consumer brand loyalty provides defence against generic competition and prolongs the product life cycle. Consistently outperforming the ethical sector globally, OTC sales are boosted by innovation, promotion of self-medication and expansion of distribution channels. Sales have accelerated in emerging markets, providing global players with a rare source of growth and a quick way to gain presence in these key markets. Consumer marketing skills are key, especially with new competition from companies such as Danone and Nestlé, who are capitalising on consumer interest in personal wellbeing by making health claims for so-called *nutraceuticals*.

Another important category of medicine is vaccines, a key industry growth driver. Prophylactic vaccines provide life-long protection against serious diseases, preventing at least three million deaths annually worldwide and saving an estimated $7–20 healthcare dollars per dollar spent on vaccines. This nearly $30bn market is highly concentrated: just five global players account for nearly 80 per cent. Global vaccine sales tripled between 2005 and 2013 with launches of high-priced vaccines for new applications such as human papilloma virus (HPV). Entry barriers are high, with specialised skills required in manufacturing, conducting large and complex clinical trials and managing surveillance programmes. Vaccines have higher development success rates and a lower risk of generic entry than conventional medicines, while offering blockbuster sales potential. Novartis, AstraZeneca and Pfizer all entered the sector through acquisitions, while Brandicourt benefited from an enviable heritage through Sanofi Pasteur.

Key markets

The majority of pharmaceutical sales originate in the USA, Japan, China, the EU and Brazil, with ten key countries contributing 75 per cent of the global market. Pharmaceutical market growth is strongly aligned with GDP growth. The USA is by far the largest market by

BOX 3 US dominance under threat?

A number of factors contributed to industry globalisation. Chief is the international convergence of medical science and practice under the influence of modern communications technology and increased travel and information exchange. Well-funded US universities and hospitals generally led their fields, while US scientific congresses provided the most prestigious platforms for new discoveries.

Leading corporations globalised, with presence in all significant markets. Production sites had a global mandate and were selected by worldwide screening. R&D was sourced from best place worldwide, which often meant the USA. Strong US market growth gave US companies a springboard in achieving global ambitions, and in 2014 they occupied six of the top ten slots (see Table 2 below).

Biotechnology companies were 'born global': from their inception they drew upon a global pool of collaborators and investors, rather than growing from small

domestic beginnings. Once again, the USA dominated: publicly-traded biotechs employed over four times more people in the USA than in the EU, with a similar ratio for R&D spend. US biotechs secured the majority of venture capital investment.

In the longer term, US pre-eminence in biomedical research could be under threat from Asia. Global companies were opening R&D sites in Asia, while closing them in the USA and EU. The Chinese government declared its intention to become a leader in the field and poured money into new universities and science parks, with the result that the number of Chinese graduates in natural sciences overtook the USA by 2004. Routine chemistry and toxicology were already often outsourced to China, but as US returnees and home-grown talent sought more innovative projects, a fully integrated life science innovation ecosystem began to emerge.

volume and value – $365bn in 2014 – nearly 40 per cent of global sales. US growth collapsed in 2010, the consequence of patent expiries, fewer new products and reduced consumer demand, but returned to a very healthy 12 per cent in 2014, as product launches picked up. Indeed, the USA remains critical to launch success: for *NCEs* launched during 2010–14, nearly 60 per cent of sales were from the USA, compared with 25 per cent from the EU.

Following regulatory changes in 1997, *direct-to-consumer* (DTC) advertising transformed the US marketplace and fuelled growth. However, companies' costs for providing healthcare benefits to employees exceeded $12,000 on average by 2012, with employees contributing a further $8500.[6] Private payers asked consumers for increasing co-payments and implemented other cost-control measures. Medicare reforms extended drug coverage for the elderly, and gave the government new pricing leverage as the largest direct purchaser of medicines. President Obama's controversial Patient Protection and Affordable Care Act significantly reduced the number of Americans without health insurance, and expanded Medicaid coverage, while increasing focus on value for money.

Gilead's 2014 introduction of Sovaldi for hepatitis C virus (HCV) put pharmaceutical pricing in the spotlight. HCV is a devastating condition that can ultimately lead to cancer, liver transplant and early death. Sovaldi eradicates the virus rapidly in many cases. Even at a list price of $84,000 for 12 weeks' therapy, cost-effectiveness is indisputable, as expensive future treatment is avoided. However, payers suffered 'sticker shock', having never seen such a price for short-term treatment of a largely asymptomatic condition. More seriously, given the enormous latent pool of patients harbouring the virus, funding Sovaldi could bankrupt smaller health plans. Rather than offering a creative solution, such as accepting annuity payments matched to future healthcare savings, Gilead chose to generate over $9bn in revenue in 2014, smashing all previous launch records. The outcry strengthened in September 2015 when Turing Pharmaceuticals, sole supplier of the old drug Daraprim for a complication of AIDS, hiked the price by 5000 per cent. Not surprisingly, during her presidential campaign Hillary Clinton vowed to tackle drug pricing, instantly deflating the 2015 'biotech bubble'. Despite all these pressures, annual US market growth to 2019 is predicted to be a healthy six to nine per cent.

Japan is the second largest market for pharmaceuticals, with sales of $116bn in 2014. The Japanese operating environment was historically quite different from the USA and EU. This divergence occurred at all levels, from medical practice, regulatory requirements, the lack of generics, distribution and the accepted approach to sales and marketing. Not surprisingly, domestic companies dominate the market. Economic recession caused tax revenues to fall, while the cost of treating the world's most rapidly ageing population rose. This resulted in changes to healthcare funding, regular price cuts and the introduction of stringent price controls, limiting annual market growth to an average below two per cent from 2010–14, with little improvement predicted to 2019.

The European pharmaceutical market, which contributed 25 per cent of global sales in 2014, is highly fragmented and driven by governments' forever-changing cost containment plans, resulting in a lack of predictability for companies' operational planning. The UK market fell from fifth to eighth position between 2006 and 2014, illustrating the strong impact of NICE decisions on reimbursement and access. European market annual growth is expected to stay well below 5 per cent up to 2019.

For industry players to maintain growth, they either have to capture a disproportionate share of established markets or focus on accessing those still in their growth phase. In contrast to the generally stagnant developed markets, top-tier emerging markets are predicted to grow at 5–12 per cent per year to 2019. These countries therefore constitute an ever larger share of the global market – reaching nearly a quarter by 2014. With its growing GDP and huge population, China alone was expected to overtake Japan to become the second largest market globally by 2018.

IMS Health identified a diverse group of 'pharmerging' markets led by China, Brazil, India and Russia. In addition to the high net worth individuals who can afford the most innovative treatments, their middle-class populations are growing more rapidly than at any time in history. The key challenge is to adapt to these countries' varied needs and environments. Some companies built their strategy on premium-priced generics, offering the reassurance of a known brand and reliable manufacturer, so-called '*branded generics*'. However, this approach is highly vulnerable to local generic competition and reference pricing reforms. Other companies expanded access to innovative medicines. For example, Roche supplied Herceptin free of charge to Chinese breast cancer patients after they had paid for a threshold number of months, and fostered health insurance schemes. Brandicourt was fortunate that Sanofi was historically strong in emerging markets, providing a much needed revenue growth driver.

Innovation

Pharmaceutical companies' key contribution to medical progress is the ability to turn fundamental research findings into proven innovative treatments that are widely available and accessible.[7] Companies with consistently high levels of R&D spending and productivity became industry leaders. For this reason, stock market valuations place as much importance on the R&D *pipeline* (i.e. the products in development) as on marketed products.

The holy grail of pharmaceutical R&D was the *blockbuster*. Blockbuster drugs are genuine advances that achieve rapid, deep market penetration. Because of their superlative market performance, blockbusters determine the fortunes of individual companies. Gilead leapt into the top rank of global pharma companies thanks to Sovaldi, which beat all records by selling $2.3bn in its first quarter. While blockbusters make immense contributions to company fortunes, they are few and far between. Andrew Witty, the CEO of GlaxoSmithKline, likened the hunt to 'finding a needle in a haystack right when you need it'.

Focusing on blockbusters exposed an already high-stakes industry to even greater levels of risk. This was dramatically brought home in September 2004 when the cardiovascular safety risks of Vioxx emerged, and Merck withdrew the brand from the market. Merck lost $2.5bn in sales, a quarter of its stock market value, and faced the prospect of numerous liability suits. Blockbusters also exacerbate the impact of patent expiries, creating a so-called 'patent cliff'. Companies were projected to lose nearly $100bn in sales due to generic erosion on small molecule drugs alone up to 2018, when the impact of *biosimilars* would also start to bite. Witty argued that the industry must move from being 'blockbuster dependent' to 'blockbuster capable'[8] – i.e. able to develop and commercialise blockbusters, but also efficient at developing and commercialising a steady stream of drugs in the $50–500m range.

Unfortunately, R&D productivity has declined and development times lengthened. The average cost to develop a new drug is estimated at $1.4bn[9] and has grown at double the rate of inflation for 20 years. Despite increasing R&D spend from 11 per cent of annual sales to 20 per cent or more, the industry struggles to replace the value lost through patent expiries. Attrition increased as companies put higher hurdles in place to address payer needs for meaningful clinical benefit. Employing thousands of in-house scientists to develop drug candidates from scratch became a billion dollar gamble that simply wasn't delivering. From 2008 onwards, industry R&D spending growth slowed rapidly, and actually declined in 2012.

Companies endeavoured to become both creative and efficient. They narrowed their areas of therapeutic focus:

for example, Novartis and GlaxoSmithKline swapped oncology and vaccine portfolios, while Brandicourt streamlined Sanofi's R&D. They invested in alliances with academic institutions, seeking depth of expertise. Strategic out-sourcing to *contract research organisations* (CROs) reduced fixed costs and leveraged lower cost geographies. Lilly created a special unit to conduct small clinical tests to quickly and cheaply shake out molecules that were not going to make it. Recognising that biopharmaceuticals had a lower attrition rate, companies acquired biologics capabilities – Sanofi through a crucial strategic partnership with Regeneron. Some reorganised their R&D to create smaller and more nimble units: GlaxoSmithKline's research centres competed for funding like internal biotechs. Many opened R&D sites in innovation 'hotspots', such as the US West coast, Boston and Asia. All sought external innovation through licensing deals and acquisitions, although with few real jewels available the cost of deals spiralled.

To better manage some of the tremendous risks involved, companies moved towards a more network-based approach to innovation. For diseases that were just too tough to tackle alone, 'pre-competitive' collaboration allows costs and insights to be shared. Companies, foundations and regulators working on Alzheimer's disease pooled data and resources to create shared understanding. Where large, long-term outcome studies were needed, companies pooled assets, moving only the best forward. In diabetes, AstraZeneca and BMS paired up to develop drugs together, sharing cost, risk and reward, as did Lilly and Boehringer Ingelheim.

There are encouraging signs that industry's focus on meaningful clinical benefit, together with the FDA's explicit support for drugs designated as 'breakthroughs', is finally delivering improved R&D productivity and desperately needed revenue. The FDA approved 41 NMEs in 2014, of which eight were expected to sell over $1bn within five years of launch.

Sales and marketing

Historically, sales and marketing capability was important to competitive advantage. A company that developed a strong global franchise with its customers could maximise return on its products and was in a good position to attract the best in-licensing candidates.

The traditional focus of drug marketing was the personal *detail* in which a sales representative (rep) discussed the merits of a drug in a face-to-face meeting with a doctor and provided free samples. Promotion is subject to industry self-regulation. For example, in the UK, reps have to pass an examination testing medical knowledge. In some countries, government regulatory agencies check that promotional claims are consistent with the data.

There were important differences in the marketing of 'primary care' and 'specialist' products. Office-based practitioners generally prescribe primary care products, whereas treatment with specialist products is typically initiated in hospitals. Sales volume, marketing spend and skills required differed for the two segments. Product-led muscle marketing was key in the primary care sector, while specialist products involved more cost-effective targeted relationship marketing.

The term 'high compression marketing' was coined to describe global launches of primary care brands. This involved near-simultaneous worldwide launches, global branding and heavy investment in promotion. The aim was to create a rapid take-off curve that maximised return by creating higher peak year sales earlier in the product life cycle. A typical example was the launch of Celebrex in 1999, which netted $1bn sales in the first nine months. In the USA, an important marketing tool was DTC advertising, where spending peaked at $5.4bn in 2006. DTC was costly because of the vast target audience and expensive television advertising, but profitable. Well-informed patients asked for drugs by brand name, creating a powerful 'pull' strategy.

Sales force size was a key competitive attribute. However, as primary care blockbusters dried up, sales force productivity declined sharply. Over 500,000 sales reps were made redundant between 2006 and 2008, while use of contract sales forces and digital channels increased. As pipelines shifted to high-unmet-need diseases treated by specialists, the era of lavish launches and massive sales forces was over. Selling became a more complex process with multiple stakeholders interested in cost-effectiveness as well as clinical arguments, requiring new skills. Crucially for big pharma, size is no longer a critical advantage: in fact, the fastest growing companies are specialty players such as Gilead, Biogen and Celgene.

Corporate social responsibility

Today's EU citizens can expect to live up to 30 years longer than they did a century ago. Much of this improvement can be attributed to pharmaceutical innovation. For example, EU deaths from AIDS fell by three quarters between 2004 and 2013. Few other industries have done as much for the well-being of mankind. Furthermore, at a global level the industry has the highest ratio of R&D to net sales, funds nearly a fifth of all industrial R&D investment, and makes a significant contribution to skilled employment.[10] So how has an industry that delivers all these benefits acquired such a tarnished image and become an easy target for government intervention?

Pharmaceuticals have the characteristics of a 'public good' – i.e. expensive to produce but inexpensive to reproduce. The manufacturing cost of drugs is often tiny compared with the cost of R&D that led to the discovery. Setting prices that attempt to recoup R&D therefore look like corporate greed in comparison with the very low prices charged for generics. This was exacerbated as sales volumes dwindled and prices spiralled.

Some companies damage the industry's overall reputation. In July 2012, GSK paid $3bn in the largest healthcare fraud settlement in US history, having pleaded guilty to promoting two drugs for unapproved uses. The Deputy US Attorney General declared the settlement 'unprecedented in both size and scope'. Even more seriously, companies were accused of putting profits before patient safety. After the withdrawal of Vioxx, Merck was accused of ignoring problems during product development, and publishing misleading scientific results. As a consequence, the FDA was empowered to demand risk evaluation and mitigation strategies (REMS) – costly additional programmes to monitor and ensure drug safety after product approval. Soon one third of new drug approvals involved REMS.

The industry also faces condemnation of its response to the enormous unmet need in developing countries. Although effective drugs and vaccines exist for many diseases affecting millions, often their cost is beyond the means of the people who need them. It is argued that companies could reallocate R&D efforts in favour of tropical diseases, sell low-priced essential drugs and provide technology transfer. In response, most global players donate medicines for neglected diseases, and a few go further, for example making molecules and patents freely available to researchers.

Industry mergers and acquisitions

The pharmaceutical market is fragmented, with very large numbers of domestic and regional players, but consolidated at the global level, with the top ten companies holding 34 per cent of the market in 2014. Table 2 shows how the industry responded to the patent cliff and declining productivity with a wave of mergers and acquisitions. Mergers resulted in the formation of Novartis, Sanofi, AstraZeneca and GlaxoSmithKline, while Pfizer acquired Warner-Lambert, Pharmacia and Wyeth. A striking development was the sudden appearance of Gilead on the leader board – clear evidence that a single blockbuster can change company fortune.

Table 2 Leading global pharmaceutical companies, 2005–14

	2005			2008			2011			2014			
Company	Company	Sales $bn	Global market share	Company	Sales $bn	Global market share	Company	Sales $bn	Global market share	Company	Sales $bn	Global market share	Sales growth 2013–14
Pfizer[1,3] (US)	Pfizer[1,3] (US)	45.9	8.1%	Pfizer[1,3] (US)	43.4	6.0%	Pfizer[1,3,6] (US)	56.4	6.6%	Novartis (CH)	51.3	4.9%	−10.6%
GlaxoSmith-Kline[2] (US)	GlaxoSmith-Kline[2] (US)	35.3	6.2%	GlaxoSmithKline[2] (US)	36.5	5.0%	Novartis (CH)	51.6	6.0%	Pfizer[1,3,6] (US)	44.9	4.2%	−13.8%
Sanofi-Aventis[4] (Fr)	Sanofi-Aventis[4] (Fr)	30.9	5.4%	Novartis(CH)	36.2	5.0%	Merck & Co[5] (US)	40.1	4.7%	Sanofi[4] (Fr)	40.0	3.8%	2.5%
Novartis (CH)	Novartis (CH)	29.6	5.2%	Sanofi-Aventis[4] (Fr)	35.6	4.9%	Sanofi[4] (Fr)	39.5	4.6%	Roche[7] (CH)	37.6	3.6%	1.5%
Johnson & Johnson (US)	Johnson & Johnson (US)	27.2	4.8%	AstraZeneca (UK)	32.5	4.5%	AstraZeneca (UK)	37.0	4.3%	Merck & Co[5] (US)	36.5	3.5%	−4.5%
AstraZeneca (UK)	AstraZeneca (UK)	24.7	4.3%	Roche (CH)	30.3	4.2%	Roche[7] (CH)	34.9	4.1%	Johnson & Johnson (US)	36.4	3.4%	4.3%
Merck & Co (US)	Merck & Co (US)	23.9	4.2%	Johnson & Johnson (US)	29.4	4.1%	Johnson & Johnson (US)	34.5	4.0%	AstraZeneca (UK)	33.3	3.2%	1.1%
Roche (CH)	Roche (CH)	20.1	3.5%	Merck & Co (US)	26.2	3.6%	GlaxoSmith-Kline[2] (US)	27.7	3.2%	GlaxoSmith-Kline[2] (US)	31.5	3.0%	−8.6%
Abbott (US)	Abbott (US)	14.8	2.6%	Abbott (US)	19.5	2.7%	Abbott (US)	25.9	3.0%	Teva (Israel)	26.0	2.5%	−1.1%
Bristol-Myers-Squibb (US)	Bristol-Myers-Squibb (US)	14.7	2.6%	Lilly (US)	19.1	2.7%	Teva (Israel)	23.9	2.8%	Gilead Sciences (US)	23.7	2.2%	121.8%

Notes

	Created	Originating companies	
1	2000	Warner-Lambert (US)	Pfizer (US)
2	2000	Glaxo Wellcome (UK)	SmithKline Beecham (UK)
3	2003	Pfizer (US)	Pharmacia (US)
4	2004	Sanofi (France)	Aventis (France)
5	2009	Merck (US)	Schering-Plough (US)
6	2009	Pfizer (US)	Wyeth (US)
7	2009	Roche (CH)	Genentech (US)

One rationale for M&A was to acquire global commercial reach. The acquisition of Nycomed transformed Takeda from a Japanese player with limited geographic reach to a global company. Companies also used M&A to access growth segments. In February 2011, Sanofi acquired Genzyme, the leading player in rare disease, one of pharma's few growth areas. Sanofi also acquired Medley, the third largest pharmaceutical company in Brazil, in 2009, and merged with the Chinese company BMP Sunstone in 2011. Other industry acquisitions increased presence in vaccines, biologics, consumer health and generics.

Buying exciting assets could also boost growth. Alongside the IPO market, M&A offered another way for venture capitalists to recover the cash invested in early stage biotechs. Those with the best programmes could command remarkable prices, as desperate big pharmas, Japanese companies seeking to globalise and newly-rich specialty players all entered the fray. Public companies were targets too: when Gilead placed its $11bn bet on what was essentially a one-drug company with its purchase of Pharmasset in late 2011, there were concerns that it had massively overpaid. Gilead was the world leader in combination therapies for HIV and saw the opportunity to repeat this success in HCV. This belief was vindicated with the highest US sales of any company in 2014, as well as the most valued pipeline product, and Gilead was forecast to capture over half the global antiviral market by 2020.

Mergers were also strongly motivated by falling revenue and the attraction of eliminating duplicated costs. Within a month of merging with Wyeth, Pfizer announced a 35 per cent reduction in R&D square footage with six site closures. Another way to cut costs was to relocate to a more attractive tax domicile. A striking example was Actavis, which first built critical mass as a generics player, cost-stripping and moving to Ireland in the process. Fuelled by very cheap debt, it acquired Forest Laboratories for $25bn in 2014, along with CEO Brent Saunders. Shifting tax domicile for Forest's US income was quickly accretive to earnings. Alongside smaller purchases, Actavis then acquired the highly respected California company Allergan (best-known for Botox), for $70bn. Saunders adopted the Allergan name, and promptly sold the generics business to Teva for $40.5bn to cement rebranding as a specialty 'growth' pharma. This dizzying series of deals culminated in November 2015 in the announcement that Allergan was to merge with venerable US giant Pfizer in a $160bn deal, with Saunders becoming President and Chief Operating Officer of the new Ireland-based Pfizer Inc. At this point, the US government lost patience and announced planned legislative changes that scuppered the deal.

Where next?

At the start of 2016, the global pharmaceutical industry faced its most positive outlook in decades, but also a greater degree of turmoil than ever before. As economies of scale no longer played a critical role, and size undermined crucial R&D productivity, industry giants were supplanted by much faster growing mid-sized players. The industry was also undergoing rapid transformation through a spate of M&A transactions. Investment in biotechs had reached record levels, thanks to a combination of scientific breakthroughs and regulatory support for meaningful advances. However, as innovative pharmaceuticals were used in ever lower volumes at ever higher prices, becoming akin to a luxury good, pharmaceutical pricing was a focus of public debate, putting the whole industry model at risk.

An intriguing response to environmental change was pioneered by Roche, who positioned themselves as operating a 'personalised healthcare' business model. Roche was the global leader in diagnostics and their strategy was to offer value through targeting treatments to patients that would benefit most. This concept appealed to regulators and payers, who endorsed the linkage of high-priced cancer drugs such as Zelboraf for melanoma with diagnostic tests to identify suitable patients. Investing in discovery and development of tests added further to cost and complexity, but offered the chance to reduce attrition, build unique competencies and secure rapid market uptake. Most of the Roche pipeline was being developed with *companion diagnostics.*

A related but more embryonic field was healthcare information technology. Other sectors were able to analyse huge data sets to generate and exploit highly personalised consumer insights, but the pharmaceutical industry was slow to harness the power of 'big data'. Electronic health records offered an opportunity to detect patterns and gain new insights. However, there were huge challenges: even simple tests were not standardised between hospitals, and adoption rates were low with poor inter-operability of medical records systems. Nevertheless, visionary players were starting to tackle these problems. In August 2015, Sanofi announced a collaboration with Google Life Science aimed at improving diabetes health outcomes. The companies planned to use data and miniaturised technology to give patients tools to self-manage their disease. The declared goal was 'to strive to shift from episodic, event-driven diabetes care to continuous, value-based care'.[11]

Brandicourt's first year

On 6 November 2015, Brandicourt held a press conference to reveal his new Sanofi strategy, comprising three pillars resting on a fundamental platform. The platform was the much-needed simplification of the complex and unwieldy organisation, with the creation of five global business units, comprising all activities from clinical proof of concept through to marketing and sales. All support functions, including R&D, were to be integrated and globalised. After many years of an unusual regionalised operating model, Sanofi would adopt a more conventional global approach, akin to Brandicourt's experience at Pfizer. The three strategic pillars were to reshape the portfolio, deliver outstanding launches and sustain innovation in R&D. Reshaping the portfolio meant focusing on those areas where Sanofi could win: Brandicourt announced a planned strategic swap of the animal health business for Boehringher Ingelheim's consumer healthcare business, and a slew of licensing deals to boost core franchises. Delivering outstanding launches of the rich late-stage pipeline was clearly crucial to establish his credibility as the new CEO. A new

R&D operating model was expected to boost productivity, together with an increased emphasis on accessing external innovation. The new blueprint for Sanofi's future had thus been laid out.

Notes and references
1. $1 = £0.6 = €0.75.
2. 'Bad medicine', *The Economist*, 13 October 2012.
3. UCL School of Pharmacy, 'Falsified medicines and the global public's health', 7 March 2013.
4. *The Pharmaceutical Industry in Facts & Figures 2015*, EFPIA.
5. *Nature Reviews Drug Discovery*, vol. 8 (2009), pp. 609–10.
6. 'Healthcare costs for insured American family top $20K in 2012: Milliman', *Insurance Journal*, 15 May 2012.
7. 'The truth about drug innovation: thirty-five summary case histories on private sector contributions to pharmaceutical science', Manhattan Institute for Policy Research, http://www.manhattan-institute.org/html/mpr_06.htm.
8. http://www.rsc.org/chemistryworld/News/2008/July/25070805.asp.
9. Tufts Center for the Study of Drug Development, 'Cost to develop and win marketing approval for a new drug is $2.6 billion', 18 November 2014.
10. *The 2011 EU Industrial R&D Investment Scoreboard*, Joint Research Centre, Directorate General Research & Innovation, European Commission.
11. http://www.news.sanofi.us/2015-08-31-Sanofi-to-Collaborate-with-Google-Life-Sciences-to-Improve-Diabetes-Health-Outcomes.

APPENDIX: Glossary

big pharma A group term for large globalised pharmaceutical companies.

biologic or biopharmaceutical Large molecules that behave like natural substances, such as therapeutic proteins and monoclonal antibodies.

biosimilar Molecules designed to mimic the therapeutic effects of an original biologic agent – similar in molecular structure but not identical.

biotech Shorthand for biotechnology, biotech companies typically discover and develop products, which may be diagnostics, therapeutics or vaccines. However, some biotechs simply provide services to other companies.

blockbuster A drug that is marketed globally and has annual sales exceeding $1bn.

branded generics Branded generics are original brands that have lost patent protection and are priced similarly to identical generic medicines, but offer the reassurance that they are produced by an established manufacturer.

companion diagnostic A diagnostic product to be used alongside a drug, to identify patients that are either best suited, or not suited, to receive the therapy.

contract manufacturing organisation (CMO) A service organisation that undertakes manufacturing activities on behalf of a pharma or biotech company, thus avoiding the need for capital investment in manufacturing plants.

contract research organisation (CRO) A service organisation that undertakes laboratory or clinical research activities on

behalf of a pharma or biotech company; this has evolved from a project-based model to more strategic relationships.

detail/detailing Detailing refers to a sales call in which a pharmaceutical sales representative ('rep') discusses the merits of a drug in a face-to-face meeting with a doctor and may provide free samples.

direct-to-consumer (DTC) DTC advertising involves communication of promotional messages directly to consumers via print, radio, television and the internet.

disease management initiatives These involve understanding the goals of the healthcare system in addressing a specific disease. The firm then aligns itself with the healthcare providers, to offer an integrated service that improves eventual disease outcomes, positioning its products as one part of the solution.

ethical Ethical medicines can only be obtained with a prescription from a qualified medical practitioner.

evidence-based medicine Basing medical decisions, and decisions to fund therapy, on objective evidence of effectiveness.

Food and Drug Administration (FDA) The FDA is responsible for approving drugs for marketing and regulating the US pharmaceutical market.

generic medicine A generic medicine contains exactly the same active ingredients as the original brand, but is typically launched at less than 60 per cent of the price.

Generics manufacturers cannot use the original manufacturers brand name. Drugs are known by both a brand and a 'generic' name, for example 'Viagra' is a Pfizer brand name; the generic name is 'sildenafil'. Generic names refer to the active ingredients and are independent of manufacturer.

HCV Hepatitis C virus

intellectual property Proprietary knowledge that can be defended against imitation using patent law.

IPO Initial public offering – launch of a company on the stockmarket.

Managed Care Organisation (MCO) MCOs operate within the US healthcare market and act as an interface between patients and healthcare providers such as hospitals. MCOs provide defined healthcare benefits for client populations in return for regular premiums, which may be paid by individuals or their employers.

market exclusivity Period during which a first-in-class drug is the only product of its type on the market and faces no class competition.

National Institute for Clinical Effectiveness (NICE) A government-funded organisation in the UK that aims to provide evidence-based guidelines on the optimal and most cost-effective use of drugs and other medical interventions.

new chemical entity (NCE) A completely new molecule launched as a medical treatment for the first time.

nutraceutical A nutrition (food) product for which health benefits are claimed.

over-the-counter (OTC) medicines OTC medicines can be purchased by consumers without a prescription.

pipeline Drugs that are in development but have not yet reached the market.

Siemens A: exploring the future

Gerry Johnson

Founded in 1847 Siemens is a multinational electrical engineering company that has developed a wide range of products and services for power generation and transmission, infrastructure, industry solutions as well as medical diagnosis. In addition to explaining their business portfolio, this case focuses on their analysis of a changing business environment for the purpose of identifying opportunities for growth.

Introduction

After a successful 30-year career within the company in August 2013, Joe Kaeser became CEO of Siemens. He faced two major challenges. The first was the challenge of improving performance. Since 2011, Siemens had not met the growth targets that had been promised to shareholders, and profit margins lagged behind major competitors such as ABB and General Electric. The *Financial Times* quoted Joe Kaeser: 'We are lagging behind in growth and we must improve here.' It went on to comment that this was not only a symptom of Siemens' complex business environment and the increasing numbers of competitors, but also the disruptive changes in Siemens' industries, not least the global influences on the demand for power affecting the core of Siemens' portfolio.[1]

Siemens (then called Siemens and Halske) was founded in 1847 by Werner von Siemens and Johann Georg Halske. The company initially produced telegraphs but soon started to expand in other electrical, communications and energy-related equipment with ground-breaking innovations in such diverse areas as pacemakers, trains and light bulbs. By 2015, Siemens explained its portfolio as being aligned along the 'value chain of electrification' with products 'designed to generate, transmit, distribute and utilize electrical energy with particularly high efficiency'. It also claimed that Siemens' 'integrated setup not only enables us to leverage opportunities in individual markets; it also allows us to exploit the potential at their interfaces'.[2]

Siemens' business portfolio

With headquarters in Germany, Siemens' businesses spanned power generation, power distribution and the

application of electrical energy. With a group turnover in 2015 of almost €76bn (£60.8bn, $98.8bn),[3] it employed 348,000 people and operated through ten divisions and 50 business units, in 100 different business fields in 190 countries throughout the world. The divisions were as follows:

- **The Power and Gas Division** offered products and solutions for the environmentally-friendly and resource-saving generation of power from fossil fuels as well as solutions for the production and the transport of oil and gas. Customers were utilities, independent power producers, engineering, procurement and construction (EPC) companies as well as the oil and gas industry. The portfolio stretched from gas and steam turbines, generators and compressors to the design and delivery of entire turnkey, integrated power plants.
- **The Wind Power and Renewables Division** was a leading supplier of offshore and onshore wind turbines around the world. The focus had been on bringing down the costs of wind power and streamlining the manufacturing and installation process. In offshore wind power, Siemens was the most experienced company within the industry, with the creation of the world's first offshore wind power plant in 1991 in Denmark.

  Siemens also operated in the hydropower sector. Here it was the only integrated energy company serving the entire energy conversion chain 'from water to wire' with products, solutions and services that required a high degree of coordination.
- **The Power Generation Services Division** provided products and services for power equipment within the utility, oil and gas, and industrial processing industries worldwide. This included factory or field service support, maintenance, repairs, replacements, modernisations and

Special thanks are due to executives of Siemens for their interest and co-operation in the writing of this case. The case was prepared by Gerry Johnson. It is intended as a basis for class discussion and not as an illustration of good or bad practice. © Gerry Johnson 2016. Not to be reproduced or quoted without permission.

upgrades of components, such as gas, steam and wind turbines as well as generators, in large-scale and industrial power plants, and compressors for the oil and gas industry. Siemens also had extensive experience with the remote monitoring and diagnostics of power equipment.

- **The Energy Management Division** was a global supplier of products, systems, solutions and services for the transmission and distribution of electrical power. This included facilities and systems for the low-voltage and distribution power grid level, smart grid and energy automation solutions, power supply for industrial plants and high-voltage transmission systems.

- **The Building Technologies Division** was a leading provider of automation technologies and services for safe, secure and efficient commercial, industrial and public buildings and infrastructures throughout their life cycles. Applications included automation, comfort, fire safety and security. For instance, the division offered a comprehensive portfolio of components, products and systems for the demand-based and efficient control of heating, ventilation and air-conditioning plants.

- **The Mobility Division** provided transportation systems for people and goods by rail and road. In so doing it was concerned with the infrastructure challenges of national economies such as the transport and logistics facilities of cities, the efficiency and safety of rail systems, the integration of rail and road traffic and the optimisation of freight transport. For example, amongst other products and services the portfolio of the Mobility Division included regional as well as intercity and high-speed trains, metro cars, streetcars and light rail, passenger coaches and locomotives but also the signal and control technology for rail-based passenger and freight traffic.

- **The Digital Factory Division** was focused on the automation of discrete manufacturing processes (as in the automotive industry). The aim was to provide a comprehensive portfolio of hardware and software products integrating product design, production engineering and automation. Siemens believed that the integration of data along industrial value chains would become a key criterion for the survival of development and manufacturing companies, so the ultimate goal of the division was the complete digital representation of the entire physical value chain of the manufacturing process. Siemens had created a solution platform for this purpose called 'Digital Enterprise'.

- **The Process Industries and Drives Division** focused on businesses in process industries (e.g. oil companies). It offered support in continuous improvement of the reliability, safety and efficiency of their products, processes and plants through automation, drive technology, industrial software, and services based on technology platforms like Totally Integrated Automation or Integrated Drive Systems.

- **Siemens Healthcare** was one of the world's largest suppliers of technology to the healthcare industry and a leader in medical imaging and laboratory diagnostics. As the healthcare industry shifted from treating illness to managing health, the division was building solutions to enable the integration of diagnostics and therapy so as to enable better planning and execution of minimally invasive treatment options. With traditional strengths in the imaging and laboratory fields, the division was complementing these with management, consulting and digital services, advanced therapy solutions and molecular in-vitro diagnostic products. Given that healthcare was *not* about industrial engineering and because the high cost of growth in the healthcare sector needed external financing, Siemens had decided to give the Healthcare Division more autonomy and manage it separately from the other Siemens divisions as a 'company within the Company'.

- **The Financial Services Division** provided business-to-business financial solutions, supporting customer investments with project and structured financing as well as leasing and equipment finance. This helped Siemens tap into new business opportunities, support the acquisition of new customers and strengthened existing business relationships with financial decision-makers. It also provided financial solutions for Siemens' projects and products, opened the way for new business ideas and public–private partnerships, and signalled confidence to the markets through long-term risk participation (equity-invest). Additionally, the division provided financial risk management services within Siemens.

Figure 1 shows this range of businesses within the divisionalised structure, together with the turnover and profits of each division. Table 1 shows Siemens' financial performance 2010–2015.

The identification of trends and megatrends

In 2006, Siemens believed that 'Recognizing relevant, long-term changes, i.e. closely studying megatrends, (was) a strategic requirement for sustainable corporate success'.[4] This still held in 2012 when Siemens undertook a major environmental scanning exercise with the aim of identifying trends that could affect Siemens' businesses over and beyond the next decade. It involved the scanning of reports on environmental change from universities, consultancies, analysts, governments and

Figure 1 Divisional structure and key performance data (as of October 2014)

	Power and gas	Wind power and renewables	Power generation services	Energy management	Building technologies	Mobility	Digital factory	Process industries and drives	Healthcare (separately managed)	Financial services
	e.g. turbines, compressors; power plant solutions	Offshore and onshore		Power transmission	Products & services for energy-efficient buildings	Locomotives, signalling & control systems	Production control	Automation & drive technology	Imaging & diagnostics	
Turnover	€13.2 bn	€5.7bn	Part of PG & WP	€11.9bn	€6.0bn	€7.5bn	€10.0bn	€9.9bn	€12.9bn	Assets €22.0bn
Op/ting profit % on equity after tax	€1.4bn 10.8%	€0.2bn 2.8%		€0.6bn 4.8%	€0.6bn 9.2%	€0.6bn 7.8%	€1.7bn 17.5%	€0.5bn 5.4%	€2.2bn 16.9%	IBIT €6.0bn

Table 1 Financial performance 2010–2015 (key figures in €bn)

	FY 2010	FY 2011	FY 2012	FY 2013	FY 2014	FY 2015
Revenue[1]	65.1	69.6	74.7	73.4	71.9	75.6
Net income	3.9	5.9	4.3	4.4	5.5	7.4
EPS (basic) in €	4.28	6.55	4.74	5.08	6.37	8.84
Free cash flow	7.1	5.3	4.7	5.3	5.2	4.7

[1]Continuing operations

international agencies such as the World Economic Forum, the World Bank, the OECD and the United Nations. It also involved over 130 interviews with internal and external experts from different regions of the world. Each trend identified was considered in terms of its likelihood, its potential impact on markets and industry structures as well as the potential impact on Siemens.

The potential impact of future trends on Siemens: the development of themes of change

The study identified 57 future trends that could impact on Siemens' businesses. These were then categorised in terms of five megatrends: demographic change, climate change, urbanisation, globalisation and digitalisation. Table 2 shows some of these trends and how they relate

Table 2 Trends and megatrends

Trends	Megatrends
• Automation, robotics and self-learning machines • Individualised manufacturing: from mass manufacturing towards individualisation • Biotech growth • Big data, information explosion • Digital integration within and across businesses	Digital transformation
• Population growth • Ageing societies • Bottom of the pyramid: increase in population with very low incomes • Connectedness via internet, mobile communication, etc. • War for talent: increasing competition in the West for scarcer talent pool • Individualisation; i.e. people's expectation of products and services to meet individual needs	Demographic change
• Growth of urban agglomerations • Infrastructure investment needs given urban development, especially in developing countries • Decentralisation of power generation and supply	Urbanisation
• Resource scarcity • Greater number of natural disasters • Alternative energy sources • Water scarcity	Climate change
• New economic growth areas • Rising global competition • Public sector under pressure	Globalisation

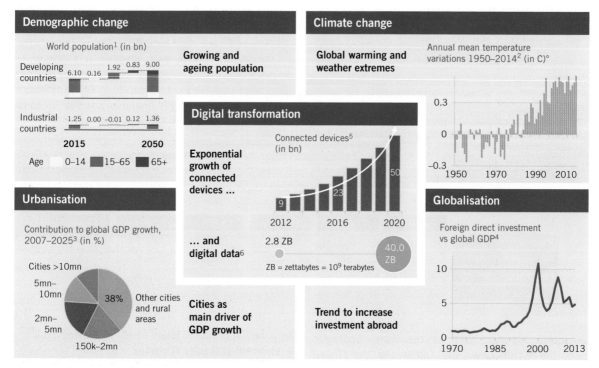

Figure 2 Five megatrends shaping our world of tomorrow

Sources: 1. UN World Population Prospects, 2015; 2. Met Office Hadley Centre observations, 2014; 3. McKinsey Global Institute Cityscope, 2011; 4. UNCTAD, 2013; 5. Cisco: The Internet of Everything, 2013; 6. IDC: The Digital Universe, 2012.

to the megatrends and Figure 2 summarises the megatrends themselves.

Arising from these trends, themes of change were derived and analysed in terms of the likelihood of their occurrence and the potential impact on the Siemens businesses. For example, trends such as alternative energy sources, the decentralisation of power generation and supply and infrastructure investment needs were considered in the context of climate change. The resulting thematic scenario was one in which there was a potential major increase in the supply of energy through renewables, but where that supply did not match the requirements of the grid, for example, in terms of the timing and fluctuations of supply in relation to the timing of demand. In such circumstances, it was recognised that there would be a major need for – and possible provision of – a facility not currently existing, identified as the theme of 'storage for renewable energy'. This theme was then considered in terms of its impact on the Siemens portfolio and the likelihood of it happening within the next decade. Impact was considered to be very high; it would provide the opportunity for

localised power generation and storage, thus vastly reducing the need for centralised power plants. It would therefore affect significant parts of the Siemens businesses. On the other hand, the likelihood of the major breakthrough of energy storage in the coming decade was considered to be low to moderate.

A second example related more specifically to the Healthcare Division. It was recognised that changes in healthcare solutions were being triggered by an ageing society: more specifically that the reduced mobility of this age group demanded new solutions adapted to their needs. The potential growth of interconnected devices could also lead to medical equipment and solutions being transportable, more localised and less costly and it could allow for data transfer and speedier consultation with medical specialists. A possibility, then, was that healthcare would be increasingly managed by individuals. The potential impact on Siemens Healthcare was high. Siemens would be expected to provide technical devices to serve the more decentralised services, but, with individuals taking more responsibility for their health, the overall need for treatment technology might decrease.

The potential impact of megatrends on Siemens: the case of digital transformation

One of the megatrends identified was that of digitalisation. Siegfried Russwurm, the Chief Technology Officer of Siemens explained its impact:[5]

'Digitalization (is) a field that is taking command of virtually every aspect of our daily lives. From connected devices in our private lives to increasingly connected complex systems in the industrial space – we all live in a more and more digitalized world. At Siemens, we are at the forefront of digitalization in our industries. We are leveraging digitalization to combine the physical and the virtual world. The *physical world* is represented by our huge installed base around the globe – ranging from gas and wind turbines to our trains and our medical imaging equipment. . . . We have become a leader in the electrification and automation of power plants and grids, transportation, buildings and production systems.

For many years now, another dimension has been added to this . . . the *virtual world* . . . for example . . . in integrating product design, production engineering and automation – including sophisticated simulation and verification capabilities . . . .

At present, more than 280,000 devices in our installed worldwide base are connected via a secure communication platform through the Internet. They generate huge amounts of condition and performance data, and we apply our . . . know-how to generate specific insights from this data. Ultimately, we use these insights to improve the resilience of electricity grids, optimize energy efficiency in buildings, help surgeons conduct image-guided therapies – or a thousand other things that keep our modern world running.

So . . . digitalisation . . . is about leveraging digital technologies like data analytics and cloud computing along our entire portfolio to create business opportunities in three ways:

- First . . . it enhances our electrification and automation business . . . . In Riyadh, for example, we just won a 1.6-billion-euro order for a driverless metro system. The trains will employ a large set of sensors, IP communication and advanced automation software . . . (to) . . . improve throughput by up to 50 per cent and at the same time deliver 15 per cent energy savings. . . . In India, . . . we won two projects to build smart distribution grids across 19 Indian cities. Several thousand smart units now collect sensor data from distribution substations and relay this data to central distribution control centers. These in turn integrate a range of IT systems to ensure fast fault elimination and improve grid availability and resilience. . . . The benefits are much more stable grid operations and at the same time up to 50 per cent reduction in losses.

- Second, . . . service is a strong lever for profit and growth at Siemens, and we have a unique advantage: the ability to leverage all the data from those 280,000 connected devices worldwide to expand our digital service offers. The 99.9 per cent on-time track record for Velaro trains in Spain or the 5.5 million euros in energy savings for a hotel group are just two examples of how our analytics-driven operations and maintenance improve our services, while saving money for our customers.

- A significant percentage of our gas turbine customers have long-term contracts . . . . We remotely monitor their machines and collect operations data. We now combine this data with our know-how of the underlying physics to build very accurate deterministic models that predict equipment and component wear and tear under different operating conditions. For example, we can predict the condition and service need of a turbine blade for a particular turbine operating 20,000 hours at peak load vs. one operating in volatile load cycles. . . .

- Using our analytics-based models, we can (also) optimize our spare parts inventory and our service technicians' scheduling by predicting replacement needs. In addition additive manufacturing helps us to provide selected spare parts with unprecedented speed.

- Third . . . is our ability to optimally leverage our leading integrated portfolio of vertical software . . . For example, one of our customers, a leading global machine tool vendor, offers its customers in addition to a real machine a virtual machine – a fully functional digital twin. Together we have developed a software solution that . . . allows its customers to simulate and optimize the production of highly complex parts using actual machine data prior to production. This highly precise simulation reflects the real time behaviour of the machine with a deviation of less than 1 per cent – and saves customers up to 80 per cent of set-up time without keeping the real machine away from productive work. This in turn translates into shorter time-to-market and lower costs.'

The result of the environmental scanning confirmed that major changes were likely to happen globally. For CEO Joe Kaeser that meant that the next decade would provide major opportunities to further develop the company. Still, important questions remained. Were these indeed the trends that Siemens' strategy needed to be built on and what were the implications for Siemens and its businesses?

Notes and references
1. C. Bryant, 'Siemens battles to close profitability gap as revenues stagnate', *Financial Times*, 6 November 2014.
2. *Vision 2020: Siemens strategy overview*, 2014, Siemens.com.
3. €1 = £0.8 = $1.3.
4. The Siemens Megatrend Report, October 2006, Siemens.com.
5. These are extracts from 'Digitalization Strategy', a presentation made on 9 December 2014 in Berlin by Professor Dr Siegfried Russwurm, Chief Technology Officer and a member of the Managing Board of Siemens AG.

The 'pub': decline of a British institution – how the brewers fought back

Stephen J. Oliver and Barry Whitehouse

This case study examines the prevailing market conditions in the UK brewing industry from the perspective of the UK's largest remaining brewers, Marston's and Greene King, both of which brew beer and operate large pub estates. They occupy the middle ground of the market between the international mega-brewers and the resurgent micro-breweries. The industry has seen significant change due to shifts in the market structure, demand and the position of the 'pub' in UK society.

The plight of the pub

Pubs (public houses) are a uniquely British institution, offering food, drink and social entertainment to the masses. The type of pub available is very varied, from idyllic thatched country pubs to backstreet 'boozers'. They all cater for a wide range of customers and for centuries have formed part of the social history of the UK. On his recent visit to the UK the Chinese President Xi Jinping insisted on visiting a pub, the 'Plough' near Chequers, with Prime Minister David Cameron to sample a pint of ale and eat a traditional fish and chips meal. Numerous surveys cite 'the pub' as one of the top tourist attractions in the UK.

As the pub market has grown more sophisticated, responding to the change in consumer habits, companies have had to adapt their strategies. The days of the 'wet-led' pub, where sales of drinks were the main source of revenue, were numbered and many of these closed. The regeneration of many urban areas, as well as societal changes in the nature of work and the traditional role of men within the family, also changed pub-going habits. In the aftermath of the smoking ban in public places in

2007, many pubs closed their doors forever. At the height of the recession in 2009, some 50 pubs per week were closing,[1] although there are still over 50,000 pubs in the UK (see Figure 1). In the place of the traditional pub came the development of a new type of pub-restaurant. These ranged from so-called gastro-pubs, which were quasi-restaurants, to large family-oriented pubs offering play areas for children, a wide range of wines and soft drinks, with a strong emphasis on food sales.

The changing industry

For many years, the UK brewing and pub industry was characterised by vertical integration, in which the brewers also owned pubs that were 'tied' to the brewery for their beer supplies. This provided the brewery with a guaranteed market for their beer and created supply chain efficiencies, albeit at the expense of consumer choice. No other major market in the world had the same system; indeed in the US it was illegal to own the means of both production and distribution.

The traditional British beer is 'ale'. This is usually dark, continues to ferment in the cellar (in a cask) and is

Figure 1 Total number of pubs in the UK
Source: British Beer and Pubs Association (BBPA).

Stephen J. Oliver is MD of TrigPoint Coaching and Development Ltd and was formerly the Managing Director of Marston's Beer Company. Barry Whitehouse is Senior Lecturer in Strategy at Wolverhampton University Business School. This case study is intended as a basis for class discussion and not as an illustration of good or bad practice.

highly hopped to give it a distinct bitter flavour. Continental beers ('beer' is a generic term) tend to be 'lagers', much lighter in colour, colder, pasteurised and bottom fermented. Stouts, e.g. Guinness, are very dark and usually strong in alcohol. The ingredients are long-standing: grain, hops, yeast, lots of water and heat!

As foreign travel made British consumers more cosmo-politan in their tastes, they demanded more interesting brands of beer as substitutes for their regular ale. Premium lagers such as Beck's Bier from Germany and Pilsner Urquell from the Czech Republic entered the UK lager market, providing a bridgehead for the entry of other inter-national brewers into the UK. Anheuser-Busch of the US brought its key brand Budweiser to the UK to capitalise on the growth in lager, which rapidly overtook ale. Big adver-tising budgets were funded from the substantial margins generated, and weaker secondary and tertiary brands failed, driven out by the power brands.

Direct government intervention in the pub and brewing sector over several decades helped create giant pub companies ('pubco's') such as Punch Taverns and Enterprise Inns, which came to own over 30 per cent of the market. In the late 1980s, the UK government introduced legislation, The Beer Orders (1989), which forced Brewers with over 2000 pubs to decide between brewing or pub ownership, by making them dispose of half of the excess. Over the course of less than a decade, multiple pub oper-ators and the new pubcos went from nowhere to controlling a third of the market. These pub groups were able to exer-cise considerable buyer power over the brewers. Profit margins in brewing businesses were under severe pressure and industry consolidation was encouraged.

Consumer habits were changing too, as people's increasingly comfortable homes became more of a focus of their social life and 'cocooning'[2] drove the significant growth in the 'take home' market. The home became a social hub instead of the pub. While in the 1980s the vast majority of beer sales were through pubs ('on trade'), by 2015 over 50 per cent of all sales were through the 'off-trade' of supermarkets and off-licenses.[3] The 'off-trade' sector is dominated by the UK's four big supermarket chains, each of which has immense buying power and where the price of alcohol is significantly cheaper, often being used as a 'loss-leader' to lure consumers into the stores, which are also engaged in a price war and a desperate battle for market share. This has led to large-scale pub closures as beer drinkers were drawn in by the off-trade price differential of around 150 per cent: based on the British Beer and Pub Association (BBPA) data, almost 15 per cent of pubs closed between 2000 and 2015, particularly 'wet-led' pubs where beer sales were the major source of income, compared to those that focused on providing drinks and food. Figure 2 shows off- and on-trade sales of beer between 2000 and 2014.

The impact of falling demand was compounded by the rising price of alcohol, largely triggered by the amount of tax and duty levied on the products of the industry by the UK government and thus beyond the control of the brewers. As can be seen from the BBPA Beer Story (2015) diagram (Figure 3), this is significantly higher than for most other European countries.

New competitors

In 2002, the government introduced progressive beer duty (PBD), which meant that smaller brewers paid significantly less beer duty than larger breweries. It was designed to encourage new start-ups. The cost of small-scale brewing technology dropped as more suppliers entered the market. In 2000, there were around 20 new start-ups nationally. This rocketed in the years after the introduction of PBD, peaking in 2013 with a total of 224 starting operations.[4] This was the peak of the micro-brewery or 'craft beer' boom that was born in the USA and imported to the UK. New entrants came to market, experimenting with new beer styles and exciting variants of old favourites. The pub market was less 'tied' than ever and they found publicans willing to stock their beers in place of established brands such as Marston's Pedigree and Greene King IPA. Some of the start-ups rapidly went on to achieve international success, such as the Scottish brewer Brewdog, and some were sold to

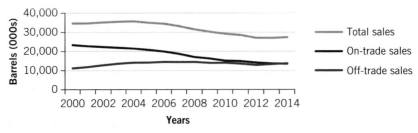

Figure 2 UK off-trade and on-trade sales of beer, 2000–2014
Source: British Beer and Pubs Association (BBPA).

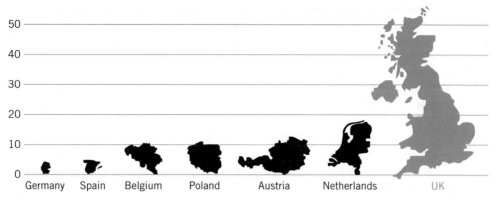

Figure 3 Beer duty rates in top six EU brewing nations (pence per pint of 5% ABV beer)

Source: British Beer and Pubs Association (BBPA).

multinationals, such as Camden Town Brewery, which was acquired by global giant AB InBev for £85m[5] in December 2015.

The break-up of traditional vertically integrated brewers also encouraged many start-up businesses into the tenanted pubco market. New chains of higher-quality managed pub groups such as Wetherspoon, Laurel, Spirit and M&B were created, as barriers to entry fell, following the change to the 'tie'. The traditional regional mid-sized vertically integrated brewer pub owners such as Marston's and Greene King faced big strategic decisions. Did they sell out part of their operations to focus on brewing or did they become pubcos? Or was there a third strategic option of remaining vertically integrated, particularly as the government had by 2002 relaxed the rules on pub ownership?

Strategic responses

Greene King and Marston's embarked on rival takeovers of other breweries. Greene King, based in eastern England, was keen to extend its geographic distribution. Founded in 1799, it has a proud brewing heritage and has built a broad-based business with breweries, pubs, restaurants and hotels. Marston's is also over 180 years old and was firmly based in the English Midlands, with very wet-led pubs and traditional ales. Marston's strategy was to grow rapidly by geographical expansion and acquiring new brands, both beer and pub, e.g. the Pitcher & Piano chain. Each company found itself often bidding against its direct competitor for a third-party target. The prevailing strategic approach became 'dog eat dog', as acquiring critical mass and generating growth through acquisition, rather than organic development, was seen as the quickest response to pressures from financial investors. Marston's bought a credible

competitor brand, Hobgoblin, in the rapidly growing premium bottled ale (PBA) sector of the off-trade[6], as well as market and category expertise in that sector, which it had lacked. It also invested in building its own bottling lines, as the costs of outsourcing bottling were becoming prohibitive, and in addition offered opportunities for contract packaging work for other brewers.

Marston's kept open most of the breweries it acquired and used the brands, distribution channels and pubs it now owned to develop new regions for sales and distribution. In contrast, Greene King followed a centralised strategy, closing down breweries and integrating the operations into its HQ in East Anglia. The multimillion pound synergies or cost-savings created were significant and were a key driver of the strategy. The Scottish Belhaven business was an exception and Greene King used its new purchase to build a Scottish distribution base. Unlike Marston's, Greene King aggressively culled its brand portfolio and pumped marketing support into its key brands such as IPA and Old Speckled Hen, to challenge Marston's for sector share.

Both companies were adopting a modern version of vertical integration. They were consolidating the regional breweries sector, focusing single-mindedly on the UK, and beginning to invest heavily in M&A (Greene King) and/or building new managed pubs. Marston's started to extend its managed portfolio by building pubs in Scotland and across the whole of the UK, well beyond its original Midlands base. Marston's raised £140m in 2009 to build around 20 pubs per year, becoming the country's largest builder of new pubs. By contrast, Greene King built its managed business mainly by buying other pub companies. Their largest acquisition was the £773m purchase of Spirit (1200 pubs) in 2015, making Greene King the UK's largest managed pub operator, with over 3000, well ahead of its rival Marston's which had 1600.

Both businesses brew and market ales as their primary products. Lager is still a significant sector in pub retailing and so key suppliers to both companies are the international brewers, which focus on well-known lager brands such as Carling, Fosters, Peroni and Stella Artois. The control of routes-to-market through their directly managed pubs gives Greene King and Marston's a degree of protection against supplier domination and strength. They are able to negotiate effective prices for the main lager brands because they hold the key to distribution through their own pubs. They can also exert more direct influence over the quality of the consumer experience.

Marston's and Greene King both set out their pub strategies to capitalise on the consumer's interest in casual dining. Preparation and cooking of food at home was becoming less popular as households found their working hours increasing and commuting times lengthening. As ready meals and convenience food offerings from supermarkets continued to grow,[7] pub restaurants found that their competitors included large food retailers such as Marks & Spencer with their 'Gastropub' convenience food range and deals such as 'Dine in for Two for £10'.

By 2014, the rate of pub closures in the UK had slowed, but some sources still estimated that 30 pubs shut their doors for good every week. Marston's strategy of building new pubs would seem counter-intuitive but their CEO Ralph Findlay stressed that 'good pubs are doing really well, whereas pubs which aren't attracting anyone will close.'[8] Findlay's 'new build strategy' is a slower way of generating incremental growth than Greene King's acquisition-led approach. Some financial analysts favoured the premium paid by Greene King to acquire ready-made pubs while others viewed Marston's as creating shareholder value through building them on greenfield sites.

Back in 2006, Marston's had conducted extensive consumer research to understand how pubs were being used, what different consumer groups wanted from the pub, and how best to develop new offerings. This led to what Marston's dubbed the F-plan, which stood for 'females, family, food and forty-to-fifty somethings', clearly defining the principal target clientele for their pub restaurants. Given that the traditional market for many pubs was beer-drinking young males, this was a significant change in approach. Longer-term demographic trends showed how consumers were growing older. Over a decade Marston's actively 'churned' its estate of pubs in response, selling off poorer quality pubs with heavy reliance on 'wet sales' and little opportunity to do food well. Consumers responded positively to the growing eating-out market. They sought pubs which offered good value, good quality and in a convenient location.

Consumers wanted an experience as well as food, so décor, customisation of meals, healthy options and flexibility of serving times, as well as customer service have become fundamental differentiators.

For both companies the pub operations now represent the bulk of corporate profits[9]. Their brewing operations are still culturally important, however. Nevertheless, despite the strong competition in the sector, including from many micro or craft brewers, Marston's share of total premium cask ale had grown to 17.6 per cent by 2015[10] and 21.7 per cent of bottled ale. In the same period Greene King's share of total ale grew by 40 basis points to ten per cent.

Significantly, the global brewing industry leader AB InBev has been acquiring successful micro-brewers to gain a foothold in this segment of the US market and also in Brazil. They have set up a 'Disruptive Growth' team which includes these micro-brewers. The development of craft beers and micro-brewers is now a global development. At the other end of the scale, AB InBev agreed a takeover of industry number two, SABMiller in 2016 (see the Megabrew case study), a deal worth £71bn which would create a 'mega-brewer' company, producing a third of all the world's beer with global brands such as Budweiser, Stella Artois, Grolsch, Peroni, Corona, Miller and Beck's.[11] In 2011, Molson Coors, another major international brewer, had moved from simply distributing Cornish brewer Sharp's ales to taking them over, and has since secured the widest distribution for any ale in the UK – another clear sign that the giants of the industry were prepared to buy their way into the ale market rather than going through organic development.

The microbrewery or craft beer revolution brought new, younger consumers into the beer market and sales of premium cask beer grew for the first time in years. Traditional breweries had to adapt to the new entrants and some, like Greene King, set up in 2013 their own craft small batch beer plant brewing beers that would appeal to 'affluent 25–40-year-old young professionals. Trend-setting early adopters with a work hard, play hard attitude to life'.[12] Marston's already had a wide range of ale brands, with its five breweries (Banks's, Marston's, Jennings, Wychwood and Ringwood) and eight brand families (beers from the above breweries plus Brakspear, Thwaites and Mansfield) but then launched a new range of craft beers under the 'Revisionist' label, playing down associations with the parent brand. In this increasingly competitive market, bottled beers became even more important and Marston's excelled in the off-trade sector, selling 55 per cent of its beers through supermarkets.[13] Marston's brewing division achieved UK sector leadership with a 20 per cent share of both premium bottled and premium cask beers. Meanwhile, Greene King focused on the larger standard ale sector and, helped by its iconic IPA brand, it has remained the UK's largest cask ale brewer and the market leader for managed pubs.

In the changing environment in which the UK brewers operate, there are still some serious questions about their future, e.g. can the vertical integration of the two indigenous players, Marston's and Greene King hold off the mega- and microbrewers and resist competitive pressures from the pubcos and supermarkets? There are also questions about the future of the pub itself, e.g. will craft beers and better food offerings save it from the increasing competition of casual dining outlets, supermarkets and particularly from the seemingly inexorable rise of the coffee shops (some of which are starting to sell alcoholic drinks too)? Although the pub has been an iconic part of British life for centuries, is it in danger of become extinct during the twenty-first century?

Notes and references
1. Institute of Economic Affairs, 'Closing time – who's killing the British pub'?, Christopher Snowdon, December 2014.
2. 'Cocooning' is used to describe people socialising less and spending time at home. The name was coined in the 1990s by Faith Popcorn, a trend forecaster and marketing consultant.
3. British Beer and Pub Association.
4. *The Brewery Manual 2015*, p. 28.
5. £1 = €1.2 = $1.5.
6. +10.5% year-on-year growth (IRI, BBPA data, Marston's PBA Report 2015).
7. +5.1% per annum to April 2015, worth £37.7bn (Institute of Grocery Distribution).
8. Interview with *This is Money*, August 2014.
9. 87% of Marston's profits from pub operations, 13% from brewing (Marston's Annual Report and Accounts 2015); Greene King 15% from brewing (Greene King Annual Report and Accounts 2015).
10. Marston's Annual Report and Accounts 2015.
11. S. Daneshkhu, 'AB InBev makes formal £71bn bid for SABMiller', *Financial Times*, 11 November 2015.
12. Greene King website.
13. Marston's Annual Report and Accounts 2015.

CASE STUDY

Ricoh Canada Inc.: printing the future or recycling the past?

Jonathan Fast and Prescott C. Ensign

Ricoh Canada Inc. (RCI) had long relied on its business model to become a national leader in digital print and imaging, but a combination of changing consumer behaviour and competition threatened the profitability of this segment. RCI was faced with the daunting task of moving away from its legacy business towards the unknown services market. Addressing the issue of strategic decision-making during a critical corporate transformation, this case is well suited to industry and competitive analysis, as well as discussions of strategic positioning: RCI had to assess itself as an organisation and its place in the market to create a sustainable growth strategy.

In January 2016, Glenn Laverty, President and CEO of Ricoh Canada Inc. (RCI), was going to meet with his executive management team to develop the company's strategy for the next three years. RCI, a wholly owned subsidiary of Ricoh Americas Corporation, had its head office in Toronto, Ontario, and employed over 2100 people in Canada. Its parent, Ricoh Company Ltd, head-quartered in Japan, was an international leader in the digital imaging and document management industry. It operated in more than 200 countries and regions and employed 108,000 people worldwide. Ricoh Company Ltd had worldwide sales of US$20bn[1] in FY2015.

RCI was facing saturation in the market segment that was its primary source of revenue – delivery and mainte-nance of printing/copying devices to customers. Canon and Xerox were both strong competitors in this segment, and Laverty was concerned: 'We will see an increasingly rapid shrinkage in our traditional market during the next five years.'[2] Areas of opportunity included document management systems and IT services. RCI defined services as a combination of on-site and off-site resources that supported business operations infrastructure. These resources included cloud computing, remote monitoring and other innovations.

Laverty openly admitted his dilemma with services by saying, 'What services to develop further and how aggressively to market them is still an unknown.' He knew that providing more services would require additional investment, but the questions of how much and to what areas were the real issues. Given RCI's current financial position, how realistic was it for RCI to transition to a services company?

Background

RCI adopted its current name in 1997, but had been operating in Canada under various names since 1924. RCI was a sales organisation that used a lease and service model with its office imaging equipment. All the equipment was manufactured in Ricoh's high-quality and efficient facilities in Japan. RCI's focus was on using its direct channel and dealer network to sell and service the inventory coming from Japan. RCI moved into digital printing in the 1990s and became a dominant player in the Canadian market. It accounted for 20 per cent of Canadian market sales in the high-end multifunction product segment in FY2015 (see Figures 1 and 2).

In August 2008, the parent company, Ricoh Company Ltd, acquired IKON Office Solutions (IKON) for US$1.6bn. IKON was the world's largest independent provider of docu-ment management systems and services. It used copiers, printers and multifunction printer technologies from leading manufacturers, and document management software and systems from companies like Captaris Inc., Kofax Ltd and Electronics for Imaging Inc. The acquisition strengthened Ricoh's North American direct sales network and gave it control of the dealer network on which its largest compet-itor, Canon Inc., relied heavily. Following the acquisition, workforce integration did not take place as rapidly as Ricoh Company Ltd management had anticipated.

Jonathan Fast and Prescott C. Ensign are at the Lazaridis School of Business & Economics, Wilfrid Laurier University, Waterloo, Ontario, Canada. Reproduced with permission from Thunderbird Case Series #A09-15-0006, Thunderbird School of Global Management, Arizona State University.

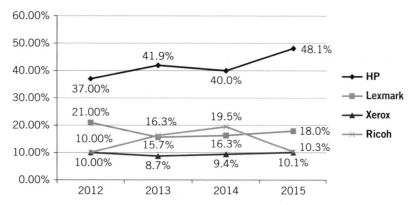

Figure 1 Laser printer market share – A4, A3, dealer and direct
Source: Internal company documents.

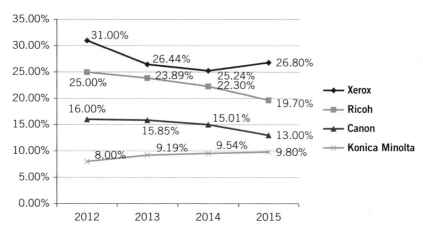

Figure 2 Multi-function product (printer, scanner, fax) market share (US$1000+)
Source: Internal company documents.

State of the market

In 2015, Laverty had asked his management team to look at the state of the services market. The way he saw it, three trends were pushing RCI towards services: shifts in technology, user behaviour and corporate behaviour. The advent of digital storage and document management technologies meant that customers were printing fewer documents. Using digital documents allowed for faster and more effective workflows as well as greater accessibility. Digital documents were available to anyone over the internet. Laverty mentioned that 'Modern businesses were striving to become paperless offices, which is a very scary thing for anyone at Ricoh to say out loud.'

The team found that the Canadian services market was worth US$24bn in 2015. By comparison, the size of the hardware/break-and-fix market – RCI's primary revenue source – was US$4.5–5bn with growth in 2015 of two per cent. It was clear that technological advancements in tablet and mobile device networks were disrupting RCI's

legacy business. By 2019, the printer/copier market was estimated to shrink by three per cent annually, and this downward trend would accelerate after that point. Glenn pointed out, 'It has never been easier not to print something, and that means trouble for everyone in the industry. We have to adapt or face extinction.' Early signs of this were already present; mergers and acquisitions activity had been rampant in the traditional market as big competitors sought to protect profits by buying competitors. As Laverty told his management team:

> **'If we stay only in the printer business, RCI will be squeezed at both ends. We will see a decline in sales and a decline in the subsequent stream of income from maintenance. Where the market will stabilize once it begins to contract is unknown. So we have to move beyond this segment. Planning for negative growth is not acceptable.'**

When the services market was broken down further, it became clear that big changes were taking place with medium-sized businesses. It could be seen that 42 per cent of services spending was going to be made by medium-sized businesses in 2016. This represented a 7.4 per cent spending increase year over year. The cost of services had come down to an inclusive price point where medium-sized businesses could take advantage of what was offered and, consequently, usage was increasing. After seeing this, VP of Services Mike Fast commented, 'What we are seeing here is the good kind of deflation which is produced by increases in efficiency allowing better products to be sold cheaper and to a wider market.' RCI had a two per cent market share in the services market for medium-sized businesses, or, in RCI terms, firms that fit into RCI's geographic/key named accounts classifications. Another major trend was small to medium-sized businesses shifting towards cloud services where IT infrastructure was handled for them. As volume on the cloud increased, cloud services were able to achieve economies of scale and flexibility. From a consumer perspective, using the cloud was much more cost-effective than upgrading an in-house server network and corresponding support resources. Finally, companies were demanding software to better share information across an organisation whether it be document management, process management or communication management.

Consumer studies of the services market indicated that consumers considered a long list of factors when assessing a provider. These included: cost-effectiveness; environmental sustainability; information security and compliance; business process streamlining; change management; worker productivity; information optimisation; and strategic infrastructure. VP of Marketing Eric Fletcher advised Glenn that all of his team's research had been pointing to one factor: 'The primary interest of consumers was a provider who could unify services in the company at a reasonable cost.'

Competition in Ricoh Canada Inc.'s market

Tier 1 competitors – Canon, Xerox and HP

Canon Canada Inc. had relied heavily on IKON for both unit sales and service infrastructure, so it was focusing on rebuilding this channel after IKON was acquired by Ricoh. In March of 2010, Canon Inc. acquired Océ N.V. (based in the Netherlands) to increase its market share in the digital space as well as to expand its research and development. Canon Inc. was positioned as a leader in managed print and content services according to Gartner Inc.'s proprietary research.

Xerox Corporation entered the services market in February 2010 with the acquisition of Affiliated Computer Services Inc. (ACS), an IT services firm based in Dallas, Texas. In Canada, Xerox was maintaining traditional core unit sales while encouraging its sales force to sell services. Its cash flow from the traditional product lines was expected to fund the expansion into services. Xerox Canada had performed well with its major accounts in healthcare and government. Recently, Xerox had launched cloud services.

Hewlett-Packard Company (HP), in Canada and world-wide, had a very strong brand and customer network for its IT hardware. It was using this reputation to move into services. HP acquired EDS (Electronic Data Systems) on 28 August 2008 to give it the ability to combine hardware and services to create holistic offerings to customers. The integration of services with hardware was ongoing.

Tier 2 competitors – Konica Minolta and others

Konica Minolta Business Solutions Canada Ltd was strong in the A3 (standard European format) printer segment, and was upgrading its current line-up. Konica Minolta products had good image quality and performance, as well as low cost on a cost per page basis, making it hard for others to compete in this segment.

Lexmark had left the inkjet printing business and turned its attention to improving its A4 (standard North American format) laser printer line-up. Lexmark was on an acquisition spree, year after year gobbling up software companies to support its growth objectives.

Within the services landscape, there were several other large competitors – specifically, Google, IBM and Amazon with highly developed cloud services.

Ricoh Canada Inc.'s customer base

RCI had sold business-to-business (B2B) with 89 per cent of sales made directly to business customers, and the remaining 11 per cent of sales made by independent dealers. RCI did not have a business-to-consumer (B2C) line, although most of RCI's primary competitors (Canon, Xerox and HP) did. Laverty did not see the B2C market providing long-term growth because it was so competitive. However, he was open to anything should sufficient evidence be presented.

Part of RCI's strategic dilemma was that the profile of its customers was morphing rapidly. Customers were changing what they wanted and discriminating more when making purchase decisions. Laverty said, 'Studies show that 57 per cent of consumers are well informed.' Given the deterioration of information asymmetry in the industry, RCI was trying to build on experience and relationships with customers. RCI top management believed that a positive customer experience would still resonate more than any other factor. Laverty felt this should

Table 1 Projected spending growth for major accounts and strategic accounts

Industry	2015	2016	2017	2018	2019	Trends
Healthcare	7%	6%	7%	6%	6%	• Paper intensive to electronically automated • Cloud-based storage and sharing • Mobile workflow
Legal	4%	4%	4%	5%	5%	• Huge growth in electronically stored information • Legal process outsourcing • Working remotely and information security
Government	–1%	–1%	2%	2%	3%	• Shared cloud hubs in 65% of provinces by 2018 • Need for more cross-government collaboration
College/University	3%	3%	3%	4%	4%	• More e-learning on smaller budgets • Looking for cost reductions and ongoing support
Public School K-12	0%	2%	3%	4%	3%	• More e-learning on smaller budgets • Looking for cost reductions and ongoing support
Private School K-12	5%	4%	4%	4%	4%	• More e-learning on smaller budgets • Looking for cost reductions and ongoing support

Source: Internal company documents.

continue to be a priority based on an assessment of the NPS (net promoter score) metric. RCI's customers could be broken down as follows:

- *Geographic accounts* were RCI's smallest customers and typically had only one location. New customers in this segment were generally targeted through cold calling by RCI's sales force. The estimated success rate of cold calling was one in ten. Most new business based on client count was generated in this manner. These customers offered the highest margins because the transactions were usually isolated, rather than drawn out business deals where RCI would be fighting on price.
- *Key named accounts* were small to medium-sized enterprises that had five or six locations. Like geographic accounts, these entities were also targeted through cold calling. Existing accounts in this segment were prime targets for off-cycle selling. That is, once under contract, they were asked to buy more from RCI. According to VP of Sales Peter Ronan, 'Marketing services would fit very well between hardware cycles because it would allow us to increase our share of a customer's wallet through a business relationship that is already established.'
- *Major accounts* included large customers like hospitals and colleges/universities. The complexity of these clients required more customisation in product and services offerings. Together with strategic accounts, this defined the key GEM (government, education and medical) market. Transactions with these entities required more internal resources, often requiring up to six months to complete. RCI was aggressively targeting healthcare accounts because it could leverage its government relationships with these clients. Some of RCI's large customers in this area included Canada's largest board of education as well as a large health-care company in eastern Canada.

- *Strategic accounts* were RCI's largest customers and included banks and substantial government units. They were also the hardest deals to close. These customers generally sent a request for proposal (RFP) to major competitors in the industry and based their decisions on a bidding process that routinely took six months or more. RCI's track record in this realm was mixed, but it had managed to win contracts with a large life insurance company, two of Canada's big five banks, and Canada's largest food retailer. Government units were an area where RCI would have liked to have focused more resources because they offered exposure into the broader public sector. For example, hospitals could buy products using the same prices set in government contracts without having to send out a separate tender.[3] See Table 1 for the projected growth in spending of major and strategic accounts.

Current service offerings

RCI's services could be broken into three segments: Technical Services (traditional break-and-fix); Professional Services; and Managed Services. Technical Services was the largest in terms of revenue, producing US$193m, or 39 per cent of the revenue in 2015, but the growth potential was limited (see Table 2). RCI's total revenue from Professional Services and Managed Services was US$52m in 2015. With regard to Professional Services and Managed Services, Laverty stated, 'Currently, we don't have a lot of volume in these areas, but we have some cool technology. We are just not completely sure how to use all of it. Also, given our relative inexperience in the services market, we need to figure out where RCI should operate relative to competitors.'

Table 2 Services revenue, market share and margin for 2015

Services revenue breakdown	2015 (US$m)	Revenue	Market share	Margin	Annual market growth
Break/fix – hardware maintenance and support	193	39%	23%*	36%	2%
Total technical	**193**				
Managed Document Services (MDS) – business process consulting	4	<1%	1%	21%	3%
Legal Document Services (LDS) – litigation support services	5	<1%	30%	60%	2%
Ricoh Document Management (RDM) – print, fulfilment and imaging	5	1%	1%	20%	–5%
Ricoh Management Services (RMS) – onsite/offsite resources	25	5%	25%	13%	1%
Total managed services	**40**				
IT/Professional Services – solution consulting, IT hardware, remote monitoring, deployment services	12	2%	0%	46%	Consulting – 18%, IT services – 5% ($900bn global market),
Cloud – software as a service (SaaS), backup as a service (BaaS)	0	0%	0%	56%	SaaS – 17.9% ($14.5bn global market), BaaS – 40% ($5.6bn global market)
Total professional services	**12**				

* Based on B2B multi-function printer market only.

Technical Services was based on the legacy business and involved servicing machines in the field. From the standpoint of a service level agreement, customers had become more demanding, and RCI had been able to grow its market share by meeting or exceeding customer expectations. The field technical team of 550 well-trained personnel was the backbone of the service agreements. VP of Services Mike Fast said, 'These guys aren't your traditional copier technicians; they are highly trained, and have competencies, like networking skills, that extend beyond the machine.'

Professional Services helped customers streamline and better integrate their work flow processes. The solutions currently offered included: Managed Document Services (MDS), IT hardware and remote monitoring and deployment services. MDS was designed to increase the efficiency of information transfer within an organisation. For example, the software could read scanned images and automatically route documents to those who approved and/or used them. This concept could extend point-to-point across an organisation using programmed rules that fit the business's structure. MDS helped a small or large company increase its work flow efficiency, manage its network, enhance its security and troubleshoot when problems arose. Revenue for MDS was reported under Managed Services due to corporate restructuring, but was controlled as a part of Professional Services.

Although not yet released, IT services included cloud services and disaster recovery support. RCI's cloud services were intended to be a gateway to critical information. Corporate planning was underway in Japan and margins for this segment of the business were expected to be 56 per cent at launch in the first quarter of 2016.

Managed Services encompassed three areas: (i) imaging print and fulfilment (Ricoh Document Management or RDM); (ii) onsite managed services (Ricoh Management Services or RMS); and (iii) litigation support services (Legal Document Services or LDS). Image print and fulfillment was just as the name suggests: items (e.g., books or posters) were printed for customers and then held in inventory. Onsite managed services were customer-specific services such as conference management, internal print room management and reception services. Legal Document Services was a niche service to support law firms during litigation through a process called electronic document discovery. RCI scanned legal documents and recorded them digitally so that law firms could search and retrieve them.

Services support teams (consultants and solution engineers) operated as an overlay structure to the sales channel, with sales owning the customer relationship. Support teams educated the sales channel and identified opportunities within the market. Furthermore,

Table 3 Sales force breakdown

Dealer operations	2
Sales – corporate	21
Sales – major accounts	84
Sales – geographic/key named accounts	175
Sales – strategic accounts	23
Sales – DDLP (document direction limited partnership)	51
Selling – dealer	15
Selling – software	9
Total	**380**

Source: Author created.

support teams also engaged in more traditional consulting activities focused on enterprise software and hardware needs. In general, the consulting service was free for customers who subsequently bought RCI products. Independent dealers were able to use these support teams to supplement operations, improve knowledge and integrate with RCI.

RCI sales team

RCI's direct sales force of 380 people was focused on maintaining existing customer relationships while hunting for new opportunities. For a breakdown of the sales force by customer segment, see Table 3. For the sales force, the time spent on repeat business versus new business was approximately at a 4 to 1 ratio. Over half of new business in any given year, based on the number of clients, came from geographic accounts that were acquired through cold calling. Overall, RCI had a reputation for treating its sales people well.

RCI's sales force would need additional training if RCI was to continue to expand its services offerings. The current estimate was $6,095 per person (this included rep costs, instructor costs, material, training sessions, a technology show and revenue lost from not selling during training). Kevin Braun, Director of Quality and Strategic Planning, believed this cost might even be too low, saying:

> 'My belief is that we do not spend enough on training our sales team. This is a new area for most of them and we are heavily relying on support staff to assist them in these early stages. This issue is of high priority for the EMT [executive management team], but it is my personal opinion this number should be close to doubled.'

RCI's independent dealer network would have to undergo significant change to address a large-scale shift to services. Most importantly, dealers would have to be interested in selling services. At many dealers, sales people were vested in their positions or near retirement so were not motivated. Glenn Laverty and Peter Ronan recognised the problem: 'We must find a way to encourage the sale of

our services or find new dealers that specialise in selling our services. Although hardware is still a very important part of RCI's business, we must figure out a way to balance the legacy business while creating growth in services.'

The financial quagmire

RCI's investment capital came from income generated by its legacy business. The current CFO, Richard Perri, said, 'The issue RCI presently faces from a financial perspective is how to allocate these funds to generate the best returns.' Laverty and Perri wondered how realistic it was for RCI to invest in services growth given RCI's current financial position. Laverty said, 'We have to make sure we have the internal resources to make a dent in the services market. A lot of these things take scale, and at the very least we need to know how much growth to plan for.' See Table 4 for the income statement and balance sheet of RCI.

Management

In the prior five years, RCI had experienced 110 per cent turnover in its executive management team; some had left voluntarily, while others had been forced out. This turnover reflected the need for creative thinking in the executive suite. The replacements were tech savvy, had fresh ideas and could think outside the box, but the high turnover had created a leadership crisis. According to Laverty.

> 'Recruiting new people and getting them up to speed as a team has not been as fast as we had hoped. It takes time for everyone to settle in. This makes it even more crucial for us to have a strategy for RCI that we can unify around.'

Performance management

Because RCI was part of a Japanese corporation, it followed the practices of its parent. RCI was heavily involved in planning, assessing past performance and revising goals. Every month, each member of the RCI executive management team had a one-on-one meeting with the head of Ricoh Americas Corporation in Caldwell, New Jersey. RCI executives also travelled to Japan biannually for week-long meetings with their counterparts from other regions to discuss the future of the company on a global scale. Laverty often told his management team, 'As an organization, we must always be actively looking for criticism from our customers that will help us refine and improve our operations.' To this end, everyone took the concept of Kaizen (continuous improvement) seriously.

Table 4 RCI financials FY2015 (000s)

Income statement	2015
Revenue	
Sales (hardware)	192,790
Key (incl. DDLP)	91,701
Major accounts	68,338
Strategic accounts	14,551
Dealer sales	18,200
Rental, affiliate and other	12,883
Parts, supplies and paper	45,728
Technical service	192,546
IT/PS services	12,402
IT Services	1,477
Professional services	10,925
Managed services	40,667
Total revenue	**497,016**
Total gross profit	**159,467**
Sales GP%	29.10%
Key (incl. DDLP) GP%	36.10%
Major accounts GP%	26.80%
Strategic accounts GP%	8.10%
Dealer sales GP%	19.20%
Expenses	
Sales	56,094
IT/PS services	3,647
Managed services	3,303
Dealer	2,780
Marketing	9,226
Other	56,370
Total expenses	**131,420**
Operating profit	**28,047**

Balance sheet	2015
Assets	
Current assets	**205,496**
Lease receivable	6,043
Property, plant and equipment, net	16,042
Goodwill	44,863
Intangibles, net	10,967
Future income tax asset	1,580
Pension asset	7,178
	87,579
Total assets	**293,075**
Liabilities	
Current liabilities	**85,276**
Lease payable	6,043
Promissory note	15,252
Other long-term liabilities	2,928
	24,223
Shareholder's equity	
Share capital	72,061
Contributed surplus	23,558
Retained earnings	87,958
	183,577
Total liabilities & shareholder's equity	**293,075**

Source: Internal company documents.

RCI placed emphasis on what it called a net promoter score (NPS). This score was based on customers' responses to the question: 'Would you recommend RCI to another company?' RCI's NPS scores were consistently high (most recent was 56 per cent), while scores from other companies that utilised an NPS assessment were often negative, indicating that more customers would not recommend that company than would. RCI's focus on NPS began because of its lease and service business model – where interactions with the customer were frequent, particularly for machine maintenance. RCI believed that a positive social experience helped promote a long-term relationship, and with 80 per cent of RCI's sales effort focused on repeat customers, it was easy to see why a long-term focus on customers was important. Employees were trained in interpersonal skills so that they handled interactions positively. Laverty often reminded everyone, 'It is amazing just how far a smile can go.'

Services growth strategies

RCI's management team was considering a number of growth strategies for Professional Services and Managed Services. These included growth by acquisitions, partnerships, alliances and/or organic growth.

Any domestic acquisition would have to be funded by RCI, but, were partnerships and alliances more critical for the transition to services than outright acquisitions? Could a partnership or alliance be used for knowledge transfer to Ricoh? How feasible was it to think that another company could provide a foundation for how RCI would compete in the services market?

Could RCI rely solely on organic growth? If history were a guide, RCI would have to rely on the head office in Japan to develop and introduce innovations in services. In this situation, RCI was limited in its ability to tailor products to the Canadian marketplace and would be on the defensive until such time. But, as Laverty told his team, 'Perhaps this isn't impossible. How different could the services in Canada be from those of businesses globally?'

Future threats

RCI management knew that they must fully understand the services market before committing to it. Laverty explained:

'Markets are always moving, and we can't be static in our approach. If we find something that works, our competitors will be right behind us, so we need to account for that. In fact, some of our competitors are already ahead of us in this area and we have to try to leapfrog them and get two steps ahead. Every market we enter will cause a ripple effect and we must plan for the outcomes.'

The final decision

As President and CEO, Laverty wrote to his management team:

'With a corporate shift to Managed and Professional Services, RCI will have to ensure that the Ricoh brand does not erode. We will have to get past the hurdle of being known as the printer guys if we intend to become more than that. Customers will need to be assured that RCI is a serious player in the Managed Services and Professional Services industries, especially when continued support in key functionalities such as cloud services is a priority for a prospective customer. RCI must also figure out a way to handle failures when delivering new services. Since this is new territory for RCI, there is no doubt that unexpected challenges will occur. We must work closely with Eric Fletcher, VP of Marketing, who may be the deciding vote on when the process will occur. With all the competition in the services area, we must move ahead and make our strategic decisions in the very near future. But the important question is still: "How can we grow in the area of services?" We must examine our strengths and come up with a sustainable growth strategy, one that we can put in place that will move us forward over the next three years.'

Having just a generic strategy of growth was not enough, the team would need to create SMART goals (specific, measurable, attainable, relevant and time-bound) as they moved forward. In his communication to the management team, Laverty reminded them: 'Our goals must be specific enough so we can measure progress and adjust. Without specific goals, we will lose sight of what is important and end up stuck between two markets.'

Whatever strategy the team formulated, Laverty would have to back it up to the Board of Directors in Japan. Laverty knew this was a tall order, but he felt his team was ready to work hard to reach this stretch goal.

Notes and references
1. $1 = £0.6 = €0.75.
2. This and other quoted material in the case study was based upon interviews. We thank the executives at Ricoh Canada Inc. for graciously meeting with us.
3. Healthcare was publically run in Canada.

H&M in fast fashion: continued success?

Patrick Regnér and H. Emre Yildiz

This case examines the role of resources and capabilities in building competitive advantage and the key issues to consider while evaluating the sustainability of competitiveness. H&M has enjoyed a leading position in the global fashion and apparel market thanks to its unique concept, business model and ability to combine elegant designs with affordable prices. Key competitors, however, have challenged that position and H&M needs to evaluate the sustainability of competitive advantage derived from its resources and capabilities. The case explores the areas and functions in which H&M has enjoyed advantage vis-à-vis competitors and how, if at all, this advantage can be sustained in the long term.

Introduction

The apparel retailer H&M has made an incredible journey, from a single store established by the founder Erling Persson in Sweden in 1947 to a pioneering 'fast fashion' business with 3700 stores in 61 countries and more than 132,000 employees worldwide. 'Fast fashion' refers to a quick response to new trends and fashion items that are made available in stores immediately thereafter. By the time Persson's 34-year-old grandson Karl-Johan Persson took over as CEO in 2009, H&M had become global leader in the 'fast-fashion' segment with a distinctive business approach that challenged most competitors. The business model, commonly referred to as 'cheap-and-chic', emphasised high fashion at prices significantly below those of competitors, with the fundamental principle being 'Fashion and quality at the best price'.

As the CEO of the company, Mr Persson emphasised the importance of maintaining the company's growth-based strategy, as he stated in the 2014 annual report:

> '2014 was a very good year for H&M, with strong sales and profitability. We are continuing to add value for our customers and to invest for an even stronger H&M. We will open a net total of 400 new stores and nine new online markets in 2015.'

H&M opened another 379 new outlets in 2014 with the addition of flagship stores in key locations such as Milan, Munich and New York, as well as expansion into new markets like Australia and the Philippines. However, H&M was being seriously challenged by Zara, the prime retail brand of Spain's Inditex, which had already overtaken H&M to become the world's biggest fashion retailer by market capitalisation, based on Zara's rapid expansion, particularly in emerging markets. The increased competition, and the fact that margins had started to erode due to increased cotton prices and rising production costs in Asia, put the H&M high-fashion/low-price formula and aggressive expansion under scrutiny. Investors had come to trust H&M's model that relied on a set of unique resources and capabilities, but Zara's success questioned the sustainability of the formula.

The increased competition for consumer spending in the fast-fashion business was further intensified by the poor economic situation. With 70 per cent of shareholder voting rights controlled by the company's founding Persson family, H&M's chief executive Karl-Johan Persson tried to calm investors and emphasised the long-term view:

> 'We have great respect for the economic climate. In this situation it is extra important to have a long-term perspective and to always make sure we give the best combination of fashion and quality for money in every market.'[1]

> '. . . we are investing for the future and we always have the customers in focus. Despite increased purchasing costs, we have continued to strengthen our customer offering – for example, by not raising our prices to customers.'[2]

H&M continued to emphasise the long-term view in its expansion strategy. For 2015, 400 new stores were planned, with China, the USA and the UK expected to be the largest growth markets. They also planned to enter new markets including Taiwan, Peru, Macau, South

---

Africa and India. Despite these aggressive expansion plans, analysts had some doubts:

'There are fears that the product is not good enough, brand appeal is fading or that prices have been undercut by an even cheaper competitor. These are big questions.'

Adam Cochrane, analyst at UBS[3]

The apparel industry

The total market size of the global apparel retail industry in 2014 was $1,317bn (£856bn, €1,014bn),[4] but with an annual growth rate of just 3.8 per cent for the period 2010–14.[5] This slow growth increased competition, which was further intensified by a large number of small players, although the large international incumbents, including Inditex (Zara), Gap and H&M, continued to be the market leaders (see Table 1). An example of the new and vibrant smaller players was the Japanese company, Uniqlo, which had started to expand aggressively. Moreover, fashion is, by its very nature, unpredictable and fickle – trends are prone to sudden changes, which makes competition uncertain. End consumers have an enormous selection of garments to choose from and will quickly adopt new trends. In the 'fast-fashion' category they are also extremely cost conscious and will seek out bargains.

Some of the players in the industry are both producers and retailers. For example, Gap Corporation and Inditex both manufacture their own products and sell them in their own stores. Other retailers have a multitude of suppliers to choose from. As international trade liberalises, the number of suppliers increases and competition

Table 1 H&M and its multinational competitors

	Positioning and segments	Business model	Key figures	Financials
H&M	H&M is a retailer of fashion apparel, cosmetics, accessories and shoes for women, men, teenagers and children. *Collection of Style (COS)* offers customers a combination of timelessness and distinctive trends, for both women and men. The *Monki* stores provide innovative collections and an inspiring fashion experience characterised by playfulness and colourful graphic design. *Weekday* sells its own brands but also commissions design collaborations with independent fashion labels. The *Cheap Monday* stores combine influences from street fashion and subcultures with a catwalk vibe. The latest addition is the luxury store concept *& Other Stories*.	The business is operated from leased store premises, through internet and catalogue sales and on a franchise basis. H&M does not own any factories. Production is outsourced to independent suppliers. H&M's growth target is to increase the number of stores by 10–15% per year, and at the same time increase sales in comparable units. This growth is entirely self-financed. The collections are created by 140 in-house designers.	At the end of 2014, the company had 3261 H&M stores, 114 *COS* stores, 92 *Monki* stores, 22 *Weekday* stores and five *Cheap Monday* stores as well as 130 franchise stores. The group outsources product manufacturing to 700 independent suppliers through its 16 local production offices in Asia and Europe. The company employs more than 132,000 people.	The company recorded revenue of $20,137m in the fiscal year ending November 2014, an increase of 3.84% compared to fiscal 2013. Its net income was $2,691m in fiscal 2014, representing a slight increase compared to a net income of $2,620m in the preceding year.
Inditex (Zara)	The flagship brand of the company is *Zara*. Zara also operates *Kiddy's Class* stores, which specialise in junior fashion. The *Pull and Bear* format offers casual clothing. It caters primarily to young males and females and offers a range that starts from sophisticated urban fashions to casual wear. *Bershka* stores are large and spacious. They are intended to be meeting points for street fashion, music and art. *Massimo Dutti* stores are located in prime retail locations and offer basic, contemporary styles in next-generation fabrics including high-quality garments. *Stradivarius* is aimed at young fashion-conscious customers, offering international fashion with the latest designs. *Oysho* offers fashion trends in women's lingerie and undergarments.	With an in-house design and a tightly controlled factory and distribution network, the company has the ability to take a design from drawing board to store shelf in just two weeks. That enables *Zara* to launch new items every week, which keeps customers coming back again and again to check out the latest styles. The company also has a policy of zero advertising and instead invests its revenues in opening up new stores.	*Zara* is present in 87 countries, with a network of 1991 stores located in major cities throughout the world. *Pull and Bear* has opened 853 shops in the main streets and shopping centres of 63 countries. *Massimo Dutti* operates 665 stores in 63 countries. The *Bershka* sales format has 954 stores in 66 countries. There are currently 858 *Stradivarius* stores in 56 countries. There are currently 549 *Oysho* stores in 39 countries.	The company recorded revenue of $20,480m in the fiscal year ending January 2015, which represents a decrease of about 10% compared to fiscal 2014. Its net income was $2,826m during 2014, compared to a net income of $3,212m in the preceding year.

(continued)

Table 1 H&M and its multinational competitors *(continued)*

	Positioning and segments	Business model	Key figures	Financials
Gap	Under the *Gap* brand, the company offers an extensive range of apparel at moderate price points. *Banana Republic* was acquired by the company in 1983. This brand offers sophisticated, fashionable collections at higher price points than the Gap brand. The Old Navy brand was launched in 1994 to address the market for value-priced family apparel. The brand *Athleta* offers customers performance-driven women's sports and active apparel and footwear for a variety of activities.	The company operates through two segments: stores and direct. The stores segment includes the results of the retail stores for each of the company's brands: Gap, Banana Republic, Old Navy and Athleta. The direct segment includes the results of the online business for each of the company's web-based brands.	By the end of fiscal year 2014, Gap had 3280 company-operated and 429 franchise stores. Of the company-operated stores, 1398 were operated under *Gap* brand, 1022 run with *Old Navy* label, 650 stores sell *Banana Republic* branded apparels and the remaining 103 stores sell *Athleta, Piperlime* and *Intermix* brands.	The company recorded revenue of $16,435m in the fiscal year ending January 2015, an increase of 1.7% compared to fiscal 2014. Its net income was $1,262m in fiscal 2015, compared to a net income of $1,280m in the preceding year.
UNIQLO	The company is a retail chain operator specialising in in-house designed casual clothing for men and women. The company operates stores under the name of *UNIQLO*. The company is the leading clothing retail chain in Japan in terms of both sales and profits. UNIQLO is a member of Fast Retailing Group, which also operates other chain stores under the franchise names *Theory* (fashionable basic clothes that suit a contemporary lifestyle), *Comptoir Des Cotonniers* (the brand nurtures a sense of natural authenticity and flattering femininity), *Princesse tam.tam* (corsetry, lounge wear and swimwear brand) and *G.U.* (an entirely new business model for a company offering extremely low-priced clothing in the Japanese market).	*UNIQLO* has established a SPA (Specialty store retailer of Private label Apparel) business model encompassing all stages of the business – from design and production to final sale. By continuously refining this SPA model, *UNIQLO* differentiates itself from the competition by developing unique products. The company quickly makes adjustments to production to reflect the latest sales environment and minimise store-operation costs, such as personnel costs and rent. This is how *UNIQLO* provides such high-quality clothing at such reasonable prices.	*UNIQLO* Japan operated a network of 852 stores at end of August 2014. UNIQLO International has a total of 633 stores. Of that total, 374 stores are located in Greater China (Mainland, Hong Kong and Taiwan), 133 in South Korea, 80 in Southeast Asia and Oceania, 42 in the USA, 9 in the UK, 8 in France and 8 in Russia. *UNIQLO* has around 70 partner factories, and roughly 75% of *UNIQLO* products are made in China.	The company recorded revenue of $13,382m by the end of August 2014, an increase of 13% compared to fiscal 2013. Its net income was $791m in fiscal 2011, compared to a net income of $2,088m in the preceding year.

Source: Company websites.

among manufacturers in low-wage regions intensifies. Switching from one supplier to another is not difficult, although it entails the risk that choosing low-cost suppliers may imply a more extended supply chain, less able to cope with sudden fluctuations in demand as the industry reacts to changes in fashion. There is also a risk that low-cost suppliers may not be up to the required quality standards.

Entry to the retail industry does not require a large capital outlay: setting up a single independent retail store is within the means of many entrepreneurs and there are plenty of suppliers to choose from. However, on a global scale, a few large corporations account for a major share of total industry revenues. Their size and economies of scale (see Table 2) enable them to build brands in multiple retail outlets, and exploit their greater buying power when negotiating with suppliers.

The spirit of Hennes & Mauritz (H&M)

H&M is an abbreviation of 'Hennes' (the name of the first women's apparel store opened by Erling Persson in 1947) and 'Mauritz' (a later acquisition of a men's clothing store). The company has undergone a tremendous transformation from having just one store and a domestic focus to become one of the world's largest fashion retailers. As argued by one of the few journalists that has access to the company: 'The story of H&M does not really concern clothing, but from the beginning one man's vision – or rather unbreakable stubbornness, devotion to a goal and knowledge of human nature.'[6]

Not unlike IKEA in furniture, the H&M philosophy is to make fashion affordable for everyone: 'Fashion and quality at the best price.' The roots of the H&M 'spirit' can be traced back to the 1940s, when Erling Persson started to conduct, what he calls, 'the primitive trade of

Table 2 Comparative financial data

	H&M[1]	Inditex (Zara)[2]	Gap[3]	UNIQLO[4]
Key figures (thousand USD)				
Operating revenue (turnover)	20,398,901	20,480,750	16,435,000	13,382,00
Income before tax	3,488,529	3,668,241	2,013,000	1,332,000
Net income	2,691,132	2,826,871	1,262,000	791,000
Cash flow	3,370,785	3,849,846	1,836,000	1,028,000
Total assets	10,184,295	17,383,705	7,690,000	9,568,000
Shareholders' funds	6,945,534	11,834,871	2,983,000	6,133,000
Price earning ratio	23.36	32.57	13.83	n.a.
Number of employees	93,351	137,054	141,000	30,448
Profitability ratios				
Return on equity (%)	38.75	23.89	42.31	12.90
Return on capital employed (%)	36.16	21.59	24.51	11.50
Return on total assets (%)	26.42	16.26	16.41	8.27
Profit margin (%)	17.10	17.91	12.25	9.96
Gross margin (%)	59.19	57.33	41.70	50.78
EBITDA margin (%)	20.23	22.69	16.05	11.02
EBIT margin (%)	16.90	17.70	12.55	9.25
Cash flow/turnover (%)	16.52	18.80	11.17	7.68
Structure ratios				
Current ratio (x)	2.11	1.90	1.93	2.63
Liquidity ratio (x)	1.15	1.40	1.09	1.81
Shareholders' liquidity ratio (x)	13.79	9.03	1.21	7.66
Solvency ratio (%)	68.20	68.08	38.79	64.10
Gearing (%)	7.25	11.95	83.61	13.06

[1]As of 11/30/2014 and for 12 months.
[2]As of 01/31/2015 and for 12 months.
[3]As of 01/31/2015 and for 12 months.
[4]As of 08/31/2014 and for 12 months.
Source: Mint Global, Bureau van Dijk.

buying and selling'[7] with the essence of 'tradesman-ship'. This was also maintained at the core of the company's culture when his son Stefan Persson took over as CEO in the 1980s. Even after Karl-Johan Persson took over in 2009, the leadership style and organisational culture still relied on Erling Persson's basic values and beliefs, based on his strong business acumen and characterised thrift, no-nonsense decision-making and delegation of responsibility. These are fundamental ingredients of 'the spirit of H&M', which retained the shared and tacit understanding of how the company does business. It is underlined by seven codified core values:[8]

- We believe in people
- We are one team
- Straightforward and open-minded
- Keep it simple
- Entrepreneurial spirit
- Constant improvement
- Cost-consciousness

Another aspect of the H&M spirit is the extraordinary focus on employee involvement. This participatory management philosophy is one of the reasons why H&M is seen as a company where experimentation, trial-and-error learning, fast decision-making and willingness to take initiatives and try new ideas define the basic pillars of organisational culture. Another key ingredient in the culture of H&M is the active encouragement of this spirit at all organisational levels.[9] Trying new things is also encouraged among purchasing managers, but while trying something new and making mistakes is acceptable, it is important that the same mistake is not repeated.

Experimentation is also present at the store level, where interior decoration, lighting, colours, clothes displays and even locations are swiftly changed depending on sales and customer preferences. However, the range within which new ideas can be tried is clearly bounded by H&M's core ideas and values. In a memo to its employees, H&M specifies this as follows: 'Our employees all contribute to making H&M what it is today. We have a strong corporate culture – the spirit of H&M – that is based on simplicity, a down-to-earth approach, entrepreneurship, team spirit, straight lines, common sense and a belief in individuals and their ability to use their initiative.'[10]

Swedish national values also play a role – including a humble, informal and non-hierarchical management style combined with the 'democratisation of fashion'. Creative advisor Margareta van den Bosch comments: 'We're a very democratic society [in Sweden] . . . We keep what we do simple and we think it's wrong that fashion should be the preserve of the rich.'[11]

Despite this humility, results are central, something which is emphasised by Erling Persson's early focus on 'takten' or 'the pace', which still remains a fundamental practice at all organisational levels. It is a straightforward and persuasive weekly list that includes sales and other key figures compared to the previous day, month and year. On this list each manager can clearly see exactly how much has been sold of each individual product. The buyers use this information to reallocate production or shipments, reducing potential overstocking problems. This itemised report also allows buyers to maintain a high level of turnover, keeping the apparel on the sales floor up to date. All employees are also made aware of these results and if sales are up from the day before the sales figures are applauded during store morning meetings.

Limited attention to titles and job descriptions is also a characteristic of H&M: 'At H&M we do not have any job descriptions. It provides considerable freedom, but it also makes it more difficult to blame someone else and claim that something is not part of your duties. Some love it, but others leave after a few weeks.'[12]

In line with this emphasis on informality, independent decision-making is celebrated and decentralisation is encouraged within the limits of the organisational culture. However, central functions like buying and logistics also have a considerable influence and the organisation is in a sense 'a peculiar mix of strong centralisation and delegation'.[12] It has been a challenge to preserve the flat and simple organisational structure during H&M's tremendous growth. The company has a matrix country/function organisation with each executive management team member being responsible for a function and for the results of work within their function in each country.

Store operations and management

The company always positions its stores in prime locations, whether in a city or a small-town shopping centre. This has been a firm principle of H&M's since the first shop opened in 1947 and the principle is still strictly adhered to. The store is the most important communication channel H&M has with its customers and it must be inviting and inspiring; strengthening the brand and offering local customers the best possible shopping experience.

Instead of owning retail properties, H&M opts for renting store premises, which increases flexibility and adaptability. By renting space, the company is able to adapt more quickly to the changing demand patterns and location attraction in its key markets.

The window display – where the customer meets H&M – is perhaps the most important ingredient of the stores. Guidelines for store design and display windows are created centrally based on a large 'test store' in Stockholm. Every two or three years a completely new interiors programme is created. Although centrally guided, every store is unique as it showcases different items in the window display, although they may come from the same collection. Displays, both in windows and inside stores, are changed frequently. This way, consumers are continually attracted to visit the stores to keep up with the latest collections.

In line with H&M values, decision-making is decentralised and store managers have considerable autonomy. The shop manager runs the business like an entrepreneur and is authorised to take independent decisions within the overall guide lines; essentially like running their own business. This increases employee loyalty and commitment to the organisation and is a great motivator.

Marketing and social media

H&M's strong brand image is associated with value and stylish collections. In addition to 200 in-house collaborations with famous designers, there is a unique approach employed by H&M over recent years. This has included signature collections designed by Stella McCartney in 2005, by avant-garde Dutch designers Viktor & Rolf in 2006, by Madonna in 2007, by the Italian designer Roberto Cavalli and Kylie Minogue in 2007, by Sonia Rykiel in 2009, by Versace in 2011, by Italian fashion label Marni in 2012, by Isabel Marant and Beyoncé in 2013 and by American designer Alexander Wang in 2014.

Highlighting the high level of brand awareness, H&M was ranked 21st among the top 100 most valuable global brands according to Interbrand in 2015, with a brand value of US$22bn. In comparison, Zara ranked 30th with US$14bn, and neither Gap nor Uniqlo made it into the top 100 list. H&M's superior brand value vis-à-vis its main competitors can partly be attributed to its long-term advertising campaigns with high-profile celebrities. To maintain and enhance the value of its brand name,

H&M spends around five per cent of its revenues on advertising.

In addition to conventional channels, H&M has also established a strong social media presence. The company aims to become part of its customers' daily lives, through its pages on Facebook, Twitter, Instagram, Google+ and YouTube, as well as the Chinese social networks Youku and Sina Weibo. Each network is updated on a regular basis. Through social media, millions of H&M followers share ideas and opinions and get quick answers to their queries. New fashion videos and reports are uploaded onto YouTube weekly and have had millions of hits. Through the H&M apps customers can explore the latest collections and campaigns, find out what's new at H&M and locate stores. At its launch in August 2010, the iPhone app was the most downloaded application in almost all of H&M's markets.

Design

Design is centralised at the Stockholm headquarters and includes a team of almost 200 designers and about 100 pattern makers. The centralisation of design allows for minimum time-to-market and the design team has direct contact with the production offices around the globe. This allows for a rapid-response manufacturing process to capitalise on design trends immediately. The design team works intensively with new trends, materials and colours from what is popularly known as the 'White Room' and is supported by the 50 production offices around the world.

Much effort is put into researching and predicting emerging market trends. H&M designers hold customer surveys, dialogue sessions and focus groups, and pick up trends from employees in the global stores and then add their own particular features. They need to have an up-to-the-minute fashion feedback focus and be conscious of the very latest trends. According to Ann-Sofie Johansson, head of H&M design department: 'We try to look out for trendsetters, what's popping, vintage looks, what's happening at music festivals. The internet is getting more important as are catwalk shows, but these are more of a confirmation of what we know is out there'.[13]

She and her team pick up inspiration in several ways: notes from travels, fashion classics offered by Paris, Milan, New York, London and Tokyo, textile fairs, street fashion and exhibitions: 'Celebrity inspiration is also important, as well as what bloggers are saying and old-fashioned sources such as music, magazines, movies and costume dramas'.[13]

However, H&M always adds its own touch to the design, creating collections that strike a good balance between the latest trends and the basics. Margareta Van den Bosch, creative adviser and former head designer says: 'We get inspiration from everywhere, but the most important thing is to make it your own way. Quality means carefully testing everything before it hits the shops, from jeans to lipstick. But it also means H&M is a fashion house in its own right, with its own trends. We do not copy'.[14]

Apart from size adjustments, for example in the Asian market, no special changes are made to to adapt the collections for specific countries. H&M argue that: 'It is important that H&M keeps its own personality in each country, and fashion has become more global, more international'.[15] Similar trends are appearing the world over. Of course this is also driven by economies of scale in buying and manufacturing.

Buying, local production offices and corporate social responsibility (CSR)

H&M does not own any factories. Instead, manufacturing is primarily outsourced to low-cost countries with some 70 per cent of production in the Far East and South Asia and the remainder in Africa, Europe and the Middle East. With the focus on economies of scale, including low-wage and high-volume production, the company maintains low input costs and often has the latest trends in its stores within a month of the initial design.[16] H&M also constantly redefines its production and distribution in response to changing market and production conditions to ensure that they continuously improve the efficiency of the production flow. This way, H&M has been able to reduce lead times by 15–20 per cent in recent years.[17] In 2011, H&M worked with 900 independent suppliers of which 150 were considered long-term strategic partners. Buying is centralised in Stockholm and has always had a central role in H&M. Managers within this function have often been the best paid in the entire organisation.

To reduce lead times, the 50 production offices are in direct contact with suppliers and report back to central procurement in Stockholm. They mediate between the large network of independent suppliers and the central purchasing office, to identify the right suppliers to place orders with, to optimise time and cost decisions, and to ensure that decisions comply with H&M's CSR policies. Each supplier owned or subcontracted multiple factories; globally 1652 factories were approved for making goods for H&M. H&M conducted a total of annual 3623 audits of suppliers in 2014. CSR has increased in importance for H&M. Being a high-profile and visible player in the textile and apparel industry, the company is under constant scrutiny in terms of working conditions and wage levels in the overseas suppliers they work with. Being fully cognisant of this, H&M pays particular attention to CSR and takes several actions throughout its value chain to keep its brand name away from the usual criticisms aimed at the textile industry. H&M also produces a special collection (Conscious Collection) using sustainable materials. The company has formulated seven commitments called 'H&M Conscious Actions'. These include adopting ethical practices, improving working conditions and using natural resources responsibly. Other projects include community investments.[18]

Logistics: distribution, warehousing and IT

Buyers and production offices are closely integrated throughout the value chain with distribution centres, warehouses and the stores around the globe. To reduce poor buying decisions and to increase flexibility in allowing stores to restock quickly during the season with best-selling products H&M made sure not to place orders too early. H&M puts more emphasis on economies of scale in its supply chain set-up compared to Zara's focus on flexibility and speed:

> 'Lead-times vary from two to three weeks up to six months. The different lead-times reflect differences in the nature of the goods. The trick is to know the right time to order each item. A short lead-time is not always the best, since the right lead-time is a matter of bringing price and quality into balance.'[19]

H&M controls virtually all logistics internally except for external contractors handling transportation. The integrated logistics function is a key business process for H&M that supports cost efficient supply of goods and generates economies of scale: 'H&M can offer the best price by avoiding middlemen, buying the right product from the right market, being cost-conscious at every stage and having efficient distribution.'[20]

This integrated direct distribution channel ensures that H&M stores receive new shipments daily, giving the company further control over supply and demand shifts. Store-keeping of merchandise is minimised and individual stores do not have backup stocks; they are replenished as required from a central warehouse. They also shift merchandise around internally depending on demand. For example, if a particular fashion proves exceptionally popular to men in a particular region, but not in another, they can shift inventory from the first region to the second. The distribution set-up also enables H&M to respond to market segment changes within a country.

To support the swift and efficient flow of goods, H&M logistics is dependent on effective information sharing and the latest IT systems that are continuously developed. These systems permit optimal supply and demand decisions, whilst also providing valuable information for understanding customer needs and the placement of products.

Taking H&M's mix of supply chain management, logistics and IT into consideration the company is considered a world leader in these areas:

> 'Its centralized logistics and warehouse system, close coordination of the procurement staff with the production offices, intelligent use of ICT [information and communication technologies] tools, purchasing flexibility and overall a central governing model, has incredibly reduced the lead time and improved logistics to have lightning-fast turnaround speed of just 20 days, making it a truly unique supply chain innovator.'[21]

Human resource management (HRM)

Key to the recipe of H&M's success is its ability to establish a strong corporate culture with well-defined values, and to make sure its employees understand and internalise these values in their job. One important element to ensure that this culture continues to be integrated into HRM is the recruitment process and training.

Internal promotion and job rotation are two central ingredients in the HRM policies, and experience, loyalty and continuity are highly regarded. These two aspects are central to cultivating and disseminating the H&M spirit and culture throughout the organisation. The company's steady growth has been providing ample opportunities for employees to take on new challenges in another store, department, role or country. Aligning corporate and individual goals with development and growth strategies are essential for H&M:

> 'The key words for continual growth are responsibility and commitment. We have committed employees and we are prepared to delegate responsibility at every level. I tell employees, if you do not grow, neither will H&M.'
>
> Head of HRM, Pär Darj[22]

A participative culture is thus central to the spirit of H&M and the leadership philosophy emphasises straightforward and direct relationships with employees. The HRM policies emphasise the core value – 'We believe in people' – and the open-door policy, granting all employees the right and possibility to discuss any work-related issue directly with management.

Consequently, H&M values personal qualities much more than formal qualifications: great school grades and all the university credits in the world are no guarantee of a job or a fast-track career. More than anything, H&M looks for people with the right personality – people can gather skills as they go along, but personality can't be taught. H&M is a fast company with a high tempo and needs employees who are self-motivated, like responsibility and decision-making, and are capable of leading. A love of fashion combined with a focus on sales is perceived as a major advantage.

Internationalisation and expansion

While H&M's skill in providing fashionable and elegant clothes at affordable prices and catering for the dynamic tastes and preferences of customers can broadly be identified as the main drivers of its success, perhaps their unique advantage lies in their ability to replicate the same business concept and 'spirit' across time and space. Since the 1990s, international expansion has been aggressive and the company has moved into Eastern European markets, the Middle East, Asian markets and Russia. By 2005, H&M had already expanded into more than 20 countries with more than 1000 stores.

Continuous growth by replicating the same business model and store concept thus defines the core of the company's expansion strategy. Prior to moving to a new country or city, H&M first conducts a thorough evaluation of market potential. This is done according to factors like demographic structure, purchasing power, economic growth, infrastructure and political risk.

H&M's policy is to recruit local people wherever they open a new store. H&M looks for those who have the 'right' personality and potential to understand and adopt the core values of the organisation. Another element is to use formal training programmes, as well as on-the-job training, to socialise employees into this culture and make sure that they understand and act according to the company's core values. These socialisation mechanisms are the means by which H&M successfully adopts a 'mental franchising' model, in which the ownership of each and every store remains in the hands of H&M whereas the shop managers often run their shop as if it were their own.

All of these initiatives are essential elements of H&M's constant growth strategy, where the ambition is to create and re-create businesses that reflect the basic and fundamental values and the overall H&M spirit. To this end, the company keeps formal rules and procedures to a minimum and prefers to equip its employees with tacit skills via experiential learning in the field. This way, H&M makes sure that those who work in new outlets are exposed to and infused with the original spirit. Combining this with the values of initiative-taking and entrepreneurship, H&M has been able to stay ahead of its competitors by moving fast and reaching large markets based on applying a simple business model universally, yet making subtle modifications and adaptations at the local level.

H&M's growth to become one of the largest global fashion retailers is an incredible success story – from one store in 1947 to 4000 in 2015. In 2016, H&M planned to open another 400 stores and to pursue aggressive growth in its new luxury label format of stores called '& Other Stories'. However, fashion-retailing history is full of companies that have confidently expanded into new international markets but later been forced to retreat and drastically curtail their growth, e.g. Marks & Spencer, C&A, Benetton. The question for H&M and its third-generation leader Karl-Johan Persson is to what extent will H&M's resources, capabilities, practices and knowledge be enough to keep up with the competition, including vigorous new players? Will these entrants be able to replicate H&M's success?

Notes and references

1. As quoted in C. MacCarthy, 'H&M continue aggressive expansion', *Financial Times*, 29 September 2011.
2. As quoted in M. Stothard, 'H&M to launch new line of stores', *Financial Times*, 29 March 2012.
3. As quoted in M. Stothard, 'H&M defend strategy as margins fall', *Financial Times*, 26 January 2012.
4. $1 = £0.6 = €0.75.
5. Marketline, Industry Profile: Global Apparel Retail, ID:MTLN5577521, 2015.
6. B. Pettersson, *Handelsmännen*, Månpocket: Stockholm, 2001, p. 21.
7. Ibid.
8. H&M website: http://about.hm.com/AboutSection/en/About/Facts-About-HM/About-HM/Business-Concept-and-Growth.html.
9. B. Pettersson, 2001, p. 91.
10. http://about.hm.com/en/About/facts-about-hm/people-and-history/working-at-hm/values.html.
11. As quoted in J. Craven, 'H&M: meet the brains behind fashion's megabrand', *Daily Mail/Mail Online*, 23 February 2010.
12. Jan Jacobsen as quoted in B. Pettersson, 2001, pp. 261–2.
13. As quoted in P. Kam, 'High street label H&M serves up inspiring fashion at affordable prices', *The Star online*, 20 September 2012.
14. As quoted in N. Mehta-Jasani, 'H&M: from the inside', *Chinadaily.com*, 29 June 2007.
15. Margareta Van den Bosch, creative adviser as quoted in N. Mehta-Jasani, *Chinadaily.com*, 'H&M: from the inside', 29 June 2007.
16. K. Capell and G. Khermouch, 'Hip H&M: the Swedish retailer is reinventing the business of affordable fashion', *Business Week*, 11 November 2002.
17. 'Industrial change in the textiles and leather sector', EMCC, http://www.eurofound.europa.eu/sites/default/files/ef_files/emcc/publications/2004/ef0465en_1.pdf.
18. http://about.hm.com/en/About/sustainability/commitments/strengthen-communities.html.
19. T. Kihlén, *On Logistics in the Strategy of the Firm*, Linköping University, 2005.
20. H&M Annual Report 2011.
21. R. Pal 'Identifying organizational distinctive competence by business mapping in a global textile context', *Journal of Textile and Apparel Technology and Management*, 7(4), 2011.
22. H&M Annual Report 2008.

Recommended videos

- http://www.youtube.com/hm (official YouTube channel of H&M where video clips on new campaigns and promotions are shared).
- http://www.youtube.com/watch?v=CHYogtRrrUY (interview with CEO Karl-Johan Persson by Bloomberg on strategy, costs and internet sales as indicated in the video clip. Please note: sign in video incorrectly names the former CEO 'Stefan Persson').

CASE STUDY

The Formula 1 constructors: capabilities for success

Mark Jenkins

This case describes four periods of dominance by particular firms in a highly competitive technological context. Formula 1 (F1) motorsport is the pinnacle of automotive technology. Highly specialised constructors design and build single-seat racing cars (and sometimes engines) to compete for annual championships which bring huge financial and reputational rewards. The case study explores the stories of four contrasting companies in different competitive time periods in terms of how they both created and lost the basis for sustained competitive advantage.

'For the most part, it's just commerce, but between two and four on a Sunday afternoon, it's still a sport.'

Frank Williams, Managing Director, Williams F1[1]

In 1945, the Fédération Internationale de l'Automobile (FIA) established Formula A as the premier level of motorsport. In the years that followed, Formula A became referred to as Formula 1 (F1) and a drivers' world championship was introduced in 1950. By the mid-sixties, F1 had moved from being a basis for car manufacturers to promote and test their products to a highly specialist business where purpose-built cars were developed through leading-edge technology. Having enjoyed exponential growth during the 1990s, F1 had become a TV sporting event which enjoyed the third highest audience in the world, surpassed only by the Olympics and World Cup Soccer.

There have been between ten and fourteen race car constructors competing in F1 at any one time. In 2015, the top three teams were Mercedes AMG F1, Ferrari and Williams, all medium-sized businesses turning over between $150m (€112m, £90m) and $500m (€375m, £300m) per annum.[2] For the first three years of their entry into F1 in 2002, Toyota was estimated to have committed $1bn on capital and running costs of which only one fifth came from sponsorship. The top teams would typically have their own testing and development equipment, which would include wind-tunnels and other facilities. The larger teams employ around 800 people, one hundred of whom travel around the world attending Grand Prix every two to three weeks throughout the F1 season (March to November). Labour costs account for around 25 per cent of the budget. All the teams would

Source: pbpgalleries/Alamy Images.

have highly qualified technical staff which would include race engineers (who work with the driver to set up the car), designers, aerodynamicists, composite experts (to work with specialised carbon-composite materials) and systems specialists.

In addition to sponsorship, revenue is provided by prize money generated by winning championship points. The prize money is a way of dividing up the royalties earned from media coverage and other revenues negotiated on behalf of the teams by the Commercial Rights Holder: Formula One Management (FOM). In 2014, Ferrari received $164m from the FOM payout – estimated to represent 38 per cent of their annual operating budget.

The Formula 1 Constructors provide a unique context to consider the competitive advantage of different multimillion-pound organisations over time. The pace of change and the basis of advantage is constantly changing, shown by the fact that since the start of the world championships, only three constructors have won the championship consecutively for four years or greater (McLaren 1988–91; Ferrari 1999–2004; Red Bull Racing 2010–13), and only Ferrari (1975–77) and Williams (1992–94) have won for three consecutive years. The remainder of the case considers the four most recent of these periods of competitive dominance in chronological order.

McLaren and Honda domination in the late 1980s

The period from 1988 to 1991 was unusual in the hyper-competitive world of F1, where the pace of change is rarely matched in any other competitive environment. This period was notable because of the dominance of one constructor. In 1988, the McLaren team won 15 of the 16 races. Such dominance had not been seen before and will almost certainly never be seen again.

Founded by New Zealander and F1 driver Bruce McLaren in 1966, the McLaren team had their first victory in the Belgian Grand Prix of 1968. Tragically, McLaren himself was killed two years later in a testing accident. Lawyer and family friend Teddy Mayer took over as team leader and in 1974 secured a long-term sponsorship from Philip Morris to promote the Marlboro brand of cigarettes. This partnership was to last until 1996, one of the most enduring relationships between a constructor and a 'flagship' sponsor. In September 1980, Ron Dennis became joint team principal with Mayer, a position which he took over solely in 1982, when Mayer was 'encouraged' by Philip Morris to take a less active role in the management of McLaren.

Dennis had been a mechanic for the highly successful Cooper team in 1966, but left to set up his own Formula Two (a smaller, less expensive formula) team in 1971. By the end of the 1970s, he had built up a reputation for professionalism and immaculate presentation. His Project Four company brought in designer John Barnard who had some radical ideas about using carbon fibre, rather than metal, as the basis for a race car chassis. These ideas were to provide the basis for the MP4 (McLaren Project Four) car. Both Dennis and Barnard were perfectionists, with Dennis's obsession with immaculate presentation and attention to detail complemented by Barnard's uncompromising quest for technical excellence.

In 1986, John Barnard left to join the struggling Ferrari team. The partnership between Dennis and Barnard had been stormy, but a huge amount had been achieved through the energy of these two individuals; Dennis providing the managerial and commercial acumen and Barnard highly innovative design skills. To replace Barnard, Brabham designer Gordon Murray was brought into the team, perhaps best known for developing the innovative 'fan car' for Brabham in 1978. Murray, like Barnard, was at the leading edge of F1 car design.

A further factor in McLaren's success had been their relationship with engine suppliers. In the mid-1980s, turbo charging became the key technology and in 1983 they used a Porsche turbo engine which was funded by the electronics' company TAG. However, the emerging force in engine development was Honda who had re-entered F1 in 1983 in partnership with Williams. Importantly, the engines were supported by a significant commitment from Honda in both people and resources. Honda used the relationship as an opportunity to develop some of their most talented engineers and to transfer F1 design and development capabilities to their production car programme. In the mid-1980s, the Williams/Honda partnership was very successful, but following Frank Williams' road accident in 1986, Honda began to have doubts about the future of the Williams team and agreed to supply both McLaren and Lotus for the 1987 season.

Halfway through 1987, McLaren announced that they had recruited two of the top drivers in F1 to their team for the 1988 season: Alain Prost and Ayrton Senna. This was unusual as most teams tended to have a clear hierarchy with a lead driver being supported by a 'number two' who was regarded as either less skilful and/or less experienced than the lead driver; this hierarchy reduced the competitive tensions between the two drivers and their respective engineering teams. However, McLaren appeared to feel that they would be able to deal with the potential problems which such a structure could cause.

Prost and Senna were real contrasts: Senna was fast, determined and ruthless. Prost was also fast, but a great tactician and adept at team politics, making sure that the whole team was behind him. It was rumoured that a key reason for Honda moving to McLaren was that they now had Alain Prost.

In 1988, the Honda-powered MP4 car was without question the fastest and most reliable car on the circuit. This meant that effectively the only real competition for Prost and Senna was each other. This competition between two highly committed and talented drivers resulted in one of the most enduring and bitter feuds the sport has ever known. In 1990, the acrimony with Senna culminated in Prost moving to Ferrari.

Ron Dennis and his professional management style was synonymous with the success of McLaren, indicating that the era of the 'one man band' Formula 1 constructor was past. His record since taking over in 1982 has been impressive. Eddie Jordan, principal of the Jordan team, held him in high regard:

'He's won that many Grand Prix, he's won that many championships, he's been on pole that many times and he's got the best drivers. Everyone hates him; but they only hate him because he's the best.'[3]

Dennis's negotiating and marketing abilities were legendary throughout Formula 1. McLaren also created their own marketing consultancy operation where the smaller teams engaged them to find sponsors. In 1991 *Management Week* had Ron Dennis on the front cover with the question: 'Is Ron Dennis Britain's best manager?' Dennis likens the management of McLaren to that of a game of chess: '. . . you've got to get all the elements right, the overall package, the budget, the designer, the engine, the drivers, the organisation'.[4]

Dennis is renowned for being hyper-competitive and once chastised a driver who was delighted with finishing second with the comment – 'just remember, second place is the first of the losers'.[5]

Dennis's ambitions went beyond F1 and in 1988 he had begun a project to build a road-going car, the McLaren F1. In many ways, this mirrored the development of Ferrari who had made the progression from producing dedicated race cars to also develop road-going cars. The McLaren F1 was launched in 1994 and with a price tag of £634,000 and a top speed of 231 mph became the most expensive and fastest road-going car in the world.

The McLaren–Honda combination had dominated F1 from 1988 through to 1991, and it was difficult to see what more could be achieved. In September 1992, Honda confirmed that they were pulling out of F1. They had been hugely successful and achieved all of their objectives; it was now time to stand back and find some new challenges. Dennis had been told about Honda's thinking earlier in the year, but it appeared that he hadn't taken it seriously enough and the team had no real engine alternatives. This meant they lost valuable winter development time as they tried to find a new engine supplier. In 1993, they competed with 'off the shelf' Ford engines available to any team who had the cash to buy them. Senna's skills still gave McLaren five victories, despite having a less than competitive car. However, at the end of 1993, Senna left the McLaren team to move to Williams, whom he saw as having the superior car and engine combination. Former world champion and adviser to Ferrari, Niki Lauda saw this as the terminal blow: 'Senna was a leader. He told them exactly what was wrong with the car. Hakkinen (Senna's replacement) is not in a position to do that, so the reaction time is much longer. Senna motivated the designers.'[6]

The mid-1990s were a particularly difficult period for McLaren. Having tried Peugeot engines in 1994, they moved to Mercedes in 1995. Mercedes had been considering a major commitment to F1 and in 1995 they concluded a deal which involved taking equity stakes in McLaren (40 per cent) and also in specialist engine builder Ilmor Engineering based near Northampton (which they subsequently purchased) who were to build the Mercedes engines used in F1.

Williams and the technological revolution: the mid-1990s

During the period 1992–94, Williams' cars won 27 out of 48 races, they secured the F1 constructors' title for all three years and the world championship for drivers was won in a Williams in 1992 (Nigel Mansell) and 1993 (Alain Prost).

Like many of the founders of F1 teams, Frank Williams began as a driver, perhaps not of the same standing as Bruce McLaren or Jack Brabham, but nonetheless someone who lived and breathed motor racing. His desire to remain in the sport led him to develop a business buying and selling racing cars and spare parts and in 1968 Frank Williams (Racing Cars) Ltd was formed. A series of triumphs, tragedies and near bankruptcies led up to the establishment of Williams Grand Prix Engineering in 1977 when Frank Williams teamed up with technical director Patrick Head. Frank Williams' approach and style owed a lot to the difficult years in the 1970s when he survived on his wits and very little else, including operating from a public telephone box near the workshop when the phones were disconnected as he hadn't paid the bill. His style could be described as autocratic, entrepreneurial and certainly frugal, despite the multimillion-pound funding he managed to extract from the likes of Canon, R.J. Reynolds and Rothmans. Williams saw his role as providing the resources for the best car to be built. His long-standing relationship with Head was pivotal to the team and brought together a blend of entrepreneurial energy and technical excellence needed to succeed in F1.

The first car from this new alliance was the FW06, designed by Patrick Head and with support from Saudi Airlines. The team enjoyed success in 1980–81 by winning the constructors' championship both years and with Alan Jones winning the drivers' title in 1980. Jones was a forthright Australian who knew what he wanted and was not afraid to voice his opinions. His approach to working with the team was very influential and coloured Frank Williams' view of drivers: 'I took a very masculine attitude towards drivers and assumed that they should behave – or should be treated – like Alan.'[7]

Further success occurred in 1986–87 with Nelson Piquet winning the drivers' title in 1987 and Williams the constructors' title in both years. This was despite the road accident in 1986 which left Frank Williams quadriplegic and confined to a wheelchair. However, 1988 was Williams' worst season, with Honda having switched to supplying McLaren, they were forced to use uncompetitive

Judd V10 engines. Williams didn't win a single race, and McLaren won 15 out of the 16 Grand Prix of 1988 and a disillusioned Nigel Mansell left and went to Ferrari. Frank Williams had to search frantically for a new engine deal which he found in 1990 with Renault. This relationship became a far reaching and durable one, with Renault putting human and financial resources into the project with Williams. They also sought to develop the relationship further and extended their activities with Renault by running their team for the British Touring Car Championship, and also provided engineering input and the Williams name for a special edition of the Renault Clio.

In 1990, a lack of driver talent meant that the team were only able to win two races. In 1991, Nigel Mansell was persuaded to return from retirement by Frank Williams and narrowly missed taking the 1991 title, but in 1992 the team dominated the circuits, effectively winning the championship by the middle of the season. Nigel Mansell went into the record books by winning the first five consecutive races of the season. However, deterioration in the relationship between Williams and Mansell led to the driver's retirement from F1 at the end of the year.

In a sport where personnel change teams frequently, the stable relationship between Williams and Head provided enviable continuity compared with the rest of the field. Head's designs had often been functional rather than innovative, but he had always been able to take a good idea and develop it further. These have included ground effect (originally developed by Lotus), carbon-composite monocoque (McLaren), semi-automatic gearbox (Ferrari) and active suspension (Lotus). The car development process was always a top priority at Williams and Head was supported by many junior designers who then went on to be highly influential in F1, such as Neil Oatley (McLaren), Adrian Newey (McLaren and Red Bull), Frank Dernie (Ligier, Lotus, Arrows and Toyota) and Ross Brawn (Benetton, Ferrari, Brawn and Mercedes).

This focus on developing the car and engine combination sometimes meant that the driver took second place in the Williams philosophy, despite the fact that a good test driver, who could help the technicians define and solve problems, was essential to the development process. There had been a number of high-profile disputes with drivers which had, in part, been attributable to Frank Williams' 'masculine' approach to dealing with drivers. In 1992, Nigel Mansell left when he felt his 'number one' driver position was threatened by the recruitment of Alain Prost for 1993 (although Prost himself left the following year for the same reason regarding the hiring of Ayrton Senna). A similar situation arose when the 1996 world champion, Damon Hill, was not retained for the 1997 season and was replaced with Heinz-Harald Frentzen.

In an interview with the *Sunday Times,* Patrick Head set out the reasons for the decision not to hold on to Hill: 'We are an engineering company and that is what we focus on. Ferrari are probably the only team where you can say the driver is of paramount importance and that is because [Michael] Schumacher is three-quarters of a second a lap quicker than anyone else.'[8]

This emphasis on the driver being only part of the equation was not lost on Paul Stewart who was concentrating on developing the Stewart Grand Prix entry to F1 in 1996: 'If you look at the Williams team, they rely on a solid framework, their organisation, their engine, their car design is all amalgamated into something that gives a platform for everyone to work on. They don't believe putting millions into a driver is going to make all the difference.'[9]

Williams' emphatic dominance in the 1992 season was due to a number of factors: the development of the powerful and reliable Renault engine was perfectly complemented by the FW15 chassis which incorporated Patrick Head's development of some of the innovations of the early 1990s, namely semi-automatic gearboxes, drive-by-wire technology and their own active suspension system. As summarised by a senior manager at Williams F1: 'I think we actually were better able to exploit the technology that was available and led that technology revolution. We were better able to exploit it to the full, before the others caught up . . . it wasn't just one thing but a combination of ten things, each one giving you another 200/300th of a second, if you add them up you a get a couple of seconds of advantage.'[10]

However, in 1993, the Benetton team made a great deal of progress with both the gearbox and suspension innovations largely attributed to the development skills of their new driver, Michael Schumacher. Williams' technical lead coupled with the tactical race skills of Alain Prost, supported by promoted test driver Damon Hill (due to Mansell's sudden exit) secured the 1993 world championship and constructors' championship for Williams F1.

The year 1994 was disastrous, although Williams won the constructors' championship for the third successive year (this was always their declared primary objective, with the drivers' championship very much a secondary aim). Frank Williams had, for some time, regarded Brazilian Ayrton Senna as the best driver around and, now with the obvious performance advantage of the FW15 chassis and the Renault V10 engine, Senna was keen to move to Williams, which he did, partnered by Damon Hill for the 1994 season. Tragically at the San Marino Grand Prix on 1 May 1994 Senna was killed in an accident, an event which not only devastated the Williams team but the sport as a whole.

In 1995, the Benetton team had eclipsed the Williams domination. Benetton had developed a car using many of the technological innovations used by Williams (with the help of ex-Williams designer, Ross Brawn). In addition, Renault's ambitions to match Honda's previous domination of the sport as an engine supplier from 1986–91, led them to end exclusive supply to Williams and also to provide Benetton with their engines. The year 1995 was when Benetton and Michael Schumacher broke the three-year domination of the Williams team. However, in 1996 Schumacher moved to the then uncompetitive Ferrari team for £27m, putting him in third place in the Forbes chart of sports top earners. This left the way clear for Williams to dominate the season, with Benetton failing to fill the gap left by Schumacher.

Ferrari: the return to glory: 1999–2004

In the 1980s, legendary F1 team Ferrari were struggling, only winning six races in the period from 1984 to 1988. A key problem was that new developments in aerodynamics and the use of composite materials had emerged from the UK's motorsport valley. Ferrari had traditionally focused on the engine as their competitive advantage, which made perfect sense given that, unlike most of the competition who outsourced their engines from suppliers such as Cosworth and Renault, Ferrari designed and manufactured their own engines. However, it appeared that these new technologies were effectively substituting superior engine power with enhanced grip due to aerodynamic downforce and improved chassis rigidity.

In 1986, British designer John Barnard was recruited to the top technical role, but was not prepared to move to Italy. Surprisingly, Enzo Ferrari allowed him to establish a design and development facility near Guildford in Surrey that became known as the Ferrari 'GTO' or Guildford Technical Office. It seemed that rather than being a unique and distinctively Italian F1 team, Ferrari were now prepared to imitate the British constructors who Enzo had previously referred to as 'garagistes' or 'assemblatori'. The concept of the GTO was that it would concentrate on the design of the following year's car, whereas in Maranello they would focus on building and racing the current car. However, the fact that Barnard was defining the technical direction of Ferrari meant that he became increasingly involved in activities at both sites.

Enzo Ferrari's death in 1988 created a vacuum which was filled by executives from Fiat S.P.A. It was written into the contract between Ferrari and Fiat that on Enzo's death Fiat's stake would be increased from 40 to 90 per cent; this led to attempts to run Ferrari as a formal subsidiary of the Fiat group. Barnard became frustrated with the politics of the situation and left to join Benetton in 1989.

In 1992, Fiat appointed Luca di Montezemolo as CEO with a mandate to take Ferrari back to the top. Montezemolo, who had been team manager for Ferrari during the mid-1970s, had subsequently taken on a range of high-profile management roles including running Italy's hosting of the Soccer World Cup in 1990. One of his first actions was to re-appoint John Barnard as technical director and re-establish GTO. 'If you want to make pasta, then you have to be in Parma. I want to make a sophisticated F1 project, so I want to be involved in England.'[11]

With an Englishman heading up design, he followed this up with the appointment of a Frenchman, Jean Todt, to handle the overall management of the team. Both appointments were clear signals to all involved in Ferrari that things were going to change. Todt had no prior experience in F1 but had been in motorsport management for many years and had led a successful rally and sports car programme at Peugeot.

But the physical separation between design and development in Guildford and the racing operation in Maranello was not a sustainable arrangement and Barnard and Ferrari again parted company in 1996. At the end of 1996, Ferrari recruited double world champion Michael Schumacher from the Benetton team and followed this by recruiting two further individuals from Benetton: Rory Byrne, who had overall responsibility for designing the car, and Ross Brawn who managed the entire technical operation. With Barnard and his UK operation gone, Byrne and Brawn faced the task of building up a new design department in Maranello of around 50 people. One of the most important tasks for the new team was to take advantage of the fact that Ferrari made their own engines, by integrating the design of the engine, chassis and aerodynamics as early in the process as possible. Ferrari's historic emphasis on the engine was replaced by a focus on integration, summarised by Ross Brawn: 'It's not an engine, it's not an aeropackage, it's not a chassis. It's a Ferrari'.[12]

At this time, Ferrari also entered into a long-term partnership with Shell to provide both financial and technical support to the team, a departure for Ferrari who had previously worked with Italian petroleum giant Agip. In these kinds of arrangements Ferrari led a trend away from selling space on cars to long-term commercial and technological arrangements, with coordinated marketing strategies for commercial partners to maximise the benefits of their investments.

This rejuvenated team provided the basis for Michael Schumacher's dominance of F1. In 1999, they won their first constructors' championship for 12 years. In 2000, Ferrari secured both championships and it was at this point that they felt they had truly returned to the glory of the mid-1970s, its having been 21 years since their last drivers' world championship. In 2002, Schumacher and Ferrari were so dominant that a series of regulation changes were introduced to try and make the racing more competitive.

Schumacher's talent as a driver and a motivator of the team (he learnt Japanese to converse with an engine technician recruited from Honda) was critical, but another key aspect in Ferrari's advantage for 2002 had been their relationship with Bridgestone tyres (other leading teams used Michelin tyres) who designed and develop their compounds specifically for Michael Schumacher in a Ferrari. Despite stronger competition from Williams, McLaren and Renault, in 2003 Ferrari won both drivers' and constructors' titles and repeated the feat again in 2004 giving them a record-breaking sixth consecutive constructors' title and Michael Schumacher a seventh world championship, breaking Juan Fangio's record which had stood since 1957.

In 2005 and 2006, the competition became much stronger and despite being competitive Ferrari lost the drivers' and constructors' titles to the Renault F1 team (formerly Benetton). Renault benefited from the rising talent of Fernando Alonso who proved himself a match for Schumacher in both driving and team motivation. In 2005, changes in the regulations meant that tyres were required to last for the whole race, which often benefited the Michelin technology used by Renault and left Ferrari struggling towards the end of the race on their Bridgestone tyres. In 2006, a more drastic change to the regulations meant that the constructors had to shift from 3.5 litre V10 engines to smaller V8s, with engine design to be frozen for three years from 2007. In many ways an engine change should have benefited Ferrari, but they struggled to get the performance in the early part of the season. Towards the end of the 2006 season, Michael Schumacher announced his intention to retire at the end of the year, Jean Todt was promoted to CEO, highly experienced engine director Paolo Martinelli moved to a job with Fiat and Ross Brawn announced he was taking a sabbatical in 2007.

Red Bull Racing: a new formula for success, 2010–2013

On Monday 15th November 2004, Ford Motor Company announced that it was selling the Jaguar Racing F1 team to the Red Bull beverage company for a 'nominal sum' and in exchange Red Bull agreed to underwrite the team for at least three years securing around 350 jobs at their facility in Milton Keynes. Nine years later in 2013, German driver Sebastian Vettel secured a fourth consecutive world championship (making him the youngest-ever double, triple and quadruple world champion) and along with it brought a fourth consecutive constructors' championship

to the team. In 2013, they won the championship with 596 points, their closest rival, Mercedes, having secured only 360 points. It was a dominant display by Red Bull Racing making them only the third constructor in the history of Formula 1 to have achieved a four-year domination of the constructors' trophy.

The man behind the purchase of Jaguar Racing was Dietrich Mateschitz, an Austrian entrepreneur who had founded Red Bull Gmbh in 1987, and effectively created a new category in beverages – energy drinks. In 2013, the *New York Times* reported that the US market alone was worth around $10bn with Red Bull holding around 40 per cent of this rapidly growing sector. Mateschitz had focused on building the Red Bull brand by association with a wide range of sports, including more extreme sports such as mountain biking, BMX biking, air racing, skydiving – and motor racing.

Red Bull's first involvement with F1 came in 1995 when they acquired a majority stake in the struggling Sauber Team, for which they received title sponsorship in a period when the television audience of F1 was doubling to over 150 million people. In 2001, Red Bull launched the Red Bull Junior team under the guidance of former sportscar racer Dr Helmut Marko. Red Bull Juniors support and develop young drivers in a range of different formulae with the intention of bringing new talent into F1. In addition to financial support, the programme provides structured driving and fitness training. In 2004, the scheme had 15 drivers under contract, including a 16-year-old German, Sebastian Vettel, who Red Bull had first supported driving karts when he was 12 years old. Marko made the following comment about him in 2004: '. . . his main difference to the other drivers is his head. When it comes to qualifying on one lap he can get his act together and do the job. He is also physically the fittest. He is competing in Formula BMW for the second year and we expect him to win.'[13]

In 2001, Dieter Mateschitz disagreed with Sauber over the choice of drivers for 2002, Mateschitz wanting Red Bull Junior driver, Enrique Bernoldi, and Peter Sauber favouring an unknown Finnish driver, Kimi Raikkonen, who went on to be world champion with Ferrari. Mateschitz sold his stake in Sauber to Credit Suisse and considered acquiring the Arrows team in 2002 in order to secure a drive for Bernoldi, that fell through and Arrows went into liquidation. In 2004, keen to find a drive for Red Bull Junior driver Christian Klien, he entered into discusssions with Jaguar Racing and discovered that Ford were considering the sale of the team; he made the purchase in November 2004.

Initially he intended for the incumbent management team, Tony Purnell and Dave Pitchforth, to run the team, but a disute over drivers for 2005 led to their leaving the company and being replaced by Christian Horner as team principal for the start of 2005. At only 31 years old, Horner was a surprising choice, particularly in terms of his age and having had no F1 experience prior to this appointment. As a racing driver, Horner, along with his father Garry, had established his own racing team, Arden, in 1997 to contest the FIA Formula 3000 championship. In 1999, he stepped out of the cockpit and concentrated entirely on managing the team. Markko already knew Horner as they had both run teams in F3000, and so had already observed Horner's management style as a competitor.

Mateschitz wanted Red Bull Racing to display some of the non-conformist values he felt were central to the Red Bull brand. At the first European race of 2005, the Red Bull Energy Station made its first appearance. An immense three-storey hospitality centre which needed 25 people to assemble it and 11 trucks to transport it, it redefined the standard in the F1 paddock. In contrast to all the other teams, the Red Bull facility was open access to everyone within the paddock; it belted out load music and served drinks and snacks for all; and it was particularly popular with the F1 media who could now use the facility to unwind or catch up on the gossip of the day. Red Bull also produced the *Red Bulletin,* available free within the paddock, a rather irreverent publication that featured many of the Red Bull sportsmen and women.

But even if Red Bull liked to be non-conformist and youthful, most of all they wanted to win. Horner recognised that a key component in bringing success to Red Bull Racing was the recruitment of a leading F1 designer. He set his sights very high, and in 2005 attempted to recruit McLaren chief designer Adrian Newey, one of the elite designers in F1 whose salary was greater than many of the drivers. This was a high-risk strategy; back in May 2001 Jaguar Racing team principal and close friend of Newey, Bobby Rahal had signed a five-year deal with Newey to secure his services as technical director; however, two days later Newey changed his mind and signed a further contract with McLaren up to the end of July 2005. Rahal subsequently ended up leaving the team at the end of 2001. Horner enlisted the help of Red Bull driver David Coulthard, who had worked with Newey at both Williams and McLaren, a meeting was set up and Newey was invited to Austria to meet with Mateschitz. In a magazine interview Horner describes how the deal was finalised:

'Adrian, we'd love to have you. Do you want to come? He stated a figure that caught my attention because it was about 70 per cent higher than I'd warned Dietrich we might have to pay. I called Dietrich, he went quiet for a few seconds, then he said, "Let's go for it." That's the great thing about Red Bull. It's his company, it belongs just to him and one other person in Thailand. No board meetings, no shareholders' approvals, just an instant decision.'[14]

The decision to bring Newey into the team was undoubtedly an expensive one, but it also marked a turn in fortunes for the team, which Horner attributes to the influence of their new technical director:

'Adrian forced a change of culture on us, because the way he works is completely different. We weren't prepared for the amount of detail he gets involved in. For starters, he still uses a drawing board. [Note: Most design F1 work is undertaken using computer-aided design, and the designs are worked up on computers.] I had to do a deal with Martin Whitmarsh to get McLaren to release his beloved board which had followed him there from Williams and is now in his office at Red Bull Racing. In F1 nowadays a technical director is usually a technical manager, someone who chairs meetings and agrees philosophy and strategic direction, but isn't involved in the actual architecture of the car. Adrian draws the surfaces of the car himself and then passes that over to the aerodynamicists and designers. He stimulates and encourages them, they feed off him, and he feeds off them.'

Although Horner is technically the man in charge, he and Newey run the team together: 'Adrian very much has an input into driver choice, he's involved in all the major decisions. Dietrich will have the final say on the big things – choice of driver, engine, strategic investment – but Adrian and I run the business day to day.'[14]

In 2007, RBR started using Renault engines, the first team outside the Renault works team to be supplied with Renault engines for some time, Renault having won the constructors' trophy in 2005 and 2006. Newey had previously worked with Renault when designing the world championship winning Williams FW14B. When the team won their first constructors' and drivers' (Sebastian Vettel) championship in 2010, it seemed that all the investment had finally paid off.

By the end of 2013, Red Bull Racing had grown to over 700 employees, and the team had enjoyed four successive world championship drivers' and constructors' championships, putting them into a very elite club of only three teams who had won the constructors' trophy four or more times in a row. However, the 2014 F1 season marked a change in fortune for Red Bull Racing. A drive to adopt 'clean' technologies had led to radical new F1 regulations for the 2014 season. The engine specification moved from a 2.4 litre normally aspirated V8 to a 1.6 litre V6 turbo-charged engine and new energy recovery systems (ERS) were allowed which would create a further 150 horse power through using kinetic and heat energy which would be stored in batteries and re-used to enhance car performance. At the end of 2012, only three suppliers remained committed to providing F1 powerplants for 2014 – Renault, Ferrari and Mercedes. In 2012, Christian Horner was concerned that these new regulations could mean a change in the established order: 'What we need to be careful of is that we don't make the engine and powerplant a key performance differentiator between teams. If you end up on the wrong or the right power-plant in 2014, that could prove crucial.'[15] His comments proved to be prophetic and in 2014 the best power unit was clearly that of the Mercedes which allowed them to take the constructors' trophy, with Renault powered Red Bull Racing finishing in second place, almost 300 points behind. At the end of 2014, Vettel announced that he was leaving Red Bull Racing to join Ferrari. In 2015, the Mercedes domination continued with Dietrich Mateschitz publically criticising engine partner Renault: 'Beside taking our time and money they have destroyed our enjoyment and motivation – because no driver and no chassis in this world can compensate for this horse-power deficit.'[16]

The changing face of Formula 1

Looking at the Formula 1 constructors raises some important questions around the challenge of sustaining successful performance in a highly competitive context. How are these teams able to sustain success after they have dominated the championships? What are the different ways in which this can be achieved in different organisations? And how does the basis for success shift over time? These four examples illustrate some of the challenges which organisations face in attempting to both create and sustain competitive advantage.

Notes and references

1. Quote taken from N. Roebuck, 'Frank Williams: The enthusiast turned realist', *The Independent*, 12 July 1992.
2. $1 = £0.6 = €0.75.
3. M. Jacques and D. McLaren Robson, 'Lose the key', *The Independent Magazine*, 9 July 1994, p. 18.
4. Ibid., p. 19.
5. A. Henry, *McLaren: The Epic Years*, Yeovil, Somerset, Haynes Publishing, 1998, p. 179.
6. M. Jacques and D. McLaren Robson, 'Lose the key', *The Independent Magazine*, 9 July 1994, p. 19.
7. Sir Frank Williams, quoted in *Autocar & Motor*, 9 March 1994, p. 78.
8. Patrick Head, quoted in *Sunday Times*, 8 September 1996, p. 14.
9. Quote from interview with the author.
10. Quote from interview with the author.
11. Interview in *Autosport*, 10 September 1992, p. 30.
12. Quote from M. Jenkins, K. Pasternak and R. West, *Performance at the Limit: Business Lessons from Formula 1 Motor Racing*, 2nd edn, Cambridge, UK: Cambridge University Press, 2008, p. 48.
13. M. Cutler, 'The future is bullish for Red Bull's youngsters', *BusinessF1*, vol. 2, no. 4 (April 2004), pp. 343–6.
14. S. Taylor, 'Lunch with Christian Horner', *Motorsport*, vol. 88, no. 1 (2012), pp. 67–72.
15. 'Horner's blueprint for Formula 1', *Autosport online*, 19 October 2012.
16. Quoted in *autosport.com*, 15 June 2015.

APPENDIX: Summary of world champions

Year	Driver	Car/engine	Constructors' Cup
1950	Giuseppe Farina	Alfa Romeo	
1951	Juan Manuel Fangio	Alfa Romeo	
1952	Alberto Ascari	Ferrari	
1953	Alberto Ascari	Ferrari	
1954	Juan Manuel Fangio	Maserati	
1955	Juan Manuel Fangio	Mercedes-Benz	
1956	Juan Manuel Fangio	Lancia-Ferrari	
1957	Juan Manuel Fangio	Maserati	
1958	Mike Hawthorn	Ferrari	Vanwall
1959	Jack Brabham	Cooper/Climax	Cooper/Climax
1960	Jack Brabham	Cooper/Climax	Cooper/Climax
1961	Phil Hill	Ferrari	Ferrari
1962	Graham Hill	BRM	BRM
1963	Jim Clark	Lotus/Climax	Lotus/Climax
1964	John Surtees	Ferrari	Ferrari
1965	Jim Clark	Lotus/Climax	Lotus/Climax
1966	Jack Brabham	Brabham/Repco	Brabham/Repco

(continued)

Year	Driver	Car/engine	Constructors' Cup
1967	Denny Hulme	Brabham/Repco	Brabham/Repco
1968	Graham Hill	Lotus/Ford	Lotus/Ford
1969	Jackie Stewart	Matra/Ford	Matra/Ford
1970	Jochen Rindt	Lotus/Ford	Lotus/Ford
1971	Jackie Stewart	Tyrrell/Ford	Tyrrell/Ford
1972	Emerson Fittipaldi	Lotus/Ford	Lotus/Ford
1973	Jackie Stewart	Tyrrell/Ford	Lotus/Ford
1974	Emerson Fittipaldi	McLaren/Ford	McLaren/Ford
1975	Niki Lauda	Ferrari	Ferrari
1976	James Hunt	McLaren/Ford	Ferrari
1977	Niki Lauda	Ferrari	Ferrari
1978	Mario Andretti	Lotus/Ford	Lotus/Ford
1979	Jody Scheckter	Ferrari	Ferrari
1980	Alan Jones	Williams/Ford	Williams/Ford
1981	Nelson Piquet	Brabham/Ford	Williams/Ford
1982	Keke Rosberg	Williams/Ford	Ferrari
1983	Nelson Piquet	Brabham/BMW	Ferrari
1984	Niki Lauda	McLaren/Porsche	McLaren/Porsche
1985	Alain Prost	McLaren/Porsche	McLaren/Porsche
1986	Alain Prost	McLaren/Porsche	Williams/Honda
1987	Nelson Piquet	Williams/Honda	Williams/Honda
1988	Ayrton Senna	McLaren/Honda	McLaren/Honda
1989	Alain Prost	McLaren/Honda	McLaren/Honda
1990	Ayrton Senna	McLaren/Honda	McLaren/Honda
1991	Ayrton Senna	McLaren/Honda	McLaren/Honda
1992	Nigel Mansell	Williams/Renault	Williams/Renault
1993	Alain Prost	Williams/Renault	Williams/Renault
1994	Michael Schumacher	Benetton/Ford	Williams/Renault
1995	Michael Schumacher	Benetton/Renault	Benetton/Renault
1996	Damon Hill	Williams/Renault	Williams/Renault
1997	Jacques Villeneuve	Williams/Renault	Williams/Renault
1998	Mika Hakkinen	McLaren/Mercedes	McLaren/Mercedes
1999	Mika Hakkinen	McLaren/Mercedes	Ferrari
2000	Michael Schumacher	Ferrari	Ferrari
2001	Michael Schumacher	Ferrari	Ferrari
2002	Michael Schumacher	Ferrari	Ferrari
2003	Michael Schumacher	Ferrari	Ferrari
2004	Michale Schumacher	Ferrari	Ferrari
2005	Fernando Alonso	Renault	Renault
2006	Fernando Alonso	Renault	Renault
2007	Kimi Raikonen	Ferrari	Ferrari
2008	Lewis Hamilton	McLaren/Mercedes	Ferrari
2009	Jenson Button	Brawn/Mercedes	Brawn/Mercedes
2010	Sebastian Vettel	Red Bull/Renault	Red Bull/Renault
2011	Sebastian Vettel	Red Bull/Renault	Red Bull/Renault
2012	Sebastian Vettel	Red Bull/Renault	Red Bull/Renault
2013	Sebastian Vettel	Red Bull/Renault	Red Bull/Renault
2014	Lewis Hamilton	Mercedes/Mercedes	Mercedes/Mercedes
2015	Lewis Hamilton	Mercedes/Mercedes	Mercedes/Mercedes

Note: Constructors' championship is based on the cumulative points gained by a team during the season. Currently each team is limited to entering two cars and drivers per race.

'Access to Healthcare': integrating a CSR programme in Coloplast

Christina Berg Johansen

The notion of 'strategic corporate social responsibility' implies an improved fit between a corporation's strategy and its responsibility activities, making these less 'philanthropic' and more relevant to business – ideally raising the status and impact of CSR in daily corporate life. Danish medical devices company Coloplast went on the journey from philanthropic CSR to strategic CSR with its programme 'Access to Healthcare' that aims to improve healthcare in emerging markets. But the journey from lofty philanthropic vision to practical impact was far from straightforward, and blurring the line between business and CSR has also changed the CSR ambition.

From 2007 until 2017, Coloplast developed, strategised and changed the most ambitious CSR initiative in its history: 'Access to Healthcare'. From its philanthropic and festive beginnings to its current policy focus, Access to Healthcare is the result of passionate project managers, constant strategic changes and a more from idealism to pragmatism. It all began in 2007, when the Danish medical devices company Coloplast celebrated its 50th anniversary with great pride. Founded in 1957 by a nurse and a plastics engineer, Coloplast had become a world leader in the business of what it called 'intimate health-care'; ostomy care,[1] continence care and advanced wound care. By 2007, Coloplast had 7000 employees, its annual revenue was DKK8.047m (£0.9m, $1.2m, €1.05m)[2] and revenue growth was 20 per cent compared to an average 8 per cent in preceding eras.

Coloplast wanted to celebrate its success by 'giving something back' to society and its stakeholders: the nurses, doctors and patients using its products. The result was the launch of 'Access to Healthcare – Coloplast Donation Programme' – a corporate social responsibility (CSR) initiative designed to improve conditions for end-users in emerging and poor markets. Access to Healthcare would spend DKK5m per year over the following ten years (2007–17), totalling DKK50m, on donations to social and educational projects within Coloplast's areas of expertise. This would improve local treatment and help underprivileged end-users to better lives.

However, over the next years, Access to Healthcare struggled with its strategy and increasingly peripheral status in the company; it came close to termination, showed meagre results and struggled to get a foothold in the emerging markets it was trying to address. From 2012, the programme was integrated with wider public affairs activities and improved its strategic relevance to Coloplast. It was, however, far from its initial CSR vision. What happened on the route from CSR to public affairs, and what was so difficult about implementing the initial strategy?

Foundation: idealistic visions

In September 2007, Access to Healthcare was an expense the company could afford. Its fundamental idea was philanthropic, and it had no business case or return on investment projections. It was a highly independent project in the organisation, conceptualised by a narrow group of managers comprising CEO Sten Scheibye, the ethics manager and a trusted marketing manager. An internal 'steering group' followed and supported the development of the programme. However, the aim and strategy of the programme was not completely clear. From the outset, steering group members disagreed on the programme's overarching objectives. Some managers saw Access to Healthcare's social objectives as a moral obligation to help poor end-users. Others tried to incorporate business aspects, such as the provision of new knowledge about customers in the emerging markets and Asia Pacific region, and relationship marketing support to subsidiaries in those markets.

An initial strategy draft stated that Access to Healthcare should be a 'commitment to the UN Global Compact and the Millennium Development Goals [. . .] extend[ing] our listening and responding abilities to include our stakeholders all over the world',[3] as well as

---

supporting the business by 'secur[ing] access and knowledge to growth in the long run'. In practice, this would be carried out by 'initiating and/or supporting projects accelerating education, training, research and development, or information within, or as a natural extension of, the healthcare areas in which we operate. The focus should be on regions where healthcare systems are less developed and/or access to qualified healthcare is limited.'

The structure of the programme was inspired by large private foundations, in which the commercial objectives of the mother business were separated from the philanthropic objectives of the foundation. Everybody involved agreed that, even if there was business potential in the programme, this should not be the *aim* of the programme. Managers were heedful of the ethical challenges in mixing benevolence and the bottom line, having seen other companies dragged through media scandals on this account. Therefore, Access to Healthcare was designed as a 'mini-version' of a foundation, granting project assessment and donation rights to a mainly external board with three representatives of nurses' and doctors' associations, and two internal high-level managers – but also keeping the programme corporate instead of making it a legally autonomous entity, as a regular foundation would be. The idea was for projects to be proposed to the board then, if granted a donation, report on their results. Projects would mainly take place in countries where Coloplast representation overlapped with the UN Industrial Development Organization's list of 'middle-income economies', and the steering group agreed to commence with China, India and selected South American economies. This was to be supported by a full-time position as 'programme manager', referring directly to the CEO. In 2008, the marketing manager from the initiator group, Jane Grant,[4] was hired for this position in the highly independent Access to Healthcare programme (see organisational structure in Figure 1), and began finding board members, creating application schemes and providing information about the programme – for example, website and information to key stakeholders.

Disruption: corporate crisis

In early August 2008, Coloplast released an announcement of reducing organic growth as well as EBIT margin expectations. Offshoring production to Hungary had not provided expected gains and there were serious management issues in the Global Operations division. Some weeks later the CEO resigned and a new and leaner top-management took over. Chief Commercial Officer Lars Rasmussen became the new CEO and his previous position was cut. Chief Financial Officer (CFO) Lene Skole stayed in place. This new two-person leadership

Figure 1 ATH structure, 2008
Source: Christina Berg Johansen.

set out to raise profitability and create a stronger and more coherent Coloplast strategy. Within a few months, the new management had eliminated several hundred jobs, initiated cost-cutting in all departments and was launching a new strategic tool: the short-term business priority strategy named *The Agenda*. Through 8–10 changing priorities, The Agenda targeted either sales generation or cost-efficiency. Corporate practices not included on The Agenda became at best peripheral, at worst officially questioned. The new CEO Lars Rasmussen repeatedly stated at organisation-wide Agenda presentations: 'If you do not see your work represented on The Agenda, you should consider if you are doing the right things.'

Raising profitability was the vital concern in Coloplast and more developmental, long-term opportunities were marginalised if not abandoned. Practices such as CSR and Access to Healthcare were not on The Agenda, neither were emerging market strategies, whose share in Coloplast profits was much lower than European markets and therefore not an immediate priority. More than that, Access to Healthcare had lost its main protector, the previous CEO, and its Steering Group was more or less haphazard, since its members now had other more pressing issues to spend their time on. The programme was generally ignored and left to programme manager Jane Grant, who worked autonomously to create projects that could be approved by the Access to Healthcare board. She later reflected on this period:

'I was just thinking that "I need to drive this." And I could see if I didn't make any changes, it would stop really. So I had to do something. And this was . . . I knew it would not be the perfect way of doing it. But I thought, "This is what I can do now. And then later on I have to look at it and maybe change it."'

To create better strategic fit, she got Access to Healthcare moved to the Communications department, but quickly learned that management there was busy with more immediate priorities such as media relations and supporting the internal turnaround. Instead she turned to her own internal network of long-time Coloplast managers for help. They facilitated contact with selected subsidiary managers in emerging markets, who were interested in finding money and time for initiatives outside immediate sales.

A series of projects were born out of these efforts, for example nurses' education in China or diabetic wound care training for doctors in India. Projects were sometimes conceived by the local Coloplast office and then formulated in collaboration with the official applicant organisations, such as the International Ostomy Association, International Spinal Cord Society, China Nursing Association and local wound care doctors' associations. By offering educational opportunities to influential doctors' and nurses' organisations, Coloplast's emerging market subsidiaries could build important relationships in their own markets – similar to what its regular marketing projects had done in core markets. The role of Coloplast was, however, not visible in the official application, since Access to Healthcare was still arms'-length to business and run as donations to independent NGOs.

Generally, the development of projects was far from the simple 'application – grant – report' process initially envisioned. It took between six and eighteen months to get from the first application to a financed and running project, involving several rounds of assessment by the board, adjustments of goals and roles, budget changes and uncertainty around contract signing. In late 2009, Access to Healthcare had only six projects either approved or in the pipeline, varying in size from US$22,000 to US$241,000 and in duration from two-day workshops to three-year educational programmes. The annual budget of DKK5m was not spent. There were no results to communicate, since projects had hardly started. Programme manager Jane Grant was exhausted, felt misunderstood and resigned, and the programme came close to termination. CFO Lene Skole, who had become the C-level manager accountable for Access to Healthcare, decided to give the programme a second chance – not least because it was initially a public commitment with positive branding, stakeholder and market development potential.

Re-orientation: legitimising the business perspective

In late 2009, a new programme manager, Paul Nissen, took over with a contracted agreement to:

- create new projects (minimum five applications and three approved in 2010);
- monitor and follow up on projects – hereunder to communicate results;
- build (internal) awareness and knowledge.

For Paul Nissen, however, this could not be done before clarifying the aim of the programme, with associated adjustments to its structure. 'What did Coloplast really want from Access to Healthcare?' he asked. It was subtitled 'Coloplast Donation Programme' but had evolved through a form of partnerships between Coloplast subsidiaries and large local healthcare NGOs. For new projects to be created, Paul would have to know which direction they should take – strategic collaborations for Coloplast subsidiaries, or arms'-length project donations? Either route would mean a changed structure and approach. But Paul was not managing an independent programme – Access to Healthcare was now at the bottom of a managerial hierarchy (see Figure 2) and his managers did not agree to change the structure of the programme; rather they wanted Access to Healthcare to be 'less troublesome' and to create positive results. The message was clear: 'Please make sure that you do only what is necessary, and focus on creating results' (External Affairs manager).

What 'results' were was not exactly clear, but building on what Access to Healthcare already seemed to be doing, and the fact that Paul was himself a marketing specialist (and headhunted from the Coloplast marketing department), he pursued the idea of strategic collaborations, regardless of the ambiguous structural set-up. He struggled to 'describe that fine line between when it is enough of a marketing program [. . .] to be of interest to Coloplast, without compromising the promise to the user' and opened up project development by networking across Coloplast headquarters and visiting emerging market offices. Working with emerging market managers in headquarters, a matrix emerged that was used for

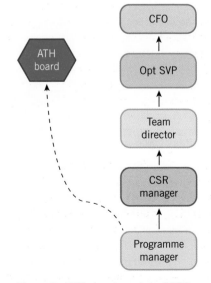

Figure 2 ATH structure, late 2009
Source: Christina Berg Johansen.

several discussions about potential Access to Healthcare projects: on one axis, project ideas were rated according to business opportunities, on the other axis according to 'promise to user'. The best projects were those that scored high on both axes (see Figure 3).

A few local Coloplast managers saw great potential for relationship marketing in Access to Healthcare, and also for development of their brand and presence in emerging markets. As their budgets were generally allocated to short-term sales efforts, Access to Healthcare was a welcoming funding opportunity for long-term market developments. However, it was difficult for local managers to invest resources for developing Access to Healthcare projects, while continuously meeting commercial performance targets. In the words of managers from the Argentinian and Chinese subsidiaries:

> **'We need to consider effort versus gains, [since we are dealing with] projects that are not impacting the sales of the coming year. . . . There is no doubt that you could do something – but we are talking long term. And we have a lot on our plates . . . '**

In 2010, only one project emerged from conversations with subsidiaries.

The other big objective in Paul Nissen's contract was to monitor existing projects, ensuring their progress and identifying and communicating their results. Most projects were behind schedule and the NGOs in charge changed both timing and content of milestones as their projects evolved. There had been very little overseeing of progress up to this point, since the function of the Access to Healthcare board had been to evaluate applications and approve projects, and not to monitor or in other ways develop the programme, and the programme manager had been too busy trying to make projects happen. Paul Nissen set out to design a detailed project management tool in which data from projects could be added and followed; however, the tool was never put to use. Getting data turned out to be challenging, and often Paul got data from emails and phone conversations, which he compiled into temporary progress reports. Data were output numbers, such as '12 workshops completed and 480 healthcare practitioners trained' (wound care training programme in India) or 'pilot studies in 8 hospitals completed' (ostomy treatment guidelines project in China), from project update March 2011, but what this meant for Coloplast or for end-users was not described. Projects were generally behind schedule or stalled entirely. As a donation programme, Access to Healthcare did not *have* to interfere with project progress – the programme could simply shut down project payments and end unsuccessful projects. Nevertheless, Paul and management deemed it better to work *with* the NGOs and help improve their work, rather than to just shut projects down and hope for new and better ones. And, as a corporate programme, Access to Healthcare was interested in creating relations with the NGOs which represented large customer groups; thus the programme manager tried to understand their needs and help create momentum.

Paul kept working to change the structure of the Access to Healthcare programme as such. He envisioned a 'partnership programme' with clear roles for all involved partners, and with less bureaucratic project development procedures. Though his managers at first opposed this 'governance discussion', because it took focus from creating and communicating results, the Steering Group eventually applauded the idea and concurrently decided that there was no need for an external, project-approving board. The Access to Healthcare board was terminated in early 2011.

Meanwhile, a last round of cost trimming was being rolled out in headquarters. The option to eliminate Access to Healthcare was, once again, seriously considered. Against the programme were its relatively high costs and little business value. In its favour were the future prospects of emerging markets, and the role it could play in these. Top management opted for continuing the programme, but with a somewhat altered strategic focus and less administrative costs.

	Good projects	Ideal projects
Promises to users ↑	(high degree of philanthropy)	(fulfil promise to patients and end-users to a high degree – and provide good business opportunities)
	Poor projects	**Business projects**
	(poor impact on access to healthcare for patients and end-users)	(projects better linked to marketing and sales, not ATH)
	Business opportunities →	

Figure 3 Presentation of social/business relevance, 2010
Source: Christina Berg Johansen.

Business integration: building healthcare policy

In mid-2011, Paul Nissen was dismissed and Access to Healthcare added to the work portfolio of Matt Danner, the Senior Public Affairs Manager in charge of emerging market geographies (Access to Healthcamp would take up around 25 per cent of his work time, although no specific measure was allocated). He related Access to Healthcare to an evolving growth strategy in Coloplast: revenue was growing and the EBIT margin had increased from 12 per cent in 2007–08 to 21 per cent in 2009–10. In 2011, emerging markets such as China reappeared on The Agenda because of their high growth rates. Since Access to Healthcare had several projects in China, positive attention was turned towards it as one of many ways to support market development and reimbursement efforts. Coloplast wanted to impact national and regional healthcare policy in geographies such as Latin America and China, to increase reimbursement opportunities for their products.

Matt Danner therefore developed a new and more policy-oriented Access to Healthcare, in which the 'partnership programme' ideas from his predecessor were elaborated upon and made to fit the new company-wide agenda to grow emerging markets with more than simple sales.

Marketing objectives were dropped along with the remnants of the 'donation' structure and tagline, and the programme's potential as a market *development* tool was buttressed, as Matt explained:

'We are trying to think a little more holistically [. . .] in terms of how do you create a system of care in these places, [. . .] making sure that these projects are also addressing the policymaking community in these countries.'

The programme focused on local healthcare organisations and political units, and subsidiaries were made responsible for reaching out to local interest groups and key opinion leaders and for building projects with them. This placed the individual and poor end-users outside most projects' scope – the aim was not to help individuals directly but to help them through changing healthcare systems, to the long-term benefit of the relevant countries (e.g. improving national health structure via standards of care), end-users (e.g. getting better care and helping them access good products via reimbursement) and the company (e.g. reimbursement and market share, stakeholder relations).

Matt Danner spent considerable time with local Coloplast managers to help them develop realistic projects that supplemented traditional training of healthcare professionals with clear advocacy and policy effects, but it was still not easy. Working with non-commercial targets and measures did not come naturally to subsidiary managers, though they were keen on strengthening this side of their business. So he focused on making the actual impacts of Access to Healthcare projects clearer, building tools and guidelines for Coloplast managers, and

visiting local country offices for more in-depth development. He encouraged local managers to consider external partners according to their policy impact and abilities, and the new application system required the roles of both partners and Coloplast to be clearly described.

By late 2012, seven new projects had been contracted, spread across China, Brazil, Argentina, India and South Africa. In 2012, Access to Healthcare for the first time managed to use all its funds for projects.

Over the following years, some of the previous Access to Healthcare projects paved the way for new developments and strengthened partnerships. For example, the ostomy treatment guidelines project in China, whose core Chinese partners opened the door to collaboration with the Chinese Ministry of Health in a new 'Go West' programme – offering stoma and wound care training for physicians in the remote Western regions of China.

Reimbursement strategies for non-Western markets gained importance in the corporate structure and budget allocations. Headquarters prompted the relevant subsidiaries to integrate Access to Healthcare projects into their business plans, such that all projects are today part of local business plans, concurrent to being contracted with local external partners. Some partner organisations such as ISCoS (International Spinal Chord Society) had continued making projects with Coloplast and others were new, e.g. the Chinese Disabled Persons Federation, an expert panel of Brazilian rehabilitation centre nurses, and the Argentinian Ostomy Patient Organization.

In 2015, the increasing focus on reimbursement and the policy work entailed (e.g. dialogues with public payers and other stakeholders) led to the move of Public Affairs (hereunder Access to Healthcare) into the Payers & Trade department, as part of a broader reorganisation of sales and marketing functions into the new strategic business unit 'Chronic Care' (see Figure 4).

Project governance is continuously based on project applications from the subsidiaries in collaboration with local partners, with design assistance from Matt Danner's team. Assessment and approval of new projects is a simple two-step process going through first a small four-person Steering Group (Matt Danner, the VP of Payers & Trade, an expert from Compliance, and the head of Corporate Responsibility) and then for final approval by EXM (Executive Management).

The strong focus to raise 'standards of care' has prompted new projects to predominantly target continence care (over ostomy care), e.g. for people with spinal chord injuries who are typically wheel-chaired. In most of Coloplast's emerging markets, ostomy care does have a certain baseline, whereas the standard of care in continence is close to non-existent. Concurrently, Coloplast's 'intermittent catheter' technologies make

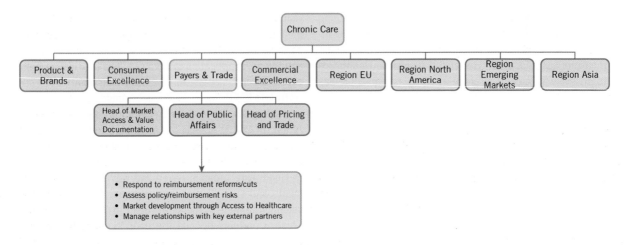

Figure 4 ATH structure, 2015–
Source: Coloplast.

strong business cases. Raising standards of care takes place on several levels, placing projects on a 'developmental' line with five steps (see Figure 5).

As the reimbursement strategy has evolved, so have the countries in which Access to Healthcare is represented. Instead of an externally defined selection of countries (the UN-defined 'middle-income economies' from the programme's early days), the level of – and impact potential on – a country's standard of care has become a core selection criterion, and the programme is now used globally. An example is the 'Promoting Intermittent Catheterization in Poland' project from 2014, aiming to 'promote an adoption of new guidelines for urinary incontinence that embrace HCIC (hydrophilic coated intermittent catheters) as a new and improved standard of care'.

Raising the standards in continence care is thus seen as developing Coloplast's commercial agenda while building the type of societal impact that Access to Healthcare symbolises. The social focus is not so much on quality of life (QOL) practices for individual end-users, as it is on improving policy and taking on responsibility as a 'market

leader', as Matt Danner expresses: 'One of the obligations you have as a market leader is to build and develop the market – even when your competitors benefit, too.'

Another ten years? The decennial evaluation

In 2017, Access to Healthcare has existed for ten years. In the spring of 2016, therefore, Matt Danner was 'expecting to evaluate the impact of the programme as we near the ten-year lifespan it was initially aiming for'. A presentation of the programme today shows three large areas of benefit (see Figure 6).

However, assessing the value of Access to Healthcare is still not easy. What will be presented are numbers from the contracted project deliverables, e.g. output numbers from training programmes, surveys on their usefulness, and assessments of improved stakeholder relations, as well as the overall success of projects in reaching their goals, e.g. 'New legislation that promotes broader access to ostomy supplies for Argentinian citizens' (in collaboration with the above-mentioned Argentinian Ostomy Patient Association).

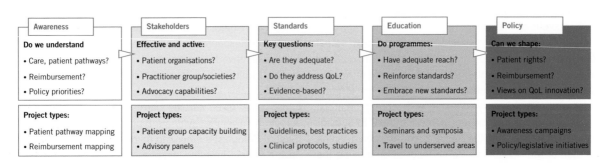

Figure 5 A developmental approach to project selection, grounded in practice
Source: Coloplast.

Improved conditions for stakeholders

- Better-trained practitioners
- Improved access to products
- More treatment options
- Reimbursement

Deeper market insight

- Standards of care
- End-user/practitioner views, priorities
- State of product technology
- Reimbursement policies

Stronger, deeper ties to stakeholders

- End-users
- Practitioners
- Policy-makers
- NGOs and others

Figure 6 How does Coloplast benefit?

Source: Coloplast.

Besides these numbers, the meaningfulness of the programme is also evaluated on a more anecdotal basis, 'checking in' with subsidiaries and their partner organisations to hear how projects are going and to see whether they are still interested and engaged in the projects.

The broader social impact is challenging and time-consuming to measure, and there is little research on social effects such as 'quality of life' measures for end-users, since, as Matt Danner reflects: 'you have to prioritize . . . there is a lot of things I don't do, because the programme has limited money.'

Across three programme managers and multiple organisational changes, Access to Healthcare has managed to survive and even to improve its relevance for and integration with the company. At its ten-year assessment, Access to Healthcare can present itself as a successful programme with 32 projects (finished and current) that has helped and still helps Coloplast raise the 'standard of care' and build partnerships in more than ten countries across the globe. According to the current programme manager, its strategic relevance will only continue and, if the company decides to continue the programme from 2017 onwards, it will be on behalf of the entire Coloplast organisation 'because it sees it as a strategic tool'. Figure 7 illustrates Coloplast's view of Access to Healthcare as having moved from the organisational periphery to being a strategic tool.

Access to Healthcare is now a recognised tool in Coloplast, which has lifted its CSR perspective from philanthropy to corporate relevance, and one with future strategic potential in developing markets and improving healthcare frameworks globally. Whether that makes for successful CSR, or is something completely different from CSR, is a discussion that Coloplast – as well as CSR practitioners and researchers in general – have yet to bring to a conclusion.

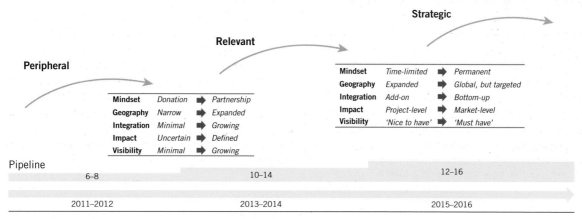

Figure 7 Access to Healthcare – evolution from peripheral to strategic

Source: Coloplast.

Notes and references

1. An ostomy pouching system (also called a bag) is a medical device that provides a means for the collection of waste from a surgically diverted biological system.
2. DKK1 = £0.11 = $0.15 = €0.13.
3. This and all subsequent quotations are taken from the author's own interviews.
4. All names other than CEO and CFO positions have been changed.

Manchester United FC: competing with Europe's elite clubs
Steve Pyle

This case describes the playing and financial issues at Manchester United in English professional football, focusing on the club's debts and the controversies concerning its ownership. Football in Europe is becoming dominated by a small number of very rich clubs – can Manchester United compete successfully with these elite clubs? Will the financial 'fair play' regulations have an impact? Will MUFC thrive or be overtaken by richer clubs? The case involves a number of issues including ownership structures, football finances, governance and the expectations of different stakeholders.

Introduction

Although Manchester United (MUFC) is the most celebrated football (soccer) club in the UK, their supremacy was in danger of coming to an abrupt end. Both Manchester City (who won the English premier league in 2012 and 2014) and Chelsea (who won the premier league in 2010 and 2015 and the European Champions League in 2012) have become major forces in English and European football. These clubs have mega-rich owners who, unlike Manchester United, have invested heavily in facilities and star players without plunging the club into massive debt.

Within Europe, Manchester United was the third biggest club behind Real Madrid and Barcelona in terms of turnover, while Manchester City was sixth and Chelsea eighth in 2014–15. Although MUFC remain relatively successful, 2013–14 was a traumatic year for the club after the retirement of long-term manager Sir Alex Ferguson and a seventh place finish under new manager David Moyes. This was the worst in many years and resulted in failure to qualify for the European Champions League. The financial position has remained a concern with high levels of debt. However, in the year to June 2014 MUFC increased revenues to a record level of $£433m (£519m, $649m)[1] and made profits (before interest and taxation) of £67.9m. MUFC remain a top team and under another new manager Louis Van Gaal (who replaced Moyes) the club moved up to fourth place in 2015 and a return to European competition. New sponsorship deals and increased TV income means that the

Source: robertharding/Alamy Images.

financial position should improve provided success on the field continues.

Football finances in Europe are coming under much greater scrutiny as UEFA have introduced a 'financial fair play' policy aimed at limiting excessive expenditure and unsustainable debt levels among European clubs. Can Manchester United compete with their domestic rivals and rise to the challenge of the elite clubs in Europe? Will MUFC's unpopular ownership by the Glazer family remain in place or will the club return to plc status? Will the club be taken over by yet another ambitious billionaire attracted by 'the beautiful game' or will the real fans get a look in?

Manchester United FC – a proud history

Manchester United's success and global brand is rooted in the club's history. The club achieved limited success

---

in the first 70 years of its existence, but since the 1950s MUFC has become increasingly successful. The club has continued to develop young and exciting teams and became the first English team to win the European Cup in 1968. Manchester United are the best supported club in the UK and their fame spreads over the globe – they claim to have 659 million fans worldwide. After the English premier league was introduced in 1992–3, Manchester United began to dominate the English game – winning the league 12 times in the first 20 years. However, this dominance has come under challenge in recent years with Chelsea and Manchester City becoming key rivals.

The club was traditionally run as a private limited company with control in the hands of the Edwards family. In 1989, the club was valued at £10m but over the next 30 years the valuation of the club rocketed as the value of an iconic football brand was realised and the commercialisation of football became greater. When live televised matches became the norm after the 1980s, it was recognised that big football clubs could be very valuable assets.

Manchester United becomes a public limited company in 1991

In 1991, the chairman, Martin Edwards, was concerned by the strategic problems of raising funds for ground improvements and improving playing success by attracting top players. The club was floated on the London Stock Exchange with an initial valuation of £40m. As a public limited company (plc), the club was able to raise further capital by share issues in 1994 and 1997. At the time of the flotation in 1991, very few football clubs had the ownership structure of a plc and it was a controversial move. The manager Alex Ferguson said: 'When the plc started there were grave doubts about it – I had them myself – but I think the supporters came round.'[2]

What brought the supporters round was the success of the team and the increased financial revenues the club was attracting. In May 1997, Peter Kenyon was recruited for his marketing and branding expertise. Later, as chief executive, he helped to build the club's global business interests. MUFC's sales of replica kits and club-related gifts continued to expand and their merchandising success became the benchmark for the industry. Increasingly, Manchester United became a well-known brand across the world. When Kenyon left to join Chelsea he was succeeded by David Gill, whose financial expertise had been instrumental in the success of the plc, and Manchester United continued to set the pace for commercial revenues.

Clean sheets or balance sheets

A public limited company has a different set of purposes and priorities compared to other forms of ownership structures that are common among football clubs. Shareholders demand profits and, although some shares were held by supporters, the vast majority were owned by financial institutions that were looking for a return on their investment. MUFC as a plc were at the forefront of the revolution that was changing football from a traditional working class sport into a multinational business. Clubs were now receiving huge sums from the media (Sky TV and more recently BT Sport have massively increased the value of football on TV) and clubs are getting a lot more income from sponsors. Some genuine football supporters began to feel alienated by the club's values and global aspirations – should a football club be striving for profits? The range of stakeholders that needed to be satisfied had got considerably wider.

In the 14 years that MUFC were a plc (1991–2005), they dominated English football (winning the premier league title eight times and the FA cup four times) and the profits were rolling in. Everyone seemed to be benefiting from the success, but there was an undercurrent of dissatisfaction among some supporters and resentment from other clubs.

The Glazer takeover – a return to private ownership

One of the disadvantages of plc status is the risk of a takeover. Manchester United was a cash-rich club and the potential to exploit the brand attracted predatory interest. In the early 2000s Malcolm Glazer (a multimillionaire with diverse business interests in the USA) began to build a shareholding stake in MUFC. Glazer had no real knowledge of soccer but had successfully acquired Tampa Bay Buccaneers – an American football team – and thought he could replicate that success. Glazer saw the potential of a strong brand and believed that he might be able to market it successfully in the USA and globally. Throughout the takeover battle many fans bitterly opposed the acquisition and initially this opposition was shared by the Board of Directors. David Gill, the CEO, cautioned against the acquisition saying: 'The Board continues to believe that Glazer's business plan assumptions are aggressive and could be damaging.'[3]

Glazer steadily built his stake – financial institutions will almost always sell at the right price. By May 2005, Glazer had increased his stake to the critical 75 per cent level. He was therefore able to de-list the club from the Stock Exchange and soon after he bought out all the remaining shares. When the final takeover was complete the valuation of MUFC was estimated at £800m. However, the Glazer family were not rich enough to finance the deal themselves and had to borrow heavily to gain control – much of this debt (approximately £275m) was secured against the football club's assets. Moreover, a significant part of this finance was obtained at high rates of interest from US Hedge Funds. After being debt free for almost 15 years as a plc, MUFC had become a privately owned company with total debts estimated at £660m incurring annual interest payments of approximately £60m.

The Glazer years

Immediately after the takeover the Glazer family began to pursue policies to dampen hostility. They pledged funds for transfers and offered new contracts to Sir Alex Ferguson and David Gill to ensure continuity. They assured fans that they were not after a quick profit. Malcolm Glazer was an old man and appointed his sons (Joel, Ave and Bryan) to the Board to oversee the business.

During the takeover, fans were worried that ticket prices would soar in order to pay the increased costs of the borrowing undertaken by the Glazers. This fear may be misplaced. Ticket prices have gone up but they are still cheaper than many premiership clubs – notably at the London clubs Chelsea and Arsenal. The stadium is full for almost every match and there is a long waiting list for season tickets

Manchester United continued to invest heavily in the stadium and its facilities – the developments completed in 2006 took ground capacity up to 75,691 making it by far the largest club ground in England. Average attendances (and match day revenues) are higher than key rivals – in 2014–15 Manchester United had an average league attendance of 75,335 compared to its next biggest UK rival Arsenal whose average attendance was 60,000. Indeed in Europe only Barcelona and Borussia Dortmund command higher average attendances. The Manchester United superstore is still by far the most lucrative club shop in the country and sponsorships together with commercial income (most importantly broadcasting fees) ensure that the revenues continue to rise. This has enabled the club to service the interest payments on the debts.

Refinancing

Clearly the financial position of the club needed attention with debts of £716m outstanding in January 2010. Later that year a bond issue generated £504m which enabled MUFC to pay off most of the debt held by international banks. The annual interest payable on these bonds – due to mature in February 2017 – was approximately £45m although this was considerably less than was previously being paid out. The club's debt prompted protests from fans – supporters started wearing green and gold scarves, the club's original colours. Banners stating 'Love United Hate Glazer' appeared around the ground. The Manchester United Supporters' Trust (who had opposed the Glazers from the start) held meetings with a group of wealthy fans, dubbed the 'Red Knights', with plans to buy out the Glazers' controlling interest. No exact figures have been published, but it seems the Red Knights were unwilling to pay more than £1.2bn whereas the Glazers valued the club at over £1.6bn. It soon became apparent that the Glazers were not going to sell out.

In July 2012, the club decided to list shares on the New York Stock Exchange – thereby diluting the Glazers ownership but without them losing control. Shares were set to go on sale at $16 but the price was cut to $14 on the day of the launch following negative comments from analysts. The shares traded poorly at first but recovered to trade at $15–$18 throughout 2015. Manchester United was valued by Forbes at $3.1bn in 2015, making it the third most valuable football club in the world – after Real Madrid and Barcelona – and predicted to be the most valuable in 2016.

On the playing side, success has continued despite the massive investments made by rivals Chelsea, Arsenal, Liverpool and particularly Manchester City. Manchester United completed a hat trick of league titles in 2009 and won again in 2011 and 2013. They also reached the European Champions League final in both 2008 and 2009 – beating Chelsea in 2008 and losing to Barcelona in 2009.

The end of an era in 2013

On 8 May 2013, Sir Alex Ferguson announced that he was retiring as club manager at the end of the season. Ferguson had proved himself to be one of the most successful football managers of all time – in his 26 years at Manchester United the club won 38 trophies. In addition the CEO, David Gill, also retired from his post (to be replaced by Ed Woodward) and took up a role with UEFA. The club appointed David Moyes as manager after he had done well as manager of Everton and hopes were high that he could continue Ferguson's success. However, 2013–14 proved to be a very poor season for the club – finishing seventh and failing to qualify for the European Champions League. Moyes was sacked despite having been on a six-year contract and many commentators feared that this once mighty club faced financial meltdown unless they quickly returned to the top. An experienced manager, Louis Van De Gaal was appointed in May 2014 on a three-year contract and a recently-retired star player, Ryan Giggs, was appointed as assistant manager – with a view to him taking over after three years. Fortunately for Manchester United there was something of a recovery in 2014–15. Although Chelsea won the league and Manchester City finished second, United managed fourth place and so qualified for the lucrative European competition. May 2014 also saw the death of Malcolm Glazer, but this had relatively little impact on the club as control of the club had already passed to his sons Joel and Avram Glazer who are co-chairmen.

Alternative ownership structures

There are alternatives to the debt-financed pattern of ownership that is now common in the English premier league. In Germany, nearly all the professional clubs have at least 51 per cent ownership by the members. In Spain the two richest clubs (Real Madrid and Barcelona) are owned and operated by the members. Nonetheless, this doesn't stop these clubs taking on debt – the seemingly irresistible drive to be successful demands that spending often exceeds income.

A further possibility would be for clubs to be supported by large firms who use the club as part of a promotion strategy and support the local club in the communities where they are located, for example Philips support PSV Eindhoven and Bayer support Bayer Leverkusen. It is also possible for local government bodies to support clubs financially and in other ways (provision of stadia), but this is not common at senior levels of football.

Some clubs are lucky enough to have rich benefactors who provide funding. Chelsea are backed by the billionaire support of Roman Abramovich. The latest clubs to receive massive financial support from mega-rich owners include Manchester City – the club is fully owned by Sheikh Mansour (part of the UAE ruling family), with an estimated individual net worth of at least £17bn. Similarly, Qatar Investment Authority acquired leading French club Paris Saint-Germain (PSG) in 2012: PSG president Nasser Al-Khelaifi announced that he expected to invest £100m to build a strong team.

A lack of continuing interest or support from the owners can leave a club in deep financial trouble – this happened to Malaga FC after the Qatari owners pulled the plug on their funding.

It was problems like this and the spiralling debt at many top clubs that persuaded UEFA and its president Michel Platini to develop a 'Financial Fair Play' policy.

Platini expressed the concerns of many when he said:

'The goal is not to win titles but to make money to pay off debts. Look at Chelsea and Manchester United. FIFA and UEFA owe it to themselves to fight this. I am very concerned by clubs being bought by foreigners. I don't see why Americans come to invest in these clubs if not to turn them into "products". It's a never ending gold rush.'[4]

The 'Financial Fair Play' (FFP) regulations

Many clubs, like MUFC, have reported repeated financial losses; moreover, the wider economic situation has created difficult market conditions for clubs in Europe. Many clubs have experienced liquidity shortfalls leading to delayed payments to other clubs, employees and social/tax authorities. With Platini as a driving force, UEFA decided to take action and set about tackling these problems. UEFA's Executive Committee unanimously approved a financial fair play concept for the game's well-being in September 2009 and published their policy in 2010[5] the principal objectives being to:

* introduce more discipline and rationality in club football finances;
* decrease pressure on salaries and transfer fees and limit inflationary effect;
* encourage clubs to compete with (in) their revenues;
* encourage long-term investments in the youth sector and infrastructure;
* protect the long-term viability of European club football;
* ensure clubs settle their liabilities on a timely basis.

One important aspect of the policy is an obligation for clubs to balance their books or 'break even'. Clubs cannot repeatedly spend more than their generated revenues, and will be obliged to meet all their transfer and employee payment commitments. Higher-risk clubs that fail to meet key indicators will be required to provide budgets detailing their strategic plans. UEFA has a range of sanctions including warnings, fines, deduction of points and disqualification from tournaments. A Financial Control Panel has been set up to monitor and ensure that clubs adhere to the financial fair play requirements.

There are, however, concerns that these regulations will not stop billionaire owners pumping funds into clubs and circumventing the regulations. For instance, if benefactors put money into a club in the form of excessive sponsorship, it may still be categorised as football-related income, so enabling the club to 'balance its books' and facilitate more spending.

Some wonder if Manchester City are already doing this. The biggest driver of revenue growth has been sponsorship. Not all of City's sponsors are suspect. However, it is striking that among its portfolio of commercial partners it counts four companies that are either owned or controlled by the UAE's government – Sheikh Mansour's family, in other words. Etihad Airline's ten-year £400m sponsorship deal with City is so astonishingly rich that in August UEFA announced that it would investigate the deal. This loophole will have to be closed as Arsenal manager Arsene Wenger noted: 'It raises the real question about the credibility of Financial Fair Play. If Financial Fair play is to have a chance, the sponsorship has to be at market price.'[6]

Nonetheless, the Financial Fair Play regulations do seem to be having some effect. In 2012–14, total transfer spending was significantly reduced in England and across Europe. Moreover, even the big spenders (notably Chelsea and Manchester City) were keen to offload some highly paid players before spending on new players. As UEFA General Secretary Gianni Infantino noted: 'Aggregate net losses of Europe's clubs have fallen from £1.7bn in 2011 to £400m in 2014.'

In 2015, UEFA relaxed the FFP regulations to allow cash injections from owners that do not involve increasing the club's debts. This is good news for clubs like Manchester City and PSG and was partly the result of lobbying by these clubs – it is also doubtful that the regulations were enforceable in law anyway. Moreover, there has been criticism that the FFP regulations tend to favour the richest clubs and reinforce their dominance by making it very difficult for clubs outside the elite group to spend the sums needed to compete with these giants.

Governance issues

Football has always had a rather poor image as regards good governance. Dubious characters seem drawn to the game and several clubs (and even governing bodies) have suffered from the bad publicity that attaches to the all-too-frequent scandals in the game. Powerful men like Silvio Berlusconi (at AC Milan) and Thaksin Shinawatra (at Manchester City) have faced charges of corruption. Several clubs have faced bans for match fixing; for example, five big clubs in Italy in 2006 (which included Juventus and AC Milan) and Fenerbahçe in Turkey in 2012. Individuals in the game have frequently been found guilty of tax evasion; for example, Uli Hoeness when President of Bayern Munich.

Perhaps the worst scandal erupted in 2015 when Sepp Blatter was suspended from his role as FIFA President after years of rumours about corruption. Shortly after, Michel Platini (UEFA President) also became involved in the scandal and was suspended from his role. Platini's fall from grace may impact on the FFP regulations as he has been their greatest supporter.

Future prospects

Manchester United have supported the FFP regulations since they are less constrained by them than their closest rivals – MUFC has much higher football revenues than rivals Manchester City, Chelsea, Liverpool or Arsenal. As of 2016, the financial future for all the English premier league clubs was looking brighter, with massive new broadcasting deals coming on stream. The new TV contract is worth £5.1bn for the three seasons 2016–19 (a 70 per cent increase on the previous deal). Moreover, Manchester United, along with many other English premier league teams, had negotiated lucrative sponsorship and marketing arrangements. The Glazer family could look back on what appeared to have been a successful gamble (to retain ownership): they could now sell the club at a huge profit and in September 2015 announced that dividends would be paid on shareholdings – this would amount to £15m per annum for the Glazer family (who still held 80 per cent of the shares). Nevertheless, the overall position remained tenuous. Without playing success, revenues would plummet – MUFC needed to keep qualifying for the Champions League. The debt level has remained high and the club (and particularly its fans) want to see this steadily reduced. Without regular profits, the interest payments on the debt would become a major threat.

Postscript

The 2015–16 season turned out to be another difficult season for Manchester United despite winning the FA cup. They just missed qualification for the European Champions League – and manager Louis Van Gaal was sacked (to be replaced by Jose Marinho who in turn was sacked by Chelsea earlier in the season). Even more surprising was the fall of Chelsea – champions in 2015 but struggled in 2016 and finished well down the league and without a trophy. Arsenal finished second and once again qualified for the Champions League but, frustratingly for their fans, failed to win a trophy. Local rivals Manchester City reached the Champions League semi-finals in April 2016 and had secured the services of top international coach Pep Guardiola for season 2016–17. However, the club only just managed to qualify for the Champions League, amidst concerns that the team was past its best and the owners would need to invest in yet more costly new players. The big surprise, however, was the success of a little known team with limited resources,

Leicester City (5000:1 outsiders at the beginning of the season!) pulling off one of the biggest shocks in soccer history by winning the Premier League in May 2016 – sometimes football really is a beautiful game. As for the other leading European clubs: Bayern Munich won their domestic league easily (but surprisingly lost in the semi-finals of the Champions League); Real Madrid won the Champions League; however, Barcelona won both league and cup in Spain. PSG dominated in France but are yet to make the major breakthrough in European competition that their owners crave.

Notes and references
1. £1 = €1.2 = $1.5.
2. MUFC website, www.manuntd.com, 22 November 2004.
3. MUFC board statement as quoted by www.joinmust.co.uk, 26 July 2005.
4. B. Archer, 'UEFA boss Platini: 'England '"cheats"', *Times*, 7 June 2008.
5. © UEFA.com 1998-2012. All rights reserved.
6. ESPN, 'Will FFP save football from itself?' 4 January 2012.
7. M. Slater, 'Michel Platini: UEFA to "ease" financial fairplay rules', *BBC Sport*, 18 May 2015.

APPENDIX 1: Profiles of the elite football clubs in Europe

Real Madrid FC (Spain)

Real Madrid are the biggest club in world football. The club is valued at over £2.5bn and generated a revenue of £577m in 2014/15. They are the most successful club side in European competitions having won the European Cup/Champions League ten times.

Real Madrid is a registered sports association which is owned by its members – there are 60,000 members (called *socios*) who elect an assembly of delegates (the governing body) and a club president. The president (Florentino Perez) is responsible for the club's strategy and managerial appointments. Head coaches come and go regularly as the president, socios and supporters expect continual success. The club is particularly sensitive to being outdone by Barcelona. TV money from football is very unevenly distributed in Spain with almost 50 per cent going to these two clubs alone. Both clubs are also guaranteed large revenues by qualifying for the European Champions League – each having qualified every year since 2004. Nevertheless, Real Madrid are still massively in debt (estimated at £590m in 2014) as they always want to buy the world's best players.

FC Barcelona (Spain)

Barcelona are Real Madrid's main rivals in both Spain and Europe. They have won the Spanish league 23 times and the Spanish cup a record 27 times. They have won the European Cup/Champions League five times – most recently in 2014/15. They are one of the most valuable sports teams in the world and the second richest football club in Europe with annual revenue of £460.8m in 2015.

Barcelona play attractive, passing football with a plethora of top players. Barcelona is a registered sports association owned by its members (170,000 socios) and controlled by an elected Board of Directors. Barcelona's financial position is not completely secure. They had debts of £578m and recorded a net loss of £12m in 2013–14. However, this level of debt is manageable as long as playing success continues. Barcelona have narrowly avoided breaking the FFP regulations. Barcelona were particularly successful from 2008–12 under Pep Guardiola who guided the club to 14 trophies in this period. However, he moved to Bayern Munich in 2013 and was recruited by Manchester City for season 2016–17.

FC Bayern Munich (Germany)

Bayern Munich are the most successful club in German football and the most financially stable club in world football. They have won the German league 25 times and the German cup 17 times. They have won the European Cup/Champions League on five occasions – second only to Real Madrid. Bayern are majority owned (75 per cent) by their members – an astonishing 231,197 of them – who elect an Executive Board and President. The other 25 per cent is owned by three large German companies (Adidas, Audi and Allianz) who are also major sponsors. This ownership model has worked well, as the club is debt free and, like all German clubs, puts a high degree of importance on the expectations of supporters. Ticket prices are relatively cheap and supporters have significant influence. Bayern attract large crowds (average attendance was 72,882 in 2014/15). Bayern are among the top five clubs in Europe in terms of revenue (£487.5m in 2013/14) and have recorded profits in nine out of ten years between 2005 and 2014. Bayern totally dominate German football and have no concerns with the FFP regulations. They seem assured of remaining at the summit of European football for the foreseeable future.

Borussia Dortmund [BVB] (Germany)

Borussia Dortmund are one of the most successful clubs in Germany having won the German league eight times and are the main rivals to Bayern Munich. Their stadium is the biggest in Germany and their average league attendance (80,463 in 2014/15) is the highest in Europe. Borussia Dortmund are part of a sports association with 115,000 members that runs the football club. The club is part of a two-tier organisation, where the other part is a public limited company. BVB is the only German club that has adopted this form of ownership.

Between 2003 and 2005, Borussia Dortmund were nearly bankrupt but gradually the finances improved – by increased sponsorship and selling players. However, it was the appointment of Jurgen Klopp as head coach in 2008 that revived the playing fortunes – BVB won the league twice and were runners-up twice between 2010 and 2014 and qualified for the European Champions League. However, Klopp joined Liverpool in 2015. In 2014/5 BVB had revenues of £261.5m (11th highest in Europe). In September 2014, BVB struck a deal with their main sponsors – injecting £114m into the club in return for an ownership stake. The club cleared most of its debt and had funds for investment.

Chelsea FC (London, UK)

Chelsea were not particularly successful in the first hundred years of their existence. However, that changed in 2003 when Russian billionaire Roman Abramovich bought the club for £140m. Abramovich invested a vast amount in new players. Transfer fees and wages rocketed at Chelsea and other clubs struggled to match this level of expenditure. Abramovich is impatient and has hired and fired 12 managers since 2003. The most successful, with two stints in charge, was Jose Mourinho with three league championships (most recently in 2015), but a poor start to the 2015/16 season led to Mourinho getting sacked. Chelsea have invested heavily in their training facilities and stadium, but it is relatively small and this limits revenue. Their average attendance in 2014/15 was 41,546 (28th in Europe) and their revenue was £420m (8th in Europe). The club plans to rebuild their stadium with a capacity of 60,000.

Chelsea itself remains debt free although the parent company, which is completely owned by Abramovich, holds an estimated £709m of debt. The FFP regulations have impacted on Chelsea. The early years of Abramovich's ownership were marked by very large financial losses, but since then increased revenues and an attempt to restrain wage costs and transfer spending have enabled Chelsea to stay close to, but within, the FFP limits. In 2014/15 the club recorded a loss of £23.1m (despite winning the league championship) but they expect their finances to improve with more sponsorship and TV money, enabling compliance with FFP regulations. However, Chelsea's finances are heavily dependent on qualification for the European Champions League. Nonetheless, as long as Roman Abramovich remains committed their financial future seems secure.

Manchester City FC (UK)

Manchester City, apart from a brief period in the late 1960s/early 1970s, struggled to achieve any sustained success. However, everything changed in 2008 when the Abu Dhabi United Group bought the club for a reported £200m. City are effectively controlled by Mansour bin Zayed Al Nahyan (called Sheikh Mansour), a member of the Abu Dhabi royal family and one of the richest men in the world. Since then several managers have come and gone, but Sheikh Mansour has consistently invested vast sums into players, staff, ground and training facilities. Manchester City's Etihad stadium is relatively new and the Etihad campus (training ground) have benefited from £150m–£200m of investment.

Although it took some time for this huge investment to result in playing success, Manchester City won the FA Cup in 2011 and the league title in 2012 and 2014. The club is now expected to qualify for the European Champions League each year. In total, Sheikh Mansour has invested over £1.15bn in the club since the takeover. This level of expenditure has led to significant trading losses, resulting in the club breaching the FFP regulations and being subject to sanctions in 2014/15. The sanctions were lifted in July 2015, once there was a marked improvement in income (up £76m in 2013/14) from increases in sponsorship and commercial revenues. The club also cut wage costs by £28m in 2013/14. However, some commentators have questioned how these improvements have been achieved: much of the sponsorship and commercial revenue comes from Abu Dhabi-based companies – are these companies paying an inflated, non-commercial rate? Nonetheless, Manchester City have avoided further sanctions and, with the immense wealth of Sheikh Mansour behind them, the club is well placed for further success.

Arsenal FC (London, UK)

Arsenal are the most consistently successful club in English football, having never been out of the top tier since 1919 and having won the league 13 times and the FA Cup a record 12 times. However, Arsenal have not won the English premier league since 2004, although they have qualified for the European Champions League in 16 successive seasons (from 2001 to 2016). In 2006, Arsenal moved into the 60,000+ Emirates stadium (named after their major sponsor) enabling increases in revenues and attendances – in 2014/15 average attendance was 59,992, second only to Manchester United in England and 7th highest in Europe. Qualification for the Champions League and increased attendances has ensured healthy revenues – €435.5m in 2015 (7th in Europe).

The stadium cost £390m and this caused the club to be relatively frugal in the transfer market while there was a significant debt. By 2015, net debts had been reduced to a relatively modest £5.7m and profit increased to £24.7m. Arsenal have consistently made profits and, although critics have suggested their spending has been too conservative to win trophies, the club is well managed and controlled – and has never broken the FFP rules.

Arsenal FC is a limited company, but its shares are not quoted on the stock exchange. There are two major shareholders – Stan Kronke (a US businessman with 67 per cent) and Alisher Usmanov (a Russian billionaire with 30 per cent) – neither seems keen to make significant changes to the way the club is run. Arsenal are well placed to compete in Europe – they were ranked the 7th most valuable football club in Europe in 2014 (worth $1,307m) and the 6th most valued brand in world football. However, their fans have become frustrated by the lack of trophies – Arsenal have never won the European Cup/Champions League, making the final only once. The question is: do they start spending similar sums as some of their rivals, or do they continue to balance playing success with financial responsibility?

APPENDIX 2: The elite clubs in Europe (statistics)

Club	Total revenue 2014/15 (€m)	Average attendance 2014/15	Total valuation 2014 ($m)	Domestic league titles	European titles
Manchester United	519.5	75,335	3,104	20	3
Manchester City	463.5	45,365	1,375	4	0
Chelsea	420.0	41,546	1,370	5	1
Arsenal	435.5	59,992	1,307	13	0
Liverpool	391.8	44,659	982	18	5
Real Madrid	577.0	73,081	3,263	32	10
Barcelona	560.8	77,632	3,163	23	5
Bayern Munich	474.0	72,882	2,347	25	5
Borussia Dortmund	280.6	80,463	700	8	1
Schalke	219.7	61,578	572	7	0
Paris SG	480.8	45,789	634	5	0
Juventus	323.9	38,553	837	31	2

Sources: Deloitte, 'Annual review of football finance', 2016; Forbes, 'The business of soccer: the world's most valuable football teams, 2016', 5 November 2016.

Adnams: a living company

Julie Verity and Kim Turnbull James

This is a case about the long-term survival and evolution of a UK-based SME, one that has an iconic brand and a strong local position. It covers all aspects of the company, providing an opportunity to discuss competitive strategy, corporate governance, strategic capabilities and core competences, customer and brand values, culture, innovation, leadership and strategy process and decision-making. Adnams is a unique company and this can make for interesting and probing discussions about the nature of strategy and strategy-making.

Adnams is a mid-sized brewing and distilling business based in Southwold in Suffolk, UK with a turnover in 2015 of about £65m.[1] Adnams also owns and operates hotels and pubs mostly in and around Suffolk and Norfolk. Roughly 435 people work at Adnams and there are about 1500 shareholders. Andy Wood joined the company in 1994 with responsibility for developing customer service and supply chain operations. He joined the Board in 2000 with the additional responsibility of sales, marketing and the wine business, becoming Managing Director in 2006 and Chief Executive in 2010.

Andy Wood describes himself as a guardian of Adnams who is privileged to share in its history and development. He doesn't believe in 'white charger leadership': 'Instead, I want to celebrate others and push them to the front.' At the time of writing, he was also aware of significant challenges:

> 'There is a lot going on – we will always be a manufacturer . . . but we are stretching the brand into long drinks, spirits, food and retail; becoming more of a broad church. The competition are demanding this, we can't compete head-on with global or micro-brewers, and the hotel and pub scene is changing fundamentally.'

Suffolk connections

> 'If you took the brewery out of Southwold you would rip its heart out.'[2]

Southwold and beer have lived together for the past 650 years. Beer was sold from the site of the current Swan Hotel in Southwold from 1345 using hops grown locally to brew the beer. The Sole Bay Brewery was moved a short distance away from The Swan in 1660 and has stood on the same site in Southwold for 450 years. In 1872, both the brewery and hotel were bought by the Adnams family and one of the Adnams brothers established the enterprise officially as Adnams & Company Ltd in 1890. The business grew as a brewery with associated inns, located mainly in Suffolk and Norfolk.

As one employee explained: 'People ask me where I work, and when I tell them – Adnams – they say: "that's in Southwold". This happens all the time – people automatically make links between the name and the place.'[3]

Southwold is a coastal town located in an area of natural beauty which is rich in wildlife. The town itself has great charm. The landscape lends much to the image and flavour of Adnams' products and hence the business. The business and its brand are closely linked to its Southwold roots and the Suffolk environment.

One example is Adnams Hotels. The Swan and The Crown are a long-established part of the portfolio, commanding prime positions in the heart of Southwold, close to the beach and the seafront with its rows of Victorian, brightly painted beach huts. A famous landmark in Southwold is the land-locked lighthouse. Sixteen of the Swan Hotel's rooms are named 'The Lighthouse Rooms', because they look out on the lighthouse.

Another example is in the visual identity of the Adnams brand. Simon Loftus (then chairman and part owner; see below) launched a new corporate identity in

This case was prepared by Julie Verity and Kim Turnbull James and was made possible because of funding from the Cranfield/Thurnham legacy. It is intended as a basis for class discussion and not as an illustration of good or bad practice. Thanks to people at Adnams who generously gave their time for interviews. Copyright © Julie Verity and Kim Turnbull James 2016. Not to be reproduced or quoted without permission.

1999. He took this further in 2003 with the launch of an iconic advertising campaign called 'Beer from the Coast'. In the same year the annual report included the following:

> 'September saw the launch of our "Beer from the Coast" marketing campaign. . . . Six illustrations depicting coastal scenes were produced by a local artist. . . . The *Daily Telegraph* named our posters "Ad of the Week" with the following comment: "You can almost smell the sea looking at these posters. They combine head and heart appeal; the product message is that Adnams is a brewer, based on the coast; the

intangible message is that Adnams is the ultimate local brewer offering a beer-drinking pleasure that the big brewers can never match." We couldn't have put it better ourselves.'[4]

Andy Wood commented in 2010:

> 'I think there are more and more consumers who are looking for products with provenance; with a sense of place that they can relate to. There are a growing number of people who are more aware of what they are eating and drinking. Their health and wellbeing is important to them and local food and drink, plus knowing and trusting it is genuine, this is all part of what the Adnams brand has at its heart.'

Source: Adnams plc.

Family connections

The Loftus family bought a stake in Adnams in 1902. This means that the two families, Adnams and Loftus, have jointly given about 250 years of service and stewardship to the company. Generations of these families have lived locally, invested locally, joined the fabric of the local society and employed thousands of local people. During the 1960s, these families were under pressure to sell out at a time of consolidation in the brewing industry and growing market demand, but they chose to retain the company's independence and local identity. Long-term commitment to Adnams is no less today, and while the company is listed with traded shares, local families retain a controlling stake.

Further family connections can be found among shareholders. Adnams' shares are relatively illiquid: shareholders form long-term connections with Adnams. Very recently, Andy noted an influx of small investors, those specifically attracted to the brand's values – of authentic craftsmanship, sustainability and the company's long-term perspective.

Customer connections

Adnams tries hard to keep close and tight connections with customers. The wine business is an early example, which Simon Loftus took control of when he first started working for the company. It was his idea to shorten the distance between suppliers, Adnams and its customers, bringing the consumer and grower into contact with each other by telling the growers' stories. This was a first among wine merchants, setting Adnams apart from the pack. The senior wine buyer at Adnams said:

> 'Simon turned a sleepy Suffolk wine merchant into one of England's premier wine merchants; not in terms of volume, but in terms of profile. We are front-edge. We

buy wines from people who are interested in something different and, therefore, are interesting. We do this rather than buy wines that are perfectly good but middle-of-the-road. It is important for Adnams to have an opinion. If we sell wines that are populist, we have no difference. So, we are looking for the superlatives on the landscape and we price them very competitively.'

The marketing activity at Adnams has evolved to suit the rural nature of Suffolk, as the head of marketing explained: 'Putting up a billboard will not work. The media opportunities to touch customers here are rare, we have to be much more targeted and direct.'

Having worked previously for one of the UK's largest multiple grocers, the constraints of the location were starkly evident to her. Learning to adapt to the demands of the situation, however, had resulted in fun, creative and cost-effective ways to engage customers. One idea was to take the brand to customers. For example, 120,000 people visit the annual Suffolk Show. There is also a Norfolk Show and other festivals in and around East Anglia which attract local people and holiday-makers. To these, Adnams send the Mobile Beach Hut or the Mobile Boat Bar from which customers can sample Adnams' products directly. Adnams also formed partnerships with the Cycling Tour of Britain, London Boat Races and Newmarket Racecourse to host events.

Adnams today is not just a local company but increasingly has a national market and is expanding its overseas opportunities.

Andy Wood commented:

'I think we were the first real beer brand to go onto Twitter and we have many (thousands of) followers. Social media and the web has extended and changed our reach considerably. We are actively looking to exploit export opportunities.'

Renewal

Early in the 2000s, Adnams committed to updating their assets. Today, the Southwold brewery is one of the most modern, energy- and water-efficient brew streams in the UK. Ninety per cent of the waste heat from the process of brewing is captured and recycled, lowering energy use dramatically. Traditionally, it took eight pints of water to make one pint of beer, but this has been reduced to 3.2 pints with the latest technology. Quality was also up, with less than 0.1 per cent (down from approx one per cent) of barrels returned because of spoiled beer. The cost of this renewal was £4m. Production capacity was increased adding new fermentation tanks, but (extraordinarily) the exterior of the building retains its original Victorian façade.

A further £6m was spent building a new distribution centre which became another Adnams' success story. *Management Today*, for example, wrote:

'The firm's bottles are the lightest – and thus the greenest – on the market. And to top it all, the new £6m distribution centre opened in October 2006 has been called the greenest warehouse in the country. Thanks to natural construction materials and a reed-covered-roof, it doesn't need heating and air-conditioning systems to maintain an even temperature and should save £500,000 on energy bills over the next ten years. It was also a low carbon build, as the hemp-and-lime block walls lock 150 tonnes of carbon into the structure.'[5]

The new distribution centre cost 20 per cent more to build than would the usual 'distribution shed'. Initial costing put the excess at much higher than this, but the huge rise in market prices for steel at the time reduced the differential. For this small/medium-sized company whose annual turnover was then about £45m and whose profits ranged between £3m and £3.5m, this extra up-front outlay could have appeared extravagant. Andy Wood explained:

'We wanted to do something of which we could be proud. Second, we all thought fossil-based fuels were going to get more expensive and that polluters would have to pay for their pollution. We needed to be better at keeping our energy consumption low for both reasons. Third, we have a framework for decision making. We look at: return on capital employed, internal capability and capacity and, our value base. If these things align we go ahead. So, in this case, spending more up-front would make our ROCE harder to meet, but the sustainable argument made it the right thing to do. Our shareholders tell us this is right and they stick with us through thick and thin.'

The investment in the distribution centre paid off. It was ten times the size of the old refrigerated store and, despite this extra capacity and escalating utility prices, running costs by 2010 were less than five years earlier. Water is collected from the roof and used for the toilets and showers.

Sustainability is one of Adnams' values, but it has not been adopted just because it became trendy to be environmentally conscious and the meaning of 'sustainability' to Adnams is not limited to being 'green'. For example, in 1981 Adnams bought a farm in order to recycle the brewery waste in an environmentally efficient way. The farm produced prize-winning beef and pork. Adnams' management argue that it is the longevity of the *enterprise* that its people value as well as having pride in what they do. The leaders at Adnams think about themselves as stewards who look after the company for a while and who want to leave it better fit for survival than when they took over. Andy said: 'We are trying to build a model for tomorrow. In the new world this will be a good way to generate wealth – one that is not rapacious.'

The company also sought to reduce carbon emissions. To achieve this, an anaerobic digester plant was opened in 2010 on the Adnams Bio Energy site. The digester is fed by food and brewing waste and the biogas produced used as fuel for Adnams' trucks that deliver wines and ales. Dual-fuel trucks (biogas and diesel) are more expensive to buy than straight diesel vehicles, but the operations director estimated that when the whole fleet was converted the diesel bill could reduce to £60k pa rather than the predicted cost of £350k.

By 2014, the carbon produced during the everyday running of the business, and measured as Kg/£1000 revenue, had reduced by 25 per cent from the 2008 level. On waste, Adnams achieved zero to landfill.

Innovation

UK consumers' attitudes about alcohol and drinking habits are volatile. The market environment generally is hard to read. Competitor moves, regulatory changes, even the weather all play a part in its up-and-down nature. Some longer-term trends are:

- A decline in the number of and sales from traditional 'wet-led pubs' (in which income is primarily from beer and drinks, not food): this trend accelerated from 2007, when smoking was banned inside public buildings in the UK.
- Consolidation among the large corporate breweries and proliferation of very small micro-breweries. In 2014, the number of micro-brewers rose to the highest ever at almost 2000, the vast majority of which were registered under the Small Breweries Relief scheme, allowing them to pay reduced tax. The amount of cask beer in the UK market in 2014 attributed to these brewers was up from 15 per cent in 2004 to about 45 per cent a decade later. As a mid-sized brewer, Adnams was not eligible for this relief, giving cost advantage to the micro-brewers since scale efficiencies did not accrue until beyond the scale of Adnams.[6]
- Increased consumption of alcohol at home. In 2014, in the UK, the total amount of beer consumed at home exceeded that drunk in pubs for the first time.
- Supermarkets taking an increasing share of wine, spirits and beer sales.
- Increasing awareness of health-related issues, and the dangers of alcohol misuse.

Adnams needed to innovate to keep pace with this challenging market. For example, as the 2011 *Good Pub Guide* said: 'Adnams stands out, with its interesting and seasonally changing range of splendid ales (good wines too), now very widely available.'

According to Fergus, the master brewer, renewal of the brewery and flexibility of the new brew stream also facilitated change:

> '**The brew house does let us do a lot that we couldn't with the old kit because the old brew stream was only designed to do an English style of brewing. Now we can respond to the market and have also led the market with new beers.'**

Andy Wood believes in and encourages innovative behaviour everywhere: 'Innovation is about the mindset of *all* our people.'

An illustration is given by the Head of Hotels about Mary, who looks after breakfast service in The Swan:

> '**I told her about a hotel in London where the boiled eggs at breakfast were served with hand-knitted, individual bobble hats – to keep them warm. Five days later, Mary brought in a prototype for our restaurant. She had made it herself, in her own time, with her own materials and so we started serving eggs with bobble hats. Now she has to keep knitting, because our customers like them so much they ask if they can have one to take home.'**

Andy had done a lot to encourage this behaviour; it had not always been like this. Long-timers at Adnams would explain that it was patriarchal and top-down: a caring organisation, but also a closed one.[7] Over the last two decades it had changed. As one employee explained:

> '**It has become a more open structure and if you want to, if you had the drive and capability, you could work your way up. Before it was all about dead-men's shoes. It is quite dramatically different in the way it has modernised itself and involved new people, but at the same time, it remains completely anchored in Southwold.'**

Portfolio

Beer is at the heart of Adnams' ecosystem, but the business is more complex than this suggests. Beer brands are sold through three channels: (i) direct through the 50+ Adnams licensed pubs, direct through Adnams' shops and hotels and to independent free-trade pubs in East Anglia and London; (ii) to large pub-owning companies and wholesalers for distribution throughout the UK, and (iii) to supermarkets and other off-trade outlets.

Wine is sold direct through the tied estate and Adnams' hotels, through shops and by mail order.

Adnams' distribution centre stocks 3000 lines, supplying the tied estate with all they need: from spirits, mixers, bottled mineral water to cordials and peanuts. All logistics are in-house. The Company have their own fleet of trucks and draymen, a customer service centre and warehouse team. While Adnams own and manage the two Southwold Hotels, the other four in the portfolio are managed by Adnams but remain on the balance sheets of their original owners.[8] The hotels are showcases for Adnams' products and skills, as well as commercial, profitable businesses.

In 2015 there were 11 'Cellar&Kitchen' shops selling Adnams' brands: beer, spirits, some foods, kitchenware and gifts. Diversification into retail started in 2006–7 which management admit, with hindsight, was a terrible time to expand any business. But, given the longer-term pressures in Adnams' traditional markets, becoming more diverse made sense to Andy Wood, even if it did start as an experiment:

'Our shareholders don't want us to dilute their holding. We need to find ways to grow without access to large amounts of capital. We have always had a small retail offer in Southwold. We have the supply chain and some products. We have some experience about how to package the offer. Expanding our retail proposition gives us the opportunity to reach a new consumer – close to 50% of all purchases from our shops are made

by women – this compares with beer which is predominately sold to men. We tried it in Holkham in North Norfolk, a shop in the middle of nowhere, and it did really well. Interestingly, and what we probably didn't anticipate, is that we sell a lot of beer from the shops as well.'

Stores were set up in the more affluent parts of East Anglia, in towns like Southwold that tend to have high proportions of second-home ownership. By mid-2012, the stores were generating sales of around £11m – just one fifth of Adnams' total turnover, and it was in 2014 that, after building significant learning into the management of the store portfolio, Adnams' shops turned profitable. Figure 1 gives a segmented analysis of Adnams' revenue and profit during 2010–15.

In 2010, Adnams was diversifying again, this time into spirits. A change in UK tax rules made it possible for brewers to distil alcohol for the first time and Adnams committed early, building a distiller in the brewery yard.

The marketing manager was excited:

'Customers are looking for quality and to escape the mass market. It is about purity and a hand-crafted product. We have the space, the raw materials, distribution channels and customers. We know that with the Adnams name on a product we sell more than if it doesn't have the brand. So it makes a lot of sense. We are going to distil vodka, gin, and oaked vodka and in time, we will sell a whisky.'

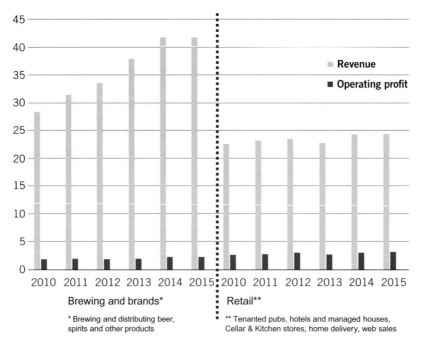

Figure 1 Segmented analysis of revenue and operating profit, 2010–2015 (£m)

Four years later, Adnams' leaders were planning the next investment in the distillery and brewery. Costed at around £7m, the alm was to accommodate their success with the Adnams' spirit brands (the company having won the International Wine and Spirits competition for their London Dry gin in 2013 and for their Longshore vodka in 2014) as well as market shifts in demand for bottled, canned, cask and keg beers.

In 2014, out of Adnams' 435 employees there were only a dozen in the brewing team and only four of them actually do the brewing. Although Andy described the business as a brewery, it has evolved into a much more complex operation than this. The brand is about provenance – the food and drink are associated with their place of origin and all its qualities; the hotels are in lovely locations where customers can retreat and be looked after; the pubs are all individual and idiosyncratic to their locale; and the stores provide outlets for Adnams' products as does the internet and traditional mail order.

Internal connections

People are proud to work at Adnams. Karen Hester started working at Adnams in 1990 as a part-time cleaner. By 1994, she was a transport clerk and in 1996 she became Transport Manager. Karen was promoted again in 2000 into Andy Wood's old job as Head of

Logistics and in 2003 added the customer services team to her remit. During this time, she led the relocation and rebuilding of the distribution centre. In 2006, after a successful move to the new site, Karen became Operations Director when she added the brewery to her team. IT and HR were added in 2008, when Andy thought these services were becoming isolated. In the same year, she won the prestigious East of England Business Woman of the Year Award. In 2010, Karen took on oversight of the tenanted pubs and in 2013 she won the CBI First Women Business of the Year title in recognition of Adnams' success in supporting women employees to reach their full potential. In 2015, she joined the Adnams Board. Karen insists she can do every one of her teams' jobs – and probably has done at some point in her career at Adnams. She is a director but, she gladly helps pick orders at Christmas when staff are at their busiest. Figure 2 summarises the revenue, operating profit and leadership during 2005–15.

Staff turnover at Adnams is low and people have a sense of belonging. For example, three weeks after a new team leader was appointed, he said:

'The really good thing about the people here is that when you ask them to do something it gets done; problems are solved between us. I was worried when I started because there was no clocking-on, but there

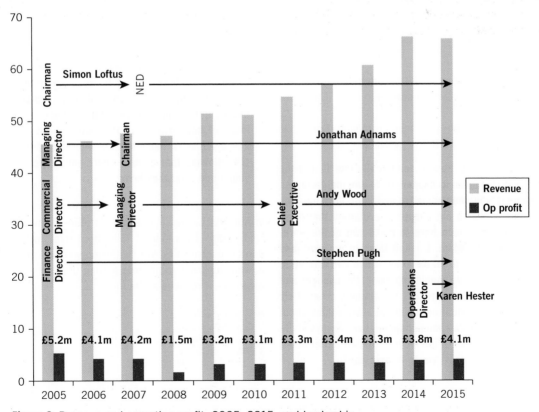

Figure 2 Revenue and operating profit, 2005–2015, and leadership

was no need because everyone is here at 6.30, the lights are on and people are working. We should finish at 4 pm, but it could be 4.30, 5 pm: we finish when the work is done and no one claims overtime. But on the days when we have done all the work, we ask Fergus if we can finish early. We do what needs to be done because here, you feel you are one of the cornerstones of the business.'

Karen believes that communication is what makes organisations succeed and, when there is a lack of it, to fail. With the redesign of the distribution centre, she insisted on one, open-plan, office where teams sit in 'pods' but where there are no dividing walls between teams. Every morning at 9 am she meets with all her managers for what she describes as: 'a quick chat about what happened yesterday, what needs putting right today and what will be done by tomorrow.' Everyone knows, at high level, what everyone else is doing.

Once a month Karen has a 'snack and chat' with her brewery staff – because they are not part of her open-plan office. This happens at 10 am in the Swan Hotel where a room is reserved, egg and bacon rolls and coffee arrive and: 'We sit and talk. I tell them what is going on and they tell me what is happening in their world and we have a chat about what is bubbling – it is an hour for airing thoughts.'

Three or four times a year she visits her draymen and takes all ten for a meal and a chat. Her customer service team sit in the distribution centre and mostly chat to customers about their orders and deliveries. Very few customers use email or fax (though this is an option) as Karen said: 'Our customers like talking to us and we like listening. We can improve our service to them if we know more about them.'

If there is a problem that needs resolving, Karen has cake and a chat with all those involved:

'We change a lot. People don't really like it, but the best way to make it happen is to be inclusive. An example is when we decided to distribute the wine from here, which was a big change. I explained that if we didn't do this I would have to make two of the warehouse staff redundant. I asked them to go away and think about it and to let me know which two wanted to go. They decided we should implement the changes and save the jobs. In the process we actually created six new jobs for the local community. I always think about how I would make a change happen, but I always invite the people involved to tell me how to do it better and if they have great ideas, we do it their way.'

Tenants among the tied estate are not employees of Adnams[9] but that does not mean their ideas are not welcomed. In the past, the most significant part of the relationship between tenants and the company was the rent level set for the pub. The process was less than transparent to the tenants. There were many stories among tenants about the unfairness of this process, which prompted one of them to write to Andy with a proposal of how to do it differently.

'I wrote to him proposing what I thought was a better way to set rents for us landlords. My point was that it didn't have to be so complex or difficult. So, Andy invited me to talk with him . . . and it has grown from there. . . . This is different from the past when there was an attitude among the senior leaders that we were here just to sell their beer and if it all goes wrong, there will always be someone else who would come and rent a pub. Now, Andy and Karen provide a support network that you can choose to opt into.'

Going forward

There is a feeling of stability at Adnams despite its mid-size, its increasingly competitive landscape and the challenge of being a family business that is opening itself up to more outside influences. Andy Wood stresses the skills of leaders and followers in equal measure that mean Adnams can constantly adapt and survive:

'We need a framework – we need to steer . . . but at the same time we need our people to bring their own intelligence to the business and for us to reinforce the great behaviours that they already display in their work – excellent customer service for instance, and having ideas of how to improve their work. So it is learning new disciplines, being clear in where you are going but still allowing that culture where you respect the individual and what they know.'

Respect and pride are two words that are heard often in Adnams' conversations and literature as one employee said: 'Lots of companies talk about this stuff, but you don't expect it to be like that when you work there. That is what took me some time getting used to – here they mean it – it really is authentic!'

Notes and references
1. £1 = €1.2 = $1.5.
2. Adnams' employee.
3. Adnams' employee.
4. Adnams' Annual Report 2003.

5. 'Changes a-brewing', *Management Today*, 1 December 2007.

6. See N. Thomas, 'Adnams calls for review of "unfair" tax breaks for micro brewer', *Telegraph*, 27 March 2013.

7. Adnams was one of the first companies to set up a profit-sharing scheme for employees – in 1960. This was followed by an employees' trust in 1977 and the employee share ownership scheme in 1992, which means that longer-serving employees can hold Adnams' shares and often do own part of the company.

8. Adnams manage these hotels. A manager and chef respond directly to Adnams, the hotels are rebranded Adnams. There is no equity ownership or financial risk, it is the brand that is extended and, ultimately, at risk.

9. Landlords pay a rent for an Adnams pub and manage it as their own business. They have to sell Adnams' 'wet' products, but they can develop the business in other ways (by selling food, for example) and retain the profits from these sales.

Widespace: managing growth and culture within a maturing technology venture

Karl Wennberg, Cecilia Lönnström and Sandra Tersluisen

This case focuses on the formation and development of an entrepreneurial business in the mobile advertising industry. Since its foundation in 2007, Widespace has grown into an international business and by 2016 was beginning to expand in the USA. The case explores several issues related to entrepreneurship and innovation including how best to structure the business, maintain an innovative culture and develop appropriate entrepreneurial strategies and relationships.

Introduction

Patrik Fagerlund, CEO of Widespace, had plenty of reasons to be happy. The mobile advertising company he had started with his Ericsson colleague, Henric Ehrenblad, had been hugely successful, winning prize after prize and growing faster than they could have imagined. Now, in June 2014, they were finally starting to reap the fruits of all their labour. As Patrik sat in Widespace's bright new offices in Stockholm, Sweden, munching on a cinnamon bun, he wondered what his next steps should be. The company was continuing to grow at a rate that was becoming hard to sustain, hiring around two new employees every week. Henrik and Patrik had worked hard to keep the entrepreneurial spirit high within the company and to develop a cohesive corporate culture at all the different Widespace offices around the world, but with the increased number of people came an increased need for routines and organisation. How could they provide the structure necessary for the company to continue to grow without destroying what had made the company so innovative in the first place?

A brief history of Widespace

Widespace was founded in 2007, around the same time Apple released the first version of the iPhone, something now recognised as a watershed moment in the mobile handset industry.

Patrik Fagerlund and Henric Erhenblad met while working at Ericsson, the Swedish mobile platforms provider. Both engineers by trade, Henric worked mainly in business development in China, the USA and in Sweden. Patrik's background at Ericsson was as a salesman, both in Sweden and in the USA. Patrik worked with the platform considered to be the future of the mobile internet – wireless application protocol (WAP). The idea for Widespace and a mobile advertising company came in 2004, but the idea was put on hold because of the still sluggish increase in mobile internet penetration. Both Patrik and Henric had worked with internal start-ups within Ericsson but found they were too constricted when working within the bounds of a big corporation. In 2007, they finally decided the business case for mobile internet advertisements was convincing enough and started Widespace.

Growth was slow in the beginning. The iPhone was just out on the market, but smartphones were not yet part of the public mindset, and less in the mindset of advertising buyers. The buyers – primarily media agencies – were headed by executives who were not usually technological pioneers themselves and most of them did not have a smartphone. This was a major challenge – how to explain the difference between an ordinary cell phone and a cell phone with rapid internet connection in a pitch to a conservative 50-something executive? Another challenge was that the Widespace founders came from a technology-oriented environment to a media-oriented environment. So while Widespace was first on the market, it took about two years for the firm to take off, and for advertising buyers to acquire their own smartphones, making them realise the potential of the medium. The two founders realised early on that they needed to create their own market in order not to get crushed by giants with established brands and technological platforms. To do that, they needed their own technologies and their own sales force. They also saw their own limitations, especially when sales started to pick up.

Neither Henric nor Patrik had worked within digital sales. They were both engineers, and had neither the language nor the networks to be able to build up the relationships needed for the firm to grow.

Consequently, they hired Sami Abidi from Swedish publisher, Schibsted, as Head of Sales, and he brought with him the current VP of Sales Toni Kaski, and several of their best colleagues from Schibsted. At first, Widespace had been financed only by the founders' own money and with that of their families and friends but, in 2012, Swedish venture capitalist firms Northzone and Industrifonden contributed €3m[1] in equity funding. It was a deliberate move by the founders as they knew that in order to scale up the technology needed to succeed internationally, and move away from the small premium market in Sweden, they would need external investors.

The mobile advertising market

'There's a huge gap [in the market] that's going to be filled. [. . .] First the eyes shift and then the money follows.'

Toni Kaski, Sales

While mobile advertising had grown exponentially since the release of the iPhone, it was still a relatively small market and, more importantly, the money spent on mobile advertising in relation to the time people spent on their mobile devices was tiny in comparison. In 2013, media budgets spent around four per cent on mobile advertising, while the average person spent 20 per cent of their media time on phones or tablets. Widespace saw this as lucrative opportunity for future market growth and predicted the mobile advertising market could grow around 100 per cent per annum, depending on the country. They had seen similar trends in the internet advertising industry, where investments only caught up in 2013. Mobile advertising consisted of ads for both smartphones and tablets, and within apps, on mobile webpages and within specially built apps for certain ad campaigns. The aim was often to continue to provide free content to an end-user (such as reading a newspaper or playing the free version of a game) in exchange for the user looking at ads. As such, mobile advertising companies needed to work with both companies who wanted to advertise and the publishers where the ads would be displayed. The main contact with the advertisers went through the big media agencies, though a small percentage of the contacts came directly from the advertisers. Big and smaller publishers, as well as popular apps producers, were the clients, all depending on the focus of the mobile advertising company. There was also

competition from some of the big publishing houses who had their own sales teams, such as Schibsted in Sweden and VG in Norway.

Generally, the market has been developing quickly, with innovative new ad formats being launched on a weekly basis. However, a common problem for all the players in this industry has been how to measure the performance of the ads. Conventional measuring methods included the number of clicks per ad or the number of views redirected to the advertiser's webpage, but these were unreliable and easy to manipulate. Widespace worked continuously to develop new and better ways to measure performance. By focusing on a high-priced premium product focusing on 'how to smoothly deliver the ad to the best recipient', Widespace was able to position itself as catering to advertisers with strong brands that were cautious of using low-cost solutions that could lead to degrading the brand value if the brand was inappropriately exposed. There was also discussion on how to harmonise mobile ads with TV and print ads, and the role mobile ads would play in the future. Were they a complement or would they completely take over the market from traditional media?

A problem which all of the mobile advertising companies encountered was the need to educate customers on both the advertising and the publishing side about what mobile advertising actually was and its potential. This was the main part of the sales process, and depended largely on establishing contacts in the businesses to get a foothold in the right places. With a technology intensive software based on advanced algorithms and machine learning capabilities, Widespace invested significant time and money to have its sales team convince customers that 'the way of the future' would be to trust machines to do their job by automatically deciding where and how to place an advertisement. Convincing the customers to trust Widespace's technology more than their own experience necessitated prolonged efforts on the part of the sales team, with success slow in the beginning and then rapidly expanding.

Business model

Widespace was primarily a technology company but employed a rather unique business model within the market as it was a sales company at the same time. The three primary functional departments in the value chain were sales, publisher sales and technology. While the technology department produced the advertising campaigns, publisher sales were responsible for building an attractive network of mobile websites and apps to sell the inventory, for example space for advertisements within the mobile applications. The overall sales department offered the combination of advertising inventory and technological solutions to media agencies that were responsible for the media plan development for advertising companies from all industries. The three distinct functions emerged simply out of the challenge that for several years in the early growth of the industry customers did not have smartphones themselves and needed to be educated. Widespace's sales force began increasingly recruiting sales people from media backgrounds instead of technology, in order to better communicate solutions 'in the customers own words'.

Premium focus

Widespace followed a strong premium strategy regarding both advertisers and publishers, counting on differentiation. The target group for advertising campaigns were large multinationals, regardless of the industry. Campaigns included a diverse customer base of companies such as McDonalds, Volkswagen, Audi, P&G, Unilever, H&M, Panasonic, IKEA, KLM, Coca Cola, 7-Eleven, and many more. The apps and sites that were part of the Widespace ad network ranged from top brand radio stations to brand name entertainment apps, sports and news. Internationally, cooperation agreements included those with Wordfeud and the Swedish radio station NRJ and other top publishers. Partners included Expressen, TV4 and Mix Megapol in Sweden, Dagbladet, TV2 and The Voice in Norway and MTV 3, Iltalehti and NettiAuto in Finland.

Network approach

Widespace sold the advertising inventory in a network approach rather than individual offerings, increasing the reach significantly. In other words, media agencies booked the campaigns with a certain budget and could not control exactly when and on which publishers' sites and apps the ads would be shown. As Josefine Vinberg from the publisher sales team explained, this approach gave Widespace a competitive advantage as it allowed them to offer the advertisers a large reach within a relevant target group. However, she pointed out that Widespace focused on premium sites and the campaigns would thus never be shown on sites that could have negative impact on the brand's image – as could be the case in open networks where no control over the content of the publishers was given (including political, violent or pornographic content). Nevertheless, advertisers were able to specifically target certain customers, not only regarding the demographic reach of different publishers but by using the unique environment of mobile devices, GPS technology enabled geographical targeting. Another feature under develop-

ment with TV4 was using synchronised ads across channels, allowing an increased impact and following the trend of second screens in media consumption.

Products

Widespace is committed to premium mobile advertising, which shows in their technology and products that not only include classical banner advertising but also strive to add real customer value to the end-user and thus to their clients. Some of the formats include:

- *The Splash*: a full-screen ad for maximum impact of about three seconds when the app was loading, and followed by a clickable ad in the app.
- *Video banner*: allows for video advertising such as TV ads to be played directly in the mobile app, opening the full screen when clicked and minimising to a banner again after finishing.
- *Store locator*: by clicking on the app a fully interactive map, that can also display a street view within the banner, shows the nearest store location using the GPS technology of smartphones.
- *Calendar*: allows the user to add a calendar event or a reminder on the phone with just one click on the ad.
- *The Swipe*: The user can easily slide over the ad and switch through an unlimited number of pictures within the original app. A partnership with the US-technology company Nuance Communications resulted in an innovative development of voice-ads, which allows the user to interact with the ads via speech.

Broadening the product offer

While the core business of delivering advertising campaigns as a service towards media agencies consumed the majority of Widespace resources in 2014, there were plans in the technology department to include innovative software that would help the publishers to increase revenues on their own. This would mean a different kind of sales model looking less like a service but more like a real, internet-based software product. The newly-developed software package provided significant analytical capability and ability for customers – primarily international publishers such as *Business Insider, Huffington Post, NY Times, BBC* and *Le Monde*. Using Widespace's new software allowed these media houses to directly deliver mobile customised advertisements from their advertisers to their readers, providing the advertisers with automatically-generated analytics as a significant value added. This provided additional potential for cost savings among the major media houses, putting a premium value on Widespace's new solution.

Organisational structure

The organisational structure of Widespace had emerged out of concrete needs rather than following a planned route. Within the company, an organisational chart did not even exist. However, roles were naturally being defined and several management layers had been introduced since the beginnings with a handful of employees. The vast majority of employees worked in the headquarters located in the city centre of Stockholm, Sweden. Most of the functional departments were centralised and the offices around Europe worked only as sales offices, employing only sales people, dealing with both media agencies and publishers, reporting to a country manager who had usually founded the office and thus started as a sales manager. An additional office had been opened in Dhaka, Bangladesh in 2012, to support the technological development. At headquarters, the technology department accounted for the majority of employment with 110 employees, underlining the main focus of technology in the company rather than a sales mediator. Within the technology department employees were organised into five functional teams, each one headed by a middle manager who reported to the CTO.

He described the development of the management structure as:

> 'We had a push in management last autumn, around eight months ago. We hired new experienced managers, as the team leaders didn't have any previous management experience. And this started to show in team co-ordination and performance as the organisation grew. So we introduced a middle layer between myself and the team managers, that are now responsible for each of the five departments.'
>
> Henric Stridsberg, CTO Widespace

The five teams are:

- *Research and development.* R&D represents the second largest department with close to 100 employees. Given the technology-intensity of Widespace's offering, continuous hiring of skilled developers continues to be a core activity for the company. In the increasingly competitive market for technology workers, a shortage of skilled developers can be foreseen if sales goals continue to be met.
- *Campaign management and studio.* Campaign management are responsible for the delivery of all orders placed by the sales department. A dozen employees in Europe plus half a dozen employees in Dhaka, Bangladesh work on bringing together the necessary organisational resources and developing the campaigns according to the customer wishes. When rich media are

used, as in about 56 per cent of all campaigns, the half dozen members of the studio team develop the media and work closely together with campaign management, covering the work that in other cases a creative advertising company would deliver.

- *Network.* The network team, currently consisting of a dozen people, supports the publisher sales team with the technical integration towards the publisher side and ensures the quality of the network.
- *Data and operations.* This department manages the data coming from every single user request, collected by permission. Derived from billions of transactions per month, analysts develop targeting algorithms and draw conclusions on how business is going. Visitors at Widespace immediately notice the obsession with real-time campaign tracking as a large screen in the entrance foyer displays the most successful ads – updated in real-time and covering all countries. Besides the dozen data management employees, the equally strong operations team ensure that the infrastructure works continuously without problems, keeping the servers up and running all the time.
- *Products.* Half a dozen product managers work on long-term development and defining new products, working together with R&D, network and data and operations on the long-term developments.

Sales and publisher sales

While the technology department is the heart of the organisation, the other two important parts in creating value are sales and publisher sales. These are separately organised teams: the publisher relations are managed by two employees, supported as described above by the network team. The sales department however is larger, led by a Head of Sales, and another management layer of Regional Heads of Sales coordinating across various countries. Sales represented the largest Widespace department with over 200 employees. Given the intensity of negotiations required to convince customers to launch a campaign using Widespace software, average contract size tends to range between €200000 and €1m. After sales successfully signs a contract, campaign management takes over customer contacts and for most contracts, studio builds the whole campaign since few customers can build the campaign with internal resources. The expansion of the sales organisation follows a key performance indicator (KPI)-logic where new staff are hired as soon as certain targets are met, to allow further expansion.

Supporting functions were initially covered by the founders and a few support employees in support function roles, but began to emerge as formalised departments in 2013. An experienced Head of Marketing was hired from Nokia to empower the brand building, supported later by an assistant. The recruiting process had previously been managed by the individual team managers and often involved informal methods and a range of interviews with the top management. However, at the beginning of 2014 a new, professionalised HR management was introduced. Again, an experienced manager with background from the media industry (MTG) was brought in:

> 'When I came in, there were just no processes and no existing HR strategy. Currently, apart from the strategies we have, I am still focusing a lot on building the structural capital and stability to support continued growth as well as designing and implementing necessary HR processes.'
>
> Suzanne Nygren, HR Director Widespace

Culture

Widespace has a distinct company culture that employees see as one of the main factors behind the company's success. They also remark that the culture emanates from Patrik and Henric. Both founders have taken care to implement the culture in all subsidiaries, even the Bangladesh office, making sure that the offices looked the same worldwide and that all new employees came to the Stockholm office for training during their initial employment and induction. It has become unwieldy due to the many new employees being hired each month, but both Henrik and Patrik considered it an essential step to preserve the culture. Neither of them liked formal processes, and considered the culture paramount rather than the processes. Widespace's culture is characterised by 'freedom under responsibility' and prides itself on having 'organised chaos' in order to keep energy levels high. Doors and communication are open, and employees are encouraged to enjoy their time together and to work proactively to come up with new solutions. The employees were all recruited on the premise that they understood and enjoyed working under stressful conditions, with a lot of hard work, but where they could get plenty of freedom to work however they liked. Employees are encouraged to want to change the world, and build a world-class company, and it is clear that those who want to work nine-to-five in a secure, stable environment will not fit in, or indeed get hired at Widespace. The employees should want to use their own initiatives rather than just taking orders, and feel ownership for their work and the

company. As CEO Patrik Fagerlund explained: 'Culture beats strategy. In the end the value of the company is in the people.'

Whilst much of the culture was emergent, brought about by hiring the type of people outlined above, Widespace has defined a number of values for the company which summarise what they want to stand for: 'The customer is the boss. We have fun. We are professional. We are proactive.' These values are painted on the walls of all Widespace offices. Commitment to these values was visible in the layout and design of all the offices – with open-plan offices for everybody, including the top management team. The facilities also include traditional IT start-up features such as big meeting rooms, whiteboard walls, ping-pong tables and video game consoles.

With rapid expansion, internationally as well as in national offices, Widespace saw a great need to maintain 'its entrepreneurial vibe' and the employee-friendly culture which had marked the company since founding. Technicians by training and profession, Patrik and Henric realised that the only way to attract skilled technology recruits and maintain their current experts would be to continuously involve the employees in decision-making, provide them with autonomy and responsibility and for Widespace to be seen as an exciting workplace. With recruitment strategies still based mainly on word-of-mouth and referrals for junior employees and executive search for senior recruits, Widespace was considering establishing closer contacts with premier engineering and business schools in order to enhance potential future staff's awareness of Widespace as an exciting company and an attractive employer.

Widespace's future expansion

Expanding into new markets encountered some difficulties due to the differences in mobile usage between countries and the costs associated with starting new offices. New offices in Sweden, Bangladesh, Finland, Norway, the Netherlands, the UK and France were added in 2013–14 and new offices in Italy, Spain and the USA were added in 2015. The main share of the company's revenues still comes from local markets, but Patrik and Henric saw that the big money would come from transnational deals, launching campaigns simultaneously across Europe. In order to achieve this, the UK office was of particular strategic importance, as many advertising efforts from the largest multinationals originated from there. Internally, the organisation had become unwieldy and, while the essential supporting departments had all been started, it would be some time before they would all be fully operational.

In early 2016, Widespace reached over 128 million users in 19 European countries, more than half of the European smartphone population. Further, via direct media partnership deals in the USA, Widespace also reached over 50 million US users, a quarter of the local smartphone base. Future US expansion would be Widespace's biggest challenge to date. With a lot of players in the US market, the market for mobile advertisements was more competitive than anything faced by Widespace to date.

Note
1. €1 = £0.8 = $1.3.

Ryanair: the low fares airline – 'always getting better'?

Eleanor O'Higgins

Ryanair, the first and largest budget airline in Europe, has enjoyed remarkable growth and success, based on a rigorously applied low-cost business model, with robust operating and financial performance even during the financial recession. However, Ryanair's prevous indifference to repeated complaints about its poor standards of customer service was suddenly reversed in 2014 with the introduction of an 'Always Getting Better' plan. The case illustrates how to analyse and deploy internal resources and capabilities to add perceived value to customers, thereby delivering sustainable strategic advantage. It also explores the difficulties of developing and extending strategic capabilities in response to changing environmental and industry conditions.

'People say the customer is always right, but you know what – they're not. Sometimes they are wrong and they need to be told so.'

Michael O'Leary, before 2014

'If I had known that being nice to customers was going to be so good for my business, I would have done it years' ago. Everyone loves a converted sinner. We have learned humility – and that we have to keep learning and listening to our customers.'

Michael O'Leary, November 2014

In November 2014, CEO Michael O'Leary predicted a full year 2016 profit growth of 20 per cent. Ryanair shares had closed at a record high of €14.66.[1] Customer traffic for the summer was over 30 million, with an average load factor of 95 per cent and over 90 per cent punctuality. In those 12 weeks, Ryanair had more customers than Air France in a full year; it became the first airline to carry over 10 million international customers in a single month. Cost discipline was evident, with fuel down five per cent and other costs expected to decline by one per cent for the year. Profits, excluding exceptional items, at €1088m for the first half exceeded the previous year by 37 per cent.

'Always getting better'

This was almost a year after the airline had turned a new leaf in its attitude to customers. Previously, Ryanair had conveyed 'The customer is usually wrong. The only time you hear from a customer is when they're complaining

Source: Philippe Huguen/AFP/Getty Images.

because they want to break our rules. Why can't I get a refund for my non-refundable ticket? Bugger off.'[2] So proclaimed Michael O'Leary in 2010.

The carrier had attracted complaints for its inflexible baggage policies and punitive charges, like hefty cancellation and change penalties, and charges for printing boarding passes. However, these customer-unfriendly practices had not appeared to daunt passengers who continued to fly Ryanair for its low fares.

However, in autumn 2013, a series of events made Ryanair sit up and listen. The airline was voted worst of the 100 biggest brands in the UK in customer relations by readers of the consumer magazine *Which?*. Its adversarial treatment of customers culminated in a wave of negative publicity after its refusal to allow a passenger to change his flight home to the UK when he learned his entire family had died in a house fire. Faced with heightened competition from other carriers offering cheap fares and recognising that some passengers were willing to pay higher fares to competitors for a better customer experience, Ryanair did an about-face, changing its historic service attitude. Perhaps the most convincing factor that a change would be worth trying was pressure on fares and profits.

Thus, in January 2014, Ryanair rolled out its 'Always Getting Better' (AGB) three-year plan. Significantly, the airline appointed its first Marketing Director, Kenny Jacobs. Heretofore, Ryanair had relied on newsworthy publicity stunts and provocative statements from Michael O'Leary as marketing tools, on the assumption that no publicity is bad publicity. Examples of Mr O'Leary's statements were that overweight people should pay extra and that passengers should have to pay a fee to use onboard toilets. Then, in January 2016, Ryanair hired its first PR head, Cristian Samoilovich, former manager of European public policy for Uber to handle relations with European governments and institutions.

The AGB programme consisted of repositioning Ryanair as 'Low Fares. Made Simple'. It centred on providing customers with more choice, an improved travel and digital experience, while maintaining budget fares. The buy-in of Michael O'Leary and the board, and staff, alongside a relatively flat organisation structure and open culture, facilitated a fast and effective execution of the plan.

The most dramatic change was Ryanair's attitude to customers, asserting that 'it starts at the top: listen to customers'. Ryanair still maintained its cost focus to continue to offer relatively lower fares than competitors. Investment in capability was part of the changes, principally in digital and technology. The company asserted that it wanted to become the leader in the industry on all things digital, and created Ryanair Labs with a team of over 150 working on a new digital platform.

Specifically the changes in the AGB consisted of:

- *Improve the flying experience.* Allowing customers to bring two bags on board and allocating seats.
- *Embrace digital.* Launching a new, simpler website, a new Ryanair app, a customer registration function called 'MyRyanair' so the airline could target and personalise its offers, communications and digital platform, improving the selling of ancillary products like car hire and reserved seats.
- *Broaden Ryanair's appeal.* Segmenting products to meet the needs of different groups. 'Family Extra' was a new product focused on families and 'Business Plus' was aimed at business customers. Groups and corporate service products were also launched.

- *Improve the product.* Changing its previous policy of concentrating on cheaper secondary airports, primary airports were added to the network. These included Brussels National, Athens, Amsterdam Schiphol, Milan Malpensa, Lisbon, Cologne, Hamburg and Glasgow International, alongside statements of improved flight times and frequencies on the most popular routes. Ryanair claimed to publish its schedules earlier than other airlines, meaning customers could plan and book flights longer in advance.

AGB phase 2

In March 2015, to celebrate its 30th anniversary, Ryanair unveiled the second phase of its AGB plan with an eight-point Customer Charter, emphasising its new image:

- Always Getting Better is the way we promise to do things.
- We promise the lowest fares.
- We promise the best choice of destinations.
- We promise to always prioritise safety.
- We promise to strive to make your travel an enjoyable experience.
- We promise we will always be Europe's most reliable airline.
- We promise to be transparent and to make travel simple for you.
- We promise to innovate to make your travel exciting.

Ryanair also announced a series of initiatives to be rolled out over the second year of the AGB programme, with a range of improved services, fee reductions and exciting digital developments to be introduced over the coming year. These included:

- New aircraft interiors, new seats with more leg room and new cabin crew uniforms.
- Lower airport check-in fees, missed departure fees and a new flight cancellation option.
- Real-time airline fare comparisons on Ryanair.com.
- A new destination content service, featuring customer reviews.
- A personalised Ryanair.com website with up to 100 versions of the homepage and personalised promotional emails with customer-specific tailored offers.
- A 24-hour 'hold the fare' feature for €5.
- Improved in-flight menus with more healthy meal choices and a hot breakfast pre-order service on key routes.
- Faster mobile apps, an improved Ryanair.com desktop and an enhanced 'My Ryanair' customer registration system.

However, as of December 2015, Ryanair retained its Skytrax 2 star rating, the worst for budget airlines in

Europe. It ranked 155 out of 160 companies on a corporate empathy index, which refers to 'being a company that relates in a human way to all its stakeholders, or emotional intelligence on a corporate scale.'[3]

Overview of Ryanair

Ryanair was founded in 1985 by the Ryan family to provide scheduled passenger services between Ireland and the UK, as an alternative to then state monopoly airline, Aer Lingus. Initially, Ryanair was a full service carrier, with two classes of seating, leasing three different types of aircraft. Despite growth in passenger volumes, by the end of 1990, the company had disposed of five chief executives and accumulated losses of IR£20 million. Its fight to survive in the early 1990s saw the airline transformed to become Europe's first low-fares, no frills carrier, built on the model of Southwest Airlines, the successful US operator. A new management team, led by Michael O'Leary, was appointed. Ryanair floated on the Dublin Stock Exchange in 1997 and is now quoted on the Dublin and London Stock exchanges and on the NASDAQ-100.

After its makeover into a budget airline, Ryanair never looked back, as it added new bases, routes and aircraft. Despite the up-and-down cycles of the airline industry over the decades, Ryanair continued its upward trajectory, among the world's most profitable airlines, leaving almost all others behind.

At its 30th birthday, as of July 2015, Ryanair offered 1600-plus flights per day from 72 bases and 190 airports across Europe, with a fleet of 315 Boeing 737-800 aircraft and six additional leased aircraft to provide extra capacity for the summer. Year-on-year traffic growth was 11 per cent from 81.7 million passengers in 2014 to 90.6 in 2015, expected to be 105 million by 2016. Load factor had increased from 83 per cent to 88 per cent.

After two profit warnings in 2013–14, net profits had recovered in its 2015 results, increasing by 66 per cent from €523m to €867m. Average fares increased by just one per cent from €46.40 to €47.05, whilst operating revenue had increased by 12 per cent from €5036.7 to €5654. Thus, much of the profit growth came from lower operating costs, especially a reduction of 11 per cent per passenger in fuel costs. (Ryanair's financial data can be viewed in the 'Investor relations' section of the Ryanair website).

Investor perspectives and the Aer Lingus saga

As of December 2015, Ryanair shares were trading in the €14.60 to €15.08 range, with a P/E ratio of 13.5. The share price had risen steadily after plummeting to a low of €1.97 in October 2008, when global equity markets tumbled. The most dramatic share price rise had occurred during the latter part of 2015 after stellar financial results, and expectations of even better to come.

After its flotation in 1996, Ryanair's policy was not to pay dividends. It retained earnings to fund its business operations, the acquisition of additional aircraft required for new markets, expansion of existing services and routine fleet replacements. However, thanks to a healthy balance sheet, the no-dividend policy changed in June 2010 when Ryanair began to pay a series of special dividends. It had also engaged in various share buybacks. The company had thereby returned over €2.9bn to shareholders over eight years, five times the €560m originally raised when Ryanair floated in 1997 and in two subsequent secondary issues.

The autumn of 2015 also saw the end of Ryanair's 29.8 per cent stake in Aer Lingus. The Aer Lingus saga began in 2007 when, in a surprise bid, Ryanair acquired a 25.2 per cent stake, a week after the flotation of the Irish national carrier. It subsequently increased its interest to 29.8 per cent, at a total aggregate cost of €407.2m. By July 2009, the investment had been written down to €79.7m. At the time of the initial bid, Ryanair declared its intention to retain the Aer Lingus brand and 'upgrade their dated long-haul product, and reduce their short-haul fares by 2.5 per cent per year for a minimum of 4 years . . . one strong Irish airline group will be rewarding for consumers and will enable both to vigorously compete with the mega carriers in Europe.'[4]

According to a *Financial Times* commentator, 'Ryanair's bid for Aer Lingus was a *folie de grandeur*'.[5] Even Michael O'Leary admitted it was 'a stupid investment. At the time, it was the right strategy to go for one combined airline but it has now proven to be a disaster.'[6] Aer Lingus rejected the Ryanair approach and two subsequent bids in 2008 and 2012, notwithstanding blocking of its bids from the EU and the UK Office of Fair Trade (OFT), and orders to divest its Aer Lingus stake.

After years of rejection from Aer Lingus shareholders and jousting with Irish, European and UK competition authorities, the matter was finally resolved in July 2015. International Airlines Group (IAG), led by Willie Walsh, a former CEO of Aer Lingus, made a successful bid to buy Aer Lingus for €1.36bn, having gained EU approval after some concessions to give up some London airport slots. The Irish government had already agreed to sell its 25 per cent stake in Aer Lingus, and the Ryanair board then agreed to dispose of its stake too. Ryanair had fully written down the value of its Aer Lingus stake. Proceeds, totalling €398m, were distributed to shareholders via a 'B' share programme at the end of 2015, bringing the amount distributed to shareholders to over €3.3bn since 2010.

Ryanair's strategy

Ryanair designates itself as Europe's favourite airline, as the world's largest international carrier by passengers. Before its conversion moment in 2013, Ryanair had stuck closely to the low-cost/low-fares model. It differed in its application of the Southwest Airlines prototype business model, and that of its main European rival, easyJet, as these two were not so frill-cutting. One observer described the difference between easyJet and Ryanair as – 'easyJet is classy cheap, rather than just plain cheap'.[7]

In its 2015 annual report, Ryanair indicated various key aspects of its strategy.

Fare and route policy

Ryanair's key selling point has been low fares designed to stimulate demand, particularly from fare-conscious leisure and business travellers. Ryanair sells seats on a one-way basis. When launching a new route, Ryanair's policy is to price the new route at its lowest fare so that it will be significantly lower than other carriers' lowest fares, but still provide a satisfactory operating margin.

Consistent with the budget model, Ryanair's routes are point-to-point only. In 2015 fiscal year, Ryanair flew an average route length of 776 miles (1250 km) and average flight duration of 1.83 hours. Short-haul routes eliminate the need to provide free in-flight meals and movies, expected on longer flights, while point-to-point flying allows Ryanair to offer direct, non-stop routes and avoid the costs of providing transfers for connecting passengers, including baggage transfer and transit passenger assistance.

In response to an operating environment characterised by high fuel prices, typically lower seasonal yields and higher airport charges and/or taxes, Ryanair has adopted a policy of grounding a portion of its fleet during the winter months. In the winters of fiscal 2014 and fiscal 2015, Ryanair grounded approximately 70 aircraft and 50 aircraft, respectively, but was planning to ground approximately only 40 aircraft during the winter 2015–16 season, due to lower fuel costs and higher anticipated demand.

Low operating costs

Low operating costs continues to be at the heart of Ryanair's strategy. There are various facets to the implementation of this low-cost cornerstone.

Aircraft fleet

Ryanair has always grown and developed its fleet to meet expansion of its routes and to acquire the most up-to-date fuel-efficient aircraft. In 2015, the principal fleet was composed of 315 Boeing 737-800 'next generation' aircraft, each having 189 seats. In 2019, when the Boeing 737-800 is scheduled to go out of production, Ryanair will become the launch customer for the new Boeing 197-seat 737-MAX-200 aircraft, designed to replace the Boeing 737-800, and will purchase up to 200 of such aircraft. It expects to have an operating fleet comprising approximately 520 Boeing 737s by 2024 comprising a mix of Boeing 737-800s and Boeing 737-MAX-200 aircraft. In its 2015 annual report, Ryanair notes satisfaction with the pricing and conditions of its aircraft purchases from Boeing.

The purchase of aircraft from a single manufacturer enables Ryanair to limit the costs associated with personnel training, maintenance and the acquisition and storage of spare parts while also affording the company greater flexibility in the scheduling of crews and equipment.

Airport costs

Up until 2013, Ryanair reduced airport charges by avoiding congested main airports, choosing secondary and regional destinations, eager to increase passenger throughput. Ryanair further reduces its airport charges by opting, when practicable, for less expensive gate locations and outdoor boarding stairs, rather than jetways.

Secondary and regional airports are significantly further from the centres of cities they serve than the main airports, 'from nowhere to nowhere' in the words of Sir Stelios Haji-Ioannou, founder of easyJet, Ryanair's biggest competitor.[8] For example, Ryanair uses Frankfurt Hahn, 123 km from Frankfurt, Torp, 100 km from Oslo, and Charleroi, 60 km from Brussels. In December 2003, the Advertising Standards Authority rebuked Ryanair, upholding a complaint of misleading advertising for attaching 'Lyon' to its advertisements for flights to St Etienne, 62 km from Lyon.

However, as part of its AGB programme, it added more primary airports to its route system. Ryanair continued to denounce charges and conditions imposed by most governments at airports in the form of air passenger duties. An example is its dispute with Athens Airport (AIA) over allegedly high charges imposed for its installations and services. Ryanair blamed pricing policy rather than the Greek economic crisis for a decline in traffic. Ryanair promised to bring ten million tourists to Greece within the next three years should AIA reduce taxes and fees from current €12 per passenger down to €5 and reduce to zero in other peripheral airports, an offer declined by the Greeks. Subsequently, the Greek government withdrew plans for the tax.

In September 2013, Ryanair made a ten-year growth agreement with Manchester Airports Group, the new owners of London Stansted, in relation to an expansion of capacity at Stansted in return for significant airport charge reductions for the incremental passenger volumes delivered. In 2015, Ryanair confirmed that it would bid for Gatwick slots which were to be sold as a condition of IAG's takeover of Aer Lingus, to develop further its capacity at the London airport.

Staff costs and productivity

By 2015, Ryanair's employee number at 9394 was up on 8992 in 2014, reflecting growth in traffic and upgraded product. Staff costs increased 1.1 per cent from €9501m to €9586m. Ryanair refuses to recognise trade unions and negotiates with employee representative committees (ERCs), regarding pay, work practices and conditions of employment. Following negotiations through this ERC system, pilots and cabin crew at all Ryanair bases are covered by long-term collective agreements. But, as seen below, various aspects of Ryanair's industrial relations continue to attract controversy.

Ryanair's employees earn productivity-based incentive payments. These include bonus payments for onboard sales of products by flight attendants and payments based on the number of hours or sectors flown by pilots and flight attendants. By tailoring rosters, the carrier maximised productivity and time off for crew members, whilst nonetheless complying with EU regulations which impose a ceiling on pilot flying hours to prevent dangerous fatigue. Its passenger-per-employee ratio of approximately 9640 was the highest in the industry. Share option plans for employees (and directors) add to staff remuneration packages.

Generally, onboard crew have to pay for their initial training and uniforms. Ryanair has licensed approved organisations in Dublin, Germany and the UK to operate pilot training courses, using Ryanair's syllabus, to grant Boeing 737 type-ratings. Based on their performance, trainee pilots may be offered a position operating on Ryanair aircraft.

Apart from employing its own staff at Dublin Airport, Ryanair outsources much of its services at other airports for ticketing, passenger and aircraft handling, and activities that can be more cost-efficiently provided by third parties. It claims that it obtains competitive rates for such services by negotiating fixed-price, multiyear contracts.

Ryanair imposes the same labour conditions, such as no unions, and pay rates on its staff operating abroad as it does in Ireland. This has led to some disagreements where it was accused of breaching local labour laws. For instance, in October 2014, Ryanair lost an appeal against a ruling that it breached French labour laws by employing 127 local staff on Irish contracts. It was fined €200,000 and €8.1m in damages to trade unions, France's social security system and pilots among others.

Having introduced a service to Copenhagen in the spring of 2015, Ryanair had come under attack from trade unions in Denmark. They accused the carrier of violating workers' rights, and threatened to go on strike after a ruling by the Danish Labour Court that Copenhagen airport staff had the right to refuse to service its flights in the dispute. Moreover, the mayor of Copenhagen banned city employees from using the airline because its low wages amounted to 'social dumping'; in general, Ryanair was subjected to a campaign of abuse in Denmark by labour protagonists, especially in social media. This included statements by Morten Windeløv, a Ryanair pilot from 2007–11, and now a leading voice in the unions' campaign to the effect that 'Ryanair's style is management by fear . . . There is a widespread disdain for employees, you are not treated with trust or respect as an individual.'[9] The dispute culminated in Ryanair's exit from its two Danish bases in Copenhagen and Billund before the unions could carry out their strike threat. The airline announced that a planned €360m investment in the Copenhagen base will instead be spread throughout other European cities, and it would continue to fly to the Danish capital but will not base any aircraft or crew there. Ryanair's reputation went steeply downhill in Denmark during the course of the row; it was ranked last in YouGov surveys of corporate reputation. However, customers were apparently indifferent, as a poll suggested more Danes would choose Ryanair than before the dispute.

Passenger service

The internet has been a source of cost savings for Ryanair in the passenger process. The development of its own internet booking facility has allowed Ryanair to eliminate travel agent commissions, although, as part of its improved service initiatives, the company has broadened its distribution base by making its fares available online to a limited number of other websites for a nominal cost. Direct sales via the Ryanair website and mobile app continue to be the prime generator of scheduled passenger revenues.

Ryanair pioneered cost-cutting/yield-enhancing measures for passenger check-in and luggage handling. One was priority boarding and web-based check-in. Charging for check-in bags encouraged passengers to travel with less or zero check-in luggage, thus saving costs and enhancing speed. Before it charged for checked-in bags, 80 per cent of passengers travelled with checked-in luggage; within two years, this had fallen to 30 per cent, and was less than 20 per cent in 2015. The airline met harsh criticism of its meagre luggage allowances and ever-rising fees for checking in bags with strict enforcement of limits on size and weight of carry-on luggage.

Passengers incurred penalties for exceeding the limits. As part of its AGB programme, it relaxed the limits by allowing two pieces of carry-on luggage, but there are reports that this has created a shortage of space in overhead lockers, with passengers forced to put their carry-on luggage in the hold.

From October 2009, Ryanair adopted a 100 per cent web check-in policy, enabling a reduction in staff numbers, calculated to save €50m per year. Hefty fees were incurred when passengers had not checked in online. This was another heavily criticised aspect of Ryanair passenger service. It was moderated as part of its new customer-friendly ethos, cutting its airport check-in fee, which applies to anyone who has not checked in online beforehand from €70 per person per flight to €45. The cost of checking in luggage at the airport (rather than online) has fallen from €60 to €30, its boarding card re-issue fee has been cut from €70 to €15, and a 24-hour post-booking 'grace' period has been introduced to correct minor errors or spelling mistakes, free of charge (after that it costs €110, or €160 at the airport).

Ancillary revenues

Ryanair provides various ancillary services, including in-flight beverage, food and merchandise, console entertainment sales and internet-related services. It distributes airport transfers, car park services, accommodation, travel insurance and car rentals through its website. Delivering these services through the internet enables Ryanair to increase sales, while reducing unit costs. As part of its website upgrade, the company declared it aimed to become the 'Amazon for travel' in Europe, with all travel services currently being provided by intermediaries available on Ryanair.com.

Over the years, ancillary revenue initiatives were constantly being introduced to raise extra revenue. It was the first airline to charge for check-in luggage and in-flight food and beverages. Virtually all budget airlines have followed suit, as they have with other Ryanair initiatives. It has continued to find ways of charging passengers for services once considered inclusive. While the airline has now changed its seating policy from open seating to allocated seats, an extra charge procures 'priority boarding' purchased in advance for £10/€10 per flight, an initiative followed by many traditional carriers, such as British Airways, charging passengers to book seats online for an extra charge. Ryanair incentivises its ground staff to levy excess baggage charges.

In July 2015, Hertz ended its long-standing contract to market its car rental services through Ryanair's website in a dispute over the airline's ticket selling arrangements using third-party agents. Hertz is believed to have viewed it as a breach of the original contract which entailed only direct ticket sales by Ryanair. Subsequently, in a change of strategy, Ryanair launched its own car hire website in a new partnership with online car rental aggregator, CarTrawler. This arrangement would offer customers a direct connection to over 1500 car rental agents in over 30,000 locations, across 174 different countries.

Ancillary services accounted for approximately 25 per cent of Ryanair's total operating revenues in the 2015 and 2014 fiscal years, increasing 11.7 per cent, from €1247.2m in the 2014 fiscal year to €1393.7m in the 2015 fiscal year. Ancillary revenues per booked passenger increased to €15.39 from €15.27. This reflects an improved product mix and fully reserved seating across the network. Revenues from non-flight scheduled operations, including excess baggage charges, administration/credit card fees, sales of rail and bus tickets, priority boarding, reserved seating, accommodation, travel insurance and car rental increased 15 per cent to €1164.4m from €1012.4m in the 2014 fiscal year. Revenues from in-flight sales increased 9.2 per cent to €128.1m from €117.3m in the 2014 fiscal year. However, revenues from internet-related services, primarily commissions received from products sold on Ryanair.com or linked websites, decreased 13.9 per cent, from €117.5m in the 2014 fiscal year to €101.2m in the 2015 fiscal year.

Further growth and development

Having become the largest international airline in Europe with respect to passengers carried, Ryanair continues its growth ambitions, declaring in its 2015 annual report that it intends to follow a growth path consistent with the way it has expanded in the past. It intends to grow by offering low fares and fare promotions, thereby achieving higher load factors. It will add additional routes and flight frequencies on existing flights, as well as new bases in the EU, and in countries party to a European Common Aviation Agreement with the EU on both international and domestic intra-country routes. It will seek opportunities to offer budget fares on routes currently served by mainstream and higher cost competitors, but expects to open new routes, not currently served by any carriers.

While it has mentioned plans to connect airports within its existing route network, it does not mention anything about offering connection services to passengers, such as luggage transfers. Ryanair was in talks with Norwegian Air Shuttle and Portugal's TAP to provide transfer connections on long-haul flights. Similar talks with Aer Lingus and Virgin Atlantic had broken down, since Ryanair did not want to be responsible for missed connections or delays. In March 2015, Michael O'Leary retracted a statement issued two days' earlier, announcing board approval to launch a transatlantic airline. Indeed, the company had talked for years about starting transatlantic services, offering one-way fares for as little as £10. However, O'Leary admitted that the logistics were not possible, as the plan was dependent on procuring long-haul, fuel-efficient, wide-bodied jets, which could take many years to obtain, as aircraft manufacturers had backed up orders from existing long-haul carriers developing their routes.

In the past, Ryanair has grown organically, with one exception, its acquisition in 2003 of Buzz, a budget airline subsidiary of KLM, the Dutch flag carrier, with headquarters at Stansted, for a bargain £15m. Buzz's operations were quickly absorbed into those of Ryanair. Of course, Ryanair had been trying for eight years to acquire Aer Lingus until the matter was concluded when it conceded in 2015. Nonetheless, it is open to acquisition opportunities. These can arise by sweeping up competitors, although, in the past, Ryanair has been more inclined to eliminate competitors through open competition rather than by acquiring them.

Safety and maintenance

Ryanair has always been conscious of safety as a critical factor, and that any safety-related harmful incidents on Ryanair or other budget carrier could adversely affect its business. It places resources into safety training of its staff and maintenance of its equipment and a board-level safety committee constantly reviews safety issues.

Ryanair carries out routine maintenance of its Boeing fleet, but contracts out overhaul engine and component services to third parties. The commonality of the fleet helps to keep down maintenance costs.

Ryanair's competitive space

Europe has a total of 168 carriers; low-cost carriers (LCCs) or budget airlines make up 45 per cent of the capacity share. The industry in Europe is fragmented, as consolidation has slowed down, forcing each airline to devise its own unique strategy. Airlines compete primarily in respect of fare levels, frequency and dependability of service, name recognition, passenger amenities (such as access to frequent flyer programs), and the availability and convenience of other passenger services. The industry is highly susceptible to price discounting, because airlines incur very low marginal costs for providing service to passengers occupying otherwise unsold seats.

Contributing to competition in 2015 was growth in short-haul capacity accelerating to 7.7 per cent in the fourth quarter. This growth was led by LCCs, especially Ryanair, contributing 20 per cent. However, the 2015 growth was also a product of buoyant demand.

The CAPA Centre for Aviation has divided European airlines into five models:

- *Major network carriers.* This model comprises the major legacy groups, such as Air France-KLM, IAG, Lufthansa.
- *Niche full-service carriers.* These are airlines from smaller countries, with less developed networks, and lower costs, such as Air Berlin.
- *Pan European LCCs.* Exemplified by easyJet, Vueling, Norwegian, these airlines are not pure LCCs as they offer some 'frills'.
- *Ultra LCCs.* Also pan-European, this group is led by Ryanair as following the pure low-cost model. Other examples are Wizz Air and Pegasus.
- *Leisure LCCs.* These airlines are smaller scale, operate mainly out of one country, concentrating on leisure travel with longer distance routes to tourist destinations. Transavia, Monarch and Jet2.com are examples.

The differences between the features and cost base of LCCs and legacy airlines have narrowed. Furthermore, the distinction between the various business models for short distances is increasingly irrelevant as traditional flag carriers' short-haul operations now compete head to head with the LCCs' point-to-point services.

The operating margins of European LCCs, especially ultra-LCCs, in 2014 compared favourably to those of full-service carriers. Five of the top six and all of the top three by operating margin are LCCs. CAPA also points out that for Europe's major network airlines, successful LCC subsidiaries are rare and require a distinct culture. Creating new lower cost platforms can cannibalise the mainline brand and present significant industrial relations challenges in realising LCC cost savings. Ryanair was the most profitable listed European airline in 2014 ranked by operating margin. The least profitable was Air Berlin. Wizz Air managed its unit cost down further while raising its unit revenues. easyJet continued to take advantage of its network of primary airports and its lead over other LCCs in terms of initiatives towards business travelers and customer service. However, some LCCs recorded falling margins in 2014, among them Vueling and Pegasus, and two were even loss-making, Norwegian and Transavia.

Risks and challenges

Although the company had been enjoying success in the 2014–15 period, it was conscious that it had to be equally vigilant about risks to sustain its exemplary record. Some of the challenges faced by Ryanair were specific to itself and some were general to the aviation industry or the budget sector.

Fuel costs

Given that fuel constitutes a key input cost, wide fluctuations in the price and availability of this commodity are a concern, since these are subject to factors beyond Ryanair's control. In these volatile circumstances, hedging is the only answer. Historically, Ryanair has entered into arrangements to provide for substantial protection against fluctuations in fuel prices, generally through forward contracts covering periods of up to 18 months of anticipated jet fuel requirements. Because oil prices could change suddenly downward, hedging could end up being costly if the price had been set before an unexpected drop. As of fiscal 2015, Ryanair was hedged at prices below contemporary spot prices. On 20 January 2016, crude oil prices fell to levels 76 per cent below the previous year's peak, down to just over $27 a barrel from $115. Ryanair's declaration of 'no fuel surcharges ever' and its reliance on low fares limit its capacity to pass on increased fuel costs, especially in the face of its planned expansion.

Risks associated with the euro

Headquartered in Ireland, Ryanair's reporting currency is the euro. With its extensive route system within eurozone countries, the company and the value of its euro-denominated assets would be adversely affected by a breakup of the euro or the exit of one or more members from it. Operating inputs purchased abroad in non-euro currencies could become more expensive, further undermining profitability. With so much of Ryanair's business conducted in the UK, the collapse of the euro against sterling could be especially difficult. Moreover, as international prices for jet fuel are denominated in US dollars, Ryanair's fuel costs are also subject to exchange rate risks, exacerbated by a continuing fall in the value of the euro against the dollar, from a 2008 high of just under $1.60 to $1.08 in 2015.

Recent strategic initiatives – the jury is still out?

The actions taken as part of Ryanair's improved customer services and AGB campaign were intended to increase passenger traffic, load factor and yields. There are additional costs associated with the initiatives, such as primary airport fees and marketing expenses, simultaneously reducing ancillary revenues previously earned from various penalty fees and charges. Although the revenues from allocated seating and premiums from its Business-Plus passengers should offset the reduction in ancillary revenues, there can be no assurance that this will occur. Ryanair recognises that factors beyond its control, such

as customer acceptance, competitive reactions and market and economic conditions could derail the potential benefits of its AGB strategy. Initial reactions to Ryanair's 'business-lite' product from corporate travellers was sceptical, as they compared it unfavourably to mainstream carriers, such as BA's business class product, especially as it does not include incentives such as loyalty programmes. Others saw Ryanair's combination of airports in its network and competitive pricing as potentially attractive for small businesses, as fares were pitched to be considerably cheaper than other carriers' business class flexi-fares, but more than its own standard fares.

It was also a matter of balancing still attractive fares with more costly service inputs. Historically, the success of Ryanair's business model depended on its ability to control costs to deliver lower fares than competitors while still earning a profit. Operating in an increasingly competitive marketplace, with a number of low-fare, traditional and charter airlines competing throughout its route network, places some pressure on Ryanair's ability to raise fares significantly.

Adapting to seasonality

Ryanair's growth has been largely dependent on increasing summer capacity, and decreasing winter capacity. The policy of seasonally grounding aircraft presents some risks. While reducing variable operating costs, it does not avoid fixed costs such as aircraft ownership costs, and it decreases Ryanair's potential to earn ancillary revenues. Decreasing the number and frequency of flights may also negatively affect Ryanair's labour relations, including its ability to attract flight personnel interested in year-round employment.

Various legal proceedings

Ryanair has been in litigation with the EU for over a decade about alleged receipt of state aid at certain airports. Although an EU ruling in 2004 that it had received illegal state aid from publicly owned Charleroi Airport was subsequently overturned on appeal, the EU launched further investigations into allegations of illegal aid, purportedly subsidising Ryanair at as many as 20-plus publicly owned airports, such as Paris Beauvais, Lubeck and Frankfurt Hahn in Germany. Competitors launched other legal challenges against the company. Ryanair has won some of these cases and lost some others, but many remain unresolved, as the losing party always appeals the decision to the EU General Court, a process that takes some years.

Frequently, Ryanair took the initiative on alleged illegal aid to rivals. It filed a complaint with the EU Commission accusing Air France-KLM of attempting to block competition after the French airline filed a case, alleging that Marseille was acting illegally by offering discount airlines cut-price fees at its second, no-frills terminal. Ryanair also called on the Commission to investigate allegations that Air France had received almost €1bn in illegal state aid, benefiting unfairly from up to 50 per cent discounted landing and passenger charges on flights within France. Adverse rulings on these airport cases would not have major costs in fines, but they could curtail Ryanair's growth if it was prevented from making advantageous deals with publicly-owned airports and was confined to the fewer privately-owned airports across Europe. It could also encourage more rivals to bring actions against Ryanair.

Three airport authorities were suing Ryanair over alleged delays in paying airport charges. After it called for an Irish presiding judge to withdraw on grounds of bias against Ryanair in previous proceedings, the judge did withdraw, though not because he admitted Ryanair's charges but to avoid delay in the case. He stood by his previous comments that 'Ryanair told untruths to and about the court and . . . that the airline and the truth made uncomfortable bedfellows'.[10]

Ryanair has vigorously opposed different continental European governments' attempts to move its staff from British or Irish employment contracts to more expensive national ones on the basis that they were protecting their own flag carriers. Ryanair accused the French government of using these contracts to protect Air France-KLM, as it continues to fight a €9m sanction imposed by a French court for breaking local labour laws. As shown above, in the Denmark case, Ryanair was ready to abandon its bases rather than succumb.

On another legal front, in the UK, Spain and Italy, Ryanair launched a legal claim against Google and online travel agent eDreams, which it accused of hosting a misleading subdomain with Ryanair branding, selling Ryanair tickets at higher prices than its own. It had already won a similar case in Germany. eDreams responded by denying any wrongdoing, but it did change its website, though not sufficiently to fully satisfy Ryanair.

Unforeseen events and passenger compensation

In the airline industry, there is always the possibility that accidents and catastrophic events may occur, due to natural or man-made causes. Among these are accidents and safety-related incidents, terrorist highjackings, outbreaks of contagious disease epidemics like swine flu, weather and natural phenomena that interfere with flights, such as the 2010 closure of a significant portion of the airspace over northern Europe caused by safety concerns from ash cloud emissions of an Icelandic volcano.

Such disturbances can entail rescheduling passengers, and disputes about compensation, since, according to EU law, passengers denied boarding or delayed for more than three hours are entitled to compensation from the airline. Only circumstances outside the airlines' control exempt it from such compensation, but Ryanair claims that the extraordinary circumstances defence has been very narrowly interpreted by the EU. Ryanair usually resists paying compensation, mindful that large-scale compensation payments are especially harmful to airlines with low fares. Ryanair was appealing a court decision in the UK that ruled that airlines could not enforce a two-year limit in its terms and conditions on passengers claiming flight delay compensation and claims could be made for up to six years. This could have implications for retrospective claims of £610m according to the law firm representing claimants, but in Ryanair's view, the sum would be up to £5m.

In August 2012, Ryanair faced an investigation by the Spanish Ministry of Public Works following emergency landings of three Ryanair aircraft at Valencia Airport after the airplanes had run out of fuel. The aircraft had been diverted to Valencia when they were prevented from landing at Madrid, due to an electrical storm. The Ryanair flights, with others, were put in a holding pattern, but only the Ryanair flights had to instigate emergency procedures because they were running low on fuel. This incident raised questions about Ryanair's fuel policy – to take on the minimum possible to save money. However, Ryanair insisted that fuel levels never fell below the permitted minima during the Valencia incidents, and that all of the company's aircraft operate with required fuel levels. If irregularities were to be found at Ryanair, it could face the loss of its operating licence for three years, with additional fines of up to €4.5m. Further, the following year, a group of pilots, deemed to be the Ryanair Pilots Group, raised safety concerns about the airline. However, Ryanair claimed that the group did not include Ryanair pilots, and was a PR front for pilot unions of their competitor airlines, including KLM, Air France and Aer Lingus.

Ryanair maintains various insurances: aviation third-party liability, passenger liability, employer liability, directors and officers' liability, aircraft loss or damage, and other business insurance, consistent with industry standards. Ryanair believes its insurance coverage is adequate, although not comprehensive. This insurance does not cover claims for losses incurred when, due to unforeseen events, airspace is closed and aircraft are grounded, such as the closures associated with the ash cloud. It is almost impossible to insure against what may be unlimited liabilities. For instance, EU legislation provides for unlimited liability of an air carrier in the event of death or injuries suffered by passengers.

Labour relations

Ryanair has been criticised for refusing union recognition and allegedly providing poor working conditions. The British Airline Pilots Association (BALPA) tried to organise Ryanair pilots in the UK, maintaining the right to ballot Ryanair pilots to join the union. In July 2006, the Irish High Court ruled that Ryanair had bullied pilots to accept new contracts, where pilots would have to pay €15,000 for re-training on new aircraft if they subsequently left the airline, or if the company was forced to negotiate with unions during the following five years. Meanwhile, Ryanair was contesting the claims of some pilots for victimisation under the new contracts.

Ryanair was ordered to pay 'well in excess' of €1m in legal costs after a court refused the airline access to the names and addresses of pilots who posted critical comments about the company, on a site hosted by British and Irish pilots' unions. It claimed anonymous pilots were using a website to intimidate and harass foreign-based pilots to dissuade them from working for the company.

In late 2015, Ryanair concluded five-year agreements of pay increases of ten per cent with all 76 of its pilot bases across Europe and was commencing a similar process with cabin crew. The Irish Airline Pilots Association responded to the news by accusing Ryanair of misrepresenting the real situation that pilots face in establishing normal industrial relations with their employer and claiming that the agreement did not cover contractors who were more than 50 per cent of all pilots.

The company maintains its right to treat its crew operating from bases in other higher paying countries as if it were on Irish territory, and therefore subject to Irish labour laws, which are less exacting than those pertaining in other European jurisdictions. This issue may be compounded by EU regulations which require the payment of employer and employee social insurance costs to be governed by the country where the employee is based. For instance, social charges in France are 40–45 per cent of wages against 10.75 per cent in Ireland.

Notwithstanding the adversarial incidents in its industrial relations history, Ryanair appears to have no problems recruiting staff, including pilots.

Other risks and challenges

As listed in its own report, Ryanair faced other risks, some specific and some generic to the industry:

- Prices and availability and financing of new aircraft.
- Dependence on key personnel (especially CEO Michael O'Leary).
- Dependence on external service providers.
- Dependence on its internet website, should it break

down, even if there are robust backup procedures in place; potential unauthorised use of information from the company's website; cyber-security risks.
- A potential rise in Irish Corporation Tax, since Ireland may be under pressure to raise its tax regime from other EU countries.
- EU regulation of carbon emissions trading.
- Risks related to ownership of the company's shares due to restrictions limiting share ownership by non-EU nationals in EU-based companies to 49 per cent. However, in late 2015, the EU was considering loosening the rule for individual countries that agree to abide by strict regulations on state subsidies.

Leading Ryanair into the future

'It is good to have someone like Michael O'Leary around. He scares people to death.' This praise of Ryanair's CEO came from fellow Irishman, Willie Walsh, then CEO of British Airways and later CEO of the International Airlines Group (IAG).[11] O'Leary has been described as 'at turns, arrogant and rude, then charming, affable and humorous, has terrorised rivals and regulators for more than a decade. So far, they have waited in vain for him to trip up or his enthusiasm to wane.'[12]

In fact, O'Leary had been pronouncing his intention to depart from the airline 'in two years' time' since 2005. He declared that he would sever all links, refusing to 'move upstairs' as chairman. However, in an apparent change of heart in 2014, he signed a contract up to 2019, replacing his previous year-on-year rolling contracts. His basic package, before bonuses, for 2015 was €2.4m, up by a third on 2014. In 2015, Michael O'Leary held 3.8 per cent of Ryanair's share capital. His fortune is worth between €750m and $1.3bn, depending on different reports.

When asked whether he would retire to focus on his stud farm, O'Leary admitted that what he enjoys most is working, and he will be involved in Ryanair as long as it is doing something interesting. Besides, he needed to keep working to finance his racehorses which were a 'money pit', and strictly a hobby. 'Jesus, I'm only 54. I'm such a beloved leader here. Can you imagine the devastation I would cause if I announced on Monday I'm leaving?' he 'joked' in an interview in late 2015.[13]

For most of Ryanair's 30-year history, Michael O'Leary had been operating with two deputy CEOs, Howard Millar, CFO and Michael Cawley, Chief Commercial Officer, part of the team that had built up Ryanair. Both retired as executives in 2014, joining the board as non-executive directors. Since then, there have been no deputy CEOs. Although O'Leary consistently praised the contributions and achievements of his management team, Ryanair was inextricably identified with him. He was credited with single-handedly transforming European air transport. In 2001, O'Leary received the European Businessman of the Year Award from *Fortune* magazine; in 2004, *The Financial Times* named him as one of 25 European 'business stars' who have made a difference, describing him as personifying 'the brash new Irish business elite' and possessing 'a head for numbers, a shrewd marketing brain and a ruthless competitive streak'.[14]

Present and former staff have lauded O'Leary's leadership style: 'Michael's genius is his ability to motivate and energise people . . . There is an incredible energy in that place. People work incredibly hard and get a lot out of it. They operate a very lean operation . . . It is without peer,' said Tim Jeans, a former sales and marketing director of Ryanair.[15]

O'Leary's publicity-seeking antics are legendary. These included his 'declaration of war' on easyJet when, wearing an army uniform, he drove a tank to easyJet's headquarters at Luton Airport. When Ryanair opened its hub at Milan Bergamo he flew there on a jet bearing the slogan 'Arrivederci Alitalia'. He has dressed as St Patrick and as the Pope to promote ticket offers. A self-confessed 'loudmouth' whose outspokenness has made him a figure of public debate, 'he is called everything from "arrogant pig" to "messiah".'[16] His avowed enemies include trade unions, politicians who impose airport taxes (calling former UK Prime Minister, Gordon Brown a 'twit' and a 'Scottish miser'[17]), environmentalists, bloggers who rant about poor service, travel agents, reporters who expect free seats, regulators and the EU Commission, and airport owners like BAA, whom he once called 'overcharging rapists'.[18] An EU Commissioner, Philippe Busquin, denounced Michael O'Leary as 'irritating . . . and insists he is not the only Commissioner who is allergic to the mere mention of the name of Ryanair's arrogant chief.'[19]

An *Irish Times* columnist suggested that 'maybe it's time for Ryanair to jettison O'Leary', asserting that he has become a caricature of himself, fulfilling all 15 warning signs of an executive about to fail.[20] Professor

Sydney Finklestein identified these signs under five headings – ignoring change, the wrong vision, getting too close, arrogant attitudes and old formulae. But having demonstrated the extent that O'Leary meets the failure criteria, the columnist concluded: 'So, is it time for Ryanair to dump Mr O'Leary? Depends whether you prefer the track record of one of the most successful businessmen in modern aviation, or the theories of a US academic from an Ivy League school.' Would Professor Finkelstein's diagnosis be proven wrong after CEO Michael O'Leary's conversion to customer service and the 'AGB' plan in 2014?

Notes and references
1. €1 = £0.8 = $1.3 (at the time of writing).
2. F. Gillette, 'Ryanair's O'Leary mulls one-euro toilets, standing passengers', Bloomberg.com., 2 September 2010.
3. R. Rigby, 'Social media is capitalism with a human face', *Financial Times*, Executive Appointments section, 26 November 2015, p. 4.
4. Statement from Ryanair's half yearly results presentation, 6 November 2006.
5. LEX, Ryanair, *Financial Times*, 3 June 2009, p. 16.
6. L. Noonan, 'O'Leary admits stake in Aer Lingus was stupid disaster', *Irish Independent*, 6 March 2009.
7. J. Guthrie, 'Sir Stelios beknighted as suits prove bolder risk takers', *Financial Times*, 30 July 2009, p. 16.
8. S. Lyall, 'No apologies from the boss of a no-frills airline', *New York Times*, 1 August 2009 (The Saturday Profile).
9. D. Crouch, 'Ryanair closes Denmark operation to head off union row', *The Guardian*, 17 July 2015.
10. M. Carolan, 'Judge pulls out of Ryanair case without altering previous findings or comments', *Irish Times*, 22 June 2010.
11. K. Done, 'O'Leary shows it is not yet the end for budget air travel', *Financial Times*, 2 August 2008, p. 11.
12. The FT ArcelorMittal Boldness in Business Awards, 2009, *Financial Times* supplement, 20 March, p. 21.
13. T. Powley, 'Michael O'Leary: 'I'm Irish so you're born with bullshit on tap', Irishtimes.com., 5 October 2015.
14. B. Groom, 'Leaders of the new Europe: business stars chart a course for the profits of the future', *Financial Times*, 20 April 2004.
15. G. Bowley, 'How low can you go?' *Financial Times Magazine*, No. 9, 21 June 2003.
16. *Ibid*.
17. S. Lyall, 'No apologies from the boss of a no-frills airline', *The New York Times*, 1 August 2009 (The Saturday Profile).
18. *Ibid*.
19. S. Creaton, 'Turbulent times for Ryanair's high-flier', *Irish Times*, 31 January 2004.
20. John McManus, 'Maybe it's time for Ryanair to jettison O'Leary', *Irish Times*, 11 August 2003.

CASE STUDY

Flight Centre Limited: competing to provide the lowest air fares

Kenneth Wiltshire

Flight Centre has grown to become one of the major players in the world travel industry building on its entrepreneurial culture and business model. The case focuses on the challenges faced by Flight Centre in a highly competitive industry and the viability of pursuing its unique business model across all markets and cultures.

Introduction

Flight Centre Limited (FLT) is one of the world's largest travel agency groups, with more than 30 brands and 2500 leisure, corporate and wholesale businesses in 11 countries. In 2015, FLT achieved a record revenue of A$2.4bn[1] and profit before tax of A$256.5m continuing the annual growth trend that FLT has established over three decades. Originally based in Australia, FLT's rapidly expanding network now extends throughout Australia, New Zealand, the USA, Canada, the UK, South Africa, Hong Kong, India, China, Singapore and the United Arab Emirates. In addition, the company's global travel management network, FCM Travel Solutions, extends to more than 75 other countries through strategic licensing agreements with independent local operators. The company employs more than 15,000 people globally, and actively pursues organic growth. FLT is a successful entrepreneurial venture that became established and grew rapidly despite considerable industry and government obstacles. FLT operates in a highly competitive environment requiring constant innovation, with a staff- and client-focused global business model. However, it constantly faces significant challenges in an intensely competitive industry including the growing capacity for clients to make their own travel arrangements online. Having become a major global operator, questions arise as to whether Flight Centre can continue to operate with one business operations model for all regions and cultures.

The early years

It all began in 1973 when a few young Australians living in the UK got the inspiration to begin a travel company called 'Top Deck Tours', using old refitted London

Source: Kumar Sriskandan/Alamy Images.

double decker buses to take tour groups around Europe. Despite harrowing experiences with bus breakdowns, snarling officialdom in many countries, shortage of working capital and back-breaking hours for the founders /drivers/operators, the tours proved very popular and the number of buses and tours grew. Along this journey the entrepreneurs, who had no experience in the industry, had to engage in improvisation, rule-bending, fudging and originality in marketing with no formal strategy.[2] However, the lessons learned stood them in good stead when they decided to explore the gap they perceived in discounted air travel and founded Flight Centre in 1981.

This turned out to be a formidable challenge. The practice of flight discounting was virtually unknown in the cosy travel industry in Australia, which was characterised by intensive government regulation of airlines which had long-established relations with existing travel agents. The industry was immediately hostile to these new upstarts, and they had to turn first to lesser known

---

airlines to obtain discount business, and also engage in intense lobbying of government to change the legislation to allow their kind of operation to be licensed.

The first retail shop was established in Sydney in 1981 and made a profit of A$93,000 in its first year from a turnover of A$2.5m. By 2012, Flight Centre operated almost 2500 shops, in 11 countries, earning a profit of A$294m from a turnover (total transaction value) of over A$13b, with 34 different brands. The core business is still arranging flights and accommodation, but the company has also diversified into arranging many other forms of travel including sea, rail, coach, bicycling and trekking, as well as related services such as insurance and currency exchange.

Leadership and philosophy

Although there were five key founders, the focus inevitably falls on Graham 'Skroo' Turner who has been CEO or Executive Chairman for all of the company's history. He began his working life as a vet in Australia and later moved to the UK. Turner has been described severally as a maverick, a larrikin, a plain speaker and an entrepreneur. A softly spoken, bearded, physical fitness fanatic (cycling 30 km before breakfast most days), his business instincts are shaped by a keen understanding of human nature and constant reading of management and leadership literature. He espouses his philosophy regularly within the organisation, especially through an annual published collection of wisdom, seminal leadership and management articles, sayings, poetry, proverbs, anecdotes and a raft of business principles practices and goals for all aspects of the business.

His strategies are based on conceptual and philosophical underpinnings which he constantly updates in a staff manual, combined with the application of common sense to emerging challenges. An innovator himself by instinct and nature, he is prepared to admit to mistakes, and he operates by placing trust in the leaders within the organisation, decentralising much decision-making to country and sectional managers, including decisions on the choice of new markets to be explored, experimentation with business systems and arranging local partnerships with suppliers and contractors of travel packages. However, he closely monitors performance across the company and travels around the world, stepping in when necessary. This has occurred on a few occasions when senior managers have made poor decisions. Described often in the media as a charismatic leader, he is now a legend in all parts of the travel industry. Despite the publicity that follows his success, Turner tries to maintain a low profile, seldom venturing into public issues or politics, although he is an environmentalist with concerns

about population growth. The company makes no political donations.

The foundation of the Flight Centre business strategy is very clear and it revolves around its people. In essence the message is: look after your people and they in turn will look after your clients. Structure and motivation are key, all based on the belief that people like to work in teams. Flight Centre's operational structure was modelled on anthropological principles inspired by Nicholson's work on hunter-gatherers[3] following this model, there are the 'family', the 'village' and the 'tribe'. The 'family' is a team usually consisting of between three and seven people; the 'village' is a group of three to seven geographic families or teams who support each other; the 'tribe' is a maximum of around 25 groups of villages with a single tribal identity who come together for celebration and interaction. Beyond this, the tribes come together to form a nation.[4]

Innovation and experimentation are encouraged and staff suggestions readily analysed and many acted upon. An egalitarian culture prevails with very few special perks for senior executives, not even car parking, and all Flight Centre offices are open plan. (Turner himself has no executive assistant or personal office.) Incentives play a key role in staff motivation; remuneration is made up of a base salary plus a commission which can be very rewarding, and this is complemented by the option of joining a share ownership and debenture scheme. The total package can be lucrative, having produced a number of employee millionaires in a relatively short space of time. There is a highly sought after 'prize and recognition/reward programme' for staff performance and improvement, which is celebrated at gala conferences held around the globe. Employees have access to in-house health and fitness and financial well-being services. Staff are carefully recruited but more for their personal qualities than any deep knowledge of the travel industry. The incentive model ensures that those who aren't performing move on fairly quickly. None of the staff at Flight Centre belongs to a trade union – according to Turner if employees feel the need to join a union it is an indication that you are not looking after them.

Strategy and the business model

When the company decided to float in 1995 the decision was largely based on a desire to facilitate greater staff ownership in the organisation in order to enhance motivation, loyalty and identification. Of course, the additional funds were welcome as the existing owners (the original founders) could not have personally financed the desired expansion of the business and did not want to borrow. Some foresaw the need to establish a potential personal exit path for them to leave the company which a float would facilitate. Indeed, the company has always eschewed borrowing, has had relatively little debt during its existence, and has a firm policy of keeping healthy cash reserves. This has often meant that the directors have placed themselves in some tight personal financial situations to fund expansion or acquisitions along the way. A failed share buy-back scheme was attempted in 2005 but only because the directors felt that the share price had fallen well below the true value of the company as a result of external conditions. Flight Centre has always operated with a small Board of Directors – four or five members, comprising the original founders for most of the company's history.

Another key element of the strategy is the price guarantee. The advertising slogan originally said 'Lowest Air Fares Guaranteed' because the company's policy is to beat any other lower published price for a fare. But this slogan met with objections from regulators and today the brand carries the slogan 'Lowest Airfare Guarantee'. This promise has caused plenty of headaches and additional costs, sometimes over A\$10m – the total cost of matching lower fares submitted by clients. It is made more precarious because of the airlines who now offer direct deals to the public themselves. However, Flight Centre has stuck religiously with this pledge and it is now a firmly entrenched part of the brand and the culture.

The fundamentals of Flight Centre's strategy are centred on organic growth and in this it has been highly successful. Some buy-outs have occurred and some related diversification (e.g. hire of bicycles), but the company is firmly grounded in the travel business and its variations. Expansion into corporate and student travel as well as the more up-market luxury products has all been positive. Behind the retail presence is an engine room of wholesale activity as deals are negotiated with a plethora of suppliers. Most travel agents operate their own wholesale sections which arrange deals and contracts with

flight, accommodation and ground travel package operators, and then make these deals available to their own retail agents. In an effort to achieve cost efficiencies through internal competition, Flight Centre introduced a purchaser–provider approach whereby their retail stores could opt not to choose to buy from the company's own suppliers if they could do better elsewhere – a cost-centre concept which was fiercely resisted at first and caused some morale problems, but has gained acceptance and introduces healthy intra-company competition. However, more in-house transactions are now happening than ever before. The FCL 'replicable small business model' contains six elements (see Box 1).

The business model is followed by a list of rules for running a project which are process-oriented. Perhaps the most interesting one is 'Perfection is banned – near enough is good enough. We want action and progress – not perfection.'

A challenging business environment

The company has faced some major challenges, many of which were very threatening to the travel business, including wars, natural disasters, global health epidemics and the global financial crisis. The sudden collapse and liquidation of Australia's Ansett airlines caught the company off guard because of loss of over-rides, super over-rides, plus credit card reversals. The closure of Heathrow Airport in December 2010 owing to its inability to cope with snow and bad weather with days of flight cancellations is an interesting case in point, where Flight Centre's own emergency helpline gave its customers up-to-the-minute information and the certainty that someone was looking after them, by comparison with the lacklustre performance of the airlines and the airport in this respect. Customer loyalty was further entrenched. Indeed the company has always been prepared to sustain extra costs to retain customer loyalty and return business.

BOX 1 The FCL global 'replicable small business model'

- Ongoing growth (organic, acquisitions and start-ups) at every level of the business.
- A flat team-based and decentralised decision-making structure and local ownership by individuals with clear roles and responsibilities.
- Individual rewards/incentives on individual outcome based, fully relevant, consistently measured and accurate KPIs.
- The teams are decentralised, multiskilled if possible, all members with directorships (alternated).

- The team leader works in the team with the same technical job as the rest of the team.
- All business team and support teams operate under the 'one best way' brand guide, business systems and operating systems (the *Systems Manual*). In FCL we have one set of values, one culture and one set of philosophies.[5]

Maintaining a healthy level of cash reserves has been an important element of risk management in a precarious industry.

Throughout the whole of its history, Flight Centre has had to deal with a great deal of inflexibility and intransigence from government officialdom. In the beginning, this applied particularly to gaining licenses to operate in almost all countries they wanted to enter. Innovative ways were found around this including using less popular airlines, operating under licenses of associates, and even occasionally beginning operations before licenses were obtained and adopting a 'crash through' approach which involved severe risk taking. This has usually been successful in the end, although initial attempts to operate in Vietnam were given up at considerable cost in the light of bureaucratic inertia. The company has baulked at bribery and corruption suggestions from officials in some countries.

Legal issues

In a very significant twist in 2012, the company was investigated by Australia's Competition Regulator for allegedly trying to collude with airlines in fixing prices and anti-competitive behaviour. This was because of an attempt it made to have an airline reveal a cheap air fare which it was offering directly to the public, and which was lower than Flight Centre had been offering for the same fare. The regulator accused Flight Centre of illegally fixing prices of international flights on six occasions between 2005 and 2009 with Singapore Airlines, Malaysia Airlines and Emirates. The Federal Court in 2013 ruled that Flight Centre had competed with airlines for the retail or distribution margin on the sale of international fares and had sought to stop them from undercutting it on these fares. The issue involved the airlines offering cheaper fares on their own websites than it made available to Flight Centre agents through its global distribution system. Because of Flight Centre's 'lowest price guarantee' – a key element in FLC's business model – it was forced to match the cheaper fares even though this inevitably meant selling at a loss. The case hinged on the question of whether travel agents are a retail extension of an airline or competitors of airlines. Clearly this ruling would have significant repercussions for accommodation and ground tour operators as well.

The initial court decision went against FLC which experienced a small dent in its share price and then had to face a strategic decision as to whether to appeal. Given the crucial importance to the business of its 'Lowest Price Guarantee' policy Flight Centre mounted an appeal; a costly and time-consuming exercise lasting over five years. In 2015, the company won the appeal;

the full bench of the Federal Court finding that the primary judge in the initial case erred in finding that 'Flight Centre and the airlines compete in a market for distribution and booking services'. The full court reasoning was that Flight Centre and the airlines do not compete in a market for booking distribution services because the airlines do not have separate internal teams doing so and the carriers also could not provide access to bookings on other airlines. FCL had the fine of A$11m refunded, together with all its legal costs plus interest. The regulator has signified that it may mount an appeal but to date there has been no action. Skroo Turner's statement at the time is instructive:

> **'For more than 30 years Flight Centre has sought to deliver cheaper airfares to the travelling public. The company is not in the business of attempting to make airfares more expensive. As an agent providing advice to the public and extensive marketing for airlines, Flight Centre has asked for appropriate commissions from suppliers and also reasonable access to all of the deals they release to the market. This is a logical and natural business request for an agent to make to ensure the customers it serves on behalf of the airlines are not disadvantaged. Given that travel agents book up to 80 per cent of international flights to Australia, it benefits consumers because it means special offers are not solely available from supplier websites.'[6]**

The complexities of competition

The highly competitive nature of the airline and travel industry was highlighted in an incident in 2015 when the company issued a profit warning as it had lost some market share to internet companies like Airbnb and Booking.com and experienced weak growth in leisure travel in Australia. The share price slumped 17 per cent. The episode had a key business analyst asking whether Flight Centre's business model had been cracked by its giant online global competitors.[7] Turner was open in conceding that this competition was a fact of life, stating that travel has become more commoditised and it has increasingly gone online where the only point of difference is price. However, the Flight Centre model is a hybrid or 'omni-channel' model with an extensive physical retail network complemented by its online offer. It is in the midst of another evolution, producing its own products together with its ability to offer person-to-person advice and service to create unique and higher margin products. Its physical presence through its international network of businesses is a differentiator.

In the event, the incident proved to be just a glitch, with the market recognising the resilience of Flight

Centre's diversity, scale and financial capacity, including the long-standing company policy of holding large cash reserves and minimal debt. However, it was instructive that this incident saw Skroo Turner take a personal A$90m wealth hit, because his private company holds a 15 per cent stake in Flight Centre.[8] It was also a reminder that the top executives of the company have taken pay cuts when performance targets have not been met. Flight Centre's executives, including Turner, have been described as being grossly underpaid, in terms of salary, in comparison with other top Australian firms; their rewards are determined more by the shareholdings they possess in the company.

Perhaps the biggest competitive challenge has come from the growth of people making direct internet bookings with airlines and accommodation venues. The Flight Centre strategy to confront this is the offering of a combined online and personal booking blended facility, where online customers get the added advantage of personal attention and follow up, along with the price guarantee, the emergency helpline, and faster refunds of cancelled bookings. Clients book online through Flight Centre, they are given the name of their consultant, they look at the fare, book it, and then hand it over to the consultant who holds it for 24 hours and personally follows up. They then receive ongoing access to all of the travel assistance facilities of the company.[9]

The strategic response

In the light of the increasingly competitive environment, including the threat posed by clients' own online bookings, Flight Centre formalised a strategic long-term planning system (two to five years). There is a heavy emphasis on leadership development, through training and recruitment, development of their own product, refining the one best way of operation, improving systems for distributing product, and significant attention to ICT and its potential. The brand strategy is focused very much on consolidation given that out of the 34 brands less than half of all business is conducted under the Flight Centre brand itself. Another goal is to create a smoother relationship between transactional, virtual and real presence to ensure smoother integration and consistency in the emerging different modalities of travel bookings in different global markets. (There are countries where Flight Centre operates with no physical presence.)

The new strategy is conceptualised in terms of key developments ('journeys') characterised as the company's 'killer theme'. Essentially these five journeys have been earmarked as keys in the evolution from travel agent to the world's best travel experience retailer:

- *Brand and specialisation*: evolving brands which truly specialise in specific areas of travel and have clear customer value propositions.
- *Unique product*: making, combining and sourcing exclusive Flight Centre Travel products, rather than simply just selling supplier's products using the tagline 'Our product – not just someone else's'.
- *Experts not agents*: ensuring each brand's people are experts in understanding the brand's specialty and that they in turn are backed by 'travel gurus' who are readily available if additional expertise is required.
- *Redefining the shop*: ensuring corporate, wholesale and retail spaces reflect the fact that Flight Centre's people are retailers first and foremost, and not office workers. (This is most observable in the new configuration in Flight Centre stores with a change from bench row seating of consultants to face customers, to individualised circular tables for each consultant to enjoy a more direct and personalised space with individual customers.)
- *Blended access*: ensuring Flight Centre's brands are always available to customers. They can touch, browse and buy Flight Centre products when and how they want – online, offline, shop, email, chat, phone or SMS.

Underpinning these five journeys is the belief that for the company, information is power through 'profiles', 'patterns' and 'predictions'. It also encompasses a sales and marketing machine that is more agile, personalised and relevant.[9]

A dynamic business model

The increasingly competitive travel industry environment has seen Flight Centre constantly re-orient its business model to acknowledge and accept the trends which are occurring, especially the growth of self-booking of travel, and offer services that enhance and enrich that experience and blend with it. This is achieved by offering more client-focused and personal attention, unique products and services, guaranteed backup and instant access for customers through a wide range of modern and traditional communication and contact modalities

In recent times, Skroo Turner has identified one big strategic challenge for the company as achieving greater productivity per employee. A number of approaches are being taken in this regard, including revision of support to the shopfront, clever use of ICT and an improved database, and introduction of more realistic performance measurement. Another is the creation of more hyperstores in some markets where various teams performing in different parts of the company will be accommodated together in the one location on different floors. The Oxford Street branch in London has been a prototype. This will be a seven-day-a-week operation. The 'village' ladder will be in the one place. There is also a vertical integration strategy to overcome the problem that occurs when the purchaser–provider principle does not fit because one part of the company cannot choose whether to purchase from another part because the margins are not suitable or the product unavailable elsewhere. The goal here is better and faster service to the customer. The pay and incentive structure for consultants has also been remodeled.

The full year net profit for 2015 was A$256.5 million, up 24 per cent from the previous year. Revenue climbed 6.8 per cent to A$2.4 billion, but the company said it faced higher costs in Australian operations owing to a new more generous and incentivised salary structure for consultants.[10] Currently, Australian business accounts for 56.5 per cent of the company's total transaction value but 81.3 per cent of its earnings before interest and tax, meaning that, despite ongoing growth in its overseas business, it remains heavily leveraged to Australia. Turner has said he would like that mix to shift over time so that overseas businesses accounted for around 30–40 per cent of EBIT (earnings before interest and taxation), at the same time as the Australian division continues to grow. The company's sights are set for more overall organic growth, having already achieved a return to its origins with a buyout of Top Deck Tours, and acquisitions currently being negotiated for five separate travel groups in Australia and internationally.[11] In addition to its dual position as Australia's largest travel retailer and Australia's largest corporate travel manager, it has successfully entered niche markets which are growing rapidly internationally, including student travel, travel money and Cruisealone (for ocean and river cruising).

The company continues to win a succession of travel awards in all categories of its operations, and Skroo Turner is very upbeat about prospects in what he describes as the current 'golden era of travel' with cheaper fares, more choice, greater comfort and less flying time.

Notes and references
1. A$1 = £0.52 = $0.74 = €0.66.
2. James Bill, *Top Deck Daze,* Halbon NSW, Avalon, 1990.
3. Nigel Nicholson, *Executive Instinct*, New York, Crown, 2000; Nigel Nicholson, 'How hard wired is human behavior?' *Harvard Business Review*, July–August 1998.
4. Mandy Johnson, *Family Village Tribe: The Story of Flight Centre Limited*, Sydney, Random House, 2005.
5. Graham Turner 'Skroo', *Business Directory and Articles Edition No. 2,* Brisbane, Flight Centre Ltd 2011.
6. *Australian Financial Review*, 1–2 August 2015.
7. *Business Spectator*, 24 June 2015.
8. *Sydney Morning Herald*, 2 July 2015.
9. *Flight Centre Annual Report*, 2015.
10. *Courier Mail*, 28 August 2015.
11. *Australian Business Review*, 23 September 2015.

CASE STUDY

Megabrew: creating an undisputed global brewing champion?

Duncan Angwin

In 2015, SABMiller was considering its strategic options for expansion. It had grown successfully upon the basis of its strength in developing markets, first in Africa and then in other parts of the world. However, on 11 November 2015 it received a bid worth $107bn from AB Inbev, the third biggest bid in history. The aim was to create an undisputed global brewing champion controlling around half the world's brewing profits. Although SABMiller had agreed to the deal, had it made the right decision? What other strategic options could SABMiller have pursued? Assuming the deal would be completed later in 2016, subject to overcoming regulatory hurdles, how could AB Inbev integrate SABMiller successfully?

Introduction

Following its acquisitions of the American brewer Miller in 2002, Grupo Empresarial Bavaria, South America's second largest brewer in 2005, and the Australian Beer Group Fosters in 2011, SABMiller had become the second largest brewer by volume and profits in the world. By 2015, its market share by volume was 12 per cent and its brand portfolio included international brands Pilsner Urquell, Peroni Nastro Azzurro, Miller Genuine Draft and Grolsch along with local country brands such as Aguila, Castle Lager, Miller Lite, VB, Snow and Tyskie.

Despite these successes, the dramatic consolidation in the brewing industry continued. In the early 1990s, the five largest brewing companies accounted for just 17 per cent of global beer sales. By 2014, the largest four brewing companies accounted for 45.7 per cent of sales and analysts estimated they had captured 80 per cent of the $33bn global profit pool. Moreover, three of SABMiller's main global competitors, Anheuser Busch, Interbrew and Ambev, had merged in 2008, to form AB InBev, to claim market leadership with a consolidated 25 per cent of global market share, although that had fallen to 20 per cent by 2014.

In September 2014, SABMiller launched a surprise takeover bid for Dutch counterpart and third placed rival, Heineken. Charlene de Carvalho-Heineken and her husband Michel de Carvalho are head of one of the richest families in Britain, with a combined fortune estimated at more than £6bn. The family controlled more than 50 per cent of Heineken and their response was swift and unequivocal. They rejected the bid and said they intended to 'preserve the heritage and identity of

Source: Douglas Carr/Alamy Images.

Heineken as an independent company'. This dealt a blow to SABMiller's ambitions and there was little point in returning with a better offer as the family wasn't motivated by money.[1]

In order to consider their position, SABMiller re-examined its four strategic priorities set out in 2010 (see Table 1). This can be seen as a synthesis of the learning the company had developed over its history, first weathering the political crises of twentieth-century South African history, then building its operations in emerging and mature markets, where it gained a reputation as 'a turnaround specialist' and subsequently an acquirer of major breweries in mature markets. These strategies had served the company well as SABMiller has shown sustained good performance compared with the London Stock Market Beverage index (see Figure 1).

Table 1 SABMiller's strategic priorities

1. Creating a balanced and attractive global spread of businesses	'Our acquisitions in recent years have given us a wide geographical spread with good exposure to emerging markets without being over-reliant on any single region. This allows us to capture new growth in developing markets and "value" growth as consumers around the world trade up from economy to mainstream and premium brands. We also look to identify and exploit opportunities for growth within our existing business portfolio. This can involve a range of activities, from entering into local joint ventures or partnerships, to buying or building breweries, to acquiring local brands to help shape a full, local, brand portfolio.'
2. Developing strong, relevant brand portfolios in the local market	'Our aim is to develop an attractive brand portfolio that meets consumers' needs in each of our markets. In many markets, growth is fastest at the top end, as shown by the increasing popularity of our international premium brands. Another rising consumer trend is the shift towards fragmentation. Affluent consumers are varying their choices and becoming more interested in speciality brands, craft beers, foreign imports and other subdivisions of the premium segment. And a third trend is the growing importance of female consumers.'
3. Constantly raising the performance of local businesses	'In order to raise our performance, we need to become more efficient, especially in our manufacturing processes. Efficiency is part of our day-to-day management and the rise in commodity costs compels us to do whatever we can to counteract the squeeze on our margins. All SABMiller operations strive to improve our products' route to market, to remove costs and to ensure that the right products reach the right outlets in the right condition.'
4. Leveraging our global scale	'As a global organisation we are constantly seeking to use the benefits of our scale while recognising that beer is essentially a local business and that local managers are in the best position to identify and exploit local opportunities. Our aim is to generate maximum value and advantage from our size without becoming over-centralised and losing our relevance and responsiveness in each market.'

Source: SABMiller.

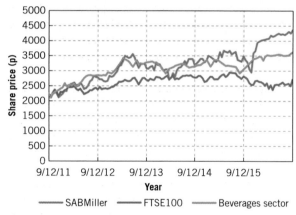

Figure 1 Five-year SABMiller share price vs FTSE 100 and Beverages indexes (rebased)

While SABMiller was pondering its options in 2015, rival beer giant AB InBev announced a formal offer to buy them for $107bn. The combined group would control 58 per cent of the global profit pool, dwarfing next rival Heineken with just 11.6 per cent and Carlsberg with only 4.6 per cent. Tense private talks between stakeholders followed until 13 October 2015 when a tentative deal was announced. There was some way to go, however, to complete the deal, scheduled for late 2016, with formidable obstacles to overcome, not least dealing with regulatory interests around the world. In the meantime, the question was whether the deal was the best strategic option for SABMiller?

Background

South African Breweries (SAB) predated the state of South Africa itself. It faced the challenge of doing business amidst the upheaval the country experienced during the twentieth century, including the 'apartheid' regime (1948–1994). Worldwide opposition to apartheid included a campaign for economic sanctions on South Africa, aiming to restrict international business from investing in, or trading with, South Africa and restricting South African business from trading with international markets. In 1950, SAB moved its head office from London to Johannesburg and southern Africa became the focus of its business expansion during the subsequent four decades.

In this time, SAB responded to business restrictions by focusing on dominating domestic beer production through acquisition of competitors and rationalisation of production and distribution facilities. By 1979, SAB controlled an estimated 99 per cent of the market in South Africa and held commanding positions in Swaziland, Lesotho, Rhodesia (now Zimbabwe) and Botswana. In 1978, SAB also diversified into hotels and gambling by acquiring the Sun City casino resort.

The establishment of a multiracial democracy in South Africa in the 1990s eased SAB's expansion through the rest of Africa. By 2000, SAB's market dominance in southern Africa provided a serious deterrent to potential competitors, but there remained little space for it to expand locally, particularly in alcoholic beverages.

Emerging onto the global market

In 1993, SAB made its first acquisition outside Africa, purchasing Hungary's largest brewery, Dreher, describing it as a 'beach-head move' into Central Europe. So began a strategy explained in the 1998 annual report: 'SAB's international focus has been on countries in which it believes it could use its expertise, which has been gained over 100 years in South Africa, to develop beer markets in emerging economies.'

The strategy of developing brewing capabilities in under-developed beer markets continued through the 1990s. SAB established operations in China in 1994, forming a joint venture with China Resources Enterprise Ltd, to add China's biggest beer brand, Snow, to its portfolio. There followed further acquisitions in Eastern Europe including Lech (1995) and Tyskie (1996) in Poland, acquisitions in Romania, Slovakia, and the Czech Republic and in 1998 SAB entered into Russia by establishing a 'greenfield' brewery in Kaluga, near Moscow.

SAB's strategy was spelled out in the 2000 report and this logic prevailed up until AB InBev's bid:

'In the less developed world, Africa and Asia and much of Europe, brewing remained highly fragmented, with beer drinkers supplied by breweries which were never more than small-scale and localised, often producing low-quality beer . . . This fragmentation presented the opportunity for SAB from the mid-1990s to create a profitable and fast-expanding business in emerging markets with huge potential. This opportunity involves, generally, taking a share in a brewery with a local partner and, transforming the business while retaining the brand, given drinkers have fierce attachments to their local brew. Transformation starts with upgrading quality and consistency to create a beer for which people are prepared to pay more and which can give us a healthy profit margin. Then comes improvement to marketing and distribution and improvement to productivity and capacity. In each country we have begun by acquiring an initial local stronghold from which we can advance into regions beyond the brewery's original catchment area. We then build critical mass in the region and progress, over time, to a national basis. This is often achieved by acquiring further brewing businesses and focusing the brand portfolio. An optimum brand portfolio gives us a better overall marketing proposition, increases total sales and delivers economies of scale in production and distribution.

This process demands, on one level, great political sensitivity in dealing with governments, partners, local communities and our workforce and, on another level, the deployment of expert operational management

skills learnt in South Africa . . . Our management structure is de-centralised, reflecting the local nature of beer branding and distribution.

Our businesses do not all advance at the same speed, or have the same potential. It is characteristic of emerging markets that growth can be variable, and we are accustomed to temporary setbacks. However, the spread of our international businesses provides a 'portfolio effect', thereby reducing the impact of setbacks in one or two individual countries.'

SAB's history of buying local companies with strong market positions had worked very well for the group. The most successful acquisitions had domestic leadership positions in under-developed beer markets. CEO Graham MacKay commented that: 'We acquire reasonably priced assets, often severely neglected under public ownership in growing markets; establish market leadership and build local mainstream brands.'

The way in which SAB could be successful with these acquisitions was through 'Operational improvement and efficiencies – to distribute beer more efficiently and drive down costs.' This could be achieved reliably through the use of seasoned leaders with deep experience from the South African business. They would parachute into new acquisitions, drawing upon SABMiller's long-standing strengths and capabilities in operational excellence in the beer industry and its distinctive people/performance management.

Analysts had also recognised, however, that SAB had been less successful with its acquisitions in developed markets, where it seemed to have less strength. This focus on local improvement was echoed in MacKay's comments that: 'We are not top down. We are very locally driven.'

This reflected a strongly held view in the group that beer is a local taste and that SABMiller can create winning brands that tap into deep local insights and win. One way in which SABMiller had been particularly effective in boosting local sales was the development of a 'shopper' marketing capability, where they worked alongside local beer retailers to help them grow their beer category, helping SABMiller sales. Amongst its major competitors, SABMiller saw itself as the most local of global brewers.

Going global

In 1999, SAB decided to list on the London Stock Exchange (LSE), justifying it in terms of:

'Giving the group greater access to world capital markets and providing it with financial resources and flexibility' [so as to] 'enhance the ability of SAB to take

advantage of increasing consolidation in the international brewing industry and to compete with other international brewers for development opportunities throughout the world.'

Initially SAB's share price lost over 15 per cent relative to the FTSE 100 as analysts argued this reflected a failure to make a major acquisition of a first-world (developed country) brand and its over-reliance on its developing markets.

SABMiller

In 2002, SAB did succeed in acquiring a major brand in a developed market: Miller Brewing Company, the second largest brewery in the USA. SAB paid Philip Morris Co. US$3.6bn in stock and assumed US$2bn of Miller's debt. The 2003 annual report claimed that this gave the group access, through a national player, to a growing beer market within the world's largest profit pool, and at the same time diversifying the currency and geographic risk of the group.

SAB became SABMiller following the acquisition and the second largest brewery by volume in the world. However, the acquisition brought with it its own problems. James Williamson, an analyst at SG Securities in London, commented: 'They didn't buy it because they thought it was a strong growth business. They bought it because they needed a mature cash cow. Unfortunately it's been losing more market share than expected.'

Indeed, following the first full year of SABMiller operating Miller, its US market share had dropped from 19.6 per cent to 18.7 per cent and by September 2003 the share price of the company had dropped from 530 pence on the day of acquisition of Miller to 456.5 pence.

SABMiller appointed Norman Adami, previously head of its South Africa Beer business, as head of Miller, and introduced the traditional SAB system of performance management that rewards strong performers and focuses on improving weaker performers. This was a considerable change from Miller's previous system of performance rating which routinely rated all staff at the highest level. SABMiller also announced that there would be a rationalisation of Miller's product portfolio from 50 brands to 11 or 12, meaning that market share would go down before it could go up again.

Continued acquisitions and international development

There followed a series of acquisitions (see Table 2).

In 2005, there followed a merger with Grupo Empresarial Bavaria, the second largest brewer in South America, consolidating SABMiller as the world number

Table 2 Main acquisitions, joint ventures and brewery investments 2001–15

2001	Takes a majority stake in the Sichuan Blue Sword Breweries Group in China. Pan-African alliance with Castel for investing in promising African countries. First international brewer to enter Central America when it acquired Honduran brewer, Cervecería Hondureña.
2002	Acquires 100% of Miller Brewing Company and changes name to SABMiller plc. Now the second largest brewer (by volume) in the world.
2003	Acquires majority interest in Birra Peroni S.p.A. developing Peroni as a global premium brand.
2004	SABMiller associate, China Resources Breweries Limited, acquires two Chinese breweries.
2005	Buyout of joint venture partner in India, Shaw Wallace & Company. Acquires 71.8% of Colombian Grupo Empresarial Bavaria, the second largest brewer in South America, for $7.8bn.
2006	Acquires the Foster's business and brand in India and in South Vietnam. Joint venture with Vinamilk to establish a brewery in Vietnam. SABMiller and Coca-Cola Amatil form Pacific Beverages Pty Ltd, a joint venture to market, distribute and sell SABMiller brands in Australia.
2007	10-year partnership with Foster's Group to brew Foster's lager in the USA. $170m invested in a new brewery in Moscow. Pacific Beverages buys Australian premium brewer Bluetongue Brewery.
2008	Acquires Royal Grolsch NV for €816m ($1.2bn). Acquires the Vladpivo brewery in Vladivostock (Russia) and Sarmat brewery in the Ukraine. Joint venture with Moulson Coors Brewing Co., named MillerCoors, to pool US interests.
2009	Acquires Bere Azuga, Romania. Acquires the remaining 50% interest in the Vietnamese business and remaining 28% in the Polish business. Acquires three further breweries in China. Investment in new plant in Juba (South Sudan), Russia, Tanzania, Mozambique and Angola.
2010	Acquires Cervecería Argentina S.A. Isenbeck ('CASA Isenbeck'), the third largest brewer in Argentina, from the Warsteiner Group. Builds US$34m brewery in Namibia. A new US$105m brewery begins operations in New South Wales, Australia. Southern Sudan Beverages Ltd (SSBL) is doubling the size of its existing brewery operations.

(continued)

Table 2 Main acquisitions, joint ventures and brewery investments 2001–15 (*continued*)

2011	Builds a new brewery in Nigeria. Establishes a new £3m research brewery in the UK. CR Snow continues expansion in China with acquisition of remaining equity interest in Hangzhou Xihu Beer and Huzhou Brewery and announces a new joint venture, Guizhou Moutai Beer, in partnership with China Kweichow Moutai Distillery Co. Ltd. SABMiller, Anadolu Group and Anadolu Efes agree a strategic alliance for Turkey, Russia, the CIS, Central Asia and the Middle East. SABMiller acquires Foster's Group, the number one brewer in Australia for A$11.8bn.
2012	Strategic alliance with Castel to takeover running of Nigerian businesses. Invests in doubling capacity in Uganda.
2014	Unsuccessful attempt to acquire Heineken International. Agreement to take a 47% stake in a new combined bottling operation for non-alcoholic ready-to-drink beverages, Coca-Cola Beverages Africa, with The Coca-Cola Company and Gutsche Family Investments. This will account for 40% of all Coca-Cola sales in Africa.
2015	Acquires Meantime Brewery in the UK.

two brewer and making Latin America the largest contributor of profits in the group (32 per cent of EBITA, ahead of South Africa). The area has performed very strongly since the acquisition in terms of top- and bottom-line growth. Reviewing the Latin American operations at that time, the CEO confirmed that SABMiller saw these markets as offering 'exciting prospects for growth' and added:

> 'Although the Bavaria businesses are well managed and profitable, we plan to create further value by applying SABMiller's operating practices and management skills. The best opportunities lie in brand portfolio development, creating good relationships with distributors and retailers, and improving merchandising at the point of sale. The Bavaria acquisition brought very strong leader positions in its markets, with 90% market share – a huge advantage in a scale-driven industry.'

In 2008, a joint venture, Miller Coors, was formed between Molson Coors and the SABMiller business in the USA for scale advantages and productivity improvements of $500m in the face of increasing cost pressures and improved logistics across the North American market. The complementarity of brands was to enable more effective competition against the dominance of Anheuser Busch in the USA. Commentators viewed the joint venture as a way of gaining market share in the profitable light beer category that accounted for 40 per cent of total US beer sales. The joint venture's profit performance has been robust.

At the group level, in 2009 profits dropped; however (see Appendix 1 financial summary), this did not diminish top management interest in making further M&A. As CEO Graham Mackay stated via Bloomberg:[2] 'Nothing is stopping us from the right acquisition . . . There is money available even if we have to raise capital. We think our shareholders would agree with it if it was the right acquisition.' He added, however, that: 'The right acquisition

means something very different in an emerging market where a brewer can capitalise on growing volumes, than it does in the developed world where cost cuts and selling more premium beer is key.'

In 2011, SABMiller made a major acquisition in Foster's Group in Australia for A$11.8bn[3]. Some industry observers were not convinced it was the right move as Foster's, the number one brewer in Australia, was competing in a mature market and its beer volumes profits and market share were all in decline compared with its main rival Anheuser-Busch InBev. In the year ended March 2012, Foster's volumes of beers were down four per cent on the year when SABMiller group saw an overall rise. Analysts worried that SABMiller's Foster's deal mirrored its Miller purchase in 2002 when SAB bought into an effective duopoly in the low-growth US market and gave the brewer a long-term headache. As one investor remarked: 'SABMiller has turned around difficult situations before but those have often been from dominant market share positions.'

As an analyst at the time remarked, 'they have to be very careful how they play their hand. SAB's big deal record hasn't been great.'[2] The Miller acquisition took longer than expected to repay the cost of capital and analysts believe the turnaround of Foster's would take some time.[4] However, the CEO Graham Mackay was reported to say that he would 'sweat the assets' and 'make the numbers work'.[5] The board also acknowledged that there were few brewers remaining that could be acquired and would really make a difference to the company going forwards.

The state of the world brewing market to 2015

Global beer volumes (excluding China) recovered to about a two per cent growth rate after the trough of 2008–10 but well below the four to five per cent achieved in 2006–7. The growth rate by region varied considerably (see Table 3). Going forwards analysts expected flat beer

Table 3 Compound annual growth rates (CAGR) by volume, by region (2013–2017)

Region	CAGR (2013–2017F)
Africa	5%
Asia	4%
Australasia	1%
East Europe	0%
Latin America	3%
Middle East North Africa	4%
North America	1%
West Europe	−1%

Source: Based on http://www.canadean.com/news/africa-to-become-fastest-growing-beer-market-in-the-world-by-2017/.

volumes in North America and Europe with decline in key markets such as Germany France and UK. The per capita consumption by Germans for instance, some of the world's biggest aficionados of beer, had fallen due to demographic change, alternative beverages such as health drinks, wine and cider, tighter regulations and global economic slowdown. There was significant growth, however, in Latin America, with China, India and Africa offering the best long-term volume prospects given their large populations and low per capita consumption. Table 4 gives market profitability estimates by region. In particular, Africa's growth rate was estimated to be 44 per cent from 2014–25, nearly three times the forecast global growth rate.

Against this backdrop of regional variation in sales (see Figure 2), the large brewing companies also faced changes in the nature of demand. There was intensifying competition in premium beer segments where high profit margins made it easier for niche providers to compete successfully. In many European countries there was a substantial increase in new beer products on retailers' shelves and in the US craft beers were making substantial inroads.

In this context, SABMiller's main competitors, focused on various geographies and had different strategies. Heineken was increasingly centralising its brands in order to have a global brand design that they could then license, allowing global advertising and the use of a mass premium model. They were determined to retain their independence. AB InBev remained focused on cost reduction through a few very large acquisitions and had generally managed to achieve between 10 and 15 per cent margin

on each one. Carlsberg was struggling due to a recession in its core Russian market, tighter regulations and conflict in Ukraine. Although it turned profitable for the first time in India in 2016, it announced a profits warning and a strategy review which could include an intention to acquire in growth markets such as Asia (see Table 5 for competitor share of global profits).

Potential new competitors, including global spirits companies, were also increasingly encroaching on beer competitors' markets with greater focus on the same consumer occasions and needs, e.g. alcopops and ready-mixed drinks. Companies such as Diageo, previously focused on developed markets, were now very active in growing rapidly through M&A in key emerging markets. Some media commentators predicted this would lead to convergence in the wine and beer market and pointed towards increased innovation in mixing beers with spirits and flavours. Heineken's flavoured beer 'Desperados' reflected an increased consumer demand for more sophisticated beverages at mixed gender occasions.

The AB InBev bid

The AB InBev bid, dubbed 'Megabrew' by analysts, would result in the world's largest consumer-staples maker by earnings, with profits around $25bn.[6] The enlarged brewer would be number 1 or number 2 in 24 of the world's 30 biggest beer markets. Analysts believe AB InBev made the bid in order to continue growing as its own growth rate was forecast to slow down over the following five years. In the US market, which accounted for 34 per cent of group revenue, its market share had already fallen from over 50 per cent to 44 per cent largely due to the rapid growth of craft brewers (see Figure 3). Its attempts to create its own craft beers such as Bud Lime had had only limited success.

Historically, AB InBev had a strong position in Latin America with 78 per cent market share in Argentina, 68 per cent in Brazil and 58 per cent in Mexico. This accounted for 30 per cent of group revenue in 2014 (see Table 6). It was an attractive area as there were low labour and raw material costs, economies of scale and production was near to market. Together with Mexico, Latin American revenue at $18,849m accounted for over 40 per cent of AB

Table 4 Market profitability estimates (2010)

Brazil	North America	S. Africa	Other Latin America	Europe	Russia	Other Africa	Other Asia	China	India
$31/hl	$31/hl	$24/hl	$20/hl	$17/hl	$13/hl	$10/hl	$10/hl	$2/hl	$2/hl

Source: Merrill Lynch report.

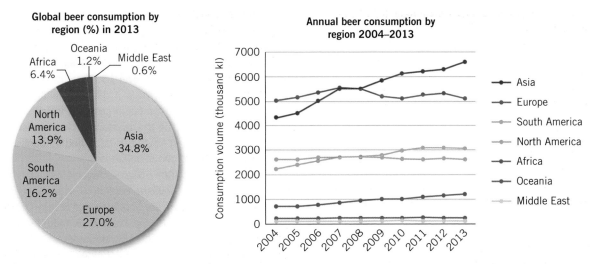

Figure 2 Global beer consumption by region

Source: www.kirinholdings.co.jp, Kirin Beer University Report Global Beer Consumption, 24 December 2014.

Going Flat

Anheuser-Busch InBev's volumes have declined in the USA in recent years as craft and imports have risen.

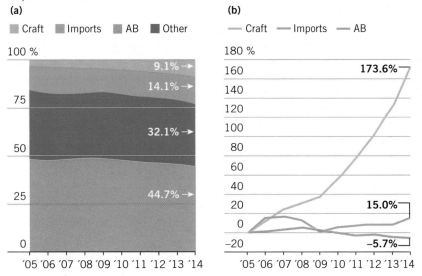

Figure 3(a) Beer market shares in the USA, 2006–2014

Source: Beer Marketer's Insights.

Figure 3(b) Change in pattern of beer shipments, 2005–2015

Source: The Wall Street Journal.

Table 5 Competitor share of global $33bn profit pool (2014)

Company	Percentage share
AB InBev	39.9
SABMiller	17.9
Heineken	11.6
Carlsberg	4.6
Asahi	3.1
Molson Coors	2.9
Others	20.0

InBev's group revenue, greater than North American sales. SABMiller also had a strong presence in Latin America although not in Brazil, Argentina and Mexico where AB InBev was dominant. SABMiller's focus upon premium branding allowed it to achieve 33 per cent higher revenue per unit volume in this region than AB InBev. The combination could increase AB InBev's Latin American volumes by 30 per cent. In developed countries AB InBev was already strong, accounting for 47 per cent of revenues (see Table 6).

AB InBev needed to make an acquisition in order 'to move the needle', to make a difference in terms of its earnings. The bid was 50 per cent above SABMiller's closing share price of £29.34 on 14 September 2015. Stock markets welcomed the news as SABMiller shares rose 1.9 per cent in London and AB InBev gained 2.2 per cent in Brussels.

In terms of control, the Belgian and Brazilian families that controlled AB InBev would have seen their ownership diluted from 50 per cent to 44 per cent and SABMiller's two biggest shareholders, Altria Group Inc. and Colombia's Santo Domingo family, would own 16.5 per cent. At the time of the bid, it was not clear if the top management team of SABMiller would remain in post. AB InBev would finance the cash part of the transaction from existing resources and third-party debt and had lined up banks to raise $75bn, a record commercial loan.

A bid of such magnitude triggers regulatory concerns as it might create monopolistic conditions in some countries. In the USA there were concerns that a very dominant company might hurt the craft beer industry and reduce consumer choice. The US regulator uses a relative market share measure, the HHI index, to determine the concentration of competitors in an industry. As a rule of thumb, the regulator prefers a score for the industry to be below 2500. With the passage of AB InBev's bid for SABMiller, without taking into account any restructuring and disposals, the new group would have 68 per cent market share and a HHI score of 5366 post-deal – significantly up from the pre-acquisition level of 2696. There were also concerns that a very dominant company might distort the market for supplies such as barley, hops and aluminium cans. In order to gain regulatory approval, the bid stated that Molson Coors Brewing Company would acquire SABMiller's 58 per cent stake in Miller Coors, the CR Snow business in China would need to be

Table 6 AB InBev revenue and gross profit (US$m) and volumes by region (hlm)

		2014	2013	% change
Group	Revenue	47,063	43,195	8.9%
	Gross profit	28,307	25,601	10.6%
	Volume	458.801	445.786	2.9%
North America	Revenue	16,093	16,023	0.4%
	Gross profit	9,702	9,504	2.1%
	Volume	121.150	122.118	−0.8%
Mexico	Revenue	4,619	4,669	9.9%
	Gross profit	3,245	3,099	4.7%
	Volume	38,800	38,185	1.6%
Latin America	Revenue	14,230	14,279	−0.03%
	Gross profit	9,409	9,518	−0.01%
	Volume	162.244	157.345	3.1%
Europe	Revenue	4,865	5,021	−0.03%
	Gross profit	2,784	2,749	1.3%
	Volume	44.278	47.030	−5.6%
Asia	Revenue	5,040	3,354	50.3%
	Gross profit	2,489	1,469	69.4%
	Volume	82.529	65.787	25.5%
Global export and holding companies	Revenue	2,216	2,138	3.6%
	Gross profit	678	589	15.1%
	Volume	9.800	15.323	−36%

Source: www.ab-inbev.com Annual Report 2014.

sold, as would the Peroni and Grolsch brands in Europe. And, an important bottler for Coca-Cola's drinks in Africa, this partner would be lost as AB InBev already worked with PepsiCo in Latin America.

AB InBev aimed to cut annual costs by $1.4bn, about 9 per cent of SABMiller's sales. As an acquisition driven company, AB InBev had a successful track record of cutting costs, e.g. by 19 per cent when it bought Anheuser-Busch in 2008 and a 21 per cent cost reduction at Mexico's Modelo in 2013. AB InBev has an impressive operating profit margin of 33 per cent compared with other competitors who struggle to reach that level. An estimated one third of savings from the SABMiller acquisition might come from overlapping head-office roles. The rest would come from restructuring although those details had not emerged at the time of writing. Some analysts even believed that AB InBev cost cuttings were being underestimated. However, others pointed out that SABMiller was already a lean operation, and its operations were dispersed, which might not provide many opportunities for amalgamation. They also pointed out that whilst AB InBev had been excellent at cutting costs on acquisition, their track record for generating subsequent organic growth was lacking.

What next?

SABMiller had agreed to the takeover by AB InBev but whether this was the best strategic option for the company was not clear. It was also important to consider other options in case the bid failed to close due to regulatory hurdles, of which there was approximately a 27 per cent chance, and SABMiller remained independent. Nonetheless, assuming the bid did close, both SABMiller and AB InBev had to consider what a successful bid might mean for the combined business going forwards. How might SABMiller be integrated effectively into the new group? Would the integration strategy destroy valuable SABMiller heritage or enhance its value? How would the new company compete in the future?

Whilst SABMiller and AB InBev wrestled with satisfying regulators and planning for integration, the beer market seemed to have fewer opportunities for expansion: large transformational deals were hard to find and with lower prospects of high financial returns. The other global brewers were increasingly looking for growth from emerging markets as beer sales slowed in more developed consumer markets. Heineken was pursuing growth in Africa and Carlsberg aimed to expand into Asia. Japanese brewers were also becoming increasingly active in the Asian market. The added complication of the economic recession had also impacted on all beer markets, albeit with different degrees of severity. For all companies there were questions about the emphasis placed on 'local vs global' brands in their portfolios. Should they consider entering more profitable beverage segments? Could there be yet another 'market changing' deal that could be shaped to win the battle in beer?

Main sources: T. Buckley, 'SABMiller buoys case for AB InBev takeover as Africa sales gain', Bloomberg.com, 21 January 2016. *The Economist*, 'The beerhemoth – SABMiller is AB InBev's toughest takeover yet. It may not be its last', Economist.com, 17 October 2015. J. Fontanella-Khan, A. Massoudi and S. Daneshkhu, 'Anheuser-Busch InBev eyes takeover of rival SABMiller', FT.com, 16 September 2015. E. Holodny, 'A Budweiser-Miller brewing company would be a monster', uk.businessinsider.com, 16 September 2015. P. Jarvis and T. Buckley, 'AB InBev buys SABMiller for $107 billion as U.S. deal agreed', www.bloomberg.com, 11 November 2015. T. Mickle, 'AB InBev defends SABMiller buy to Senate: questions asked about deal's potential impact on craft brewers, rival beer makers', www.wsj.com, 8 December 2015. Trefis Team, 'Anheuser–Busch InBev: what the SABMiller acquisition could mean', Forbes.com, 18 September 2014. Trefis Team, 'How the potential AB InBev–SABMiller deal focuses on Africa', Trefis.com, 14 December 2015. E. Rutishauser, S. Rickert and F. Sänger, 'A perfect storm brewing in the global beer business', Mckinseyonmarketingandsales.com, June 2015.

Notes and references

1. B. Marlow and N. Thomas, 'Billion dollar beer war is brewing', *The Telegraph*, 20 September 2014.
2. A. Cleary, 'SABMiller chief says he's ready for M&A, predicts slow recovery', Bloomberg.com, 11 August 2009.
3. AUD$1.00 = £0.52 = $0.74 = €0.66.
4. D. Jones, 'Analysis: SABMiller faces long haul to turnaround Foster's', *Reuters*, 31 May 2012.
5. N. Hue, 'SAB fosters beer brands in Australia', FT.com, 26 May 2013.
6. Exane BNP Paribas, quoted in Bloomberg news, 11 November 2015.

APPENDIX: SABMiller financial summary (US$m) for years ended 31 March

	2015	2014	2013	2012	2011[1]	2010	2009	2008	2007	2006	2005
Income statements											
Group revenue	33,558	34,087	34,487	31,388	28,311	26,350	25,302	23,828	20,645	17,081	14,543
Revenue	22,130	22,311	23,213	21,760	19,408	18,020	18,703	21,410	18,620	15,307	12,901
Operating profit	4,384	4,242	4,192	5,013	3,127	2,619	3,148	3,448	3,027	2,575	2,547
Net finance costs	−637	−645	−726	−562	−525	−563	−706	−456	−428	−299	−143
Share of associates' and joint ventures' post-tax results	1,083	1,226	1,213	1,152	1,024	873	516	272	205	177	148
Taxation	−1,273	−1,173	−1,192	−1,126	1,069	−848	−801	−976	−921	−779	−823
Minority interests	−258	−269	−237	−256	−149	−171	−276	−265	−234	−234	−208
Profit for the year	**3,299**	**3,381**	**3,250**	**4,221**	**2,408**	**1,910**	**1,881**	**2,023**	**1,649**	**1,440**	**1,521**
Adjusted earnings	**3,835**	**3,865**	**3,772**	**3,400**	**3,018**	**2,509**	**2,065**	**2,147**	**1,796**	**1,497**	**1,224**
Balance sheets											
Non-current assets	40,552	48,366	50,588	50,998	34,870	33,604	28,159	31,947	25,683	24,286	12,869
Current assets	4,359	5,385	5,683	4,930	4,244	3,895	3,460	4,135	3,053	2,829	2,778
Total assets	**44,911**	**53,751**	**56,294**	**55,928**	**39,114**	**37,499**	**31,619**	**36,082**	**28,736**	**27,115**	**15,647**
Derivative financial instruments	−111	−115	−86	−109	−135	−321	−142	−531	−209	−178	–
Borrowings	−12,544	−17,047	−18,548	−19,226	−8,460	−9,414	−9,618	−9,658	−7,231	−7,602	−3,340
Other liabilities and provisions	−8,012	−9,222	−10,286	−10,554	−7,760	−7,171	−5,746	−7,649	−6,295	−5,750	−3,552
Total liabilities	**−20,556**	**−26,269**	**−28,834**	**−29,896**	**−16,355**	**16,906**	**−15,506**	**−17,838**	**−13,735**	**−13,530**	**−6,892**
Net assets	**24,355**	**27,482**	**27,460**	**26,032**	**22,759**	**20,593**	**16,113**	**18,244**	**15,001**	**13,585**	**8,755**
Total shareholders' equity	23,172	26,319	26,372	25,073	22,008	19,910	15,375	17,545	14,406	13,043	8,077
Minority interests in equity	1,183	1,163	1,088	959	751	683	738	699	595	542	678
Total equity	**24,355**	**27,482**	**27,460**	**26,032**	**22,759**	**20,593**	**16,113**	**18,244**	**15,001**	**13,585**	**8,755**
Cash flow statements											
EBITDA	**5,680**	**5,677**	**5,758**	**4,979**	**4,502**	**3,974**	**4,164**	**4,518**	**4,031**	**3,348**	**2,736**
Net working capital movements	132	93	−204	258	66	563	−493	−242	−13	−57	56
Net cash generated from operations	5,812	5,770	5,554	5,237	4,568	4,537	3,671	4,276	4,018	3,291	2,792
Net interest paid (net of dividends received)	756	385	230	610	271	175	−116	−410	−385	−248	−79
Tax paid	−1439	−1596	−683	−893	−885	−620	−766	−969	−801	−869	−625
Net cash inflow from operating activities	**3,722**	**3,431**	**4,101**	**3,937**	**3,043**	**3,277**	**2,789**	**2,897**	**2,832**	**2,174**	**2,088**

	2015	2014	2013	2012	2011[1]	2010	2009	2008	2007	2006	2005
Net capital expenditure	-1,503	-1,416	-1,440	-1,522	-1,245	-1,483	-2,072	-1,927	-1,351	-984	-738
Net investments in subsidiaries, joint ventures and associates	755	-338	-223	-11095	-183	-504	-555	-1,439	-429	-2,644	-897
Net other investments							-10	5	-2	-2	456
Net cash inflow/(outflow) before financing and dividends	**4,381**	**2,805**	**3,438**	**-7663**	**2,526**	**2,105**	152	-464	1,050	-1,456	909
Net cash inflow/(outflow) from financing	-3,677	-1195	-517	8,819	-1,214	-804	620	1,240	-455	1,733	-271
Dividends paid	-1705	-1640	-1517	-1,324	-1,113	924	-877	-769	-681	-520	-412
Effect of exchange rates	-117	-61	-51	-39	25	90	26	-113	-18	11	-56
(Decrease)/increase in cash and cash equivalents	**-1118**	**-91**	**1353**	**-207**	**224**	**467**	**-79**	**-106**	**-104**	**-232**	**170**
Per share information (US cents per share)											
Basic earnings per share	205.7	211.8	204.3	266.6	152.8	122.6	125.2	134.9	110.2	105	125.5
Diluted earnings per share	203.5	209.1	202	263.8	151.8	122.1	124.7	134.2	109.5	104.3	121.2
Adjusted basic earnings per share	239.1	242	237.2	214.8	191.5	161.1	137.5	143.1	120	109.1	101
Net asset value per share[2]				1,506.50	1,326.60	1,203.20	969.8	1,108.30	912	828	599.9
Total number of shares in issue (millions)	1,675.7	1,672.6	1,669.7	1,664.30	1,659	1,654.70	1,585.40	1,583.10	1,579.60	1,575.20	1,346.50
Other operating and financial statistics											
Return on equity (%)[3]	16.6	14.7	14.3	13.6	13.7	12.6	13.4	12.2	12.5	11.5	15.2
EBITA margin (%)[4]	24.2	24.2	23.7	17.9	17.8	16.6	16.3	17.4	17.4	17.2	16.4
EBITDA margin (%)[5]	31.7	31.4	30	23	22.9	21.7	22.3	21.1	21.6	21.9	21.2
EBITDA interest cover (times)	10.7	10.3	8.9	11.4	10.8	9.3	6.6	9.2	9.2	11.4	19.1
Total borrowings to total assets (%)	27.9	31.7	32.9	34.5	21.6	25.1	30.4	26.8	25.2	28	21.3
Cash flow to total borrowings (%)	45.3	33.3	31.0	27.2	54	48.2	38.2	44.3	55.6	43.3	83.6
Revenue per employee (US$000's)	321.6	318.9	329.3	305.9	280.4	256.9	272.5	309.8	278.1	284.7	315.5
Average monthly number of employees	68,808	69,947	70,486	71,144	69,212	70,131	68,635	69,116	66,949	53,772	40,892
Group revenue											
Primary segmental analysis (numbers are restated for 2012–2015)											
Latin America	5,768	5,745	5,802	5,315	6,335	5,905	5,495	5,251	4,392	2,165	521
Europe	4,398	4,574	4,300	4,235	5,394	5,577	6,145	5,248	4,078	3,258	2,909
North America	4,682	4,665	4,656	4,544	5,223	5,228	5,227	5,120	4,887	4,912	4,892
Africa and Asia*	11,329	11,365	11,770	10,434	5,280	4,457	4,132	3,367	2,674	2,221	1,937
South Africa:											
– Beverages				5,815	5,598	4,777	3,955	4,446	4,274	4,204	3,995
– Hotels and Gaming	111	370	404	421	481	406	348	396	340	321	289
	26,288	26,719	26,932	31,388	28,311	26,350	25,302	23,828	20,645	17,081	14,543

(continued)

APPENDIX *(continued)*

	2015	2014	2013	2012	2011[1]	2010	2009	2008	2007	2006	2005
Operating profit (excluding share of associates and joint ventures)											
Primary segmental analysis											
Latin America	2,110	2,069	1,983	1,736	1,497	1,270	1,057	953	810	387	90
Europe	548	576	652	804	857	840	900	947	730	567	482
North America	14	9	7	–	16	12	230	462	366	454	487
Africa and Asia	1,909	1,946	1,952	546	343	280	352	330	272	257	249
South Africa: Beverages				1,091	997	826	704	962	1,043	1,011	906
Corporate	-122	-161	-202	-190	-147	-139	-97	-94	-101	-86	-82
Group operating profit – before exceptional items	**4,459**	**4,439**	**4,392**	**3,987**	**3,563**	**3,091**	**3,146**	**3,560**	**3,120**	**2,590**	**2,132**
Exceptional credit/(charge)											
Latin America	–	47	-63	-119	-106	-156	45	-61	-64	-11	–
Europe	–	-11	-64	1,135	-261	-202	-452	–	-24	–	-51
North America	–			92	-4		409	-51			111
Africa and Asia	-407	-111	-47	-41	-188	-3					103
South Africa: Beverages						-53					
Corporate	-69	-122	-26	-41	123	-58			-5	-4	252
	-476	-197	-200	1,026	-436	-472	2	-112	-93	-15	415
Group operating profit – after exceptional items	**4,384**	**4,242**	**4,192**	**5,013**	**3,127**	**2,619**	**3,148**	**3,448**	**3,027**	**2,575**	**2,547**
EBITA											
Primary segmental analysis											
Latin America	2,224	2,192	2,112	1,865	1,620	1,386	1,173	1,071	915	436	90
Europe	700	703	784	836	887	872	944	952	733	569	482
North America	858	804	740	756	741	619	581	477	375	454	487
Africa and Asia	2,675	2,799	2,811	1,064	739	636	642	568	467	422	383
South Africa: included in aggregate figures 2012–15											
– Beverages				1,168	1,067	885	764	1,026	1,102	1,062	956
– Hotels and Gaming				135	137	122	122	141	100	84	73
Corporate	-122	-161	-202	-190	-147	-139	-97	-94	-101	-86	-82
Group	**6,335**	**6,337**	**6,245**	**5,634**	**5,044**	**4,381**	**4,129**	**4,141**	**3,591**	**2,941**	**2,389**

[1] Restated for the adjustments made to the provisional fair values relating to the CASA Isenbeck and Crown Beverage Ltd acquisitions.

[2] Net asset value per share is calculated by dividing total shareholders' equity by the closing number of shares in issue.

[3] This is calculated by expressing adjusted earnings as a percentage of total shareholders' equity.

[4] EBITA margin is % of group 2013–2015.

[5] EBITDA margin is % of group 2013–2015.

* Africa and Asia revenue figures are not split out in the accounts summary, but 2015 figures were $7,462m and $3,867m, respectively.

Source: www.sabmiller.com Annual Report 2015.

CASE STUDY

AirAsia and the Tune Group: diversifying across industries

Julie Verity, Mark Jenkins and Tazeeb Rajwani

Introduction

In 2001, Tony Fernandes and Dato Kamarudin Meranum bought the failing government-owned Malaysian Airline – AirAsia – for one Ringgit (MYR).[1] They launched their new venture as a short-haul, low-cost Malaysian carrier, with just two aircraft and a lot of debt.

Fifteen years later AirAsia, with its sister long-haul airline AirAsia X, was the largest low-cost carrier in the Asean region and the founding company of the Tune Group, a corporate portfolio under the ownership and guidance of the original founders – Fernandes and Meranum. Other ventures in the Group include: Tune Hotels, Tune Talk, Tune Money, Tune Sport, Tune Labs, Tune Protect, Tune Studios, Epsom College and Caterham Cars, among others (see Figure 1).

Fernandes and, to a lesser extent, Meranum were highly visible owners who appeared regularly on websites and in the media promoting the group, its services and philosophy. Always smiling and sporting baseball caps the founders set out to serve the rising class of the less well-off in Asia by offering relentlessly low prices without comprising on service quality. According to the group website, the philosophy behind their winning formula was constant innovation on the service offer, through an intimate understanding of what would appeal locally, plus efficient, low-cost use of the internet as a channel to engage with potential consumers. All this was achieved through a fun, high-energy attitude reflecting Fernandes, media personality (and his baseball cap), with the purpose of changing the lives of Asia's under-served customers – an ambition that appeared achievable as after a little more than a decade, Tune Group planes were carrying around 32 million customers a year.

AirAsia operated alone until 2007 when the Tune Group was officially created after AirAsia X was launched as a franchise to AirAsia under the Tune Air Company and Fernandes, along with his fellow investors, diversified into the hotel and financial services industries. Tune Hotels were built to offer a 'limited service hotel chain that provides 5 star beds at 1 star prices'[2] and to accommodate travellers when at their flight destinations. Tune Money sought to enrich lives by 'offering affordable prepaid and loyalty cards as well as life and general insurance products.'[3]

Despite a turbulent year in 2008, Fernandes and his co-Tune Group investors continued diversifying, adding:

- Tune Talk, a mobile phone operator, giving customers 'super low calling rates at the lowest flat rate nationwide' (i.e. Malaysia).[4]
- Tune Sport, a Formula 1 racing team and sports car manufacturer (Caterham) and a professional basketball league.
- Tune Studios, which engaged in promoting local Asian and international talent through concerts, audio productions and event management.

Figure 1 Tune Group in 2015
Source: http://tunegroup.com/about.html.

This case was prepared by Mark Jenkins, Tazeeb Rajwani and Julie Verity, Cranfield School of Management. It is intended as a basis for class discussion and not as an illustration of good or bad practice. © Mark Jenkins, Tazeeb Rajwani and Julie Verity 2016. Not to be reproduced or quoted without permission.

Towards the end of the same year, the Group took a controlling interest in the Malaysian company: Oriental Capital Assurance (OCA). Commentators predicted that this might become the seventh company in the family group, and indeed it was – Tune Protect. Then, Fernandes announced a joint venture partnership between Caterham and Renault – the French car manufacturer – the aim of which was to produce and sell classic roadsters in Asia. In 2013, Fernandes concluded successful negotiations with the Indian conglomerate Tata Sons with a view to setting up a new domestic airline for India. Finally, in 2015, Fernandes and his team of entrepreneurs added another venture to the Group – Tune Labs.

After more than a decade of phenomenal success, questions were being raised about the future of the group and its figurehead – Fernandes. So far, the doubters about Tune Group's success have been subdued by the resilience of the group, its continued growth and the lure of the potential markets across Asia. The questions that were rumbling in the background, however, were about the number of ventures Fernandes had under his corporate Tune Group. How could he manage so many disparate businesses, especially since he had also bought the majority stake in a UK football team and he loved spending time at the Formula 1 track? There were also persistent murmurs about AirAsia X, which were strengthened after flights to Europe and India were withdrawn in 2012. No other long-haul, low-cost airline had succeeded in the past. How could Fernandes make this a success when all others had failed? Also, how does a roadster and an expensive F1 team fit with the vision Fernandes and Meranum started out with – of serving the 'under-served' with affordable services? Finally, why did this Group make sense over the longer term – why were these ventures better together than apart?

Tune Air

Tune Air was the first company the two entrepreneurs launched to run an airline – AirAsia – with the slogan 'Now Everyone Can Fly'.[5] The idea of serving potential travellers who had never flown before was one which Tony Fernandes had coveted for a long time. Born in Malaysia, he was packed off to school in the UK as a youngster and when he asked his mother if he could go home for Christmas, she declined because they couldn't afford the air ticket. So, in 2001, before Fernandes had reached his 40th birthday, with $250,000 ready to invest and a great friend – Kamarudin – in a similar position, he took the opportunity to buy AirAsia – a failing government-owned Malaysian airline. The price was 1 Ringgit plus a significant amount of the airline's debt.

Growth came easily and swiftly to the Malaysian operation (see Appendix). The Malaysian government was generally helpful, appreciating that low-cost travel around the country (one where transport infrastructure – road and rail was immature or non-existent) could stimulate and support economic activity. Economic growth rates were, in themselves, highly attractive at about seven per cent. The market was significantly under-developed; in 2001, only six per cent of the Malaysian population ever bought a plane ticket and this small percentage of fliers was typical among the population region-wide. Routes were limited, both locally and internationally, creating potential for growth. AirAsia ticket prices, at between 40 per cent and 60 per cent less than the traditional full-service fares, provided a stimulus to market growth as flying became a realistic alternative to taking the bus.

There were few competitors in the market space that were able to deliver and sustain the low-cost culture that Fernandes created at AirAsia. Competitors were often low-cost offshoots of full-service airlines whose culture simply didn't transfer into the energetic and entrepreneurial drive required to find new ways to drive prices down and profits up, at the same time.

There were also the European and American low-cost airline business models; tried-and-tested and ready to copy. While learning from these,[6] Fernandes insisted he tailored the AirAsia offering to his local market needs and created some 'no-frills' tricks of his own. These included selling advertising space within the cabin and in the annual reports to generate extra revenue.

Realising a dream

Fernandes started his 'dream' enterprise in 2001, but as a regional carrier, resisted the lure of the highly competitive long-haul sector. But nearly six years later, when AirAsia had 30 aircraft, was making revenues of MYR1,094m and profits of MYR 38.9m (see Table 1), Fernandes decided the time was right to extend his ambitions and create the long-haul, low-cost service that would be affordable to the masses. He branded his new enterprise: AirAsia X.

Fernandes believed that low-cost, long-distance was possible because he could leverage many of the resources and skills AirAsia had already developed. However, long-haul flying is a deceptively different business. Larger planes are required. The legal issues are complex because planes have to cross into different national governments' air spaces. Most countries have their own national carriers and any new entrant is a direct competitor. So, whereas the Malaysian government was supportive of AirAsia's local service, they perceived a long-haul product to be in direct competition with their own Malaysian Airlines. Landing slots, certificates,

Table 1 AirAsia financials (Tune Air activities are consolidated)

MYR million	2007	2008	2009	2010	2011	2012	2013	2014
Net cash flow	−184	−269	598	757	616	152	−876	−73
Revenue	1094	2855	3133	3948	4495	4946	5112	5416
Net total expenses	875	3207	2220	2881	3332	3919	4194	4562
EBIT	219	−352	913	1067	1163	1027	918	854
Net profit (after tax)	426	−496	506	1061	555	790	362	83
Net profit margin	38.9		16.2	26.9	12.3	16	7.1	1.5
Operating statistics								
Passengers carried (m)	5.2	11.8	14.2	16	17.9	19.6	21.8	22.1
Load factor (%)	78	75	75	78	80	80	80	79
Size of fleet (Malaysia)	39	44	48	53	57	64	72	81
Size of fleet (group)	65	78	84	90	97	118	154	172
No of employees	3474	3799	4593	4702	5137	5644	6089	6304
% revenue via internet	65	70	76	77	78	79	85	84
Market capitalisation (Rmbn)	3.8	2	3.8	7	10.5	7.6	6.1	7.6

Source: Annual Reports.

approvals and the complications of time zones and cultural differences multiply the challenges and the differences compared with local air travel.

For these reasons and because it was taken for granted that the long-distance offer needed to be a 'more comfortable' one for customers, i.e. food, baggage services, onboard entertainment and seat allocation were a must-have inclusion, it was widely believed that low-cost, long-haul was an unsustainable business concept. Fernandes was undeterred. Created as a franchise to the sister brand, AirAsia 'X' was able to use the AirAsia website to market and sell tickets and share the brand halo, giving the new venture a significant head start: AirAsia and AirAsia X operate synergistically, with both feeding guests into the other's network. The Company's 2009 Annual Report stated: 'Around 40% of guests on AirAsia X flights are being fed into our network, which shows how vital they are to our vision to be the world's best low fare airline.'[7]

AirAsia maintenance engineers and flight crews were trained to service and fly larger Airbus planes and provide cover when the fledgling airline needed support. The AirAsia low-cost model was transferred to the X offer. Seat prices were advertised clearly – differentiated from airport taxes and unbundled from any 'extras'. Different from the AirAsia offer, however, the 'extras', such as a pre-allocated seat, excess baggage, onboard food and drinks, flight transfers, pillows, blankets and inflight entertainment, *were* available, but at a price. With 'X', the seat price to fly between Kuala Lumpur and

international destinations appeared affordable to a wide audience and, with this proposition, 'X' ignored the warnings from previous failed attempts at low-cost, long-haul flying and took off to a successful start.

Buffeting against turbulence

2008 was a hard year for Tune Air. Jet fuel prices escalated at a terrifying rate during the early months. Projections suggested that the oil price might reach the unprecedented level of US$200 per barrel. As a result, management took the decision to forward-buy fuel on hedged contracts. This, the 2009 annual report described, was an insurance policy that became a liability as the financial crisis bit and oil prices tumbled in the second half of the same year. AirAsia leaders decided to unwind their hedges (at a price) and return to the spot market. This proved a powerful, early lesson: that a low-cost business, dependent on the supply of a commodity with a highly volatile and unpredictable price, is not profit-robust. Leaders at AirAsia looked for additional revenue streams to increase the resilience of their business model and recognised the potential in extending the 'extras' from 'X' to its short-haul sister brand and, at the same time, growing the 'extras' offer. These revenue streams were grouped together under the banner of 'Ancillary' products and services.

In 2009, the revenues from 'Ancillary' had increased to MYR 413m (13 per cent of total revenues), up by 34.4 per cent in one year. In 2010, ancillary income rose to

18 per cent of total income. In 2014, ancillary income grew 31.6 per cent year-on-year to MYR 432.8m.[8] Ancillaries included:

- super-size baggage
- inflight food (under the brand 'AirAsia Café')
- 'AirAsia Courier' (a door-to-door cargo service)
- pick a seat
- 'AirAsiaGo.Com' (a holiday booking portal)
- merchandise and duty free (from the AirAsia Megastore)
- e-gift vouchers
- charter flights
- membership of the Junior Jet Club
- 'AirAsia RedTix' (ticket-booking portal for sporting events, concerts, theatre and more)
- 'AirAsia Insure' (travel insurance)
- AirAsia Credit Card
- Airspace Advertising

In 2010, AirAsia X became an independent company within Tune Air. At the creation of the stand-alone company, a 30-year brand licence agreement was set up allowing X to continue using the AirAsia brand name. Separating the two airlines helped manage shareholder concerns, but this division of companies would not help relieve the tensions that were rumoured between the propositions of the two brands. Since launching, X had introduced reclining seats and flat beds to its cabin in order to stretch its appeal to those customers who wanted (and could afford) a comfortable long-hop. It was also adding Red Carpet 'Ancillary' services. However, these services did not naturally align with the original AirAsia low-price, 'under-served' proposition, making it difficult for X marketers to touch their (different) target customers with a message that didn't conflict with the brand values of AirAsia.

Beyond great expectations

'The cynics said it couldn't be done . . . Five years on, AirAsia X has shown not only that it can be done, but also that it can be done so successfully as to spawn imitators in the region and beyond.'[9]

The statistics were impressive. In 2011, AirAsia X was reporting a 45 per cent increase in revenues over 2010, to RM1.9bn, driven by a 32 per cent growth in passenger numbers, which in turn was driven by its 30–50 per cent lower prices compared to rivals and the world's lowest unit cost at US$3.6c per available-seat-km. As a percentage of AirAsia's total customers in 2011, AirAsia X accounted for nearly 14 per cent.

By 2011, routes extended to China, Taiwan, India, Australia, South Korea, Iran and Japan. However, in the same year, Air Asia management announced that flights to Europe and Northern India would stop as they refocused their attention on a new strategy of prioritising resources in the most profitable markets of East Asia and Oceania. High fuel prices and the EU's carbon taxes were reported to be making the Paris and London flights loss-making. As of March 2016, AirAsia X serves 19 destinations across Asia (Sapporo, Tokyo, Osaka, Seoul, Busan, Taipei, Xian, Beijing, Hangzhou, Chengdu, Shanghai, New Delhi and Kathmandu), Australia (Sydney, Melbourne, Perth and Gold Coast), New Zealand (Auckland) and the Middle East (Jeddah).[10]

Nearer to home, the strategy was to overcome rising costs with:

- the addition of more ancillary products and services (e.g. preferential services like a premium lounge);
- charging more for some existing services (e.g. pick a seat);
- charging for services AirAsia wanted to stop providing (e.g. assisted check-in).

Biggies for loyalty

2011 saw the launch of AirAsia's loyalty programme called Big Shots. Customers were invited to collect 'biggies' (or points) on their purchases of AirAsia products and services plus those from merchant partners. Accumulating points would earn free flights. The airline expected to benefit from the programme by:[11]

1. using the programme strategically to increase passenger load on flights;
2. driving sales of ancillary products and services;
3. promoting new or underutilised routes;
4. clearing 'distressed inventory' – with special promotions;
5. creating two new revenue streams:
   - (i) by selling points to credit card partners and local retail partners
   - (ii) by targeting specific customer segments with attractive 'biggie' rates.

Merchant partners were companies wishing to align with the AirAsia brand and access its massive customer base. Ancillary spend by customers was encouraged through offering more 'biggies' when additional services such as 'pick a seat' were purchased with the flight.

The Big Shots programme was launched as a 50:50 joint venture with Tune Money, another company in the Tune Group (see below). Operational responsibilities were split between the two companies; Tune Air was responsible for redemptions against points and transfer pricing rules, while Tune Money issued BIG cards, found merchant partners and took care of regional administration. Tune Money also launched a 'first' prepaid MasterCard tied to the Big Shots loyalty programme. In 2014, BIG membership increased to 12.6 million from 870,000 in December 2013, representing 150,000 new members every month.[12]

Also during 2011, two new joint ventures with Expedia Inc. and CAE were created to complement AirAsia's travel and aviation businesses. Another new structure – called Adjacency businesses – was created within the group to accommodate these partners and the revenue streams they were expected to generate. The new partners would, according to the AirAsia 2011 annual report: 'monetise our database and/or physical assets and turn these from cost centres to profit centres'. In 2014, Redbox – a courier service – was launched to provide swift and consistent shipment and delivery services within and across borders. In the same year, Asia Aviation Capital (AAC) was incorporated to manage all aircraft leased to associate airlines by AirAsia.

100m passengers in 8.5 years

The speed of growth of the AirAsia brand outstripped that experienced by other successful low-cost airlines including South West Airlines in the USA and Ireland's Ryanair. Fernandes attributed much of this speedy success to Tune Air's corporate structure and the associate network. Setting up separate joint venture companies in Thailand, Indonesia and later in the Philippines (see Appendix) allowed AirAsia to transfer its low-cost business model to other countries and set up new hubs, routes and destinations rapidly without having to operate them day-by-day. This meant that by 2011 AirAsia had 14 hubs established in four countries, with 154 routes (including X) and 80 destinations (including X), connecting people in 10 Asean nations. By 2014, the number of routes increased to 199. In February 2013, AirAsia signed a partnership with Tata Sons and Telestra Tradeplace to set up a low-cost airline in India, with the former holding 30 per cent and the latter 21 per cent equity in the tripartite venture, leaving AirAsia with the major share of 49 per cent.

Tune Hotels

Tune Hotels was launched in 2007 six years after the founding entrepreneurs launched AirAsia with the slogan '5 Star Beds at 1 Star Prices'.[13] Tune Hotels was funded through the holding company Tune Ventures, which was owned by Fernandes (45 per cent), Kamarudin (30 per cent) and Denis Melka (25 per cent) (a former Credit Suisse investment banker). These partners made a start-up investment in Tune Hotels of US$3.5m. A further $2m was raised from individual investors and employees.

The philosophy behind spending a night at a Tune Hotel mirrored exactly that of taking a Tune Air flight: the experience was guaranteed to be safe and clean, stripped of almost everything that might be described as a 'comfort' (a towel, a window) and to be very low priced. What appealed to customers at Tune Hotels was the ability to be in the best locations, be safe and secure and sleep well (something that was not guaranteed in the Asean region at a hotel that was less than 'luxury'). Any other 'needs', like towels, soap, hair shampoo, air conditioning, TV viewing, internet connection, daily room cleaning, were available, but at an additional price. Another appealing feature and, again, matching the brand promise of Tune Group flights was the authentic description of what was 'in' and what was 'out' of the room price. There were no surprises at a Tune Hotel (but toilet paper was free!).

Also borrowing from the AirAsia formula, room reservations could only be made online and early booking was rewarded with lower prices. Like the AirAsia planes, the exterior of the signature hotel in Kuala Lumpur was painted all over – red and white. Floor space within the hotels was leased to fast-food restaurants and, for example, Lavazza coffee stations, and lobby and corridor wall space was sold to advertisers.

Early in 2016, the group had hotels in six countries, mostly in destinations where AirAsia fliers were likely to land: Malaysia (12), Indonesia (2), India (1), Australia (1), Kenya (1) and the UK (8).

Tune Money

Tune Money was launched in 2007 six years after the founding entrepreneurs launched AirAsia. In 2007, when the partners in Tune Ventures were opening the first Tune Hotel, they were also laying the foundations for Tune Money. This company, which was the third to shelter under the corporate umbrella of the Tune Group, was to cater for 'value-seeking consumers' wanting 'payment, loyalty and insurance products at affordable prices'.[14] The strategy behind Tune Money was to offer financial products to potential customers directly through the Tune Group website, 'as most of them don't have their own credit card'.[15] When CIMB – a Malaysian financial services firm – took a 25 per cent stake in the venture and Aviva (the global insurance company) agreed to act as lead underwriter, Tune Money took a step closer to being granted the first new license from the Malaysian government for a prepaid MasterCard.

Four years later, the BIG prepaid MasterCard was launched by Tune Money through a 50:50 joint venture partnership with sister company AirAsia. This was heralded as a first in the Asean region – a prepaid Visa card that also carried a loyalty function. The card allowed customers to collect loyalty points when buying any AirAsia product or service, or from merchant partners to the programme. Points were then redeemable against AirAsia flights or other specified rewards. Tune Money issued the cards and recruited business partners to join the loyalty programme. In 2011, some of the partners were: Concorde Hotel and Hathaway Medical in Singapore, K Bank and DTAC in Thailand, Petronas and CIMB Bank in Malaysia. Early in 2016, the number of partners increased to include MayBank, RHB, Public Bank, Bank Islam and Hong Leong Bank.[16]

Tune Money also sold home insurance, motor and personal accident insurance and travel insurance. The company also served as the insurance manager for AirAsia's direct insurance business, selling two products: a travel and a lifestyle protection plan.

Tune Protect Malaysia Berhad

Late in 2012, the media announced the launch of Tune Insurance. This followed Tune Group's acquisition of a controlling interest in OCA – Oriental Capital Assurance – in May of the same year. With new management in place, the new company aimed to sell more to Tune Group customers. The CEO of OCA said:[17]

> 'Fostering an alliance with AirAsia and the Tune Group is a strategic decision. . . . With our entry into the Tune Group we are better placed and with stronger financial and technological backing to be more competitive in the insurance market. . . . Our strategy moving forward is to leverage on these strong foundations to satisfy the insurance needs of an extensive base of customers. That is our key competitive strength.'

In February 2013, Tune Insurance raised MYR283.5m (US$91m) from a public listing of shares. This exceeded the $65m Fernandes told reporters that he planned to raise.[18] Fernandes was reported to have said that Tune Insurance's potential for growth was stronger than that seen for either Tune Hotels or Tune Talk. In March 2014, Tune Insurance entered the Middle East through a joint venture agreement with Cozmo Travel LLC and in 2015, Tune Insurance was rebranded to Tune Protect.

Tune Talk

Tune Talk was launched in 2008, seven years after the founding entrepreneurs launched AirAsia. Tune Talk was launched in 2009 as the fourth company within the corporate embrace of the Tune Group. It was preceded and enabled by a partnership deal in 2008 with Celcom Axiata Berhad, the oldest telecommunications company in Malaysia.

The Tune Talk website introduces itself as the youngest mobile virtual network operator (MVNO) in Malaysia: 'meeting consumer's demand for a simple, value for money product with easy accessibility', and answers the question about its distinctiveness: 'Why are we better than others'? Tune Talk promises:

- the lowest call rates in the country;
- free personal accident insurance to all subscribers who spend more than MYR30 each month on their phone; and
- 'biggie' loyalty points, which can be redeemed against concert and movie tickets, e-gift vouchers from the Tune Group website and offers on AirAsia flights.

Tune Sport

Tune Sport was launched in 2009 eight years after the founding entrepreneurs launched AirAsia. Tune Sport was a relatively late, formal addition to the Tune Group portfolio, but sport had been integral to the business since the time when AirAsia only had seven planes in the sky. As with many aspects of the Tune Group's business, this was widely suspected to be because of Fernandes and his love of sport generally, football more specifically. He has a controlling stake in London-based Queen Park Rangers (QPR) football club.

In 2005, Fernandes signed a sponsorship deal with Manchester United (see Table 2). The sponsorship deal allowed him to paint his planes not just red and white, but also with images of superstars from Manchester United's stable – Wayne Rooney and Cristiano Ronaldo. 'Branding with a buzz and to reinforce our youthful and fun organisation', was how the group explained their investment in sport sponsorship, which by 2012 had grown to include Formula 1, the Asean Basketball League and MotoGP. These sponsorships allowed the AirAsia brand to be emblazoned on F1 and MotoGP circuits, on sports jerseys and baseball caps and captured by media cameras for global consumption.

Fernandes found a new way to sponsor soccer in 2010 when AirAsia became the official shirt sponsor for referees and match officials in the English Premier League, Football League and FA Cup. The partnership allowed Fernandes access to 2000 professional football matches and an estimated global TV audience of (cumulatively) more than three billion. In exchange for a six-figure sum, AirAsia branding could be placed on the shirt sleeves and training wear of all professional match referees, assistant referees and officials and all PGMO[19] governing body websites, as well as match official and refereeing inventory. In 2011, AirAsia established its own football club – AirAsia Allstars FC – to compete in the Malaysian domestic league.

Making dreams come true

The Tune Group's involvement with sport was not just about branding or corporate entertaining. It was also

Table 2 Tune Group's involvement with sport

2005	AirAsia signs a one-year sponsorship deal with Manchester United Football club
2006	AirAsia extends its partnership with Manchester United
2009	AirAsia X sponsors the Oakland Raiders National Football Team in the USA
	Tune Sport co-founds the Asean Basketball League
	Tune Sport buy the licence to Lotus Racing and the company – Caterham Cars
2010	Tune Group sign a deal to become the principle partner for PGMO – a three-year deal taking them to the 2013/14 season.
2011	Fernandes takes a controlling (66%) stake in Queen Park Rangers, a UK premier league football team from Bernie Ecclestone and Flavio Briatore
	AirAsia starts a football club, AirAsia FC
2012	Caterham cars form a partnership with Renault to build road-going sports cars for sale in Asia.
2014	Caterham cars is sold to Swiss and Middle Eastern investors
	Caterham cars goes into administration

about corporate social responsibility. Sponsoring sport allowed the group to promote Malaysia and the region's sporting heroes as well as giving a helping hand to local youthful talent. The group promoted Asia by co-founding (in 2009) and sponsoring the ASEAN Basketball League (ABL) – the first international, professional league in Southeast Asia.

After moving into F1, the company also created a development programme for aspiring, young Asian driving talent. This programme was led by the former Malaysian F1 driver Alex Yoong and in its first year invited talented drivers from Malaysia, Thailand and Singapore to join. In its second year young people from the UK and USA were also invited in. Initiatives like this were described as AirAsia spreading its people-empowering philosophy more broadly than just being able to fly: 'we also empower people to make their dreams come true'.

Fernandes also wanted to get more Malaysians into F1 and when he became the proud owner of his own team (racing in 2010 as Lotus Racing) 10 per cent of the team were Malaysian. As a top-ten finisher in 2010, Lotus Racing took approximately US$30m in prize money, some compensation for the estimated $100m it cost to set up a team and a car from scratch just five months before the season started. Despite performing well on the track again in 2011, Group Lotus (the company holding the licence to the name – Lotus Racing) and Fernandes became embroiled in a legal battle over the use of the iconic racing name. As a result, Fernandes walked away from Lotus and bought the UK company Caterham Cars which produced a small light-weight sports/racing car based on the original design of the Lotus 7.

The 2012 Formula 1 season for Fernandes and his renamed Team Caterham was not good. Problems with the car put Caterham well behind the pack and without any championship points for the majority of the season; F1 can be costly and risky advertising. However, Fernandes came back fighting, saying it was not just about promotion, it was also about Caterham road cars, which had the potential to bring affordable sports/racing cars to a wider audience. This was the reason he was in discussion with Renault (the French car manufacturer) to up-scale production of the Caterham roadsters ready for sale in Asia. Fernandes said:

'We will make affordable sports cars with F1 technology that sell for much less than Ferrari and McLaren road cars. There are a lot of people who watch F1 and want to own a piece of it. . . . We understand how to market to that [Asian] population which is made up of three billion people. That is why Renault are attracted to us.'[20]

In July 2014, Tony Fernandes and his partners announced that they had sold the team to a consortium of Swiss and Middle Eastern investors. This was a major divestiture within the Tune Group. In October 2014, Caterham cars entered administration and 230 staff were made redundant.[21]

The failure of Caterham cars did not discourage Fernandes. He continued to launch new ventures, with the latest being Tune Labs, a Kuala Lumpur-based start-up created in 2015 to identify, mentor and fund entrepreneurs across the Asean region. The venture aims to support aspiring entrepreneurs achieve their visions of creating market-leading and innovative businesses through two programmes – the Incubator and the Accelerator.[22]

Notes and references
1. MYR1 = £0.175 = $0.256 = €0.224.
2. www.tunegroup.com/tunehotels.html.
3. www.tunegroup.com/tune_money.html.
4. www.tunetalk.com.
5. www.flyairasia.com.au.
6. In his earlier career, Fernandes worked for the Virgin Group.
7. Air Asia 2009 Annual Report and Accounts.
8. Air Asia, 'AirAsia X records revenue of 16.2% to RM698.8 million In third quarter 2014 and re-strategizes for 2015', press release, 19 November 2014.
9. Air Asia 2011 Annual Report and Accounts.

10. http://www.airasiasx.com.
11. Air Asia 2011 Annual Report and Accounts.
12. Air Asia 2014 Annual Report and Accounts.
13. www.tunehotels.com.
14. www.tunegroup.com.
15. J. Doebele, 'Proletariat capitalist', Forbes Asia, vol. 3, no. 10 (2007), p. 30.
16. www.bigprepaid.com.
17. 'Oriental Capital Assurance Berhad is renamed Tune Insurance Malaysia Berhad', Media release, 27 September 2012.
18. Euroweek, IPO Investors Like that Tune, 8/2/2013, Iss.1291.
19. PGMO: Professional Game Match Officials – formed in 2001 to improve refereeing standards.
20. 'Fernandes wants faster route to car sales', Financial Times, 15 November 2012.
21. 'Struggling Caterham team confirm 230 staff will be made redundant', Caterham News, 17 November 2014.
22. www.thetunelabs.com.

APPENDIX: The Tune Air story

2001 Tune Air Sdn Bhd is founded when Tony Fernandes and his partner buy the Malaysian government-owned AirAsia, 1 week before 9/11 for 1 Ringgit and US$11m debt.

2002 Airline is branded AirAsia, the first low-cost carrier in Asia. Ticketless offer flights paid by credit card over the telephone or online.

2003 AirAsia introduces first airline SMS booking.
AirAsia has 7 planes.

2004 AirAsia goes public in November. IPO raises US$188.8m.
AirAsia Berhad was listed on the Main Market of Bursa Malaysia Securities Berhad in November 2004.
AirAsia sets up a 49% owned subsidiary – Thai AirAsia. Thai AirAsia commenced its inaugural commercial flight on 4 February 2004 from Bangkok to Hat Yai.

2005 AirAsia signs a one-year deal with Manchester United Football club.

2006 AirAsia sets up a 49% owned subsidiary – Indonesia AirAsia.
AirAsia has 42 planes.
AirAsia extends its partnership with Manchester United.

2007 Tune Group Sdn Bhd is established.
AirAsia X commences operations as a franchise of AirAsia with just one plane. Richard Branson takes a 20% ownership stake.
AirAsia expands into transporting cargo through collaboration with Leisure Cargo.

2008 AirAsia loses $63m (mishedging oil prices).

2009 AirAsia X makes first flights into India and the UK.
AirAsia X sponsors the Oakland Raiders National Football Team in the USA.
AirAsia wins the Skytrax award for the second year.

2010 AirAsia is the region's largest low-cost carrier with 100 planes and 8000 employees. Together, the short and long haul operations passed the 100 million passengers carried in October.
Tune Air restructures – AirAsia X becomes an independent company, but continues to use the AirAsia brand name.
AirAsia form an alliance with Jetstar, the Australian low-fare subsidiary of Qantas.
AirAsia announce a JV holding of 40% in new airline – Philippines AirAsia.

2011 IPOs offered for Indonesian and Thai AirAsia.
Tune Group enter into a partnership with state-owned Malaysian Airlines.
Tune Group take a 30% stake in VietJet. Within the year, the deal is called off as Vietnamese government do not grant permission for the new airline – VietJet AirAsia.
AirAsia forms a joint venture with Expedia, establishing a travel agency covering the Asia–Pacific region, offering a complete range of great value flights, hotels and holiday packages.
AirAsia in a 50:50 joint venture with Tune Money launches the 'BIG Shots' loyalty programme with other merchant suppliers. This includes the first Visa Prepaid card tied to a loyalty function in the Asian region. The JV company is called: Think Big Digital Sdn Bhd.
AirAsia forms an alliance with CAE inc. to set up an aviation training centre that offers training to airlines throughout Asia.

2012 AirAsia builds a new office in Jakarta and proposes buying Batavia Air a local Indonesian carrier.
AirAsia X ceases flights to Europe and India.
Asia Aviation was listed on the Stock Exchange of Thailand in May 2012 and is the investment holding company of Thai AirAsia Co. Ltd.
AirAsia in negotiations to form a JV with All Nipon Airways to form a Tokyo-based low-cost carrier.

2013 AirAsia X places its largest order with Airbus for 25 A330-300s airplanes.
AirAsia X announces its third destination in Japan – Nagoya – and commences a new route to Adelaide, Australia.
AirAsia named as 'Best managed company overall in Malaysia' and 'Best managed company in Asia – Airlines/Aviation'.

2014 AirAsia X suspends services to Male, Maldives due to challenging business conditions.
AirAsia X receives approval to start its associate company, Thai AirAsia X, in Thailand.
AirAsia suspends Miri–Terengganu route.

2015 AirAsia wins three awards at the World Travel Awards 2015.
AirAsia inaugurates flights to new destinations in China and Japan.

2016 Air Asia launches flights to New Zealand.

Severstal: growth and consolidation strategies in a turbulent global steel industry

Eustathios Sainidis

This case study offers an overview of the global steel industry, a highly dynamic, volatile and fragmented sector. It describes how one of the largest Russian steel producers, Severstal, has developed its international strategy through a number of overseas acquisitions during the booming years up until the Great Recession of 2008 and how the steel industry, markets and Severstal have developed since. With a strong vision to become one of the major global players in its industry the company successfully developed its global presence. However, the post-great recession business environment has had a detrimental impact on global steel demand, with high levels of volatility and uncertainly to which Severstal have responded by taking a new strategic direction defined by consolidation and divestment.

Introduction

Lakshmi Mittal, Chairman and CEO of the world's largest-by-volume steel producer ArcelorMittal, confidently announced in November 2013: 'The bottom of the cycle is behind us'.[1] During the same month, Alexey Mordashov the Chairman of the Russia's second-largest steel producer Severstal, in an interview with the *Financial Times* voiced a somehow more pessimistic view:

'Without solving the problem of supply and demand, without optimising the industry, we are doomed to be in a struggle for survival in the best-case scenario. That is, if there aren't mass cases of bankruptcies and industry enterprises shutting down. Excess capacity is a serious problem for the whole global sector and without a solution the industry risks falling into a deep crisis like it was 10 to 15 years ago when one in four US steel producers went into bankruptcy.'[2]

Although Alexey Mordashov was expressing his concerns for the future of the global steel industry, his own firm 'Severstal' sustained its profitability even though its US and European competitors were reporting losses for another financial year. Severstal's focus on staying competitive and sustaining a positive balance sheet has been based on a consolidation and divestment strategy, by selling off its loss-making business units and strengthening its vertically-integrated business model.

Historically, the global steel market is subject to high market volatility and since the Great Recession of 2008 has suffered a supply:demand imbalance with excess capacity. Chinese over-supply of steel on the global market has made things even tougher for steel producers around the world: 2015 alone saw an increase in Chinese export-destined steel 26 per cent. The main cause of this substantial export rise was a slowing domestic Chinese market; consequently, the only way for Chinese steel

Source: E. Sainidis.

This case was prepared by Dr Eustathios Sainidis, Senior Lecturer at Newcastle Business School, Northumbria University. It is intended as a basis for class discussion and not as an illustration of good or bad practice. © Eustathios Sainidis 2016. Not to be reproduced or quoted without permission.

producers to reduce their stock levels was by flooding their export markets. A global steel over-supply had driven down steel prices, exacerbating the already-high levels of competitive rivalry within the industry. Due to a fall in profit margins, steel producers embarked on reducing their investment and acquisitions expenditure, a stark contrast from the booming years prior to the 2008 recession. The World Steel Association was expecting a challenging market well into 2016 with sluggish growth from 2017 and beyond. An overall slow growth in consumer markets in both developed and emerging economies, coupled with a decline in oil prices and other steel-related supply chains, a deceleration of the Chinese economy and resultant nervousness in global financial markets, were dampening business confidence.

World Steel's Economics Committee Chairman Hans Jürgen Kerkhoff blamed the ongoing uncertainty on Eurozone's financial uncertainty and the unexpected slowdown in Chinese industrial output and consumer demand. As he put it:

> 'These factors have weighed heavily on business confidence and manufacturing activities around the world. As a result momentum in both developed and emerging parts of the world weakened considerably [. . .] Since the 2008 economic crisis, uncertainty and volatility has become the norm for the steel industry but it is worth noting that world steel demand has maintained positive growth despite all the headwinds and lingering difficulties.'[3]

With the excess Chinese steel-making capacity being redirected to export markets, prices for crude steel products continued to fall in 2016. With no short-term improvements likely, several leading producers took the drastic decision of shutting down or selling off steel plants, rather than continuing to fund loss-making operations. The Indian steel giant Tata Steel was slow to react to the economic challenges posed by the Great Recession era when it decided in the spring of 2016 to sell its unprofitable steel plant in Wales, UK, that had been acquired in the Corus deal less than a decade earlier.

However, some steel producers were managing to maintain a relatively positive balance sheet despite the headwinds. By the end of 2015, Severstal, one of Russia's largest steel producers, reported net profits of $1.7bn (£1bn, €1.3bn) on revenues of $6.3bn (£3.8bn, €4.7bn).[4] The company's aggressive divestment strategy, based on the sale as its overseas steel and mining plants (US, Italy and UK), was paying dividends. By the end of 2015, Severstal showed an improved financial performance from 2014 and 2013 and substantially better than the recessionary years of 2009 and 2010 when significant losses were being reported. Severstal's

majority shareholder and Chairman, Alexey Mordashov, remained bullish and confident about the company's future despite the difficult recent years. His approach was to stay flexible and cautiously optimistic about Severstal's new strategic direction: the company's new strategic plan was to maintain its vertically integrated business model and further consolidate its business units, driven by a strong focus on cost reduction and operational improvement programmes. At the end of 2015, Vadim Larin, CEO of Severstal, made the following statement:

> 'This year [2015] we have made further progress in our strategy to be one of the most efficient steelmakers globally and, in an uncertain climate, have delivered another set of strong financial results. We have maintained our relentless focus on improving production efficiency at all our business units and have continued to benefit from our asset structure which has underpinned our flexibility and resilience. Despite limited visibility in both domestic and export markets, the company is consistent in the execution of its stated strategy to focus on customer care and product quality improvement, cost efficiency, and investment optimisation. This combined with a strong financial position enables the company to constantly deliver long-term shareholder value.'[5]

A challenging and dynamic industry

Steel is an alloy, made out of iron and small amounts of carbon, and is one of the most widely used materials. Its main applications are within the construction, shipping, automotive and energy markets. Its success as a product is based on its strong, resilient, versatile and recyclable properties.

Since the late 1980s, the steel industry has become more global both in terms of competition and markets. Steel producers continued to invest in production and energy efficiencies leading to higher profit margins. Foreign direct investment opportunities and the rapid growth of the emerging economies of China, Eastern Europe, Russia and South America created a financially rewarding business environment. Steel production in 2015 reached almost 1.54 billion metric tonnes (mt), with China by far the largest consumer and producer (711 million mt), followed by the European Union (147m mt), and North American Free Trade Association (NAFTA) countries (145m mt). Demand for steel had been increasing year on year since the 1990s until the third quarter of 2008 when the steel industry was one of the first to experience the severe impact of the longest global economic slowdown since World War II, a recession

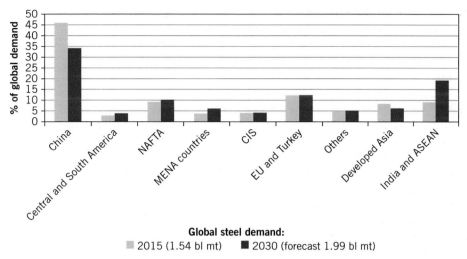

Global steel demand:
■ 2015 (1.54 bl mt)   ■ 2030 (forecast 1.99 bl mt)

Figure 1 Steel consumption outlook, 2015–2030
Source: World Steel Association.

termed as the Great Recession. Figure 1 illustrates steel consumption of each major geographical market and how they are expected to grow between 2015 and 2030, evidencing a shift in demand from the Chinese market to other Asian markets.

Major players in the industry include ArcelorMittal, which is by far the largest producer of steel products and is led by the Indian-born Lakshmi Mittal, followed by the Japanese firm Nippon Steel and Sumitomo Metal Corporation in second place (2014 data). ArcelorMittal was the result of the acquisition of Luxembourg-based Arcelor by Mittal in 2006. The acquisition has become a milestone in the consolidation process of the steel industry. The company is nearly twice the size of the Nippon Steel and Sumitomo Metal Corporation with a production capacity sufficient to supply the entire world automotive market. Table 1 offers an illustration of how the competition has changed from 2011 to 2014, providing evidence of industry consolidation and the rise of steel producers based in emerging economies.

Although the industry has seen significant merger and acquisition (M&A) activity, it still remains highly fragmented in comparison to other global manufacturing sectors. Steel producers use M&A as their preferred strategic method to achieve rapid growth and market penetration. Organic development is relatively slow and expensive. Tough environmental regulations often act as a barrier to obtaining planning permission and finance for the construction of new steel plants. In contrast, acquisitions offer a fast-track path to growth and niche market penetration, allowing for differentiation strategies and strategic or product synergies. Similar to the

Mittal–Arcelor deal, the acquisition of British–Dutch steel producer Corus by Indian-based Tata Steel in 2007 was a celebrated example at the time. Professor Phanish Puram from London Business School commented on the acquisition: 'The Tata-Corus deal is different because it links low-cost Indian production and raw materials and growth markets to high-margin markets and high technology in the West.'[6]

Such vertical acquisitions (in other words the linking of iron ore producers and steel makers) resulted in increased negotiating power for steel producers in relation to their suppliers and buyers. Although prices of raw materials (iron ore and metallurgical coke) continued to increase, steel producers saw their supply chains as sources of value creation through improved productivity and reduced costs, implying stronger financial returns and a basis for investment in quality and service with the aim of producing differentiated steel products for which premium prices could be charged.

The most resourceful steel producers also saw opportunities in related and unrelated acquisitions in order to expand their product portfolio. The privatisation of government-owned assets in the emerging economies of the BRIC countries and the Middle East offered strong opportunities for foreign direct investment. Owning a steel plant close to construction sites, ship-building facilities and automotive manufacturers based in these locations offered a first-mover advantage and access to local supply chains. Exchange rates were also in favour of Russian and Chinese steel producers with a weakening US dollar since the mid-2000s assisting cross-border acquisitions.

Table 1 World steel producers 2014 by volume

Companies	HQ	Tonnage (mt)				Rank 2014
		2011	2012	2013	2014	
ArcelorMittal	Luxembourg	97.248	93.575	96.096	98.088	1
Nippon Steel and Sumitomo Metal Corp.	Japan	33.388	47.858	50.128	49.300	2
Hebei Steel Group	China	44.360	42.840	45.786	47.094	3
Baosteel Group	China	43.340	42.700	43.908	43.347	4
POSCO	South Korea	39.118	39.875	38.261	41.428	5
Shagang Group	China	31.920	32.310	35.081	35.332	6
Ansteel Group	China	29.750	30.230	33.687	34.348	7
Wuhan Steel Group	China	37.680	36.420	39.311	33.053	8
JFE Steel Corporation	Japan	29.902	30.409	31.161	31.406	9
Shougang Group	China	30.040	31.420	31.523	30.777	10
Tata Steel Group	India	23.820	22.974	25.272	26.202	11
Shandong Steel Group	China	24.020	23.010	22.793	23.336	12
Nucor Corporation	USA	19.892	20.125	20.162	21.411	13
HYUNDAI Steel Company	South Korea	16.292	17.124	17.303	20.576	14
United States Steel Corporation	USA	21.990	21.444	20.380	19.732	15
Gerdau S.A.	Brazil	20.501	19.807	18.966	19.001	16
Maanshan Steel	China	16.680	17.340	18.794	18.903	17
Tianjin Bohai Steel	China			19.326	18.488	18
ThyssenKrupp AG	Germany	17.936	14.461	15.864	16.271	19
Benxi Steel	China	16.490	15.080	16.826	16.261	20
Novolipetsk Steel (NLMK)	Russia	12.112	14.923	15.468	16.108	21
Evraz Group, S.A.	Russia	16.773	15.945	16.109	15.536	22
China Steel Corporation	Taiwan, China	14.010	12.729	14.288	15.399	23
Valin Group	China	15.890	14.110	14.988	15.383	24
Jianlong Group	China	12.360	13.760	14.295	15.256	25
IMIDRO	Iran	12.584	13.613	14.292	14.420	26
Severstal JSC	*Russia*	*15.293*	*15.140*	*15.691*	*14.232*	27
Fangda Steel	China	2.619	3.283	13.164	13.643	28
Steel Authority of India Ltd. (SAIL)	India	13.498	13.504	13.519	13.565	29
Magnitogorsk Iron & Steel Works (MMK)	Russia	12.195	13.037	11.941	13.031	30

Source: World Steel Association.

On the other hand, customers of steel producers were also pushing for structural changes in their own supply chain. Automotive manufacturers in particular wanted to see steel producers having a greater role in the production of their vehicles with the early stages of car assembly (e.g. stamping) taking place within the steel mills. Steel producers that invested in such production facilities to fabricate custom-made parts would offer differentiated products attracting higher prices.

The steel industry experiences production output (supply) cycles which follow the economic cycles of the global economy (GDP), and Figure 2 provides a graphical representation of this pattern. Examining Figure 2, there is evidence of the steel industry reaching a tipping point even before the Great Recession arrived. Gradually increasing pricing pressures, gaps in product mix and asset concentration were signalling that the industry had reached maturity by 2006. Industry analysts were already talking about evidence of hyper-competition from as early as 2002. The industry was changing rapidly with

the dominant steel producers based in the USA, Japan and Germany now under attack from new players in South Korea, Russia and more recently China and India. The industry has been experiencing a constant cycle of global consolidation and fragmentation, and opportunistic short-term counter-attack strategies. The Great Recession and the global economic downturn which followed were wake-up calls for steel trading speculators and investors, making shareholders of steel producers much more cautious and asking their CEOs to take more calculated risks and become more market-focused in their business ventures.

After a good eight years of growth in the metals industry, September 2008 proved to be a turning point for steel producers. The global financial crisis and subsequent economic downturn had a severe effect on the industry and its markets. At the start of the Great Recession in 2008, demand for steel had fallen by 60 per cent and prices dropped to 2002 levels, a 70 per cent fall relative to their peak in 2007. With many steel

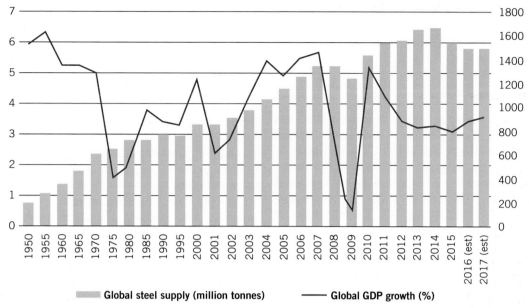

Figure 2 Global steel production output (supply) vs global GDP (1950–2017)

Source: International Monetary Fund (IMF) and World Steel Association datasets.

plants continuing to operate at full capacity, very soon over-supply resulted in plummeting steel prices due to low plant capacity utilisation. Between 2013 and 2015, the capacity utilisation ratio (CUR) within steel plants lingered around 70 per cent, a stark contrast to the 88 per cent CUR prior to the Great Recession. Although by the end as 2015 there were positive signs of growth in the USA and the UK, albeit a mixed picture in the emerging economies of China, India and South America, banks and other finance providers were still very risk-averse in providing credit to industrial consumers, resulting in very slow growth in global steel demand.

Global market opportunities and challenges

The emerging economies of South America, Asia and the Middle East are seen as the main growth markets for steel products, expected to continue growing at higher rates than the mature markets of North America, the European Union (EU-28) and Japan. The steel market is very cyclical with short 'peak to peak' periods. Large demand variations exist between regional markets which makes forecasting very difficult. Industry experts have projected an annual increase of about five per cent in global construction, automotive and other transport markets by 2021, based on future growth in Asia-Pacific, Africa and the Middle East. The US and European markets were expected to stay only at 2012 levels, if not decline. None of these regions is currently dominated by one single steel producer with all the major international

steel players constantly seeking the most appropriate strategy to enter the next prospective market.

China has become the largest consumer of steel products and at the same time a major producer, with Chinese domestic production increasing by 15 per cent year on year up to 2014 but taking a reverse direction in 2015 with a drop of three per cent in overall Chinese supply. Although there are only a small number of efficient high-volume Chinese producers capable of exporting steel, their historic tendency to over-produce puts further pressures on global steel prices. In contrast, non-Chinese steel producers have seen the lower product quality of some Chinese steel as a market opportunity and driver for establishing joint ventures in China.

The USA has a high level of steel consumption, mainly in the automotive, machine tooling and construction markets and at the same time has several steel producing companies. As a market, the USA has been attractive for its high demand, with the low value of the US dollar leading to an increase in inward foreign direct investment. On the other hand, perceived barriers to investment in the USA have been the powerful trade unions and occasional federal protectionist measures.

South Korea has evolved as one of the major steel exporters with an increasing market share in the USA, Japan and China. Significantly, South Korea is the biggest indirect exporter of steel, because of its growing domestic demand for steel-based products supplying the country's rapidly expanding automotive, shipping and electronic industries. The country exports almost 60 per cent of its automotive production, 90 per cent of its shipping products and 60 per cent of its electronics. This is almost ten times more than the EU countries and three times more than Japan.

Severstal Group

Severstal was founded in 1955 as Cherepovets Steel Mill and remained under government ownership until the collapse of the Soviet Union in 1991. It was privatised in 1993, under the ownership and leadership of Alexey Mordashov, when it was registered as the open joint stock company 'Severstal'. The city of Cherepovets, located in north-west Russia, 600 km from Moscow, remains the global headquarters of the company under its latest form as the Severstal Group.

Severstal's core businesses are steel and mining products, but its portfolio also includes unrelated assets such as a domestic airline and the Cherepovets local port. Since its privatisation in the 1990s, it has become one of the most internationally-minded Russian companies with extensive overseas exports, activity and ownership of foreign assets. The company is listed in the Russian Exchange (MICEX) and London Stock Exchange (LSE). Together with its Russian steel and mining operations, Severstal owns production facilities in the USA, Italy, Africa and CIS countries. The range of products includes raw materials such as iron ore and coking coal which are supplied for in-house production of flat, rolled and long steel products as well as downstream products of steel pipes, wire ropes and metalware. Business ventures include the acquisition of a gold mining business (Nordgold) in West Africa, and a joint venture with Arcelor producing galvanised steel products (Severgal).

At the start of the Great Recession in 2008, Severstal produced 19.2 million mt of steel, positioning it as the third largest producer by volume in Russia and number 14 in the world, with revenues reaching $22.4bn ($5.4bn EBITDA). The group employed over 100,000 staff with the majority based in its Cherepovets steel mill. By 2014, however, Severstal had dropped to number 27 on the list of global steel producers by production volume, with an output of 14.2 million mt of steel.

From 2002, Severstal shifted its focus towards high value-added steel products and in particular the lucrative but also extremely demanding automotive steel market. To do so, the company embarked on a series of acquisitions outside Russia, starting with the acquisition of Rouge in the USA, a historic but by then unprofitable supplier to the automotive giant Ford. Rouge was rebranded as Dearborn and became part of the Severstal

North America subdivision. The steel plant Severstal Columbus in Mississippi, USA, was an organic development built in 2007 at a cost of $880m which was subsequently sold in 2014 for $1.63bn. The US steel facilities were all strategically located near major customers producing highly efficient, low-cost, high-margin products. Severstal also made a number of acquisitions in Europe, most notably the Franco–Italian steelmaker Lucchini and Carrington Wire in the UK, both acquired at the height of the steel market bubble in the mid-2000s. Severstal pulled out of all its European steel assets by the end of 2010.

This turnaround strategy, driven by the sale of Severstal's US, European and other overseas assets described above, was the result of the Great Recession and subsequent severe slowdowns in all major geographical and industrial markets. By the end of 2014, all US assets owned by Severstal had been sold for $2.33bn. The closure of the Severstal North America subdivision marked the company's completion of its overseas divestment strategy. All remaining Severstal steel plants, mostly now only located in Russia, embarked on a firm consolidation and cost efficiency programme.

Within Russia, Severstal enjoys a very good relationship with the Russian government, access to capital for upgrading and extending its production facilities, and a very positive public image in its hometown Cherepovets. Substantial investment was also put towards promoting the international image of the company with a strong emphasis on corporate governance and sustainability.

Severstal group business units

With the aim of reducing cost and concurrently facilitating a simplified and more efficient corporate reporting system, Severstal embarked on a major corporate restructuring programme. Until 2014, Severstal Group was operated as a corporate parent (holding company) and three divisions: Severstal Russian Steel, Severstal Resources (mining assets) and Severstal International. Following the July 2014 sale of its US assets, Severstal Group comprised just two major business units: Severstal Russian Steel and Severstal Resources. Both those business units employed a vertically-integrated business model, with a global reach of related diversified products. Further corporate restructuring and fine tuning was expected in the future, including divestment of low-margins production assets and a stronger focus on emerging markets, where demand for steel products was expected to continue growing, albeit at a modest rate.

Evolution of Severstal's international strategy

In 2004, Severstal Group had embarked on a series of international and domestic acquisitions. Alexey Mordashov is a strong believer in the consolidation of the steel industry and his vision was to make the company a globally recognised player, in particular in the automotive market and other high-value niche markets. Under Mordashov's leadership and vision, the company had aggressively pursued a number of high-risk offshore acquisitions in the USA and Europe, taking over loss-making steel mills with the objective of turning them into profitable businesses and expanding the global profile and brand of Severstal.

Although the company had good experience in acquisitions as a method of pursuing its strategic direction, the lack of shared common management knowledge within the company when integrating newly-acquired assets meant missed opportunities for further growth during the favourable years up to the Great Recession of 2008. There was strong dependency on the skills and knowledge of a small group of senior managers who were able to negotiate and manage newly-acquired businesses but, at a broader organisational level, there was a lack of shared understanding and culture on how to incorporate such management competences and create synergies. The strong leadership in certain business units contributed to their efficient and rapid growth, whereas other units that lacked similar management competences conspicuously underperformed. Coordination of global activities was heavily centralised, allowing for moderate flexibility, although this was an area that Mordashov sought to improve with continuous investment in his managers' competences, e.g. management development training programmes to act as enablers for a common 'Severstal culture and thinking'. For a number of years senior Severstal managers embarked on further training and upskilling, most noticeably through collaborations with Northumbria University and Cranfield University in the UK, and Skolkovo School of Management in Moscow, as well as internal Severstal leadership programmes.

Severstal has continued to invest in its corporate governance, corporate social responsibility and sustainability as part of its strategy to raise global awareness of the Severstal brand and attract investment capital. In Russia, Severstal and its leader Alexey Mordashov were seen as the modern face of healthy and transparent Russian enterprises that could stand as equals with the established Western companies. The company's investment into a best-practice corporate governance reporting system, which preceded a successful London Stock Exchange listing in November 2006 (worth $1.1bn), contributed to raising multimillion-dollar funding from Russian and foreign creditors to support the company's global expansion strategy.

The future

The steel industry is under pressure to act upon environmental concerns and to improve energy efficiency and cut harmful emissions. Even though the Kyoto protocol is unlikely to have the desired impact, the imperatives of dealing with climate change are bound to affect the industry. In view of these concerns over the effects of global warming on the environment and humanity the United Nations Conference on Climate Change 2015 (COP15/COP21) produced the Paris Agreement which legally binds at least 55 countries (including China and Russia) to the ambitious target of reducing carbon emissions per capita by nine per cent by 2030 and aims to reduce global warming to no more than two degrees Celsius by 2100.

In response, the World Steel Association, the industry's trade body, has proactively launched the Steel in a Sustainable World series led by the CEOs of seven leading steel producers. The initiative aims to stimulate a sustainable common strategy for steel producers globally and to promote a positive image of steel as a product and manufacturing process. The Director General of the World Steel Association captured the notion behind the initiative with the following quote:

> **'As an industry, our belief is that sustainable development must meet the needs of the present without compromising the ability of future generations to meet their own needs. We are committed to a vision in which steel is recognised as a key element in a sustainable world. The properties of steel alone demonstrate its significance in this area – steel is 100% recyclable and is in fact the most recycled material in the world.'[7]**

Steel as a product faces competition from other environmentally-friendly materials and inter-material substitutes. Nevertheless, steel has proved to be a remarkably versatile material, with a strong track record of materials technology development and process innovation, leading to improved properties and cost efficiencies – albeit sometimes requiring less 'bulk steel'. That trend, coupled with the effects of an ageing population in the developed economies, China and Russia, will likely contribute to reducing steel demand in the long term. Growth rates in national economies and in the typical steel markets of construction, shipping and automotive are also subject to volatility, influenced by macro-economic trends and geopolitical instabilities, e.g. in the Middle East and North Africa. As a result of the uncertain outlook, steel business executives have been predicting lower levels of investment in innovation through to 2020, perhaps beyond too. On the other hand, the expected increase in urbanisation – 70 per cent of the global population is predicted to live in cities by 2050 – and consequent demand for residential and office buildings, public transport infrastructure, energy grids and utility pipelines – should sustain the demand for steel as a necessary material to enable such development projects. Severstal's strategy will necessarily be adapted accordingly.

Main sources: Bloomberg.com, Severstal, *Annual Reports* (2013, 2014, Q4 2015). *Financial Times*. World Steel Association (http://www.world-steel.org/).

Notes and references
1. J. Fontanella-Khan, 'ArcelorMittal cautiously optimistic about 2014', *Financial Times*, 7 November 2013.
2. C. Weaver, 'Severstal call for global steel agreement', *Financial Times*, 14 November 2013.
3. World Steel Association, 'World steel short range outlook', 11 October 2012.
4. $1 = £0.6 = €0.75.
5. Severstal reports Q4 & FY 2015, financial results, February 2016.
6. Knowledge@Wharton, 'Pedal to the metal: challenges of Tata Steel's Corus takeover', 31 October 2006.
7. World Steel Association, 'Steel CEO's insights on steel's role in a sustainable future', press release, 26 October 2015.

Indian Premier League: glitz, glamour and globalisation

Steve Henderson

This case draws together two influential business trends, namely, globalisation and the increasing market for sporting entertainment. Using the Indian Premier League as an example, the case explores issues that drive internationalisation in the market for short format cricket and the chances of success for IPL.

The cricketing context

Sports such as soccer, tennis and motor racing have developed large, international fan bases that help turn the individuals and teams involved into worldwide sporting superstars. Alongside such development, the business world has recognised the commercial opportunity in attracting fans to spend money via their involvement in these sporting endeavours. At the heart of each of these sports, there are leagues or knock-out competitions that are central to the development of the stories that generate their legendary status. The Indian Premier League (IPL) is one of those leagues having developed over a relatively short period of time into a cricket competition that attracts 'Bollywood' style glitz and glamour as well as some controversy. Its 2014 brand value has been estimated at $7.2bn (£4.3bn, €5.4bn),[1] demonstrating the dramatic rise made since its formation in 2008.

Before leagues can be formed, an interest in a sport has to develop. Nobody is really sure where cricket comes from though it is widely accepted as having started as a children's game in England or France before being later adopted by adults in the early part of the seventeenth century. The game developed in England in the eighteenth and nineteenth centuries and was taken by the English to North America and, afterwards, the British colonisation of the West Indies, India, Australia, New Zealand and South Africa meant that the game spread across the world.

Those who encounter cricket for the first time often find it to be a baffling game, but it is the complexity and subtlety that gives its fans the most to discuss. At its heart, the game is simple in that two teams compete to score the most 'runs'. Those runs are scored by the batsmen when the opposing team bowls the ball to

Source: Dinodia Photos/Alamy Images.

This case was prepared by Steve Henderson, Leeds Beckett University. It is intended as a basis for class discussion and not as an illustration of good or bad practice. © Steve Henderson 2016. Not to be reproduced or quoted without permission.

them. However, the skills of batsmen mean that the game could last for many days. Hence, those baffled by the game also found it lasted too long which added to their boredom. By offering a short format variation of the game, limiting the time played by applying a restriction on bowling – termed 'limited-overs' cricket – the modern game has increased its appeal by allowing such limited-overs matches to run for one day or even just a few hours in the afternoon or evening. The international teams within the International Cricket Council (ICC) competition quickly added this short format cricket alongside the longer format international competition (known as 'test cricket' and generally lasting up to five days).

Whilst cricket developed as an international game, its early days not only involved the long format of the game but also revolved around players who were either unpaid amateurs or, at best, poorly-paid professionals. There was friction created between the national cricketing authorities and players who felt that they were underpaid for playing but were offered payment from newspapers for their involvement in writing articles. All this came to head in the 1970s when the Australian Kerry Packer decided to form a World Series Cricket competition based on paying cricketers significantly more to play. At a stroke, he also achieved his main purpose of holding the worldwide broadcasting rights for the competition. Through his television network (Packer owned Channel 9 in Australia), the competition successfully recruited cricketers looking to make an improved income. It made enemies of the national cricket authorities who hitherto had seen it as their sole right to manage national competitions and organise international games with their colleagues within the ICC.

The globalisation of short form cricket

After Kerry Packer broke the mould, many other sporting organisations recognised that producing a successful league could bring enormous reward. For example, soccer's English Premier League was reported to have increased broadcasting income alone by a massive 29 per cent in the 2014–15 season to £3.3bn. So, the format of bringing sporting stars with a global reputation to your league and broadcasting the competition back to the world was established.

Bringing this thinking together with the short form of cricket that emerged, a number of competing countries (see Table 1) began to offer competitions known as 'Twenty 20' or 'T20', a name derived from the limitation of 20 overs per side, to achieve a shorter match time. Each competing league had to attract teams and choose the months where the competition could be run without being impacted by either the local weather or competitor leagues.

Indian Premier League

In creating enemies of the national cricket authorities, Packer planted the seed of a new idea about how to form cricketing competitions in the minds of other sports organisers. It is hardly surprising, then, to find that the Board of Control for Cricket in India (BCCI) looked to adopt this model when forming the IPL in 2008. Furthermore, they looked to design the league in a way that would enhance its global appeal in a world that had moved on from the 1970s technology of Packer's time. Indeed, India had become something of a global hub for many organisations to base their communications due to the plentiful availability of cheap IT skills. Moreover,

Table 1 T20 leagues

Country	Domestic competition	Year started	Competition months*	Broadcast internationally
Australia	Big Bash League	2011	December–January	Yes
Bangladesh	Bangladesh Premier League	2012	November–December	Yes
England	NatWest T20 Blast	2014	May–August	Yes
India	Indian Premier League	2008	April–May	Yes
Ireland	Inter-Provincial Trophy	2013	July	No
Nepal	Nepal Premier League	2014	May	No
Netherlands, Scotland	North Sea Pro Series	2014	May–June	No
New Zealand	Georgie Pie Super Smash	2014	November–December	No
Pakistan	Pakistan Super League	2016	February	No
South Africa	Ram Slam T20 Challenge	2003	November–December	Yes
Sri Lanka	Sri Lanka Premier League	2012	August	Yes
West Indies	Caribbean Premier League	2013	June–July	No

* Some of these have varied year to year.

watching cricket on TV (often on pay-to-view channels) had become widespread throughout India and indeed in all cricket's major markets.

Cricket being the most popular game in India, teams were asked to bid for the franchise of having a team competing in a new league bringing in $723.59m for the BCCI. In April and May of each year, around eight teams based in the major Indian cities now compete for this Twenty 20 trophy. The teams look to conjure up an image of an exciting league and impress cricket fans with glamorous names like Rajasthan Royals and Chennai Super Kings.

However, the BCCI hadn't been quite as proactive as it may seem as the IPL was developed in response to a private cricket league, the Indian Cricket League (ICL), funded by the broadcaster Zee Entertainment Enterprises. The ICL ran for just two years between 2007 and 2009. Its demise followed the BCCI increasing prize money in its own competitions and placing lifetime bans on players who joined the ICL league. In this way, the BCCI was not only offering more money but also clearly attempting to stop players from joining the competing ICL league.

The IPL's appeal to fans was increased by the introduction of the player auction as a route to building a team squad. The franchises are limited in terms of how they can put together their squad and must fit within limitations such as the number of players in the squad, whether they are home (Indian) or foreign players, and an allowance for young players. However, the very high fees on offer to the top international players makes the league very attractive to them. This creates an opportunity for gossip and rumour amongst fans, which becomes rife on social media before culminating in the live streaming of the auction itself.

After all the excitement around the auction, around 60 matches take place with attendance at these matches averaging close to 60,000 spectators. Spectacle is added to the game with the traditional white clothing of the players abandoned for colours suited to each team's brand. Music and dancing in short bursts are added to spice up the experience too. All this played between teams full of the biggest name players in the sport makes for an atmosphere that can reach fever pitch.

Broadcasting to the world

Modern capabilities to gather and analyse data have led to a wide range of facts, figures and instant replays being available to sports fans. In cricket, this means the umpires who referee the game can use this to check that their decisions are accurate; the commentators have tools to aid their analysis and fans can immerse themselves in as much of the detail of the game as they like.

This provides information to fans at the match and at home creating tension at key moments of the game. The TV broadcasters make the most of this opportunity to focus on key parts of the match by having studio debates around replays of the action.

Over recent years, the broadcasting opportunities have grown massively with a greater ability to transmit an increased data bandwidth at a faster speed to a global audience that may watch on their TV, tablets or even mobile phones. This change in the broadcasting reach has opened up the broadcasting of major sporting competitions around the world with fans watching live at any time of day or using 'catch up' TV just a short time later.

For the IPL, the rise in broadcasting interest has offered a worldwide opportunity to present their matches (see Table 2). Broadcasting rights may move between different broadcasters as contracts come up for renewal, but the international coverage reflects the areas where cricket is played. Ironically, where free-to-air broadcasting of the IPL on ITV4 in the UK boosted popularity ten-fold, this meant there was an increased interest from the subscription-based services leading to Sky Sports winning the 2015 contract.

As Table 2 shows, there are a number of large corporations who hold broadcasting rights for the IPL and some are able to broadcast in different countries. However, managing such rights can cause difficulties when, for example, members of the public seek to access broadcast services from another country. Nevertheless, the IPL can be seen to be generally successful in the spread of broadcasting to different national audiences.

It is clear that the race is on to bring the IPL to the forefront and others are visibly active in the Twenty 20 cricket market. The autumn of 2015 found cricketing legends, Shane Warne and Sachin Tendulkar, taking their Cricket All-Stars Team to play in the huge baseball stadiums of New York, Houston and Los Angeles. Whilst the relatively modest 60,000 attendance across the three games reflected locals originally from countries where cricket is already popular, the cricketing pair are still hopeful of providing the spark for cricket in the USA which David Beckham has provided with his soccer activities in the country.

Other income mired in controversy for the IPL

Sponsorship within sports has seen a massive increase over recent years due to a greater number of fans accessing related broadcasts and the consequent increased reach for sponsors. Whilst the value of sponsorship deals varies with the success of particular sports competitions and teams, as well as the influence of the

Table 2 IPL broadcasters in 2014

Location	Broadcast rights holders
Africa (Sub-Saharan)	SuperSport
Bangladesh	Maasranga Television
Bhutan	SET Max (Hindi)
Brunei	Astro
Canada	Sportsnet One
Caribean	SportsMax
Hong Kong	PCCW
India	Sony MAX (Hindi)
Malaysia	Astro
Middle East and North Africa	Arab Digital Distribution (Cric One)
Nepal	Sony MAX (Hindi)
New Zealand	Sky Sport
Pakistan	GEO Super
Singapore	StarHub
Sri Lanka	Carlton Sports Network
United Kingdom	ITV4
United States	NEO Cricket
Worldwide	The Times Group
	Sony SIX (English)
	Sportsnet World
	ATN-Asian Radio (radio)
	Sony SIX (English)
	Willow

economy on marketing budgets, the income stream remains of high value to major sport competitions.

Sponsorship finds its way into sports via either the rights offered by the clubs themselves or direct to the IPL. Individual teams allow sponsors to fund brand images on their clothing. Like Formula 1, the TV close-ups of those involved and the surface area of visible clothing in the IPL has allowed for multiple sponsors. In addition to this, the merchandising of the team clothing offers another revenue stream that the league and its teams are able to develop.

Pepsi signed a five-year sponsorship deal with the IPL in 2012 worth $62m. However, they abruptly terminated this agreement in the autumn of 2015 leaving the IPL to announce that the Chinese phone manufacturer Vivo Electronics would take over the deal for the final two years. It is believed that Pepsi's termination of the contract resulted from some of the controversies that have surrounded the IPL.

In mid-2015, there was an investigation into the IPL by Rajendra Mal Lodha, a retired Indian Supreme Court Chief Justice, which resulting in the suspension for two years of a pair of the biggest teams in the league, Chennai Super Kings and Rajasthan Royals. The investigation followed up on some of the activities in the 2013 competition when players for the Rajasthan Royals team were accused of match fixing. This led to the arrest of those players and some of the bookmakers who were claimed to have bribed them in order to fix the match. As the investigations continued, the network of those involved was found to be extensive and included the Chennai Super Kings too. This suspension led to last minute changes to the teams involved in the 2016 competition. Accusations of match fixing, especially in the Indian sub-continent, have been common in cricket for some time and the high profile of the IPL has made it especially vulnerable to this threat.

With such betting scandals calling the governance within the IPL into question, not only are sponsors concerned that they may become tainted by the unethical behaviour of their partners in sponsorship but also fans have started to question whether they are really watching a true competition between their sporting heroes. The future of the IPL and its ability to penetrate the international market is now being called into question by scandals which seem set to stain one of cricket's most exciting spectacles.

Note
1. $1 = £0.6 = €0.75.

Handelsbanken: banking done differently

Olof Brunninge

Handelsbanken, one of the key players in the Scandinavian banking market, has chosen a strategic path that has been significantly different from those of its competitors. The bank follows a process of decentralisation, making the 800+ local branches the most important units in its structure. Handelsbanken is one of Scandinavia's most profitable banks with operating profit of SEK20,475m (£1740.1m, $2517.4m, €2235.5m)[1] at the end of 2015 and a return on equity of 13.5 per cent, having a strong financial standing even in times of financial unrest. Success has led to international expansion most notably in the UK. The key question is can Handelsbaken maintain its success in the face of new developments in banking and increasing levels of competition in many of its international markets?

The beginnings

Handelsbanken started its operations in Stockholm in 1871 and grew throughout Sweden by acquiring local banks in different parts of the country. The bank prides itself on not having changed its name for almost 100 years. This underlines Handelsbanken's emphasis on continuity and differentiates it from competitors that have gone through various name changes due to mergers, acquisitions and branding projects.

Nonetheless, during the following decades, Handelsbanken developed much in line with its competitors. International business was done through a network of foreign correspondent banks serving Handelsbanken customers abroad. The bank also took over a number of indebted industrial companies in Sweden. These were managed under a newly-created holding company called 'Industrivärden' and gave rise to the so-called 'Handelsbanken sphere', one of the ownership spheres that still dominate Swedish industry today. Handelsbanken and Industrivärden are major shareholders in one another, protecting Handelsbanken against hostile takeovers.

Handelsbanken continued expanding in Sweden by acquiring smaller competitors. Further internationalisation was not an option, as regulated national banking markets were closed for foreign entrants. However, Handelsbanken was doing well financially and had established itself as one of the major players in the Swedish market. The return on equity in 2015 was 13.5 per cent, one of the highest in the banking sector. The bank's success is often attributed to its culture emphasising decentralisation, cost-consciousness and a conviction that a company that wants to outperform its competitors must be different from the mainstream.

Jan Wallander introduces a new concept of banking

In the late 1960s, Handelsbanken's standing would have been strong, had there not been a scandal relating to the currency regulations prevailing in Sweden at the time. Sweden was financially closed in the sense that cross-border currency transactions required authorisation by the banking authorities. This created trouble for Swedish companies doing international business and some cooperated with their banks in inventing creative, not always entirely legal, solutions to circumvent the problem. Handelsbanken was alleged to have been involved in illegal transactions and Managing Director Rune Höglund was forced to leave his position in 1970. The board hired Jan Wallander who was, at the time, the Managing Director of Sundsvallsbanken, a provincial bank in north Sweden, to lead a turnaround. As the board felt very uncomfortable with the allegations, Wallander had free reign to undertake revolutionary changes. A drastic decentralisation of Handelsbanken's operations was to become the cornerstone of his change programme.

Wallander left no doubt that he was serious about making changes. One of his first actions was to close down the bank's marketing department. In Wallander's

This case was prepared by Olof Brunninge, Jönköping International Business School, Sweden. It is intended as a basis for class discussion and not as an illustration of good or bad practice © Olof Brunninge 2016. Not to be reproduced or quoted without permission.

opinion, marketing departments pushed products onto customers, initiating sales campaigns without caring enough about customer needs. In the new Handelsbanken, it was the branches themselves that should decide what to sell after carefully listening to their customers. Several high-ranking officials at Handelsbanken were either fired immediately or chose to resign from their posts. Wallander wanted to downsize the head office and reducing the number of central managers and getting rid of potential adversaries did not hurt in this situation. Wallander also cancelled the celebrations of the bank's centenary anniversary that had been planned for the following year. While the money Handelsbanken saved through this step was a minor amount, the cancelled celebration still had a major impact. It created a sense of urgency and provided Wallander's reforms with momentum. Moreover, it sent a signal that, from now on, Handelsbanken would not spend money on unnecessary things that did not create value for the customers.

When Jan Wallander took over, Handelsbanken was a modern bank in the sense that it was at the forefront of introducing computers and following the ideas of sophisticated long-range planning processes and the marketing management philosophy that was on the rise. However, both long-range plans and centrally organised sales campaigns were prohibited by Wallander. Based on his experience as an economist he believed that long-range plans, including budgets, were unrealistic. He had observed that reality often turned out differently from professional forecasts. What annoyed Wallander about most sales campaigns was that they aimed at pushing the bank's products based on centrally decided priorities. He believed that these campaigns, inspired by consumer goods marketing, did not fit the banking business. There was a risk that customers ended up buying services they did not need. In banking, offers had to be adapted to the individual customer's needs and that was best done at the local branch office.

Another change he initiated was less spectacular, but perhaps even more important. The accounting system was changed in such a way that costs and revenues, as far as possible, were allocated to the local branches. In a decentralised bank, the branches should directly take all the positive and negative consequences a customer relationship resulted in, in terms of costs and revenues. Each customer, from individuals to large multinational businesses, was assigned to a local branch. There was no special unit dedicated to large customers and business was divided according to the 'church tower principle', i.e. customers belonged to the branch that was closest to their own location. At least metaphorically speaking, the branch manager should have an overview of all his or her customers when looking down from the local 'church

tower'. Overall, the organisational structure introduced by Wallander was flat. It consisted of three levels; the branches, a number of regional head offices and corporate headquarters in Stockholm. In Wallander's view, the branch level was the core level, as it was here that the bank met its customers. To underline this, he introduced the so-called 'Managing Director's visits'. Even today, the Managing Director annually visits a couple of branches in each region to talk about business with the branch manager and other staff.

At least in principle, managers at higher levels were not allowed to interfere with the branch managers' decisions concerning their local customers. Each branch decided which products they wanted to promote given their knowledge of the local market and each branch was evaluated based on their own financial results. The accounting system enabled Handelsbanken to monitor profits and losses on a branch by branch basis and Wallander introduced a benchmarking system to evaluate performance and set targets. He did not believe in forecasts and budgeting with absolute goals; his idea was that comparing oneself to the performance of others was the best way of measuring success. Branches set their targets relating to the performance of comparable branches and Handelsbanken as a whole aimed at exceeding the average return on equity of its competitors. This target made sense regardless of business cycles. Although the competitors have changed, and Handelsbanken includes banks in its markets outside Sweden, the bank has succeeded in outperforming the competition with a higher return on capital than the average of its peer banks for 44 successive years

One of the strengths Handelsbanken is renowned for is its cost-consciousness. Branch managers are eager to keep their costs low in order to succeed in the internal benchmarking with other Handelsbanken branches. In addition, employees feel that they can contribute to cost consciousness and be rewarded for success. When he took over the bank, Jan Wallander introduced a unique reward system for all staff. Each year Handelsbanken reaches its goal of exceeding the profitability of its competitors, the bank gives part of the profit to a pension foundation, called the 'Octagon' (alluding to Handelsbanken's traditional logo). This bonus is distributed equally among all employees, meaning that each full-time member of staff gets the same amount, regardless of whether the person is the Managing Director or a secretary. This signals that each member of staff's contribution to the bank's financial goals is important. The money is paid out when the person retires and long-term employees can receive more than a million SEK. Handelsbanken employees sometimes say in day-to-day talk, 'I have saved some money for the Octagon again', when they have found a cost-efficient solution for an everyday business issue. The Octagon foundation invests its money on the stock exchange, to a large extent in Handelsbanken shares, meaning that the foundation is one of the largest shareholders in the bank. The system creates a sense of working towards a common goal and provides a very long-term incentive for success.

Overall, Wallander succeeded in accomplishing major cultural change that still has a lasting impact more than 40 years later. Stories about Wallander's reforms are told at staff training programmes and many Handelsbanken managers have read the books Wallander has written about the changes he initiated at Handelsbanken. Today, the bank still stands out as being more decentralised and more cost-conscious than its peers. At the same time there is a reluctance to follow industry trends quickly, particularly if these are not in line with Handelsbanken's culture. There is a saying in the bank that rather than following the competitors, looking to see if the 'grass is greener on the other side', Handelsbanken should reflect on whether things cannot simply be done differently. For instance, internet banking was introduced at Handelsbanken more than a year later than some of its competitors, which is a very long time in an IT context. Handelsbanken was not willing to introduce online services until a decentralised online banking solution had been found, meaning that each branch got its own website. While the overall design and functionality are standardised, each customer is automatically directed to the site of his/her branch, where the branch manager can decide to promote offers that fit the clientele of that particular branch. Decentralisation is also mirrored in the continuously large branch network of Handelsbanken. Until 2015, Handelsbanken opened new branches in Sweden while the competitors were reducing their networks. Then finally in 2016, Handelsbanken announced that, due to digitalisation and changing customer behaviour, 50–60 branches would be closed down in the coming two years. Even after this reduction, Handelsbanken would retain the largest branch network in Sweden. In order to follow the idea of decentralisation, the regional head offices in different parts of Sweden rather than the corporate head office in Stockholm, were to decide which branches to close.

Only two major aspects of business remain centralised at Handelsbanken. One is the non-negotiable corporate culture – managers are internally recruited whenever possible and proven ability to comply with Handelsbanken's culture is an essential criterion for a successful career. Internal training progammes as well as the more subtle reproduction of culture in everyday work situations ensures that Handelsbanken's ideas of decentralisation and cost-consciousness stay alive. The other centralised business aspect is the credit process, meaning that central management remains in control of larger loans to customers. This does not mean, however, that top management would be allowed to grant a loan that had been denied by the branch manager in charge. While central managers can stop a risky loan on the local level they can never force local managers to invest in a business they do not believe in.

Handelsbanken goes international

Handelsbanken's internationalisation was limited by banking regulations until the late 1980s. The existing international business was primarily a complement to the domestic operations, helping Swedish customers to do international business. Swedish companies internationalised rapidly after World War II. It was Handelsbanken, Stockholm's Enskilda Bank and Gothenburg-based Skandinaviska Banken (the two latter later merging to form Skandinaviska Enskilda Banken or in short SEB) that helped Swedish firms to do business abroad. Initially, this happened through the existing pre-war networks with foreign banks but, in 1961, Handelsbanken was the first Swedish bank to offer a representative office abroad. The office was based in São Paolo in Brazil, a city where many Swedish firms had established production facilities. Additional representative offices followed in New York, Paris and Beirut.

While Handelsbanken established its first foreign operations on its own, the recipe soon shifted towards consortia with other Scandinavian banks. Similar strategies were pursued by Handelsbanken's competitors – Kansallis from Finland, Köpenhamns Handelsbank from Denmark and Den Norske Kreditbank from Norway. The logic behind this approach was simple; the banks could share costs and at the same time learn more about international markets. As they all saw the consortia as service organisations to their respective domestic customers, there was no internal competition within each consortium. However, differing opinions about the aim and operations of the consortia meant that they were dissolved after several years and the banks returned to a strategy of wholly-owned representative offices. These were typically located in the main markets of domestic customers as well as in international financial centres such as New York, London and Frankfurt. At the time, it was still not legally possible for Swedish banks to direct any business towards the domestic markets of the countries where they had operations. Likewise, the Swedish market was closed to foreign competitors. This changed in the 1980s, when Sweden, in common with many other European countries, liberalised their financial markets, dropped currency regulations and opened up for full-scale cross-border banking operations.

Doing local business outside Sweden

The Swedish banks did not undertake any revolutionary moves but prepared to go international when the borders opened. SEB was an early mover, establishing the 'Scandinavian Banking Partners', an alliance with one partner each from Norway, Denmark and Finland. The idea behind the alliance went clearly beyond that of the consortia in the 1970s. The four banks established cross-holdings of shares, creating a pan-Scandinavian constellation. This implied that SEB had established itself in the other Scandinavian markets, although not under its own brand, but through ownership in local banks. Handelsbanken felt pressure to counter this move.

As the bank was not happy with its experience from its previous consortium activities, it was reluctant to buy shares in a local bank. Instead, Björn-Åke Wilsenius, an experienced Handelsbanker was sent to Oslo to start up a representative office in Norway. The office opened in 1986, still on a small scale and serving Sweden-related business rather than engaging in the local banking market. In parallel, Handelsbanken opened a representative office in the Finnish capital Helsinki, while Denmark had to wait until 1990 when the representative office in Copenhagen opened. It was not clear initially if the representative offices in the neighbouring Scandinavian countries would ever go beyond serving cross-border trade with Sweden.

However, true to its idea of decentralisation, Handelsbanken was open for local initiatives. When Norway suffered from a financial crisis in the late 1980s, Björn-Åke Wilsenius saw an opportunity for a newcomer to challenge the local banks. He convinced Managing Director Tom Hedelius to apply for a Norwegian banking license and Handelsbanken's representative office was formally converted into a wholly-owned subsidiary in 1988. The following year, Handelsbanken began offering its services in the local market, starting with corporate customers. In 1990, Wilsenius saw an opportunity to speed up growth by acquiring the small, one-branch Oslo Handelsbank (despite the similar names the banks had no relationship before the takeover). The deal came with a portfolio of private customers, so Handelsbanken now had a foot in both the private and the corporate markets in Norway.

Handelsbanken was now established in Sweden, Norway, Finland and Denmark. Like Handelsbanken, Swedish competitors also looked primarily at neighbouring countries as a starting point for their international expansion, as the SEB example demonstrates. The Swedish savings banks, who at the time were still a network of mutually-owned local or regional banks, showed interest in opening offices in Poland which was emerging as a potential market after the fall of communism in Europe and the introduction of a market economy. However, a deep financial crisis that hit Sweden in the early 1990s abruptly put a halt to the expansion plans of the Swedish banks. As a result of the liberalised financial sector in Sweden, banks had been able to dramatically increase their loan portfolios. Soaring real estate prices resulted in a speculative bubble that burst in 1990. Real estate prices fell sharply, many owners went bankrupt and the banks that had financed the real estate boom of the 1990s suddenly found themselves with customers that could not repay their loans. Depreciation of the Swedish currency in 1992 made things even worse as many bank customers had taken loans in foreign currencies.

Most Swedish banks made huge losses and several had to fight for survival. The government supported the banking sector and took over Nordbanken (today Nordea) that had itself acquired two other bankrupt banks. SEB applied for government support, but eventually the bank managed to survive on its own. While fighting for survival at home, the Swedish banks had to cancel their international expansion plans. It was only Handelsbanken that survived the crisis without any major problems, making a moderate loss in 1991, which in itself was very unusual for the bank, but returning to profitability the next year. This was partly attributed to the cautiousness and the cost-consciousness of the local branch managers that had prevented the bank from financing overly risky real estate deals. Thanks to the 'church tower principle', the branch managers knew their customers well and understood which deals were too risky to engage in. With the competition temporarily paralysed, Handelsbanken was able to continue its international expansion in a relatively undisturbed manner. However, typically for Handelsbanken, this expansion was carried out cautiously and without taking huge risks.

Growing the foreign operations

Another small bank in Norway, Stavanger bank, was acquired in 1991, moving the Norwegian operations beyond Oslo. In parallel, Handelsbanken also started opening entirely new branches in Norway. The Finnish and Danish representative offices were converted into subsidiaries that started serving local corporate customers before moving into the market for private customers. All new branches in Finland were directly opened by Handelsbanken themselves. However, the bank was able to acquire the credit portfolio of Skopbank that was closed down as a result of the financial crisis that had also hit Finland. Customers in Finland had lost confidence in much of their domestic banking system during the crisis which opened up the market for a newcomer like Handelsbanken.

Denmark was the last of the Nordic markets where Handelsbanken started full-scale local banking operations. This was done in 1992 with a focus on corporate customers, with private customers served from 1996 onwards. In contrast to Norway and Finland, Handelsbanken had trouble identifying suitable local banks to acquire. Danish customers were also more loyal to their domestic banks that were usually well-anchored locally. Handelsbanken grew slowly by establishing one new branch after another. It was not until 2001 that a suitable acquisition target, Midtbank, was found. The deal added 23 branches to the existing seven, being an untypically large acquisition for Handelsbanken and giving it a strong position in the central Jutland region of Denmark.

What was challenging with the takeover of Midtbank was its relative size compared to the existing operations in Denmark. As Handelsbanken was keen to reproduce its culture based on decentralisation and cost-consciousness, taking over an existing structure with its own established culture was more difficult than establishing new branches from scratch. Small acquisitions, like those in Norway, were also easier to handle as experienced Handelsbankers could be sent to the acquired units and serve as ambassadors. Overall, Handelsbanken has always been reluctant to engage in large takeovers for this reason. When Handelsbanken acquired the Swedish mortgage bank Stadshypotek in the 1990s, this was a huge acquisition in terms of balance sheet, but a relatively moderate step in terms of the personnel concerned, thus less of a concern. Stadshypotek employees were assimilated by distributing them across Handelsbanken's branches.

Following a similar logic, Handelsbanken's international expansion has mainly been characterised by opening entirely new branches and complementing this organic growth with relatively minor acquisitions. Of course, the possibility to engage in acquisitions differed from market to market. If no suitable targets were available, Handelsbanken had to rely on organic growth only. The bank has never entered a market by buying a local bank. The first step was always to open an office on its own to ensure that the operations in the new market were characterised by the Handelsbanken culture from the very beginning.

While Handelsbanken refrained from large acquisitions, the Swedish competitors like SEB, Nordbanken and Swedbank prioritised speed in their international expansion. Having recovered from the financial crisis, these banks once again moved towards foreign markets. Nordbanken went for the most radical strategy, engaging in mergers with some of the largest banks in Finland, Denmark and Norway, eventually resulting in the creation of Nordea as a pan-Scandinavian bank. There was no intention in this process to extend the culture and identity of Nordbanken to the new markets. Rather the mergers were seen as an opportunity to create something new.

SEB took an opportunity to acquire Bank für Gemeinwirtschaft (BfG) as a means to enter the German retail banking market. Around the year 2000, SEB had rather optimistic plans for international expansion. SEB, a traditionally centralised bank focusing on large corporate customers and wealthy individuals, saw an opportunity of acquiring banks in various countries and then expanding rapidly through internet banking. This strategy did not succeed. SEB did not manage to make its retail operations outside Sweden and the Baltic states profitable. The German retail operations suffered from a high cost structure that SEB had inherited from BfG. In addition, high levels of competition in the German market made it difficult to increase revenues. Eventually, the German retail operations were sold to the Spanish bank Santander. Today, SEB offers universal banking only in Sweden and the three Baltic states of Estonia, Latvia and Lithuania.

Among the major Swedish banks, it was only Handelsbanken that did not take the step across the Baltic Sea and enter the former Soviet republics after they regained independence in 1991. Sweden had historical ties with Estonia, Latvia and Lithuania, considering them almost as an extension of Scandinavia so SEB, Nordea and Swedbank perceived it as a more or less natural step to enter these markets. They did so by acquiring local banks that were mushrooming in the Baltic countries after the introduction of their market economies. Only Handelsbanken was hesitant. In line with its traditionally cautious attitude, the bank feared that the emerging economies in the former Soviet republics would suffer from significant backlashes on their way to prosperity. This pessimistic prognosis proved true in 2008, when the global financial crisis hit the booming Baltic economies and the local operations of Swedbank, Nordea and SEB suffered dramatic financial losses.

Going beyond the Nordic countries

While the Swedish competitors had invested in the emerging banking markets of Eastern Europe, Handelsbanken had been looking westward instead. Since the early 1970s, the bank had run an operation in

BOX 1 The Swedish banking industry

The Swedish banking industry is dominated by four banks, offering universal banking services through a nationwide branch network combined with online services (see Table 1). SEB (Skandinaviska Enskilda Banken), Handelsbanken, Nordea and Swedbank together have a market share of almost two thirds of household deposits. SEB and Handelsbanken have traditionally been major actors in the Swedish market, while Nordea is a result of mergers of four major Scandinavian banks, including Swedish Nordbanken. Nordea has only a small part of its market in Sweden. Swedbank was created from a series of mergers of savings and cooperative banks. The Swedbank group closely cooperates with local savings banks that are still independent.

In addition to the big four, there is a variety of smaller banks that mainly offer their services online. Some of those are linked to insurance companies or other firms in the financial sector. The product range of these small banks varies from niche market providers to broader offerings, addressing both private and corporate customers. Since 1997, Danske Bank, a large Danish Bank, has been established in Sweden. Danske Bank is the only foreign bank so far offering universal banking in Sweden and it has been particularly successful among corporate customers and wealthy individuals.

A major turning point in the development of the Swedish banking market was the financial crisis the country went through in the early 1990s. The market consolidated, resulting in the formation of Nordea and Swedbank among others. From the mid-1990s onwards, the Swedish banks have internationalised. Apart from Handelsbanken that chose its own way, the Baltic states (Estonia, Latvia and Lithuania) have been the main focus of international expansion. Attempts by some banks to expand to Germany, Poland and Ukraine were not successful. Nordea has minor branch operations in Russia. Only Handelsbanken and Nordea have substantial pan-Scandinavian branch networks offering a full-range banking services today.

Table 1 The Swedish universal banks compared

	Nordea	SEB	Handelsbanken	Swedbank
Operating income	£9.964	£2.287	£2.24	£223
ROE	12.2%	12.2%	13.5%	13.5%
Employees	29,815	15,605	11,819	13,542
Cost/income ratio	47%	50%	45%	43%
Branches	713 (2014)	277 (2014)	845	419
Branches Sweden	231 (2014)	164 (2014)	463	275
Major markets	Sweden, Norway, Denmark, Finland, Estonia, Latvia, Lithania, Russia	Sweden, Estonia, Latvia, Lithuania (mainly corporate customers in Germany, Norway, Denmark, Finland)	Sweden, Norway, Denmark, Finland, UK, Netherlands	Sweden, Estonia, Latvia, Lithuania

Note: €1 = SEK 9,135 3 December (2015).

Source: 2014 reports for SEB and Nordea, 2015 reports for Swedbank and Handelsbanken.

London under different formats. The UK capital was not only a major financial centre, but also played an important role in trade between Sweden and the UK. Parts of the London operations were converted into a branch in 1987 and branches in Manchester and Birmingham were added in 1989 and 1994, respectively. Still the purpose was limited to serving business between the UK and Sweden as well as the other emerging Scandinavian operations of Handelsbanken. The operations did not aim at serving the local UK market. The UK was not an obvious market for a Swedish bank to enter as the market was mature and dominated by large domestic banks. These national players had consolidated the market by acquiring smaller banks and by rationalising their own operations.

Handelsbanken successfully ran its Scandinavia-focused business. However, although the UK Handelsbanken staff realised that their UK customers were very satisfied with the service they got, there were only limited opportunities to grow based on business with the Nordic countries. Ulf Sylvan, who was in charge of the operations in the UK, approached his managers in Stockholm and convinced them to try serving the local market based on the three existing branches. Managing Director Arne Mårtensson announced the launch of universal banking operations in the UK in 1999.

Growth in the UK had to rely on opening Handelsbanken branches from scratch. There were no suitable acquisition targets available. So management in the UK started to look for places that might be suitable for establishing a new branch. In terms of population, the UK market was larger than all the existing Scandinavian markets put together. Essentially, there would have been potential customers anywhere, but Handelsbanken wanted to start with relatively large cities where it was possible to choose among the most attractive customers. In places with many potential customers, Handelsbanken had enough choice to proactively target companies and wealthy individuals who were likely to generate profits for the bank. Many of the new customers appreciated the decentralised concept of banking. UK banks were increasingly centralising their operations, using their branches as mere outlets for financial products, without delegating much decision-making authority to local staff. In contrast, at a Handelsbanken branch, customers could have a direct relationship with the local branch and only larger credit decisions had to be approved by Handelsbanken in London.

Regarding the new branches, there was an idea to establish a basic geographic coverage of England to start with. As the bank did not have enough employees of its own to staff the new branches, new recruitment would be required. In order to ensure that the new branches developed in line with Handelsbanken's philosophy, they were supposed to receive support from existing branches in the beginning. However, when choosing new branch locations, what was even more important than geography was the availability of a suitable branch manager. Handelsbanken would even postpone entry into an attractive local market, if they did not find a branch manager who wholeheartedly identified with the culture of running a bank in a decentralised manner. Following Handelsbanken's concept of decentralisation, the branch manager would be expected to run his or her branch with a large degree of independence, while at the same time ensuring a cost-conscious and relatively risk-averse approach to banking.

Handelsbanken's management in the UK put a lot of time into selecting the right branch managers. They were particularly interested in experienced bankers from the large clearing banks or from medium-sized banks that were frustrated about the increasing centralisation of their own organisations. The individuals who were eventually recruited saw Handelsbanken as an opportunity to revive the independence they once had had in their previous banks and to be able to take more responsibility at a local level. At Handelsbanken they were able to decide how to manage their local business rather than being driven by directives and targets set by a faraway head office. This was particularly emphasised in the start-up process of new branches. A branch manager was typically recruited to open a branch in a specific city where he or she had experience of the local banking market. However, the city was basically the only thing that was determined beforehand. All other decisions, including the choice of the location, were to be made by the branch manager him or herself.

Many of the new branch managers embraced the decentralisation idea wholeheartedly and took pride in recruiting their co-workers and in making practical arrangements for the office. The manager starting up the Leeds branch, for instance, took the cost-conscious culture of Handelsbanken very seriously. He bought the office furniture for a bargain price and decorated the office with paintings made by his wife, rather than buying expensive artwork from a gallery. His story came to be told throughout the UK operations as a good example of putting Handelsbanken's culture of cost-consciousness and localised decision-making into practice. While it would not have been against the Handelsbanken culture as such to take some more help from the regional head office in London, for example for buying office furniture, the new UK managers took pride in doing as much as possible themselves. Their peers in other markets were more pragmatic. For instance, the Norwegian operations for a while had a dedicated support team, helping new branches with practicalities rather than just advice on business issues and the Handelsbanken culture.

During the start-up phase, all branch managers received close support from an experienced Handelsbanken manager, whose role it was to give advice but also to make sure that the new branches developed within the framework of the Handelsbanken culture. However, in most cases the latter was not a problem. The news spread in Handelsbanken that the UK colleagues who had 'converted' from other banks were more zealous about the Handelsbanken culture than long-time Handelsbanken employees in Sweden who had started taking their bank's approach to business too much for granted. As the bank did not acquire any existing banking operations in the UK, the Handelsbanken branches had more freedom than their Nordic peers to develop their operations without being bound to existing customers' expectations.

While Handelsbanken's profile in the Nordic countries is that of a mass-market provider, with street-level branches, Handelsbanken in the UK positioned itself more like an old style private bank. Customers are hand-picked, i.e. the branches systematically look for profitable businesses and wealthy individuals to approach. By proactively searching for customers rather than waiting for customers to approach the bank, Handelsbanken in the UK reduces the risk of ending up with a portfolio of non-profitable clients (e.g. struggling businesses or individuals that are not well off). This is already signalled by the choice of office locations, typically on the upper floors of an office building. Instead of attracting transaction customers from the street in a more random manner, the branches are supposed to serve selected customers who visit the branch as a part of an in-depth relationship with the bank.

Speeding up international growth

Business in the UK was successful and Handelsbanken realised that the UK branches usually reached break-even after approximately two years. At the same time, there was a continued expansion of the operations in the other Nordic countries, including two acquisitions in Norway – the medium-sized Bergensbanken in 1999 and Lokalbanken i Nordsjælland in 2008. Meanwhile competitors were growing quickly and questions were being raised about Handelsbanken, not least from the stock market, whether the strategy of organic and relatively slow international growth was sufficient in the long term. Handelsbanken had to take a stance how to prioritise between markets in order to speed up growth. Even

organic growth was costly and had to use the equity of the bank. This meant that it was not possible to push for growth with equal speed everywhere.

Major strategic decisions about priorities, such as new market entry, are made centrally even in a decentralised bank. However, top management at Handelsbanken want the local managers to come up with initiatives for strategic development, such as starting to reach out for local customers or for increasing the speed of growth. As the UK branches became profitable so quickly and the market seemed almost unlimited, Handelsbanken's management decided in 2006 to triple the speed of opening new branches for the coming year. The speeding up of organic growth led to a tremendous expansion in the UK. The UK operations grew from 20 branches in 2005 to 83 by 2010 and 178 by 2014, including branches in Scotland and Wales. In 2013, Handelsbanken eventually made its first acquisition in the UK when it took over the asset management company Heartwood. With about 90 employees, Heartwood managed assets amounting to £1.6bn and advanced the bank's position in the UK savings and wealth management markets.

Handelsbanken's international expansion has not come to an end with growth in the UK and the Nordic countries. New markets have been tested, again based on existing representative offices. During the last ten years, operations in Poland, Germany and the Netherlands have expanded beyond just serving business related to Handelsbanken's home markets (see Figure 1 and Table 2). Poland seemed to be a promising market in 2005 and the bank started opening branches outside Warsaw. A few years later, operations in the Netherlands and in Germany were also expanded.

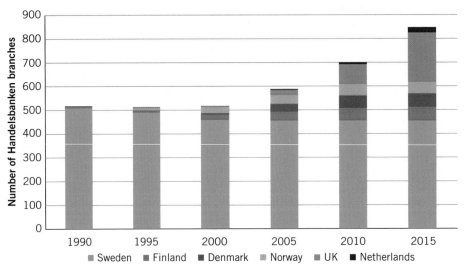

Figure 1 The development of Handelsbanken's branch network

Source: Annual reports of Handelsbanken for the respective years.

Table 2 Number of Handelsbanken branches

	1990	1995	2000	2005	2010	2015
Sweden	511	488	460	455	461	463
Finland	1	7	20	36	45	36
Denmark	1	2	7	35	53	57
Norway	1	12	25	37	49	50
UK	2	3	4	20	83	206
Netherlands	0	0	0	1	7	23
Total	516	512	516	584	698	835

Again, the approach was cautious. The new branches often started with limited investments in office buildings and did not move to larger premises until their business started generating sufficient income. Local managers spent a lot of time recruiting branch managers that they believed fitted the Handelsbanken approach to banking. Besides being experienced bankers with knowledge of the local market, they needed to be entrepreneurial and willing to run their local business with a large degree of independence.

Teaching the new staff Handelsbanken's decentralised concept of banking has been a cornerstone each time Handelsbanken entered a new market. Experienced Handelsbanken managers from existing markets always play an important role when setting up operations in another country. They often hold key positions, such as credit managers, as the process of granting loans mirrors the balancing act between granting autonomy to local branches and ensuring cost-consciousness and risk adversity with some centralised control. However, while experienced Handelsbankers have played an important role in spreading culture, relatively few of them have been needed. Today, there are hardly any Swedes left in the Norwegian, Finnish and Danish operations and a Dane is now the first non-Swede to be appointed managing director. Local staff have been very enthusiastic about the decentralised banking idea, sometimes even unconsciously pushing it further than the Stockholm head office initially wanted. For instance, the Finnish operations allowed branch managers to decide about local staff numbers shortly after the bank had entered the country. A few years later, when the head office gave all branches permission to decide about staff levels, the Finns realised that they had

decentralised even more than they had actually been allowed to.

Despite its success, Handelsbanken's international expansion has not happened without setbacks. The Polish branches struggled as a result of the financial crisis so the operations there were scaled back in 2010 with several branches being closed down. Handelsbanken in Germany experienced the tough local banking market. The branch network was consolidated at the level of ten branches and then scaled down to five in 2015. Operations in the Netherlands, on the other hand, developed positively so this market seemed to be the most attractive option for Handelsbanken to develop further. In 2013, when the Dutch operations had reached a level of 15 branches, Handelsbanken formally declared that the Netherlands now were one of the home markets of the bank, along with Sweden, Denmark, Norway, Finland and the UK. Three years later the bank's presence in the Netherlands had grown to 24 branches. In 2015, Handelsbanken had major local operations in six countries that are primarily managed by local staff. In 2015, Frank Vang-Jensen became the first non-Swede to be CEO of Handelsbanken. He came to the bank as an employee of Danish Midtbank with the takeover in 2001.

Notes

1. SEK1 = £0.085 = $0.123 = €0.109.
2. This case primarily builds on the author's dissertation and his own empirical work. Additional information has been obtained from the bank's own publications, its website, and media reports. For additional material on the historical background of the case as well as a comprehensive list of references, please refer to the author's dissertation: Brunninge, O. (2005). Organisational self-understanding and the strategy process. Strategy Dynamics in Scania and Handelsbanken. JIBS Dissertation Series No. 027. Jönköping: Jönköping International Business School www.diva-portal.org/smash/get/diva2:3867/FULLTEXT01.pdf.

Ningbo Smarter Logistics: innovating in partnership with IBM in China

Shameen Prashantham

This case study focuses on Ningbo Smarter Logistics, a new venture in a mid-sized city in China. The venture was established with the purpose of creating technological solutions in the logistics sector in close collaboration with IBM's research unit in Ningbo. In typical Chinese fashion, the city government was heavily involved in creating the venture although it was set up as a private new venture. The case highlights the growing aspiration for innovation in emerging economies, the importance of partnerships involving new ventures and large multinationals, and the crucial role that the government plays in China.

Background: the Ningbo Smart City Initiative

Ningbo is a mid-sized Chinese port city with an urban population of about two million, and the second city of the prosperous Zhejiang province, which has a reputation for its entrepreneurship (particularly traditional family businesses). In a country dominated by state-owned enterprises, Ningbo (like the wider Zhejiang province), has many private firms – many of them small entrepreneurial companies – that serve both the domestic and international markets in manufacturing-based industries such as textiles, light electronics and automotive parts. In recent years, the Ningbo city government has sought to improve its technology-based industries as China seeks to move beyond low-cost manufacturing to increase the level of its innovation output. An important effort in this regard was the establishment of the 'Ningbo smart city initiative'.

Smart city initiatives can be increasingly found around the world. For example, in recent years the UK government has announced various initiatives to support smart cities in the UK. According to the UK government website:[1]

'A smart city uses intelligent technology to enhance our quality of life in urban environments. Cities can use the data in a variety of ways; to save money, minimise waste, measure domestic water usage and manage transport routes. Allowing the public access to real time information enables people to make more informed choices, such as planning a journey by checking for available room on trains and buses or even identifying car parking spaces before leaving the house.'

The Ningbo smart city initiative was established in 2010 under the auspices of the Ningbo Economy and Information Committee, a local governmental unit, with a remit to facilitate the creation and use of digital technologies to enhance the welfare of the city's citizens. This is one of numerous such initiatives in China that seek to utilise information technology to improve the efficacy of services in education, healthcare, logistics, commerce and transportation, to name but a few potential applications.

This type of initiative exists in almost every major city in China, and helps to improve the services provided to local citizens through the effective utilisation of information technology. However, in Ningbo it was seen as more than that. Specifically, the Ningbo city government rather creatively regarded the initiative as an opportunity to attract high-quality multinational corporations (MNCs) to establish a local presence and to facilitate relationship-building between such companies and local new ventures with innovative ideas but lacking the wherewithal to commercialise them.

Ningbo city pursued these twin objectives through its initial five-year plan (2011–15) by dividing up the smart city initiative into a small number of substantial segments such as logistics, healthcare and transportation. Atypically among Chinese cities, large companies were invited to tender for the contract to handle an entire segment (e.g. logistics, healthcare, transport). The rationale for this was that only a substantial piece of business would attract large companies to establish a presence in a city lacking a strong high-tech reputation. Moreover, government officials were confident that no single company would be able to deliver the entire set of services by themselves and would perforce end up working with local partners, including new ventures and older small and medium-sized enterprises (SMEs), which possessed the requisite local knowledge to customise and implement smart city solutions in Ningbo. City officials tended to informally encourage collaborations although the final decision on partner selection would be with the large company.

In the event, Ningbo City was successful in accomplishing this. For example, in the case of 'smart healthcare', the contract was awarded to Huawei, a large Chinese multinational company. Huawei worked closely with King-T, a local SME specialising in health information technology and with an in-depth knowledge of local healthcare systems. Huawei also worked with a small Norwegian company with the help of Ningbo smart city government officials who, in turn, were introduced to this start-up by the Nordic Industrial Park in Ningbo.

Similarly, in the area of 'smart manufacturing', SAP, a large German multinational company, worked closely with a small local new venture called Chinajey. This local company developed enterprise resource planning (ERP) solutions in collaboration with SAP and the local government subsidised numerous Ningbonese manufacturing SMEs to adopt these solutions. However, such collaborations built on the initial success of a new venture partnering with a large multinational in the area of 'smart logistics'. This was Ningbo Smarter Logistics.

The origins of Ningbo Smarter Logistics

The first facet of the smart city programme to be put out to tender was the smart logistics segment. This partly reflected one of Ningbo city's priority areas viz. its port, which according to the Ningbo government[2] is the world's busiest in terms of volume (tonnage) of cargo. IBM was awarded the smart logistics contract in Ningbo, resulting in a research centre being established in Ningbo in 2010–11 – a major, and highly improbable, accomplishment for a city lacking a strong reputation for its high-tech industries – with oversight from IBM's Shanghai research centre. At the time, it was IBM's only greenfield research unit in mainland China outside of Beijing or Shanghai.

IBM's early analysis, based on preliminary investigations in Ningbo and the wider company's extensive experience with smart city solutions across the world, rapidly led to the conclusion that it would be prudent for any information technology-based logistics solution to involve 'cloud computing' which involves storing data on offsite

locations available through the internet and which can be accessed on internet-enabled devices such as smartphones and computers. Cloud computing has led to the creation of more efficient and flexible solutions because many substantial fixed costs in information technology infrastructure are no longer required. While Ningbo Smart City officials readily accepted the logic of adopting a cloud computing-based approach to logistics solutions, there was a legal obstacle to be addressed in that the Chinese government prohibits foreign companies from hosting cloud-based platforms in China.

The solution arrived at was the creation of a new venture that would host and develop cloud computing solutions in close collaboration with IBM and Smart City officials. This venture, which was to be called Ningbo Smarter Logistics, would be housed on the ground floor of the same building as IBM's development lab in Ningbo. The physical, and symbolic, proximity to IBM was intended to facilitate day-to-day interactions between the venture and its larger partner. Although ostensibly a private venture backed by a wealthy local entrepreneur, the active day-to-day running of the company was to be entrusted to a suitable professional manager with the requisite technical expertise and capacity to engage with IBM.

The Ningbo city government believed the ideal candidate to become CEO of Ningbo Smarter Logistics was Mr Larry Qin, the IBM senior manager leading its smart city activities in Ningbo and also heading research labs in the Greater China region. Mr Qin, who was based over 1000 miles to the north in Beijing, agreed to relocate with his family to Shanghai, a closer city, from where he commuted to Ningbo each week. This was viewed as a major breakthrough in Ningbo's fledgling attempt to attract top talent to its information technology sector.

Key strategic decisions

Upon taking over as CEO in 2013, Mr Qin turned his attention to developing a few viable pilot projects. One of them involved a cloud computing-based solution to ensure secure and trackable transportation of seafood from Ningbo to inland regions of China. If successful, such a solution could be deployed to the transportation of other cargoes from the port to other parts of China. To deliver on this plan, Mr Qin developed a three-pronged strategy for Ningbo Smarter Logistics.

First, strenuous efforts were made to gain IBM's attention at multiple levels. Here, Mr Qin's high-level contacts within, and knowledge of, IBM was a great help. He continuously engaged with key members of the IBM research unit in Ningbo – greatly facilitated by the venture's physical proximity to the IBM facility – and other IBM managers in Shanghai. Furthermore, he made sure that IBM's top management based in Beijing was kept abreast of developments in Ningbo. He knew that only if the wider China subsidiary of IBM supported the initiative could the Ningbo-based initiative be ultimately successful.

Second, a group of high-quality managers and technologists was assembled to form the top management team of Ningbo Smarter Logistics. Given the limitations of access to top technical talent in Ningbo, Mr Qin actively sought to hire professionals from more reputed technological hubs such as Shanghai and Hangzhou. He also activated his personal networks. For instance, he persuaded a manager with whom he had done business before to come onboard. He also co-opted a senior technologist on secondment, as the venture's chief technology officer (CTO). In addition to these senior appointments, Mr Qin was also conscious that the more junior managers and technologists had an important role to play and sought to actively mentor this young team.

Third, local relationships were actively cultivated with government officials, prospective partners and the wider community. In mapping out what a cloud-based logistics solution might look like, it became apparent that neither IBM nor Ningbo Smarter Logistics possessed all the inputs that would be required for such a solution. For example, important hardware components were required. As a result, Ningbo Smarter Logistics would have to be not only a close partner of IBM's but also an interface between IBM and local companies possessing the missing ingredients in the solution being created. As is always the case in China, this would only be possible through the support of local government officials. In addition to actively networking with local businesses and government officials, Mr Qin also made it a point to raise the profile of his organisation among other influential local entities such as Zhejiang University and the Ningbo-based China campus of Nottingham University from where he was able to hire a number of the most capable interns to provide further support.

An interesting example of how these local relationships bore fruit was the incorporation of an important component (an internet-controlled locking device) into the pilot solution being developed by Ningbo Smarter Logistics. This device was created by a very small new venture – with fewer than 20 employees at the time – called Delian Technology. This venture's innovation was brought to the attention of Ningbo Smarter Logistics through a Ningbo High-Tech Zone government officer.

This led to close interactions between the venture and Mr Qin's team, and ultimately Delian's technology became part of IBM's smart logistics pilot solution.

Establishing credibility, looking ahead

The efforts described above bore fruit, and by early 2014 a pilot solution was put together. The demonstration of the pilot, housed within the IBM facility in Ningbo, drew a favourable response from the local government and logistics companies associated with the seafood industry. This was a significant development because it meant that Ningbo Smarter Logistics had now developed credibility in the eyes of several stakeholders including the local government, local partners, prospective customers and importantly IBM itself, which views the Chinese market as a high priority.

Indeed, not only was the IBM research unit in Ningbo suitably impressed but also, remarkably, the Board of IBM China also expressed appreciation for the project because they saw it as representing technology that could be deployed elsewhere with other clients. They saw it as embodying an innovative and effective way of working with a municipal government in China, an approach that could be replicated in other Chinese cities. The climax of this process of validation by IBM, which further evidenced how much IBM was impressed by this achievement, was a visit from Steve Mills, one of the highest-ranking executives at IBM's global headquarters, along with Dr Matt Wang, the globally respected head of the research division in Shanghai. By personally visiting the demo in Ningbo, these executives signalled not only IBM's satisfaction with the pilot but also their belief in the long-term potential of Ningbo Smarter Logistics as an IBM partner.

By the end of 2015, Ningbo Smarter Logistics had become the first joint innovation collaboration established in China under the auspices of IBM's newly introduced 'Technology Partnership' initiative, and had won awards at multiple smart city expos and other industry forums.

Mr Qin, while quietly satisfied with the initial success of Ningbo Smarter Logistics, knew full well that the key stakeholders would now have even higher expectations of him and his organisation. Despite the clear sense of a big opportunity due to China's rising aspirations to enhance its innovation capacity, the road ahead will not necessarily be smooth. In establishing itself as a viable partner of a large multinational company while at the same time aligning itself with local government priorities, Ningbo Smarter Logistics could be particularly vulnerable to having to deal with shifting priorities on the part of either of these entities. Moreover, its own identity is a multifaceted one – as an IBM partner in one sense, a Ningbo local government partner in another, and an interface between IBM and external actors in yet another. The challenge of coping with these multiple identities is exacerbated by the Chinese government's inherently complex stances vis-à-vis foreign companies – welcoming them with open arms on the one hand and restricting them (e.g. in terms of cloud computing) on the other.

But then, Mr Qin knows as well as anyone that any entity seeking success in this market filled with both promise and peril has to learn the art of embracing contradictory tensions.

Notes
1. Department for Business Innovation and Skills, 'New initiative to support $40 billion smart cities in the UK', press release, 9 October 2013.
2. 'Port in Ningbo', 24 October 2013, http://english.ningbo.gov.cn/art/2013/10/24/art_87_644254.html.

Leadership and innovation at Apple Inc.: entering the post-Jobs era

Loizos Heracleous and Angeliki Papachroni

This case looks at the development and success of Apple as an innovative company under the leadership of Steve Jobs and Tim Cook. After Jobs' unique approach and record of achievement, Apple transitioned to a new era where it faced unique challenges. What are the key elements of Apple's innovative culture and how does the company maintain its leadership position in innovation? Will the new leadership maintain this record of achievement under new competitive pressures?

Apple Computer Inc. was founded in 1976 by Steve Jobs and two close colleagues. However, in 1985, after a major bust up with the then CEO, Jobs left the company he had founded and started a new venture (NeXT Inc). In the next decade, Apple went through many changes searching for success and eventually decided to acquire NeXT Inc. in 1997 thus bringing Steve Jobs back into Apple (initially as an advisor). Within months, the board of Apple replaced the CEO and reinstated Jobs to the position he had held in the early days of Apple. In 1997, when Steve Jobs returned to the company, few would have thought that the failing, niche Apple Computers would one day be recognised as one of the most innovative companies in the world, transcending the barriers of the computer industry to compete in the consumer electronics, telecommunications and music industries. Since 1997 Apple's market capitalisation increased from $2bn to $741.8 billion[1] in 2015,[2] becoming the world's most valuable company.[3] By 2015, Apple was first by almost any measure, including the largest sales, profits and assets among the world's technology companies.[4] On top of this, Apple was the world's most valuable brand according to Interbrand's 2015 report (estimated at around $170.3bn) for the third year in a row, after pushing Coca-Cola off the top in 2013.[5] Building on innovative products that have redefined their markets (such as the iPod, the iPhone and the iPad), a consumer base as loyal as a fan club, and a business model characterised by integration and synergies that no competitor could easily imitate, Apple continued its extraordinary performance. Under the leadership of Tim Cook (who took over from Jobs as CEO in 2011) Apple reported sales of $200bn, net profit of $45bn and assets of $260bn in April 2015 (for more financial information see Table 1).[6] The key question is, 'can Apple maintain this extraordinary success?' Declining iPhone sales during 2016 led to the first year-over-year decline in revenue in 13 years for Apple,[7] raising serious concerns about the growth of the company in the future.

Jobs' turnaround and rebuilding an innovative organisation

However, things haven't always been that rosy for the company once known as the underdog of the computer industry. During the time when Steve Jobs was away from the organisation (1985–1997), Apple's performance progressively deteriorated to the point where it was struggling for survival despite the effort of three different CEOs to reverse the decline. Jobs' return to Apple as Interim CEO in 1997 and CEO in 2000 marked the beginning of a new era for the company. He worked for a salary of $1 per year for 30 months (but held plenty of stock options), leading Apple's successful turnaround. His priority was to revitalize Apple's innovation capability. As he noted in an interview, 'Apple had forgotten who Apple was',[6] stressing that it was time for Apple to return to its core values and build on them. Upon taking charge, Jobs axed 70 per cent of the new products in development, kept the 30 per cent that he believed were 'gems', and added some new projects that he believed could offer breakthrough potential. He also revamped the marketing message to take advantage of the maverick, creative Apple brand, and employed stock-based incentives to retain talented employees.[8] In parallel, Jobs

Table 1 Selected Apple financial data (2011–2015)

	2015	2014	2013	2012	2011
Net sales	$233,715	$182,795	$170,910	$156,508	$108,249
Net income	$53,394	$39,510	$37,037	$41,733	$25,922
Earnings per share:					
Basic	$9.28	$6.49	$5.72	$6.38	$4.01
Diluted	$9.22	$6.45	$5.68	$6.31	$3.95
Cash dividends declared per share	$1.98	$1.82	$1.64	$0.38	$0
Shared used in computing earnings per share:					
Basic	5,753,421	6,085,512	6,477,320	6,543,726	6,469,806
Diluted	5,793,069	6,122,663	6,521,634	6,617,483	6,556,514
Total cash, cash equivalents and marketable securities	$205,666	$155,239	$146,761	$121,251	$81,570
Total assets	$290,479	$231,839	$207,000	$176,064	$116,371
Commercial paper	$8,499	$6,308	$0	$0	$0
Total term debt[2]	$55,963	$28,987	$16,960	$0	$0
Other long-term obligations[1]	$33,427	$24,826	$20,206	$16,664	$10,100
Total liabilities	$171,124	$120,292	$83,451	$57,854	$39,756
Total shareholders' equity	$119,355	$111,547	$123,549	$118,210	$76,615

[1] Other long-term obligations exclude non-current deferred revenue.

[2] Includes current and long-term portion of term debt.

Source: Apple Inc.

proceeded to simplify Apple's product mix in terms of four lines of desktop and portable computers designed for both the professional and consumer markets. Whereas most of Apple's innovations led to even more 'closed Apple archipelagos'[9] (software and hardware integration), at the same time Jobs decided to loosen control in other areas, for example the use of standard interfaces, such as the USB port.

Growing the Apple ecosystem: breakthrough innovation in the consumer electronics and entertainment industries

In 2001, Apple introduced its first iPod, launching a new era for the company as it entered the consumer electronics industry. Capitalising on the emerging trend of MP3 music, and despite being a relatively late entrant in this market (rival systems like Winamp and MPMan were released in 1997 and 1998 respectively), Apple's iPod soon became synonymous with the MP3 music player category. By the end of 2003, more than one million iPods were sold marking the first substantial stream of revenues apart from the iconic Apple Macintosh computers. Since then the iPod product range has been often renewed and the company announced in 2007 that it sold the 100 millionth iPod, making the device the fastest selling music player in history. One of Apple's

most important innovations was the launch of the iTunes Music store in 2003, a service through which consumers could access and purchase online music for only $0.99 per song. The iTunes Music Store was compatible with all iPods (running on both Macs and Windows-based computers) and served as Apple's Trojan horse to what Jobs had envisioned as the digital hub where digital content and Apple devices would be seamlessly interconnected. The downloaded songs had royalty protection and could only be played by iPods, bringing the inter-operability between Apple's hardware, software and content to a new level and creating higher barriers to entry into this ecosystem (as well as exit from it). iPods had the capacity to display videos and through them Apple became a significant distributor of movies and TV shows.

Apple's next ground-breaking innovation, the iPhone, was launched in 2007, six years after Palm's first smartphone in the USA. A year later, Apple launched the App Store, the only authorised service for loading programmes onto the iPhone. The App Store was based on the same principle of seamless integration between hardware and software, giving Apple 30 per cent of third-party developers' revenues along the way. The Apple ecosystem was further reinforced in 2010 with the introduction of the iPad, a tablet computer that galvanised what had, for ten years, been a commercially failure-ridden product category. Consumers could play games, read books, load all sorts of applications and access the internet through their iPad. In October 2011, Apple introduced iCloud, a cloud service for storing music, photos, applications, calendars and documents that can be wirelessly transferred to multiple iOS devices, Macs and Windows-based computers. By providing a means of integrating the use of multiple Apple devices, iCloud was a significant move towards a mobile Apple ecosystem.

Apple has also developed a series of strategic alliances in the course of its efforts to become the centre of the digital hub, where digital content would be easily created and transferred to any Apple device. Development of the iPod, iTunes and iPhone has necessitated this collaborative approach, since entry in the entertainment and consumer electronics markets would not have been as successful without some key strategic partners (for example, the big record labels such as EMI, Sony BMG, Universal and Warner Brothers for iTunes, or YouTube for the iPhone). At the same time, Apple proceeded with a number of acquisitions of relatively small, innovative firms in fields such as video creation and microprocessor production intended to strengthen its own technological core competencies. In 2014, the company acquired headphone maker Beats Electronics for $3bn, marking its biggest acquisition in its history.[10]

Playing with different rules

Deep collaboration

Long before Apple was first recognised as the world's most innovative company in 2005 by the Boston Consulting Group, Apple had placed its trademark on a long list of technological breakthroughs including the mouse, the graphical user interface, colour graphics, built-in sound, networking and wireless LAN, FireWire and many more. Some of these, such as the graphical user interface, were seen by Jobs on visits to research facilities such as Xerox's Palo Alto Research Center, and adapted for broader use in Apple's offerings. Apple's approach over the years had been to make the use of a personal computer as easy and intuitive as possible through developing a highly responsive operating system, establishing standard specifications to which all applications' software packages were expected to conform, strict control of outside developers, and delivering computers with high performance.[11] Apple practises what employees call 'deep collaboration', 'cross-pollination' or 'concurrent engineering'. This refers to products not developed in discrete stages but by 'all departments at once – design, hardware, software – in endless rounds of interdisciplinary design reviews'.[12] Other companies have outsourced most, or all, of their product design

function, relying on outsourced design manufacturers (ODMs) to develop the products that with minor adaptations will fit into their product lines. Apple, however, believes that having all the experts in one place – the mechanical, electrical, software and industrial engineers, as well as the product designers – leads to a more holistic perspective on product development; and that a critical mass of talent makes existing products better and opens the door to entirely new products. According to Jobs:

> **'You can't do what you can do at Apple anywhere else. The engineering is long gone in the PC companies. In the consumer electronics companies they don't understand the software parts of it. There's no other company that could make a MacBook Air and the reason is that not only do we control the hardware, but we control the operating system. And it is the intimate interaction between the operating system and the hardware that allows us to do that. There is no intimate interaction between Windows and a Dell computer.'[13]**

Sticking with a proprietary ecosystem

Since the introduction of the iPhone and iTunes, the Apple ecosystem has been growing steadily with the introduction of new products like the iPad, the Apple Watch and Apple TV, all of which share the same operating system. Buying and sharing content between devices becomes a seamless experience, increasing users' dependence on Apple's iOS and ecosystem of devices. Job's vision of integration between hardware and software has followed Apple throughout the years, offering a superior consumer experience. As a result, Apple has managed to attract a high-value customer base. According to the industry estimates, Google's Android OS accounted for 83.6 per cent of smartphone shipments in the third quarter of 2014 while Apple's iOS accounted for only 12.3 per cent of the shipments. However, Apple's smartphone is much more lucrative as it attracted a high-value customer base and its smartphones accounted for 60 per cent of mobile web usage in 2014.[14]

Over the years, there have been some notable exceptions to this proprietary approach. In late 2003, in order to reach a broader consumer base, Apple offered a Windows-compatible version of iTunes not only allowing Windows users to use the iPod but more importantly familiarising them with Apple products. Another milestone came with the company's switch from PowerPC processors made by IBM to Intel chips, a decision announced in mid-2005. This decision allowed Macs to run Windows software, implied lower switching costs for new Mac consumers and also allowed software developers to adapt their programs for Apple more easily. A previous alliance with Microsoft occurred in 1997 when Microsoft agreed to invest $150m in Apple, reaffirming its commitment to develop core products such as Microsoft Office for the Mac.

Steve Jobs' leadership and Apple's corporate culture

'Some leaders push innovations by being good at the big picture. Others do so by mastering details. Jobs did both, relentlessly.'[15]

Many believe that Jobs' reputation as one of the greatest technology entrepreneurs is not based so much on his knowledge of technology (he was not an engineer or a programmer, neither did he have an MBA or college degree) but on his innate instinct for design, the ability to choose the most talented team and 'the willingness to be a pain in for what matters for him most', such as great design and user-friendliness.[16] Strategically speaking, Jobs understood that to be different as a company, you have to make tough choices; in Apple's case, this was clearly reflected in the product-markets it decided to pursue, as compared for example to large competitors. Referring to Apple's focus, he noted, 'I'm as proud of what we don't do as I am of what we do.'[17] For many years, Jobs stimulated thinking out of the box and encouraged employees to experiment and share with others 'the coolest new thing' they had thought of. It may not be accidental that Apple's emblem of corporate culture is a pirate flag with an Apple rainbow coloured eye patch, designed after a famous Jobs' quote: 'It's better to be a pirate than join the navy.' This flag was hanging over the Macintosh building as Apple's team was working on the first iMac, to act as a reminder of their mission.[18] Jobs could be inspirational, but also experienced by employees as scary. According to Guy Kawasaki (celebrated author and ex-Apple employee):

'Working for Steve was a terrifying and addictive experience. . . . Watching him crucify someone scared you into working incredibly long hours. . . . Working for Steve was also ecstasy. Once in a while he would tell you that you were great and that made it all worth it.'[19]

Apple's organisation design was flat and simple. Even though Apple did not have an official organisation chart, one interpretation of its design was that the organisation radiated around the CEO, with 15 senior vice presidents and 31 vice presidents overseeing the main functions. In terms of this structure, the CEO would only be two levels away from any key part of the company; and financial management was centralised, with the only executive responsible for costs and expenses being the Chief Financial Officer.[20] Apart from ensuring confidentiality, other aspects of Apple's organisational design provide the necessary agility and focus. Small teams bear responsibility for crucial projects, a characteristic that is reminiscent of start-up companies. Committees are not prevalent at Apple. As Jobs said: 'We are organised like a startup. . . . We are the biggest startup on the planet. And we all meet for three hours once a week and we talk about everything we are doing, the whole business.'[21]

In addition to secrecy and a start-up mentality, Apple's culture focuses on intense work, creativity and perfectionism. Each manufacturing and software detail is worked and reworked until a product is considered perfect, aiming for seamless integration of software and hardware. Apple's employees are not paid significantly more than those in other technology companies nor are they pampered, nor do they enjoy unique privileges beyond what most large companies offer, yet Apple recruited talent of the highest calibre. Specialisation and clear specification of responsibilities at Apple was a way of employing the best people for particular roles, reflecting Jobs' aversion towards a general management approach.[22]

In August 2011, Jobs resigned from his position as CEO and Tim Cook, former chief operating officer, was appointed as CEO. Cook's leadership role in Apple's operations since 1998 had given him a deep understanding of the company and a prominent position, being the only person to have a vast area of responsibility apart from Jobs (and he replaced him during his medical absences). Jobs remained at Apple as chairman until his death in October 2011.

Entering a new Apple era

'In the 26 years that *Fortune* has been ranking America's Most Admired Companies never has the corporation at the head of the list so closely resembled a one-man show.'[23]

This inextricable link between Apple and its visionary founder Steve Jobs was one of the main reasons analysts thought that the future of Apple under a new leader would never recreate past glories. Upon becoming Apple's CEO, Tim Cook maintained a low profile and focused on managing the transition to the post-Jobs era as smoothly as possible. In stark contrast to his predecessor's flamboyant personality, Cook is known as a low-key and soft-spoken workaholic, who guards his privacy closely. At the same time he is known to have a tough side: 'He could skewer you with a sentence' a colleague reported.

During Cook's first 16 months as CEO, Apple introduced the next generation of iPhones and iPads and saw its share price rise by 43 per cent.[24] In an industry characterised by declining prices, Apple maintained a strategy of keeping high selling prices attracting a high-value customer base. The iPhone was expected to maintain its price of around $600 when by 2018 Android phones were expected to be sold at around $200. Similarly, Macs were sold at a premium average price of $1300 in a PC market where the company's main competitors sell PCs at an average price point of $311.[25] In one of his rare interviews Tim Cook underlined his belief that Apple should remain focused on having a small number of high-quality products that seemingly integrate software, hardware and services.[26] To Cook, the mobile industry doesn't race to the bottom, it splits: 'There's a segment of the market that really wants a product that does a lot for them, and I want to compete like crazy for those customers.'[27]

Building Apple's future

Despite Apple's financial success under Cook's leadership, the chances that Apple could revive its past glories seemed rather slim when Cook took over. Apple's reliance on the iPhone (accounting for more than half of Apple's revenue and gross profit), at the time when phones running on free Android software were on the rise, had left Apple with a shrinking share of the smartphone market.[28] At the same time, Cook inherited a decentralised company of specialised groups (hardware, software design, marketing, and finance) all tussling for turf after Job's passing.[29]

For some time, changes within the company remained largely invisible to the public. The decisive moment for Cook came at the end of his first year as CEO when he decided to fire Scott Forstall, one of Jobs' most trusted employees, head of software development for the iPad and iPhone but also responsible for the poorly received Apple Maps and Siri voice recognition service. When the dismissal was announced, Cook immediately arranged meetings with senior managers to explain the new structure: Jonathan Ive, Apple's head of design, was given control over the look and feel of iOS while development of the mobile operating system was consolidated with Mac software under Craig Federighi, the senior vice president for software engineering. Ive had joined Apple in 1992 and was appointed senior vice president of industrial design in 1997 shortly after Jobs returned to Apple, and he had a brilliant track record as a designer. Ive's promotion marked an important shift in the company's structure as previously only Steve Jobs held those same responsibilities. Analysts explained Cook's decision in view of intensifying competition by Samsung and Google:

'Tim is a supply-chain expert and he needs to rely on people like Jon to be able to make the right decisions,' said David Yoffie, a professor at Harvard Business School,[30] while others noted that by letting Ive lead Apple's design Cook mitigated speculation that Apple was falling short on innovation.[31] Following his promotion, Ive worked closely with Federighi, in designing Apple's operating system, iOS 7, which was the biggest overhaul of the OS ever. In the following years, Apple also went on a hiring spree of accomplished professionals such as Patrick Pruniaux, the chief salesman at watchmaker Tag Heuer, Paul Deneve, the former CEO of 'haute couture' house Yves Saint Laurent, and Angela Ahrendts, Burberry's former chief executive – all of which added a diversity of views within Apple.

In 2014, Apple presented the large-screen iPhone 6 (and its even bigger iPhone 6 Plus), a new payment system (Apple Pay) and Apple Watch (the first product since Jobs passing that put Apple in a new product category). These launches also marked an effort to increase inter-device integration. Embedded in the iPhone 6, the iOS 8 and Mac OS X Yosemite operating system, a feature called 'Continuity' allowed users to start an email or any other task on their Mac, pick it up on their iPhone, and then move it to their iPad or even the Apple Watch. 'We would never have gotten there in the old model. . . . These new products are reminders of why we exist. The things we should be doing at Apple are things that others can't,' Cook said.[32] Another illustration of Cook's focus on products that combine hardware, software and services was the introduction of Apple Pay, a service that enables users to touch their finger to the Touch ID finger scanner on their iPhone, tap their handset against a credit card terminal, and make a payment without having to turn on their phone or open an app.[33] The new iPhones put Apple back on its upward trajectory: 'Sales for iPhone 6s and iPhone 6s Plus have been phenomenal, blowing past any previous first weekend sales results in Apple's history,' said Tim Cook.[34] Apple Pay was also embraced by major banks (Bank of America, Capital One, JPMorgan Chase among others) and key credit card companies as well as by a number of retailers.[35]

Building on the app-store experience, the new Apple TV, launched in 2015, turned content providers into apps allowing users to search for a movie, a TV show title, genre or even the names of individual actors across all the video apps they have installed using Siri.[36] 'Our vision for television is simple and perhaps a little provocative,' said Tim Cook. 'We believe the future of TV is apps.' According to analysts, by opening up the hardware for third-party apps, the Apple TV could transform (through an Apple TV App Store) to a new platform that could move Apple into new opportunities.[37] Under Tim Cook, Apple has also been eager to promote its devices into corporate environments, through strategic partnerships with IBM and Cisco. As consumer demand for iPads hit a plateau in 2014 with slower replacement cycles, demand for tablets in business enterprises was on the rise, with the percentage of tablets in use for business set to increase from 14 per cent in 2015 to 20 per cent by 2018.[38] With the launch of the iPad Pro in 2015, Apple aimed to appeal to hyper-mobile workers who value ease of use and mobility but need a bigger screen, for conducting corporate training, conferencing or consuming a lot of content, whereas the Apple Pencil companion increased the appeal for professional designers. The advanced, bigger and faster iPad Pro was presented with representatives of Microsoft and Adobe who highlighted its usability in the professional market. These outside partnerships were well received by analysts who saw in Cook an ability to keep an open mind and a clear vision. Ginni Rometty, IBM's chief executive, called Cook the 'hallmark of a modern-day CEO. . . . It's all about clarity of vision and knowing what to do and what not to do.'[39]

Future challenges

With Apple reaching new profit and sales records under his leadership, Tim Cook is under more pressure than ever to maintain Apple's performance. By the end of 2015, Apple had set a pace for itself that was hard to keep up. Already the second half of 2016 marked the end of Apple's streak of 51 consecutive quarters of uninterrupted sales growth as fewer consumers upgraded to the latest iPhones and revenues from China, Apple's second most important region, fell by 26 per cent compared to 2015.[40] At the same time, consumers had not yet issued their verdict on the Apple Watch, Cook's biggest bet as chief executive. If consumers are confused or hesitant, the questions about his strategic decisions, and Apple's ability to innovate, will return with a new ferocity.[41] Leading the most scrutinised and successful company in the world has put Cook in a challenging position.

Notes and references

1. $1 = £0.69 = €0.89.
2. http://www.forbes.com/companies/apple/.
3. C. Liyan, 'The world's largest tech companies: Apple beats Samsung, Microsoft, Google', *Forbes*, 5 November 2015.
4. Ibid.
5. N. McAlone, 'Apple is the most valuable brand in the world – for the third year in a row', *Business Insider*, 5 October 2015.
6. P. Burrows, 'The seed of Apple's innovation'. Interview with Steve Jobs, *Business Week*, 12 October 2004.
7. A. Pressman, 'Why Apple shares just hit a near two-year low', *Fortune*, 6 May 2016.
8. C. Booth, 'Steve's job: restart Apple', *Time*, 18 August 1997.
9. Technology that makes Apple products separate from other companies' technologies and hence difficult, if not impossible, to integrate with non-Apple products.
10. B. Solomon, 'It's official: Apple adds Dr. Dre with $3 billion beats deal', *Forbes*, 28 May 2014.
11. J. Cruikshank, *The Apple Way*, McGraw Hill, New York, 2006.
12. L. Grossman, 'How Apple does it', *Time*, 16 October 2005.
13. B. Morris, 'What makes Apple golden', *Fortune*, 17 March 2008.
14. Apple Inc. Company Profile, 25 May 2015. Reference Code: 5B0A0C20-9BB6-4284-A575-AC0F2261F45C.
15. W. Isaacson, 'American icon', *Time*, 17 October 2011.
16. L. Grossman, 'How Apple does it', *Time*, 16 October 2005.
17. P. Burrows and R. Grover, 'Steve Jobs' magic kingdom', *Business Week*, 6 February 2006.
18. A. Lashinsky, 'How Apple works: Inside the world's biggest startup', *Fortune*, 25 August 2011.
19. G. Kawasaki, *The Mackintosh Way*, Scott Foresman Trade, 1989.
20. A. Lashinsky, 'How Apple works: Inside the world's biggest startup', *Fortune*, 25 August 2011.
21. P. Kafka, 'Apple CEO Steve Jobs at D8: the full uncut interview', 7 June 2010, http://allthingsd.com/20100607/steve-jobs-at-d8-the-full-uncut-interview/.
22. A. Lashinsky, 'How Apple works: Inside the world's biggest startup', *Fortune*, 25 August 2011.
23. P. Elkind, 'the trouble with Steve Jobs', *Fortune*, 5 March 2008.
24. 'Cook says lives enriched matter more than money made', *Bloomberg*, 6 December 2012.
25. Apple Inc. Company Profile, 25 May 2015. Reference Code: 5B0A0C20-9BB6-4284-A575-AC0F2261F45C.
26. S. Grobart, 'Tim Cook: the complete interview', *Bloomberg*, 20 September 2013.
27. S. Grobart, 'Apple chiefs discuss strategy, market share – and the new iPhones', *Bloomberg*, 20 September 2013.
28. B. Stone and A. Satariano, 'Tim Cook interview: the iPhone 6, the Apple Watch, and remaking a company's culture', *Bloomberg*, 17 September 2014.
29. B. Stone and A. Satariano, 'Tim Cook interview: the iPhone 6, the Apple Watch, and remaking a company's culture', *Bloomberg*, 17 September 2014.
30. Satariano 'Apple's Ive seen risking iOS 7 delay on software overhaul', *Bloomberg*, 1 May 2013.
31. C. Thompson, 'How Apple has changed since Steve Jobs', *CNBC*, 4 October 2013.
32. B. Stone and A. Satariano, 'Tim Cook interview: the iPhone 6, the Apple Watch, and remaking a company's culture', *Bloomberg*, 17 September 2014.
33. B. Stone and A. Satariano, 'Tim Cook interview: the iPhone 6, the Apple Watch, and remaking a company's culture', *Bloomberg*, 17 September 2014.
34. T. Bradshaw, 'Apple iPhone 6s beats high end of sales', *Financial Times*, 28 September 2015.
35. B. Stone and A. Satariano, 'Tim Cook interview: the iPhone 6, the Apple Watch, and remaking a company's culture', *Bloomberg*, 17 September 2014.
36. M. Ingram, 'Apple TV continues the unbundling of traditional television', *Fortune*, 10 September 2015.
37. A. Tilley, 'New Apple TV hardware gets major overhaul, but big price hike will make it a difficult sell', *Forbes*, 9 September 2015.
38. A. Konrad, 'With new iPad Pro, Apple makes its move to dominate the enterprise mobility market', *Forbes*, 9 September 2015.
39. B. Stone and A. Satariano, 'Tim Cook interview: the iPhone 6, the Apple Watch, and remaking a company's culture', *Bloomberg*, 17 September 2014.
40. A. Webb, 'Apple forecasts second sales drop as iPhone woes deepen', *Bloomberg*, 26 April 2016.
41. B. Stone and A. Satariano, 'Tim Cook interview: the iPhone 6, the Apple Watch, and remaking a company's culture', *Bloomberg*, 17 September 2014.

CASE STUDY

All change at Teva

Justin Boag and Sarah Holland

This case explores the growth strategies of Teva, an Israel-based company which is now the world's largest 'generic' pharmaceuticals producer. Under the direction of CEO Shlomo Yanai, Teva followed an aggressive inorganic growth programme until 2010, becoming a more diversified pharmaceutical company with markets all over the world. However, the resulting complexity led to a period of reduced profitability and failure to achieve the bold revenue growth targets, creating boardroom tensions and investor unease. A series of top management changes followed, each associated with a new strategy but with disappointing performance. By 2015, those strategies were being discarded in favour of a return to the principles that had served Teva so well in the past: growth through M&A and strategic partnerships, with rapid integration and rationalisation of production capacity.

Introduction

After less than 18 tumultuous months as the head of Teva, the world's largest generic pharmaceuticals company, in October 2013 Jeremy Levin stepped down as CEO. He had been brought into the company in January 2012 to change Teva's strategy from that of the outgoing CEO and President Shlomo Yanai, a former high-ranking army officer, when it seemed clear that the target of achieving global sales of US$D 33bn[1] by 2015 was no longer achievable, and the share price had subsequently collapsed. Its third CEO within two years was appointed in 2014: Erez Vigodman, a company insider, who announced that Teva would introduce its third new global strategy in three years with a focus on product rationalisation, organic growth and cost saving.

Teva in a nutshell

- World's number one generic company
- 15th largest pharmaceutical company
- Sales of $19.7bn in 2015
- Product portfolio of over 1000 molecules
- Active in 120 countries
- 73 manufacturing sites
- 45,000 employees

Teva's operating results for the years 2011–2015 are shown in the Appendix at the end of the case.

Source: Clynt Garnham Medical/Alamy Images.

Founding of Teva

Teva was founded in 1901 in Jerusalem as a small drug wholesale business that distributed imported medications. It moved to manufacturing pharmaceuticals in the 1930s and had a considerable boost in the Second World War supplying allied troops with medical supplies. By 1951, it was being listed on the Israeli stock exchange.

Expansion under Eli Hurvitz and Shlomo Yanai

After a series of consolidations within the Israeli home market, in 1976 the company became Teva Pharmaceutical Industries Ltd, Israel's largest healthcare company, and appointed Eli Hurvitz as the first CEO and President, a role he was to keep until 2002, when he took on the role of Chairman until his departure from ill health in 2010. Under Hurvitz's control Teva's revenue would grow from $30m in 1976 to $16bn in 2010, strongly focused on generic pharmaceuticals. Hurvitz identified the huge opportunity for generic medicines in the USA and Europe when the USA passed laws in 1984 encouraging the sale of generic drugs after patents had expired, if the manufacturer could prove they were equivalent to the original molecule. This rapid growth was achieved through a series of European and US acquisitions focused on generic pharmaceutical companies, moving Teva away from dominating the local Israeli market to eventually becoming the world's largest generic pharmaceutical company.

In the 1980s, a series of collaborations with Israeli university research departments, saw Teva beginning to develop non-generic or branded pharmaceuticals. By the mid-1990s, Teva's first non-generic drug, Copaxone® for the treatment of multiple sclerosis (MS), was approved in Europe and in the USA. Copaxone® still accounted for around 20 per cent of Teva's turnover and 50 per cent of profit in 2015. One of the cornerstones for the successful expansion strategy was a strong focus on cost savings and the very rapid integration of acquired companies.

In April 2002, Hurvitz took on the role of Chairman and appointed another Teva insider, Israel Makov, who had joined Teva in 1995, as CEO. Although some acquisitions were made by Makov, it was a period of relative quiet for the company – albeit with rumours of board room disagreements between Hurvitz and Makov. According to the journalist Mina Kimes, Eli Hurvitz still has a significant influence over Teva: '. . . black and white portraits of him hang on the walls. Employees quote his favoured aphorisms, such as, "It's better to get a speeding ticket than a parking ticket." The company maintains an empty office in Hurvitz's memory at its Jerusalem facility.'[2]

Following the resignation of Israel Makov in 2007, Teva recruited a high-ranking member of the Israeli defence forces, Shlomo Yanai, as Teva's President and CEO. Working with Hurvitz as Chairman, Yanai stated that Teva's aim was to achieve a sales revenue of around $33bn by 2015. Together they oversaw a doubling of sales revenue in just three years, from $8bn in 2007 to $16bn in 2010. This was achieved by a dual approach of aggressive acquisition of competitor generic companies and diversifying the company into over-the-counter (OTC) medicines and looking for branded pharmaceuticals to replace the aging Copaxone®. Aggressive growth in generics was accomplished by the acquisition of Barr in the USA, Ratiopharm in Europe and Taisho and Taiyo in Japan. The company also announced an OTC joint venture with Procter & Gamble.

Purchase of Cephalon and share price collapse

After a period of ill health, Hurvitz stepped down in 2010 and the first non-Israeli Chairman, Philip Frost, a US-based billionaire, was appointed in his place. In May 2011, after a short bidding war, Teva successfully trumped a rival hostile bid from Valeant Pharmaceuticals to acquire Cephalon, a research-based pharmaceutical company of around 4000 employees located in Pennsylvania, USA, in a deal worth $6.8bn.

Cephalon posted sales of $2.76bn in 2010, up 28 per cent, and adjusted net income of $657m, an increase of 40 per cent. Growth was driven by the sleep disorder drug Provigil® and its follow-up long-acting drug Nuvigil®, the cancer drug Treanda® and the cancer painkiller Fentora®. Cephalon also boasted a large research portfolio in several key areas – central nervous system ('CNS'), oncology, respiratory and women's health, the most promising but highest risk being its proprietary stem cell technology.

Valeant, an aggressively acquisitive Canadian pharmaceutical company, had seen in Cephalon's established products an opportunity for further revenue growth and increased profitability, and had bid $5.7bn, but had discounted the value of the therapies in development. The takeover by Teva was welcomed by the board of Cephalon, which saw Teva as an organisation that valued their pipeline and would support their ambitious research and development plans. As Cephalon CEO Kevin Buchi said at the time: 'Teva shares our strong commitment to R&D, and we believe our pipeline will thrive under their leadership.'[3] Mr Yanai added:

> **'Our newly-expanded portfolio in CNS, Oncology, Respiratory and Women's Health along with our robust pipeline of more than 30 late-stage products truly cements our position as a leader in specialty pharma. . . . We are welcoming many of Cephalon's talented employees into the Teva family. The combination of our two winning teams will position Teva to create maximum value for our patients and customers.'[4]**

Teva and Cephalon executives said they saw particular potential in a stem cell therapy for congestive heart failure under development with Mesoblast Ltd, in reslizumab for asthma and in the lung-cancer treatment obatoclax. Ori Hershkovitz, a partner at Sphera Global Healthcare Fund in Tel Aviv commented in an interview at the time: 'Teva's making four or five shots on goal with a very high-risk, high-reward kind of profile. If they pull off the stem-cell product, they're in the clear. But if they pull off two or three of the others, it would also be a very good deal.'[5]

The company, however, had a number of significant challenges: the rapid inorganic expansion in generic pharmaceuticals from 2007–10 meant that the manufacturing base was not consolidated, with over 100 manufacturing sites spread across a large number of countries. Supply chain and quality-control issues had also meant that, in the USA, crucial supplies of two generic drugs had not been made in 2009. The patent protection on Copaxone® was nearing expiry and, ironically for a generics company, around 20–30 per cent of the sales revenue and a significant amount of profit was at risk in the next two to three years of generic erosion with no obvious replacement in view.

The share price began to slide and a number of shareholders called for a significant reduction in costs and expressed dissatisfaction with the decision to purchase Cephalon. In response to this criticism and the falling share price, Philip Frost accepted the resignation of Shlomo Yaniv and appointed Jeremy Levin, a South African born, UK-educated pharmaceutical executive with a highly successful track record at two major pharmaceutical companies. For the first time since its creation, Teva was headed by two outsiders, both non-Israeli citizens and with no previous experience of Teva.

Levin's short tenure

On the announcement of his appointment, Teva's share price increased, major shareholders seeing Levin's strong pharmaceutical background as a good fit for the company. Levin told journalists on his appointment:

'Teva is a company with a unique culture. In the time I have been here, I have had the opportunity to meet the leadership and talent that has made Teva the successful company that it is today. In my experience, Teva has some of the best people in the industry with a level of drive, determination and innovation that is second to none. . . . We will continue to be innovative by focusing not only on how we commercialise but also on how we discover, develop and manufacture – all of which start from the same point – world-class R&D.'[6]

The new CEO started to develop a new strategy aimed at moving Teva towards a business focus on profitability versus one based on revenue growth. There would be a focus on cutting production costs significantly and

actively seeking new products as a replacement for Copaxone®. This strategy it was claimed would reshape the company into 'the most indispensable medicines company in the world' and provide significant value to shareholders.[7]

Teva began a series of rationalisations and economies. aimed at reducing costs by around $2bn per year, involving around 700 job losses in Israel. With the CEO working alongside the new Chairman, it appeared the company had moved into a new era. As Philip Frost stated: 'Teva also must act like a global pharmaceutical company. There's a lot of nostalgia for the good old days when it was a family company and the board got together for a little lunch. That's not what Teva is nowadays.'[8] Levin said Teva would sustain 'profitable growth' but confirmed that the company would not achieve the ambitious previous target of $33bn revenue by 2015.

Key elements of the new strategy included:

- Tailoring the product offering to address regional needs. With its diversified portfolio, Teva was well placed to focus on high-value generics in the USA and Japan, but consumer OTC products in Latin America and Russia, for example.
- Rationalisation of the marketed generic product portfolio. Less profitable products were to be culled, while price increases were implemented for others.
- Globalising key functions to streamline operations and gain economies of scale, cutting costs by $1.5 to $2bn per year.
- New R&D focus on high-value generics. Teva planned to leverage its huge portfolio of over 1400 medicines, and its extensive formulation and drug delivery expertise, to create new combination products that would be harder to imitate than traditional generics. These would offer medical value through improved efficacy or compliance, or reduced side-effects, in order to justify higher prices. For the first time, Teva would incorporate formal medical input to its generics business.
- Refocusing the R&D pipeline, with a strong emphasis on CNS and respiratory products. The oncology product obatoclax developed by Cephalon was discontinued.
- Formation of a drug discovery network comprising all the academic centres in Israel.

The announcement did not meet with shareholder approval and the share price dropped by nearly seven per cent. Cost cutting and consolidation continued, mostly without major workplace disruption, except in Israel where a number of sites threatened strike action.

Throughout Levin's tenure there were rumours of disputes between board members and the new CEO's management team. Dispute apparently came from two directions:

- The Israeli board members who felt that the new CEO working alongside the Chairman failed to understand the unique culture of Teva.
- Rumoured disputes between Frost and Levin over the size and speed of cost cutting.

The relationship between board and directors was often challenging and at one point there were even stories that Levin had hired a private detective agency, which had used a polygraph test on board members to identify the source of boardroom leaks to the press.[9]

Levin departs and Teva enters a new era

In October 2013, following further press speculation and a press story that the management team had sent a memo to the controlling board asking them not to intervene so heavily in management decisions, Jeremy Levin left Teva and the Finance Director was appointed as temporary CEO. The already-lowered share price reduced by a further seven per cent. In an investor call shortly after Levin's departure, Philip Frost stated: 'Since Levin's arrival, the board and management saw eye to eye when formulating the strategy. . . . However, differences of opinion arose between us as to how the strategy will be implemented. In the last few weeks we had talks with Levin and decided that it would be better for our ways to part.'[10]

Other insiders reported that the problems for Levin ran much deeper, not least a failure to understand the unique Israeli character of Teva. As Eldad Tamir, from an Israel-based investment group stated:

'Levin entered a difficult situation. The need for a cultural and communicational connection to Israeli society is critical for Teva. This company is among the cornerstones of the local industry and its products can be found in every home. . . . Teva had an open relationship with its investors, employees and Israeli society. Instead of continuing the cultural tradition they brought in someone else, and it didn't work. There was no continuity for the rootedness. Everything became cold and alienated. Teva needs a local leader.'[11]

Erez Vigodman: a new/old strategy for Teva?

After an extensive international search, a local leader, the Israeli turnaround specialist Erez Vigodman, became Teva's President and CEO in February 2014. He had joined Teva's Board of Directors in 2009. Shortly afterwards, following rumours of disagreements with the new CEO, Frost resigned and a new Chairman was appointed in his place: Yitzhak Peterburg, an Israeli citizen who had worked with Teva in the past. In July 2014, Teva announced a new commercial structure, effectively dividing the company into two business units, the Global Specialty Medicines group and the Global Generic Medicines group. They stated that this would bring a heightened focus on profitable and sustainable business, driven through organic growth of it two business units and in defending Copaxone® from generic competitors by launching a new higher dose formulation. They also stated they would increase their focus on key markets and on key products. The company stated that it would continue its cost-saving drive but would also look for appropriate business development opportunities.

In April 2015, Teva launched a $40bn hostile bid to buy Mylan, a Netherlands-based rival generic pharmaceutical manufacturer. The combined companies would have a turnover of around $30bn and a profitability of around $8bn. Teva argued that cost-saving synergies of around $2bn could be achieved by the acquisition. Teva believed that: 'The combined company would leverage its significantly more efficient and advanced infrastructure, with enhanced scale, production network, end-to-end product portfolio, commercialization capabilities and geographic reach'.[12] Mylan rejected Teva's offer and took the unusual step of publishing the text of a letter sent from its CEO, Robert Coury, to Teva's Erez Vigodman, saying that he hoped Teva's culture would change and they would have more credibility in their future business dealings but that the Mylan board did not want to inflict Teva's problems on Mylan's shareholders. Coury went on to say:

'Since 2007, your Board has churned through three different Chief Executive Officers, running the only one with the global pharmaceutical experience, which we think is critical to the position, out of town within 18 months of being on the job. Any investor should be gravely concerned that an experienced lead executive could be dismissed over "slight differences" of opinion with the Board. We believe that these rapid changes in a short period of time have left the company with a complete lack of long-term strategic focus. While I recognize that you are fairly new to your position, I cannot ignore the fact that you were present on Teva's Board during some of the company's most turbulent and "dysfunctional" times. . . . Ten years of acquisitions and a flip-flopping strategy have left Teva with a smattering of assets in specialty, generics, biotech and consumer. You claim to want to "redefine the generics industry", but what faith can we have that you have any clear vision for the industry at all? And how can investors be assured this "redefinition" will not be abandoned for yet another new strategy?'[13]

The board of Teva replied that they rejected many of the statements in the letter and reiterated their interest in the purchase of Mylan.

Teva buys Allergan's generic business

In a surprise move in July 2015, Teva announced that they were dropping the attempt to buy Mylan, as they had instead entered into a definitive agreement to acquire Allergan's global generic pharmaceuticals business for $40.5bn, with Allergan receiving $33.75bn in cash and $6.75bn in Teva stock. Under the agreement, Teva would acquire Allergan's global generics business, including the US and international generic commercial units, a third-party supplier, global generic manufacturing operations, the global generic R&D unit, the international over-the-counter (OTC) commercial unit (excluding OTC eye-care products) and some established international brands. The acquisition would mean that around 70 per cent of future turnover would be from the sale of generics.

The deal, the largest in Israel's corporate history, was generally welcomed by shareholders and stock market analysts: 'Allergan's business is more high-end [than Mylan]. It's a more interesting business . . . a profitable business and it's well managed,' said Gilad Alper, an analyst at brokerage Excellence Nessuah.[14]

Yitzhak Peterburg said:

'This acquisition will result in significant and sustained value creation for our stockholders, reinforces our strategy, accelerates the fulfilment of a new business model, strongly supports top-line growth and opens a new set of possibilities for Teva. Together with Allergan Generics, Teva will have a much stronger, more efficient platform to achieve our goals – both financially and strategically – with the right platform for future organic and inorganic growth.'[15]

Teva's strategic future?

Following the acquisition of Allergan's generic business, Teva appears to have returned to the business model of expansion in generic pharmaceuticals through aggressive acquisition of competitor manufacturers, as originally laid down by Eli Hurvitz. With closely cooperating Israeli Chairman and CEO, and a stock market eager for further growth, further inorganic growth in the coming years was anticipated. Time will tell, however, if Teva is able to follow the other part of Hurvitz's former strategy: rapid integration of new companies and consolidation and rationalisation of the manufacturing capacity.

Notes and references
1. $1 = £0.6 = €0.75.
2. M. Kimes, 'Teva returns to roots after outside CEO faces "nuthouse"', *Bloomberg*, 4 March, 2014.
3. Teva, 'Teva to acquire Cephalon in $6.8 billion transaction', press release, 2 May 2011.
4. Teva, 'Teva completes acquisition of Cephalon', press release, 14 October 2011.
5. N. Kresge and R. Langreth, 'Teva bets on stem cells, cancer in $6.2 billion bid for Cephalon', *Bloomberg*, 3 May 2011.
6. S. Griver, 'Meet Jeremy Levin, the new head of drugs firm Teva', *Jewish Chronicle*, 17 May 2012.
7. B. Berkrot, 'Teva CEO promises to reshape, refocus company', *Reuters*, 11 December 2012.
8. D. Wainer, 'Billionnaire doctor prescribes small Teva deals for Israeli giant', *Bloomberg*, 5 March 2013.
9. T. Staton, 'Teva's ex-Ceo reportedly forced polygraph tests on board to plug media leaks', *FiercePharma*, 5 November 2013.
10. A. Weisberg, 'Teva chairman: "the company is stronger than ever"', 30 October 2013, http://www.jerusalemonline.com/finance/teva-chairman-the-company-is-stronger-than-ever-2162.
11. N. Zommer, 'Can foreign CEO make it here?', *Ynetnews*, 11 March, 2013.
12. Teva, 'Teva proposes to acquire Mylan for $82.00 per share in cash and stock', press release, 21 April 2015.
13. Mylan, 'Mylan board unanimously rejects unsolicited expression of interest from Teva', press release, 27 April, 2015.
14. M. de la Merced and C. Bray, 'Teva pharmaceuticals to buy Allergan's generics business', *New York Times*, 27 July 2015.
15. Teva, 'Teva to acquire Allergan generics for $40.5 billion dollars creating a transformative generics specialty company well positioned to win in global healthcare', press release, 27 July 2015.

APPENDIX: Teva's operating data

	For the year ended 31 December				
	2015	2014	2013	2012	2011
	US$m (except share and per share amounts)				
Net revenues	19,652	20,272	20,314	20,317	18,312
Cost of sales	8,296	9,216	9,607	9,665	8,797
Gross profit	11,356	11,056	10,707	10,652	9,515
Research and development expenses	1,525	1,488	1,427	1,356	1,095
Selling and marketing expenses	3,478	3,861	4,080	3,879	3,478
General and administrative expenses	1,239	1,217	1,239	1,238	932
Impairments, restructuring and others	1,131	650	788	1,259	430
Legal settlements and loss contingencies	631	(111)	1,524	715	471
Operating income	3,352	3,951	1,649	2,205	3,109

Source: 2015 Annual Report of Teva Pharmaceutical Industries Ltd.

Mondelēz International: 'Are you going to stick around, Irene?' Acquisition, de-merger, divestment and governance in the growth strategy of Mondelēz International

Eric Cassells

This case explores corporate strategy as it emerges over time, through the example of Mondelēz International. The origins of Mondelēz lie in the long-term growth strategy to create a global snacks business within what was the Kraft food group. The case focuses on the initial major acquisition of Cadbury PLC by Kraft as a means to achieve scale and global coverage in snacks, the subsequent de-merger from Kraft's slow-growing grocery business, and the divestment of the more volatile coffee business into an equity alliance ('JDE') to allow the creation of a focused Mondelēz snacks business. All of these events occur against the backdrop of pressures to deliver against corporate forecasts built on expectations of growth in a volatile marketplace, and the pressures on the corporate managers dealing with activist and short-term investors is also considered in some detail.

The ChicagoBusiness.com line on 6 August 2015 was attempting to put Irene Rosenfeld in play, with the question: 'Are Mondelēz CEO Irene Rosenfeld's days numbered?' It followed a period of market speculation over whether PepsiCo (or another competitor) would acquire Mondelēz, and the announcement of a 7.5 per cent stake acquisition in Mondelēz by 'activist' shareholder William Ackman and his Pershing Square Capital Management on 5 August. Come 23 December, Irene was very much still in place at Mondelēz, and CNNMoney nominated her as one of their top ten 'Best CEOs of the year' for 'coping with activists'. A few days earlier in the UK, the arena of her bitter acquisition of Cadbury in 2009–10, the *Independent* newspaper profiled her as 'the (. . .) chocolate boss with a hard centre'.

The rise of Irene Rosenfeld

Born in 1953, Ms Rosenfeld spent the first decade of her career accumulating degrees (including a PhD in Marketing and Statistics) from Cornell University. After a brief spell in advertising, she joined General Foods, at the start of a 30-year plus career in the food and beverage industry. In time, General Foods was acquired by Kraft, and Ms Rosenfeld has largely stayed within this one evolving group ever since. Arguably, her key career break came on the one occasion she ventured outside the Kraft group in 2004, to become chair and CEO of PepsiCo's large snacks business – Frito-Lay. By June 2006, Kraft had wooed her back to become CEO of the

entire Kraft group. In 2011, Kraft announced it would de-merge, with its North American grocery business retaining the Kraft name, and its larger international snacks and confectionery business being named Mondelēz. Irene Rosenfeld chose to stay as the CEO of Mondelēz.

Ms Rosenfeld is recognised as a powerful businesswoman (ranked 17 in 2014 in Forbes' annual list of 'The World's 100 Most Powerful Women'). Less welcome recognition, perhaps, is her honourable mention in 2013 in *FT* columnist Lucy Kellaway's annual business Golden Flannel Awards, in the Chief Obfuscation Champion category. Her profile in the *Independent* (December 2014), however, notes her 'legendary' reputation for attention to detail, an ultra-competitive streak derived in part from a sporting background, her boldness in making brave moves, and her willingness to 'face off . . . formidable foes.' It also reports views that she can be 'remote and clinical'.

Transforming Kraft – the acquisition of Cadbury PLC

Prior to the de-merger of the Kraft Corporation in 2011, Irene Rosenfeld was at the centre of one of the most controversial hostile acquisitions of recent decades. Between August 2009 and February 2010, Kraft fought a hard battle to acquire the UK confectionery giant, Cadbury PLC, eventually acquiring it for £11.5bn (€13.8bn, $17.3bn).[1] Cadbury was a pillar of the British

---

The case was prepared by Eric Cassells, of the Business and Management Department at Oxford Brookes University Business School, UK. It is intended as a basis for class discussion and not as an illustration of good or bad practice. © Eric Cassells, 2016. Not to be reproduced or quoted without permission.

Table 1

Kraft strategic priorities	The importance of the Cadbury acquisition
Focus on growth categories to transform Kraft into a leading snack, confectionery and quick meal company.	A combined global portfolio of 40 leading confectionery brands, each with sales in excess of $100m.
Expand its footprint and scale in growing developing markets.	Cadbury offers Kraft a complementary presence in developing markets, with Kraft strength and channels in Brazil, China and Russia, and Cadbury in India, Mexico and South Africa.
Increase presence in 'instant consumption' channels as they continued to grow relative to traditional grocery channels in the established US and EU markets.	Kraft's strength lay in traditional grocery channels, whereas Cadbury was well placed in 'instant consumption' channels.
Pursue margin growth, through improved portfolio mix, reducing costs and investing in quality.	The higher exposure to confectionery of a post-acquisition Kraft would provide Kraft shareholders with an improved portfolio of higher-margin growth products.

business establishment and had a history as a benevolent employer, noted, for example, for pioneering employee pensions. The company was rooted in the communities it operated in (notably at Cadbury's headquarters in Bourneville, south of Birmingham, where a model village was constructed after 1893 to show how employees could be better housed in the factory age).

Kraft's rationale for acquiring Cadbury was laid out in its bid offer documents (see Table 1).

Kraft's bid did not attract the uniform support of its own investors. The largest shareholder in Kraft was Berkshire Hathaway, led by the prominent investor Warren Buffet, arguably the most influential and best-known investor in the world, and a favourite of the US financial news channels. On 16 September 2009, Buffet warned that Kraft must not 'overpay' for Cadbury, expressing concern at the offer to Cadbury of an 'attractive' EBITDA multiple of 13.9 times. Buffet was a long-term supporter of the Kraft corporation, holding 9.4 per cent of shares. More provocatively, perhaps, on Bloomberg's business news channel on 19 January, whilst describing Kraft CEO Irene Rosenfeld as a 'good person', Buffet described the increased final takeover offer as a 'bad deal'. He dismissed the potential synergy benefits identified in Kraft's offer document, saying he was distrustful of unrealised benefits. He stated that, 'If I had a chance to vote on this, I'd vote no'. Referring to the proposed acquisition of Cadbury, he concluded, 'I feel poorer'. Kraft's shares fell two per cent on his intervention.[2] Irene Rosenfeld was asked about Buffet's intervention on Bloomberg TV. Refusing to be drawn, she stated that she believed Buffet was evaluating the deal from the basis of existing cash flow and that he was ignoring the potential transformational synergies that were at the heart of the strategy to acquire Cadbury.

In addition to the 'transformational' rationale put forward by Kraft for the deal, the offer documents identified potential cost savings of $625m. The $625m was to come from savings and scale economies in procurement,

manufacturing, customer service, logistics and R&D ($300m), general and administrative costs ($200m), and marketing and selling costs ($125m). These savings estimates were in line with historic transaction experience for the sector at 6.5 per cent of revenues.

Resistance to the deal in the UK was led by the trade unions (concerned that up to 7000 jobs might be lost as part of those 'savings'), by the nationalist heritage lobby (concerned by the impact on Cadbury's communities, and concern for national prestige with the loss of a large global corporation headquartered in the UK), and by Cadbury family members (concerned that a distinctive 'values-led' corporation would be destroyed). Local and UK national governments also expressed their concern that Cadbury's base in the UK (including its R&D centres), and its status as a global leader in confectionery, might be subverted.

In the event, Kraft was forced to raise its offer for Cadbury by over 12 per cent (Warren Buffet's 'bad deal') to secure the recommendation of the Cadbury board, and concluded the deal in late January 2010. Their case may have been helped in no small measure by the interventions of short-term traders and hedge funds, increasing their aggregate holdings in Cadbury from about five per cent in August 2009 at the start of the bid, to an estimated 40 per cent by the end. Cadbury argued that the actions of these short-term arbitraging investors effectively de-stabilised Cadbury's defence. Concerns over their behaviour and interests were also raised by UK politicians during and after the acquisition.

Political and regulatory concerns over the Cadbury acquisition – 'Where's Irene?'

The Cadbury takeover process caused consternation in the press, trade unions, politicians, regulators and general public in the UK. So much so, that the Business, Innovation and Skills (BIS) Committee of the UK's House of Commons issued a report on 6 April 2010 which stated that: 'The Kraft takeover of Cadbury has proved to be an event which is likely to shape future public policy towards takeovers and corporate governance.'[3] The report was highly critical of the behaviour of Kraft, and bloggers gleefully described MPs as 'fighting each other to lay into Kraft.' MP Lindsay Hoyle, at one point queried whether Kraft is 'remote, smug, and . . . duplicitous'.

The more measured tones of the Committee's report focused on two issues primarily:

1. Kraft made a promise (made during the takeover battle) to reverse Cadbury's recent announced decision to close its Somerdale factory and move that production to Poland. The promise (to reverse the closure) was subsequently withdrawn by Kraft less than three weeks after it took control of Cadbury, and production moved to Poland regardless. The Committee's formal conclusion was measured but damning, opining that: 'Kraft acted both irresponsibly and unwisely in making its original statement . . . (and) has left itself open to the charge that either it was incompetent in its approach . . . or that it used a "cynical ploy" to improve its public image during its takeover of Cadbury.'[3]

2. The Committee also expressed their 'disappointment' that: 'Irene Rosenfeld, the Chairman and CEO of Kraft Foods Inc. did not give evidence in person. Her attendance at our evidence session would have given an appropriate signal of Kraft's commitment to Cadbury in the UK and provided the necessary authority to the specific assurances Kraft have now given to the future of Cadbury.'[3]

Indeed, during the proceedings, MPs simply demanded 'where's Irene?' and lambasted Kraft's senior representative at the hearing, Marc Firestone, as an 'apologist' for her, calling her absence a 'sizeable discourtesy'.[3] The *Daily Telegraph* newspaper quoted Ms Rosenfeld's robust response that: 'Attendance would not be the best use of my personal time.'

As to the commitments Kraft made to the BIS, in December 2010 a plan to shed 200 jobs at Cadbury's Bourneville plant was announced. At the same time, Kraft announced a £17m investment in research at its designated sole global 'Centre of Excellence for Chocolate', now located in Bourneville. The BIS Committee revisited events in April 2011 to monitor Kraft's commitments. Concern was expressed at poor engagement between Kraft and the trade unions, and the perception that strategic decisions over the Cadbury brands were being made in Kraft's European headquarters in Zurich. More personal criticism followed for Ms Rosenfeld: 'In a repeat of our predecessors' experience, Irene Rosenfeld (. . .) refused to give evidence despite repeated requests from us that she should appear.

Neither that refusal to attend, nor the manner of it, reflected well on Kraft . . . '[4]

The Cadbury acquisition as part of a longer-term strategy

Warren Buffet reduced his holding in Kraft from 9.5 per cent to nearer 6 per cent in the immediate aftermath of the bid. His comments at the time reflected the belief that bidders often overpay to the detriment of their shareholders, and that Kraft would suffer the 'winner's curse' (of having paid too much for synergies that would take much longer to deliver, or of ignoring the real costs of post-acquisition integration).

On the release of Kraft's fourth quarter results for 2010, commentators believed that shareholders were still 'wondering whether they bit off more than they could chew when they put up £11.5bn for Cadbury last year.'[5] Net profits had fallen 24 per cent to $540m in the quarter, reflecting the scale of integration costs, and a 'disappointing' 2.2 per cent rise in Cadbury's like-for-like sales, well behind the 5 per cent sales growth that Cadbury had posted in its last period of independence. The deal had certainly not yet shown itself to be the transformational move that Ms Rosenfeld staked her reputation on. Kraft's next move to transform itself was less expected.

When interviewed on Bloomberg TV on 16 September 2010, Ms Rosenfeld re-affirmed that Cadbury was 'a critical piece of the puzzle we have been trying to complete.' On 4 August 2011, Kraft announced its intention to split into two separate corporations, and the criticality of the Cadbury acquisition became more obvious.

Kraft said these two businesses, 'differ in their future strategic priorities, growth profiles and operational focus.'[6] The lower-growth North American grocery foods business was to include brands such as Kraft cheeses, Maxwell house coffee and Capri Sun, with revenues of $16bn. At the same time, a more focused but globally spread snacks and confectionery business (including Trident gum, Oreo cookies, Milka chocolate and Cadbury) would have estimated revenues of $36bn, with over 100,000 employees in 80 countries. This snacks business was poised to take advantage of the perceived shifts in consumer behaviour towards snacking, rather than cooking two or three meals each day.

Within the confectionery arm of that global snacks business, Cadbury brands represented over 80 per cent of revenues. The rationale for the global snacks business remained that which drove the Cadbury acquisition: to move into higher growth segments as a 'snack, confectionery, and instant consumption' company, and to increase footprint and 'white space' synergies for 'iconic brands' in fast-growing emerging markets.

The de-merger took place on 1 October 2012 when the North American grocery business started trading as Kraft Foods Group Inc., whilst the global snacks business became Mondelēz International, with Ms Irene Rosenfeld firmly at its helm. Benefits from the Kraft de-merger were to be 'evident in the first year'.[7] The Kraft Foods Group commenced trading on NASDAQ, and gained 2.99 per cent in the day's trading to reach $45.42. On the same day, shares in Mondelēz International opened at $28.42, before softening to $28.01.

Mondelēz strategy after de-merger

The name 'Mondelēz' was coined by two of the company's employees in response to a naming competition, a composite of Romance/Latin words for 'world' and 'delicious'. It was chosen to evoke the global ambitions needed to take on the 'global titans' of PepsiCo's snacks business, Frito-Lay, and Nestlé SA. The name was intended only as a 'small print' label, with the famous brand names such as Ritz, Oreo, Cadbury and Milka taking prominence for consumers. Despite the intention that it was not to be a consumer brand, some queried the failure to spend money to use a professional naming agency, and others criticised the chosen name as having meaning only in the Mediterranean Latin countries of France, Spain, Italy and Portugal: 'I doubt that its connotations are going to be so obvious to English, German, Japanese, or Chinese speakers . . . it's saving grace is that it's just a name for a corporate entity.'[8]

The two main strands of the Mondelēz strategy were laid out by Tim Cofer, European president at Mondelēz International, speaking in October 2012: 'Forty-four per cent of our revenue will come from the emerging markets, benefitting from the growth there,' with Europe accounting for 37 per cent, and North America less than 20 per cent. Further, Mondelēz was poised to take advantage of a significant change in the world's eating habits: 'Snacking is a behaviour that is growing, and we have a strong leadership position in this area. Snacking categories are growing much faster than non-snacking businesses, and it's a great position to be in.'[9]

Mondelēz having divorced itself from the low margin, slow-growing North American grocery business, many analysts approved.[10] Particular comments were made on Mondelēz's focus on emerging markets, with their three-cluster priority strategy of targeting: first, the BRIC markets, followed by 'next wave' markets (Indonesia, Middle East and Africa), and finally 'scale' market opportunities in Australia, Japan, Mexico and Central Europe. Whilst Cadbury had provided much-needed presence in the Indian market, strength in the Chinese market came from the dominance of the Oreo cookie in the biscuit/cookies market. In May 2013, it was reported that $600m was to be channelled into advertising and supply chain improvements in these markets over the following three years.

Writing about the wider 'packaged foods' sector in March 2014, Skelly[11] noted that Mondelēz (with 2.2 per cent global maket share) faced strong competitors in Nestlé (3.4 per cent), PepsiCo (2.1 per cent), Unilever (1.7 per cent), Danone (1.4 per cent), Mars (1.4 per cent) and others such as Kraft Foods, Kellogg, General Mills and Lactalis, all of which were aware of the importance of the emerging markets. Mondelēz's key strengths were seen as: a more even global distribution of their key brands (see Figure 1); owning nine globally recognised 'power brands' (see Figure 2); expertise and potential for 'cross-branding' to leverage those power brands and fill in the market 'white space'; a strong supporting network of manufacturing and distribution facilities in Latin

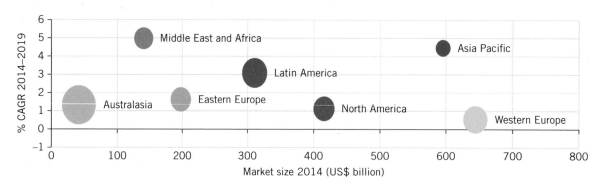

Figure 1 Mondelēz's balanced geographic portfolio 2014 and growth 2014–2019 by region

Note: Bubble size shows company shares of region in 2014; range displayed 0.4–3.1%.

Source: Skelly/*Euromonitor*, 2014.

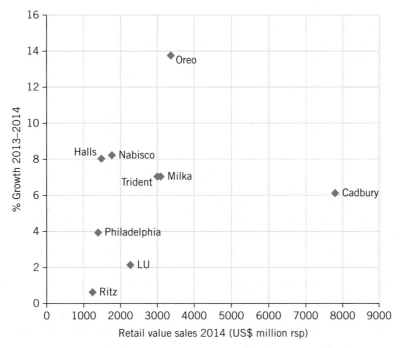

Figure 2 Mondelēz billion dollar brands: retail value sales 2014 vs percentage growth 2013–14
Source: Skelly/*Euromonitor*, 2014.

America, Asia Pacific, Eastern Europe, Middle East and Africa; and a strong position to exploit future biscuit growth in India. Set against these competitive strengths, however, they had weaknesses in the US chocolate confectionery market (where the historic rights to manufacture Cadbury products lay instead with Hershey), a virtually complete reliance on sweet (rather than savoury) snacks, and greater exposure to volatile cocoa and coffee commodity prices.

The Mondelēz power brands in the 'packaged foods' sector were concentrated in the two categories, confectionery and biscuits (see Figure 3). Mondelēz was the dominant manufacturer of biscuits in the world, with 18 per cent market share (six times larger than Kellogg in second place), and with four of the top five labels (Oreo, TUC, LU and Nabisco). With Cadbury, Milka and Trident, it also accounted for the largest 14 per cent global market share in confectionery.

This narrowed product portfolio (by 'packaged food' sector standards) was, of course, the very result of the de-merger, and in pursuing these higher growth businesses, Mondelēz had arguably increased its dependence on the performance of the confectionery and biscuits markets. Within these categories, the heightened

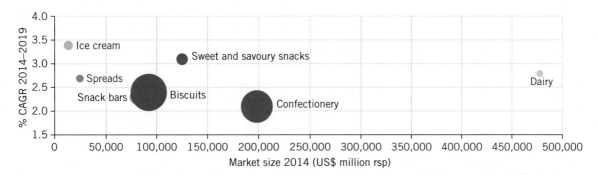

Figure 3 Mondelēz product category portfolio 2014 and growth prospects 2014–2019 by category
Note: Bubble size shows company share of category in 2013; range displayed 0.4–18.0%.
Source: Skelly/*Euromonitor*, 2014.

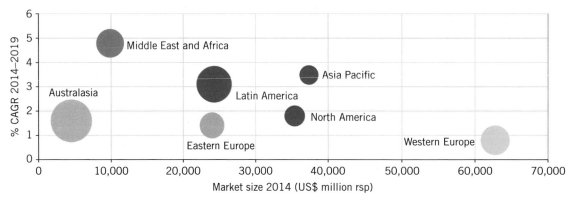

Figure 4 Mondelēz International Inc.: confectionery growth prospects by region 2014–19

Note: Bubble size shows region's proportion of Mondelēz % value share in confectionery from 7.5% for Asia Pacific to 33.2% for Australasia.

Source: Skelly/*Euromonitor*, 2014.

importance of the emerging markets can be seen by, for example, the market growth prospects by region for confectionery (see Figure 4).

How did Mondelēz fare in the emerging markets?

The risks inherent in running an international business had already been acknowledged by Kraft in September 2012, prior to the de-merger, where it was noted, for example, that reported earnings in 2013 for Mondelēz would likely be lower than some forecasts due to the strengthening of the US dollar (Mondelēz's reporting currency) against a basket of other international currencies. At the same time, Tim Cofer had suggested that Mondelēz was 'well positioned to cope with volatile commodity prices'.

Revenues from emerging markets had been soaring by 23 per cent in 2011, as GDP in the BRICs countries increased by 6.9 per cent. With US GDP growing at only 1.8 per cent, the de-merger and divestment of Kraft's slow-growing North American grocery business from Mondelēz made 'Ms Rosenfeld look genius'.[12] The growth rating that Mondelēz was attracting has, however, faltered in the short term, as emerging market GDP growth dipped to 5.2 per cent in 2013 (recovering to 5.3 per cent in 2014, before dipping once more to 4.4 per cent in 2015, with an estimate of 4.9 per cent for 2016). At the same time, the developed world GDP (led to some extent by the USA) showed slightly enhanced growth in the 2.0 to 2.4 per cent range.[13] In addition, Mondelēz suffered from a poor competitive performance with the failure of expected sales growth in Brazil and Russia specifically, and sales of the key Oreos cookies brand faltering in 2013–14 in China. This change in the balance of

economic growth played directly against Mondelēz's intended strategy and, for example, led to Mondelēz's revenue growth from the emerging markets slowing to only 8 per cent in 2012, with operating income from these markets down 22 per cent. Further difficult years were recorded in 2013 and 2014, with Ms Rosenfeld noting in February 2014 that, 'frankly, we're very disappointed that our performance was below what we and our shareholders originally expected.'[12] Michael Silverstein of Boston Consulting Group hinted at this dilemma: 'Everyone knows the growth is there, but there is high year-to-year variability. One year of turmoil does not really break long-term trends. No company should be choosing to invest in developing markets for a short-term bump. It's about riding the 10-year doubling, tripling of market size.'[12]

Investor pressures to improve profit margins

Persuading all investors that a highly focused snacks and confectionery business, geared to the growth of the emerging markets, is a good investment, at the same time as results deteriorate, has not been a straightforward task. According to data from the *Wall Street Journal* (see also Figure 5), Mondelēz's shareholders had seen a 68 per cent total return in the period from October 2012 (the de-merger) to December 2015. The equivalent return for the Standard & Poor 500 index was 55 per cent, and sector returns were even less at 52 per cent. Investors looking to the promise of emerging market growth that failed to materialise appeared to want more. In a September report by Sanford C. Bernstein & Co., analyst Alexia Howard wrote: 'If Mondelēz fails to live up to the expectations of investors, or leaves money on the table with respect to the potential for further cost-cutting

Pressure Cooker

Snack-food maker Mondelēz International, after its split from Kraft Foods, has been under pressure from two activist investors to improve performance.

$50 a share

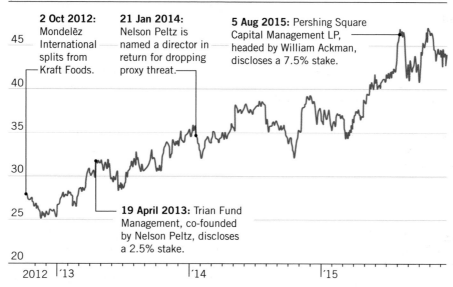

Figure 5 Mondelēz share price performance, October 2012–December 2015
Source: WSJ Market Data Group.

and margin improvement, the company runs the risk of becoming a target.'[14]

These comments were not new for 2015. This pressure to improve operating margins and reduce overheads has been a near constant after Mondelēz's de-merger from Kraft was completed, since it became clear that emerging market growth was more muted than expected. Whilst Warren Buffet reduced his exposure to Kraft in the wake of the Cadbury acquisition, one of the supporters of that deal has proved more persistent. Nelson Peltz (and his investment company, Trian Fund Management) liked the idea of a global snacks and confectionery business so much that on 17 July 2013 he announced his belief that PepsiCo should acquire Mondelēz (which he criticised for poor profit margins), merge it with its own Frito-Lay snacks subsidiary, and divest its own slow-growing soft drinks business (including its iconic 'Pepsi' brands). Trian was a shareholder in both companies (at 2.5 per cent, the fourth largest Mondelēz shareholder), but the initial reaction from the market and other PepsiCo shareholders was less than enthusiastic.

The intervention was unwelcome to Ms Rosenfeld, regardless, effectively underlining the questions about Mondelēz's performance and seeking to put the company 'in play'. Peltz's campaign to persuade PepsiCo to launch a bid for Mondelēz persisted until January 2014, when, under pressure, Mondelēz offered him a seat on the board of the company. In exchange, Peltz dropped his campaign, his threat of a proxy fight against the board to put the company up for sale, and concentrated instead on trying to persuade PepsiCo to sell its drinks business.

The manoeuvre of offering Mr Peltz a seat on the board seemed consistent with Ms Rosenfeld's strategy of trying to engage with activists without ceding authority to them – in her words, keeping them 'inside the tent'. Mr Peltz was not a 'typical board member', however, asking for detailed information about company spending by country, and interviewing Ms Rosenfeld about expected return on investment (ROI) data on large investments in global plant modernisation.

Even as Ms Rosenfeld invited Mr Peltz onto the board, others were lining up to pressure Mondelēz management into further cuts. In April 2014, for example, Ralph Whitworth of Relational Investors LLC, stated he was joining Trian in pressing for better margins:[15] 'We're working behind the scenes to try to urge change there . . . Does the current management have the ability to get the job done? That's a question mark. If they don't, I think that you'll probably see some changes there.' When asked in interview to respond to Mr Whitworth's threat, Irene Rosenfeld responded that, 'I run this company for the benefit of all of our shareholders, [and] I am pleased by the progress we have made to date.'[15]

Out of all this (including the weaker results from emerging markets), Mondelēz has, nevertheless, embarked upon a series of efforts, inter alia, to improve margin and shareholder value:

1. Introducing a share buy-back scheme, which has gradually increased to a plan to buy $13.7bn of shares by 31 December 2018.
2. Introducing a zero-based budgeting system, of the type championed by 3GCapital, and intended to produce $1.5bn of annual savings.
3. A further scheme to save $1.5bn through headcount cuts and supply chain improvements.
4. Consolidating its headquarters in Illinois.
5. Selling the corporate jet.
6. A series of budget cuts in order to maintain and increase advertising budgets.

Selling coffee

While these actions might be more typical examples of financial engineering, Mondelēz has also moved decisively with the divestment of its coffee business (including such innovative brands as Millicano) to form part of JDE, a joint venture with JAB Holding's subsidiary Douwe Egbert. The coffee business accounted for approximately 11 per cent of Mondelēz's global revenues, and had relatively high margins and growth prospects. The coffee sector is potentially even more exposed to commodity price volatility, however, and predictions of world shortages of coffee beans are potentially even more damaging than possible cocoa bean volatility for the chocolate business. In addition, it had been argued that Mondelēz's global snacks supply chain would be more easily integrated without the coffee business, eliminating parallel activities and potentially leading to further cost savings.

This new venture created a clear number two pureplay coffee competitor to Nestlé globally, with $7bn revenues, a number one market position in over 24 countries, stronger synergies and purchasing economies of scale. The deal with JAB Holding, provided $5bn in cash to Mondelēz, whilst allowing Mondelēz to retain a 44 per cent equity interest in JDE. The transaction, intended to produce a stronger competitor to vie with Nescafe, also removes a 'volatile asset' from Mondelēz's balance sheet. The deal was announced on 7 May 2014, and Mondelēz's shares rose 8.2 per cent that day.

Improving margins and incremental growth opportunities

Taken together, these actions helped to drive operating profit margin to 13.4 per cent in 2014, up from 12 per

cent in 2012. The target for operating margin by 2018 is 15–16 per cent.[16] In Ms Rosenfeld's vision,[17] the goal is to: '. . . aggressively reduce costs to expand margins and provide the fuel for incremental investments in our Power Brands . . . and route-to-market capabilities to drive sustainable revenue growth and improve market shares.' One of the examples of such incremental investment is the acquisition in July 2015 of an 80 per cent stake in Kinh Do, Vietnam's leading snacks and biscuits business, recognising the potential of the country's 90 million consumers.

Whatever happened to Kraft Foods? (. . . or, what is Warren Buffett up to?)

The de-merged North American grocery business of Kraft found itself on the receiving end of an acquisition bid from H.J. Heinz, and succumbed on 2 July 2015, to become a major part of Kraft Heinz Co. This was a new company with about $28bn of annual revenue, with eight 'power brands' (each with global revenues of over $1bn each), and counting as the fifth largest food and beverage company worldwide.

Familiar names play a part in this story, as Heinz itself had earlier been acquired in 2013 by a consortium of Berkshire Hathaway (Warren Buffett's investment company) and 3G Capital. Whereas Buffett has been well known in the US investment community over many years, 3G Capital has built up its reputation through a methodology of acquiring consumer brand corporations (such as Budweiser and Burger King), and eliminating costs through the introduction of techniques such as zerobased budgeting, elimination of duplicate overhead expenses, and other 'synergies'. This joint investment partnership repeated 3G's pattern of margin improvement with Heinz from 2013–15, before launching the larger deal to acquire Kraft Foods, promising potential savings of $1.5bn of cost synergies. This deal (largely based on a 'paper' offer of shares in the new Kraft Heinz Co) would leave 3G and Buffett with a controlling 51 per cent stake of shares, and majority control of the board. Importantly, analysts also saw the potential to replicate this model of applying Buffett's financial engineering skills in acquisition, with 3G's ability to find cost-saving synergies integrating businesses throughout the sector: '. . . with Buffet's cash-gushing Berkshire Hathaway as a linchpin investor and financier to the combined company, there's no telling where 3G may strike next. In a foods industry where companies like PepsiCo, Campbell's Soup, General Mills and Kellogg are struggling and brand conglomerates like Proctor & Gamble are divesting assets, Kraft Heinz could emerge as an empire-building consolidator.'[18]

Equally, it did not take long for some to propose Mondelēz as a potential target for the synergy-seeking 3G Capital, and imagine a proposed (and possibly ironic) re-integration of its snack businesses with the wider foods and grocery businesses of Kraft Heinz. By 12 August 2015, Kraft Heinz had announced the first wave of synergies in its Kraft businesses, eliminating 2500 jobs from its 46,000 strong workforce in North America, and downsizing Kraft's Illinois headquarters.

. . . and more investor pressure

Shortly after Heinz's acquisition of Kraft (on 7 August 2015), Bill Ackman of Pershing Square Capital Management announced his 7.5 per cent stake in Mondelēz, purchased for $5.57bn. Ackman rapidly got to work to further pressurise Mondelēz's management with a reported agenda to either (i) grow revenues faster, (ii) cut costs more aggressively, or (iii) sell itself to the newly-formed Kraft Heinz or to PepsiCo.

Within days of Pershing Capital's stake acquisition (and its attempt to put a 'for sale' sign up on Mondelēz), Warren Buffett had, however, indicated that Kraft Heinz already had a significant post-acquisition integration task on its hands, and, more significantly, that – poorer margins or not – the biggest hurdle to any takeover of Mondelēz is its 'rich valuation'. According to Bloomberg, in August 2015 Mondelēz's enterprise value was already $92.4bn, with a value multiple of 17.1 times revenue, making it difficult for another peer company such as PepsiCo, General Mills or Nestlé to contemplate a take-over bid.[19]

Which leaves Pershing Capital's profit margin improvement agenda. It was assumed that, like Peltz and Trian, Ackman (or his nominee) would seek a seat on the Mondelēz board to push for margin improvement initiatives. According to Ackman's colleague Ali Namvar:[20] 'We think Mondelēz has by far the greatest cost saving opportunity among its peers . . . we think the whole industry is under change . . . 3G Capital is setting new benchmarks for efficiency, organizational structure and profitability.' The new benchmarks produced by 3G Capital's methods were believed by many to offer savings that could increase industry margins by up to eight per cent (Peter Brabeck-Letmathe, chairman of Nestlé, quoted in FT.com).[16] Alexia Howard of Bernstein credits 3G with squeezing an extra seven per cent of margin out of Heinz between 2013 and 2015, 'more than twice Mondelēz's own ambitions at the time.' Some of the most ambitious targets suggest Mondelēz could even pursue an operating margin of 20 per cent by 2020.

Ms Rosenfeld met Mr Ackman directly on 21 September, where he urged her to improve operating margin more aggressively, reduce the number of suppliers, reduce its portfolio of products, reduce prices paid to retailers to stock product lines, and reduce advertising from a planned ten per cent of revenue to eight per cent. Ms Rosenfeld reportedly resisted the proposed new wave cutting, and, in particular, the advertising cuts that might impact revenue growth: 'all of our investors, even Nelson [Peltz], support an increase in advertising'.[14] Ms Rosenfeld said that she 'chafes' at the increasing pressure on her to further boost the stock price (share value) and profit margins quickly, while she is simultaneously trying to increase sales for the long term.

Managing the activist shareholders

Despite the resistance to Mr Ackman's demands, Irene Rosenfeld did respond by ordering deeper cuts for 2016 operating budgets, and by accelerating savings originally planned for 2018. Responding to Mr Ackman's request to nominate a new board member to pursue his interests, she agreed to look for a 'proven cost-cutter' who would be acceptable to both Ackman and herself. Ms Rosenfeld now claims to be on 'speed dial' for other CEOs learning to deal with activist shareholders (keep them 'inside the tent' and avoid proxy fights, is her main advice). She states that dealing with the detailed concerns of her two principal activist shareholders now takes up about 25 per cent of her time as CEO, to the extent that she was looking to appoint a new 'Chief Commercial Officer' in late 2015, to focus entirely on the marketing and sales oversight she has previously undertaken as CEO. She reportedly told her senior management that she was 'doing everything in my power to handle the distractions so you can stay focused on the business.' She implies, however, that there is no ceding of authority to the activists: 'I'm frustrated by investors' fascination with activists. I'm successfully running Mondelēz for all shareholders – without the activists help'.[14] The activities of the activist do seem to have some impact, however, as reported in the *Wall Street Journal*'s in-depth study of Mondelēz. From interviews with senior directors, they note the instance where, in seeking to hire a new director with a proven record to revive the global chocolate business, Ms Rosenfeld was told by the target executive that there was a 'cloud' over Mondelēz, and was asked 'Are you going to stick around, Irene?'

Notes and references
1. £1 = €1.2 = $1.5.
2. Z. Wood, S. Carrell and R. Wachman, 'Buffett blasts Kraft bid for Cadbury', *Guardian*, 20 January 2010.
3. House of Commons BIS Committee, 'Mergers, acquisitions and take-overs: the takeover of Cadbury by Kraft', 9th report of session 2009–10, London, Stationery Office, 2010.
4. House of Commons BIS Committee, 'Is Kraft working for Cadbury?' 6th report of session 2010–12, London, Stationery Office, 2011.

5. A. Webb and A. Wilson, 'Was Cadbury a sweet deal for Kraft?', *Telegraph*, 24 April 2011.

6. 'Kraft to split into two companies', *BBC News*, 4 August 2011.

7. E. Thomasson, 'Demerged Kraft unit sees consumers hungry for snacks', *Reuters*, 2 October 2012.

8. S. Strom, 'For Oreo, Cadbury, and Ritz, a new parent company', *New York Times*, 24 May 2012.

9. S. Ahmed, 'Emerging markets key to Kraft spinoff's success', *CNBC*, 2 October 2012.

10. A. Nieburg, 'Mintel analyst lauds Mondelez geographic choices', Confectionerynews.com, 13 September 2012.

11. Skelly/*Euromonitor*, 'Mondelez International Inc. in packaged Food World', 2014.

12. L. Yue, 'Mondelez gets a lesson global economics', Chicagobusiness.com, 15 February 2014.

13. '2016 Macroeconomic outlook', Goldman Sachs, accessed 8 July 2016.

14. M. Langley, 'Activists put Mondelez CEO Irene Rosenfeld on the spot', *Wall Street Journal*, 15 December 2015.

15. D.D. Stanford, M. Boyle and C. Perri, 'Master blenders to buy Mondelez coffee unit for $5B', *Bloomberg*, 7 May 2014.

16. L. Whipp and S. Foley, 'Pressure on Mondelez to take a bit out of costs', *Financial Times*, 6 August 2015.

17. S. Neuwirth, 'Not so sweet: Cadbury owner Mondelez posts eighth consecutive quarterly revenue decline', *CityA.M.*, 28 October 2015.

18. A. Gara, 'Why the Heinz–Kraft food merger is a rare kind of Warren Buffett deal', *Forbes*, 25 March 2015.

19. R. Collings, 'Mondelez too expensive for Nestle, General Mills to acquire?', *TheStreet*, 14 August 2015.

20. A. Gara, 'Bill Ackman didn't buy Mondelez just to dish it off to Warren Buffett and 3G Capital', *Forbes*, 13 August 2015.

CRH plc: leveraging corporate strategy for value creation and global leadership

Mike Moroney

Corporate strategy can be the driver of value generation, growth and development, notwithstanding a challenging industry environment and a lean corporate centre. These issues are explored in this case study on CRH, which places acquisition-led corporate strategy at the heart of its value creation model.

In March 2016, CRH plc, the second largest building materials company in the world with a stock market valuation over €20bn (£16bn, $26bn)[1] released financial results for 2015. Albert Manifold, Group CEO since the start of 2014, could reflect with satisfaction on the first two years of his tenure. EBITDA[2] was ahead strongly, margins continued to expand across the Group and 2015 marked the second consecutive year of improvement from trough levels of the severe global recession. In addition, in a spin-off deal following the merger of two of the largest industry players, Lafarge and Holcim, CRH had acquired certain assets with a value of €6.5bn (the 'LH Assets'), the Group's biggest ever transaction. Furthermore, the Group had initiated a programme of dynamic capital management, which had released almost €1.4bn in capital in two years from targeted disposals to fund future acquisition-led growth. Moreover, cost reduction initiatives in recent years had yielded cumulative annualised cost savings of over €2.5bn. At the same time, Albert Manifold and his management team were acutely aware of the many challenges that lay ahead in the next phase of CRH's development as the Group sought to realise its ambition of becoming the world's leading building materials company. Success would depend on CRH's corporate strategy, leadership and actions.

The building materials industry

The industry involves the extraction, manufacture and supply of building materials, products and services for construction activity. These include primary materials (such as cement, aggregates, crushed stone, sand and gravel), ready mixed concrete (RMC) and asphalt products), 'heavyside' building products (for example, structural

and architectural concrete products), 'lightside' building products (for example, glass and glazing systems, construction accessories, shutters and awnings, fencing and network access products) and distribution (builders' merchanting and DIY). Industry outputs have their own external, intermediate markets. However, building materials also serve as inputs to higher-level and final products across integrated industry value chains. Sectors served are residential, industrial/commercial and infrastructure/public works. End-uses comprise new work in the early phases of construction activity and repair, maintenance and improvement (RMI) in later phases.

Core industry characteristics

Building materials are characterised by several distinguishing features. *Cyclicality* derives from the fact that construction cycles reflect general economic cycles. Construction/building materials cycles are longer in duration and larger in amplitude, while their timing varies between countries. In developing economies, construction demand tends to lead GDP growth, in contrast to a lagged relationship in mature economies. Cyclicality is most pronounced for 'heavyside' products such as cement, aggregates and concrete products. These products involve intensive capital investment which is characterised by long-term, large-scale commitments and significant lead times, and for which additions to capacity are sizeable and occur only periodically.

Building materials manifest a dual *mature/dynamic* geographically based character. In developed markets (North America, Western Europe and Australasia) where the bulk of buildings and infrastructure is already in place, construction is stable with modest growth and is largely (late cycle) RMI-based. Population and public

---

This case was prepared by Mike Moroney, Lecturer in Strategic Management at the J.E. Cairnes School of Business and Economics, National University of Ireland Galway. It is intended as a basis for class discussion and not as an illustration of good or bad practice. © Mike Moroney, 2016. Not to be reproduced or quoted without permission.

investment are the prime drivers of activity.[3] By contrast, in developing markets (Asia, Central and Eastern Europe, Latin America) and in some Western countries at an earlier stage of economic development, construction output is high growth and predominantly new build, reflecting above average economic growth.

In general, building materials and products are *commodities,* have long life cycles, are similar across markets and largely stable over time, with price-based competition predominant. Production processes are standard. Technology is non-proprietary and, for some products, relatively unsophisticated. Innovation focuses on enhancing manufacturing processes, improving ease of product use and installation, and providing value-added services and solutions to customers.

Traditionally, the building materials industry is *fragmented.* Production is linked to the location of appropriate reserves, with proximity to the end market key. Because building materials and products are characterised by a high weight to value ratio, high transport costs rapidly outweigh scale economies, with the result that the radius of economic activity and competition often can be 150 kilometres or less. Moreover, many markets are local in nature due to differences in building regulations, construction practices and product standards. Success is often determined by micro-market factors like locality, quality, reliability of service and price.[4] As a result, the industry developed over time as a large number of small/medium-sized firms, often family-owned and run.

Strategic and cyclical trends

Structurally, consolidation was ongoing (particularly in primary materials and merchanting) reflecting supply side concentration and significant merger and acquisition (M&A) activity. During the two decades to mid-2009, there were 20 large corporate deals involving total consideration of US$125bn at an average value to EBITDA multiple of 10.3 times,[5] financed mainly by borrowing. Major transactions largely ceased during the severe sector downturn of 2007–13 as firms reduced debt. However, there were several large deals involving industry leaders and ambitious medium-sized players. Over time, large international building materials companies, including CRH, had leveraged strong local market positions and/or product competences to increase scale and to expand into other regions and areas of activity. There was also erosion of local differences between geographic markets, driven by institutional harmonisation of regulations, standards and tendering, convergence in building practices, consolidation of customers and homogenisation of their needs.

These developments resulted in considerable changes in the industry. Several large, established players (many household names) went out of existence, particularly in the UK. A number of large, often global, players emerged, especially in 'heavyside' markets. Rationalisation was ongoing, as smaller, independent operators merged into larger groups. CRH was a leader in these developments. Nonetheless, the underlying logic of fragmentation prevailed. Notwithstanding corporate activity, globally concentration ratios in 'heavyside' markets such as cement, aggregates and asphalt were comparatively low, while a significant proportion of capacity remained privately held.

In 2016, the sector was recovering following the severe global downturn from 2007, which was unprecedented since the 1930s in severity and extent and in its synchronised nature. In general the outlook was positive. US construction had enjoyed several years of growth, with sector output expanding at six per cent p.a. After six years of consecutive declines[6] European markets exhibited modest volume growth of over two per cent in 2015, although the picture was mixed across countries. In all markets, recovery was from a low base, presaging significant upside potential. US construction output was still depressed relative to GDP, new build markets in Europe remained at trough levels[7] and UK house-building and mortgage approvals were considerably lower than sustainable demand.[8] However, macro uncertainties continued to prevail. Economic growth in China, the engine of the global economy for two decades, was slowing. Recovery was likely to be gradual, evidenced by expectations for only modest rises in interest rates. Moreover, certain structural trends were not favourable, such as the shift to multi-family homes with lower building material intensity.[9]

Profile of CRH

Headquartered in Dublin, Ireland, CRH is a top two, leading global diversified building materials group with annual revenues of €24bn in 2015, employing 89,000 people at over 3900 operating locations in 31 countries worldwide. CRH's prominence is recognised by many industry awards for corporate governance,[10] financial reporting, investor relations, and excellence/innovation in environmental and safety practices.

CRH plc was formed in 1970 through the merger of two leading Irish public companies, Irish Cement Limited (established in 1936) and Roadstone (established in 1949). At that time, CRH was the sole producer of cement and principal producer of aggregates, concrete products and asphalt in the country, with Group sales of €27m, 95 per cent in Ireland. Since that time, CRH has developed new geographic platforms in its core businesses while taking advantage of complementary product opportunities. This has enabled the Group to achieve strategic balance and to establish multiple platforms from which to deliver superior, sustained performance and growth. Since its formation in 1970, CRH has delivered annual Total Shareholder Return of 16 per cent. In 45 years of operation, the Group has undergone major growth through several phases of development:

- organic market penetration in Ireland (from 1970);
- acquisition-led overseas expansion (from the late 1970s);
- product focus, larger acquisitions (from the late 1990s);
- developing value-based growth platforms (from the early 2010s).

In general, change has been evolutionary, involving a managed, learning process of building, augmenting and layering competences.

Products and markets

CRH served the spectrum of construction activity, delivering superior building materials and products for use in housing, buildings, roads, public spaces, infrastructure and commercial projects. The Group manufactured and distributed a range of building materials products from the fundamentals of heavy materials and elements to construct the frame, through value-added products that complete the building envelope, to distribution channels which service construction fit-out and renewal. CRH was engaged in three closely related core businesses: primary materials (not including steel and timber); value-added building products (primarily 'heavyside' concrete-based, with selected 'lightside'), and building materials distribution

(through builders' merchants and DIY stores). CRH's main product concentration was in primary materials and 'heavyside' products (cement, aggregates, asphalt, RMC and concrete products).

Geographically, CRH is a top two building materials company globally and the largest in North America. The Group has leadership positions in Europe as well as established strategic leadership positions in the emerging economic regions of Asia and South America. In the long-term, CRH's businesses were underpinned by a high level of increasingly scarce reserves of materials totalling 20 billion tonnes. In aggregates, CRH's reserves were equivalent to over 80 years of production and were among the highest in the sector.[11] In 2014, CRH had 700 quarries/pits in the US and 400 in Europe.[12]

CRH strategy[13]

CRH's vision is to be the global leader in building materials. To achieve this vision CRH had developed a Group-wide, integrated, multi-level strategy to create value and deliver superior, sustainable shareholder returns.

Value-based strategic imperatives (see Figure 1)

Reflecting long-standing core values, strategic imperatives guided Group action:

- **Continuous business improvement** through operational, commercial and financial excellence, as manifested in return on net assets (RONA).

- **Disciplined and focused growth.** Financial discipline maintained through working capital management and capital expenditure controls. Use of the Group's strong balance sheet, cash generation capability, active portfolio management and focused allocation of capital to achieve optimum growth.

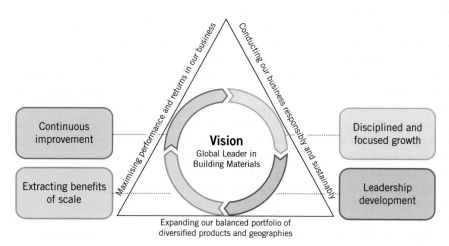

Figure 1 CRH vision and strategic imperatives
Source: CRH plc.

Table 1 The CRH business model

Balanced portfolio	Group businesses are diversified across a number of product, geographies and end uses, while also spanning multiple different demand cycles, thereby reducing exposure to any single driver. Enterprise risk management (ERM) framework involves three lines of defence across all levels in the Group.
Making businesses better	Proven track record in delivery of stronger returns on capital invested by applying collective Group knowledge and experience to acquired new businesses to produce improvements in performance. Supported through targeted investment to improve capacity, quality and efficiency.
Proven acquisition model	Identifying and acquiring strong businesses that complement the Group's existing portfolio of operations. Acquisition typically of small and medium-sized companies, releasing value through synergies and network optimisation. Larger transactions where strategic rationale is compelling. Excellence in integration of appropriately positioned and resourced businesses to realise their full potential.
Dynamic capital management	Constant monitoring of how capital is employed to ensure it is recycled from low growth areas into core business offering potential for stronger growth and returns. Allocation of capital to businesses best positioned to take advantage of developing growth cycles and areas offering improved value creation and growth potential.
Financial strength	Constant focus on financial discipline and strong cash generation enabling efficient funding of value-adding investments and acquisitions. Reduced cost of capital.

Sources: CRH Annual Reports, www.crh.com.

- **Leadership development** of performance-oriented, innovative and entrepreneurial leaders. Attract best-in-market talent. Empowerment, mobility opportunities and promotion from within of talented individuals for career and personal development. Development of high performers through leadership development programmes.

- **Extracting the benefits of scale** to fund expansion by acquisition and to build leadership positions in local markets.

The CRH business model

CRH's strategy was underpinned by a proven business model over decades providing long-term value creation which was straightforward and systematic (see Table 1). The Group's business model had five key components.

In terms of *balanced portfolio*, CRH assiduously maintained strategic balance across operations, at corporate, group and regional levels. Balance was managed for both legacy businesses and acquisitions, with the latter often reinforcing overall portfolio balance (as in the purchase of the Lafarge–Holcim (LH) assets). Regarding CRH's *unique acquisition model*, 'investment and acquisition [are] the drivers of value creation in our business'.[14] In 2015, CRH spent almost €8bn on acquisitions, including the €6.5bn Lafarge-Holcim transaction and the $1.3bn purchase of C.R. Lawrence (North America's leading supplier of glass and glazing custom hardware) both of which enhanced earnings in the first year following acquisition.

In *making businesses better*, CRH adopted a rigorous approach to evaluation, approval and review. The twin requirements of performance and growth were reinforced continually. Entities had to demonstrate a track record of achievement in order to earn the right to grow. Planning was formalised and interactive, with goals and objectives reflecting leading practice benchmarks. Performance measurement was timely, formal and rigorous, facilitating early critical review of underperformance, allowing appropriate corrective measures to be put in place and enabling senior management to draw broader lessons. Continuous improvement was relentless, with ongoing programmes of benchmarking and best practice. *Dynamic capital management* became a cornerstone of the Group's business model from 2014. By the end of 2015, cumulative proceeds from CRH's multi-year divestment and disposal programme amounted to almost €1.4bn, with €1bn accruing during the year. In general, businesses were divested by CRH at multiples of ten times EBITDA and acquired at multiples of eight times, resulting in value augmentation.

CRH was noted for its *financial strength*, characterised by extensive business knowledge, value contribution and prudence. CRH had the best balance sheet in the sector across cycles, reflecting strong debt metrics, robust liquidity, a well-balanced profile of future debt maturities and the highest long-term investment grade credit rating in the sector: BBB+ (Standard & Poors).[15] Operations were required to earn a mid-teen percentage return on invested capital through the cycle. A cash generative mentality pervaded operations, evaluation and control processes. In 2015, CRH increased operating cash flow by 47 per cent to €1.3bn, in part due to tight working capital management. In addition, the Group raised over €2.5bn in debt capital markets at record low interest rates.

Region and division strategy and KPIs

CRH's vision, values and business model provided a strategic framework for the Group as a whole. Consistent with this, clear strategies were articulated for the major regions: Europe, Americas, China and India, and (in respect of 2015) the LH Assets. Moreover, specific strategies were also developed for each product group. For the largest product group, Americas Materials, the strategy was 'to build strong regional leadership positions underpinned by well-located, long-term reserves'.[16]

Strategic goals and objectives were operationalised in key performance indicators (KPIs) reflecting a philosophy that measurement fosters positive behaviour and performance improvement. Reflecting CRH's strategic focus on continuous business improvement, KPIs were used to measure progress across a range of financial and non-financial dimensions (from operating cash flow and EBITDA interest cover to greenhouse gas emissions and gender diversity).

Corporate strategy at CRH

CRH was organised as a federal group structure, with a small central headquarters and seven regionally focused business segments supported by a lean Group centre (see Figure 2). To capitalise on local market knowledge, a high degree of individual responsibility was devolved to experienced operational managers, within Group guidelines and controls. CRH's corporate headquarters employed approximately 200 people in Dublin, with around 350 people in total across the Group engaged in headquarters-type activities. CRH's senior executive management team of ten was similarly small and tightly focused. Notwithstanding the centre's relatively small size, corporate strategy was pivotal to value creation, growth and development in CRH.

CRH regarded its people as its most important asset and engaged actively in talent management. The Group's management was characterised by experience, stability and continuity. In 45 years, there had been only seven chief executives, all of whom (like many senior managers) were internal appointments. In 2016, key corporate, divisional and operational managers numbered around 500. Managers were drawn from internally developed operating managers, highly qualified and experienced professionals, and owner–entrepreneurs from acquired companies, providing a healthy mix and depth of skills and backgrounds. Management turnover was low, reflecting CRH's long-term success through industry cycles, a market-driven, performance-related remuneration policy and a range of formal and informal mechanisms to promote integration (see below). Collectively, low turnover, rotation and promotion from within resulted in a wealth of in-house industry knowledge and expertise.

Scope and diversification (footprint)

In 2016, CRH was a world-leading, diversified building materials Group with extensive and integrated exposure to construction markets globally which had developed gradually over time. Strategic balance was most evident across the Group's businesses in North America and Western Europe. 'Heavyside' operations gave exposure to new build, infrastructure and RMI construction. 'Lightside' and distribution businesses were mainly exposed to residential and non-residential markets, where the Group had positions of scale, global brands and potential for growth.

Strategic priorities for growth differed by the stage of development of markets. In mature markets in developed economies, CRH sought to develop existing businesses further through dynamic reallocation of capital, investment

Figure 2 CRH group organisation
Source: CRH plc.

in greenfield projects and acquisitions. Criteria for success included achieving vertical integration, adding to reserves and expanding regional and product positions. In developing regions, CRH sought premium entry platforms, involving an initial local or regional position in primary materials, backed by sizeable reserves. The acquired footprint was usually in cement and often involved partnership with strong local established businesses, providing valuable learning for a relatively low investment. CRH targeted businesses with the potential to develop further downstream into integrated building materials business (often with national presence) capitalising on industrialisation, urbanisation and population growth.

Corporate parenting

Senior management continually reinforced CRH's business model. Management training and meetings were used to restate key messages, from the performance-based 'right to grow' strategic mantra, to the minutiae of operational best practice. Value-creating performance was buttressed by formal and rigorous measurement, evaluation and control processes, ensuring early intervention and appropriate corrective measures. Communications opportunities were exploited to the full. CRH's expertise in market and investor relations is replicated internally. The CEO and senior management team engage regularly with all employees through face-to-face meetings and communications technologies including: emails, blogs, intranets, video, apps and other social media with a constant focus on values, performance, strategic priorities and knowledge share.

CRH operated a Group-wide management development system to ensure systematic requisite exposure to the wide range of CRH's operations, particularly when managers were mobile, in their 20s and 30s. A key element was the management database, on which the core 500 managers in the Group were profiled formally. In addition, there were a variety of development programmes for managers, many of which involved inputs and presentations on strategy from senior management, including the chief executive. These included the Management Seminar, Development Forum, Leadership Development Programmes and Business Leadership Programme. Promotion, rotation and mentoring were also instruments of manager development. HR measures to ensure greater cohesion and consistency of policies were designed to foster coordination and a culture of interdependence.

Divisional and Group-wide mechanisms facilitated delivery of business model elements. Ongoing best practice and knowledge exchange activities involved meetings by small teams of experts facilitated by technical advisors in each of the six regionally focused divisions. These resulted in highly innovative ideas and exchanges of products, delivering significant synergies. There were also long-standing Group-wide best practice programmes (e.g. cement, development) in addition to more recent initiatives, such as in procurement and commercial excellence. Best practice was supplemented by benchmarking exercises and common systems platforms. Divisions also sponsored formal systematic programmes to improve operational performance and increase efficiency in a range of areas, including health and safety, recycling and energy recovery.

Informal mechanisms underpinned performance. Corporate culture was nurtured and sustained constantly. The supportive team orientation was evident in informal mentoring, hands-on assistance and individual and team coaching within and across entities. Flexibility prevailed regarding hierarchy and job descriptions. Core values were continually reinforced through corporate folklore and subtle mechanisms including leading by example and clear norms of acceptable behaviour. Strong informal networks existed among managers, even between far-flung regions of the Group's activities, arising from organisational mechanisms of interaction and from a social dimension to formal events (such as the annual Management Seminar).

Acquisition-led expansion

Acquisitions were the engine of corporate growth and development. Historically, acquisitions accounted for 70 per cent of CRH's profit growth (with organic growth contributing one quarter, and currency movements the remainder).[17] Traditionally, CRH's acquisitions were bolt-on in nature (three to four deals per month at an average value of less than €20m) augmented from time to time with larger deals where there was compelling value and a strong strategic rationale. In general, CRH acquired on favourable terms, reflecting the Group's 'valuation discipline'. Purchase price/EBITDA multiples ranged between 6 and 8.

CRH's rigorous and comprehensive acquisition strategy was singular in conception and execution and had 'proven very difficult to replicate'.[18] For identification of prospects, CRH resourced multiple development teams spread across the Group seeking opportunities and maintaining contact with an extensive database of potential targets accumulated over 45 years. At any one time, dozens of acquisitions were under active consideration, ensuring a steady deal flow. Each purchase gave rise to further opportunities, in other markets.

Courtship in these deals involved a patient and often long process of familiarisation and coaching. CRH took time to assess suitability and strategic fit, and to know management and their evolving needs. Much effort was spent appraising the target of CRH's strategy, management, values and expectations, including up-front clarity on post-acquisition priorities. It was not unusual for CRH to walk away from a deal, on grounds of timing, price or compatibility. Sometimes acquisitions were completed at a later date.

To enhance best practice in deal execution, CRH had codified, in a classified, proprietary document, the best practice, knowledge and processes involved in making an acquisition, gleaned from many years of experience. This was full of collected wisdom and practical advice on deal-making. An experienced operational manager guided each acquisition team. At the appropriate time, a senior-level 'ambassador' was introduced to close the deal. Before completion, each deal underwent rigorous evaluation, including qualitative operational review, due diligence, strict cash flow testing and Board approval.

Traditionally, CRH's acquisitions shared many common characteristics:

- medium-sized, private, often family-run businesses;
- geographic/product market leaders, with potential to enhance existing Group operations, fill a gap or provide a platform for growth;
- careful structuring of deals, often involving initial stakes with buy options (and/or joint ventures) in new regions/product areas;
- retention of owner–managers to ensure continuity and maintain human capital.

Post-acquisition integration to boost returns was rapid and well-practiced. RONA typically rose to the benchmark level of 15 per cent within two to three years from purchase.[19] Group financial, management information and control systems were implemented immediately. Revenue and cost synergies were captured through benchmarking, best practice programmes and targeted capital investment. The central expertise and coordination of CRH's superstructure delivered procurement economies of scale, enhanced customer access and greater network density and synergies. After three years, a formal look back review was carried out. Although more complex, the acquisition process for larger deals was similar in principle.

Acquisition of the LH assets

During 2015, CRH acquired for €6.5bn assets from major industry players Lafarge and Holcim (the 'LH assets'), involving 'heavyside' businesses with leading market positions across 700 locations in 11 countries with 15,000 employees. The deal doubled CRH's cement capacity to become the second largest building materials company in the world and the number two provider of aggregates globally. Strategically, the acquisition provided significant value creation potential and strategic fit with CRH's legacy businesses, providing four new regional platforms for growth in cement, aggregates and RMC. Moreover, the deal widened the Group's global footprint and was expected to have a considerable impact on CRH's future growth trajectory. Under the leadership of a specific committee of the Board, CRH immediately put in place a thorough plan for integration of the LH Assets.

In announcing its 2015 results, CRH reported considerable progress in relation to the LH Assets. The integration programme was largely complete, with both sales and EBITDA ahead of expectations. Moreover, arising largely from higher than anticipated process operating efficiencies, the Group upgraded its expected synergies over three years from completion of the acquisition from €90m to €120m. Going forward, external commentators estimated that €150m in synergy savings was within the Group's capability.[20]

Outlook

For the first time in many years, the outlook for CRH for 2016 and beyond was favourable in a number of areas. The macro-economic backdrop boded well for ongoing cyclical recovery and a return to peak levels of margins and returns. Moreover, the 'transformative' Lafarge–Holcim deal reinforced expectations for robust earnings growth arising from integration of acquired businesses, synergies and increased development opportunities from enhanced platforms. At the same time, financial discipline and prudent financial management highlighted CRH's commitment to restore debt metrics to normalised levels. Market expectations reflected a fall in the Group's net debt/EBITDA ratio from a post-deal high of 3.5x to 1.8x by 2016 year-end. Importantly, CRH retained its firepower for further transactions, with an estimated capacity to spend €12bn on acquisitions over five years.[21] Albert Manifold and his management team knew that achieving the Group vision of global leadership in building materials would require sustained delivery on all fronts.

Notes and references
1. €1 = £0.8 = $1.3.
2. Earnings before interest, tax, depreciation and amortisation.
3. J.P. Morgan Cazenove, 'On the turn. We initiate on the sector', 21 April 2011, p. 128.
4. Bank of America-Merrill Lynch, 'Cement Handbook: Time for more selective stock picking', 22 June 2009, p. 14.
5. J.P. Morgan Cazenove, 'On the turn. We initiate on the sector', 21 April 2011, p. 27.
6. Euroconstruct, 'EC-Summary Report', presented at the 80th Euroconstruct Conference, Budapest, Hungary, 3–4 December 2015.

7. Goodbody Stockbrokers, 'Building Materials: Building on a solid H1', 16 July 2015.

8. Goodbody Stockbrokers, 'Building Materials: Preference for UK distributors into H1 results', 23 July 2014.

9. Goodbody Stockbrokers, 'Building Materials: Preference for UK distributors into H1 results', 23 July 2014.

10. UBS, 'European building materials: Significant upside to mid cycle valuations', 13 July 2009, p. 7.

11. J. P. Morgan Cazenove, 'On the turn. We initiate on the sector', 21 April 2011, p. 108 and 109.

12. CRH Annual Report on Form 20-F in respect of the year ended December 31, 2014.

13. CRH Annual Report 2015.

14. CRH Annual Report 2014, 'Strategy review: Chief Executive's introduction', p. 4.

15. M. Lee, 'CRH Presentation', Sanford C. Bernstein Strategic Decisions Conference, September 2012, slide 3.

16. CRH Annual Report 2015, p. 38.

17. Goodbody Stockbrokers, 'CRH: still to play its "trump card"', 13 July 2005, p. 7.

18. Merrill Lynch, 'Adding value or hot air?', 25 October 2005, p. 12.

19. Goodybody Stockbrokers, 'CRH: still to play its "trump card"', 13 July 2005, p. 10.

20. Goodbody Stockbrokers, 'CRH: investment case firmly intact', 4 March 2016, cover page.

21. Goodbody Stockbrokers, 'CRH: building blocks to doubling of profits', 11 September 2015.

CASE STUDY

Evaluating the Mexican narco-trafficking problem

Sophia O. Kerridge and Clive Kerridge

This case study looks at examples of 'successful' international crime organisations, Mexican drug trafficking cartels. These illegal businesses are often just as structured, organised and strategically managed as legal corporations. This case gives an opportunity to evaluate strategic options, from the point of view of Mexican government policy advisors, as the state attempts to better understand the strategies used by drug trafficking organisations, in order to counteract them.

'Mission accomplished: We got him' tweeted a relieved Mexican President Enrique Peña Nieto in early 2016, after the dramatic recapture of 'El Chapo' Guzman, leader of the notorious Sinaloa Federation, a narco-trafficking organisation (NTO) that controlled a vast illegal drug trade in the Americas and beyond. Powerful businesses frequently try to influence government policy, notably by lobbying. Equally, governments seek to limit or control the behaviour of big businesses, mainly through legislation and taxation. However, when they are large illegal businesses, this is more complex, difficult, and often dangerous.

The problem

Back in 2006, in an effort to tackle the growing strength of NTOs, the previous Mexican President, Felipe Calderón (PAN Party) had deployed the military onto the streets. Little did he know that he would be unleashing a 'drug war' of huge proportions, destabilising the illegal narcotics trade and instigating violent battles, not only between the military and NTOs but also amongst the NTOs themselves. When President Peña Nieto (PRI party) came into power in December 2012, he vowed to crack down on the country's notorious drug cartels.[1]

To his credit, by the end of 2015 he was able to show that many of the major cartel leaders were under arrest or had been killed, and drug-related deaths decreased from over 12,000 in 2012 to around 8000 in 2014.[2] On the other hand, various scandals had rocked his administration: in 2014 alone there had been a conflict-of-interest scandal involving the President himself; the disappearance and presumed death of 43 students at the hands of NTOs and state officials; and the brazen

escape from a high-security prison of 'El Chapo', Mexico's most powerful cartel leader. Several regions also saw the development of vigilante groups in response to ongoing NTO violence and the state's inability to protect civilians.[3] The President continued to face strong diplomatic pressure, the threat of declining international business investment as the economy stagnated (especially in the US border area), a serious threat to national security, and recognition that:

'. . . the organisations now pose a multi-faceted organised criminal challenge to governance in Mexico no less threatening to the rule of law than the challenge that faced Peña Nieto's predecessor.'[4]

Despite much dissatisfaction, Peña Nieto's PRI party kept a bare majority after the mid-term elections of 2015. As he went into the second half of his term, policy advisors needed to analyse the NTOs' activities and redefine the government's strategic options – and quickly.

The business

Peña Nietos' government was facing more than just a problem of widespread violence. Much of the violence was orchestrated by an increasing number of varied and complex organisations that ran very profitable businesses in the trade of narcotics – an industry worth billions of dollars and employing thousands of people.

In 2010, the United Nations Office on Drugs and Crime (UNODC) estimated the value of the illegal global drug trade at $320bn (£192bn, €240bn)[5] per year, with profits from the US cocaine market alone constituting $35bn. In comparison, immigrant smuggling from Latin America to the USA was valued at $6.6bn a year and the

---

Clive Kerridge, INSEAD AMP graduate and former international executive with Foseco and Castrol/BP, teaches strategic management at Aston Business School and at the University of Gloucestershire, UK. Sophia Kerridge (daughter), after completing her Oxford University postgrad thesis on Mexican and Colombian drug-trafficking violence, worked as an International Observer for PBI in Colombia before training as a Barrister in the UK. © SO Kerridge & CR Kerridge 2016

illicit arms trade from the USA to Mexico was worth just $20m a year (see Figure 1b).[6]

The cocaine trade is a particularly profitable undertaking due to its non-labour-intensive production, simple technology and compact transportation. The value added to cocaine at each stage of the manufacturing and distribution process reflects not the production costs but the varying levels of risk and complexity required to transport it. For example, a kilo of cocaine that in Colombia would cost around $2000 has a value of $10,000 in Mexico and, after crossing the US border, would sell wholesale at $30,000. Once broken down, mixed and split among street dealers the value per kg is $100,000.[7]

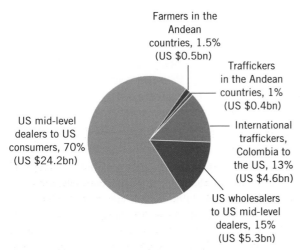

Figure 1a Distribution of gross profits (in %) of the US$35bn US cocaine market, 2008

Source: UNODC World Drug Report 2010, Figure 39.

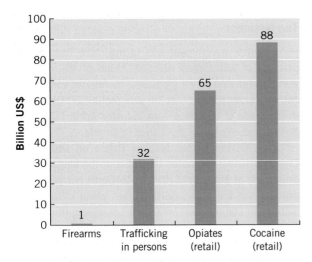

Figure 1b Estimated annual value of some global criminal markets in the 2000s

Source: UNODC World Drug Report 2010, Figure 4.

As can be seen from the UNODC pie chart (Figure 1a), most of the profits from the drug trade are at the distribution level (to final consumers). However, the fragmented and decentralised nature of end-level distribution means that concentrated wealth is at the international trafficking level. So, although 70 per cent of gross income goes to dealers selling to consumers (Figure 1a), there are thousands of street-level drug dealers in the USA who share those profits. In their celebrated book *Freakonomics*,[8] Levitt and Dubner encapsulate this fragmentation and low 'retail' profitability in the title of Chapter 3: 'Why do drug dealers still live with their moms?'. At production level, there are various supply sources and little value has yet been added, so gross profits are small compared to those made by the international drug-trafficking organisations. This smuggling or trafficking is undertaken by a select number of groups that specialise in complex operations, coordinating products from many sources and delivering them to numerous destinations. Through this bottleneck, wealth and power are concentrated. It has been estimated that the Colombian Cali and Medellín Cartels, which dominated the cocaine trade during the 1980s, each made close to $5bn annually just from cocaine trafficking.[9]

The illicit drug trade is not a static or stable industry. For decades, Latin America has been the main supply source for the US market, the world's largest consumer of marijuana, opiates, cocaine and ATS (amphetamine-type stimulants). However, the dominant criminal organisations and the type of drugs being trafficked have changed: whereas earlier traffickers primarily dealt with marijuana, Colombians became the world's principal cocaine traffickers. Colombia has continued to be a major cocaine-producing source, but Mexican NTOs are now the dominant traffickers, also involved in the marijuana, opiate and ATS trades. These evolutions in market control or dominance occur due to factors such as changes in an NTO's ability to operate or fluctuations in demand. By 2016, demand in the USA for Mexican ATS was increasing, whereas cocaine had stagnated and marijuana demand decreased; in contrast, cocaine demand in Europe was on the rise (see Figure 2).

Legal and illegal businesses: the law enforcement effect

The illicit nature of the industry means drug trafficking is always at risk of interruption by law enforcement. Therefore, NTOs are often organised to keep a low profile and avoid the state's attention. Yet they maintain the capacity for violence and to co-opt or corrupt state employees so they can guarantee impunity and protection over their activities. NTOs face additional operational

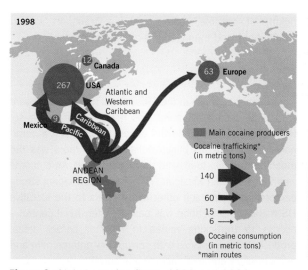

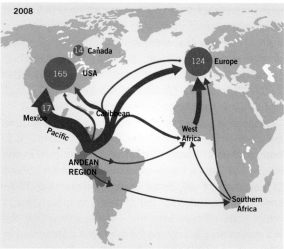

Figure 2 Global cocaine flows, 1998 and 2008

Source: UNODC World Drug Report, 2009, and UNODC calculations informed by US ONDCP, *Cocaine Consumption Estimates Methodology*, September 2008 (internal paper).

costs because, unlike legal businesses, agreements cannot be enforced or arbitrated by the law. NTOs have to enforce their own contracts and settle their own disputes, with violence if necessary.

Like legal businesses, however, the drug trade benefits from economies of scale. Organisations seek to expand and integrate various stages of the industry, where possible monopolising the market, to maximise profitability. Low barriers to entry, and the attraction of quick and high profits, ensure constant new competition that, can potentially destabilise the market. Stability and control may be achieved via NTO alliances (though such alliances are often temporary) or with the division of territories and markets. The unpredictability of operating under such conditions inevitably requires NTOs to be adaptable: for example, if leaders are arrested it must be possible to substitute them quickly. This supports the observation by a high-level panel of the United Nations that, 'organised crime is increasingly operating through fluid networks rather than more formal hierarchies. This form of organisation provides criminals with diversity, flexibility, low visibility and longevity.'[10] Such adaptability can also be seen through novel trafficking mechanisms, which are introduced to remain ahead of the competition and law enforcement, for example via tunnels under (and catapults over) the US-Mexican border or small submarines operating in the Caribbean; also through the development of new generations of drugs which are easier to transport, less complex to produce, and harder to detect. As for longevity, however, life-expectancy for the people involved in NTOs is often short (with prison as the most likely alternative), as the police and military attack the NTOs' organisational structures.

'Balloons' and 'Mercury'

NTOs do not benefit from the legal and other protections enjoyed by legitimate businesses. However, they are not constrained by the legislation and state bureaucracy that can slow down business growth and development. In some senses, NTOs are operating in a completely 'free market'. To survive in such fast-changing environments, NTOs have to be dynamic entrepreneurial organisations. For example, if the state suppresses drug production in a certain part of the country, NTOs will often transfer these activities to another area, or even abroad, where law-enforcement is less effective (the 'balloon effect': squeeze a balloon and the air moves to the parts with less pressure).[11] When counter-narcotics efforts in Colombia during the late 1980s reduced the NTOs' capacity to manage complex international smuggling routes, Mexican groups began taking over cocaine trafficking. Additionally, when the state puts pressure on the senior levels of large NTOs, these organisations tend to split into many smaller units (the 'mercury effect'). This occurred in Colombia once the Cali and Medellín cartels had been destroyed. It is worth noting that none of these measures resulted in the termination of international trafficking or the illicit drug trade.

The growth of the Sinaloa Cartel

Perhaps most embarrassing for the Mexican authorities prior to 2016 had been the continued dominance of the Sinaloa Cartel, often referred to as the world's leading organised crime or 'mafia' business. Its infamous leader, Joaquin 'El Chapo' Guzmán, heralded in various *narcocorridos* (modern Mexican folk songs) for his legendary outlaw status, humiliated Mexico internationally in 2015 when videos were released showing his successful escape from a maximum security prison, through a large tunnel stretching more than a mile underground. Nor was this Guzmán's first escape: he had already fled prison in 2001, thereafter directing the Sinaloa Cartel to dominate the illicit trafficking industry in Mexico and much of the Americas.

Over the years El Chapo amassed a personal fortune which *Forbes* magazine valued at $1bn in 2012. In 2013, Forbes ranked El Chapo 67th most powerful man in the world, given that he was responsible for between 25 and 50 per cent of all illegal drugs entering the USA. Rumours about this NTO and its ability to influence and corrupt state officials were rife – to the extent that the PAN government felt compelled to release a statement in 2010 that it was not co-operating with the Sinaloa Cartel to bring down the competing NTOs. With El Chapo back in the field, it was expected that the Sinaloa Cartel would be as strong as ever.

The Sinaloa organisation has strong local roots and was one of the original cartels, dating back to long before the 1980s. Based in Sinaloa State, it controlled marijuana production and trafficking in much of north-west Mexico, mostly destined for the US market. When the Colombian NTOs, which had dominated the twentieth-century cocaine trade, were subjected to heavy government and US pressure, they started to lose their ability to manage complex international trafficking operations. They were already working with Mexican crime gangs so the Colombian groups started to sell cocaine directly to the Mexican NTOs, which then independently managed transportation and supply to the US market.

The political stability during the many years of the PRI party's control up until 2000 meant that the Sinaloa Cartel had embedded itself into the political structure, protecting its activities and members. Often called the Sinaloa Federation, it comprises various large and small NTOs that work closely on its multinational trafficking operations. As its most visible leader, Guzman was the local 'patrón', somewhat similar to the figure of *The Godfather*,[12] enforcing his own law among the local population and giving out favours, buying him a strong local support base that served to protect him during his many years as a fugitive.

Although the Mexican state had previously been able to limit or informally manipulate NTO activity through their links with the cartels, in the early twenty-first century the changes between PAN and PRI governments made this less effective, thereby leaving NTOs to operate with more freedom. The US cocaine market was a huge opportunity for the cartels, with enormous profits to be made. Consequently, Mexican NTOs started to develop their structures to accommodate the international trafficking of cocaine, leading to new transport routes, connections and management of supply chains.

NTO diversification

After dramatic growth in the 1980s and 1990s, by the year 2000 US cocaine demand was reaching saturation so, while Mexican NTOs had the opportunity to take a dominant position in this billion dollar market, there was not much opportunity to expand the market itself. An outcome was that the main Mexican NTOs were soon facing strong competition from each other over access to the lucrative US market. Competition was based on territorial control – access to trafficking routes in Mexico, border areas, production areas, places with corrupt law enforcement and ports of entry and exit (including airports).

As the competition became fiercer, several NTOs looked for ways to diversify – moving into new markets, such as cocaine for Europe, or supplying new illicit drugs (principally methamphetamines) into North America via their established routes and contacts. Others took the opportunity to reinforce their local territorial control by developing the domestic consumer market, in this way involving more local people in their business model and increasing local dependency on (and thus loyalty to) that NTO.

The Sinaloa Cartel, for example, building on its existing dominance of the Mexican drug trafficking market and its relationships with US distributors and Colombian suppliers, expanded international operations to almost all of the Americas and started to develop trafficking networks through western Africa as a route to penetrating the European market. Their presence has been noted in as many as 50 countries worldwide. Strategically located on the western US border, it also developed various complex but effective drug corridors for all types of illegal narcotics making their way into the USA, gaining particular fame for their underground tunnels. Such was their territorial dominance that anyone involved in any part of the drug trade in their territory had to do it under the watchful eye of the Sinaloa Cartel, paying 'taxes'. Although these groups were not directly affiliated, their activities got absorbed into the Sinaloa Cartel's network (see Figure 3).

With the extra income generated from this new era of trafficking, the Sinaloa Cartel had to find new ways of investing and protecting their cash. One was money laundering, the creation of new legal businesses where they could hide and reinvest their drug profits, in order to present them as legitimate funds. Involvement in legal business presented new markets that the Sinaloa Cartel could seek to monopolise, using a mixture of legal and illegal methods. Looking to increase its market position further, the cartel also pursued an aggressive strategy of

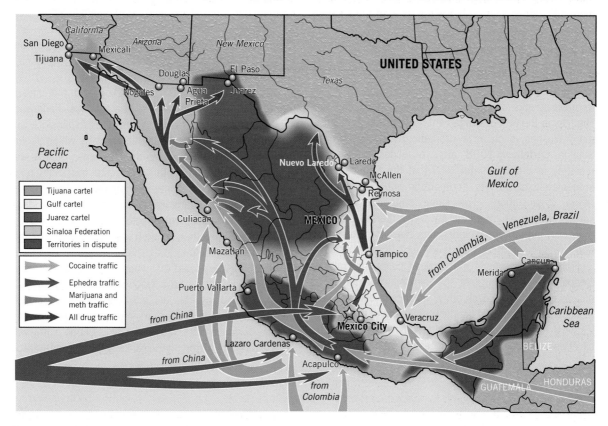

Figure 3 Cartel territories and drug routes, 2008
Source: Strategic Forecasting Inc., www.stratfor.com.

territorial expansion from 2005 onwards, seeking to control the entire west coast of Mexico from Guatemala up to California and the US border states. This brought it into direct territorial conflict with other NTOs, notably the Gulf Cartel, its main historic competitor on the East Coast, resulting in a series of bloody turf battles.

A changing competitive landscape . . .

The Gulf Cartel had expanded in much the same way in the early 2000s but had also developed a new wing to its operations: a paramilitary section that came to be known as the Zetas. The Zetas served to enforce the Gulf Cartel's 'law', collect debts and generally ensure territorial control and the protection of assets. Through extreme violence, the Gulf Cartel was able to take control over the entire eastern coast by 2008.

In response, and in order to expand into new areas, the Sinaloa Cartel did much the same, creating various armed groups or allying with local crime gangs. To build up those enforcement operations, the Sinaloa Cartel increased its investment in areas such as weapons procurement and trafficking, recruitment and corruption of military and police.

This led to further diversification in cartels' activities: to keep their paramilitaries busy, and to enforce territorial control, these groups dedicated their time not only to supporting and protecting the narco-trafficking operations and assets, but also moved into extortion, human trafficking and other criminal activities that benefit from the presence of armed 'protection'. These new activities meant that the government of Mexico was faced with highly competitive and successful criminal business organisations, willing to compete violently and now developing military capabilities.

Although tackling the cartels with force became harder for the state, these more diverse NTOs also developed a weakness: they could not survive without the capability to deploy force against the competition, which in turn could not survive without the huge income from trafficking, which was needed to fund arms procurement and increased personnel numbers. Managing the multifaceted nature of these organisations (legal and illegal business, together with military elements) meant expanding management capabilities. Expansion inevitably implied more difficulty in keeping below the radar of the state.

... and changing alliances

As the NTOs rapidly became stronger and more diverse, internal tensions and frictions increased, aggravated by frequent attacks from competing NTOs, causing constant changes in the NTO management hierarchies. This led to many clashes, such as a dramatic rupture within the Sinaloa Cartel in 2008 after a leadership dispute, resulting in a new splinter NTO that the Sinaloa Cartel immediately came into competition with (the Beltràn Leyva Organization). The same happened in other cartels, as the new paramilitary wings started to assert their own authority and undermine the parent organisations' traditional 'modus operandi' (see Figure 4).

From 2006 onwards, the Mexican police and military stepped up strikes against the cartels, while the NTOs increasingly attacked each other: violence levels exploded, resulting in thousands of deaths every year and huge organisational instability for many of the NTOs. While the aim for all of them was to manage successful international traf-

ficking operations, for which they prefer a relatively stable environment, survival was now based on eroding their main competitors. As a result, many NTOs were no longer able to manage both turf wars and leadership challenges, and thus saw their market share, and their capacity to manage complex trafficking operations, diminish.

Despite the inter-NTO competition and the government's 'drug war' initiatives, the Sinaloa Federation continued its strategy of aggressive expansion and attacking its rivals, including those with which it was once allied. While it suffered defections, deaths and arrests, its ability to maintain successful trafficking operations allowed it to continue dominating the market. Arguably, the continuing leadership and legendary status of El Chapo, was the management glue that held the Sinaloa Cartel together, giving it stability despite changes to the hierarchy below.

It had been expected that when El Chapo was arrested in 2014 there would be a leadership contest within the cartel. Surprisingly, this did not occur. In spite of being behind bars in one of Mexico's most secure prisons, the Sinaloa Cartel continued to be run by El Chapo jointly with other leaders of historic importance within the drug trade.

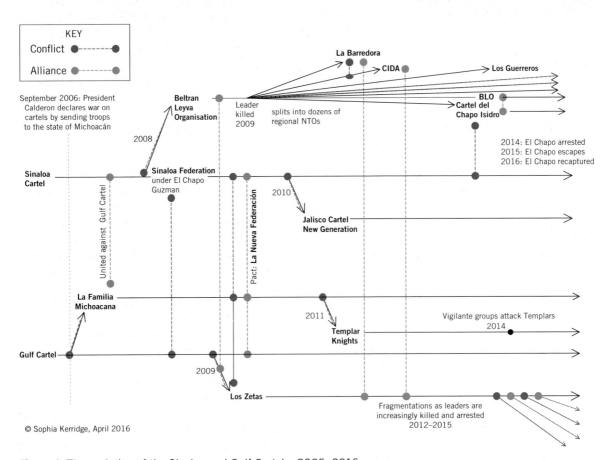

© Sophia Kerridge, April 2016

Figure 4 The evolution of the Sinaloa and Gulf Cartels, 2005–2016

The Sinaloa Cartel continued to successfully undermine lesser organisations, through street battles and bombings, and by organising the arrest or death of their leaders – and through the successful corruption and co-option of state agents. This did not stop factions from breaking off, as the rapid rise of the Jalisco Cartel demonstrated. Nevertheless, this did not significantly reduce the Sinaloa Cartel's market share, given the space left by other NTOs throughout Mexico fragmenting at an even faster rate.

A threat to the stability of the state?

2009 saw a new dynamic, as the Zetas broke away from the Gulf Cartel (the Sinloa Cartel's main rivals) and expanded control dramatically through eastern Mexico and into Central America, using extreme levels of violence and brutality when dealing with opponents. The Zetas are formed principally of people with some form of military training, which is clearly reflected in their organisational structure. Their military chain of command and strict discipline has meant that when leaders were removed, there was initially a clear line of succession. The organisation's reputation for violence and lack of 'second chances' allowed them to assert authority over new business activities despite their rapid organisational and operational expansion throughout Mexico and into Central America. The Zetas, unlike the more traditional NTOs, were more opportunistic: they had no need to win over the local population, and their principal motivation was income and gaining control over as many illegal industries in as large an area as possible.

As the Zetas grew, they came into direct competition with the Sinaloa Cartel. The resulting clash between the Zetas and the Sinaloa Cartel is also a clash of business models. Sinaloa and the older drug cartels focus on exploiting their core competences (international trafficking capabilities) and maintaining their brand reputation (for quality and reliability) in the industry. Embedding their activities in local economies is central to their survival and, at the highest levels, family and personal ties reinforce the networks. In contrast, the Zetas were more involved across a range of local criminal businesses and were less dependent upon international trafficking operations. Although risks are spread across various operations, those local businesses have much lower barriers to competitive entry and are more susceptible to fragmentation. Furthermore, their rapid expansion and excessive use of violence attracted the attention of various state forces and competitors, and forced Zeta units to adapt constantly. Blood rather than political corruption was their currency.

However, the Zeta model seems to have hastened its own demise. The brazen violence attracted a strong response from the state, with power struggles leading to fractures in the structure, and all four leaders being killed or arrested between 2012 and 2015. Its rapid expansion made any centralised control impossible and it seems that the Zetas have lost their power in the international trafficking market, instead dominating localised criminal networks in the areas in which they operate.

In this unstable competitive environment the violence continued: frictions caused divisions; divisions led to several new organisations and new alliances. Meanwhile the Mexican state, through police and military responses, continued trying to break the NTOs' power and influence by attacking their organisational hierarchies. While this has served to destabilise the NTOs, it does little to limit the business of drug trafficking, as the organisations merely adapt and continue supplying drugs to their customers. Analysts have noted that many NTOs such as the Zetas are too fragmented to manage international trafficking operations, whereas a few, such as the Sinaloa Federation, still do through their network of various specialised operations (see Figure 5).

In his mid-term address, President Peña espoused the successes he had had in targeting the NTOs, arguing that. 'We're not just capturing them, we're undermining their organisations and financial capacities.' While some of the NTOs, like the Zetas, were notably weaker as a result of this policy, the evidence of NTO violence and corruption implied that the market as a whole was not significantly affected, with Mexico continuing to be the main route for drugs into the USA. The need for a more comprehensive approach was evident. This was the challenge for President Peña Nieto and his policy advisors.

A new strategy in the war on drugs

By 2016, it was clear that the state's strategy was not having the desired results. Despite some successes, there was widespread anxiety about personal and public security, particularly in the main cities, and increasing mistrust of public institutions. The run-up to the next election in 2018 was Peña Nieto's last opportunity for a new approach in the war against the cartels, perhaps confronting them from an altogether different position.

In theory, the change in political leadership when Peña Nieto came into power should have affected the NTOs negatively, since previous political linkages would end and fresh ones would have to be established within the new political system. Although rumours of a possible return to the previous system of 'co-habitation' between the PRI and NTOs was fiercely denied, the pervasive violence meant that such options surely would be considered if they might guarantee better public safety.[13] It would not be the first time that a state chose to allow an

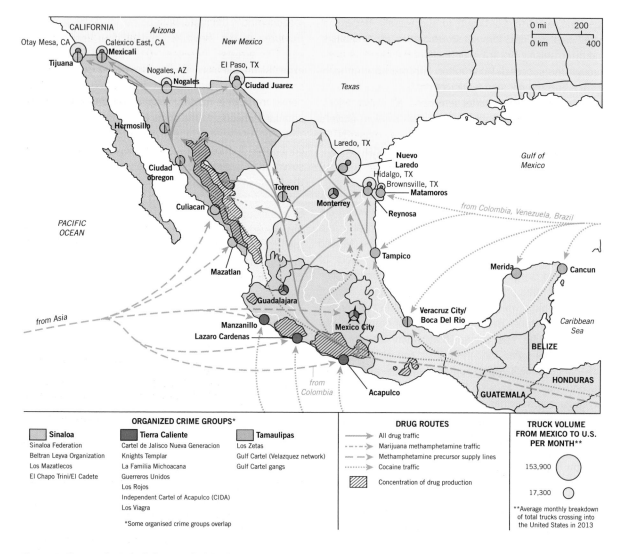

Figure 5 Areas of cartel influence in Mexico
Source: Strategic Forecasting Inc., www.stratfor.com.

NTO the freedom to operate in order to target other, more violent groups.[14]

At the same time, the Mexican state also has to respond to various national and international influences. In a democracy, where the President has just a few years to turn things around, there have to be visible improvements if there is any hope for the party to be re-elected. There are also external influences that need to be considered, such as foreign investment, US political pressure, and the impact on neighbouring countries as the NTOs expand across beyond Mexico's borders.

Evidently, the policy of armed attacks on the NTO hierarchies and short-term disruptions of drug routes had not produced the desired results. In part, this was because that strategy had not attacked the root of the problem, the *business* of drug trafficking.

To develop an effective strategy, the state needs to understand how the NTOs grew to be so large and wealthy; what strategies NTOs used to develop their markets and fight their competition. Much like other companies may look at competitors and try to evaluate their strategies, as a means to improve or adapt their own, the state can also do this to identify the cartels' business weaknesses and vulnerabilities. By analysing how an NTO has developed its business model, the state can evaluate its likely strategy in future scenarios – and try to act pre-emptively. Not least, instead of fighting the symptoms of the NTO problem, notably violence and the widespread influence of wealthy criminal families or organisations, it may be more productive to beat the NTOs at their own game: by changing conditions for the *business* of trafficking.

The President's policy advisors were well aware that suitable counter-NTO strategies would have to be acceptable to a range of stakeholders, in Mexico and abroad. For implementation to be feasible, it would be imperative that the government had sufficient and appropriate capabilities. Undoubtedly the recapture of El Chapo was a great boost to the Peña Nieto administration – but only one step forward in what was going to be a long and arduous path. The tough task now was to propose and implement an effective strategy to curtail these powerful NTO businesses.

Further information:

For further information, see the following videos:

The business model
- DNA Info, DEA's New York Chief explains the 'business model' of drug trafficking, http://www.youtube.com/watch?v=k2bFO-VY1ps

Violence as a marketing strategy
- Al Jazeera, Mexican drug gangs' public relations campaign, https://www.youtube.com/watch?v=MFasg-6ql1TY

The Sinaloa Cartel
- BBC, This World: Mexico's Drug War, https://www.youtube.com/watch?v=WxGAFbRfYtM
  CBS News, El Chapo's Escape, https://www.youtube.com/watch?v=zNsXEpWOriw

Zetas
- Insight Crime, Steven Dudley on the Zetas internal crisis, http://www.youtube.com/watch?v=wUm564EE-IT8&list=UUhEvdHcQEGdoKTsLFeNdb7g

The rise of self-defence forces
- Vice, Fighting Mexico's Knights Templar Cartel https://www.youtube.com/watch?v=dzalpuffwFI

Investment and diversification
- Insight Crime, Drug Gangs and Human Smuggling, http://www.youtube.com/watch?v=JH9GNd5AR-mU&list=UUhEvdHcQEGdoKTsLFeNdb7g&index=3
- Al Jazeera, How Mexico Drug Lords spend their ill-gotten gains, http://www.youtube.com/watch?v=BY-1dcqgEG2I
- Vice, Mexican Oil and Drug Cartels: Cocaine and Crude, https://www.youtube.com/watch?v=mPE-fArQU7tc

Notes and references
1. Note that this term, used in reference to large drug trafficking organisations, does not mean that they control and determine market prices.
2. K. Heinle, C. Molzahn and D. Shirk, *Drug Violence in Mexico: Data and Analysis Through 2014*, Justice in Mexico Project: University of San Diego, 2015, p. 10.
3. For further details see the 2015 documentary *Cartel Land*, https://www.youtube.com/watch?v=xC5bpPfltOI
4. June S. Beittel, CRS Report to the United States Congress, Mexico: Organised Crime and Drug Trafficking Organisations, R41576, 22 July 2015.
5. $1 = £0.6 = €0.75.
6. UNODC, *The Globalization of Crime: A transnational organized crime threat assessment*, 2010, p. 16.
7. Patrick Radden Keefe, 'Cocaine Incorporated', *New York Times Magazine*, 15 June 2012.
8. Steven D. Levitt and Stephen J. Dubner, *Freakonomonics: a rogue economist explores the hidden side of everything*, New York, William Morrow, 2005.
9. Sophia O. Kerridge, Oxford University Dept of Latin American Studies, MPhil thesis, 2011.
10. United Nations High-Level Panel on Threats, Challenges and Change in 2001, quoted in UNODC, *The Globalization of Crime: A transnational organized crime threat assessment*, 2010, p. 27.
11. Michael Shifter, 'Latin America's drug problem', *Current History*, February 2007, p. 62.
12. As epitomised in *The Godfather* movies, based on a novel by Mario Puzo.
13. *El Mundo*, 'Queremos tener tranquilo el pueblo. Todo está en su mano', 2 October 2012.
14. In Colombia during the early 1990s, the priority was to capture Pablo Escobar, leader of the Medellin Cartel, who had declared violent war on the state and also escaped from prison. Meanwhile the rival Cali Cartel remained unchallenged by the state until after the Medellin Cartel's downfall. It is believed that the Cali Cartel assisted the police and army in their efforts against the Medellin Cartel.

Where should the beds go? Infrastructure planning in NHS England

Paul Walley

This case looks at the strategic planning in one health community within NHS England, which provides healthcare to the population in England free at the point of access. The case examines the underlying financial structure and the control and measurement systems put into place by central government. It considers the challenges faced by managers focusing on the strategic planning within one hospital system, South Warwickshire NHS Foundation Trust (SWFT), and its aims to meet performance targets whilst maintaining financial stability. SWFT operates within the NHS and hence provides healthcare free at the point of consumption. SWFT's attempts to maintain its emergency care performance from 2007 onwards and the strategy decisions it faced at key points in time are tracked.

Background

The NHS is funded through taxation, and the HM Treasury in 2014–15 financial year provided £98.3bn[1] for the NHS England. Eighty per cent of all contact with the NHS is in primary care and £12bn of the total budget is spent on primary care services that provide access to the general practitioners (GPs) in local family practices. One of the big resource allocation issues is to decide how much money should go into other services and which organisations should receive it. The bulk of the money (about 60 per cent) is given to 209 *clinical commissioning groups* (CCGs). CCGs, each of which typically serves a local population of around 250,000, are led by an elected body and are responsible for the local purchase of mental health services, urgent and emergency care, elective hospital services and community care. Local GPs comprise 41 per cent of members of CCGs, but other professions are represented. The CCG's representative body states:

'Commissioning is about getting the best possible health outcomes for the local population, by assessing local needs, deciding priorities and strategies, and then buying services on behalf of the population from providers such as hospitals, clinics, community health bodies, etc. It is an ongoing process, and CCGs must constantly respond and adapt to changing local circumstances. CCGs are responsible for the health of their entire population, and are measured by how much they improve outcomes.'[2]

The money is spent by CCGs on a wide range of providers, including hospitals, GPs, dentists, opticians, private and third-party providers. A high proportion of the money is currently spent on hospital care, but not all hospitals are directly controlled by NHS England. Hospital Foundation Trusts, like SWFT, are

'independent legal entities and have unique governance arrangements. They are accountable to local people, who can become members and governors. They are set free from central government control and are no longer performance managed by health authorities. As self-standing, self-governing organisations, NHS foundation trusts are free to determine their own future. They have financial freedoms and can raise capital from both the public and private sectors within borrowing limits determined by projected cash flows, and are therefore based on affordability. They can retain financial surpluses to invest in the delivery of new NHS services'[3]

From the hospital manager's perspective, foundation status offers the opportunity to operate like a private company in many respects, but within a tight regulatory framework where many prices for the services it offers are largely fixed by NHS England in a tariff system. To achieve foundation status a hospital has to meet strict criteria and make a formal application.

As a result of increases in the UK population, increases in the average age of the population and more patients surviving longer with chronic diseases and degenerative conditions, the NHS is facing an increase in demand and an increase in the resources (staff time and money) required per patient. In addition, as scientific knowledge progresses, the complexity and hence costs of treatment are increasing. For example, the cost of new drugs is increasing due to higher development costs. This has often led the National Institute for Care Excellence (NICE), which produces evidence-based guidance on treatment and drug effectiveness, to reject recommendation for the use of new drugs as they offer poor value for the NHS.

Measuring performance in the NHS

It is clearly essential that a budget, as large and significant as that of the NHS, is spent wisely, with the government putting into place checks and balances to ensure that the system works as efficiently as possible. To assist in this process, a wide range of government departments and independent bodies are tasked with setting standards, reviewing practice and auditing providers. With over 1600 separate measures collected by different parts of the NHS and government, the NHS is probably one of the most measured organisations in the world. *The Care Quality Commission* is the independent regulator of health and social care in England that monitors, inspects and regulates services to ensure they meet standards of quality and safety. *Monitor* is a non-departmental body sponsored by the Department of Health that is 'required to support patient interests by promoting the provision of healthcare services that is economic, efficient and effective, and maintains or improves their quality.'[4] (In April 2016, Monitor was moved to become part of a larger organisation, *NHS Improvement*, bringing together several support groups.) The *National Audit Office* also gets involved, looking for cost savings in public bodies, including the NHS.

CCGs are guided by the NHS Outcomes framework which specifies five domains of efficiency, effectiveness and safety for organisations to achieve (see Figure 1).

Secondary care hospitals provide the majority of more complex surgical and medical procedures within the NHS, ranging from routine heart operations, orthopaedic treatment, cancer treatments, treatment for respiratory conditions and emergency care. Partly due to this extensive variety of care offered, each hospital trust has to report on a series of over 200 performance targets. There are several mandatory targets that every hospital strives to achieve:

1. 92% of patients must be seen within 18 weeks of referral, to ensure their treatment is not excessively delayed.
2. A 31-day diagnosis-to-treatment target for anyone diagnosed with cancer.
3. A 62-day referral-to-treatment target for anyone suspected of having cancer.
4. A *'c difficile'* infection reduction target.[5]
5. An *MRSA* infection reduction target.[6]
6. A four-hour waiting time target for accident & emergency (A&E) cases.

Senior hospital managers have to devise their own strategy for the ways in which they achieve these targets whilst maintaining the viability of the organisation in the longer term. The CCG pays for the care it commissions through a system called 'payment by results' where payment is based around standard tariffs for each type of treatment. Every time a patient is admitted to hospital for treatment, or attends A&E, their 'health resource group' (HRG) code will be recorded and this dictates how much money the hospital can claim for treating the patient. The HRG codes are determined by assessment of what work and resources should be used to complete treatment. A hospital that completes treatment very efficiently might make a slight surplus, but one that is a high cost provider could make a loss.

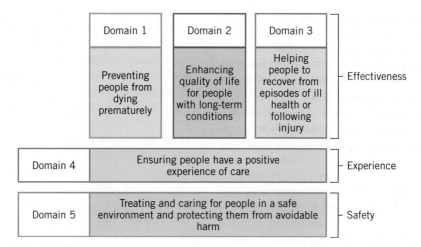

Figure 1 The five domains of the NHS Outcomes framework
Source: The NHS Outcomes Framework 2015/16, NHS England, Department of Health.

Meeting the four-hour target in South Warwickshire

It can be argued that the four-hour A&E target is the most challenging of these targets. The hospital is tasked with discharging or admitting 95 per cent of all patients that attend A&E within four hours of their arrival. For patients with minor injuries such as sprained ankles or simple cuts and bruises this should, in theory, be an easy target to achieve. Such treatment should take less than 30 minutes in many cases, but hospitals need to ensure that the medical staff are available and on duty at all times for this treatment to take place. The more serious cases such as patients suffering heart attacks, car accidents or serious falls present a bigger challenge. Dr Kate Silvester, an expert in designing healthcare systems, explains some of the challenges for the health community:

'The A&E waiting time target is a very good indicator of the health of the care system in a region as it is affected by the performance of every single provider and the interaction, coordination and cooperation between them. If we take a look at the services needed by an elderly patient, who maybe has had a fall at home or in a care facility, we can see that they use almost every part of the local healthcare system. The organisations involved could include the local GP, the out-of-hours primary care system, emergency call numbers (999 and 111), the ambulance service, the local hospital and its A&E department, community hospitals and care homes which may take the patient once their emergency care is over and community support services including community nurses, occupational therapists and social care. Some of these latter services may be provided by the local council or even voluntary groups.

Each of these providers may have a number of challenges of their own. For example, general practices are privately owned by a partnership of general practitioners whose services are commissioned and managed by NHS South Warwickshire Clinical Commissioning Group. Since it is very difficult for a small general practice of 3 to 6 doctors to provide 24/7 care 365 days a year to their list of patients who are registered with them, an "out of hours" service has to be commissioned. If either access to GP appointments or out-of-hours services becomes difficult this may encourage patients to simply attend their local A&E department where treatment is "guaranteed" within four hours.

When a patient arrives at the A&E department they will be assessed by a nurse and prioritised again to wait in the waiting room. If there is no bed or trolley available for ill patients, then they will wait on the ambulance's trolley, cared for by the ambulance crew until the A&E staff have the space and time to take over the patients care. This creates problems for the ambulance services because ambulances cannot get back out to deal with new patients until they have properly handed patients over to A&E.

If the patient requires care to be administered in hospital they will be transferred to a ward, and their care taken on by the on-take clinician rotated to take the emergencies for that day (or week). The patient may then need to be transferred to another specialist. For example, a patient may be initially seen by a respiratory specialist but they have a gastric problem. Once the patient is stable and no longer needs in-hospital care they will be discharged back home to be managed and monitored by their GP or as an outpatient.

For some patients a period of rehabilitation is required and they will be transferred to another hospital (often called a community hospital) or a nursing/residential care home where this care takes place until and if the patient is physically fit enough to go home. Community hospital staff, in this case managed by CCGs, also provides nursing and physiotherapy services into the patient home.

If the patient does not require nursing care, but social care, social care services and funds for privately run nursing homes and residential care are provided by the Social Service department managed by the local County Council which are not part of the NHS.

This system goes wrong whenever the flow of patients working their way through this complex, multi-organisation journey becomes disrupted or the system infrastructure becomes unbalanced. The main problem occurs when hospital beds become full because of delays to care and discharge. Slow in-hospital processes are one cause of these delays. Often there is also no opportunity for existing patients to be safely discharged into community facilities or care homes after their acute care is complete. This leaves no room for the new A&E arrivals to be admitted, eventually resulting in "trolley waits" where A&E patients can't even be given a cubicle and they have to wait on trolleys in hospital corridors. Ambulances are then unable to unload patients because A&E becomes full. This type of crisis still happens surprisingly often as few people really understand how to address the problems and implement solutions.'

Figure 2 is a representation of the healthcare system that Kate is describing, showing how patients might flow from Primary Care, through the hospital emergency department and hospital wards, to out-of-hospital services and back into the care of their GP.

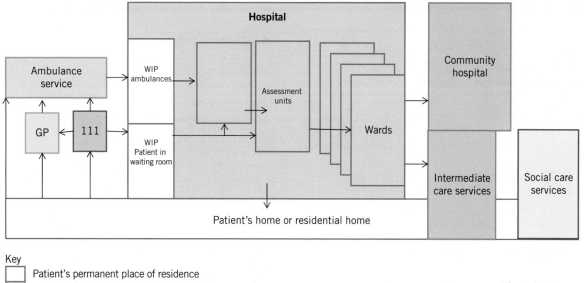

Figure 2 A typical emergency patient flow (based on South Warwickshire in 2009)
Source: Paul Walley/Kate Silvester, based on NHS data.

Addressing the four-hour wait target

The emergency care target has been an intense political issue since 2001 and remains a problem to the present day. The complexity of the system reflects the numerous interventions and re-organisations that have taken place in the NHS to achieve the A&E target. Demand into A&E is increasing and patients presenting to A&E often have chronic, not emergency, conditions. Many of the infrastructure developments such as the relatively new 111 telephone assistance service, the GP out-of-hours services and minor injury units were implemented with the objective to reduce the demand on A&E and reduce the number of emergency admissions to hospital, thus reducing the overall cost of the emergency service to the tax payer. However, those patients initially given a low priority, particularly the elderly, have learnt to go straight to A&E if they are acutely ill. Nationally, the emergency target performance has been steadily declining for the last few years, resulting in frequent 'winter crises' where the system appears to completely break down.

To look at the challenges faced by the Chief Executive of SWFT in meeting this target it is useful to take a longitudinal look at the trust's performance and the actions taken to address issues. Figure 3 shows the A&E performance at the trust from April 2007 to the end of October 2013. The chart shows that the SWFT A&E hasn't been able to hit the 98 per cent target consistently, with a number of periods over time when the trust suffered significant drops in performance. In November 2008, performance dropped suddenly and dramatically and then recovered in the summer of 2009, only to fall again in November 2011 and thereafter deteriorated with worsening performance particularly in the winter periods.

The A&E performance was the one target that the trust was failing to meet, so the trust started a major improvement programme in April 2009. The performance drop in November 2008 was highly significant as A&E performance is a factor that can affect a hospital's achievement of Foundation Status. Senior managers consider the achievement of foundation status a key part of their strategy because of the advantages it provides in being able to raise their own capital for investment, the ability to reinvest surpluses and less central government interference. Hence delays to achieving the A&E target were delaying all their independent investment decisions.

At this time two other critical factors came to the attention of the executive.

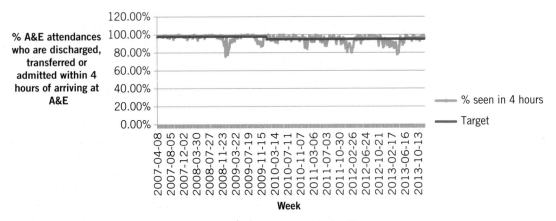

Figure 3 A&E performance in South Warwickshire NHS Foundation Trust

Source: Paul Walley/Kate Silvester, based on NHS data.

The hospital standardised mortality ratios

The comparable mortality data was published for all hospitals in England, now called rate adjusted morality index (RAMI) and produced and published publically by the private company, Dr Foster. The death rates for all hospitals in England are compared statistically and are indexed so that the death rate for the average hospital is equal to 100. In June 2009, the executive and population of South Warwickshire learned that their hospital's mortality rate for emergency patients was considerably above the 100 average figure. Checks suggested this was not a coding problem.

Was the mortality high in Warwick due to the delays in the emergency care system? Were the delays due to a shortage of resources or the very inefficient processes that staff had unwittingly created over the years of practice?

A patient's experience

In June 2009, a patient wrote to the hospital CEO with a detailed and factual account of his experience of being admitted with a serious emergency over the Easter bank holiday. The CEO invited the patient to talk to the clinical staff who had been involved in his care. As the patient explained what happened, a member of staff mapped what had happened to him. This value map showed that he lay in bed for ten days waiting for care which should have only taken 34 hours, a crucial part of his care was delayed for five days and he lost one third of his blood volume over this time which went unnoticed by the staff on the three wards between which he was moved. The doctors involved in the care were shocked by the story and after a period of discussion accepted the system had problems. The patient accepted the public apology by the A&E consultant (whose department had done an excellent job) on behalf of all the hospital's staff, there was agreement that the current system could not be

allowed to continue. This emotional event was exactly what was needed to ensure that the clinicians and managers engaged, perhaps unwillingly to start with, in addressing the delays in their system of care – even though they still believed that the poor care and flow was due to a lack of resources not the internal working and scheduling of the hospital, which had been beautifully observed and monitored by the patient.

Crisis in September 2009

A&E performance suddenly deteriorated again in September 2009. No-one could understand why as demand was normal for the time of year. An improvement programme created fortnightly 'big room' meetings in which clinicians and senior managers from organisations across the local health and social care system were encouraged to attend and learn about changes to the wider system (not just inside the acute hospital). For the first time they were given the opportunity to observe the impact of these changes on the South Warwickshire's health and social care system performance.

At the October 2009 'big room' meeting, the public health doctors working for the CCG revealed that a local 40-bed community hospital in Alcester had been closed on 1 September 2009 in order to reduce the CCG's costs. The remaining residents had been transferred into other NHS community hospitals or into private residential nursing homes funded by the patients privately or through social services. Although this had been part of the CCG's strategy for many years, the focus of attention had been on implementation of the physical changes to the system and not the impact on the system as a whole. From the CCG's perspective, the closure of Alcester's community beds was a straightforward decision from a financial and strategic point of view. A typical hospital bed costs £400 a day to keep open and even though community hospital beds are usually cheaper, they are often in small facilities where there are no economies of scale. In the case of Alcester, the site occupied by these facilities was of tremendous value and its closure also facilitated the demolishing of older buildings to be replaced by a brand new £6.8m primary care centre. This was intended to provide better value healthcare with more care delivered in the primary care system and elderly patients treated at home by an 'integrated health and social care' (IHSC) team. This would eventually use a new delivery concept called the 'virtual ward' where the systems and staffing found in a hospital ward are re-created in a home setting.[7] The expansion and integration of the primary care facilities in Alcester would also allow further non-NHS activity to be provided at the same location. This includes private treatments for acupuncture, trauma counselling, podiatry, hypnotherapy, coaching and sports therapy.

The impact of this closure became apparent to everyone in the 'big room'. The staff at Warwick hospital were unable to discharge any of their patients who required community hospital rehabilitation care, so the backlog of patients waiting for discharge suddenly and significantly increased inside the acute hospital. The flow from A&E reduced – with an accompanying spike in the death rate that no-one else had noticed because of the way in which these statistics are compiled.

The change in culture across the organisations represented in the 'big room' was profound. Instead of each organisation and department focusing on their own efficiency and cost, everyone began to realise that they were part of a complex interdependent system. A well-intentioned change in one part of the system could have profound and unintended consequences in another part of the system. In this case, we have a change imposed by central government, implemented by an independent funding body, but the chief executive of the local hospital is blamed for the poor A&E performance that happens as a consequence.

The CCG and acute hospital staff all recognised that they had to increase the bed capacity to cope with the increased delays to discharge. Since the community hospital had been sold to the private sector and couldn't be reopened, two temporary wards were built at the acute hospital and opened just before Christmas 2009. A&E performance improved for one week, and then it deteriorated again as these 40 beds filled up. The outflow constraint still had not been addressed. Again there was the spike in the death rate over the Christmas 2009 holiday period.

By the end of March 2010, internal policy constraints that impacted on mortality were being addressed at the hospital – in particular the change to the working schedules of all the staff. Junior doctor capacity was pooled across A&E and the assessment units so patients were examined and investigated within two hours of arrival, the prioritisation policies abandoned and lead times for laboratory and imaging investigations were improved. Senior medical and surgical staff were scheduled in the hospital from 08:00 to 22:00, seven days a week, 365 days a year, to ensure that all patients had a clear diagnosis, prognosis and their care plan on their day of attendance. Although these changes didn't impact on the flow constraint downstream of the hospital, the impact on mortality was dramatic. Despite the poor A&E performance, Monitor recognised the outstanding process improvements and the impact on mortality and the South Warwickshire NHS Foundation Trust was confirmed in April 2010.

What happened between April 2011 and November 2012?

Having reduced the overburden on the staff and thus improved morale and the mortality rate, the hospital continued to struggle against the constraint caused by closing the beds in the community trust without first improving the lead times for the community and social care services to discharge patients from all the hospitals in the system to home or to residential care.

In April 2011, SWFT took over the community hospitals and services from the CCG, but the social care services and funding was still managed by the local government. Over the next two years the combined teams reorganised themselves around the work so that all patients who no longer needed hospital care could be transferred either directly to community rehabilitation hospital or a nursing home in which the rehabilitation care would be provided. The first six weeks in a private facility were paid by South Warwickshire NHS Foundation Trust. Six weeks is enough time to assess whether a patient will recover sufficiently to return home and six weeks is the lead time for family and social care to sort out the finances for private residential care if they can't. Community services delivered into the patient's home were also reorganised and the lead times reduced by eliminating the prioritisation policies. In October 2012, the social care budget was cut and the policies governing social care financial support for patients changed. The impact of this system change is visible in the A&E performance. By April 2012, 7/7 working had been agreed and re-contracted for all staff in the parts of the system now managed by SWFT. Figure 4 shows the last recorded measure for A&E performance and mortality and indicates that A&E flow had improved

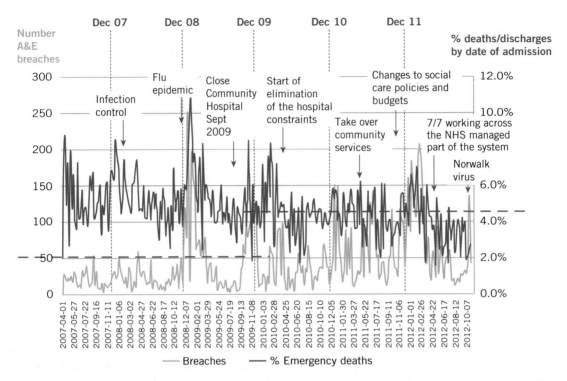

Figure 4 Summary of the main changes and their temporal relationship to A&E performance and mortality
Source: Paul Walley/Kate Silvester, based on NHS data.

dramatically until the impact of the norovirus outbreak in October 2012. Norovirus does not respond to alcohol and alcoholic hand rubs – the mainstay of the hospitals infection control policy is now ineffective. The figure highlights the journey that managers and clinicians have been on in their efforts to achieve targets and maintain outcomes whilst keeping within financial constraints.

Postscript

In December 2014, the UK NHS had one of the biggest winter crises in its history. A&E target achievement collectively fell to below 90 per cent and most hospitals failed to maintain their own target achievement. SWFT was one of the very few that managed to maintain its A&E flow throughout the winter period.

Notes and references
1. £1 = €1.2 = $1.5.
2. http://www.nhscc.org/ccgs/ This page takes you to the NHS Clinical Commissioners website which is an independent membership organisation for Clinical Commissioning Groups (CCGs).

3. http://www.nhs.uk/NHSEngland/thenhs/about/Pages/authoritie-sandtrusts.aspx This is the 'NHS Choices' website that provides information to patients and other members of the public about the NHS in England. There is some useful background information about the structure of the NHS in England and the 2013 restructuring of the NHS.
4. https://www.gov.uk/government/organisations/monitor/about This provides a link to the reports and description of Monitor activities. Monitor was moved to become part of NHS Improvement in April 2016.
5. *C. difficile* is a bacterium that is present in 3% of adults and 66% of babies. Patients weakened by other conditions can be made more seriously ill if they suffer from *C. difficile* and so hospitals have to demonstrate good hygiene practice and a reduction in *C. difficile* cases. For example in 2012 the target was to reduce infections by 17% (16,000 cases per year).
6. There is a significant increase of antibiotic-resistant bacteria globally. In 2012, for example, the target was to reduce NHS MRSA bloodstream infections by 29% to around 880 cases per year.
7. http://www.nuffieldtrust.org.uk/our-work/projects/examining-effectiveness-virtual-wards provides a summary of a report; G.H. Lewis, T. Georghiou, A. Steventon *et al.*, *Impact of 'Virtual Wards' on hospital use: a research study using propensity matched controls and a cost analysis*, National Institute for Health Research Service Delivery and Organisation Programme, November 2013, HMSO.

Strategic planning at King Faisal Hospital and Research Centre Saudi Arabia

Paul Walley

This case examines the strategic planning processes inside a public-sector organisation. PESTEL analysis can be conducted to highlight some of the unique features of the environment in which the hospital operates. Senior managers have embarked on a formal planning process and the effectiveness of both the process of strategy development and the outcome can be explored and critiqued. The case highlights how political processes influence the outcome and demonstrates that even within the public sector, organisations can be seen to compete with each other for market share and a share of the resource pool.

Introduction

The King Faisal Specialist Hospital and Research Centre (KFSH & RC) is a tertiary care health facility and research centre with two main sites in Riyadh and Jeddah, Saudi Arabia. The organisation has nearly 7000 staff, 46 per cent of whom are expats comprising 63 different nationalities, and a total operating budget of some £1bn (€1.2bn, $1.5bn)[1] across all sites. There are 18 medical departments including oncology, cardiology, neuroscience, genetics and transplants. Staff offer highly advanced types of care in specialist disciplines but also offer primary care, secondary care and emergency services to staff and to those patients accepted for tertiary care.

Built in the 1970s, the hospital was one of the first modern facilities in the country. Initially used exclusively by the royal family, as it expanded it gradually served the general population for specialist care in areas such as cancer and organ transplantation. It sits outside the main Health Ministry hospital system and exists as a special organisation within government. Consequently, it can operate largely independently. It was the first hospital in Saudi Arabia to produce its own formal five-year strategic plan, from 2008–12. This case considers the process for the revised plan from 2013 onwards – producing a 'Vision 2020'.

The strategic plan

We join Dr Paul Walley, head of the Project Management Office in the Department of Planning and Monitoring, who explains the nature of the organisation's strategic plan and the planning process itself:

'The first strategic plan had a number of very useful elements in that it helped the hospital's senior managers to develop clear guidelines and vision, mission and values statements that can largely be carried forward to the next strategic plan. The current plan has detailed over 80 separate strategic projects that are mostly still underway and that collectively work towards the aims and objectives within the original plan, with a total planned capital spend somewhere around £1bn. My role is to monitor the progress of these projects and to report progress to the director of strategic planning and to a larger planning committee, chaired by the chief executive, once a month. I then try to encourage more activity on projects that are making slow progress and assist the project managers in achieving project completion. The projects are diversified, ranging from small IT developments through to large construction projects, including the new King Abdullah Cancer Centre, which is going to be a 22-storey new hospital within the existing Riyadh site that we hope will be opening within the next two years. When the Cancer Centre is finished this should really be a flagship development within the country. Like most of the other buildings at the hospital, it will not only have the most up-to-date medical equipment, but also lavish interiors. In the main buildings the public areas have marble floors and walls. The budget for furniture and equipment has just been doubled to

£150m, and when we appoint new department heads they will come with their own shopping lists of new items of equipment adding further to the expenditure.

I have been working on the development of the next strategic plan for the last nine months and we are hoping that we will be able to produce the new full document in time for its official start in January 2013. Things never really happen on time as there is always much discussion and consultation, with last-minute changes, so it will be a challenge to bring everything together. This week we have reached a real peak in our activity. The hospital has engaged two external consultants, one from the University of Oklahoma and one from Johns Hopkins University, to come over in a relatively short visit to help produce the document. They have expertise in health planning and understand the trends in healthcare globally. One consultant is also on the Advisory Board to the Saudi Health Ministry and so has an inside track on what developments are happening in the rest of the country. We also have to understand trends in health research and what governments are doing across the Middle East. Most of the oil-rich countries, including Saudi Arabia, are continuing to invest and grow their health services, which is obviously a good thing, but it creates additional issues for the supply of qualified staff, for example.

Our process for producing the report is quite formal and we now have a series of meetings and events to put some final touches to the plan for Riyadh. Our site in Jeddah has more complex issues because we are waiting for the sign-off of a massive new development on a brand new two million square metre site not far from Jeddah airport. You can imagine the budget for an entire new hospital, with all support services including shops and accommodation for thousands of doctors and nurses, will be huge. We've found that people cannot really think beyond this at the moment so this is proving to be a bit of a mental block. Today my 8.30 am meeting is with the consultants to go through the findings from prior meetings with senior officials from different public organisations in Saudi Arabia. Next we have a quick catch-up with my three Saudi colleagues in the planning department, who are organising a workshop in Jeddah for about 150 senior staff. We have just held an almost identical workshop in Riyadh, at the nearby Ritz Carlton Hotel. At these meetings we present our findings on the external analysis, staff surveys and strategic project progress reviews so that we can get all department heads and other important individuals to discuss and hopefully agree on the priorities and programmes for the next seven years. At 11.00 am I have to go with the team to the monthly project review meeting where I will report on the progress of the current projects. This meeting will finish at about midday, just as prayers are called.[2] This will give us time for a quick lunch before we get out on the road to visit more officials and VIPs. These external visits are vital. They provide us with valuable information about health policy, progress on existing projects, where future money is likely to be spent, etc. and we can gauge the level of support the hospital has amongst some very influential people. Our plans will not be supported by anyone who feels they have been left out of the consultation process, so we have to be very thorough. Over the last few days we have met with Dr Abdullah Al-Sharif, the Secretary General of the Council of Cooperative Health Insurance, Dr Abdulrahman Muammar, Vice Rector of King Saud University Medical Affairs, Professor Saleh Bawazir, from the Saudi Food and Drug Authority, and Dr Yagoub Al Mazrou, from the Council for Health Services. Today's meetings are the most important as we are meeting Dr Mohammed Khushaim, from the Health Ministry, and then His Excellency Dr Abdullah Al Rabiah, Minister of Health. Our strategic plan cannot happen without the support of the Minister of Health and we need to approach the meeting carefully. The Minister is a well-known surgeon who has worked at other hospitals, including the National Guard hospital and is on the Executive Board of another major hospital in Saudi.'

The first meeting starts and the team discuss the findings of their early interviews. It is clear that some other hospitals within the country are gaining a better reputation in some clinical areas. Consequently, support for funding King Faisal Hospital to offer the same care could be threatened. They process this data and then systematically work through the slides they are intending to present at the forthcoming workshop. Table 1 shows the results of a simple poll amongst the senior leaders of all the main health organisations, showing which hospitals had the best reputation for care in the kingdom.

The external analysis initially looks at changes in demand for healthcare. The Saudi population is expected to grow from the current (estimated) 29 million to nearly 32 million by 2020, but it is the demographic balance which is providing a number of possible challenges. The number of Saudis aged 60 or above will double by 2020, putting pressure on health services. There is also a larger group of younger people who, potentially, could cause an increase in the birth rate in a few years' time. However, this may be counter-balanced by a drop in the number of children each family chooses to have. Another factor is the potential for poor health amongst the population caused by low levels of exercise, dietary changes and

Table 1 Who provides the best care? (Number of votes from senior leaders in face-to-face interviews)

	King Faisal Hospital	Prince Sultan Military Medical City	King Fahd Medical City	National Guard	King Khalid University Hospital	Suliaman Habib (private)
Cardiology	0	6	1	3	0	2
Neuroscience	1	0	5	0	2	0
Oncology	4	0	1	1	0	0
Genetics	4	0	0	0	0	0
Transplants	6	1	0	4	0	0

genetic predisposition towards some inherited diseases. Somewhat ironically, the level of consanguinity in marriages that raises levels of genetic disease also makes living donor organ transplant much more feasible than in most other countries as the likelihood of finding a perfect genetic match within a family is much greater. In this respect the hospital is well-placed to take advantage of new medical technologies and advanced clinical practices in some areas.

The planning team also consider the likelihood of continued public spending within Saudi Arabia. As the country with the largest reserves of crude oil in the world, the King has been able to provide very generous budgets and ambitious growth plans for many parts of the public sector. However, the money supply is becoming more vulnerable as oil prices fluctuate, oil reserves decrease and the country starts to consume more of its own oil output in activities such as electricity generation and water desalination.

The results from staff surveys form a major part of the internal analysis. Results show good knowledge and support for the organisation's mission and values: 67 per cent of staff believe the organisation is ready for further change; 75 per cent of managers believe they are able to identify problem areas and help make improvements, but fewer than half non-managers agree that managers provide this capability. These results highlight some of the implementation challenges. This data is put onto slides and approved by Khalid Al Rasheed, the Director of Strategy and Planning.

The team is joined by the rest of the planning department mainly to work on the logistics for the Jeddah workshop which will be held at the Hilton hotel on the Corniche (seafront). Buses will be arranged to transport staff there and there are housekeeping issues, such as the likelihood of segregation of male and female staff at the conference which clearly affects seating plans and discussion groups. Jeddah is more liberal than Riyadh, so there are likely to be fewer restrictions. In the Riyadh workshop female senior nurses and doctors, including the Executive Director of Nursing, were not able to sit with other senior staff in case the hotel was inspected by the religious police. Paul explains the intended approach for the Jeddah workshop:

> **'Our plan is to present the analysis and then ask teams to work on the strategic priorities, with an electronic voting system in place so that the levels of support for the plans can be determined. We have five proposed strategic priorities, adapted from those in the existing plans. We still aim to have the development of world-leading care as our first priority, focusing on areas such as cancer and transplant surgery. Some areas, such as cardiology, need development but there are other good providers in the Kingdom. All section heads inevitably want their department to expand, but we must make some difficult and politically sensitive choices. Capacity is still short across the Kingdom so expansion is still a priority in many areas and it also needs to become more efficient. We still judge recruitment and retention of staff difficult and in need of considerable attention over the next few years. We must also do better to obtain funding from both government and non-government sources. There are many potential donors out there and the trick is to find those prepared to fund sensible developments that have a strategic fit.'**

The planning team make their way to the top-floor grand meeting room near the Chief Executive's office in the main building for the project review meeting. Paul presents his findings. About half of the programmes are progressing very well, especially the construction projects where there are extensive project plans. Related projects, such as those dealing with the recruitment and mobilisation of staff, are not happening as quickly. Paul gently warns that they could end up with a fully fitted-out new cancer hospital and no-one to work the equipment or treat the patients. The one programme that needs greater impetus (a red flag on the report) is the programme to improve revenue generation and fundraising. The Chief Executive cuts the discussion short and issues an instruction that only programmes should be discussed at the meeting and not individual projects. The meeting finishes at prayer time and the team go to the staff social club for an early lunch.

Meeting the ministers

Two cars arrive outside the planning office and the team bundle into them to get to the Ministry of Health on time. The journey is a short distance but takes time in the traffic-clogged streets. The first meeting, with Dr Khushaim, starts off informally, but the conversation moves quickly to the Ministry of Health plans. Much of this information is published within government five-year planning documents, but changes always occur quite rapidly as new money is found for additional projects and progress is haphazardly made on existing efforts. Dr Khushaim is well-informed and explains his plans:

> 'We are aware of the dissatisfaction in the population with the current state of healthcare in the Kingdom, as many people struggle for a hospital bed when they need care. We currently have 59,000 beds for a population of 29 million (two beds per thousand) and we need to expand this so that we have 3.9 beds per thousand people . . . King Faisal Hospital still has an important role in the country, but it must focus on its areas of strength in tertiary and quaternary care. We also need you to coordinate services well with the Health Services Council. The shortage of facilities in Jeddah should allow you to expand services there to match those in Riyadh . . . Our big challenge is to produce the doctors you will need in your hospitals and we are moving from four to 26 new medical schools to produce 16,000 new medical students. We are also looking outside the Kingdom to academic medical centres for new staff.'

The team are suddenly called through to meet Dr Rabiah so they thank Dr Khushaim for his important input to the plan and move to the waiting area for the Minister's office. They go into a large office and sit informally at tables. Staff bring in Arabic coffee in large dallahs and fresh dates, followed later by mint tea. The Minister arrives and the conversation starts. The team deliver a draft copy of the strategic plan working document and ask the Minister for his advice in finalising the work. The Minister is clear in his opinion:

> 'The Health Ministry is making large investments in five medical cities and in community hospitals across the country. King Faisal Hospital does not need to replicate services that these organisations can provide and so you should focus on quaternary[3] care and care for those conditions that the country cannot otherwise provide. We send 1500 people abroad each year for care in other countries where we don't have a capability ourselves. King Faisal Hospital should develop capabilities to stop this from happening. I would also like to see you develop better community outreach

services. You are located in a part of Riyadh where very few local people can access your services.'

The discussion moves on to the national referral system which goes live in two months' time. This system will allocate patients to hospitals based upon availability and need.

> 'King Faisal Hospital cannot be integrated into the referral system as it is too late to do so now. The opportunity was given years ago and was not taken. We can coordinate with you to ensure that you receive the patients you should be treating.'

The meeting finishes when the Minister is called to another meeting. The team thank him for his valuable input and leave. Paul explained their interpretation of this last meeting and the inference for support for the plan:

> 'Things have definitely changed since last time. Five years ago our hospital didn't have much internal competition for funding from other secondary or tertiary centres. Now we have the Prince Sultan Military Hospital, amongst others, with expertise in cardiology and three other major centres with comparable or better expertise in neuroscience. We still have the best reputation for oncology, genetics and transplants which still makes us a most valuable provider of care in these areas. However, the level of support for us is falling as political allegiances move towards the Military Hospital. This is affecting our funding and may influence the scope of our plans. For example, we have a proposal for an £80m experimental proton carbon-ion therapy unit for the treatment of tumours but another hospital has seen our plans and submitted exactly the same request. Given there are only three of these units in the rest of the world it would not make sense for two to be located within eight miles of each other in Riyadh, so one organisation is likely to lose out. I have my concerns that the Minister is favouring other hospitals. There is a lot of tribal allegiance within the culture and this is reflected in the ways allegiances to organisations can be established.'

By the time they arrive back at the hospital there is another prayer time called so they finish for the day. Tomorrow will be just as busy putting the final arrangements in place for the Jeddah workshop.

Trip to Jeddah

The following week the team arrive late one evening at the Jeddah Hilton and check on the progress in the meeting room where the workshop will be held. Paul helps put the workshop folders around each table and then loads the presentations onto the room computer. Everything seems to be in place, so he retires to his suite. Next day, the breakfast meeting is more animated than expected. They had all received their complimentary copies of the *Arab News* outside their rooms and, on page 2, there was an extensive article about the Health Ministry's plans, including an interview with the Health Minister. The Minister explained a new strategy for the National Guard hospital. There were plans to develop world-leading services, expand capacity and make recruitment of staff a priority. There were striking similarities between this press release and the report the team had left with the Minister just a few days before. Was this just a coincidence?

Notes

1. £1 = €1.2 = $1.5.

2. Muslim prayers are called five times a day, normally twice during a daytime shift, and all muslim staff are obliged to attend. Prayers are called via the local mosques and the hospital tannoy. Doctors can continue with surgical operations during prayers. You can also finish a meal or journey before you pray. Western staff often buy food and drink just before the shops close and wait out the 20–30 minutes. The times of the prayers varies slightly each day dependent on the location, lunar calendar and time of year.

3. Quaternary healthcare is usually defined as 'highly specialised and advanced medical procedures, such as specialised surgery, including activities such as rarely-practised organ transplants, or experimental treatments'.

Mormor Magda's ice cream: can you be hot in a cool market?

Adele Berndt and Anders Melander

In this case Angela Hafström reflects on her dream of producing tasty ice cream and all that had happened since she started out in 2010. Despite all the challenges, she knew she had made a difference to the market. The key issue now is to translate this difference into a profitable growth!

Angela was polite while speaking on the phone, but inside she felt frustration grow. She knew this was not going to be the last time. And in some ways, it was flattering, but why should she receive so many calls from unknown people asking her about how to develop an ice cream business? Why couldn't people develop their own ideas?

In the autumn of 2015, Angela Hafström and her company, Mormor (Grandma) Magdas[1] made it into the news again. This time they had launched an innovative new product – dairy-free ice cream entirely based on natural ingredients and with no nuts. Once again they were among the first on the Swedish market with such an innovation and again the idea was inspiring to many other organisations.

Any frustration about the phone calls from unknown people soon disappeared when Angela remembered the father who came in and bought six tubs of ice cream from their small factory in Taberg, Sweden. He almost cried as he explained – this was going to be the first time his daughter, suffering from a severe nut allergy, would be able to taste ice cream.

The background

In spring 2010, Angela Hafström was on parental leave with her third child and without a job to return to. Educated in marketing/public relations and with a keen interest in food and cooking, she decided to search for new opportunities. With few job opportunities in Jönköping (a city of about 130,000 inhabitants), the search for a new job had become tiring. Home on the sofa, she realised that there wasn't a quality ice cream made in Sweden that could compete with international brands (such as Ben and Jerrys®). Her husband initially thought this was just a phase, but when a few days later Angela had produced a business plan, he realised that he either had to support her or find himself divorced. He chose the supportive strategy and soon Angela, together with two of their closest friends and her brother in Stockholm (a successful entrepreneur), began to plan intensively for this new business. One of Angela's first moves was to set up a blog that soon became a success. The intention was that after some time she would reveal her plan to start an ice-cream factory on the blog. 'By making my plan public, I could not abandon the project. I had to go through with it,' Angela explained.

None of those involved knew how to make ice cream or had experience from the ice cream industry. Where to find a suitable location for the factory? How to make ice cream? How many employees? How to sell the ice cream? The only way to raise capital was for Angela to take a mortgage on the house she and her husband owned.

Following her brother's advice, Angela began to conduct market research. Therefore she began conducting cold calls. One such speculative call was to one of Sweden's most successful food store owners, who happened to be situated in Jönköping. To her surprise, he spent more than an hour explaining the mysteries of the ice cream business to her. He concluded by saying that logistics was the key to success and she probably had no chance in succeeding in that area. However, if she made a success of it, he promised to sell her ice cream in his stores. Five years later he still sells Mormor Magda's ice cream and Angela continues to use him as a sounding board.

A vertical take-off

About a year later in July 2011, Angela's dream became a reality when her factory opened in Taberg, a very small town where space could be found at a reasonable cost, situated several kilometres south of Jönköping. The opening of the 118-square-metre factory was a success. Angela's blog and other activities had resulted in articles in both national and local media – as a result, on the opening day there was a queue on about 650 people outside the small factory. The overwhelming success, however, created problems. All the ice cream was sold out within two days. On Friday night, Angela and her husband closed the factory, put their three children to sleep in the office and made ice cream until four in the morning. By Saturday morning they could once again offer the customers freshly made ice cream!

By the autumn of 2011, sales at the factory had stabilised, a couple of employees were hired and ice cream was distributed to local stores in the immediate vicinity. Soon afterwards, a large investment was made to create a freezing room, which made it possible to expand distribution to Stockholm, three hours' driving distance away, and its surrounds. Angela explained, 'I wanted to go to Stockholm. It is my hometown and my brother lives there. And, that is the place to be if you are going national.'

On social media there were a lot of potential customers that wanted to buy the Mormor Magda's ice cream in Stockholm. Angela has actively used social media to engage with actual and potential customers. This included not only Facebook but also Instagram and her own blog. Her goal is to post three to five times per week on Facebook/Instagram, showing where the ice cream is available and building connections with customers.

In the summer of 2012, Angela experimented with selling ice cream in waffle cones. In a few months, turnover was more than SEK1mn (€95,000)[2] at just one mobile sales outlet in Jönköping. Sales were a success, but if she had paid regular salaries to herself and her family the profit would have been low. As with most small business owners, she invested a lot of her own time into the business. The 2012 annual report commented on this, concluding that waffle cone sales was very different from the company's original business idea and that perhaps a franchising concept could be more suitable for this product in the future.

In terms of the main ice cream business, business was expanding, albeit slowly. However, without the waffle cone business turnover halved in 2013 and the company made a loss. As a result, there was a need for new ideas on how to expand. In 2014, Angela's brother joined the business as a board member, bringing one of his friends with him. Both were experienced entrepreneurs from the travel agency industry. Additionally two of Angela's friends, a successful web-designer and an art director, also joined the group, extending the board to six people (including Angela and her husband and brother). The board meet once a year and have phone meetings every third month. Angela is the only one in the board with working experience from the ice cream business; 'The board is really supportive, but sometimes they are perhaps too entrepreneurial. Realities in the ice-cream business are tough!' Angela concludes.

The board soon decided that there was a need for more capital if the business was to expand. More marketing and the instalment of branded fridges in food stores were two of the urgent needs. Branded fridges are a common way of increasing exposure in food stores and avoiding the battle over space with competitors.

Crowdfunding to manage growth

Soon the idea was raised to test 'crowdfunding' in order to afford these investments. As a contributor to an entrepreneurship magazine *Entreprenor*, Angela raised the issue faced by many entrepreneurs in her column, namely access to funds. The editor suggested making contact with Daniel Daboczy, the founder of Fundedbyme, a Scandinavian equity crowdfunding platform. Equity crowdfunding provides investors with the opportunity to invest money in return for shares in the organisation. In the first two weeks, 33 people invested in the campaign, but it did not continue like this in the following weeks. Then suddenly, when the campaign was about to close, investments flooded in (98 in the last two weeks). 'I was really disappointed as I thought we would not meet our objective,' says Angela, 'but we got there in the end. I learnt so much from the campaign – I almost want to do it again.' The campaign was considered a success and SEK1.4M was raised by the time it closed in April 2015. Now Mormor Magda had 142 new shareholders owning 20.5 per cent of the company. Most of these investors had invested SEK2,000–10,000 (€220–1100). There was one big exception in the campaign, a local resident with a background as a financial controller who invested a significant sum and thus expected a seat on the board, so extending the board to seven.

In the investment prospectus, Angela presented ownership as 'doing something fun and different' to potential shareholders, a key reason she believes people were initially keen to invest. The reason Angela decided to pursue crowdfunding was the perceived ability to create brand ambassadors from those who invested in the business – those who bought shares would tell others about the business and help to spread the word about the ice cream and the company itself. Analysis of those who invested through the crowdfunding campaign showed that the majority were first-time investors. In general, people who invest in crowdfunding campaigns want to help other people in their attempts at success. In the case of equity crowdfunding, this includes an investment in a local business with the potential for getting a return on the sum invested.

As of 2015, Mormor Magda has a stable business. Production facilities are up to standard and four employees run the business. The Mormor Magda product is stocked in about 70 food stores, ranging from the biggest supermarkets to smaller local shops, across Sweden. Mainly due to her social media strategy, Mormor Magda is becoming well known. Recently, Mormor Magda's ice cream appeared in a Swedish TV series. The belief that social media can drive the brand and brand awareness throughout Sweden seems to be paying off.

The ambition now is to increase distribution to about 200 food stores, but growth has been more difficult than expected as stores demand high levels of sales to provide free space for Mormor Magda's branded fridges. Innovations such as adding new flavours and developing ice cream that is dairy-free and made only with natural ingredients are believed to be one way forward. Using road trips to help build local demand is another attempt to increase penetration. When a road trip to a number of towns is decided on, Mormor Magda announces this on its blog and on Facebook, and encourages followers to spread the word and place orders. Deliveries are then made outside local food stores. With this presence the aim is to create an interest in carrying Mormor Magda's ice cream into the chosen shops.

The product and branding

Mormor Magda early on added the word '*Därproducerad*' ('there produced' implying local, additive-free production) in the company name. The ice cream is not 'home-made' – it is made in a factory – and when it is sold outside Jönköping, it is no longer 'locally produced'. The solution was to add 'Därproducerad' – 'there produced' – to the name of the company to stress that the ice cream manufactured by Mormor Magda is made from natural, locally-sourced ingredients and that the products are totally free of additives. Natural ingredients that are added in the production process include Swedish strawberries (for the strawberry ice cream) and cookie dough, which is made in the factory. Obviously the source of the ingredients added is regarded as important to consumers, hence this is clearly stated on the packaging. The range produced includes strawberry, mint, chocolate and vanilla as well as salted caramel, popcorn and toffee and

cookie dough. The range was expanded in 2015 to include egg-, nuts- and preservative-free ice cream.

Product quality is very important in the manufacture of ice cream, with an emphasis on aspects such as creaminess and taste. In the crowdfunding prospectus from 2015 you could read that the brand values of the ice cream include the following aspects: 'genuine' (like you would make at home), 'traditional', 'high-quality', 'stylish', 'luxurious' and 'unique'. These values are incorporated in all the aspects associated with the product, its design as well as the flavours that have been developed. As a result of the production process, Mormor Magda's ice cream contains lower amounts of air, making it heavier than competitor's ice cream. This results in a better-tasting ice cream and, consequently, better value for money for consumers. But it also makes it more expensive to produce as supplies are paid per kilo.

Distribution takes place in a number of different ways, depending on the location. Local outlets are reached through the Mormor Magda's own distribution system while a distribution company assists in other areas. The pricing of the product varies based on when the product is purchased as well as the size of the product. Buying from a retailer results in a higher price being charged while it is also possible to visit the factory and purchase directly at a lower price.

The organisation is also committed to socially responsible behaviour. One example is that Mormor Magda works with the Swedish employment agency to employ young workers in order to assist in the development of skills within this group. The company also takes a clear stand on issues like sexuality, where a rainbow ice cream was launched – an initiative that has resulted in very positive feedback. Obviously the strategy of using locally-produced ingredients in the 'there-produced' ice cream can be included under the social responsibility umbrella.

The ice cream business

Ice cream has varying popularity levels around the world. In New Zealand, it is estimated that average consumption is 28 litres per person per year, followed by the USA (20 litres), Australia (18 litres) and Finland (14 litres). Sweden is fifth in per capita ice cream consumption in the world with 11 litres per person per year (about 100 million litres in total), ahead of countries like Italy (eight litres) and the UK (seven litres). Due to the climate, this Swedish SEK4bn market is highly seasonal. In the summer time the sale of single-wrapped ice cream is at its highest, but sales of the packaged ice cream (in consumer packages from 250 ml to two litres) are more evenly distributed over the year. On the list of Swedes' favourite flavours are the classic flavours of vanilla and chocolate, as well as flavours like liquorice, pecan and pistachio. The trends in the Swedish ice cream market are that premium ice cream is a growing segment and that people are generally becoming more aware of the health aspects of what they eat. In terms of products, the popularity of frozen yoghurt is increasing rapidly.

Generally, consumers know that ice cream is 'not good' for them to eat. It is a 'reward product'. This means that consumers 'indulge' in ice cream, placing the emphasis on the quality of ice cream ('when I eat it, it must be good'). There has also been an increase in the number of consumers searching for healthier alternatives (such as yoghurt ice cream and fruit-based flavours). There has also been an increase in the number of people with allergies of various kinds (lactose, nuts, gluten and other additives). This has enabled Mormor Magda to develop new products to satisfy the needs of this market. Regarding gender differences, women marginally consume more ice cream compared to men while older consumers enjoy the highest number of ice cream occasions.

Competitors

Of course, with the popularity of ice cream in Sweden, there are many competitors. The largest competitor is the multinational Unilever. Unilever is public company listed in England and in the Netherlands. In 2014, the turnover from more than 400 well-known brands was €48.4bn. In Sweden the most popular ice cream brands are GB Glace®, Magnum®, Daim® and Carte d'Or®. Overall Unilever has a 47 per cent share of the total Swedish market. However, they dominate the single-wrapped ice cream market with a market share of approximately about 80 per cent, making them less dominant in the packed ice cream market. Ben & Jerrys® (owned by Unilever since 2000) is of most interest as this brand's position on the market has been highly inspirational for Mormor Magda. The premium segment of the market is about five per cent in volume but about ten per cent in market value.

In 2014, there were 71 Swedish ice cream manufacturers listed. Only four of those had more than 20 employees and 52 were in the category of zero to four employees. Most of these small manufacturers are farm based and compete on a regional basis. One interesting concept is known as farmhouse ice cream (*Gårdsglass* in Swedish). This is a concept from the Netherlands that appeals to dairy farmers directly to help them produce ice cream from their excess milk production. This gives farmers the opportunity to expand their product range. Farmers purchase a starter-kit from a company, including the machinery and equipment to begin producing ice cream using standard recipes. The concept has spread to several countries.

Other competitors include store brands and brands such as SIA Glass® (family-owned, with about 20 per cent of the total market), and premium brands as Lejonet och® Björnen®, Pipersglace®, Djurgårdsglace®, Järnaglass® and Guteglass®. They are all agile and can respond quickly to changes in the market and to new product launches of other ice cream manufacturers. Many of the ice cream packages look rather similar, illustrating the inability to sustain the differentiation of products.

Mormor Magda's financial performance

In the first half year (2011), Mormor Magda's turnover was about SEK300,000 (€33,000), which resulted in a loss of SEK335,000 (€36,000). In 2012, turnover increased to SEK1.8m (€195,000) and the company made a profit of SEK120,000 (€13,000). The sharp increase was mainly due to the seasonal sale of ice cream in waffle cones. Abandoning mobile waffle sales in 2013 for strategic reasons, turnover was only SEK950,000 (€103,000) and the company made a loss of SEK159,000 (€17,200). In 2014, turnover again increased to the level of SEK1.7m (€184,000), but still the company made a loss. This was due to several investments, listed below. For 2015, breakeven was projected at the level of SEK5.5–5.8m (€600,000) in turnover.

The company has continued to develop making many Important investments in the period 2011–15 including:

- completion of the rebuilding/renovation of production facilities in Taberg;
- installation of cooling equipment at the factory, with the possibility to keep the ambient temperature during manufacturing down to 16°C during warm summer days;
- purchase of a new vehicle for transporting the ice cream;
- purchase of equipment for sales of ice cream at locations away from the factory and used in Jönköping;
- purchase of a pasteurising machine which is used to heat and treat the dairy products prior to production at ice-cream machines.

As a result, the company is now ready to produce up to 250,000 packages (half litre) a year, which translates into about SEK6.5–7m (€750,000) in turnover.

The company was initially owned by Angela (50 per cent) and Micael Hafström (50 per cent). In 2014, five private investors entered as owners and, after the crowdfunding campaign in 2015, the company had 148 shareholders. Today the Hafström family owns about 40 per cent, the board another 40 per cent and the remaining 142 shareholders about 20 per cent.

In the crowdfunding prospectus in 2015, the venture was valued at SEK7.3m (€790,000), indicating a prospective price/earnings ratio of 18 in 2017. The aim was to distribute the ice cream in more than 200 stores in 2017, compared to 70 in mid-2015 (and eventually to reach 400 stores). Given this, it was projected that sales will reach SEK6.8m (€735,000) in 2017 and an after-tax profit of SEK402,000 (€45,000). The initial financial goal is to generate sales of SEK5.8m (€630,000) in 2016, as this is the point as which profits can be generated. The gross profit margin is projected to be 60 per cent (excluding labour costs) and 40 per cent (including labour costs). In 2012–13, labour costs were artificially low, amounting to approximately 20 per cent of sales, reflecting the investment in time made by the owners.

The future for Mormor Magda

There are a number of challenges in the market, primarily concerning changing market conditions. A high likelihood of new competitors coming in means that Mormor Magda will have to think about doing some things differently in the future. While the new dairy-free ice cream has attracted a large number of new customers, this doesn't change the potential challenge of the competitors in the marketplace. Perhaps they will also soon be offering the same product? The question facing Mormor Magda now is, what to do next?

Notes
1. The full name of the company is Mormor Magdas Därproducerade Mat och Glass AB (Grandma Magdas 'there produced' Ice Cream and Food Company). The meaning of 'there produced' is discussed further in the case.
2. SEK1 = £0.086 = $0.124 = €0.109.

Further reading
Blog (Swedish): http://mormormagdas.se/blogg/.
Website (Swedish): http://www.darproducerat.se/category/mormor-magdas-events/.
Website (English): https://www.fundedbyme.com/en-us/campaign/5367/mormor-magda-ice-cream/?type=e.

Recommended video
• You can get a flavour for Mormor Magda Ice Cream in the following short video: https://www.youtube.com/watch?v=7SuYEFsMsTY

Sources: '149 owner of the ice cream', *JP.se,* 27 June 2015, http://www.jp.se/article/149-agare-av-glassen/. 'Ice cream and frozen desserts in Sweden', *Euromonitor International,* October 2015. 'Ice cream market in Sweden to 2017: market size, distribution and brand share, key events and competitive landscape', *ReportLinker,* February 2014. 'Much air and little glass', *Dagens Nyheter,* 6 July 2013. Fundedbyme.com, Mormor magda's ice cream, https://www.fundedbyme.com/en/campaign/5367/mormor-magda-ice-cream/. http://www.gardsglass.com/html/concept.html (in Swedish). K. Magnusson, M. Starkenberg and N. Åman, *Customer Engagement and Loyalty Cultivation through Social Media: A Small Business Perspective,* Unpublished Bachelor These, Jönköping International Business School, 2013.

CASE STUDY

Academies and Free Schools: the future of education?

Kevan Scholes

The public sector continues to face dilemmas as to how far strategic management should be centralised or devolved. This case looks at one example – the extension of devolved control of schools in England and Wales through the creation of Academies and Free Schools. But the principles and issues involved in this case would apply to many other public services and private-sector organisations.

'We want everyone to have a chance to succeed, and education is the best way of ensuring that. This means schools with strong standards and discipline. It also means giving head teachers the freedom to run their own schools with the ability to set their own curriculum and pay their staff properly. Academy schools were created to do exactly that. . . . I want teachers, not bureaucrats, deciding how best to educate our children.'[1]

This was the British Prime Minister, David Cameron, speaking in August 2015, 100 days after his general election victory. This followed a period of five years in coalition government when controversial changes had been introduced to turn most schools into Academies and to establish Free Schools. Both Academies and Free Schools received state funding but were semi-independent and outside local authority control.[2]

Disagreement over both political and management control of schools was certainly not a new issue. Indeed, there had been many significant changes over the previous 150 years. Since 1833, when British governments first took a role in the provision of education, through financial grants to support the work of voluntary bodies (including churches), there had been a progressive involvement of the state in policy, funding and the management of education in the UK. From 1870, elementary education became compulsory and partially state-funded. The 'Balfour' Education Act of 1902 created Local Education Authorities (LEAs). The act allowed for all schools, including religious denominational schools, to be funded by the LEA through local taxation.[3]

City of London Academy School, London

Source: VIEW Pictures Ltd/Alamy Images.

The 'Butler' Education Act of 1944 established the Ministry of Education, headed by a single minister responsible for education policy and delivering state education through LEA-funded schools. The most significant change in the following 50 years was the introduction of comprehensive (as against 'selective') schools from the mid-1960s. By 2005, about 93 per cent of English schoolchildren attended the state-funded school system.[4] This was financed from national taxation and was free between the ages of three and 18.

In January 2015, there were 20,200 state funded schools (16,800 primary and 3400 secondary) in England and Wales educating some 7.7 million pupils (4.5 million primary and 3.2 million secondary).[5] There were five main types of state-funded school in England:[6]

- *Community schools* (formerly county schools) (about 44 per cent of schools/40 per cent of pupils), in which the LEA employed the schools' staff, owned the schools' lands and buildings, and had primary responsibility for admissions.
- *Voluntary controlled schools* (about 11 per cent of schools/six per cent of pupils), which were almost always church schools, with the lands and buildings often owned by a charitable foundation. However, the LEA employed the schools' staff and had primary responsibility for admissions.
- *Voluntary aided schools* (about 18 per cent of schools / 13 per cent of pupils), linked to a variety of organisations. They could be faith schools (often the Church of England or the Roman Catholic Church) or non-denominational schools. A charitable foundation contributed towards the capital costs of the school and appointed a majority of the school governors. The governing body employed the staff and had primary responsibility for admissions.
- *Foundation schools* (about five per cent of schools/six per cent of pupils), in which the governing body employed the staff and had primary responsibility for admissions. School land and buildings were owned by the governing body or by a charitable foundation. The Foundation appointed a minority of governors. Many of these schools were formerly grant-maintained schools. In 2005, the Labour government proposed allowing all schools to become Foundation schools if they wished. From 2010 this type of school was overtaken by Academies and Free Schools.
- *Academies and Free Schools* (see below). These had grown rapidly to 22 per cent of schools/35 per cent of pupils.

What are Academies and Free Schools?

Academies were first introduced by the Labour government in 2005 as secondary schools funded and monitored *directly* by the Department for Education (DfE). Academies could also accept funding from private sources such as individuals or companies. The policy of running schools with the types of freedoms to be offered to Academies and Free Schools was well established in other countries. They were often called Charter Schools. The English changes were inspired by the example of Sweden[7] which had 'charter' schools dating back to 1992. The Labour government thought such changes would be particularly important in areas of social deprivation where traditional schools were seen to be 'failing' – as reflected in the academic performance of pupils and through Ofsted[8] inspections. Following the general election of 2010, when Labour

lost to a Conservative/Liberal Democrat coalition, Academies became a main plank of government policy for *all* existing schools – not just as a replacement for failing schools. Over the next five years, a high proportion of schools judged to be 'excellent' by Ofsted opted for Academy status. These schools were called converter Academies. Whereas in 2010 there were only about 200 Academies, by 2015 the number was almost 4800 as 61 per cent of secondary schools and 15 per cent of primary schools had converted to Academy status or started as a free school in England and Wales (out of a total of 20,200 state funded schools – about 16,800 primary and 3400 secondary). Following the 2015 election victory the government introduced legislation to change all failing schools into Academies and for the first time took powers to convert 'coasting' schools to Academies, but for all other schools conversion remained optional.

What is different about Academies[9]

Academies are independent, state-funded schools, which receive their funding directly from central government, rather than through a local authority.

Freedoms

Academies benefit from greater freedoms to innovate and raise standards. These include:

- freedom from local authority control;
- the ability to set their own pay and conditions for staff;
- freedoms around the delivery of the curriculum;
- the ability to change the lengths of terms and school days.

Sponsors

Some Academies, generally those set up to replace underperforming schools, have a sponsor. Sponsors come from a wide range of backgrounds including successful schools, businesses, universities, charities and faith bodies. Sponsors are held accountable for improving the performance of their schools. They do this by challenging traditional thinking on how schools are run and what they should be like for students. They seek to make a complete break with cultures of low aspiration and achievement. The sponsor's vision and leadership are vital to each project.

Funding

Academies receive their funding directly from the Education Funding Agency (an agency of the Department for Education) rather than from local authorities. Academies receive the same level of per-pupil funding as they would receive from the local authority as a maintained school, plus additions to cover the services that are no longer provided for them by the local authority (usually about ten per cent extra). However, Academies have greater freedom over how they use their budgets to best benefit their students. Some large Academy chains run schools creating economies of scale themselves.[10] Multi-Academy Trusts were being created and by 2015, there were 20 such chains managing 240 schools.[11]

Governance[12]

The principles of governance are the same in Academies as in maintained schools, but the governing body has greater autonomy. Academies are required to have parent governors on the governing body.

What is the same?

Admissions, special educational needs and exclusions

Academies are required to follow the law and guidance on admissions, special educational needs and exclusions as if they were maintained schools.

Collaboration

Academies have to ensure that the school will be at the heart of its community, collaborating and sharing facilities and expertise with other schools and the wider community.

There are expectations that all high-performing schools will be willing to partner a weaker school. Collaboration and partnership are now embedded in the school system, and this is also the case for Academies.

Selection

Schools which already selected some or all of their pupils were able to continue to do so if they became Academies, but schools becoming Academies could not decide to become newly selective schools.

What additional differences do Free Schools have?

First introduced in 2010, there were 80 Free Schools by 2012 and 252 by 2015. The DfE website[13] in 2012 explained the *additional* freedoms that Free Schools have (compared with Academies):

> **'(Whereas Academies were mainly 'conversions' from existing state schools) . . . a Free School could be set up by any suitable proposer, where there is evidence of parental demand such as a petition or declaration from interested parents and a clear and compelling business case. This could include one or more of the following groups: teachers, charities, Academy sponsors,**

> **universities, independent schools, community and faith groups, parents, businesses (on a not-for-profit basis).**
>
> **. . . Free Schools will have some additional freedoms. For example, teachers in Free Schools will not necessarily need to have Qualified Teacher Status. They will be subject to the same Ofsted inspections as all state schools and will be expected to maintain the same rigorous standards.'**

Reaction of different stakeholders

Since education policy has always been a major political battleground and is close to the hearts of many individuals and groups, any changes tend to receive a mixed reaction from these 'stakeholders'. The rapid growth in the number of Academies and Free Schools was not universally welcomed! Here are some reactions from different stakeholders:

Local Education Authorities, such as Leicestershire County Council, said that they would receive reduced funding because Academies got money directly from central government. Council leader David Parsons said he disagreed with the scheme because the county had 'some of the best schools' and 'some of the best results' in the country. 'Because of the Academies programme the government is effectively putting a tax on local authorities of about £100 per pupil, per year,' the Conservative leader said.[14]

Many *head teachers,* like Hamid Patel in Blackburn, were convinced that Free Schools had been a force for good. 'When you have these new places and new schools, they do lead to innovation within those new schools. But it also means – and I've seen it – that schools around you raise their standards . . . there are challenges, but I think the whole town is better as a result of the programme. You don't only see good provision in these Free Schools, but I think across [Blackburn's] stock of schools, our community and state schools, there has been a step change. I'm confident that all my head teacher colleagues . . . would agree.'[15]

Some *parents and teachers* mounted public protests such as at Montgomery Primary School, in the Sparkbrook area of Birmingham. They claimed there had been a lack of consultation and that Academy status was being imposed by the government. They also claimed that parents would have less say in how the school was run and how money was spent if Montgomery gained Academy status.[16]

Teachers' Unions, such as the National Union of Teachers, said that school communities and their local authorities, and not an external sponsor, were best placed to judge what support any particular school needed. They also expressed concerns that external sponsorship could be the beginnings of the privatisation of England's schools.[17]

School Leaders, through their Association of School and College Leaders (ASCL), said that the key to success in schools remained excellent teaching and leadership rather than their governance 'status'. There were many successful schools that remained working within the local authority system of governance.[18] In 2015 a leader article on their website commented: 'Since change is happening so rapidly, we need to re-examine our thinking and structures now, as our members are already finding new roles and responsibilities in a dynamic educational world that is re-inventing itself before our eyes . . . it is a wonderful opportunity for ASCL to place itself ahead of the curve by ensuring that we are the first choice professional association for the leaders of both today and tomorrow.'[19]

In turn the Department for Education was keen to broadcast good news about Academies and Free Schools on its website:[20] 'Maura Regan OBE, CEO of Carmel Education Trust, which has seven schools in the Tees Valley area, said: "It is vital that there are as few obstacles as possible in the way between education experts and struggling schools. In my experience the Academy model allows fresh and innovative approaches to reach consistently struggling schools, allowing pupils' education to be improved at an often rapid pace."'[20]

International comparisons

As mentioned above, the policy of running schools with the types of freedoms offered to Academies and Free Schools was well established in other countries. They were often called Charter Schools. For example, Sweden[21] had more than 1000 such schools dating back to 1992. Indeed in 2010, the Swedish Kunskapskolen became the lead sponsor in converting Hampton Community College in Richmond Surrey into an Academy.[22] In the USA, the Charter Schools programme (started in 1991) was regarded as a major success with more than two million pupils attending 6000 charter schools across 42 states and the District of Columbia by 2013.[23] This represented about six per cent of publicly funded schools. In Canada (from 1995), charter schools were established in Alberta but not in other provinces (there were 22 schools by 2010). In 2015, there was still a debate in other provinces.[24] In New Zealand, following the general election in 2011, the National-ACT coalition government announced plans to establish Charter Schools, but by 2015 only five were in operation with a further four approved.[25] Interestingly, Chile had a long history of 'voucher schools' dating back to the 1980's with about 54 per cent of pupils studying in these private schools state funded through vouchers by 2014.[26]

Alarm bells from abroad?

'It's a political failure: how Sweden's celebrated schools system fell into crisis' ran a headline in *The Guardian* in June 2015.[27] Gustav Fridolin, Sweden's education minister, described the relative international decline in the performance of Sweden's schools. He said that it was not one single change that caused the problems, but a combination that helped create a 'fragmentary school system' which lacked steering and sowed the seeds for growing inequality. *The Guardian* asked Andreas Schleicher, the OECD's director for education and skills, what lessons the UK might learn from the Swedish experience. He said:

'When establishing school autonomy and choice, the Swedish system did not strengthen oversight and intervention functions (which were traditionally weak in Sweden). So the system had no means to learn from successful schools and scale their success, and it had no means to detect and address educational underperformance. I think the UK needs to watch out for that as well, unless it is willing and able to upscale Ofsted by dimensions. Successful school systems are more than a collection of independent schools.'

Future plans

In the budget statement on 16 March 2016[28] the government announced that *all* schools should become Academies by 2020 or have plans to do so by 2022. However, Fasna (the national forum for self-governing schools and Academies) described this as a risky timetable because of the challenge of having sufficient leadership capacity in the system by then.[29]

Notes and references
1. 'Conservative ideas can shape the next decade', *Daily Telegraph*, 15 August 2015, p. 23.
2. Local authorities in the UK run local government at city or county levels. This includes both the political process of local councils and the provision of local services (including schools).
3. 'The history of education in England', Wikipedia, 2012.
4. Approximately 7% of schoolchildren in England attend privately run, fee charging, independent schools which do not have to follow the National Curriculum, and their teachers are not required or regulated by law to have official teaching qualifications. However, they are registered with and inspected by the state.
5. 'Schools, pupils and their characteristics', Department for Education, January 2015.
6. 'Education in England', Wikipedia, 2015.
7. Liz MacKean, 'Can Sweden really teach British schools a lesson?', BBC website, 8 February 2010.
8. All state-funded schools are regularly inspected by the Office for Standards in Education (Ofsted) who publish reports on the quality of education at each school. Schools judged by Ofsted to be providing an inadequate standard of education may be subject to special measures, which could include replacing the governing body and senior staff.
9. 'Policy Paper: Academies and Free Schools', Department for Education, 22 April 2013, updated 8 May 2015. Also: 'Academies – old and new explained', BBC website, Education and Family, 3 June 2015.

10. 'The growth of academy chains: implications for leaders and leadership', National College for School Leadership, 2012.

11. Patrick Wintour, 'Academy chains', *The Guardian*, 24 March 2015; also Peter Kent, 'Changing Landscape', *Leader*, 2 April 2015, http://www.leadermagazine.co.uk/articles/changing_landscape1/.

12. Alison Powell, 'How academy governance works', *Governing Matters*, NGA, Nov/Dec 2011, pp 16–17.

13. www.education.gov.uk.

14. 'Leicestershire MPs challenge academy school funding', *BBC News*, 19 January 2012.

15. Richard Adams, 'Should the Free Schools be extended?', *Guardian*, 9 March 2015.

16. 'Montgomery primary school teachers strike over academy plan', *BBC News*, 25 January 2012.

17. Angela Harrison, 'Michael Gove: Academy school critics happy with failure', *BBC News*, 4 January 2012; also 'Academies: old and new explained', *BBC News*, 3 June 2015.

18. Angela Harrison, 'Michael Gove: Academy school critics happy with failure', *BBC News*, 4 January 2012.

19. Peter Kent, 'Changing Landscape', *Leader*, 2 April 2015, http://www.leadermagazine.co.uk/articles/changing_landscape1/.

20. www.education.gov.uk.

21. Liz MacKean, 'Can Sweden really teach British schools a lesson?', BBC website, 8 February 2010.

22. Richard Garner, 'For these new pupils, the first question is: Who am I?' *The Independent*, 3 September 2010.

23. 'Charter Schools', Wikipedia, 2015; 'Charter Schools fast facts', National Center for Education Statistics, 2015.

24. J. Freedman and F. McMahon, 'Charter Schools in Atlantic Canada: an idea whose time has come', Atlantic Institute for Market Studies, 2015.

25. 'Charter Schools in New Zealand', Wikipedia, 2015.

26. 'Education in Chile', Wikipedia, 2015.

27. Sally Weale, '"It's a political failure": how Sweden's celebrated schools system fell into crisis', *Guardian*, 10 June 2015.

28. Katherine Sellgren, 'Budget sets out Academies plan and longer school day', *BBC News*, 16 March 2016.

29. Hannah Richardson, 'Speedy academisation plan risky, says school body', *BBC News*, 22 March 2016.

Siemens B: implementing the strategy

Gerry Johnson

As a result of their 2014 strategy review, Siemens identified significant future opportunities for business development but associated challenges to achieve this. This case study focuses on how the corporate strategists set about planning the implementation of strategy so as to achieve the changes required for profitable growth.

A key role for Torsten Ende in the Corporate Strategy Department was to help ensure the implementation of Siemens' strategy in its ten divisions and about 50 business units throughout the world. (See the Siemens A case for a fuller explanation of Siemens' product and global scope and financial performance.) By 2015, Torsten had worked in Siemens for 14 years. After graduating in business economics in 2001, he became a management consultant with the company. Following this, in 2004, he became assistant to a member of the management team of the Siemens IT Solutions and Services Division. Later in 2005 he joined the division's strategy team where he managed a transformation programme of the business in the USA as well as mergers and acquisitions and a global restructuring programme. In 2010, he came into the corporate centre of Siemens, working on strategy projects at headquarters, regional levels and in businesses including the design and implementation of strategy. In 2015, however, he knew he faced some of the most significant challenges of his career over the next few years.

Strategy roles at Siemens

Dr Horst J. Kayser was Chief Strategy Officer at Siemens. There were about 400 people involved in strategy in Siemens, 70 of whom worked in corporate strategy roles. At corporate level, the focus was on the management of the portfolio, coordinating strategic planning, establishing targets for the businesses and monitoring performance against these. There were two main corporate strategy roles:

- **Strategic planning and portfolio management** was concerned with the collection of data from businesses about likely growth and performance within their markets and the examination of these against the corporate views and aspirations. It was this that the strategic plan was built upon (see Illustration 13.2, Strategic planning at Siemens). This strategic plan was revised annually for a period of five years. It was on the basis of this plan that Siemens developed views on their portfolio and policy on mergers, acquisitions and disposals. Wolfram Seiler was head of this department.

- **Strategy development** was responsible for the development and execution of strategic choices. This involved working with and, if necessary, guiding the businesses on projects for the development, implementation and communication of strategy. Joachim Kraege was head and Torsten was based in this department.

There were also strategists at divisional and business unit levels, where they reported to the CEOs of those divisions or business units. Here the focus was more on how to compete within markets; so the identification of market opportunities and bases of competitive advantage. Joachim Kraege explained, however, that there had been a move to more centrally planned strategy since the 1990s: 'Because of pressure to focus on profits and also the consolidation of competitors. We had to start thinking harder about how to shape the company for the benefit of shareholders.'[1]

Siemens' strategy

With corporate headquarters in Germany, Siemens had a group turnover in 2015 of almost €76bn (£60.8bn, $98.8bn).[2] With businesses that spanned power generation, power distribution and the application of electrical energy, it was one of the world's largest producers of energy-efficient, resource-saving technologies, a leading

Special thanks are due to executives of Siemens for their interest and co-operation in the writing of this case. The case was prepared by Gerry Johnson. It is intended as a basis for class discussion and not as an illustration of good or bad practice. © Gerry Johnson 2016. Not to be reproduced or quoted without permission.

supplier of systems for power generation and transmission as well as medical diagnosis. (For more information on the range of businesses together with the turnover and profits of each division see Figure 1 in Siemens A.)

Joe Kaeser took over as chief executive in 2013 on the back of a concern by investors and analysts about the failure of Siemens to meet its growth and profitability targets. In 2014, he announced 'Vision 2020' which set out the Siemens strategy. It explained the core business logic of the business portfolio as aligned along the 'value chain of electrification' with products 'designed to generate, transmit, distribute and utilize electrical energy with particularly high efficiency'. It also claimed that Siemens' 'integrated setup not only enables us to leverage opportunities in individual markets; it also allows us to exploit the potential at their interfaces.'[3]

The strategic priorities

Vision 2020 emphasised three strategic priorities:

- In the short term, to drive performance by 're-tailoring . . . structures and responsibilities . . . focusing on business excellence', getting underperforming businesses 'back on a successful track and mak(ing) them competitive again'. Or, as Joachim Kraege observed, 'by selling them or setting up joint ventures' if there was a better owner for that business.[4] It was expected that payoff from this would be evident by 2016. The target on cost savings alone was to take €1bn of costs out of the company by 2016.
- In the medium term, the aim was to strengthen the core: 'to focus on the things that make you strong and put other things aside . . . we intend to strengthen our successful businesses along the value chain of electrification. Among other things we want to allocate resources in a more rigorous way in order to expand in strategic growth fields.' Payoff from this would be evident by 2017.
- The long-term aim was to 'intensify our efforts to seize further growth opportunities and tap new fields.'

Dr Horst J. Kayser commented further on the background to the major thrusts of the future strategy of Siemens as follows:

'It was evident by 2014 that there were a number of key issues that needed addressing. Our previous strategy, especially with regard to growth, had not materialised: so, we needed to focus on profitable growth and innovation in areas of electrification, automation and digitalisation. There was a mixed picture with regard to performance and major profit imbalances: so, we needed to strengthen our operating excellence and productivity. There was a loss of market share in some areas; so we needed to improve market and customer centricity. Fifty per cent of our managers believe we are not innovative enough, so we needed to improve innovation management and improve our time to market with regard to innovation. The costs of our project execution have been too high so we needed to improve our operations in project management through improved corporate memory and better technical risk management. The complexity of the organisation has been increasing and, together with this, our level of overhead. So, we have flattened the hierarchy, reducing management layers. We also believe we have not sufficiently recognised strategic threats and opportunities for the future: so, there has been more attention to addressing global changes in demand and what competitors are doing. There also needs to be a more active acquisition strategy with regard to this.'

The reduction in layers of management involved doing away with the sector structure introduced by Joe Kaeser's predecessor Peter Loescher. Loescher's approach had been to consolidate the activities of Siemens under four broad sectors: Industry, Energy, Healthcare and Infrastructure and Cities. The sectors provided the home for the various Siemens divisions. The stated objective of the sector structure was to unlock the growth potential of global trends and the various markets Siemens operated in. Table 1 provides an overview of the sectors and divisions as they had been in 2012. However, the sectors

Table 1 The sector structure

Energy	Healthcare	Industry	Infrastructure and cities
Energy service	Clinical products	Customer services	Building technologies
Fossil power generation	Diagnostics	Drive technologies	Low and medium voltage
Oil & gas power transmission	Imaging and therapy systems	Industry automation	Mobility and logistics
Wind power	Audiology solutions	Metals technologies	Rail systems
			Smart grid

Source: Siemens Annual Report 2012.

each had a chief executive and chief finance officer with the same roles at both divisional and business levels. In 2014, the sector level was eliminated with the stated purpose of reducing bureaucracy, cutting costs and accelerating the speed of decision-making within the company.

With regard to the third strategic priority of long-term growth, the emphasis was on identifying opportunities for profitable growth. Here the work that the corporate strategists had undertaken to identify megatrends and future growth fields provided a basis for assessing both the threats and also the opportunities the business would face over the next decade. The megatrends included climate change, demographic change, urbanisation, globalisation and digital transformation (see Siemens A for a fuller explanation). Future growth fields identified included, among others, business analytics and data-driven services, digital-twin software and offshore wind power. Siemens saw the potential of two to three per cent market growth in electrification, the historical base of the business, four to six per cent in automation, where they were market leaders globally and seven to nine per cent in digitalisation, the trend that they believed would provide the main future growth opportunity.

Digitalisation

Vision 2020 highlighted the threat, but also the opportunity and 'the paradigm shift' that digitalisation would hold in store: 'By the year 2000 some two billion gigabytes of data had been accumulated worldwide. Today, the same volume of information is generated in a single day. And, driven by the ongoing merger of real and virtual worlds, this trend is increasing.' There would be an exponential growth in the number of connected devices over the next decade or so. Siemens estimated that by 2016 there would be 23 billion connected devices and that this would more than double by 2020.

Siemens saw the opportunity in combining the physical and virtual world in areas as diverse as operations analytics, fleet management, efficient buildings, imaging software and the digital factory. Wolfram Seiler gave some examples:

'We believe Siemens has strong offerings in the digitalisation arena. For example with regard to industy-specific software, the digital factory can offer streamlined products to automation design, strengthened by simulation. In energy management optimised grid automation can provide 50 per cent loss reduction. In wind power data driven and self-learning algorithms can provide major output increases. In healthcare image guided therapy can provide a basis for novel surgery procedures. Digital services can help achieve trains with almost 100 per cent on-time track record via predictive maintenance. In building technology, energy optimisation and remote monitoring can provide massive energy savings. In all this, however, the emphasis has to be on understanding customer processes and needs rather than driving the business on the basis of technical innovation in traditional areas.'

Joachim Kraege explained digitalisation as an integrative theme because:

'So many of our devices have sensors that generate data. However, to turn this into an opportunity means integrated data analysis and data driven services across domains driven off an understanding of customer processes. So we need the ability to provide synergies across businesses. For example virtual imaging can apply to healthcare, trains, oil platforms and so on. But, we need to recognise that the speed of digitalisation and connectivity is not driven by us and is moving very fast. Moreover, it is not being driven by our typical competitors but by other firms which have capabilities that can change our markets and threaten our business models and subsequently our market positions.'

The digitalisation opportunities were being addressed both at corporate level and business level. For example, the corporate technology department was looking at areas of potential digitalisation together with executives from businesses. The belief was that there was potential to learn across the Siemens businesses about how such opportunities might be taken.

Wolfram Seiler added:

'We were slow to pick up on digitalisation in communications business in the past and lost out to competitors as a result. We are facing similar challenges on energy generation and in other areas. We also need to make the businesses aware that there are likely to be new competitors; but to be aware that digitalisation is not just a threat but most of all an opportunity. So, we have to change our mindset to accept digitalisation within businesses but, also, across businesses. We need to find cross-divisional competences.'

An ownership culture

In order to achieve the strategic priorities and, in particular, Siemens' growth opportunities, Joe Kaeser was convinced that a change towards 'an ownership culture', typical of well-run family businesses, was needed. This was explained in Vision 2020 as the need to encourage 'every individual in our company to give his or her best in his or her position in order to help Siemens long term success'. Joe Kaeser believed that, as in a family business, this would require 'entrepreneurial behaviour (to) be the standard and foundation for how we act'. It also meant that it was important to foster diversity of experience and expertise and for employees to identify fully with Siemens, its values – not least of innovation to achieve long-term success – and act in line with these values.

Joe Kaeser emphasised a number of characteristics of such a culture.[5]

'This means, first, a modern understanding of leadership. We expect managers to think long-term, to act like entrepreneurs, and to inspire and motivate employees . . . Second, it means employee orientation. That entails communicating management decisions transparently, encouraging employees to ask questions, promoting an open dialogue, and standing by employees with the promise . . . Third, our employee stock ownership program is turning Siemens employees into Siemens shareholders . . . in over 60 countries worldwide . . . Our maxim is therefore: "Always act as if it were your own company." . . . Seek opportunities and seize them rather than being content to stay in your comfort zone. And in doing so, always focus on what creates value for customers and society.'

He further emphasised characterisitics of the company that helped foster such a culture:

'As in family enterprises, Siemens gives financial solidity priority over short-term profit. That is reflected by financial targets oriented toward the creation of sustainable value. . . . Werner von Siemens (Siemens' founder) had financial sustainability in mind when he said: "I will not sacrifice the future for short-term gain." We at Siemens follow that principle to this day.

The model of a family-run business shapes our customer relationships. We nurture close and trusted partnerships with customers, often over generations. . . . And that's why we want our sales employees, wherever they work around the globe, to devote 30 per cent more time to customers. Customer proximity also means reducing bureaucracy and paperwork.'

The strategic challenges

Torsten summarised the strategic priorities:

'The driving of performance and the strengthening of the core of the business through its portfolio may be regarded as fairly typical challenges for the strategist.

However, the other priorities are not. Developing an ownership culture and tackling the threats and opportunities of digitalisation are big challenges.'

Joachim Kraege added:

'The biggest challenge is not the analysis when developing a new strategy: it is getting 'movement': in other words, the implementation of strategy and change. It is imperative that we do not only analyse, but also constantly follow up and get things done.'

Further, given that many senior managers inherited a wealth of experience in the company's heritage in electrical engineering, the future opportunities did not just mean challenges in the businesses but, as Joachim Kraege explained: 'To implement elements of the strategy and create impact within the company also means getting people aligned at all levels, from managing board to business unit level and within 190 countries . . .'

Apart from the dismantling of the sector structure, by 2015 there had already been changes at managing board level. There was a new managing board member responsible for the Energy business, Lisa Davis, who had been appointed from Shell; and a new board member responsible for HR and labour, Janina Kugel, who had joined Siemens in 2001 from Accenture and, since then, had worked for Siemens in Germany, China and Italy.

Joachim Kraege also commented:

'We aspire to be global and, indeed, operate globally; but we are, by origin, a German company and most of our global business headquarters are located in Germany. Whereas currently we have most people in Germany, most of our revenue is from outside Germany. [Figure 1 summarises the global scope of Siemens]. Our target is that more than 30 per cent of our division and business unit managers should be based outside Germany: for example the oil & gas HQ is now in Houston in the US. This is also, of course, to get closer to customers.'

Wolfram Seiler saw an increasing need, not only for the future strategy to be embedded at business level, but also for a quite different approach to how Siemens' businesses were managed. In particular there was a need to be more aware of market needs rather than technical advances – to begin thinking strategically from 'outside in' rather than 'inside out'. This needed to be accompanied by more emphasis on services rather than products. As Torsten explained:

'Siemens has built its reputation on the basis of excellence in the design and manufacturing of engineered products. Moving from a focus on manufacturing to additional service provision is a challenge we have to

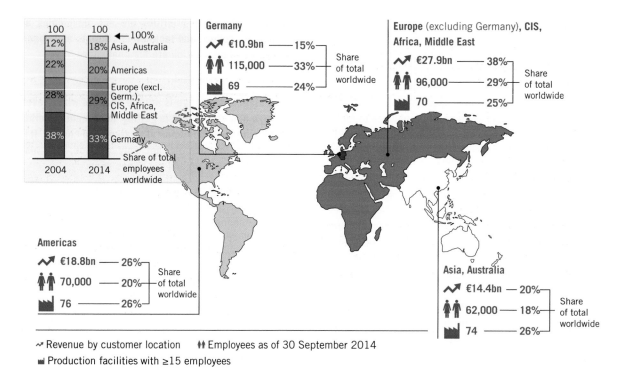

Figure 1 Siemens' global presence

Notes: All figures refer to continuing locations. CIS: Commonwealth of Independent States.

Source: Siemens Annual Reports from 2004 to 2014, as reported.

face; but is not easy for a traditional equipment manufacturer to cover the full value chain including integrated service provision, given both the investments and change involved and the heritage of the business.'

There was also a need for much more collaboration across businesses, not least on digitalisation. Torsten explained:

'The collaboration of the individual divisions is crucial for business success. For example in the next year or so the three divisions Power Generation, Wind Power and Renewables and Energy Management have to deliver jointly into an 8bn EUR customer contract in Egypt. Siemens has undergone several attempts to encourage such collaboration in both organizational changes through an additional Sector layer and through changed management processes in terms of incentive schemes.'

Such collaboration, in turn, would mean clarifying decision-making. Wolfram gave an example:

'If we take decentralised power generation, who is responsible for developing future answers to this? Is it our power and gas businesses, our energy management businesses, corporate technology or cooperation across all of them?'

Implementing the strategy

By 2015, the corporate strategists had begun a range of projects to implement the strategy and address the main strategic challenges. On capitalising on digitalisation Torsten explained:

'We have set up a community of Siemens business CEOs, to address the opportunities and challenges brought about by digitalization and to ensure everyone is on the same page. Digitalization requires them to change the way they look at their businesses. We steer this community by leveraging internal expertise as well as external perspectives through workshops and conferences. These are attended by key executives at all levels, from managing board members through division CEOs to business CEOs.'

Wolfram Seiler also explained:

'We are also more intensively partnering with other firms. For example, we are selectively cooperating with the leading IT players. We might see them as a threat, for example, with regard to 'smart' healthcare or digital factories but, we also might be able to work with them in other areas to best address our customers' needs. It is a kind of "co-opetition".'

Joachim Kraege added:

'We are working on encouraging ownership of the digitalization strategy at the business level. For example, we have set up a strategic alliance between Siemens and Atos, which has grown to be the largest alliance between a global engineering company and a global IT provider. This is supported by a joint investment fund of €150 million, set up by corporate to drive joint innovation in areas such as data analytics, cyber security and device connectivity. There are a number of businesses that are actively partnering with Atos and are leveraging the joint investment fund. We have set up a structure in which they present the progress and opportunities to board level executives, with our guidance. Other business units that were not previously involved are seeing the success of the partnership and joining in.'

Torsten also explained that since 2010 there had been an emphasis on communicating and highlighting strategic priorities by means of key performance indicators (KPIs), each of which was broken down to measurable performance data:

'It took us some months to agree the strategic direction we have adopted with the board and there are ongoing discussions as to what the right key performance indicators are. There is a lot to consider here. We have defined strategic KPIs and linked them to financial KPIs in the operating system. We had to link KPIs to incentive system. We have to decide an 'owner' of each KPI on the Managing Board. We also have to consider how to communicate targets internally to executives and employees and to external stakeholders such as the business press and capital markets. Then there is a need to monitor the results so that we can measure the sustainability of the strategy and again the communication of achievements to internal and external stakeholders as well as any consequences for underperformance.'

There was also the potential for intervention in businesses from the centre if the strategic direction at the business level was not in line with corporate strategy priorities.

Wolfram believed that collaboration across businesses and divisions would also be aided by the remuneration structure for executives:

'In the past top management was incentivized on the basis of business level performance. Now a percentage of top management remuneration is on the basis of collaboration across businesses. So, incentives are not only based on the level an executive is responsible for but on Siemens overall performance. The higher up an executive is in the hierarchy the higher the percentage that is variable in this way.'

For example, the compensation at main board level was structured around base compensation, a variable bonus and long-term stock-based compensation, each of about one third. The variable bonus was based on performance in terms of board members' individual responsibilities on financial performance but also on measures of customer and employee satisfaction and innovation. And the stock-based compensation was of course based on corporate-level rather than individual performance.

As he looked forward to 2016 and beyond, Torsten pondered on the challenges ahead. He knew Siemens' success would to a large extent depend on the successful implementation of the strategy. That meant linking the corporate strategy to the strategy of divisions and business units and making sure it was acted upon. So what should be the priorities at which stage of the strategy development and transformation process? And were there aspects of strategy implementation he – and his colleagues – had not considered?

Notes and references
1. This and other quotations based on interviews carried out by the author with Siemens executives.
2. €1 = £0.79 = $1.13.
3. *Vision 2020; Siemens strategy overview*, 2014, Siemens.com.
4. Wolfram Seiler: 'We have divested businesses in the past that did not fit with our competences: for example, we made washing machines and hearing aids. But, these were too focused on end users which is not our core.'
5. Joe Kaeser, 'Ownership culture: the code for sustainable success', *St Gallen Business Review*, Summer 2015, pp. 18–23.

Paul Polman: turnaround and development of strategy at Unilever

D. Jan Eppink

This case focuses on the changes that Paul Polman initiated to make Unilever a much better performing company than it was in the years before he took over as CEO. As a background to this, the case starts with a brief history of the company, followed by an analysis of the strategy which Unilever pursued and how the company's performance improved. The challenge is how to maintain and improve on this.

Introduction

At the publication of the 2014 full year results on 20 January 2015, Paul Polman, Unilever's CEO since January 2009, remarked that the company had to deal with, 'significant economic headwinds and weak markets'. Underlying sales growth was up almost three per cent, but turnover had declined, mainly due to the negative effect of currency changes.

Commenting on the results in the Annual Report 2014 Polman said:

> 'For the first time in many years, for example, we had to confront the reality of largely flat developed markets and markedly slowing emerging markets. Indeed, markets slowed from some 3.5% growth in 2013, to around 2.5% in 2014.'

Looking forward through 2015 he said:

> 'We expect the economic pressures to continue. Consumer demand in emerging markets is likely to remain subdued for some time to come. There is still little sign of recovery in Europe and, while conditions in North America have improved, any increase in consumer demand is likely to be slow and shoppers will remain focused on value.'

The challenge facing Unilever, then, was to maintain progress and improve on it, despite the economic pressures.

A brief history of Unilever

Unilever was created in 1930 when Margarine Unie from the Netherlands and Lever Brothers from the UK started to work with one another. Both companies had been well established long before 1930 and saw the advantage of cooperation. Legally, it still consists of two separate entities, Unilever NV in the Netherlands and Unilever PLC in the UK with two headquarters, one in the centre of Rotterdam and one in the centre of London. Special provisons in the Articles of Association and three agreements between the two entities enable them to operate as a single economic entity.

Strategy of Unilever

Product scope

The strategy of Unilever focuses on having leading positions and being in high growth markets.[1] In 2014, Unilever segmented its portfolio into four distinct groups: Personal Care, Foods, Refreshments (ice cream and tea) and Home Care. Well known brands are Axe and Dove in Personal Care; Knorr and Blue Band in Foods; Magnum and Lipton in Refreshments, and Omo and Cif in Home Care.

Unilever sells its products to a variety of retailers. In the developed world there is an increasing reliance on supermarket groups, often multinational, e.g. Wal-Mart (USA) and Carrefour (France). In the developing countries its products are sold in smaller shops when there are no supermarkets.

International scope

From the start, Unilever has been an international company. Its two parent companies were already very active in sourcing raw materials and serving foreign markets. Early on, markets were often protected by trade barriers. Then as now, preferences in taste – in particular for food products – differ a great deal. These factors explain the historically high degree of decentralisation of decision-making as well as production and marketing at Unilever.

Business-level strategy

The 2007 annual report describes the ways in which Unilever competes and delivers value. The three elements are:

- continual development of new and improved products that address relevant consumer needs and aspirations;
- rolling out innovations and brand concepts across the businesses around the world;
- lowering the cost of sourcing, manufacturing and distribution processes whilst ensuring product quality.

These three elements continue to be relevant driving forces at Unilever, demonstrating that the same basics of strategy, with differing implementation, can yield very different results.

Performance

The Appendix gives an overview of the most important financial data from 2005 through 2014. It shows that turnover from 2004 to 2008 grew far less than net profit. In 2009, turnover and profit declined but grew in the years 2010 through 2012. In 2013 and 2014 showed lower absolute turnover, but there was an increase in profit. The data also show the differences in sales growth in the various regions and categories.

Indications for relative performance are found in Unilever's annual reports. These mention the Total Shareholder Return[2] ranking of Unilever compared to its chosen peer group. This is summarised in Table 1 and shows that in 2006 Unilever was part of the lowest third of the group. After Polman's arrival Unilever's position in the peer group was highest in 2009, but worsened in the later years.

Every year *Fortune Magazine* publishes a list of the most admired companies. In the 2008 global list, Unilever's competitors were ranked as follows: Procter & Gamble 5th, Nestlé 27th and L'Oréal 37th. Unilever was not ranked in the top 50. However, in the 2015 rankings Unilever had risen to number 36, just below Nestlé (33rd); Procter & Gamble was placed 17th. In 2008, Unilever was not on *Fortune's* list of most-desired companies to work for, which is a must if a company wants to attract the best employees. Furthermore, analysts suggested that the elements of business strategy shown above were more of a wish than a reality. At that time, questions were being asked about the rationale for a company like Unilever. Were there any synergies between food and personal care products and, if so, where were they? What did the corporate centre do to make these real? Was it better to split up the company?

At the AGM held in May 2005 there was criticism of Anthony Burgmans (Head of Unilever NV) from the Dutch shareholders' association (VEB) because of the disappointing performance of the company. VEB asked investors to vote against the appointment of Mr Burgmans as non-executive chairman. VEB mentioned the failure of Unilever's five-year growth strategy for which he was partially held responsible.[3]

Worries about such questions and a further decline in performance led the board of directors to decide in 2008 that the new CEO should come from outside Unilever.

Table 1 Composition of and ranking in peer group in 2014

Peer group	
Avon	Kao
Beiersdorf	Kellogg
Campbell Soup	Kimberley-Clark
Coca-Cola	L'Oreal
Colgate-Palmolive	Nestle
Danone	Pepsico
General Mills	Proctor and Gamble
Estee lauder	Reckitt Bensicker
Henkel	Shisheido

Ranking in peer group 2006–2014								
2006	2007	2008	2009	2010	2011	2012	2013	2014
13	8	9	5	na	8	9	10	14

Note: Since 2006, eight companies have been taken off the list because they were acquired and six new companies have been added. Of the group of 20 companies in 2006, 12 companies are still in the peer group.

Paul Polman with a long history in the business of fast-moving consumer goods was chosen. Polman had worked for many years at Procter & Gamble and was Nestlé's CFO and head of the Americas before his appointment at Unilever.

Polman's reforms

First few months

In his first speech at the Annual General Meeting of shareholders on 13 May 2009, Polman said that in his first few months he had spent time understanding the portfolio of brands and categories, the businesses across countries and regions, the innovation capabilities and the organisational strengths while meeting many of the key people in the company.

He was encouraged by what he had seen. The elements were there to succeed consistently. There were great brands, leading global positions, strong innovative capabilities, a depth of organisational quality and great values on which the company had been built. Another statement at the AGM was: 'Although we will undoubtedly fine-tune and sharpen the strategy as we move forward, our main priority is now to put electricity through the wires, to get consistent business results. It requires making the company increasingly externally focused, with a passion for winning.' Having worked for two of Unilever's largest competitors he was in a very good position to make such a judgement.

In an interview for this case in 2012, Polman said his plans for the future had two stages, the aim of the first was to close the gap with better-performing competitors in the fast-moving consumer goods business, and the second to bring Unilever into a leading position compared to those competitors. His approach had four elements: a change in strategy, a change in personnel, a change in organisational structure, and a change in culture. Polman's reasoning behind this sequence was that you first have to decide what the change in strategy should be, find the right people that fit with the new strategy, align the structure with the strategy, and work on a change in culture from the start.

Polman's new strategy

Polman said that a succesful strategy: 'must make clear choices, have an aligned activity system and be made possible by a high performance organisation. A good strategy also has a flywheel effect.' Looking at the phrasing of the strategy in the Annual Report of 2014, compared with that in the report for 2007, one can see similarities. Both highlight growth and the importance of innovation in products. Yet the results are quite different when looking at the regions and the categories. Implementation of strategy was more focused on performance than previously.

The period from 2008 to 2014 saw an increase in the sales of products in developing and emerging countries. This reflected the presence of Unilever in high-growth markets. Over this period, the percentage of turnover in Europe decreased from 36 per cent in 2008 to 27 per cent of total turnover in 2014. Turnover in the Americas as a whole remained the same in 2014 as in 2008 (32 per cent). Interestingly, the annual reports of 2013 and 2014 both note a stronger performance in Latin America than in North America, where there was a decline in 2013. The percentage of turnover in Asia, Africa, Middle East, Turkey, Russia, Ukraine and Belarus rose from 32 per cent in 2008 to 41 per cent in 2014. Sales in emerging markets in 2014 were 57 per cent of total revenue.

Looking at the change in categories, it is clear from the Appendix that as a percentage of total turnover, Foods decreased from 35 to 25 per cent between 2008 and 2014. In the same period, turnover of Home Care increased from 18 to 19 per cent, whereas Personal Care categories increased from 28 to 37 per cent.

The changes in the composition of turnover can be explained in part by underlying growth, but also by acquistions and divestments. Recent acquisitions include several premium skin care companies. In 2015, Unilever also acquired Talenti Gelato & Sorbetto and Grom, an Italian premium ice cream company with some 60 shops, most in Italy, but also abroad – for instance in Paris, Dubai and New York. Divestments included the frozen meal business in North America, consumer tomato products in Brazil, Unipro bakery and industrial oil products, two dressing brands, three pasta sauce brands, a snack business and Slim-Fast.

Right from the start, Polman stressed the importance of profitable volume growth. Until then, taking account of input cost inflation and disposals of non-core businesses, turnover of the company had remained almost at the same level for years. In contrast, other companies in the fast-moving consumer goods sector had shown considerable growth. Consequently, a priority amongst the nine objectives for 2009 was to return to profitable volume growth, as a prerequisite to return to improved performance.

Following his first year as CEO, Polman's new approach could be summarised as the 'Compass Strategy', detaling how the company would win in four ways:

- winning with brands and innovation: superior products, widespread appeal, and bigger, better and faster innovation;

- winning in the marketplace: lead market development, win with winning customers, be an execution power-house;
- winning through continuous improvement: fast and flexible and increasingly competitive, advantages of global scale, best return on brand and customer investment;
- winning with people: develop a team fit for growth, a place to succeed.

The launch of the 'Unilever Sustainable Living Plan' in 2010 introduced a renewed business purpose which drew on Unilever's history and values. Unilever's ambition (to double its turnover without increasing its environmental footprint) whilst increasing overall social impact, required a novel, sustainable and equitable approach.

By 2020, the company aims to complete the three main objectives of the Unilever Sustainable Living Plan: to help a billion people take action to improve their health and well-being; to halve the environmental cost involved in the manufacture and use of its products; and to enhance the livelihood of hundreds of thousands of people while growing the business, for example by sourcing 100 per cent of its agricultural raw materials sustainably. The corporate brand is growing fast and Unilever is again a preferred employer in most countries it operates in and is credited for driving a more responsible business model.

In an interview for *Harvard Business Review*[4] Polman answered the question about how sustainability benefits the Unilever business:

'I always turn the question around: How would you make the case that not doing this could help society and mankind? For proper long-term planning, you've got to take externalities into account, in order to be closer to society. It's clear that if companies build this thinking into their business models and plan carefully, it will accelerate growth.'

The 2014 Annual Report visualises the integration of the Unilever Sustainability Plan, the (slightly rephrased) elements of the Compass Strategy and the virtuous circle of growth in the Unilever Business Model as shown in Figure 1.

Change of people

Just as the board of directors had looked outside Unilever for a new CEO, Polman extended this to some other positions as well. For a company that is admired for its excellent management development programmes, this was a remarkable step. Polman succeeded Patrick Cescau as CEO in January 2009. Jean-Marc Huët was recruited from Bristol-Myers Squibb as CFO and Pier-Luigi Sigismondi joined Unilever in mid 2009 as Chief Supply Chain Officer, after a career in Nestlé. In 2012 Ritva Sotamaa was appointed Chief Legal Officer after positions at General Electric Company and Siemens AG.

The changes not only affected the top levels in Unilever; there was also a 'management shuffle' after Polman's arrival. Polman remarked that managers of major divisions and locations must:

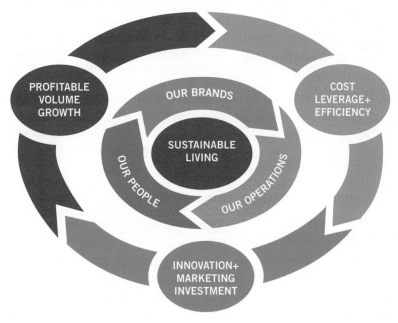

Figure 1 Unilever's business model

Source: Unilever Annual Report and Accounts 2014 (Strategic Report), p. 14.

'. . . deeply understand the power of bringing innovation to the market place. Increasingly a strong customer development and/or marketing background will be required from our cluster leaders to ensure that brand and category positions are built again and we constantly grow share.'

As far as total headcount is concerned, there was a slight reduction after 2008 (see Table 2). Then, total headcount was 174,000, whereas at the end of 2014 it stood at 173,000. It should be noted that in that period there were a number of acquisitions and disposals that affected the number of employees, as well as the composition of the product portfolio.

Change of organisation structure

In 2011, Unilever transformed its organisational structure. Following an earlier change from a highly decentralised structure to a multi-country organisation with 22 regional centres, operating in 11 categories, the change put the focus on four categories and eight geographical clusters in order to significantly speed up decision-making and improve resource allocation. It also allowed for identification of business opportunities faster, allowed trade-offs to be made more quickly and transferred best practices across regions and categories more rapidly, all supporting the key drivers of growth. In Rotterdam, a European Marketing and Innovation Hub was opened. Here, some 270 employees from nine countries work together to speed up decision-making and share best practices. This structural change was supported by several projects and tools. Among these are 'Project Half for Growth' (which follows the principle of half the time, half the process, and double the speed) and 'Project Sunset' (which is an IT tool that speeds up decisions and which has been rolled out across 103 countries).

One of the themes of 'Winning in the marketplace' is to win with customers. One way of achieving this is through the introduction of 'Customer Insight and Innovation Centres'. The first one was opened in New Jersey (USA), followed by the opening of a centre in London in 2009 and centres in Paris, Shanghai and Sao

Paulo in 2010. The centres, now in 11 locations, enable Unilever to work directly with customers on issues such as merchandising, store lay-out, displays and packaging. New concepts can be designed and tested without the expense of in-store pilots. In 2011, working closely with customers in the pharmacy segment resulted in underlying sales growth of 9.2 per cent in that channel.

'Winning with people' requires providing staff with the opportunity for self-development, enabling them to reach their full potential. The top international high-potential personnel were traditionally trained at Unilever's International Management Training Centre in Kingston upon Thames, UK. However, in 2011 the Unilever Learning Academy was introduced, for e-learning and classroom courses. In its first year, 128,000 employees followed one or more of the 7600 training courses on offer. In 2013, the Global Leadership Training Centre in Singapore was opened. In the years before Polman, budgets for employee development were an easy target when profit targets had to be reached. Recruiting was even outsourced, but this has now been brought in-house again. Moreover, morale was not as high as it should have been at that time for 'winning in the market place'.

The history of Unilever, in common with other companies that were early to internationalise, demonstrates that regional managers had a high level of decision-making power. National markets were so different that it was not always possible for managers at a central level to have the right information about local circumstances to make the best decisions. At Unilever, geographical clusters have profit responsibility which may add to the desire for decentralisation in decision-making. The changes in the composition of the leadership suggest a change to a more category-driven company, with decision-making now more centralised than before. As decentralisation carries the risk of less coordination it can, for example, lead to fragmented introduction of products in various countries and consequently higher marketing and production costs. This is especially relevant in categories where brands and products have a global reach, such as in parts of the personal care business.

Table 2 Number of employees per region (average during the year, 000s)

	2005	2006	2007	2008	2009	2010	2011	2012	2013	2014
Western Europe				32	29	29	29			
Europe	51	47	44					35	34	32
The Americas	46	46	44	42	41	40	42	43	43	42
Asia/Africa/CEE[1]			87	100	98	96	98			
Asia/AMET/RUB[2]								94	97	99
Asia Africa	115	96								
Total	212	189	175	174	168	165	169	172	174	173

[1] CEE: Central and Eastern Europe.

[2] AMET: Africa, Middle East and Turkey; RUB: Russia, Ukraine and Belarus.

Change in culture

Culture in Polman's words is 'how you bring the values to life in the company'. One aspect of this is how you change systems to change the behaviour of people at all levels in the organisation. In this section, attention is paid to the changes in two systems: performance target setting and remuneration.

Performance target setting

The Board of Directors is ultimately responsible for target approval. These targets are then cascaded throughout the organisation. The main key performance indicators over the years from 2006 to 2014 are summarised in Table 3. They remain quite constant over the period, with very few changes (some having been made in order to simplify definitions and communications). Polman mentioned in interview that the move from, 'underlying operating profit' to 'core operating profit' at the beginning of 2012 introduced more discipline and rigour to restructuring spending with the objective of improving prioritisation of resources, between competing restructuring projects and other investments.

Targets are becoming more long-term, whereas operational control seems to be done more frequently. Early in his tenure as CEO, Polman made the decision to abandon earnings guidance – he stopped quarterly reporting and changed the compensation system to encourage better 'long-term behaviours'. At the same time he sharpened the performance culture, putting focus on 'winning the consumer' squarely back into the business model with the ultimate goal that this will be to the benefit of the shareholders as well. He actively encourages shareholding with a longer term focus, aligned with the business model and purpose.

In line with what Polman stated about being more cost-competitive, there is a focus on short-term performance indicators too, such as cash flow, cost levels and market share. To support the objective of refocusing on consumers and customers and to make profitable volume growth the number one priority, the company has taken

decisive steps. From 2009 to the end of 2011, Unilever spent around €300m[3] on improving product formulations. This resulted in over 90 per cent of its formulations being equal to, or better than, the competition in blind testing. This is reflected in market share gains across its businesses. Furthermore, the company invested €850m more into advertising and promotion from €302m in 2009 to €6832m in 2013. Additionally, research and development spend increased from €891m in 2009 to €1040m in 2013 (but in 2014 this amount decreased to €955m). In order to support renewed growth, capital expenditure grew from 2.7 to 4.2 per cent of turnover between 2008 and 2014.

Moreover, Unilever changed its innovation programme from many relatively small projects to fewer, bigger and better projects that could be rolled out faster (and globally). The company has also started to invest in supply chain capabilites and capital investment, with the aim to transfom an under-invested, decentralised structure into a highly efficient, more centralised and consumer focused global supply chain.

Remuneration arrangements

The 2013 Annual Report states that the remuneration systems are designed to support the business vision and the implementation of the strategy. The business vision is:

'. . . to double the size of Unilever, while reducing our environmental footprint and increasing our positive social impact through a focus on our brands, our operations and our people and the Unilever Susatinable Living Plan (USLP).'

The principles of the remuneration systems are:

- paying for performance;
- aligning performance measures with strategy;
- delivering sustainable performance;
- alignment with shareholder interests;
- paying competitively;
- preventing inappropriate risk-taking.

Table 3 Key performance indicators 2006–2014

2006	2007	2008	2009	2010	2011	2012	2013	2014
USG	USG	USG	USG	USG	USG	USG	USG	USG
			UVG	UVG	UVG	UVG	UVG	UVG
OM	OM	OM	OM	UOM	UOM	COM	COM	COM
UFCF	UFCF	UFCF	UFCF	FCF	FCF	FCF	FCF	FCF
ROI	ROI	ROI	ROI					
TSR rank	TSR rank	TSR ranking	TSR rank					

Note:

USG: underlying sales growth (underlying: excludes effects of acquisitions and disposals and is based on constant exchange rates); UVG: underlying volume growth; OM: operating margin; UOM: underlying operating margin; COM: core operating margin; UFCF: ungeared free cash flow; FCF: free cash flow; ROI: return on investment; TSR: total shareholder return.

The executive directors' remuneration has two elements: fixed and performance-related. Fixed elements are the base salary and fixed allowances and other benefits. Performance-related elements are annual bonuses, and a longer-term Management Co-Investment Plan (MCIP) and Global Share Incentive Plan (GSIP). A 'claw back' of the performance-related elements is possible in 'in the event of a significant downward restatement of the financial results of the Group'. Top executives are required to build and retain a personal shareholding in Unilever. Under the Management Co-Investment Plan 2015, executive directors are required to invest 25 per cent of their gross bonus in shares, but may invest up to 60 per cent of their gross bonus. They are awarded an equal number of MCIP matching shares.

In line with the objectives, the annual bonus measures for the executive directors for 2015 are underlying sales growth, free cash flow and core operating margin improvement. For the two share plans (the Global Share Incentive Plan and the Management Co-investment Plan), four performance targets are used: underlying sales growth, core operating margin improvement, cumulative operating cash flow and total shareholder return, relative to the peer group. Both underlying sales growth and core operating margin improvement must reach threshold performance levels before any payout in respect of either target is made. In 2014, relative Total Shareholder Return rank in the peer group (14, Table 1) was below target (10th) and no shares were awarded under the two share plans.

Over the 2014 fiscal year, over 70 per cent of the total remuneration for the executive directors was linked to performance, with the majority of this linked to shareholder-aligned longer-term performance. The remuneration structure is generally consistent for the executive directors and senior management of Unilever.

Furthermore, targets are now set more strictly than before. In 2011, for example, the bonus payout was reduced by 25 per cent as a result of under-achievement on the margin target even though growth was outperforming industry average and the stock was the best performing on the Amsterdam Stock Exchange. Targets are set realistically but are challenging.

As far as Polman himself is concerned, as he said in an interview for *Management Today*:

'. . . My decisions are made for the long-term interest of the company. It would be easy for me to jack up the share price, collect a bonus and go sailing in the Bahamas, but in five or 10 years Unilever would not be in good shape.'[6]

Before Polman, for those below top executive level, historically, there was little differentiation between top and mediocre performers and almost no opportunity for most managers to boost their income through sizeable bonuses. After Polman's arrival, the organisation made changes to improve focus, speed and efficiency. As a consequence, performance targets are clearer, more aligned and more differentiated. While performance rewards bring the opportunity to earn more than in the past, the percentage of fixed income is lower.

What's next?

After six years at the helm, Polman had appeared to have transformed Unilever into a more successful company – certainly the share price had responded positively to the changes, rising from €17.34 on 31 December 2008 to €39.05 on 11 December 2015. Despite this, its rank in the peer group was down from number 5 in 2009 to number 14 in 2014.

The investment community appears to have mixed feelings about the performance of Unilever. In August 2015, Goldman Sachs signalled a 'structurally lower growth rate' in developing markets. And whilst positive in terms of the luxury personal care products, it noted that it accounted for just one per cent of total turnover. Goldman Sachs also lowered its target share price from €38 to €37 in October of 2015. However, at around the same time, Berenberg raised its target from €43.59 to €45.78, noting that, whilst markets were difficult, Unilever was performing solidly and that margins were improving and earnings per share were growing at double digit pace.

In addition to its financial performance, the *Financial Times* in February 2015 wrote that Unilever was socially very responsible 'but falls short on growth'.[7] In an interview with *The Guardian,* Polman noted that in the end embedding sustainability is good for profitability, increasing turnover and reducing costs.[8] In September 2015, the United Nations Environment Programme recognised Polman's 'exceptional achievements in the service of the planet' awarding him the title of 'Champion of the Earth, 2015'.[9]

In 2016, Polman will reach the age of 60, the customary retirement age within Unilever. Polman will have to show that the changes he brought about can be sustained in volatile economic conditions, with a slowdown in market growth and increased competition. For the latest financial data, Unilever's annual report can be viewed at the company's website.

Main sources: Unilever Annual Reports, 2006, 2007, 2008, 2009, 2010, 2011, 2012, 2013, 2014. Unilever (2016) *Charts 2015,* www.unilever. com/images/charts_2006-2015_ar15_tcm244-477385_en.pdf. D. Arnoldus, *Family, Family Firm and Strategy. Six Dutch family firms in the food industry 1880–1970,* Oegstgeest/Amsterdam, Aksant Academic Publishers, 2002. Chartered Management Institute, *Paul Polman: Unilever's clean winner in leadership*, 2015, http://www.managers.org. uk/insights/news/2015/february/paul-polman-unilevers-clean-winner-incorporate-governance. S. Daneshku, 'Frustrated Unilever investors call for shake-up', *Financial Times*, 1 March 2015. *Economist*, 'Fighting for the next billion shoppers', 30 June 2012. *Economist*, 'Consumer goods in Africa. A continent goes shopping', 18 August 2012, pp. 49–50. FD, 'Beursblik: Berenberg verhoogt koersdoel Unilever', http://fd.nl/beurs/1112555/beursblik-berenberg-verhoogt-koersdoel-unilever (27 July) 2015. FD, 'Goldman Sachs negatief over Unilever', http://fd.nl/beursblik/1114697/goldman-sachs-negatief-over-unilever (12 August) 2015. *Fortune* (2008). List of global most admired companies, http://money.cnn.com/magazines/fortune/globalmostadmired/top50/index.html. G. Jones, *Renewing Unilever: Transformation and Tradition*, 'Oxford', Oxford University Press, 2009. G. Ruddick, 'Unilever boss Paul Polman in management reshuffle', *The Telegraph*, 21 February 2009.

Notes and references
1. Unilever Annual Report 2006.
2. TSR measures the return received by shareholders and captures changes in share price and dividend income.

3. C. Muspratt, 'Unilever's Dutch head fends off rebel vote', *The Telegraph*, 11 May 2005.
4. A. Ignatius, 'Captain Planet. Interview with Unilever CEO Paul Polman', *Harvard Business Review*, vol. 90, no. 6 (2012), pp. 112–18.
5. €1 = £0.8 = $1.3.
6. A. Saunders, 'The MT interview: Paul Polman of Unilever', *Management Today*, 1 March 2011.
7. S. Daneshku and D. Oakley, 'Paul Polman's socially responsible Unilever falls short on growth', *Financial Times*, 9 February 2015.
8. J. Confino, 'Embedding sustainability drives greater profitability, says Unilever CEO Polman, *Guardian*, 27 May 2014.
9. UNEP, 'Transformative business leader to receive United Nations Champion of the Earth award', press release, 18 September 2015.

APPENDIX

		2005	2006	2007	2008	2009	2010	2011	2012	2013	2014
Group											
Turnover (€m)		38,401	39,642	40,187	40,523	39,823	44,262	46,467	51,324	49,797	48,436
Operating profit (€m)		5,074	5,408	5,245	7,167	5,020	6,339	6,433	6,989	7,517	7,980
Net profit (€m)		3,975	5,015	4,136	5,285	3,659	4,598	4,623	4,948	5,236	5,515
Share price NV year end (€)		19.28	20.70	25.15	17.34	22.75	23.30	26.57	28.84	29.28	32.64
Geographical area											
Asia/AMET/RUB	% total turnover	28	29	31	32	35	37	38	40	40	41
	% total operating profit	26	25	30	23	37	34	33	38	37	33
The Americas	% total turnover	34	35	33	32	32	33	33	33	33	32
	% total operating profit	34	40	38	41	37	34	35	35	38	40
Europe	% total turnover	38	36	36	36	33	30	29	27	27	27
	% total operating profit	40	35	32	36	26	32	32	27	25	27
Categories											
Foods	% total turnover	35	35	35	35	33	32	30	28	27	25
	% total operating profit	40	37	39	45	37	45	42	37	41	45
Refreshments[1]	% total Turnover	20	19	19	19	20	19	19	19	19	19
	% total operating profit	12	17	16	13	14	11	11	13	11	7
Personal care	% total turnover	27	28	28	28	30	31	33	35	36	37
	% total operating profit	35	35	34	25	37	36	39	42	41	41
Home care	% total turnover	18	18	18	18	17	18	18	18	18	19
	% total operating profit	13	11	11	17	12	8	8	8	7	7

[1] Before 2011; Ice cream and beverages.
Sources: Unilever Annual Reports 2005–2014; Unilever Charts 2014 (www.unilever.com/search.html?search=charts+2014).

Aurizon: managing change in a complex environment

Kenneth Wiltshire

Aurizon is Australia's largest national rail freight operator and an internationally competitive freight business. It is now a top-50 Australian public company with earnings of A$851m[1] and one of the world's largest transporters of coal, hauling on average nearly 600,000 tonnes a day. It also ships a wide range of products from agricultural commodities to containerised freight. Aurizon was privatised in 2010 (under the original name of QR National) and has had to adapt its strategies accordingly. This case raises a number of key questions regarding strategy in government business settings and issues leading strategic change. Is it possible for a government-owned business to operate strategically and in an entrepreneurial manner given the political context in which it has to function? Is risk-taking compatible with public-sector accountability regimes? How important is leadership from a CEO in a very challenging and complex context, and to what extent can a board and CEO devise and implement a strategy in endeavouring to influence its government owner?

Queensland Rail (QR) achieved its early success, whilst in government ownership, through strategic decisions on competition and investment, and the formation of alliances. However, in response to the impact of the global financial crisis on public finances after 2007, the Queensland Government announced plans to privatise the freight component of Queensland Rail, giving rise to a major protest campaign from unions, the media, the public and some coal companies. Privatised in 2010, the freight arm became 'QR National', with the passenger arm remaining as a government-owned corporation. QR National was rebranded as 'Aurizon' in 2012 due to brand confusion with the passenger business. In recent times, the conditions imposed on the privatisation, particularly those relating to employment, have expired and the company has faced some hostile press over its move to introduce redundancies. Additionally, falling prices for world commodities, especially coal, have forced efforts to find new markets and new strategic directions.

Australia is an extremely large continent, larger than either the USA or Western Europe, but with a relatively small population. Consequently, it fell in the past to governments to provide the major transport and communication infrastructure, because private enterprise found the task uneconomic, especially as the population was very scattered across the nation. Another factor is the Australian belief, embedded in the nation's value system, that every citizen is entitled to the same standard of public services wherever they may live – a very costly goal for governments to deliver. Establishment of railways in the nineteenth century faced all of these challenges.

Queensland is the most decentralised state in Australia and the railways were a major element in opening up of the vast frontier. Indeed, the railways were seen as the key element of land settlement policy. The Queensland track was built to a gauge of only three foot six inches (narrow gauge), rather than the standard gauge of four foot eight inches, to save costs in the construction, and the railway remained the single largest cost item in the government's budget throughout the nineteenth century.

Over time, a number of community service obligations were forced upon QR including concessional freight rates

Source: Image courtesy of Aurizon.

This case was prepared by Kenneth Wiltshire, J.D. Story Emeritus Professor of Public Administration at the University of Queensland Business School. It is intended as a basis for class discussion and not as an illustration of good or bad practice. © Ken Wiltshire 2016. Not to be reproduced or quoted without permission.

for particular commodities or regions, concessions to some passengers such as pensioners and school children, and free travel for politicians for life. Organisational change has been a constant theme. QR has been through several institutional forms. It began as a government department operating under its own piece of legislation, *The Railways Act.* In 1991, QR began the commercialisation process with the creation of an independent board of directors (non-executive), appointed by the government to set strategic direction. In 1995, the entity was corporatised as a statutory Government Owned Corporation (GOC) and on 1 July became a company GOC which is very close to a private company in corporation law, with two ministers as shareholders – the State Treasurer and the Minister Responsible for Transport. In 2010, the company was split in two, with the freight arm being privatised to become 'QR National', and the passenger arm remaining as a government corporation, 'QR'.

In government ownership QR had always confronted the classic governance dilemma of trying to run as a business but also remain a service to the public, with the main issue being how to maintain an 'arm's length' relationship with its owner, the Queensland Government. The role of the board had never been clear – it set strategic directions which the government noted, but in reality there was disconnect between plan and execution.

QR was required to pay an annual dividend to the government, which was set in a rather arbitrary fashion depending on annual results. It needed government approval for its capital-raising – a delicate aspect since competitive strategies in rail require large outlays on track and rolling stock. For most of its existence QR was subject to full public-sector accountability controls including Auditor-General, Parliamentary Committee scrutiny, Freedom of Information, etc. In its government corporate forms QR's board comprised people with business expertise, but the discretionary areas for the board were somewhat limited with the government retaining control over most aspects. QR was highly unionised, which caused tensions regarding the introduction of modern business practices and had been a major force in keeping the railway in public ownership.

However, the dominant policy matter had been the need to cross-subsidise an unprofitable passenger network (especially in the urban areas) from profitable freight operations, especially haulage of coal. QR was also subject to regulation of its network access prices, often a source of tension. The same regulator, the Queensland Competition Authority, also oversees the ports, which have become bottlenecks in recent times, hindering QR's own freight haulage operations.

So in summary, QR had a board of non-executives, two shareholder ministers, service agreements with the

state government, a requirement to pay a dividend, funded community service obligations and it reported to a public regulatory and accountability regime.

In 2009, QR had six operating divisions:[2]

- QR National: coal and bulk logistics, transport and general freight business.
- Passenger Services: community, long distance and tourist passenger network.
- Network Access: management of the Queensland railway network – including access and operations on it.
- Infrastructure Services: construction, maintenance and management of the rail network.
- Rolling Stock and Component Services: manufacture, heavy repair and overhaul of most of QR's rolling stock fleet.
- Shared Services: internal business support across QR operations.

In the last part of the twentieth century, as a result of sweeping national reforms to Australian competition policy, the 'business areas' of the public sector lost the traditional 'shield of the crown' and were forced to engage in open competition, including payment of full taxes, total transparency and a requirement to provide third-party access to their infrastructure. This had a major impact on Australian railways which now faced competition from private freight companies who had to be given access to the track for their rolling stock at competitive prices.

Rather than take a defensive stance, QR took strategic advantage of this situation and won contracts in other Australian states (e.g. coal contracts in the Hunter Valley of New South Wales) and overseas, in competition with private bidders. This was quite an achievement for an organisation with a longstanding public service culture. A large part of the credit is given to the entrepreneurial skills of the CEO of the period of the 1990s and early 2000s, Bob Scheuber, who had a long career in QR, having worked his way up the ladder. He had always retained his union membership, and the trust he had generated with the staff is considered to have been a vital factor in being able to introduce the new corporate and strategic focus which required some job cutting. It was also a key aspect of his leadership of a railway which had the usual run of accidents which affect railways the world over. He has commented that in his major media appearances during such crises he regarded the interviews as a key avenue for communicating to his own workforce, just as much as to the public.

In 2006, QR signalled a more commercial future with the appointment of former BHP CEO John Prescott as Chairman. In 2007, leading steel executive Lance

Hockridge (formerly of Bluescope and BHP) was appointed CEO to replace Bob Scheuber, whose contract had expired.

QR's success had been aided by a set of strategic partnerships it formed with linked operators in the transport and logistics supply chain. It has also had active corporate social responsibility programmes with several community, not for profit, organisations.

In 2008, in a shock announcement, the State Labour government revealed that the global financial crisis had caused a major dent in the state's finances, so much so that Queensland lost its longstanding Triple A credit rating and was facing intense difficulties in raising loans in the face of already mounting debt levels. In response to this crisis, the government announced a privatisation programme which would include government forests, ports and parts of QR including its freight division and coal network. This immediately produced a public outcry since privatisation had not even been mentioned during the election campaign. The unions mounted a major protest campaign against privatisation in general, but especially at the proposals for QR. This campaign gathered intensity and was backed by substantial media commentary, particularly when it became obvious that the government had not carefully thought through the privatisation goals or process and its likely ramifications.

Business generally welcomed the privatisation moves, citing various reasons why rail freight should be in private hands. The debate, it was argued, was about who would be the best owner of QR's freight business: the government or private sector – not an argument about individual managers but about structure and governance.

The question being asked was, 'Do we want QR's freight business owned by a government, which has a complex array of political and policy objectives, or do we want it owned by an entity with only a commercial focus?'[3]

Three reasons for privatisation advanced at the time were:

1. The freight business is capital intensive and it is extremely important that the required investments are made to transport Queensland's growing coal exports. A commercial entity that is well capitalised will generally invest when it sees sufficient demand for the services, but a government owner must weigh the more immediate political benefits of investing in possibly schools or hospitals instead.
2. It is more difficult for a government to run QR efficiently given that it is constantly lobbied by customers, unions and other stakeholders making demands that they would not do to a private operator.

3. QR needs to be responsive to commercial opportunities and such decisions with customers, who might be prepared to pay, should not have to pass through a political filter.

On the other hand, a group of leading economists attacked the privatisation plan saying that the measures of costing and return had overstated the financial returns, given the costs of dressing up the assets for sale, and undervalued the dividend stream that would have kept flowing to the government if the asset remained in public ownership. The coal industry expressed concerns at the plan to sell both QR track and rolling stock as one entity (i.e. an integrated operator like the Class 1 railways in the USA) which they claimed might lead to anti-competitive pricing and access decisions that would create inefficiencies and delay upgrades. The argument effectively complained that this would amount to replacing a public monopoly with a private one.

QR itself conducted a study of rail privatisations around the world and was unimpressed by experiences in the UK and New Zealand, but regarded Canadian experience more favourably. The British experience was believed to have brought some benefits, including possibly lower rail fares, but it also seemed that crowded trains, allegations of profiteering by the multitude of new rail service providers, paralysing crashes and endless political friction had led to a bigger British government subsidy than had been the case when rail was in full British government ownership. Many argued that the splitting of the UK's train operating services from control of the track – i.e. 'above-rail' (the locomotives and rolling stock), from 'below-rail' assets (construction and maintenance of the track) was the source of many of the problems, because it led to a multitude of small train operators squabbling over access to lines that were controlled by a company that had no financial incentive to maintain or improve the infrastructure.

The main Australian competitor group to QR, Asciano, which operates the Pacific National group, an 'above-rail' operator, expressed concerns to the competition regulator that the sale of a vertically-integrated QR would give it incentives to discriminate against above-rail competitors, because it could set the price and access conditions for such competitors.

As the debate wore on, it became clear that the government had not taken many of these factors into account, especially the question of which body would have responsibility for track maintenance. Some 5000 workers in QR had this responsibility. It was not clear what the interface between the newly privatised parts of QR and the rest would be, and particularly why a government would continue to subsidise one part but not the other. The actual valuation of the assets and their split was another very difficult task. Moreover, QR had an enviable safety record, a reputation for good technical excellence, a sound customer /commercial balance and a sense of corporate responsibility – the damage which could be done to this brand needed to be considered.

Consequently it became progressively clear to incumbent CEO Lance Hockridge and the board that a series of strategic moves would be required to handle a very complex situation which included:

- A Labour government forced to consider privatisation, though ideologically opposed to it and without an electoral mandate to take such action and bound to alienate its own supporters including the unions.
- Strong opposition from the state Treasury to any combined integration of 'above' and 'below' rail based on their belief that this was in breach of competition policy and would lower returns to the state coffers.
- Competition from mining companies for the purchase of the rail company led by a high-profile former premier of New South Wales.

All of these challenges were addressed and facilitated by the close and constant relationship which Hockridge and his team had maintained throughout with the key relevant government ministers and their opposition counterparts. The key example was the constant feeding of supportive information to the minister who was facing considerable hostility from his own party and colleagues, including supportive arguments which he could emphasise to placate them, such as retention of controlling share ownership, assurances that the head office would remain in Queensland and the potential to ensure no sackings or industrial disruption in the early stages of privatisation. According to a detailed comprehensive account written by a key insider in the company this was a crucial factor[4]. In particular, the strategy of bringing Paul Martin, the former Canadian Rail Minister (later Prime Minister), to Queensland to explain the Canadian process of rail privatisation proved a vital element in impressing the government and allaying their doubts about the company's preferred model of privatisation, and suggesting some ways forward. The Treasury arguments about competition were met by hiring the former head of Australia's Consumer and Competition Commission to demonstrate that combining 'above' and 'below' rail would be more effective overall. Another study was commissioned by one of Australia's leading experts on regulation to demonstrate that effective regulation of the preferred operational model was possible.

For the government, the strong political opposition to the privatisation would be countered by using all this material, especially the Canadian experience. Key aspects would be the maintenance of the head office of the company in Queensland, the offering of parcels of shares to Queensland citizens and to workers, imposition of conditions on the company for three to five years regarding employment, including no forced redundancies, and particularly the most controversial aspect (not of the company's choosing), which was the government's retention of a controlling shareholding in the company which somewhat appeased the Labour Party but created extreme difficulties for the company in attracting private-sector investment in Australia.

In the event, the government responded to union and public concerns about ownership by announcing that the sale of QR's freight operations and coal network would be by a public float, with parcels of shares reserved for QR staff, and preferential access to shares for the Queensland public. The government offered QR National employees A\$1000 worth of free shares, and an additional A\$4000 worth on a discounted basis. The government would also retain a 25–40 per cent initial shareholding which would be sold down over time. The rolling stock workshops, which service the freight rolling stock, and the track maintenance staff who build new track or maintain current track were included in the new privatised freight entity called 'QR National'. Therefore QR National was planned to be a fully integrated freight operator and track owner.

With the split of freight from passenger operations, the plan also created a new entity called Queensland Rail which would become a government-owned passenger business offering the suite of passenger services which were currently provided.

Owing mainly to the government's remaining and controlling share in the company, there was cynicism in the Australian stock market. Faced with this, and recognising that, as a result, there would be less than sufficient interest in Australia, Hockridge moved quickly to undertake an exhaustive worldwide trade show. In the event, the privatisation could not have succeeded without overseas investment. Whilst the original share price was set at A\$2.40, the price quickly rose to A\$4.00 then settled at A\$3.40. The irony is that the Australian investors who had had little faith in the venture were now forced to buy in at a higher price than they could have had earlier. The fact that both the Labour government and the opposition pledged to sell down the government share eventually gave some certainty although it was reported that some potential investors in the company remained wary given the government retention of an ownership stake.

QR National became listed in the top 30 companies in Australia by market capitalisation at A\$8.5bn – bigger than Qantas. Unlike experience with other privatisations around the world, there were few staff redundancies, numbers falling from 9500 to 9000 through voluntary redundancies (staff have employment guaranteed for three years under the enterprise agreement). In the words of a senior official, 'Compulsory redundancy is the last resort of the bad manager'. QR National embarked on a policy of creating more indigenous employment and now employs more indigenous workers than was the case under government ownership. It has also tripled the number of apprenticeships it has offered.

The government retained 34 per cent of ownership but had no seat on the new board and did not issue any directions to the company. Some community service obligations remain in place relating mainly to regional freight concessions, which are government funded. The rail freight operator owns 3000 km of track, with the government retaining ownership of 7000 km. Ownership of the track facilitates a focus on supply chains and vertical integration means a strong incentive to maintain the track and address safety concerns, especially during natural disasters such as floods which have caused severe damage. The company is recognised as having an excellent record in this domain.

Since privatisation, the company's activities have continued to be heavily associated with mineral haulage in Queensland, the intensely mineral-rich north west region of Western Australia, and the Hunter Valley of New South Wales. It is the major Australian player in resource infrastructure. It also still carries general freight across Australia on the interstate freight node and provides consulting and technical services overseas. The philosophy is now one of growth for it believes that without growth it will not have a strategy. That strategy can be summed up as 'supply chain management' which will be vital, both to address the competition and to achieve innovation. Different modes beckon including ownership of track, using others' tracks and building new tracks.

Competition comes in many forms including:

- Other Australian rail operators also pursuing supply chain control.
- Overseas interests currently receiving minerals and other freight who want full and certain supply chain control.
- Many mining companies who want to establish their own track and rail operations.
- Gaining access to existing tracks owned by competitors under the access rules laid down by National Competition Policy, despite these existing operators claiming their track is fully utilised.

- Opportunities presented by new smaller mining companies amenable to suggestions of combining to establish new rail lines.

The strategy of supply chain control and management covers a broad spectrum of possibilities and alliances including vertical integration of rail, suppliers such as miners and farmers, ports and overseas purchasers. It also means the company will need to become closer to its customers, understand their industries and the factors unique to them, and closely follow the development of new and growing industries such as carbon capture and storage. There is also the matter of re-engaging with customers who were formerly at odds with the company before privatisation and who were trying to take over their track.

In other words, QR National decided to pursue a growth strategy based on its core business, with any diversification not straying too far from its core business. It committed itself to maintaining a good corporate citizen record through employment policies, strategic sponsorships and other corporate social responsibility programmes. Safety and indigenous employment have become key priorities. This privatisation, therefore, appeared to have unleashed a new dynamic in performance and growth without much of the downside often experienced elsewhere, proving the sceptics wrong.

There was a strong performance in 2012, with a growth of 52 per cent in underlying earnings before interest and tax to A$584mn. This was achieved despite lower coal haulage due to the slowness of large coal projects coming on stream, and partly caused by losses of exports to the USA during the severe Queensland floods. The company predicted modest growth and the cut of another 750 jobs through voluntary redundancies. With much debate occurring in Australia about the prospective length of the resources boom, CEO Lance Hockridge commented that, 'It is a more cautious world.'

In 2012, the Queensland government, as a result of a major Commission of Audit into state debt-laden finances, announced that it was going to progressively sell down its remaining stake in QR National. With the share price rising to A$3.30 from the listing price of A$2.55, the media declared that the sceptics had been silenced because QR National had performed. Additionally, late in 2012, as a result of continuing brand confusion between QR National and Queensland Rail (including amongst politicians themselves), the company announced that it was changing its name to 'Aurizon', combining the iconic word images of Australia and Horizon.

The expiry of labour employment conditions which had been part of the privatisation agreement allowed Hockridge, in 2014 and 2015, to meet cost pressures from falling world commodity prices by entering new enterprise bargaining arrangements with unions. This involved offering redundancies and abolition of restrictive rostering arrangements. There was some bitterness from the unions involved and press comments about him being a 'toe-cutter' – a ruthless and intimidating type of person.[5] The press trawled through previous examples where he had taken cost-cutting measures in former CEO positions. However, the general consensus was that this description did not fit his personality, or management style. He stated that he saw himself as a 'change manager', though he conceded that this had involved a no-nonsense approach to cutting costs throughout his career. He noted that restructuring a business may be destabilising but it can eventually result in a stronger and more resilient organisation. Reflecting on the criticism he had endured:

'When I came to QR National the pace was slow, bureaucratic, non-commercial, overly responsive to political stimulus, over governed, over regulated, and over influenced by the unions. On the other hand, all the raw material was there – we had great people and great assets.'[5]

In the event, new enterprise agreements for all workers on the railway were satisfactorily concluded by mid-2015, in some cases involving more pay and continuation of the same working conditions. Unions had arranged strikes and taken Aurizon to the Fair Work Commission, but the commission allowed Aurizon to terminate expired enterprise agreements on the grounds that the business needed to remain competitive.

As a result of declining markets for commodities, especially coal in China, Hockridge went to India in 2015 to build relationships and open new partnerships in a country facing increasing requirements for coal transport infrastructure and logistics networks. He remarked: 'Our agenda is simple to explore growth markets where Aurizon can leverage our capability in rail-based integrated supply chains.'[6]

In more recent times, Hockridge has become more high profile in social causes and in being prepared to criticise governments, especially over his belief that Australia is slipping behind Asia in terms of productivity because of the lack of a cohesive infrastructure plan. Asian neighbours by contrast were boosting investments in rail and ports. He has said that such short-term political thinking meant reduced productivity as transportation links became increasingly congested.

A new Chairman, Tim Poole, was appointed in 2015 to replace veteran John Prescott. Poole is a 46-year-old infrastructure expert whom the board see as having the expertise to introduce more efficient use of capital and apply keen financial analysis of vulnerable projects like the potential West Pilbara project in Western Australia which is of concern to shareholders because of the risk involved. It will also help that he chaired Asciano (Aurizon's main competitor) from 2007–9. It will be his immediate task to balance investors' concerns about commodity price risk with the need to invest long term.[7]

Notes and references
1. A$1 = £0.54 = $0.78 = €0.69.
2. QR Annual Report 2009.
3. Australian Financial Review, 30 November 2009.
4. Stephen Baines, *Steel on Steel*, UQP, St Lucia, 2014.
5. G. Norris, 'Queensland Business Monthly: Aurizon chief Lance Hockridge not done shaking up rail giant', *The Courier Mail*, 28 May 2015.
6. G. Norris, 'Freight giant Aurizon eyes Indian railways and logistics market', *The Courier Mail*, 6 November 2015.
7. *Boss Magazine*, 13 November 2013.

In the boardroom at HomeCo

Gerry Johnson

This case is concerned with how strategy might be determined in practice. It explains the strategic issues facing a (fictitious) company producing plastic homeware products and the strategic options being advocated to tackle them. Profiles of the board members are provided so the case lends itself to a role-play exercise in which they discuss the options as well as the underlying purpose of HomeCo and the objectives it should be pursuing.

HomeCo[1] is probably best known for its range of plastic goods, such as buckets and bowls, sold through supermarkets and hardware shops throughout the UK where it has built a substantial market share. Their products can also be found in various countries in Europe to a lesser extent. It does not have much international presence beyond that. Recently, however, its growth has been challenged by an American multinational firm on the back of much higher marketing expenditure.

The growth of HomeCo

HomeCo was founded some 40 years ago as a family-owned industrial plastics firm. This original interest in industrial products was superseded by growth in consumer products sold through retailers, which now comprise the bulk of the turnover and profit of the Plastics Division of HomeCo. The family influence on the business gradually declined as the business went public in 1995. Its current ownership structure is shown in Table 1. Prior to the flotation of the business, the then family owner also sold shares to employees. This tradition has been continued with an employee share ownership scheme now accounting for some ten per cent of the shares.

Table 1 Ownership structure of HomeCo

	Percentage of shares
Family	15
Employees	10
Institutional shareholding	60
Other individual (non-institutional) shareholders	15

In addition to the Plastics Division, a second division was established in the late-1990s. This was based on two acquisitions; one of a business specialising in plastic storage units for offices and the second in sleeves for products such as CDs and DVDs. Initially these businesses were run within the overall business, but in 2001 it was decided to set up a separate division to use the technology available from these business units to develop a wider range of plastic storage and leisure goods; and so a separate 'Homeware Division' was created. Table 2 shows the breakdown in turnover and profit contribution of each of the businesses.

After its flotation the company, then just a plastics business, grew rapidly and profitably; and this was reflected in its growth in share price. In 1998, the board decided that if future growth was to be maintained, diversification was necessary and this led to the acquisition of the other plastics businesses over the next fifteen years. However, financial analysts believe that the company paid too much for these acquisitions and their performance has never really

Table 2 Turnover and profit contribution of each business

	Turnover		Percentage of total group operating profits
	£mn[*]	%	
Plastics Division			
- Consumer	205	40	52
- Industrial	80	16	14
Homeware Division	210	44	34
Total	495		

[*] £1 = €1.2 = $1.5.

justified the optimism voiced at the time. There is also scepticism as to just what HomeCo, as a corporate parent, can add to these businesses. In addition, the growth in the plastics business, though continuing, has slowed down; and financial analysts believe that the growing interest of multinational firms in this area will inevitably threaten nationally-based firms with limited markets. The result has been a declining share price and disquiet amongst investment managers with interests in the firm.

However, there is a belief held by some in the firm itself that inadequate attention has been paid in the past to the competences developed in retail markets. They argue that the lessons learned in marketing to major retail chains could be transferred to the new Homeware Division more effectively than they have been. The argument here is that the company has not sufficiently sought, or managed, synergies effectively.

HomeCo's future

Michael has been chairman and group chief executive for the last five years. He has announced that he intends to retire as group CEO and become a part-time non-executive chairman. The board has decided that his successor will be Brian, the existing chief executive of the Plastics Division.

The board now has to decide what should be done. They appear to have a number of options:

1. Expand the international operations of the plastics business, i.e. focus on traditional strengths but grow internationally. If capital is required for this, arguably look for buyers for the industrial plastics business or for all or some of the Homeware Division, which some argue has failed to deliver against original expectations. Of course this would mean a loss of jobs, something that the employee shareholders and perhaps family shareholders would object to considerably, as well as some members of management.
2. Realise capital from selling off some of the Homeware Division activities and absorb the activities with a more obvious retail plastics emphasis into an expanded consumer plastics business unit.
3. Pursue the strategy advocated by the Homeware Division. Namely invest further in that division, expand its product range and its distribution.
4. Sell the whole company. A multinational plastics business has already expressed their interest in a potential takeover and at a price well above the existing share price.

However, prior to a discussion on such strategic options, Michael, the chairman, believes that there needs to be clarity on other issues:

'We have to be clear about our strategy: that is true. But first we have to decide who the strategy is for. If we are not, then the debate on strategy will lack any clear focus. At the extreme it can just be an exercise in self interest.'

With this in mind the brief of the board is to discuss and decide upon what Michael sees as a set of related issues:

- To whom are the board responsible in deciding the future strategy of the group and for the performance of the group.
- Is there a rationale for the group: if so what is it? As Michael puts it: 'It is becoming increasingly clear that some influential shareholders and industry analysts are unclear what the group is about, what its logic is and why it has the businesses it has: and this is depressing the share price.'
- What business units should HomeCo have?
- And what should their strategies be?

Members of the board

Chairman and Group CEO (Michael)

Group Finance Director (Paula)

CEO – Plastics Division and Group Chief Executive Designate (Brian)

CEO – Chemicals Division (Charles)

Family Non-Executive Director (James)

Employee Non-Executive Director (Arthur)

Two Non-Executive Directors (Julia and Derek)

Michael: Chairman

Michael has been Chief Executive and Chairman of the HomeCo Group for five years: he is now relinquishing the post of Chief Executive and moving to a part-time Chairman's role. He was recruited into HomeCo at the time of its public flotation.

Michael has become convinced that some major changes have to be made at HomeCo and that 'they probably need someone other than me to do this'. He is open-minded about what should be done, but within the last few years has become more and more convinced that, whatever the strategy, it has to be targeted towards increasing shareholder value. This conviction has come about for two linked reasons. The first is the sluggish share price; and the second is the consequent pressure he has come under from financial institutions to improve returns to shareholders and the long-term prospects for shareholders. Although he recognises the heritage of the company, its family traditions and its responsibility to employees, he has become convinced that, whilst their interests are important, it is the wider shareholding community, particularly as represented in the institutional investors, who have to be the primary concern.

He sat on the board at the time of the acquisition of the businesses now forming the Homeware Division, though these were primarily driven by the previous chairman. He supported them at that time, but is more questioning now about their worth and their future prospects. He acknowledges that this could be because he is by history a 'plastics man' and that his primary interest in the past has been the development of the consumer plastics business.

> 'I acknowledge that achieving greater synergies with the Homeware Division should be possible but, based on experience so far, they are more difficult to realise than was thought. Or to put it another way, do we really need different divisions? We have ended up with an infrastructure above our businesses – a corporate centre – and I am being asked what that adds to the businesses; what is it there for? If we aren't clear on that then the centre is at risk of just being a costly overhead: and our investors would have every right to be unhappy about that.'

His overriding concern, however, is that there should be a full debate within the board on what should be done. He knows there are different views about the future strategy of the business. He believes strongly that the way forward, therefore, is to address an overarching question before details of the strategy are discussed: Who is the strategy for? Or, as Michael puts it: 'Who are we answerable to? I didn't think as a board we are clear enough on it. And I don't see how we can discuss future strategy without being clearer. If we are not, debating strategy is unfocused.'

He sees his primary role in the meeting as insisting on clarity on this issue and then ensuring that strategies are examined and evaluated in terms of that focus.

Brian: Chief Executive of the Plastics Division and Chief Executive Designate of the Group

Brian was recruited to HomeCo to run the Plastics Division when Michael took over as Group CEO. By background he is a consumer products man, having spent most of his time with Unilever, mainly in marketing jobs. He believes that, in the end, it is success in the market-

place that will provide the best return for shareholders. He sees the priorities as defending the market share in the UK for the plastics business and growing it internationally.

He has had less direct exposure to pressure from the institutions and shareholder groups than has Michael. His view is that Michael may be unduly concerned about such pressure and that it is likely to be a short-term reflection of a downturn in the growth rate of the business. The answer is to go for growth.

He understands concerns about the Homeware Division. His view is: 'If both Plastics and Homeware are growing and developing their markets profitably, then there is no issue. Shareholders and managers alike would be satisfied.' However, he is unsure of the current approach with regard to Homeware, though he believes the appointment of Charles as CEO of Homeware has been a good one.

> 'Charles has been recruited to grow the Homeware Division. If he is successful he will have done his job and as Chief Executive of HomeCo I will be satisfied. But I am less sure about the current structure. Now I am taking over as Group CEO, I can see an argument for pulling all retail plastics businesses together, selling off some of the non-retail businesses in Homeware, and just having two divisions – Consumer and Industrial. That seems much more clear-cut: the two divisions would each have clearly different market focuses; and surely that makes sense.'

He then added: 'Could Charles run an enlarged consumer business? I don't know. I would like to see evidence of success in what he is doing just now.'

In the meantime, he sees that his new role as Chief Executive of the Group is to ensure that the growth and profit targets for each of the divisions and their constituent businesses are met: 'That is the primary role of the corporate centre. The businesses manage their strategy: the centre makes sure they achieve the results.'

As for the shareholders, particularly the institutional investors, he believes that the new and separate role of Group Chairman for Michael is primarily to provide an interface with them: 'My responsibility is the businesses: Michael's responsibility is the shareholders.'

As for the takeover interest by the multinational competitors, he is worried that this would result in his not getting the chance to manage the HomeCo Group – something he has been aspiring to for years.

Charles: Chief Executive of the Homeware Division

Charles was appointed just two years ago to take over the Homeware Division. He also has a background in consumer goods marketing. He believes that, paradoxically,

HomeCo's plastics heritage has marginalised the businesses in the Homeware Division.

> **'HomeCo has never realised the potential of Homeware. The major reason for this is it doesn't know how to do so. Selling buckets and bowls to retail chains is not the most sophisticated marketing you can imagine. Sure we could benefit from the contacts and the supply chain. But it's not the marketing expertise we need: its resources – investment in marketing and good people – that would help. The problem is the Group is too concerned with its buckets and bowls to see this.'**

He acknowledges the logic of bringing together all the retail businesses together in one division but also has concerns:

> **'Okay, but there are two problems. First, I think it could end up just being an emphasis on the existing consumer plastics business – just buckets and bowls again. There is no more growth to be had there. Second, although I think I could do a good job heading that enlarged business, I am not sure the rest of the board would back my appointment, so I would be out.'**

Like Brian he believes that the answer to the current problems is to build profitable growth by concentrating on the existing businesses. He wants to get down to discussing the strategies for achieving this. Whilst he understands Michael's concern about shareholder pressure, he believes that this can be alleviated by ensuring improved performance of the businesses through growth. He also believes there is a good potential for cost savings in the businesses through greater efficiency. He knows this would mean losing jobs and believes that the company has been 'soft' on this issue because of the historical influence of both the family and the employees.

He would prefer that the Homeware Division stays as it is for the time being and is concerned about the takeover interest by the plastics multinational. As he sees it, a takeover from them would inevitably result in a break up of HomeCo. Privately he will admit that whether this makes sense or not, this is his first job running a business at this level and he wants to make it work.

Paula: Finance Director

Paula was recruited as Finance Director of the firm eight years ago. She used to be with the auditors of HomeCo. As well as being Finance Director of the group, Paula is the major contact, other than Michael, with the various investors and has a responsibility for maintaining good relationships with investment managers. She is, perhaps, the most exposed to current criticisms and concerns about the share performance of the firm. She summarises this as follows:

> **'There are three main issues that investors are concerned about. One is the sluggish performance of the shares in recent years. The second reason is that they believe we paid too much for the businesses we acquired. The third reason is that they do not understand why we made those acquisitions. They believe that fundamentally this is a basic plastics business and wonder if we really understand some of the businesses we have got into. They want to see evidence that we can make them work. In the absence of such evidence they would prefer us to dispose of them. Indeed some argue that the Homeware businesses would benefit by being owned by someone who would understand them better than us. In any case they want us to focus much more on answering the question of how we will provide greater value to our shareholders than currently.'**

Paula is therefore 100 per cent behind Michael in asking for clarity in the board about who the firm is answerable to before getting down to the details of the strategy debate. And she sees it starkly:

> **'It is the institutional investors: they are the majority shareholders. It is vital we all recognise that. If we do not, the destiny of the business may be removed from our hands by them. We have to start taking their interests much more seriously.'**

Because of this she is determined to support Michael's insistence on a debate on this issue before moving on to a discussion of strategic options.

Personally Paula is neutral as to whether there should be a Homeware Division as well as a Plastics Division. She has some sympathy with Charles' view that the company has never really focused on the Homeware businesses and its markets. However, she has some sympathy with city analysts' belief that HomeCo is inherently a fairly simple plastics business:

> **'There is an argument to say that we should focus on what we know best. That inherently HomeCo is a single product plastics business. That's where our capabilities lie. The danger, however, is that, as such, we may be even more vulnerable to a takeover. Ironically a buyer may be less attracted to us with our Homeware businesses than without. So in some respects I think the issue of the portfolio logic of the business gets in the way of a real debate about how we act in the best interests of our shareholders. I suspect that if we do the numbers (and I have) the most logical answer of what is best for most shareholders is to negotiate the best offer we can for the sale of the business. I also think that we could probably maximise the price if we dispose of Homeware first. That is what I intend to argue.'**

Arthur: Employee Director

At the time of the public flotation of HomeCo, the family insisted that the employees should retain ten per cent of the shares and have the right to have a non-executive director on the board. For the last ten years this non-executive director has been Arthur.

Arthur is now retired from HomeCo but used to be a senior trade union official for 25 years when he worked for the company. He was proud to build up good working relationships between the employees and the family in his time and believes that that has been one of the strengths of the firm in the past. Indeed he is concerned that some recent appointments at senior management level have eroded this strength.

He also takes seriously the legacy of what the family intended:

> 'It was always intended that HomeCo be a caring employer. The whole point of giving the employees the right to own shares was to give them an interest in the commercial success of the business. We have built that interest and have a good employee relations track record as a result. It is all very well the directors talking about maximising shareholders' returns: they need to remember we are shareholders. They should also remember that there are thousands of shareholders just like our employees who have invested in pension funds and insurance policies which in turn have invested in HomeCo.'

Arthur sees himself representing the interest of the employees; and that this is about getting a good return on their shares as well as ensuring job security.

As a director of the firm, he is aware of the current takeover interest and opposes it because he believes that it would result, inevitably, in significant job losses and a short-term rather than long-term view.

Although he does not approve of Charles' attitude towards the employees, he does believe that developing Homeware, rather than disposing of it, is a good argument. Disposal would again result in job losses: development means job security.

He knows that he has a battle on his hands in the board but sees his role not only to fight on behalf of the employees as shareholders but to 'fight for the small shareholder' who do not just invest in businesses for short-term gain, but because they believe in the viability of those businesses.

Julia: non-executive director

Julia is a non-executive director who joined the board four years ago at the request of two of the most significant institutional investors. She sees her role as taking a measured view about the future of the business, with a priority interest in developing returns for shareholders.

Her brief on appointment was to encourage the board to address some key issues which the investment community found problematic. These were (and remain) the following:

- How to maximise long-term shareholder benefit?
- Whether this is best done by focusing on a plastics business alone or a diversified business?
- Within either option, how to minimise costs?
- Related to both the logic of the portfolio and to reducing costs, to determine just what the corporate centre adds in terms of value to the businesses. Her personal view is that the corporate centre is unclear on what it adds and, as a result, is destroying value and lowering returns to shareholders. Indeed she wonders if it is really needed.

She has tried to remain dispassionate and objective over the last few years in following this brief. She believes she has influenced Michael and Paula to take seriously the needs of shareholders but is concerned that Brian and Charles have not really thought through the implications of this for the future of the business:

> 'Brian and Charles are, essentially, managers and see their responsibilities as being down in the businesses. I believe they need to lift their sights to look at the interests of the shareholders and then decide the strategies of the businesses in that light.'

She is delighted that Michael is asking that these issues, which she sees as central, need to be clarified and will give Michael support in ensuring this happens.

The recent expression of interest by the multinational plastics firm is one about which, again, she has tried to remain objective. Her focus is on wanting to be convinced about how growing returns to shareholders in the future can be achieved. Her intention is to challenge the executives to demonstrate they can develop a strategy that does provide such an increase in shareholder value:

> 'I want to hear from them how they expect to be able to create real value from these businesses. It is not good enough to simply say we should grow them. I want to hear a much more convincing story about building bases of competitive advantage. Moreover I don't see that as an easy matter in the market conditions they are facing. I am, however, open to being convinced. But if they don't convince me of this, I believe the sale of the company may be in shareholders' interests.'

Derek: non-executive director

Derek has a number of non-executive positions in firms related to plastics, oils and chemicals businesses. He is regarded as an industry expert in some of these sectors. He joined the board at the invitation of Michael whom he knows well. Derek has a clear view about what should now be done. He believes that the firm has done well in the past but probably made a mistake in acquiring the Homeware businesses since the senior management at the time knew very little about them. He has a good deal of confidence in Charles and believes that, given time, Charles could sort them out and maybe achieve the sort of growth required. However, he explains the current situation as follows:

> 'The fact is we now have a choice. Do we go for a long term strategy which could require a good deal of invest-ment in Homeware as well as a plastics business faced with multinational competition? I can see why the management of the business might see this as a chal-lenge they would like to take on: but I see it as a risk. The alternative is to try and maximise the offer price in a takeover. I think we should do this for two reasons. First, because I think there is a window of opportunity here. I think we can get a good price now; but I am not sure we will be able to do so in a year or so. Second, I think the Homeware businesses can be used to enhance that offer. I think our share price is depressed because of our Homeware businesses and that we should get rid of them. If we do, I think it will make us more attractive to a take-over, but at a higher offer price than currently. So I think we have a short-term opportunity that we need to be following which is in the best interests of most of the shareholders. The problem is it is not in the interest of all the shareholders or in the career interest of the managers.'

He understands why Michael wants a debate about the centrality of shareholders but has his reservations on this:

> 'Look, Michael has come under a lot of pressure recently from institutional investors; and he knows that Brian and Charles don't understand this entirely. I understand his concerns but I think he is being some-what academic in all this. The fact is we have a short-term opportunity to get a really good price for this business and we should take it. If we don't I fear the time will pass. I also believe that if we follow Michael's logic and place the shareholder first we will come to the same conclusion anyway. It is in their best interest to take the short-term opportunity to maximise the value of their shares through a sale. I know there are those around the table who won't like that but I intend to push hard to get them to see the logic of such a sale.'

James: non-executive director

James is the grandson of the founder of HomeCo. He is a non-executive director. For some years he worked within the firm but left a few years after it went public. He was elected as a Labour party member of parliament for a local constituency. He describes himself, politically, as: 'New Labour, socially responsible and commercially aware.'

James takes seriously the family heritage of the firm and supports the strong belief of his father in the employee shareholder scheme, which he had set up. Indeed he believes the interest of the family and employees are closely aligned. He explains:

> 'The family set up this firm with the long term in mind. It was there to benefit the interests of the family over decades. I believe this is also the interest of the employees and, indeed, the wider shareholders. The family, employees and the ultimate shareholders are interested in the prosperity of this firm over decades, not a few years. The perspective I want to see this firm taking is to ensure its growth and prosperity over those time periods. I am well aware that since we have gone public the board, and Michael in particular, have come under all sorts of pressure that might lead to short-term decisions. I am very much against these.'

James believes that it is the responsibility of the board, to take a long-term view in the interests of all shareholders. In the board, and in parliament, he is scornful of professional investment managers (who publicly he has referred to as 'wide boys') whose primary interest, he argues, is their own careers rather than the long-term interest of firms or the real shareholders.

> 'We have created an industry of financial advisers and investment houses that have created a reality of their own. The shareholder is virtually isolated from the firms they invest in. They know virtually nothing about them, they are not encouraged to know about them and have become reliant on sometimes spurious advice from so-called specialists.'

He does not have a firm view as to what should be done at HomeCo except that he is determined to oppose its sale. Beyond that he intends to listen to the argu-ments. He does have doubts as to whether the firm has really thought through its diversification programme, but is open to persuasion if there is a long-term future there. He is, however, concerned that a decision to dispose of the Homeware businesses might in turn expose the group to a takeover bid to which he would be opposed.

Note:
1. HomeCo is a fictitious name for the case study. The description of the business is not intended to represent or be based on any specific exist-ing business.

GUIDE TO THE CLASSIC CASES ON THE COMPANION WEBSITE*

CASES	Introduction to strategy	The environment	Strategic capability	Strategic purpose	Culture and strategy	Business level strategy	Directions and corporate level strategy	International strategy	Innovation and entrepreneurship	Mergers, acquisitions and alliances	Strategy evaluation	Strategy development processes	Organising for success	Managing strategic change	The practice of management	Public sector/not-for-profit management	Small business strategy
The Lego Group: adopting a strategic approach	●●																
Vodafone: developing communications strategy in the UK market		●●			●												
European Tour Operators: confronting competition in the tourism industry		●●						●									
A source of cheap energy or a source of problems – the potential benefits and costs of **shale gas**		●●														●	
Amazon.com 2007–early 2009			●●				●										
Inside **Dyson** – a distinctive company?			●●														
Sheffield Theatres: strategy formulation for a wide audience of public and commercial stakeholders				●●												●●	
(RED)				●●													
Iona				●●												●●	
Hermes Fund Management, Total and Premier Oil: the responsibility and accountability of business				●●													
Marks and Spencer (A): can new initiatives and new management reverse a decline?					●●												
Cultural Turnaround at **Club Med**					●●												
Cordia LLP: service reform in the public sector					●●												
Thorntons: a variety of strategies in the manufacture and retail of chocolates						●●											
Madonna: the reigning queen of pop						●●											
Marks and Spencer plc (C): where next for the icon of British retailing						●	●●										
News Corporation: corporate logic and corporate management in a worldwide media business							●●										

*Classic cases are available at **www.pearsoned.co.uk/johnson**

CASES	Introduction to strategy	The environment	Strategic capability	Strategic purpose	Culture and strategy	Business level strategy	Directions and corporate level strategy	International strategy	Innovation and entrepreneurship	Mergers, acquisitions and alliances	Strategy evaluation	Strategy development processes	Organising for success	Managing strategic change	The practice of management	Public sector/not-for-profit management	Small business strategy
Lenovo computers: East meets West								●									
Sustaining the magic of Bang & Olufsen					●	●		●		●		●		●			
Coopers Creek: developments in domestic and international collaboration for a New Zealand winery			●					●									●
Skype: innovator and entrepreneurs									●								
Eden Project (A): inspiration, innovation and entrepreneurship to create a new 'wonder of the world'									●								
Eden Project (B): latest developments in a successful tourist attraction									●								
Where's Irene and just exactly what is she up to? The acquisition of **Cadbury plc** by **Kraft Foods** 2010										●							
Police Mergers: are mergers the best way forward in tackling major crime?										●						●	
Alliance Boots: a major merger in the pharmaceutical distribution and retailing sector										●							
TNK-BP: from Russia without love - a joint venture that almost fell apart					●					●							
Final Fantasy captures Lara Croft										●							
International HIV/AIDS Alliance				●						●	●		●			●	
Doman Synthetic Fibres plc (B)			●								●						
Ericsson: innovation from the periphery – the development of mobile telephone systems												●					
Direct & Care: strategy development in the multi-stakeholder context of public sector services												●				●	
Hurricane Katrina: human made disaster?													●				
Arts Council: changes in structure and responsibilities in funding the arts in the UK													●			●	

771

CASES	Introduction to strategy	The environment	Strategic capability	Strategic purpose	Culture and strategy	Business level strategy	Directions and corporate level strategy	International strategy	Innovation and entrepreneurship	Mergers, acquisitions and alliances	Strategy evaluation	Strategy development processes	Organising for success	Managing strategic change	The practice of management	Public sector/not-for-profit management	Small business strategy
BBC: structural changes to deliver a better service														●●		●●	
Managing change at **Faslane**														●●			
Marks and Spencer (B): turnaround at the high street legend														●●			
Forestry Commission: from forestry management to service provider: the challenge of managing change					●●									●●			
UNHCR: managing change in a global not-for-profit organisations			●●										●●		●●		
Ray Ozzie: software strategist															●●		
NHS Direct: managing in difficult times																●●	

*Classic cases are available at **www.pearsoned.co.uk/johnson**

GLOSSARY

acceptability expected performance outcomes of a proposed strategy to meet the expectations of the stakeholders (p. 387)

acquisition is achieved by purchasing a majority of shares in a target company (p. 341)

Ansoff's growth matrix is a classic corporate strategy framework for generating four basic directions for organisational growth (p. 244)

BCG matrix uses market share and market growth criteria to determine the attractiveness and balance of a business portfolio (p. 262)

Blue Oceans new market spaces where competition is minimised (p. 86)

business case provides the data and argument in support of a particular strategy proposal, for example investment in new equipment (p. 520)

business-level strategy how an individual business competes in its particular market(s) (p. 11)

business model describes a value proposition for customers and other participants, an arrangement of activities that produces this value, and associated revenue and cost structures (p. 229)

CAGE framework emphasises the importance of cultural, administrative, geographical and economic distance (p. 290)

capabilities the ways in which an organisation may deploy its assets effectively (p. 98)

co-evolution underlines the way in which partners, strategies and capabilities need to evolve in harmony in order to reflect constantly changing environments (p. 355)

collaborative advantage is about managing alliances better than competitors (p. 351)

collective strategy how the whole network of alliances, of which an organisation is a member, competes against rival networks of alliances (p. 351)

competitive advantage how a company, business unit or organisation creates value for its users both greater than the costs of supplying them and superior to that of rivals (p. 210)

competitive strategy how a company, business unit or organisation achieves competitive advantage in its domain of activity (p. 210)

complementor(s) an organisation is your complementor if it enhances your business attractiveness to customers or suppliers (p. 69)

configurations the set of organisational design elements that fit together in order to support the intended strategy (p. 458)

corporate entrepreneurship refers to radical change in an organisation's business, driven principally by the organisation's own capabilities (p. 348)

corporate governance is concerned with the structures and systems of control by which managers are held accountable to those who have a legitimate stake in an organisation (p. 141)

corporate-level strategy is concerned with the overall scope of an organisation and how value is added to the constituent businesses of the organisation as a whole (p. 10)

corporate social responsibility the commitment by organisations to behave ethically and contribute to economic development while improving the quality of life of the workforce and their families as well as the local community and society at large (p. 150)

cost-leadership strategy involves becoming the lowest-cost organisation in a domain of activity (p. 211)

critical success factors those factors that are either particularly valued by customers or which provide a significant advantage in terms of costs. (Sometimes called key success factors (KSF)) (p. 85)

cultural systems aim to standardise norms of behaviour within an organisation in line with particular objectives (p. 453)

cultural web shows the behavioural, physical and symbolic manifestations of a culture (p. 175)

deliberate strategy involves intentional formulation or planning (p. 412)

differentiation strategy involves uniqueness along some dimension that is sufficiently valued by customers to allow a price premium (p. 215)

diffusion is the process by which innovations spread amongst users (p. 324)

disruptive innovation creates substantial growth by offering a new performance trajectory that, even if initially inferior to the performance of existing technologies, has the potential to become markedly superior (p. 328)

distinctive resources and capabilities are required to achieve competitive advantage (p. 100)

diversification (related and unrelated/conglomerate) increasing the range of products or markets served by an organisation (p. 244)

divestiture when a business no longer fits the corporate strategy it may be sold (p. 350)

divisional structure is built up of separate divisions on the basis of products, services or geographical areas (p. 442)

dominant logic the set of corporate-level managerial competences applied across the portfolio of businesses (p. 250)

dynamic capabilities an organisation's ability to renew and re-create its strategic capabilities to meet the needs of changing environments (p. 119)

economies of scope efficiency gains made through applying the organisation's existing resources or competences to new markets or services (p. 250)

emergent strategy a strategy that develops as a result of a series of decisions, in a pattern that becomes clear over time, rather than as a deliberate result of a 'grand plan' (p. 419)

entrepreneurship is a process by which individuals, teams or organisations identify and exploit opportunities for new products or services that satisfy a need in a market (p. 310)

entrepreneurial life cycle progresses through start-up, growth, maturity and exit (p. 315)

Exploring Strategy **Framework** includes understanding *the strategic position* of an organisation (context); assessing *strategic choices* for the future (content); and managing *strategy in action* (process) (p. 11)

feasibility whether a strategy can work in practice (p. 399)

first-mover advantage where an organisation is better off than its competitors as a result of being first to market with a new product, process or service (p. 327)

focus strategy targets a narrow segment or domain of activity and tailors its products or services to the needs of that specific segment to the exclusion of others (p. 216)

forcefield analysis provides an initial view of change problems that need to be tackled by identifying forces for and against change (p. 476)

forecasting takes three fundamental approaches based on varying degrees of certainty: single-point, range and multiple-futures forecasting (p. 47)

functional strategies how the components of an organisation deliver effectively the corporate- and business-level strategies in terms of resources, processes and people (p. 11)

functional structure divides responsibilities according to the organisation's primary specialist roles such as production, research and sales (p. 440)

game theory encourages an organisation to consider competitors' likely moves and the implications of these moves for its own strategy (p. 226)

gap analysis compares actual or projected performance with desired performance (p. 377)

global–local dilemma the extent to which products and services may be standardised across national boundaries or need to be adapted to meet the requirements of specific national markets (p. 286)

global integration encourages organisations to coordinate their activities across diverse countries to gain efficient operations (p. 286)

global sourcing purchasing services and components from the most appropriate suppliers around the world, regardless of their location (p. 284)

global strategy involves high coordination of extensive activities dispersed geographically in many countries around the world (p. 278)

governance chain shows the roles and relationships of different groups involved in the governance of an organisation (p. 143)

hybrid strategy a hybrid strategy combines different generic strategies (p. 219)

hypothesis testing a methodology used particularly in strategy projects for setting priorities in investigating issues and options; widely used by strategy consulting firms and members of strategy project teams (p. 518)

industry a group of firms producing products and services that are essentially the same (p. 63)

inimitable resources and capabilities are those resources and capabilities that competitors find difficult and costly to imitate or obtain or substitute (p. 102)

innovation the conversion of new knowledge into a new product, process or service *and* the putting of this new product, process or service into actual commercial use (p. 317)

international strategy a range of options for operating outside an organisation's country of origin (p. 278)

key drivers for change are the environmental factors likely to have a high impact on industries and sectors, and the success or failure of strategies within them (p. 47)

leadership the process of influencing an organisation (or group within an organisation) in its efforts towards achieving an aim or goal (p. 470)

learning organisation an organisation that is capable of continual regeneration from the variety of knowledge, experience and skills within a culture that encourages questioning and challenge (p. 420)

legitimacy is concerned with meeting the expectations within an organisational field in terms of assumptions, behaviours and strategies (p. 171)

local responsiveness implies a greater need to disperse operations and adapt to local demand (p. 286)

logical incrementalism the development of strategy by experimentation and learning (p. 419)

macro-environment broad environmental factors that impact to a greater or lesser extent many organisations, industries and sectors (p. 33)

market a group of customers for specific products or services that are essentially the same (e.g. a particular geographical market) (p. 63)

market segment a group of customers who have similar needs that are different from customer needs in other parts of the market (p. 84)

market systems these typically involve some formalised system of 'contracting' for resources or inputs from other parts of an organisation and for supplying outputs to other parts of an organisation (p. 456)

matrix structure combines different structural dimensions simultaneously, for example product divisions and geographical territories or product divisions and functional specialisms (p. 444)

merger the combination of two previously separate organisations in order to form a new company (p. 341)

mission statement aims to provide the employees and stakeholders with clarity about what the organisation is fundamentally there to do (p. 7)

network effects there are network effects in an industry when one customer of a product or service has a positive effect on the value of that product for other customers (p. 71)

objectives are statements of specific outcomes that are to be achieved (often expressed in financial terms) (p. 8)

open innovation involves the deliberate import and export of knowledge by an organisation in order to accelerate and enhance its innovation (p. 321)

opportunity recognition means recognising an opportunity, circumstances under which products and services can satisfy a need in the market or environment (p. 310)

organic development is where a strategy is pursued by building on and developing an organisation's own capabilities (p. 340)

organisational ambidexterity the ability of an organisation simultaneously to exploit existing capabilities and to search for new capabilities (p. 481)

organisational culture the taken-for-granted assumptions and behaviours of an organisation's members (p. 171)

organisational field a community of organisations that interact more frequently with one another than with those outside the field (p. 40)

organisational fit refers to the match between the management practices, cultural practices and staff of characteristics between the target and the acquiring firms (p. 346)

organisational identity refers to what members believe and understand about who they specifically are as an organisation (p. 172)

organisational knowledge the collective intelligence, specific to an organisation, accumulated through both formal systems and the shared experience of people in that organisation (p. 105)

outsourcing activities that were previously carried out internally are subcontracted to external suppliers (p. 254)

paradigm is the set of assumptions held in common and taken for granted in an organisation (p. 172)

parental developer seeks to employ its own central capabilities to add value to its businesses (p. 261)

parenting advantage is the value added to businesses by corporate-level activities (p. 244)

path dependency where early events and decisions establish 'policy paths' that have lasting effects on subsequent events and decisions (p. 164)

performance targets focus on the *outputs* of an organisation (or part of an organisation), such as product quality, revenues or profits (p. 454)

PESTEL analysis categorises environmental influences into six main types: political, economic, social, technological, environmental and legal (p. 34)

planning systems plan and control the allocation of resources and monitor their utilisation (p. 451)

political view of strategy development strategies develop as the outcome of bargaining and negotiation among powerful interest groups (and stakeholders) (p. 442)

Porter's Diamond suggests that locational advantages may stem from local factor conditions; local demand conditions; local related and supporting industries; and from local firm strategy structure and rivalry (p. 282)

Porter's Five Forces Framework helps identify the attractiveness of an industry in terms of five competitive forces: the threat of entry; the threat of substitutes; the power of buyers; the power of suppliers; and the extent of rivalry between competitors (p. 64)

portfolio manager he or she operates as an active investor in a way that shareholders in the stock market are either too dispersed or too inexpert to be able to do so (p. 258)

power the ability of individuals or groups to persuade, induce or coerce others into following certain courses of action (p. 136)

profit pools the different levels of profit available at different parts of the value network (p. 112)

project-based structure teams are created, undertake a specific project (e.g. internal or external contracts) and are then dissolved (p. 448)

rare resources and capabilities are those resources and capabilities that are possessed uniquely by one organisation or by a few others (p.102)

recipe a set of assumptions, norms and routines held in common within an organisational field about the appropriate purposes and strategies of field members (p. 170)

resource-based view states that the competitive advantage and superior performance of an organisation is explained by the distinctiveness of its capabilities (p. 97)

resources and capabilities of an organisation contribute to its long-term survival and potentially to competitive advantage (p. 98)

returns a measure of the financial effectiveness of a strategy (p. 390)

risk the extent to which strategic outcomes are unpredictable, especially with regard to possible negative outcomes (p. 388)

S-curve the shape of the curve reflects a process of initial slow adoption of an innovation, followed by a rapid acceleration in diffusion, leading to a plateau representing the limit to demand (p. 325)

situational leadership strategic leaders are able to adjust their style of leadership to the context they face (p. 471)

social entrepreneurs individuals and groups who create independent organisations to mobilise ideas and resources to address social problems, typically earning revenues but on a not-for-profit basis (p. 316)

staged international expansion model proposes a sequential process whereby companies gradually increase their commitment to newly entered markets as they build market knowledge and capabilities (p. 295)

stakeholder mapping identifies stakeholder expectations and power, and helps in the understanding of political priorities (p. 136)

stakeholders those individuals or groups that depend on an organisation to fulfil their own goals and on whom, in turn, the organisation depends (p. 134)

statements of corporate values communicate the underlying and enduring core 'principles' that guide an organisation's strategy and define the way that the organisation should operate (p. 8)

strategic alliance where two or more organisations share resources and activities to pursue a common strategy (p. 351)

strategic business unit supplies goods or services for a distinct domain of activity (p. 209)

strategic choices involve the options for strategy in terms of both the *directions* in which strategy might move and the *methods* by which strategy might be pursued (p. 13)

strategic drift the tendency for strategies to develop incrementally on the basis of historical and cultural influences, but fail to keep pace with a changing environment (p. 180)

strategic entrepreneurship combines strategy and entrepreneurship and includes both advantage-seeking strategy activities and opportunity-seeking entrepreneurial activities to create value (p. 309)

strategic fit the extent to which the target firm strengthens or complements the acquiring firm's strategy (p. 346)

strategic groups organisations within an industry or sector with similar strategic characteristics, following similar strategies or competing on similar bases (p. 81)

strategic issue-selling the process of gaining attention and support of top management and other important stakeholders for strategic issues (p. 509)

strategic lock-in is where users become dependent on a supplier and are unable to use another supplier without substantial switching costs (p. 71)

strategic plan provides the data and argument in support of a strategy for the whole organisation (p. 520)

strategic planners (also known as strategy directors or corporate managers) managers with a formal responsibility for coordinating the strategy process (p. 501)

strategic planning systematic analysis and exploration to develop an organisation's strategy (p. 413)

strategic position the impact on strategy of the external environment, the organisation's strategic capability (resources and competences), and the organisation's goals and culture (p. 12)

strategy the long-term direction of an organisation (p. 4)

strategy canvas compares competitors according to their performance on key success factors in order to establish the extent of differentiation (p. 85)

strategy in action this is about how strategies are formed and how they are implemented (p. 14)

strategy lenses ways of looking at strategy issues differently in order to generate additional insights (p. 21)

strategy projects involve teams of people assigned to work on particular strategic issues over a defined period of time (p. 517)

strategy statements should have three main themes: the fundamental *goals* that the organisation seeks, which typically draw on the organisation's stated mission, vision and objectives; the *scope* or domain of the organisation's activities; and the particular *advantages* or capabilities it has to deliver all of these (p. 8)

strategy workshops (also called strategy away-days or offsites) these involve groups of executives working intensively for one or two days, often away from the office, on organisational strategy (p. 515)

structures give people formally defined roles, responsibilities and lines of reporting with regard to strategy (p. 439)

suitability assessing which proposed strategies address the *key opportunities and threats* an organisation faces (p. 380)

SWOT provides a general summary of the Strengths and Weaknesses explored in an analysis of resources and capabilities and the Opportunities and Threats explored in an analysis of the environment (p. 115)

synergy the benefits gained where activities or assets complement each other so that their combined effect is greater that the sum of their parts (p. 251)

synergy manager is a corporate parent seeking to enhance value for business units by managing synergies across business units (p. 259)

systems support and control people as they carry out structurally defined roles and responsibilities (p. 439)

three-horizons framework suggests organisations should think of themselves as comprising three types of business or activity, defined by their 'horizons' in terms of years (p. 6)

threshold resources and capabilities those that are needed for an organisation to meet the necessary requirements to compete in a given market and achieve parity with competitors in that market (p. 100)

transactional leaders emphasise 'hard' levers of change such as designing systems and controls (p. 471)

transformational leaders emphasise building a vision for their organisations (p. 471)

transnational structure combines local responsiveness with high global coordination (p. 446)

trust becomes highly important to the success of alliances over time (p. 355)

turnaround strategy here the emphasis is on speed of change and rapid cost reduction and/or revenue generation (p. 479)

valuable resources and capabilities are those which create a product or a service that is of value to customers and enables the organisation to respond to environmental opportunities or threats (p. 101)

value chain describes the categories of activities within an organisation which, together, create a product or service (p. 107)

value system comprises the set of inter-organisational links and relationships that are necessary to create a product or service (p. 107)

value net a map of organisations in a business environment demonstrating opportunities for value-creating cooperation as well as competition (p. 70)

vertical (forward and backward) integration entering into activities where the organisation is its own supplier or customer (p. 253)

vision statement is concerned with the desired future state of the organisation (p. 8)

VRIO analysis helps to evaluate if, how and to what extent an organization or company has resources and capabilities that are (i) valuable, (ii) rare, (iii) inimitable and (iv) supported by the organisation (p. 107)

Yip's globalisation framework sees international strategy potential as determined by market drivers, cost drivers, government drivers and competitive drivers (p. 280)

NAME INDEX

GENERAL INDEX

Page numbers in bold refer to definitions in the Glossary.

ACKNOWLEDGEMENTS

We are grateful to the following for permission to reproduce copyright material:

Figures

Figure 1.2 from *The Alchemy of Growth*, Texere Publishers (Baghai, M., Coley, S. and White, D. 2000) figure 1.1, p, 5, copyright 2000, reprinted by permission of Texere Publishers, a member of the Perseus Books Group and copyright © 1999, 2000 McKinsey & Company. All rights reserved. Reprinted by permission; Figure on page 52 after *Last Call For Datatopia Boarding Now! Four Future Scenarios On The Role of Information and Technology in Society, Business and Personal Life, 2030,* Gartner, Inc. (2014) figure 1, p. 6; Figures 3.2 and 7.8 from *Competitive Strategy: Techniques for Analyzing Industries and Competitors,* The Free Press (Porter, M.E. 1998), with the permission of The Free Press, a Division of Simon & Schuster, Inc. Copyright © 1998 by M.E. Porter. All rights reserved; Figure 3.3 from The Right Game, *Harvard Business Review,* July-August, pp. 57–64 (Brandenburger, A. and Nalebuff, B. 1996), copyright © 1996 by the Harvard Business School Publishing Corporation. All rights reserved; Figures 4.4, 4.5 and 7.2 adapted from *Competitive Advantage: Creating and Sustaining Superior Performance,* The Free Press (Porter, M.E. 1985), with the permission of The Free Press, a Division of Simon & Schuster, Inc. Copyright © 1985 by M.E. Porter. All rights reserved; Figure 4.6 from Bjorn Haugstad, 'Strategy as the international structuration of practice. Translation of formal strategies into strategies in practice', Doctoral dissertation submitted to Said Business School, University of Oxford, 2009; Figure 5.3 adapted from From client to project stakeholders: a stakeholder mapping approach, *Construction Management and Economics,* 21(8), pp. 841–8 (Newcombe, R. 2003), figure 3, reprinted by permission of the publisher, Taylor & Francis Ltd, http://www.tandfonline.com; Figure 5.5 adapted from David Pitt-Watson, Hermes Fund Management; Figure 6.5 after *Turnaround: Managerial Recipes for Strategic Success,* Associated Business Press (Grinyer, P. and Spender, J.C. 1979) p. 203, reprinted with permission of Peter H. Grinyer and J.C. Spender; Figure 7.5 adapted from *The Essence of Competitive Strategy,* Prentice Hall (Faulkner, D. and Bowman, C. 1995), with permission from Pearson Education Ltd; Figure 7.6 adapted from *Hypercompetition: Managing the Dynamics of Strategic Maneuvering,* The Free Press (D'Aveni, R. and Gunther, R. 1994) p. 50, with the permission of The Free Press, a Division of Simon & Schuster, Inc. Copyright © 1994 by R. D'Aveni and R. Gunther. All rights reserved; Figure 7.7 from A framework for responding to low-cost rivals, *Harvard Business Review,* December (Kumar, N. 2006), copyright © 1996 by the Harvard Business School Publishing Corporation. All rights reserved; Figure 8.2 adapted from *Corporate Strategy,* Penguin (Ansoff, H.I. 1988), reprinted by permission from the Ansoff Family Trust; Figures 8.5 and 8.8 adapted from *Corporate Level Strategy,* Wiley (Goold, M., Campbell, A. and Alexander, M. 1994), © 1994 Wiley. Reproduced with permission of John Wiley & Sons, Inc.; Figure 9.3 adapted from *The Competitive Advantage of Nations,* The Free Press (Porter, M.E. 1990), with the permission of The Free Press, a Division of Simon & Schuster, Inc. Copyright © 1990 by M.E. Porter. All rights reserved; Figure on page 269 from *The New Corporate Strategy,* John Wiley & Sons, Inc. (Ansoff, H. 1988), reprinted by permission of John Wiley & Sons, Inc., and the Ansoff Family Trust; Figure 9.5 from In the eye of the beholder: cross-cultural lessons in leadership from Project GLOBE, *Academy of Management Perspectives,* February, pp. 67–90 (Javidan, M., Dorman, P., de Luque, M. and House, R. 2006), figure 4, p. 82, Academy of Management; Figure 9.6 adapted from Global gamesmanship, *Harvard Business Review,* May (MacMillan, I., van Putter, S. and McGrath, R. 2003), copyright © 2003 by the Harvard Business School Publishing Corporation. All rights reserved; Figure 9.7 from *Managing across Borders: The Transnational Solution,* Harvard Business School Press (Bartlett, C.A. and Ghoshal, S. 1989) pp. 105–11, copyright © 1989 by the Harvard Business School Publishing Corporation. All rights reserved; Figure 10.5 adapted from A dynamic model of process and product innovation, *Omega,* 3(6), pp. 639–56 (Abernathy, J. and Utterback, U. 1975), copyright 1975, with permission from Elsevier; Figure on page 323 from *Making the Transition to Cloud*, Fujitsu Services Ltd (Gentle, D. 2011), with permission from Fujitsu Limited UK; Figure 10.7 adapted from *The Innovator's Solution*, Harvard Business School Press (Christensen, C. and Raynor, M.E. 2003), copyright © 2003 by the Harvard Business School Publishing Corporation. All rights reserved; Figure 10.8 from *The Entrepreneurial Mindset*, Harvard Business School Press (MacMillan, I. and McGrath, R.G. 2000) p. 176, copyright © 2000 by the Harvard Business School Publishing Corporation. All rights reserved; Figure 11.3 from New integration strategies for post acquisition management, *Long Range Planning*, 48(4), pp. 235–51 (Angwin, D. N. and Meadows, M. 2015), copyright 2015, with permission from Elsevier; Figure 11.5 adapted from Strategic alliances: gateway to the new Europe, *Long Range Planning*, 26, pp. 102–11 (Murray, E. and Mahon, J. 1993), p. 109, copyright 1993, with permission from Elsevier; Figure 1 on page 406 from Broadcasters' Audience Research Board Ltd (BARB); Figure 2 on page 407 from ITV Annual Report (2015), p. 39; Figure 13.1 adapted from Of strategies, deliberate and emergent, *Strategic Management Journal*, 6(3), p. 258 (Mintzberg, H. and Waters, J.A. 1985), with permission from John Wiley & Sons Ltd; Figure 14.5 adapted from *Managing Across Borders: The Transnational Corporation*, 2nd ed., Harvard Business School Press (Bartlett, C.A. and Ghoshal, S. 1998), copyright © 1998 by the Harvard Business School Publishing Corporation. All rights reserved; Figure on page 447 from One chart that explains Alphabet, Google's new parent company, *Business Insider*, 11 August (2015), Wright's Media, LLC; Figure 14.7 from Achieving strategy with scorecarding, *Journal of Corporate Accounting and Finance*, 16(3), p. 64 (Lawson, R., Stratton, W. and Hatch, T. 2005), exhibit 1, with permission from John Wiley & Sons Ltd; Figure 14.8 from Structure is not organization, *Business Horizons*, 23, pp. 14–26 (Waterman, R., Peters, T.J. and Phillips, J.R. 1980), McKinsey & Company, reproduced with permission; Figure 1 on page 465 from Yahoo! Finance; Figure 2 on page 466 and Figure 3 on page 467 adapted from www.sony.net; Figure 15.2 adapted from *Exploring Strategic Change*, 3rd ed., Prentice Hall (Balogun, J. and Hope Hailey, V. 2008) and Figure 15.4 adapted from *Exploring Strategic Change*, 4th ed., Prentice Hall (Balogun, J., Hope Hailey, V. and Gustafsson, S. 2016) p. 23, © Pearson Education Ltd; Figure 16.3 adapted from An attention-based theory of strategy formulation: linking micro and macro perspectives in strategy processes, *Advances in Strategic Management*, 22, pp. 39–62 (Ocasio, W. and Joseph, J. 2005), copyright © 2005, with permission from Elsevier; Figure 1 on page 546 from *Medicines in Development – Biotechnology*, Pharmaceutical Research and Manufacturers of America (2006) p. 51; Figure 1 on page 559 and Figure 2 on page 260 from Siemens AG; Figure 1 on page 563, Figure 2 on page 564 and Figure 3 on page 565 from http://www.beerandpub.com/statistics, British Beer and Pubs Association; Figures on page 609 from Adnams plc; Figure 3 on page 645 from AB InBev defends SABMiller buy to Senate, *The Wall Street Journal*, 8th December 2015 (Mickle, T.), reprinted with permission of The Wall Street Journal, Copyright © 2015 Dow Jones & Company, Inc. All Rights Reserved Worldwide. License number 3950140214420 and 3950140333272; Figure 1 on page 661 from World Steel Association, www.worldsteel.org; Figure 1 on page 698, Figures 2 and 3 on page 699 and Figure 4 on page 700 from Skelly/Euromonitor, 2014, Euromonitor International; Figure 5 on page 701 from Activists Put Mondelez CEO Irene Rosenfeld on the Spot; Mondelez boss Irene Rosenfeld hears often from investors Nelson Peltz and Bill Ackman, *The Wall Street Journal*, 15th December 2015 (Rosenfeld, I.), reprinted with permission of The Wall Street Journal, Copyright © 2015 Dow Jones & Company, Inc. All Rights Reserved Worldwide. License number 3950141291990 and 3950141434555; Figure 1 on page 707 and Figure 2 on page 709 from CRH plc; Figure 1a on page 714 from *UNODC World Drug Report 2010*, figure 39, p. 79, copyright © 2010 United Nations. Reprinted with the permission of the United Nations; Figure 1b on page 714 from *UNODC World Drug Report 2010*, figure 4, p. 33, copyright © 2010 United Nations. Reprinted with the permission of the United Nations; Figure 2 on page 715 from *The Transatlantic Cocaine Market*, United Nations Office on Drugs and Crime (2011) figure 6, p. 12, copyright © 2011 United Nations. Reprinted with the permission of the United Nations; Figure 3 on page 717 from Stratfor, reproduced with permission; Figure 5 on page 720 from Areas of cartel influence in Mexico, https://www.stratfor.com/interactive/areas-cartel-influence-mexico, courtesy of Stratfor.com; Figure 1 on page 723 from NHS Outcomes Framework, https://www.england.nhs.uk/resources/resources-for-ccgs/out-frwrk/, contains public sector information licensed under the Open Government Licence v3.0; Figure 1 on page 748 from Siemens AG; Figure 1 on page 753 from Unilever 2014 Annual Report and Accounts – Strategic Report, p. 14, Unilever.

Tables

Table 1 on page 93 after Zenith, January 2016; Table 3 on page 94 after Zenith, September 2015; Table 4 on page 94 after eMarketer.com; Table on page 128 from Attack of the clones, *The Economist*, 06/08/2011, © The Economist Newspaper Limited, London, 2011; Table 12.4 adapted from Arthur D. Little; Table 1 on page 408 from ITV Annual Report (2015), p. 107; Table 16.1 from How to pick a good fight, *Harvard Business Review*, December, pp. 48–57 (Joni, S.A. and Beyer, D. 2009), copyright © 2009 by the Harvard Business School Publishing Corporation. All rights reserved; Table 1 on page 559 from Siemens AG; Table on page 648 from SABMiller Annual Report 2015, SAB-Miller plc; Table 6 on page 646 from AB Inbev Annual Report 2014, Anheuser-Busch InBev; Table 1 on page 662 from World Steel Association, www.worldsteel. org; Table on page 694 from Annual Report 2015, Teva Pharmaceutical Industries Ltd.

Text

Illustration 1.2 from Samsung Electronics, www.samsung. com, and The University of Southampton Simply Better: The University Strategy, www.southampton.ac.uk/about/ strategy.page, reproduced with permission; Illustration 4.1 from Tony Hall, Chief Executive of the Royal Opera House Royal Opera House Annual Review, 2005–6, p. 11, reprinted by permission of Royal Opera House; Illustration 7.2 from Volvo takes a lead in India, *Financial Times*, 31/08/2009 (Leahy, J.), © The Financial Times Limited. All Rights Reserved; Illustration 8.4 from Berkshire Hathaway, extracts from Annual Reports, the material is copyrighted and used with permission of the author; Quote on page 561 from "Digitalization Strategy", by Professor Dr Siegfried Russwurm, Chief Technology Officer and a member of the Managing Board of Siemens AG, 9th December 2014; Case Study on page 568 from Thunderbird Case Series #A09-15-0006, Thunderbird School of Global Management, Arizona State University; Quote on page 641 from SABMiller Annual Report 2000 and quote on page 643 from SABMiller Annual Report 2003, SABMiller plc; Extracts on page 697 from House of Commons BIS Committee (2010), Mergers, acquisitions and takeovers: the takeover of Cadbury by Kraft, 9th report of session 2009–10, London, the Stationery Office, contains public sector information licensed under the Open Government Licence (OGL) v3.0. http://www. nationalarchives.gov.uk/doc/open-government-licence; Quote on page 724 from Dr Kate Silvester; Extract on page 741 from Department of Education, www. education.gov.uk, contains public sector information licensed under the Open Government Licence (OGL) v3.0. http://www.nationalarchives.gov.uk/doc/open-government-licence; Newspaper headline on page 742 from It's a political failure: how Sweden's celebrated schools system fell into crisis, *The Guardian*, 10/06/2015 (Weale, S.), copyright Guardian News & Media Ltd 2016; Quote on page 744 from Joachim Kraege, Siemens AG; Quote on page 745 from Horst J. Kayser, Siemens AG; Quote on page 746 from Wolfram Seiler, Siemens AG; Quote on page 747 from Joe Kaeser, Siemens AG; Quote on page 747 from Torsten Ende, Siemens AG.

Photos

Alamy Images: Clynt Garnham Medical 690, Dinodia Photos 667, Douglas Carr 639, Jim West 5, Kumar Sriskandan 633, pbpgalleries 584, RichardBakerFarnborough 271, robertharding 600, Roger Cracknell 01/ classic 543, Russell Hart 24, VIEW Pictures Ltd 739; **Aurizon:** 758; **Dieter Mayr Photography:** 128; **Eustathios Sainidis:** 659; **Funders and Founders:** image courtesy of Anna Vital 25; **Getty Images:** Jerome Favre/Bloomberg 187, Simon Dawson/Bloomberg 202, Philippe Huguen/AFP 622; **Press Association Images:** Ng Han Guan 304; **Rex Shutterstock:** Bloxham/LAT 495, Imaginechina 305; **Rufus Curnow:** xxv.